Our Favorite Recipes

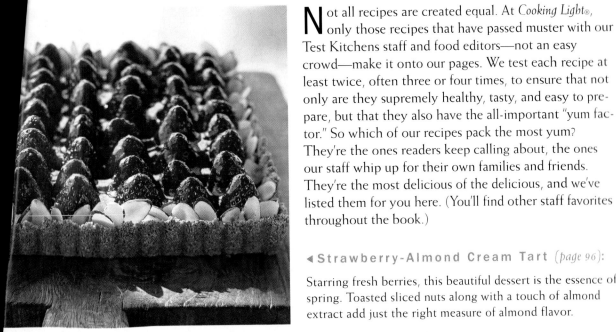

Not all recipes are created equal. At *Cooking Light®*, only those recipes that have passed muster with our Test Kitchens staff and food editors—not an easy crowd—make it onto our pages. We test each recipe at least twice, often three or four times, to ensure that not only are they supremely healthy, tasty, and easy to prepare, but that they also have the all-important "yum factor." So which of our recipes pack the most yum? They're the ones readers keep calling about, the ones our staff whip up for their own families and friends. They're the most delicious of the delicious, and we've listed them for you here. (You'll find other staff favorites throughout the book.)

◄ **Strawberry-Almond Cream Tart** *(page 96)*:

Starring fresh berries, this beautiful dessert is the essence of spring. Toasted sliced nuts along with a touch of almond extract add just the right measure of almond flavor.

◄ **Bulgogi** *Korean Beef Barbecue (page 68)*:

Paper-thin strips of sirloin steak emerge extremely tender and saturated with salty-sweet flavors after marinating only one hour and spending just five minutes on the grill.

◄ **Chicken Breasts Stuffed with Artichokes, Lemon, and Goat Cheese** *(page 116)*:

On the table in less than an hour, this chicken dish is as worthy for a weekend with company as it is for a Wednesday night.

◄ **Chicken Tetrazzini** *(page 51)*:

This family favorite is a great way to use leftover chicken or turkey. The recipe makes two casseroles, so you can feed a crowd or freeze one for a supereasy weeknight supper.

◄ **Spaghetti with Parmesan and Bacon** *(page 108)*:

Not only does this dish come together in a flash, but it also boasts a creamy egg sauce that coats every strand of pasta for serious richness.

◄ **Shallot-Rubbed Steak with Roasted Potatoes and Pickled Onions** *(page 98)*:

The subtle and ginlike flavor of juniper berries complements hearty beef. The pickled onions contribute a tangy touch.

◄ **Hot Browns** *(page 165)*:

This scrumptious open-faced turkey sandwich melds tomatoes, smoky bacon, and lots of Cheddar cheese for the ultimate quick comfort food.

Banana-Raspberry Cake with Lemon
Frosting, page 45

Sesame Beef and Asian Vegetable
Stir-Fry, page 25

Rustic White Bread, page 30

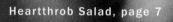
Heartthrob Salad, page 7

Chocolate Fudge Pie,
page 15

All-American Chili, page 18

The Mod Pod

Edamame—young green soybeans—turn up in surprising and flavorful places.

The Japanese have long snacked on edamame (eh-dah-MAH-meh), or fresh soybeans. But Americans are just now catching on to their charms.

Not least among their merits is a buttery, nutty flavor and wonderfully crisp texture that makes edamame a fun snack food that's addictive to eat. You simply use your teeth to squeeze the beans out of the salted pods, which are picked while young and look like large, fuzzy sugar snap peas. The beans themselves are similar in color to fresh fava or lima beans.

Thanks to edamame's new-found popularity, the beans—which are sold frozen as well as fully cooked and ready to eat, in or out of the pods—are now available at many grocery stores and are appearing as a featured ingredient in some of America's top restaurants. Try these recipes and see for yourself what all the fuss is about.

QUICK & EASY
Edamame-Garlic Purée

Michel Nischan, chef at Heartbeat in New York City, makes a versatile edamame purée that's a perfect side dish for grilled fish or chicken. With the addition of tofu, it's creamy and packed with soy protein.

- 4 cups frozen blanched shelled edamame (green soybeans)
- 10 garlic cloves, peeled
- ¼ cup soft silken tofu
- 1½ teaspoons lemon juice
- ¾ teaspoon salt
- ⅛ teaspoon black pepper

1. Bring 2 quarts water to a boil in a medium saucepan over medium-high heat; add edamame and garlic. Cook 5 minutes. Drain in a colander over a bowl, reserving ½ cup liquid.
2. Combine edamame, garlic, ½ cup cooking liquid, and tofu in a food processor, and process until smooth (about 3 minutes). Add lemon juice, salt, and pepper, and pulse to combine. Yield: 5 servings (serving size: ⅔ cup).

CALORIES 176 (27% from fat); FAT 5.2g (sat 0.6g, mono 0.9g, poly 3g); PROTEIN 13.8g; CARB 16.9g; FIBER 6.6g; CHOL 0mg; IRON 2.8mg; SODIUM 402mg; CALC 95mg

Sesame Beef and Asian Vegetable Stir-Fry
(pictured on page 22)

Chinese black vinegar has a sweet flavor and a rich, dark color that sets it apart from commonly used clear rice vinegars. You can find it at Asian markets, or order it from www.ethnicgrocer.com.

- ¼ cup low-sodium soy sauce, divided
- ¼ cup Chinese black (Chinkiang) vinegar or rice vinegar, divided
- 4 teaspoons dark sesame oil
- ½ teaspoon five-spice powder
- ¾ pound top round, cut into ¼-inch strips
- ⅓ cup water
- 1 teaspoon cornstarch
- 2 teaspoons peanut oil, divided
- 3 tablespoons sesame seeds, toasted and divided
- 1 tablespoon minced peeled fresh ginger
- 2 garlic cloves, minced
- 2 cups red bell pepper strips
- 1½ cups frozen blanched shelled edamame (green soybeans), thawed
- 1 cup sliced shiitake mushroom caps
- 1 (15-ounce) can whole baby corn, drained
- ½ cup diagonally cut green onions
- 3 cups hot cooked jasmine rice

1. Combine 2 tablespoons soy sauce, 2 tablespoons vinegar, sesame oil, and five-spice powder in a medium bowl, stirring with a whisk. Add beef; toss to coat. Let stand 10 minutes. Remove beef from bowl; discard marinade.
2. Combine 2 tablespoons soy sauce, 2 tablespoons vinegar, water, and cornstarch, stirring with a whisk.
3. Heat 1 teaspoon peanut oil in a large nonstick skillet over medium-high heat. Add beef; stir-fry 1 minute. Remove beef from pan. Add 1 teaspoon peanut oil, 2 tablespoons sesame seeds, ginger, and garlic to pan; stir-fry 30 seconds. Add bell pepper, edamame, mushrooms, and corn; stir-fry 2 minutes. Add beef and cornstarch mixture; stir-fry 3 minutes or until sauce thickens. Remove from heat; stir in 1 tablespoon sesame seeds and onions. Serve over rice. Yield: 6 servings (serving size: 1 cup stir-fry and ½ cup rice).

CALORIES 434 (30% from fat); FAT 14.4g (sat 3.3g, mono 4.8g, poly 3.5g); PROTEIN 21.7g; CARB 55.9g; FIBER 6.3g; CHOL 36mg; IRON 3.7mg; SODIUM 318mg; CALC 62mg

Roasted Chile-Spiced Edamame

A slight crunch on the outside gives way to a meaty texture inside. We used authentic New Mexico chile powder, which is made from pure dried chiles and has a slightly bitter taste; but regular chili powder is also good.

- 1 (14-ounce) package frozen blanched shelled edamame (green soybeans), thawed
- Cooking spray
- 1 tablespoon New Mexico red chile powder or chili powder
- 1 teaspoon onion powder
- ¾ teaspoon sea salt
- ½ teaspoon ground ginger
- ½ teaspoon ground red pepper

1. Preheat oven to 350°.
2. Arrange edamame in a single layer on a baking sheet, and coat with cooking spray. Combine chile powder and remaining 4 ingredients. Sprinkle over edamame; toss to coat.

Continued

3. Bake edamame at 350° for 1 hour, stirring every 30 minutes. Yield: 5 servings (serving size: about ¼ cup).

CALORIES 113 (28% from fat); FAT 3.5g (sat 0.4g, mono 0.7g, poly 1.7g); PROTEIN 8.7g; CARB 10.9g; FIBER 4.8g; CHOL 0mg; IRON 2mg; SODIUM 393mg; CALC 59mg

QUICK & EASY • MAKE AHEAD

Edamame Hummus with Pita Crisps

If the hummus seems too thick, add more water to reach the desired consistency. Each serving has 4 grams of soy protein. Broken pita chips create a rustic presentation.

6   (6-inch) pitas, split in half horizontally
1½ cups frozen blanched shelled edamame (green soybeans)
4   teaspoons extravirgin olive oil, divided
½   teaspoon salt
½   teaspoon ground cumin
¼   teaspoon ground coriander
2   garlic cloves, peeled
½   cup fresh flat-leaf parsley leaves
3   tablespoons tahini (sesame-seed paste)
3   tablespoons water
3   tablespoons fresh lemon juice
½   teaspoon paprika

1. Preheat oven to 350°.
2. Arrange pita halves in a single layer on oven rack. Bake at 350° for 15 minutes or until crisp, and cool completely on a wire rack. Break each pita half into about 6 chips.
3. Prepare edamame according to package directions, omitting salt. Place 1 tablespoon oil, salt, cumin, coriander, and garlic in a food processor, and pulse 2 or 3 times or until coarsely chopped. Add edamame, parsley, tahini, water, and juice; process 1 minute or until smooth. Spoon hummus into a serving bowl. Drizzle with 1 teaspoon oil, and sprinkle with paprika. Serve with pita crisps. Yield: 12 servings (serving size: 2 tablespoons hummus and about 6 pita crisps).

CALORIES 147 (30% from fat); FAT 4.9g (sat 0.6g, mono 2.2g, poly 1.9g); PROTEIN 5.6g; CARB 20.3g; FIBER 2.2g; CHOL 0mg; IRON 1.5mg; SODIUM 268mg; CALC 48mg

Edamame Succotash with Shrimp

Edamame stand in for lima beans in this one-dish meal. If you like your food spicy, use 2 jalapeño peppers.

1½ cups frozen blanched shelled edamame (green soybeans)
3   bacon slices
½   cup chopped celery
¼   cup chopped red onion
3   garlic cloves, minced
1   to 2 jalapeño peppers, split lengthwise and cut crosswise into thin strips
2   cups fresh corn kernels (about 2 ears)
3   tablespoons white wine
1   pound medium shrimp, peeled and deveined
½   teaspoon salt
¼   teaspoon freshly ground black pepper
2   tablespoons chopped fresh parsley

1. Prepare edamame according to package directions, omitting salt. Drain.
2. Cook bacon in a large nonstick skillet over medium-high heat until crisp. Remove from pan, reserving 1 tablespoon drippings in pan; crumble bacon.
3. Reduce heat to medium; add celery, onion, garlic, and jalapeño to pan; cook 2 minutes, stirring frequently. Stir in edamame, corn, and wine; cook 4 minutes, stirring frequently. Add shrimp; cook 5 minutes or until shrimp are done, stirring frequently. Remove from heat. Stir in salt and pepper; sprinkle with crumbled bacon and parsley. Serve immediately. Yield: 4 servings (serving size: 1¼ cups).

CALORIES 365 (28% from fat); FAT 11.2g (sat 2.9g, mono 4g, poly 3.7g); PROTEIN 33.8g; CARB 31.7g; FIBER 6.2g; CHOL 180mg; IRON 5.4mg; SODIUM 599mg; CALC 118mg

Edamame-Avocado Soup

Chef Andrew Meek of Sage, in Des Moines, Iowa, serves this refined yet hearty soup as an appetizer. It's packed with soy protein, fiber, and mono- and polyunsaturated fats.

1½ pounds frozen shelled edamame (green soybeans)
2   cups fat-free, less-sodium chicken broth, divided
¼   cup chopped shallots
2   peeled avocados, cut into quarters
4   cups water
3   tablespoons lemon juice
1   teaspoon salt
¼   teaspoon white pepper
Chopped fresh parsley (optional)
Lemon wedges (optional)

1. Place edamame in a large saucepan. Cover with water to 2 inches above beans; bring to a boil, and cook 10 minutes or until soft. Drain.
2. Place half of edamame, ½ cup broth, and shallots in a blender; process until smooth. Pour puréed shallot mixture into a large bowl. Combine remaining edamame, ¾ cup broth, and avocados in blender or food processor; process until smooth. Add puréed avocado mixture to puréed shallot mixture; stir to combine. Add ¾ cup broth, water, juice, salt, and pepper to puréed mixture; stir well with a whisk. Cover and chill. Serve with parsley and lemon wedges, if desired. Yield: 9 servings (serving size: 1 cup).

CALORIES 182 (49% from fat); FAT 9.9g (sat 1.1g, mono 5.3g, poly 3.4g); PROTEIN 9.8g; CARB 13.8g; FIBER 6.3g; CHOL 0mg; IRON 2.2mg; SODIUM 396mg; CALC 58mg

QUICK & EASY

Edamame Mashed Potatoes

Serve these green-tinted potatoes with salmon for a meal rich in omega-3 fatty acids and isoflavones.

3   cups frozen blanched shelled edamame (green soybeans)
5   cups peeled baking potato, cut into 2-inch pieces (about 2 pounds)
1   (14-ounce) can fat-free, less-sodium chicken broth
¾   cup warm 2% reduced-fat milk (100° to 110°)
2   tablespoons olive oil
1¼ teaspoons salt
⅛   teaspoon white pepper

1. Place edamame in a large saucepan. Cover with water to 2 inches above edamame, and bring to a boil. Cook 10 minutes or until soft. Drain edamame, and set aside.

2. Place potato and chicken broth in a large saucepan; add water to cover potatoes. Bring to a boil. Reduce heat; simmer 15 minutes or until tender. Drain in a colander over a bowl, reserving ½ cup cooking liquid.

3. Place edamame in a food processor; process 1 minute or until finely chopped. With food processor on, slowly pour reserved cooking liquid through food chute; process until smooth.

4. Place edamame mixture, potato mixture, milk, oil, salt, and pepper in a large bowl, and mash with a potato masher to desired consistency. Yield: 8 servings (serving size: about 1 cup).

CALORIES 194 (29% from fat); FAT 6.2g (sat 1g, mono 3g, poly 1.3g); PROTEIN 8.5g; CARB 25.8g; FIBER 4.3g; CHOL 2mg; IRON 1.5mg; SODIUM 419mg; CALC 70mg

MAKE AHEAD
Orzo Salad with Marinated Mushrooms and Edamame

This is a great make-ahead salad that's good with pork or chicken.

- ½ cup white wine vinegar
- 2½ tablespoons olive oil
- 1 tablespoon dry sherry
- 1 tablespoon brown sugar
- 1 tablespoon fresh thyme leaves
- 1½ teaspoons salt
- 1 teaspoon dry mustard
- ½ teaspoon freshly ground black pepper
- 2 garlic cloves, minced
- 1 bay leaf
- 7 cups quartered mushrooms (about 1 pound)
- 2 cups frozen blanched shelled edamame (green soybeans), thawed
- 1 cup chopped red bell pepper
- 2 cups cooked orzo (about 1 cup uncooked rice-shaped pasta)

1. Combine first 10 ingredients in a large saucepan; bring to a boil. Reduce heat, and simmer 10 minutes. Stir in mushrooms, edamame, and bell pepper; cook 1 minute. Place mushroom mixture in a large bowl; cool to room temperature. Discard bay leaf. Add pasta, and toss to combine. Cover and refrigerate overnight. Yield: 8 servings (serving size: about ¾ cup).

CALORIES 201 (29% from fat); FAT 6.5g (sat 0.7g, mono 3.7g, poly 1.9g); PROTEIN 8.9g; CARB 27.7g; FIBER 3.6g; CHOL 0mg; IRON 2.5mg; SODIUM 456mg; CALC 37mg

QUICK & EASY
Soba with Herbed Edamame Sauce

You can use walnuts instead of cashews.

- 1 cup frozen blanched shelled edamame (green soybeans)
- 6 tablespoons chopped dry-roasted cashews, divided
- 1 cup loosely packed basil leaves
- 1 cup loosely packed cilantro leaves
- 6 tablespoons (1½ ounces) grated fresh pecorino Romano cheese
- ¼ cup fresh lemon juice
- ¼ cup extravirgin olive oil
- 1 teaspoon salt
- ¼ teaspoon freshly ground black pepper
- 3 garlic cloves, peeled
- 1 cup hot water
- 6 cups hot cooked soba (about 1 pound uncooked buckwheat noodles)
- Cilantro sprigs (optional)
- Lime wedges (optional)

1. Prepare edamame according to package directions, omitting salt.

2. Place edamame, ¼ cup cashews, basil, and next 7 ingredients in a food processor; process 1 minute or until finely chopped.

3. With food processor on, slowly pour hot water through food chute; process 2 minutes or until smooth. Serve over soba, and sprinkle with 2 tablespoons cashews. Garnish with cilantro sprigs and lime wedges, if desired. Yield: 7 servings (serving size: about 1 cup noodles, about ⅓ cup sauce, and about 1 teaspoon cashews).

CALORIES 408 (30% from fat); FAT 13.8g (sat 2.6g, mono 8.1g, poly 2.1g); PROTEIN 18g; CARB 58.6g; FIBER 4.5g; CHOL 5mg; IRON 2.5mg; SODIUM 562mg; CALC 112mg

Chicken Noodle Bowl with Edamame and Straw Mushrooms

You also can use cellophane noodles in this Asian chicken noodle soup. Each serving provides 13 grams of soy protein—which is more than half of the recommended daily amount. Substitute 2 (2-inch) pieces julienne-cut lemon rind in place of the lemongrass, if you prefer.

- 2 peeled fresh lemongrass stalks
- 6 cups fat-free, less-sodium chicken broth
- 1 (1-inch) piece peeled fresh ginger, thinly sliced
- 5 ounces uncooked wide rice sticks (rice-flour noodles)
- 12 ounces skinless, boneless chicken thighs, cut into ¼-inch strips
- 2 cups frozen blanched shelled edamame (green soybeans), thawed
- ⅓ cup diagonally cut carrot
- 1 tablespoon low-sodium soy sauce
- 1 (15-ounce) can straw mushrooms, drained
- ½ cup loosely packed cilantro leaves
- ⅓ cup diagonally sliced green onions
- Lime wedges (optional)

1. Lightly crush lemongrass using side of a knife; cut stalks into 2-inch pieces. Combine lemongrass pieces, broth, and ginger in a large saucepan; bring to a boil. Reduce heat to low, and simmer 45 minutes. Remove lemongrass pieces and ginger using a slotted spoon; discard.

2. Cook noodles according to package directions; drain and set aside.

3. Add chicken strips to broth; increase heat to medium, and cook 5 minutes. Add edamame, carrot, soy sauce, and mushrooms; cook 5 minutes or until chicken is done. Remove from heat; stir in cilantro and green onions.

4. Place rice noodles in each of 5 soup bowls. Ladle chicken mixture over noodles. Garnish with lime wedges, if desired. Yield: 5 servings (serving size: about ¾ cup noodles and about 1¼ cups chicken mixture).

CALORIES 318 (18% from fat); FAT 6.3g (sat 0.8g, mono 1.7g, poly 3g); PROTEIN 26.4g; CARB 36.6g; FIBER 5.8g; CHOL 0mg; IRON 2.7mg; SODIUM 860mg; CALC 62mg

All About Baking Bread

Learn how to make terrific homemade bread—and,
in the process, knead in fun and creativity.

Before You Get Started

Equipment: A baker's most important tool is observation. After your first few loaves, you'll begin to "read the bread"—you'll be able to tell how your recipe is developing by the bread's texture and appearance. Aside from that, all you need are measuring cups and spoons, a large glass bowl, a wooden spoon, a flat surface on which to knead the bread, an oven, and a wire cooling rack. (Glass bowls and wooden spoons are preferable to metal, which can react with the dough and affect the bread's flavor.)

Ingredients: As with any type of cooking, quality ingredients help produce quality food. But that doesn't mean you have to spend a lot of money. Common-sense steps will help ensure a tasty loaf: Check the expiration date when you purchase yeast; be sure to buy exactly the type of flour called for in a recipe (bread flour, for example), and use bottled water if your local tap water has any unpleasant smells or flavors.

Measuring: Careful measuring of ingredients is essential to making good bread. Don't rely on guesswork. When measuring the flour, be sure to follow our instructions to lightly spoon it into the measuring cup (don't scoop!), and level off the excess using a knife. Be sure to use dry measuring cups for dry ingredients like flour and sugar, and liquid measuring cups for any liquid.

Let's Get Started: Dissolving the Yeast

In this first step, dry yeast and a little sugar are dissolved (or proofed) in a liquid that's usually warmed to 100° to 110°. First-timers take note: It's always a good idea to use a thermometer until you feel comfortable

recognizing the target temperature. You can also test the warmth of the liquid on the inside of your wrist—it should feel no warmer than a hot shower.

About five minutes after mixing the yeast and sugar with liquid, the moisture and warmth bring the yeast out of the dormant stage and cause it to begin reproducing. As yeast grows, it consumes the sugar and emits carbon dioxide and alcohol, which appear as bubbles on the surface of the dissolved yeast; those bubbles mean the yeast is alive and well, and it's safe to go on to the next stage. If no bubbles are present, then the liquid used to proof the yeast was either too hot and killed it, or it was too cold and inhibited the yeast growth. Another possibility is that the yeast in the package has expired due to time or exposure to differing temperatures. (Store unopened dry yeast in the refrigerator.)

Mixing

Within this stage there are 2 methods:
1. For simple mixing, often called the straight dough method, the remaining ingredients are added to the dissolved yeast to form a dough.
2. In the sponge method, a small amount of flour (and sometimes sugar) is added to the yeast mixture to create a batter that's allowed to ferment for a period of time. Later, the remaining ingredients are added to form a dough. This method is often used to develop interesting flavors or to create a lighter texture in otherwise heavy breads (such as whole grain).

Kneading

Kneading is the process of repeatedly folding the dough onto itself. It's a vital part of making bread because it distributes the yeast evenly throughout the dough, forming long, stretchy strands of protein called gluten.
1. Place the dough on a lightly floured surface. It's important to use only enough flour to keep the dough from sticking. Adding too much flour will prevent the loaf from rising properly and create a dense crumb. If small bits of dough begin sticking to your hands, take a moment to wash and dry your hands. Clean, dry hands help prevent the dough from sticking and tearing as you knead.

2. Using the heels of your hands, push the dough away from you.

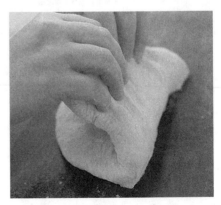

3. Lift the edge farthest away from you, and fold it toward you.

4. Give the dough a quarter turn.

5. Repeat Steps 2 through 4 until the dough feels smooth and elastic; this usually takes 8 minutes. (Using a timer is a good way to ensure adequate kneading.)

Some recipes call for adding ingredients, such as dried fruit, at the end of the kneading stage. In that case, gently press the dough until it's about 1 inch thick, sprinkle the chosen ingredient over the surface, then fold the dough in half. Knead as you did before until the ingredients are evenly distributed (about 1 to 2 minutes).

Be patient with yourself as you learn to knead. Before long you'll find yourself falling into a pleasantly rhythmic motion—and what might have once seemed a chore becomes a soothing exercise.

Rising (First)

During rising, the yeast continues to grow and emit carbon dioxide. The carbon dioxide becomes trapped by the gluten strands and pushes up on them like hot air in a balloon; this is what causes the bread to rise. Much of a bread's flavors are developed during its rising stages. Most recipes have 2 rising stages, while some have 3 or more.

For the first rising, the dough is placed in a bowl coated with cooking spray and turned so all sides of the dough are coated. Then the bowl is covered (plastic wrap or a clean towel works well). These are precautions against the dough drying out as it rises. If the surface of the dough dries, the dough won't stretch and therefore can't rise.

The best environment for rising is a humid, draft-free area that's about 85°. An easy way to create this environment is to place the dough in a cool, closed oven alongside a 1- to 2-cup glass measure filled with boiling water.

The dough needs to rise until doubled in size. Depending on the dough and the environment, this can take from 30 minutes to 2 hours. To check for effective rising, gently press 2 fingers about an inch into the dough. If the dough springs back immediately, it hasn't risen enough; if the indentations remain, the dough is ready. If the dough begins to collapse, though, it has

risen too much. In that case, punch the dough down, shape it into a ball, and repeat the first rising stage.

Be patient—you can encourage bread to rise by controlling its environment, but don't rush it. Dough that hasn't risen enough results in dense, overly chewy bread.

Punching Down

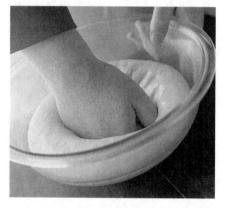

Punch down the dough between rising stages by pressing into the center with a closed fist. This action releases excess carbon dioxide and redistributes the yeast for its next stage of growth.

Shaping

After a 5-minute rest that makes the dough easier to handle, it's formed into the desired shape (loaf, rolls, etc.) in preparation for the final rise.

Rising (Final)

For the final rising stage, the shaped dough is placed on a baking sheet or in a pan. The dough should be lightly coated

with cooking spray and covered, just as it was for its first rising. The rising procedure and method of checking for doneness remain the same as in the first rise.

Some recipes call for slashing or cutting into the dough. Originally done to identify the type of bread, slashing is still done for cosmetic reasons, and to allow the bread to expand as it bakes without tearing or cracking. Be sure to use a very sharp knife or sharp scissors to slash the dough.

An egg wash (egg white and water) is sometimes brushed on the dough before baking to create a glossy, crusty surface.

Baking

Remember to preheat your oven. In the early minutes of baking, the yeast goes through a final growth spurt called oven-spring (in a well-lit oven, you can actually see the surface of the dough move) before it begins to die. The trapped carbon dioxide that was holding up the gluten strands evaporates just as the heat causes the gluten to harden in place. This series of events determines the bread's final shape and size—and all depends on an accurate oven temperature.

Completely baked bread will have a beautiful golden-brown color and sound hollow when tapped on the bottom. If you are baking bread in a loaf pan, cover both hands with oven mitts and remove the loaf from the pan to tap the bottom. You should always begin checking your bread 10 minutes before the end of the recommended baking time, in case your oven tends to run hot.

Storing

Cool freshly baked bread on a wire rack (to prevent steam from softening the crust) for at least 10 minutes before slicing. Cool completely before wrapping. Wrap bread in a clean kitchen towel or several layers of cheesecloth. Store at room temperature. Keeping bread in the refrigerator will cause it to dry out. You can wrap most breads in heavy-duty foil and freeze them up to 2 months.

Rustic White Bread

(pictured on page 22)

Shape the bread into a free-form round instead of a traditional loaf.

    1   package dry yeast (about 2¼ teaspoons)
    1   cup warm water (100° to 110°)
    3   cups bread flour, divided
    1   teaspoon salt
  Cooking spray
    1   teaspoon cornmeal
    1   teaspoon water
    1   large egg white, lightly beaten

1. Dissolve yeast in 1 cup warm water in a large bowl, and let stand 5 minutes.

2. Lightly spoon flour into dry measuring cups; level with a knife. Add 2¾ cups flour and salt to yeast mixture; stir until a soft dough forms. Turn dough out onto a floured surface. Knead until smooth and elastic (about 8 minutes); add enough of remaining flour, 1 tablespoon at a time, to prevent dough from sticking to hands (dough will feel tacky).

3. Place dough in a large bowl coated with cooking spray, turning to coat top. Cover and let rise in a warm place (85°), free from drafts, 45 minutes or until doubled in size. (Gently press 2 fingers into dough. If indentation remains, dough has risen enough.)

4. Punch dough down. Cover and let rest 5 minutes. Shape dough into a 6-inch round; place on a baking sheet sprinkled with cornmeal. Lightly coat surface of dough with cooking spray. Cover and let rise 45 minutes or until doubled in size.

5. Preheat oven to 450°.

6. Uncover dough. Combine 1 teaspoon water and egg white, stirring with a whisk; brush over dough. Make 3 (4-inch) cuts ¼ inch deep across top of dough using a sharp knife.

7. Bake at 450° for 20 minutes or until bread is browned on bottom and sounds hollow when tapped. Remove from pan; cool on a wire rack. Yield: 12 servings (serving size: 1 slice).

CALORIES 128 (4% from fat); FAT 0.6g (sat 0.1g, mono 0.1g, poly 0.3g); PROTEIN 4.6g; CARB 25.3g; FIBER 1g; CHOL 0mg; IRON 1.6mg; SODIUM 201mg; CALC 6mg

Sunflower-Wheat Loaf

A quick sponge method works well to keep this bread from becoming too dense. Dried blueberries make for a tasty breakfast bread; use chopped dried apples or apricots, if you prefer. Or, if you'd like a more straight-forward multigrain bread, omit the fruit.

    1   package dry yeast (about 2¼ teaspoons)
    1   cup warm water (100° to 110°)
    2   cups whole wheat flour
    ¼   cup honey
    2   tablespoons vegetable oil
    1   tablespoon dark molasses
    1   teaspoon salt
    ¼   cup wheat germ
    2   tablespoons cornmeal
  1¼   cups bread flour, divided
    ⅓   cup raw unsalted sunflower seeds
    ¼   cup dried blueberries
  Cooking spray

1. Dissolve yeast in warm water in a large bowl; let stand 5 minutes.

2. Lightly spoon whole wheat flour into dry measuring cups; level with a knife. Add whole wheat flour, honey, oil, molasses, and salt to yeast mixture, stirring well. Cover and let stand at room temperature 1 hour to create a sponge.

3. Add wheat germ and cornmeal to sponge. Lightly spoon bread flour into dry measuring cups; level with a knife. Add 1 cup flour to sponge; stir until a soft dough forms. Turn dough out onto a floured surface. Knead until smooth and elastic (about 8 minutes); add enough of remaining flour, 1 tablespoon at a time, to prevent dough from sticking to hands (dough will feel tacky). Knead in sunflower seeds and blueberries.

4. Place dough in a large bowl coated with cooking spray; turn to coat top. Cover; let rise in a warm place (85°), free from drafts, 1 hour or until doubled in size. (Gently press 2 fingers into dough. If indentation remains, dough has risen enough.)

5. Punch dough down. Cover and let rest 5 minutes. Roll into a 14 x 7-inch rectangle on a floured surface. Roll up tightly, starting with a short edge, pressing firmly to eliminate air pockets; pinch seam and ends to seal. Place roll, seam side down, in an 8 x 4-inch loaf pan coated with cooking spray. Coat dough with cooking spray. Cover and let rise 45 minutes or until doubled in size.

6. Preheat oven to 375°.

7. Uncover dough; bake at 375° for 45 minutes or until loaf is browned on bottom and sounds hollow when tapped. Remove from pan; cool on a wire rack. Yield: 16 servings (serving size: 1 slice).

CALORIES 157 (22% from fat); FAT 3.8g (sat 0.5g, mono 0.7g, poly 2.2g); PROTEIN 4.7g; CARB 27.9g; FIBER 2.9g; CHOL 0mg; IRON 1.8mg; SODIUM 149mg; CALC 23mg

Parmesan and Cracked Pepper Grissini

Grissini are thin, crisp breadsticks that are irresistibly good. This recipe builds on the Rustic White Bread (recipe at left). Flavorings are added and a different shaping technique is used, but the dough is basically the same. Use a sharp knife, pastry wheel, or pizza cutter to quickly cut the dough, and use a ruler as a guide to make dividing the dough easier.

    1   package dry yeast (about 2¼ teaspoons)
    1   cup warm water (100° to 110°)
    3   cups bread flour, divided
  1¼   teaspoons salt
  Cooking spray
    1   teaspoon water
    1   large egg white, lightly beaten
    ½   cup (2 ounces) grated fresh Parmesan cheese
    1   tablespoon cracked black pepper
    2   teaspoons cornmeal

1. Dissolve yeast in 1 cup warm water in a large bowl; let stand 5 minutes.

2. Lightly spoon flour into dry measuring cups; level with a knife. Add 2¾ cups flour and salt to yeast mixture; stir until a soft dough forms. Turn dough out onto a floured surface. Knead until smooth and elastic (about 8 minutes); add enough of remaining flour, 1 tablespoon at a time, to prevent dough from sticking to hands (dough will feel tacky).

3. Place dough in a large bowl coated with cooking spray, turning to coat top. Cover and let rise in a warm place (85°), free from drafts, 45 minutes or until doubled in size. (Gently press 2 fingers into dough. If indentation remains, dough has risen enough.)

4. Punch dough down. Cover and let rest 5 minutes. Turn dough out onto a lightly floured surface; roll into a 12 x 8-inch rectangle.

5. Combine 1 teaspoon water and egg white, stirring with a whisk; brush evenly over dough. Sprinkle dough with cheese and pepper. Lightly coat dough with cooking spray; cover with plastic wrap. Gently press toppings into dough; remove plastic wrap.

6. Sprinkle each of 2 baking sheets with 1 teaspoon cornmeal. Cut dough in half lengthwise to form 2 (12 x 4-inch) rectangles. Cut each rectangle crosswise into 12 (1-inch-wide) strips.

7. Working with 1 strip at a time (cover remaining strips to prevent drying), gently roll strip into a log. Holding ends of log between forefinger and thumb of each hand, gently pull log into a 14-inch rope, slightly shaking it up and down while pulling. (You can also roll each strip into a 14-inch rope on a lightly floured surface.) Place rope on a prepared pan, curving into a series of shapes so that rope fits on pan.

8. Repeat procedure with remaining strips, placing 12 on each pan. Lightly coat ropes with cooking spray. Cover and let rise 20 minutes or until doubled in size.

9. Preheat oven to 450°.

10. Uncover dough; bake at 450° for 6 minutes with 1 pan on bottom rack and 1 pan on second rack from top. Rotate pans; bake an additional 6 minutes or until golden brown. Remove breadsticks from pans; cool completely on wire racks. Yield: 12 servings (serving size: 2 breadsticks).

CALORIES 148 (12% from fat); FAT 1.9g (sat 0.9g, mono 0.4g, poly 0.3g); PROTEIN 6.4g; CARB 25.9g; FIBER 1.1g; CHOL 3mg; IRON 1.8mg; SODIUM 326mg; CALC 64mg

MAKE AHEAD
Fontina and Red Pepper-Stuffed Garlic Focaccia

Roasted garlic is mashed into a paste and added to the dough so that every bite of the savory bread is infused with its flavor. An overnight sponge creates complex flavor in the bread.

    1 package dry yeast (about 2¼
       teaspoons)
    1 cup warm water (100° to 110°)
 3¼ cups bread flour, divided
    1 whole garlic head
 1½ tablespoons extravirgin olive oil,
       divided
 1¼ teaspoons salt, divided
    Cooking spray
    1 teaspoon cornmeal
   ¼ cup chopped fresh basil
   ¾ cup chopped bottled roasted red
       bell peppers
   ½ cup (2 ounces) shredded fontina
       cheese

1. Dissolve yeast in 1 cup warm water in a large bowl; let stand 5 minutes.

2. Lightly spoon flour into dry measuring cups; level with a knife. Add 1 cup flour to yeast mixture, stirring well. Cover and let stand at room temperature 8 hours or overnight to create a sponge (mixture will become very bubbly).

3. Preheat oven to 350°.

4. Remove papery skin from garlic head (do not peel or separate cloves). Wrap in foil. Bake at 350° for 1 hour; cool 10 minutes.

5. Separate cloves; squeeze to extract garlic pulp. Discard skins. Place garlic pulp, 1 tablespoon oil, and 1 teaspoon salt in a small bowl, and mash with a fork until smooth. Stir into sponge.

6. Add 2 cups flour to sponge; stir until a soft dough forms. Turn dough out onto a floured surface. Knead until smooth and elastic (about 8 minutes); add enough of remaining flour, 1 tablespoon at a time, to prevent dough from sticking to hands (dough will feel tacky).

7. Place dough in a large bowl coated with cooking spray, turning to coat top. Cover and let rise in a warm place (85°), free from drafts, 45 minutes or until doubled in size. (Gently press 2 fingers into dough. If indentation remains, dough has risen enough.)

8. Punch dough down. Cover and let rest 5 minutes. Divide dough in half; roll each half into a 10-inch round.

9. Place 1 dough round on a baking sheet sprinkled with cornmeal. Arrange basil over dough, leaving a ¼-inch border; top with bell peppers. Sprinkle evenly with cheese. Top with other dough round; pinch edges to seal. Lightly coat with cooking spray. Cover and let rise 45 minutes or until dough is doubled in size.

10. Preheat oven to 400°.

11. Uncover dough. Make indentations in top of dough with a knife. Gently brush dough with 1½ teaspoons oil, and sprinkle with ¼ teaspoon salt. Bake at 400° for 30 minutes or until focaccia is browned on bottom and sounds hollow when tapped. Remove from pan; cool on a wire rack. Yield: 14 servings (serving size: 1 wedge).

CALORIES 150 (20% from fat); FAT 3.3g (sat 1.1g, mono 1.5g, poly 0.5g); PROTEIN 5.3g; CARB 24.4g; FIBER 1g; CHOL 5mg; IRON 1.6mg; SODIUM 265mg; CALC 33mg

MAKE AHEAD • FREEZABLE
Buttered Sweet Potato Knot Rolls

Enriched with egg yolks, sweet potato, milk, and butter, these rolls have a sweeter, richer taste and softer texture than other breads. Unlike a loaf bread, these dinner rolls can stand up to more elegant foods.

    1 package dry yeast (about 2¼
       teaspoons)
    1 cup warm 2% reduced-fat milk
       (100° to 110°)
   ¾ cup canned mashed sweet
       potatoes
    3 tablespoons butter, melted and
       divided
 1¼ teaspoons salt
    2 large egg yolks, lightly
       beaten
    5 cups bread flour, divided
    Cooking spray

Continued

1. Dissolve yeast in 1 cup warm milk in a large bowl; let stand 5 minutes.

2. Add sweet potatoes, 1 tablespoon butter, salt, and egg yolks; stir with a whisk.

3. Lightly spoon flour into dry measuring cups; level with a knife. Add 4½ cups flour to potato mixture; stir until a soft dough forms.

4. Turn dough out onto a floured surface. Knead until smooth and elastic (about 8 minutes); add enough of remaining flour, 1 tablespoon at a time, to prevent dough from sticking to hands (dough will feel very soft and tacky).

5. Place dough in a large bowl coated with cooking spray, turning to coat top. Cover and let rise in a warm place (85°), free from drafts, 45 minutes or until doubled in size. (Gently press 2 fingers into dough. If indentation remains, dough has risen enough.) Punch dough down. Cover and let rest 5 minutes.

6. Line 2 baking sheets with parchment paper. Divide dough into 24 equal portions. Working with 1 portion at a time (cover remaining dough to prevent drying), shape portion into a 9-inch rope. Carefully shape rope into a knot; tuck top end of knot under roll. Place roll on a prepared pan.

7. Repeat procedure with remaining dough, placing 12 rolls on each pan. Lightly coat rolls with cooking spray; cover and let rise 30 minutes or until doubled in size.

8. Preheat oven to 400°.

9. Uncover rolls. Bake at 400° for 8 minutes with 1 pan on bottom rack and 1 pan on second rack from top. Rotate pans; bake an additional 7 minutes or until rolls are golden brown on top and sound hollow when tapped.

10. Remove rolls from pans; place on wire racks. Brush rolls with 2 tablespoons butter. Serve warm or at room temperature. Yield: 24 servings (serving size: 1 roll).

CALORIES 134 (17% from fat); FAT 2.6g (sat 1.2g, mono 0.7g, poly 0.3g); PROTEIN 4.3g; CARB 23g; FIBER 0.9g; CHOL 22mg; IRON 1.4mg; SODIUM 147mg; CALC 21mg

How To Make Knot Rolls

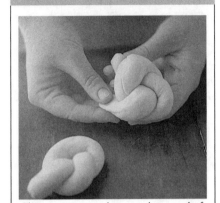

Shape rope into a knot, tuck top end of knot under roll.

Sandwich Night Menu
serves 4

Rich Tomato Bread makes a tasty multipurpose loaf. Try toasting some to create an extraordinary sandwich. You can round out the menu with baked chips and fresh fruit.

Turkey on Rich Tomato Bread*

Baked tortilla chips

Grapes

*Combine ¼ cup low-fat mayonnaise, 1 teaspoon fresh lemon juice, and 1 minced garlic clove. Toast 8 (½-inch-thick) slices Rich Tomato Bread. Top each of 4 bread slices with 1 (1-ounce) slice provolone cheese, 1 ounce roasted deli turkey, 1 lettuce leaf, 1 (⅛-inch-thick) red onion slice, and 2 (⅛-inch-thick) tomato slices. Spread each of remaining 4 bread slices with about 1 tablespoon mayonnaise mixture; place on top of tomato slices.

MAKE AHEAD • FREEZABLE
Rich Tomato Bread

Sun-dried tomatoes give the loaf a savory quality. And because the water used to rehydrate the tomatoes is the liquid for the bread, the tomatoes' flavor (and color) permeates the loaf. Enriched with olive oil and an egg, the bread takes on a moist texture. It's excellent for sandwiches—try it with turkey and Brie. Or toast it and add a little smear of butter.

1 cup boiling water
20 sun-dried tomato halves, packed without oil
1 package dry yeast (about 2¼ teaspoons)
3½ cups bread flour, divided
2 tablespoons extravirgin olive oil
1 teaspoon salt
1 large egg, lightly beaten
Cooking spray
1 tablespoon butter, melted

1. Combine boiling water and tomatoes in a small bowl. Cover and let stand 30 minutes.

2. Drain tomato mixture through a sieve over a bowl, reserving liquid. Finely chop tomatoes. Heat reserved liquid to 100° to 110°. Place liquid in a large bowl, and stir in yeast. Let stand 5 minutes.

3. Lightly spoon flour into dry measuring cups; level with a knife. Add 3 cups flour, chopped tomatoes, oil, salt, and egg to yeast mixture; stir until a soft dough forms.

4. Turn dough out onto a floured surface. Knead until smooth and elastic (about 8 minutes); add enough of remaining flour, 1 tablespoon at a time, to prevent dough from sticking to hands (dough will feel tacky).

5. Place dough in a large bowl coated with cooking spray, turning to coat top. Cover and let rise in a warm place (85°), free from drafts, 45 minutes or until doubled in size. (Gently press 2 fingers into dough. If indentation remains, dough has risen enough.)

6. Punch dough down; cover and let rest 5 minutes. Roll dough into a 14 x 7-inch rectangle on a lightly floured surface. Roll up rectangle tightly, starting with a short edge, pressing firmly to eliminate air pockets; pinch seam and ends to seal. Place roll, seam side down, in an 8 x 4-inch loaf pan coated with cooking spray.

7. Lightly coat dough with cooking spray. Cover and let rise 30 minutes or until doubled in size.

8. Preheat oven to 350°.

9. Uncover dough; bake at 350° for 40 minutes or until loaf is browned on bottom and sounds hollow when tapped. Remove from pan; place on a wire rack.

Brush with melted butter. Yield: 16 servings (serving size: 1 slice).

CALORIES 145 (20% from fat); FAT 3.3g (sat 0.9g, mono 1.7g, poly 0.5g); PROTEIN 4.7g; CARB 23.9g; FIBER 1.3g; CHOL 15mg; IRON 1.8mg; SODIUM 233mg; CALC 11mg

MAKE AHEAD

Three-Seed Epi

Traditionally known in France as *pain d'épi*, this beautiful bread gets its name from the wheat stalk it resembles. It works as an edible centerpiece. The recipe can also be made as rolls: Divide the dough into 14 equal portions, shape each into a ball, arrange on a baking sheet, and proceed as the recipe directs in Step 6.

  1 package dry yeast (about 2¼ teaspoons)
  1 cup warm water (100° to 110°)
  3 cups bread flour, divided
  1 tablespoon extravirgin olive oil
1¼ teaspoons salt
   Cooking spray
  1 teaspoon cornmeal
  1 teaspoon water
  1 large egg white, lightly beaten
  1 teaspoon poppy seeds
  1 teaspoon sesame seeds
  ½ teaspoon mustard seeds

1. Dissolve yeast in 1 cup warm water in a large bowl; let stand 5 minutes.
2. Lightly spoon flour into dry measuring cups, and level with a knife. Add 2¾ cups flour, oil, and salt to yeast mixture, and stir until a soft dough forms. Turn dough out onto a floured surface. Knead until smooth and elastic (about 8 minutes); add enough of remaining flour, 1 tablespoon at a time, to prevent dough from sticking to hands (dough will feel tacky).
3. Place dough in a large bowl coated with cooking spray, turning to coat top. Cover and let rise in a warm place (85°), free from drafts, 45 minutes or until doubled in size. (Gently press 2 fingers into dough. If indentation remains, dough has risen enough.)
4. Punch dough down. Cover and let rest 5 minutes. Shape dough into a 21-inch rope; place on a baking sheet sprinkled with cornmeal. (If your pan isn't

long enough, form rope into a slight semicircle until it fits.)
5. Using a pair of sharp scissors held almost horizontally, make diagonal cuts on both sides of loaf about three-fourths of the way through dough, leaving about 1½ inches between cuts. Cuts will form triangular pieces; gently pull pieces away from center on alternating sides.
6. Combine 1 teaspoon water and egg white; stir with a whisk. Combine poppy, sesame, and mustard seeds. Brush dough evenly with egg white mixture, and sprinkle evenly with seeds. Cover and let rise 30 minutes or until doubled in size.
7. Preheat oven to 400°.
8. Uncover dough, and bake at 400° for 20 minutes or until bread is browned on bottom and sounds hollow when tapped. Remove from pan, and cool on a wire rack. Yield: 14 servings (serving size: 1 slice).

CALORIES 121 (13% from fat); FAT 1.7g (sat 0.2g, mono 0.9g, poly 0.4g); PROTEIN 4.1g; CARB 21.8g; FIBER 0.9g; CHOL 0mg; IRON 1.5mg; SODIUM 214mg; CALC 11mg

MAKE AHEAD • FREEZABLE

Stout-Chocolate-Cherry Bread

An overnight sponge made with stout creates a rich, complex flavor that matches well with bittersweet chocolate and dried tart cherries. Because yeast feeds on the sugar in the beer, keep the sponge in the refrigerator to control the yeast's growth. A sprinkling of pearl sugar (available at gourmet stores and large supermarkets) adds texture.

4¼ cups bread flour, divided
  1 (12-ounce) bottle Guinness Stout
  1 package dry yeast (about 2¼ teaspoons)
  1 tablespoon granulated sugar
  1 teaspoon salt
  ½ cup dried tart cherries
  4 ounces bittersweet chocolate, coarsely chopped
   Cooking spray
  1 teaspoon water
  1 large egg white, lightly beaten
  1 teaspoon pearl sugar (optional)

1. Lightly spoon flour into dry measuring cups; level with a knife. Combine 2 cups flour, beer, and yeast in a large bowl, stirring with a whisk. Cover and refrigerate 8 hours or overnight.
2. Remove mixture from refrigerator; let stand 1 hour.
3. Add 2 cups flour, granulated sugar, and salt; stir until a soft dough forms. Turn dough out onto a floured surface. Knead until smooth and elastic (about 8 minutes); add enough of remaining flour, 1 tablespoon at a time, to prevent dough from sticking to hands (dough will feel tacky). Knead in cherries and chocolate.
4. Place dough in a large bowl coated with cooking spray, turning to coat top. Cover and let rise in a warm place (85°), free from drafts, 1 hour or until doubled in size. (Gently press 2 fingers into dough. If indentation remains, dough has risen enough.)
5. Punch dough down; cover and let rest 5 minutes. Shape dough into a 9-inch round; place on a baking sheet lined with parchment paper. Lightly coat dough with cooking spray. Cover and let rise 1 hour or until doubled in size.
6. Preheat oven to 350°.
7. Uncover dough. Combine water and egg white, stirring with a whisk, and brush over dough. Sprinkle dough with pearl sugar, if desired. Make a ¼-inch-deep cut across center of dough using a sharp knife.
8. Bake at 350° for 30 minutes or until bread is browned on bottom and sounds hollow when tapped. Remove from pan; cool on a wire rack. Yield: 20 servings (serving size: 1 slice).

CALORIES 156 (14% from fat); FAT 2.4g (sat 1.3g, mono 0.2g, poly 0.2g); PROTEIN 4.3g; CARB 28.1g; FIBER 1.3g; CHOL 0mg; IRON 1.4mg; SODIUM 121mg; CALC 5mg

dinner tonight

Get Comfortable

If you long for comfort food like Mom used to make, look no further.

Meat Loaf Menu

serves 4

Mini Meat Loaves

Steak house-style lettuce wedges*

Mashed potatoes

*Combine 2 tablespoons crumbled blue cheese, 1 tablespoon fat-free buttermilk, 2 tablespoons fat-free sour cream, 1 tablespoon light mayonnaise, ¾ teaspoon white vinegar, and ¼ teaspoon salt, stirring well with a whisk. Cut a small head of iceberg lettuce into 4 wedges; place 1 wedge on each of 4 plates. Drizzle each wedge with about 1½ tablespoons dressing.

Game Plan

1. While oven heats for meat loaves:
- Combine ketchup and mustard
- Chop onion

2. While meat loaves bake:
- Prepare lettuce wedges
- Prepare mashed potatoes

QUICK & EASY
Mini Meat Loaves

TOTAL TIME: 35 MINUTES

QUICK TIP: Using seasoned breadcrumbs rather than the plain, dry variety reduces the need for extra spices in the ingredient list.

½ cup ketchup
1½ tablespoons Dijon mustard
1 pound ground sirloin
¾ cup finely chopped onion
¼ cup seasoned breadcrumbs
½ teaspoon salt
½ teaspoon dried oregano
⅛ teaspoon black pepper
1 large egg, lightly beaten
Cooking spray

1. Preheat oven to 400°.
2. Combine ketchup and mustard, stirring well with a whisk. Reserve 2½ tablespoons ketchup mixture. Combine remaining ketchup mixture, beef, and next 6 ingredients in a large bowl, stirring to combine.
3. Divide beef mixture into 4 equal portions. Shape each portion into a 4 x 2½-inch loaf; place loaves on a jelly roll pan coated with cooking spray.
4. Spread about 2 teaspoons reserved ketchup mixture evenly over each loaf. Bake at 400° for 25 minutes or until done. Yield: 4 servings (serving size: 1 loaf).

CALORIES 255 (28% from fat); FAT 7.9g (sat 2.8g, mono 3.2g, poly 0.4g); PROTEIN 27.4g; CARB 15.7g; FIBER 0.9g; CHOL 120mg; IRON 2.7mg; SODIUM 944mg; CALC 31mg

---

Stuffed Peppers Menu

serves 4

Stuffed Peppers

Sautéed cabbage*

Sugar snap peas

*Heat 1 teaspoon olive oil and 1 teaspoon butter in a large nonstick skillet over medium-high heat. Add ½ cup thinly sliced onion; sauté 3 minutes. Add 4 cups shredded napa (Chinese) cabbage and ½ teaspoon salt; cook 3 minutes or until cabbage is tender, stirring frequently.

Game Plan

1. While rice cooks:
- Cut tops off peppers, and remove seeds and membranes
- Microwave peppers
- Chop onion and parsley for peppers
- Preheat oven

2. While meat mixture cooks:
- Grate cheese for peppers
- Bring wine mixture to a boil

3. While peppers bake:
- Prepare cabbage
- Prepare snap peas

Stuffed Peppers

TOTAL TIME: 45 MINUTES

QUICK TIP: Bring the sauce mixture to a boil before adding it to the dish.

1 (3½-ounce) bag boil-in-bag long-grain rice
4 red bell peppers
¾ pound ground sirloin
1 cup chopped onion
½ cup chopped fresh parsley
1 teaspoon paprika
½ teaspoon salt
⅛ teaspoon ground allspice
2 cups bottled tomato-and-basil pasta sauce (such as Classico), divided
½ cup (2 ounces) grated fresh Parmesan cheese
½ cup dry red wine
Cooking spray

1. Preheat oven to 450°.
2. Cook rice according to package directions, omitting salt and fat. Set aside.
3. While rice cooks, cut tops off bell peppers; reserve tops. Discard seeds and membranes. Place peppers, cut sides down, in an 8-inch square baking dish; cover with plastic wrap. Microwave at HIGH 2 minutes or until peppers are crisp-tender. Cool.
4. Heat a large nonstick skillet over medium-high heat. Add beef and next 5 ingredients; cook 4 minutes or until beef is lightly browned, stirring to crumble. Remove from heat. Add rice, ½ cup pasta sauce, and cheese to beef mixture, stirring to combine.
5. While beef cooks, combine 1½ cups pasta sauce and wine in a small saucepan; bring to a boil.
6. Spoon about ¾ cup beef mixture into each pepper. Place peppers in a 2-quart baking dish coated with cooking spray; add wine mixture to dish. Cover with foil.
7. Bake at 450° for 20 minutes. Uncover; bake an additional 5 minutes or until lightly browned. Serve peppers with sauce. Garnish with pepper tops. Yield: 4 servings (serving size: 1 stuffed pepper and ⅓ cup sauce).

CALORIES 347 (20% from fat); FAT 7.9g (sat 3.9g, mono 2.6g, poly 0.7g); PROTEIN 26.6g; CARB 39.9g; FIBER 4.6g; CHOL 55mg; IRON 4.1mg; SODIUM 747mg; CALC 284mg

Creamed Chicken Menu

serves 4

Creamed Chicken

Broiled tomatoes*

Hot cooked rice

*Combine 2 tablespoons seasoned bread-crumbs, 1 tablespoon grated Parmesan cheese, ¼ teaspoon salt, and ¼ teaspoon freshly ground black pepper, stirring to combine. Add 1½ teaspoons water and ½ teaspoon olive oil, stirring until moist. Halve 4 plum tomatoes lengthwise; sprinkle evenly with breadcrumb mixture. Place tomato halves, cut sides up, in a baking pan coated with cooking spray. Broil 2 minutes or until golden brown.

Game Plan

1. While water for rice comes to a boil and broiler heats for tomatoes:
- Chop chicken
- Prepare topping for tomatoes

2. While rice cooks:
- Prepare chicken
- Broil tomatoes

QUICK & EASY
Creamed Chicken

Serve over the rice.

TOTAL TIME: 25 MINUTES

QUICK TIP: If you can't find roasted skinless, boneless chicken breast, buy a whole roasted chicken and substitute 2¼ cups chopped cooked breast meat. Add the leftover chicken to soup, pasta, or a salad later in the week.

- ½ cup all-purpose flour
- 2¼ cups whole milk, divided
- 1 cup frozen green peas, thawed
- 2 teaspoons chopped fresh sage
- 1 teaspoon butter
- 1 (10-ounce) package roasted skinless, boneless chicken breast (such as Perdue Short Cuts), chopped
- 1 tablespoon fresh lemon juice
- ¼ teaspoon freshly ground black pepper
- Sage sprigs (optional)

1. Lightly spoon flour into a dry measuring cup, and level with a knife. Combine flour and ½ cup milk in a large saucepan over medium heat, stirring with a whisk until smooth. Stir in 1¾ cups milk. Cook 4 minutes or until thick, stirring constantly with a whisk.

2. Stir in peas, sage, butter, and chicken. Cook 2 minutes or until thoroughly heated. Remove from heat; stir in juice and pepper. Garnish with sage sprigs, if desired. Yield: 4 servings (serving size: about ¾ cup).

CALORIES 232 (23% from fat); FAT 6g (sat 3.6g, mono 1.8g, poly 0.4g); PROTEIN 20.9g; CARB 25.4g; FIBER 2.1g; CHOL 53mg; IRON 2.2mg; SODIUM 1,001mg; CALC 164mg

Turkey Tetrazzini Menu

serves 6

Turkey Tetrazzini

Green beans with almonds*

Garlic bread

*Trim 1 pound green beans; cook in boiling water 2 minutes or until crisp-tender. Drain. Toast 2 tablespoons sliced almonds in a nonstick skillet over medium-high heat 2 minutes, stirring frequently. Add 2 teaspoons butter to pan; cook 30 seconds or until lightly browned. Add green beans, ½ teaspoon salt, and ¼ teaspoon black pepper, tossing to coat.

Game Plan

1. While water for pasta and water for green beans come to a boil:
- Trim green beans
- Heat skillet for turkey

2. While pasta and beans cook:
- Cook turkey
- Cook mushroom mixture
- Preheat oven

3. While pasta mixture bakes:
- Prepare garlic bread
- Toast almonds
- Finish green beans

MAKE AHEAD • FREEZABLE
Turkey Tetrazzini

TOTAL TIME: 43 MINUTES

- 10 ounces uncooked vermicelli
- 2 teaspoons vegetable oil
- 1 pound turkey breast cutlets
- ¾ teaspoon onion powder, divided
- ½ teaspoon salt, divided
- ¼ teaspoon black pepper, divided
- 2 tablespoons dry sherry
- 2 (8-ounce) packages presliced mushrooms
- ¾ cup frozen green peas, thawed
- ¾ cup fat-free milk
- ⅔ cup fat-free sour cream
- ⅓ cup (about 1½ ounces) grated fresh Parmesan cheese
- 1 (10¾-ounce) can reduced-fat cream of chicken soup (such as Healthy Choice)
- Cooking spray
- ⅓ cup dry breadcrumbs
- 2 tablespoons butter, melted

1. Preheat oven to 450°.

2. Cook pasta according to package directions, omitting salt and fat. Drain.

3. Heat oil in a large nonstick skillet over medium-high heat. Sprinkle turkey with ½ teaspoon onion powder, ¼ teaspoon salt, and ⅛ teaspoon pepper. Add turkey to pan; cook 2 minutes on each side or until done. Remove turkey from pan.

4. Add ¼ teaspoon onion powder, sherry, and mushrooms to pan. Cover and cook 4 minutes or until mushrooms are tender.

5. Combine peas and next 4 ingredients in a large bowl. Chop turkey. Add ¼ teaspoon salt, ⅛ teaspoon pepper, pasta, turkey, and mushroom mixture to soup mixture, tossing gently to combine. Spoon mixture into a 13 x 9-inch baking dish coated with cooking spray.

6. Combine breadcrumbs and butter in a small dish, tossing to combine. Sprinkle breadcrumb mixture over pasta mixture. Bake at 450° for 12 minutes or until bubbly and thoroughly heated. Yield: 6 servings (serving size: about 1⅔ cups).

CALORIES 459 (29% from fat); FAT 14.8g (sat 5.9g, mono 4.4g, poly 2.8g); PROTEIN 30.5g; CARB 48.1g; FIBER 3.1g; CHOL 69mg; IRON 4mg; SODIUM 716mg; CALC 199mg

Get 'Em While They're Hot

Heat up your breakfast repertoire with whole-grain cereals studded with fruits, nuts, cheese, and spices.

Mention hot cereal, and many people immediately think of oatmeal. But a host of other grains—including wheat bran, pearl barley, oat bran, and cracked wheat—make great hot cereals. Add a handful of dried fruits and nuts along with a dash of seasonings, from brown sugar to chili powder, and you have some seriously satisfying cereals.

Muesli

Muesli, when soaked overnight in milk or yogurt, has the same creaminess and stick-to-your-ribs quality as hot cereal. If you prefer a crunchy consistency, just pour milk over the dry mix and eat it immediately. You can store the combined dry ingredients in a zip-top plastic bag. Make a single serving by adding ½ cup milk to ¾ cup cereal.

- 1 cup whole wheat flake cereal (such as Wheaties)
- 1 cup rolled oats
- ¾ cup slivered almonds
- ⅔ cup sweetened dried cranberries
- ⅔ cup chopped pitted dates
- ½ cup untoasted wheat germ
- ½ cup dried figs, chopped
- ¼ cup unsweetened coconut, toasted
- ¼ cup oat bran
- ¼ cup brown sugar
- 2 tablespoons sunflower seed kernels
- 1 teaspoon salt
- ¼ teaspoon ground ginger
- 3 cups 2% reduced-fat milk

1. Combine first 13 ingredients in a large bowl. Stir in milk.
2. Cover and refrigerate overnight. Yield: 7 servings (serving size: ¾ cup).

CALORIES 364 (29% from fat); FAT 11.8g (sat 2.6g, mono 4.9g, poly 3.2g); PROTEIN 12.9g; CARB 58g; FIBER 8.8g; CHOL 2.5mg; IRON 4.1mg; SODIUM 352mg; CALC 257mg

Five-Grain Cereal with Apricots, Apples, and Bananas

Store this dry cereal in a zip-top plastic bag in the freezer. To make the cereal a batch at a time, add ½ cup dry cereal mix to 1½ cups boiling water for each serving.

- ⅓ cup flaxseed
- 1¼ cups steel-cut (Irish) oats
- ⅔ cup dried apricots, coarsely chopped
- ⅔ cup dried apple, coarsely chopped
- ⅔ cup dried banana chips
- ½ cup cracked wheat
- ½ cup uncooked regular grits
- ½ cup oat bran
- ⅓ cup wheat bran
- ¾ teaspoon salt
- 13½ cups water

1. Place flaxseed in a spice or coffee grinder; process until coarsely ground. Combine flaxseed, oats, and next 8 ingredients in a large bowl, stirring well.
2. Bring water to a boil in a large saucepan. Add cereal; cover, reduce heat, and simmer 15 minutes, stirring occasionally. Uncover and cook 2 minutes or until thick, stirring constantly. Serve immediately. Yield: 9 servings (serving size: 1½ cups).

CALORIES 271 (22% from fat); FAT 6.5g (sat 2.5g, mono 1.1g, poly 2g); PROTEIN 8g; CARB 51g; FIBER 8.9g; CHOL 0mg; IRON 3.2mg; SODIUM 205mg; CALC 38mg

Southwestern Barley "Grits"

This savory cereal—imagine cheese grits infused with chiles—will take the chill off the coldest mornings.

- 1¼ cups uncooked pearl barley
- 3 cups water
- 3 cups 1% low-fat milk
- 1 tablespoon honey
- ¾ teaspoon salt
- 1 cup (4 ounces) shredded sharp Cheddar cheese
- 1 teaspoon chili powder
- 1 (4.5-ounce) can chopped green chiles, drained
- 6 tablespoons reduced-fat sour cream

Hot sauce (optional)

1. Place ⅓ cup barley in a blender; process until coarsely ground (about 15 to 20 seconds). Place ground barley in a large saucepan. Repeat procedure with remaining barley. Cook barley over medium heat 4 minutes or until toasted, stirring frequently.
2. Add water, milk, honey, and salt; bring to a boil. Reduce heat; simmer 25 minutes or until barley is soft, stirring frequently. Add cheese, chili powder, and chiles; cook 5 minutes or until cheese melts, stirring constantly. Top each serving with 1 tablespoon sour cream. Serve with hot sauce, if desired. Yield: 6 servings (serving size: 1 cup).

CALORIES 314 (29% from fat); FAT 10g (sat 6.1g, mono 2.2g, poly 0.5g); PROTEIN 13.8g; CARB 43.7g; FIBER 6.9g; CHOL 32mg; IRON 1.4mg; SODIUM 739mg; CALC 327mg

---

As Close as Oatmeal

Most whole grains are as close as your local supermarket, thanks to such national brands as Bob's Red Mill and Arrowhead Mills. You can also find whole grains in health-food and natural foods stores. Or order directly from Bob's Red Mill of Milwaukie, Oregon (800-349-2173 or www.bobsredmill.com).

Three-Grain Cereal with Sunflower Seeds and Fruit

Combine dry ingredients, and store them in a zip-top plastic bag in the freezer. Add ½ cup dry cereal mix to 1½ cups boiling water per serving. You can also microwave 3½ minutes at HIGH, stirring occasionally.

- ¼ cup flaxseed
- 1½ cups steel-cut (Irish) oats
- ½ cup golden raisins
- ½ cup dried sweet cherries
- ⅓ cup oat bran
- ⅓ cup untoasted wheat germ
- ⅓ cup sunflower seed kernels
- ¾ teaspoon salt
- ½ teaspoon ground cinnamon
- ½ teaspoon ground nutmeg
- 9 cups water

1. Place flaxseed in a spice or coffee grinder; process until coarsely ground. Combine flaxseed, oats, and next 8 ingredients in a large bowl, stirring well.
2. Bring water to a boil in a large saucepan; add cereal. Cover, reduce heat, and simmer 15 minutes; stir occasionally. Uncover and cook 2 minutes or until thick; stir constantly. Serve immediately. Yield: 6 servings (serving size: 1½ cups).

CALORIES 327 (25% from fat); FAT 9.1g (sat 1.1g, mono 2g, poly 4.8g); PROTEIN 11g; CARB 56g; FIBER 9.3g; CHOL 0mg; IRON 3.7mg; SODIUM 300mg; CALC 61mg

Fruited Breakfast Barley

Grind and toast the barley ahead of time; store in an airtight container.

- 1¼ cups uncooked pearl barley
- 5 cups water
- ⅓ cup packed brown sugar
- 1 teaspoon salt
- 1 cup 1% low-fat milk
- ½ cup raisins
- ½ cup dried apricots, quartered
- ½ cup slivered almonds, toasted and coarsely chopped

1. Place ⅓ cup barley in a blender; process until coarsely ground (about 15 to 20 seconds). Place ground barley in a large saucepan. Repeat procedure with remaining barley. Cook barley over medium heat 4 minutes or until toasted, stirring frequently.
2. Add water, sugar, and salt; bring to a boil. Reduce heat; simmer 25 minutes or until barley is soft, stirring frequently. Add milk; cook 5 minutes or until thick, stirring constantly. Stir in raisins, apricots, and almonds. Serve immediately. Yield: 6 servings (serving size: 1 cup).

CALORIES 329 (15% from fat); FAT 5.6g (sat 0.8g, mono 3.1g, poly 1.4g); PROTEIN 8.2g; CARB 65.8g; FIBER 9.6g; CHOL 2mg; IRON 2.6mg; SODIUM 425mg; CALC 105mg

for one

Supper and the Single Cook

Solo dinners made simple—and without endless leftovers.

Solo Supper Pointers

- Buy only what you need for a few days at a time—half a bunch of bananas, a single fish fillet, a bag of baby spinach.
- Use your ingredients wisely. If the red bell pepper you bought on Tuesday is looking a little deflated by Friday, roast it and use it as a pizza topping.
- Be wise. If you're craving mashed potatoes, just prepare a single serving; that way you aren't eating leftovers all week.

We know that one of the biggest frustrations of cooking for one is the little bits of this and that left lingering in the fridge—half a can of beans, 12 cherry tomatoes, half a package of shiitake mushrooms. That's why the meals we offer here connect throughout the week, utilizing ingredients left over from a previous night's meal. With recipes as flavorful as these, you may decide that they're too good not to share. That's the best part: Should the meal plan change from solo to duo, just double the ingredient quantities.

Mini Red Pepper-Mushroom Pizza

Although you only use half of the bell pepper in this pizza, go ahead and roast both halves; use the other half in a sandwich.

- ½ red bell pepper
- ½ teaspoon fresh lemon juice
- 1 garlic clove, minced
- Cooking spray
- ½ cup thinly sliced shiitake mushroom caps
- 1 tablespoon sliced shallots
- ½ teaspoon balsamic vinegar
- 1 (6-inch) Italian cheese-flavored pizza crust (such as Boboli)
- 1 tablespoon thinly sliced fresh basil
- ¾ cup torn spinach
- 6 tablespoons (1½ ounces) shredded fresh mozzarella cheese
- ¼ teaspoon freshly ground black pepper
- Dash of salt

1. Preheat broiler.
2. Place bell pepper half, skin side up, on a foil-lined baking sheet; flatten with hand. Broil 15 minutes or until blackened. Place in a zip-top plastic bag; seal. Let stand 10 minutes. Peel and finely chop. Combine bell pepper, juice, and garlic, stirring well.
3. Preheat oven to 450°.
4. Heat a small nonstick skillet coated with cooking spray over medium-high heat. Add mushrooms and shallots; sauté 2 minutes or until tender. Remove from heat; stir in vinegar.
5. Place crust on a baking sheet coated with cooking spray. Spread bell pepper mixture evenly over crust, leaving a ½-inch border. Sprinkle basil evenly over bell pepper mixture; top with spinach. Spoon mushroom mixture evenly over spinach; sprinkle with cheese.
6. Bake at 450° for 4 minutes or until cheese melts. Sprinkle with black pepper and salt. Yield: 1 serving.

CALORIES 467 (30% from fat); FAT 15.5g (sat 8.1g, mono 5.4g, poly 1.5g); PROTEIN 22.4g; CARB 58.7g; FIBER 2.6g; CHOL 33mg; IRON 4.8mg; SODIUM 829mg; CALC 589mg

Quick Coconut Soup

Serve this soup with Asian Cucumber Salad (recipe on page 39). Use the remaining canned coconut milk as a marinade for fish or to boost the flavor of rice or couscous.

- 2 teaspoons chopped peeled fresh ginger
- 1 teaspoon fish sauce
- ½ teaspoon minced garlic
- ½ teaspoon grated lime rind
- ¼ teaspoon chile paste with garlic
- 3 ounces medium shrimp, peeled and deveined
- 1 (14-ounce) can fat-free, less-sodium chicken broth
- ¾ cup light coconut milk
- 1 tablespoon chopped green onions
- 1½ teaspoons chopped fresh cilantro
- 1 teaspoon fresh lime juice
- ⅓ cup hot cooked basmati rice

1. Combine first 7 ingredients in a medium saucepan; bring to a boil. Reduce heat; simmer, uncovered, 10 minutes.
2. Remove from heat; stir in coconut milk, onions, chopped cilantro, and lime juice. Spoon rice into a soup bowl; ladle soup over rice. Yield: 1 serving (serving size: about 2½ cups).

CALORIES 340 (28% from fat); FAT 10.7g (sat 6.3g, mono 0.6g, poly 0.7g); PROTEIN 30g; CARB 27.3g; FIBER 1.1g; CHOL 129mg; IRON 7.3mg; SODIUM 995mg; CALC 92mg

Chicken with Black Bean Salsa

Serve this as is, or for chicken fajitas.

SALSA:
- ½ cup canned black beans, rinsed and drained
- ¼ cup fresh corn kernels
- 1 tablespoon chopped red onion
- 1 teaspoon chopped seeded jalapeño pepper
- 1 teaspoon fresh lime juice
- 1 teaspoon extravirgin olive oil
- ⅛ teaspoon salt
- ⅛ teaspoon ground coriander
- 4 grape or cherry tomatoes, quartered

CHICKEN:
- 1 teaspoon butter
- Cooking spray
- 1 (6-ounce) skinless, boneless chicken breast half
- Dash of salt
- Dash of freshly ground black pepper
- Lime slice (optional)

1. To prepare salsa, combine first 9 ingredients, tossing well to combine.
2. To prepare chicken, heat butter in a small nonstick skillet coated with cooking spray over medium-high heat. Sprinkle chicken with dash of salt and black pepper. Add chicken to pan; cook 6 minutes on each side or until done. Serve with salsa and lime slice, if desired. Yield: 1 serving (serving size: 1 chicken breast half and ¾ cup salsa).

CALORIES 425 (26% from fat); FAT 12.2g (sat 3.7g, mono 5.1g, poly 2.3g); PROTEIN 48.4g; CARB 29.1g; FIBER 9.2g; CHOL 109mg; IRON 4.6mg; SODIUM 867mg; CALC 69mg

Garlic Mashed Red Potatoes

If you like your mashed potatoes smooth, a hand mixer works well. Otherwise, a potato masher or the back of a spoon or fork will do the trick.

- ½ pound small red potatoes, quartered
- 1 teaspoon butter
- 1 garlic clove, minced
- 3 tablespoons fat-free milk
- ⅛ teaspoon salt

1. Place potatoes in a small saucepan, and cover with water. Bring to a boil. Reduce heat; simmer 13 minutes or until tender. Drain.
2. Combine butter and minced garlic in a medium microwave-safe bowl. Microwave at HIGH 30 seconds or until butter melts. Add potatoes, milk, and salt. Mash mixture with a potato masher or fork to desired consistency. Yield: 1 serving (serving size: ¾ cup).

CALORIES 208 (17% from fat); FAT 3.9g (sat 2.5g, mono 1.2g, poly 0.2g); PROTEIN 7.9g; CARB 43.1g; FIBER 4.7g; CHOL 11mg; IRON 1.7mg; SODIUM 357mg; CALC 94mg

Everything-But-the-Kitchen-Sink Frittata

Here's a great way to use up leftovers—you can swap out any beans, cheese, or vegetable in this dish.

- ½ cup (1-inch) sliced asparagus
- 2 tablespoons fat-free milk
- ⅛ teaspoon salt
- Dash of freshly ground black pepper
- 4 large egg whites
- 1 large egg
- Cooking spray
- ¼ cup canned black beans, rinsed and drained
- 1 tablespoon chopped red onion
- 2 teaspoons chopped fresh basil
- 2 tablespoons shredded fresh mozzarella or Asiago cheese
- 2 grape or cherry tomatoes, quartered

1. Preheat broiler.
2. Place sliced asparagus in a small microwave-safe bowl; cover. Microwave at HIGH 20 seconds.
3. Combine milk and next 4 ingredients, stirring with a whisk.
4. Heat an 8-inch nonstick skillet coated with cooking spray over medium-high heat. Add beans and onion; sauté 30 seconds. Add egg mixture; reduce heat to medium, and cook 1 minute. Sprinkle asparagus and basil evenly over egg mixture; cook 1 minute. Sprinkle with cheese.
5. Wrap handle of pan with foil. Broil 4 minutes or until top is set and cheese melts. Sprinkle with tomatoes. Yield: 1 serving.

CALORIES 278 (29% from fat); FAT 8.9g (sat 3.7g, mono 2g, poly 1.3g); PROTEIN 29.5g; CARB 18.7g; FIBER 5.8g; CHOL 224mg; IRON 3.1mg; SODIUM 749mg; CALC 193mg

Filet Mignon with Lemon Asparagus

This simple steak gets its flavor from the smoked paprika. Look for it in Latin markets, or order it through www.tienda.com. You can use Hungarian sweet paprika, but the flavor won't be as deep.

  1 (4-ounce) beef tenderloin steak, trimmed (1 inch thick)
  ⅛ teaspoon salt
  ⅛ teaspoon hot smoked paprika
Dash of freshly ground black pepper
  4 ounces asparagus spears
  1 teaspoon fresh lemon juice
Dash of salt

1. Heat a small, heavy skillet over medium-high heat. Sprinkle both sides of steak with ⅛ teaspoon salt, paprika, and pepper. Add steak to pan, and cook 3 minutes on each side or until desired degree of doneness.
2. Snap off tough ends of asparagus. Steam asparagus, covered, 3 minutes. Drizzle juice evenly over asparagus, and sprinkle with dash of salt. Serve with steak. Yield: 1 serving.

CALORIES 219 (42% from fat); FAT 10.3g (sat 4.1g, mono 4g, poly 0.6g); PROTEIN 26.2g; CARB 5.7g; FIBER 2.4g; CHOL 70mg; IRON 4.2mg; SODIUM 503mg; CALC 32mg

Asian Cucumber Salad

This salad gets even better the longer it marinates. So make a double batch, eat it once with Quick Coconut Soup (recipe on page 38), and have it again with a stir-fry or fried rice that uses the extra rice you prepared with the coconut soup.

  1 cup thinly sliced peeled English cucumber
  ¼ cup vertically sliced red onion
  1 tablespoon rice wine vinegar
  ½ teaspoon sugar
  ½ teaspoon fish sauce
  ⅛ teaspoon chile paste with garlic

1. Combine all ingredients, tossing well to combine. Cover salad, and chill at least 30 minutes. Yield: 1 serving (serving size: 1½ cups).

CALORIES 41 (4% from fat); FAT 0.2g (sat 0g, mono 0g, poly 0.1g); PROTEIN 1.2g; CARB 8.1g; FIBER 0.7g; CHOL 0mg; IRON 0.4mg; SODIUM 269mg; CALC 22mg

Penne with Shiitakes, Olives, and Asiago

Here, we've used the remaining shiitake mushrooms from Mini Red Pepper-Mushroom Pizza (recipe on page 37). They add richness to this pasta dish, but any other type of mushrooms will work, too.

Cooking spray
  ½ cup thinly sliced shiitake mushroom caps
  1 tablespoon chopped shallots
  1 garlic clove, minced
  1½ cups torn spinach
  1 tablespoon chopped fresh basil
  1 teaspoon rice wine vinegar
  ½ cup fat-free, less-sodium chicken broth
  2 tablespoons sliced ripe olives
  1½ cups hot cooked pasta (about ¾ cup uncooked tube-shaped pasta)
  1½ teaspoons extravirgin olive oil
  ⅛ teaspoon freshly ground black pepper
Dash of salt
  ¼ cup (1 ounce) grated Asiago cheese

1. Heat a small nonstick skillet coated with cooking spray over medium-high heat. Add mushrooms, shallots, and garlic, and sauté 2 minutes or until mushrooms are tender. Stir in spinach, basil, and vinegar, and cook 1 minute or until spinach wilts, stirring frequently. Add broth and olives; cook 15 seconds.
2. Combine mushroom mixture, pasta, oil, pepper, and salt, tossing gently to coat. Spoon pasta mixture onto a plate; top with cheese. Yield: 1 serving (serving size: 2 cups).

CALORIES 543 (30% from fat); FAT 18g (sat 6.4g, mono 8.5g, poly 1.7g); PROTEIN 23.4g; CARB 72g; FIBER 5g; CHOL 26mg; IRON 5.8mg; SODIUM 636mg; CALC 363mg

reader recipes

Salsa with an Edge

A good knife and fresh produce are all you need for this sharp salsa.

Corey Milligan invented this salsa while working as a rafting guide in Jackson Hole, Wyoming. But it wasn't until he founded his own company—New West Knifeworks in Ventura, California—that he truly began to appreciate its versatility. Corey uses this chopping-intensive salsa recipe to put his hand-crafted blades to the test.

New West Salsa

Corey Milligan makes many variations of this recipe. "I'll change the fruit from apple to peach to mango. And the salsa is good on lots of things or by itself with chips." Corey is particularly fond of it with black bean tacos or shrimp with goat cheese.

  2 cups chopped plum tomato (about 3 tomatoes)
  1 cup chopped Granny Smith apple
  ½ cup chopped cucumber
  ½ cup fresh corn kernels
  ½ cup chopped red bell pepper
  ¼ cup chopped green onions
  ¼ cup chopped red onion
  2½ tablespoons chopped fresh cilantro
  1½ tablespoons fresh lime juice
  1 tablespoon chopped seeded jalapeño pepper
  1 tablespoon balsamic vinegar
  1½ teaspoons sugar
  ¾ teaspoon salt
  ½ teaspoon freshly ground black pepper

1. Combine all ingredients, stirring well. Serve at room temperature or chilled. Yield: 4½ cups (serving size: ½ cup).

CALORIES 33 (8% from fat); FAT 0.3g (sat 0.1g, mono 0.1g, poly 0.1g); PROTEIN 0.8g; CARB 7.7g; FIBER 1.4g; CHOL 0mg; IRON 0.3mg; SODIUM 196mg; CALC 8mg

Classic Apple and Blue Cheese Salad

"I first tasted this salad at a luncheon given by a friend of mine. I love the flavor combination of tart-sweet apples, crunchy walnuts, and pungent blue cheese."

—Joy Beck, Cincinnati, Ohio

  2 tablespoons fresh lemon juice
  2 teaspoons sugar
  2 teaspoons Dijon mustard
1½ teaspoons extravirgin olive oil
  ¼ teaspoon salt
  ¼ teaspoon freshly ground black pepper
  6 cups torn Bibb lettuce leaves (about 2 heads)
  1 cup chopped Granny Smith apple
  2 tablespoons crumbled blue cheese
  2 tablespoons chopped green onions
  1 tablespoon chopped toasted walnuts

1. Combine first 6 ingredients in a large bowl, stirring with a whisk. Add lettuce and remaining ingredients, tossing gently to coat. Yield: 6 servings (serving size: about ¾ cup).

CALORIES 54 (48% from fat); FAT 2.9g (sat 0.6g, mono 1.2g, poly 0.8g); PROTEIN 1.7g; CARB 6.5g; FIBER 1.3g; CHOL 1.8mg; IRON 0.3mg; SODIUM 176mg; CALC 35mg

Spanish Rice with Shrimp

"We enjoy this healthy dish immensely and wanted to share this recipe with other *Cooking Light* readers."

—Laura Olken, Standish, Maine

  1 tablespoon olive oil
  1 cup chopped onion
  2 garlic cloves, minced
  5 cups chopped plum tomato (about 7 tomatoes)
  1 cup chopped green bell pepper
  ½ cup chopped celery
  2 cups water
  1 cup uncooked medium-grain rice
  ½ teaspoon salt
  1 pound medium shrimp, peeled and deveined

1. Heat oil in a large nonstick skillet over medium-high heat. Add onion and garlic; sauté 4 minutes. Add tomato, pepper, and celery; sauté 6 minutes.
2. Stir in water, rice, and salt, and bring to a boil. Cover, reduce heat, and simmer 15 minutes.
3. Add shrimp; cook 4 minutes or until shrimp are done. Yield: 4 servings (serving size: 1¾ cups).

CALORIES 378 (15% from fat); FAT 6.1g (sat 1g, mono 2.9g, poly 1.3g); PROTEIN 28.2g; CARB 51.6g; FIBER 3.6g; CHOL 173mg; IRON 5.7mg; SODIUM 487mg; CALC 89mg

Smoky Black Bean and Vegetable Soup

"Canned vegetable broth saves time, and the soup freezes well."

—Lisa Rebelli, Oakland, California

  1 (7-ounce) can chipotle chiles in adobo sauce
Cooking spray
  2 cups coarsely chopped onion
  1 cup chopped carrot
  ¾ cup thinly sliced celery
  4 garlic cloves, minced
  2 teaspoons ground cumin
  2 teaspoons dried basil
  1 teaspoon dried oregano
  1 teaspoon chili powder
  2 bay leaves
  2 cups water
  3 (15-ounce) cans black beans, rinsed and drained
  2 (14½-ounce) cans vegetable broth
  2 (14.5-ounce) cans no-salt-added plum tomatoes, undrained and chopped
  ½ cup plain fat-free yogurt
  ¼ cup chopped fresh cilantro
  8 lime wedges

1. Remove 2 chiles from can; reserve remaining chiles and sauce for another use. Finely chop chiles. Heat a large Dutch oven coated with cooking spray over medium-high heat. Add onion, carrot, celery, and garlic; sauté 8 minutes or until onion and carrot are tender. Stir in chiles, cumin, and next 4 ingredients; cook 1 minute, stirring constantly. Stir in water, beans, broth, and tomatoes; bring to a boil. Partially cover, reduce heat, and simmer 2 hours, stirring occasionally.
2. Remove from heat; discard bay leaves. Place 3 cups soup mixture in a blender. Let stand 5 minutes; process until smooth. Return puréed mixture to pan, stirring to combine. Ladle 1¼ cups soup into each of 8 bowls; top each serving with 1 tablespoon yogurt and 1½ teaspoons cilantro. Serve with lime wedges. Yield: 8 servings.

CALORIES 162 (6% from fat); FAT 1g (sat 0.1g, mono 0.1g, poly 0.1g); PROTEIN 10.1g; CARB 36.9g; FIBER 10.9g; CHOL 0mg; IRON 3.8mg; SODIUM 740mg; CALC 145mg

Fettuccine with Bacon and Roasted Red Peppers

"Sometimes I substitute prosciutto for the bacon."

—Kerry Caparco, Charlestone, Rhode Island

  1 (7-ounce) bottle roasted red bell peppers, drained
  2 bacon slices (raw), chopped
  1 cup sliced onion
  3 garlic cloves, minced
  1 cup frozen green peas, thawed
  ¼ cup fat-free, less-sodium chicken broth
  4 cups hot cooked fettuccine (about 8 ounces uncooked pasta)
  2 tablespoons grated fresh Parmesan cheese
  ½ teaspoon salt
  ¼ teaspoon black pepper

1. Cut bell peppers into ¼-inch-wide strips.
2. Cook bacon in a large Dutch oven over medium-high heat until crisp (about 2 minutes). Add onion and garlic; sauté 1 minute. Add bell peppers, peas, and broth; simmer 1 minute. Stir in pasta, cheese, salt, and black pepper. Yield: 4 servings (serving size: 1⅓ cups).

CALORIES 332 (25% from fat); FAT 9.4g (sat 3.1g, mono 3.3g, poly 1.1g); PROTEIN 12.7g; CARB 51.3g; FIBER 5.2g; CHOL 10mg; IRON 2.9mg; SODIUM 804mg; CALC 68mg

Sausage and Peppers

"This is my lightened version of a favorite dish. I usually have all of these ingredients on hand, and I can make the entire dish in the time it takes to boil the water and cook the pasta."

—Heather Godine, York, Pennsylvania

Cooking spray
6 (4-ounce) links turkey Italian
    sausage
2 cups (¼-inch strips) green bell
    pepper
1 cup (¼-inch strips) red bell
    pepper
1 cup (¼-inch strips) yellow bell
    pepper
6 garlic cloves, thinly sliced
1 (26-ounce) bottle fat-free
    pasta sauce (such as Healthy
    Choice)
½ cup (2 ounces) shredded
    part-skim mozzarella cheese
6 cups hot cooked penne (about
    ¾ pound uncooked tube-shaped
    pasta)
2 tablespoons grated fresh Parmesan
    cheese

1. Heat a large nonstick skillet coated with cooking spray over medium-high heat. Add sausage to pan; cook 8 minutes or until lightly browned, turning occasionally. Remove from pan; cool slightly. Cut sausage into ½-inch-thick slices.
2. Wipe pan with paper towels; recoat with cooking spray. Place pan over medium-high heat. Add peppers; sauté 6 minutes. Add sausage; sauté 2 minutes. Add garlic; sauté 2 minutes. Add sauce; bring to a simmer. Reduce heat; cook 5 minutes, stirring occasionally. Remove from heat.
3. Add mozzarella, stirring until melted. Place 1 cup pasta in each of 6 shallow bowls; spoon about 1 cup sausage mixture over each serving. Sprinkle each serving with 1 teaspoon Parmesan. Yield: 6 servings.

CALORIES 483 (26% from fat); FAT 13.9g (sat 4.8g, mono 3.2g, poly 3.7g); PROTEIN 33g; CARB 55.7g; FIBER 5g; CHOL 102mg; IRON 3.4mg; SODIUM 1,150mg; CALC 158mg

inspired vegetarian

Blast from the Past

Vegetarian cooking has changed over the years. Here are a few traditional dishes that have been updated with flavor, freshness, and seasonal produce.

Miso Vegetable Noodle Bowl

Asian vegetables are barely cooked in simmering broth so they remain crisp and their vibrant colors stay intact. Yellow miso, milder than red, keeps the flavor mellow.

4 ounces uncooked udon noodles
    (thick, round fresh Japanese wheat
    noodles) or spaghetti
3 cups water
3 cups vegetable broth
1½ cups frozen shelled edamame,
    thawed
1 cup thinly sliced napa (Chinese)
    cabbage
1 cup (⅛-inch) diagonally cut
    carrot
1 cup thinly sliced red bell pepper
1 cup diagonally cut snow peas
1 cup thinly sliced shiitake
    mushroom caps
½ cup finely chopped green onions
2 tablespoons fresh lime juice
1 tablespoon minced peeled fresh
    ginger
3 tablespoons yellow miso (soybean
    paste)
2 teaspoons chile paste with garlic
2 tablespoons minced fresh
    cilantro
Lime wedges (optional)

1. Cook noodles in a Dutch oven according to package directions, omitting salt and fat. Rinse with cold water; drain.
2. Bring water and broth to a boil in pan. Add noodles, edamame, and next 6 ingredients. Remove from heat.

3. Combine juice, ginger, miso, and chile paste, stirring with a whisk; stir into soup. Sprinkle with cilantro; serve with lime wedges, if desired. Yield: 6 servings (serving size: 1½ cups).

CALORIES 214 (25% from fat); FAT 5.9g (sat 0.5g, mono 1.2g, poly 2.7g); PROTEIN 14.2g; CARB 29.5g; FIBER 5.8g; CHOL 0mg; IRON 3.6mg; SODIUM 948mg; CALC 158mg

Firecracker Vegetable Roast

Indian flavors meld with Italian herbs to season vegetables. Unless you prefer milder food, leave the seeds in the jalapeño so the dish befits its name.

1 cup loosely packed fresh basil
    leaves
¼ cup loosely packed fresh mint
    leaves
2 tablespoons olive oil
1 tablespoon low-sodium soy
    sauce
1 teaspoon dried Italian seasoning
1 teaspoon curry powder
½ teaspoon salt
3 garlic cloves, halved
1 jalapeño pepper, halved
2 cups cauliflower florets
2 cups broccoli florets
1½ cups thinly sliced fennel bulb
    (about 1 small bulb)
1 cup red bell pepper strips
1 cup yellow bell pepper strips
1 cup thinly sliced red onion
Cooking spray
1 tomato, cut into 12 wedges
1 (15½-ounce) can chickpeas
    (garbanzo beans), rinsed and
    drained
6 cups hot cooked basmati rice

1. Preheat oven to 450°.
2. Place first 9 ingredients in a food processor; process until smooth.
3. Combine basil mixture, cauliflower, and next 5 ingredients, tossing well to coat. Arrange vegetable mixture on a jelly roll pan coated with cooking spray.
4. Bake at 450° for 15 minutes or until lightly browned. Add tomato and *Continued*

chickpeas; bake an additional 5 minutes. Serve over rice. Yield: 6 servings (serving size: 1⅓ cups vegetable mixture and 1 cup rice).

CALORIES 343 (17% from fat); FAT 6.4g (sat 0.8g, mono 3.9g, poly 1.3g); PROTEIN 9.1g; CARB 63.2g; FIBER 6.5g; CHOL 0mg; IRON 4mg; SODIUM 430mg; CALC 92mg

Tofu and Swiss Chard Stacks

Marinated, broiled tofu and a spicy chard mixture are layered for free-form individual lasagnas. Use water-packed tofu; its firm texture holds up well. Serve with fried rice that's been tossed with steamed edamame.

TOFU:
   2 tablespoons low-sodium soy
      sauce
   1 tablespoon mirin (sweet rice wine)
   2 teaspoons rice vinegar
   1 teaspoon honey
   1 (12.3-ounce) package
      water-packed reduced-fat
      firm tofu, drained
Cooking spray

GREENS:
   1 teaspoon dark sesame oil
   1 cup thinly sliced shiitake
      mushroom caps
1½ teaspoons minced peeled fresh
      ginger
   ¼ teaspoon crushed red pepper
   2 garlic cloves, minced
   4 cups thinly sliced Swiss chard
   ½ teaspoon sesame seeds, toasted
   2 teaspoons low-sodium soy
      sauce

1. To prepare tofu, combine first 4 ingredients, stirring with a whisk. Cut tofu lengthwise into 4 equal slices. Carefully place tofu in an 11 x 7-inch baking dish. Pour soy sauce mixture over tofu. Cover and refrigerate 30 minutes, carefully turning once.
2. Preheat broiler.
3. Remove tofu from dish; discard marinade. Place tofu on a baking sheet coated with cooking spray. Broil 10 minutes on each side or until tofu is lightly browned.

4. To prepare greens, heat oil in a large nonstick skillet over medium heat. Add mushrooms, ginger, pepper, and garlic; cook 1 minute, stirring frequently. Add chard and sesame seeds; cook 3 minutes or until chard wilts, stirring frequently. Stir in 2 teaspoons soy sauce.
5. Place ¼ cup chard mixture on each of 2 plates; top each serving with 1 tofu slice. Repeat layers with remaining chard and tofu. Yield: 2 servings.

CALORIES 155 (29% from fat); FAT 5g (sat 0.4g, mono 1.2g, poly 2.8g); PROTEIN 13.8g; CARB 12.4g; FIBER 2.1g; CHOL 0mg; IRON 3.9mg; SODIUM 754mg; CALC 130mg

Mashed Potatoes with Zucchini Ragoût

Mashed potatoes laced with spinach and infused with olive oil are topped with a savory vegetable ragoût. Black olive paste lends a salty, meaty quality to the ragoût.

POTATOES:
   2 pounds cubed Yukon gold
      potato
   2 tablespoons extravirgin olive
      oil
   ½ teaspoon salt
   ¼ teaspoon freshly ground black
      pepper
   ¾ cup 2% reduced-fat milk
   4 cups torn spinach
   ½ cup minced green onions

RAGOÛT:
   2 teaspoons extravirgin olive oil
1½ cups thinly sliced onion
   1 teaspoon dried oregano
   2 garlic cloves, minced
   1 pound cremini mushrooms,
      quartered
   3 cups (½-inch) cubed zucchini
   2 cups water
   ¼ cup chopped fresh basil
   2 teaspoons black olive paste
   ½ teaspoon salt
   ¼ teaspoon freshly ground black
      pepper
   1 (14.5-ounce) can diced tomatoes,
      undrained
   6 tablespoons (1½ ounces) grated
      fresh Parmesan cheese

1. To prepare potatoes, place potatoes in a large saucepan; cover with water. Bring to a boil. Reduce heat; simmer 15 minutes or until tender. Drain.
2. Return potatoes to pan; add 2 tablespoons oil, ½ teaspoon salt, and ¼ teaspoon pepper. Mash mixture with a potato masher to desired consistency. Cover and keep warm.
3. Heat milk over medium heat in a large nonstick skillet to 180° or until tiny bubbles form around edge (do not boil). Stir in spinach; cook 1 minute or until spinach wilts. Add milk mixture and green onions to potato mixture, stirring until well combined.
4. To prepare ragoût, wipe skillet with paper towels. Heat 2 teaspoons oil in pan over medium heat. Add sliced onion, oregano, and garlic; cook 5 minutes or until lightly browned, stirring frequently. Add mushrooms; cook 7 minutes or until mushrooms are tender, stirring frequently. Add zucchini; cook 2 minutes, stirring frequently.
5. Stir in water and next 5 ingredients; simmer, uncovered, 15 minutes, stirring occasionally. Serve ragoût over potatoes, and sprinkle with cheese. Yield: 6 servings (serving size: about 1 cup potatoes, 1 cup ragoût, and 1 tablespoon cheese).

CALORIES 307 (28% from fat); FAT 9.6g (sat 2.4g, mono 5.2g, poly 0.7g); PROTEIN 12.1g; CARB 45.1g; FIBER 8.1g; CHOL 7mg; IRON 3.7mg; SODIUM 703mg; CALC 189mg

A Cross-Cultural Affair Menu
serves 8

Root Vegetable Tagine with Lentils

Sautéed spinach with garlic

Ginger-mango lassi*

*Place 3 cups chopped peeled ripe mango, ½ cup water, ⅓ cup sugar, 3 tablespoons chopped peeled fresh ginger, 1 tablespoon fresh lemon juice, and 1 (16-ounce) carton low-fat vanilla yogurt in a blender; process until smooth.

Root Vegetable Tagine with Lentils

This version of a Moroccan tagine features lentils with aromatic spices and winter vegetables. Although the ingredient list is long, the preparation is simple.

SPICE BLEND:
½ teaspoon salt
½ teaspoon ground cumin
½ teaspoon paprika
¼ teaspoon ground cinnamon
¼ teaspoon ground turmeric
¼ teaspoon curry powder
¼ teaspoon black pepper
⅛ teaspoon ground red pepper
⅛ teaspoon ground allspice

TAGINE:
1 tablespoon olive oil
3 cups chopped green cabbage
2 cups (1-inch) cubed peeled sweet potato (about 12 ounces)
1 cup coarsely chopped onion
1 cup (1-inch) slices parsnip
1 cup (1-inch) slices carrot
1 cup (1-inch) cubed peeled turnip
1 cup dried lentils
½ cup chopped dried apricots
1 tablespoon minced peeled fresh ginger
2 teaspoons grated lemon rind
2 (14½-ounce) cans vegetable broth
1 (14.5-ounce) can diced tomatoes, undrained
1 tablespoon fresh lemon juice
6 cups hot cooked couscous

1. To prepare spice blend, combine first 9 ingredients.
2. To prepare tagine, heat oil in a Dutch oven over medium heat. Add cabbage and next 8 ingredients; cook 3 minutes, stirring frequently. Stir in spice blend; cook 1 minute, stirring constantly. Add rind, broth, and tomatoes; bring to a boil.
3. Reduce heat; simmer, uncovered, 40 minutes or until lentils are tender. Stir in juice. Serve over couscous. Yield: 8 servings (serving size: 1¼ cups tagine and ¾ cup couscous).

CALORIES 343 (7% from fat); FAT 2.7g (sat 0.3g, mono 1.3g, poly 0.4g); PROTEIN 13.4g; CARB 68.4g; FIBER 10.3g; CHOL 0mg; IRON 3.1mg; SODIUM 691mg; CALC 85mg

happy endings

Desserts By the Bunch

No matter the season, this fruit is ripe for dessert.

The only criteria for selecting bananas is the color of the peel. Green-tipped bananas—which are perfectly suited for baking in recipes such as our Banana-Mango Crisp (recipe below)—signal a firm flesh and slightly green flavor. A skin that has turned completely yellow or has begun to speckle brown will yield a creamy, mellow sweet banana.

Because they tend to ripen better off the tree, bananas are picked and shipped while still green. Often still underripe in the supermarket, they may need a few more days at room temperature to ripen completely. You can slow the ripening process by storing bananas in the refrigerator. The peels may darken a bit, but the insides will stay pale. Should you find yourself with a bunch of overripe bananas and no time to make banana bread, freeze them peeled on a tray, then transfer them to freezer bags and store them for future smoothies and shakes.

MAKE AHEAD
Banana-Mango Crisp

Green bananas work well in this recipe. Serve warm or at room temperature.

5 cups sliced banana (about 6 bananas)
3 cups chopped peeled mango (about 3 mangos)
¼ cup dark rum
Cooking spray
¼ cup all-purpose flour
¾ cup regular oats
½ cup flaked sweetened coconut, toasted
6 tablespoons brown sugar
3 tablespoons chopped crystallized ginger
¼ teaspoon salt
3 tablespoons chilled butter, cut into small pieces

1. Preheat oven to 375°.
2. Combine first 3 ingredients in an 11 x 7-inch baking dish coated with cooking spray. Lightly spoon flour into a dry measuring cup; level with a knife. Combine flour, oats, coconut, sugar, ginger, and salt in a bowl; cut in butter with a pastry blender or 2 knives until mixture resembles coarse meal.
3. Add ⅓ cup oat mixture to banana mixture, stirring gently to combine. Sprinkle remaining oat mixture over banana mixture.
4. Bake at 375° for 30 minutes or until lightly browned and bubbly. Yield: 8 servings (serving size: about 1 cup).

CALORIES 276 (23% from fat); FAT 6.9g (sat 4.3g, mono 1.5g, poly 0.5g); PROTEIN 3g; CARB 50g; FIBER 4.4g; CHOL 12mg; IRON 1.2mg; SODIUM 134mg; CALC 27mg

STAFF FAVORITE
Banana Pudding

This pudding has a mile-high meringue and will easily feed a crowd. Although we think using a vanilla bean infuses superior flavor, you can substitute ½ teaspoon vanilla extract; stir it into the cooked custard.

⅔ cup all-purpose flour
2 cups sugar, divided
½ teaspoon salt
4 cups 2% reduced-fat milk
1 (4-inch) vanilla bean, split lengthwise
2 large eggs, lightly beaten
8 large egg whites
80 vanilla wafers (about 1 [12-ounce] box)
5 cups sliced banana (about 6 bananas)

1. Preheat oven to 325°.
2. Lightly spoon flour into a dry measuring cup; level with a knife. Combine flour, 1¼ cups sugar, and salt in a large saucepan; stir with a whisk. Gradually add milk; stir until smooth. Scrape seeds from vanilla bean; add seeds and bean to milk mixture.
3. Cook over medium heat 12 minutes or until thick and bubbly, stirring constantly.
4. Place eggs in a large bowl, and gradually add hot milk mixture, stirring
Continued

constantly. Place mixture in pan; cook over medium heat 2 minutes or until thick and bubbly, stirring constantly. Discard vanilla bean.

5. Place egg whites in a large bowl; beat with a mixer at high speed until foamy. Add ¾ cup sugar, 1 tablespoon at a time, beating until stiff peaks form.

6. Arrange half of vanilla wafers in bottom of a 13 x 9-inch baking dish. Arrange half of banana slices over wafers. Pour half of custard over banana. Repeat procedure with remaining wafers, banana, and custard.

7. Top with meringue, spreading evenly to edges of dish.

8. Bake at 325° for 20 minutes or until lightly browned. Serve pudding warm or chilled. Yield: 16 servings (serving size: about ¾ cup).

CALORIES 289 (16% from fat); FAT 5.1g (sat 1.6g, mono 1.5g, poly 0.2g); PROTEIN 6.1g; CARB 57.1g; FIBER 1.2g; CHOL 33mg; IRON 1.2mg; SODIUM 202mg; CALC 94mg

---

MAKE AHEAD • FREEZABLE
Banana Split Ice Cream Pie

Make this simple recipe up to 3 days ahead, and keep it frozen until you're ready to serve it. Use firm yellow bananas. You can substitute canned pineapple tidbits for the garnish. To soften the ice cream for spreading, let it stand at room temperature for 30 minutes.

1¼ cups chocolate wafer crumbs (about 25 cookies; such as Nabisco's Famous Chocolate Wafers)
2 tablespoons butter, melted
¾ cup fat-free chocolate sundae syrup, divided
4 cups sliced banana (about 5 bananas)
1 (1.75-quart) container vanilla low-fat ice cream, softened
1 (18-ounce) jar strawberry sundae topping
1 cup coarsely chopped pineapple
5 tablespoons chopped dry-roasted peanuts
16 maraschino cherries with stems (optional)

1. Combine crumbs and butter, stirring with a fork until moist. Press crumb mixture into bottom and ½ inch up sides of a 10-inch springform pan. Spread ½ cup chocolate syrup evenly over crust; top with banana. Spread ice cream evenly over banana. Cover and freeze 3 hours or until firm.

2. Spread strawberry sundae topping evenly over ice cream. Cover and freeze 1 hour.

3. Let stand at room temperature 5 minutes. Cut into 16 wedges. Drizzle each serving with about ¾ teaspoon chocolate sundae syrup, and top each with 1 tablespoon chopped pineapple, about 1 teaspoon chopped peanuts, and, if desired, 1 maraschino cherry. Serve immediately. Yield: 16 servings.

CALORIES 313 (18% from fat); FAT 6.1g (sat 2.5g, mono 1.6g, poly 0.7g); PROTEIN 4.6g; CARB 61.6g; FIBER 2.7g; CHOL 9mg; IRON 0.6mg; SODIUM 156mg; CALC 94mg

---

MAKE AHEAD
Banana Roulade with Hazelnut Cream

Roulade [roo-LAHD] refers to a sponge cake that's rolled jelly roll fashion with a creamy filling. Use very ripe bananas for this recipe to ensure a moist cake.

¼ cup chopped hazelnuts
Cooking spray
1 tablespoon all-purpose flour
1½ cups all-purpose flour
6 large egg yolks
1 cup granulated sugar, divided
1½ cups mashed ripe banana (about 3 bananas)
6 large egg whites
2 tablespoons powdered sugar, divided
½ cup (4 ounces) ⅓-less-fat cream cheese
¼ cup hazelnut-chocolate spread (such as Nutella)
1 teaspoon vanilla extract
1½ cups powdered sugar, sifted

1. Preheat oven to 375°.

2. Place hazelnuts on a baking sheet. Bake at 375° for 8 minutes or until lightly browned. Turn nuts out onto a towel.

Roll up towel; rub off skins. Cool. Place nuts in a food processor; process until finely ground.

3. Increase oven temperature to 400°.

4. Coat a 15 x 10-inch jelly roll pan with cooking spray; line bottom with wax paper. Coat wax paper with cooking spray; dust with 1 tablespoon flour.

5. Lightly spoon 1½ cups flour into dry measuring cups, and level with a knife. Combine flour and nuts, stirring well with a whisk. Beat egg yolks in a large bowl with a mixer at high speed 4 minutes. Add ⅓ cup granulated sugar, beating until thick and pale (about 2 minutes). Add flour mixture, beating just until combined. Stir in banana.

6. Beat egg whites with a mixer at high speed until soft peaks form using clean, dry beaters. Gradually add ⅔ cup granulated sugar, 1 tablespoon at a time, beating until stiff peaks form. Gently stir one-fourth of egg white mixture into banana mixture; gently fold in remaining egg white mixture.

7. Gently spread batter into prepared pan. Bake at 400° for 12 minutes or until cake springs back when touched lightly in center. Loosen cake from sides of pan; turn out onto a dishtowel dusted with 1 tablespoon powdered sugar.

8. Carefully peel off wax paper; cool cake 1 minute. Starting at a long end, roll up cake and towel together. Place, seam side down, on a wire rack; cool completely.

9. Combine cream cheese, hazelnut-chocolate spread, and vanilla; beat with a mixer at medium speed until smooth. Gradually add 1½ cups powdered sugar, beating just until blended.

10. Unroll cake carefully, and remove towel. Spread cream cheese mixture over cake, leaving a ½-inch border.

11. Reroll cake, and place, seam side down, on a platter. Cover and chill 2 hours. Sprinkle with 1 tablespoon powdered sugar. Cut cake into 14 slices. Yield: 14 servings.

CALORIES 257 (23% from fat); FAT 6.7g (sat 2.3g, mono 2.3g, poly 0.5g); PROTEIN 5.6g; CARB 45.2g; FIBER 1.2g; CHOL 97mg; IRON 1.3mg; SODIUM 62mg; CALC 25mg

Banana-Raspberry Cake with Lemon Frosting
(pictured on page 21)

CAKE:
Cooking spray
1 tablespoon all-purpose flour
1⅓ cups granulated sugar
¼ cup butter, softened
3 large eggs
1¾ cups all-purpose flour
2 teaspoons baking powder
½ teaspoon salt
1 cup low-fat buttermilk
1 cup mashed ripe banana (about 2 bananas)
1 teaspoon vanilla extract

FROSTING:
¾ cup (6 ounces) ⅓-less-fat cream cheese, chilled
2 tablespoons butter, softened
2 teaspoons grated lemon rind
½ teaspoon vanilla extract
Dash of salt
2½ cups powdered sugar, sifted
1½ cups fresh raspberries (optional)

1. Preheat oven to 350°.
2. To prepare cake, coat 2 (8-inch) round cake pans with cooking spray; line bottoms with wax paper. Coat wax paper with cooking spray; dust each pan with 1½ teaspoons flour.
3. Place granulated sugar and ¼ cup butter in a large bowl; beat with a mixer at medium speed until well blended (about 3 minutes). Add eggs, 1 at a time, beating well after each addition.
4. Lightly spoon 1¾ cups flour into dry measuring cups, and level with a knife. Combine flour, baking powder, and ½ teaspoon salt, stirring well with a whisk.
5. Combine buttermilk, banana, and 1 teaspoon vanilla. Add flour mixture and buttermilk mixture alternately to sugar mixture, beginning and ending with flour mixture (mix after each addition just until blended). Pour batter into prepared pans.
6. Bake cake at 350° for 25 minutes or until a wooden pick inserted in center comes out clean. Cool in pans 10 minutes on a wire rack; remove from pans.

Peel off wax paper. Cool layers completely on wire rack.
7. To prepare frosting, combine cream cheese and next 4 ingredients in a large bowl. Beat with a mixer at high speed until fluffy. Gradually add powdered sugar; beat at low speed just until blended (do not overbeat).
8. Place 1 cake layer on a plate, and spread with ⅓ cup frosting. Arrange raspberries in a single layer over frosting, if desired, and top with remaining cake layer. Spread remaining frosting over top and sides of cake. Store cake loosely covered in refrigerator. Garnish with fresh raspberries, if desired. Yield: 14 servings (serving size: 1 slice).

CALORIES 289 (25% from fat); FAT 8g (sat 4.6g, mono 2.4g, poly 0.4g); PROTEIN 4.5g; CARB 51.7g; FIBER 1.2g; CHOL 60mg; IRON 1mg; SODIUM 247mg; CALC 65mg

superfast

... And Ready in Just About 20 Minutes

Hot Garlic Shrimp and Asparagus

8 (½-inch-thick) slices diagonally cut French bread baguette
2 tablespoons olive oil
2½ cups (1-inch) sliced asparagus (about 1 pound)
2 teaspoons bottled minced garlic
½ teaspoon salt
¼ teaspoon crushed red pepper
¼ teaspoon freshly ground black pepper
1½ pounds peeled and deveined large shrimp
1 cup Chardonnay or other dry white wine
2 tablespoons lemon juice

1. Preheat oven to 400°.
2. Place bread slices in a single layer on a baking sheet. Bake at 400° for 6 minutes or until toasted.
3. While bread toasts, heat oil in a large nonstick skillet over medium heat. Add asparagus, garlic, salt, and peppers; cook 2 minutes, stirring frequently. Add shrimp, and cook 4 minutes, stirring frequently.
4. Stir in wine and juice; bring to a boil. Remove from heat; serve with bread slices. Yield: 4 servings (serving size: 1½ cups shrimp mixture and 2 bread slices).

CALORIES 324 (25% from fat); FAT 9.1g (sat 1.5g, mono 5.6g, poly 1.4g); PROTEIN 30.6g; CARB 20.3g; FIBER 2.7g; CHOL 242mg; IRON 5.5mg; SODIUM 747mg; CALC 97mg

Ginger-Glazed Salmon

Fillets that are more than an inch thick will take longer than 15 minutes to cook.

4 (6-ounce) salmon fillets (about 1 inch thick)
Cooking spray
½ cup pineapple preserves
1½ tablespoons lime juice
1 tablespoon Dijon mustard
1½ teaspoons bottled ground fresh ginger (such as Spice World)
1 teaspoon bottled minced garlic
1 teaspoon low-sodium soy sauce
¼ teaspoon salt
¼ teaspoon black pepper

1. Preheat oven to 425°.
2. Place fillets in a 13 x 9-inch baking dish coated with cooking spray. Combine preserves and remaining 7 ingredients; pour over fillets.
3. Bake at 425° for 15 minutes or until fish flakes easily when tested with a fork. Yield: 4 servings (serving size: 1 fillet).

CALORIES 336 (29% from fat); FAT 10.9g (sat 2.5g, mono 4.7g, poly 2.6g); PROTEIN 31.4g; CARB 29.5g; FIBER 0.1g; CHOL 80mg; IRON 0.7mg; SODIUM 372mg; CALC 23mg

Turkey Philly Sandwiches

You can also add sliced mushrooms to the pan with the onion and bell pepper. Serve with dill pickles and chips.

    2   teaspoons butter
    1   cup thinly sliced onion
    1   cup thinly sliced green bell pepper
    ¼   teaspoon black pepper
    ¾   pound thinly sliced deli turkey breast
    4   (2-ounce) sandwich rolls
    4   (1-ounce) slices low-sodium
        mozzarella or provolone cheese

1. Preheat oven to 375°.
2. Melt butter in a large nonstick skillet over medium-high heat. Add onion and bell pepper; sauté 5 minutes or until tender. Stir in black pepper.
3. Divide onion mixture and turkey evenly among bottom halves of rolls; top each serving with 1 cheese slice. Cover with top halves of rolls.
4. Place sandwiches on a baking sheet. Bake at 375° for 5 minutes or until cheese melts. Yield: 4 servings (serving size: 1 sandwich).

CALORIES 380 (30% from fat); FAT 12.9g (sat 6.9g, mono 2.7g, poly 1.4g); PROTEIN 28.5g; CARB 40.6g; FIBER 2.6g; CHOL 52mg; IRON 2.2mg; SODIUM 1,042mg; CALC 277mg

Veal Marsala

Veal scaloppine is a superthin veal cutlet. Serve over egg noodles or a blend of white and wild rice.

    1   pound veal scaloppine
    ¼   cup all-purpose flour, divided
    ⅔   cup beef consommé
    1   tablespoon butter
    ½   cup dry Marsala wine
    1   cup presliced mushrooms
    ¼   teaspoon salt
    1   tablespoon chopped fresh parsley

1. Dredge veal in 3 tablespoons flour. Combine 1 tablespoon flour and consommé, stirring with a whisk; set aside.
2. Melt butter in a large nonstick skillet over medium-high heat. Add veal; cook 1½ minutes. Turn veal over; cook 1 minute. Remove veal from pan.
3. Add wine to pan, scraping pan to loosen browned bits. Add consommé mixture, mushrooms, and salt; bring to a boil. Reduce heat; simmer 3 minutes or until thick. Return veal to pan; sprinkle with parsley. Yield: 4 servings (serving size: 3 ounces veal and about 2 tablespoons sauce).

CALORIES 193 (28% from fat); FAT 6.1g (sat 3g, mono 1.1g, poly 0.4g); PROTEIN 26g; CARB 7.5g; FIBER 0.4g; CHOL 102mg; IRON 1.9mg; SODIUM 481mg; CALC 24mg

Chicken with Artichokes and Olives

Serve over buttered bow tie pasta.

    1   tablespoon olive oil
    4   (6-ounce) skinless, boneless
        chicken breast halves
    ¼   teaspoon salt
    ¼   teaspoon black pepper
    ½   cup dry white wine
    ¼   cup fat-free, less-sodium chicken
        broth
    2   teaspoons Dijon mustard
    1   teaspoon cornstarch
    ⅓   cup pitted kalamata olives
    1   (14-ounce) can quartered artichoke
        hearts, drained
    2   tablespoons minced fresh parsley

1. Heat oil in a large nonstick skillet over medium-high heat. Sprinkle chicken with salt and pepper. Add chicken to pan; cook 5 minutes on each side. Remove chicken from pan; keep warm.
2. Combine wine, broth, mustard, and cornstarch. Add to pan, scraping pan to loosen browned bits. Bring to a boil; cook 1 minute. Stir in olives and artichokes; cook 1 minute. Spoon sauce over chicken; sprinkle with parsley. Yield: 4 servings (serving size: 1 chicken breast half and ¼ cup sauce).

CALORIES 323 (28% from fat); FAT 10.1g (sat 1.6g, mono 6.1g, poly 1.4g); PROTEIN 42.4g; CARB 10.1g; FIBER 3.8g; CHOL 99mg; IRON 2.1mg; SODIUM 788mg; CALC 50mg

Greek Lamb Chops

Try this with couscous tossed with chopped tomato, cucumber, and feta cheese.

    2   tablespoons lemon juice
    1   tablespoon bottled minced garlic
    1   tablespoon dried oregano
    ½   teaspoon salt
    ¼   teaspoon black pepper
    8   (4-ounce) lamb loin chops,
        trimmed
    Cooking spray

1. Preheat broiler.
2. Combine first 5 ingredients; rub over both sides of chops. Place chops on a broiler pan coated with cooking spray; broil 4 minutes on each side or until desired degree of doneness. Yield: 4 servings (serving size: 2 lamb chops).

CALORIES 192 (39% from fat); FAT 8.4g (sat 3g, mono 3.6g, poly 0.6g); PROTEIN 25.8g; CARB 1.7g; FIBER 0.1g; CHOL 81mg; IRON 1.8mg; SODIUM 367mg; CALC 36mg

Pecan-Crusted Tilapia

Serve with rice and coleslaw, or cheese grits and sautéed greens.

    ½   cup dry breadcrumbs
    2   tablespoons finely chopped pecans
    ½   teaspoon salt
    ¼   teaspoon garlic powder
    ¼   teaspoon black pepper
    ½   cup low-fat buttermilk
    ½   teaspoon hot sauce
    3   tablespoons all-purpose flour
    4   (6-ounce) tilapia or snapper fillets
    1   tablespoon vegetable oil, divided
    4   lemon wedges

1. Combine first 5 ingredients in a shallow dish. Combine buttermilk and hot sauce in a medium bowl; place flour in a shallow dish. Dredge 1 fillet in flour. Dip in buttermilk mixture; dredge in breadcrumb mixture. Repeat procedure with remaining fillets, flour, buttermilk mixture, and breadcrumb mixture.
2. Heat 1½ teaspoons oil in a large nonstick skillet over medium-high heat.

Add 2 fillets; cook 3 minutes on each side or until fish flakes easily when tested with a fork. Repeat procedure with remaining oil and fillets. Serve with lemon wedges. Yield: 4 servings (serving size: 1 tilapia fillet).

CALORIES 302 (27% from fat); FAT 9.1g (sat 1.1g, mono 3.9g, poly 2.6g); PROTEIN 38.4g; CARB 14.2g; FIBER 0.9g; CHOL 64mg; IRON 1.3mg; SODIUM 530mg; CALC 98mg

Turkey Cutlets with Rosemary-Tomato Sauce

Serve the turkey and sauce over pasta.

- 4 teaspoons olive oil, divided
- 8 (2-ounce) turkey cutlets
- ¾ teaspoon salt, divided
- ½ teaspoon black pepper, divided
- 1 tablespoon chopped fresh rosemary
- 1 teaspoon bottled minced garlic
- 1½ cups chopped tomato
- 1 tablespoon white wine vinegar

1. Heat 2 teaspoons oil in a large nonstick skillet over medium-high heat. Sprinkle turkey with ¼ teaspoon salt and ¼ teaspoon pepper. Add turkey to pan; cook 2 minutes on each side or until done. Remove from pan; keep warm.
2. Add 2 teaspoons oil, rosemary, and garlic to pan; sauté 1 minute. Add tomato; cook 1 minute, stirring frequently. Stir in ½ teaspoon salt, ¼ teaspoon pepper, and vinegar. Serve over turkey. Yield: 4 servings (serving size: 2 turkey cutlets and ¼ cup sauce).

CALORIES 182 (27% from fat); FAT 5.5g (sat 0.9g, mono 3.5g, poly 0.7g); PROTEIN 28.6g; CARB 3.6g; FIBER 0.9g; CHOL 70mg; IRON 1.8mg; SODIUM 498mg; CALC 19mg

Red Snapper Salad with Green Peppercorn-Tarragon Vinaigrette

Use bagged prewashed baby greens to save on preparation time. Serve with baked breadsticks or focaccia from the bakery. We liked the green peppercorns, but you can also use a mixed peppercorn blend.

Cooking spray
- 4 (6-ounce) red snapper or other firm whitefish fillets
- 1 tablespoon olive oil, divided
- ½ teaspoon salt, divided
- 2 tablespoons white wine vinegar
- 2 tablespoons water
- 2 tablespoons honey
- 2 tablespoons Dijon mustard
- 1 tablespoon minced fresh or 1 teaspoon dried tarragon
- 1 teaspoon dried green peppercorns, crushed
- 6 cups mixed baby greens

1. Heat a large nonstick skillet coated with cooking spray over medium-high heat. Drizzle fish with 2 teaspoons oil; sprinkle with ¼ teaspoon salt. Add fish to pan; cook 4 minutes on each side or until fish flakes easily when tested with a fork.
2. While fish cooks, combine 1 teaspoon oil, ¼ teaspoon salt, vinegar, and next 5 ingredients, stirring with a whisk. Drizzle ¼ cup vinaigrette over greens; toss gently to combine. Arrange about 1¼ cups greens on each of 4 plates. Top each serving with 1 fillet; drizzle each serving with 1 tablespoon vinaigrette. Yield: 4 servings.

CALORIES 269 (23% from fat); FAT 6.8g (sat 1g, mono 3.2g, poly 1.4g); PROTEIN 39.2g; CARB 12.9g; FIBER 2g; CHOL 67mg; IRON 1.7mg; SODIUM 583mg; CALC 117mg

Seared Pork with Cranberry-Orange Sauce

Serve over rice with steamed broccoli.

- ½ cup whole-berry cranberry sauce
- 3 tablespoons low-sodium soy sauce
- 2 tablespoons orange juice
- 1 tablespoon honey
- 1 teaspoon bottled ground fresh ginger (such as Spice World)
- ¼ teaspoon salt, divided
- 1 tablespoon olive oil
Cooking spray
- 4 (4-ounce) boneless center-cut loin pork chops (about ½ inch thick)
- ½ teaspoon dried rosemary
- ¼ teaspoon black pepper
- ⅓ cup dry white wine

1. Combine first 5 ingredients and ⅛ teaspoon salt.
2. Heat oil in a large skillet coated with cooking spray over medium-high heat. Sprinkle pork with ⅛ teaspoon salt, rosemary, and pepper. Add pork to pan, and cook 4 minutes on each side. Remove from pan.
3. Add wine to pan, scraping pan to loosen browned bits. Stir in cranberry mixture; return pork to pan. Bring to a simmer; cook 2 minutes or until pork is done. Yield: 4 servings (serving size: 1 pork chop and about 2 tablespoons sauce).

CALORIES 250 (27% from fat); FAT 7.6g (sat 1.9g, mono 4.4g, poly 0.8g); PROTEIN 25.7g; CARB 19.1g; FIBER 0.5g; CHOL 78mg; IRON 1.2mg; SODIUM 907mg; CALC 29mg

Gorgonzola Topped Pork Tenderloin

Serve over instant polenta or microwaved frozen mashed potatoes.

- 1 (1-pound) pork tenderloin, trimmed and cut crosswise into 4 pieces
- 1 teaspoon vegetable oil
Cooking spray
- 2 teaspoons bottled minced garlic
- ½ teaspoon black pepper
- ¼ teaspoon salt
- ½ cup beef broth
- ¼ cup dry red wine
- 2 tablespoons crumbled Gorgonzola or other blue cheese

1. Place pork between 2 sheets of heavy-duty plastic wrap; pound to 1-inch thickness using a meat mallet or rolling pin.
2. Heat oil in a large skillet coated with cooking spray over medium-high heat. Combine garlic, pepper, and salt; rub over both sides of pork. Add pork to pan, and cook 5 minutes on each side or until done. Remove pork from pan, and keep warm.
3. Add broth and wine to pan, scraping pan to loosen browned bits. Increase heat to high, and cook until reduced to ⅓ cup (about 6 minutes). Spoon sauce over pork; sprinkle with cheese. Yield: 4 servings (serving size: 3 ounces pork, *Continued*

about 1 tablespoon sauce, and 1½ teaspoons cheese).

CALORIES 170 (27% from fat); FAT 5.1g (sat 1.8g, mono 1.6g, poly 1g); PROTEIN 28.3g; CARB 1.1g; FIBER 0.1g; CHOL 71mg; IRON 1.6mg; SODIUM 341mg; CALC 32mg

QUICK & EASY
Mussels in Spicy Coconut Broth

½ cup light coconut milk
¼ cup thinly sliced peeled fresh ginger
2 tablespoons lemon juice
1 tablespoon sugar
2 teaspoons red curry powder (such as McCormick)
Dash of salt
1 (14-ounce) can fat-free, less-sodium chicken broth
2 pounds mussels, scrubbed and debearded
¼ cup chopped fresh basil

1. Combine first 7 ingredients in a Dutch oven, and bring to a boil. Add mussels; cover and cook 5 minutes or until shells open.
2. Remove from heat; discard any unopened shells. Spoon 1½ cups broth mixture into each of 2 soup bowls. Divide mussels evenly between bowls. Garnish with chopped basil. Yield: 2 servings.

CALORIES 241 (27% from fat); FAT 7.1g (sat 2.8g, mono 1g, poly 1.1g); PROTEIN 22.9g; CARB 20.3g; FIBER 1g; CHOL 46mg; IRON 7.8mg; SODIUM 940mg; CALC 66mg

QUICK & EASY
Balsamic Glazed Pork Chops with Red Pepper Grits

3 cups water
¾ teaspoon salt, divided
¾ cup uncooked quick-cooking grits
2 tablespoons butter
½ teaspoon bottled minced garlic
1 (7-ounce) bottle roasted red bell peppers, drained and chopped
Cooking spray
4 (4-ounce) boneless center-cut loin pork chops (about ¾ inch thick)
⅛ teaspoon black pepper
¼ cup balsamic vinegar
2 tablespoons honey

1. Bring water and ½ teaspoon salt to a boil. Add grits, butter, and garlic, stirring with a whisk. Reduce heat, and simmer, uncovered, 5 minutes. Remove from heat; stir in bell pepper.
2. While grits cook, heat a large nonstick skillet coated with cooking spray over medium-high heat. Sprinkle pork with ¼ teaspoon salt and black pepper. Add pork to pan; cook 4 minutes on each side or until done. Remove pork from pan. Stir in vinegar and honey, scraping pan to loosen browned bits. Bring to a boil; cook 1 minute or until thick, stirring constantly with a whisk. Return pork to pan; turn to coat. Serve pork and sauce over grits. Yield: 4 servings (serving size: 1 pork chop and 1 cup grits).

CALORIES 397 (30% from fat); FAT 13.1g (sat 6.7g, mono 3.2g, poly 0.6g); PROTEIN 28.8g; CARB 40.5g; FIBER 0.8g; CHOL 88mg; IRON 2.2mg; SODIUM 592mg; CALC 26mg

QUICK & EASY
Tomato-Chicken Pasta

1 (9-ounce) package fresh fettuccine
¼ cup boiling water
2 tablespoons sun-dried tomato sprinkles
2 teaspoons olive oil
Cooking spray
½ cup finely chopped shallots
1 pound chicken breast tenders, cut into 1-inch pieces
½ cup dry white wine
⅓ cup whipping cream
½ cup chopped fresh basil, divided
¼ cup (1 ounce) preshredded fresh Parmesan cheese
½ teaspoon salt
¼ teaspoon freshly ground black pepper

1. Cook pasta according to package directions, omitting salt and fat.
2. While pasta cooks, combine water and tomato sprinkles in a small bowl; let stand 5 minutes. Drain.
3. While tomato soaks, heat oil in a large nonstick skillet coated with cooking spray over medium-high heat. Add shallots and chicken, and sauté 5 minutes. Reduce heat to medium; stir in wine and cream. Cook 3 minutes, stirring occasionally.

4. Combine pasta, tomato, chicken mixture, ¼ cup basil, cheese, and salt, tossing well to coat. Sprinkle with ¼ cup basil and pepper. Yield: 4 servings (serving size: 1½ cups).

CALORIES 426 (21% from fat); FAT 10.2g (sat 4.1g, mono 3.7g, poly 1.3g); PROTEIN 37g; CARB 40.2g; FIBER 3.1g; CHOL 129mg; IRON 3.7mg; SODIUM 537mg; CALC 133mg

QUICK & EASY
Barley Pilaf with Chickpeas and Artichoke Hearts

Starting out with warm or hot water ensures the preparation of this dish takes no more than 20 minutes. Chickpeas are sturdy beans that hold up well, but you can use cannellini beans, if you prefer.

2 cups warm water
1 cup uncooked quick-cooking barley
¼ teaspoon salt
2 tablespoons commercial pesto
1 (15-ounce) can chickpeas (garbanzo beans), drained and rinsed
1 tablespoon fresh lemon juice
1 tablespoon olive oil
1 teaspoon bottled minced garlic
1 (14-ounce) can quartered artichoke hearts, drained and rinsed
½ cup (2 ounces) preshredded fresh Parmesan cheese

1. Combine first 3 ingredients in a medium saucepan. Bring to a boil; cook 3 minutes. Cover, reduce heat, and simmer 8 minutes or until barley is tender and liquid is absorbed. Stir in pesto and chickpeas; cook 1 minute or until thoroughly heated. Stir in lemon juice.
2. While barley cooks, heat oil in a large nonstick skillet over medium-high heat. Add garlic and artichokes; sauté 3 minutes or until lightly browned.
3. Place 1 cup barley mixture into each of 4 bowls, and top each serving with ¼ cup artichoke mixture. Sprinkle each serving with 2 tablespoons cheese. Yield: 4 servings.

CALORIES 371 (30% from fat); FAT 12.3g (sat 4g, mono 6g, poly 1.4g); PROTEIN 16.1g; CARB 51.4g; FIBER 7.5g; CHOL 12mg; IRON 3.1mg; SODIUM 845mg; CALC 260mg

The Big Chill

Five entrées, 10 dinners—eat one now, freeze one for later.

With the recipes that follow, you can have the best of both worlds—the benefit of a homemade dinner now *and* later with a frozen entrée. It's easy to make a double batch of each of these recipes, without requiring extra time or effort in the kitchen.

Cold Truths

• Disposable foil pans are good for freezing casseroles, so your baking dishes won't be occupied in the freezer. Foil pans can be a bit flimsy, though; place them on a baking sheet before you fill them with hot food. That way you can move them to the refrigerator to cool without worrying about spilling.

• Wrap the casserole in plastic wrap to eliminate as much air space as possible, so there's less chance for freezer burn. Then wrap it in heavy-duty foil to give the food an extra layer of protection.

• In most cases, going straight from freezer to oven causes uneven baking. The outer edges tend to overcook, while the middle is uncooked. So we suggest you thaw all but one of the casseroles— Four-Cheese Stuffed Shells with Smoky Marinara (recipe on page 50)—in the refrigerator first.

MAKE AHEAD • FREEZABLE

Sun-Dried Tomato Meat Loaf with Red Currant-Wine Sauce

Red currant jelly and wine make a quick, rich sauce that is a nice change from the typical ketchup topping. Serve with mashed potatoes. If you decide to freeze one of the meat loaves for later, make half the amount of Red Currant-Wine Sauce now and half when you bake the frozen meat loaf.

MEAT LOAF:
    Cooking spray
  3 (1-ounce) slices white bread
  1 cup finely chopped onion
  1 cup (4 ounces) grated fresh
     Parmesan cheese
  ½ cup thinly sliced fresh basil
  ⅓ cup sun-dried tomato sprinkles
  ¼ cup chopped fresh parsley
  4 garlic cloves, minced
  2 large eggs, lightly beaten
2½ pounds ground turkey breast

RED CURRANT-WINE SAUCE:
  ½ cup red currant jelly
  ¼ cup dry red wine
  1 teaspoon all-purpose flour

1. Preheat oven to 400°.
2. Coat 2 (8 x 4-inch) loaf pans with cooking spray; set aside.
3. To prepare meat loaves, place bread in food processor; pulse 10 times or until coarse crumbs form. Combine crumbs, onion, and next 7 ingredients. Divide mixture in half. Press each portion into a prepared pan. Bake at 400° for 55 minutes or until a meat thermometer registers 180°.
4. To prepare sauce, combine jelly, wine, and flour in a small saucepan. Bring to a boil; cook 5 minutes or until jelly melts. Serve with meat loaf. Yield: 10 servings, 5 per pan (serving size: 5 ounces meat loaf and about 1 tablespoon sauce).

TO FREEZE UNBAKED MEAT LOAF: Prepare through Step 3. Cover with plastic wrap, pressing to remove as much air as possible. Wrap with heavy-duty foil. Store in freezer up to 2 months.

TO PREPARE FROZEN UNBAKED MEAT LOAF: Thaw completely in refrigerator (about 24 hours). Preheat oven to 400°. Remove foil; reserve foil. Remove plastic wrap; discard wrap. Cover meat loaf with reserved foil; bake at 400° for 45 minutes. Uncover and bake an additional 45 minutes or until a meat thermometer registers 180°. Prepare half of red currant-wine sauce; serve over meat loaf.

CALORIES 271 (19% from fat); FAT 5.6g (sat 2.8g, mono 1.6g, poly 0.5g); PROTEIN 35.2g; CARB 18.4g; FIBER 0.8g; CHOL 122mg; IRON 2.3mg; SODIUM 435mg; CALC 193mg

MAKE AHEAD • FREEZABLE

Savory Breakfast Casserole

The vegetarian sausage adds a lot of sage flavor to the casserole and doesn't need to be precooked. The sausage often comes in a tube and is usually located in the refrigerated area of the produce section, near the tofu. Although we call this dish a breakfast casserole, you can serve it for dinner with sautéed greens or roasted red-skinned potatoes.

  2 cups 2% reduced-fat milk
  1 cup (4 ounces) shredded
     reduced-fat Cheddar cheese,
     divided
  ½ cup chopped green onions
  ½ teaspoon dry mustard
  ¼ teaspoon salt
  ¼ teaspoon freshly ground black
     pepper
  8 large egg whites, lightly
     beaten
  4 large eggs, lightly beaten
 14 ounces meatless fat-free
     sausage, crumbled (such as
     Gimme Lean!)
  4 cups (½-inch) cubed white bread
     (about 4½ ounces)
    Cooking spray

1. Preheat oven to 350°.
2. Combine milk, ½ cup Cheddar cheese, green onions, and next 5 ingredients, stirring with a whisk.

Continued

3. Divide sausage and bread evenly between 2 (8 x 4-inch) loaf pans coated with cooking spray. Pour egg mixture evenly into pans. Top each pan with ¼ cup cheese.

4. Cover each pan with foil. Bake at 350° for 20 minutes. Uncover and bake an additional 40 minutes or until a wooden pick inserted in center comes out clean. Yield: 2 casseroles, 3 servings per pan.

TO FREEZE UNBAKED CASSEROLE: Prepare through Step 3. Cover with plastic wrap, pressing to remove as much air as possible. Wrap with heavy-duty foil. Store in freezer up to 2 months.

TO PREPARE FROZEN UNBAKED CASSEROLE: Thaw completely in refrigerator (about 24 hours). Preheat oven to 350°. Remove foil; reserve foil. Remove plastic wrap; discard wrap. Cover casserole with reserved foil; bake at 350° for 40 minutes. Uncover and bake an additional 50 minutes or until bubbly.

CALORIES 316 (26% from fat); FAT 9.2g (sat 4.3g, mono 2g, poly 0.6g); PROTEIN 30g; CARB 26.7g; FIBER 2.2g; CHOL 162mg; IRON 3.2mg; SODIUM 864mg; CALC 347mg

MAKE AHEAD • FREEZABLE
Smoky Marinara

Look for fire-roasted tomatoes (we used Muir Glen) in the organic section or with the canned tomatoes in your supermarket.

- 1 tablespoon olive oil
- 3 garlic cloves, minced
- ¼ cup chopped fresh basil
- 2 tablespoons chopped fresh parsley
- 2 tablespoons chopped fresh or 2 teaspoons dried oregano
- 2 teaspoons balsamic vinegar
- ⅛ teaspoon salt
- ⅛ teaspoon black pepper
- 1 (28-ounce) can crushed fire-roasted tomatoes, undrained
- 1 (28-ounce) can crushed tomatoes, undrained

1. Heat oil in a large saucepan over medium heat. Add garlic, basil, parsley, and oregano; sauté 1 minute, stirring frequently. Stir in vinegar and remaining ingredients. Reduce heat, and simmer

10 minutes. Yield: 6 cups (serving size: ½ cup).

CALORIES 55 (20% from fat); FAT 1.2g (sat 0.2g, mono 0.8g, poly 0.1g); PROTEIN 2.3g; CARB 9g; FIBER 2.3g; CHOL 0mg; IRON 0.9mg; SODIUM 350mg; CALC 49mg

MAKE AHEAD • FREEZABLE
Butternut Squash Lasagna

You can make the marinara in advance, and store it in the refrigerator up to 2 days.

- Cooking spray
- 3 cups chopped onion
- 10 cups fresh spinach
- ¾ cup (3 ounces) shredded sharp provolone cheese
- ½ cup chopped fresh flat-leaf parsley
- 1 teaspoon salt
- ½ teaspoon freshly ground black pepper
- 2 large eggs, lightly beaten
- 1 (15-ounce) carton part-skim ricotta cheese
- 1 (15-ounce) carton fat-free ricotta cheese
- 3 cups diced peeled butternut squash
- 6 cups Smoky Marinara (recipe at left), divided
- 12 oven-ready lasagna noodles (such as Barilla), divided
- 1 cup (4 ounces) grated fresh Parmesan cheese, divided

1. Preheat oven to 375°.

2. Heat a large Dutch oven coated with cooking spray over medium-high heat. Add onion; sauté 4 minutes or until tender. Add spinach; sauté 1½ minutes or until spinach wilts. Combine provolone, parsley, salt, pepper, eggs, and ricotta cheeses in a large bowl.

3. Place squash in a microwave-safe bowl. Cover and cook at HIGH 5 minutes or until tender.

4. Coat bottom and sides of 2 (8-inch-square) baking dishes with cooking spray. Spread ½ cup Smoky Marinara sauce in bottom of one prepared dish. Arrange 2 noodles over sauce; spread 1 cup cheese mixture over noodles. Arrange 1½ cups squash over cheese mixture; spread ¾ cup sauce over squash.

5. Arrange 2 noodles over sauce; spread 1 cup cheese mixture over noodles. Arrange 1½ cups spinach mixture over cheese mixture; spread ¾ cup sauce over spinach mixture.

6. Arrange 2 noodles over sauce; spread 1 cup sauce evenly over noodles. Sprinkle with ½ cup Parmesan. Repeat procedure with remaining ingredients in remaining dish. Cover each dish with foil.

7. Bake at 375° for 30 minutes. Uncover and bake an additional 30 minutes. Yield: 2 lasagnas, 6 servings per dish.

TO FREEZE UNBAKED LASAGNA: Prepare through Step 6. Cover with plastic wrap, pressing to remove as much air as possible. Wrap with heavy-duty foil. Store in freezer up to 2 months.

TO PREPARE FROZEN UNBAKED LASAGNA: Thaw completely in refrigerator (about 24 hours). Preheat oven to 375°. Remove foil; reserve foil. Remove plastic wrap; discard wrap. Cover lasagna with reserved foil; bake at 375° for 1 hour. Uncover and bake an additional 30 minutes or until bubbly.

(Totals include Smoky Marinara) CALORIES 254 (30% from fat); FAT 8.5g (sat 4.5g, mono 2.2g, poly 0.3g); PROTEIN 18.6g; CARB 27.6g; FIBER 3.3g; CHOL 69mg; IRON 3.2mg; SODIUM 560mg; CALC 414mg

MAKE AHEAD • FREEZABLE
Four-Cheese Stuffed Shells with Smoky Marinara
(pictured on page 57)

This dish goes straight from freezer to oven—no thawing required. The fire-roasted tomatoes in the marinara sauce give the dish a subtle smoky flavor. You can also easily vary the filling by adding basil or oregano and a different cheese. (We tried fontina instead of mozzarella and threw in some arugula for a peppery bite.) Make some garlic bread and a green salad, and dinner's on.

QUICK TIP: The only downside to stuffed shells or manicotti is getting the filling into the pasta. Using a heavy-duty zip-top plastic bag as a pastry bag works great. Simply spoon the filling into the plastic bag, squeeze out the air, snip a 1-inch hole in one corner of the bag, and pipe the filling into the shells. Snip a small hole to start with; you can always make it bigger.

1 pound uncooked jumbo shell pasta
  (40 shells)
Cooking spray
1 (12-ounce) carton 1% low-fat
  cottage cheese
1 (15-ounce) carton ricotta cheese
1 cup (4 ounces) shredded Asiago
  cheese
¾ cup (3 ounces) grated fresh
  Parmesan cheese
2 tablespoons chopped fresh chives
2 tablespoons chopped fresh parsley
¼ teaspoon black pepper
¼ teaspoon salt
1 (10-ounce) package frozen
  chopped spinach, thawed,
  drained, and squeezed dry
6 cups Smoky Marinara (recipe on
  page 50), divided
1 cup (4 ounces) shredded part-skim
  mozzarella cheese, divided

1. Cook pasta according to package directions, omitting salt and fat. Drain and set aside.
2. Preheat oven to 375°.
3. Coat 2 (13 x 9-inch) baking dishes with cooking spray; set aside.
4. Place cottage cheese and ricotta cheese in a food processor; process until smooth. Combine cottage cheese mixture, Asiago, and next 6 ingredients.
5. Spoon or pipe 1 tablespoon cheese mixture into each shell. Arrange half of stuffed shells, seam sides up, in one prepared dish. Pour 3 cups Smoky Marinara over stuffed shells. Sprinkle with ½ cup mozzarella. Repeat procedure with remaining stuffed shells, 3 cups Smoky Marinara, and ½ cup mozzarella in remaining prepared dish.
6. Cover with foil. Bake at 375° for 30 minutes or until thoroughly heated. Yield: 2 casseroles, 5 servings per dish (serving size: about 4 stuffed shells and about ½ cup Smoky Marinara).

TO FREEZE UNBAKED CASSEROLE: Prepare through Step 5. Cover with plastic wrap, pressing to remove as much air as possible. Wrap with heavy-duty foil. Store in freezer up to 2 months.

TO PREPARE FROZEN UNBAKED CASSE-ROLE: Preheat oven to 375°. Remove foil; reserve foil. Remove plastic wrap; discard wrap. Cover frozen casserole

with reserved foil; bake at 375° for 1 hour and 10 minutes or until shells are thoroughly heated.

(Totals include Smoky Marinara) CALORIES 470 (30% from fat); FAT 15.7g (sat 8.8g, mono 4.7g, poly 0.9g); PROTEIN 28.3g; CARB 52.7g; FIBER 5.3g; CHOL 47mg; IRON 3.8mg; SODIUM 916mg; CALC 508mg

STAFF FAVORITE • MAKE AHEAD
FREEZABLE
Chicken Tetrazzini

This dish is a great way to use leftover cooked chicken or turkey.

1 tablespoon butter
Cooking spray
1 cup finely chopped onion
⅔ cup finely chopped
  celery
1 teaspoon freshly ground
  black pepper
¾ teaspoon salt
3 (8-ounce) packages presliced
  mushrooms
½ cup dry sherry
⅔ cup all-purpose flour
3 (14-ounce) cans fat-free,
  less-sodium chicken broth
2¼ cups (9 ounces) grated fresh
  Parmesan cheese, divided
½ cup (4 ounces) ⅓-less-fat cream
  cheese
7 cups hot cooked vermicelli (about
  1 pound uncooked pasta)
4 cups chopped cooked chicken
  breast (about 1½ pounds)
1 (1-ounce) slice white bread

1. Preheat oven to 350°.
2. Melt butter in a large stockpot coated with cooking spray over medium-high heat. Add onion, celery, pepper, salt, and mushrooms, and sauté 4 minutes or until mushrooms are tender. Add sherry; cook 1 minute.

3. Lightly spoon flour into a measuring cup; level with a knife. Gradually add flour to pan; cook 3 minutes, stirring constantly with a whisk (mixture will be thick). Gradually add broth, stirring constantly. Bring to a boil. Reduce heat; simmer 5 minutes, stirring frequently. Remove from heat.
4. Add 1¾ cups Parmesan cheese and cream cheese, stirring with a whisk until cream cheese melts. Add pasta and chicken, and stir until blended. Divide pasta mixture between 2 (8-inch square) baking dishes coated with cooking spray.
5. Place bread in a food processor; pulse 10 times or until coarse crumbs form. Combine breadcrumbs and ½ cup Parmesan cheese; sprinkle evenly over pasta mixture.
6. Bake at 350° for 30 minutes or until lightly browned. Remove from oven; let stand 15 minutes. Yield: 2 casseroles, 6 servings each (serving size: about 1⅓ cups).

TO FREEZE UNBAKED CASSEROLE: Prepare through Step 5. Cool completely in refrigerator. Cover with plastic wrap, pressing to remove as much air as possible. Wrap with heavy-duty foil. Store in freezer up to 2 months.

TO PREPARE FROZEN UNBAKED CASSE-ROLE: Thaw casserole completely in refrigerator (about 24 hours). Preheat oven to 350°. Remove foil; reserve foil. Remove plastic wrap; discard wrap. Cover casserole with reserved foil; bake at 350° for 30 minutes. Uncover and bake an additional 1 hour or until golden and bubbly. Let stand 15 minutes.

CALORIES 380 (29% from fat); FAT 12.2g (sat 6.6g, mono 3.4g, poly 0.7g); PROTEIN 33g; CARB 32.7g; FIBER 2g; CHOL 66mg; IRON 2.8mg; SODIUM 964mg; CALC 319mg

---

The best thing about these comforting meals is knowing another one is waiting for you.

All About Sugars

Common white sugar has many cousins, from brown sugar to corn syrup. Here's a guide for knowing which form to use when.

We tend to think of sugar only as the white grains we stir in coffee or sprinkle on cereal. But there are many different kinds of sugars and other natural sweeteners. Some are solid (granulated, brown, turbinado), while others are liquid (molasses, corn syrup, honey). What all sugars have in common is sweetness, but different sugars play different roles in cooking, and the success of a recipe often depends on using the right one at the right time.

QUICK & EASY

Spinach, White Bean, and Bacon Salad with Maple-Mustard Dressing

Maple syrup is a good sweetener for salad dressings. Here, it gives body to the dressing and pairs well with the creamy beans and salty bacon. Grilled salmon fillets are a fine accompaniment to the salad.

    ¼   cup maple syrup
    3   tablespoons cider vinegar
    1   tablespoon extravirgin olive oil
    1   tablespoon Dijon mustard
    ¼   teaspoon salt
    ¼   teaspoon freshly ground black
        pepper
    1   (15.5-ounce) can Great Northern
        beans, rinsed and drained
    ½   cup thinly sliced green onions
    ½   cup finely chopped red bell pepper
    5   bacon slices, cooked and crumbled
        (drained)
    2   (7-ounce) packages fresh baby
        spinach

1. Combine first 6 ingredients in a microwave-safe bowl, stirring with a whisk; microwave at HIGH 1 minute or until hot. Place beans in a 2-cup glass measure; microwave at HIGH 1 minute or until hot.
2. Combine onions, bell pepper, bacon, and spinach in a large bowl. Add syrup mixture and beans; toss well to combine. Serve immediately. Yield: 8 servings (serving size: about 1¾ cups).

CALORIES 124 (30% from fat); FAT 4.2g (sat 1g, mono 2.3g, poly 0.5g); PROTEIN 5.5g; CARB 17.6g; FIBER 2.7g; CHOL 3mg; IRON 2.2mg; SODIUM 227mg; CALC 79mg

Triple-Play Cinnamon Rolls

Use dental floss to make easy work of cutting the dough.

DOUGH:

    1   package dry yeast (about 2¼
        teaspoons)
    ¼   cup warm water (100° to 110°)
    ½   cup warm 1% low-fat milk
        (100° to 110°)
    ⅓   cup granulated sugar
    ¼   cup butter, softened
    1   teaspoon vanilla extract
    ¾   teaspoon salt
    1   large egg, lightly beaten
    3½ cups all-purpose flour, divided
        Cooking spray

FILLING:

    ¾   cup raisins
    ⅔   cup packed brown sugar
    1   tablespoon ground cinnamon
    2   tablespoons butter, melted

GLAZE:

    1   cup powdered sugar
    2   tablespoons 1% low-fat milk
    ½   teaspoon vanilla extract

1. To prepare dough, dissolve yeast in warm water in a large bowl; let stand 5 minutes. Add ½ cup warm milk and next 5 ingredients; stir with a wooden spoon until combined (batter will not be completely smooth).
2. Lightly spoon flour into dry measuring cups; level with a knife. Add 3 cups flour to yeast mixture; stir until a soft dough forms. Turn dough out onto a lightly floured surface. Knead until smooth and elastic (about 8 minutes); add enough of remaining flour, 1 tablespoon at a time, to prevent dough from sticking to hands (dough will feel slightly tacky).
3. Place dough in a large bowl coated with cooking spray; turn to coat top. Cover and let rise in a warm place (85°), free from drafts, 1 hour or until doubled in size. (Press two fingers into dough. If indentation remains, dough has risen enough.)
4. To prepare filling, combine raisins, brown sugar, and cinnamon. Roll dough into a 15 x 10-inch rectangle; brush with 2 tablespoons melted butter. Sprinkle filling over dough, leaving a ½-inch border. Beginning with a long side, roll up dough jelly roll fashion; pinch seam to seal (do not seal ends of roll). Wrap roll in plastic wrap; chill 20 minutes.
5. Unwrap roll, and cut into 20 (¾-inch) slices. Arrange slices, cut sides up, 1 inch apart on a jelly roll pan coated with cooking spray. Cover and let rise in a warm place (85°) free from drafts, 1 hour and 15 minutes or until doubled in size.
6. Preheat oven to 350°.
7. Uncover dough. Bake at 350° for 20 minutes or until rolls are golden brown.
8. To prepare glaze, combine powdered sugar, 2 tablespoons milk, and ½ teaspoon vanilla, stirring well with a whisk. Drizzle glaze over warm rolls. Yield: 20 servings (serving size: 1 roll).

CALORIES 200 (18% from fat); FAT 4g (sat 2.3g, mono 1.1g, poly 0.3g); PROTEIN 3.2g; CARB 38.3g; FIBER 1.1g; CHOL 20mg; IRON 1.5mg; SODIUM 134mg; CALC 28mg

Types of Sugar

Granulated Sugar

At the market you'll find two kinds of granulated sugar: cane, derived from sugarcane, and beet, made from sugar beets. They're chemically identical (they're the same sucrose molecule), and they sell equally well in American markets.

Granulated, or white, sugar is the most refined. The juices from sugarcane or sugar beets are processed to remove the molasses and then filtered through charcoal, crystallized, and dried into fine granules that are made of more than 99.9% pure sucrose.

Granulated sugar contributes sweetness and moisture to baked goods. It also helps them brown and gives them structure. That means granulated sugar makes pastries tender, gives crunch to some cookies, and is essential in cake batters for aeration. When beaten with butter, sugar granules create tiny bubbles that expand during baking, causing cakes to rise even without chemical leaveners.

Superfine sugar is an ultrafine granulated sugar. It's useful in making meringues and angel food cakes. To make your own, simply process granulated sugar in a food processor for a minute or two.

Powdered (or Confectioners') Sugar

Powdered sugar is pulverized granulated sugar. Older cookbooks call it 10X sugar, meaning it's 10 times finer than granulated sugar. It's used mostly to make icings and frostings (since it dissolves quickly) and to dust over baked cookies, cakes, and cupcakes. A small amount of absorbent cornstarch is usually added before packaging to keep the sugar dry.

Brown Sugar

Brown sugar owes its moist, pliable texture and caramel-like flavor to molasses, a small amount of which is added to granulated sugar to create brown sugar.

Dark brown sugar has more molasses, and so has a deeper, richer, more assertive taste than light brown sugar. For a delicate molasses-like flavor, use light brown sugar in recipes. For a stronger toffee-like flavor, use the dark variety. Many recipes that call for brown sugar specify which to use. (For any *Cooking Light* recipe that calls for brown sugar, use light brown sugar.)

Raw Sugar

Raw sugar comes from the residue left after sugarcane has been processed to remove the molasses. Some familiar names are Demerara and turbinado, which are both coarse, dry, and golden, and Muscovado and Barbados, both fine, moist, and dark brown. In general, raw sugar is coarser in texture than granulated or brown sugar; use it when you want extra crunch—atop cookies or in a crisp or crumble.

Corn Syrup

Available in light and dark varieties, corn syrup is created by combining cornstarch with an enzyme that converts the starch to sugar. Pancake syrups are often made with corn syrup and flavoring. Corn syrup contributes silky smoothness and adds moisture and chewiness to such baked goods as cakes and cookies. When cooked with granulated sugar to make syrups and fondants, it helps prevent crystallization. Dark corn syrup is a mixture of light corn syrup and a darker syrup produced during the refining of sugar; it's often used in pecan pie fillings to provide a deep butterscotch taste. The flavor of light corn syrup is more neutral.

Honey

Honey has a sweet intensity all its own, because its flavor is determined by the source of flower nectar. In general, the darker the honey, the stronger the flavor. Orange blossom, clover blossom, sage blossom, and buckwheat are some of the most common types. Like corn syrup, honey adds moisture to cakes and cookies. Unlike corn syrup, which is fairly neutral, honey imparts a distinctive flavor. Be sure to taste honey before you use it to make sure the flavor is appropriate. A strong buckwheat honey, for example, might overwhelm the Honey Gelato (recipe on page 54).

Maple Syrup

The boiled-down sap from the sugar maple tree adds moisture and a unique flavor to cakes, cookies, and frostings. It comes in different grades, ranging in color from light golden to dark brown. As with honey, the lighter the syrup, the milder the flavor. Use light syrups for anything from pouring over waffles or pancakes to baking in cookies and cakes. The darker grades—more amber in color—are also suitable for eating and baking, but the darkest kind is best used in baking when you want to add intense maple flavor—it works wonderfully in soft ginger cookies and in gingerbread. Be sure the label says "pure maple syrup"; syrups labeled "maple flavored" are usually just corn syrup with artificial maple flavoring. Always refrigerate maple syrup after opening to ensure freshness.

Molasses

Molasses is a by-product of the sugar-refining process. Boiling the juices extracted from sugarcane and sugar beets transforms them into a syrup from which sugar crystals are extracted. The liquid left behind is molasses. Light molasses, as its name implies, is light in both color and flavor; it's often used to top pancakes. Dark molasses—used in gingerbread, shoofly pie, barbecue sauces, and Boston baked beans—is darker, thicker, stronger in flavor, and less sweet than light molasses. Blackstrap molasses (also called black treacle) has a strong bitter flavor. Popular with some health-conscious people because of its mineral content, blackstrap is more commonly used as cattle feed.

Honey Gelato

We liked mild clover and lavender honeys in this recipe. Store the gelato in an airtight container in the freezer up to 1 week. Purchased piroline cookies are a delicate accompaniment to this rich dessert.

½ cup honey
⅓ cup nonfat dry milk
1 (12-ounce) can evaporated fat-free milk
⅛ teaspoon salt
4 large egg yolks
1 cup 2% reduced-fat milk
Mint sprigs (optional)

1. Combine first 3 ingredients in a medium, heavy saucepan. Heat mixture over medium heat until honey dissolves; stir frequently (do not boil). Remove from heat.

2. Combine salt and egg yolks in a large bowl; stir with a whisk. Gradually add honey mixture to egg mixture; stir constantly with a whisk. Place honey mixture in pan; cook over medium heat until mixture reaches 180° (about 3 minutes); stir constantly (do not boil). Remove from heat; stir in 2% milk. Cool completely.

3. Pour mixture into freezer can of an ice-cream freezer; freeze according to manufacturer's instructions. Spoon gelato into a freezer-safe container. Cover and freeze 2 hours or until firm. Garnish with mint sprigs, if desired. Yield: 8 servings (serving size: ½ cup).

CALORIES 153 (19% from fat); FAT 3.3g (sat 1.2g, mono 1.2g, poly 0.4g); PROTEIN 6.7g; CARB 25.4g; FIBER 0g; CHOL 111mg; IRON 0.5mg; SODIUM 121mg; CALC 208mg

Clumping, Lumping, and Crystallizing

• Honey and syrup crystallize after long storage. To reliquefy, leave it in the jar and place in a saucepan of water over low heat until crystals dissolve. Or remove the metal lid and microwave at HIGH 15 to 60 seconds.

• Powdered sugar contains cornstarch, but can still clump, especially in high humidity. If it's lumpy, sift before measuring.
• To soften brown sugar, add a cut apple to the container, close it, and wait a day. Or smash the dried sugar into clumps, put them into a shallow pan, and spritz lightly with water. Cover the pan lightly with foil and heat in a warm oven (about 225°) for 15 minutes or until the sugar has regained its softness. Cool before using.

Taking Appropriate Measures

• To measure both granulated and powdered sugar, lightly spoon into a dry measuring cup, and level off the excess with a knife.

• Brown sugar is moist and clumpy; measure by packing it into a dry measuring cup. The sugar should hold its shape when unmolded.
• Coat a liquid measuring cup with cooking spray before measuring honey or syrup; that way the gooey liquid will slide out of the cup without clinging.

Pear, Apple, and Cherry Crumble

½ cup dried tart cherries
⅓ cup apricot preserves
1 teaspoon grated lemon rind
2 tablespoons fresh lemon juice
2 pounds Bosc pears, peeled, cored, quartered, and cut crosswise into ½-inch-thick slices (about 4½ cups)
1 pound Braeburn apples, peeled, cored, quartered, and cut crosswise into ½-inch-thick slices (about 2¼ cups)
Cooking spray
1 cup all-purpose flour
1 teaspoon ground cinnamon
¼ teaspoon salt
¼ teaspoon ground mace (optional)
6 tablespoons chilled butter, cut into small pieces
1 cup regular oats
¾ cup turbinado sugar

1. Preheat oven to 375°.
2. Combine first 6 ingredients in a large bowl, tossing well to coat. Spoon mixture into an 11 x 7-inch baking dish coated with cooking spray.
3. Lightly spoon flour into a dry measuring cup, and level with a knife. Place flour, cinnamon, salt, and mace, if desired, in a food processor; pulse 5 times or until well combined. Add butter, and pulse 20 times or until mixture resembles coarse crumbs. Add oats and sugar; pulse 5 times or until well combined.
4. Sprinkle oat mixture over pear mixture. Bake at 375° for 1 hour or until topping is golden and filling is bubbly. Cool on a wire rack 10 minutes. Serve warm or at room temperature. Yield: 10 servings.

CALORIES 304 (24% from fat); FAT 8.1g (sat 4.5g, mono 2.3g, poly 0.6g); PROTEIN 3.3g; CARB 59.2g; FIBER 4.5g; CHOL 19mg; IRON 1.7mg; SODIUM 140mg; CALC 37mg

Chocolate Fudge Snack Cake

Granulated sugar allows the pure chocolate flavor to shine through in this easy-to-make cake. Dutch process cocoa imbues the cake with a deep chocolate taste.

Cooking spray
2 teaspoons all-purpose flour
1 cup all-purpose flour
½ cup Dutch process cocoa
½ teaspoon baking soda
¼ teaspoon salt
5 tablespoons butter, softened
1 teaspoon vanilla extract
1¼ cups granulated sugar
2 large eggs
⅔ cup fat-free buttermilk
½ teaspoon powdered sugar (optional)

1. Preheat oven to 350°.

2. Coat an 8-inch square baking pan with cooking spray; dust with 2 teaspoons flour. Lightly spoon 1 cup flour into a dry measuring cup; level with a knife. Combine flour, cocoa, baking soda, and salt, stirring with a whisk.

3. Place butter in a large bowl; beat with a mixer at medium speed until smooth. Add vanilla; beat well. Add granulated sugar, ¼ cup at a time, beating well after each addition. Beat at medium-high speed 3 minutes. Add eggs, one at a time, beating well after each addition.

4. Beating at low speed, add flour mixture and buttermilk alternately to sugar mixture, beginning and ending with flour mixture; beat just until smooth.

5. Pour batter into prepared pan. Bake at 350° for 32 minutes or until a wooden pick inserted in center comes out clean. Cool in pan 10 minutes on a wire rack; remove from pan. Cool completely on wire rack. Sift powdered sugar over top of cake, if desired. Yield: 9 servings.

CALORIES 251 (29% from fat); FAT 8.2g (sat 4.7g, mono 2.5g, poly 0.5g); PROTEIN 4.5g; CARB 42.6g; FIBER 1.8g; CHOL 65mg; IRON 1.6mg; SODIUM 233mg; CALC 37mg

MAKE AHEAD
Bittersweet Chocolate Sauce

Light corn syrup gives this sauce a silky-smooth texture. Because corn syrup is about half as sweet as granulated sugar, it's necessary to add a little of the latter to prevent the sauce from becoming too bitter. Although thin when taken off the stove, the sauce thickens as it chills. Store it in an airtight container in the refrigerator up to 2 weeks.

1 cup light-colored corn syrup
¾ cup Dutch process cocoa
½ cup water
¼ cup granulated sugar
¼ cup evaporated fat-free milk
⅛ teaspoon salt
2 teaspoons vanilla extract

1. Combine first 6 ingredients in a small saucepan, stirring with a whisk until blended. Bring to a simmer over medium heat. Reduce heat; simmer 6 minutes, stirring occasionally. Remove from heat; stir in vanilla. Cover and chill. Yield: 2¼ cups (serving size: 2 tablespoons).

CALORIES 74 (6% from fat); FAT 0.5g (sat 0.3g, mono 0.2g, poly 0g); PROTEIN 0.9g; CARB 19.2g; FIBER 1.1g; CHOL 0mg; IRON 0.6mg; SODIUM 43mg; CALC 15mg

MAKE AHEAD • FREEZABLE
Graham Cracker Brown Bread
(pictured on page 60)

Graham cracker crumbs take the place of whole wheat flour. Molasses is the only sweetener and is in part responsible for the unique flavor. The texture is moist, and the bread is not too sweet. Store the loaf for a few days at room temperature in a zip-top plastic bag, or wrap it tightly and freeze for up to 1 month. Serve as is, toasted, or with a drizzle of honey.

Cooking spray
4 teaspoons graham cracker crumbs
1 cup all-purpose flour
1 teaspoon baking soda
1 teaspoon ground nutmeg
½ teaspoon salt
¼ cup butter, softened
1 cup graham cracker crumbs
1 large egg
⅓ cup dark molasses
1 cup fat-free buttermilk
1 cup raisins

1. Preheat oven to 350°.

2. Coat an 8 x 4-inch loaf pan with cooking spray; dust with 4 teaspoons crumbs.

3. Lightly spoon flour into a dry measuring cup; level with a knife. Combine flour, baking soda, nutmeg, and salt in a large bowl, stirring with a whisk.

4. Place butter in a large bowl; beat with a mixer at medium speed until smooth (about 1 minute). Gradually add 1 cup crumbs; beat until well combined (about 2 minutes). Add egg, and beat 1 minute. Add molasses, and beat until well combined.

5. Beating at low speed, add flour mixture and buttermilk alternately to butter mixture, beginning and ending with flour mixture; beat just until blended. Stir in raisins. Pour batter into prepared pan.

6. Bake at 350° for 1 hour or until a wooden pick inserted in center comes out clean. Cool in pan 15 minutes on a wire rack; remove from pan. Cool completely on wire rack. Yield: 12 servings (serving size: 1 slice).

CALORIES 180 (27% from fat); FAT 5.4g (sat 2.8g, mono 1.6g, poly 0.6g); PROTEIN 3.3g; CARB 30.8g; FIBER 1g; CHOL 29mg; IRON 1.5mg; SODIUM 319mg; CALC 54mg

Blueberry-Lime Parfaits

Berries, lime juice, and maple syrup form a compelling trio of flavors. Since there are no granules to dissolve, rich maple syrup makes this recipe as easy as it is delicious. You can make and refrigerate the blueberry mixture up to 2 days ahead.

4 cups fresh blueberries, divided
⅓ cup Riesling or other slightly sweet white wine
⅓ cup maple syrup
2 tablespoons fresh lime juice
½ cup (4 ounces) ⅓-less-fat cream cheese
⅓ cup sifted powdered sugar
1 teaspoon grated lime rind
½ teaspoon vanilla extract
1 cup fat-free sour cream
Grated whole nutmeg (optional)

1. Place 2 cups blueberries in a large, heavy saucepan; press berries 2 times with a potato masher to slightly crush. Add wine, syrup, and juice; bring to a boil over medium-high heat, stirring occasionally. Cook 5 minutes, stirring occasionally. Reduce heat to medium; cook 3 minutes or until mixture thickens, stirring frequently. Remove from heat; cool to room

Continued

temperature. Stir in 2 cups blueberries. Cover and chill at least 2 hours.

2. Place cream cheese in a medium bowl; beat with a mixer at low speed until smooth. Add sugar, rind, and vanilla; beat well. Add sour cream; beat at low speed just until combined.

3. Spoon about 2½ tablespoons berry mixture into each of 6 (6-ounce) parfait glasses; top with about 1½ tablespoons cream cheese mixture. Repeat layers with remaining berry and cream cheese mixtures. Sprinkle each serving with nutmeg, if desired. Yield: 6 servings.

CALORIES 218 (22% from fat); FAT 5.4g (sat 3.2g, mono 1.4g, poly 0.3g); PROTEIN 4.6g; CARB 40g; FIBER 2.7g; CHOL 18mg; IRON 0.5mg; SODIUM 115mg; CALC 94mg

---

MAKE AHEAD
Rum Crème Brûlée

    1 cup evaporated fat-free milk
    1 cup 2% reduced-fat milk
   ⅔ cup nonfat dry milk
   ¼ cup sugar
    1 teaspoon sugar
   ⅛ teaspoon salt
    5 large egg yolks
  1½ tablespoons dark rum
    3 tablespoons sugar

1. Preheat oven to 300°.
2. Combine first 4 ingredients in a medium, heavy saucepan. Heat mixture over medium heat to 180° or until tiny bubbles form around edge (do not boil), stirring occasionally. Remove from heat.
3. Combine 1 teaspoon sugar, salt, and egg yolks in a medium bowl, stirring well with a whisk. Gradually add hot milk mixture to egg mixture, stirring constantly with a whisk. Stir in rum.
4. Divide milk mixture evenly among 6 (4-ounce) ramekins or custard cups. Place ramekins in a 13 x 9-inch baking pan; add hot water to pan to a depth of 1 inch. Bake at 300° for 50 minutes or until center barely moves when ramekin is touched. Remove ramekins from pan; cool completely on a wire rack. Cover and chill 4 hours or overnight.
5. Sift 1½ teaspoons sugar evenly over each custard. Holding a kitchen blow torch about 2 inches from the top of each custard, heat sugar, moving torch back and forth, until sugar is completely melted and caramelized (about 1 minute). Serve immediately or within 1 hour. Yield: 6 servings.

CALORIES 197 (24% from fat); FAT 5.2g (sat 1.9g, mono 1.9g, poly 0.6g); PROTEIN 9.6g; CARB 26.3g; FIBER 0g; CHOL 183mg; IRON 0.7mg; SODIUM 166mg; CALC 285mg

---

MAKE AHEAD
Butterscotch Pie

Make the pie a day ahead; the filling needs time in the refrigerator to set properly.

CRUST:

    1 cup all-purpose flour
    1 tablespoon powdered sugar
   ¼ teaspoon salt
  3½ tablespoons vegetable shortening
    3 tablespoons ice water
   ¾ teaspoon cider vinegar

FILLING:

    2 tablespoons butter
   ¾ cup plus 2 tablespoons packed
       dark brown sugar
    1 cup evaporated fat-free milk, divided
   ⅓ cup cornstarch
   ⅛ teaspoon salt
    3 large egg yolks, lightly beaten
    2 cups 2% reduced-fat milk
    2 teaspoons vanilla extract
  1½ cups frozen fat-free whipped
       topping, thawed

1. To prepare crust, lightly spoon flour into a dry measuring cup; level with a knife. Combine flour, powdered sugar, and ¼ teaspoon salt in a medium bowl; cut in shortening with a pastry blender or 2 knives until mixture resembles coarse meal. Combine water and vinegar. Sprinkle surface of flour mixture with water mixture, 1 tablespoon at a time; toss with a fork until moist. Gently press mixture into a 4-inch circle on plastic wrap, and cover. Chill 1 hour.
2. Preheat oven to 400°.
3. Slightly overlap 2 (15-inch) sheets of plastic wrap on a slightly damp surface. Unwrap chilled dough, and place on plastic wrap. Cover with 2 additional (15-inch) sheets of overlapping plastic wrap. Roll dough, still covered, into a 12-inch circle. Place dough in freezer 10 minutes or until plastic wrap can be easily removed.

4. Let stand 1 minute. Remove 2 sheets of plastic wrap. Fit dough, plastic wrap side up, into a 9-inch pie plate; remove remaining plastic wrap. Press dough against bottom and sides of pie plate. Fold edges under, and flute. Freeze 10 minutes.
5. Line bottom of dough with a piece of foil; arrange pie weights or dried beans on foil. Bake at 400° for 20 minutes or until pastry edge is lightly browned. Remove pie weights and foil; bake an additional 8 minutes or until done. Cool completely on a wire rack.
6. To prepare filling, melt butter in a large, heavy saucepan over medium heat. Add brown sugar; cook 2 minutes or until mixture resembles wet sand, stirring constantly with a wooden spoon. Add ¼ cup evaporated milk, 1 tablespoon at a time, stirring after each addition. Bring to a boil, stirring constantly; cook 30 seconds. Remove from heat.
7. Combine ¾ cup evaporated milk, cornstarch, ⅛ teaspoon salt, and egg yolks in a medium bowl, stirring with a whisk. Heat 2% milk in a small saucepan over medium heat to 180° or until tiny bubbles form around edge (do not boil), stirring frequently. Gradually add hot milk to cornstarch mixture, stirring constantly with a whisk.
8. Gradually add cornstarch mixture to brown sugar mixture, stirring with a whisk. Cook over medium heat 11 minutes or until thick, stirring constantly with a wooden spoon. Cook 2 minutes; remove from heat. Stir in vanilla. Place pan in a large ice-filled bowl 20 minutes or until mixture comes to room temperature, stirring occasionally.
9. Remove pan from ice. Spoon mixture into prepared crust. Cover and refrigerate 8 hours or overnight. Spread whipped topping evenly over filling just before serving. Yield: 10 servings.

CALORIES 280 (30% from fat); FAT 9.4g (sat 3.7g, mono 3.6g, poly 1.6g); PROTEIN 5.7g; CARB 42g; FIBER 0.4g; CHOL 75mg; IRON 1.3mg; SODIUM 182mg; CALC 159mg

Grilled Adobo Pork,
page 88

Four-Cheese Stuffed Shells with
Smoky Marinara, page 50

Raspberry-Almond Torte with Chocolate Ganache, page 84

Citrus-Couscous Salad, page 84

Asparagus with Black Pepper, Bacon, and Goat Cheese Sauce, page 83

Cold Poached Salmon with Fennel-Pepper Relish, page 83

Bourbon Fudge Brownies,
page 81

Chicken and Roast
Beef Muffulettas,
page 81

Graham Cracker Brown Bread,
page 55

Bibimbop
Rice and Vegetable Medley,
page 71

Fusion of Favorites

Armed with coconut milk, curry paste, and barley, a New York reader gets creative with Thai cuisine.

JeAnne Swinley recently lost 140 pounds and redesigned her eating habits in the process. "I really do love cooking, so I knew I had to develop the skills to satisfy my cravings for certain fatty ethnic foods," she says. Thai food is a favorite of JeAnne and her husband, Chaz. An avid *Cooking Light* reader, she credits the magazine with the recent addition of fish sauce, five-spice powder, and light coconut milk to her pantry. She came up with Thai Chicken-Barley Risotto while craving something both Thai and comforting.

Thai Chicken-Barley Risotto

1 tablespoon sesame oil, divided
1½ cups chopped green onions, divided
2 tablespoons minced garlic, divided
½ cup uncooked pearl barley
½ cup chopped fresh cilantro, divided
½ teaspoon salt
⅛ teaspoon black pepper
1 (14-ounce) can fat-free, less-sodium chicken broth, divided
2 jalapeño peppers, seeded and minced
¼ cup fresh lime juice
1 tablespoon brown sugar
1 tablespoon water
1½ teaspoons rice vinegar
1 teaspoon low-sodium soy sauce
½ teaspoon red curry paste
1 tablespoon chopped peeled fresh lemongrass
1 teaspoon grated peeled fresh ginger
3 cups shredded cooked chicken breast (about 1 pound)
1¼ cups red bell pepper strips
1 cup sugar snap peas, trimmed
1 cup light coconut milk
4 teaspoons chopped peanuts

1. Heat 1½ teaspoons oil in a medium saucepan over medium-high heat. Add ½ cup onions and 1 tablespoon garlic; sauté 1 minute. Stir in barley, ¼ cup cilantro, salt, black pepper, ½ cup broth, and jalapeños; bring to a boil. Cook 3 minutes or until liquid is nearly absorbed, stirring constantly. Add remaining broth, ½ cup at a time, stirring constantly until each portion is absorbed before adding next (about 15 minutes).
2. Combine juice and next 5 ingredients; set aside.
3. Heat 1½ teaspoons oil in a large non-stick skillet over medium-high heat. Add 1 cup onions, 1 tablespoon garlic, lemongrass, and ginger; sauté 1 minute. Add chicken, bell pepper, and peas; sauté 2 minutes. Stir in barley mixture, juice mixture, and milk; bring to a boil. Reduce heat; simmer 5 minutes or until sauce thickens, stirring occasionally. Stir in ¼ cup cilantro. Sprinkle each serving with 1 teaspoon nuts. Yield: 4 servings (serving size: 1¼ cups).

CALORIES 434 (26% from fat); FAT 12.4g (sat 3.9g, mono 3.7g, poly 3g); PROTEIN 41.6g; CARB 37.4g; FIBER 7.8g; CHOL 96mg; IRON 3mg; SODIUM 691mg; CALC 65mg

Sweet-and-Sour Carrot Salad

"I'm constantly looking for something new and outside the box of traditional Mexican offerings. This salad is a frequent addition to our regular menu throughout the seasons. Its refreshing crispness will heighten the flavor of any meal, and the colors will brighten your plate."
—Rochelle Taylor, Green Valley, Arizona

4 cups fresh bean sprouts
¾ cup shredded carrot
½ cup thinly sliced green bell pepper
½ cup thinly sliced red bell pepper
¼ cup sliced green onions
¼ cup chopped banana pepper
½ cup white vinegar
3 tablespoons sugar
1 tablespoon sesame oil
¼ teaspoon salt
⅛ teaspoon hot sauce
1 garlic clove, crushed

1. Combine first 6 ingredients in a medium bowl, tossing well. Combine vinegar and remaining 5 ingredients, stirring well with a whisk. Pour vinegar mixture over sprout mixture, tossing gently to coat. Cover and chill. Yield: 4 servings (serving size: 1 cup).

CALORIES 217 (15% from fat); FAT 3.7g (sat 0.6g, mono 1.4g, poly 1.5g); PROTEIN 3.8g; CARB 44.8g; FIBER 3.6g; CHOL 0mg; IRON 1.5mg; SODIUM 189mg; CALC 32mg

Family Night Menu
serves 4

For an easy weeknight meal, this menu is the answer. Make the potatoes while the pork cooks.

Curried Pork

Garlic mashed potatoes*

Gingersnap cookies

*Place 1½ pounds chopped peeled baking potato and 4 minced garlic cloves in a large Dutch oven. Cover with water; bring to a boil. Cook 15 minutes or until potato is tender; drain. Return to pan. Add ½ cup 2% reduced-fat milk, ¼ cup low-fat sour cream, 1 tablespoon butter, ½ teaspoon salt, and ½ teaspoon freshly ground black pepper. Mash to desired consistency; cook over medium heat 1 minute or until thoroughly heated.

Curried Pork

"I have been in America for nine years, my native country being England. I love Indian food, which is popular in my country. This is one of my favorite recipes that I cook."
—Jane Jordan, Englewood, Florida

Cooking spray
1½ cups finely chopped onion
1 cup chopped green bell pepper
1½ cups sliced mushrooms
¼ cup all-purpose flour
1 teaspoon curry powder
½ teaspoon salt
½ teaspoon black pepper
1½ pounds boneless pork loin, cut into ½-inch cubes
1 (14.5-ounce) can no-salt-added diced tomatoes, undrained

Continued

1. Preheat oven to 350°.

2. Heat a large nonstick skillet coated with cooking spray over medium-high heat. Add onion and bell pepper; sauté 3 minutes. Add mushrooms; sauté 2 minutes. Place onion mixture in an 11 x 7-inch baking dish coated with cooking spray.

3. Combine flour, curry powder, salt, and black pepper in a medium bowl, stirring with a whisk. Add pork; toss to coat. Recoat skillet with cooking spray; place over medium-high heat. Add pork mixture; cook 5 minutes, browning on all sides. Add pork mixture to onion mixture. Pour tomatoes over pork mixture. Cover and bake at 350° for 1 hour or until pork is done. Yield 4 servings (serving size: 1½ cups).

CALORIES 325 (28% from fat); FAT 10.1g (sat 3.4g, mono 4.4g, poly 1.2g); PROTEIN 40.1g; CARB 17.6g; FIBER 3.1g; CHOL 100mg; IRON 3.1mg; SODIUM 395mg; CALC 79mg

QUICK & EASY

Warm Chicken and Rice Salad

"This is a beautiful dish I came up with while trying to jazz up a grilled chicken salad. Currants add a unique flavor that goes nicely with the tarragon dressing while the cashews provide a refreshing crunch."

—Judy Kaplan, Forest Hills, New York

DRESSING:
- ¼ cup seasoned rice vinegar
- 1 tablespoon extravirgin olive oil
- 2 teaspoons finely chopped fresh tarragon
- ½ teaspoon Dijon mustard
- ¼ teaspoon black pepper

SALAD:
- 4 (6-ounce) skinless, boneless chicken breast halves
- ¼ teaspoon salt
- ¼ teaspoon black pepper
- Cooking spray
- 6 cups gourmet salad greens
- 2 cups hot cooked brown and wild rice blend
- 1 cup (4 ounces) crumbled feta cheese
- ½ cup dried currants
- 2 tablespoons dry-roasted cashews, salted

1. To prepare dressing, combine first 5 ingredients, stirring well with a whisk.

2. To prepare salad, sprinkle chicken with salt and ¼ teaspoon pepper. Heat a nonstick grill pan coated with cooking spray over medium-high heat. Add chicken; cook 5 minutes on each side or until done. Cut chicken into thin slices, and keep warm.

3. Place greens in a large bowl. Drizzle ¼ cup dressing over greens; toss gently to coat. Combine rice and remaining dressing, tossing to coat.

4. Divide greens evenly among 4 plates, and spoon ½ cup rice mixture over each serving. Top each serving with 1 chicken breast half, and sprinkle each serving with ¼ cup cheese, 2 tablespoons currants, and 1½ teaspoons nuts. Yield: 4 servings.

CALORIES 452 (30% from fat); FAT 15.3g (sat 6.9g, mono 5.8g, poly 1.3g); PROTEIN 37.3g; CARB 42.5g; FIBER 3.7g; CHOL 99mg; IRON 3.8mg; SODIUM 1,001mg; CALC 278mg

Chicken Souvlaki with Tzatziki Sauce

"My husband and I love the fresh-tasting combination of lemon juice, garlic, and olive oil that is so prevalent in Greek cuisine. Inspired by these flavors, I created this recipe. We serve it alongside a Greek salad of chunked tomatoes, cucumber, red onion, and feta cheese. *Tzatziki* is a traditional Greek yogurt-based sauce flavored with lemon, garlic, and crisp cucumbers."

—Lindsay Evans, Twisp, Washington

SOUVLAKI:
- 3 tablespoons fresh lemon juice
- 2 teaspoons olive oil
- 1½ teaspoons chopped fresh or ½ teaspoon dried oregano
- ½ teaspoon salt
- 4 garlic cloves, minced
- ½ pound skinless, boneless chicken breast, cut into 1-inch pieces
- 1 zucchini, quartered lengthwise and cut into (½-inch-thick) slices
- Cooking spray

TZATZIKI SAUCE:
- ½ cup cucumber, peeled, seeded, and shredded
- ½ cup plain low-fat yogurt
- 1 tablespoon lemon juice
- ¼ teaspoon salt
- 1 garlic clove, minced

1. To prepare souvlaki, combine first 5 ingredients in a zip-top plastic bag; seal and shake to combine. Add chicken to bag; seal and shake to coat. Marinate in refrigerator 30 minutes, turning once.

2. Remove chicken from bag; discard marinade. Thread chicken and zucchini alternately onto 4 (8-inch) skewers.

3. Heat a grill pan coated with cooking spray over medium-high heat. Add skewers; cook 8 minutes or until chicken is done, turning once.

4. To prepare tzatziki sauce, combine cucumber and remaining 4 ingredients, stirring well. Serve tzatziki sauce with souvlaki. Yield: 2 servings (serving size: 2 skewers and about ¼ cup tzatziki sauce).

CALORIES 219 (19% from fat); FAT 4.7g (sat 1.3g, mono 2.3g, poly 0.6g); PROTEIN 30.9g; CARB 12.3g; FIBER 2.4g; CHOL 69mg; IRON 1.4mg; SODIUM 705mg; CALC 161mg

Grilled Chicken with Fruit Salsa

"I made this recipe for a family reunion, and it's a good thing I doubled the salsa—it was gone in 30 minutes, and everyone wanted the recipe. This salsa is also good with salmon and tuna."

—Sarah Parslow, Providence, Utah

CHICKEN:
- ½ cup fresh lemon juice (about 4 lemons)
- ½ cup low-sodium soy sauce
- 1 tablespoon minced peeled fresh ginger
- 1 tablespoon lemon pepper
- 2 garlic cloves, minced
- 6 (6-ounce) skinless, boneless chicken breast halves
- Cooking spray

1½ cups cubed pineapple
¾ cup cubed peeled kiwifruit (about 3 kiwifruit)
¾ cup coarsely chopped orange sections
½ cup chopped peeled mango
½ cup chopped red onion
2 tablespoons chopped fresh cilantro
1½ teaspoons ground cumin
¼ teaspoon salt
⅛ teaspoon black pepper
1 small jalapeño pepper, seeded and chopped

1. To prepare chicken, combine first 5 ingredients in a large zip-top plastic bag. Add chicken to bag; seal and shake to coat. Marinate in refrigerator 1 hour, turning once.
2. Prepare grill or broiler.
3. Remove chicken from bag; discard marinade. Place chicken on grill rack or broiler pan coated with cooking spray; cook 5 minutes on each side or until chicken is done.
4. To prepare salsa, combine pineapple and remaining 9 ingredients, tossing gently. Serve with chicken. Yield: 6 servings (serving size: 1 chicken breast half and ½ cup salsa).

CALORIES 257 (9% from fat); FAT 2.6g (sat 0.6g, mono 0.6g, poly 0.6g); PROTEIN 40.9g; CARB 16.7g; FIBER 2.7g; CHOL 99mg; IRON 2mg; SODIUM 683mg; CALC 49mg

on hand

Noodling Around

Native to Asia, rice noodles translate well into many culinary uses.

Once available only at specialty grocers, rice noodles can now be found in mainstream markets. Rice noodles offer an entirely different "bite" than pasta. They aren't served al dente, but are cooked to sleek smoothness throughout. We suggest that you closely observe the cooking times, because they're easily overcooked.

Tandoori Shrimp Spring Rolls with Pineapple Sauce

Delicate rice sticks, a natural filling for spring rolls, are paired with tender rice paper wrappers.

ROLLS:
1 tablespoon finely chopped peeled fresh ginger
½ teaspoon crushed red pepper
½ teaspoon ground turmeric
1 pound medium shrimp, peeled and deveined
2 garlic cloves, minced
1 (8-ounce) carton plain fat-free yogurt
2 teaspoons olive oil
2 cups finely shredded napa (Chinese) cabbage
1½ cups fresh bean sprouts
½ cup cooked skinny rice stick noodles (about 1 ounce uncooked *py mai fun*)
¼ cup chopped green onions
2 tablespoons chopped fresh cilantro
½ teaspoon salt
1 tablespoon cornstarch
1 tablespoon water
6 (8-inch) round sheets rice paper

SAUCE:
⅓ cup pineapple preserves
¼ cup orange juice
1 tablespoon red wine vinegar
1 tablespoon low-sodium soy sauce
2 teaspoons prepared horseradish
1 teaspoon dark sesame oil
Green onion strips (optional)

1. To prepare rolls, combine first 6 ingredients in a large zip-top plastic bag. Seal and marinate in refrigerator 30 minutes. Remove shrimp from bag, discarding marinade.
2. Heat olive oil in a large nonstick skillet over medium-high heat. Add shrimp; sauté 4 minutes or until done. Stir in cabbage and next 5 ingredients; cook 2 minutes, stirring occasionally. Combine cornstarch and 1 tablespoon water in a small bowl. Stir cornstarch mixture into shrimp mixture; cook 1 minute or until slightly thickened.
3. Add hot water to a large, shallow dish to a depth of 1 inch. Place 1 rice paper sheet in dish. Let stand 30 seconds or just until soft.
4. Place sheet on a flat surface. Arrange about ½ cup shrimp mixture to cover half of sheet, leaving a ½-inch border. Fold sides of sheet over filling; starting with filled side, roll up jelly roll fashion. Gently press seam to seal; place, seam side down, on a serving platter (cover to keep from drying). Repeat procedure with remaining sheets and shrimp mixture. Cut each roll in half crosswise.
5. To prepare sauce, combine pineapple preserves and next 5 ingredients in a small bowl, stirring with a whisk. Serve with spring rolls. Garnish with green onion strips, if desired. Yield: 6 servings (serving size: 1 spring roll and 2 tablespoons sauce).

CALORIES 240 (17% from fat); FAT 4.4g (sat 1g, mono 1.8g, poly 1g); PROTEIN 20.1g; CARB 30.2g; FIBER 1g; CHOL 117mg; IRON 2.6mg; SODIUM 448mg; CALC 151mg

---

Guide to Rice Noodles

There are three basic types of rice noodles. The trickiest part of using them is that they frequently come in packages without cooking instructions. But happily, a saucepan, boiling water, and a few minutes are all you need. The big three:
• Skinny rice stick noodles also labeled *py mai fun*. Cook 3 minutes in boiling water.
• Rice vermicelli also labeled *bún giang tây*. Cook 6 minutes in boiling water.
• Wide rice stick noodles, also labeled *bánh pho*, have a width similar to fettuccine. Cook 5 minutes in boiling water.

To order rice noodles and other Asian ingredients, go to www.thaikitchen.com or call 800-967-8424.

Indian-Style Lamb Curry with Rice Noodles

Instead of serving this curry over the traditional bed of rice, try using rice noodles, which are more tender and better absorb the savory sauce.

1¼ pounds lamb stew meat, trimmed and cut into 1-inch cubes
¼ teaspoon kosher salt
¼ cup all-purpose flour
1½ cups chopped onion
1 tablespoon minced peeled fresh ginger
2 garlic cloves, minced
1 tablespoon curry powder
2 teaspoons ground cumin
2 teaspoons ground coriander
½ cup whipping cream
¼ cup mango chutney
2 (14-ounce) cans fat-free, less-sodium chicken broth
1 (15½-ounce) can chickpeas (garbanzo beans), drained
1 (14.5-ounce) can diced tomatoes, undrained
½ pound uncooked wide rice stick noodles (*bánh pho*)
½ cup chopped fresh cilantro

1. Heat a nonstick Dutch oven over medium-high heat. Sprinkle lamb with salt. Add lamb to pan; sauté 4 minutes or until browned.
2. Lightly spoon flour into a dry measuring cup; level with a knife. Add flour, onion, ginger, and garlic to lamb mixture; sauté 2 minutes. Stir in curry, cumin, and coriander; cook 1 minute. Add cream and next 4 ingredients; bring to a boil. Reduce heat; simmer 1 hour.
3. Cook noodles in boiling water 5 minutes or until done. Drain well. Place 1 cup noodles in each of 8 soup bowls. Spoon about 1 cup lamb mixture over each serving. Top each serving with 1 tablespoon cilantro. Yield: 8 servings.

CALORIES 387 (25% from fat); FAT 10.7g (sat 4.9g, mono 3.5g, poly 1.1g); PROTEIN 21.5g; CARB 51.1g; FIBER 3.5g; CHOL 67mg; IRON 4.6mg; SODIUM 543mg; CALC 83mg

Hot-and-Sour Chicken Noodle Soup

We added rice noodles to this Thai-inspired version of chicken noodle soup.

¼ pound uncooked wide rice stick noodles (*bánh pho*)
2 teaspoons olive oil
2 cups thinly sliced onion
2 cups water
1 teaspoon grated lime rind
¼ cup fresh lime juice
2 tablespoons brown sugar
1 tablespoon fish sauce
1 teaspoon green curry paste
2 (14-ounce) cans fat-free, less-sodium chicken broth
1 (15-ounce) can whole peeled straw mushrooms, drained
1 (14-ounce) can light coconut milk
1 (8-ounce) can sliced bamboo shoots, drained
2 tablespoons cornstarch
2 tablespoons water
1¼ pounds skinless, boneless chicken breast, cut into ¼-inch strips
2 tablespoons minced fresh cilantro

1. Cook noodles in boiling water 5 minutes or until done. Drain and rinse with cold water; drain well. Set aside.
2. Heat oil in a large Dutch oven over medium-high heat. Add onion; sauté 4 minutes or until tender. Stir in 2 cups water and next 9 ingredients. Bring to a boil; reduce heat, and simmer 30 minutes.
3. Combine cornstarch and 2 tablespoons water in a small bowl. Stir cornstarch mixture into soup. Bring to a boil; cook 1 minute, stirring constantly. Stir in chicken; cook 3 minutes or until chicken is done. Place ⅓ cup noodles and 1½ cups soup into each of 6 large soup bowls. Sprinkle 1 teaspoon cilantro over each serving. Yield: 6 servings.

CALORIES 258 (13% from fat); FAT 3.8g (sat 1.3g, mono 1.4g, poly 0.5g); PROTEIN 25.9g; CARB 28.5g; FIBER 1.4g; CHOL 55mg; IRON 1.9mg; SODIUM 1,014mg; CALC 37mg

Florentine Rice Noodle Gratin

Serve with French bread and a side salad.

½ pound uncooked wide rice stick noodles (*bánh pho*)
1¼ cups 2% reduced-fat milk
1 cup (4 ounces) grated Swiss cheese, divided
1 teaspoon chopped fresh rosemary
¼ teaspoon salt
¼ teaspoon ground nutmeg
¼ teaspoon black pepper
2 vegetable-flavored bouillon cubes
1 (8-ounce) block ⅓-less-fat cream cheese
1 teaspoon olive oil
1½ cups chopped onion
1 (10-ounce) package frozen chopped spinach, thawed, drained, and squeezed dry
Cooking spray

1. Preheat oven to 375°.
2. Cook noodles in boiling water 5 minutes or until done. Drain and rinse with cold water; drain well.
3. Combine milk, ½ cup Swiss cheese, rosemary, and next 5 ingredients in a blender or food processor, and process until smooth.
4. Heat oil in a large Dutch oven over medium heat. Add onion; cook 5 minutes or until tender, stirring frequently. Remove from heat; stir in noodles, cheese mixture, and spinach.

5. Place mixture in an 8-inch square baking dish coated with cooking spray; sprinkle with ½ cup Swiss cheese. Bake at 375° for 20 minutes or until bubbly and lightly browned. Yield: 6 servings (serving size: about 1¼ cups).

CALORIES 302 (23% from fat); FAT 7.6g (sat 4.2g, mono 2.3g, poly 0.6g); PROTEIN 14.7g; CARB 42.8g; FIBER 2.9g; CHOL 29mg; IRON 2mg; SODIUM 839mg; CALC 424mg

Vegetarian Pad Thai

We love this meatless version of Thailand's popular noodle dish.

⅔ cup chili sauce (such as Heinz)
¼ cup packed brown sugar
2 tablespoons water
2 tablespoons fish sauce
1½ teaspoons grated peeled fresh ginger
1 teaspoon chopped seeded serrano chile
½ pound uncooked wide rice stick noodles (*bánh pho*)
4 teaspoons vegetable oil, divided
1 (12.3-ounce) package extrafirm tofu, drained and cut into ½-inch cubes
2 large egg whites
1 large egg
3 garlic cloves, minced
2 cups fresh bean sprouts
¾ cup diagonally cut green onions
½ cup minced fresh cilantro, divided
⅓ cup coarsely chopped dry-roasted peanuts
6 lime wedges

1. Combine first 6 ingredients; set aside.
2. Cook noodles in boiling water 5 minutes or until done. Drain and rinse with cold water; drain well.
3. Heat 2 teaspoons oil in a large nonstick skillet over medium heat. Add tofu; cook 7 minutes or until browned, stirring occasionally. Remove from pan.
4. Combine egg whites and egg, stirring well with a whisk.
5. Heat 2 teaspoons oil in pan over medium-high heat. Add garlic, and sauté 10 seconds. Add egg mixture, and cook 30 seconds or until soft-scrambled,

stirring constantly. Stir in chili sauce mixture and noodles; cook 2 minutes. Stir in tofu, bean sprouts, onions, and ¼ cup cilantro, and cook 3 minutes or until thoroughly heated.
6. Sprinkle ¼ cup cilantro and peanuts over noodle mixture. Serve with lime wedges. Yield: 6 servings (serving size: 1⅓ cups noodle mixture, 2 teaspoons cilantro, about 1 teaspoon peanuts, and 1 lime wedge).

CALORIES 347 (25% from fat); FAT 9.6g (sat 1.6g, mono 3.5g, poly 3.5g); PROTEIN 10.9g; CARB 56.7g; FIBER 2.5g; CHOL 37mg; IRON 2.4mg; SODIUM 935mg; CALC 80mg

Clam-and-Shiitake Marsala Sauce over Rice Noodles

This is definitely not a typical clam sauce. The shiitake mushrooms give the sauce an earthy flavor; finishing with crème fraîche makes it creamy.

½ pound uncooked rice vermicelli (*bún giang tây*)
4 teaspoons olive oil, divided
4 cups thinly sliced shiitake mushroom caps
¼ teaspoon black pepper
2 cups chopped onion
2 tablespoons chopped garlic
1¼ cups dry Marsala wine
3 tablespoons all-purpose flour
3 (8-ounce) bottles clam juice
2 (6-ounce) cans chopped clams, drained
¾ cup (3 ounces) grated fresh Parmesan cheese
⅓ cup chopped fresh parsley
¼ cup (2 ounces) crème fraîche

1. Cook noodles in boiling water 6 minutes or until done. Drain and rinse with cold water; drain well.
2. Heat 2 teaspoons oil in a large saucepan over medium-high heat. Add mushrooms and pepper; sauté 4 minutes. Remove mushroom mixture from pan.
3. Add 2 teaspoons oil to pan. Add onion and garlic; sauté 4 minutes or until tender. Add wine. Reduce heat, and simmer 8 minutes or until liquid almost evaporates.

4. Sprinkle with flour; stir to combine. Add clam juice and clams; bring to a boil. Reduce heat; simmer until slightly thick (about 15 minutes). Stir in noodles, mushroom mixture, cheese, parsley, and crème fraîche. Yield: 6 servings (serving size: 1⅓ cups).

CALORIES 345 (29% from fat); FAT 11g (sat 5.2g, mono 4.5g, poly 0.7g); PROTEIN 11.9g; CARB 48.9g; FIBER 2.6g; CHOL 36mg; IRON 4.3mg; SODIUM 685mg; CALC 271mg

Rice Noodles with Shrimp and Basil-Mint Pesto

Rice noodles do a fabulous job of absorbing the pesto flavor. When measuring the basil and mint, don't pack the leaves, or you'll end up with a thick paste instead of a juicy pesto.

1⅓ cups loosely packed fresh basil leaves
⅓ cup loosely packed fresh mint leaves
⅓ cup macadamia nuts
2 tablespoons water
2 tablespoons fresh lime juice
1 tablespoon olive oil
1 tablespoon fish sauce
1½ teaspoons green curry paste
1 teaspoon minced garlic
½ pound uncooked skinny rice stick noodles (*py mai fun*)
Cooking spray
3 cups peeled and deveined small shrimp (about 1½ pounds)
2 cups chopped tomato
5 mint sprigs (optional)

1. Place first 9 ingredients in a food processor; process until smooth.
2. Cook noodles in boiling water 3 minutes or until done. Drain and rinse with cold water; drain well.
3. Place a large skillet coated with cooking spray over medium-high heat. Add shrimp; sauté 3 minutes or until done. Stir in pesto, noodles, and tomato; cook until thoroughly heated. Garnish with mint sprigs, if desired. Yield: 5 servings (serving size: about 1⅓ cups).

CALORIES 377 (28% from fat); FAT 11.6g (sat 1.8g, mono 7.6g, poly 1.2g); PROTEIN 22.6g; CARB 46.1g; FIBER 2.1g; CHOL 155mg; IRON 4.3mg; SODIUM 468mg; CALC 94mg

Beyond Burgers

Ground meats gain intrigue beyond burgers when they take on international flavors.

Thai Menu

serves 2

Larb

Hot cooked rice

Spicy sesame snow peas*

*Heat ½ teaspoon sesame oil in a nonstick skillet over medium-high heat. Add ½ pound trimmed snow peas; sauté 1 minute. Add 1 tablespoon rice vinegar, 1½ teaspoons low-sodium soy sauce, and ¼ teaspoon crushed red pepper, stirring to combine; cook 4 minutes or until peas are crisp-tender. Sprinkle with 2 teaspoons sesame seeds.

Game Plan

1. While water for rice comes to a boil:
- Combine juice mixture for larb
- Chop mint
- Core and halve cabbage
- Heat skillet for larb

2. While rice and turkey cook:
- Prepare snow peas

QUICK & EASY

Larb

Larb is a traditional Thai dish of spicy ground chicken, but ground turkey breast is leaner and just as tasty. Place the cooked turkey mixture in cabbage leaves for a delicious wrap.

TOTAL TIME: 25 MINUTES

QUICK TIP: If you can't find ground turkey breast, you can use ground chicken breast.

- 2 teaspoons grated lime rind
- 1 teaspoon grated lemon rind
- ¼ cup fresh lime juice
- 1 tablespoon fresh lemon juice
- 1 tablespoon fish sauce
- 2 teaspoons brown sugar
- ½ teaspoon finely chopped serrano chile
- ¼ teaspoon crushed red pepper
- 1 teaspoon vegetable oil
- 12 ounces ground turkey breast
- 1 tablespoon chopped shallots
- ½ cup coarsely chopped fresh mint
- ½ head green cabbage, cored and halved

1. Combine first 8 ingredients, stirring with a whisk until sugar dissolves.

2. Heat oil in a large nonstick skillet over medium-high heat. Add turkey and shallots; sauté 5 minutes or until done, stirring to crumble. Drizzle with juice mixture, stirring to coat. Sprinkle with mint. Serve with cabbage. Yield: 2 servings (serving size: about ⅔ cup larb and 1 cabbage wedge).

CALORIES 305 (12% from fat); FAT 4.2g (sat 0.9g, mono 1.3g, poly 1.4g); PROTEIN 46.6g; CARB 21.3g; FIBER 7.3g; CHOL 105mg; IRON 6.3mg; SODIUM 829mg; CALC 184mg

---

Greek Menu

serves 4

Gyros

Greek salad*

Vanilla yogurt with honey

*Combine 2 teaspoons olive oil, 1 teaspoon fresh lemon juice, ½ teaspoon salt, and ¼ teaspoon freshly ground black pepper, stirring well with a whisk. Combine 6 cups mixed salad greens, 2 cups chopped tomato, and ¼ cup (1 ounce) crumbled feta cheese in a large bowl. Add oil mixture; toss gently to coat. Serve immediately.

Game Plan

1. While broiler heats:
- Prepare meat mixture
- Drain cucumber and onion for sauce

2. While meat cooks:
- Prepare sauce for gyros
- Prepare salad

QUICK & EASY

Gyros

A Greek specialty, *gyros* are traditionally made from spiced, spit-roasted lamb. Here, we mold a ground lamb mixture into loaves. The yogurt dressing is a variation on traditional *tzatziki*.

TOTAL TIME: 19 MINUTES

QUICK TIP: Lemon juice is used in the meat mixture, sauce, and salad, so squeeze enough for all at one time.

LOAVES:

- 1 teaspoon onion powder
- 1 teaspoon garlic powder
- 1 teaspoon dried oregano
- 2 teaspoons fresh lemon juice
- ¼ teaspoon salt
- 3 garlic cloves, minced
- 6 ounces ground lamb
- 6 ounces ground sirloin
- Cooking spray
- ⅛ teaspoon ground red pepper

SAUCE:

- 1 cup shredded peeled cucumber
- ¼ cup vertically sliced red onion
- 1 tablespoon chopped fresh mint
- ½ teaspoon garlic powder
- ½ teaspoon fresh lemon juice
- ⅛ teaspoon salt
- ⅛ teaspoon black pepper
- 1 (8-ounce) carton plain fat-free yogurt

REMAINING INGREDIENT:

- 4 pocketless pitas

1. Preheat broiler.

2. To prepare loaves, combine first 8 ingredients, stirring well. Divide mixture in half, forming each half into a 6 x 3-inch loaf. Place loaves on a broiler pan coated with cooking spray; broil 7 minutes on each side or until done.

3. Sprinkle loaves with red pepper. Cut each loaf crosswise into ⅛-inch slices.

4. To prepare sauce, place cucumber and onion on several layers of heavy-duty paper towels. Cover with additional paper towels; let stand 5 minutes.

5. Combine cucumber mixture, mint, and next 5 ingredients, stirring well.

Divide meat slices evenly among pitas; top each serving with about ¼ cup sauce. Yield: 4 servings.

CALORIES 375 (28% from fat); FAT 11.6g (sat 4.4g, mono 4.7g, poly 1g); PROTEIN 25g; CARB 42.4g; FIBER 2.3g; CHOL 61mg; IRON 3.5mg; SODIUM 627mg; CALC 158mg

Ragù Menu
serves 4
Pork and Fennel Ragù

Romaine salad*

Focaccia

*Combine 2 tablespoons light mayonnaise, 1 tablespoon Dijon mustard, 2 teaspoons fresh lemon juice, 1 teaspoon red wine vinegar, ½ teaspoon Worcestershire sauce, and 2 minced garlic cloves in a large bowl, stirring with a whisk. Add 8 cups torn romaine lettuce, tossing gently to coat.

Game Plan

1. While ragù cooks:
  • Bring water for pasta to a boil
  • Prepare salad dressing
2. While pasta cooks:
  • Toss salad
  • Warm focaccia

Pork and Fennel Ragù

The flavor of this traditional meat sauce is reminiscent of Italian sausage.
TOTAL TIME: 38 MINUTES

Cooking spray
1 cup finely chopped onion
1 cup finely chopped fennel bulb
2 garlic cloves, minced
1 tablespoon fennel seeds
2 teaspoons sugar
1 teaspoon dried oregano
½ teaspoon salt
½ teaspoon crushed red pepper
¼ teaspoon ground red pepper
¼ teaspoon freshly ground black pepper
8 ounces lean ground pork

2 cups chopped tomato
½ cup fat-free, less-sodium chicken broth
4 cups hot cooked rigatoni (about 8 ounces uncooked pasta)
Fennel fronds (optional)

1. Heat a large nonstick skillet coated with cooking spray over medium-high heat. Add onion, chopped fennel, and garlic; sauté 5 minutes. Add fennel seeds and next 7 ingredients, stirring to combine; sauté 3 minutes.
2. Add tomato and broth; bring to a boil. Reduce heat, and simmer 15 minutes, stirring occasionally. Serve over pasta. Garnish with fennel fronds, if desired. Yield: 4 servings (serving size: 1 cup ragù and 1 cup pasta).

CALORIES 408 (30% from fat); FAT 13.7g (sat 4.7g, mono 5.7g, poly 1.6g); PROTEIN 18.6g; CARB 52.8g; FIBER 5g; CHOL 41mg; IRON 3.5mg; SODIUM 405mg; CALC 64mg

Meatballs Menu
serves 4
Meatballs and Rice Noodles

Sweet-and-spicy cucumbers*

Fresh mango with toasted coconut

*Combine 4 cups thinly sliced cucumber, 3 tablespoons red wine vinegar, ¾ teaspoon sugar, ¼ teaspoon salt, and ¼ teaspoon crushed red pepper, tossing gently to coat.

Game Plan

1. While water for noodles comes to a boil:
  • Prepare meatballs
  • Prepare cucumbers
  • Peel and slice mango
2. While meatballs cook:
  • Prepare sauce for meatballs and noodles
  • Chop herbs
  • Toast coconut

Meatballs and Rice Noodles

An Asian spin on spaghetti and meatballs, these pork and beef balls are nestled atop spicy rice noodles flavored with lime, garlic, and fish sauce. Try grinding ⅔ pound shrimp as a substitute for the pork mixture; the shrimp cooks in just 6 minutes.
TOTAL TIME: 30 MINUTES

3 tablespoons chopped shallots
2 teaspoons fish sauce
1 teaspoon fresh lime juice
2 garlic cloves, minced
1 bacon slice
6 ounces ground sirloin
6 ounces lean ground pork
Cooking spray
10 ounces uncooked rice vermicelli or thin rice stick noodles
½ cup warm water
6 tablespoons sugar
¼ cup fresh lime juice
1½ tablespoons fish sauce
2 teaspoons chili garlic sauce (such as Lee Kum Kee)
4 garlic cloves, minced
1 tablespoon chopped fresh basil
1 tablespoon chopped fresh cilantro
1 tablespoon chopped fresh mint

1. Combine first 5 ingredients in a food processor; process until smooth. Add beef and pork; pulse to combine.
2. Divide meat mixture into 12 equal portions, shaping each into a 1-inch ball. Heat a large nonstick skillet coated with cooking spray over medium-high heat. Add meatballs; cook 10 minutes or until meatballs are done, browning on all sides.
3. Cook noodles in boiling water 6 minutes; drain. Combine ½ cup warm water and next 5 ingredients, stirring with a whisk until sugar dissolves. Combine basil, cilantro, and mint. Divide noodles evenly among 4 plates; top each serving with 3 meatballs. Drizzle each serving with about ⅓ cup sauce; sprinkle with about 2 teaspoons herb mixture. Yield: 4 servings.

CALORIES 487 (28% from fat); FAT 15.1g (sat 5.6g, mono 6.6g, poly 1.2g); PROTEIN 19.1g; CARB 66.7g; FIBER 2.1g; CHOL 59mg; IRON 1.9mg; SODIUM 905mg; CALC 36mg

My Korean Kitchen

Cooking Light Assistant Food Editor Ann Taylor Pittman embraces the food of her mother's native country.

Growing up in Mississippi, Ann Taylor Pittman wanted to be like everyone else. That included eating what everyone else ate—fried okra, black-eyed peas, corn bread, chicken-fried steak, and mashed potatoes and gravy. But as she matured, she began to embrace the foods of her mother's native country. Here is a sampling of some of the recipes that she has grown to love.

Pork and Kimchi Dumplings

Serve *mandu* (a.k.a. dumplings) as an appetizer—the recipe doubles easily if you're expecting lots of guests. You can use wonton wrappers in place of *gyoza* skins.

DUMPLINGS:
- ½ cup finely chopped shiitake mushroom caps
- ½ cup finely chopped Shang Kimchi (recipe on page 69)
- ¼ cup finely chopped green onions
- 2 teaspoons mirin (sweet rice wine)
- 2 teaspoons low-sodium soy sauce
- 1 teaspoon cornstarch
- 1 teaspoon minced peeled fresh ginger
- ½ teaspoon dry mustard
- ½ teaspoon dark sesame oil
- 4 ounces ground pork
- 24 gyoza skins
- 1 teaspoon cornstarch
- Cooking spray

SAUCE:
- 3 tablespoons low-sodium soy sauce
- 1½ tablespoons mirin (sweet rice wine)
- 1½ tablespoons rice vinegar
- 1 tablespoon minced green onions
- 1 teaspoon sesame seeds, toasted
- ½ teaspoon dark sesame oil

1. To prepare dumplings, combine first 10 ingredients. Working with 1 gyoza skin at a time (cover remaining skins to prevent drying), spoon about 1½ teaspoons pork mixture into center of each skin. Moisten edges of skin with water. Fold in half, pinching edges together to seal. Place dumplings, seam sides up, on a baking sheet sprinkled with 1 teaspoon cornstarch (cover loosely with a towel to prevent drying).

2. Arrange half of dumplings in a single layer in a bamboo or vegetable steamer coated with cooking spray. Steam dumplings, covered, 10 minutes. Remove dumplings from steamer; keep warm. Repeat procedure with remaining dumplings.

3. To prepare sauce, combine 3 tablespoons soy sauce and remaining 5 ingredients. Serve sauce with dumplings. Yield: 8 servings (serving size: 3 dumplings and about 2 teaspoons sauce).

(Totals include Shang Kimchi) CALORIES 131 (24% from fat); FAT 3.5g (sat 1g, mono 1.4g, poly 0.8g); PROTEIN 5.8g; CARB 17.7g; FIBER 1.2g; CHOL 12mg; IRON 1.3mg; SODIUM 466mg; CALC 29mg

Bulgogi
Korean Beef Barbecue

- 1 pound top sirloin steak, trimmed
- 3 tablespoons low-sodium soy sauce
- 1 tablespoon mirin (sweet rice wine)
- 1 tablespoon brown sugar
- 1 teaspoon minced peeled fresh ginger
- 1 teaspoon dark sesame oil
- 3 garlic cloves, minced
- Cooking spray

1. Wrap beef in plastic wrap; freeze 1 hour or until firm. Remove plastic wrap; cut beef diagonally across the grain into 1/16-inch-thick slices.

2. Combine beef, soy sauce, and next 5 ingredients in a large zip-top plastic bag. Seal and marinate in refrigerator 1 hour, turning bag occasionally.

3. Prepare grill.

4. Place a wire grilling basket on grill rack. Remove beef from bag; discard marinade. Place beef on grilling basket coated with cooking spray; grill 5 minutes or until desired degree of doneness, turning frequently. Yield: 4 servings (serving size: 3 ounces).

CALORIES 208 (33% from fat); FAT 7.6g (sat 2.7g, mono 3.2g, poly 0.7g); PROTEIN 26.1g; CARB 6.4g; FIBER 0.2g; CHOL 76mg; IRON 3.1mg; SODIUM 457mg; CALC 19mg

---

Korean Barbecue Tips

Bulgogi, Korean barbecue, is one of Korea's most famous dishes. At Korean restaurants and in many Korean homes, you'll find people seated around the tabletop grill, which is used to quickly sear thin slices of marinated meat. The meat is often wrapped with short-grain rice in red-leaf lettuce leaves with fresh *shiso* (perilla leaves).

• The key to bulgogi is to slice the meat paper-thin so it absorbs the flavors of the marinade and cooks quickly. Freezing it briefly first makes this task easier. Use a very sharp knife or mandoline to create 1/16-inch-thick slices.

• Although Koreans cook bulgogi on tabletop grills, we've developed these recipes for standard backyard grills. Because the meat is sliced very thinly, you'll need to cook it on a wire grilling basket. For best results, allow the basket to heat on the grill a few minutes before adding the meat.

• The raw meat tends to clump on the basket. Just spread it out as best you can, and toss with tongs.

• You can also cook the meat in a large, heavy skillet (cast-iron works great) or grill pan over high heat for 3 to 5 minutes.

Ingredient Roundup

These recipes use mostly everyday ingredients, but there are a few authentic items you may have to get by going to an Asian market.

• Traditional Korean recipes are quite spicy—*sambal oelek* or crushed red pepper supplies heat in these recipes. Sambal oelek, unlike some other chile sauces, is neither sweetened nor seasoned with garlic, so the pure taste and fiery heat of chiles really come through. If you'd like to tame the flame, start by using only about half the amount of chile sauce or crushed red pepper called for. You can always add more, but it's hard to take it back.

• Many of these recipes call for toasted sesame seeds. Save yourself the time and trouble of toasting your own by purchasing pretoasted seeds, available in most Asian markets.

• The Rice Cake Soup (recipe below) calls for sliced rice cakes, which you'll find either in the freezer case or vacuum-packed on the shelves of your local Asian market. (They're sometimes labeled "rice ovaletts.") Sliced rice cakes are about the size and shape of sliced water chestnuts. When thawed and tossed into soup, they become soft but retain a pleasant resilience.

• *Mirin* is a low-alcohol, golden-hued rice wine that adds subtle sweetness to some of these dishes. Many large supermarkets carry it in the Asian foods section.

STAFF FAVORITE
Daeji Bulgogi
Spicy Korean Pork Barbecue

The caramel notes of brown sugar balance the heat of *sambal oelek* and crushed red pepper.

 1 pound pork tenderloin, trimmed
 2 tablespoons brown sugar
 2 tablespoons low-sodium soy sauce
 1½ tablespoons sambal oelek or Thai chile paste
 1 teaspoon minced peeled fresh ginger
 1 teaspoon dark sesame oil
 ½ teaspoon crushed red pepper
 3 garlic cloves, minced
Cooking spray

1. Wrap pork in plastic wrap; freeze 1½ hours or until firm. Remove plastic wrap; cut pork diagonally across the grain into ¹⁄₁₆-inch-thick slices.
2. Combine pork, sugar, and next 6 ingredients in a large zip-top plastic bag. Seal and marinate in refrigerator 1 hour, turning bag occasionally.
3. Prepare grill.
4. Place a wire grilling basket on grill rack. Remove pork from bag; discard marinade. Place pork on grilling basket coated with cooking spray; grill 5 minutes or until desired degree of doneness, turning frequently. Yield: 4 servings (serving size: 3 ounces).

CALORIES 205 (29% from fat); FAT 6.6g (sat 2.1g, mono 2.7g, poly 1g); PROTEIN 26.5g; CARB 8.9g; FIBER 0.3g; CHOL 80mg; IRON 1.6mg; SODIUM 471mg; CALC 16mg

---

MAKE AHEAD
Shang Kimchi
Summer, or Raw, Kimchi

Most *kimchi* is fermented for days or weeks. Although this recipe skips fermentation, it tastes authentic. Save some for the Pork and Kimchi Dumplings (recipe on page 68).

 14 cups coarsely chopped napa (Chinese) cabbage (about 2 pounds)
 3 tablespoons kosher salt
 2½ tablespoons sambal oelek or Thai chile paste
 2 tablespoons minced fresh garlic
 1 tablespoon sesame seeds, toasted
 2 teaspoons dark sesame oil

1. Place cabbage and salt in a bowl; toss gently to combine. Weigh down cabbage with another bowl. Let stand at room temperature 3 hours; toss occasionally. Drain; rinse with cold water. Drain; squeeze dry.
2. Combine cabbage, sambal oelek, and remaining ingredients. Cover and refrigerate at least 4 hours. Yield: 4 cups (serving size: ¼ cup).

CALORIES 19 (47% from fat); FAT 1g (sat 0.2g, mono 0.4g, poly 0.4g); PROTEIN 0.9g; CARB 2.5g; FIBER 1.9g; CHOL 0mg; IRON 0.3mg; SODIUM 302mg; CALC 51mg

---

D'uk Gook
Rice Cake Soup

To garnish the rice, toast seasoned nori sheets and cut them into quarters. Store them in an airtight container if you're not serving immediately. If you're using vacuum-packed rice cakes, don't presoak them; cook for 10 minutes instead of 5.

 1 nori (seaweed) sheet
 1½ teaspoons dark sesame oil, divided
 2 teaspoons vegetable oil
 1 tablespoon minced peeled fresh ginger
 4 garlic cloves, minced
 1 pound skinless, boneless chicken breast, cut into bite-sized pieces
 1 cup water
 2 teaspoons low-sodium soy sauce
 2 (14-ounce) cans fat-free, less-sodium chicken broth
 2½ cups frozen sliced rice cakes (rice ovaletts)
 1 large egg, lightly beaten
 ¼ cup thinly sliced green onions
 2½ teaspoons sesame seeds, toasted

1. Preheat broiler.
2. Rub 1 side of nori with ½ teaspoon sesame oil; broil, oiled side up, 30 seconds. Turn nori; broil 30 seconds or until browned (or a dark green color). Crumble nori; set aside.
3. Heat vegetable oil in a large Dutch oven over medium-high heat. Add
Continued

ginger and garlic, and stir-fry 30 seconds. Add chicken, and stir-fry 4 minutes. Add water, soy sauce, and broth, and bring to a boil. Cover, reduce heat, and simmer 15 minutes.

4. Soak rice cake slices in cold water 10 minutes; drain. Add to broth mixture. Increase heat to medium; cook, uncovered, 5 minutes or until rice cake slices are tender.

5. Reduce heat to low. Slowly drizzle egg into soup, stirring constantly. Cook 1 minute, stirring constantly. Stir in onions and 1 teaspoon sesame oil. Sprinkle with nori and sesame seeds. Yield: 5 servings (serving size: about 1½ cups soup, about 1 tablespoon nori, and ½ teaspoon sesame seeds).

CALORIES 308 (19% from fat); FAT 6.6g (sat 1.2g, mono 2.1g, poly 2.5g); PROTEIN 27.8g; CARB 32.4g; FIBER 1.3g; CHOL 95mg; IRON 2.2mg; SODIUM 458mg; CALC 25mg

Om Rice

Start with cold cooked rice (leftovers work great) so the oil will coat the grains and prevent clumping.

PORK:

1 teaspoon sambal oelek or Thai chile paste
1 teaspoon low-sodium soy sauce
½ teaspoon dark sesame oil
8 ounces boneless center-cut loin pork chops, trimmed and cut into ½-inch cubes
Cooking spray

RICE:

3 tablespoons low-sodium soy sauce
2 teaspoons to 1 tablespoon sambal oelek or Thai chile paste
2 teaspoons dark sesame oil
1 tablespoon vegetable oil
2 teaspoons minced peeled fresh ginger
4 garlic cloves, minced
¼ cup finely chopped carrot
1 cup sliced shiitake mushroom caps
1 cup chopped zucchini
¾ cup chopped green onions
½ cup chopped red bell pepper
3 cups cold cooked short-grain rice

CRÊPES:

1 teaspoon dark sesame oil
½ teaspoon kosher salt
3 large eggs, lightly beaten
4 large egg whites, lightly beaten

1. To prepare pork, combine first 4 ingredients in a small zip-top plastic bag. Seal and marinate in refrigerator 30 minutes. Heat a large nonstick skillet or wok coated with cooking spray over medium-high heat. Add pork mixture; stir-fry 2 minutes or until pork loses its pink color. Remove pork from pan. Cover and keep warm.

2. To prepare rice, combine 3 tablespoons soy sauce, 2 teaspoons sambal oelek, and 2 teaspoons sesame oil, stirring with a whisk; set aside.

3. Heat vegetable oil in pan over medium-high heat. Add ginger and garlic; stir-fry 30 seconds. Add carrot; stir-fry 1 minute. Add mushrooms, zucchini, onions, and bell pepper; stir-fry 3 minutes. Add rice; stir-fry 2 minutes or until thoroughly heated. Add pork. Drizzle soy sauce mixture over rice mixture; stir well to combine. Cover and keep warm.

4. To prepare crêpes, combine 1 teaspoon sesame oil, salt, eggs, and egg whites, stirring with a whisk. Heat an 8-inch nonstick skillet coated with cooking spray over medium-high heat. Pour about ¼ cup egg mixture into pan; quickly tilt pan in all directions so egg mixture covers pan with a thin film. Cook about 1 minute. Carefully lift edge of crêpe with a spatula to test for doneness. Turn crêpe over when it can be shaken loose from pan and underside is lightly browned; cook 30 seconds on other side. Place crêpe on a towel. Repeat procedure until all of egg mixture is used. Stack crêpes between single layers of wax paper or paper towels to prevent sticking.

5. Spoon about 1 cup rice mixture down center of each of 5 plates. Top each serving with a crêpe; tuck edges of crêpe under rice mixture. (The dish will look like a burrito.) Yield: 5 servings.

CALORIES 351 (30% from fat); FAT 11.7g (sat 2.7g, mono 4.3g, poly 3.7g); PROTEIN 20.6g; CARB 38.9g; FIBER 2.8g; CHOL 152mg; IRON 3.1mg; SODIUM 733mg; CALC 40mg

MAKE AHEAD
Radish and Carrot Salad

You'll almost always see some version of this dish at a Korean meal. It's traditionally made with *moo* (sweet Korean radish), but daikon radish is more readily available and makes a fine substitute.

2 cups (3-inch) julienne-cut peeled daikon radish
1 teaspoon kosher salt
1 cup (3-inch) julienne-cut carrot
1 tablespoon rice vinegar
2 teaspoons sugar
1 teaspoon mirin (sweet rice wine)

1. Combine daikon and salt, tossing well to coat. Let stand at room temperature 30 minutes. Rinse with cold water; drain. Combine daikon and carrot.

2. Combine vinegar, sugar, and mirin, stirring until sugar dissolves. Drizzle over daikon mixture; toss to combine. Cover and chill. Yield: 10 servings (serving size: ¼ cup).

CALORIES 13 (0% from fat); FAT 0g; PROTEIN 0.2g; CARB 3g; FIBER 0.7g; CHOL 0mg; IRON 0.1mg; SODIUM 55mg; CALC 8mg

Chapchae
Noodles with Beef and Mixed Vegetables

Chapchae is the most popular noodle dish in Korea. Adding a little cornstarch helps the marinade adhere to the beef mixture so that a little beef goes a long way. To make this easier to stir together and serve, snip the noodles after they've softened.

BEEF:

1 teaspoon cornstarch
8 ounces eye of round steak, trimmed and thinly sliced
1 tablespoon low-sodium soy sauce
2 teaspoons sambal oelek or Thai chile paste
1½ teaspoons minced peeled fresh ginger
½ teaspoon dark sesame oil
3 garlic cloves, minced
Cooking spray

NOODLES:
- 1 (3.75-ounce) package uncooked bean threads (cellophane noodles)

VEGETABLES:
- 1 teaspoon dark sesame oil
- 1 teaspoon vegetable oil
- ½ teaspoon crushed red pepper
- 5 garlic cloves, minced
- 3 cups sliced shiitake mushroom caps (about 6 ounces mushrooms)
- 1 cup (2-inch) diagonally sliced green onions
- 1 cup (2-inch) julienne-cut carrot
- 1 (10-ounce) bag fresh spinach

REMAINING INGREDIENTS:
- ⅓ cup low-sodium soy sauce
- 1 tablespoon brown sugar
- 1 tablespoon rice vinegar
- 1 tablespoon dark sesame oil
- 1 tablespoon sesame seeds, toasted

1. To prepare beef, sprinkle cornstarch over beef; toss to combine. Add 1 tablespoon soy sauce and next 4 ingredients; toss well to coat. Cover and refrigerate 30 minutes to 1 hour.

2. Heat a large nonstick skillet or wok coated with cooking spray over medium-high heat. Add beef mixture; stir-fry 3 minutes or until done. Remove mixture from pan. Cover and keep warm.

3. To prepare noodles, pour boiling water over noodles; let stand 10 minutes or until tender. Drain and rinse with cold water. Drain. Snip noodles several times with kitchen shears.

4. To prepare vegetables, wipe skillet or wok clean with paper towels. Heat 1 teaspoon sesame oil and vegetable oil in pan over medium-high heat. Add red pepper and 5 garlic cloves; stir-fry 30 seconds. Add mushrooms, onions, and carrot; stir-fry 3 minutes. Add half of spinach; stir-fry 2 minutes or until spinach wilts. Add remaining spinach; stir-fry 2 minutes or until spinach wilts.

5. Reduce heat to medium-low. Add beef mixture and noodles to pan, stirring well to combine. Combine ⅓ cup soy sauce, brown sugar, vinegar, and 1 tablespoon sesame oil, stirring with a whisk. Drizzle over noodle mixture; stir well to combine. Cook over medium-low heat 3

minutes or until thoroughly heated. Sprinkle with sesame seeds. Yield: 4 servings (serving size: 1¾ cups).

CALORIES 372 (26% from fat); FAT 10.9g (sat 2.2g, mono 4g, poly 3.6g); PROTEIN 26.1g; CARB 41.3g; FIBER 5g; CHOL 51mg; IRON 5.5mg; SODIUM 1,020mg; CALC 102mg

Bibimbop
Rice and Vegetable Medley
(pictured on page 60)

Bibimbop is a popular one-dish lunch of piping hot rice, an assortment of vegetables, often a small bit of meat, and always an egg on top. Koreans like this dish spicy, so they usually add at least 2 teaspoons chile paste per serving after cooking. It's customary to stir everything together before eating, but you can omit that step if you'd like to taste each element independently.

- 2 teaspoons low-sodium soy sauce
- ½ teaspoon minced peeled fresh ginger
- 1 garlic clove, minced
- 4 ounces eye of round or top round steak, thinly sliced
- Cooking spray
- 1 cup (2-inch) julienne-cut carrot
- 1 cup (2-inch) julienne-cut English cucumber
- ½ teaspoon sesame seeds, toasted
- ½ teaspoon rice vinegar
- ⅛ teaspoon kosher salt
- ⅛ teaspoon dark sesame oil
- 1 garlic clove, minced
- 4 large eggs, divided
- ¼ teaspoon kosher salt
- 3 cups hot cooked short-grain rice
- 1 cup thinly sliced shiitake mushroom caps
- 1 cup Seasoned Spinach (recipe at right)
- 4 teaspoons sambal oelek or Thai chile paste

1. Combine first 4 ingredients in a zip-top plastic bag. Seal and marinate in refrigerator 30 minutes. Heat a small nonstick skillet coated with cooking spray over medium-high heat. Add beef mixture; stir-fry 3 minutes or until done. Remove from pan. Cover and keep warm.

2. Cook carrot in boiling water 1 minute or until crisp-tender. Drain. Rinse with cold water; drain and set aside.

3. Combine cucumber and next 5 ingredients; set aside.

4. Heat skillet coated with cooking spray over medium-high heat. Break 1 egg into hot skillet. Cook egg 1 minute; carefully turn over. Sprinkle with dash of salt. Cook 1 minute or until desired degree of doneness. Remove from pan. Cover and keep warm. Repeat procedure with remaining eggs and salt.

5. Spoon ¾ cup rice into each of 4 bowls. Arrange ¼ cup each of beef, carrot, cucumber mixture, mushrooms, and Seasoned Spinach over each serving. Top each serving with 1 egg and 1 teaspoon sambal oelek. Yield: 4 servings.

(Totals include Seasoned Spinach) CALORIES 374 (20% from fat); FAT 8.3g (sat 2.4g, mono 3g, poly 1.4g); PROTEIN 23.8g; CARB 50.6g; FIBER 5.6g; CHOL 238mg; IRON 6.9mg; SODIUM 699mg; CALC 138mg

MAKE AHEAD
Seasoned Spinach

You will need to steam the raw spinach in two batches, since there is so much of it. Combining the cool ingredients with your hands is easiest.

- 2 (10-ounce) packages fresh spinach, divided
- ¼ cup finely chopped green onions
- 2 teaspoons low-sodium soy sauce
- 1 teaspoon sesame seeds, toasted
- ½ teaspoon dark sesame oil
- ¼ teaspoon kosher salt
- 2 garlic cloves, minced

1. Steam half of spinach, covered, 5 minutes or until spinach wilts; place steamed spinach in a colander. Repeat procedure with remaining spinach. Cool slightly, and squeeze dry.

2. Place spinach in a bowl. Add onions and remaining ingredients; toss mixture well to combine. Serve chilled or at room temperature. Yield: 6 servings (serving size: about ¼ cup).

CALORIES 31 (26% from fat); FAT 0.9g (sat 0.1g, mono 0.3g, poly 0.4g); PROTEIN 2.9g; CARB 4.2g; FIBER 2.8g; CHOL 0mg; IRON 2.7mg; SODIUM 214mg; CALC 96mg

Casseroles Redefined

Simple and wholesome, these recipes may change your view about one-dish meals.

In the 1950s, the casserole made its way into American kitchens and has held a place of dubious honor ever since. In the 1980s and 90s, however, as Americans became increasingly sophisticated about food and cooking, its reputation deteriorated.

But comfort food and home cooking are back, and it's time to reassess the casserole's potential. With fresh, colorful produce, flavorful cheeses, ethnic flavorings, exotic pastas, and healthful grains replacing cans of soup and vegetables, casseroles are an easy dinnertime solution for busy, health-conscious cooks.

These five recipes, filled with fresh, wholesome ingredients, are easy enough for weeknight meals—they're quick to throw together, and they don't dirty many dishes. All you need is a simple side salad to complete the meal.

Baked Barley with Shiitake Mushrooms and Caramelized Onions

Slow baking allows the barley to absorb the woodsy flavor of the mushrooms and the sweetness of the caramelized onion.

- 2 tablespoons butter
- 4½ cups chopped onion (about 3 medium)
- 1 teaspoon sugar
- 3 cups sliced button mushrooms (about 9 ounces)
- 3 cups sliced shiitake mushroom caps (about 8 ounces)
- 1½ cups uncooked pearl barley
- 1 tablespoon low-sodium soy sauce
- ¼ teaspoon salt
- ¼ teaspoon black pepper
- ⅛ teaspoon dried thyme
- 4 cups vegetable broth
- Thyme sprigs (optional)

1. Melt butter in a Dutch oven over medium heat. Add onion and sugar; cover and cook 25 minutes or until golden brown, stirring frequently. Add mushrooms; cook 10 minutes or until browned, stirring frequently. Add barley; cook 2 minutes, stirring frequently. Remove from heat. Stir in soy sauce, salt, pepper, and dried thyme.
2. Preheat oven to 350°.
3. Bring broth to a boil in a medium saucepan. Pour broth over barley mixture; cover and bake at 350° for 1 hour or until barley is tender. Let stand 10 minutes. Garnish with thyme sprigs, if desired. Yield: 6 servings (serving size: about 1⅔ cups).

CALORIES 292 (17% from fat); FAT 5.4g (sat 2.6g, mono 1.2g, poly 0.6g); PROTEIN 9.5g; CARB 55.1g; FIBER 10.7g; CHOL 10mg; IRON 2.4mg; SODIUM 908mg; CALC 42mg

QUICK & EASY
Couscous with Chickpeas, Tomatoes, and Edamame

Substitute thawed frozen green peas for the *edamame*, if you prefer.

- 1 tablespoon olive oil
- 1 cup fresh or frozen shelled edamame (green soybeans)
- ½ teaspoon crushed red pepper
- 4 garlic cloves, minced
- 2¼ cups water, divided
- ¼ cup chopped fresh basil
- 1 (16-ounce) can chickpeas (garbanzo beans), drained and rinsed
- 1 (14.5-ounce) can diced tomatoes, undrained
- ¾ teaspoon salt
- 1 cup uncooked couscous
- 2 cups coarsely chopped green onions
- 1 cup (4 ounces) crumbled feta cheese

1. Heat oil in a large skillet over medium heat. Add edamame, pepper, and garlic; cook 3 minutes, stirring frequently. Stir in ½ cup water, basil, chickpeas, and tomatoes; simmer 15 minutes. Add 1¾ cups water and salt; bring to a boil. Gradually stir in couscous. Remove from heat; cover and let stand 5 minutes. Stir in onions and feta; toss well. Yield: 5 servings (serving size: 1⅓ cups).

CALORIES 454 (28% from fat); FAT 13.9g (sat 5.4g, mono 4.3g, poly 2.6g); PROTEIN 20.7g; CARB 62.4g; FIBER 11g; CHOL 27mg; IRON 4mg; SODIUM 990mg; CALC 307mg

Orzo with Zucchini, Tomatoes, and Goat Cheese

For a make-ahead meal, cook the orzo, then toss with the rest of the ingredients in a 2½-quart casserole dish. Store, covered, in the refrigerator for up to 24 hours. Bake at 375° for 30 minutes or until thoroughly heated.

- 1 (16-ounce) package orzo (rice-shaped pasta)
- 1 tablespoon olive oil, divided
- 2 zucchini, quartered lengthwise and thinly sliced
- 1 garlic clove, minced
- ¼ cup minced fresh parsley
- 1 teaspoon minced fresh or ¼ teaspoon dried oregano
- ½ teaspoon salt
- ¼ teaspoon black pepper
- 1 (14.5-ounce) can diced tomatoes with garlic and oregano
- 1 (7-ounce) jar roasted red bell peppers, drained and chopped
- ½ cup (2 ounces) grated fresh Parmesan cheese
- ½ cup (2 ounces) crumbled goat cheese

1. Cook pasta in a Dutch oven according to package directions, omitting salt and fat. Drain; toss with 2 teaspoons oil.
2. Heat 1 teaspoon oil in pan over medium heat. Add zucchini, and cook 7 minutes, stirring frequently. Add garlic, and cook 3 minutes, stirring frequently. Stir in parsley and next 5 ingredients. Cook 5 minutes or until thoroughly heated. Remove from heat; stir in pasta and cheeses. Yield: 6 servings (serving size: 1⅓ cups).

CALORIES 429 (20% from fat); FAT 9.3g (sat 4.3g, mono 3.3g, poly 0.9g); PROTEIN 17.4g; CARB 67.5g; FIBER 3.9g; CHOL 15mg; IRON 4.2mg; SODIUM 781mg; CALC 228mg

Black Bean Burrito Bake

Half of the beans are finely chopped to give the filling a thick, creamy consistency. This dish can be made up to 8 hours in advance and chilled; just bring it back to room temperature before baking.

  1 (7-ounce) can chipotle chiles in adobo sauce
  ½ cup reduced-fat sour cream
  1 (15-ounce) can black beans, rinsed, drained, and divided
  1 cup frozen whole-kernel corn, thawed
  4 (8-inch) flour tortillas
  Cooking spray
  1 cup bottled salsa
  ½ cup (2 ounces) shredded Monterey Jack cheese

1. Preheat oven to 350°.
2. Remove one chile from can. Chop chile. Reserve remaining adobo sauce and chiles for another use. Combine sour cream and chile in a medium bowl; let stand 10 minutes.
3. Place half of beans in a food processor; process until finely chopped. Add chopped beans, remaining beans, and corn to sour cream mixture.
4. Spoon ½ cup bean mixture down center of each tortilla. Roll up tortillas; place, seam sides down, in an 11 x 7-inch baking dish coated with cooking spray. Spread salsa over tortillas; sprinkle with

cheese. Cover and bake at 350° for 20 minutes or until thoroughly heated. Yield: 4 servings (serving size: 1 burrito).

CALORIES 365 (29% from fat); FAT 11.7g (sat 5.8g, mono 2.8g, poly 0.8g); PROTEIN 15.7g; CARB 55.3g; FIBER 7.2g; CHOL 28mg; IRON 3.5mg; SODIUM 893mg; CALC 311mg

QUICK & EASY
Smoked Gouda Macaroni and Cheese

This American classic has been updated for heightened flavor. You can use regular Gouda or any other cheese that melts well.

  1 (1-ounce) slice whole wheat bread
  1 tablespoon butter
  ¼ cup thinly sliced green onions
  2 garlic cloves, minced
  2 tablespoons all-purpose flour
  2 cups fat-free milk
  ½ teaspoon salt
  ¼ teaspoon black pepper
  ½ cup (2 ounces) shredded smoked Gouda cheese
  ⅓ cup (about 1½ ounces) grated fresh Parmesan cheese
  5 cups coarsely chopped fresh spinach
  4 cups hot cooked elbow macaroni (about 2 cups uncooked)
  Cooking spray

1. Preheat oven to 350°.
2. Place bread in a food processor, and pulse 10 times or until coarse crumbs measure ½ cup.
3. Melt butter in a large saucepan over medium heat. Add onions and garlic; cook 1 minute. Add flour; cook 1 minute, stirring constantly. Gradually add milk, salt, and pepper, stirring constantly with a whisk until blended. Bring to a boil; cook until thick (about 2 minutes). Add cheeses; stir until melted.
4. Add spinach and macaroni to cheese sauce, stirring until well blended. Spoon mixture into a 2-quart baking dish coated with cooking spray. Sprinkle with breadcrumbs. Bake at 350° for 15 minutes or until bubbly. Yield: 4 servings (serving size: 1¼ cups).

CALORIES 399 (25% from fat); FAT 10.9g (sat 6.2g, mono 3g, poly 0.8g); PROTEIN 20.1g; CARB 54.9g; FIBER 3.7g; CHOL 33mg; IRON 3.6mg; SODIUM 725mg; CALC 421mg

well equipped

Blending Possibilities

No food processor? No problem. Break out the blender. It's good for bartending and more.

QUICK & EASY
Mango-Mint-Rum Slush

Fresh mint brightens the flavor of this cooler.

  3 cups coarsely chopped peeled mango
  1 cup ice cubes
  1 cup mango nectar
  ¾ cup white rum
  ¼ cup fresh lime juice
  2 tablespoons sugar
  1 tablespoon chopped fresh mint

1. Place mango in freezer 1 hour. Combine mango, ice cubes, and remaining ingredients in a blender; process until smooth. Serve immediately. Yield: 4 servings (serving size: about 1 cup).

CALORIES 242 (2% from fat); FAT 0.4g (sat 0.1g, mono 0.1g, poly 0.1g); PROTEIN 0.8g; CARB 34.8g; FIBER 2.4g; CHOL 0mg; IRON 0.3mg; SODIUM 5mg; CALC 17mg

QUICK & EASY • MAKE AHEAD
Blueberry-Balsamic Barbecue Sauce

Try this sweet and tangy sauce the next time you grill chicken, pork, or tuna. Add some sauce right at the end of cooking, and pass the rest at the table. If fresh blueberries aren't available, use 2 cups of thawed frozen blueberries.

  2 cups fresh blueberries
  ¼ cup balsamic vinegar
  3 tablespoons sugar
  3 tablespoons ketchup
  ½ teaspoon garlic powder
  ¼ teaspoon salt

Continued

1. Place all ingredients in a saucepan. Bring to a boil; reduce heat, and simmer 15 minutes or until slightly thick. Remove from heat; cool. Place blueberry mixture in a blender; process until smooth. Yield: 6 servings (serving size: about ¼ cup).

CALORIES 67 (3% from fat); FAT 0.2g (sat 0g, mono 0g, poly 0.1g); PROTEIN 0.5g; CARB 16.9g; FIBER 1.4g; CHOL 0mg; IRON 0.2mg; SODIUM 194mg; CALC 8mg

---

QUICK & EASY • MAKE AHEAD

Bean, Bacon, and Blue Cheese Dip

Serve with warm pita wedges or toasted baguette slices.

¼ cup chopped onion
1 tablespoon chopped fresh parsley
1 teaspoon chopped fresh or ¼ teaspoon dried thyme
¼ teaspoon salt
¼ teaspoon freshly ground black pepper
1 (15-ounce) can navy beans, drained
1 garlic clove, chopped
½ cup (2 ounces) crumbled blue cheese
3 bacon slices, cooked and crumbled (drained)

1. Place first 7 ingredients in a blender; process until smooth. Combine bean mixture, cheese, and bacon in a small bowl. Yield: 1½ cups (serving size: 2 tablespoons).

CALORIES 71 (33% from fat); FAT 2.6g (sat 1.4g, mono 0.8g, poly 0.2g); PROTEIN 4.4g; CARB 7.8g; FIBER 1.9g; CHOL 6mg; IRON 0.7mg; SODIUM 230mg; CALC 49mg

---

QUICK & EASY • MAKE AHEAD

Shallot and Grapefruit Dressing

Drizzle this zesty, citrusy dressing over mixed gourmet greens topped with goat cheese and roasted corn. You can squeeze your own grapefruit juice or look for fresh grapefruit juice in the produce section of the grocery store.

1 teaspoon olive oil
½ cup chopped shallots
2 cups fresh grapefruit juice (about 3 grapefruits)
2 tablespoons chopped fresh cilantro
2 teaspoons sugar
¼ teaspoon freshly ground black pepper
2 tablespoons olive oil

1. Heat 1 teaspoon oil in a large non-stick skillet over medium heat. Add shallots; cook 5 minutes or until golden brown. Stir in juice. Bring to a boil over medium-high heat, and cook until reduced to 1 cup (about 6 minutes). Remove from heat; cool.
2. Place grapefruit juice mixture, cilantro, sugar, and pepper in a blender; process until smooth. With blender on, slowly add 2 tablespoons oil; process until smooth. Yield: 1 cup (serving size: 1 tablespoon).

CALORIES 35 (51% from fat); FAT 2g (sat 0.3g, mono 1.5g, poly 0.2g); PROTEIN 0.3g; CARB 4.2g; FIBER 0.1g; CHOL 0mg; IRON 0.1mg; SODIUM 1mg; CALC 4mg

---

What to Look for in a Blender:

- **Multiple speeds.** If you're only going to make milk shakes or frozen drinks, a blender with one or two speeds will work fine. But for more versatility, choose a blender with several speeds (a pulse option is great, too). If you'll be making lots of frozen beverages, look for an ice-crushing mode.
- **Clear glass jar.** Stainless-steel jars look sleek and retro, but they don't allow you to see what you're blending. And although plastic jars won't break, they hold odors; blending a slushy drink after whipping up a garlicky sauce in one may not yield appetizing results.
- **Not-too-deep base.** You'll want this for three reasons: It makes cleanup easier, food won't get caught beneath the blades during blending, and when you blend a small amount, the food is mixed by the blades instead of being whirled to the sides.

Garden Greens Gazpacho

2 cups chopped peeled cucumber, divided
1 cup chopped spinach
4 cups low-fat buttermilk, divided
1 cup chopped green bell pepper, divided
2 tablespoons minced fresh cilantro
1 tablespoon chopped seeded jalapeño pepper
2 tablespoons fresh lime juice
¾ teaspoon salt
½ teaspoon freshly ground black pepper
½ cup sliced green onions
¾ cup reduced-fat sour cream
Cilantro leaves (optional)

1. Place 1 cup cucumber, spinach, 2 cups buttermilk, ½ cup bell pepper, and next 5 ingredients in a blender; process until smooth.
2. Pour puréed mixture into a large bowl; stir in 1 cup cucumber, 2 cups buttermilk, ½ cup bell pepper, and onions. Ladle soup into bowls; top with sour cream. Garnish with cilantro leaves, if desired. Yield: 6 servings (serving size: about 1 cup soup and 2 tablespoons sour cream).

CALORIES 132 (30% from fat); FAT 4.4g (sat 3g, mono 0.4g, poly 0.1g); PROTEIN 9g; CARB 14.9g; FIBER 1.2g; CHOL 20mg; IRON 0.6mg; SODIUM 497mg; CALC 246mg

---

QUICK & EASY

Cilantro-Pumpkinseed Sauce

Serve at room temperature with grilled flank steak or chicken. Or spoon over fish or chicken before baking. Pumpkinseeds are in produce sections of grocery stores or Latin markets.

¾ cup cilantro leaves
¼ cup chopped onion
2 tablespoons unsalted pumpkinseed or sunflower seed kernels, toasted
2 tablespoons chopped fresh parsley
1 tablespoon chopped seeded jalapeño pepper
¼ teaspoon salt
2 garlic cloves, peeled
2 mint sprigs
1 (7-ounce) can salsa verde

1. Place all ingredients in a blender; process until well blended. Yield: 1¼ cups (serving size: 1 tablespoon).

CALORIES 24 (49% from fat); FAT 1.3g (sat 0.2g, mono 0.4g, poly 0.6g); PROTEIN 1.4g; CARB 2g; FIBER 0.4g; CHOL 0mg; IRON 0.7mg; SODIUM 176mg; CALC 10mg

---

MAKE AHEAD • FREEZABLE
Romesco Sauce

Serve this sauce over pasta, and garnish with parsley sprigs.

  4 cups (1-inch) pieces red bell pepper
  1 cup fat-free, less-sodium chicken broth
  2 teaspoons olive oil
  ¾ cup (1-inch) cubed white bread (about 1 [1-ounce] slice)
  ¼ cup slivered almonds
  1 tablespoon sherry vinegar
  1 (14.5-ounce) can diced tomatoes, undrained

1. Combine bell pepper and broth in a large saucepan; bring to a boil. Cover, reduce heat, and simmer 15 minutes or until very tender.
2. Heat oil in a large nonstick skillet over medium heat. Add bread; cook 2 minutes or until lightly browned, stirring frequently. Add almonds; sauté 1 minute or until nuts are lightly browned. Place bell pepper mixture, nut mixture, vinegar, and tomatoes in a blender; process until smooth. Pour puréed mixture into pan, and cook 3 minutes or until

---

thoroughly heated. Yield: 4½ cups (serving size: ¼ cup).

NOTE: Store in refrigerator up to 1 week or in freezer up to 1 month.

CALORIES 29 (40% from fat); FAT 1.3g (sat 0.1g, mono 0.8g, poly 0.2g); PROTEIN 1g; CARB 3.6g; FIBER 0.9g; CHOL 0mg; IRON 0.2mg; SODIUM 64mg; CALC 11mg

---

superfast

. . . And Ready in Just About 20 Minutes

Italian-Style Hash Browns and Steak is just one of the tasty but quick dinners featured here.

  For a decidedly more adventurous meal, choose Duck Breast with Double-Cherry Sauce or Southern-Style Shrimp. Or, if you're craving classic comfort food, try our Rotini and Cheese with Broccoli and Ham or Turkey Soup Provençal.

QUICK & EASY
Duck Breast with Double-Cherry Sauce

Keep the duck warm by tenting it with foil after you remove it from the pan. If you can plan a day ahead, thaw the cherries in the refrigerator. You can also thaw them under warm running water while the duck cooks. Serve with rice pilaf.

  2 teaspoons vegetable oil
  4 (5-ounce) boneless duck breast halves, skinned
  ½ teaspoon salt, divided
  ¼ cup finely chopped shallots
  ¼ cup black cherry preserves
  2 tablespoons brandy
  1 (16-ounce) bag frozen pitted dark sweet cherries, thawed

1. Heat oil in a large nonstick skillet over medium-high heat. Sprinkle duck with ¼ teaspoon salt. Add duck to pan;

---

cook 3½ minutes on each side or until medium-rare or desired degree of doneness. Remove from pan; keep warm.
2. Add shallots to pan, and sauté 1 minute. Add ¼ teaspoon salt, preserves, brandy, and cherries, and cook 2 minutes or until slightly thick. Serve duck with sauce. Yield: 4 servings (serving size: 1 duck breast half and ⅓ cup sauce).

CALORIES 379 (24% from fat); FAT 9.9g (sat 2.6g, mono 3.8g, poly 1.5g); PROTEIN 30.2g; CARB 36.4g; FIBER 6.1g; CHOL 109mg; IRON 8.1mg; SODIUM 381mg; CALC 45mg

---

QUICK & EASY
Seared Sesame Tuna with Orange Sauce

There's no need to toast the sesame seeds before rubbing them on the tuna because they brown in the skillet while the tuna cooks. Serve this entrée with steamed snow peas or broccoli.

  1 cup water
  ½ teaspoon salt, divided
  ⅔ cup uncooked couscous
     Cooking spray
  ¼ cup sesame seeds
  1 tablespoon all-purpose flour
  ¼ teaspoon black pepper
  4 (6-ounce) Bluefin tuna steaks (about ¾ inch thick)
  ½ cup fresh orange juice (about 2 oranges)
  1 tablespoon honey
  1 tablespoon low-sodium soy sauce
  1 teaspoon dark sesame oil
  ½ teaspoon bottled minced ginger
  ½ teaspoon bottled minced garlic
  1 tablespoon water
  2 teaspoons cornstarch

1. Bring 1 cup water and ¼ teaspoon salt to a boil in a medium saucepan; gradually stir in couscous. Remove from heat; cover and let stand 5 minutes. Fluff with a fork.
2. While couscous stands, heat a large nonstick skillet coated with cooking spray over medium-high heat. Combine ¼ teaspoon salt, sesame seeds, flour, and black pepper. Dredge both sides of tuna steaks in sesame seed mixture. Add fish
Continued

to pan, and cook 4 minutes on each side or until desired degree of doneness. Remove fish from pan, and keep warm.

3. While fish cooks, combine orange juice and next 5 ingredients in a small saucepan, and bring to a boil over medium-high heat. Combine 1 tablespoon water and cornstarch, stirring with a whisk until smooth. Add cornstarch mixture to pan, and cook 2 minutes or until sauce is thickened, stirring frequently. Serve fish with couscous and sauce. Yield: 4 servings (serving size: 1 steak, about ½ cup couscous, and 2½ tablespoons sauce).

CALORIES 460 (28% from fat); FAT 14.3g (sat 3g, mono 4.1g, poly 4.9g); PROTEIN 45.7g; CARB 35.2g; FIBER 1.6g; CHOL 65mg; IRON 3.6mg; SODIUM 513mg; CALC 118mg

Lamb Chops with Sautéed Apples

Slice the apples while the chops cook.

Cooking spray
- 8 (4-ounce) lamb loin chops, trimmed
- 1 teaspoon butter
- 2 cups sliced Braeburn apple (about 2 medium)
- 2 tablespoons brown sugar
- 1 tablespoon water
- ½ teaspoon salt
- ¼ teaspoon ground cinnamon
- ⅛ teaspoon ground cloves

1. Heat a large skillet coated with cooking spray over medium-high heat. Add lamb chops, and cook 5 minutes on each side or until desired degree of doneness. Remove lamb chops from pan, and keep warm.

2. Add butter to pan, scraping pan to loosen browned bits. Add apple; sauté 5 minutes. Add brown sugar, water, salt, cinnamon, and cloves; cook 2 minutes or until sugar dissolves, stirring constantly. Serve with lamb. Yield: 4 servings (serving size: 2 chops and about ½ cup apples).

CALORIES 202 (32% from fat); FAT 7.1g (sat 2.8g, mono 3g, poly 0.4g); PROTEIN 18.8g; CARB 15.5g; FIBER 2.6g; CHOL 62mg; IRON 1.5mg; SODIUM 355mg; CALC 18mg

Turkey Soup Provençal

- 1 pound ground turkey breast
- ½ teaspoon dried herbes de Provence, crushed
- 1 (15-ounce) can cannellini beans or other white beans, drained
- 1 (14-ounce) can fat-free, less-sodium chicken broth
- 1 (14.5-ounce) can diced tomatoes with garlic and onion, undrained
- 4 cups chopped fresh spinach

1. Cook turkey in a large saucepan over medium-high heat until browned, stirring to crumble.

2. Add herbes de Provence, beans, broth, and tomatoes to pan; bring to a boil. Reduce heat, and simmer 5 minutes. Stir in spinach; simmer 5 minutes. Yield: 4 servings (serving size: 1¼ cups).

CALORIES 294 (12% from fat); FAT 3.8g (sat 1.5g, mono 0.8g, poly 0.4g); PROTEIN 40g; CARB 25.4g; FIBER 5.4g; CHOL 75mg; IRON 6.1mg; SODIUM 890mg; CALC 206mg

Mushroom Pasta

To make this dish vegetarian, use vegetable broth instead of chicken broth.

- 12 ounces uncooked medium egg noodles
- 1 tablespoon olive oil
- 1½ teaspoons all-purpose flour
- 3 cups sliced cremini mushrooms
- 2 (8-ounce) packages presliced button mushrooms
- 1 cup fat-free, less-sodium chicken broth
- ½ cup white wine
- 1 tablespoon fresh lemon juice
- ½ teaspoon salt
- 2 tablespoons butter
- ¾ teaspoon black pepper
- ½ cup (2 ounces) preshredded fresh Parmesan cheese

1. Cook noodles according to package directions, omitting salt and fat.

2. While noodles cook, combine oil and flour in a large Dutch oven over medium-high heat, and sauté 1 minute. Add

mushrooms; sauté 2 minutes. Add broth, wine, juice, and salt; cook 8 minutes or until sauce is slightly thick.

3. Stir in butter and pepper. Add noodles; toss to coat. Stir in cheese. Yield: 5 servings (serving size: 2 cups).

CALORIES 434 (29% from fat); FAT 13.9g (sat 6.1g, mono 5.2g, poly 1.4g); PROTEIN 19.2g; CARB 55.1g; FIBER 3.8g; CHOL 86mg; IRON 4.6mg; SODIUM 613mg; CALC 187mg

Pork and Cheese Quesadillas

Ask for ground pork loin at your grocer's meat counter. To vary the flavor of the quesadillas, buy the skinless, boneless chicken breasts, and grind them in a food processor.

Cooking spray
- ½ cup chopped onion
- 2 teaspoons bottled minced garlic
- 1 pound ground pork loin
- 1 (4.5-ounce) can chopped green chiles, undrained
- 8 (6½-inch) flour tortillas (such as Mission)
- 1½ cups (6 ounces) preshredded light Mexican cheese blend (such as Sargento)
- ¼ cup chopped green onions
- ½ cup fat-free sour cream
- ½ cup bottled salsa

1. Preheat broiler.

2. Heat a large nonstick skillet coated with cooking spray over medium-high heat. Add onion, garlic, pork, and chiles; cook 6 minutes or until browned, stirring to crumble.

3. Place 4 tortillas in a single layer on a baking sheet. Spread about ⅓ cup pork mixture over each tortilla; top each with about ⅓ cup cheese, 1 tablespoon green onions, and 1 tortilla.

4. Broil quesadillas 1½ minutes on each side or until crisp. Cut each quesadilla into 4 wedges. Serve with sour cream and salsa. Yield: 4 servings (serving size: 4 wedges, 2 tablespoons sour cream, and 2 tablespoons salsa).

CALORIES 472 (23% from fat); FAT 12g (sat 6.2g, mono 3.3g, poly 0.7g); PROTEIN 46g; CARB 44.6g; FIBER 3.7g; CHOL 98mg; IRON 3.9mg; SODIUM 972mg; CALC 434mg

Southern-Style Shrimp

Bottled real bacon bits add smoky flavor without the hassle of frying. Serve over rice or with corn bread.

  1 tablespoon butter
  2 tablespoons bottled real bacon bits, divided
  1 teaspoon bottled minced garlic
1½ pounds peeled and deveined large shrimp
  1 (8-ounce) package presliced mushrooms
  ½ cup sliced green onions
  ¼ teaspoon salt
  ½ teaspoon hot pepper sauce
  ¼ cup chopped fresh parsley
  1 tablespoon lemon juice

1. Melt butter in a large nonstick skillet over medium-high heat. Add 1 tablespoon bacon bits and garlic; sauté 1 minute. Add shrimp; sauté 3 minutes. Add mushrooms; cook 1 minute or until mushrooms are tender and shrimp is done, stirring frequently. Stir in onions, salt, and hot sauce; remove from heat. Stir in parsley and lemon juice. Sprinkle with 1 tablespoon bacon bits. Yield: 4 servings (serving size: about 1 cup).

CALORIES 245 (24% from fat); FAT 6.5g (sat 2.6g, mono 1.6g, poly 1.3g); PROTEIN 38.6g; CARB 5.3g; FIBER 1.9g; CHOL 269mg; IRON 4.9mg; SODIUM 570mg; CALC 97mg

Turkey Paprikash

You can also use chicken tenders.

  8 ounces uncooked medium egg noodles
  2 teaspoons vegetable oil
  1 cup reduced-fat sour cream
  2 tablespoons paprika, divided
  ½ teaspoon salt, divided
  ¼ teaspoon black pepper
  1 cup vertically sliced onion
  1 pound turkey breast cutlets, cut into ¼-inch-wide strips
  ½ cup fat-free, less-sodium chicken broth

1. Cook noodles according to package directions, omitting salt and fat.
2. While noodles cook, heat oil in a large nonstick skillet over medium-high heat. Combine sour cream, 1 tablespoon paprika, ¼ teaspoon salt, and pepper in a bowl; set aside.
3. Combine 1 tablespoon paprika, ¼ teaspoon salt, onion, and turkey, tossing to coat. Add turkey mixture to pan; sauté 4 minutes or until turkey is done. Add broth; cook 2 minutes or until liquid almost evaporates. Reduce heat to medium-low.
4. Add sour cream mixture; cook 1 minute or until thoroughly heated, stirring constantly (do not boil). Serve over noodles. Yield: 4 servings (serving size: about ½ cup turkey mixture and 1 cup egg noodles).

CALORIES 477 (25% from fat); FAT 13.3g (sat 5.9g, mono 3.6g, poly 2.8g); PROTEIN 39.5g; CARB 48.4g; FIBER 3.1g; CHOL 154mg; IRON 3.2mg; SODIUM 452mg; CALC 143mg

Italian-Style Hash Browns and Steak

No need to peel and dice potatoes, onions, or peppers. Buy frozen precut potatoes with chopped onion and bell pepper, such as Ore-Ida Potatoes O'Brien, to save several prep steps. If you don't have a mortar and pestle, you can grind the fennel seeds in a spice or coffee grinder, then combine them with the salt, pepper, and garlic.

  1 tablespoon olive oil
1¼ teaspoons salt, divided
  1 teaspoon dried oregano
  ½ teaspoon black pepper, divided
  1 (28-ounce) package frozen hash brown potatoes with onions and peppers (such as Ore-Ida Potatoes O'Brien)
  1 teaspoon fennel seeds
  ½ teaspoon bottled minced garlic
  1 (1-pound) boneless sirloin steak
Cooking spray

1. Heat oil in a large nonstick skillet over medium-high heat. Add ¾ teaspoon salt, oregano, ¼ teaspoon pepper, and potatoes; cook 10 minutes or until

potatoes are browned, stirring occasionally. Remove from pan.
2. While potatoes cook, combine ½ teaspoon salt, ¼ teaspoon pepper, fennel seeds, and garlic in a mortar. Mash to a paste with a pestle; rub over steak.
3. Heat a nonstick skillet coated with cooking spray over medium-high heat. Add steak; cook 3 minutes on each side or until desired degree of doneness. Thinly slice steak; serve with potatoes. Yield: 4 servings (serving size: 3 ounces steak and 1 cup potatoes).

CALORIES 350 (27% from fat); FAT 10.4g (sat 3.1g, mono 5.5g, poly 0.6g); PROTEIN 28.7g; CARB 31.5g; FIBER 5.2g; CHOL 77mg; IRON 3.3mg; SODIUM 826mg; CALC 24mg

Breaded Veal Topped with Tomatoes, Spinach, and Lemon

  ½ cup all-purpose flour
  2 large eggs, lightly beaten
  1 cup dry breadcrumbs
  4 (4-ounce) veal cutlets (about ¼ inch thick)
  ½ teaspoon salt
  ¼ teaspoon black pepper
  4 teaspoons olive oil, divided
Cooking spray
  2 teaspoons balsamic vinegar
  ⅛ teaspoon salt
  3 cups fresh spinach
  1 cup grape tomatoes, halved (about ¼ pound)
  1 lemon, quartered

1. Place flour in a shallow dish. Place eggs in another shallow dish. Place dry breadcrumbs in another shallow dish. Sprinkle veal with ½ teaspoon salt and black pepper. Working with 1 cutlet at a time, dredge veal in flour, turning to coat; shake off excess flour. Dip veal in egg, and dredge in breadcrumb mixture.
2. Heat 2 teaspoons oil in a large nonstick skillet coated with cooking spray over medium-high heat. Add veal; cook 4 minutes. Turn veal over; cook 3 minutes or until done.
3. While veal cooks, combine 2 teaspoons oil, vinegar, and ⅛ teaspoon salt

Continued

in a large bowl. Add spinach and tomatoes; toss gently to coat. Top veal with spinach mixture; serve with lemon wedges. Yield: 4 servings (serving size: 1 cutlet, ¾ cup spinach mixture, and 1 lemon wedge).

CALORIES 384 (29% from fat); FAT 12.5g (sat 2.9g, mono 6.2g, poly 2.8g); PROTEIN 32.5g; CARB 33.8g; FIBER 2.4g; CHOL 197mg; IRON 4.2mg; SODIUM 730mg; CALC 97mg

---

Rotini and Cheese with Broccoli and Ham

Serve this creamy dish with a tossed green salad or a fruit salad.

QUICK TIP: Whenever you're using frozen vegetables in a pasta dish, go ahead and toss them in with the pasta while it's cooking so both are done at the same time.

    4   quarts water
    8   ounces uncooked rotini
        (corkscrew pasta)
    1   (10-ounce) package frozen
        chopped broccoli
    ¼   cup all-purpose flour
    2   cups fat-free milk
    1½ cups (6 ounces) cubed light
        processed cheese (such as
        Velveeta Light)
    2   teaspoons Dijon mustard
    ½   teaspoon salt
    ¼   teaspoon garlic powder
    ¼   teaspoon black pepper
    1   cup chopped reduced-fat ham

1. Bring water to a boil in a large stockpot. Add pasta; cook 5 minutes. Add broccoli; cook 5 minutes or until pasta is done; drain.
2. While pasta cooks, lightly spoon flour into a dry measuring cup; level with a knife. Place flour in a medium saucepan; gradually add milk, stirring with a whisk until blended. Cook over medium heat 8 minutes or until mixture is thick; stir frequently.
3. Remove from heat; stir in cheese and next 4 ingredients. Combine pasta mixture, cheese sauce, and ham. Yield: 6 servings (serving size: 1¾ cups).

CALORIES 288 (15% from fat); FAT 4.7g (sat 2.5g, mono 0.6g, poly 0.4g); PROTEIN 19.1g; CARB 42.6g; FIBER 2.6g; CHOL 23mg; IRON 2.5mg; SODIUM 937mg; CALC 296mg

---

technique

The Slow Lane

Simmer down. The antidote to a fast-forward life may already be in your kitchen: the slow cooker.

What made the slow cooker successful in the '70s holds true today: You can use the slow cooker to make family meals and company fare alike while you save valuable time and energy. With practically no effort at all, you can create succulent braised or simmered dishes (and ingredients for other dishes) that will make you glad that there are extra electrical outlets in your kitchen. Ready? Then slow down with these recipes.

Tiny French Beans with Smoked Sausage

Find flageolets, tiny French kidney beans, in specialty food stores. For a nice presentation, garnish with thyme sprigs.

    2   pounds smoked turkey sausage,
        cut into 1½-inch pieces
    1   tablespoon vegetable oil
    ⅓   cup minced shallots
    3   garlic cloves, minced
    2   cups dried flageolets or other dried
        white beans (about 1 pound)
    2   cups water
    ¼   cup minced fresh or 1 tablespoon
        dried thyme
    1   teaspoon celery seeds
    ¼   teaspoon freshly ground black
        pepper
    2   (14-ounce) cans fat-free,
        less-sodium chicken broth

1. Heat a large nonstick skillet over medium heat. Add sausage; sauté 5 minutes or until browned. Remove from pan, and place in an electric slow cooker. Heat oil in pan over medium heat. Add shallots and garlic; sauté 1 minute.
2. Sort and wash beans. Add beans, shallot mixture, water, and remaining ingredients to slow cooker. Cover and cook on HIGH 8 hours or until beans are tender. Yield: 8 servings (serving size: 1¼ cups).

CALORIES 397 (30% from fat); FAT 13.1g (sat 3.7g, mono 4.3g, poly 3.7g); PROTEIN 29.7g; CARB 41.4g; FIBER 8.6g; CHOL 75mg; IRON 5.2mg; SODIUM 1,105mg; CALC 143mg

---

Stewed Dried Plums in Marsala

Marsala is a deep, robust fortified wine from Sicily. It comes in both dry and sweet varieties. For the best flavor, marinate the dried plums overnight, then let them reach room temperature before serving.

    1   orange
    1   lemon
    3   cups pitted dried plums (about
        1 pound)
    2   cups orange juice
    1   cup sweet Marsala wine
    1   (3-inch) cinnamon stick
    Yogurt Cream

1. Carefully remove rinds from orange and lemon using a vegetable peeler, making sure to avoid white pith; discard orange and lemon.
2. Place rinds, plums, juice, Marsala, and cinnamon in an electric slow cooker; stir to combine. Cover and cook on LOW 4 hours or until plums are very tender. Discard rinds and cinnamon stick. Cover and chill plum mixture overnight. Serve at room temperature with Yogurt Cream. Yield: 8 servings (serving size: ½ cup plum mixture and 2 tablespoons Yogurt Cream).

(Totals include Yogurt Cream) CALORIES 272 (5% from fat); FAT 1.4g (sat 0.6g, mono 0.5g, poly 0.1g); PROTEIN 5.2g; CARB 60.8g; FIBER 4.7g; CHOL 4mg; IRON 1.9mg; SODIUM 48mg; CALC 151mg

---

YOGURT CREAM:

Called yogurt cheese when it's unsweetened, this thick, tangy condiment is a snap to make. In fact, it's likely to become one of your favorite kitchen staples.

    1   (16-ounce) carton plain low-fat
        yogurt
    ⅓   cup packed brown sugar

1. Place a colander in a 2-quart glass measure or medium bowl. Line colander with 4 layers of cheesecloth, allowing cheesecloth to extend over outside edges. Spoon yogurt into colander. Cover colander loosely with plastic wrap, and refrigerate 12 hours.

2. Spoon yogurt cheese into a bowl; discard liquid. Stir in brown sugar. Cover and refrigerate. Yield: 1 cup (serving size: 2 tablespoons).

CALORIES 58 (14% from fat); FAT 0.9g (sat 0.6g, mono 0.2g, poly 0g); PROTEIN 3g; CARB 9.8g; FIBER 0g; CHOL 3mg; IRON 0.2mg; SODIUM 42mg; CALC 109mg

Tamarind-Sweet Potato Bisque

The pods of the tamarind tree yield a sweet-sour pulp that flavors many Dutch, Indonesian, and East Indian dishes. You can find tamarind paste in specialty food stores or online at www.spicesgalore1.com and www.quickspice.com. A little goes a long way, so measure carefully.

3¼ cups (1-inch) cubed peeled sweet potato
  3 cups vegetable broth
  1 cup water
  ½ cup chopped onion
  ½ cup orange juice
  2 tablespoons plum vinegar
  2 tablespoons low-sodium soy sauce
1½ teaspoons minced peeled fresh ginger
1½ teaspoons dark sesame oil
  1 teaspoon tamarind paste
  ¼ teaspoon black pepper
  1 fresh lemongrass stalk, halved lengthwise

1. Place all ingredients in an electric slow cooker. Cover and cook on HIGH 5 hours. Discard lemongrass. Place half of potato mixture in a blender, and process until smooth. Pour puréed potato mixture into a large bowl. Repeat procedure with remaining potato mixture. Yield: 5 servings (serving size: about 1 cup).

CALORIES 133 (14% from fat); FAT 2.1g (sat 0.3g, mono 0.6g, poly 0.7g); PROTEIN 3g; CARB 27.2g; FIBER 3.1g; CHOL 0mg; IRON 0.8mg; SODIUM 627mg; CALC 27mg

Guinness-Braised Beef Brisket

Tender from gentle cooking, this entrée is a classic preparation made without the usual pot watching. Serve it with grainy, coarse-ground mustard. Use the leftovers in classic Rueben sandwiches: sliced corned beef with Thousand Island dressing, Swiss cheese, and sauerkraut on sourdough, rye, or pumpernickel bread.

  2 cups water
  1 cup chopped onion
  1 cup chopped carrot
  1 cup chopped celery
  1 cup Guinness stout
  ⅔ cup packed brown sugar
  ¼ cup tomato paste
  ¼ cup chopped fresh or 1 tablespoon dried dill
  1 (14½-ounce) can low-salt beef broth
  6 black peppercorns
  2 whole cloves
  1 (3-pound) cured corned beef brisket, trimmed

1. Combine first 11 ingredients in a large electric slow cooker, stirring until well blended; top with beef. Cover and cook on HIGH 8 hours or until beef is tender. Remove beef; cut diagonally across the grain into ¼-inch slices. Discard broth mixture. Yield: 6 servings (serving size: 3 ounces).

CALORIES 226 (39% from fat); FAT 9.7g (sat 3.2g, mono 4.7g, poly 0.4g); PROTEIN 17.9g; CARB 15.2g; FIBER 0.9g; CHOL 87mg; IRON 2.2mg; SODIUM 1,105mg; CALC 28mg

Caramelized Onions

Serve these delicate cooked onions as a side or as a pizza topping. Or toss them with pasta, shredded Asiago cheese, and fresh herbs. They also make a fantastic addition to risotto. Use the skimmed onion-scented butter to flavor stocks or stews, or to spread over toasted slices of French or Italian bread. To ensure maximum flavor, cook the onions the full 24 hours.

  ½ cup butter
  3 pounds Vidalia or other sweet onions (about 4 medium), peeled

1. Combine butter and onions in an electric slow cooker. Cover and cook on LOW 24 hours.

2. Remove onions with a slotted spoon.

3. Pour cooking liquid into a bowl. Cover and chill.

4. Skim solidified fat from surface; reserve for another use (see recipe blurb). Discard liquid. Yield: 4 servings (serving size: about 1 onion).

CALORIES 180 (32% from fat); FAT 6.3g (sat 3.7g, mono 1.8g, poly 0.4g); PROTEIN 4g; CARB 29.4g; FIBER 6.1g; CHOL 16mg; IRON 0.8mg; SODIUM 69mg; CALC 70mg

Thai-Spiced Braised Chicken

To serve, spoon the aromatic cooking liquid over the chicken and vegetables, and offer a lime wedge with each serving.

  2 cups water
  1 cup chopped onion
  ⅓ cup julienne-cut peeled fresh ginger
  ¼ cup rice vinegar
  2 tablespoons Thai fish sauce
  2 teaspoons freshly ground black pepper
  2 teaspoons Thai paste
  8 chicken thighs (about 3 pounds), skinned
  1 (1-pound) bag baby carrots
  1 (14-ounce) can fat-free, less-sodium chicken broth
  3 garlic cloves, halved
  1 (8-inch) stalk fresh lemongrass, cut in half lengthwise
  ½ cup coarsely chopped fresh cilantro
  2 cups hot cooked jasmine rice
  ½ cup sliced green onions
  4 lime wedges

1. Place first 12 ingredients in an electric slow cooker. Cover and cook on HIGH 7 hours or until chicken is done. Discard lemongrass; stir in cilantro.

2. Place ½ cup rice and 2 chicken thighs into each of 4 large bowls. Ladle 1¾

Continued

cups broth mixture over each serving; sprinkle each with 2 tablespoons green onions. Serve with lime wedges. Yield: 4 servings.

CALORIES 465 (18% from fat); FAT 9.5g (sat 2.6g, mono 2.5g, poly 2.3g); PROTEIN 45g; CARB 47.8g; FIBER 4.4g; CHOL 163mg; IRON 3.5mg; SODIUM 1,005mg; CALC 89mg

Osso Buco with Gremolata

Inexpensive veal shanks become a succulent meal in the slow cooker. Even if you aren't an anchovy lover, don't omit the anchovy paste—it adds immeasurably to the flavor. Use the remaining broth mixture in soups and stews.

OSSO BUCO:

- ⅔ cup all-purpose flour
- ¾ teaspoon freshly ground black pepper, divided
- ½ teaspoon kosher salt, divided
- 6 veal shanks, trimmed (about 5 pounds)
- 2 teaspoons butter, divided
- 2 teaspoons olive oil, divided
- 2 cups coarsely chopped red onion
- 1½ cups chopped celery
- 6 garlic cloves, minced
- 4 cups beef broth
- 2 cups dry white wine
- 1 tablespoon chopped fresh rosemary
- 1 tablespoon anchovy paste

GREMOLATA:

- ½ cup chopped fresh flat-leaf parsley
- 1 tablespoon grated lemon rind
- 2 garlic cloves, minced

REMAINING INGREDIENT:

- 8 cups hot cooked pappardelle pasta (about 1 pound uncooked pasta)

1. To prepare osso buco, combine flour, ¼ teaspoon pepper, and ¼ teaspoon salt in a shallow dish. Dredge veal in flour mixture.
2. Heat 1 teaspoon butter and 1 teaspoon oil in a large skillet over medium heat. Add half of veal; cook 6 minutes, browning on both sides. Place browned veal in a large electric slow cooker.

Repeat procedure with 1 teaspoon butter, 1 teaspoon oil, and remaining veal.
3. Add onion and celery to pan; sauté over medium-high heat 5 minutes or until tender. Add 6 garlic cloves to pan; sauté 1 minute. Stir in broth, wine, rosemary, and anchovy paste, scraping pan to loosen browned bits. Bring to a boil; cook 4 minutes. Pour over veal.
4. Cover and cook on LOW 9 hours or until done. Sprinkle veal with ½ teaspoon pepper and ¼ teaspoon salt. Remove veal from cooker; cool slightly. Remove veal from bones, and cut up.
5. To prepare gremolata, combine parsley, lemon rind, and 2 garlic cloves. Place 1 cup pasta in each of 8 pasta bowls. Top each serving with ⅔ cup veal and ½ cup broth mixture. Reserve remaining broth mixture for another use. Sprinkle each serving with 1 tablespoon gremolata. Yield: 8 servings (serving size: 3 ounces veal, ½ cup broth mixture, and 1 tablespoon gremolata).

CALORIES 443 (25% from fat); FAT 12.2g (sat 4.1g, mono 4.9g, poly 1.1g); PROTEIN 54.9g; CARB 15.9g; FIBER 1.8g; CHOL 200mg; IRON 3.3mg; SODIUM 485mg; CALC 94mg

season's best

Corned Beef and Cabbage Dinner

Imported from the Emerald Isle, corned beef with cabbage is a Saint Patrick's Day staple.

Before the days of refrigeration, the Irish cured beef with "corns" of salt to preserve it. They most often enjoyed the unique flavors and textures of the beef and cabbage dish on important holidays and at large celebrations. In modern times, corned beef has fallen in popularity in Ireland, but the dish is still enjoyed by Irish Americans on Saint Pat's Day as a nostalgic way of preserving their heritage. We've updated the classic by tossing pungent horseradish with breadcrumbs to create a flavorful crust.

Corned Beef and Cabbage Dinner

- 1 (4-pound) cured corned beef brisket, trimmed
- 16 cups water
- 2 cups chopped onion
- 1 cup chopped celery
- 1 cup chopped carrot
- 1½ teaspoons pickling spice
- 3 garlic cloves, peeled
   Cooking spray
- 1 tablespoon caraway seeds
- 1 (2½-pound) head green cabbage, cored and cut into 1-inch strips
- 4 pounds small red potatoes, quartered
- 2 tablespoons chopped fresh parsley
- 2 teaspoons butter
- 2 teaspoons grated lemon rind
- 2 teaspoons fresh lemon juice
- ⅛ teaspoon black pepper
- ½ cup dry breadcrumbs
- 1 (5-ounce) jar prepared horseradish, drained and squeezed dry
- 3 tablespoons Dijon mustard

1. Place brisket in a large stockpot; add water and next 5 ingredients. Bring to a boil. Cover, reduce heat, and simmer 3 hours. Remove brisket from pot.
2. Place brisket on rack of a broiler pan or roasting pan coated with cooking spray; place rack in pan. Strain cooking liquid through a colander into 2 large bowls; discard solids. Return liquid to pot. Add caraway seeds and cabbage; bring to a boil. Reduce heat; simmer 20 minutes. Drain.
3. While cabbage is cooking, place potatoes in a large Dutch oven. Cover with water. Bring to a boil; cook 20 minutes or until tender. Drain. Return potatoes to pan. Stir in parsley, butter, rind, juice, and pepper; toss to coat.
4. Preheat broiler.
5. Combine breadcrumbs and horseradish. Spread mustard over one side of brisket. Press breadcrumb mixture onto mustard. Broil 3 minutes or until lightly browned. Serve brisket with cabbage and potatoes. Yield: 8 servings (serving size: 3 ounces beef, about 1½ cups cabbage, and about 1⅓ cups potatoes).

CALORIES 321 (41% from fat); FAT 14.5g (sat 4.6g, mono 6.5g, poly 0.8g); PROTEIN 22.8g; CARB 27.6g; FIBER 10g; CHOL 86mg; IRON 4.3mg; SODIUM 927mg; CALC 11mg

Hoops & Hoopla

Whether it's ball games or ball gowns you celebrate in March, we have your menu.

To satisfy your appetite while awaiting the winners of the NCAA basketball tournament and the Academy Awards, try these menus suited to each occasion.

Final Four Party Menu
serves 12

Designed for those who crave net games, we have a full court press of a menu set up for watching college basketball. Our team's star starter is Honey-Ginger Chicken Bites (recipe on page 82). Score with a winning play of muffulettas or a slam dunk of Black Bean and Chorizo Chili (recipe at right). And the bourbon brownies will keep everybody hoping for overtime.

Chicken and Roast Beef Muffulettas

Bourbon Fudge Brownies

Black Bean and Chorizo Chili

Honey-Ginger Chicken Bites

MAKE AHEAD
Chicken and Roast Beef Muffulettas
(pictured on page 59)

Although classic muffulettas include layers of ham, salami, and provolone cheese, olive salad is the hallmark of the real thing. Wrapping the sandwich tightly with plastic wrap and refrigerating it helps the flavors meld.

OLIVE SALAD:
- ½ cup kalamata olives, pitted
- ¼ cup chopped fresh basil
- 2 tablespoons capers, drained
- 2 tablespoons balsamic vinegar
- 2 teaspoons olive oil
- 1 (14-ounce) can artichoke hearts, drained and coarsely chopped
- 1 (7-ounce) bottle roasted red bell peppers, drained and chopped
- 1 garlic clove, minced

MUFFULETTA:
- 12 (1½-ounce) French bread rolls
- 6 (1-ounce) slices Swiss cheese
- 6 cups gourmet salad greens
- 12 (1-ounce) slices deli roast beef
- 12 (1-ounce) slices roasted breast of chicken

1. To prepare olive salad, combine first 8 ingredients in a food processor. Process 30 seconds or until finely chopped; chill.
2. To prepare muffuletta, cut rolls in half horizontally. Cut each cheese slice in half crosswise. Spread about 2½ tablespoons olive mixture onto top half of each roll. Layer ½ cup greens, ½ cheese slice, 1 roast beef slice, and 1 chicken slice on each roll bottom; cover with top of roll.
3. Wrap each sandwich tightly in plastic wrap; chill up to 8 hours. Yield: 12 servings.

CALORIES 288 (28% from fat); FAT 9g (sat 4.3g, mono 2.3g, poly 0.8g); PROTEIN 23.3g; CARB 27.9g; FIBER 2.5g; CHOL 49mg; IRON 2.4mg; SODIUM 795mg; CALC 181mg

MAKE AHEAD
Bourbon Fudge Brownies
(pictured on page 59)

Use hot milk in place of bourbon, if you prefer.

- ¼ cup bourbon
- ¼ cup semisweet chocolate chips
- 1½ cups all-purpose flour
- ½ cup unsweetened cocoa
- 1 teaspoon baking powder
- ½ teaspoon salt
- 1⅓ cups sugar
- 6 tablespoons butter, softened
- ½ teaspoon vanilla extract
- 2 large eggs
- Cooking spray

1. Preheat oven to 350°.
2. Bring bourbon to a boil in a small saucepan; remove from heat. Add chocolate chips, stirring until smooth.
3. Lightly spoon flour into dry measuring cups, and level with a knife. Combine flour, cocoa, baking powder, and salt, stirring with a whisk.
4. Combine sugar and butter in a large bowl; beat with a mixer at medium speed until well combined. Add vanilla and eggs; beat well. Add flour mixture and bourbon mixture to sugar mixture, beating at low speed just until combined.
5. Spread batter into a 9-inch square baking pan coated with cooking spray. Bake at 350° for 25 minutes or until a wooden pick inserted in center comes out clean. Cool in pan on a wire rack. Yield: 20 servings.

CALORIES 148 (30% from fat); FAT 5g (sat 2.9g, mono 1.5g, poly 0.2g); PROTEIN 2.2g; CARB 23.2g; FIBER 1g; CHOL 31mg; IRON 1.5mg; SODIUM 121mg; CALC 20mg

FREEZABLE
Black Bean and Chorizo Chili

- 1 (7-ounce) can chipotle chiles in adobo sauce
- Cooking spray
- 2½ cups chopped onion, divided
- 1½ cups chopped green bell pepper
- 1½ cups chopped red bell pepper
- 5 garlic cloves, minced
- 3 links Spanish chorizo sausage (about 6½ ounces), diced
- 1½ tablespoons chili powder
- 1 tablespoon ground cumin
- 1 tablespoon fresh lime juice
- 1½ teaspoons dried oregano
- ⅛ teaspoon ground cinnamon
- 3 (15-ounce) cans black beans, drained
- 3 (14-ounce) cans whole peeled tomatoes, undrained and chopped
- 1 (8½-ounce) can no-salt-added whole-kernel corn, drained
- 1½ ounces semisweet chocolate, chopped
- ¾ teaspoon salt
- ½ teaspoon black pepper
- ¾ cup fat-free sour cream
- Baked tortilla chips (optional)

Continued

1. Remove 2 chiles from can; finely chop, reserving remaining chiles and sauce for another use.

2. Heat a large Dutch oven coated with cooking spray over medium-high heat. Add chiles, 1¾ cups onion, bell peppers, garlic, and chorizo; sauté 5 minutes or until tender. Add chili powder and next 7 ingredients, stirring to combine. Bring to a boil. Reduce heat, and simmer, covered, 30 minutes, stirring occasionally. Remove from heat; stir in chocolate, salt, and black pepper.

3. Ladle 1 cup chili into each of 12 bowls. Top each serving with 1 tablespoon sour cream and 1 tablespoon onion. Serve with tortilla chips, if desired. Yield: 12 servings.

CALORIES 311 (24% from fat); FAT 8.4g (sat 3.2g, mono 3.4g, poly 1g); PROTEIN 16.5g; CARB 43.9g; FIBER 12.9g; CHOL 13mg; IRON 4.1mg; SODIUM 888mg; CALC 95mg

Honey-Ginger Chicken Bites

These bite-sized appetizers are steeped in a mixture of garlic, soy sauce, ginger, citrus, and honey. The marinade is then reduced and used to glaze the chicken.

⅔ cup honey
2 tablespoons minced peeled fresh ginger
2 tablespoons fresh lemon juice
2 tablespoons cider vinegar
2 tablespoons low-sodium soy sauce
2 teaspoons dark sesame oil
1 teaspoon grated orange rind
1 teaspoon Worcestershire sauce
4 garlic cloves, minced
1¼ pounds skinless, boneless chicken thighs (about 16 thighs), cut into bite-sized pieces
Cooking spray
1 teaspoon salt
¼ teaspoon black pepper
2 teaspoons cornstarch
2 teaspoons water
2 teaspoons sesame seeds, toasted (optional)

1. Combine first 9 ingredients in a large zip-top plastic bag; seal and shake well. Add chicken; seal and toss to coat. Refrigerate at least 2 hours or overnight, turning occasionally.

2. Preheat oven to 425°.

3. Remove chicken from bag, reserving marinade. Arrange chicken in a single layer on rack of a broiler pan coated with cooking spray. Sprinkle chicken with salt and pepper. Bake at 425° for 20 minutes, stirring once.

4. While chicken is cooking, strain marinade through a sieve into a bowl; discard solids. Place marinade in a saucepan; bring to a boil. Cook 3 minutes; skim solids from surface. Combine cornstarch and water in a small bowl; stir with a whisk. Add cornstarch mixture to pan, stirring with a whisk; cook 1 minute. Remove from heat; pour glaze into a large bowl.

5. Preheat broiler.

6. Add chicken to glaze; toss well to coat. Place chicken mixture on a jelly roll pan; broil 5 minutes or until browned, stirring twice. Sprinkle with sesame seeds, if desired. Yield: 12 servings (serving size: about 1½ ounces).

CALORIES 179 (22% from fat); FAT 4.4g (sat 1g, mono 1.4g, poly 1.2g); PROTEIN 18.2g; CARB 17g; FIBER 0.1g; CHOL 76mg; IRON 1.1mg; SODIUM 430mg; CALC 14mg

Oscar Party Menu
serves 8

For an evening filled with stars, we have a menu that says "yes" to the egotistical, the elegant, the refined. In the leading role, we have coral salmon fillets with a fennel and pepper relish. The supporting cast features emerald asparagus accompanied by a goat cheese-bacon sauce and a pistachio-studded couscous salad.

Pickled Shrimp

Mushroom Ravioli with Lemon-Caper Mayonnaise

Cold Poached Salmon with Fennel-Pepper Relish

Asparagus with Black Pepper, Bacon, and Goat Cheese Sauce

Citrus-Couscous Salad

Raspberry-Almond Torte with Chocolate Ganache

MAKE AHEAD
Pickled Shrimp

In this impressive buffet appetizer, sautéed shrimp marinates with vegetables in a tangy vinaigrette. The taste gets even better as it steeps in the flavorful mixture, so make it up to 2 days before your party.

1 tablespoon olive oil, divided
1½ pounds jumbo shrimp, peeled, deveined, and divided
¾ cup julienne-cut red bell pepper
⅔ cup cider vinegar
½ cup vertically sliced onion
⅓ cup julienne-cut carrot
2 tablespoons sliced jalapeño pepper
1 tablespoon sugar
1 teaspoon ground cumin
¾ teaspoon salt
¼ teaspoon crushed red pepper
2 bay leaves
2 tablespoons chopped fresh cilantro

1. Heat 1½ teaspoons oil in a large nonstick skillet over medium-high heat. Add half of shrimp; sauté 3 minutes or until done. Place shrimp in a large bowl. Repeat procedure with 1½ teaspoons oil and remaining shrimp.

2. Combine bell pepper and next 9 ingredients in a medium saucepan over medium-high heat; bring to a boil. Cover, reduce heat, and simmer 8 minutes or until tender.

3. Pour pepper mixture over shrimp; add cilantro, stirring to combine. Cover and chill 8 hours or up to 2 days, stirring occasionally. Discard bay leaves. Yield: 8 servings (serving size: 1½ ounces).

CALORIES 124 (24% from fat); FAT 3.3g (sat 0.5g, mono 1.5g, poly 0.7g); PROTEIN 17.6g; CARB 5.6g; FIBER 0.7g; CHOL 129mg; IRON 2.4mg; SODIUM 349mg; CALC 52mg

Mushroom Ravioli with Lemon-Caper Mayonnaise

We used a mixture of shiitake and button mushrooms, but you can use any combination of mushrooms. Make the ravioli ahead, and freeze it up to 2 weeks. You can make the mayonnaise up to 2 days ahead.

MAYONNAISE:
¾ cup low-fat mayonnaise
2 tablespoons fresh lemon juice
2 teaspoons capers
2 teaspoons anchovy paste or 4 anchovy fillets, mashed

RAVIOLI:
4 cups sliced shiitake mushroom caps (about 1 pound)
4 cups sliced button mushrooms (about 1 pound)
Cooking spray
½ cup finely chopped shallots
1½ teaspoons chopped fresh thyme
3 garlic cloves, minced
⅓ cup dry sherry
2 tablespoons grated fresh Parmesan cheese
½ teaspoon salt
⅛ teaspoon black pepper
¼ cup fat-free sour cream
48 wonton wrappers

1. To prepare mayonnaise, combine first 4 ingredients, stirring until smooth; cover and chill.
2. To prepare ravioli, place shiitake mushrooms in a food processor; pulse 6 times or until finely chopped. Remove from processor. Place button mushrooms in food processor; pulse 10 times or until finely chopped.
3. Heat a large nonstick skillet coated with cooking spray over medium-high heat. Add mushrooms, shallots, thyme, and garlic; sauté 15 minutes or until tender. Add sherry; bring to a boil. Cook 8 minutes or until liquid almost evaporates. Remove from heat; stir in Parmesan, salt, and pepper. Place mushroom mixture in a bowl; let stand 10 minutes. Stir in sour cream.
4. Preheat oven to 425°.
5. Coat 2 baking sheets with cooking spray. Working with 1 wonton wrapper at a time (cover remaining wrappers to prevent drying), spoon 2 teaspoons mushroom mixture into center of wrapper. Moisten edges of wrapper with water; bring 2 opposite corners together. Press edges with a fork to seal, forming a triangle.
6. Place ravioli in a single layer on prepared baking sheets; spray tops lightly with cooking spray. Bake at 425° for 14 minutes or until golden brown, turning once. Serve with mayonnaise. Yield: 16 servings (serving size: 3 ravioli and about 1 tablespoon mayonnaise).

CALORIES 136 (29% from fat); FAT 4.4g (sat 0.8g, mono 1.2g, poly 2.1g); PROTEIN 4.4g; CARB 19.2g; FIBER 1g; CHOL 7mg; IRON 1.7mg; SODIUM 404mg; CALC 39mg

MAKE AHEAD

Cold Poached Salmon with Fennel-Pepper Relish

(pictured on page 58)

You can do all of the chopping and cooking for this dish the day before the party. Keep it refrigerated until you're ready to serve, and top the salmon with the relish just before you put it on the buffet.

RELISH:
¾ cup finely chopped red bell pepper
¾ cup finely chopped fennel bulb
¼ cup finely chopped onion
3 tablespoons white wine vinegar
1 tablespoon finely chopped fresh or 1 teaspoon dried tarragon
1 tablespoon sugar
2 teaspoons capers
¼ teaspoon salt

SALMON:
1 cup chopped onion
½ cup chopped carrot
⅓ cup chopped celery
2 (8-ounce) bottles clam juice
1 (12-ounce) bottle dark ale (such as Liberty)
1 bay leaf
8 (6-ounce) salmon fillets (about 1 inch thick), skinned

1. To prepare relish, combine first 8 ingredients, stirring well. Cover and chill.
2. To prepare salmon, combine 1 cup onion and next 5 ingredients in a Dutch oven; bring to a simmer. Cover and cook 20 minutes. Strain liquid through a sieve into a bowl; discard solids.
3. Return liquid to pan; bring to a simmer. Add salmon; cover and cook 5 minutes. Remove from heat; let stand 5 minutes. Remove salmon from pan; chill. Discard cooking liquid. Serve relish over salmon. Yield: 8 servings (serving size: 1 fillet and 3 tablespoons relish).

CALORIES 338 (35% from fat); FAT 13.2g (sat 3.1g, mono 5.7g, poly 3.2g); PROTEIN 37.3g; CARB 12.7g; FIBER 1.3g; CHOL 88mg; IRON 1mg; SODIUM 315mg; CALC 45mg

QUICK & EASY • MAKE AHEAD

Asparagus with Black Pepper, Bacon, and Goat Cheese Sauce

(pictured on page 58)

Cook the asparagus in salted water to maintain its bright green color. You can vary the dressing by adding your favorite crumbled cheese, such as feta or blue cheese.

1 teaspoon salt
2 pounds asparagus spears, trimmed
¾ cup (3 ounces) crumbled goat cheese, softened
¼ cup fat-free mayonnaise
1 teaspoon lemon juice
¼ teaspoon freshly ground black pepper
2 bacon slices, cooked and crumbled (drained)
¼ cup fat-free milk

1. Bring 1 gallon water and salt to a boil in a Dutch oven; add asparagus. Cook 2 minutes or until crisp tender. Drain and rinse with cold water. Pat dry with paper towels; chill.
2. Combine goat cheese, mayonnaise, juice, pepper, and bacon in a medium bowl; stir with a whisk. Add milk, 1 tablespoon at a time, stirring until smooth.
3. Arrange asparagus on a platter; drizzle with sauce. Yield: 8 servings (serving size: about ¼ pound asparagus and 1½ tablespoons sauce).

CALORIES 69 (39% from fat); FAT 3g (sat 1.9g, mono 0.5g, poly 0.2g); PROTEIN 5.4g; CARB 7.3g; FIBER 2.4g; CHOL 7mg; IRON 1.2mg; SODIUM 161mg; CALC 48mg

Citrus-Couscous Salad
(pictured on page 58)

Serve this chilled or at room temperature. It pairs nicely with fish, chicken, or shrimp.

 2 cups fresh orange juice, divided
 ½ cup water
 1 teaspoon salt
 1 (10-ounce) package couscous (about 1⅔ cups)
 ½ cup dried apricots, sliced
 ½ cup dried currants
 2 tablespoons red wine vinegar
 1 cup chopped seeded cucumber
 ¾ cup chopped green onions
 ½ cup coarsely chopped pistachios
 ¼ cup chopped fresh mint
 ¼ cup fresh lemon juice
 2 tablespoons extravirgin olive oil

1. Bring 1½ cups orange juice, water, and salt to a boil in a medium saucepan; gradually stir in couscous. Remove from heat; cover and let stand 5 minutes. Fluff with a fork. Place couscous in a large bowl.
2. Combine ½ cup orange juice, apricots, currants, and vinegar in a small saucepan; bring to a boil. Remove from heat; let stand 15 minutes. Drain and discard cooking liquid.
3. Add apricot mixture, cucumber, and remaining ingredients to couscous, tossing to combine. Yield: 8 servings (serving size: about 1 cup).

CALORIES 295 (23% from fat); FAT 7.4g (sat 1g, mono 4.4g, poly 1.5g); PROTEIN 7.7g; CARB 51.4g; FIBER 5g; CHOL 0mg; IRON 2mg; SODIUM 302mg; CALC 43mg

Raspberry-Almond Torte with Chocolate Ganache
(pictured on page 58)

CAKE:
 Cooking spray
 6 tablespoons butter, softened
 2 tablespoons almond paste
 1 cup granulated sugar, divided
 3 large eggs
 ¾ cup all-purpose flour
 ¼ teaspoon salt
 4 large egg whites

FILLING:
 ¼ cup fresh lemon juice
 1 (10-ounce) jar seedless raspberry preserves
 ½ cup sifted powdered sugar

GANACHE:
 ½ cup granulated sugar
 ¼ cup unsweetened cocoa
 ⅓ cup fat-free milk
 1 (4-ounce) bar semisweet chocolate, chopped

1. Preheat oven to 350°.
2. Coat a 15 x 10-inch jelly roll pan with cooking spray; line bottom with parchment paper. Coat parchment paper with cooking spray.
3. To prepare cake, place butter and almond paste in a large bowl; beat with a mixer at medium speed 2 minutes or until blended. Add ½ cup granulated sugar, beating until well blended (about 3 minutes). Add eggs, 1 at a time, beating well after each addition.
4. Lightly spoon flour into a dry measuring cup; level with a knife. Combine flour and salt, stirring with a whisk. Add flour mixture to butter mixture, beating just until combined.
5. Place egg whites in a large bowl. Using clean, dry beaters, beat egg whites with a mixer at high speed until foamy. Gradually add ½ cup granulated sugar, 1 tablespoon at a time, beating until stiff peaks form. Fold egg whites into batter; pour batter into prepared pan.
6. Bake at 350° for 18 minutes or until cake springs back when touched lightly. Cool. Invert cake onto a wire rack. Remove parchment paper. Cut cake into 4 (10 x 3¾-inch) rectangles.
7. To prepare filling, combine juice and raspberry preserves, stirring with a whisk. Add powdered sugar, stirring until smooth. Reserve ¾ cup raspberry mixture. Place 1 cake rectangle on a cake platter; spread with ¼ cup raspberry mixture, leaving a ¼-inch border. Repeat procedure with remaining cake and ½ cup raspberry mixture, ending with cake.
8. To prepare ganache, combine ½ cup granulated sugar, cocoa, and milk in a medium saucepan over medium heat; bring mixture to a boil, stirring frequently.

Cook 1 minute, stirring constantly. Remove from heat, and add chocolate, stirring until smooth. Spread ganache evenly over top and sides of cake; let stand 20 minutes or until set. Serve reserved raspberry mixture with torte. Yield: 12 servings (serving size: 1 torte slice and 1 tablespoon raspberry mixture).

CALORIES 313 (30% from fat); FAT 10.3g (sat 5.7g, mono 2.9g, poly 0.5g); PROTEIN 4.7g; CARB 52.5g; FIBER 1.6g; CHOL 69mg; IRON 2.1mg; SODIUM 149mg; CALC 69mg

in season

Fish for Friday

Simply superb fish dishes that suit the season.

Manhattan-Style Fish Chowder

You can use any firm white fish in this classic tomato-based soup.

 2 tablespoons butter
 2¾ cups chopped onion
 1 cup chopped carrot
 ¾ cup chopped celery
 3 garlic cloves, minced
 ¼ cup tomato paste
 1 cup dry white wine
 2 cups chopped peeled red potato
 2 cups water
 1 tablespoon chopped fresh or 1 teaspoon dried thyme
 1 teaspoon salt
 ½ teaspoon freshly ground black pepper
 2 (8-ounce) bottles clam juice
 1 (28-ounce) can diced tomatoes, undrained
 1 bay leaf
 2 pounds halibut fillets, skinned and cut into 1-inch pieces

1. Melt butter in a Dutch oven over medium-high heat. Add onion, carrot, celery, and garlic to pan; sauté 10 minutes or until lightly browned. Stir in tomato paste; cook 1 minute. Stir in wine; cook 1 minute. Add potato and next 7 ingredients; bring to a boil. Reduce heat; simmer 30 minutes.

2. Add fish. Cover and simmer 10 minutes or until fish flakes easily when tested with a fork. Discard bay leaf. Yield: 6 servings (serving size: 2 cups).

CALORIES 323 (21% from fat); FAT 7.6g (sat 2.9g, mono 2.3g, poly 1.5g); PROTEIN 35.9g; CARB 27.7g; FIBER 5.5g; CHOL 61mg; IRON 3.1mg; SODIUM 878mg; CALC 144mg

Fish Tacos with Tomatillo Salsa

A simple tomatillo salsa brightens these soft tacos. Use a commercial variety such as Herdez, if you're in a rush.

TOMATILLO SALSA:

- 8 tomatillos, halved (about ¾ pound)
- 1 onion, peeled and quartered
- Cooking spray
- ½ cup fresh cilantro leaves
- ¼ cup fresh lime juice
- ¼ teaspoon salt
- 1 garlic clove, chopped
- 1 chopped seeded jalapeño pepper

TACOS:

- 12 (6-inch) corn tortillas
- 1½ pounds tilapia fillets, cut into 24 pieces
- ½ teaspoon salt, divided
- ¼ cup all-purpose flour
- 1 teaspoon ground cumin
- 1 tablespoon vegetable oil
- ½ cup fresh cilantro leaves
- ¾ cup finely chopped onion
- ¾ cup diced peeled avocado

1. Preheat broiler.

2. To prepare salsa, remove husks and stems from tomatillos. Place tomatillos and quartered onion, cut sides down, on a baking sheet coated with cooking spray. Broil 10 minutes or until tomatillos begin to blacken. Place tomatillos, onion, ½ cup cilantro, and next 4 ingredients in a food processor; process until puréed. Pour salsa into a bowl; cool completely.

3. Preheat oven to 350°.

4. To prepare tacos, wrap tortillas in foil; bake at 350° for 10 minutes or until thoroughly heated; keep warm.

5. Sprinkle fish with ¼ teaspoon salt. Combine ¼ teaspoon salt, flour, and cumin in a medium bowl; dredge fish in flour mixture.

6. Heat oil in a large nonstick skillet over medium-high heat, and add fish. Cook 2 minutes on each side or until fish flakes easily when tested with a fork. Place 2 pieces of fish down center of each tortilla; top each taco with 2 teaspoons cilantro, 1 tablespoon onion, and 1 tablespoon avocado. Fold tacos in half; serve with salsa. Yield: 6 servings (serving size: 2 tacos and about ⅓ cup salsa).

CALORIES 327 (28% from fat); FAT 10.3g (sat 1.8g, mono 4.8g, poly 2.3g); PROTEIN 23.6g; CARB 37.2g; FIBER 5.8g; CHOL 66mg; IRON 2.3mg; SODIUM 355mg; CALC 131mg

QUICK & EASY
Catfish with Dill Sauce

Unlike tartar sauce, this sauce contains honey, a sweet contrast for the dill.

- ¾ cup fat-free sour cream
- ½ cup fresh parsley leaves
- ½ cup fresh dill
- ½ cup chopped green onions
- 3 tablespoons rice vinegar
- 1 tablespoon honey
- 1 garlic clove, chopped
- ¾ teaspoon salt, divided
- 1 tablespoon vegetable oil, divided
- 6 (6-ounce) catfish fillets
- ¼ teaspoon freshly ground black pepper

1. Combine first 7 ingredients in a food processor; add ½ teaspoon salt. Process until puréed.

2. Heat 1½ teaspoons oil in a large nonstick skillet over medium-high heat. Sprinkle fish with ¼ teaspoon salt and pepper. Add 3 fillets to pan; cook 3 minutes on each side or until fish flakes easily when tested with a fork. Remove from pan, and keep warm. Repeat procedure with 1½ teaspoons oil and remaining fillets; serve with sauce.

Yield: 6 servings (serving size: 1 fillet and about 2 tablespoons sauce).

CALORIES 231 (29% from fat); FAT 7.5g (sat 1.8g, mono 3.1g, poly 1.7g); PROTEIN 29.7g; CARB 9.2g; FIBER 0.4g; CHOL 102mg; IRON 1.1mg; SODIUM 395mg; CALC 85mg

Classic Fish Sandwiches with Tartar Sauce

FISH:

- ⅓ cup cornmeal
- ⅓ cup all-purpose flour
- 1 tablespoon water
- ¼ teaspoon salt
- ⅛ teaspoon black pepper
- 1 garlic clove, minced
- 1 large egg, lightly beaten
- 6 (5-ounce) grouper fillets (1 inch thick)
- Cooking spray

SAUCE:

- ½ cup light mayonnaise
- ⅓ cup sweet pickle relish
- ¼ cup finely chopped shallots
- 2 tablespoons capers
- 1 tablespoon Dijon mustard
- 2 teaspoons grated lemon rind

REMAINING INGREDIENTS:

- 6 (2-ounce) hamburger buns, split and toasted
- 3 cups thinly sliced iceberg lettuce

1. Preheat oven to 400°.

2. To prepare fish, combine cornmeal and flour in a shallow dish, stirring with a whisk. Combine water and next 4 ingredients in another shallow dish, stirring with a whisk.

3. Dip 1 fillet in egg mixture; dredge in cornmeal mixture. Place fillet on a jelly roll pan coated with cooking spray. Repeat procedure with remaining fillets, egg mixture, and cornmeal mixture. Bake at 400° for 25 minutes or until fish flakes easily when tested with a fork, turning once.

4. To prepare sauce, combine mayonnaise and next 5 ingredients. Spread about 2 tablespoons sauce over bottom half of each bun; top each serving with ½
Continued

cup lettuce and 1 fillet. Cover with top halves of buns. Yield: 6 servings (serving size: 1 sandwich).

CALORIES 464 (25% from fat); FAT 12.9g (sat 3.4g, mono 3.4g, poly 5.2g); PROTEIN 36.7g; CARB 49.9g; FIBER 2.9g; CHOL 95mg; IRON 4.1mg; SODIUM 901mg; CALC 131mg

Baked Flounder with Fresh Lemon Pepper

Use fresh lemons, good olive oil, freshly ground peppercorns, and garlic, and you'll never look at lemon pepper the same way again. Serve with steamed asparagus.

    2 tablespoons grated lemon rind (about 3 lemons)
    1 tablespoon extravirgin olive oil
 1¼ teaspoons black peppercorns, crushed
    ½ teaspoon salt
    2 garlic cloves, minced
    4 (6-ounce) flounder fillets
Cooking spray
Lemon wedges (optional)

1. Preheat oven to 425°.
2. Combine first 5 ingredients. Place fillets on a jelly roll pan coated with cooking spray. Rub lemon pepper mixture evenly over fillets. Bake at 425° for 8 minutes or until fish flakes easily when tested with a fork. Serve with lemon wedges, if desired. Yield: 4 servings.

CALORIES 189 (26% from fat); FAT 5.4g (sat 0.9g, mono 2.9g, poly 0.9g); PROTEIN 32.2g; CARB 1.2g; FIBER 0.4g; CHOL 82mg; IRON 0.8mg; SODIUM 432mg; CALC 39mg

Garlic-Studded Mahimahi with Sage Butter

    4 garlic cloves, thinly sliced
    4 (6-ounce) mahimahi or other firm white fish fillets
Cooking spray
    5 teaspoons butter, softened
 1½ tablespoons finely chopped fresh sage
    ½ teaspoon salt
    ¼ teaspoon freshly ground black pepper

1. Preheat oven to 475°.
2. Place garlic in a small saucepan, and cover with water. Bring to a boil; remove from heat. Drain and cool slightly. Make several small slits on outside of fillets; stuff with garlic. Place fillets on a broiler pan coated with cooking spray.
3. Combine butter, sage, salt, and pepper; spread evenly over fillets. Bake at 475° for 13 minutes or until fish flakes easily when tested with a fork. Yield: 4 servings (serving size: 1 fillet).

CALORIES 193 (28% from fat); FAT 6g (sat 3.3g, mono 1.6g, poly 0.5g); PROTEIN 31.8g; CARB 1.2g; FIBER 0.1g; CHOL 137mg; IRON 2mg; SODIUM 492mg; CALC 38mg

lighten up

Creamy Custard-Fruit Pie

A few changes bring a Colorado reader's favorite dessert back to the table.

Geri Johnson of Aurora, Colorado, has always been "intrigued with buttermilk and any recipe that uses it." That's why when she first saw the recipe for Warm Apple-Buttermilk Custard Pie in a magazine, she rushed to make it.

But Geri felt that serving the pie was a disservice because of its poor nutritional value. We agreed that it was a good candidate for lightening.

We ditched the quarter-cup of butter from the custard without sacrificing the taste or texture. It's still creamy and flavorful, but it's 402 calories and 45.4 grams of fat lighter. We also unloaded a quarter-cup of butter, which was originally used to sauté the apples, by using a nonstick skillet and cooking spray. This cut another 45.4 grams of fat and 402 calories from the recipe. Since butter is essential for creating a crisp topping, removing it from the apples and the custard meant we could keep a reasonable two-and-a-half tablespoons for the streusel. Our lightened version has half the fat of the original recipe, but it maintains all its mellow flavors and textures.

BEFORE	AFTER
SERVING SIZE	
1 wedge	
CALORIES PER SERVING	
469	317
FAT	
20.4g	10.1g
PERCENT OF TOTAL CALORIES	
39%	29%

Warm Apple-Buttermilk Custard Pie

The key to both a flaky piecrust and crisp streusel topping is to keep them as cold as possible before putting them into the oven.

CRUST:
    ½ (15-ounce) package refrigerated pie dough (such as Pillsbury)
Cooking spray

STREUSEL:
    ⅓ cup all-purpose flour
    ⅓ cup packed brown sugar
    ½ teaspoon ground cinnamon
 2½ tablespoons chilled butter, cut into small pieces

FILLING:
    5 cups sliced peeled Granny Smith apple (about 2 pounds)
    1 cup granulated sugar, divided
    ½ teaspoon ground cinnamon
    2 tablespoons all-purpose flour
    ¼ teaspoon salt
    3 large eggs, lightly beaten
 1¾ cups fat-free buttermilk
    1 teaspoon vanilla extract

1. To prepare crust, roll dough into a 14-inch circle; fit into a 9-inch deep-dish pie plate coated with cooking spray. Fold edges under; flute. Place pie plate in refrigerator until ready to use.
2. To prepare streusel, lightly spoon ⅓ cup flour into a dry measuring cup; level with a knife. Combine ⅓ cup flour, brown sugar, and ½ teaspoon cinnamon

in a medium bowl; cut in butter with a pastry blender or 2 knives until mixture resembles coarse meal. Place streusel in refrigerator.

3. Preheat oven to 325°.

4. To prepare filling, heat a large nonstick skillet coated with cooking spray over medium heat. Add sliced apple, ¼ cup granulated sugar, and ½ teaspoon cinnamon; cook 10 minutes or until apple is tender, stirring occasionally. Spoon into prepared crust.

5. Combine ¾ cup granulated sugar, 2 tablespoons flour, salt, and eggs; stir with a whisk. Stir in buttermilk and vanilla. Pour over apple mixture. Bake at 325° for 30 minutes. Reduce oven temperature to 300° (do not remove pie from oven); sprinkle streusel over pie. Bake at 300° for 40 minutes or until set. Let stand 1 hour before serving. Yield: 10 servings.

CALORIES 317 (29% from fat); FAT 10.1g (sat 4.6g, mono 3g, poly 1.2g); PROTEIN 5g; CARB 52.6g; FIBER 1.3g; CHOL 76mg; IRON 0.8mg; SODIUM 230mg; CALC 73mg

passport

Wholly Mole

South-of-the-border salsas and sauces combine the best of both worlds—Old and New.

In the United States, we usually think of salsa as something served with tortilla chips and perhaps a bowl of nacho cheese. South of the border, salsa (Spanish for "sauce") can translate into a simple condiment, a tangy marinade, or an elaborate stew. See firsthand salsa's endless versatility.

Sources

www.mexgrocer.com offers both Mexican kitchen equipment and ingredients.
1-888-7-TIERRA Tierra Vegetables sells farm-grown chiles in fresh, dried, and smoked form.

Butterflied Shrimp with Habanero-Tomatillo Salsa

Butterflying the shrimp gives it an attractive appearance and more surface area for the marinade to penetrate. Handle habaneros with care. They're among the hottest chiles, but marinating them in vinegar and sugar softens their bite.

SALSA:

- 2 tablespoons lime juice
- 2 tablespoons cider vinegar
- 1 tablespoon fresh orange juice
- 1 tablespoon sugar
- ⅛ teaspoon salt
- ⅛ teaspoon freshly ground black pepper
- ¼ cup finely chopped red onion
- 1 habanero pepper, cored, seeded, and finely chopped
- 1 tomatillo, finely chopped

SHRIMP:

- 1 pound large shrimp
- 1 tablespoon lime juice
- 2 teaspoons olive oil
- 1 garlic clove, minced
- Dash of salt
- Cooking spray

1. To prepare salsa, combine first 6 ingredients, stirring well with a whisk. Stir in onion, habanero, and tomatillo. Cover and let stand at room temperature 30 minutes.

2. Prepare grill.

3. To prepare shrimp, peel shrimp, leaving tails intact. Starting at tail end, butterfly each shrimp, cutting to, but not through, backside of shrimp. Combine 1 tablespoon lime juice, 2 teaspoons oil, garlic, and dash of salt in a large bowl. Add shrimp; toss well. Cover and marinate in refrigerator 10 minutes.

4. Place shrimp, cut sides down, on grill rack coated with cooking spray, and grill 5 minutes or until shrimp are done, turning once. Serve with salsa. Yield: 4 servings (serving size: 4 ounces shrimp and 2 tablespoons salsa).

CALORIES 136 (26% from fat); FAT 3.9g (sat 0.6g, mono 1.9g, poly 0.8g); PROTEIN 17.6g; CARB 7.5g; FIBER 0.5g; CHOL 129mg; IRON 2.2mg; SODIUM 237mg; CALC 51mg

Pollo Mole Verde

In Mexico, a pumpkinseed mole is called *mole pipian*, and foods are often cooked in the sauce. We've adapted it into a green sauce to dress grilled chicken cutlets and rice.

- 6 tablespoons shelled unsalted raw pumpkinseed kernels
- ¼ teaspoon salt
- ⅛ teaspoon ground cumin
- ⅛ teaspoon ground cinnamon
- Dash of freshly ground black pepper
- 1¼ cups fat-free, less-sodium chicken broth, divided
- 2 tomatillos
- 1 small serrano chile, stem removed
- 1 garlic clove
- ½ small onion, peeled and root end intact
- 1 tablespoon chopped fresh cilantro
- 2 large romaine lettuce leaves
- ½ teaspoon vegetable oil
- 4 (4-ounce) skinless, boneless chicken breast halves
- Cooking spray
- 3 cups hot cooked rice

1. Heat a large, heavy skillet over medium heat; add pumpkinseeds. Cook 3 minutes or until lightly browned, shaking pan frequently. Remove from heat; cool completely.

2. Place pumpkinseeds, salt, cumin, cinnamon, and black pepper in a spice or coffee grinder; process until finely ground. Place spice mixture in a small bowl; stir in ½ cup broth. Set aside.

3. Remove husks and stems from tomatillos. Heat skillet over medium-high heat; add tomatillos, chile, garlic, and onion. Cook 5 minutes or until browned, turning frequently. Remove from heat; cool. Quarter tomatillos. Trim root from onion half; discard root.

4. Place tomatillos, chile, garlic, and onion in a blender or food processor; process until coarsely chopped. Add ¼ cup broth, cilantro, and lettuce; process until smooth.

5. Prepare grill.

6. Heat ½ teaspoon oil in skillet over medium heat. Add puréed tomatillo mixture; reduce heat to low, and cook 5

Continued

minutes or until slightly thick, stirring occasionally. Stir in spice mixture and ¼ cup broth; simmer 10 minutes, stirring frequently. Add ¼ cup broth, stirring with a whisk. Remove from heat; keep warm.

7. Place each chicken breast half between 2 sheets of heavy-duty plastic wrap; pound to ½-inch thickness using a meat mallet or rolling pin. Place chicken on grill rack coated with cooking spray; grill 3 minutes on each side or until done. Top chicken with mole. Serve with rice. Yield: 4 servings (serving size: 1 chicken breast half, about ⅓ cup sauce, and ¾ cup rice).

CALORIES 467 (22% from fat); FAT 11.6g (sat 2.3g, mono 3.4g, poly 4.9g); PROTEIN 38.8g; CARB 49.6g; FIBER 2.3g; CHOL 66mg; IRON 4.6mg; SODIUM 368mg; CALC 46mg

Know Your Chiles

Chiles are an integral part of Latin American cooking. The heat of each type of chile can vary dramatically. Your best bet is to use the amount listed in the recipe as a guideline. If you prefer mild food, start with half the amount called for and add to your liking.

Ancho: Anchos are dried poblano chiles with a maroon luster. They have a rich, almost mochalike flavor, with a slow heat.

Chipotle: Chipotle chiles are actually dried, smoked jalapeño peppers. In the U.S., we most often see them canned "in adobo," meaning in a marinade. Their smoky, sweet heat can be deceptively alluring. Beware: These are hotter than they seem at first bite.

Habanero: A tiny, superhot, bright orange chile shaped like a Chinese lantern, the habanero is one to be reckoned with.

Jalapeño: Dark green jalapeño chiles are popular in the U.S. They can be up to a few inches long, and their heat varies from chile to chile.

Serrano: Narrow serrano chiles may be smaller than the similar jalapeño, but they're about twice as fierce. Serrano chiles have crisp heat, which mellows beautifully when roasted to lend a high note to salsas and sauces.

Grilled Adobo Pork
(pictured on page 57)

The word *adobo* comes from the Spanish verb *adobar*, meaning "to season or marinate"—usually in a tangy, vinegary sauce. Serve this pork alongside steamed long-grain rice mixed with corn and cilantro.

Cooking spray
3 ancho chiles
1 garlic clove
¼ small onion, peeled
1 cup fat-free, less-sodium chicken broth
¼ teaspoon ground oregano
¼ teaspoon freshly ground black pepper
⅛ teaspoon ground cumin
Dash of ground allspice
2 tablespoons cider vinegar, divided
½ teaspoon brown sugar
¼ teaspoon salt
4 (6-ounce) bone-in center-cut pork chops (about ½ inch thick), trimmed
2 tablespoons fresh orange juice
1 tablespoon fresh lime juice

1. Heat a large skillet coated with cooking spray over medium heat. Remove stems and seeds from chiles. Tear chiles into large pieces; place in skillet. Cook 15 seconds or until thoroughly heated, turning pieces occasionally (be careful not to burn chiles); remove from pan. Add garlic and onion to pan; cook 5 minutes or until browned, turning frequently.

2. Combine chiles, garlic, onion, broth, and next 4 ingredients in a small saucepan over medium heat. Stir in 1 tablespoon vinegar. Bring to a simmer; cook 5 minutes or until chiles are soft. Remove from heat; cool slightly. Place half of chile mixture in a blender; process until smooth. Pour puréed mixture into a small bowl; repeat procedure with remaining chile mixture.

3. Heat skillet coated with cooking spray over medium-high heat. Add chile mixture; cook 5 minutes, stirring constantly. Remove from heat; stir in sugar and salt. Cool completely.

4. Combine ½ cup chile mixture and 1 tablespoon vinegar in a large zip-top plastic bag. Add pork to bag; seal bag. Marinate in refrigerator 8 hours or overnight, turning bag occasionally. Combine remaining chile mixture, orange juice, and lime juice; cover and refrigerate.

5. Prepare grill.

6. Place orange juice mixture in a small saucepan; cook over medium heat 5 minutes or until thoroughly heated.

7. Remove pork from bag, reserving marinade. Place pork on grill rack coated with cooking spray; grill 4 minutes on each side or until thermometer registers 160° (slightly pink), basting frequently with reserved marinade. Remove from heat; top with warm juice mixture. Yield: 4 servings (serving size: 1 pork chop and about 1½ tablespoons sauce).

CALORIES 224 (32% from fat); FAT 7.9g (sat 2.6g, mono 3.1g, poly 1.1g); PROTEIN 27.9g; CARB 10.1g; FIBER 3.1g; CHOL 69mg; IRON 2.3mg; SODIUM 316mg; CALC 42mg

MAKE AHEAD
Mexican Molcajete Sauce

Roasted vegetables in the colors of the Mexican flag combine for a sauce that complements grilled chicken or fish. If you have a *molcajete* (or mortar), use it to mash the sauce, then serve it right from the stone bowl.

½ small onion, peeled
3 serrano chiles, stems removed and seeded
2 plum tomatoes
1 garlic clove, peeled
¼ teaspoon kosher salt

1. Cut onion half into quarters.

2. Heat a skillet over medium-high heat. Add onion, chiles, tomatoes, and garlic; cook 5 minutes or until blackened, turning frequently. Cool.

3. Trim root from onion wedges; discard root. Core tomatoes. Finely mince onion, chiles, tomatoes, and garlic together until mixture is almost pastelike. Sprinkle with salt; stir well. Yield: 4 servings (serving size: ¼ cup).

CALORIES 30 (3% from fat); FAT 0.1g (sat 0g, mono 0g, poly 0.1g); PROTEIN 0.5g; CARB 3.4g; FIBER 0.7g; CHOL 0mg; IRON 0.2mg; SODIUM 152mg; CALC 7mg

Black Bean-Mango Salsa

Think of this refreshing salsa as a side salad. Its smoky, earthy flavors—jalapeño, chipotle, and Tabasco—enhance grilled pork or beef.

  ¼ cup finely chopped red onion
  2 tablespoons chopped fresh cilantro
  2 teaspoons finely chopped canned chipotle chile in adobo sauce
  1½ teaspoons finely chopped jalapeño pepper
  ½ teaspoon hot sauce (such as Tabasco)
  ¼ teaspoon salt
  1 mango, peeled and chopped
  1 (15-ounce) can black beans, rinsed and drained

1. Combine all ingredients in a bowl; toss well. Yield: 5 servings (serving size: ½ cup).

CALORIES 118 (5% from fat); FAT 0.6g (sat 0.1g, mono 0.1g, poly 0.2g); PROTEIN 6g; CARB 23.5g; FIBER 6.6g; CHOL 0mg; IRON 1.5mg; SODIUM 299mg; CALC 26mg

Salsamole

Half salsa and half guacamole, this tasty mixture is a great companion for tacos, burritos, and tortilla chips.

  ¼ cup finely chopped red onion
  1 tablespoon fresh lime juice
  1 tablespoon cider vinegar
  ¼ teaspoon salt
  1 garlic clove, minced
  1 serrano chile, seeded and finely chopped
  ¼ cup chopped fresh cilantro
  1 ripe peeled avocado, seeded and coarsely mashed
  1 tomato, chopped

1. Combine first 6 ingredients in a medium bowl. Add cilantro, avocado, and tomato; stir well. Serve immediately. Yield: 1 cup (serving size: 2 tablespoons).

CALORIES 49 (70% from fat); FAT 3.8g (sat 0.6g, mono 2.4g, poly 0.5g); PROTEIN 0.8g; CARB 3.4g; FIBER 0.4g; CHOL 0mg; IRON 0.4mg; SODIUM 79mg; CALC 6mg

Brewing a Perfect Match

How to bring out the best in your food *and* your beer.

Twenty or so years ago, typical dinner party fare consisted of steak, potatoes, and a good bottle of wine. But today, as we explore more adventurous cuisines, we're discovering that the most appropriate libation for many foods is beer.

The United States now has about 1,500 regional specialty breweries, microbreweries, and brewpubs. These "craft" brewers compose only about 3 percent of the U.S. beer market, but they're nevertheless a $3 billion industry—one that's growing even as large breweries see their volume decline.

With an increased presence on supermarket shelves, craft beers are finding a place on more and more dining tables as well. According to Brooklyn Brewery brewmaster Garrett Oliver, that's in part because we're discovering that beer enhances many foods, and that its carbonation refreshes the palate between bites.

"It's a matter of people knowing the choices that are out there," says Oliver, author of *Brewmaster's Table*, a guide to beer and food. "By learning more about beer, we can have a much more enjoyable food life."

A multitude of beer styles offer profuse flavor options. From the fruity undertones of a pale ale to the dark chocolate overtones of a stout, craft beers are successfully being matched with everything from Texas barbecue to New York cheesecake.

How do you figure out which beer goes best with which food? Although every region in the country offers uniquely flavored craft beers, these brews are made in common styles that can be matched to certain kinds of foods. In the guide on page 90, we tell you what those styles of beer taste like and offer recipes (beginning on page 91) that make them sparkle.

How to Match Beer with Food

Beer and food should taste better together than either would separately. Neither the food nor the beer should overwhelm the other; rather, the flavors should balance.

Beer's slightly sweet malty flavors (with undertones of bitter hops and bready yeast) complement many foods. That said, beer pairs particularly well with strong flavors. Hence, beer is the beverage of choice for foods with vinegary, smoky, spicy hot, and pungent tastes. It's also sensational with deep-fried foods.

It's no accident that beer is popular with much Mexican, Thai, Indian, and German cuisine. Usually the best beer to enjoy with these dishes is one from the country where the food originated. Soothing Singha beer from Thailand is ideal with Thai food, while Bohemia from Mexico is ideal with chile-laden food, for example.

When choosing beer to pair with a particular dish, match like with like—mild lagers and lighter ales with delicate and subtle foods, and full-flavored ales and even stouts with stronger foods. (See "Your Beer Primer" on page 90 for a glossary of beer styles.) For example, try a pilsner with a light dish like Stuffed Shrimp with Lemon-Pomegranate Glaze (recipe on page 92), or a full-flavored amber ale with the assertive Roasted Garlic and Shallot Potato Soup with Cheesy Croutons (recipe on page 91).

Beer is made with malted grain (usually barley), water, yeast, and a flavoring. That flavoring is usually hops (the dried cone-shaped flowers of a vining plant), whose bitterness counters the sweetness of the malt. Different flavors and beer styles are achieved by using malts that have been roasted to various degrees, by choosing different types of yeasts and hops, and by controlling when the hops are added. The taste of beer also can be changed by using other grains, such as wheat, in addition to barley. Many American beers include corn and/or rice to lighten the taste and lower the price.

Beer is divided into two basic types: lagers and ales. Lagers are made with special strains of yeast that sink to the bottom of the brewing tank. Lagers are fermented and stored at cold temperatures. They tend to be light in color, with a subtle crisp, clean taste.

Ales often are fermented with yeasts that sit atop the tank and prefer warmer temperatures. These yeasts ferment more quickly and produce beer with fruitier flavors and more yeasty and malty aromas. Ales are made with more hops and have an earthier, stronger, more complex taste than lagers. There are many styles of both lagers and ales.

LAGER STYLES

Bock: These German-style dark beers are often high in alcohol. Full-bodied with low-to-medium hoppiness and good malty taste, they're usually made in the spring to be served in the fall. Serve bock with smoked meat, sausages, and sauerkraut. Try Aass Beer or Shiner Bavarian Bock.

Doppelbock: Stronger and even more intense than regular bock, doppelbocks are high in alcohol (7.4%). They taste great with strong cheese, pickled herring, and raw onions. Celebrator Doppelbock is a good choice.

Lambic: Brewed only in Belgium, lambics are made with wild, rather than brewer's, yeast. These beers are less hoppy and can be sour, sweet, or fruity. Often they're infused with cherry or raspberry extract. Fruited lambics are ideal with fruity desserts like pies, compotes, and fresh berries. Traditional lambics also go well with dark chocolate.

Märzenbier/Oktoberfest: Originating in Germany, these lagers were historically brewed in March to last until the next brewing season. They have an amber color, full malt flavor, and medium hoppiness. Oktoberfest beer is an example of a Märzenbier; it goes well with smoked meats and vinegary potato salad. Try Samuel Adams Oktoberfest and Paulaner Oktoberfest Märzen Amber.

Pilsner: Originally brewed in Plzen, Czech Republic, pilsners have a golden color with a flowery aroma, lots of malt flavor, and a dry finish with a bitter taste. American pilsners, such as Budweiser, are light in color and have less hoppiness and malt flavor than European pilsners, like Pilsner Urquell. Pair these with pork or seafood.

ALE STYLES

American Ale: Pale to amber in color, American ales have medium body, medium to high hops, and aren't high in alcohol. Nuts and slightly sweet foods such as coleslaw, roast lamb, and beef are good with American ales. Try Sierra Nevada Pale Ale.

Bitter: These English ales have lots of malt and hops, low carbonation, and good body. Extra special bitter (ESB) has a higher alcohol and more body than other bitters. Try with roast duck, roast beef, and well-aged Cheddar and Stilton cheeses. Try Boddington's Pub Ale, Fuller's ESB, and Redhook ESB.

India Pale Ale (IPA): Because this ale was originally made in England for shipping to India, it needed high alcohol content and lots of hoppiness to survive the long trip. It has a pleasing malty flavor with a full-bodied taste. The high bitterness balances slightly sweet foods. Try it with barbecued ribs, glazed ham, or Hoisin-Marinated Chicken (recipe on page 91). Hop Devil IPA and Harpoon IPA are good choices.

Pale Ale: Ales made with lighter roasted malt have a pale to amber color, medium hops, and maltiness with a drier taste. Try them with steak, salmon, or other fatty fish. Bass makes a good English-style pale ale.

Porter: Dark brown and full-bodied with high alcohol and chocolate tastes, porters are moderate-to-high hoppiness beers that can be enjoyed with bittersweet chocolate desserts. Try Samuel Smith, the Famous Taddy Porter.

Stout: Very dark and made with toasted malt, stouts are full-bodied and hoppy. Ireland's Guinness is the most famous stout. Bitter coffee and chocolate flavors make stout great with oysters, rich meats, such as braised short ribs, and game, such as grouse.

Wheat Beers (Hefeweizen, Weissbier, Weizen, Weizenbock): Beers containing wheat are often cloudy and slightly tart with high carbonation. They're also very refreshing and are ideal with spicy foods like curry. The tartness and wheaty flavors go well with fried food, such as fish and chips. Try Sierra Nevada Wheat Beer and Pyramid Hefeweizen.

A stout best rounds out the meal for the sweet and pungent Roasted Garlic and Shallot Potato Soup.

Roasted Garlic and Shallot Potato Soup with Cheesy Croutons

The strong cheeses provide a good opportunity to enjoy a full-flavored ale that doesn't dominate the food. Try Fuller's ESB from London, or Dock Street Ale from Philadelphia. The caramel flavors of Guinness stout would also work well.

SOUP:
- 5 whole garlic heads, unpeeled
- 3½ tablespoons olive oil, divided
- 1¼ teaspoons salt, divided
- 1 teaspoon freshly ground black pepper, divided
- 10 shallots, unpeeled (about ¾ pound)
- 2 cups coarsely chopped onion
- 1 cup dry white wine
- 3 cups fat-free, less-sodium chicken broth
- 2 cups (½-inch) cubed peeled baking potato (about ¾ pound)
- 1 teaspoon chopped fresh thyme
- 1 cup 2% reduced-fat milk

CROUTONS:
- 16 (½-inch-thick) slices French bread baguette
- Cooking spray
- ¾ cup (3 ounces) crumbled blue cheese
- 2 tablespoons grated fresh Parmesan cheese

1. Preheat oven to 400°.
2. To prepare soup, remove white papery skins from garlic heads (do not peel or separate cloves); cut off tops, leaving root ends intact. Place garlic in a shallow roasting pan. Drizzle 1 tablespoon oil over garlic; sprinkle with ¼ teaspoon salt and ¼ teaspoon pepper. Cover with foil. Bake at 400° for 20 minutes. Add shallots to pan. Drizzle 1 tablespoon oil over shallots; sprinkle with ¼ teaspoon salt and ¼ teaspoon pepper. Cover and bake at 400° for 25 minutes or until tender and browned. Cool. Squeeze garlic to extract pulp; peel shallots. Discard skins. Set garlic pulp and shallots aside.
3. Heat 1½ tablespoons oil in a Dutch oven over medium heat; add onion. Cover and cook 15 minutes or until lightly browned, stirring occasionally. Add garlic pulp, peeled shallots, and wine. Reduce heat; simmer, uncovered, 5 minutes.
4. Stir in broth, potato, and thyme; bring to a boil. Cover, reduce heat, and simmer 20 minutes or until potato is tender. Cool slightly. Place half of potato mixture in a blender; process until smooth. Pour puréed mixture into a large bowl. Repeat procedure with remaining potato mixture.
5. Return puréed mixture to pan; stir in milk, ¾ teaspoon salt, and ½ teaspoon pepper. Cook over medium heat 5 minutes or until thoroughly heated.
6. Preheat oven to 400°.
7. To prepare croutons, place bread slices in a single layer on a large baking sheet. Lightly coat tops of bread with cooking spray. Bake at 400° for 8 minutes or until lightly browned. Sprinkle cheeses evenly over bread slices. Bake 3 minutes or until cheese melts. Serve warm with soup. Yield: 8 servings (serving size: 1 cup soup and 2 croutons).

CALORIES 290 (30% from fat); FAT 9.6g (sat 3.5g, mono 4.7g, poly 0.8g); PROTEIN 11.1g; CARB 41g; FIBER 3.3g; CHOL 12mg; IRON 2mg; SODIUM 806mg; CALC 202mg

Hoisin-Marinated Chicken

Serve this with an Asian beer, such as Sapporo Draft Beer or 33 Export.

- ½ cup hoisin sauce
- ¼ cup low-sodium soy sauce
- 2 tablespoons dark sesame oil
- 1 tablespoon rice vinegar
- 1 tablespoon dry sherry
- 1 tablespoon minced peeled fresh ginger
- 4 garlic cloves, minced
- 8 (6-ounce) skinless, boneless chicken breast halves
- Cooking spray

1. Combine first 7 ingredients, stirring with a whisk. Place chicken in a large shallow dish; pour half of hoisin mixture over chicken, turning to coat. Reserve remaining hoisin mixture. Cover and chill chicken mixture 3 hours, turning occasionally.
2. Prepare grill or broiler.
3. Remove chicken from dish; discard marinade. Place chicken on grill rack or broiler pan coated with cooking spray; cook 4 minutes on each side or until done, basting occasionally with reserved hoisin mixture. Yield: 8 servings.

CALORIES 243 (19% from fat); FAT 5.2g (sat 0.9g, mono 1.5g, poly 1.6g); PROTEIN 40.1g; CARB 6.1g; FIBER 0g; CHOL 99mg; IRON 1.3mg; SODIUM 525mg; CALC 21mg

Balsamic-Steeped Fruit with Yogurt

A quality balsamic vinegar will add depth to this simple dessert. Don't make it too far in advance because the fruit can water out. Traditional lambics, such as Oudbeitje and Cuvée René, are best with this dessert. Oudbeitje is sour with sweet undertones; Cuvée René is more mellow.

- 3 cups cubed peeled ripe mango
- 2 cups fresh raspberries
- 3 tablespoons brown sugar
- 1 tablespoon balsamic vinegar
- 1½ cups vanilla low-fat yogurt

Continued

1. Combine first 4 ingredients. Spoon ½ cup fruit mixture into each of 8 bowls; top each serving with 3 tablespoons yogurt. Serve immediately. Yield: 8 servings.

CALORIES 109 (7% from fat); FAT 0.9g (sat 0.4g, mono 0.2g, poly 0.1g); PROTEIN 2.9g; CARB 24g; FIBER 3.2g; CHOL 2mg; IRON 0.4mg; SODIUM 33mg; CALC 95mg

Tandoori-Marinated Red Snapper

We really liked this dish with Pyramid Hefeweizen, but any wheat beer should be a great match for this fish. You could also play off the tandoori flavors with a thirst-quenching Taj Mahal.

SNAPPER:
1½ cups plain low-fat yogurt
¼ cup fresh lemon juice
2 tablespoons garam masala (such as McCormick)
2 tablespoons Hungarian sweet paprika
1 tablespoon minced peeled fresh ginger
1 tablespoon minced garlic
1½ teaspoons salt
1½ to 2 teaspoons ground red pepper
1 teaspoon ground turmeric
½ teaspoon freshly ground black pepper
6 (6-ounce) red snapper or other firm white fish fillets

SALAD:
½ cup vertically sliced red onion
2 tablespoons fresh lemon juice
½ teaspoon salt
⅛ teaspoon garam masala
2 cups plain low-fat yogurt
1 cup finely chopped English cucumber
½ cup chopped fresh cilantro
⅛ teaspoon freshly ground black pepper

REMAINING INGREDIENT:
Cooking spray

1. To prepare snapper, combine first 10 ingredients in a 13 x 9-inch baking dish,

stirring with a whisk. Add fish, turning to coat. Cover and marinate in refrigerator 2 hours.
2. To prepare salad, combine onion, 2 tablespoons juice, ½ teaspoon salt, and ⅛ teaspoon garam masala in a medium bowl; let stand 1 hour. Add 2 cups yogurt, cucumber, cilantro, and ⅛ teaspoon black pepper, tossing gently to combine.
3. Preheat broiler.
4. Remove fish from dish; discard marinade. Place fish on a broiler pan coated with cooking spray. Broil 10 minutes or until fish is firm to touch with a fork, turning once. Serve salad with fish. Yield: 6 servings (serving size: 1 fillet and ½ cup salad).

CALORIES 279 (15% from fat); FAT 4.7g (sat 1.9g, mono 0.5g, poly 0.9g); PROTEIN 43.2g; CARB 15g; FIBER 1.3g; CHOL 77mg; IRON 1.2mg; SODIUM 606mg; CALC 351mg

Dry-Rub Steak with Fresh Fruit Salsa

Serve with Bohemia or Negra Modelo, Mexican beers that will complement the Latin spices. Or try Gordon Biersch, a full-flavored Märzenbier that goes well with beef. The salsa is best if prepared just before the sirloin is grilled.

STEAK:
1 tablespoon fresh lime juice
1½ teaspoons salt
1½ teaspoons minced garlic
1 teaspoon chili powder
1 teaspoon finely chopped fresh or ¼ teaspoon dried oregano
1 teaspoon freshly ground black pepper
½ teaspoon ground cumin
1 (2-pound) boneless sirloin steak

SALSA:
½ cup finely chopped red onion
2 tablespoons fresh lime juice
½ teaspoon kosher salt
1½ cups finely chopped peeled mango
1 cup finely chopped peeled kiwifruit
½ cup quartered cherry tomatoes

¼ cup chopped green onions
2 tablespoons minced fresh cilantro
1 tablespoon chopped fresh mint
1 teaspoon sugar
1 jalapeño pepper, seeded and minced

REMAINING INGREDIENT:
Cooking spray

1. To prepare steak, combine first 7 ingredients; rub evenly over steak. Cover and refrigerate 2 hours or overnight.
2. Prepare grill or broiler.
3. To prepare salsa, combine red onion, 2 tablespoons juice, and kosher salt, tossing to coat. Let stand 30 minutes. Combine mango and next 7 ingredients in a medium bowl. Add onion mixture; toss gently to combine.
4. Place steak on grill rack or broiler pan coated with cooking spray; cook 6 minutes on each side or until desired degree of doneness. Place steak on a platter; let stand 5 minutes. Cut diagonally across the grain into ¼-inch-thick slices. Serve with salsa. Yield: 8 servings (serving size: 3 ounces beef and about ⅓ cup salsa).

CALORIES 229 (36% from fat); FAT 9.1g (sat 3.4g, mono 3.6g, poly 0.4g); PROTEIN 24.7g; CARB 12.1g; FIBER 2.1g; CHOL 66mg; IRON 2.7mg; SODIUM 535mg; CALC 29mg

Stuffed Shrimp with Lemon-Pomegranate Glaze

This sweet-tart appetizer pairs best with a classic pilsner, such as Pilsner Urquell from the Czech Republic, Redhook ESB, or a Thai beer, such as Singha.

SAUCE:
1½ teaspoons grated lemon rind
⅓ cup fresh lemon juice
3 tablespoons pomegranate molasses
3 tablespoons olive oil
¼ teaspoon salt
¼ teaspoon freshly ground black pepper
1 garlic clove, minced

SHRIMP:

24 unpeeled jumbo shrimp
(about 1½ pounds)
½ cup finely chopped onion
¾ pound skinless, boneless
chicken breast
1 tablespoon Hungarian sweet
paprika
1 tablespoon chopped fresh cilantro
1 tablespoon chopped fresh mint
2 teaspoons tomato paste
1 teaspoon ground cumin
1 teaspoon ground coriander
¾ teaspoon salt
½ teaspoon ground turmeric
½ teaspoon freshly ground black
pepper
¼ teaspoon grated peeled fresh ginger
¼ teaspoon ground red pepper
2 garlic cloves, minced
Cooking spray
Cilantro sprigs (optional)

1. To prepare sauce, combine first 7 ingredients, stirring with a whisk. Remove 2 tablespoons sauce; set aside. Reserve remaining sauce for dipping.
2. Preheat oven to 425°.
3. To prepare shrimp, peel and devein shrimp, leaving tails intact.
4. Cook onion in boiling water 2 minutes or until tender. Drain and rinse with cold water; drain. Place onion in a large bowl.
5. Place chicken in a food processor; process until coarsely chopped. Add chicken, paprika, and next 11 ingredients to onion; stir well.
6. Place shrimp in a single layer on a large baking sheet coated with cooking spray. Arrange shrimp on their sides, so that each forms a "C" shape. Spoon a heaping tablespoon of chicken mixture into center of each shrimp. Gently press chicken mixture until it touches sides of shrimp.
7. Brush shrimp with 2 tablespoons sauce. Bake at 425° for 10 minutes or until shrimp are done and stuffing is firm. Serve with reserved sauce. Garnish with cilantro sprigs, if desired. Yield: 12 servings (serving size: 2 shrimp and 2 teaspoons sauce).

CALORIES 145 (30% from fat); FAT 4.9g (sat 0.8g, mono 2.7g, poly 0.8g); PROTEIN 18.4g; CARB 6.4g; FIBER 0.6g; CHOL 103mg; IRON 2.2mg; SODIUM 263mg; CALC 52mg

---

MAKE AHEAD
Couscous Salad with Dried Fruits

Wheat beer complements this hot and sweet side dish. Give it a try with Pyramid Hefeweizen. Add sliced grilled chicken and apple sausage to transform this dish into a main course.

2 tablespoons olive oil, divided
¾ cup chopped onion
1 teaspoon Hungarian hot
paprika
½ teaspoon salt
½ teaspoon ground cumin
½ teaspoon ground coriander
¼ teaspoon ground turmeric
⅛ teaspoon ground ginger
Dash of ground cinnamon
Dash of ground allspice
1½ cups fat-free, less-sodium
chicken broth
1 cup uncooked couscous
1 cup halved cherry tomatoes
¼ cup golden raisins
¼ cup chopped pitted dates
¼ cup chopped dried apricots
¼ cup coarsely chopped fresh mint
¼ cup slivered almonds, toasted
3 tablespoons fresh lemon juice
2 tablespoons chopped green
onions
2 tablespoons chopped green
olives
⅛ teaspoon freshly ground black
pepper

1. Heat 1 tablespoon oil in a medium saucepan over medium-high heat. Add ¾ cup onion; sauté 5 minutes or until tender. Add paprika and next 7 ingredients; sauté 30 seconds. Add broth; bring to a boil. Gradually stir in couscous. Remove from heat. Cover and let stand 5 minutes. Fluff couscous with a fork. Place couscous in a large bowl. Add 1 tablespoon oil, tomatoes, and remaining ingredients; toss well. Serve warm or at room temperature. Yield: 6 servings (serving size: about 1 cup).

CALORIES 258 (26% from fat); FAT 7.5g (sat 0.9g, mono 5g, poly 1.1g); PROTEIN 6.7g; CARB 42.9g; FIBER 4.6g; CHOL 0mg; IRON 1.8mg; SODIUM 359mg; CALC 45mg

---

How to Serve and Taste Beer

Serve beer in glasses large enough to hold a 12-ounce bottle so you can pour the entire contents at once. Sloping pilsner flutes are nice, as are the large, slightly tapered English-style pint glasses. The head on beer, especially lagers and bubbly ales, is important. A good inch to inch-and-a-half head of foam is ideal. Begin pouring with your glass slightly tilted, and gradually straighten it as you pour, carefully building the head. Serve most beer well chilled but not icy (about 40° to 45°). Stouts and British-style ales such as extra special bitter (ESB) can be served at cellar temperature (about 50°).

Before you taste the beer, notice its appearance. The head should hold for a while, indicating good body and malty character. As you drink, the foam should cling to the glass. Carbonation varies based on beer style and producer, but some beers—such as typical American pilsners—can be overly fizzy from high levels of carbon dioxide. Aromas should be hoppy, malty, or fruity, depending on the beer style. Beware of sour, skunky, stale odors, which indicate outdated beer.

Mollie Katzen in the Kitchen

The noted cookbook author shares some of her personal recipe favorites.

Scalloped Potatoes with Shallots, Mushrooms, Roasted Garlic, and Thyme

This recipe, adapted from Katzen's book *Vegetable Heaven*, uses roasted garlic rather than cheese to flavor the white sauce.

- 4 whole garlic heads, unpeeled
- 2 teaspoons olive oil
- 2⅓ cups minced shallots (about 15 medium)
- 3 cups chopped mushrooms (8 ounces)
- 2 tablespoons balsamic vinegar
- 2½ cups 2% reduced-fat milk
- 2 tablespoons all-purpose flour
- 2 tablespoons chopped fresh or 2 teaspoons dried thyme
- 1 teaspoon salt
- ¼ teaspoon freshly ground black pepper
- 2 pounds Yukon Gold potatoes, thinly sliced
- Cooking spray
- ½ cup (2 ounces) grated Pecorino Romano cheese

1. Preheat oven to 350°.
2. Remove white papery skins from garlic heads (do not peel or separate cloves). Discard skins. Wrap each head separately in foil. Bake at 350° for 1 hour; cool 10 minutes. Separate cloves; squeeze to extract garlic pulp (you should have about ¼ cup).
3. Preheat oven to 375°.
4. Heat oil in a large nonstick skillet over medium-high heat. Add shallots; sauté 3 minutes or until softened. Add mushrooms; sauté 5 minutes. Stir in vinegar; cook 1 minute or until liquid almost evaporates. Remove from heat.

5. Place garlic pulp, milk, flour, thyme, salt, and pepper in a food processor; process until smooth.
6. Arrange one-third of potatoes in a 13 x 9-inch baking dish coated with cooking spray. Spread half of shallot mixture over potatoes. Repeat procedure with remaining potato slices and shallot mixture, ending with potato slices. Pour milk mixture evenly over potatoes.
7. Cover with foil; bake at 375° for 30 minutes. Remove foil; bake, uncovered, 30 minutes. Sprinkle with cheese; bake 15 minutes or until cheese is golden. Let stand 10 minutes before serving. Yield: 8 servings (serving size: 1 cup).

CALORIES 163 (26% from fat); FAT 4.7g (sat 2.3g, mono 1.8g, poly 0.3g); PROTEIN 9.9g; CARB 22.3g; FIBER 3.5g; CHOL 13mg; IRON 2.5mg; SODIUM 433mg; CALC 224mg

Asparagus in Warm Tarragon Vinaigrette with Pecans and Bacon

This side dish originally appeared in *Vegetable Heaven*. For this new version, Katzen decreased the total amount of pecans for an overall reduction in fat.

- 1 tablespoon olive oil
- Cooking spray
- 1 tablespoon minced garlic
- 1½ pounds asparagus cut into 1½-inch pieces
- 2 tablespoons balsamic vinegar
- 2 teaspoons sugar
- 1½ teaspoons minced fresh tarragon
- ¾ teaspoon salt
- ⅛ teaspoon freshly ground black pepper
- 2 tablespoons chopped pecans, toasted
- 2 bacon slices, cooked and crumbled (drained)

1. Heat oil in a nonstick skillet coated with cooking spray over medium-high heat. Add garlic; sauté 1 minute. Add asparagus; sauté 4 minutes or until tender.
2. Combine vinegar and sugar in a small bowl. Add vinegar mixture, tarragon, salt, and pepper to asparagus mixture; stir well. Cook 2 minutes, stirring frequently. Sprinkle with pecans and bacon. Yield: 4 servings (serving size: 1 cup).

CALORIES 134 (50% from fat); FAT 7.4g (sat 1.2g, mono 4.6g, poly 1.2g); PROTEIN 5.1g; CARB 11.8g; FIBER 4g; CHOL 3mg; IRON 0.9mg; SODIUM 489mg; CALC 47mg

MAKE AHEAD
White Bean and Black Olive Soup

- 1 cup dry white beans
- 2 teaspoons olive oil
- 1¼ cups chopped onion
- 4 garlic cloves, minced
- ½ cup chopped celery
- ½ cup chopped carrot
- ½ cup chopped red bell pepper
- ⅓ cup tomato paste
- ¼ cup dry red wine
- 2 cups vegetable broth
- 2 cups water
- 1 cup chopped zucchini
- 2 cups sliced escarole
- ¾ cup sliced pitted kalamata olives
- ¼ cup chopped fresh parsley
- 2 tablespoons chopped fresh or 2 teaspoons dried basil
- 1 tablespoon fresh lemon juice
- 1 teaspoon salt
- ¼ teaspoon freshly ground black pepper

1. Sort and wash beans; place in a large saucepan. Cover with water to 2 inches above beans; bring to a boil. Cook 2 minutes; remove from heat. Cover and let stand 1 hour. Drain beans.
2. Heat oil in a Dutch oven over medium-high heat. Add onion and garlic; sauté 5 minutes or until lightly browned. Add celery, carrot, and bell pepper; sauté 10 minutes. Add tomato paste; cook 5 minutes, stirring constantly. Stir in wine, scraping pan to loosen browned bits. Add broth and water to pan, and stir well. Add beans; bring to a boil. Cover, reduce heat to medium-low, and simmer 1½ hours or until beans are tender.
3. Stir in zucchini; cook 5 minutes. Add escarole and remaining ingredients; stir well. Yield: 7 servings (serving size: 1 cup).

CALORIES 183 (18% from fat); FAT 3.7g (sat 0.5g, mono 2.1g, poly 0.5g); PROTEIN 9g; CARB 30g; FIBER 10g; CHOL 1mg; IRON 3.7mg; SODIUM 860mg; CALC 100mg

Simple Spring Brunch

This mix-and-match menu makes the most of fresh ingredients.

Here's a menu that's as easily applied to Easter as it is to Mother's Day. And it can gracefully accommodate all the graduation, wedding, and birthday fetes in between. It features the season's tender best: delicate asparagus spears, luscious strawberries, and the refreshing flavor of lemon. Both entrées—a salmon pilaf and a spinach-leek frittata—have make-ahead components and can be finished in short order the morning of the brunch. The crust and filling for the dessert, a strawberry-almond tart, can be made two days ahead, and the topping can be added the night before. You need only step outside for cuttings to create a stunning centerpiece. All of which leaves you free to enjoy your guests—and a Raspberry Sparkler.

Brunch for Six Menu

Raspberry Sparkler

Field Salad with Snow Peas, Grapes, and Feta

Spring Pilaf with Salmon and Asparagus
or
Frittata with Spinach, Potatoes, and Leeks

Strawberry-Almond Cream Tart

Lemon-Blueberry Muffins

QUICK & EASY
Raspberry Sparkler

For a nonalcoholic variation, use club soda or sparkling water in place of the Champagne.

    3 cups cran-raspberry juice
       (such as Ocean Spray), chilled
    1 tablespoon fresh lime
       juice
    1 (750 milliliter) bottle
       brut Champagne, chilled
    6 thin slices lime

1. Combine cran-raspberry juice and lime juice in a pitcher; stir well. Pour ½ cup juice mixture into each of 6 Champagne glasses; top with chilled Champagne. Garnish with lime slices. Serve immediately. Yield: 6 servings.

CALORIES 172 (0% from fat); FAT 0g; PROTEIN 0.5g; CARB 23.6g; FIBER 0.3g; CHOL 0mg; IRON 0.6mg; SODIUM 13mg; CALC 21mg

Field Salad with Snow Peas, Grapes, and Feta

Make the dressing up to 2 days ahead. Toss the salad the day of the brunch.

    5   tablespoons white wine
         vinegar
    5   tablespoons fresh orange
         juice
    2   tablespoons extravirgin olive
         oil
    2½   teaspoons sugar
    ½   teaspoon salt
    ¼   teaspoon freshly ground black
         pepper
    8   cups gourmet salad greens
    2   cups snow peas, trimmed and
         cut lengthwise into thin strips
    2   cups seedless red grapes, halved
    ½   cup (2 ounces) crumbled feta
         cheese

1. Combine first 6 ingredients in a small bowl; stir well with a whisk. Combine greens and remaining 3 ingredients in a large bowl. Drizzle dressing over salad; toss well. Yield: 6 servings.

CALORIES 151 (44% from fat); FAT 7.9g (sat 2.6g, mono 4.2g, poly 0.7g); PROTEIN 4.3g; CARB 18.6g; FIBER 3g; CHOL 11mg; IRON 2mg; SODIUM 354mg; CALC 123mg

Spring Pilaf with Salmon and Asparagus

This version of stir-fried rice is a fine use for leftover salmon. You can make preparation even simpler by cooking the rice and salmon a day ahead. Just warm both in the microwave before completing the dish.

    4   cups water
    4   (6-ounce) salmon fillets (about 1
         inch thick)
    1   tablespoon butter
    2   cups (1-inch) diagonally cut
         asparagus
    3   cups hot cooked long-grain rice
    1   cup fresh or frozen peas, thawed
    ½   cup vegetable broth
    2   tablespoons chopped fresh flat-leaf
         parsley
    2   tablespoons chopped fresh chives
    1   tablespoon fresh lemon juice
    ½   teaspoon salt
    ¼   teaspoon freshly ground black
         pepper

1. Bring water to a boil in a large skillet; add salmon (skin side up). Return to a boil. Reduce heat, cover, and simmer 10 minutes or until fish flakes easily when tested with a fork. Remove fish with a slotted spoon, and discard water; cool fish slightly. Remove and discard skin; break fish into large pieces.
2. Return pan to heat; melt butter over medium-high heat. Add asparagus; cook 6 minutes or until tender, stirring occasionally. Stir in rice, peas, and broth; cook 1 minute. Add salmon, parsley, and remaining ingredients; stir well to combine. Cook 2 minutes or until thoroughly heated. Yield: 6 servings (serving size: 1⅓ cups).

CALORIES 391 (29% from fat); FAT 12.8g (sat 3.4g, mono 4.3g, poly 4g); PROTEIN 24.7g; CARB 42.9g; FIBER 2.7g; CHOL 61mg; IRON 3.2mg; SODIUM 385mg; CALC 43mg

Frittata with Spinach, Potatoes, and Leeks

Make the leek mixture and cook the potatoes a day ahead, or use store-bought diced cooked potatoes (such as Simply Potatoes). Whisk the eggs, combine everything, and bake the morning of the brunch.

      1 teaspoon butter
      2 cups thinly sliced leek (about 2 large)
      1 (10-ounce) package fresh spinach
    ⅓ cup fat-free milk
      2 tablespoons finely chopped fresh basil
    ½ teaspoon salt
    ¼ teaspoon black pepper
      4 large eggs, lightly beaten
      4 large egg whites, lightly beaten
      2 cups cooked peeled red potato (about ¾ pound)
        Cooking spray
  1½ tablespoons dry breadcrumbs
    ½ cup (2 ounces) shredded provolone cheese

1. Preheat oven to 350°.
2. Melt butter in a Dutch oven over medium heat. Add leek; sauté 4 minutes. Add spinach; sauté 2 minutes or until spinach wilts. Place mixture in a colander, pressing until barely moist.
3. Combine milk and next 5 ingredients; stir well with a whisk. Add leek mixture and potato. Pour into a 10-inch round ceramic baking dish or pie plate coated with cooking spray. Sprinkle with breadcrumbs, and top with cheese. Bake at 350° for 25 minutes or until center is set.
4. Preheat broiler.
5. Broil frittata 4 minutes or until golden brown. Cut into wedges. Yield: 6 servings (serving size: 1 wedge).

CALORIES 185 (35% from fat); FAT 7.1g (sat 3g, mono 1.5g, poly 0.6g); PROTEIN 12.5g; CARB 18.9g; FIBER 2.8g; CHOL 150mg; IRON 3mg; SODIUM 429mg; CALC 176mg

STAFF FAVORITE • MAKE AHEAD
Strawberry-Almond Cream Tart

(pictured on page 110)

CRUST:

    36 honey graham crackers (about 9 sheets)
      2 tablespoons sugar
      2 tablespoons butter, melted
      4 teaspoons water
        Cooking spray

FILLING:

    ⅔ cup light cream cheese
    ¼ cup sugar
    ½ teaspoon vanilla extract
    ¼ teaspoon almond extract

TOPPING:

      6 cups small fresh strawberries, divided
    ⅔ cup sugar
      1 tablespoon cornstarch
      1 tablespoon fresh lemon juice
      2 tablespoons sliced almonds, toasted

1. Preheat oven to 350°.
2. To prepare crust, place crackers in a food processor; process until crumbly. Add 2 tablespoons sugar, butter, and water; pulse just until moist. Place in an 8 x 12-inch rectangular removable-bottom tart pan coated with cooking spray; press into bottom and ¾ inch up sides of pan. Bake at 350° for 10 minutes or until lightly browned. Cool on a wire rack.
3. To prepare filling, combine cream cheese and next 3 ingredients; stir until smooth. Spread over bottom of tart shell.
4. To prepare topping, place 2 cups strawberries in food processor; process until puréed. Combine strawberry purée, ⅔ cup sugar, and cornstarch in a small saucepan over medium heat, stirring with a whisk. Bring to a boil, stirring constantly. Reduce heat to low; cook 1 minute. Remove glaze from heat, and cool to room temperature, stirring occasionally.
5. Combine 4 cups strawberries and juice; toss to coat. Arrange berries, bottoms up, in a rectangular pattern over filling. Spoon half of glaze evenly over berries (reserve remaining glaze for another use). Sprinkle nuts around edge. Cover and chill 3 hours. Yield: 10 servings.

NOTE: You can use either 9-inch round removable bottom tart pan or a 9-inch springform pan. The recipe also works with a 9-inch round tart pan or a 10-inch pie plate.

CALORIES 289 (28% from fat); FAT 8.9g (sat 4.2g, mono 1.7g, poly 0.5g); PROTEIN 4.5g; CARB 48.7g; FIBER 3g; CHOL 15mg; IRON 1.3mg; SODIUM 242mg; CALC 59mg

MAKE AHEAD
Lemon-Blueberry Muffins

(pictured on page 109)

      2 cups all-purpose flour
    ½ cup sugar
      1 teaspoon baking powder
    ½ teaspoon baking soda
    ½ teaspoon salt
    ⅛ teaspoon ground nutmeg
    ¼ cup butter
  1¼ cups low-fat buttermilk
      1 tablespoon grated lemon rind
      1 large egg, lightly beaten
      1 cup blueberries
        Cooking spray
      1 tablespoon fresh lemon juice
    ½ cup powdered sugar

1. Preheat oven to 400°.
2. Lightly spoon flour into dry measuring cups; level with a knife. Combine flour and next 5 ingredients in a medium bowl; cut in butter with a pastry blender or 2 knives until mixture resembles coarse meal.
3. Combine buttermilk, rind, and egg; stir well with a whisk. Add to flour mixture; stir just until moist. Gently fold in blueberries.
4. Spoon batter into 12 muffin cups coated with cooking spray. Bake at 400° for 20 minutes or until muffins spring back when lightly touched. Remove muffins from pans immediately, and place on a wire rack to cool.
5. Combine lemon juice and powdered sugar in a small bowl. Drizzle glaze evenly over cooled muffins. Yield: 1 dozen (serving size: 1 muffin).
NOTE: Make muffins up to 2 days ahead; glaze them the morning of the brunch.

CALORIES 187 (23% from fat); FAT 4.8g (sat 2.7g, mono 1.4g, poly 0.3g); PROTEIN 3.7g; CARB 32.6g; FIBER 1g; CHOL 30mg; IRON 1.1mg; SODIUM 264mg; CALC 59mg

All About Onions & Family

Onions, garlic, leeks, green onions, chives, and shallots lend distinctive fragrance and flavor to savory dishes.

Alliums—onions, garlic, chives, leeks, shallots, and green onions—make up one of the most important culinary plant families. There are more than 300 species of alliums, and many of these have, at one time or other, been used in cooking. Yet we often take members of the allium family for granted. We value their flavors but overlook them as noble ingredients in their own right. Onions are about as omnipresent in cooking as salt. And garlic—well, imagine pesto, aïoli, or hummus without it. All of the alliums featured in this Cooking Class can and do take center stage. For more information on the six most popular alliums, listed in order of potency, turn to page 101.

Ragoût of Cipollini Onions with Tomato, Cinnamon, and Cumin

This recipe, full of North African flavors, is good served as part of a mixed hors d'oeuvre, such as tapas, or over basmati rice. Roasting the tomatoes yields a richer flavor than you'd get by cooking them on the stovetop.

2 garlic cloves, chopped
Cooking spray
1¼ pounds tomatoes, cut in half crosswise (about 3 large)
½ teaspoon salt, divided
¼ teaspoon freshly ground black pepper, divided
2 pounds cipollini onions, peeled
1 teaspoon ground coriander
¼ teaspoon ground cumin
1 (2-inch) cinnamon stick
1 cup vegetable broth
¼ cup dried currants
3 thyme sprigs
2 bay leaves
1 (3-inch) orange rind strip
2 tablespoons fresh orange juice
1 teaspoon brown sugar
2 tablespoons chopped fresh cilantro

1. Preheat oven to 375°.
2. Sprinkle garlic evenly in bottom of a 13 x 9-inch baking dish coated with cooking spray. Arrange tomato halves, cut sides down, over garlic. Sprinkle with ¼ teaspoon salt and ⅛ teaspoon pepper; lightly spray tomato halves with cooking spray. Bake at 375° for 55 minutes or until tender. Remove from oven; cool in dish.
3. Place tomato mixture in a blender or food processor, reserving liquid in baking dish. Process tomato mixture until smooth; strain through a sieve into a large bowl. Discard solids. Add reserved liquid to bowl.
4. Heat a large nonstick skillet coated with cooking spray over medium-high heat. Add onions, and sauté 8 minutes. Remove onions from pan. Add coriander, cumin, and cinnamon to pan, and sauté 1 minute. Add onions, puréed tomato mixture, ¼ teaspoon salt, ⅛ teaspoon pepper, broth, and next 4 ingredients to pan. Bring to a simmer over medium heat, and cook 30 minutes or until onions are tender and sauce is thick, stirring occasionally. Remove from heat, and stir in orange juice and sugar.

Remove cinnamon stick, bay leaves, and orange rind. Sprinkle with cilantro. Yield: 6 servings (serving size: ⅔ cup).

CALORIES 143 (5% from fat); FAT 0.8g (sat 0g, mono 0.1g, poly 0.1g); PROTEIN 3.4g; CARB 32.2g; FIBER 2.3g; CHOL 0mg; IRON 1.4mg; SODIUM 397mg; CALC 55mg

Allium Info and Tips

- Onions, shallots, and garlic will keep for months in a cool, dry, dark place. Leeks, green onions, and chives all need to be refrigerated. Keep them tightly wrapped so their flavors don't permeate milk, cheese, eggs, and butter.
- Chives are easy to grow. They do well in a pot on the windowsill.
- Stored garlic cloves can develop green shoots in the center; remove them before cooking, since they can taste bitter and burn easily.
- For a dramatic look, cut green onions diagonally before sautéing.
- Use scissors to snip chives; chopping with a knife can tear them.
- Be careful when you sauté garlic; burnt garlic will add an acrid, bitter flavor to the finished dish. When cooking onions and garlic together, add the garlic after the onions have begun to soften.
- Sometimes an onion browns quickly or exudes lots of juice when sautéed. This is due to its high sugar content—the sweeter the onion, the quicker it will brown and caramelize.
- To make short work of peeling small onions and shallots, place them in a large bowl, cover with boiling water for 3 minutes, then drain. The skins should come off easily.
- Dirt is sometimes trapped between the layers of leeks. To clean, cut the root end, then slit the leek lengthwise. Fan layers out, and rinse under cold water.
- When peeling a shallot, remove a couple of the outer layers along with the peel. You might need an extra shallot to make up for the discarded layers, but this method is a lot faster than removing only the thin peel.

Grilled Onion, Beef, and Sweet Potato Salad

This warm main-course salad is best served with bread to mop up the delicious dressing. Grill the onion slices on skewers or in a grill basket so they won't fall apart when turned. If the sweet potatoes aren't tender by the time they've browned on the grill, microwave them at HIGH for 20-second intervals until they're done. You can also broil them in the oven on a broiler pan coated with cooking spray.

SALAD:
    1   teaspoon coriander seeds, crushed
  1⅛   teaspoons freshly ground black pepper, divided
    1   teaspoon chopped fresh thyme
    ¼   teaspoon salt, divided
    1   (1-pound) flank steak, trimmed
    2   large white onions, cut into ½-inch-thick slices
        Cooking spray
    2   large sweet potatoes (about 1 pound), peeled and cut lengthwise into ½-inch-thick slices

DRESSING:
    ⅓   cup fresh orange juice
    ¼   cup finely chopped shallots
    1   tablespoon chopped fresh parsley
    1   tablespoon extravirgin olive oil
    2   teaspoons low-sodium soy sauce
    1   teaspoon stone-ground mustard
    ¼   teaspoon salt

REMAINING INGREDIENT:
    4   cups trimmed arugula or baby spinach

1. To prepare salad, combine coriander, 1 teaspoon pepper, thyme, and ⅛ teaspoon salt; rub over both sides of steak.
2. Prepare grill.
3. Sprinkle onion slices with ⅛ teaspoon pepper and ⅛ teaspoon salt; spray with cooking spray. Thread onion slices onto skewers or arrange in grilling basket. Place skewers or grilling basket on grill rack coated with cooking spray, and grill onions 5 minutes on each side

or until tender. Remove from skewers or basket; place in a large bowl.
4. Lightly coat sweet potato with cooking spray. Place on grill rack coated with cooking spray; grill 5 minutes on each side or until lightly browned. Cool slightly; cut potato into ¼-inch strips. Add to onion; toss to combine.
5. To prepare dressing, combine orange juice and next 6 ingredients, stirring with a whisk.
6. Place steak on grill rack coated with cooking spray; grill 4 minutes on each side or until desired degree of doneness. Place steak on a cutting board; let rest 5 minutes. Cut steak diagonally across the grain into thin slices.
7. Place arugula in a large bowl; drizzle with ¼ cup dressing, tossing gently to coat. Place 1 cup arugula mixture on each of 4 plates; top each serving with 1 cup onion mixture. Arrange 3 ounces steak over each serving; drizzle each serving with 1 tablespoon dressing. Serve immediately. Yield: 4 servings.

CALORIES 390 (30% from fat); FAT 13.1g (sat 4.4g, mono 6.1g, poly 0.9g); PROTEIN 28.3g; CARB 40.4g; FIBER 6.6g; CHOL 59mg; IRON 3.9mg; SODIUM 498mg; CALC 107mg

---

STAFF FAVORITE

Shallot-Rubbed Steak with Roasted Potatoes and Pickled Onions

Lime juice turns the red onions a uniform deep pink. For the best flavor, prepare the onions a day ahead. Juniper berries are crushed to release their ginlike flavor. The scented marinade and piquant onions work well with venison, too. To ensure the steak and potatoes will be done at the same time, start preparing the potatoes while the steak is marinating.

PICKLED ONIONS:
    4   cups thinly sliced red onions
    ⅓   cup fresh lime juice
    2   tablespoons rice vinegar
    1   teaspoon sugar
    ½   teaspoon juniper berries, crushed
    ½   teaspoon chopped fresh thyme
    ⅛   teaspoon salt
        Dash of crushed red pepper

BEEF:
    2   teaspoons olive oil
    ½   cup finely chopped shallots
    1   garlic clove, chopped
    1   teaspoon juniper berries, crushed
    1   teaspoon chopped fresh thyme
        Dash of crushed red pepper
    5   tablespoons dry red wine
    ½   teaspoon cracked black pepper
    1   (1-pound) boneless sirloin steak

POTATOES:
    2   teaspoons chopped fresh thyme
    ¼   teaspoon salt
    ⅛   teaspoon cracked black pepper
    ⅛   teaspoon crushed red pepper
    2   garlic cloves, chopped
        Cooking spray
    2   pounds Yukon Gold potatoes, quartered
  1½   cups vegetable broth

REMAINING INGREDIENT:
    ¼   teaspoon salt

1. To prepare pickled onions, place onion in a bowl. Add boiling water to just cover onion; let stand 2 minutes. Drain; return to bowl. Combine juice and next 6 ingredients; add to onion, tossing well. Cool to room temperature. Cover and chill overnight.
2. To prepare beef, heat oil in a saucepan over medium heat. Add shallots and 1 garlic clove, and cook 5 minutes or until tender, stirring frequently. Stir in 1 teaspoon juniper, 1 teaspoon thyme, and dash of red pepper; cook 1 minute. Remove from heat; stir in wine and ½ teaspoon black pepper. Cool to room temperature. Rub shallot mixture over both sides of steak. Cover and chill 2 hours.
3. Preheat oven to 400°.
4. To prepare potatoes, combine 2 teaspoons thyme and next 4 ingredients in a roasting pan coated with cooking spray. Add potatoes; toss well to combine. Add broth to pan. Bake at 400°, uncovered, 1 hour and 15 minutes or until potatoes are brown and liquid has almost evaporated, stirring once.
5. Prepare grill or grill pan.
6. Sprinkle steak with ¼ teaspoon salt, and lightly coat with cooking spray. Cook steak 5 minutes on each side or

until desired degree of doneness. Remove from heat; let stand 5 minutes. Cut steak diagonally across the grain into thin slices. Serve steak with onions and potatoes. Yield: 4 servings (serving size: 3 ounces steak, ¾ cup onions, and about 1 cup potatoes).

CALORIES 433 (24% from fat); FAT 11.7g (sat 4.1g, mono 5.1g, poly 0.6g); PROTEIN 31.4g; CARB 50.3g; FIBER 4.8g; CHOL 76mg; IRON 4.8mg; SODIUM 740mg; CALC 52mg

Tilapia with Coconut, Mint, and Chive Relish

Jalapeño and coconut give the refreshing relish some heat and sweetness.

RELISH:
- 1 cup chopped seeded peeled cucumber
- ¾ teaspoon salt, divided
- ¾ cup chopped fresh chives
- ½ cup chopped sweetened flaked coconut
- 2 tablespoons finely chopped fresh mint
- 2 tablespoons finely chopped fresh cilantro
- 2 jalapeño peppers, seeded and minced
- 2 tablespoons fresh lime juice
- ½ teaspoon ground cumin
- 1 teaspoon peanut oil
- 1 teaspoon mustard seeds

FISH:
- 2 teaspoons grated lime rind
- 1½ tablespoons fresh lime juice
- 1 teaspoon peanut oil
- ½ teaspoon ground cumin
- ½ teaspoon crushed red pepper
- 6 (6-ounce) tilapia or red snapper fillets
- ¼ teaspoon salt
- ¼ teaspoon freshly ground black pepper
  Cooking spray
- 6 lime wedges

1. To prepare relish, place cucumber in a colander; sprinkle with ½ teaspoon salt. Toss well. Drain 30 minutes. Rinse and drain; pat dry.

2. Preheat broiler.

3. Combine cucumber, chives, coconut, mint, cilantro, and jalapeño. Stir in ¼ teaspoon salt, 2 tablespoons juice, and ½ teaspoon cumin. Heat 1 teaspoon oil in a skillet over medium-high heat. Add mustard seeds; sauté 30 seconds or until seeds begin to pop. Add to cucumber mixture.

4. To prepare fish, combine rind and next 4 ingredients; rub evenly over cut sides of fillets. Sprinkle fillets with ¼ teaspoon salt and black pepper.

5. Place skin sides down, on broiler pan coated with cooking spray; cook 7 minutes or until fish flakes easily when tested with a fork. Serve with relish and lime wedges. Yield: 6 servings (serving size: 1 fillet, ⅓ cup relish, and 1 lime wedge).

CALORIES 238 (26% from fat); FAT 7g (sat 3.2g, mono 1.4g, poly 1.4g); PROTEIN 35.8g; CARB 6.7g; FIBER 1.1g; CHOL 63mg; IRON 0.8mg; SODIUM 523mg; CALC 72mg

Chicken and Leeks Braised in Wine

Cut diagonally into 2-inch pieces, the leeks soften and develop a delicate flavor but remain intact for a nice presentation. A salad of crisp lettuce, cucumber, tomato, and feta topped with a lemon-mint dressing. Rice or oven-baked potatoes completes the meal.

  Cooking spray
- 8 chicken thighs, skinned (about 2 pounds)
- ¾ teaspoon salt, divided
- ½ teaspoon freshly ground black pepper, divided
- 4 leeks (about 2¼ pounds), cut diagonally into 2-inch pieces
- 1 teaspoon ground coriander
- 1 (3-inch) cinnamon stick
- 2 cups Riesling or other slightly sweet white wine
- 1 teaspoon sugar
- 2 bay leaves
- 2 oregano sprigs
- 2 garlic cloves, peeled
- 1 (1 x 5-inch) orange rind strip
- 3 cups chopped seeded peeled tomato
- 1 tablespoon chopped fresh oregano
- 1 tablespoon chopped fresh parsley

1. Heat a large nonstick skillet coated with cooking spray over medium-high heat. Sprinkle chicken with ½ teaspoon salt and ¼ teaspoon pepper. Add chicken to pan; sauté 4 minutes on each side. Remove from pan. Add leeks to pan; sauté 4 minutes or until browned, turning once. Remove from pan.

2. Add coriander and cinnamon to pan; cook 30 seconds. Add wine and next 5 ingredients, and bring to a boil. Cover, reduce heat, and simmer 3 minutes. Add leeks. Cover and cook 5 minutes. Add chicken. Cover and cook 8 minutes.

3. Add tomato; bring to a boil. Uncover and cook 10 minutes, stirring frequently. Remove cinnamon, bay leaves, and rind.

4. Stir in ¼ teaspoon salt, ¼ teaspoon pepper, and chopped oregano. Sprinkle each serving with parsley. Yield: 4 servings (serving size: 2 thighs, about 2 leek pieces, and ½ cup sauce).

CALORIES 357 (17% from fat); FAT 6.6g (sat 1.5g, mono 1.8g, poly 1.9g); PROTEIN 30.9g; CARB 46.7g; FIBER 6.8g; CHOL 107mg; IRON 8.2mg; SODIUM 624mg; CALC 199mg

Marinated Duck Breasts with Shallot and Beet Relish

The shallots and sweet onion pair well with earthy beets in this sweet-sour relish. You can use chicken thighs in place of duck, and quartered regular beets for the baby beets.

DUCK:
- ½ teaspoon grated orange rind
- 3 tablespoons fresh orange juice
- 1 tablespoon low-sodium soy sauce
- 2 teaspoons honey
- 1 teaspoon ground coriander
- 1 tablespoon minced peeled fresh ginger
- 4 rosemary sprigs
- 1 garlic clove, minced
- 4 (6-ounce) boneless duck breast halves, thawed and skinned

Continued

14 ounces baby beets
Cooking spray
 1 pound (about 15) small shallots, peeled and quartered
 2 cups chopped Oso or other sweet onion
 ¼ cup dry red wine
 1 cup fat-free, less-sodium chicken broth
 2 tablespoons chopped fresh parsley
 ½ teaspoon salt, divided
 ½ teaspoon black pepper, divided

GARNISH:

Rosemary sprigs (optional)

1. To prepare duck, combine first 9 ingredients in a zip-top plastic bag. Seal and chill 2 hours; turn bag occasionally. Remove duck breast halves from bag. Reserve marinade; discard rosemary.
2. To prepare relish, leave root and 1-inch stem on beets; scrub with a brush. Place in a medium saucepan; cover with water. Bring to a boil; cover, reduce heat, and simmer 30 minutes or until tender. Drain and rinse with cold water. Drain and cool. Trim off beet roots; rub off skins. Coarsely chop beets.
3. Heat a large nonstick skillet coated with cooking spray over medium-high heat. Add shallots; sauté 2 minutes. Add onion; sauté 5 minutes. Stir in reserved marinade and wine; cook 1 minute or until liquid almost evaporates. Add broth; cook 6 minutes or until liquid almost evaporates. Remove from heat. Stir in beets, parsley, ¼ teaspoon salt, and ¼ teaspoon pepper.
4. Sprinkle duck with ¼ teaspoon salt and ¼ teaspoon pepper. Heat a large nonstick grill pan coated with cooking spray over medium-high heat. Add duck; cook 4 minutes on each side or until done. Serve with relish; garnish with rosemary sprigs, if desired. Yield: 4 servings (serving size: 1 duck breast half and 1¼ cups relish).

CALORIES 329 (11% from fat); FAT 4g (sat 0.8g, mono 1.2g, poly 0.6g); PROTEIN 41g; CARB 32g; FIBER 5g; CHOL 182mg; IRON 7.9mg; SODIUM 764mg; CALC 82mg

Green Onion Pancakes with Tomato-Avocado Salsa

Serve these fluffy pancakes and their lively salsa as a first course or as a side dish. The provolone cheese brings out the flavor of the green onions.

SALSA:

1⅔ cups chopped seeded plum tomato
 ½ cup finely chopped red onion
 ½ cup diced peeled avocado
 2 tablespoons finely chopped seeded jalapeño pepper
 2 tablespoons red wine vinegar
 1 teaspoon minced fresh oregano
 ⅛ teaspoon salt
 ⅛ teaspoon freshly ground black pepper
Dash of sugar

PANCAKES:

1½ cups all-purpose flour
 2 teaspoons sugar
 1 teaspoon baking powder
 1 teaspoon baking soda
 ½ teaspoon salt
 ⅛ teaspoon freshly ground black pepper
1½ cups low-fat buttermilk
 1 large egg, beaten
 1 cup chopped green onions
 6 tablespoons (1½ ounces) shredded sharp provolone cheese
Cooking spray

1. To prepare salsa, combine first 9 ingredients in a bowl. Cover and chill.
2. To prepare pancakes, lightly spoon flour into dry measuring cups; level with a knife. Combine flour and next 5 ingredients in a large bowl; make a well in center of mixture. Combine buttermilk and egg in a bowl; add to flour mixture. Stir just until moist. Let stand 10 minutes. Fold in green onions and cheese.
3. For each pancake, spoon about ¼ cup batter onto a hot nonstick griddle or nonstick skillet coated with cooking spray. Turn pancakes when tops are covered with bubbles and edges look cooked (about 3 minutes). Serve salsa over warm pancakes. Yield: 12 servings (serving size: 1 pancake and 3 tablespoons salsa).

CALORIES 128 (23% from fat); FAT 3.2g (sat 1.1g, mono 0.9g, poly 0.3g); PROTEIN 4.8g; CARB 20.5g; FIBER 2g; CHOL 23mg; IRON 1.2mg; SODIUM 352mg; CALC 99mg

QUICK & EASY

Pasta with Leek, Pepper, and Chive Sauce

Peel the bell peppers with a vegetable peeler; the pepper strips will become softer and adhere to the pasta better without the peel. We suggest that you use ear-shaped *orecchiette*, but any small pasta will work in this recipe.

 1 tablespoon olive oil
3½ cups thinly sliced leek (about 3 large)
 3 yellow bell peppers, peeled and cut into ¼-inch strips
 1 cup fat-free, less-sodium chicken broth
 1 teaspoon grated lemon rind
 1 tablespoon fresh lemon juice
 ½ cup (4 ounces) ⅓-less-fat cream cheese
 3 cups hot cooked orecchiette pasta (about ¾ pound uncooked)
 ½ teaspoon salt
 ¼ teaspoon freshly ground black pepper
 ½ cup (2 ounces) grated fresh Parmesan cheese
 ¼ cup chopped fresh chives
 ¼ cup thinly sliced fresh basil
 3 tablespoons pine nuts, toasted

1. Heat oil in a large nonstick skillet over medium-high heat. Add leek and pepper strips; sauté 4 minutes. Stir in broth, rind, and juice; cook 3 minutes. Add cream cheese. Reduce heat to medium-low; cook until cream cheese melts (about 2 minutes), stirring constantly. Add pasta, salt, and black pepper, and cook 2 minutes or until thoroughly heated. Stir in Parmesan and remaining ingredients. Serve immediately. Yield: 4 servings (serving size: 2 cups).

CALORIES 394 (29% from fat); FAT 12.6g (sat 5.2g, mono 3.4g, poly 2.2g); PROTEIN 16.3g; CARB 56.4g; FIBER 4.1g; CHOL 20mg; IRON 3.7mg; SODIUM 518mg; CALC 185mg

The Allium Family

Garlic (allium sativum)

Garlic is the most pungent of all alliums, and the more it's chopped, the stronger it tastes. For subtle garlic flavor, add whole unpeeled cloves to pot roasts and roasted vegetable dishes. Asian stir-fries use sliced garlic, which adds warm, toasty flavor. Finely chopped and crushed garlic add strong, "hot" flavor, especially when uncooked.

There are many types of garlic, some purple-skinned, others pearly white. Some produce huge, fat cloves with more subtle flavor than smaller-cloved garlics. So-called "elephant" garlics, with huge, mild-tasting bulbs as long as three inches, are related to the wild leek (allium ampelopra-sum). Young, or green, garlic is a mild seasonal treat that usually arrives in markets in early summer. Both young garlic and elephant garlic can be baked whole in foil then squeezed out of their skins to yield a deeply flavored paste that's good in pasta sauces and dips, with goat cheeses, or spread on toasted sourdough. Garlic stores well—you can keep it hung as a rope or a braid in a cool place for several months.

Onions (allium cepa)

This allium's bulb keeps it alive during dormancy. As onions age, they become sweeter and milder. Red onions and sweet onions, including Vidalia, Walla Walla, Oso, and Yellow Bermuda, contain more sugars than brown- or white-skinned Spanish varieties. Freshly harvested onions of any variety have a much stronger taste than stored onions.

Onions are the workhorses of the allium family, yet some varieties are more suitable for specific uses than others. Sweet onions are great raw in salads and for making quick pickles. Hotter brown- and white-skinned onions are best for soups and stews, and for baking or roasting whole or in wedges. Red onions cook to an unappetizing grayish brown, so use them only in salads or quick-cook dishes that allow them to maintain their glorious color. Small onions are useful for cooking whole in stews and ragoûts, and for pickling. Cipollini onions are small and pale yellow, and their flatness allows them to cook quickly and evenly.

Shallots (allium cepa varieties)

Shallots differ from onions in that many varieties produce a cluster of several bulbs to a plant. Shallots also have finer layers and less water. Because of the low water content, their flavor is more concentrated than that of onions, but they can also burn and toughen easily, so use caution when sautéing.

Use shallots when you want full allium flavor but not the bulk of a full-sized onion. Traditionally, shallots are used to flavor the reductions in some French sauces, including béarnaise, bordelaise, and duxelles. Shallots are also delicious cooked whole—try them caramelized with sugar and a few tablespoons of cognac, port, or sherry, or oven-roasted with rosemary or thyme. Finely chopped shallots are good in salad dressings and as a classic accompaniment to fresh oysters or beef dishes.

Leeks (allium ampeloprasum or allium porrum)

Although leeks resemble large green onions, they're milder and sweeter, and they don't cause any tears when they're chopped. Unlike other alliums, leeks are almost always enjoyed cooked since they're very fibrous when raw. The tougher, green part usually has a coarser flavor than the white part. Use the green part to flavor soups and stocks; add the white part (which is tender and needs only brief cooking) to soups and stews toward the end of cooking.

Leek soups rank among the world's favorites: from vichyssoise, created by Chef Louis Diat at New York's Ritz-Carlton almost a century ago, to the more provincial potage bonne femme, a creamy vegetable soup. Leeks are also delicious in potato, rice, and pasta dishes, such as Pasta with Leek, Pepper, and Chive Sauce (recipe on page 100). In some markets you may find finger-slim "baby" or "miniature" leeks. These are great for cooking whole; try them grilled with an herb salsa or vegetable dip, or in a tomato sauce or red wine reduction that includes Greek flavors like coriander, bay, and oregano.

Green Onions (allium cepa varieties and allium fistulosum)

These are also known as scallions, spring onions, or salad onions. They derive from several different types of wild alliums. And they can vary in thickness and length. Choose slender green onions for stir-fries, salsas, or salads; cook the thicker ones whole, or add them sliced to dishes that cook quickly. Look for red spring onions in farmers' markets—they add flavor and color to salads.

Served raw, green onions have a sweet, delicate flavor that's excellent in potato or rice salads and in salsas with chiles. Cooked green onions are great for fast recipes such as pasta, omelettes, pancakes, and stir-fries. In Catalonia, in northeastern Spain, green onions known as calcots are grilled over charcoal and served with a chili, garlic, and hazelnut romesco sauce.

Chives (allium schoenoprasum)

Chives are among the mildest culinary alliums. We use them primarily as an herb or garnish, but their subtle onion flavor can add just the right note of freshness to an otherwise lackluster dish. Chives are especially delicious with potatoes, eggs, rice, and smoked or pickled fish. The edible lilac-pink flowers of homegrown chives are attractive scattered over salads or omelettes. If you cook with chives, keep it brief to preserve their flavor.

Chives vary from grass-fine to pencil-thick. The thicker the chive, the more flavor it packs. In Asian markets you may find Chinese or Asian chives (allium tuberosum), also known as ku chai, gow choy, or garlic chives. They have a definite garlic kick; try them stir-fried with chicken or whitefish, or cook them with rice. Always use chives fresh: Dried chives lack the bright flavor that's the key to chives' charm.

Garlic-Roasted Potatoes and Fennel

2 large fennel bulbs with stalks, (about 2 pounds)
2 pounds small red potatoes, halved
Cooking spray
1 tablespoon olive oil
1 whole garlic head, unpeeled
2 large green bell peppers, cut into ½-inch strips
1 teaspoon fennel seeds, lightly crushed
1 teaspoon coriander seeds, crushed
½ teaspoon Spanish smoked paprika or sweet paprika
½ teaspoon salt
⅛ teaspoon freshly ground black pepper
1½ cups vegetable broth
⅛ teaspoon saffron threads
1 tablespoon sherry vinegar

1. Preheat oven to 375°.
2. Trim tough outer leaves from fennel; reserve fennel fronds for garnish, if desired. Remove and discard stalks. Cut fennel bulbs in half lengthwise; discard core. Cut bulb halves in half lengthwise.
3. Arrange potatoes in a single layer in a jelly roll pan or large roasting pan coated with cooking spray; drizzle with oil. Remove white papery skin from garlic head. Separate and peel cloves. Finely chop 1 garlic clove; sprinkle over potatoes. Add peeled garlic cloves, pepper strips, and next 5 ingredients to potatoes; toss well to combine.
4. Heat broth in a small saucepan over medium heat until warm. Remove from heat; stir in saffron. Let stand 10 minutes. Stir in vinegar; drizzle broth mixture over potato mixture. Bake at 375° for 30 minutes. Remove from oven, and arrange fennel wedges over potato mixture. Return to oven; bake an additional 50 minutes or until broth mixture almost evaporates and potatoes begin to brown, stirring once. Garnish with reserved fennel fronds, if desired. Yield: 6 servings (serving size: 1½ cups).

CALORIES 177 (15% from fat); FAT 2.9g (sat 0.3g, mono 1.7g, poly 0.3g); PROTEIN 6.5g; CARB 38.9g; FIBER 6.8g; CHOL 0mg; IRON 2.2mg; SODIUM 489mg; CALC 80mg

---

Entertaining Menu
serves 6

Prepare the fish packets a few hours ahead; keep them refrigerated. You also can make the breadsticks ahead.

Fish in Paper Parcels with Leeks, Fennel, Chives, and Vanilla

Fontina breadsticks*

Green salad

*Combine ¼ cup finely shredded fontina cheese and ½ teaspoon black pepper. Unroll 1 (11-ounce) can refrigerated breadstick dough; cut dough along perforations to form 12 breadsticks. Sprinkle cheese mixture over dough, gently pressing into dough. Twist each breadstick, and place on a baking sheet coated with cooking spray. Bake at 375° for 13 minutes or until lightly browned.

MAKE AHEAD
Fish in Paper Parcels with Leeks, Fennel, Chives, and Vanilla

This is an excellent dish for entertaining; you can prepare it in advance, store it in the refrigerator, then pop it in the oven. Substitute fillets of salmon, bass, haddock, or mullet for the red snapper.

6 (6-ounce) red snapper or other firm white fish fillets
¾ teaspoon salt
¼ teaspoon freshly ground black pepper
Cooking spray
2½ cups thinly sliced leek (about 3 large)
2½ cups thinly sliced fennel bulb (about 2 small bulbs)
2½ cups (2-inch) julienne-cut carrot
½ cup fat-free, less-sodium chicken broth
1 tablespoon low-sodium soy sauce
¼ cup chopped fresh chives, divided
2 tablespoons fresh lemon juice, divided
3 (6-inch) vanilla beans, split lengthwise and halved crosswise

1. Preheat oven to 400°.
2. Sprinkle fish with salt and pepper.

3. Heat a large nonstick skillet coated with cooking spray over medium-high heat. Add leek, fennel, and carrot; sauté 4 minutes or until carrot is crisp-tender. Add broth and soy sauce; cook 3 minutes or until liquid evaporates. Stir in 3 tablespoons chives and 1 tablespoon lemon juice.
4. Cut 6 (14-inch) squares of parchment paper. Fold each square in half; open each. Place 1 cup vegetable mixture near fold of each paper. Place 1 fish fillet on vegetable mixture on each paper; top each with ½ teaspoon chives, ½ teaspoon lemon juice, and 2 pieces vanilla bean. Fold papers; seal edges with narrow folds. Place 3 packets on each of 2 baking sheets.
5. Bake at 400° for 18 minutes or until puffy and lightly browned, rotating baking sheets after 9 minutes. Place on plates, and cut open. Serve immediately. Yield: 6 servings.

CALORIES 271 (9% from fat); FAT 2.8g (sat 0.5g, mono 0.4g, poly 1g); PROTEIN 38.1g; CARB 23.2g; FIBER 6g; CHOL 63mg; IRON 2.6mg; SODIUM 610mg; CALC 153mg

---

Creamy Roasted-Onion Soup

1¼ pounds Oso or other sweet onions, peeled and quartered
Cooking spray
1 whole garlic head, unpeeled
1 tablespoon water
⅛ teaspoon saffron threads (optional)
2 (14-ounce) cans fat-free, less-sodium chicken broth
1 bay leaf
¼ cup dry sherry or Madeira wine, divided
¼ teaspoon freshly ground black pepper
⅛ teaspoon salt
1 teaspoon fresh lemon juice
½ cup (2 ounces) shredded Swiss cheese
Chopped fresh parsley (optional)

1. Preheat oven to 375°.
2. Place quartered onion on a baking sheet coated with cooking spray, and lightly coat onion with cooking spray.

3. Remove white papery skin from garlic head (do not peel or separate cloves). Place garlic on a piece of aluminum foil. Drizzle with water; wrap in foil. Place wrapped garlic on baking sheet with onion. Bake at 375° for 1 hour or until onion is soft and lightly browned, turning after 30 minutes. Cool.

4. Place onion in a large saucepan. Unwrap garlic; separate cloves, and squeeze to extract pulp into pan. Discard garlic skins. Add saffron (if desired), broth, and bay leaf to pan. Bring to a simmer over medium heat. Stir in 3 tablespoons sherry, pepper, and salt. Reduce heat, and simmer 15 minutes. Discard bay leaf.

5. Place half of onion mixture in a blender or food processor; process until smooth. Pour puréed mixture into a large bowl; repeat procedure with remaining onion mixture. Return onion mixture to pan; cook over low heat until thoroughly heated. Stir in 1 tablespoon sherry and juice. Ladle 1 cup soup into each of 4 bowls; top each serving with 2 tablespoons cheese. Sprinkle with parsley, if desired. Yield: 4 servings.

CALORIES 157 (24% from fat); FAT 4.2g (sat 2.6g, mono 1.1g, poly 0.3g); PROTEIN 9.2g; CARB 18.9g; FIBER 2.9g; CHOL 13mg; IRON 0.7mg; SODIUM 496mg; CALC 194mg

inspired vegetarian

Cosmic Combinations

Two menus show how contrasting flavors can elevate any meal.

A six-pointed star illuminates good cooking the world over. Four of its points are the tastes of sweet, sour, bitter, and salty. The other two? Heat and coolness—both the temperature at which a dish is served and its level of spiciness, whether chile-hot or minty cool. These six components light up the experience of eating. To illustrate this principle, we have chosen two very different cuisines, Indian and French, for two decidedly distinct vegetarian menus.

Indian Menu

serves 6

Split Pea-Spinach Dal with Cauliflower

Stuffed Zucchini with Potatoes and Peas

Tomato Pachadi

Basmati rice

Purchased lime pickle

Golden Compote of Pineapple, Cardamom, and Rose Water

MAKE AHEAD

Split Pea-Spinach Dal with Cauliflower

Throughout India, a meal isn't complete without some variation of this spice-tempered legume dish. Cumin and turmeric provide slightly bitter notes, but the dish has an overall salty-savory flavor. The dal is more of a stew than a soup; for a thinner version, decrease the final simmering time.

3½ cups water, divided
1 cup dried yellow split peas
1 bay leaf
2 cups chopped cauliflower florets
1½ teaspoons salt
1 tablespoon butter
1 teaspoon vegetable oil
1 cup chopped onion
1½ teaspoons minced peeled fresh ginger
2 garlic cloves, minced
1 tablespoon cumin seeds
1 tablespoon brown mustard seeds
1½ teaspoons ground coriander
1 teaspoon ground turmeric
½ teaspoon ground red pepper
⅛ teaspoon ground cloves
4 cups torn spinach

1. Combine 2½ cups water, peas, and bay leaf in a large saucepan; bring to a boil. Reduce heat, and simmer, partially covered, 50 minutes or until tender. Add 1 cup water, cauliflower, and salt, and bring to a boil. Reduce heat, and simmer, uncovered, 20 minutes or until cauliflower is very tender, stirring occasionally. Remove from heat; discard bay leaf.

2. Heat butter and oil in a small skillet over medium-high heat until butter

melts. Add onion, ginger, and garlic; sauté 3 minutes. Add cumin and next 5 ingredients; cook over low heat 2 minutes, stirring frequently. Add onion mixture to pea mixture. Simmer, uncovered, 15 minutes or until thick. Stir in spinach; cook 3 minutes or until spinach wilts. Yield: 6 servings (serving size: ⅔ cup).

CALORIES 183 (18% from fat); FAT 3.7g (sat 1.4g, mono 0.9g, poly 0.6g); PROTEIN 11.4g; CARB 28.8g; FIBER 2.6g; CHOL 5mg; IRON 3.4mg; SODIUM 649mg; CALC 75mg

Stuffed Zucchini with Potatoes and Peas

(pictured on page 110)

If you're sensitive to spicy foods, seed the chile. A small amount of chickpea flour, also called *besan* or gram flour, acts as a binder and provides a delicate nutty flavor. Look for it in Indian or Asian markets, or substitute whole wheat flour.

6 zucchini (about 3 pounds)
1¼ teaspoons salt, divided
1½ cups chopped peeled baking potato
2 teaspoons butter
2 teaspoons vegetable oil
2½ cups chopped onion
1½ tablespoons minced peeled fresh ginger
2 garlic cloves, crushed
1 serrano chile, minced
2 tablespoons chickpea (garbanzo bean) flour
1 teaspoon ground coriander
¼ teaspoon ground turmeric
¼ teaspoon ground red pepper
¼ teaspoon ground cumin
1½ cups frozen green peas, thawed
2 tablespoons finely chopped fresh cilantro

1. Cut each zucchini in half lengthwise; scoop out pulp, leaving ¼-inch-thick shells. Place zucchini halves, cut sides up, in a shallow roasting pan. Sprinkle with ½ teaspoon salt. Discard pulp.

2. Preheat oven to 375°.

3. Cook potato in boiling water 2 minutes or until crisp-tender; drain.

Continued

4. Heat butter and oil in a nonstick skillet over medium-high heat until butter melts. Add onion, ginger, garlic, and chile, and sauté 3 minutes. Stir in flour and next 4 ingredients. Cook over medium-low heat 5 minutes, stirring frequently. Stir in ¾ teaspoon salt, potato, peas, and cilantro.

5. Pat zucchini dry with paper towels; spoon about ⅓ cup potato mixture into each zucchini half. Cover and bake at 375° for 20 minutes or until zucchini is tender. Yield: 6 servings (serving size: 2 zucchini halves).

CALORIES 145 (22% from fat); FAT 3.5g (sat 1.1g, mono 0.8g, poly 1.2g); PROTEIN 5.7g; CARB 24.9g; FIBER 6g; CHOL 3mg; IRON 1.7mg; SODIUM 552mg; CALC 55mg

Tomato Pachadi

(pictured on page 110)

A *pachadi* is a south Indian dish that falls Somewhere between curry, salad, and condiment, this dish is more like a chutney and goes well with the rice and dal. Fire-roasted tomatoes give the dish some smokiness. There's a bit of heat from the chiles, but the main flavors are sweet from the coconut and sugar, and sour-cool from the yogurt.

 ½ cup water
 1 tablespoon dark brown sugar
 2 bay leaves
 1 (28-ounce) can crushed fire-roasted tomatoes, undrained
 1 teaspoon vegetable oil
 2¼ teaspoons brown mustard seeds
 2 dried hot red chiles
 ¼ cup flaked sweetened coconut
 1 serrano chile, seeded and minced
 ¼ cup plain fat-free yogurt

1. Combine first 4 ingredients in a large saucepan; bring to a boil. Reduce heat, and simmer 20 minutes. Spoon into a bowl; cool to room temperature. Discard bay leaves.

2. While tomato mixture cools, heat oil in a small nonstick skillet over medium heat. Add mustard seeds and red chiles. Cook, partially covered, 3 minutes or until seeds begin to pop, shaking pan

frequently. Cool mustard mixture, and discard red chiles. Add mustard mixture, coconut, and serrano to tomato mixture. Stir in yogurt. Serve immediately. Yield: 6 servings (serving size: about ¼ cup).

CALORIES 82 (22% from fat); FAT 2g (sat 1g, mono 0.2g, poly 0.5g); PROTEIN 3g; CARB 13.7g; FIBER 2.7g; CHOL 0mg; IRON 1mg; SODIUM 340mg; CALC 64mg

---

MAKE AHEAD
Golden Compote of Pineapple, Cardamom, and Rose Water

Sweet, sour, and cool sensations combine in this intoxicatingly perfumed dessert. Look for rose water and cardamom pods in natural-foods stores or Indian markets. If you can't find cardamom pods, substitute ⅛ teaspoon ground cardamom.

 6 (¼-inch-thick) lime slices, each cut into quarters
 ¾ cup water
 ¼ cup sugar
 8 cardamom pods
 3 cups (1-inch) cubed fresh pineapple
 ½ cup golden raisins
 1½ teaspoons rose water
 3 cups vanilla low-fat ice cream
 ¼ cup chopped pistachios

1. Cook lime slices in boiling water 1 minute; drain.

2. Combine ¾ cup water, sugar, and cardamom in a medium saucepan. Bring to a boil; cook 1 minute or until sugar dissolves. Add lime slices to pan; reduce heat, and simmer 10 minutes. Remove from heat; let stand 1 hour. Discard cardamom pods.

3. Combine pineapple, raisins, and rose water in a large bowl. Pour lime mixture over pineapple mixture, and toss gently to combine. Cover and chill up to 24 hours. Serve with ice cream and pistachios. Yield: 6 servings (serving size: ⅔ cup compote, ½ cup ice cream, and 2 teaspoons pistachios).

CALORIES 248 (17% from fat); FAT 4.8g (sat 1.3g, mono 1.3g, poly 0.9g); PROTEIN 4.8g; CARB 48.6g; FIBER 3.1g; CHOL 5mg; IRON 0.7mg; SODIUM 47mg; CALC 118mg

---

French Menu
serves 6
White Bean Salad Niçoise
Mushroom Crêpes Chasseur
French bread
Bittersweet Chocolate Mousse à l'Orange

White Bean Salad Niçoise

The dressing combines contrasting flavors: Dijon mustard, black pepper, and garlic provide hot sensations, while lemon juice offers sour notes. Salty olives and bitter greens round out the tastes of this salad. *Haricots verts*—thin French green beans— work well here. If you can't find them, use regular green beans.

SALAD:
 4 ounces haricots verts, trimmed and cut in half crosswise
 ¼ cup kalamata olives, pitted and sliced
 ¼ cup thinly sliced green onions
 4 ounces trimmed arugula
 1 (16-ounce) can cannellini beans or other white beans, rinsed and drained
 1 (7-ounce) bag fresh baby spinach

DRESSING:
 ¼ cup fresh lemon juice
 2 tablespoons chopped fresh flat-leaf parsley
 2 tablespoons chopped fresh basil
 1 tablespoon Dijon mustard
 2 teaspoons extravirgin olive oil
 ¼ teaspoon salt
 ¼ teaspoon freshly ground black pepper
 2 garlic cloves, minced

1. To prepare salad, cook haricots verts in boiling water 2 minutes or until crisp-tender. Drain and plunge into ice water; drain. Place haricots verts in a large bowl. Add olives and next 4 ingredients, and toss gently to combine.

2. To prepare dressing, combine lemon juice and remaining 7 ingredients, stirring with a whisk. Drizzle dressing

over salad, and toss gently to coat. Yield: 6 servings (serving size: 2 cups).

CALORIES 86 (30% from fat); FAT 2.9g (sat 0.3g, mono 1.7g, poly 0.6g); PROTEIN 3.9g; CARB 12.1g; FIBER 4g; CHOL 0mg; IRON 2.3mg; SODIUM 338mg; CALC 94mg

MAKE AHEAD
Mushroom Crêpes Chasseur

Chasseur (French for "hunter") often refers to a brown sauce of mushrooms, shallots, and wine that's served with game. Here, the hunter is in search of mushrooms. Use any combination of mushrooms you like. With red wine, honey, and vegetable broth, the sauce takes on sour, sweet, and salty tones. To make ahead, stack cooled crêpes between sheets of wax paper and freeze in a zip-top plastic bag up to 3 months. You can make the filling and sauce a day ahead.

1 cup all-purpose flour
1 cup chickpea (garbanzo bean) flour
½ teaspoon salt
2 cups warm water
2 tablespoons olive oil
Cooking spray
4 cups vegetable broth
½ cup water
½ cup dried porcini mushrooms (about ½ ounce)
¾ cup dry red wine
2 tablespoons honey
2 tablespoons olive oil
2 cups chopped onion
2 (8-ounce) packages button mushrooms, coarsely chopped
8 ounces shiitake mushroom caps, coarsely chopped
½ teaspoon freshly ground black pepper
¼ teaspoon ground nutmeg
⅛ teaspoon salt
6 garlic cloves, minced
2 tablespoons water
2 teaspoons cornstarch
¼ cup finely chopped fresh flat-leaf parsley

1. Lightly spoon flours into dry measuring cups; level with a knife. Combine flours and ½ teaspoon salt in a medium bowl. Add 2 cups water and 2 tablespoons oil, stirring with a whisk until smooth. Let stand 20 minutes.

2. Heat an 8-inch crêpe pan or nonstick skillet coated with cooking spray over medium-high heat. Remove pan from heat. Pour a scant ¼ cup batter into pan; quickly tilt pan in all directions so batter covers pan with a thin film. Cook about 40 seconds. Carefully lift edge of crêpe with a spatula to test for doneness. Turn crêpe when it can be shaken loose from pan and underside is lightly browned; cook 30 seconds on other side.

3. Place crêpe on a towel; cool. Repeat procedure until all of batter is used to make 12 crêpes. Stack crêpes between single layers of wax paper to prevent sticking.

4. Bring broth and ½ cup water to a boil in a medium saucepan; remove from heat, and stir in porcini. Let stand 30 minutes. Strain mixture through a sieve into a bowl; reserve broth mixture and porcini. Chop porcini; set aside. Return broth mixture to saucepan. Add red wine and honey; set aside.

5. Heat 2 tablespoons oil in a large nonstick skillet over medium-high heat. Add onion; sauté 3 minutes. Add reserved porcini; sauté 1 minute. Add button and shiitake mushrooms; cook 4 minutes or until mushrooms release moisture, stirring occasionally. Reduce heat to medium; stir in pepper, nutmeg, ⅛ teaspoon salt, and garlic. Cook 1 minute, stirring frequently. Add ¾ cup broth mixture; reduce heat, and simmer 15 minutes, stirring occasionally.

6. Bring remaining broth mixture to a boil; cook until reduced to 1½ cups (about 12 minutes). Combine 2 tablespoons water and cornstarch, stirring with a whisk. Stir cornstarch mixture into boiling broth mixture. Return to a boil; cook 2 minutes or until sauce thickens.

7. Spoon ⅓ cup mushroom mixture in center of a crêpe; fold sides and ends over, and place, seam sides down, on a plate. Repeat procedure with remaining mushroom mixture and crêpes, placing 2 crêpes on each of 6 plates. Top each serving with about ¼ cup sauce; sprinkle with 2 teaspoons parsley. Yield: 6 servings.

CALORIES 339 (30% from fat); FAT 11.4g (sat 1.4g, mono 7g, poly 1.5g); PROTEIN 11.7g; CARB 46g; FIBER 5.1g; CHOL 0mg; IRON 4.1mg; SODIUM 939mg; CALC 37mg

MAKE AHEAD
Bittersweet Chocolate Mousse à l'Orange

Fresh orange sections are topped with a thick chocolate mousse for a unique presentation. The mild bitterness of orange rind and bittersweet chocolate temper the sweetness of this easy dish. You can prepare the dessert up to a day ahead.

½ cup sugar
7 tablespoons unsweetened cocoa
2 tablespoons Grand Marnier (orange-flavored liqueur)
1 teaspoon grated orange rind
½ teaspoon vanilla extract
Dash of salt
2 (12.3-ounce) packages reduced-fat silken tofu, drained
3 ounces bittersweet chocolate, chopped
3 oranges, peeled and sectioned

1. Combine first 7 ingredients in a blender or food processor; process until smooth.

2. Place chopped chocolate in a small microwave-safe bowl. Microwave at HIGH 1 minute or until almost melted; stir until smooth. Add chocolate to tofu mixture; process until smooth.

3. Divide orange sections evenly among 6 bowls or parfait glasses; top each serving with ½ cup mousse. Cover and chill at least 1 hour. Yield: 6 servings.

CALORIES 241 (27% from fat); FAT 7.1g (sat 3.6g, mono 1g, poly 0.9g); PROTEIN 9.5g; CARB 35.9g; FIBER 4.1g; CHOL 1mg; IRON 2mg; SODIUM 124mg; CALC 79mg

A Family That Bakes Together

Three generations mix it up with a delicious Cheese Pie.

Ann Bliss-Pilcher of Jamesville, New York, learned the original recipe for Cheese Pie from baking with her mother.

Now that Ann is a mother of two, she spends time with her children in the kitchen, as well. Jamie, 10, and Hannah, 13, both love to cook and have been making Cheese Pie for several years (with a little help on the crust). "It's very straightforward and pretty hard to mess up," Ann says. She likens the flavor to that of cheesecake, "but it's much lighter in texture."

MAKE AHEAD
Cheese Pie

CRUST:

1¼ cups low-fat graham cracker crumbs (about 8 cookie sheets)
2½ tablespoons butter, melted
¼ cup sugar
Cooking spray

FILLING:

1½ cups fat-free cottage cheese
½ cup (4 ounces) ⅓-less-fat cream cheese
½ cup sugar
¼ cup vanilla fat-free yogurt
2 tablespoons all-purpose flour
1 teaspoon vanilla extract
⅛ teaspoon salt
2 large eggs
2 large egg yolks
2 large egg whites
2 tablespoons sugar

SAUCE:

2 cups chopped strawberries
3 tablespoons sugar
½ teaspoon cornstarch

1. Preheat oven to 325°.
2. To prepare crust, combine first 3 ingredients; toss with a fork until moist. Press into bottom and up sides of a 10-inch pie plate coated with cooking spray; chill.
3. To prepare filling, combine cottage cheese and next 8 ingredients in a blender, and process until smooth. Place cheese mixture in a large bowl. Place egg whites in a second large bowl; beat with a mixer until soft peaks form. Add 2 tablespoons sugar, beating until stiff peaks form. Gently fold egg white mixture into cheese mixture; pour into prepared crust. Bake at 325° for 45 minutes or until center barely moves when pan is touched. Cool to room temperature. Cover and chill at least 4 hours.
4. To prepare sauce, combine strawberries, 3 tablespoons sugar, and cornstarch in a saucepan; bring to a boil. Cook 1 minute, stirring constantly. Cool slightly. Place strawberry mixture in a blender; process until smooth. Strain. Serve with pie. Yield: 10 servings (serving size: 1 wedge and 3 tablespoons sauce).

CALORIES 259 (30% from fat); FAT 8.7g (sat 4.2g, mono 2.8g, poly 0.9g); PROTEIN 8.9g; CARB 36.6g; FIBER 1.1g; CHOL 103mg; IRON 0.9mg; SODIUM 328mg; CALC 58mg

MAKE AHEAD
Root Vegetable Soup

"This soup was invented on a chilly evening as a way to use root vegetables."
—Chris Underhill, Cary, North Carolina

3 cups chopped peeled baking potato
2½ cups chopped peeled turnips (about 1¼ pounds)
1½ cups chopped peeled rutabaga
1¼ cups chopped peeled butternut squash
1 cup chopped onion
½ cup chopped carrot
1½ teaspoons dried rubbed sage
¼ teaspoon salt
2 (14-ounce) cans fat-free, less-sodium chicken broth
2 cups 2% reduced-fat milk

1. Combine first 9 ingredients in a Dutch oven; bring to a boil. Reduce heat, and simmer 30 minutes. Remove from heat; let stand 10 minutes. Place one-third of vegetable mixture in a blender; process until smooth. Pour puréed soup into a large bowl. Repeat procedure with remaining vegetable mixture. Return soup to pan; stir in milk. Cook over medium heat until thoroughly heated. Yield: 8 servings (serving size: 1¼ cups).

CALORIES 124 (10% from fat); FAT 1.4g (sat 0.8g, mono 0.4g, poly 0.1g); PROTEIN 5.7g; CARB 23.2g; FIBER 3.9g; CHOL 5mg; IRON 1mg; SODIUM 330mg; CALC 120mg

QUICK & EASY
Chicken Stroganoff

"A friend gave me this recipe, and I modified it to be a bit healthier."
—Carrie Kohler, Olympia, Washington

4 turkey-bacon slices
1½ cups chopped onion
1 pound skinless, boneless chicken breast, cut into ¼-inch strips
1½ cups fat-free, less-sodium chicken broth
½ teaspoon salt
½ teaspoon black pepper
¼ teaspoon paprika
2 garlic cloves, minced
1 (8-ounce) carton reduced-fat sour cream
2 tablespoons all-purpose flour
4 cups hot cooked medium egg noodles

1. Cook bacon in a large nonstick skillet over medium heat until crisp. Remove bacon from pan; crumble. Add onion and chicken to drippings in pan; sauté 6 minutes. Add bacon, broth, salt, pepper, paprika, and garlic; bring to a boil. Cover, reduce heat, and simmer 10 minutes.
2. Combine sour cream and flour, stirring until smooth. Add sour cream mixture to pan, and bring to a boil. Reduce heat, and simmer 2 minutes, stirring constantly. Serve over egg noodles. Yield: 4 servings (serving size: 1 cup stroganoff and 1 cup noodles).

CALORIES 514 (25% from fat); FAT 14.1g (sat 6.4g, mono 4.3g, poly 1.7g); PROTEIN 41.1g; CARB 53.3g; FIBER 3.1g; CHOL 162mg; IRON 2.4mg; SODIUM 770mg; CALC 154mg

Zucchini and Basil Lasagna

"The idea for this recipe came one summer when we had an excess of zucchini and fresh basil. Although I usually use ricotta in my lasagna, I only had cottage cheese, so I used that. The oven-ready noodles and bottled sauce make this a quick recipe to put together. It's great to have a tasty and healthier version of a longtime family favorite."

—Carolyn Marck, Seattle, Washington

2 cups fat-free cottage cheese
1 cup chopped fresh basil
1 large egg
Cooking spray
4 cups chopped zucchini
½ cup chopped onion
2 cups bottled spicy tomato pasta sauce (such as Newman's Own)
9 oven-ready lasagna noodles (such as Barilla)
1½ cups (6 ounces) shredded part-skim mozzarella cheese

1. Preheat oven to 350°.
2. Combine first 3 ingredients in a food processor; process until smooth.
3. Heat a large nonstick skillet coated with cooking spray over medium-high heat. Add zucchini and onion; sauté 5 minutes or until tender. Stir in sauce; remove from heat.

4. Spread ¼ cup zucchini mixture in bottom of a 13 x 9-inch baking dish coated with cooking spray. Arrange 3 noodles over zucchini mixture; top with one-third cottage cheese mixture, one-third zucchini mixture, and one-third mozzarella. Repeat layers with remaining noodles, cottage cheese mixture, zucchini mixture, and mozzarella.
5. Cover and bake at 350° for 45 minutes. Uncover and bake an additional 15 minutes or until lasagna is thoroughly heated. Yield: 8 servings.

CALORIES 227 (24% from fat); FAT 6g (sat 3.1g, mono 0.8g, poly 0.6g); PROTEIN 17.8g; CARB 26.4g; FIBER 2.9g; CHOL 40mg; IRON 1.4mg; SODIUM 537mg; CALC 251mg

De-lish Oatmeal

"I love breakfast almost more than I love dessert. I was inspired to experiment with oatmeal after visiting one of my favorite breakfast places. I vary the recipe a little almost every time I make it, using whatever fresh fruit is in season. It always tastes 'de-lish'—thus, the name. I like organic oats because they keep their shape and taste better, but regular oats will do."

—Sonja Elias, Minneapolis, Minnesota

¾ cup water
¾ cup apple cider
1 cup organic rolled oats
½ teaspoon salt
½ cup diced pear
¼ cup sweetened dried cranberries
½ teaspoon ground cinnamon
¼ teaspoon vanilla extract
¼ cup chopped pecans, toasted
¼ cup fat-free milk

1. Bring water and apple cider to a boil in a large saucepan. Stir in oats and salt; reduce heat to low, and cook 3 minutes, stirring occasionally.
2. Add pear, cranberries, cinnamon, and vanilla, stirring gently to combine; cook 3 minutes or until oats are tender. Stir in pecans and milk. Yield: 3 servings (serving size: about ¾ cup).

CALORIES 256 (30% from fat); FAT 8.4g (sat 0.9g, mono 4.2g, poly 2.6g); PROTEIN 6.2g; CARB 40.6g; FIBER 5g; CHOL 0mg; IRON 1.5mg; SODIUM 403mg; CALC 56mg

MAKE AHEAD
Snickerdoodles

"I am 17 and recently discovered my passion for cooking. I try to keep all of my cooking as light as possible, and *Cooking Light* has been a huge help. By modifying another cookie recipe from *Cooking Light*, I came up with this recipe, which my family adores."

—Lauren Harwick, Tumwater, Washington

1¾ cups all-purpose flour
½ teaspoon baking soda
½ teaspoon cream of tartar
1 cup sugar
¼ cup butter, softened
1 tablespoon corn syrup
1 teaspoon vanilla
1 large egg
3 tablespoons sugar
2 teaspoons ground cinnamon
Cooking spray

1. Preheat oven to 375°.
2. Lightly spoon flour into dry measuring cups; level with a knife. Combine flour, baking soda, and cream of tartar, stirring with a whisk.
3. Combine 1 cup sugar and butter in a large bowl, and beat with a mixer at medium speed until well blended. Add corn syrup, vanilla, and egg; beat well. Gradually add flour mixture to sugar mixture, beating just until combined. Cover and chill 10 minutes.
4. Combine 3 tablespoons sugar and cinnamon, stirring with a whisk.
5. With moist hands, shape dough into 42 (1-inch) balls. Roll balls in sugar mixture. Place balls 2 inches apart onto baking sheets coated with cooking spray. Flatten balls with bottom of a glass. Bake at 375° for 5 minutes (cookies will be slightly soft). Cool on baking sheets 2 minutes. Remove cookies from pans; cool completely on wire racks. Yield: 42 cookies (serving size: 1 cookie).

CALORIES 54 (22% from fat); FAT 1.3g (sat 0.7g, mono 0.1g, poly 0.4g); PROTEIN 0.7g; CARB 10.1g; FIBER 0.2g; CHOL 8mg; IRON 0.3mg; SODIUM 28mg; CALC 3mg

Garlic- and Herb-Crusted Lamb

Roast leg of lamb is a traditional seasonal offering for special spring dinners—even though lamb is now available year-round.

Garlic- and Herb-Crusted Lamb

4   whole garlic heads, unpeeled
1   tablespoon Dijon mustard
1   tablespoon olive oil
1   tablespoon thinly sliced fresh chives
1   tablespoon fresh thyme leaves, coarsely chopped
1   (8-pound) leg of lamb
12 fresh garlic slices
1¼ teaspoons salt, divided
½   teaspoon freshly ground black pepper
2   cups fresh French breadcrumbs (about 4 ounces)
2¼ cups low-salt beef broth
½   cup Merlot or other dry red wine
2½ tablespoons cornstarch
    Thyme sprigs (optional)

1. Preheat oven to 350°.
2. Remove white papery skin from garlic heads (do not peel or separate cloves). Cut off top portions of garlic heads. Wrap garlic heads in foil. Bake at 350° for 1 hour; cool 10 minutes. Squeeze garlic heads to extract pulp. Discard skins. Place garlic pulp, mustard, and oil in a food processor; process until smooth. Stir in chives and thyme leaves.
3. Increase oven temperature to 425°.
4. Trim fat from lamb. Cut 12 (¾-inch) slits in lamb; place a garlic slice in each slit. Sprinkle lamb with ½ teaspoon salt and pepper; rub with roasted garlic paste mixture. Press breadcrumbs over surface of lamb. Place on a broiler pan. Insert meat thermometer into thickest part of lamb, making sure not to touch bone.

5. Bake at 425° for 10 minutes. Decrease oven temperature to 325°. Bake an additional 2 hours and 10 minutes or until thermometer registers 140° (medium-rare) to 155° (medium). Remove lamb from rack; place on a shallow serving platter. Lightly cover with foil; let stand 15 minutes.
6. Drain fat from bottom of pan (do not scrape pan). Place broiler pan on stovetop over medium-high heat. Add broth, and bring to a boil, scraping to loosen browned bits.
7. Combine red wine and cornstarch, and stir with a whisk. Add to beef broth; return to a boil. Cook 1 minute or until mixture is slightly thick, stirring constantly. Stir in ¾ teaspoon salt, and serve immediately with lamb. Garnish with thyme sprigs, if desired. Yield: 20 servings (serving size: 3 ounces lamb and 2 tablespoons sauce).

CALORIES 211 (28% from fat); FAT 6.6g (sat 2.1g, mono 2.9g, poly 0.7g); PROTEIN 25.4g; CARB 9.9g; FIBER 0.4g; CHOL 73mg; IRON 2.9mg; SODIUM 337mg; CALC 40mg

lighten up

Spaghetti Appeal

We looked to a classic technique to lighten a Maryland family's favorite pasta recipe.

As a registered dietitian, Lesley Vogel of Westminister, Maryland, felt uncomfortable serving Spaghetti with Parmesan and Bacon to her family.

So to lighten Lesley's recipe, we took our cue from spaghetti carbonara and created a sauce of milk and eggs to maintain the pasta's creamy appeal. Whereas Lesley's recipe called for provolone cheese to thicken a whipping cream sauce, we used eggs to create a creamy sauce with a base of 2% milk. This change made the biggest difference, removing 129 grams of fat. We wanted to keep the flavor of the bacon, so we only slightly reduced it. We nixed the provolone cheese, but increased the amount of flavorful Parmesan cheese. The lightened recipe has almost two-thirds less fat than the original.

BEFORE	AFTER
SERVING SIZE	
1¼ cups	
CALORIES PER SERVING	
560	359
FAT	
30.2g	11.2g
PERCENT OF TOTAL CALORIES	
49%	28%

STAFF FAVORITE

Spaghetti with Parmesan and Bacon
(pictured on page 109)

1   pound uncooked spaghetti
12   bacon slices, chopped
3   garlic cloves, minced
1   cup 2% reduced-fat milk
1   teaspoon salt
1   teaspoon freshly ground black pepper
3   large eggs, lightly beaten
1   cup frozen petite green peas, thawed
1½   cups (6 ounces) grated fresh Parmesan cheese

1. Cook pasta according to package directions. Drain in a colander over a bowl, reserving ½ cup cooking liquid.
2. While pasta cooks, cook bacon in a large nonstick skillet over medium heat until crisp. Remove bacon from pan, reserving 1 tablespoon drippings in pan. Discard remaining drippings; set bacon aside. Add garlic to drippings in pan; cook 30 seconds, stirring constantly.
3. Combine milk, salt, pepper, and eggs, stirring with a whisk. Gradually add reserved cooking liquid to milk mixture, stirring constantly with a whisk. Add pasta, milk mixture, and peas to pan; cook over low heat 3 minutes or until sauce thickens. Add bacon and cheese; stir to combine. Yield: 8 servings (serving size: 1¼ cups).

CALORIES 359 (28% from fat); FAT 11.2g (sat 5.6g, mono 3.6g, poly 1g); PROTEIN 18.9g; CARB 44.6g; FIBER 3.3g; CHOL 99mg; IRON 2.8mg; SODIUM 721mg; CALC 315mg

Lemon-Blueberry Muffins,
page 96

Spaghetti with Parmesan and
Bacon, page 108

Stuffed Zucchini with Potatoes and Peas, page 103, accompanied by Tomato Pachadi, page 104

Strawberry-Almond Cream Tart, page 96

Crunchy Vegetable Salad, page 125

Chicken Scallopini, page 116

Spinach, Caramelized Onion, and
Bacon Pizza, page 114

Dinner On a Dime

Five weeknight meals that cost $10 or less.

With tax season around the corner, money is on everyone's mind. But just because you're on a budget doesn't mean you can't afford a little flavor. To that end, we offer five delicious and satisfying dinners that cost less than $10 apiece. Forget peanut butter sandwiches and pasta with tomato sauce—these flavorful dishes are sure to keep you well fed through any tight times ahead.

Calculating Costs

The cost for each meal is based on the amount of the products used in the recipe. We considered some ingredients as staples and didn't count them in the costs. These include herbs, spices, mustard, milk, eggs, butter, sugar, flour, and cornmeal.

Slow Cooker Red Beans and Rice

This recipe is the ultimate in thriftiness and convenience. You can also cook it on LOW heat for 8 hours. Sweet-and-Sour Slaw (recipe at right) is a choice complement.

TOTAL FOR MEAL: $5.13

- 3 cups water
- 1 cup dried red kidney beans
- 1 cup chopped onion
- 1 cup chopped green bell pepper
- ¾ cup chopped celery
- 1 teaspoon dried thyme
- 1 teaspoon paprika
- ¾ teaspoon ground red pepper
- ½ teaspoon black pepper
- ½ (14-ounce) package turkey, pork, and beef smoked sausage (such as Healthy Choice), thinly sliced
- 1 bay leaf
- 5 garlic cloves, minced
- ½ teaspoon salt
- 3 cups hot cooked long-grain rice
- ¼ cup chopped green onions

1. Combine first 12 ingredients in an electric slow cooker. Cover with lid; cook on HIGH 5 hours. Discard bay leaf; stir in salt. Serve over rice; sprinkle servings with green onions. Yield: 4 servings (serving size: 1 cup bean mixture, ¾ cup rice, and 1 tablespoon green onions).

CALORIES 413 (5% from fat); FAT 2.5g (sat 0.7g, mono 0.2g, poly 0.5g); PROTEIN 21.1g; CARB 76.3g; FIBER 10.1g; CHOL 18mg; IRON 6mg; SODIUM 749mg; CALC 102mg

Sweet-and-Sour Slaw

Try varying the slaw by adding slices of Granny Smith or Pink Lady apples to give it a slightly sweet-tart flavor and a crunchy bite.

- 1 tablespoon sugar
- 3 tablespoons cider vinegar
- 2 teaspoons vegetable oil
- ¼ teaspoon salt
- 4½ cups packaged cabbage-and-carrot coleslaw (about 8 ounces)
- ¼ cup chopped green onions

1. Combine first 4 ingredients in a large bowl, stirring with a whisk until sugar dissolves. Add coleslaw and onions to vinegar mixture; toss to combine. Serve chilled or at room temperature. Yield: 4 servings (serving size: 1 cup).

CALORIES 50 (43% from fat); FAT 2.4g (sat 0.4g, mono 0.5g, poly 1.4g); PROTEIN 0.8g; CARB 7.4g; FIBER 1.6g; CHOL 0mg; IRON 0.4mg; SODIUM 158mg; CALC 28mg

Ham and Swiss Bread Pudding

Toasting gives the delicate bread a firmer texture so the milk and eggs don't make it mushy. You can also use toasted French bread cubes, but the slight sweetness of the Hawaiian bread brings out the salty ham and nutty cheese flavors. Use the remaining rolls to make mini ham and cheese sandwiches.

TOTAL FOR MEAL: $5.02

- Cooking spray
- 1¼ cups chopped green onions
- ¾ cup chopped ham (about 3 ounces)
- 2 garlic cloves, chopped
- 7 (1-ounce) Hawaiian bread rolls, cut into ½-inch cubes
- 1¾ cups fat-free milk
- ¾ cup egg substitute
- 2 tablespoons Dijon mustard
- ¼ teaspoon salt
- ¼ teaspoon freshly ground black pepper
- ⅛ teaspoon ground nutmeg
- ¾ cup (3 ounces) shredded Swiss cheese, divided

1. Preheat oven to 350°.
2. Heat a small nonstick skillet coated with cooking spray over medium-high heat. Add onions, ham, and garlic; sauté 5 minutes. Remove from heat; cool.
3. Arrange bread cubes on a baking sheet. Bake at 350° for 15 minutes or until lightly browned, turning occasionally.
4. Combine milk and next 5 ingredients in a large bowl, stirring with a whisk until well blended. Stir in ham mixture. Add bread, tossing gently to coat.
5. Arrange half of bread mixture in an 8-inch square baking dish coated with cooking spray. Sprinkle with half of cheese; top with remaining bread mixture. Bake at 350° for 25 minutes. Sprinkle with remaining cheese; bake an additional 20 minutes or until set. Yield: 4 servings.

CALORIES 353 (30% from fat); FAT 11.9g (sat 5.7g, mono 3.9g, poly 1.1g); PROTEIN 23.9g; CARB 35.9g; FIBER 1.4g; CHOL 50mg; IRON 2.9mg; SODIUM 993mg; CALC 384mg

Beef and Bok Choy Hot Pot

You'll need a fork *and* a spoon to enjoy this meal. You can use most any greens in place of the bok choy, including spinach or Napa cabbage.

TOTAL FOR MEAL: $6.72

2¼   cups water
 ¾   cup low-salt beef broth
 ⅓   cup rice vinegar
 ⅓   cup low-sodium soy sauce
 2   tablespoons brown sugar
 ¼   teaspoon ground cinnamon
 1   tablespoon vegetable oil
 1   pound beef stew meat, cut into
      bite-sized pieces
1¼   cups chopped green onions
 1   garlic clove, minced
 1   teaspoon minced peeled fresh
      ginger
 2   cups thinly sliced bok choy
1½   cups thinly sliced carrot
 2   cups hot cooked wide rice noodles
      or fettuccine

1. Combine first 6 ingredients, stirring with a whisk; set aside.
2. Heat oil in a large Dutch oven over medium-high heat; add beef, browning on all sides. Add broth mixture, green onions, garlic, and ginger; bring to a boil.
3. Cover, reduce heat, and simmer 1 hour and 30 minutes or until beef is tender. Stir in bok choy and carrot, and cook 5 minutes or until tender. Serve beef mixture over noodles. Yield: 4 servings (serving size: 1½ cups beef mixture and ½ cup noodles).

CALORIES 369 (29% from fat); FAT 11.7g (sat 3.5g, mono 4.2g, poly 2.4g); PROTEIN 26.3g; CARB 36.6g; FIBER 3.5g; CHOL 71mg; IRON 3.8mg; SODIUM 931mg; CALC 90mg

Spinach, Caramelized Onion, and Bacon Pizza

(pictured on page 112)

A tender homemade crust is topped with a garlic-enhanced white sauce, which is then embellished with fresh sautéed spinach, caramelized onions, bacon, and Parmesan.

TOTAL FOR MEAL: $7.90

DOUGH:

 1   cup bread flour, divided
 1   cup warm water (100° to 110°)
 1   teaspoon sugar
 1   package dry yeast (about 2¼
      teaspoons)
1¾   cups all-purpose flour, divided
 ½   teaspoon salt
      Cooking spray

TOPPING:

 4   bacon slices, chopped
 1   (10-ounce) package fresh spinach
 2   cups (¼-inch-thick) sliced onion
 2   teaspoons sugar
 1   tablespoon butter
 2   garlic cloves, minced
 3   tablespoons all-purpose flour
 ½   teaspoon freshly ground black
      pepper
 1   cup 2% reduced-fat milk
 1   tablespoon cornmeal
 1   cup (4 ounces) grated fresh
      Parmesan cheese

1. To prepare dough, lightly spoon bread flour into a dry measuring cup; level with a knife. Combine ½ cup bread flour, warm water, 1 teaspoon sugar, and yeast; stir with a whisk. Let stand 15 minutes.
2. Lightly spoon 1¾ cups all-purpose flour into dry measuring cups; level with a knife. Combine 1½ cups all-purpose flour, ½ cup bread flour, and salt in a large bowl, stirring with a whisk.
3. Make a well in center of mixture. Add yeast mixture to flour mixture; stir well. Turn dough out onto a lightly floured surface. Knead until smooth and elastic (about 10 minutes); add enough of remaining all-purpose flour, 1 tablespoon at a time, to prevent dough from sticking to hands (dough will feel tacky).
4. Place dough in a large bowl coated with cooking spray, turning to coat top. Cover and let rise in a warm place (85°), free from drafts, 45 minutes or until doubled in size. (Gently press two fingers into dough. If indentation remains, the dough has risen enough.) Punch dough down; cover and let rest 20 minutes.
5. To prepare topping, cook bacon in a large nonstick skillet over medium heat until crisp. Remove bacon from pan, reserving 2 teaspoons drippings. Set bacon aside. Add spinach to drippings in pan; sauté 2 minutes or until wilted. Place spinach in a colander, pressing until barely moist. Add onion and 2 teaspoons sugar to pan; cook 12 minutes or until golden brown, stirring frequently. Remove from heat; cool.
6. Melt butter in a medium saucepan over medium heat. Add garlic; cook 2 minutes, stirring frequently. Add 3 tablespoons flour and pepper, stirring with a whisk; cook 30 seconds. Gradually add milk, stirring constantly with a whisk. Cook 5 minutes or until thick and bubbly, stirring constantly with a whisk.
7. Preheat oven to 475°.
8. Roll dough into a 12-inch circle on a floured surface. Place on a 12-inch pizza pan or baking sheet coated with cooking spray and sprinkled with cornmeal. Crimp edges of dough with fingers to form a rim. Spread milk mixture evenly over dough; top with spinach and onion.
9. Bake at 475° for 20 minutes. Sprinkle evenly with bacon and cheese; bake an additional 5 minutes or until golden brown. Cut pizza into 8 wedges. Yield: 4 servings (serving size: 2 wedges).

CALORIES 529 (29% from fat); FAT 17.3g (sat 9.3g, mono 5.9g, poly 1g); PROTEIN 26g; CARB 71.4g; FIBER 4.4g; CHOL 39mg; IRON 6.3mg; SODIUM 981mg; CALC 503mg

Italian Potato Torta

This *torta* makes a great vegetarian entrée.

TOTAL FOR MEAL: $4.12

 6   cups cubed peeled baking potato
      (about 1¾ pounds)
 ½   cup all-purpose flour
 2   teaspoons olive oil
 ⅛   teaspoon salt
 1   large egg, lightly beaten
      Cooking spray
 ¼   teaspoon dried Italian seasoning
 2   garlic cloves, minced
 1   (14.5-ounce) can diced Italian-style
      tomatoes, drained
 1   cup (4 ounces) shredded part-skim
      mozzarella cheese
 ¾   cup (3 ounces) grated fresh
      Parmesan cheese
      Thyme sprigs (optional)

1. Preheat oven to 450°.
2. Place potato in a saucepan; cover with water. Bring to a boil; cook 15 minutes or until tender. Drain. Return potato to pan; add flour, oil, salt, and egg. Mash potato mixture with a potato masher until smooth.
3. Spread potato mixture into a 9-inch round cake pan coated with cooking spray. Combine seasoning, garlic, and tomatoes; spread evenly over potato mixture. Combine cheeses, and sprinkle over tomato mixture. Bake at 450° for 25 minutes or until golden. Let stand 20 minutes. Cut torta into 4 wedges. Garnish with thyme, if desired. Yield: 4 servings (serving size: 1 wedge).

CALORIES 459 (29% from fat); FAT 14.6g (sat 7.7g, mono 5.3g, poly 0.7g); PROTEIN 23.1g; CARB 59.6g; FIBER 3.7g; CHOL 86mg; IRON 2.4mg; SODIUM 927mg; CALC 533mg

dinner tonight

The Versatile Chicken

From scallopini to grilled tostadas, the versatile chicken breast takes on new guises.

Chicken Tostadas Menu
serves 6
Grilled Chicken Tostadas
Brown rice

Pineapple refresher*

*Combine 3 cups pineapple chunks, 1 cup water, and 6 mint leaves in a blender; process until smooth. Transfer pineapple mixture to a pitcher. Add 2 cups cold water, stirring to combine. Serve over ice.

Game Plan

1. While rice cooks:
   • Season chicken
   • Combine slaw and green salsa
   • Combine tomato and olives
   • Toast pumpkinseed kernels
2. While chicken cooks:
   • Prepare pineapple refresher

QUICK & EASY
Grilled Chicken Tostadas

Fried tortillas usually form the shells for tostadas, but grilling lowers the fat. Prepared salsa, canned beans, and preshredded coleslaw make this recipe a snap to prepare.
TOTAL TIME: 35 MINUTES

    4 (6-ounce) skinless, boneless
       chicken breast halves
    1 tablespoon fresh lime juice
    1 tablespoon 40%-less-sodium taco
       seasoning (such as Old El Paso)
  ½ teaspoon sugar
  Cooking spray
    6 (8-inch) flour tortillas
    6 cups packaged coleslaw
    1 (7-ounce) can green salsa
    4 cups chopped tomato
  ¼ cup sliced ripe olives, chopped
  1¼ cups fat-free refried beans
  ½ cup (2 ounces) crumbled feta
       cheese
    6 tablespoons reduced-fat sour cream
  ¼ cup fresh cilantro leaves
  ¼ cup unsalted pumpkinseed kernels,
       toasted (optional)

1. Prepare grill, or heat a grill pan over medium-high heat.
2. Brush chicken with juice; sprinkle with seasoning and sugar. Place chicken on grill rack or grill pan coated with cooking spray; grill 4 minutes on each side or until done. Cool slightly. Cut chicken into ¼-inch strips; set aside. Place tortillas on grill rack or grill pan coated with cooking spray; grill 30 seconds on each side or until golden brown.
3. Combine coleslaw and salsa; toss to coat. Combine tomato and olives; toss gently.
4. Spread about 3 tablespoons beans over each tortilla; divide chicken evenly among tortillas. Top each serving with about ⅔ cup slaw mixture, ⅔ cup tomato mixture, 4 teaspoons cheese, 1 tablespoon sour cream, and 2 teaspoons cilantro. Sprinkle each serving with 2 teaspoons pumpkinseeds, if desired. Yield: 6 servings (serving size: 1 tostada).

CALORIES 361 (23% from fat); FAT 9.2g (sat 3.6g, mono 1.5g, poly 1.2g); PROTEIN 28.7g; CARB 43g; FIBER 6.8g; CHOL 65mg; IRON 3.7mg; SODIUM 844mg; CALC 221mg

---

Curried Chicken Menu
serves 4
Curried Chicken with Mango Relish
Minted cucumber salad*

Basmati rice

*Combine 2 cups chopped seeded cucumber, ¼ cup chopped red onion, 2 tablespoons rice vinegar, 1 teaspoon sugar, ½ teaspoon salt, and ½ teaspoon freshly ground black pepper; toss well. Add 1 cup plain fat-free yogurt and 3 tablespoons chopped fresh mint, stirring well to combine.

Game Plan

1. While chutney cooks:
   • Cook rice
   • Marinate chicken
   • Chop cucumber and red onion
2. While chicken cooks:
   • Prepare cucumber salad

QUICK & EASY
Curried Chicken with Mango Chutney

Using a grill pan scores the chicken nicely, but a skillet also works. You can substitute fresh or frozen peaches, plums, or nectarines for the mango in the chutney.
TOTAL TIME: 38 MINUTES
QUICK TIP: Look for jars of mango in the refrigerated section of your grocery store.

MANGO CHUTNEY:
    2 cups chopped peeled mango
    1 cup apple juice
  ⅓ cup diced dried apricots
    2 teaspoons cider vinegar
    1 teaspoon grated peeled fresh ginger
  ¼ teaspoon ground allspice
  ⅛ teaspoon ground red pepper

CHICKEN:
  ⅓ cup low-sodium soy sauce
  ⅓ cup fresh lime juice
    1 teaspoon curry powder
    4 (6-ounce) skinless, boneless
       chicken breast halves
  Cooking spray
  Lime wedges (optional)

Continued

1. To prepare chutney, combine first 7 ingredients in a saucepan, and bring to a boil. Reduce heat, and simmer 20 minutes, stirring occasionally.

2. To prepare chicken, combine soy sauce, juice, curry, and chicken in a zip-top plastic bag; seal and shake. Marinate in refrigerator 10 minutes, turning once. Heat a grill pan coated with cooking spray over medium-high heat.

3. Remove chicken from bag; discard marinade. Add chicken to pan; cook 5 minutes on each side or until chicken is done. Serve with chutney. Garnish with lime wedges, if desired. Yield: 4 servings (serving size: 1 chicken breast half and about ½ cup chutney).

CALORIES 257 (7% from fat); FAT 1.9g (sat 0.5g, mono 0.5g, poly 0.4g); PROTEIN 29.6g; CARB 30.6g; FIBER 2.8g; CHOL 68mg; IRON 1.7mg; SODIUM 880mg; CALC 35mg

Stuffed Chicken Breast Menu

serves 4

Chicken Breasts Stuffed with Artichokes, Lemon, and Goat Cheese

Wilted spinach

Bulgur pilaf with pine nuts*

*Heat 2 teaspoons olive oil in a medium skillet over medium-high heat. Add 1 cup coarse bulgur, ⅓ cup sliced green onions, ⅓ cup chopped shiitake mushrooms, and ⅛ teaspoon salt; sauté 5 minutes. Stir in 1 (14-ounce) can fat-free, less-sodium chicken broth; bring to a boil. Cover, reduce heat, and simmer 15 minutes. Remove from heat; let stand, covered, 5 minutes. Stir in 2 tablespoons pine nuts and 2 tablespoons chopped fresh parsley.

Game Plan

1. While bulgur cooks:
   • Combine cheese mixture
   • Pound chicken
   • Stuff chicken
2. While chicken cooks:
   • Finish pilaf
   • Prepare spinach

Chicken Breasts Stuffed with Artichokes, Lemon, and Goat Cheese

Browning the chicken on the stovetop and finishing it in the oven frees you to put the final touches on the pilaf. Wilt the spinach just before the chicken is done.

TOTAL TIME: 43 MINUTES

QUICK TIP: You can stuff the chicken breasts and chill up to 4 hours before serving.

2½ tablespoons Italian-seasoned breadcrumbs
  2 teaspoons grated lemon rind
  ¼ teaspoon salt
  ¼ teaspoon freshly ground black pepper
  1 (6-ounce) jar marinated artichoke hearts, drained and chopped
  1 (3-ounce) package herbed goat cheese, softened
  4 (6-ounce) skinless, boneless chicken breast halves
Cooking spray

1. Preheat oven to 375°.
2. Combine first 6 ingredients; stir well.
3. Place each chicken breast half between 2 sheets of heavy-duty plastic wrap; pound to ¼-inch thickness using a meat mallet or rolling pin. Top each breast half with 2 tablespoons cheese mixture; roll up jelly-roll fashion. Tuck in sides; secure each roll with wooden picks.
4. Heat a large nonstick skillet coated with cooking spray over medium-high heat. Add chicken to pan, and cook 3 minutes on each side or until browned. Wrap handle of pan with foil, and bake at 375° for 15 minutes or until chicken is done. Yield: 4 servings.

CALORIES 234 (30% from fat); FAT 7.8g (sat 3.5g, mono 1.4g, poly 0.5g); PROTEIN 33g; CARB 7.2g; FIBER 1.5g; CHOL 78mg; IRON 1.6mg; SODIUM 545mg; CALC 49mg

Chicken Scallopini Menu

serves 4

Chicken Scallopini

Orzo, tomato, and zucchini toss*

Garlic bread

*Heat 1 teaspoon olive oil in a medium skillet over medium-high heat. Add 1 cup halved cherry tomatoes, 1 cup chopped zucchini, and 2 minced garlic cloves; sauté 2 minutes. Stir in ½ teaspoon Italian seasoning and ¼ teaspoon red pepper flakes; sauté 1 minute or until zucchini is crisp-tender. Combine tomato mixture, 3 cups hot cooked orzo, and ¼ teaspoon salt; toss well.

Game Plan

1. While orzo cooks:
   • Pound chicken
   • Season and dredge chicken in breadcrumbs
   • Chop tomatoes and zucchini
2. While chicken cooks:
   • Cook tomato mixture
   • Heat garlic bread

Chicken Scallopini

(pictured on page 111)

Pounding the chicken breast halves to thin "scallops" cuts the cooking time in half but leaves the chicken moist and tender. If you don't have orzo, substitute rice in the side dish.

TOTAL TIME: 22 MINUTES

  4 (6-ounce) skinless, boneless chicken breast halves
  2 teaspoons fresh lemon juice
  ¼ teaspoon salt
  ¼ teaspoon black pepper
  ⅓ cup Italian-seasoned breadcrumbs
Cooking spray
  ½ cup fat-free, less-sodium chicken broth
  ¼ cup dry white wine
  4 teaspoons capers
  1 tablespoon butter

1. Place each chicken breast half between 2 sheets of heavy-duty plastic wrap; pound to ¼-inch thickness using a meat mallet or rolling pin. Brush chicken with juice, and sprinkle with salt and pepper. Dredge chicken in breadcrumbs.

2. Heat a large nonstick skillet coated with cooking spray over medium-high heat. Add chicken to pan; cook 3 minutes on each side or until chicken is done. Remove from pan; keep warm.

3. Add broth and wine to pan, and cook 30 seconds, stirring constantly. Remove from heat. Stir in capers and butter. Yield: 4 servings (serving size: 1 chicken breast half and 1 tablespoon sauce).

CALORIES 206 (20% from fat); FAT 4.6g (sat 2.2g, mono 1.3g, poly 0.5g); PROTEIN 29.2g; CARB 7.7g; FIBER 0.6g; CHOL 76mg; IRON 1.6mg; SODIUM 657mg; CALC 27mg

meatless mains

Feeling Saucy

Veggie pizzas and lasagnas are so satisfying and creative you'll never miss the meat.

Former *Cooking Light* magazine managing editor Hillari Dowdle has a boyfriend who is nutty for Italian food. He just can't get enough of the stuff. He adores sauces of all sorts; tomato sauce is his stated favorite, though she's never known him to reject an Alfredo.

That means Italian fare graces their table at least once a week. Among the following recipes are meals that have freed them from the chains of spaghetti with plain bottled sauce. Polenta Lasagna provides a change of pace in both flavor and texture. Both of the more traditional lasagnas offer enough meaty textures and flavors to make them forget all about Italian sausage and prosciutto. And both freeze beautifully, which means they can either save leftovers or double up and have a quick ready-made dinner for a busy weeknight. Faster still is Rustic Grilled Pizza, which makes best use of premade, refrigerated dough. But their favorite remains the Turnip Green and Shiitake Mushroom Calzone with Smoked Cheddar.

Potato and Pepper Pizza with Goat Cheese

The dough recipe yields two crusts, so you can either double the rest of the ingredients to make two pizzas or freeze the remaining dough for later. If you freeze the dough, thaw it in the refrigerator overnight.

1½ cups thinly sliced fingerling or red potatoes (about 6 ounces)
 1 large red bell pepper
 1 teaspoon olive oil
 ½ teaspoon dried oregano
 ¼ teaspoon salt
 ¼ teaspoon coarsely ground black pepper
 ½ recipe Whole Wheat Pizza Dough Cooking spray
 1 tablespoon yellow cornmeal
 ⅓ cup (3 ounces) soft goat cheese
 3 tablespoons chopped pitted kalamata olives

1. Preheat broiler.
2. Cook potato in boiling water 5 minutes, and drain.
3. Cut bell pepper in half lengthwise; discard seeds and membranes. Place pepper halves, skin sides up, on a foil-lined baking sheet; flatten with hand. Broil 15 minutes or until blackened. Place in a zip-top plastic bag; seal. Let stand 15 minutes. Peel and cut into strips. Combine potato, bell pepper, oil, oregano, salt, and black pepper, tossing well to coat.
4. Preheat oven to 500°.
5. Roll pizza dough into a 12-inch circle on a lightly floured surface. Place pizza dough on a 12-inch pizza pan or baking sheet coated with cooking spray and sprinkled with cornmeal. Crimp edges of pizza dough with fingers to form a rim. Arrange potato mixture over crust. Drop goat cheese by teaspoonfuls onto potato mixture. Sprinkle with olives.
6. Bake at 500° for 15 minutes or until browned. Remove from oven. Cut pizza into 4 wedges. Yield: 4 servings (serving size: 1 wedge).

(Totals include Whole Wheat Pizza Dough) CALORIES 332 (25% from fat); FAT 9.2g (sat 3.9g, mono 3.7g, poly 1g); PROTEIN 10.8g; CARB 52.4g; FIBER 4.6g; CHOL 19mg; IRON 3.9mg; SODIUM 725mg; CALC 132mg

MAKE AHEAD • FREEZABLE

WHOLE WHEAT PIZZA DOUGH:
 1 package dry yeast (about 2¼ teaspoons)
 ¼ teaspoon sugar
 1½ cups warm water (100° to 110°)
 2½ to 2¾ cups all-purpose flour, divided
 1 cup whole wheat flour
 1 tablespoon olive oil
 1½ teaspoons salt
 Cooking spray

1. Dissolve yeast and sugar in warm water in a large bowl; let stand 5 minutes. Lightly spoon flours into dry measuring cups; level with a knife. Add 2¼ cups all-purpose flour, wheat flour, oil, and salt to yeast mixture; stir until well blended. Turn dough out onto a floured surface. Knead until smooth and elastic (about 10 minutes); add enough of remaining flour, 1 tablespoon at a time, to prevent dough from sticking to hands (dough will feel tacky).

2. Place dough in a large bowl coated with cooking spray, turning to coat top. Cover and let rise in a warm place (85°), free from drafts, 45 minutes or until doubled in size. (Gently press two fingers into dough. If indentation remains, dough has risen enough.) Punch dough down; cover and let rest 5 minutes. Divide in half; roll each dough half into a 12-inch circle on a floured surface. Yield: 2 (12-inch) pizza crusts.

NOTE: To freeze, follow directions for kneading dough. Before rising, shape into 2 balls. Coat with cooking spray, and place in freezer in a zip-top plastic bag. To use dough, thaw overnight in refrigerator. Cover and let rise in a warm place (85°), free from drafts, 1½ hours or until doubled in size. (Gently press two fingers into dough. If indentation remains, dough has risen enough.) Shape as instructed.

(Totals are for 1 [12-inch] Pizza Crust) CALORIES 847 (11% from fat); FAT 9.9g (sat 1.4g, mono 5.4g, poly 1.9g); PROTEIN 25.7g; CARB 165g; FIBER 12.7g; CHOL 0mg; IRON 10.2mg; SODIUM 1,764mg; CALC 47mg

Polenta Lasagna

The pepper-studded polenta needs to chill overnight so it will be firm enough to stand in for the typical lasagna noodles.

POLENTA:

    2   large red bell peppers
    2   large yellow bell peppers
    8   cups water
    1   teaspoon salt
 1½   cups dry polenta
    ¾   cup (3 ounces) grated fresh
         Parmesan cheese
          Cooking spray

FILLING:

    ¼   cup water
    1   tablespoon chopped garlic
    2   (10-ounce) packages fresh spinach
    ¼   teaspoon salt
    ¼   teaspoon freshly ground black
         pepper
    ½   cup fat-free ricotta cheese
    ⅛   teaspoon ground nutmeg
    2   large egg whites, lightly beaten
    2   cups fat-free marinara sauce
         (such as Muir Glen Organic)
    6   ounces part-skim mozzarella cheese,
         thinly sliced (about 1½ cups)
    ¾   cup (3 ounces) grated fresh
         Parmesan cheese

1. Preheat broiler.

2. To prepare polenta, cut bell peppers in half lengthwise; discard seeds and membranes. Place pepper halves, skin sides up, on a foil-lined baking sheet; flatten with hand. Broil 15 minutes or until blackened. Place in a large zip-top plastic bag; seal. Let stand 15 minutes. Peel and cut into ¼-inch pieces.

3. Combine 8 cups water and 1 teaspoon salt in a large saucepan; bring to a boil. Add polenta, stirring with a whisk until polenta begins to absorb water (about 2 minutes). Reduce heat to low; cook 25 minutes, stirring frequently. Add pepper pieces and ¾ cup Parmesan; stir until well blended. Spoon onto an 18 x 12-inch jelly roll pan coated with cooking spray; spread into an even layer using a spatula coated with cooking spray. Cool to room temperature on a wire rack. Cover and refrigerate overnight.

4. Place a large cutting board on top of polenta. Turn over, and remove polenta from pan; cut polenta in half crosswise. Set aside.

5. To prepare filling, heat a large non-stick skillet over medium-high heat. Add ¼ cup water and garlic, and cook 1 minute. Add half of spinach; cover and cook 1 minute or until spinach begins to wilt. Stir in remaining spinach, ¼ teaspoon salt, and black pepper. Cover and cook 3 minutes. Place spinach mixture in a colander, and drain well. Combine spinach mixture, ricotta, nutmeg, and egg whites.

6. Preheat oven to 375°.

7. Spread ½ cup marinara into bottom of a 13 x 9-inch baking dish coated with cooking spray. Place 1 polenta sheet half over marinara. Spread ½ cup marinara over polenta. Arrange sliced mozzarella and spinach mixture over marinara, and top with ½ cup marinara. Place remaining polenta sheet half over sauce. Top with remaining marinara; sprinkle with ¾ cup Parmesan. Cover and bake at 375° for 35 minutes. Uncover and bake an additional 20 minutes. Let lasagna stand 15 minutes. Yield: 9 servings.

CALORIES 279 (30% from fat); FAT 9.4g (sat 6g, mono 1.6g, poly 0.6g); PROTEIN 19.1g; CARB 30.9g; FIBER 5.6g; CHOL 25mg; IRON 3.4mg; SODIUM 950mg; CALC 463mg

---

FREEZABLE

Eggplant Lasagna

Usually lasagna feeds a crowd, but this one makes just enough for two.

SAUCE:

    ½   teaspoon vegetable oil
    ½   cup chopped onion
    1   garlic clove, minced
    ½   cup dry red wine
    1   cup no-salt-added diced tomatoes,
         undrained
    ⅛   teaspoon dried thyme
    ⅛   teaspoon dried rosemary
    ⅛   teaspoon freshly ground black
         pepper
          Dash of salt
    1   (8-ounce) can no-salt-added
         tomato sauce

EGGPLANT:

    1   (¾-pound) eggplant, cut crosswise
         into ⅛-inch-thick slices
    ⅛   teaspoon salt
 1½   teaspoons water
    1   teaspoon vegetable oil
    1   large egg white
    ⅓   cup Italian-seasoned breadcrumbs
          Cooking spray

REMAINING INGREDIENTS:

    ½   cup (2 ounces) shredded part-skim
         mozzarella cheese
    2   tablespoons shredded fresh
         Parmesan cheese
    ⅛   teaspoon freshly ground black
         pepper
    3   oven-ready lasagna noodles
         (such as Barilla)

1. To prepare sauce, heat ½ teaspoon oil in a small saucepan over medium-high heat. Add onion; sauté 5 minutes or until lightly browned. Add garlic, and sauté 30 seconds. Add wine; cook 1 minute. Add tomatoes and next 5 ingredients. Reduce heat, and simmer 20 minutes.

2. Preheat oven to 450°.

3. To prepare eggplant, arrange slices in a single layer on paper towels. Sprinkle ⅛ teaspoon salt on both sides of eggplant. Let stand 15 minutes, and pat dry. Combine water, 1 teaspoon oil, and egg white in a shallow bowl, stirring with a whisk. Place breadcrumbs in another shallow bowl. Dip eggplant in egg white mixture, and dredge in breadcrumbs. Place breaded slices on a baking sheet coated with cooking spray. Bake at 450° for 24 minutes or until eggplant is golden and crisp, turning after 12 minutes. Cool on a wire rack.

4. Combine cheeses and ⅛ teaspoon pepper. Spoon ¼ cup sauce into bottom of an 8 x 4-inch loaf pan. Place one noodle over sauce. Arrange a single layer of eggplant slices over noodle; top with ¼ cup sauce and about 3 tablespoons cheese mixture. Repeat layers twice, ending with cheese. Cover and bake at 450° for 40 minutes. Yield: 2 servings.

CALORIES 442 (24% from fat); FAT 11.6g (sat 5g, mono 3g, poly 2.8g); PROTEIN 22.3g; CARB 62.7g; FIBER 9g; CHOL 20mg; IRON 3.9mg; SODIUM 989mg; CALC 373mg

Rustic Grilled Pizza

3 large red bell peppers
1 tablespoon minced fresh oregano
1 tablespoon olive oil, divided
¾ teaspoon salt, divided
3 cups thinly sliced onion
¼ teaspoon sugar
7 ounces shiitake mushrooms, stems removed
1 (10-ounce) can refrigerated pizza crust dough
Cooking spray
⅔ cup (about 2½ ounces) crumbled goat cheese
1 tablespoon chopped fresh parsley
¼ teaspoon freshly ground black pepper

1. Preheat broiler.
2. Cut bell peppers in half lengthwise, and discard seeds and membranes. Place pepper halves, skin sides up, on a foil-lined baking sheet; flatten with hand. Broil 15 minutes or until blackened. Place in a zip-top plastic bag, and seal. Let stand 15 minutes. Peel and cut bell peppers into ½-inch strips. Combine bell peppers, oregano, 1 teaspoon oil, and ¼ teaspoon salt.
3. Heat 1 teaspoon oil in a large non-stick skillet over medium heat. Add onion and ¼ teaspoon salt; cook 15 minutes, stirring frequently. Increase heat to medium-high. Sprinkle onion with sugar; sauté 5 minutes or until lightly browned. Remove from pan.
4. Heat 1 teaspoon oil in pan over medium-high heat. Add mushrooms; cover and cook 2 minutes. Uncover and sauté 1 minute or until tender. Combine onion, mushrooms, and ¼ teaspoon salt.
5. Prepare grill.
6. Roll dough into a 12-inch circle. Place dough on grill rack coated with cooking spray; grill 3 minutes or until browned. Turn crust. Arrange onion mixture and bell pepper mixture on crust. Top with cheese. Cover and grill 3 minutes. Sprinkle with parsley and black pepper. Yield: 4 servings.

CALORIES 338 (27% from fat); FAT 10g (sat 3.2g, mono 3.4g, poly 0.6g); PROTEIN 12.4g; CARB 49.4g; FIBER 5.5g; CHOL 9mg; IRON 3.6mg; SODIUM 955mg; CALC 62mg

Mushroom Lasagna

You can substitute shredded mozzarella cheese for the fontina. To vary the flavor, use a variety of mushrooms.

9 uncooked lasagna noodles (about 8 ounces)
¼ cup all-purpose flour
3 cups 1% low-fat milk
1 cup (4 ounces) grated fresh Parmesan cheese, divided
1 cup 1% low-fat cottage cheese
¾ teaspoon salt
¼ teaspoon freshly ground black pepper
⅛ teaspoon ground nutmeg
1 (10-ounce) package frozen chopped spinach, thawed, drained, and squeezed dry
2 teaspoons butter
1½ cups thinly sliced leek (about 2 large)
2 (8-ounce) packages button mushrooms, thinly sliced
⅓ cup chopped fresh flat-leaf parsley
½ teaspoon dried oregano
2 garlic cloves, minced
Cooking spray
½ cup (2 ounces) shredded fontina cheese

1. Cook pasta according to package directions, omitting salt and fat.
2. Preheat oven to 400°.
3. Place flour in a medium saucepan. Gradually add milk, stirring with a whisk until blended. Bring to a boil over medium heat; cook until thick (about 5 minutes), stirring constantly. Remove from heat; stir in ½ cup Parmesan, cottage cheese, and next 4 ingredients.
4. Melt butter in a large nonstick skillet over medium heat. Add leek and mushrooms; sauté 7 minutes or until tender. Drain well; return to pan. Stir in parsley, oregano, and garlic. Spread 1 cup spinach mixture onto bottom of a 13 x 9-inch baking dish coated with cooking spray. Arrange 3 noodles over spinach mixture; top with 1½ cups mushroom mixture. Repeat layers, ending with noodles. Top with ½ cup spinach mixture.
5. Cover and bake at 400° for 25 minutes. Uncover and sprinkle with ½ cup

Parmesan and fontina. Bake an additional 15 minutes or until golden brown. Let stand 10 minutes. Yield: 9 servings.

CALORIES 262 (29% from fat); FAT 8.5g (sat 5g, mono 1g, poly 0.5g); PROTEIN 18.2g; CARB 30.9g; FIBER 2.8g; CHOL 30mg; IRON 2.8mg; SODIUM 561mg; CALC 353mg

Turnip Green and Shiitake Mushroom Calzones with Smoked Cheddar

Use any smoked cheese or other greens, such as spinach or kale. You can serve this with warmed chunky marinara sauce.

1 cup boiling water
⅓ cup yellow cornmeal
1 package dry yeast (about 2¼ teaspoons)
¼ cup warm water (100° to 110°)
2 cups all-purpose flour
1 teaspoon salt, divided
½ teaspoon dried thyme
1 tablespoon honey
1½ teaspoons olive oil
Cooking spray
¾ pound turnip greens
4 cups water
3 cups sliced shiitake mushroom caps
2 garlic cloves, minced
1 tablespoon balsamic vinegar
¼ teaspoon freshly ground black pepper
¼ teaspoon crushed red pepper
2 teaspoons yellow cornmeal
1 cup (4 ounces) grated smoked Cheddar or mozzarella cheese
1½ teaspoons water
1 large egg white

1. Combine boiling water and ⅓ cup cornmeal; let stand 20 minutes, stirring occasionally. Dissolve yeast in warm water; let stand 5 minutes.
2. Lightly spoon flour into dry measuring cups; level with a knife. Combine cornmeal mixture, flour, ½ teaspoon salt, and thyme in a food processor; pulse 4 times or until blended. With processor on, slowly add yeast mixture, honey, and oil through food chute; process until

Continued

dough forms a ball. Process 1 additional minute. Turn dough out onto a floured surface; knead lightly 4 or 5 times (dough will feel tacky).

3. Place dough in a bowl coated with cooking spray, turning to coat top. Cover and let rise in a warm place (85°), free from drafts, 1 hour or until doubled in size. (Gently press two fingers into dough. If indentation remains, dough has risen enough.)

4. While dough is rising, remove stems from greens. Wash and coarsely chop. Bring 4 cups water to a boil in a Dutch oven. Add greens, and cook 1 minute, stirring constantly. Remove greens from water with a slotted spoon. Plunge into ice water, and drain. Squeeze out any remaining liquid.

5. Heat pan coated with cooking spray over medium-high heat. Add mushrooms and garlic; sauté 5 minutes or until just tender. Add greens, ½ teaspoon salt, vinegar, black pepper, and red pepper; cook 1 minute.

6. Preheat oven to 450°.

7. Punch dough down. Cover and let rest 5 minutes. Divide dough into 4 equal portions. Working with one portion at a time (cover remaining dough to prevent drying), shape each portion into a ball. Roll out into a 7-inch circle. Place on a baking sheet lightly dusted with 2 teaspoons cornmeal.

8. Place ½ cup greens mixture on half of each circle leaving a 1-inch border; sprinkle each circle with ¼ cup cheese. Fold dough over filling until edges almost meet. Bring bottom edge over top edge, and crimp edges with fingers to form a rim. Place calzones on a baking sheet coated with cooking spray. Combine 1½ teaspoons water and egg white, stirring with a whisk. Brush calzone tops with egg mixture. Bake at 450° for 12 minutes or until golden brown. Yield: 4 servings (serving size: 1 calzone).

CALORIES 468 (25% from fat); FAT 13g (sat 6.4g, mono 4.1g, poly 1g); PROTEIN 18.5g; CARB 70.2g; FIBER 5.6g; CHOL 30mg; IRON 5.8mg; SODIUM 813mg; CALC 388mg

Heaven-Sent Angel Food Cakes

These divine recipes made us rethink this classically light cake.

We've traditionally shied away from angel food cake in the pages of *Cooking Light.* It was, we reasoned, too ordinary. But we've changed our minds.

These angel food cakes are light in all aspects but flavor; we've revved them up by adding coffee, chocolate, coconut, tropical fruits, nuts, and even five-spice powder. Follow our how-to tips, and you'll be able to whip up angel food cake that's perfect every time. These recipes will convince you—as they did us—that angel food cake can be not only inventive, flavorful, and satisfying but also devilishly good.

STAFF FAVORITE • MAKE AHEAD
Classic Angel Food Cake

This master recipe is good as is, but it's also easy to modify to suit any craving (see "Endless Variations" on page 123).

    1   cup sifted cake flour
    1½ cups sugar, divided
    12 large egg whites
    1   teaspoon cream of tartar
    ¼   teaspoon salt
    1½ teaspoons vanilla extract
    1½ teaspoons fresh lemon juice
    ½   teaspoon almond extract

1. Preheat oven to 325°.
2. To prepare cake, combine flour and ¾ cup sugar, stirring with a whisk.
3. Place egg whites in a large bowl; beat with a mixer at high speed until foamy. Add cream of tartar and salt; beat until soft peaks form. Add ¾ cup sugar, 2 tablespoons at a time, beating until stiff peaks form. Beat in vanilla, juice, and almond extract.
4. Sift ¼ cup flour mixture over egg white mixture; fold in. Repeat with remaining flour mixture, ¼ cup at a time.
5. Spoon batter into an ungreased 10-inch tube pan, spreading evenly. Break air pockets by cutting through batter with a knife. Bake at 325° for 55 minutes or until cake springs back when

lightly touched. Invert pan; cool completely. Loosen cake from sides of pan using a narrow metal spatula. Invert cake onto a plate. Yield: 12 servings (serving size: 1 slice).

CALORIES 146 (0% from fat); FAT 0.1g (sat 0g, mono 0g, poly 0.1g); PROTEIN 4.2g; CARB 31.8g; FIBER 0.1g; CHOL 0mg; IRON 0.6mg; SODIUM 104mg; CALC 4mg

Angel Food Shortcakes

This light, delicate angel food cake is a refreshing change from your typical biscuit shortcake. You can also try serving this dessert with fresh, ripe strawberries.

CAKE:
    ½   cup sifted cake flour
    ¾   cup granulated sugar, divided
    6   large egg whites
    ½   teaspoon cream of tartar
    ⅛   teaspoon salt
    ¾   teaspoon fresh lemon juice
    ¾   teaspoon vanilla extract
    ½   teaspoon almond extract
    3   tablespoons slivered almonds
    1   tablespoon powdered sugar
    Cooking spray

SAUCE:

2 tablespoons granulated sugar
2 tablespoons brandy
2 teaspoons fresh lemon juice
1 (10-ounce) package frozen unsweetened raspberries, thawed

FRUIT:

1½ cups fresh blackberries or raspberries
1½ cups fresh blueberries
3 tablespoons granulated sugar
2 tablespoons brandy

GLAZE:

¼ cup seedless raspberry jam
2 teaspoons water

1. Preheat oven to 325°.
2. Line bottom of a 13 x 9-inch baking pan with wax paper; set aside.
3. To prepare cake, combine flour and 6 tablespoons granulated sugar, stirring with a whisk.
4. Place egg whites in a large bowl; beat with a mixer at high speed until foamy. Add cream of tartar and salt; beat until soft peaks form. Add 6 tablespoons granulated sugar, 2 tablespoons at a time, beating until stiff peaks form. Beat in ¾ teaspoon juice and extracts.
5. Sift ¼ cup flour mixture over egg white mixture; fold in. Repeat with remaining flour mixture, ¼ cup at a time. Gently spread batter into prepared pan; sprinkle with almonds. Bake at 325° for 25 minutes or until cake springs back when lightly touched.
6. Place a clean dishtowel over a large wire rack; dust towel with powdered sugar. Loosen cake from sides of pan; turn out onto dishtowel. Carefully peel off wax paper. Lightly coat another large wire rack with cooking spray; place over cake. Invert cake; remove first rack and towel. Cool completely.
7. To prepare sauce, combine 2 tablespoons granulated sugar, 2 tablespoons brandy, 2 teaspoons juice, and raspberries in a food processor. Process until well blended. Press mixture through a sieve into a bowl, reserving ¾ cup. Discard solids.
8. To prepare fruit, combine blackberries, blueberries, 3 tablespoons granulated

sugar, and 2 tablespoons brandy. Let stand 1 hour.
9. To prepare glaze, combine jam and water in a 1-cup glass measure. Microwave at HIGH 30 seconds or until jam melts, stirring once.
10. Cut cake into 12 rectangles using a serrated knife. Place 1 cake rectangle on each of 6 dessert plates. Drizzle each serving with 2 teaspoons glaze, and top each serving with ½ cup fruit mixture and 1 cake rectangle. Drizzle 2 tablespoons sauce around each shortcake. Yield: 6 servings.

CALORIES 310 (6% from fat); FAT 2.1g (sat 0.2g, mono 1.1g, poly 0.6g); PROTEIN 5.6g; CARB 63.5g; FIBER 4.5g; CHOL 0mg; IRON 1.4mg; SODIUM 106mg; CALC 32mg

---

MAKE AHEAD

Five-Spice Toasted-Coconut Cake Roll with Tropical Fruit Compote

Freeze the rolled cake up to 2 days before serving it with the compote. To soften the sorbet for spreading on the cake, let it stand at room temperature for 30 to 45 minutes.

CAKE:

½ cup sifted cake flour
¾ cup granulated sugar, divided
¾ teaspoon five-spice powder
6 large egg whites
½ teaspoon cream of tartar
Dash of salt
1 teaspoon fresh lemon juice
1 teaspoon vanilla extract
½ teaspoon coconut extract
⅓ cup flaked sweetened coconut
2 tablespoons powdered sugar
1 pint mandarin orange with passionfruit sorbet (such as Edy's Whole Fruit Sorbet), softened

COMPOTE:

1 cup (½-inch) cubed peeled ripe mango
1 cup (½-inch) cubed fresh pineapple
1 cup (½-inch) cubed peeled kiwifruit
2 tablespoons brown sugar
2 tablespoons dark rum

REMAINING INGREDIENT:

¼ cup flaked sweetened coconut, toasted

1. Preheat oven to 325°.
2. Line bottom of a 15 x 10-inch jelly roll pan with wax paper; set aside.
3. To prepare cake, combine flour, 6 tablespoons granulated sugar, and five-spice powder, stirring with a whisk.
4. Place egg whites in a large bowl; beat with a mixer at high speed until foamy. Add cream of tartar and salt, and beat until soft peaks form. Add 6 tablespoons granulated sugar, 2 tablespoons at a time, beating until stiff peaks form. Beat in juice and extracts.
5. Sift ¼ cup flour mixture over egg white mixture; fold in. Repeat with remaining flour mixture, ¼ cup at a time. Spread batter into prepared pan. Sprinkle with ⅓ cup coconut. Bake at 325° for 20 minutes or until cake springs back when lightly touched.
6. Place a clean dish towel over a large wire rack; dust with powdered sugar. Loosen cake from sides of pan; turn out onto towel. Carefully peel off wax paper; cool 3 minutes. Starting at narrow end, roll up cake and towel together. Place, seam side down, on wire rack; cool cake completely. Unroll cake, and remove towel. Spread sorbet over cake, leaving a ½-inch border around outside edges. Reroll cake. Wrap cake in plastic wrap; freeze 1 hour or until firm.
7. To prepare compote, combine mango and next 4 ingredients; let stand 20 minutes. Cut cake into 16 slices, and place 2 slices on each of 8 plates. Spoon about ¼ cup compote over each serving, and sprinkle each serving with 1½ teaspoons toasted coconut. Yield: 8 servings.

CALORIES 245 (8% from fat); FAT 2.1g (sat 1.6g, mono 0.1g, poly 0.1g); PROTEIN 4g; CARB 51.6g; FIBER 1.7g; CHOL 0mg; IRON 1.2mg; SODIUM 80mg; CALC 22mg

Maple-Brown Sugar Angel Cake with Walnuts

Look for brown sugar that is granulated; it dissolves better in the batter. Otherwise, sift brown sugar before using.

CAKE:

1   cup sifted cake flour
1   cup granulated sugar, divided
⅓   cup packed brown sugar
⅛   teaspoon ground nutmeg
12 large egg whites
1   teaspoon cream of tartar
¼   teaspoon salt
2   teaspoons vanilla extract
1   teaspoon maple extract

TOPPING:

6   tablespoons powdered sugar
3   tablespoons maple syrup
¾   cup coarsely chopped walnuts, toasted

1. Preheat oven to 325°.

2. To prepare cake, combine flour, ½ cup granulated sugar, brown sugar, and nutmeg; stir with a whisk. Place egg whites in a bowl; beat with a mixer at high speed until foamy. Add cream of tartar and salt; beat until soft peaks form. Add ½ cup granulated sugar, 2 tablespoons at a time; beat until stiff peaks form. Beat in extracts.

3. Sift ¼ cup flour mixture over egg white mixture; fold in. Repeat with remaining flour mixture, ¼ cup at a time.

4. Spoon batter into an ungreased 10-inch tube pan, spreading evenly. Break air pockets by cutting through batter with a knife. Bake at 325° for 50 minutes or until cake springs back when lightly touched. Invert pan; cool completely. Loosen cake from sides of pan using a narrow metal spatula. Invert onto a plate.

5. To prepare topping, combine powdered sugar and maple syrup in a small bowl, stirring with a whisk until smooth. Drizzle sugar mixture over top of cake; sprinkle with walnuts. Yield: 12 servings (serving size: 1 slice).

CALORIES 214 (21% from fat); FAT 5g (sat 0.5g, mono 0.7g, poly 3.6g); PROTEIN 5.3g; CARB 37.6g; FIBER 0.6g; CHOL 0mg; IRON 1mg; SODIUM 107mg; CALC 19mg

---

Secrets to Great Angel Food Cake

- Separate the eggs while they're still cold from the refrigerator—the yolks and whites will be more firm and separate more easily. Use an egg separator, if you like, but pouring the egg into your hand and letting the whites slip through your fingers works just as well (and saves washing a utensil).

- Don't allow any pieces of yolk to mix with the whites, or the whites won't beat to maximum volume. To ensure that the whites do stay free of any yolks, separate each egg over a small bowl, then pour the whites into a scrupulously clean large bowl (free of even the faintest trace of grease).

- Beat the whites with a mixer on high speed until they're foamy, then add the cream of tartar and salt.

- Continue to beat the egg whites on high speed until soft peaks form, then add the sugar gradually. (Add more sugar only when the previous addition is dissolved.)

- When stiff peaks form, the whites will look shiny, moist, and snowy, and the peaks will hold high when you lift the beater. Be careful not to overbeat the whites—lightly underbeaten egg whites will work, but overbeaten whites will make a tough cake.

- Sift or sprinkle the flour a little at a time over the beaten egg whites. Then, with a large spatula, use large sweeping motions to fold the flour into the whites. The goal is to work in the dry ingredients without deflating the whites.

- Gently scrape the batter into an ungreased pan—preferably an angel food tube pan with a removable bottom. Don't bother to use a nonstick pan—the batter needs to cling to the sides of the pan as it cooks, and will do so despite the surface. Smooth the top of the batter evenly. If you're using an angel food pan, run a knife through the batter to break up any air pockets that may have formed when the batter was poured into the pan.

- Place the cake in the center of the oven for even baking. Don't open the oven door until the baking time is up (or very nearly so); the fragile egg whites may begin to deflate as cool air rushes into the oven.

- Cool the cake upside down so that the weight of the batter doesn't deflate the cake while it's still warm. If your pan does not have "feet," invert it by placing the center hole on the neck of a wine bottle.

- To remove the cooled cake from the pan, run a narrow metal spatula or thin knife around the edges, including the center tube; take care to dislodge as little golden crust as possible. If your pan has a removable bottom, push it up to dislodge the cake, then use the same spatula method to loosen the cake from the bottom of the pan. If not, or if you're using another kind of pan—such as a jelly roll pan—line the bottom with parchment paper or wax paper before spooning the batter into it.

- Cut the cooled cake with a serrated knife using a gentle sawing motion. There's no need to bother with pronged cutters made especially for angel food cake—they don't work nearly as well.

- Store angel food cake, tightly covered, at room temperature up to 2 days, or freeze up to 4 weeks.

Margarita Angel Cake

Tart lime is an ideal match for the sweet cake. Triple Sec, tequila, and lime juice give the glaze the flavor of a margarita. Use wooden skewers to poke holes in the cake large enough to let the glaze soak into it.

CAKE:

  1 cup sifted cake flour
1½ cups sugar, divided
 12 large egg whites
  1 teaspoon cream of tartar
 ½ teaspoon salt
  2 tablespoons grated lime rind
  2 teaspoons vanilla extract
1½ teaspoons fresh lime juice

GLAZE:

  3 tablespoons sugar
  3 tablespoons fresh lime juice
  3 tablespoons tequila
  3 tablespoons Triple Sec (orange-flavored liqueur)
  3 tablespoons water

1. Preheat oven to 325°.
2. To prepare cake, combine flour and ¾ cup sugar, stirring with a whisk.
3. Place egg whites in a large bowl; beat with a mixer at high speed until foamy. Add cream of tartar and salt; beat until soft peaks form. Add ¾ cup sugar, 2 tablespoons at a time, beating until stiff peaks form. Beat in rind, vanilla, and 1½ teaspoons juice.
4. Sift ¼ cup flour mixture over egg mixture; fold in. Repeat with remaining flour mixture, ¼ cup at a time.
5. Spoon batter into an ungreased 10-inch tube pan, spreading evenly. Break air pockets by cutting through batter with a knife. Bake at 325° for 50 minutes or until cake springs back when lightly touched. Invert pan; cool completely. Loosen cake from sides of pan using a narrow metal spatula. Invert onto a plate.
6. To prepare glaze, combine 3 tablespoons sugar and remaining 4 ingredients in a small saucepan; bring to a boil. Reduce heat; simmer 3 minutes or until sugar dissolves, stirring occasionally. Pierce entire surface of cake liberally with a skewer; drizzle glaze over cake.

Let stand 10 minutes. Yield: 12 servings (serving size: 1 slice).

CALORIES 181 (0% from fat); FAT 0.1g (sat 0g, mono 0g, poly 0.1g); PROTEIN 4.2g; CARB 37.1g; FIBER 0.3g; CHOL 0mg; IRON 0.6mg; SODIUM 154mg; CALC 5mg

Marbled Devil's Food Angel Cake

CAKE:

  1 cup sifted cake flour
1½ cups sugar, divided
 12 large egg whites
  1 teaspoon cream of tartar
 ¼ teaspoon salt
  2 teaspoons vanilla extract
1½ teaspoons fresh lemon juice
  2 tablespoons unsweetened cocoa

GLAZE:

  2 ounces bittersweet chocolate, chopped
 ¼ cup hot water

1. Preheat oven to 325°.
2. To prepare cake, combine flour and ¾ cup sugar, stirring with a whisk.
3. Place egg whites in a large bowl; beat with a mixer at high speed until foamy. Add cream of tartar and salt; beat until soft peaks form. Add ¾ cup sugar, 2 tablespoons at a time, beating until stiff peaks form. Beat in vanilla and juice.
4. Sift ¼ cup flour mixture over egg white mixture; fold in. Repeat with remaining flour, ¼ cup at a time. Gently spoon half of cake batter into a large bowl. Sift cocoa over half of batter; gently fold in.
5. Spoon half of plain batter into an ungreased 10-inch tube pan, spreading evenly. Top with half of chocolate batter; repeat layers. Swirl batters together with a knife. Bake at 325° for 50 minutes or until cake springs back when lightly touched. Invert pan; cool completely. Loosen cake from sides of pan using a narrow metal spatula. Invert onto a plate.
6. To prepare glaze, place chocolate and hot water in a small glass bowl. Microwave at HIGH 1 minute or until almost melted; stir until smooth. Drizzle

glaze over cake. Chill cake 10 minutes. Yield: 12 servings (serving size: 1 slice).

CALORIES 174 (9% from fat); FAT 1.8g (sat 1.1g, mono 0.2g, poly 0g); PROTEIN 4.7g; CARB 35.1g; FIBER 0.8g; CHOL 0mg; IRON 0.8mg; SODIUM 105mg; CALC 5mg

Endless Variations

Angel food cake can be modified with just about any flavoring to go from afternoon snack to dinner party dessert, as our recipes illustrate. Here are more ideas.

Chocolate: Add ¼ cup sifted unsweetened cocoa to the flour mixture.

Chocolate-glazed: Whisk together 3 tablespoons unsweetened cocoa, 1 cup powdered sugar, ½ teaspoon vanilla extract, and about 3 tablespoons water or cold coffee. Drizzle over cooled cake.

Chocolate malt: Add 2 tablespoons malted milk powder and 2 tablespoons unsweetened cocoa powder to the flour mixture.

Citrus-glazed: Whisk together 2 tablespoons lime, lemon, or orange juice and 1 cup powdered sugar until smooth. Drizzle over cooled cake.

Ice cream: Cut the cake horizontally into 3 layers, then spread each layer with 1 cup of softened ice cream or sorbet. Reassemble the cake, then freeze it until ready to serve.

Nutty: Fold ½ cup finely chopped toasted nuts—such as almonds, walnuts, or hazelnuts—into the batter with the flour.

Orange: Fold 2 tablespoons grated orange peel and 1 teaspoon orange extract into the batter.

Pink peppermint: Add ¼ teaspoon red food coloring to the batter and fold in ¼ cup finely crushed hard peppermint candies.

Spiced: Add 1½ teaspoons pumpkin pie spice to the flour mixture.

Chocolate Chip Angel Cupcakes with Fluffy Frosting

These individual angel food cakes are a good choice for a birthday party or shower.

CUPCAKES:
½ cup sifted cake flour
¾ cup sugar, divided
6 large egg whites
½ teaspoon cream of tartar
⅛ teaspoon salt
1 teaspoon vanilla extract
¾ teaspoon fresh lemon juice
⅓ cup semisweet chocolate minichips

FROSTING:
½ cup sugar
2 tablespoons water
⅛ teaspoon cream of tartar
Dash of salt
2 large egg whites
½ teaspoon vanilla extract

REMAINING INGREDIENT:
¼ cup flaked sweetened coconut, toasted

1. Preheat oven to 325°.

2. To prepare cupcakes, combine flour and 6 tablespoons sugar, stirring with a whisk.

3. Place 6 egg whites in a large bowl; beat with a mixer at high speed until foamy. Add ½ teaspoon cream of tartar and ⅛ teaspoon salt; beat until soft peaks form. Add 6 tablespoons sugar, 2 tablespoons at a time, beating until stiff peaks form. Beat in 1 teaspoon vanilla and juice.

4. Sift ¼ cup flour mixture over egg white mixture; fold in. Repeat with remaining flour mixture, ¼ cup at a time. Fold in chocolate chips.

5. Place 24 paper muffin cup liners in muffin cups. Spoon about 3 heaping tablespoons batter into each muffin cup. Bake at 325° for 15 minutes or until cupcakes spring back when lightly touched. Remove from pans; cool on a wire rack.

6. To prepare frosting, combine ½ cup sugar and next 4 ingredients in top of a double boiler; place mixture over barely simmering water. Beat with a mixer at high speed until stiff peaks form and candy thermometer registers 160°. Beat in ½ teaspoon vanilla. Spoon 1 heaping tablespoon frosting over each cupcake. Sprinkle evenly with coconut. Yield: 2 dozen (serving size: 1 cupcake).

CALORIES 69 (13% from fat); FAT 1g (sat 0.7g, mono 0.3g, poly 0g); PROTEIN 1.5g; CARB 14.1g; FIBER 0.2g; CHOL 0mg; IRON 0.3mg; SODIUM 39mg; CALC 2mg

Café au Lait Angel Food Cake

The custard, a versatile dessert sauce that's also great with fresh fruit, makes use of some of the extra egg yolks. For a fitting garnish, arrange a few chocolate-covered coffee beans around the cake.

CAKE:
1 cup sifted cake flour
1½ cups sugar, divided
¼ teaspoon ground cinnamon
2 tablespoons instant espresso granules or instant coffee granules
2 tablespoons hot water
12 large egg whites
1 teaspoon cream of tartar
¼ teaspoon salt
1½ teaspoons vanilla extract

SAUCE:
3 large egg yolks, lightly beaten
½ cup sugar
1 tablespoon cornstarch
⅛ teaspoon salt
3 cups 2% reduced-fat milk, divided
1 vanilla bean, split lengthwise
3 tablespoons Frangelico (hazelnut-flavored liqueur)

REMAINING INGREDIENT:
½ cup chopped hazelnuts, toasted

1. Preheat oven to 350°.

2. To prepare cake, combine flour, ¾ cup sugar, and cinnamon, stirring with a whisk; set aside. Combine espresso and hot water, stirring until espresso dissolves; set aside.

3. Place egg whites in a large bowl; beat with a mixer at high speed until foamy. Add cream of tartar and ¼ teaspoon salt; beat until soft peaks form. Add ¾ cup sugar, 2 tablespoons at a time, beating until stiff peaks form.

4. Beat in espresso mixture and vanilla extract. Sift ¼ cup flour mixture over egg white mixture; fold in. Repeat with remaining flour mixture, ¼ cup at a time.

5. Spoon batter into an ungreased 10-inch tube pan, spreading evenly. Break air pockets by cutting through batter with a knife. Bake at 350° for 50 minutes or until cake springs back when lightly touched. Invert pan; cool completely. Loosen cake from sides of pan using a narrow metal spatula. Invert cake onto a plate.

6. To prepare sauce, place egg yolks in a large bowl; set aside. Combine ½ cup sugar, cornstarch, and ⅛ teaspoon salt in a medium saucepan. Gradually add ½ cup milk, stirring with a whisk until smooth. Stir in remaining milk. Scrape seeds from vanilla bean into milk mixture; add bean to mixture. Bring to a boil over medium heat. Remove from heat; gradually add hot milk mixture to egg yolks, stirring constantly with a whisk.

7. Return milk mixture to pan. Cook mixture over medium heat until thick and bubbly (about 4 minutes), stirring constantly. Remove from heat. Spoon milk mixture into a bowl; place bowl in a large ice-filled bowl 10 minutes or until milk mixture comes to room temperature, stirring occasionally. Remove bowl from ice; stir in liqueur. Cover and chill completely.

8. Remove and discard vanilla bean. Serve angel food cake with sauce, and sprinkle with toasted hazelnuts. Yield: 12 servings (serving size: 1 cake slice, about 3 tablespoons sauce, and 2 teaspoons hazelnuts).

CALORIES 271 (18% from fat); FAT 5.5g (sat 1.4g, mono 3g, poly 0.6g); PROTEIN 7.7g; CARB 46.8g; FIBER 0.6g; CHOL 58mg; IRON 1.1mg; SODIUM 162mg; CALC 90mg

Memories of West Africa

Jessica Harris, cookbook author and culinary historian, reveals the secrets of West African hospitality: Keep it informal, cook plenty, and offer what you have with a giving heart.

Benin, the Ivory Coast, and Senegal are three of Jessica Harris' favorite West African countries. Here are her hints on how to evoke the exotic feel and create the (almost) familiar foods of these countries for your own friends and family.

Crunchy Vegetable Salad

(pictured on page 111)

Traditional West African meals aren't served in courses. Some families borrow a French custom and start meals with a plate of crudités—crisp vegetables that add color to the meal. The dipping sauce, similar to Thousand Island dressing, combines light mayonnaise and cocktail sauce.

SALAD:

1 cup (¾-inch) cubed peeled Yukon gold potato
1 cup (¾-inch) cubed peeled sweet potato
4 cups water
1 cup cauliflower florets
1 cup broccoli florets
4 carrots, peeled
3 small beets (about 8 ounces)
10 Bibb lettuce leaves
10 small red cabbage leaves

VINAIGRETTE:

2 tablespoons fresh lemon juice
2 tablespoons red wine vinegar
1 tablespoon Dijon mustard
1 tablespoon chopped fresh thyme
⅛ teaspoon sugar
⅛ teaspoon freshly ground black pepper
2 teaspoons extravirgin olive oil

DIPPING SAUCE:

2 dried habanero chiles
½ cup prepared cocktail sauce
¼ cup light mayonnaise
¼ teaspoon salt
¼ teaspoon freshly ground black pepper
Dash of ground ginger

1. To prepare salad, place potato in a medium saucepan; cover with water. Bring to a boil. Reduce heat; simmer 10 minutes or until tender. Drain; rinse with cold water. Drain. Place potato in a large bowl. Bring 4 cups water to a boil in a medium saucepan; add cauliflower and broccoli. Cook 1 minute or until crisp-tender. Drain; rinse with cold water. Drain. Add cauliflower mixture to potato. Using a vegetable peeler, scrape carrots from tip to stem to make long ribbons. Add carrot to potato mixture, tossing gently to combine. Leave root and 1-inch stem on beets; scrub with a brush.

Place in a medium saucepan; cover with water. Bring to a boil. Cover, reduce heat, and simmer 25 minutes or until tender. Drain; rinse with cold water. Drain; cool. Trim off beet roots; rub off skins. Cut beets into ¼-inch-thick slices. Arrange lettuce and cabbage leaves alternately on a large platter.

2. To prepare vinaigrette, combine lemon juice and next 5 ingredients, stirring with a whisk. Add oil, stirring well to combine; drizzle vinaigrette over lettuce and cabbage leaves. Spoon potato mixture over lettuce and cabbage leaves; top with beets.

3. To prepare dipping sauce, place chiles in a spice or coffee grinder; process until finely ground. Place ⅛ to ¼ teaspoon ground chile in a medium bowl (reserve remaining ground chile for another use). Add cocktail sauce and remaining 4 ingredients, stirring well to combine. Serve with vegetables. Yield: 8 servings (serving size: about 1 cup salad, 1½ teaspoons vinaigrette, and about 1½ tablespoons dipping sauce).

CALORIES 125 (30% from fat); FAT 4.2g (sat 0.6g, mono 0.9g, poly 0.3g); PROTEIN 2.7g; CARB 20.7g; FIBER 3.7g; CHOL 3mg; IRON 1.1mg; SODIUM 425mg; CALC 41mg

Grilled Apple-Smoked Striped Bass

The key to this simple dish, which earned our Test Kitchen's highest rating, is high-quality fresh fish. It's served in many of the open-air restaurants of Benin's major city, Cotonou, and is always grilled over a wood fire. Wood chips infuse a similar smoky flavor. You can substitute red snapper, which cooks in about 8 minutes.

¼ cup apple wood chips
2 dried habanero chiles
1 tablespoon peanut or vegetable oil
1 teaspoon salt
½ teaspoon freshly ground black pepper
1 (3-pound) striped bass fillet (about 1 inch thick)
Cooking spray
1 lemon, thinly sliced

Continued

1. Cover apple wood chips with water, and soak 1 hour. Drain well.

2. Place chiles in a spice or coffee grinder; process until finely ground. Place ⅛ teaspoon ground chile in a small bowl (reserve remaining ground chile for another use). Add oil, salt, and pepper, stirring to combine. Rub spice mixture over fillet; refrigerate 30 minutes.

3. Prepare grill.

4. Place wood chips on hot coals. Coat a large piece of heavy-duty aluminum foil with cooking spray; pierce foil several times with a fork. Place foil on grill rack coated with cooking spray. Place fish on foil; arrange lemon slices over fish. Grill 20 minutes or until fish flakes easily when tested with a fork. Serve immediately. Yield: 8 servings (serving size: about 5 ounces).

CALORIES 229 (24% from fat); FAT 6.1g (sat 1.4g, mono 1.7g, poly 2.2g); PROTEIN 40.3g; CARB 0.8g; FIBER 0.1g; CHOL 90mg; IRON 0.7mg; SODIUM 442mg; CALC 30mg

QUICK & EASY • MAKE AHEAD
Tropical Fruit Salad

Like appetizers, dessert is a recent addition to the traditional West African table. Often ripe fruit—or a combination like this—serves as dessert.

    4 cups (½-inch) cubed fresh
       pineapple
    2 cups diced peeled ripe mango
       (about 2 medium)
 1½ cups (½-inch) sliced banana
       (about 2 medium)
    ¾ cup orange sections (about 2
       medium)
    2 tablespoons dark brown sugar
    2 tablespoons fresh lime juice
    1 cup shredded unsweetened
       coconut, toasted

1. Combine first 6 ingredients in a medium bowl, tossing gently to combine. Cover and chill 1 hour. Sprinkle with coconut. Yield: 8 servings (serving size: about ¾ cup).

CALORIES 186 (30% from fat); FAT 6.3g (sat 5.4g, mono 0.3g, poly 0.1g); PROTEIN 2g; CARB 34.8g; FIBER 4.7g; CHOL 0mg; IRON 0.8mg; SODIUM 12mg; CALC 40mg

Ginger-Zapped Lemonade

Most West Africans don't drink with their meals, preferring a glass of water before or after. This cooling beverage might be served on warm days when friends come for a visit.

    6 cups water, divided
    1 cup sugar
    ¼ cup grated peeled fresh ginger
 1½ cups fresh lemon juice (about 8
       lemons)

1. Combine 1 cup water and sugar in a small saucepan over medium-high heat; cook 5 minutes or until sugar dissolves, stirring with a whisk.

2. Place ginger on a double layer of cheesecloth. Gather edges of cheesecloth together; tie securely. Place cheesecloth bag in a large pitcher, and add lemon juice. Add sugar mixture and 5 cups water to pitcher, and stir well. Refrigerate lemonade 2 hours or until chilled. Discard cheesecloth bag. Yield: 8 servings (serving size: 1 cup).

CALORIES 109 (0% from fat); FAT 0g; PROTEIN 0.2g; CARB 29.1g; FIBER 0.2g; CHOL 0mg; IRON 0mg; SODIUM 1mg; CALC 4mg

> ## Ivorian Menu
> serves 8
> **Ivory Coast Chicken**
> **Pineapple Sorbet**
> **Gingered Pineapple Juice**

Ivory Coast Chicken

This traditional slow-cooked dish, *kedjenou*, adapts easily to American kitchens. A terra-cotta pot called a *canari* is used in the Ivory Coast, but a Dutch oven does the job perfectly. Cover the pot with a tight lid to prevent steam from escaping. To keep the moisture in, shake the pan periodically. This dish is normally served over hot cooked white rice.

    4 chicken breast halves (about 2
       pounds), skinned
    4 chicken leg quarters (about 2
       pounds), skinned
    6 cups coarsely chopped onion
       (about 3 pounds)
    5 cups chopped seeded plum tomato
    1 cup water
    1 tablespoon grated peeled fresh
       ginger
 1½ teaspoons finely chopped seeded
       jalapeño pepper
    1 teaspoon salt
    ½ teaspoon freshly ground black
       pepper
    5 garlic cloves, minced
    1 bay leaf

1. Combine all ingredients in a large Dutch oven. Cover and bring to a simmer over medium heat. Reduce heat to medium-low; cook 1 hour or until chicken is done, gently shaking pan every 10 minutes. Discard bay leaf. Yield: 8 servings (serving size: about 4 ounces chicken and ¾ cup vegetable mixture).

CALORIES 250 (15% from fat); FAT 4.1g (sat 1g, mono 1.1g, poly 1.1g); PROTEIN 36.4g; CARB 16.5g; FIBER 3.5g; CHOL 104mg; IRON 2.1mg; SODIUM 422mg; CALC 51mg

MAKE AHEAD • FREEZABLE
Pineapple Sorbet

If you don't have an ice-cream freezer, use a covered metal bowl. Freeze the mixture 3 hours or until it's hard on the outside but slushy in the middle. Remove it from the freezer, beat with a whisk until smooth, and return to the freezer, covered, for 4 hours or until firm.

    1 small pineapple, peeled and cored
    2 tablespoons fresh lemon juice
    1 cup plus 2 tablespoons sugar
       Mint sprigs (optional)

1. Cut pineapple into 2-inch pieces. Place pineapple and lemon juice in a food processor; process until smooth. Add sugar; process 1 minute or until sugar dissolves.

2. Pour mixture into freezer can of an ice-cream freezer; freeze according to manufacturer's instructions. Spoon sorbet

into a freezer-safe container. Cover and freeze 1 hour or until firm. Garnish with mint sprigs, if desired. Yield: 9 servings (serving size: ½ cup).

CALORIES 116 (2% from fat); FAT 0.2g (sat 0g, mono 0.1g, poly 0.1g); PROTEIN 0.2g; CARB 30g; FIBER 0.5g; CHOL 0mg; IRON 0.2mg; SODIUM 1mg; CALC 3mg

Gingered Pineapple Juice

Making this sweet and spicy beverage—known as *gnamacoudji*—is a thrifty way of using leftover pineapple skins. A tablespoon of grated lemon rind may be substituted for lemongrass.

    2 whole unpeeled pineapples
   10 cups water, divided
    1 (3-inch) piece peeled fresh ginger, coarsely chopped (about 3 ounces)
    ¼ cup coarsely chopped peeled fresh lemongrass
    2 tablespoons water
    1 cup powdered sugar
  Mint sprigs (optional)

1. Remove peel from pineapples; cut peel into 3-inch pieces (reserve pulp for another use). Combine peels and 6 cups water in a Dutch oven; bring to a boil. Reduce heat; simmer 30 minutes. Drain in a colander, reserving 4 cups cooking liquid; press peels to release moisture. Discard peels.
2. Combine ginger, lemongrass, and 2 tablespoons water in a food processor; process until finely chopped. Place ginger mixture on a dampened double layer of cheesecloth. Gather edges of cheesecloth together; tie securely. Place cheesecloth bag and 4 cups water in a medium bowl; let stand 30 minutes. Strain reserved pineapple cooking liquid and ginger mixture into a large pitcher; discard cheesecloth bag. Add sugar; stir well. Chill. Serve over ice. Garnish with mint sprigs, if desired. Yield: 8 servings (serving size: 1 cup).

CALORIES 67 (1% from fat); FAT 0.1g (sat 0g, mono 0g, poly 0.1g); PROTEIN 0.1g; CARB 17.1g; FIBER 0.2g; CHOL 0mg; IRON 0.1mg; SODIUM 1mg; CALC 2mg

Pan-Fried Fish Balls

In Senegal, these round little fish cakes are known as *boulettes de poisson*. You can make and shape the balls ahead, then cover them and keep refrigerated until you're ready to cook them. Double the recipe if you plan to serve 8 people.

    2 tablespoons water
    ¾ teaspoon chili powder, divided
    ½ teaspoon salt
    ¼ teaspoon black pepper
    2 large eggs, lightly beaten
    1 (1-ounce) slice white bread
    1 pound cod or other flaky whitefish fillets, chopped
    1 tablespoon chopped fresh parsley
    2 garlic cloves, minced
    2 teaspoons vegetable oil
    ½ cup all-purpose flour
    ½ cup prepared cocktail sauce

1. Combine water, ¼ teaspoon chili powder, salt, pepper, and eggs in a small bowl, stirring well with a whisk.
2. Place bread in a food processor; pulse 5 times or until coarse crumbs measure ½ cup. Add 2 tablespoons egg mixture, fish, parsley, and garlic; process until a thick dough forms. Shape dough into 16 (1-inch) balls.
3. Heat oil in a large nonstick skillet over medium-high heat. Dredge fish balls in flour and dip in remaining egg mixture. Add fish balls to pan, and sauté 10 minutes or until browned on all sides, turning frequently.
4. Combine ½ teaspoon chili powder and cocktail sauce. Serve with fish balls. Yield: 4 servings (serving size: 4 fish balls and 2 tablespoons sauce).

CALORIES 136 (19% from fat); FAT 2.9g (sat 0.7g, mono 0.1g, poly 0.7g); PROTEIN 13.1g; CARB 13.8g; FIBER 0.3g; CHOL 74mg; IRON 0.9mg; SODIUM 452mg; CALC 16mg

Senegalese Lemon Chicken

This chicken stew is called *yassa* in Senegal.

    6 cups sliced onion (about 3 pounds)
    ⅓ cup fresh lemon juice
    1 teaspoon salt
    ½ teaspoon black pepper
    1 jalapeño pepper, seeded and minced
    4 chicken breast halves (about 2 pounds), skinned
    4 chicken leg quarters (about 2 pounds), skinned
  Cooking spray
  1½ tablespoons peanut oil
    2 cups thinly sliced carrot
  1½ cups fat-free, less-sodium chicken broth
    ½ cup pimiento-stuffed olives
    ½ cup water
    1 tablespoon Dijon mustard
    1 Scotch bonnet pepper, pierced with a fork
    4 cups hot cooked long-grain rice

1. Combine first 5 ingredients; divide evenly between 2 (1-gallon) heavy-duty zip-top plastic bags. Divide chicken evenly between bags; seal bags. Toss each bag well to coat. Refrigerate 3 hours, turning bags occasionally.
2. Preheat broiler.
3. Remove chicken from bags, reserving marinade. Place chicken on broiler rack coated with cooking spray; broil 6 minutes on each side or until lightly browned.
4. Strain marinade through a colander over a bowl, reserving marinade and onion. Heat oil in a Dutch oven over medium-high heat. Add onion to pan; sauté 5 minutes. Add reserved marinade; bring to a boil. Cook 1 minute; add chicken, carrot, and next 5 ingredients. Bring to a boil; cover, reduce heat, and simmer 1 hour or until chicken is done. Discard Scotch bonnet. Serve over rice. Yield: 8 servings (serving size: about 4 ounces chicken, ⅔ cup stew, and ½ cup rice).

CALORIES 422 (29% from fat); FAT 13.6g (sat 3g, mono 5.5g, poly 3.6g); PROTEIN 32.7g; CARB 40.4g; FIBER 3.6g; CHOL 99mg; IRON 3mg; SODIUM 704mg; CALC 48mg

MAKE AHEAD
Hibiscus Punch

If you enjoy the tart floral flavor of hibiscus tea, you'll like this unique punch called *bissap rouge* in Senegal. You can find dried hibiscus (also called roselle or sorrel) in Asian, Mexican, and Caribbean specialty markets, or order online at www.mexgrocer.com.

    8 cups water
    1 cup hibiscus pods
    ⅔ cup superfine sugar

1. Combine water and hibiscus in a large nonaluminum Dutch oven. Cover and let stand 2 hours. Bring to a boil. Reduce heat and simmer, uncovered, 5 minutes. Strain through a sieve, reserving punch; discard solids. Add sugar, stirring until sugar dissolves; chill. Yield: 8 cups (serving size: 1 cup).

CALORIES 66 (0% from fat); FAT 0g; PROTEIN 0.2g; CARB 16.9g; FIBER 0g; CHOL 0mg; IRON 0mg; SODIUM 0mg; CALC 4mg

cooking light profile

When in Rome

Nutrition expert Claudia Probart explores how the Mediterranean lifestyle translates into good health.

For Claudia K. Probart, these simple pleasures—a glass of wine, a bit of cheese, and a pleasant chat—are the stuff of a healthy lifestyle. No one knows that better than residents of the Mediterranean region, which stretches from the shores of Spain and France to Italy and Greece to Turkey and North Africa. Probart, an associate professor of nutrition at Pennsylvania State University, spends part of each year in Italy investigating the science of the Mediterranean diet in its cultural setting. She believes that Italy is the ideal classroom for students to study—and experience—the intersection of cuisine, health, and culture. Following are some ways to incorporate a Mediterranean diet into your life.

---

5 Ways to Bring the Mediterranean Diet Home

1. Cook with heart-healthy and vitamin E-rich olive oil.
2. Shop for simple, high-quality ingredients, including locally grown fresh produce.
3. Cook and enjoy dried semolina pasta often, and serve it al dente with sauces made from ingredients like greens, beans, and herbs.
4. Treat yourself to a leisurely midday meal with friends or family. If possible, fit in a short stroll after lunch.
5. Bring joy to every meal.

QUICK & EASY
Pasta with Pomodoro Sauce

Pomodoro is Italian for tomato. Claudia prepares this light, simple pasta dish at least once a week. She adds any flavorful ingredients she has on hand, such as chopped black or green olives.

    2 tablespoons olive oil
    4 garlic cloves, minced
    ½ teaspoon freshly ground black
       pepper
    ¼ teaspoon salt
    1 (28-ounce) can whole tomatoes,
       undrained and coarsely chopped
    ¼ cup finely sliced fresh basil
    8 cups hot cooked penne (about 1
       pound uncooked tube-shaped
       pasta)

1. Heat oil in a large nonstick skillet over medium heat. Add garlic; cook 2 minutes, stirring constantly (do not brown). Stir in pepper, salt, and tomatoes; bring to a boil. Reduce heat; simmer 7 minutes or until slightly thick, stirring occasionally. Remove from heat; stir in basil. Serve over pasta. Yield: 6 servings (serving size: ⅔ cup sauce and 1⅓ cups pasta).

CALORIES 346 (15% from fat); FAT 5.6g (sat 0.9g, mono 3.3g, poly 0.4g); PROTEIN 11.6g; CARB 61.5g; FIBER 3.6g; CHOL 0mg; IRON 3.3mg; SODIUM 342mg; CALC 43mg

---

taste of america

Sensational Soft-Shell Crabs

Typically considered restaurant-only fare, soft-shell crabs are surprisingly easy to prepare at home.

Because soft-shell crabs need direct heat to give them their characteristic outer crispness, they shouldn't be boiled or steamed like hard-shell crabs. Soft-shell crabs take only minutes to cook, so they're traditionally simply fried or sautéed. But they do lend themselves nicely to the broiler or grill, as well. From there they can be taken in any direction, from sushi to a salad. They're most commonly served sandwiched between two slices of bread such as in Cajun-Spiced Soft-Shell Crab Sandwiches with Yellow Pepper and Caper Aïoli (recipe on page 130).

When buying soft-shell crabs, live ones are the best but they're not always easy to find. To select the tastiest, use your nose. When fresh, they smell clean and astringent.

Herb-Stuffed Soft-Shell Crabs with Fresh Corn Spoon Bread

The herb mixture is rubbed under the crab shells so it can flavor the delicate meat.

SPOON BREAD:

    ½ cup all-purpose flour
    2 tablespoons cornmeal
 1½ cups 2% reduced-fat milk
    1 cup fresh white corn kernels
       (about 2 ears)
    1 tablespoon sugar
    1 teaspoon salt
    1 tablespoon butter
    ⅛ teaspoon freshly ground black
       pepper
    2 large egg yolks, lightly
       beaten
    4 large egg whites
       Cooking spray

CRABS:

- ¼ cup finely chopped fresh basil
- 2 tablespoons finely chopped fresh tarragon
- 2 tablespoons finely chopped fresh chives
- 1 tablespoon butter
- ¼ teaspoon salt
- 2 garlic cloves, minced
- 6 (6-ounce) soft-shell crabs, cleaned

1. Preheat oven to 400°.

2. To prepare spoon bread, lightly spoon flour into a dry measuring cup; level with a knife. Combine flour, cornmeal, and milk in a medium saucepan, stirring with a whisk until smooth. Stir in corn, sugar, and 1 teaspoon salt. Bring to a boil over medium-high heat, stirring often. Reduce heat; simmer 3 minutes or until very thick (mixture will begin to lift up from bottom of pot when stirred). Remove from heat; stir in 1 tablespoon butter and pepper.

3. Spoon corn mixture into a large bowl; stir in egg yolks. Place egg whites in a large bowl, and beat with a mixer at high speed until stiff peaks form. Gently stir one-third of beaten egg white into corn mixture; gently fold in remaining egg white. Spoon mixture into a 2-quart baking dish coated with cooking spray. Bake at 400° for 30 minutes or until top is browned and center is set. Cool on a wire rack 10 minutes.

4. Preheat broiler.

5. To prepare crabs, combine basil and next 5 ingredients; spread 1½ teaspoons herb mixture under shells of each crab. Rub outside of crabs with remaining herb mixture. Coat tops of crabs with cooking spray; place crabs on a baking sheet lightly coated with cooking spray. Place baking sheet 8 inches away from broiler, and cook 7 minutes or until crabs are done. Serve stuffed crabs with spoon bread. Yield: 6 servings (serving size: 1 stuffed crab and ⅔ cup spoon bread).

CALORIES 310 (27% from fat); FAT 9.4g (sat 4g, mono 2.6g, poly 1.4g); PROTEIN 33.7g; CARB 23.5g; FIBER 1.2g; CHOL 86mg; IRON 4.5mg; SODIUM 610mg; CALC 87mg

How to Clean Soft-Shell Crabs

1. *To clean soft-shell crabs, hold the crab in one hand, and using a pair of kitchen shears, cut off the front of the crab, about ½ inch behind the eyes and mouth. Squeeze out the contents of the sack located directly behind the cut you just made.*

2. *Lift one pointed end of the crab's outer shell. Remove and discard the gills.*

3. *Lift the other pointed end of the crab's outer shell. Remove and discard the gills.*

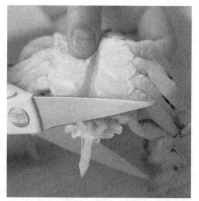

4. *Turn the crab over and snip off the small flap known as the apron. Rinse the entire crab well, and pat dry. Once cleaned, crabs should be cooked or stored immediately.*

Sautéed Soft-Shell Crabs

Here's a basic recipe for soft-shell crabs. You can vary it by adding cayenne pepper, garlic powder, or other seasonings.

- 4 (3½-ounce) soft-shell crabs, cleaned
- ½ teaspoon salt
- ¼ teaspoon freshly ground black pepper
- ¼ cup all-purpose flour
- 1 tablespoon butter

1. Sprinkle crabs with salt and pepper. Place flour in a shallow bowl. Dredge each crab in flour, turning to coat; shake off excess flour.

2. Melt butter in a large nonstick skillet over medium-high heat. Add crabs to pan, top sides down; cook 3 minutes. Turn crabs over; cook 2 minutes. Yield: 4 servings (serving size: 1 crab).

CALORIES 124 (30% from fat); FAT 4.2g (sat 2g, mono 1g, poly 0.6g); PROTEIN 16g; CARB 5.8g; FIBER 0.2g; CHOL 8mg; IRON 2.4mg; SODIUM 320mg; CALC 2mg

Grilled Soft-Shell Crab and Pineapple Salad with Watercress

Peppery watercress is tamed by the sweet-tart dressing and the creamy avocado.

    2   cups pineapple juice
    ¼   cup maple syrup
    ¼   cup spiced rum (such as Captain
        Morgan)
    ½   cup plain low-fat yogurt
    2   tablespoons white wine vinegar
    ¼   teaspoon salt
    ¼   teaspoon freshly ground black
        pepper
    1   small pineapple, peeled, cored,
        halved lengthwise, and cut into
        12 slices
Cooking spray
    6   (5 to 6-ounce) soft-shell crabs,
        cleaned
    6   cups baby spinach
    4   cups trimmed watercress (about
        2 bunches)
    2   cups thinly sliced red onion,
        separated into rings
    2   cups diced peeled avocado

1. Prepare grill.
2. Combine first 3 ingredients in a large saucepan. Bring to a boil, and cook until reduced to ½ cup (about 20 minutes). Cool. Combine one-fourth of pineapple juice mixture, yogurt, vinegar, salt, and pepper in a small bowl. Chill dressing.
3. Place pineapple on grill rack coated with cooking spray, and grill 2 minutes on each side.
4. Place crab on grill rack coated with cooking spray. Grill 5 minutes; turn and baste frequently with remaining juice mixture.
5. Divide spinach and watercress evenly among 6 plates. Top each serving with 2 pineapple pieces, ⅓ cup onion, ⅓ cup avocado, and 1 crab; drizzle each with 2 tablespoons dressing. Yield: 6 servings.

CALORIES 385 (25% from fat); FAT 10.7g (sat 1.8g, mono 5.3g, poly 2.1g); PROTEIN 30.2g; CARB 38.9g; FIBER 5.3g; CHOL 1mg; IRON 5.4mg; SODIUM 156mg; CALC 122mg

Cajun-Spiced Soft-Shell Crab Sandwiches with Yellow Pepper and Caper Aïoli

This is a great first recipe for those timid about cooking soft-shell crabs.

    2   yellow bell peppers
    ⅓   cup light mayonnaise
    ¼   cup basil leaves
    2   tablespoons capers
    ¼   teaspoon salt
    2   garlic cloves, peeled
    1   tablespoon vegetable oil
    4   (5 to 6-ounce) soft-shell crabs,
        cleaned
    1   tablespoon salt-free Cajun
        seasoning (such as Spice Hunter)
    ¼   cup cornmeal
    4   (3-ounce) pieces Italian bread, cut
        in half lengthwise and toasted
    4   curly leaf lettuce leaves
    4   (¼-inch-thick) slices red onion

1. Preheat broiler.
2. Cut bell peppers in half lengthwise, and discard seeds and membranes. Place bell pepper halves, skin sides up, on a foil-lined baking sheet, and flatten with hand. Broil 15 minutes or until blackened. Place in a zip-top plastic bag; seal. Let stand 15 minutes. Peel.
3. Place bell pepper, mayonnaise, basil, capers, salt, and garlic in a food processor; process until smooth.
4. Heat oil in a large nonstick skillet over medium-high heat. Sprinkle crabs with Cajun seasoning. Dredge crabs in cornmeal. Add crabs to pan; cook 3 minutes on each side, gently pressing body and legs against pan.
5. Spread 1 tablespoon mayonnaise mixture over each slice of bread. Arrange 1 crab over each bottom half of bread. Top each crab with 1 lettuce leaf and 1 onion slice. Cover with top halves of bread. Yield: 4 servings.

CALORIES 474 (27% from fat); FAT 14.4g (sat 2.2g, mono 3.8g, poly 6.7g); PROTEIN 34g; CARB 52g; FIBER 1.4g; CHOL 7mg; IRON 6.2mg; SODIUM 813mg; CALC 80mg

Coconut-Crusted Soft-Shell Crab with Mango Chutney

The crabs are sautéed first to crisp them, then broiled to brown the coconut topping. Serve over jasmine rice.

    2   cups chopped peeled ripe mango
    ½   cup finely chopped onion
    ½   cup water
    ¼   cup dried currants
    ¼   cup cider vinegar
    3   tablespoons sugar
    2   tablespoons chopped crystallized
        ginger
    ½   teaspoon chili powder
    ¼   teaspoon ground red pepper
    4   teaspoons vegetable oil, divided
    8   (3-ounce) soft-shell crabs, cleaned
    ½   cup flaked sweetened coconut,
        toasted
    2   tablespoons brown mustard seeds
    ¼   teaspoon salt
    1   large egg white, lightly beaten
Cooking spray

1. Combine first 9 ingredients in a medium skillet over medium-high heat. Bring to a boil; reduce heat, and simmer 15 minutes or until thick. Set mango chutney aside.
2. Preheat broiler.
3. Heat 2 teaspoons oil in a large skillet over medium-high heat. Place 4 crabs in pan, top sides down; cook 2 minutes on each side, gently pressing body and legs against pan. Place sautéed crabs, top sides up, on a baking sheet. Repeat procedure with 2 teaspoons oil and remaining crabs.
4. Combine coconut, mustard seeds, salt, and egg white. Divide evenly, and press coconut mixture on top of crabs, leaving a ⅛-inch margin around edges of shells. Lightly spray crabs with cooking spray. Place baking sheet 8 inches away from broiler; broil 5 minutes or until coconut mixture is browned and crisp. Yield: 4 servings (serving size: 2 crabs and ¼ cup mango chutney).

CALORIES 382 (29% from fat); FAT 12.4g (sat 4.7g, mono 1.7g, poly 3.6g); PROTEIN 29.5g; CARB 42.6g; FIBER 4.4g; CHOL 0mg; IRON 5.3mg; SODIUM 201mg; CALC 54mg

Spider Rolls

With the legs extending outside the sushi roll, this appetizer has a spidery look to it. Serve with wasabi and soy sauce.

1½ cups short-grain rice
1½ cups water
2 tablespoons seasoned rice vinegar
4 (4½-ounce) soft-shell crabs, cleaned
¼ teaspoon salt
¼ teaspoon black pepper
¼ cup all-purpose flour
1 tablespoon butter
4 nori (seaweed) sheets
1 peeled avocado, cut into 16 slices
½ cup thinly sliced green onions
4 teaspoons sesame seeds

1. Bring rice and water to a boil in a medium saucepan. Cover, reduce heat, and simmer 15 minutes. Remove from heat; let stand, covered, 15 minutes.
2. Place rice in a large bowl, and gently stir in rice vinegar with a spoon until combined. Cover rice mixture, and let rest 30 minutes.
3. Sprinkle crabs with salt and black pepper. Dredge crabs in flour, shaking off excess flour.
4. Melt butter in a large nonstick skillet over medium-high heat. Add crabs, top sides down; cook 3 minutes, gently pressing body and legs against pan. Turn crabs over; cook 3 minutes. Cut each crab into quarters, leaving legs attached.
5. For each roll, place nori, shiny side down, on a sushi mat covered with plastic wrap, with a short end toward you. Pat ¾ cup rice over nori with moist hands, leaving a 1-inch border on short end of nori closest to you.
6. Arrange 4 crab pieces and 4 avocado slices horizontally over rice, allowing crab legs to extend over long edges of nori. Sprinkle each sheet with 2 tablespoons green onions and 1 teaspoon sesame seeds.
7. Lift short edge of nori closest to you; fold over filling. Lift bottom edge of sushi mat; roll toward top edge, pressing firmly. Continue rolling to top edge; press mat to seal sushi roll. Slice each roll into 8 pieces with a sharp knife. Yield: 8 servings (serving size: 4 pieces).

CALORIES 265 (24% from fat); FAT 7.1g (sat 1.7g, mono 3.2g, poly 1g); PROTEIN 13.8g; CARB 36.3g; FIBER 2.8g; CHOL 4mg; IRON 3.7mg; SODIUM 168mg; CALC 28mg

Soft-Shell Crab with Fresh Thai Green Curry

The hotness of this dish depends on the number of chiles used. You can buy bottled Thai green curry paste, but it isn't as good as this bright, hot fresh sauce.

CURRY:
2 cups cilantro sprigs
½ cup coarsely chopped shallots
1 tablespoon grated lime rind
8 to 12 serrano chiles, seeded
3 garlic cloves, peeled
1 (3-inch) piece fresh ginger, peeled
1 teaspoon vegetable oil
2 cups sliced red bell pepper
1½ cups (1-inch) cubed Japanese eggplant
1½ cups water
½ cup diagonally cut carrot
2 tablespoons brown sugar
1 (13.5-ounce) can light coconut milk
2 tablespoons fresh lime juice
1 teaspoon salt

CRABS:
¼ cup cornstarch
¼ teaspoon salt
6 (5 to 6-ounce) soft-shell crabs, cleaned
4 teaspoons vegetable oil, divided
3 cups hot cooked jasmine rice

REMAINING INGREDIENTS:
6 lime wedges (optional)
Cilantro sprigs (optional)

1. To prepare curry, combine first 6 ingredients in a food processor; process 3 minutes or until a paste forms.
2. Heat 1 teaspoon oil in a large Dutch oven over medium-high heat. Add chile mixture; sauté 3 minutes. Add bell pepper and next 5 ingredients; bring to a boil. Cover, reduce heat, and simmer 10 minutes. Uncover and simmer 10 minutes. Stir in lime juice and 1 teaspoon salt, and keep warm.
3. To prepare crabs, combine cornstarch and ¼ teaspoon salt in a shallow dish. Dredge crabs in cornstarch mixture.
4. Heat 2 teaspoons oil in a large nonstick skillet over medium-high heat. Place 3 crabs in pan, top sides down; cook 3 minutes, gently pressing body and legs against pan. Turn crabs; cook 2 minutes. Remove from heat. Repeat procedure with 2 teaspoons oil and remaining crabs.
5. Place ½ cup jasmine rice into each of 6 shallow bowls; spoon ¾ cup curry mixture over each serving. Top each serving with 1 crab. Garnish with lime wedges and cilantro sprigs, if desired. Yield: 6 servings.

CALORIES 406 (22% from fat); FAT 9.8g (sat 3.1g, mono 1.5g, poly 3.3g); PROTEIN 30.5g; CARB 49.2g; FIBER 3.3g; CHOL 0mg; IRON 4.9mg; SODIUM 519mg; CALC 43mg

Soft-Shell Crab Sizes

Soft-shell crabs come in five sizes. The smallest, called **mediums**, weigh about 2 ounces and measure 3½ to 4 inches across the top. **Hotels** (2.5 ounces; 4 to 4½ inches), **primes** (about 3 ounces; 4½ to 5 inches), and **jumbos** (4½ ounces; 5 to 5½ inches) are the more commonly found sizes. **Whalers** (about 6 ounces; 5½ to 6 inches), the largest soft-shell crabs available, are reputed to be a bit on the tough side.

How to Store Soft-Shell Crabs

Soft-shell crabs are often stored at very cold temperatures to keep the shell from hardening and to prevent decomposition if they die. Store cleaned crabs wrapped in plastic wrap in the coldest part of the refrigerator up to two days.

. . . And Ready in Just About 20 Minutes

Soup, salads, and sandwiches are just a few great choices for fast suppers with international flair.

QUICK & EASY

Egg Noodles with Chicken and Escarole

You can also try farfalle or another short, wavy pasta in place of the egg noodles.

3½ cups uncooked wide egg noodles (about 6 ounces)
1 pound skinless, boneless chicken thighs, cut into bite-sized pieces
2 bacon slices, chopped
½ teaspoon crushed red pepper
1½ teaspoons bottled minced garlic
1 cup fat-free, less-sodium chicken broth
½ teaspoon salt
1 small head of escarole, cut into large pieces (about ¾ pound)

1. Cook noodles according to package directions, omitting salt and fat.
2. While noodles cook, heat a large nonstick skillet over medium-high heat. Add chicken and bacon to pan; cook 5 minutes or until chicken is done, stirring frequently. Add red pepper and garlic; sauté 30 seconds. Add broth, salt, and escarole. Cover and cook 3 minutes or until escarole wilts, stirring occasionally. Combine chicken mixture and noodles. Yield: 4 servings (serving size: about 1¾ cups).

CALORIES 374 (27% from fat); FAT 11.1g (sat 3.2g, mono 4.2g, poly 2.2g); PROTEIN 33.1g; CARB 33.9g; FIBER 3.9g; CHOL 143mg; IRON 4mg; SODIUM 684mg; CALC 72mg

QUICK & EASY

Panzanella with Crab

Whole wheat bread adds a nice texture, but regular French bread will work, too. Serve this salad as soon as you toss in the bread, so it doesn't get soggy.

1½ tablespoons chopped fresh basil
1½ tablespoons extravirgin olive oil
2 teaspoons chopped fresh mint
2 teaspoons red wine vinegar
¼ teaspoon salt
¼ teaspoon fennel seeds
2½ cups chopped tomato
½ cup vertically sliced red onion
4½ ounces whole wheat French bread, torn into 1-inch pieces (about 4 cups)
2 (6-ounce) cans lump crabmeat (such as Chicken of the Sea), drained and shell pieces removed

1. Combine first 6 ingredients in a large bowl, stirring with a whisk. Add tomato, onion, bread, and crab; toss gently to coat. Serve immediately. Yield: 4 servings (serving size: about 1¾ cups).

CALORIES 247 (27% from fat); FAT 7.5g (sat 1.2g, mono 4.4g, poly 1.2g); PROTEIN 21.5g; CARB 23.2g; FIBER 2.6g; CHOL 76mg; IRON 2.3mg; SODIUM 634mg; CALC 123mg

QUICK & EASY

Asian Pork Medallions

Serve with steamed sugar snap peas and sliced carrots. You can find bottled ground fresh ginger in the produce section of the grocery store.

QUICK TIP: For quicker prep, preheat the skillet as you assemble the ingredients.

Cooking spray
1 pound pork tenderloin, trimmed and cut crosswise into 8 pieces
½ teaspoon salt
1 tablespoon bottled minced garlic
1 tablespoon bottled ground fresh ginger
2 teaspoons dark sesame oil
½ cup water
2 tablespoons orange marmalade
1 teaspoon low-sodium soy sauce

1. Heat a large nonstick skillet coated with cooking spray over medium-high heat. Sprinkle pork with salt. Combine garlic, ginger, and oil in a large bowl. Add pork; toss to coat. Add pork to pan; sauté 3 minutes on each side or until done. Remove pork from pan; keep warm.
2. Add water, marmalade, and soy sauce to pan; bring to a boil. Reduce heat; simmer 3 minutes. Spoon sauce over pork. Yield: 4 servings (serving size: 2 pork medallions and 1 tablespoon sauce).

CALORIES 186 (30% from fat); FAT 6.2g (sat 1.7g, mono 2.7g, poly 1.4g); PROTEIN 24.1g; CARB 7.7g; FIBER 0.1g; CHOL 74mg; IRON 1.5mg; SODIUM 401mg; CALC 14mg

QUICK & EASY

Lamb Burgers

Serve with microwave-roasted potatoes: Toss quartered red-skinned potatoes with minced garlic, salt, and butter, and microwave at HIGH, covered, 15 minutes or until tender.

¼ cup minced fresh cilantro
3 tablespoons crumbled feta cheese
2 tablespoons minced red onion
½ teaspoon ground cumin
¼ teaspoon salt
¼ teaspoon ground coriander
¼ teaspoon ground red pepper
¼ teaspoon black pepper
1 pound lean ground lamb
Cooking spray
4 (2-ounce) hamburger buns, toasted
4 red leaf lettuce leaves
4 (¼-inch-thick) slices tomato

1. Prepare broiler or grill pan.
2. Combine first 9 ingredients. Divide lamb mixture into 4 equal portions, shaping each into a ¾-inch-thick patty. Place patties on broiler or grill pan coated with cooking spray. Cook 4 minutes on each side or until done.
3. Line bottom halves of buns with lettuce leaves. Top each with 1 tomato slice, 1 patty, and top half of bun. Yield: 4 servings (serving size: 1 burger).

CALORIES 336 (26% from fat); FAT 9.7g (sat 3.6g, mono 2.9g, poly 2g); PROTEIN 29.6g; CARB 30.9g; FIBER 2.3g; CHOL 79mg; IRON 4.3mg; SODIUM 617mg; CALC 134mg

Grilled Turkey and Goat Cheese Sandwiches

Use a spreadable soft goat cheese.

Cooking spray
½   cup (4 ounces) goat cheese
1   (10-ounce) Italian cheese-flavored pizza crust (such as Boboli), cut in half horizontally
½   cup chopped fresh basil
1   (7-ounce) bottle roasted red bell peppers, drained
¾   pound thinly sliced cooked turkey breast

1. Heat a large nonstick skillet coated with cooking spray over medium heat.
2. Spread cheese over one half of crust. Arrange basil, peppers, and turkey over cheese. Top with remaining half of crust, and cut into 4 wedges. Add sandwiches to pan; cook 3 minutes on each side or until browned. Yield: 4 servings (serving size: 1 sandwich).

CALORIES 369 (30% from fat); FAT 12.3g (sat 6.2g, mono 1.8g, poly 1g); PROTEIN 27.4g; CARB 38.3g; FIBER 1g; CHOL 45mg; IRON 3.3mg; SODIUM 1,296mg; CALC 238mg

Warm Shrimp and Potato Salad

Select the smallest red potatoes you can find for the fastest cooking time. While the potatoes cook, peel and devein the shrimp, and prepare the dressing.

1   pound small red potatoes, quartered
¾   pound large shrimp, peeled and deveined
¼   cup light mayonnaise
¼   cup 1% low-fat milk
1   tablespoon capers, drained
2   teaspoons white wine vinegar
½   teaspoon salt
½   teaspoon Dijon mustard
¼   teaspoon freshly ground black pepper
¼   cup thinly sliced red onion
1   (5-ounce) bag gourmet salad greens

You can count on these superfast dinners to be simple, fresh, natural, and inspired...and on your table in just about 20 minutes.

1. Place potatoes in a medium saucepan, and cover with water; bring to a boil. Reduce heat, and simmer 12 minutes or until tender. Add shrimp; cook 2 minutes or until done. Drain and rinse with cold water; drain.
2. Combine mayonnaise and next 6 ingredients in a large bowl, stirring with a whisk. Add potatoes, shrimp, and onion; toss to coat. Serve over greens. Yield: 4 servings (serving size: 1¼ cups salad and 1¼ cups greens).

CALORIES 241 (26% from fat); FAT 6.9g (sat 1.2g, mono 1.7g, poly 3.2g); PROTEIN 21.1g; CARB 23.5g; FIBER 2.9g; CHOL 135mg; IRON 4.2mg; SODIUM 643mg; CALC 102mg

Salsa-Bean Soup

To streamline your preparation, chop the cilantro and grate the cheese while the soup cooks. You can vary the heat with your choice of salsa. Serve with baked tortilla chips.

1   teaspoon vegetable oil
1   tablespoon bottled minced garlic
2   cups water
½   teaspoon chipotle chile powder
3   (15-ounce) cans black beans, rinsed and drained
1   (8-ounce) bottle salsa
1   tablespoon fresh lime juice
½   cup chopped fresh cilantro
½   cup (2 ounces) shredded Monterey Jack cheese

1. Heat oil in a large saucepan over medium-high heat. Add garlic; sauté 1 minute. Stir in water, chipotle powder, beans, and salsa. Bring to a boil; reduce heat, and simmer 1 minute.
2. Place 3 cups bean mixture in a blender; process until smooth. Return puréed mixture to pan. Stir in lime juice; simmer 10 minutes. Remove from heat; stir in cilantro. Sprinkle each serving with cheese. Yield: 4 servings (serving size: 1¼ cups soup and 2 tablespoons cheese).

CALORIES 213 (24% from fat); FAT 5.7g (sat 2.9g, mono 1.5g, poly 0.9g); PROTEIN 13.8g; CARB 36g; FIBER 12.6g; CHOL 13mg; IRON 4mg; SODIUM 957mg; CALC 215mg

Mexican Steak with Chile Rice

Chipotle chile powder gives the steak a smoky-hot flavor. Serve with sour cream, shredded lettuce, and flour tortillas to make a weeknight wrap.

1   (3½-ounce) bag boil-in-bag long-grain rice
2   teaspoons ground cumin
1   teaspoon garlic powder
1   teaspoon dried oregano
1   teaspoon chipotle chile powder
¼   teaspoon salt
1   (1-pound) sirloin steak, trimmed
Cooking spray
1   (10-ounce) can diced tomatoes and green chiles, drained
4   lime wedges

1. Preheat broiler.
2. Prepare rice according to package directions, omitting salt.
3. While rice cooks, combine cumin and next 4 ingredients; rub mixture over both sides of steak. Place steak on a broiler pan coated with cooking spray. Broil steak 4 minutes on each side or
Continued

until desired degree of doneness. Cut steak across the grain into thin slices.

4. Combine rice and tomatoes. Serve with beef and lime wedges. Yield: 4 servings (serving size: 3 ounces beef, ½ cup rice mixture, and 1 lime wedge).

CALORIES 255 (19% from fat); FAT 5.5g (sat 1.8g, mono 2g, poly 0.3g); PROTEIN 26.8g; CARB 22.3g; FIBER 1.8g; CHOL 69mg; IRON 4.6mg; SODIUM 521mg; CALC 42mg

QUICK & EASY

Chicken with Roasted Red Pepper Sauce

Serve this entrée over orzo.

 1 tablespoon olive oil
 4 (6-ounce) skinless, boneless chicken breast halves
 1 teaspoon Italian seasoning
 ¼ teaspoon salt
 ⅛ teaspoon black pepper
 ¼ cup fat-free, less-sodium chicken broth
 1 teaspoon red wine vinegar
 1 (7-ounce) bottle roasted red bell peppers, drained
 ¼ cup (1 ounce) grated Parmesan cheese
 Parsley sprigs (optional)

1. Heat oil in a large nonstick skillet over medium-high heat. Sprinkle chicken with Italian seasoning, salt, and black pepper. Add chicken to pan, and cook 3 minutes on each side.

2. While chicken cooks, place broth, vinegar, and bell peppers in a food processor; process until smooth. Add bell pepper mixture to pan; bring to a boil. Cover, reduce heat, and simmer 3 minutes. Uncover and simmer 3 minutes or until chicken is done. Sprinkle each serving with cheese. Garnish with parsley, if desired. Yield: 4 servings (serving size: 1 chicken breast half, 3 tablespoons sauce, and 1 tablespoon cheese).

CALORIES 261 (26% from fat); FAT 7.5g (sat 2.2g, mono 3.6g, poly 0.9g); PROTEIN 42.7g; CARB 3.1g; FIBER 0.4g; CHOL 103mg; IRON 1.7mg; SODIUM 528mg; CALC 116mg

QUICK & EASY

Apple Adobo Pork and Couscous

 1 teaspoon olive oil
 1 cup chopped peeled Granny Smith apple
 1 cup finely chopped onion, divided
 ¼ teaspoon cumin seed
 1½ cups fat-free, less-sodium chicken broth, divided
 1 cup apple juice, divided
 1 teaspoon cider vinegar
 ½ teaspoon salt, divided
 ¾ cup uncooked couscous
 Cooking spray
 1 (1-pound) pork tenderloin, trimmed
 ¼ teaspoon black pepper
 1 (7-ounce) can chipotle chile in adobo sauce

1. Heat oil in a medium saucepan over medium-high heat. Add apple and ½ cup onion; sauté 7 minutes or until tender. Add cumin; sauté 20 seconds. Add ¾ cup broth, ½ cup juice, vinegar, and ¼ teaspoon salt; bring to a boil. Gradually stir in couscous. Remove from heat; cover and let stand 5 minutes. Fluff with a fork.

2. While couscous stands, heat a large nonstick skillet coated with cooking spray over medium-high heat.

3. Cut pork crosswise into 12 pieces. Sprinkle both sides of pork with ¼ teaspoon salt and black pepper. Add pork to pan; cook 3 minutes on each side or until done. Remove from pan; keep warm.

4. Add ½ cup onion to pan, and sauté 1 minute. Remove 1 chile from can; reserve remaining chiles and sauce for another use. Finely chop chile. Add chopped chile, ¾ cup broth, and ½ cup juice to pan, and bring to a boil. Cook 2 minutes or until sauce is reduced to ⅔ cup. Serve pork and sauce over couscous. Yield: 4 servings (serving size: 3 pork pieces, ¾ cup couscous, and 2 tablespoons sauce).

CALORIES 339 (15% from fat); FAT 5.5g (sat 1.6g, mono 2.6g, poly 0.7g); PROTEIN 29.7g; CARB 40.8g; FIBER 3g; CHOL 74mg; IRON 2.2mg; SODIUM 543mg; CALC 30mg

Easy Weeknight Supper Menu
serves 4

Pepper Steak

Asian rice pilaf*

Steamed sugar snap peas

Fortune cookies

*Heat 1 teaspoon vegetable oil and 1 teaspoon dark sesame oil in a large nonstick skillet over medium-high heat. Add ¼ cup chopped green onions, 1 teaspoon minced peeled fresh ginger, and 2 minced garlic cloves, and sauté 2 minutes. Stir in 4 cups hot cooked white long-grain rice and 2 tablespoons low-sodium soy sauce.

QUICK & EASY

Pepper Steak

You can toss in other vegetables, such as sliced onion or water chestnuts, when you add the green bell pepper. You can find bottled ground fresh ginger in the produce section of the grocery store.

 Cooking spray
 2 tablespoons all-purpose flour
 2 tablespoons bottled minced garlic
 2 tablespoons bottled ground fresh ginger
 ¼ teaspoon salt
 ⅛ teaspoon black pepper
 1 pound sirloin steak, trimmed and cut across the grain into ¼-inch-thick strips
 1 cup green bell pepper strips
 ½ cup beef consommé
 1 teaspoon low-sodium soy sauce
 1 teaspoon dark sesame oil

1. Heat a large nonstick skillet coated with cooking spray over medium-high heat. Combine flour and next 5 ingredients, tossing to coat. Add beef mixture to pan; sauté 3 minutes. Add bell pepper and remaining ingredients to pan; cover and cook 7 minutes or until peppers are crisp-tender, stirring occasionally. Yield: 4 servings (serving size: 1 cup).

CALORIES 197 (28% from fat); FAT 6.2g (sat 1.9g, mono 2.5g, poly 0.8g); PROTEIN 26.5g; CARB 7.7g; FIBER 0.9g; CHOL 69mg; IRON 3.7mg; SODIUM 419mg; CALC 22mg

Mind Your Peas

No Qs about it: Field peas are delicious, nutritious, and thanks to inventive chefs across the land, newly stylish.

White acre peas and their field pea kin—crowder peas, black-eyed peas, pink-eyed peas, and zipper peas, to name just a few—are native to Africa and were cultivated since prehistoric times in Asia and India. However, they're also culinary survivors from a day, not too long past, when an afternoon spent rocking and shelling was viewed as welcome respite from other more demanding chores. Today, cooks of all kinds prize field peas. Field peas are high in protein and fiber and virtually fat free.

MAKE AHEAD
Field Pea Dip

A take on Middle Eastern hummus, this dip uses field peas instead of chickpeas. Serve it with baked pita chips.

    2 cups fresh pink-eyed peas
    2 (14-ounce) cans fat-free,
       less-sodium chicken broth
    6 tablespoons low-fat mayonnaise
    2 tablespoons tahini (sesame-seed
       paste)
    2 tablespoons hot pepper vinegar
       (such as Crystal)
    1 tablespoon fresh lemon juice
    2 teaspoons paprika
    2 garlic cloves, minced
    2 tablespoons chopped fresh chives
       (optional)

1. Combine peas and broth in a large saucepan; bring to a boil. Reduce heat; simmer, partially covered, 30 minutes or until tender. Drain peas. Place peas in a food processor; pulse 10 times or until coarsely chopped.
2. Combine peas, mayonnaise, and next 5 ingredients in a bowl, stirring until blended. Garnish with chives, if desired. Yield: 16 servings (serving size: 2 tablespoons).

CALORIES 109 (27% from fat); FAT 3.3g (sat 0.5g, mono 1.6g, poly 1g); PROTEIN 5.5g; CARB 15.2g; FIBER 2.5g; CHOL 2mg; IRON 1.9mg; SODIUM 53mg; CALC 28mg

STAFF FAVORITE
Lady Peas with Artichoke Hearts

Don't use canned artichokes—they'll ruin both the texture and flavor of this dish.

ARTICHOKES:

    2 cups water
    6 tablespoons fresh lemon juice,
       divided
   12 artichokes
    4 cups fat-free, less-sodium chicken
       broth
   ¼ teaspoon salt

PEAS:

    4 cups water
    2 cups fat-free, less-sodium chicken
       broth
 4½ cups fresh lady peas
    2 teaspoons olive oil
    1 cup sliced shallots
    2 garlic cloves, minced
   ¾ teaspoon salt
   ¼ teaspoon black pepper
    3 tablespoons fresh lemon juice
    1 tablespoon finely chopped fresh
       parsley

1. To prepare artichokes, combine 2 cups water and 3 tablespoons lemon juice in a bowl. Cut off stem of each artichoke to within 1 inch of base; peel stem. Remove bottom leaves and tough outer leaves of each artichoke, leaving tender heart and bottom. Remove fuzzy thistle from bottom with a spoon. Cut each artichoke into quarters lengthwise. Place artichoke quarters in lemon water, and drain.
2. Combine 4 cups broth, ¼ teaspoon salt, and 3 tablespoons lemon juice in a medium saucepan; bring to a boil. Add artichoke quarters; cook 20 minutes or until tender. Drain through a fine sieve over a bowl, reserving artichokes and ½ cup cooking liquid. Cover and set aside.
3. To prepare peas, combine 4 cups water, 2 cups broth, and peas in a medium saucepan; bring to a boil over medium-high heat. Reduce heat; simmer, partially covered, 30 minutes or until peas are tender. Drain.
4. Heat oil in a nonstick skillet over medium-high heat. Add shallots; sauté 3 minutes. Add garlic; sauté 1 minute. Add reserved cooking liquid, artichokes, peas, ¾ teaspoon salt, and pepper. Bring to a boil, and cook 1 minute. Stir in 3 tablespoons lemon juice and parsley. Yield: 8 servings (serving size: about ¾ cup).

CALORIES 198 (9% from fat); FAT 1.9g (sat 0.4g, mono 0.9g, poly 0.4g); PROTEIN 9.7g; CARB 41g; FIBER 10.6g; CHOL 0mg; IRON 3.7mg; SODIUM 493mg; CALC 200mg

QUICK & EASY
Basic Pot of Peas

    2 teaspoons olive oil
   ½ cup chopped onion
    2 garlic cloves, minced
    3 cups fresh pink-eyed peas
    3 cups water
    3 bacon slices
   ½ teaspoon salt
   ½ teaspoon black pepper

1. Heat oil in a large saucepan over medium-high heat. Add onion and garlic; sauté 2 minutes. Add peas, water, and bacon; bring to a boil. Reduce heat; simmer, partially covered, 30 minutes or until tender. Discard bacon. Stir in salt and pepper. Yield: 6 servings (serving size: ½ cup).

CALORIES 167 (28% from fat); FAT 5.3g (sat 1.6g, mono 2.8g, poly 0.6g); PROTEIN 4.1g; CARB 26.1g; FIBER 6.3g; CHOL 3mg; IRON 1.4mg; SODIUM 588mg; CALC 157mg

Black-Eyed Peas with Greens

For a more peppery flavor, substitute turnip or mustard greens for the Swiss chard in this recipe.

  4 cups vegetable broth
  3 cups water
  2 cups fresh black-eyed peas
  2 tablespoons butter
  2 cups finely chopped red onion
  6 cups coarsely chopped Swiss chard (about 1 pound)
  ½ teaspoon black pepper
  1 tablespoon hot pepper vinegar (such as Crystal)

1. Combine first 3 ingredients in a Dutch oven; bring to a boil. Reduce heat; simmer, partially covered, 30 minutes or until tender. Remove from heat.
2. Heat butter in a large skillet over medium-high heat. Add onion; sauté 5 minutes. Add Swiss chard and pepper. Sauté 3 minutes or until wilted; stir in vinegar. Add onion mixture to peas; stir. Yield: 9 servings (serving size: 1 cup).

CALORIES 185 (18% from fat); FAT 3.6g (sat 1.7g, mono 0.8g, poly 0.4g); PROTEIN 11g; CARB 30g; FIBER 5.4g; CHOL 7mg; IRON 4.1mg; SODIUM 586mg; CALC 75mg

QUICK & EASY
Sautéed Duck Breast with Peas

Try this recipe using pork chops or chicken breast halves in place of duck breasts.

  2 teaspoons vegetable oil
  4 (6-ounce) duck breast halves, skinned
  ½ teaspoon salt
  ¼ teaspoon black pepper
  3 tablespoons balsamic vinegar
  2 cups Basic Pot of Peas (recipe on page 135)
  2 tablespoons chopped fresh parsley (optional)

1. Heat oil in a large nonstick skillet over medium-high heat. Sprinkle duck with salt and pepper. Add duck to pan; sauté 5 minutes. Turn and sauté an additional 2 minutes or until desired degree of doneness. Add vinegar; cook 1 minute. Remove from heat; let stand 10 minutes. Cut duck diagonally across the grain into thin strips.
2. Spoon ½ cup peas onto each of 4 plates; place 1 breast half on each plate. Drizzle with vinegar sauce; garnish with parsley, if desired. Yield: 4 servings.

CALORIES 312 (27% from fat); FAT 9.5g (sat 2.4g, mono 3.7g, poly 2.2g); PROTEIN 37.6g; CARB 16.9g; FIBER 0.3g; CHOL 185mg; IRON 6.7mg; SODIUM 839mg; CALC 112mg

Crowder Pea Stew with Cornmeal Dumplings

Corn bread is a traditional accompaniment for field peas; cornmeal dumplings echo that tradition in this stew.

STEW:
  1 tablespoon olive oil
  1 cup finely chopped onion
  1 cup finely chopped celery
  ½ teaspoon salt
  1 (8-ounce) package presliced mushrooms
  3 cups fat-free, less-sodium chicken broth
  2 cups fresh crowder peas
  1 tablespoon chopped fresh or 1 teaspoon dried oregano
  ½ teaspoon black pepper
  1 bay leaf
  3½ cups chopped peeled tomatoes (about 1½ pounds)

DUMPLINGS:
  ½ cup yellow cornmeal
  ½ cup all-purpose flour
  ½ teaspoon baking powder
  ½ teaspoon salt
  ½ teaspoon sugar
  ⅓ cup low-fat buttermilk
  1 tablespoon butter, melted
  1 large egg, lightly beaten
  1 tablespoon chopped fresh parsley (optional)

1. To prepare stew, heat oil in a large Dutch oven over medium heat. Add onion; cook 5 minutes or until golden, stirring frequently. Add celery, ½ teaspoon salt, and mushrooms; cook 3 minutes, stirring frequently. Add broth, peas, oregano, pepper, and bay leaf; bring to a boil. Reduce heat, and simmer, partially covered, 45 minutes or until peas are tender. Add tomatoes; return to a boil. Reduce heat, and simmer, partially covered, 15 minutes. Discard bay leaf.
2. To prepare dumplings, while stew is simmering, combine cornmeal and next 4 ingredients in a bowl, stirring with a whisk. Stir in buttermilk, butter, and egg; let stand 10 minutes.
3. Drop dough by tablespoonfuls into stew to form 15 dumplings. Cover and

cook 15 minutes. Garnish with parsley, if desired. Yield: 5 servings (serving size: about 1 cup stew and 3 dumplings).

CALORIES 292 (26% from fat); FAT 8.4g (sat 2.9g, mono 3.3g, poly 1g); PROTEIN 11g; CARB 45.8g; FIBER 4.5g; CHOL 52mg; IRON 2.9mg; SODIUM 675mg; CALC 167mg

Chile and Lime-Marinated Snapper with Roasted Corn and Black-Eyed Pea Salsa

Grouper, tilapia, and different varieties of snapper all work in this recipe. For a great snack, double the salsa, and eat it with baked tortilla chips. You can serve the salsa chilled or at room temperature.

SALSA:
1 cup fresh black-eyed peas
1 cup water
1 (14-ounce) can fat-free, less-sodium chicken broth
2 ears corn, husks removed
Cooking spray
½ cup chopped red onion
⅓ cup chopped fresh cilantro
2 tablespoons apple cider vinegar
1 tablespoon olive oil
½ teaspoon salt
2 jalapeño peppers, seeded and minced
1 garlic clove, minced

FISH:
½ cup fresh lime juice (about 4 limes)
½ cup chopped red onion
2 tablespoons honey
1 tablespoon olive oil
2 jalapeño peppers, seeded and minced
4 (6-ounce) red snapper or other firm white fish fillets
¾ teaspoon salt
¼ teaspoon black pepper

1. To prepare salsa, combine first 3 ingredients in a small saucepan; bring to a boil. Reduce heat; simmer, partially covered, 30 minutes or until tender. Drain.
2. Preheat broiler.
3. Place corn on a broiler pan coated with cooking spray; broil 6 minutes or

until lightly browned, turning every 2 minutes. Cool. Cut kernels from ears of corn to measure 2 cups. Combine corn, peas, ½ cup onion, cilantro, and next 5 ingredients in a medium bowl; toss to combine. Chill.
4. To prepare fish, combine lime juice and next 4 ingredients in a large zip-top plastic bag; add fish. Seal and marinate in refrigerator 20 minutes, turning bag once. Remove fish from bag; discard marinade.
5. Preheat broiler.
6. Sprinkle ¾ teaspoon salt and black pepper evenly over fish. Place fish on a broiler pan coated with cooking spray, and broil 10 minutes or until fish flakes easily when tested with a fork. Yield: 4 servings (serving size: 1 snapper fillet and 1 cup salsa).

WINE NOTE: A fresh fish dish like this is crisply complemented by a white wine that's snappy and clean tasting and has a bit of fruit to balance the chile. Try the Smith Madrone Riesling 2001 (Napa Valley) $17.

CALORIES 323 (23% from fat); FAT 8.2g (sat 1.4g, mono 4.3g, poly 1.6g); PROTEIN 38.2g; CARB 24.5g; FIBER 2g; CHOL 63mg; IRON 1.2mg; SODIUM 860mg; CALC 114mg

---

Southern-Style Menu
serves 5

Quinoa is a light, chewy grain that takes the place of rice in this classic Southern dish.

Peas and Quinoa Hoppin' John

Sautéed zucchini and onions*

Tomato slices

Corn muffins

*Heat 1 teaspoon vegetable oil in a large nonstick skillet over medium-high heat. Add 4 cups sliced zucchini and 1 cup chopped onion; sauté 6 minutes or until tender. Add ½ teaspoon dried oregano, ½ teaspoon salt, and ¼ teaspoon black pepper; toss to coat. Sprinkle with ¼ cup grated Parmesan cheese.

Peas and Quinoa Hoppin' John

Eaten on New Year's Day in the South, Hoppin' John (black-eyed peas and rice) is said to bring good luck in the year ahead. Although any field pea will work, this adaptation uses pink-eyed peas in place of black-eyed peas and quinoa instead of rice.

1 tablespoon olive oil
2¾ cups chopped onion
4 bacon slices, cut into ¼-inch pieces
3 cups fresh pink-eyed peas
2 cups water
1 cup dry white wine
2 garlic cloves, minced
1 bay leaf
1¼ cups fat-free, less-sodium chicken broth
1 cup uncooked quinoa, rinsed
1 teaspoon salt
½ teaspoon black pepper
2 tablespoons thinly sliced green onions
1 tablespoon chopped fresh parsley

1. Heat oil in a Dutch oven over medium-high heat. Add chopped onion; sauté 2 minutes. Add bacon; sauté 5 minutes. Add peas and next 4 ingredients; bring to a boil. Reduce heat; simmer, partially covered, 30 minutes or until tender. Discard bay leaf.
2. Combine broth, quinoa, salt, and pepper in a saucepan; bring to a boil over medium-high heat. Cover, reduce heat, and simmer 30 minutes or until done. Add quinoa mixture to pea mixture, and stir. Sprinkle with green onions and parsley. Yield: 5 servings (serving size: about 1¼ cups).

CALORIES 339 (29% from fat); FAT 10.2g (sat 2.4g, mono 5g, poly 1.8g); PROTEIN 10.2g; CARB 48.9g; FIBER 3.8g; CHOL 8mg; IRON 4.6mg; SODIUM 667mg; CALC 156mg

All About Grilling

Be it burger, steak, or veggie, here's
how to grill like a pro.

Barbecued Pork Tenderloin

This pork tenderloin has a flavor that's reminiscent of slow-smoked Kansas City ribs.

½ cup strong brewed coffee
2 tablespoons cider vinegar
1 tablespoon spicy brown mustard
1 tablespoon dark molasses
2 (1-pound) pork tenderloins, trimmed
¼ cup finely ground coffee
2 tablespoons sugar
2 tablespoons paprika
2 tablespoons coarsely ground black pepper
1½ teaspoons sea or kosher salt
¼ cup barbecue sauce
1 tablespoon cider vinegar
Cooking spray

1. Combine first 4 ingredients in a large zip-top plastic bag; add pork. Seal and marinate in refrigerator 2 to 12 hours, turning bag occasionally. Remove pork from bag; discard marinade.
2. Prepare grill, heating one side to medium and one side to high heat (see "How Hot?," on page 141).
3. Combine ground coffee and next 4 ingredients; rub over pork. Let stand at room temperature 15 minutes.
4. Combine ¼ cup barbecue sauce and 1 tablespoon cider vinegar. Reserve 2 tablespoons barbecue sauce mixture, and set aside.
5. Place pork on grill rack coated with cooking spray over high heat; grill 3 minutes, turning pork to sear on all sides. Place pork over medium heat; grill 15 minutes, turning pork occasionally. Baste

with 3 tablespoons barbecue sauce mixture; grill 5 minutes or until thermometer registers 160° (slightly pink), turning pork occasionally.
6. Place pork on a platter; brush with reserved 2 tablespoons barbecue sauce mixture. Cover with foil; let stand 5 minutes. Yield: 8 servings (serving size: about 3 ounces pork).

CALORIES 196 (21% from fat); FAT 4.5g (sat 1.5g, mono 1.8g, poly 0.6g); PROTEIN 28.9g; CARB 8.4g; FIBER 1.3g; CHOL 80mg; IRON 2.4mg; SODIUM 566mg; CALC 24mg

STAFF FAVORITE
Maple-Glazed Salmon
(pictured on page 145)

Find ancho chile powder in the spice section of most supermarkets (substitute 2 teaspoons regular chili powder if you can't find it). Use a spatula to separate the fish from its skin after grilling. Round out the salmon with a simple spring salad.

2 teaspoons paprika
1 teaspoon chili powder
1 teaspoon ancho chile powder
½ teaspoon ground cumin
½ teaspoon brown sugar
1 teaspoon sea or kosher salt
4 (6-ounce) salmon fillets
Cooking spray
1 teaspoon maple syrup

1. Prepare grill, heating to medium (see "How Hot?," on page 141).
2. Combine first 5 ingredients. Sprinkle fish with salt; rub with paprika mixture.
3. Place fish on grill rack coated with cooking spray; grill 7 minutes. Drizzle fish with syrup; grill 1 minute or until fish flakes easily when tested with a fork.

Yield: 4 servings (serving size: 1 salmon fillet).

CALORIES 286 (42% from fat); FAT 13.5g (sat 3.2g, mono 5.7g, poly 3.4g); PROTEIN 36.5g; CARB 2.9g; FIBER 0.6g; CHOL 87mg; IRON 1.1mg; SODIUM 670mg; CALC 30mg

Whole Snapper with Fennel and Lemon

Look for a fish no thicker than about 1¼ inches at its roundest point and about two pounds—enough for two servings. Fish are relatively easy to handle at that size and provide an optimum proportion of grilled surface to moist interior.

4 teaspoons olive oil, divided
½ cup vertically sliced onion
1 cup thinly sliced fennel bulb
2 (2-pound) cleaned whole red snappers
1 teaspoon fennel seeds, toasted and crushed
2 teaspoons grated lemon rind
¾ teaspoon sea or kosher salt
¾ teaspoon freshly ground black pepper
1 lemon, cut into 8 slices
Cooking spray
Fennel fronds (optional)

1. Prepare grill, heating to medium-high (see "How Hot?," on page 141).
2. Heat 1 teaspoon oil in a nonstick skillet over medium heat. Add onion and fennel bulb, and cook 3 minutes, stirring constantly. Set aside.
3. Score skin of each fish with 3 diagonal cuts. Combine fennel seeds, rind, salt, and pepper. Rub each fish with 1½ teaspoons oil and half of fennel seed mixture. Stuff half of onion mixture and 4 lemon slices into each fish cavity.
4. Place fish on grill rack coated with cooking spray, and grill 8 minutes. Carefully roll fish over; grill 8 minutes or until fish flakes easily when tested with a fork. Garnish with fennel fronds, if desired. Yield: 4 servings (serving size: about 4½ ounces).

CALORIES 218 (28% from fat); FAT 6.9g (sat 1.1g, mono 3.8g, poly 1.2g); PROTEIN 34.1g; CARB 3.5g; FIBER 1.3g; CHOL 60mg; IRON 0.7mg; SODIUM 517mg; CALC 74mg

Grilling 101

*The following tips on grilling are from Cheryl Alters Jamison and Bill Jamison,
James Beard Award-winners and coauthors of* Born to Grill.

Charcoal, Gas, or Wood

We cook at home on both charcoal and gas grills, and we like both methods equally well. Some people claim to detect a taste advantage with charcoal, but we really haven't found that to be the case, as long as the two fuels provide a similar temperature range. The manufacturing process for charcoal eliminates its original wood flavor and adds nothing positive in return.

The only advantage with charcoal over the others comes from its firepower. It generates high heat, even with the lid open, which isn't normally true of the gas burners in grills. You have to shop carefully to find a gas grill with the same heat range as any inexpensive charcoal model. We've cooked on several good gas grills, and the results are always just as tasty as those from charcoal.

The only fuel that seems to us to make a difference in flavor is wood chunks or logs. Although a few wood chips added to a charcoal or gas fire aren't enough to flavor food, cooking entirely with wood has an impact. A few manufacturers offer grills meant for wood cooking, and some charcoal models adapt well to the purpose.

The choice between fuels is mainly a matter of mood and personality. We opt for gas for everyday grilling because of its speed and convenience, and use charcoal or wood for entertaining. If you don't want to deal with more than one grill, pick the kind that fits your personal style and budget. Bear in mind: Gas models that get as hot as charcoal grills are pricey.

Mastering a Charcoal Fire

Many people choose a fuel for grilling based on experience with building charcoal fires. All the attributes of gas—such as quick start-up, ease of temperature adjustment, and lack of residual heat—are an industrial curse to the first group and a modern blessing to the second.

For charcoal fans, fire building is an outdoor art. It begins with the selection of coal, which comes in briquettes or lump hardwood. We prefer lump hardwood because it ignites more easily and burns hotter and cleaner. We light our coals in a charcoal chimney, but most of the new non-polluting starters also work well.

The charcoal has reached cooking temperature when it's coated in gray ash. Arrange the bed of coals to get the right heat level for the food that you're grilling (see "The Right Fire for the Food" on page 142). If the food cooks best at a steady temperature, spread the charcoal evenly below the cooking area. A single layer of coals just touching one another produces a medium to medium-high fire. To increase or decrease the heat, add or subtract charcoal. If the food grills better on a two-level fire, stack the coals several deep in one area and spread them in a single layer elsewhere.

Direct and Indirect Heat

As long as your grill has a cover, you can cook on it with direct and indirect heat. In the case of direct heat, the food is positioned directly over a hot to moderately hot fire to sear and crisp its surface. Most of the world considers cooking food directly over an open fire to be the only form of grilling. *Bistecca alla fiorentina* in Tuscany, shrimp from the barby in Australia, and *satay* in Southeast Asia are all cooked in that manner.

With indirect grilling, the food is positioned away from the fire, and the grill cover is kept closed, reducing the cooking temperature and allowing the heat reflected from the cover to do the cooking. The indirect method is the only way to cook a turkey breast, pork roast, or other large cut of meat on a grill.

Considering everything cooked on a grill as "grilled" is akin to thinking that every dish prepared on a kitchen burner is "stoved," regardless of whether you've deep-fried, sautéed, or boiled. Indirect cooking on a grill is really a form of oven roasting, a perfectly fine method of cooking, but one that yields neither the flavor nor the texture that's characteristic of direct grilling. That's why all of these recipes use direct heat. Also, for best results, keep the cover open for these recipes—unless, of course, you're grilling in rainy or windy weather.

The Two-Level Fire

Many foods reach their peak when you grill them at two different temperatures, usually starting at a high level and then finishing at a lower level. Both porterhouse and tuna steaks, for example, are best when seared first on a hot fire and then moved to medium heat for cooking through.

On gas grills you can make temperature adjustments with nothing more than the turn of a knob. With smaller models that have one or two burners, simply turn down the heat at the appropriate time and move food temporarily to a cooler edge of the grate to speed the temperature transition. With gas grills that have three or more burners, you can usually keep a hot fire and a medium fire going simultaneously from the beginning.

Creating a two-level fire on a charcoal grill isn't much more difficult. On models that include an adjustable grate or firebox, lower the heat by increasing the distance between the coals and the food. In the case of more common conventional grills that lack that feature, build two similarly sized cooking areas on opposite sides of the grill by stacking and spreading the charcoal differently. For the hot section, pile coals between two and three deep; for the medium area, scatter them in a single layer so that they're just touching one another.

Other Grilling Basics

Good ingredients matter. Grilling accentuates the natural flavor of food. No amount of seasoning will change the essential quality of the ingredients you use. So always start with fresh vegetables and the best cuts of meat and fish.

Think grate. Make sure before you start that the cooking grate is hot, lightly oiled, and clean. Preheat the grate with the cover down, coat it with cooking spray right before you cook, and then scrape it clean with a wire brush before it cools.

Get it together. Have everything in place and handy before you begin.

Time the cooking. Know in advance how long you expect to grill the food, and set a timer to alert you to check it.

Control flare-ups. When dripping fat produces a leaping flame in one spot, move food to a different area, at least temporarily. Prevent problems by maintaining a clean grate, trimming excess fat from meat, and keeping oil in marinades to the minimum needed. Keep a spray bottle of water by the grill to put out accidental flare-ups.

Spice is nice. For bold seasoning, use dry-rub spice blends rather than marinades. Go light on sugar in homemade rubs, and avoid buying commercial versions. For a less assertive touch, salt and pepper alone often work well.

Peek for the pink. With steaks and chops, it's OK to make a small cut and peek inside just before you're ready to serve. Or use an instant-read meat thermometer to gauge doneness for poultry and large cuts of meat.

Take the chill off. Remove marinated meats from the refrigerator, and let them stand at room temperature for 10 to 15 minutes before grilling to make sure you don't end up with a cold center.

Use basic tools. Other than a timer, the only major grill tools you need are long, strong spatulas and tongs for turning food. Don't use a fork for grilling, since puncturing the food will release its juices.

Portobello Burgers

Portobello mushrooms make great burgers. Half of a roasted bell pepper is stirred into mayonnaise for the sandwich spread. Use the leftover bell pepper as a pizza topping, or in a salad or a pasta dish.

- ¼ cup low-sodium soy sauce
- ¼ cup balsamic vinegar
- 2 tablespoons olive oil
- 3 garlic cloves, minced
- 4 (4-inch) portobello mushroom caps
- 1 small red bell pepper
- Cooking spray
- ¼ cup low-fat mayonnaise
- ½ teaspoon olive oil
- ⅛ teaspoon ground red pepper
- 4 (2-ounce) onion sandwich buns
- 4 (¼-inch-thick) slices tomato
- 4 curly leaf lettuce leaves

1. Combine first 4 ingredients in a large zip-top plastic bag; add mushrooms to bag. Seal; marinate at room temperature 2 hours, turning bag occasionally. Remove mushrooms from bag; discard marinade.

2. Prepare grill, heating to medium (see "How Hot?," on page 141).

3. Cut bell pepper in half lengthwise; discard seeds and membranes. Place pepper halves on grill rack coated with cooking spray; grill 15 minutes or until blackened, turning occasionally. Place in a zip-top plastic bag; seal. Let stand 10 minutes. Peel. Reserve 1 pepper half for another use. Finely chop 1 pepper half; place in a small bowl. Add mayonnaise, ½ teaspoon oil, and ground red pepper; stir well.

4. Place mushrooms, gill sides down, on grill rack coated with cooking spray; grill 4 minutes on each side. Place buns, cut sides down, on grill rack coated with cooking spray; grill 30 seconds on each side or until toasted. Spread 2 tablespoons mayonnaise mixture on top half of each bun. Place 1 mushroom on bottom half of each bun. Top each mushroom with 1 tomato slice and 1 lettuce leaf; cover with top halves of buns. Yield: 4 servings.

CALORIES 251 (30% from fat); FAT 8.4g (sat 2.3g, mono 3.7g, poly 2.1g); PROTEIN 7.3g; CARB 37.9g; FIBER 2.4g; CHOL 0mg; IRON 2.2mg; SODIUM 739mg; CALC 81mg

Rum-Marinated Chicken Breasts with Pineapple Relish

CHICKEN:
- ½ cup dark rum
- ¼ cup barbecue sauce
- 3 tablespoons fresh lime juice
- 1 tablespoon Caribbean hot sauce (such as Pickapeppa Sauce)
- 1 teaspoon sea or kosher salt
- 2 teaspoons vegetable oil
- 4 (8-ounce) bone-in chicken breast halves

RELISH:
- 1 small pineapple, peeled, cored, and cut into ½-inch-thick rings (about 12 ounces)
- Cooking spray
- ½ cup finely chopped red bell pepper
- 1 teaspoon grated lime rind
- 2 tablespoons fresh lime juice
- 1 teaspoon dark rum
- ¼ teaspoon Caribbean hot sauce
- ⅛ teaspoon sea or kosher salt
- 4 lime wedges

1. To prepare chicken, combine first 6 ingredients in large zip-top plastic bag. Add chicken to bag; seal. Marinate in refrigerator 1 to 2 hours, turning bag occasionally. Remove chicken from bag, reserving marinade; set chicken aside. Let marinade stand at room temperature 10 minutes. Strain through a sieve into a bowl; discard solids. Set marinade aside.

2. Prepare grill, heating to medium (see "How Hot?," on page 141).

3. To prepare relish, place pineapple on grill rack coated with cooking spray; grill 3 minutes on each side or until soft and browned around edge. Cool slightly; chop. Combine pineapple, bell pepper, and next 5 ingredients; set aside.

4. Place chicken on grill rack coated with cooking spray; grill 30 minutes or until done, turning occasionally. Remove and discard skin.

5. Bring reserved marinade to a boil in a small saucepan; cook 1 minute. Drizzle cooked marinade over chicken. Serve chicken with relish and lime wedges. Yield: 4 servings (serving size: 1 chicken breast half, ½ cup relish, 2 tablespoons sauce, and 1 lime wedge).

CALORIES 288 (14% from fat); FAT 4.5g (sat 0.6g, mono 1.8g, poly 1.2g); PROTEIN 29.6g; CARB 15.6g; FIBER 1.9g; CHOL 72mg; IRON 1.5mg; SODIUM 971mg; CALC 28mg

Simply Great Steak with Grilled Fries

A superior steak for grilling needs to be an inch or more thick. Keep the smaller, more tender tip of the steak angled away from the hottest part of the fire to prevent it from cooking too quickly. To test for doneness, cut into the steak with the tip of a knife and peek, or insert an instant-read meat thermometer into the side of the steak—medium rare will register 145°. If you have a large enough grill, start grilling the potatoes with the steak so everything will be done at the same time. Otherwise, tent the beef with foil to keep it warm.

STEAK:

- 1 (2-pound) porterhouse steak (about 1½ inches thick)
- 2 tablespoons Worcestershire sauce
- 1 teaspoon sea or kosher salt
- 1 teaspoon coarsely ground black pepper
  Cooking spray
- 1 teaspoon unsalted butter, softened

FRIES:

- 2 teaspoons paprika
- 1 teaspoon sea or kosher salt
- 1 teaspoon coarsely ground black pepper
- ½ teaspoon garlic powder
- ½ teaspoon onion powder
- ½ teaspoon chili powder
- 1 teaspoon olive oil
- 2 baking potatoes, each cut into 12 wedges (about 1½ pounds)
- 2 sweet potatoes, each cut into 12 wedges (about 1½ pounds)

1. To prepare steak, coat steak with Worcestershire. Cover; marinate in refrigerator 30 minutes, turning occasionally.
2. Prepare grill, heating one side to medium and one side to high heat (see "How Hot?," at right).

3. Remove steak from Worcestershire; discard Worcestershire. Sprinkle steak with 1 teaspoon salt and 1 teaspoon pepper; let stand at room temperature 15 minutes. Place steak on grill rack coated with cooking spray over high heat; grill 3 minutes on each side. Turn steak, and place over medium heat; grill 3 minutes on each side or until desired degree of doneness. Place steak on a platter. Rub butter over top of steak; let stand 10 minutes.
4. To prepare fries, combine paprika and next 5 ingredients. Combine oil and potatoes in a large bowl, tossing to coat. Sprinkle potatoes with paprika mixture; toss gently to coat.
5. Place potatoes on grill rack coated with cooking spray over medium heat; grill 18 minutes or until sweet potatoes are tender, turning occasionally. Remove sweet potatoes; keep warm. Grill baking potatoes an additional 6 minutes or until tender. Yield: 6 servings (serving size: 3 ounces beef and 8 fries).

WINE NOTE: Steak and Cabernet Sauvignon make a classic American combo. The char and meatiness of the steak are beautifully offset by the structure of the wine. Try Sebastini Cabernet Sauvignon (Sonoma County, California); it tastes like it costs much more than $17.

CALORIES 446 (29% from fat); FAT 14.6g (sat 5.1g, mono 6.6g, poly 0.7g); PROTEIN 33.1g; CARB 45g; FIBER 5.5g; CHOL 79mg; IRON 6.6mg; SODIUM 898mg; CALC 47mg

QUICK & EASY
Grilled Plantains

Although immature green-skinned plantains are used in many Latin American dishes, ripe plantains are necessary here. Because they're tender, they're grilled in their skins to keep them in one piece. Try with Rum-Marinated Chicken Breasts with Pineapple Relish (recipe on page 140).

- 3 soft black plantains, unpeeled (about 1½ pounds)
- 2 tablespoons butter, melted
- 1 teaspoon brown sugar
- ⅛ teaspoon ground red pepper
  Cooking spray
- 6 lime wedges

1. Prepare grill, heating to medium (see "How Hot?," below).
2. Cut plantains in half lengthwise. Cut plantain halves in half crosswise. Combine butter, sugar, and pepper; brush evenly over cut sides of plantain sections.
3. Place plantain sections, cut sides up, on grill rack coated with cooking spray; grill 7 minutes or until flesh is soft and skins begin to pull away from the flesh. Turn plantain sections over; grill 3 minutes. Serve warm with lime wedges. Yield: 6 servings (serving size: 2 plantain sections and 1 lime wedge).

CALORIES 174 (22% from fat); FAT 4.3g (sat 2.6g, mono 1.2g, poly 0.2g); PROTEIN 1.5g; CARB 36.7g; FIBER 2.6g; CHOL 10mg; IRON 0.7mg; SODIUM 44mg; CALC 5mg

How Hot?

The best way to measure the temperature of an open fire is the time-honored hand test. Simply hold your hand about 3 inches above the grate, then time how long you can keep your hand there before you're forced to withdraw it:

- 1 to 2 seconds—the fire is hot and perfect for searing a steak or grilling shrimp.
- 3 seconds—indicates medium-high heat, great for most fish.
- 4 to 5 seconds—signifies a medium range, ideal for most chicken and vegetables.
- 7 to 8 seconds—indicates the temperature is low and perfect for grilling delicate vegetables and fruit.

Thermometers that come with most grills measure only oven temperatures inside the grill when the cover is closed. If you cook with direct heat with the cover down, you get a measurement of the reflected heat that contributes to the cooking process but not the actual grilling temperature on the grate where the food sits. The top side of the food is cooked at the oven temperature indicated, while the bottom side directly above the fire is grilled at a higher temperature.

Marjoram-Lemon Lamb Kabobs

 1 cup dry red wine
 ¾ cup finely chopped onion
 2 tablespoons olive oil
 4 garlic cloves, minced
 1½ pounds boneless leg of lamb, trimmed and cut into 1-inch cubes
 12 small boiling onions, peeled
 1½ tablespoons dried marjoram or oregano
 1 tablespoon grated lemon rind
 1 teaspoon sea or kosher salt
 ½ teaspoon ground cumin
 ½ teaspoon coarsely ground black pepper
 1 green bell pepper, cut into 1-inch pieces
 1 yellow bell pepper, cut into 1-inch pieces
    Cooking spray

1. Combine first 4 ingredients in a large zip-top plastic bag; add lamb to bag. Seal and marinate in refrigerator 2 to 12 hours, turning bag occasionally. Remove lamb from bag; discard marinade. Place lamb in a large bowl; set aside.
2. Cook boiling onions in boiling water 2 minutes or until tender. Drain; cool slightly.
3. Prepare grill, heating to medium-high (see "How Hot?," on page 141).
4. Add marjoram, rind, salt, cumin, and black pepper to lamb; toss gently to coat.
5. Let stand at room temperature 10 minutes. Thread lamb, boiling onions, and bell pepper pieces alternately onto each of 6 (12-inch) skewers. Place kabobs on grill rack coated with cooking spray; grill 8 minutes or until desired degree of doneness, turning once. Yield: 6 servings (serving size: 1 kabob).

CALORIES 228 (34% from fat); FAT 8.7g (sat 2.6g, mono 4.2g, poly 0.9g); PROTEIN 25.1g; CARB 8.7g; FIBER 1.9g; CHOL 77mg; IRON 2.9mg; SODIUM 453mg; CALC 40mg

---

Easy Fish Dinner Menu
serves 4

Peppered Halibut Fillets

Balsamic-shallot asparagus*

White and wild rice blend

Lemonade

*Prepare grill. Snap off tough ends of 1 pound of asparagus. Combine asparagus, 3 tablespoons balsamic vinegar, 1 tablespoon olive oil, 2 tablespoons finely chopped shallots, ½ teaspoon salt, and ¼ teaspoon black pepper; marinate 30 minutes. Remove asparagus; discard marinade. Place asparagus on grill rack coated with cooking spray. Grill 5 minutes on each side or until done.

QUICK & EASY
Peppered Halibut Fillets

Most fish can be grilled to perfection over a fairly hot fire. Moist, fresh halibut, in particular, stands up well to medium-high heat, which sears the surface and cooks the flesh through. If there is any sticking when you turn the fish, recoat the grill rack with cooking spray.

 1 tablespoon coarsely ground black pepper
 1 tablespoon fresh lemon juice
 1½ teaspoons vegetable oil
 4 (6-ounce) halibut fillets
 ¾ teaspoon sea or kosher salt
    Cooking spray
 4 lemon wedges

1. Prepare grill, heating to medium-high (see "How Hot?," on page 141).
2. Combine first 3 ingredients; rub over fish. Cover; let stand at room temperature 10 minutes. Sprinkle fish with salt.
3. Place fish on grill rack coated with cooking spray; grill 4 minutes on each side or until fish flakes easily when tested with a fork. Serve with lemon wedges. Yield: 4 servings (serving size: 1 fillet and 1 lemon wedge).

CALORIES 207 (25% from fat); FAT 5.7g (sat 0.7g, mono 2.3g, poly 1.8g); PROTEIN 35.6g; CARB 1.4g; FIBER 0.4g; CHOL 54mg; IRON 1.9mg; SODIUM 524mg; CALC 88mg

---

The Right Fire for the Food

Medium heat:
- Bell peppers, corn on the cob (shucked), eggplant, and most other vegetables
- Chicken breasts and halves
- Duck breasts
- Pork chops and most other pork cuts
- Pork ribs (after tender)
- Turkey fillets
- Veal chops (also on medium-low)

Medium-high heat:
- Most fish and shellfish

High heat:
- Salmon fillets and steaks
- Shrimp (peeled), scallops, and calamari

Sear on high; finish on medium:
- Beef and pork tenderloin
- Chicken thighs and drumsticks
- Hamburgers (switch to medium after searing each side 1 minute)
- Hot dogs (switch to medium when deeply brown all over)
- Lamb chops and butterflied leg of lamb
- Steak
- Tuna steaks
- Uncooked sausage
- Venison steaks

---

season's best

Strawberries Romanoff

This is our interpretation of the classic recipe invented by French chef Marie Antoine Carême for the Russian aristocracy in the early 19th century.

This dessert is one of the best uses for truly fresh strawberries, which are at their peak most everywhere in May. We've increased the amounts of the berries, sugar, and Cointreau, and subtracted a touch of cream to keep the focus where it belongs: on the fruit. The name and history may sound a bit distant, but this simple dessert is as close to home as your next basket of berries.

Strawberries Romanoff

Cointreau is a clear liqueur with an intense orange flavor. Its presence here—along with real whipping cream—makes this dessert truly authentic. If you would rather not use alcohol, substitute orange juice.

- 3 cups quartered fresh strawberries
- 3 tablespoons granulated sugar
- 3 tablespoons Cointreau or other orange-flavored liqueur
- ¼ cup whipping cream
- 3 tablespoons powdered sugar

1. Combine first 3 ingredients in a large bowl; cover and refrigerate 30 minutes.

2. Combine whipping cream and powdered sugar in a small bowl, and beat with a mixer at high speed until stiff peaks form.

3. Spoon ¾ cup strawberry mixture into each of 4 dessert bowls. Top each serving with 1 tablespoon whipping cream mixture. Yield: 4 servings.

CALORIES 139 (7% from fat); FAT 1.3g (sat 0.6g, mono 0.1g, poly 0.2g); PROTEIN 1.8g; CARB 33.7g; FIBER 2.7g; CHOL 18mg; IRON 0.5mg; SODIUM 10mg; CALC 33mg

new ingredient

Great Grain

Spelt (also called "farro") is one of the first cultivated grains and is making a comeback.

Resources

Look for spelt—often labeled "spelt berries"—at health food stores, or order spelt berries, flours, and pastas online at www.purityfoods.com or www.bobsredmill.com.

Insalata di Farro
Spelt Salad

This salad is delicious served chilled or at room temperature. Make it a day ahead to let the flavors blend and bloom. It can be part of a light lunch with some crusty bread and fresh fruit or can work as a side dish for a simple meat or poultry entrée.

DRESSING:
- 2 tablespoons chopped fresh flat-leaf parsley
- 2 tablespoons vegetable broth
- 1½ tablespoons extravirgin olive oil
- 1 tablespoon fresh lemon juice
- 1 tablespoon red wine vinegar
- 1 tablespoon Dijon mustard
- ½ teaspoon salt
- ¼ teaspoon black pepper
- 1 garlic clove, crushed

SALAD:
- 1¼ cups uncooked spelt (farro), rinsed and drained
- 1½ cups vegetable broth
- 1 cup water
- 1 cup (1-inch) cut green beans
- ¾ cup (¼-inch) sliced carrots
- ½ cup frozen green peas, thawed
- ½ cup frozen whole-kernel corn, thawed
- ½ cup marinated artichoke hearts, drained and chopped
- ¼ cup pitted ripe olives
- ¼ cup pitted green olives
- 1 (7-ounce) bottle roasted red bell peppers, drained and chopped

1. To prepare dressing, combine first 9 ingredients in a small bowl, stirring well with a whisk.

2. To prepare salad, combine spelt, 1½ cups broth, and 1 cup water in a saucepan, and bring to a boil. Reduce heat, and simmer 25 minutes. Drain.

3. While spelt is cooking, bring water to a boil in a medium saucepan, and add beans and carrots. Cook until crisp-tender. Drain and plunge into cold water. Drain again. Combine spelt, beans, carrots, peas, and remaining 5 ingredients in a large bowl. Add dressing, and toss well to coat. Let stand 30 minutes, stirring

---

occasionally. Yield: 6 servings (serving size: 1 cup).

CALORIES 234 (29% from fat); FAT 7.6g (sat 0.7g, mono 3.7g, poly 0.7g); PROTEIN 7.8g; CARB 40.5g; FIBER 9.4g; CHOL 0mg; IRON 2.8mg; SODIUM 837mg; CALC 41mg

Vegetable-Bean Soup with Spelt

You can substitute barley or wheat berries for the spelt.

- 2 teaspoons olive oil
- 1½ cups chopped onion
- 1½ cups chopped leek
- ½ cup chopped carrot
- 3 garlic cloves, chopped
- ½ cup chopped country ham (about 1 ounce)
- 2 cups water
- 1 cup uncooked spelt (farro), rinsed and drained
- ½ teaspoon salt
- ½ teaspoon freshly ground black pepper
- ¼ teaspoon crushed red pepper
- 2 (14-ounce) cans fat-free, less-sodium chicken broth
- 2 bay leaves
- 1 thyme sprig
- 2 cups chopped beet greens
- 2 (16-ounce) cans cannellini beans, rinsed and drained
- 1 (14.5-ounce) can diced tomatoes, undrained
- ¼ cup (1 ounce) grated Parmigiano-Reggiano cheese

1. Heat oil in a Dutch oven over medium-high heat. Add onion, leek, carrot, and garlic; sauté 5 minutes. Add ham; sauté 2 minutes. Stir in water and next 7 ingredients; bring to a boil.

2. Cover, reduce heat, and simmer 30 minutes. Add greens, beans, and tomatoes; bring to a boil. Reduce heat; simmer 5 minutes. Discard bay leaves, and garnish each serving with cheese. Yield: 8 servings (serving size: 1¼ cups soup and 1½ teaspoons cheese).

CALORIES 238 (14% from fat); FAT 3.6g (sat 0.9g, mono 1.3g, poly 0.2g); PROTEIN 12.3g; CARB 42.8g; FIBER 13.1g; CHOL 5mg; IRON 1.9mg; SODIUM 412mg; CALC 90mg

Farrotto with Greens and Parmesan

This spin on Italian risotto uses spelt, or farro, instead of rice.

    1   tablespoon olive oil
    2¼   cups chopped red onion
    4   garlic cloves, minced
    1   cup uncooked spelt (farro), rinsed
         and drained
    1   cup Chardonnay or other dry
         white wine
    1   (14½-ounce) can vegetable broth
    2   cups water
    ¼   teaspoon freshly ground black
         pepper
    4   cups chopped gourmet salad greens
    ½   cup (2 ounces) grated Parmigiano-
         Reggiano cheese

1. Heat oil in a large saucepan over medium-high heat. Add onion and garlic; sauté 7 minutes or until golden brown. Add spelt; sauté 2 minutes. Stir in wine; cook 3 minutes. Add broth; cook 12 minutes or until liquid is nearly absorbed, stirring frequently. Stir in water and pepper; cook 12 minutes or until liquid is nearly absorbed, stirring frequently. Remove from heat. Stir in greens and cheese. Yield: 4 servings (serving size: 1 cup).

CALORIES 283 (28% from fat); FAT 9g (sat 2.9g, mono 3.6g, poly 0.4g); PROTEIN 12.1g; CARB 44.8g; FIBER 10.2g; CHOL 15mg; IRON 3.1mg; SODIUM 605mg; CALC 220mg

MAKE AHEAD
Baked Spelt Pudding

This unique dish is a rustic take on baked rice pudding. The long stint in the oven (3½ hours) gives the pudding a rich, creamy texture.

    ½   cup uncooked spelt (farro), rinsed
         and drained
    4   cups 2% reduced-fat milk
    ½   cup sugar
    ¼   teaspoon salt
    ⅛   teaspoon ground cardamom
    1   vanilla bean, split lengthwise
         Cooking spray
         Dash of ground cinnamon

1. Place spelt in a medium saucepan. Cover with water to 2 inches above spelt; bring to a boil. Cook 2 minutes; remove from heat. Cover and let stand 1 hour. Drain. Place spelt in a food processor; process 45 seconds or until spelt resembles coarse meal.

2. Preheat oven to 275°.

3. Combine spelt, milk, sugar, salt, cardamom, and vanilla in a 2-quart casserole coated with cooking spray. Bake at 275° for 3½ hours, stirring every hour to prevent a skin from forming. Remove vanilla bean. Let stand 5 minutes. Sprinkle with cinnamon. Serve warm or chilled. Yield: 6 servings (serving size: ⅔ cup).

CALORIES 211 (17% from fat); FAT 3.9g (sat 2g, mono 1g, poly 0g); PROTEIN 7.4g; CARB 39g; FIBER 2.6g; CHOL 13mg; IRON 0.8mg; SODIUM 185mg; CALC 185mg

MAKE AHEAD
Lamb and Green Bean Stew with Spelt

You can substitute pork or beef for the lamb.

         Cooking spray
    1   pound lamb stew meat
    1½   cups vertically sliced onion
    2   garlic cloves, crushed
    ½   cup dry red wine
    2   cups water
    ¾   cup uncooked spelt (farro),
         rinsed and drained
    ½   cup tomato sauce
    ¾   teaspoon salt
    ¼   teaspoon black pepper
    1   pound green beans, trimmed
    1   (14.5-ounce) can diced tomatoes,
         undrained
    1   bay leaf
    2   tablespoons thinly sliced fresh
         basil

1. Heat a Dutch oven coated with cooking spray over medium-high heat. Add lamb; cook 5 minutes, browning on all sides. Add onion and garlic; sauté 8 minutes. Add wine, scraping pan to loosen browned bits. Add water and next 7 ingredients; bring to a boil. Reduce heat, and simmer 1½ hours or until lamb is tender. Discard bay leaf; sprinkle servings evenly with basil. Yield: 4 servings (serving size: 2 cups).

CALORIES 398 (20% from fat); FAT 8.8g (sat 2.7g, mono 3g, poly 0.8g); PROTEIN 36.8g; CARB 47.8g; FIBER 10.9g; CHOL 92mg; IRON 6mg; SODIUM 823mg; CALC 99mg

cooking light profile

Martha's Moms

One of the country's most remarkable rowing crews—known as Martha's Moms—has the reputation for cooking good food, too. Here's one of the team's favorite recipes.

MAKE AHEAD
Marinated Onion Rings

Martha's Moms crew member Lynne Robbins brought this dish to one of the group's potlucks. It was an instant hit. Add it to your next cookout menu.

    6   cups thinly sliced Walla Walla or
         other sweet onion (about 2 large)
    2   cups thinly sliced peeled English
         cucumber (about 2 cucumbers)
    ¾   cup white vinegar
    ⅔   cup sugar
    ½   cup water
    1   tablespoon salt
    1   teaspoon dried dill

1. Combine onion and cucumber in a large bowl. Combine vinegar and remaining 4 ingredients in a small saucepan. Bring to a boil; cook 1 minute or until sugar dissolves, stirring occasionally. Pour hot vinegar mixture over onion mixture, tossing to coat. Cover and chill at least 8 hours or overnight. Yield: 24 servings (serving size: ⅓ cup).

CALORIES 60 (2% from fat); FAT 0.1g (sat 0g, mono 0g, poly 0.1g); PROTEIN 0.5g; CARB 14.7g; FIBER 0.7g; CHOL 0mg; IRON 0.2mg; SODIUM 211mg; CALC 12mg`

Maple-Glazed Salmon, page 138

Spicy Thai Chicken Salad,
page 164

Shrimp Po'boy with Spicy Ketchup,
page 160

Peaches and Blackberries in Balsamic-Pepper Syrup
with Pound Cake, page 149

Cate's Springtime Risotto Soup,
page 163

Mushroom Tamales, page 156 and
Roasted Tomato Salsa, page 155

Fast, Fabulous Fruit Desserts

In less than 15 minutes, you can enjoy dessert as sweet as a summer evening.

Sweet summer fruit is terrific served straight up—or you can put in just a little effort and harness the season's wildest flavors to create sophisticated desserts. Here are ways to complement textures with crunchy or creamy additions, and ways to spotlight intense natural tastes with tart or piquant notes, like balsamic vinegar, peppermint, red wine, pepper, and ginger.

Summer Cherries Jubilee

A cherry pitter will save you preparation time and prevent a red-stained thumb. If you don't want to use the wine, cranberry juice produces a beautiful color and a delicious, albeit different, result.

1½ cups pitted sweet cherries
½ cup Cabernet Sauvignon or other dry red wine
¼ cup cherry preserves
1 tablespoon amaretto (almond-flavored liqueur) (optional)
2 teaspoons fresh lemon juice
2 cups vanilla low-fat frozen yogurt

1. Combine first 3 ingredients in a small saucepan, and bring to a boil. Reduce heat, and simmer 5 minutes, stirring frequently. Stir in liqueur and lemon juice. Serve warm over yogurt. Yield: 4 servings (serving size: about ⅓ cup cherry sauce and ½ cup yogurt).

CALORIES 231 (7% from fat); FAT 1.9g (sat 1g, mono 0.5g, poly 0.2g); PROTEIN 5.2g; CARB 43.5g; FIBER 1.5g; CHOL 5mg; IRON 0.5mg; SODIUM 67mg; CALC 168mg

Chocolate-Raspberry Tiramisu

To make this tiramisu even fancier, use a mixture of red, gold, and black raspberries.

¼ cup powdered sugar
¼ cup (2 ounces) mascarpone cheese, softened
¼ cup raspberry-flavored liqueur, divided
1 (8-ounce) block fat-free cream cheese, softened
12 cake-style ladyfingers, split
1½ tablespoons unsweetened cocoa
2 cups fresh raspberries
Mint sprigs (optional)

1. Place powdered sugar, mascarpone cheese, 1½ tablespoons liqueur, and cream cheese in a large bowl; beat with a mixer at high speed until well blended.
2. Brush cut sides of ladyfingers with 2½ tablespoons liqueur. Spread about 1½ tablespoons mascarpone mixture over bottom half of each ladyfinger; cover with tops.
3. Arrange 3 filled ladyfingers spokelike on each of 4 dessert plates. Sprinkle evenly with cocoa. Arrange ½ cup raspberries over each serving. Garnish with mint sprigs, if desired. Yield: 4 servings.

CALORIES 348 (27% from fat); FAT 10.3g (sat 4.8g, mono 3.5g, poly 0.9g); PROTEIN 13.6g; CARB 46g; FIBER 5.2g; CHOL 144mg; IRON 1.8mg; SODIUM 331mg; CALC 209mg

Peaches and Blackberries in Balsamic-Pepper Syrup with Pound Cake

(pictured on page 147)

For the best result, use a high-quality balsamic vinegar and a fragrant honey.

¼ cup honey
3 tablespoons balsamic vinegar
¼ teaspoon freshly ground black pepper
2 cups sliced peeled peaches
2 cups blackberries
6 (2-ounce) slices commercial pound cake (such as Pepperidge Farm)

1. Combine first 3 ingredients in a large bowl, stirring with a whisk. Add peaches and berries; toss gently to coat. Let stand 5 minutes. Serve with cake slices. Yield: 6 servings (serving size: 1 cake slice and ⅔ cup fruit mixture).

CALORIES 311 (28% from fat); FAT 9.8g (sat 5.2g, mono 3.6g, poly 0.7g); PROTEIN 4.5g; CARB 54g; FIBER 4.5g; CHOL 81mg; IRON 1mg; SODIUM 209mg; CALC 51mg

Raspberry Melba

Peach melba is reversed with puréed peaches and whole raspberries.

¼ cup peach nectar
2 tablespoons sugar
2 teaspoons fresh lemon juice
1 pound peeled ripe peaches, coarsely chopped
2 cups raspberry sorbet
1 cup fresh raspberries

1. Combine first 4 ingredients in a food processor; process until smooth. Let stand at room temperature 5 minutes.
2. Spoon ¼ cup peach purée into each of 4 parfait glasses; top each serving with ¼ cup sorbet and 2 tablespoons raspberries. Repeat layers with remaining purée, sorbet, and raspberries. Yield: 4 servings.

CALORIES 179 (2% from fat); FAT 0.4g (sat 0g, mono 0.1g, poly 0.2g); PROTEIN 2.3g; CARB 45g; FIBER 4.3g; CHOL 0mg; IRON 0.5mg; SODIUM 5mg; CALC 18mg

Chocolate Strawberries with Mint Dip

Be sure the berries are completely dry so the chocolate will adhere. Dipped strawberries need to be refrigerated for a few minutes so the chocolate can set, but they're best served at room temperature.

    16 strawberries with stems
     3 ounces bittersweet chocolate,
        coarsely chopped
    ¼ teaspoon peppermint extract
     1 (8-ounce) carton vanilla fat-free
        yogurt

1. Rinse berries; pat dry.
2. Place chocolate in a medium microwave-safe glass bowl. Microwave at HIGH 45 seconds or until almost melted; stir until smooth. Dip bottom half of each strawberry into melted chocolate; let excess chocolate drip off. Place on a wax paper-lined baking sheet. Chill strawberries 5 minutes or until set.
3. Combine peppermint extract and yogurt. Yield: 4 servings (serving size: 4 strawberries and ¼ cup dip).

CALORIES 204 (34% from fat); FAT 7.7g (sat 4.5g, mono 0.7g, poly 0.3g); PROTEIN 5g; CARB 29.7g; FIBER 4.1g; CHOL 2mg; IRON 0.6mg; SODIUM 41mg; CALC 117mg

Plum and Candied-Ginger Sundaes

     1 tablespoon butter
    ¼ cup Grand Marnier (orange-
        flavored liqueur)
     3 tablespoons sugar
     1 pound plums, pitted and thinly
        sliced
     2 tablespoons finely chopped
        crystallized ginger
     2 cups orange sherbet

1. Melt butter in a nonstick skillet over medium heat. Add liqueur, sugar, and plums, stirring until sugar dissolves. Reduce heat to medium-low; cook 4 minutes or until plums are tender and liquid is slightly thick, stirring frequently. Stir in ginger; simmer 2 minutes.

2. Spoon warm plum sauce over sherbet. Serve immediately. Yield: 4 servings (serving size: ½ cup sauce and ½ cup sherbet).

CALORIES 256 (13% from fat); FAT 3.6g (sat 1.9g, mono 1.3g, poly 0.3g); PROTEIN 1.4g; CARB 56g; FIBER 1.9g; CHOL 8mg; IRON 1.2mg; SODIUM 40mg; CALC 21mg

Fruited Apricots with Lemon-Amaretto Sauce

     2 tablespoons amaretto (almond-
        flavored liqueur)
    1½ teaspoons grated lemon rind
     1 teaspoon fresh lemon juice
     1 (8-ounce) carton lemon low-fat
        yogurt
     6 apricots, halved and pitted
        (about 1½ pounds)
     1 cup blackberries or other berries
    ¼ cup slivered almonds, toasted

1. Combine first 4 ingredients.
2. Arrange 3 apricot halves on each of 4 plates. Spoon 1 tablespoon blackberries into center of each apricot half. Spoon 3 tablespoons yogurt mixture over each serving; sprinkle each serving with 1 tablespoon blackberries and 1 tablespoon almonds. Yield: 4 servings.

CALORIES 170 (29% from fat); FAT 5.4g (sat 0.8g, mono 3.1g, poly 1.1g); PROTEIN 5.6g; CARB 23.3g; FIBER 3.8g; CHOL 3mg; IRON 0.9mg; SODIUM 39mg; CALC 138mg

Macerated Mixed Melon

Any melon except watermelon, which is too watery, can be used in this recipe. To get thickly grated lemon rind, use a channel knife or a zester with large holes.

    ⅓ cup brandy
    ¼ cup sugar
     2 tablespoons thickly grated lemon
        rind
     2 tablespoons fresh lemon
        juice
     2 cups honeydew melon balls or
        cubes
     2 cups cantaloupe balls or cubes
    ¼ cup slivered almonds, toasted
     4 (⅛-inch) slices lemon

1. Combine first 4 ingredients in a large bowl, stirring with a whisk until sugar dissolves. Add honeydew and cantaloupe; toss gently to coat. Let stand 10 minutes. Sprinkle each serving with toasted almonds, and serve with lemon slices. Yield: 4 servings (serving size: 1 cup melon mixture, 1 tablespoon almonds, and 1 lemon slice).

CALORIES 211 (19% from fat); FAT 4.5g (sat 0.4g, mono 2.8g, poly 1g); PROTEIN 2.7g; CARB 31.5g; FIBER 2.2g; CHOL 0mg; IRON 0.5mg; SODIUM 19mg; CALC 37mg

from the pantry

Get Crackin'

The power of freshly ground black pepper will boost your recipes' flavor factor.

It's easy to understand why pepper is found on nearly every tabletop. Pepper makes food livelier and engages the palate as do few other ingredients.

East Asian Pork Strips

The freshly ground pepper in the marinade releases an intense aroma when the pork chops are seared in a hot skillet. Rice with toasted sesame seeds pairs nicely with the Bourbon-spiked flavor of the pork chops.

    ½ cup chopped onion
     2 tablespoons bourbon
    ½ teaspoon freshly ground black
        pepper
     4 (4-ounce) boneless center-cut loin
        pork chops, trimmed and cut into
        ½-inch strips
    ¼ cup low-sodium soy sauce
    1½ tablespoons white vinegar
     4 teaspoons sugar
     4 teaspoons chopped peeled fresh
        ginger
    ½ teaspoon cornstarch
    ½ teaspoon honey
     3 tablespoons thinly sliced green
        onions
    1½ teaspoons vegetable oil

1. Combine first 3 ingredients in a large zip-top plastic bag, and add pork to bag. Seal and marinate in refrigerator 30 minutes.

2. Combine soy sauce and next 5 ingredients in a blender, and process until smooth. Pour soy mixture into a small saucepan, and bring to a boil. Cook 1 minute, stirring constantly. Remove mixture from heat; stir in green onions.

3. Heat oil in a large nonstick skillet over medium-high heat. Add pork mixture to pan; cook 6 minutes or until pork loses its pink color, stirring frequently. Serve pork with sauce. Yield: 4 servings (serving size: 3 ounces meat and about 1½ tablespoons sauce).

CALORIES 229 (28% from fat); FAT 7.2g (sat 2.3g, mono 3.3g, poly 0.9g); PROTEIN 26g; CARB 13.9g; FIBER 0.8g; CHOL 63mg; IRON 1.4mg; SODIUM 675mg; CALC 34mg

QUICK & EASY • MAKE AHEAD
Nouveau French Potato Salad

Make this salad a day in advance, but toss in the radishes just before serving to keep them from discoloring the potatoes. Serve the salad alongside grilled lamb chops and steamed asparagus.

  2 pounds small red potatoes
  ½ cup minced shallots
  6 tablespoons white wine vinegar, divided
  ¼ cup chopped fresh parsley
  2 tablespoons olive oil
  ¾ teaspoon salt
  ¼ teaspoon freshly ground black pepper
  ½ cup sliced radishes
  3 tablespoons chopped fresh chives

1. Place potatoes in a saucepan, and cover with water; bring to a boil. Reduce heat; simmer 10 minutes or until tender. Drain and rinse with cold water. Cool. Cut potatoes into ¼-inch-thick slices. Place potatoes in a large bowl; add shallots, 2 tablespoons vinegar, and parsley. Toss gently.

2. Combine ¼ cup vinegar, oil, salt, and pepper in a small bowl; stir well with a whisk. Pour dressing over potato mixture;

toss gently to coat. Add radishes; toss gently. Sprinkle with chives. Yield: 6 servings (serving size: 1 cup).

CALORIES 150 (29% from fat); FAT 4.8g (sat 0.6g, mono 3.3g, poly 0.4g); PROTEIN 4g; CARB 22.2g; FIBER 3g; CHOL 0mg; IRON 1.4mg; SODIUM 302mg; CALC 21mg

Measure of a Mill

When using freshly ground pepper, most cooks don't actually measure. They simply grind away and stop instinctively. But in the *Cooking Light* Test Kitchens, we strive for results you can repeat at home. Accuracy counts. So before testing begins, *CL* Test Kitchen staffers crank away on the pepper mills, accumulating enough freshly ground pepper for the recipes. Based on our experience, 10 full cranks of the mill produces about ¼ teaspoon of coarsely ground pepper.

QUICK & EASY
Mesclun Salad with Cucumber and Feta

Mesclun is a mix of delicate, small salad greens; it's sometimes sold in bags labeled "gourmet salad greens."

DRESSING:
  2 tablespoons tomato juice
  1 tablespoon rice vinegar
  1 teaspoon extravirgin olive oil
  ½ teaspoon sugar
  ¼ teaspoon salt
  ⅛ teaspoon freshly ground black pepper

SALAD:
  6 cups mesclun (gourmet salad greens)
  ⅓ cup thinly sliced peeled English cucumber
  2 tablespoons crumbled feta cheese
  2 tablespoons thinly sliced green onions

1. To prepare dressing, combine first 6 ingredients in a small bowl, stirring with a whisk.

2. To prepare salad, combine mesclun and remaining 3 ingredients in a large bowl. Drizzle dressing over salad, tossing gently to coat. Yield: 4 servings (serving size: 1½ cups).

CALORIES 44 (49% from fat); FAT 2.4g (sat 0.9g, mono 1.1g, poly 0.2g); PROTEIN 2.1g; CARB 4.1g; FIBER 2.1g; CHOL 4mg; IRON 1.2mg; SODIUM 247mg; CALC 71mg

QUICK & EASY
Pasta with Sautéed Tomatoes, Olives, and Artichokes

Because this dish cooks quickly, assemble all the ingredients before you begin. Pass the pepper mill around the table for those who prefer even more of the spice.

  1 teaspoon olive oil
  2 cups halved cherry tomatoes
  ½ cup thinly sliced pitted kalamata olives
  1 (14-ounce) can quartered artichoke hearts, drained
  4 cups hot cooked ziti (about 8 cups uncooked short tube-shaped pasta)
  ½ cup chopped fresh basil
  ⅓ cup (1¼ ounces) shredded Asiago cheese
  ¼ teaspoon salt
  ¼ teaspoon freshly ground black pepper

1. Heat oil in a large nonstick skillet over medium-high heat. Add tomatoes, olives, and artichokes; sauté 5 minutes or until thoroughly heated. Place pasta in a large bowl. Add tomato mixture, basil, cheese, salt, and pepper; toss well. Yield: 6 servings (serving size: 1 cup).

CALORIES 287 (17% from fat); FAT 5.4g (sat 1.6g, mono 2.1g, poly 1g); PROTEIN 12.5g; CARB 48.2g; FIBER 6.1g; CHOL 55mg; IRON 2.5mg; SODIUM 626mg; CALC 85mg

From Mother's, with Love

At a popular Portland, Oregon, restaurant, every day is Mother's Day.

Meet Sophia Damiani, Rose Hassin, Therese Dieringer, and Jan Boccuzzi—all moms to chef Lisa Schroeder. In Lisa's opinion, you can never have too many. That idea provided the concept for Mother's Bistro and Bar, the restaurant she founded in January 2000. Twelve times a year, she celebrates a different mother—and that mom's favorite dishes—with the bistro's "Mother of the Month" (M.O.M.) award.

QUICK & EASY • MAKE AHEAD
Mother's Cioppino

CROSTINI:

- 1 (1-pound) loaf French bread baguette, cut into 16 slices
- 1 tablespoon olive oil

CIOPPINO:

- 2 teaspoons olive oil
- ½ to 1 teaspoon crushed red pepper
- 4 garlic cloves, finely chopped
- 3 cups clam juice
- 1 cup water
- ½ cup finely chopped fresh parsley
- ½ teaspoon dried basil
- ¼ teaspoon dried thyme
- 1 (26-ounce) bottle tomato-and-basil pasta sauce (such as Bertolli)
- 16 littleneck clams
- 16 small mussels, scrubbed and debearded
- ½ cup dry white wine
- ½ teaspoon salt
- ¼ teaspoon black pepper
- 1 pound cod or other lean whitefish fillets, cut into 1-inch pieces
- ½ pound medium shrimp, peeled and deveined
- 2 cups torn spinach

1. Preheat oven to 350°.
2. To prepare crostini, place bread slices on a large baking sheet; brush with 1 tablespoon olive oil. Bake at 350° for 15 minutes or until lightly browned.

3. To prepare cioppino, heat 2 teaspoons oil in a Dutch oven over medium-high heat. Add red pepper and garlic; sauté 30 seconds. Stir in clam juice and next 5 ingredients. Add clams and mussels. Cover and cook 10 minutes or until shells open. (Discard any unopened shells.) Add wine and next 4 ingredients; simmer 5 minutes or until fish and shrimp are done. Stir in spinach. Serve with crostini. Yield: 8 servings (serving size: 1¼ cups cioppino and 2 crostini).

CALORIES 467 (24% from fat); FAT 12.4g (sat 1.7g, mono 4g, poly 3.6g); PROTEIN 31g; CARB 53g; FIBER 9.8g; CHOL 89mg; IRON 9.3mg; SODIUM 1,182mg; CALC 87mg

Pastitsio

Sophia Damiani likes to freeze and then reheat individual squares of this Greek lasagna in the microwave.

FILLING:

- 1 pound uncooked bucatini pasta or spaghetti
- 1 pound ground sirloin
- ½ cup finely chopped onion
- 3 garlic cloves, minced
- ½ cup dry white wine
- 1 (15-ounce) can tomato sauce
- ½ teaspoon salt
- ½ teaspoon ground nutmeg
- ½ teaspoon black pepper

WHITE SAUCE:

- 3 tablespoons all-purpose flour
- ½ teaspoon salt
- 3 cups 2% reduced-fat milk
- 2 large eggs, lightly beaten
- 2 large egg whites, lightly beaten
- 5 tablespoons shredded kasseri or aged white Cheddar cheese, divided

Cooking spray
- ¼ cup (1 ounce) grated fresh pecorino Romano cheese

1. To prepare filling, cook pasta according to package directions, omitting salt and fat. Rinse with cold water; set aside.
2. Cook beef, onion, and garlic in a large nonstick skillet over medium-high heat until browned; stir to crumble. Add wine, tomato sauce, ½ teaspoon salt, nutmeg, and pepper; bring to a boil. Reduce heat; simmer 10 minutes or until thick.
3. Preheat oven to 350°.
4. To prepare white sauce, place flour and ½ teaspoon salt in a medium saucepan over medium heat. Gradually add milk, stirring constantly with a whisk until blended; bring to a boil. Reduce heat; simmer 10 minutes or until slightly thick, stirring constantly. Remove from heat; set aside. Combine eggs and egg whites in a large bowl. Gradually add hot milk mixture to egg, stirring constantly with a whisk. Stir in 1 tablespoon kasseri cheese until blended.
5. Spread 1 cup beef mixture in bottom of a 13 x 9-inch baking dish coated with cooking spray. Arrange half of pasta over beef mixture. Top with 1½ cups beef mixture. Repeat layers with remaining pasta and beef mixture. Top with white sauce. Sprinkle with 4 tablespoons kasseri and Romano cheese. Bake at 350° for 30 minutes. Let stand 15 minutes before serving. Yield: 8 servings.

WINE NOTE: A red wine with earthy flavors and good acidity makes a wonderful counterpoint to this casserole. One of the earthiest reds around is Chianti. Try Fonterutoli Chianti Classico 2000 (about $26), which has flavors of earth, dried leaves, and espresso.

CALORIES 416 (19% from fat); FAT 8.9g (sat 4.1g, mono 2.7g, poly 0.9g); PROTEIN 27g; CARB 54g; FIBER 2.4g; CHOL 97mg; IRON 4mg; SODIUM 790mg; CALC 207mg

Fashoulakia

Sophia's classic Greek green bean side is traditionally served at room temperature.

- 2 tablespoons olive oil
- 1 cup finely chopped onion
- ⅓ cup finely chopped fresh parsley
- 1 tablespoon finely chopped fresh mint
- 1 tablespoon finely chopped fresh or 1 teaspoon dried dill
- 2 garlic cloves, minced
- 2 pounds green beans, trimmed
- ½ teaspoon salt
- ½ teaspoon black pepper
- 2 (14.5-ounce) cans stewed tomatoes, undrained

1. Heat oil in a stockpot over medium-high heat. Add onion, and sauté 3 minutes. Add herbs and garlic; sauté 4 minutes. Add beans and remaining ingredients; bring to a boil. Cover, reduce heat, and simmer 30 minutes or until beans are tender. Yield: 8 servings (serving size: 1 cup).

CALORIES 105 (34% from fat); FAT 3.7g (sat 0.5g, mono 2.5g, poly 0.4g); PROTEIN 3.5g; CARB 17.5g; FIBER 5.4g; CHOL 0mg; IRON 2.4mg; SODIUM 382mg; CALC 93mg

Chicken Oreganata

This dish is best marinated overnight.

- 1 cup fresh lemon juice (about 5 lemons)
- 2 tablespoons olive oil
- 1½ tablespoons minced garlic
- 1½ teaspoons dried oregano
- 2 pounds skinless, boneless chicken thighs (about 8)
- Cooking spray
- ¼ teaspoon salt
- ⅛ teaspoon black pepper

1. Combine first 4 ingredients in a zip-top plastic bag; add chicken. Seal and marinate in refrigerator 3 hours or overnight, turning occasionally.
2. Preheat oven to 350°.
3. Remove chicken from bag; discard marinade. Place chicken in a single layer on a broiler pan coated with cooking spray; sprinkle with salt and pepper. Bake at 350° for 45 minutes or until chicken is done. Yield: 4 servings (serving size: 2 thighs).

CALORIES 356 (40% from fat); FAT 15.6g (sat 3.1g, mono 7.7g, poly 2.8g); PROTEIN 45g; CARB 8g; FIBER 1g; CHOL 188mg; IRON 2.8mg; SODIUM 342mg; CALC 40mg

Apple Strudel

This is one of Rose Hassin's specialties.

- 4 ounces day-old French bread or other firm white bread, coarsely chopped
- 3 tablespoons butter, divided
- 5 cups finely chopped peeled McIntosh apples (about 1¼ pounds)
- 1 cup sugar
- ½ cup golden raisins
- 1 teaspoon ground cinnamon
- 8 sheets frozen phyllo dough, thawed
- Cooking spray

1. Preheat oven to 375°.
2. Place bread in a food processor, and pulse 10 times or until coarse crumbs measure 1¼ cups.
3. Melt 1 tablespoon butter in a large skillet over medium-high heat; add breadcrumbs. Cook 4 minutes or until lightly browned; stir frequently. Combine breadcrumbs, apple, sugar, raisins, and cinnamon in a medium bowl; toss to combine.
4. Lightly coat each of 4 phyllo sheets with cooking spray, placing one on top of the other. Cover with plastic wrap; press gently to seal sheets together. Discard plastic wrap. Spoon 3 cups apple mixture along 1 long edge of stacked phyllo; leave a 2-inch border. Fold short edges of phyllo to cover 2 inches of apple mixture on each end. Start at long edge with 2-inch border; roll up jelly-roll fashion. (Do not roll tightly, or strudel may split.) Place strudel, seam side down, on a jelly roll pan coated with cooking spray. Repeat procedure with remaining phyllo dough, cooking spray, and apple mixture.
5. Melt 2 tablespoons butter, and brush over strudels. Bake at 375° 25 minutes or until golden. Cool on a wire rack 20 minutes before serving. Yield: 8 servings (serving size: 1 [3-inch] slice).

CALORIES 302 (18% from fat); FAT 6.1g (sat 3.1g, mono 2g, poly 0.5g); PROTEIN 3.1g; CARB 61g; FIBER 2.7g; CHOL 11mg; IRON 1.2mg; SODIUM 223mg; CALC 25mg

Cauliflower Soup

Rose's soup is best eaten right away.

- 2 tablespoons butter
- 2 cups finely chopped onion
- 4½ cups cauliflower florets (about 1 head)
- 3 cups chopped peeled baking potato
- ½ cup finely chopped carrot
- 1 teaspoon caraway seeds
- 6 cups fat-free, less-sodium chicken broth
- ½ teaspoon salt
- ⅛ teaspoon freshly ground black pepper

1. Melt butter in a Dutch oven over medium-high heat; add onion. Cook 4 minutes or until lightly browned; stir occasionally. Add cauliflower florets, potato, carrot, and caraway seeds. Cook 6 minutes or until cauliflower begins to brown; stir frequently. Add broth; bring to a boil. Reduce heat; simmer 20 minutes or until vegetables are tender. Stir in salt and pepper. Yield: 6 servings (serving size: 1½ cups).

CALORIES 166 (33% from fat); FAT 5.7g (sat 3g, mono 1.1g, poly 0.3g); PROTEIN 6.6g; CARB 24g; FIBER 4.2g; CHOL 14mg; IRON 0.8mg; SODIUM 371mg; CALC 52mg

Mother's Souvlakia

MARINADE:

- ½ cup thinly sliced onion
- 2 tablespoons olive oil
- 1½ teaspoons fresh lemon juice
- 1½ teaspoons finely chopped fresh parsley
- ¼ teaspoon dried oregano
- 1 bay leaf
- 1 pound skinless, boneless chicken breast, cut into 32 bite-sized pieces

Continued

½ red onion, cut into 8 (1-inch) pieces
½ large green bell pepper, cut into 8 (1-inch) pieces
8 button mushrooms
8 large cherry tomatoes
¼ teaspoon salt
¼ teaspoon black pepper
Cooking spray

1. To prepare marinade, combine first 6 ingredients in a large zip-top plastic bag; add chicken. Seal and marinate in refrigerator 3 hours; turn occasionally.
2. Prepare grill.
3. Remove chicken from bag; discard marinade. Thread 4 chicken pieces, 1 piece each red onion and bell pepper, 1 mushroom, and 1 tomato alternately onto each of 8 (10-inch) skewers. Sprinkle with salt and black pepper.
4. Place kabobs on grill rack coated with cooking spray; grill 12 minutes or until chicken is done, turning once. Serve with Tzatziki Sauce. Yield: 4 servings (serving size: 2 skewers and 2 tablespoons Tzatziki Sauce).

(Totals include Tzatziki Sauce) CALORIES 143 (31% from fat); FAT 4.8g (sat 0.9g, mono 2.9g, poly 0.5g); PROTEIN 16.5g; CARB 8.5g; FIBER 1.7g; CHOL 35mg; IRON 1mg; SODIUM 277mg; CALC 69mg

TZATZIKI SAUCE:

1 cup finely chopped seeded peeled cucumber
¼ teaspoon salt
1 (8-ounce) carton plain low-fat yogurt
1½ teaspoons chopped fresh parsley
½ teaspoon fresh lemon juice
½ teaspoon olive oil
⅛ teaspoon black pepper
1 garlic clove, minced

1. Place cucumber in a colander over a bowl; sprinkle with salt. Toss gently to coat. Cover; chill 1 hour. Rinse with cold water; drain well. Squeeze until barely moist.
2. Spoon yogurt onto several layers of heavy-duty paper towels; spread to ½-inch thickness. Cover with additional paper towels; let stand 5 minutes. Scrape into a bowl using a rubber spatula.
3. Combine cucumber, yogurt, parsley, and remaining ingredients in a bowl.

Serve with Mother's Souvlakia. Yield: 1 cup (serving size: 2 tablespoons).

CALORIES 21 (29% from fat); FAT 0.6g (sat 0.3g, mono 0.2g, poly 0g); PROTEIN 1.5g; CARB 2g; FIBER 0.1g; CHOL 3mg; IRON 0.1mg; SODIUM 91mg; CALC 53mg

MAKE AHEAD
Chicken Paprikas

Therese Dieringer makes this dish for family get-togethers. It's great to make ahead and reheat.

2 chicken breast halves (about 1 pound), skinned
2 chicken drumsticks (about ½ pound), skinned
2 chicken thighs (about ½ pound), skinned
½ teaspoon salt, divided
½ teaspoon black pepper, divided
Cooking spray
2 cups chopped onion
½ cup fat-free, less-sodium chicken broth
1½ tablespoons Hungarian sweet paprika
2 tablespoons all-purpose flour
1 cup low-fat sour cream
4 cups cooked medium egg noodles (about 2¾ cups uncooked pasta)

1. Sprinkle chicken with ¼ teaspoon salt and ¼ teaspoon pepper. Heat a Dutch oven coated with cooking spray over medium-high heat. Add chicken; cook 6 minutes or until lightly browned. Remove chicken from pan.
2. Add onion to pan; sauté 5 minutes or until lightly browned. Return chicken to pan. Stir in broth and paprika; bring to a boil. Cover, reduce heat, and simmer 30 minutes or until chicken is done. Remove from heat.
3. Place flour in a small bowl. Add sour cream, stirring well with a whisk. Gradually stir sour cream mixture, ¼ teaspoon salt, and ¼ teaspoon pepper into chicken mixture. Cook over low heat 5 minutes or until thick, stirring occasionally. Serve over noodles. Yield: 4 servings (serving size: about 4 ounces chicken, ½ cup sauce, and 1 cup noodles).

WINE NOTE: Paprika is bold and piquant, but not hot. Dishes with the spice work well with red wines that have a lot of fruit to cushion it. Try Wolf Blass "Red Label" Shiraz/Cabernet 1998 (South Australia, Australia; about $12). With juicy ripe blackberry flavors, it's perfect.

CALORIES 600 (20% from fat); FAT 13g (sat 6g, mono 2.3g, poly 2g); PROTEIN 62g; CARB 54g; FIBER 3.4g; CHOL 229mg; IRON 3.3mg; SODIUM 573mg; CALC 141mg

Jan's Ragù

This is Jan Boccuzzi's simple, but classic, ragù—rich with wine, herbs, beef, and pork.

1 pound boneless Boston Butt pork roast, cut into ½-inch pieces
2 cups chopped onion
1 pound ground sirloin
¼ cup dry red wine
1 cup water
2 tablespoons chopped fresh basil
1 teaspoon sugar
½ teaspoon salt
2 (28-ounce) cans crushed tomatoes, undrained
8 cups hot cooked rigatoni (about 5 cups uncooked large tube-shaped pasta)
Thinly sliced basil (optional)

1. Heat a Dutch oven over medium-high heat; add pork. Cook 3 minutes, browning on all sides. Add onion; cook 4 minutes. Add beef; cook 3 minutes or until beef loses its pink color, stirring to crumble. Add wine; cook 7 minutes or until liquid almost evaporates.
2. Add water and next 4 ingredients; bring to a boil. Cover, reduce heat, and simmer 30 minutes. Uncover and cook 1 hour or until pork is tender. Serve with pasta. Garnish with basil, if desired. Yield: 8 servings (serving size: 1 cup pasta and 1 cup sauce).

CALORIES 449 (29% from fat); FAT 14.2g (sat 4.7g, mono 5.7g, poly 1.9g); PROTEIN 30g; CARB 51g; FIBER 6.7g; CHOL 107mg; IRON 5mg; SODIUM 556mg; CALC 59mg

inspired vegetarian

Cinco de Mayo

Celebrate America's favorite Mexican holiday with a festive meatless menu.

Cinco de Mayo traditionally involves elaborate preparations, including many meat-centered dishes. This menu, though, maintains the authentic feel and flavors of Cinco de Mayo with meat-free dishes.

Cinco de Mayo Menu
serves 8

Easy Sangría

Guacamole with Chipotle Tortilla Chips

Roasted Tomato Salsa

Watermelon Gazpacho

Mushroom Tamales, Tofu Mole Enchiladas, or **Chiles Rellenos Gratin**

Coconut Flan

MAKE AHEAD
Easy Sangría

After the last of the sangría has been poured, enjoying the wine-infused orange wedges is a special treat.

1   (1.5-liter) bottle dry red wine, divided
2   tablespoons brandy
2   tablespoons Triple Sec (orange-flavored liqueur)
⅓   cup sugar
⅔   cup fresh orange juice
2   tablespoons fresh lime juice
2   tablespoons fresh lemon juice
5   whole cloves
3   whole allspice
1   (3-inch) cinnamon stick
2   cups sparkling water, chilled
8   orange wedges
5   lemon slices
5   lime slices

1. Combine ½ cup wine, brandy, liqueur, and sugar in a 2-quart glass measure.

Microwave at HIGH 1 minute or until mixture is warm; stir to dissolve sugar. Stir in remaining wine, juices, cloves, allspice, and cinnamon. Chill at least 2 hours.
2. Strain mixture into a pitcher, and discard spices. Just before serving, stir in sparkling water and remaining ingredients. Yield: 8 servings (serving size: about ¾ cup).

CALORIES 199 (0% from fat); FAT 0.1g (sat 0g, mono 0g, poly 0.1g); PROTEIN 0.6g; CARB 15.8g; FIBER 0.1g; CHOL 0mg; IRON 0.9mg; SODIUM 10mg; CALC 18mg

---

QUICK & EASY
Guacamole with Chipotle Tortilla Chips

Chipotle chile powder gives the crunchy chips a smoky kick that pairs well with the buttery guacamole. Use ground cumin or regular chili powder in its place, if you prefer. Prepare the chips up to a day ahead, and store in a zip-top plastic bag.

CHIPS:
8   (6-inch) corn tortillas
Cooking spray
½   teaspoon salt
½   teaspoon chipotle chile powder (such as McCormick)

GUACAMOLE:
3   tomatillos
⅓   cup chopped onion
⅓   cup chopped plum tomato
3   tablespoons chopped fresh cilantro
1   tablespoon fresh lime juice
¾   teaspoon salt
2   ripe peeled avocados, seeded and coarsely mashed
2   jalapeño peppers, seeded and finely chopped
1   garlic clove, minced

1. Preheat oven to 375°.
2. To prepare chips, cut each tortilla into 8 wedges; arrange tortilla wedges in a single layer on 2 baking sheets coated with cooking spray. Sprinkle wedges with ½ teaspoon salt and chile powder; lightly coat wedges with cooking spray. Bake at 375° for 12 minutes or until

wedges are crisp and lightly browned. Cool 10 minutes.
3. To prepare guacamole, peel papery husk from tomatillos; wash, core, and finely chop. Combine tomatillos, onion, and remaining 7 ingredients; stir well. Serve guacamole with chips. Yield: 16 servings (serving size: 2 tablespoons guacamole and 4 chips).

CALORIES 57 (41% from fat); FAT 2.6g (sat 0.4g, mono 1.5g, poly 0.5g); PROTEIN 1.2g; CARB 8.3g; FIBER 1.7g; CHOL 0mg; IRON 0.4mg; SODIUM 207mg; CALC 27mg

---

QUICK & EASY • MAKE AHEAD
Roasted Tomato Salsa
(pictured on page 148)

Blackening the tomatoes, jalapeños, and garlic in a cast iron skillet imbues the salsa with a smoky flavor. Leave in the jalapeño seeds for even more bite. Serve with baked tortilla chips or as a topping for Mushroom Tamales (recipe on page 156). You can make the salsa up to 2 days ahead.

2   large ripe tomatoes (about 1¼ pounds)
2   to 3 jalapeño peppers
1   garlic clove, unpeeled
⅓   cup finely chopped Vidalia or other sweet onion
¼   cup chopped fresh cilantro
2   tablespoons fresh lime juice
½   teaspoon salt

1. Heat a large cast iron skillet over medium heat. Add tomatoes, jalapeños, and garlic; cook 15 minutes or until tomatoes are blackened, turning frequently. Remove from pan; cool slightly.
2. Peel, seed, and chop tomatoes; place in a medium bowl. Remove and discard stems and seeds from jalapeños, and finely chop. Add to tomatoes. Peel garlic, and finely chop. Add to tomato mixture. Add onion, cilantro, lime juice, and salt to tomato mixture, and toss well to combine. Yield: 2 cups (serving size: ¼ cup).

CALORIES 15 (12% from fat); FAT 0.2g (sat 0g, mono 0g, poly 0.1g); PROTEIN 0.6g; CARB 3.5g; FIBER 0.8g; CHOL 0mg; IRON 0.3mg; SODIUM 151mg; CALC 6mg

QUICK & EASY • MAKE AHEAD
Watermelon Gazpacho

The flavors of this cold soup are incredibly refreshing. It's easy to make in a food processor; just be sure not to purée the mixture. Use short pulses to finely chop the ingredients so the soup retains some texture. Prepare earlier in the day, and chill thoroughly.

　6　cups cubed seeded watermelon
　1　cup coarsely chopped seeded peeled English cucumber
　½　cup coarsely chopped yellow bell pepper
　⅓　cup chopped green onions
　3　tablespoons chopped fresh mint
　3　tablespoons fresh lime juice
　1　tablespoon extravirgin olive oil
　¾　teaspoon salt
　½　teaspoon hot sauce
　1　garlic clove, minced
　1　cup cranberry-raspberry juice

1. Combine first 10 ingredients. Place half of watermelon mixture in a food processor, and pulse 3 or 4 times or until finely chopped. Spoon into a large bowl. Repeat procedure with remaining watermelon mixture. Stir in cranberry-raspberry juice. Chill thoroughly. Yield: 8 servings (serving size: ¾ cup).

CALORIES 81 (24% from fat); FAT 2.2g (sat 0.3g, mono 1.4g, poly 0.3g); PROTEIN 1g; CARB 15.6g; FIBER 1.1g; CHOL 0mg; IRON 0.4mg; SODIUM 226mg; CALC 18mg

FREEZABLE
Mushroom Tamales
(pictured on page 148)

Making tamales can be a group activity. If you can arrange it, have your guests join you to fill and roll them. Just make the filling and dough beforehand (up to a day) so everything's ready. Coarse-ground *masa harina*, available at Latin markets and in some large supermarkets, gives the best texture to the tamales. Dried *pasilla* chiles are medium-hot and contribute some heat to the dish. These are great topped with Roasted Tomato Salsa (recipe on page 155).

FILLING:

　4　garlic cloves, unpeeled
　3　pasilla chiles, stemmed and seeded
　¼　cup dried porcini mushrooms (about ¼ ounce)
　3　sun-dried tomatoes, packed without oil
　2　cups boiling water
　1　large ripe tomato (about 10 ounces)
Cooking spray
　½　cup finely chopped onion
　2　cups chopped portobello mushroom caps (about 4 ounces)
　½　teaspoon dried oregano
　1½　tablespoons chopped fresh cilantro
　1　tablespoon fresh lime juice
　½　teaspoon salt
　20　large dried cornhusks

DOUGH:

　⅔　cup fresh corn kernels
　2½　cups coarse-ground masa harina
　1　teaspoon baking powder
　½　teaspoon salt
　2¼　cups warm vegetable broth, divided
　3　tablespoons vegetable shortening

1. To prepare filling, heat a large cast iron skillet over medium heat. Add garlic; cook 15 minutes or until blackened, turning occasionally. Remove garlic from pan. Cool and peel.
2. Add chiles to pan; flatten with a spatula. Cook 20 seconds on each side or until blackened.
3. Place chiles, porcini, and sun-dried tomatoes in a large bowl. Pour boiling water over chile mixture. Cover and let stand 30 minutes or until tender. Drain in a colander over a bowl, reserving 2½ tablespoons soaking liquid. Place garlic, chile mixture, and reserved liquid in a food processor; process 1 minute or until smooth. Set aside.
4. While chiles soak, heat pan over medium heat. Add large tomato; cook 15 minutes or until blackened, turning frequently. Remove tomato from pan; cool slightly. Peel, core, and chop tomato. Wipe pan clean with paper towels; coat with cooking spray. Heat pan over medium-high heat. Add onion; sauté 4 minutes or until tender. Stir in chile mixture, chopped tomato, portobello mushrooms, and oregano; cook over medium heat 15 minutes or until thick. Stir in cilantro, juice, and ½ teaspoon salt; set aside.
5. Place cornhusks in a large bowl of hot water; weigh down husks with another bowl. Soak at least 30 minutes. Drain husks; rinse with cold water. Drain and pat dry. Tear 4 cornhusks lengthwise into 16 (½-inch-wide) strips.
6. To prepare dough, place corn in a food processor; process until smooth. Combine masa, baking powder, and ½ teaspoon salt. Add 2 cups broth; stir until well blended. Place shortening in a large bowl, and beat with a mixer at medium speed 1 minute or until fluffy. Add puréed corn and ¼ cup broth; beat at medium speed until well blended. Add masa mixture; beat 2 minutes or until well blended.
7. Open 1 cornhusk, curved side up. Place 3 tablespoons dough in center of husk, and spread evenly into a 4 x 2-inch rectangle. Arrange about 1½ tablespoons filling down center of dough. Take 1 long side of husk, and roll dough around filling, making sure dough seals around filling. Fold empty tapered end of husk over bundle. Tie 1 husk strip around tamale and over folded end to secure (top of tamale will be open). Repeat procedure with remaining husks, dough, and filling.
8. Stand tamales upright (open end up) in a vegetable steamer in a large Dutch oven. Add water to pan to a depth of 1 inch; bring water to a boil. Cover and steam tamales 1½ hours or until husks pull away cleanly; add additional water to

bottom of pan as necessary. Remove tamales from steamer, and let stand 5 minutes. Remove tamales from cornhusks. Yield: 8 servings (serving size: 2 tamales).

CALORIES 242 (29% from fat); FAT 7.7g (sat 1.5g, mono 2.6g, poly 2.4g); PROTEIN 6.9g; CARB 40.4g; FIBER 5.5g; CHOL 0mg; IRON 2.7mg; SODIUM 648mg; CALC 119mg

How to Make Mushroom Tamales

1. *Spread 3 tablespoons dough in center of cornhusk, leaving a small border.*

2. *Make sure dough seals around filling as you roll.*

3. *Fold up tapered end, and tie with cornhusk strip.*

Tofu Mole Enchiladas

Dried chiles are at the heart of this heady mole—ancho chiles add a rich, fruity flavor, while *guajillo* chiles spice it up.

    8 garlic cloves, unpeeled
    3 large tomatoes (about 2 pounds)
    3 tablespoons slivered almonds, toasted
 1½ tablespoons toasted sesame seeds, divided
    4 ancho chiles, stemmed and seeded
    4 guajillo chiles, stemmed and seeded
    2 cups boiling water
    1 teaspoon dried oregano
   ½ teaspoon ground cumin
   ¼ teaspoon ground cloves
    2 teaspoons vegetable oil
    2 cups chopped onion
    3 cups vegetable broth, divided
   ¼ cup fresh cilantro leaves
    2 tablespoons unsweetened cocoa
   ½ teaspoon ground cinnamon
    2 (1-ounce) slices white bread, toasted and torn
   ½ cup raisins
   ¼ cup fresh lime juice
    1 tablespoon sugar
   ½ teaspoon salt
    4 (6-ounce) packages smoked tofu, cut into ½-inch pieces
  16 (6-inch) corn tortillas

1. Heat a large cast iron skillet over medium heat. Add garlic and tomatoes; cook 15 minutes or until tomatoes are blackened, turning frequently. Remove from pan; cool slightly. Peel garlic; set aside. Peel and core tomatoes. Place tomatoes, almonds, and 1 tablespoon sesame seeds in a food processor, and process until smooth. Set aside.
2. Wipe pan clean with paper towels. Heat pan over medium-high heat. Place 2 ancho chiles in pan; flatten with a spatula. Cook 10 seconds on each side or until blackened. Repeat procedure with remaining ancho chiles. Place 2 guajillo chiles in pan; flatten with a spatula. Cook 20 seconds on each side or until blackened. Repeat procedure with remaining guajillo chiles. Combine ancho chiles, guajillo chiles, and boiling water in a medium bowl; let stand 30

minutes. Strain chiles through a sieve into a bowl, reserving ⅓ cup soaking liquid. Place chiles, reserved liquid, garlic, oregano, cumin, and cloves in food processor; process until smooth.
3. Heat oil in pan over medium-high heat. Add onion; sauté 8 minutes or until browned. Place onion, 1 cup broth, cilantro, cocoa, cinnamon, and bread in food processor; process until smooth.
4. Return onion mixture to pan. Add chile mixture; cook over medium heat 5 minutes. Stir in tomato mixture and 2 cups broth. Cook 30 minutes or until mixture is slightly thick. Stir in raisins, juice, sugar, and salt. Stir in tofu, and simmer 20 minutes.
5. Heat tortillas according to package directions. Arrange about ⅓ cup mole down center of each tortilla; roll up. Place rolled tortillas, seam-sides down, on a platter. Top with any remaining mole, and sprinkle evenly with 1½ teaspoons sesame seeds. Yield: 8 servings (serving size: 2 enchiladas).

CALORIES 422 (26% from fat); FAT 12.4g (sat 1.9g, mono 3.2g, poly 5.6g); PROTEIN 27.2g; CARB 59.9g; FIBER 9.7g; CHOL 0mg; IRON 4.5mg; SODIUM 789mg; CALC 180mg

Chiles Rellenos Gratin

    8 poblano chiles
  Cooking spray
    1 cup finely chopped red bell pepper
 1½ cups fresh corn kernels
   ½ cup chopped green onions
    2 tablespoons pine nuts, toasted
    2 garlic cloves, minced
   ¾ cup (3 ounces) crumbled queso fresco, divided
    2 tablespoons chopped fresh cilantro
    1 teaspoon salt, divided
   ¼ teaspoon ground red pepper, divided
    1 (15-ounce) can black beans, drained and divided
    2 tablespoons butter
   ½ teaspoon ground cumin
   ⅛ teaspoon ground nutmeg
    2 tablespoons all-purpose flour
    2 cups 2% reduced-fat milk
    1 tablespoon fresh lime juice
   ½ cup dry breadcrumbs

Continued

1. Preheat broiler.

2. Place chiles on a foil-lined baking sheet; broil 3 inches from heat 8 minutes or until blackened, turning after 4 minutes. Place in a zip-top plastic bag; seal. Let stand 15 minutes. Peel and discard skins. Cut a lengthwise slit in each chile; discard seeds, leaving stems intact.

3. Preheat oven to 350°.

4. Heat a large nonstick skillet coated with cooking spray over medium heat. Add bell pepper; cook 4 minutes, stirring frequently. Add corn, onions, nuts, and garlic; cook 2 minutes, stirring frequently. Remove from heat; stir in ½ cup cheese, cilantro, ½ teaspoon salt, and ⅛ teaspoon ground red pepper.

5. Place half of beans in a bowl; mash with a fork. Add mashed beans and whole beans to corn mixture. Spoon about ⅓ cup bean mixture into each chile; fold sides of chile over filling. Arrange stuffed chiles in an 8-inch square baking dish coated with cooking spray; set aside.

6. Melt butter in a medium saucepan over medium-low heat; add ⅛ teaspoon ground red pepper, cumin, and nutmeg, and stir with a whisk. Sauté 30 seconds. Gradually add flour, and stir constantly with a whisk 5 minutes. Gradually add milk. Stir with a whisk until blended.

7. Increase heat to medium. Cook milk mixture 8 minutes or until thick. Remove from heat; stir in ½ teaspoon salt and lime juice. Pour milk mixture over stuffed chiles.

8. Combine ¼ cup cheese and breadcrumbs; sprinkle over milk mixture. Bake at 350° for 20 minutes or until sauce is bubbly.

9. Preheat broiler.

10. Broil 1 minute or until top is golden brown. Yield: 8 servings (serving size: 1 stuffed chile).

CALORIES 216 (30% from fat); FAT 7.1g (sat 3.3g, mono 1.9g, poly 0.8g); PROTEIN 9.1g; CARB 33.1g; FIBER 5.9g; CHOL 16mg; IRON 2.3mg; SODIUM 574mg; CALC 148mg

Coconut Flan

Coconut milk delicately flavors this flan and gives it a denser, more custardy texture than traditional versions.

  1 cup sugar
  ¼ cup water
  Cooking spray
  2 tablespoons dark rum
  ½ teaspoon vanilla extract
  ¼ teaspoon ground cinnamon
  ⅛ teaspoon ground nutmeg
  4 large eggs, lightly beaten
  1 (14-ounce) can fat-free sweetened condensed milk
  1 (14-ounce) can light coconut milk

1. Preheat oven to 350°.

2. Combine sugar and water in a small, heavy saucepan. Cook over medium-high heat until sugar dissolves, stirring frequently. Continue cooking 3 minutes or until golden, stirring constantly. Immediately pour into 8 (6-ounce) custard cups coated with cooking spray, tipping quickly until caramelized sugar coats bottom of cups. Cool completely.

3. Combine rum and remaining 6 ingredients; stir with a whisk until well blended. Divide egg mixture evenly among prepared custard cups (about ½ cup each).

4. Place cups in a 13 x 9-inch baking pan; add hot water to pan to a depth of 1 inch. Bake at 350° for 30 minutes or until center barely moves when custard cup is touched. Cool completely in water bath. Remove cups from pan; cover and chill at least 4 hours or overnight.

5. Loosen edges of custards with a knife or rubber spatula. Place a dessert plate, upside down, on top of each cup, and invert onto plates. Drizzle any remaining caramelized syrup over custards. Yield: 8 servings.

CALORIES 313 (15% from fat); FAT 5.2g (sat 2.5g, mono 1.1g, poly 0.3g); PROTEIN 7.5g; CARB 57.1g; FIBER 0.1g; CHOL 110mg; IRON 0.7mg; SODIUM 103mg; CALC 153mg

dinner tonight

Sandwich Night

Make sandwich night more exciting with these simple international recipes.

Italian Sandwich Menu
serves 4

Turkey and Cheese Panini

Tomato-bread salad*

Low-fat ice cream with sliced peaches

*Combine 2 tablespoons each water and light mayonnaise, 1 tablespoon fresh lemon juice, and ¼ teaspoon hot sauce, stirring with a whisk. Combine 2 cups toasted French bread cubes, 4 cups halved cherry tomato, ½ cup each chopped fresh parsley and finely chopped red onion, ⅓ cup diced peeled avocado, and ½ teaspoon salt; toss with mayonnaise mixture.

Game Plan

1. While oven preheats:
   • Halve cherry tomatoes
   • Chop parsley, onion, and avocado
   • Prepare mayonnaise mixture
2. While French bread toasts:
   • Slice tomato
   • Prepare pesto mixture
   • Heat grill pan
3. While panini cook:
   • Assemble salad
   • Slice peaches

Turkey and Cheese Panini

In Italian, *panini* means small bread and refers to a pressed sandwich. Using a grill pan gives the sandwich a nice appearance, but the recipe works just as well in a regular nonstick skillet. If you don't have provolone cheese, you can use mozzarella.

TOTAL TIME: 18 MINUTES

QUICK TIP: You can find prepared pesto in jars, tubs, or tubes at most supermarkets.

2 tablespoons fat-free mayonnaise
4 teaspoons basil pesto
8 (1-ounce) thin slices sourdough bread
8 ounces sliced cooked turkey breast
2 ounces thinly sliced provolone cheese
8 (⅛-inch-thick) slices tomato
Cooking spray

1. Combine mayonnaise and pesto, stirring well. Spread 1 tablespoon mayonnaise mixture on each of 4 bread slices; top each slice with 2 ounces turkey, ½ ounce cheese, and 2 tomato slices. Top with remaining bread slices.

2. Preheat grill pan or large nonstick skillet coated with cooking spray over medium heat. Add sandwiches to pan; top with another heavy skillet. Cook 3 minutes on each side or until golden brown. Yield: 4 servings.

CALORIES 257 (29% from fat); FAT 8.2g (sat 2.9g, mono 0.2g, poly 0.1g); PROTEIN 18.4g; CARB 30.4g; FIBER 4.1g; CHOL 30mg; IRON 2.4mg; SODIUM 1,208mg; CALC 204mg

---

Seaside Sandwich Menu

serves 4

Baked Cornmeal-Crusted Grouper Sandwiches with Tartar Sauce

Asian-style coleslaw*

Lemon sorbet

*Combine 3 cups shredded cabbage, 1 cup snow peas, ½ cup julienne-cut red bell pepper, and 3 tablespoons chopped green onions in a large bowl. Combine 1½ tablespoons rice vinegar, 1 teaspoon vegetable oil, 1 teaspoon dark sesame oil, 1 teaspoon less-sodium soy sauce, ¼ teaspoon sugar, and ⅛ teaspoon pepper, stirring with a whisk. Add to cabbage mixture, tossing well to coat.

Game Plan

1. While oven preheats:
  • Bread fish fillets
2. While fish cooks:
  • Prepare tartar sauce
  • Prepare coleslaw

QUICK & EASY
Baked Cornmeal-Crusted Grouper Sandwiches with Tartar Sauce

TOTAL TIME: 35 MINUTES

QUICK TIP: To save time if preparing the Seaside Sandwich Menu, buy bagged preshredded cabbage.

GROUPER:
½ cup yellow cornmeal
½ teaspoon salt
¼ teaspoon ground red pepper
¼ cup 2% reduced-fat milk
4 (6-ounce) grouper fillets
Cooking spray

TARTAR SAUCE:
½ cup low-fat mayonnaise
2 tablespoons chopped green onions
1 tablespoon sweet pickle relish
1½ teaspoons capers
1½ teaspoons fresh lemon juice
½ teaspoon Worcestershire sauce

ADDITIONAL INGREDIENT:
4 (1½-ounce) hamburger buns, split

1. Preheat oven to 450°.

2. To prepare grouper, combine cornmeal, salt, and red pepper in a shallow dish, stirring well with a fork. Place milk in a shallow bowl.

3. Dip each fillet in milk; dredge in cornmeal mixture. Place fish on a baking sheet coated with cooking spray. Bake at 450° for 10 minutes or until fish is done, turning once.

4. To prepare tartar sauce, combine mayonnaise and next 5 ingredients, stirring with a whisk.

5. Spread about 2 tablespoons tartar sauce over cut sides of each bun; place one fish fillet on bottom half of each bun. Top fillets with remaining bun halves. Yield: 4 servings.

CALORIES 443 (29% from fat); FAT 14.3g (sat 2.6g, mono 4.5g, poly 6.6g); PROTEIN 38.5g; CARB 38.3g; FIBER 2.5g; CHOL 75mg; IRON 3.2mg; SODIUM 961mg; CALC 110mg

---

French Sandwich Menu

serves 4

Salad Niçoise in Pita Pockets

Potato salad*

Lemonade

*Combine 2 tablespoons fresh lemon juice, 2 tablespoons light mayonnaise, 2 tablespoons fat-free sour cream, ½ teaspoon salt, and ¼ teaspoon pepper in a large bowl, stirring with a whisk. Add 2 pounds cooked quartered small red potato, ½ cup chopped green onions, and 2 strips of bacon, cooked and crumbled; stir to combine.

Game Plan

1. While potato cooks:
  • Chop green onions
  • Cook bacon
  • Combine mayonnaise mixture
  • Pit and chop olives
2. While green beans cool:
  • Combine tuna, olives, and capers
  • Prepare dressing

QUICK & EASY
Salad Niçoise in Pita Pockets

TOTAL TIME: 20 MINUTES

QUICK TIPS: Cooking the beans in the microwave will save you time.

1 cup (1-inch) cut fresh green beans (about 4 ounces)
1 tablespoon water
¼ cup niçoise olives, pitted and chopped (about 18 olives)
1 tablespoon capers
1 (12-ounce) can solid white tuna in water, drained
1 tablespoon extravirgin olive oil
1 tablespoon fresh lemon juice
½ teaspoon salt
2 (6-inch) whole wheat pita rounds, cut in half
4 curly leaf lettuce leaves

1. Combine beans and water in a small microwave-safe bowl; cover with plastic

Continued

wrap. Microwave at HIGH 1½ minutes or until beans are crisp-tender; drain. Rinse with cold water. Drain well, and cool. Combine beans, olives, capers, and tuna.

2. Combine oil, juice, and salt, stirring with a whisk. Pour oil mixture over tuna mixture; toss gently to coat.

3. Line each pita half with 1 lettuce leaf; spoon about ½ cup tuna mixture into each lettuce-lined pita half. Yield: 4 servings (serving size: 1 pita half).

CALORIES 253 (30% from fat); FAT 8.3g (sat 1.5g, mono 4.4g, poly 1.7g); PROTEIN 24.1g; CARB 21.6g; FIBER 4.2g; CHOL 36mg; IRON 2.6mg; SODIUM 702mg; CALC 48mg

---

New Orleans Sandwich Menu

serves 4

Shrimp Po'boy with Spicy Ketchup

Corn salad*

Fresh strawberries

*Heat a nonstick skillet over medium heat. Add 2 cups fresh corn kernels; cook 5 minutes, stirring frequently. Combine corn, ½ cup chopped red bell pepper, 2 tablespoons chopped fresh parsley, 2 tablespoons chopped red onion, 1½ tablespoons fresh lime juice, 1 teaspoon olive oil, ¼ teaspoon salt, and ⅛ teaspoon pepper, tossing gently.

Game Plan

1. Prepare corn salad
2. While broiler heats:
  • Prepare breadcrumb mixture
  • Toss shrimp in oil
  • Coat shrimp in breadcrumb mixture
3. While shrimp cooks:
  • Prepare ketchup mixture
  • Slice rolls
  • Tear lettuce and slice onion
  • Wash and halve strawberries

Shrimp Po'boy with Spicy Ketchup

(pictured on page 146)

A New Orleans specialty, this sandwich is often made with deep-fried shrimp. Broiling the shrimp, which is coated in garlicky breadcrumbs, delivers big flavor without the fat.

TOTAL TIME: 34 MINUTES

QUICK TIP: You'll save time in the kitchen if you buy peeled and deveined shrimp.

3 tablespoons dry breadcrumbs
¼ teaspoon salt
¼ teaspoon black pepper
1 garlic clove, minced
1 tablespoon olive oil
1 pound large shrimp, peeled and deveined
¼ cup ketchup
1½ teaspoons fresh lemon juice
½ teaspoon Worcestershire sauce
¼ teaspoon chili powder
¼ teaspoon hot sauce
2 (10-inch) submarine rolls, split
2 cups torn curly leaf lettuce
½ cup thinly sliced red onion

1. Preheat broiler.
2. Line a baking sheet with heavy-duty aluminum foil. Combine first 4 ingredients in a medium bowl, stirring with a fork. Combine oil and shrimp; toss well. Place half of shrimp in breadcrumb mixture; toss well to coat. Place breaded shrimp in a single layer on prepared baking sheet. Repeat procedure with remaining shrimp and breadcrumb mixture. Broil 4 minutes or until shrimp are done.
3. Combine ketchup and next 4 ingredients in a small bowl, stirring with a whisk.
4. Spread 2 tablespoons ketchup mixture over cut side of each roll half. Place 1 cup lettuce over bottom half of each roll; top with ¼ cup onion. Arrange 1 cup shrimp on each sandwich; top with remaining roll halves. Cut sandwiches in half. Yield: 4 servings (serving size: 1 sandwich half).

CALORIES 401 (20% from fat); FAT 9.1g (sat 1.7g, mono 4.6g, poly 1.7g); PROTEIN 30g; CARB 48.9g; FIBER 3g; CHOL 172mg; IRON 5.3mg; SODIUM 864mg; CALC 183mg

---

baking

Smart Tarts

No-fuss crusts and a variety of fillings make these as easy as pie.

If baking a tart sounds fussy to you, these recipes will convince you otherwise.

Fresh Tomato and Zucchini Tart with Mozzarella and Basil

1 tablespoon yellow cornmeal
1 (10-ounce) can refrigerated pizza crust dough
1 cup (⅛-inch-thick) diagonally sliced zucchini
4 plum tomatoes, seeded and cut into ¼-inch-thick slices (about ½ pound)
¼ teaspoon kosher salt
¼ teaspoon freshly ground black pepper
4 ounces fresh mozzarella cheese, sliced
1 teaspoon extravirgin olive oil
½ cup torn fresh basil leaves

1. Preheat oven to 400°.
2. Line a baking sheet with parchment paper; secure with masking tape. Sprinkle paper with cornmeal. Unroll dough onto paper; let stand 5 minutes. Pat dough into a 12-inch square. Arrange zucchini and tomato over dough, leaving a 1-inch border. Sprinkle evenly with salt and pepper. Fold edges of dough over zucchini and tomato (dough won't cover zucchini and tomato).
3. Bake at 400° for 15 minutes or until dough is lightly browned. Top with cheese; bake 5 minutes or until cheese melts. Drizzle with oil; sprinkle with basil. Cool on baking sheet 10 minutes on a wire rack. Yield: 4 servings.

CALORIES 304 (30% from fat); FAT 10.1g (sat 4.3g, mono 3.8g, poly 1.4g); PROTEIN 12.9g; CARB 40.1g; FIBER 2.5g; CHOL 22mg; IRON 2.5mg; SODIUM 702mg; CALC 164mg

Red Wine-Poached Fig and Ricotta Tarts

The wine mixture used as a poaching liquid for the figs is reduced to create a rich sauce that is drizzled over the finished tarts. Briefly poaching the figs infuses flavor and makes them even more tender, but you can skip this step, and just make a sauce to drizzle over raw figs. You can also make this tart in a 9-inch round removable-bottom tart pan, and increase the baking time to 10 minutes or until lightly browned.

    1   cup Zinfandel or other fruity dry
        red wine
    1   cup water
    ½   cup sugar
    ¼   cup fresh orange juice
    1   tablespoon fresh lemon juice
   12   fresh figs, halved (about ¾ pound)
    ½   (15-ounce) package refrigerated
        pie dough (such as Pillsbury)
    ¾   cup part-skim ricotta cheese
    2   tablespoons honey
  Mint sprigs (optional)

1. Combine first 5 ingredients in a large saucepan; bring to a boil. Add figs. Reduce heat; simmer 2 minutes. Remove figs with a slotted spoon, and place in a shallow dish. Cover and chill. Bring cooking liquid to a boil, and cook 15 minutes or until reduced to ½ cup. Cover and chill.
2. Preheat oven to 450°.
3. Roll dough into a 12-inch circle on a lightly floured surface; cut dough into 8 (4-inch) circles, rerolling dough scraps as necessary. Fit each dough circle into a 3½-inch tart pan. Bake at 450° for 7 minutes or until lightly browned. Cool completely on a wire rack.
4. Combine ricotta and honey. Spread about 1½ tablespoons ricotta mixture into each tart shell. Arrange 3 fig halves, cut sides up, inside each shell. Drizzle each tart with 1 tablespoon wine mixture. Garnish with mint, if desired. Yield: 8 servings.

CALORIES 286 (28% from fat); FAT 9g (sat 4g, mono 3.7g, poly 1g); PROTEIN 4.3g; CARB 46.6g; FIBER 2.5g; CHOL 12mg; IRON 0.5mg; SODIUM 131mg; CALC 92mg

Leek, Potato, and Fontina Tart

This meatless recipe is a fine choice for brunch or supper.

    2   tablespoons butter, divided
    3   cups chopped leek (about 4 large)
   2½   cups cubed peeled baking potato
    3   garlic cloves, halved
    ½   cup (2 ounces) shredded fontina
         cheese, divided
    1   tablespoon chopped fresh chives
    2   tablespoons 2% reduced-fat milk
    ¼   teaspoon kosher salt
    ¼   teaspoon freshly ground black
         pepper
    1   large egg, lightly beaten
  Cooking spray
    1   (10-ounce) can refrigerated pizza
         crust dough

1. Preheat oven to 375°.
2. Melt 1 tablespoon butter in a large nonstick skillet over medium heat. Add leek; sauté 7 minutes or until tender and lightly browned. Set aside.
3. Place potato and garlic in a large saucepan; cover with water. Bring to a boil; cook 10 minutes or until potato is very tender. Drain. Place 1 tablespoon butter, potato mixture, ¼ cup cheese, chives, and next 4 ingredients in a large bowl; mash with a potato masher.
4. Lightly coat a 10½-inch round removable-bottom tart pan with cooking spray. Unroll dough onto a lightly floured surface; let rest 5 minutes. Pat dough into bottom and up sides of pan. Spread potato mixture into dough. Spread leek over potato mixture, and sprinkle with ¼ cup cheese.
5. Bake at 375° for 20 minutes or until puffed and set. Cool in pan 5 minutes on a wire rack. Yield: 4 servings.

CALORIES 430 (30% from fat); FAT 14.4g (sat 7.2g, mono 4.6g, poly 1.7g); PROTEIN 14.4g; CARB 61g; FIBER 3.4g; CHOL 86mg; IRON 3.8mg; SODIUM 799mg; CALC 144mg

Corn, Bacon, and Green Onion Tart

Refrigerated pizza dough tends to draw up when it's first removed from the can. Let the dough rest a few minutes before you begin to work with it so it will be more pliable.

    2   slices applewood-smoked bacon
         (such as Nueske's), chopped
    2   cups fresh corn kernels
    ½   cup chopped green onions
    1   cup 2% reduced-fat milk
    ¼   cup (1 ounce) grated fresh
         Parmesan cheese, divided
    ½   teaspoon kosher salt
    ½   teaspoon freshly ground black
         pepper
    2   large egg whites, lightly beaten
    1   large egg, lightly beaten
  Cooking spray
    1   (10-ounce) can refrigerated pizza
         crust dough

1. Preheat oven to 375°.
2. Cook bacon slices in a large non-stick skillet over medium-high heat 3 minutes or until bacon is lightly browned. Add corn and onions; sauté 3 minutes. Place corn mixture in a large bowl. Add milk, 2 tablespoons cheese, salt, pepper, egg whites, and egg; stir until well blended.
3. Coat a 10½-inch round removable-bottom tart pan lightly with cooking spray. Unroll dough onto a lightly floured surface, and let rest 5 minutes. Pat dough into bottom and up sides of prepared pan. Place pan on a baking sheet. Pour bacon mixture into dough, and sprinkle with 2 tablespoons cheese. Bake at 375° for 25 minutes or until set. Cool tart in pan 10 minutes on a wire rack. Yield: 4 servings.

CALORIES 397 (29% from fat); FAT 13g (sat 5.1g, mono 5g, poly 2.1g); PROTEIN 18g; CARB 52.9g; FIBER 3.6g; CHOL 70mg; IRON 2.6mg; SODIUM 997mg; CALC 182mg

Peach Crème Brûlée Tart

This simple but impressive-looking dessert can be made up to 1 hour before serving.

½ (15-ounce) package refrigerated pie dough (such as Pillsbury)
¼ cup sugar
3½ tablespoons all-purpose flour
⅛ teaspoon salt
2 cups 2% reduced-fat milk
1 (4-inch) piece vanilla bean, split lengthwise
1 large egg, lightly beaten
2 cups sliced peeled ripe peaches
⅓ cup sugar

1. Preheat oven to 450°.
2. Fit dough into a 9-inch round removable-bottom tart pan, and pierce dough with a fork; bake at 450° for 10 minutes or until lightly browned. Cool completely on a wire rack.
3. Place ¼ cup sugar, flour, and salt in a medium, heavy saucepan. Gradually add milk, stirring with a whisk. Scrape seeds from vanilla bean; add seeds and bean to milk mixture. Cook over medium heat until thick and bubbly (about 5 minutes), stirring constantly.
4. Place egg in a large bowl. Gradually stir hot milk mixture into egg. Return milk mixture to pan. Cook 2 minutes or until thick and bubbly, stirring constantly. Spoon custard into a small bowl. Place bowl in a larger bowl filled with ice. Cool 20 minutes or until thoroughly chilled, stirring occasionally. Discard vanilla bean.
5. Spread chilled custard into bottom of prepared crust. Arrange peach slices spoke-like on top of chilled custard. Sprinkle ⅓ cup sugar evenly over peach slices. Holding a kitchen blow torch about 2 inches from top of peach slices, heat sugar, moving torch back and forth, until sugar is melted and caramelized (about 3 minutes). Yield: 8 servings.

CALORIES 247 (32% from fat); FAT 8.8g (sat 3.7g, mono 3.7g, poly 1g); PROTEIN 4.5g; CARB 37.9g; FIBER 0.9g; CHOL 36mg; IRON 0.3mg; SODIUM 175mg; CALC 80mg

Raspberry-Amaretto Cream Tart

Delicate raspberries are ideal for this dessert, but blackberries, blueberries, or sliced strawberries would work, too.

CRUST:
30 vanilla wafers
2 tablespoons butter, melted
Cooking spray

CREAM:
⅓ cup all-purpose flour
3 tablespoons sugar
⅛ teaspoon salt
1½ cups 2% reduced-fat milk
1 (4-inch) piece vanilla bean, split lengthwise
1 large egg, lightly beaten
2 tablespoons amaretto (almond-flavored liqueur)

REMAINING INGREDIENTS:
2½ cups fresh raspberries
2 tablespoons red currant jelly
1½ teaspoons amaretto

1. Preheat oven to 350°.
2. To prepare crust, place cookies in a food processor, and process until finely ground. Add butter; pulse just until combined. Press crumb mixture into bottom and up sides of a 9-inch round removable bottom tart pan coated with cooking spray. Bake at 350° for 10 minutes or until lightly browned. Cool completely on a wire rack.
3. To prepare cream, lightly spoon flour into a dry measuring cup; level with a knife. Place flour, sugar, and salt in a medium, heavy saucepan. Gradually add milk, stirring with a whisk. Scrape seeds from vanilla bean; add seeds and bean to milk mixture. Cook over medium heat until thick and bubbly (about 5 minutes), stirring constantly.
4. Place egg in a large bowl. Gradually stir hot milk mixture into egg. Return milk mixture to pan. Cook 2 minutes or until thick and bubbly, stirring frequently. Remove from heat. Stir in 2 tablespoons liqueur. Spoon mixture into a small bowl. Place in a larger bowl filled with ice. Cool 20 minutes or until thoroughly chilled, stirring occasionally. Discard vanilla bean. Spread chilled cream into bottom of prepared crust.
5. To prepare remaining ingredients, arrange raspberries over chilled cream. Cover and chill 2 hours or until set. Combine jelly and 1½ teaspoons liqueur in a small microwave-safe bowl. Microwave at HIGH 20 seconds or until jelly melts, stirring once. Brush over raspberries. Yield: 6 servings.

CALORIES 276 (30% from fat); FAT 9.3g (sat 4g, mono 2.8g, poly 0.5g); PROTEIN 4.9g; CARB 42.5g; FIBER 4g; CHOL 52mg; IRON 1.5mg; SODIUM 195mg; CALC 104mg

Plum Tatin

Use red, purple, green, or a combination of plums in this upside-down tart.

½ (15-ounce) package refrigerated pie dough (such as Pillsbury)
¼ cup packed brown sugar
1 tablespoon all-purpose flour
¼ teaspoon ground cinnamon
¼ teaspoon ground nutmeg
10 small plums, pitted and cut in half (about 2½ pounds)
½ cup granulated sugar
1 teaspoon lemon juice
1 tablespoon chopped pecans

1. Preheat oven to 425°.
2. Roll dough into a 10-inch circle on a lightly floured surface; set aside.
3. Combine brown sugar and next 4 ingredients. Combine granulated sugar and lemon juice in a 10-inch cast iron skillet, and cook over medium-high heat just until mixture begins to turn golden.
4. Remove from heat; stir until completely golden. Sprinkle with pecans, and add plum mixture. Place dough over plum mixture, tucking dough around plums.
5. Bake at 425° for 25 minutes or until bubbly. Immediately place a plate over pan. Carefully invert tart onto plate. Yield: 6 servings.

CALORIES 328 (30% from fat); FAT 11.1g (sat 3.8g, mono 4.6g, poly 1.3g); PROTEIN 2.4g; CARB 57g; FIBER 1.9g; CHOL 7mg; IRON 0.3mg; SODIUM 136mg; CALC 8mg

Roasted-Onion Tart with Maytag Blue Cheese

Using a touch of honey yields supersweet, buttery-soft roasted garlic, onions, and shallots that contrast well with the pungent cheese. If you're not a fan of blue cheese, try goat cheese, feta, or another sharp-flavored cheese.

- 1 Vidalia or other sweet onion, peeled
- 10 shallots, peeled and halved (about ½ pound)
- 10 large garlic cloves, peeled and halved
- 3 tablespoons balsamic vinegar
- 1 tablespoon butter, melted
- 2 teaspoons honey
- ¼ teaspoon dried thyme
- 1 tablespoon yellow cornmeal
- 1 (10-ounce) can refrigerated pizza crust dough
- ½ teaspoon freshly ground black pepper
- ¼ teaspoon kosher salt
- ⅔ cup (about 2½ ounces) crumbled Maytag blue cheese
- 1 tablespoon chopped fresh parsley

1. Preheat oven to 425°.
2. Cut onion into 8 wedges, leaving root intact. Place onion wedges, shallots, and garlic in a 13 x 9-inch baking dish. Combine balsamic vinegar, butter, honey, and thyme in a small bowl, and drizzle over onion mixture, tossing to coat. Bake at 425° for 30 minutes or until tender, stirring occasionally.
3. Line a baking sheet with parchment paper, and secure with masking tape. Sprinkle paper with cornmeal. Unroll dough onto paper; let stand 5 minutes. Pat dough into a 14 x 12-inch rectangle. Arrange onion mixture over dough, leaving a 1-inch border. Sprinkle evenly with pepper and salt. Fold edges of dough over onion mixture (dough will not cover onion mixture). Sprinkle with crumbled cheese.
4. Bake at 425° for 15 minutes or until lightly browned. Cool on baking sheet

10 minutes on a wire rack. Sprinkle with parsley. Yield: 4 servings.

CALORIES 358 (28% from fat); FAT 11.1g (sat 5.7g, mono 3.4g, poly 1.3g); PROTEIN 12.6g; CARB 51.9g; FIBER 2.9g; CHOL 22mg; IRON 2.8mg; SODIUM 892mg; CALC 145mg

reader recipes

Super Simple Soup

As a busy professional, Catherine Bishir is always on the lookout for quick, healthful meals.

This soup, which she named after her granddaughter, Cate, fits that bill. Catherine's approach to cooking is to fix food that is simple and low in fat. Although our recipe has been streamlined with canned broth, Catherine uses fresh chicken stock to bring out the flavors.

Cate's Springtime Risotto Soup
(pictured on page 148)

- 1 tablespoon olive oil
- 2 cups chopped onion
- 2 teaspoons grated lemon rind
- ¾ cup Arborio rice or other short-grain rice
- 3 (14-ounce) cans fat-free, less-sodium chicken broth
- 2 cups (1-inch) sliced asparagus (about 1 pound)
- 2 cups coarsely chopped spinach
- ¼ teaspoon ground nutmeg
- ½ cup (2 ounces) grated fresh Parmesan cheese

1. Heat oil in a large saucepan over medium-high heat. Add onion; sauté 2 minutes. Add lemon rind; sauté 2 minutes. Add rice; sauté 3 minutes.
2. Stir in broth, and bring to a boil. Cover, reduce heat, and simmer 10 minutes. Stir in asparagus, spinach, and nutmeg; cook, uncovered, 2 minutes or until asparagus is crisp-tender. Top each

serving with cheese. Serve immediately. Yield: 4 servings (serving size: 1¾ cups soup and 2 tablespoons cheese).

CALORIES 320 (21% from fat); FAT 7.5g (sat 2.9g, mono 3.6g, poly 0.5g); PROTEIN 14.9g; CARB 46.2g; FIBER 4.1g; CHOL 10mg; IRON 1.6mg; SODIUM 815mg; CALC 234mg

Turkey-Spinach Lasagna

"My husband and I stopped eating red meat and foods high in fat about 15 years ago. We love lasagna, so I lightened our favorite recipe in every way possible then added spinach for color and taste."

—Shelia Laiks, Parsippany, New Jersey

- Cooking spray
- 1 pound ground turkey breast
- 1½ cups chopped onion
- 2 garlic cloves, chopped
- 2 (26-ounce) jars low-fat marinara sauce, divided
- 1 (16-ounce) carton fat-free cottage cheese
- ¼ cup egg substitute
- ¼ cup (1 ounce) preshredded fresh Parmesan cheese
- 1 tablespoon dried parsley flakes
- ¼ teaspoon black pepper
- 1 (10-ounce) package frozen chopped spinach, thawed, drained, and squeezed dry
- 8 cooked lasagna noodles
- 2 cups (8 ounces) shredded part-skim mozzarella cheese

1. Preheat oven to 350°.
2. Coat a large skillet with cooking spray, and place over medium-high heat until hot. Add turkey, onion, and garlic; cook until meat is browned, stirring to crumble. Add 5¾ cups marinara sauce; cook 5 minutes, stirring occasionally. Remove from heat.
3. Combine cottage cheese and next 5 ingredients; stir well.
4. Spread remaining marinara sauce in bottom of a 13 x 9-inch baking dish coated with cooking spray. Arrange 4 noodles over marinara, and top with cottage cheese mixture and half of *Continued*

mozzarella. Spoon half of turkey mixture over mozzarella. Arrange remaining noodles over turkey mixture. Top with remaining turkey mixture and mozzarella.
5. Bake at 350° for 50 minutes or until cheese melts and sauce is bubbly. Let stand 10 minutes before serving. Yield: 9 servings (serving size: 1 square of lasagna).

CALORIES 352 (27% from fat); FAT 10.6g (sat 4.5g, mono 3.4g, poly 2.2g); PROTEIN 28.3g; CARB 35.6g; FIBER 4.6g; CHOL 57mg; IRON 3.8mg; SODIUM 969mg; CALC 436mg

---

QUICK & EASY

Spicy Thai Chicken Salad

(pictured on page 146)

"I had something similar to this at my favorite restaurant in San Francisco. The red pepper and ginger add a nice kick."
—Alicia Brennan, San Francisco, California

SALAD:
  2 cups chopped cooked chicken breast (about 1 pound)
  2 cups red bell pepper strips
  1 cup sliced celery
  1 cup thinly sliced red onion
  1 cup sliced cucumber
  ½ cup coarsely chopped fresh cilantro leaves
  1 (7-ounce) package Italian-blend salad greens

DRESSING:
  3 tablespoons fresh lemon juice
  2 tablespoons fish sauce
  1 tablespoon sesame seeds, toasted
  1 teaspoon sugar
  1 teaspoon ground ginger
  ½ teaspoon crushed red pepper

1. To prepare salad, combine first 7 ingredients in a bowl.
2. To prepare dressing, combine lemon juice and remaining 5 ingredients, stirring with a whisk. Drizzle dressing over salad, and toss well. Yield: 5 servings (serving size: about 3 cups).

CALORIES 152 (21% from fat); FAT 3.5g (sat 0.8g, mono 1.2g, poly 1.1g); PROTEIN 19g; CARB 11.7g; FIBER 3.7g; CHOL 44mg; IRON 3.1mg; SODIUM 595mg; CALC 85mg

---

QUICK & EASY • MAKE AHEAD

Mediterranean Hummus

—Karen Chan, Boston, Massachusetts

  ¼ cup chopped bottled roasted red bell peppers
  ¼ cup pitted kalamata olives
  3 tablespoons fresh lemon juice
  2 teaspoons extravirgin olive oil
  ¼ teaspoon salt
  ⅛ teaspoon black pepper
  2 garlic cloves
  1 (15½-ounce) can chickpeas (garbanzo beans), rinsed and drained

1. Place all ingredients in a food processor; process until smooth, scraping sides of processor bowl once. Store in an airtight container in refrigerator. Yield: 1¾ cups (serving size: 2 tablespoons).
NOTE: Serve with pita triangles or fresh vegetables.

CALORIES 49 (24% from fat); FAT 1.3g (sat 0.2g, mono 0.8g, poly 0.3g); PROTEIN 1.7g; CARB 7.9g; FIBER 1.5g; CHOL 0mg; IRON 0.5mg; SODIUM 171mg; CALC 14mg

---

MAKE AHEAD • FREEZABLE

Banana Bread Lite

"Banana bread seems like a light choice to serve my dessert-phobic friends and ever-dieting coworkers. This one is low in fat, so it's an even better option."

—Joyce Thomas, Cincinnati, Ohio

  1 cup sugar
  1 (8-ounce) package fat-free cream cheese
  1 cup mashed ripe banana (about 2 medium)
  2 large eggs
  2 cups reduced-fat baking mix (such as Bisquick)
  ½ cup chopped walnuts
     Cooking spray

1. Preheat oven to 350°.
2. Place sugar and cream cheese in a large bowl; beat with a mixer at medium speed until light and fluffy. Add banana and eggs; beat until well blended. Add baking mix and walnuts, and stir just until moist.
3. Pour batter into a 9-inch loaf pan coated with cooking spray; bake at 350° for 45 minutes. Tent bread with foil, and bake an additional 15 minutes or until a wooden pick inserted in center comes out clean. Cool in pan 10 minutes on a wire rack; remove from pan. Cool completely on wire rack. Yield: 16 servings (serving size: 1 slice).

CALORIES 161 (24% from fat); FAT 4.3g (sat 0.8g, mono 0.6g, poly 1.9g); PROTEIN 4.6g; CARB 26.7g; FIBER 0.7g; CHOL 28mg; IRON 0.8mg; SODIUM 260mg; CALC 49mg

---

Lime-Marinated Broiled Salmon

"This recipe came from a good friend. I'm always on the lookout for a new fish recipe. Using a blender to make the marinade is a good time-saver."
—Connie Mudore, Black Earth, Wisconsin

  ⅓ cup low-sodium soy sauce
  ¼ cup fresh lime juice
  1 teaspoon minced peeled fresh ginger
  ½ teaspoon chopped fresh thyme
  2 garlic cloves, chopped
  4 (6-ounce) skinless salmon fillets (about 1 inch thick)
     Cooking spray
  4 lime wedges

1. Place first 5 ingredients in a blender; process until smooth. Pour into a large zip-top plastic bag. Add salmon; seal and marinate in refrigerator 1 hour, turning bag occasionally.
2. Preheat broiler.
3. Remove salmon from bag, discarding marinade. Place salmon on a broiler pan coated with cooking spray; broil 8 minutes. Turn and broil an additional 4 minutes or until fish flakes easily when tested with a fork. Serve with lime wedges. Yield: 4 servings (serving size: 1 fillet and 1 lime wedge).

CALORIES 281 (42% from fat); FAT 13.1g (sat 3.1g, mono 5.7g, poly 3.2g); PROTEIN 36.8g; CARB 7.9g; FIBER 0.1g; CHOL 87mg; IRON 0.8mg; SODIUM 414mg; CALC 25mg

Derby Day Favorites

Celebrate the Run for the Roses with these lightened Kentucky classics.

On derby day, while others focus on thoroughbreds and rolling pastures, Lynn Winter—a restaurateur in Louisville—considers her fondness for classic Kentucky recipes. So when she challenged us to lighten three of her favorites, we raced ahead.

MAKE AHEAD

Cookie-Crusted Derby Pie

If you don't have a food processor, place the vanilla wafers in a heavy-duty zip-top plastic bag, and crush with a mallet, rolling pin, or wine bottle. To toast the nuts, place in a 350° oven for about 10 minutes.

CRUST:

40 reduced-fat vanilla wafers
2   tablespoons brown sugar
1   tablespoon butter, melted
1   large egg white, lightly beaten
Cooking spray

FILLING:

½   cup coarsely chopped pecans, toasted
⅓   cup semisweet chocolate chips
⅔   cup dark corn syrup
½   cup packed brown sugar
3   tablespoons bourbon
1   teaspoon vanilla extract
¼   teaspoon salt
3   large eggs, lightly beaten

1. Preheat oven to 350°.
2. To prepare crust, place cookies in a food processor; process until finely ground. Add 2 tablespoons brown sugar, butter, and egg white; pulse 2 or 3 times or just until moistened. Press mixture into bottom and up sides of a 9-inch pie plate coated with cooking spray. Bake at 350° for 5 minutes. Cool on a wire rack.

3. To prepare filling, sprinkle pecans and chocolate chips into bottom of prepared crust. Combine syrup and remaining 5 ingredients; stir well with a whisk. Pour into crust. Bake at 350° for 27 minutes or until set. Cool on a wire rack. Yield: 10 servings (serving size: 1 wedge).

CALORIES 288 (30% from fat); FAT 9.6g (sat 2.5g, mono 4.1g, poly 1.6g); PROTEIN 3.5g; CARB 46.8g; FIBER 0.9g; CHOL 67mg; IRON 1.3mg; SODIUM 187mg; CALC 40mg

BEFORE	AFTER
CALORIES PER WEDGE	
553	288
FAT	
30.2g	9.6g
PERCENT OF TOTAL CALORIES	
49%	30%

Baked Garlic-Cheese Grits

Adding milk to the cooked grits makes them fluffy and creamy. A touch of hot pepper sauce is added to enhance the sharp flavor of the cheese.

4   cups water
1¼ teaspoons salt
1   cup uncooked quick-cooking grits
1½ cups (6 ounces) shredded reduced-fat extrasharp Cheddar cheese, divided
1   tablespoon butter
¾   cup 2% reduced-fat milk
2   teaspoons garlic powder
½   teaspoon hot pepper sauce (such as Tabasco)
2   large eggs, lightly beaten
Cooking spray

1. Preheat oven to 350°.
2. Bring water and salt to a boil in a medium saucepan. Gradually add grits, stirring constantly. Cover and simmer 8 minutes or until thick, stirring frequently. Remove pan from heat. Add 1 cup cheese and butter, stirring until cheese melts.
3. Combine milk and next 3 ingredients, stirring with a whisk. Stir milk mixture into grits mixture. Pour into an 8-inch square baking dish coated with cooking spray. Bake at 350° for 45 minutes. Sprinkle with ½ cup cheese; bake an additional 15 minutes or until cheese melts. Let stand 10 minutes before serving. Yield: 8 servings (serving size: ¾ cup).

CALORIES 162 (27% from fat); FAT 4.9g (sat 2.3g, mono 1.5g, poly 0.3g); PROTEIN 6.7g; CARB 23g; FIBER 1.3g; CHOL 66mg; IRON 0.9mg; SODIUM 560mg; CALC 223mg

BEFORE	AFTER
CALORIES PER SERVING	
373	162
FAT	
26.7g	4.9g
PERCENT OF TOTAL CALORIES	
64%	27%

STAFF FAVORITE

Hot Browns

Use leftover chicken in place of the turkey. Broiling the sandwiches browns and melts the Parmesan cheese that tops them.

SAUCE:

1½ tablespoons butter
2   tablespoons all-purpose flour
¼   teaspoon salt
⅛   teaspoon paprika
⅛   teaspoon black pepper
1   cup 2% reduced-fat milk
½   cup (2 ounces) shredded reduced-fat extrasharp Cheddar cheese
½   teaspoon Worcestershire sauce
⅛   teaspoon dry mustard

REMAINING INGREDIENTS:

12 (1-ounce) slices white bread, toasted
3   cups shredded cooked turkey (about 6 ounces)
12 (¼-inch-thick) slices tomato
5   bacon slices, cooked and crumbled (drained)
¼   cup (1 ounce) grated fresh Parmesan cheese

Continued

1. Preheat broiler.

2. To prepare sauce, melt butter in a saucepan over medium heat; stir in flour, salt, paprika, and pepper. Cook 30 seconds, stirring constantly. Gradually add milk, stirring with a whisk. Cook 3 minutes or until thick, stirring constantly. Remove from heat. Add Cheddar, Worcestershire, and mustard; stir with a whisk until smooth. Keep warm.

3. Arrange toast on a large baking sheet. Arrange turkey evenly over toast. Drizzle sauce evenly over turkey; top each serving with 1 tomato slice. Sprinkle evenly with bacon and Parmesan. Broil 7 minutes or until thoroughly heated and lightly browned. Serve immediately. Yield: 6 servings (serving size: 2 open-faced sandwiches).

CALORIES 440 (30% from fat); FAT 14.9g (sat 6.2g, mono 4g, poly 1.6g); PROTEIN 34.6g; CARB 44.3g; FIBER 4.5g; CHOL 79mg; IRON 3.2mg; SODIUM 815mg; CALC 255mg

BEFORE	AFTER
CALORIES PER SANDWICH	
739	440
FAT	
44.7g	14.9g
PERCENT OF TOTAL CALORIES	
54%	30%

enlightened cook

Tastes for Life

When Drew Nieporent began to focus on healthful foods, so did the chefs and clients of his influential restaurants.

During the last year, Drew Nieporent, owner of some of New York City's finest establishments—Nobu, Tribeca Grill, and Montrachet—lost 135 pounds. Thanks to his determination and the culinary inventions of Chef Stephen Lewandowski of Tribeca Grill, Nieporent and the many patrons of his world-renown restaurants are improving their health. And now you can, too!

Thyme-Scented Salmon with Tuscan White Bean Salad

Chef Stephen Lewandowski of Tribeca Grill uses fresh herbs in this best-selling dish. At the restaurant, he serves it over arugula dressed with salt, pepper, and lemon juice.

BEAN SALAD:

1 tablespoon extravirgin olive oil
½ cup finely chopped carrot
½ cup finely chopped shallots
⅓ cup finely chopped celery
2 garlic cloves, minced
3 tablespoons lemon juice
2 teaspoons chopped fresh mint
2 teaspoons chopped fresh parsley
2 teaspoons chopped fresh basil
2 tablespoons water
1 (15-ounce) can cannellini beans or other white beans, drained

SALMON:

2 teaspoons chopped fresh thyme
1 teaspoon chopped fresh parsley
½ teaspoon salt
⅛ teaspoon black pepper
4 (6-ounce) salmon fillets (about 1-inch thick)
3 tablespoons lemon juice

1. Preheat oven to 375°.

2. To prepare bean salad, heat oil in a medium nonstick skillet; add carrot, shallots, celery, and garlic. Cook 4 minutes or until tender; add 3 tablespoons juice, mint, and next 4 ingredients. Cook bean mixture 2 minutes or until thoroughly heated, stirring constantly. Remove from heat; cover.

3. To prepare salmon, combine thyme, 1 teaspoon parsley, salt, and pepper in a small bowl; sprinkle evenly over fish. Place fish on a baking sheet or broiler pan lined with aluminum foil. Bake at 375° for 14 minutes or until fish flakes easily when tested with a fork. Remove from oven; sprinkle evenly with 3 tablespoons juice. Serve with bean salad. Yield: 4 servings (serving size: 1 salmon fillet and ½ cup bean salad).

CALORIES 414 (37% from fat); FAT 17g (sat 3.6g, mono 8.2g, poly 3.9g); PROTEIN 41g; CARB 22g; FIBER 5g; CHOL 87mg; IRON 2.6mg; SODIUM 616mg; CALC 78mg

Chicken with Stone Fruit Panzanella

Chef Lewandowski uses the bright flavors of fresh fruit and herbs inventively to make this unusual bread salad, which is served at Tribeca Grill.

PANZANELLA:

4 (1-ounce) slices French bread, cut into ½-inch cubes (about 2 cups)
Cooking spray
1 cup finely chopped peeled peach (about 1 peach)
1 cup finely chopped peeled nectarine (about 1 nectarine)
3 tablespoons sugar, divided
1 cup (½-inch) chopped plum tomato (about 3 tomatoes)
¼ cup pitted kalamata olives, halved (about 8 olives)
¼ cup thinly sliced fresh basil
2 tablespoons chopped red onion
1 tablespoon capers
3 tablespoons extravirgin olive oil
2 tablespoons red wine vinegar
¼ teaspoon salt
⅛ teaspoon black pepper

CHICKEN:

⅔ cup minced shallots
¼ cup fresh lemon juice
1 tablespoon chopped fresh parsley
1 tablespoon chopped fresh thyme
½ teaspoon salt
⅛ teaspoon black pepper
4 (6-ounce) skinless, boneless chicken breast halves
Thyme sprigs (optional)

1. Preheat oven to 450°.

2. To prepare panzanella, place bread in a single layer on a baking sheet. Bake at 450° for 4 minutes or until toasted.

3. Heat a nonstick skillet coated with cooking spray over medium-high heat; add peach, nectarine, and 1 tablespoon sugar. Cook 2 minutes or until fruit is lightly browned, stirring frequently.

4. Combine fruit mixture, tomato, olives, basil, onion, and capers in a large bowl. Combine 2 tablespoons sugar, oil, and next 3 ingredients in a small bowl, stirring with a whisk. Add vinegar mixture to peach mixture; toss gently to combine.

Let stand 30 minutes. Toss with bread just before serving.

5. To prepare chicken, combine shallots and next 5 ingredients in a large zip-top plastic bag; add chicken. Seal and marinate in refrigerator 30 minutes. Remove chicken from bag; discard marinade. Heat a large nonstick skillet over medium-high heat; add chicken, and sauté 7 minutes on each side. Cut across the grain into thin slices; serve with panzanella. Garnish with thyme sprigs, if desired. Yield: 4 servings (serving size: 1 chicken breast and 1 cup panzanella).

CALORIES 429 (31% from fat); FAT 15g (sat 2.3g, mono 10g, poly 1.8g); PROTEIN 30g; CARB 43g; FIBER 3.5g; CHOL 65mg; IRON 2.5mg; SODIUM 892mg; CALC 70mg

---

QUICK & EASY
Halibut Provençal

Nieporent's Montrachet restaurant serves this Mediterranean dish in a big shallow bowl to hold all the delicious juices.

  1   tablespoon olive oil
  2   garlic cloves, sliced
2½   cups slivered onion
  ½   teaspoon salt, divided
  2   cups chopped peeled plum tomato
       (about 4 tomatoes)
1¾   cups thinly sliced fennel bulb
       (about 1 small bulb)
  1   cup dry white wine
  ⅓   cup chopped fresh basil
  ¼   cup chopped pitted kalamata
       olives
  1   tablespoon tomato paste
  ⅛   teaspoon crushed red pepper
  2   teaspoons capers
  1   bay leaf
  ½   cup water
  ⅛   teaspoon black pepper
  6   (6-ounce) halibut or cod fillets

1. Preheat oven to 450°.
2. Heat oil in a large ovenproof skillet over medium-high heat, and add garlic. Sauté 30 seconds; add onion and ¼ teaspoon salt. Cook 2 minutes, stirring occasionally. Add tomato and next 8 ingredients; cook 10 minutes. Stir in water.
3. Sprinkle ¼ teaspoon salt and black pepper over fish; place fish on top of onion mixture. Cover and bake at 450° for 10 minutes or until fish flakes easily when tested with a fork. Discard bay leaf. Yield: 6 servings (serving size: 1 halibut fillet and ⅔ cup onion mixture).

CALORIES 279 (23% from fat); FAT 7g (sat 0.9g, mono 3.4g, poly 1.6g); PROTEIN 37g; CARB 10g; FIBER 2.6g; CHOL 54mg; IRON 2.4mg; SODIUM 392mg; CALC 119mg

---

on hand
Pasta Presto

These Mediterranean-style pasta tosses provide quick suppers with minimal cooking.

   Pasta—it's the food we all love to eat. Presto—means it's ready so fast it's almost instant. Inspired by the rustic Italian summer pasta "sauce" of chopped juicy ripe tomatoes, fresh basil, garlic, and extravirgin olive oil, these recipes capitalize on high-quality ingredients. And all the dishes—from Pasta Shells with Tuscan Tuna to Orecchiette with Sausage, Peppers, and Feta—can be tossed together in mere minutes for a robust Mediterranean meal tonight.

QUICK & EASY
Orecchiette with Sausage, Peppers, and Feta

If you can't find orecchiette, substitute penne or farfalle.

  8   ounces uncooked orecchiette
       ("little ear" pasta; about 2 cups)
  1   teaspoon olive oil
  3   cups (¼-inch-thick) slices red bell
       pepper, each cut in half
       crosswise
  ½   teaspoon salt, divided
  8   ounces turkey Italian sausage
  1   teaspoon dried oregano
  1   garlic clove, minced
  ¾   cup (3 ounces) crumbled feta
       cheese
  ¼   cup sliced pitted kalamata
       olives
  ¼   teaspoon freshly ground black
       pepper

1. Cook pasta according to package directions, omitting salt and fat. Drain pasta in a colander over a bowl, reserving ½ cup cooking liquid.
2. Heat oil in a large nonstick skillet over medium-high heat. Add bell pepper and ¼ teaspoon salt; sauté 2 minutes. Remove casings from sausage. Add sausage, oregano, and garlic to pan; cook 4 minutes or until sausage is done, stirring to crumble sausage. Add pasta, reserved cooking liquid, ¼ teaspoon salt, cheese, olives, and black pepper; cook 2 minutes or until thoroughly heated, stirring frequently. Yield: 4 servings (serving size: 1½ cups).

CALORIES 393 (29% from fat); FAT 12.8g (sat 5.3g, mono 4.6g, poly 2g); PROTEIN 21.6g; CARB 48.6g; FIBER 3.6g; CHOL 67mg; IRON 3.4mg; SODIUM 947mg; CALC 137mg

---

QUICK & EASY
Fusilli with Tomatoes, Spinach, and Prosciutto

Draining the hot pasta over the spinach is an easy, no-cook wilting method.

  8   ounces uncooked long fusilli
       (long twisted spaghetti)
  1   (6-ounce) bag baby spinach
  4   cups chopped tomato
  1   tablespoon extravirgin olive
       oil
  ¾   teaspoon salt
  ¼   teaspoon crushed red pepper
  1   garlic clove, minced
  2   ounces thinly sliced prosciutto,
       cut into strips
  ½   cup (2 ounces) shaved
       Parmigiano-Reggiano cheese

1. Cook pasta according to package directions, omitting salt and fat. Place spinach in a large colander. Drain pasta over spinach; place pasta mixture in a large bowl. Add tomato, oil, salt, pepper, and garlic; toss well. Add prosciutto; toss gently to combine. Sprinkle with cheese. Yield: 4 servings (serving size: 2 cups pasta mixture and 2 tablespoons cheese).

CALORIES 370 (24% from fat); FAT 10g (sat 3.4g, mono 4.4g, poly 1.2g); PROTEIN 18.3g; CARB 53g; FIBER 3.8g; CHOL 18mg; IRON 4.5mg; SODIUM 934mg; CALC 232mg

QUICK & EASY
Linguine with Garlic and Cheese

Substitute crushed red pepper for the black pepper if you'd like a bit more heat.

    8 ounces uncooked linguine
 1½ tablespoons olive oil
    3 garlic cloves, minced
  ¾ cup (3 ounces) grated fresh
       Parmesan cheese
  ½ teaspoon salt
  ¼ teaspoon black pepper

1. Cook pasta according to package directions, omitting salt and fat. Drain.
2. Heat oil in a small, heavy saucepan over low heat. Add garlic; sauté 5 minutes or until lightly browned. Remove from heat. Add pasta, cheese, salt, and pepper to pan; toss well to coat. Yield: 4 servings (serving size: about 1 cup).

CALORIES 338 (30% from fat); FAT 11.4g (sat 4.4g, mono 5.3g, poly 0.6g); PROTEIN 15.5g; CARB 43.8g; FIBER 1.9g; CHOL 14mg; IRON 2.1mg; SODIUM 637mg; CALC 267mg

QUICK & EASY
Chicken, Corn, and Green Onion Rotini

In this simple dish, the sweetness of fresh corn plays off the gentle heat of a seeded serrano chile. This dish also provides a perfect use for leftover chicken.

    8 ounces uncooked rotini
       (corkscrew pasta; about 4
       cups)
    2 cups chopped roasted skinless,
       boneless chicken breast (about
       2 breasts)
    2 cups fresh corn kernels
 1¼ cups thinly sliced green
       onions
    1 cup chopped plum tomato
  ½ cup (2 ounces) grated fresh
       Parmesan cheese
    2 tablespoons balsamic vinegar
    2 tablespoons extravirgin olive
       oil
  ½ teaspoon salt
    1 serrano chile, seeded and minced

1. Cook pasta according to package directions, omitting salt and fat. Drain pasta; return to pan. Add chicken and remaining ingredients; toss well. Yield: 6 servings (serving size: 1⅓ cups).

CALORIES 338 (25% from fat); FAT 9.4g (sat 2.9g, mono 4.6g, poly 1g); PROTEIN 22.7g; CARB 42.6g; FIBER 3.8g; CHOL 39mg; IRON 1.8mg; SODIUM 637mg; CALC 132mg

QUICK & EASY
Cavatappi with Vodka Sauce

Luscious, creamy vodka sauce gets into every nook and cranny of the spiral-shaped cavatappi. You can also use fusilli or penne.

    8 ounces uncooked cavatappi
       (about 3 cups)
    1 tablespoon butter
  ⅔ cup finely chopped onion
    1 garlic clove, minced
    1 (8-ounce) can tomato sauce
    4 teaspoons all-purpose flour
    1 tablespoon water
  ¾ cup half-and-half
  ½ cup 2% reduced-fat milk
  ⅓ cup vodka
  ¼ teaspoon salt
  ⅛ teaspoon ground red pepper
  ½ cup (2 ounces) grated fresh
       Parmesan cheese
    2 tablespoons finely chopped basil

1. Cook pasta according to package directions, omitting salt and fat. Drain.
2. Melt butter in a medium saucepan over medium heat. Add onion and garlic; cover and cook 3 minutes or until tender. Add tomato sauce; simmer, partially covered, 8 minutes or until thick. Combine flour and water, stirring with a whisk until smooth. Add flour mixture to pan; cook 1 minute. Add half-and-half, milk, vodka, salt, and pepper; bring to a boil. Stir in cheese. Reduce heat to low; cook 3 minutes or until cheese melts, stirring frequently. Add pasta; toss to coat. Sprinkle with basil. Yield: 4 servings (serving size: about 1⅓ cups).

CALORIES 449 (27% from fat); FAT 13.3g (sat 8g, mono 3.4g, poly 0.5g); PROTEIN 16.6g; CARB 55g; FIBER 3.2g; CHOL 36mg; IRON 2.7mg; SODIUM 784mg; CALC 275mg

Quick Pasta Tip

• Fill the pasta pot with very hot tap water (about 4 quarts of hot water for the amount of pasta in these recipes). Keep the pot covered as the water heats so that it comes to a boil quickly.
• Cook the pasta until it's al dente—chewy but not soft. Begin testing for doneness about 1 minute before the indicated cooking time.
• When draining pasta, reserve about ¼ cup cooking water. After the other ingredients are tossed in, some water may need to be added to loosen the sauce and allow the components to bind. Also, don't rinse the pasta: The starch that clings to it will help thicken the sauce.
• Experiment with pasta shapes in these dishes. Just make sure you stick to either long or short, according to the recipe.

QUICK & EASY
Pasta Shells with Tuscan Tuna

Tuna and red onion crostini are a favored snack at Florentine wine bars. The combination is tossed here with pasta shells. Look for tuna that's vacuum-sealed in bags—it's firmer than canned tuna and doesn't require draining.

    8 ounces uncooked medium seashell
       pasta (about 3 cups)
  ½ cup chopped red onion
  ¼ cup thinly sliced fresh basil
    2 tablespoons capers
    2 tablespoons extravirgin olive oil
    2 teaspoons grated lemon rind
  ½ teaspoon salt
  ¼ teaspoon freshly ground black
       pepper
    2 (7-ounce) bags white albacore
       tuna in water

1. Cook pasta according to package directions, omitting salt and fat. Drain pasta in a colander over a bowl,

168   May

reserving 2 tablespoons cooking liquid. Return pasta to pan. Add reserved cooking liquid, onion, and remaining ingredients; toss well. Yield: 4 servings (serving size: 1½ cups).

CALORIES 402 (24% from fat); FAT 10.6g (sat 1.9g, mono 5.8g, poly 1.7g); PROTEIN 31.8g; CARB 44.4g; FIBER 2.4g; CHOL 42mg; IRON 3.1mg; SODIUM 829mg; CALC 37mg

Almost everyone loves macaroni and cheese, but pasta's possibilities are almost endless. Be adventurous and give one of these dishes a try.

QUICK & EASY
Tomato Fettuccine with Shrimp and Arugula

A splash of half-and-half is combined with some of the pasta's cooking water to create a silky sauce. If you can't find arugula, use spinach in its place.

    8   ounces uncooked fettuccine
    1   tablespoon olive oil
    1   cup finely chopped Vidalia or
        other sweet onion
    2   cups grape or cherry tomatoes,
        halved lengthwise
    ¾   teaspoon salt, divided
    ¾   pound large shrimp, peeled and
        deveined
    ⅓   cup half-and-half
    ¼   teaspoon freshly ground black
        pepper
    5   cups trimmed arugula (about
        2 ounces)

1. Cook pasta according to package directions, omitting salt and fat. Drain pasta in a colander over a bowl, reserving ½ cup cooking liquid.
2. Heat oil in a large nonstick skillet over medium-high heat. Add onion; sauté 3 minutes or until tender. Add tomatoes and ¼ teaspoon salt; cook 2 minutes, stirring occasionally. Add shrimp; cook 2 minutes, stirring frequently. Add pasta, reserved cooking liquid, ½ teaspoon salt, half-and-half, and pepper; toss well. Cook over medium-low heat 3 minutes or until thoroughly heated and shrimp are done. Add arugula; toss well. Yield: 4 servings (serving size: 1½ cups).

CALORIES 393 (19% from fat); FAT 8.2g (sat 2.4g, mono 3.4g, poly 1.1g); PROTEIN 27.5g; CARB 52.1g; FIBER 3.9g; CHOL 139mg; IRON 4.8mg; SODIUM 594mg; CALC 134mg

QUICK & EASY
Spaghetti with Smoked Mozzarella

Smoked mozzarella creates the flavor of pasta carbonara without the bacon. Shred the mozzarella as finely as possible so it will melt quickly. Juicy tomato slices drizzled with sweet-tart balsamic vinegar are ideal on the side.

    8   ounces uncooked spaghetti
    2   cups (1-inch) sliced asparagus
    ¾   cup 2% reduced-fat milk
    ¾   teaspoon salt
    ¼   teaspoon freshly ground black
        pepper
    2   large eggs, lightly beaten
    2   garlic cloves, minced
    ⅓   cup (1½ ounces) finely shredded
        smoked mozzarella cheese
    ⅓   cup (1½ ounces) grated fresh
        Parmesan cheese
    ⅓   cup chopped fresh flat-leaf parsley
    ¼   teaspoon crushed red pepper

1. Cook pasta in boiling water 7 minutes. Add asparagus; cook 2 minutes or until pasta is al dente and asparagus is crisp-tender. Drain.
2. Combine milk, salt, black pepper, eggs, and garlic in a Dutch oven, stirring with a whisk until well blended. Add pasta mixture; cook over medium heat 3 minutes or until slightly thick and creamy, stirring constantly. Add cheeses, parsley, and red pepper; cook 1½ minutes or until cheese melts, stirring constantly. Serve immediately. Yield: 4 servings (serving size: 1¼ cups).

CALORIES 363 (24% from fat); FAT 9.5g (sat 4.8g, mono 2.7g, poly 1g); PROTEIN 19.4g; CARB 49.5g; FIBER 3.1g; CHOL 125mg; IRON 3.7mg; SODIUM 688mg; CALC 290mg

QUICK & EASY
Farfalle, Zucchini, and Bell Peppers in Pesto

Shredded zucchini contributes both moisture and texture to this pesto-based sauce.

    8   ounces uncooked farfalle (bow tie
        pasta; about 4 cups)
    3   tablespoons commercial pesto
    2   cups shredded zucchini
    1   cup finely chopped red bell
        pepper
    ½   cup thinly sliced red onion
    1   tablespoon fresh lemon juice
    ¾   teaspoon salt
    ¼   teaspoon crushed red pepper
    ¼   teaspoon freshly ground black
        pepper
    ½   cup (2 ounces) grated Parmigiano-
        Reggiano cheese, divided

1. Cook pasta according to package directions, omitting salt and fat. Drain pasta; return to pan. Add pesto; stir well. Add zucchini and next 6 ingredients; toss well. Stir in ¼ cup cheese. Top with remaining cheese. Yield: 4 servings (serving size: 2 cups pasta mixture and 1 tablespoon cheese).

CALORIES 346 (27% from fat); FAT 10.2g (sat 4.1g, mono 4.4g, poly 0.5g); PROTEIN 15.6g; CARB 14.5g; FIBER 4g; CHOL 19mg; IRON 2.9mg; SODIUM 705mg; CALC 261mg

. . . And Ready in Just About 20 Minutes

These recipes will take you around the world in record time.

The Chinese-inspired In-a-Pinch Moo Shu Chicken and the "Fried" Chicken with Cucumber and Fennel Raita from India feature authentic flavors with ingredients truly easy to find. The same goes for Garlic-Rosemary Lamb Chops and Grouper with Tomato, Olive, and Wine Sauce—both classic European dishes that call for ingredients available at most grocers. When your appetite drifts back home, try Smothered Pork Chops with Onions and Cheddar Grits.

QUICK & EASY
Huevos Rancheros with Zucchini and Green Pepper

Entertain at brunch with this casual main dish. Serve a pineapple and melon compote on the side tossed with fresh mint sprigs.

    1   teaspoon olive oil
    Cooking spray
    1½ cups cubed zucchini
    ½   cup cubed green bell pepper
    ¼   cup water
    ¼   teaspoon salt
    ¼   teaspoon ground cumin
    ⅛   teaspoon freshly ground black
        pepper
    1   (10-ounce) can diced tomatoes
        with green chiles, undrained
    4   (6-inch) corn tortillas
    4   large eggs
    ⅓   cup (1¼ ounces) preshredded
        reduced-fat Cheddar cheese
    2   teaspoons chopped fresh cilantro

1. Heat oil in a large nonstick skillet coated with cooking spray over medium-high heat. Add zucchini and bell pepper;

sauté 6 minutes or until lightly browned. Stir in water and next 4 ingredients. Cover and simmer 3 minutes.
2. Warm tortillas according to package directions.
3. Break 1 egg into a small custard cup. Slip egg onto tomato mixture; repeat procedure with remaining eggs. Cover and simmer 3 minutes or until eggs are done. Sprinkle with cheese. Cover and cook 30 seconds or until cheese melts.
4. Place 1 tortilla on each of 4 plates. Spoon 1 egg and ¾ cup tomato mixture onto each tortilla. Sprinkle each with ½ teaspoon cilantro. Yield: 4 servings.

CALORIES 248 (31% from fat); FAT 8.5g (sat 2.1g, mono 2.9g, poly 0.9g); PROTEIN 13.2g; CARB 31.5g; FIBER 4.1g; CHOL 214mg; IRON 2.6mg; SODIUM 679mg; CALC 155mg

QUICK & EASY
Shrimp Salad with Banana Peppers and Black Beans

Serve with baked tortilla chips.

    1   cup water
    2   teaspoons liquid crab boil
    40 large shrimp, peeled and deveined
        (about 1½ pounds)
    ¼   cup chopped fresh cilantro
    3   tablespoons fresh lemon juice
    ½   teaspoon salt
    1   banana pepper, seeded and thinly
        sliced
    1   (15-ounce) can black beans,
        rinsed and drained
    12 (¼-inch-thick) slices tomato
        (about 2 large tomatoes)
    1   peeled avocado, cut into 16
        wedges

1. Bring water and crab boil to a boil in a large skillet. Add shrimp; cook 3 minutes or until done. Drain and rinse with cold water. Chill.
2. Combine shrimp, cilantro, and next 4 ingredients in a large bowl. Arrange 3 tomato slices and 4 avocado wedges on each of 4 plates; top each serving with 1 cup shrimp salad. Yield: 4 servings.

CALORIES 333 (33% from fat); FAT 12.2g (sat 2g, mono 5.9g, poly 2.8g); PROTEIN 39.3g; CARB 16.8g; FIBER 7.1g; CHOL 259mg; IRON 6mg; SODIUM 720mg; CALC 121mg

QUICK & EASY
Garlic-Rosemary Lamb Chops

Commit this simple rub mixture to memory, and use it on pork chops, too. Serve with buttered pasta garnished with parsley.

    1   tablespoon bottled minced
        garlic
    1½ teaspoons dried rosemary,
        crushed
    ¼   teaspoon salt
    ¼   teaspoon black pepper
    8   (4-ounce) lamb rib chops,
        trimmed
    Cooking spray

1. Preheat broiler.
2. Combine first 4 ingredients; rub over lamb. Place lamb on a broiler pan coated with cooking spray; broil 5 minutes on each side or until desired degree of doneness. Yield: 4 servings (serving size: 2 chops).

CALORIES 231 (49% from fat); FAT 12.6g (sat 4.5g, mono 5g, poly 1.2g); PROTEIN 26.9g; CARB 1.1g; FIBER 0.3g; CHOL 88mg; IRON 2.3mg; SODIUM 229mg; CALC 25mg

QUICK & EASY
Cajun Flank Steak

Slice the steak with your sharpest knife on a cutting board that has a "well" around the edges to collect the flavorful juices; spoon them over the steak. Bake thick-cut fries to serve on the side.

    1   tablespoon garlic powder
    1   tablespoon onion powder
    2   teaspoons sugar
    2   teaspoons paprika
    1   teaspoon chili powder
    ¾   teaspoon salt
    ½   teaspoon black pepper
    ¼   teaspoon ground red pepper
    1   pound flank steak, trimmed
    Cooking spray

1. Combine first 8 ingredients in a small bowl. Rub spice mixture over both sides of steak.
2. Heat a large nonstick grill pan coated with cooking spray over medium-high

heat. Add steak, and cook 5 minutes on each side. Cut steak diagonally across the grain into thin slices. Yield: 4 servings (serving size: 3 ounces steak).

CALORIES 195 (42% from fat); FAT 9g (sat 3.6g, mono 3.3g, poly 0.5g); PROTEIN 22.7g; CARB 6.1g; FIBER 0.9g; CHOL 54mg; IRON 2.6mg; SODIUM 512mg; CALC 19mg

In-a-Pinch Moo Shu Chicken

Authentic Chinese moo shu uses thin homemade pancakes. Flour tortillas make a fast substitute. Serve with fresh fruit.

Cooking spray
½ cup egg substitute
1½ pounds skinless, boneless chicken breast
2 teaspoons vegetable oil
2 teaspoons bottled minced garlic
1½ teaspoons minced peeled fresh ginger
4 cups packaged cabbage-and-carrot coleslaw
1 cup chopped zucchini
¾ cup chopped green onions
¼ teaspoon salt
¼ teaspoon crushed red pepper
½ cup hoisin sauce
10 (6-inch) flour tortillas

1. Heat a small nonstick skillet coated with cooking spray over medium heat. Add 2 tablespoons egg substitute; cook 1 minute or until done. Remove egg to a cutting board. Repeat procedure with remaining egg substitute. Cut egg into thin strips; set aside.
2. Place chicken in a food processor; pulse until finely ground. Heat oil in a large nonstick skillet over medium-high heat. Add chicken, garlic, and ginger; cook 3 minutes, stirring to crumble. Stir in coleslaw, zucchini, onions, salt, and pepper; cook 3 minutes or until tender, stirring frequently. Stir in hoisin.
3. Warm tortillas according to package directions. Spoon ¾ cup chicken mixture down center of each tortilla; top each with about 1 tablespoon egg strips.

Roll up. Yield: 5 servings (serving size: 2 tortilla wraps).

CALORIES 322 (20% from fat); FAT 7.2g (sat 1.6g, mono 2.1g, poly 3g); PROTEIN 26.6g; CARB 36.1g; FIBER 2.5g; CHOL 50mg; IRON 3.1mg; SODIUM 762mg; CALC 111mg

"Fried" Chicken with Cucumber and Fennel Raita

Coating the chicken with cooking spray helps the breadcrumbs adhere and creates a crisp crust.

1 cup plain fat-free yogurt
½ cup (½-inch) cubed cucumber
½ cup (½-inch) cubed fennel bulb
1 teaspoon finely chopped fresh mint
¼ teaspoon salt
¼ teaspoon coarsely ground black pepper
4 (6-ounce) skinless, boneless chicken breast halves
⅛ teaspoon salt
Cooking spray
⅓ cup Italian-seasoned breadcrumbs
1 tablespoon olive oil

1. Combine first 6 ingredients in a medium bowl. Cover and chill.
2. Place each chicken breast half between 2 sheets of heavy-duty plastic wrap; pound to ¼-inch thickness using a meat mallet or rolling pin. Sprinkle chicken with ⅛ teaspoon salt; lightly coat both sides with cooking spray. Dredge in breadcrumbs.
3. Heat oil in a large nonstick skillet over medium-high heat. Add chicken; cook 2 minutes on each side or until done. Serve with yogurt mixture. Yield: 4 servings (serving size: 1 chicken breast half and about ⅓ cup raita).

CALORIES 213 (26% from fat); FAT 6.1g (sat 1.5g, mono 3.3g, poly 0.7g); PROTEIN 30g; CARB 7.9g; FIBER 0.6g; CHOL 70mg; IRON 1.1mg; SODIUM 358mg; CALC 140mg

Grouper with Tomato, Olive, and Wine Sauce

Serve with crusty bread to soak up the fresh tomato and wine sauce.

Cooking spray
½ cup chopped onion
2 teaspoons bottled minced garlic
½ cup dry white wine
⅓ cup fat-free, less-sodium chicken broth
1 cup quartered cherry tomatoes
¼ cup pitted ripe olives, halved
1 tablespoon chopped fresh herbs, such as basil, parsley, or oregano
1 tablespoon olive oil
4 (6-ounce) grouper fillets (about ½-inch thick)
¼ teaspoon salt
¼ teaspoon black pepper

1. Heat a medium saucepan coated with cooking spray over medium-high heat. Add onion and garlic, and sauté 3 minutes. Add wine and broth; reduce heat, cover, and simmer 3 minutes. Stir in tomatoes, olives, and herbs; cover and cook 3 minutes. Remove from heat; keep warm.
2. Heat oil in a large nonstick skillet over medium-high heat. Sprinkle both sides of fish with salt and pepper. Add fish to pan; cook 4 minutes on each side or until fish flakes easily when tested with a fork. Top with tomato mixture. Yield: 4 servings (serving size: 1 grouper fillet and ¼ cup tomato mixture).

CALORIES 268 (31% from fat); FAT 9.3g (sat 1.9g, mono 4.2g, poly 1.9g); PROTEIN 28.9g; CARB 6.9g; FIBER 1.9g; CHOL 82mg; IRON 1.6mg; SODIUM 717mg; CALC 63mg

Shepherd's Pie

Prepared mashed potatoes are located in the refrigerated section of larger grocers.

2 cups prepared mashed potatoes (such as Simply Potatoes)
¾ pound ground sirloin
¾ cup picante sauce
⅓ cup water
1 tablespoon ground cumin
2 teaspoons sugar
⅛ teaspoon salt
1 (15-ounce) can kidney beans, drained and rinsed
½ cup (2 ounces) preshredded reduced-fat extrasharp Cheddar cheese

1. Prepare mashed potatoes according to package directions; keep warm.
2. Cook beef in a large nonstick skillet over medium-high heat until browned, stirring to crumble. Stir in picante sauce and next 5 ingredients; bring to a boil. Reduce heat; simmer until mixture thickens (about 5 minutes).
3. Remove from heat. Spoon mashed potatoes over meat mixture, and sprinkle with cheese. Cover and let stand 2 minutes or until cheese melts. Yield: 4 servings (serving size: 1 cup).

CALORIES 279 (19% from fat); FAT 6g (sat 2.2g, mono 2.2g, poly 0.5g); PROTEIN 25.7g; CARB 30.5g; FIBER 8g; CHOL 48mg; IRON 2.2mg; SODIUM 699mg; CALC 88mg

Broccoli and Smoked Turkey Focaccia Sandwiches

Serve with tomato soup and melon wedges.

¾ cup broccoli florets
¼ cup (2 ounces) tub-style light cream cheese
2 tablespoons fat-free Italian dressing
½ teaspoon dried Italian seasoning
6 ounces thinly sliced smoked turkey breast
⅓ cup chopped bottled roasted red bell peppers
1 (8-ounce) round focaccia loaf

1. Steam broccoli, covered, 5 minutes or until crisp-tender.
2. While broccoli cooks, combine cream cheese, dressing, and Italian seasoning in a bowl.
3. Combine broccoli, cream cheese mixture, turkey, and bell peppers in a medium nonstick skillet; cook turkey mixture over medium-high heat until thoroughly heated, stirring frequently.
4. Preheat broiler.
5. Cut focaccia in half horizontally; place halves, cut sides up, on a baking sheet. Broil 1 minute or until toasted. Spread turkey mixture evenly over bottom half of focaccia; top with remaining focaccia half. Cut into 4 wedges. Yield: 4 servings (serving size: 1 wedge).

CALORIES 256 (25% from fat); FAT 7g (sat 3.3g, mono 1.1g, poly 1.1g); PROTEIN 14.3g; CARB 34.4g; FIBER 1.6g; CHOL 27mg; IRON 1.6mg; SODIUM 864mg; CALC 38mg

Baked Snapper with Chipotle Butter

For a side salad, toss diced cucumbers and tomatoes with reduced-fat sour cream.

½ teaspoon ground cumin
½ teaspoon paprika
¼ teaspoon salt
⅛ teaspoon black pepper
4 (6-ounce) red snapper or other firm white fish fillets
Cooking spray
1 tablespoon butter, softened
1 canned chipotle chile in adobo sauce, finely chopped
Lemon wedges

1. Preheat oven to 400°.
2. Combine first 4 ingredients; sprinkle evenly over fish. Place fish on a baking sheet coated with cooking spray; bake at 400° for 15 minutes or until fish flakes easily when tested with a fork.
3. While fish bakes, combine butter and chile. Spread butter mixture evenly over fish. Serve with lemon wedges. Yield: 4 servings (serving size: 1 snapper fillet).

CALORIES 203 (24% from fat); FAT 5.4g (sat 2.3g, mono 1.3g, poly 0.9g); PROTEIN 35.2g; CARB 1.6g; FIBER 0.4g; CHOL 71mg; IRON 0.5mg; SODIUM 317mg; CALC 63mg

Tortellini-Pepperoncini Salad

The shredded Parmesan cheese in this salad isn't powdery like finely grated Parmesan.

1 (9-ounce) package fresh cheese tortellini
2 cups halved cherry tomatoes
2 cups fresh spinach leaves, coarsely chopped
½ cup chopped pepperoncini peppers
6 tablespoons (1½ ounces) preshredded fresh Parmesan cheese
¼ cup capers
¼ cup chopped fresh basil
1 (16-ounce) can navy beans, rinsed and drained
2 tablespoons fresh lemon juice
1½ tablespoons extravirgin olive oil

1. Cook pasta according to package directions, omitting salt and fat.
2. While pasta cooks, combine tomatoes and next 6 ingredients in a large bowl. Drain pasta; rinse with cold water. Add pasta, juice, and oil to tomato mixture; toss gently. Serve immediately. Yield: 7 servings (serving size: 1 cup).

CALORIES 208 (30% from fat); FAT 7g (sat 2.3g, mono 2.8g, poly 0.6g); PROTEIN 10.8g; CARB 26.7g; FIBER 4.8g; CHOL 9mg; IRON 2.4mg; SODIUM 955mg; CALC 112mg

Curried Fruit Salad with Scallops

8 large Bibb lettuce leaves
1 tablespoon orange juice
1 tablespoon lime juice
2 teaspoons extravirgin olive oil
¼ teaspoon dark brown sugar
⅛ teaspoon salt
⅛ teaspoon curry powder
Dash of black pepper
2 cups chopped peeled mango
½ cup chopped red onion
1 teaspoon minced fresh cilantro
1½ pounds sea scallops
1 tablespoon lime juice
¼ teaspoon black pepper
⅛ teaspoon salt
Cooking spray

1. Arrange 2 lettuce leaves on each of 4 plates. Combine orange juice and next 6 ingredients in a medium bowl, stirring well with a whisk. Add mango, onion, and cilantro to juice mixture; toss gently to coat. Spoon mango mixture evenly onto lettuce leaves.

2. Drizzle scallops with 1 tablespoon lime juice; sprinkle with ¼ teaspoon pepper and ⅛ teaspoon salt. Heat a large nonstick skillet coated with cooking spray over medium-high heat. Add scallops; cook 4 minutes on each side or until lightly browned. Arrange scallops over salads. Yield: 4 servings (serving size: 5 ounces scallops and 2 cups salad).

CALORIES 241 (15% from fat); FAT 4g (sat 0.5g, mono 2g, poly 0.8g); PROTEIN 29.7g; CARB 22g; FIBER 2.3g; CHOL 56mg; IRON 0.8mg; SODIUM 423mg; CALC 65mg

QUICK & EASY
Turkey Cheeseburger

Shredded zucchini boosts the size and moistness of these patties. Cut the remaining zucchini into spears, and serve alongside the burgers.

1 tablespoon fat-free mayonnaise
1 tablespoon honey mustard
¾ pound ground turkey breast
⅓ cup shredded zucchini
1 tablespoon minced fresh cilantro
2 teaspoons low-sodium soy sauce
¼ teaspoon coarsely ground black pepper
Cooking spray
2 (1-ounce) slices reduced-fat Cheddar cheese, halved
4 English muffins, split and toasted
4 large green leaf lettuce leaves

1. Combine mayonnaise and mustard in a small bowl.

2. Combine turkey, zucchini, cilantro, soy, and pepper. Divide turkey mixture into 4 equal portions, shaping each into a ¼-inch-thick patty.

3. Heat a large nonstick skillet coated with cooking spray over medium-high heat. Add patties; cook 4 minutes. Turn

patties over; cook 3 minutes or until done. Top patties with cheese; cover and cook 1 minute or until cheese melts.

4. Spread 1½ teaspoons mayonnaise mixture over cut side of each of 4 muffin halves. Top with patties, lettuce leaves, and muffin tops. Yield: 4 servings (serving size: 1 burger).

CALORIES 337 (36% from fat); FAT 13.4g (sat 4.7g, mono 3.1g, poly 2.5g); PROTEIN 23.7g; CARB 30.2g; FIBER 0.4g; CHOL 82mg; IRON 3mg; SODIUM 515mg; CALC 194mg

QUICK & EASY
Chicken, Mint, and Coleslaw Wraps

You'll find bottled ground fresh ginger in the produce section. It gives these wrap sandwiches a fiery bite that's balanced by the cooling effect of fresh mint.

4 (6-ounce) skinless, boneless chicken breast halves
⅛ teaspoon salt
Cooking spray
⅓ cup fresh lemon juice
1 tablespoon bottled ground fresh ginger (such as Spice World)
2 teaspoons sugar
¼ teaspoon crushed red pepper
3 cups angel hair coleslaw
½ cup chopped fresh mint
1 poblano chile, halved lengthwise, seeded, and thinly sliced
6 (8-inch) flour tortillas

1. Place each chicken breast half between 2 sheets of heavy-duty plastic wrap; pound to ¼-inch thickness using a meat mallet or rolling pin. Sprinkle chicken with salt. Heat a large nonstick skillet coated with cooking spray over medium-high heat. Add chicken; sauté 4½ minutes on each side or until done. Remove chicken to a cutting board, and cut into thin strips.

2. Combine juice, ginger, sugar, and red pepper in a large bowl. Add chicken strips, coleslaw, mint, and chile, tossing well to coat. Warm tortillas according to package directions. Divide chicken mixture evenly among tortillas; roll up. Cut

each rolled tortilla in half crosswise. Yield: 6 servings (serving size: 2 tortilla halves).

CALORIES 304 (18% from fat); FAT 6.1g (sat 1.6g, mono 0.8g, poly 1.1g); PROTEIN 32.6g; CARB 31.2g; FIBER 3g; CHOL 71mg; IRON 1.9mg; SODIUM 121mg; CALC 78mg

QUICK & EASY
Smothered Pork Chops with Onions and Cheddar Grits

Serve mashed potatoes in place of the cheese grits, if you prefer. Round out the meal with steamed green beans.

2⅔ cups water
⅔ cup uncooked quick-cooking grits
¼ cup (1 ounce) preshredded sharp Cheddar cheese
½ teaspoon salt, divided
⅛ teaspoon garlic powder
Dash of ground red pepper
4 (4-ounce) boneless center-cut loin pork chops, trimmed
½ teaspoon garlic powder
⅛ teaspoon black pepper
3 tablespoons all-purpose flour
2 teaspoons butter
1 cup chopped onion
½ cup fat-free, less-sodium chicken broth
¼ cup water

1. Bring 2⅔ cups water to a boil; stir in grits. Reduce heat, and cook 5 minutes, stirring frequently. Remove from heat. Stir in cheese, ¼ teaspoon salt, ⅛ teaspoon garlic powder, and red pepper. Keep warm.

2. While grits cook, sprinkle pork with ¼ teaspoon salt, ½ teaspoon garlic powder, and black pepper. Dredge in flour. Melt butter in a large nonstick skillet over medium-high heat. Add pork and onion; sauté 6 minutes, turning pork over after 3 minutes. Add broth and ¼ cup water; bring to a boil. Cover, reduce heat, and simmer 4 minutes. Serve with grits. Yield: 4 servings (serving size: 1 pork chop and ½ cup grits).

CALORIES 394 (40% from fat); FAT 17.6g (sat 7.3g, mono 6.3g, poly 1.5g); PROTEIN 27.8g; CARB 29.3g; FIBER 1.4g; CHOL 83mg; IRON 1.9mg; SODIUM 427mg; CALC 82mg

Season Opener

Set the picnic table and welcome summer with a backyard cookout made for Memorial Day.

The calendar may say that summer doesn't start until mid-June, but nearly everybody in America knows better: The season really starts three weeks earlier with Memorial Day weekend. Officially, Memorial Day—the last Monday in May—honors the men and women who have fought in American wars. Informally, it's a time to contemplate our country's past while anticipating the season ahead.

Indeed, almost all the traditions of the long holiday weekend blend both a respect for history and the desire to celebrate with star-spangled parades, outdoor concerts of patriotic music, even the Rolling Thunder motorcycle rally on the Capitol Mall in Washington.

Most of us, though, make our Memorial Day traditions close to home. For us, the weekend ushers in the moment to inaugurate both the grill and the picnic table in the first backyard cookout of the season. To that end, this menu offers sizzling steak or chicken, a few salads you can prepare ahead, and a lemony ice cream so refreshing you'll want to make it all summer long.

MAKE AHEAD
Sweet-Spicy Cucumbers over Tomatoes

Be sure to use pickling cucumbers, which are shorter and thinner-skinned than regular cucumbers. Though 4 days is the maximum, the longer the cucumbers marinate, the spicier and more garlicky they'll become.

    2   cups thinly sliced pickling
        cucumber (about 2 cucumbers)
    1   cup thinly sliced Vidalia or other
        sweet onion
    ½   cup cider vinegar
    ¼   cup sugar
    ½   teaspoon salt
    ½   teaspoon mustard seeds
    4   garlic cloves, minced
    2   whole dried red chiles
   16   (¼-inch-thick) slices tomato
    ⅛   teaspoon salt
    ⅛   teaspoon freshly ground black
        pepper

1. Arrange half of cucumber in a 9-inch pie plate. Top with half of onion. Repeat procedure with remaining cucumber and onion.

2. Combine vinegar and next 5 ingredients in a small saucepan. Bring to a boil; cook 1 minute or until sugar dissolves, stirring occasionally. Pour hot vinegar mixture over cucumber mixture. Cover and marinate in refrigerator 1 to 4 days.

3. Arrange tomato slices on a platter; sprinkle evenly with ⅛ teaspoon salt and black pepper. Remove cucumber mixture from marinade with a slotted spoon; arrange over tomato slices. Yield: 8 servings (serving size: 2 tomato slices and about ⅓ cup cucumber mixture).

CALORIES 32 (6% from fat); FAT 0.2g (sat 0g, mono 0g, poly 0.1g); PROTEIN 0.8g; CARB 7.7g; FIBER 1g; CHOL 0mg; IRON 0.4mg; SODIUM 115mg; CALC 11mg

QUICK & EASY
White Bean and Bacon Dip with Rosemary Pita Chips

The homemade rosemary-flecked chips are a great complement to the garlicky dip, but store-bought pitas or bagel chips are a fine stand-in.

CHIPS:

    ½   teaspoon dried crushed rosemary
    ¼   teaspoon salt
    ¼   teaspoon garlic powder
    ⅛   teaspoon freshly ground black
        pepper
    3   (6-inch) pitas, each cut into
        8 wedges
        Cooking spray

DIP:

    2   applewood-smoked bacon slices,
        chopped (such as Nueske's)
    4   garlic cloves, minced
    ⅓   cup fat-free, less-sodium chicken
        broth
    1   (19-ounce) can cannellini beans,
        drained
    ¼   cup chopped green onions
    1   tablespoon fresh lemon juice
    ½   teaspoon hot sauce
    ⅛   teaspoon salt
    ⅛   teaspoon paprika

1. Preheat oven to 350°.

2. To prepare chips, combine first 4 ingredients. Arrange pita wedges in a single layer on a baking sheet. Lightly coat pita wedges with cooking spray; sprinkle evenly with rosemary mixture. Lightly recoat pita wedges with cooking spray. Bake at 350° for 20 minutes or until golden.

3. To prepare dip, cook bacon in a small saucepan over medium heat until crisp. Remove bacon from pan with a slotted spoon; set aside. Add garlic to drippings in pan; cook 1 minute, stirring frequently. Add broth and beans; bring to a boil. Reduce heat, and simmer, uncovered, 10 minutes.

4. Combine bean mixture, onions, and remaining 4 ingredients in a food processor, and process until smooth. Spoon mixture into a bowl; stir in 1 tablespoon reserved bacon. Sprinkle dip with remaining bacon just before serving. Serve with pita chips. Yield: 8 servings (serving size: 3 pita chips and 3 tablespoons dip).

CALORIES 137 (25% from fat); FAT 3.8g (sat 1.3g, mono 1.5g, poly 0.7g); PROTEIN 4.7g; CARB 20.5g; FIBER 2.6g; CHOL 3.8mg; IRON 1.4mg; SODIUM 397mg; CALC 39mg

Spice-Rubbed Flank Steak with Spicy Peach-Bourbon Sauce

Canned peach nectar, located near the bottled fruit juices in the grocery, is the base for a slightly sweet sauce that pairs well with highly seasoned beef. You can make and refrigerate the sauce up to a day ahead; bring it to room temperature just before serving.

SAUCE:
- 1 teaspoon vegetable oil
- ¾ cup chopped Vidalia or other sweet onion
- 2 garlic cloves, minced
- 1½ cups peach nectar
- 3 tablespoons brown sugar
- 2 tablespoons cider vinegar
- 3 tablespoons bourbon
- 2 tablespoons ketchup
- 1½ teaspoons Worcestershire sauce
- ½ teaspoon crushed red pepper
- 1 tablespoon fresh lime juice

Enjoy the smoky, creamy white bean dip as the entrées sizzle on the grill.

STEAK:
- 1 tablespoon brown sugar
- 1¼ teaspoons garlic powder
- 1¼ teaspoons ground cumin
- 1 teaspoon salt
- 1 teaspoon ground coriander
- 1 teaspoon paprika
- ¾ teaspoon dry mustard
- ¾ teaspoon freshly ground black pepper
- 2 (1-pound) flank steaks, trimmed
Cooking spray

1. To prepare sauce, heat oil in a medium saucepan over medium-high heat. Add onion and garlic; sauté 5 minutes or until tender. Add nectar, 3 tablespoons sugar, and vinegar. Bring to a boil; cook until reduced to 1 cup (about 15 minutes). Add bourbon, ketchup, Worcestershire, and red pepper; cook over medium heat 2 minutes, stirring occasionally. Remove from heat, and stir in lime juice. Cool slightly. Pour sauce into a blender, and process until smooth.
2. Prepare grill.
3. To prepare steak, combine 1 tablespoon sugar and next 7 ingredients; rub over both sides of steak. Place steak on grill rack coated with cooking spray, and grill 7 minutes on each side or until desired degree of doneness. Cut steak diagonally across the grain into thin slices. Serve with sauce. Yield: 8 servings (serving size: 3 ounces steak and about 2 tablespoons sauce).

CALORIES 265 (32% from fat); FAT 9.5g (sat 3.8g, mono 3.6g, poly 0.7g); PROTEIN 23.8g; CARB 17.4g; FIBER 1.1g; CHOL 57mg; IRON 2.9mg; SODIUM 425mg; CALC 28mg

Grilled Chicken with White Barbecue Sauce

The chicken is seared over direct heat then moved to the cooler side of the grill. If using a charcoal grill, stack the coals on the right side of the grill.

CHICKEN:
- 8 (8-ounce) bone-in chicken breast halves
- 1 teaspoon salt
- 1 teaspoon onion powder
- 1 teaspoon garlic powder
- 1 teaspoon paprika
- 1 teaspoon chipotle chile powder
Cooking spray

SAUCE:
- ½ cup light mayonnaise
- ⅓ cup white vinegar
- 1 tablespoon coarsely ground black pepper
- ½ teaspoon ground red pepper
- 1½ teaspoons fresh lemon juice
Dash of salt

1. Prepare grill, heating to medium-hot using both burners.
2. To prepare chicken, loosen skin from breasts by inserting fingers, gently pushing between skin and meat. Combine salt and next 4 ingredients; rub under loosened skin.
3. Turn left burner off (leave right burner on). Coat grill rack with cooking spray. Place chicken on grill rack over right burner; grill 5 minutes on each side or until browned. Move chicken to grill rack over left burner. Cover and cook 35 minutes or until done, turning once. Remove chicken from grill; discard skin.
4. To prepare sauce, combine mayonnaise and remaining 5 ingredients, stirring with a whisk. Serve with chicken. Yield: 8 servings (serving size: 1 breast half and about 2 tablespoons sauce).

WINE NOTE: The tangy bold white sauce and the char of the grilled chicken call for an assertive white that's crisp and refreshing. Try the Trinchero Sauvignon Blanc 2001 from California (about $12).

CALORIES 252 (25% from fat); FAT 6.9g (sat 1.3g, mono 1.4g, poly 3.4g); PROTEIN 34.4g; CARB 10.9g; FIBER 0.6g; CHOL 91mg; IRON 1.5mg; SODIUM 536mg; CALC 26mg

Succotash Salad

SALAD:
- 1 (16-ounce) bag frozen baby lima beans
- 3 cups fresh corn kernels
- 1 cup chopped red bell pepper
- ¾ cup chopped green onion
- ½ cup finely chopped red onion
- ¼ cup chopped fresh flat-leaf parsley
- 2 tablespoons chopped fresh oregano

DRESSING:
- ⅓ cup fresh lemon juice
- 2 tablespoons Dijon mustard
- 2 tablespoons olive oil
- ¾ teaspoon salt
- ¾ teaspoon freshly ground black pepper

1. To prepare salad, cook beans in boiling water 12 minutes. Drain; rinse with cold water. Drain. Combine beans, corn, and next 5 ingredients.

2. To prepare dressing, combine lemon juice and remaining 4 ingredients, stirring with a whisk. Drizzle over salad and, toss to coat. Yield: 8 servings (serving size: 1 cup).

CALORIES 164 (26% from fat); FAT 4.7g (sat 0.6g, mono 2.8g, poly 0.8g); PROTEIN 6.5g; CARB 27g; FIBER 6.3g; CHOL 0mg; IRON 1.9mg; SODIUM 344mg; CALC 34mg

Two-Potato Salad with Crème Fraîche

Look for crème fraîche near the gourmet cheeses in gourmet markets; if you can't find it, substitute full-fat sour cream. You can prepare this dish a day ahead; stir gently before serving.

- 1½ pounds small red potatoes, halved
- 1½ pounds peeled sweet potatoes, cut into 1-inch pieces
- 3 tablespoons white vinegar
- ¾ cup crème fraîche
- ¼ cup chopped fresh chives
- ¾ teaspoon salt
- ¼ teaspoon freshly ground black pepper

1. Place potatoes in a large Dutch oven; cover with water. Bring to a boil; reduce heat, and simmer 18 minutes or until tender. Drain. Place potatoes in a large bowl. Drizzle with vinegar; toss gently to coat. Cool to room temperature.

2. Combine crème fraîche and remaining 3 ingredients, stirring with a whisk. Add to potatoes, tossing gently to coat. Yield: 8 servings (serving size: 1 cup).

CALORIES 253 (29% from fat); FAT 8.2g (sat 5g, mono 2.3g, poly 0.4g); PROTEIN 3.9g; CARB 41.3g; FIBER 3g; CHOL 18mg; IRON 1.2mg; SODIUM 255mg; CALC 70mg

Lemon-Buttermilk Ice Cream

Three different kinds of milk provide a rich, creamy consistency. The ice cream is at its peak served as soon as it's firm.

- 1½ cups sugar
- 1 cup fresh lemon juice (about 10 lemons)
- 2 cups half-and-half
- 2 cups whole milk
- 2 cups fat-free buttermilk

1. Combine sugar and juice in a large bowl, stirring with a whisk until sugar dissolves. Add half-and-half, whole milk, and buttermilk. Pour mixture into freezer can of an ice-cream freezer; freeze according to manufacturer's instructions. Spoon ice cream into a freezer-safe container. Cover and freeze 1 hour or until firm. Yield: 18 servings (serving size: ½ cup).

CALORIES 130 (25% from fat); FAT 3.6g (sat 2.3g, mono 1.2g, poly 0g); PROTEIN 2.8g; CARB 21.4g; FIBER 0.1g; CHOL 18mg; IRON 0mg; SODIUM 54mg; CALC 93mg

Summer Savory

This fabulous Mediterranean lunch could quite possibly turn into an all-day affair.

To enjoy a meal the Mediterranean way means dining at a table laden with simple, fresh foods and lined with friends and family.

Find a space dappled with shade—a patio, a deck, a corner of the yard—and bring your dining room table outside. Set it with fine yet simple linens, glasses, and plates. And whether you serve your meal in courses or put it on the table all at once, these dishes are sure to be savored.

Garden Party Menu
serves 8

Yellow Tomato Gazpacho

Summer Bean Salad

Zucchini Custards with Tomatoes and Basil

Potato Salad with Olives, Capers, and Parmesan

Grilled Herbed Chicken

Blueberry Granita with Berry Compote

Cardamom-Lemon Polenta Cookie

WINE NOTE: Take Italy as your vinous *alfresco* inspiration. Begin with a dry, refreshing Italian white like San Quirico Vernaccia di San Gimignano 2001 from Tuscany, about $12. If you'd like to have a red on hand, Washington State's Covey Run Winery makes a steal of a Syrah at just $9. It's full of juicy blackberry flavor. Finally, finish in grand form with the beautiful apricot flavors and intense, irresistibly rich fruitiness of Robert Mondavi Winery's Moscato d'Oro, about $16 for a half bottle. It's a wonderful mate for granita.

MAKE AHEAD
Yellow Tomato Gazpacho

A few ripe tomatoes and bell peppers, be they yellow, orange, or red, are the keys to this marvelous Mediterranean soup.

GAZPACHO:

1½ cups chopped seeded peeled cucumber
1 cup chopped Vidalia or other sweet onion
1 cup coarsely chopped yellow bell pepper
6 tablespoons white wine vinegar
1 tablespoon extravirgin olive oil
½ teaspoon salt
¼ teaspoon freshly ground black pepper
2 pounds chopped seeded peeled yellow tomatoes (about 6 large)
1 garlic clove, minced

GARNISH:

2 (1-ounce) slices French bread, torn into ½-inch pieces
1 teaspoon extravirgin olive oil
1 cup quartered grape or cherry tomatoes
½ cup chopped seeded peeled cucumber

1. To prepare gazpacho, combine first 9 ingredients. Place one-third of vegetable mixture in a food processor; process until smooth. Pour puréed mixture into a large bowl. Repeat procedure with remaining vegetable mixture. Cover and chill.
2. Preheat oven to 375°.
3. To prepare garnish, place bread in a small bowl; drizzle with 1 teaspoon oil, tossing gently to coat. Spread bread mixture in a single layer on a baking sheet. Bake at 375° 10 minutes or until golden brown, stirring occasionally. Cool to room temperature. Place ¾ cup gazpacho in each of 8 soup bowls. Top servings evenly with a few croutons, 2 tablespoons quartered tomatoes, and 1 tablespoon cucumber. Yield: 8 servings.

CALORIES 89 (31% from fat); FAT 3.1g (sat 0.5g, mono 2g, poly 0.5g); PROTEIN 2.4g; CARB 13.8g; FIBER 2.6g; CHOL 0mg; IRON 1mg; SODIUM 203mg; CALC 24mg

MAKE AHEAD
Summer Bean Salad
(pictured on page 184)

Savory is a slightly bitter, minty herb. If you can't find it, increase the amount of thyme to 1½ tablespoons. Scarlett runner peas take a bit longer to cook than other shelled peas, so if you use them, allow a few extra minutes of cooking time before adding the beans.

1¼ cups fresh shelled peas (such as black-eyed, lima, or scarlett runner; about 3 pounds unshelled)
¾ pound green beans, trimmed and cut in half crosswise
¾ pound wax beans, trimmed and cut in half crosswise
¼ cup minced shallots
3 tablespoons chopped fresh chives
1½ tablespoons chopped fresh or 1 teaspoon dried savory
3 tablespoons white wine vinegar
2 tablespoons extravirgin olive oil
2 teaspoons chopped fresh thyme
¾ teaspoon salt
¼ teaspoon freshly ground black pepper
1 garlic clove, minced

1. Cook peas in boiling water 15 minutes. Add beans; cook 5 minutes or until crisp-tender. Drain; rinse with cold water. Drain; place bean mixture in a large bowl.
2. Combine shallots and remaining 8 ingredients. Pour over bean mixture; toss well. Serve at room temperature or chilled. Yield: 8 servings (serving size: about 1 cup).

CALORIES 118 (31% from fat); FAT 4g (sat 0.6g, mono 2.7g, poly 0.5g); PROTEIN 5.2g; CARB 16.8g; FIBER 6.5g; CHOL 0mg; IRON 2.6mg; SODIUM 226mg; CALC 61mg

Zucchini Custards with Tomatoes and Basil

You can make the custards earlier in the day, store them in the refrigerator, and bring them to room temperature before serving.

1⅓ pounds zucchini, coarsely grated
 ¾ teaspoon salt, divided
Cooking spray
 ¼ cup minced shallots
 ¼ cup all-purpose flour
1⅓ cups fat-free milk, divided
 1 tablespoon chopped fresh basil
 2 teaspoons chopped fresh oregano
 ¼ teaspoon freshly ground black
     pepper
Dash of nutmeg
Dash of ground red pepper
 4 large eggs, lightly beaten
 3 large egg whites, lightly beaten
 ¼ cup (1 ounce) finely grated
     Parmigiano-Reggiano cheese
 2 cups chopped seeded peeled tomato
Basil sprigs (optional)

1. Preheat oven to 350°.
2. Spread zucchini on several layers of paper towels; sprinkle with ¼ teaspoon salt. Cover with additional paper towels. Let stand 15 minutes, pressing occasionally until barely moist. Set aside.
3. Heat a saucepan coated with cooking spray over medium heat. Add shallots, and cook 5 minutes or until soft, stirring frequently. Remove pan from heat.
4. Lightly spoon flour into a dry measuring cup; level with a knife. Combine flour and ⅓ cup milk; stir with a whisk. Add 1 cup milk; stir with a whisk. Add milk mixture to pan; cook over medium heat 3 minutes or until thick; stir constantly.
5. Place milk mixture, ½ teaspoon salt, basil, and next 6 ingredients in a food processor; process until well blended. Add cheese, and process until well blended. Add zucchini; pulse until combined.
6. Divide zucchini mixture evenly among 8 (4-ounce) ramekins or custard cups coated with cooking spray. Place ramekins in a shallow roasting pan; add hot water to pan to a depth of 1 inch. Bake at 350° for 30 minutes or until puffed and brown and a wooden pick

inserted in center comes out clean. Remove ramekins from pan; run a knife around edges. Invert custards onto plates. Top with tomato; garnish with basil sprigs, if desired. Yield: 8 servings (serving size: 1 custard and ¼ cup tomato).

CALORIES 111 (32% from fat); FAT 3.9g (sat 1.6g, mono 1.3g, poly 0.5g); PROTEIN 9.1g; CARB 10.7g; FIBER 1.9g; CHOL 110mg; IRON 1.2mg; SODIUM 364mg; CALC 130mg

Potato Salad with Olives, Capers, and Parmesan

(pictured on page 184)

Cook the potatoes and make the olive mixture a day ahead; combine them before serving.

POTATOES:
 3 pounds small red potatoes
 2 tablespoons water
 ½ teaspoon salt
 ¼ teaspoon freshly ground black
     pepper

OLIVE MIXTURE:
 ½ cup green olives, pitted and
     halved lengthwise
 ½ cup chopped red bell pepper
 ½ cup chopped yellow bell pepper
 ½ cup thinly sliced green onions
 3 tablespoons capers
 2 tablespoons extravirgin olive oil
 1 tablespoon grated lemon rind
 2 teaspoons chopped fresh oregano
 2 garlic cloves, minced
 2 ounces Parmigiano-Reggiano
     cheese, shaved (about ½ cup)

1. Preheat oven to 375°.
2. To prepare potatoes, place potatoes in a 13 x 9-inch baking dish. Drizzle with water; sprinkle with salt and pepper. Cover with aluminum foil; bake at 375° for 55 minutes or until tender. Uncover and cool 5 minutes. Cut in half.
3. To prepare olive mixture, combine olives and next 8 ingredients. Add potatoes and cheese; toss gently to combine. Yield: 8 servings (serving size: about 1 cup).

CALORIES 210 (30% from fat); FAT 7g (sat 1.9g, mono 4.1g, poly 0.7g); PROTEIN 7.1g; CARB 31.2g; FIBER 3.5g; CHOL 6mg; IRON 2.7mg; SODIUM 506mg; CALC 131mg

Grilled Herbed Chicken

(pictured on page 184)

 2 (3½-pound) whole chickens
 ½ cup chopped fresh parsley
 ¼ cup chopped fresh chives
 2 tablespoons chopped fresh thyme
 2 tablespoons chopped fresh
     oregano
 2 teaspoons chopped fresh rosemary
 2 teaspoons olive oil
 ¾ teaspoon salt
 ½ teaspoon freshly ground black
     pepper
 2 cups water
Cooking spray
Lemon wedges (optional)
Oregano sprigs (optional)

1. Remove and discard giblets and necks from chickens. Rinse chickens with cold water; pat dry. Trim excess fat. Place each chicken, breast side down, on a cutting surface. Cut each chicken open along backbone, using kitchen shears; flatten chickens. Turn chickens over. Starting at neck cavity, loosen skin from breast and drumsticks by inserting fingers, gently pushing between skin and meat.
2. Combine parsley and next 7 ingredients. Rub parsley mixture under skin of breast and thighs of each chicken. Gently press skin to secure. Cut a 1-inch slit in skin at bottom of each breast half; insert tip of drumstick into slit.
3. To prepare grill for indirect grilling, place a disposable aluminum foil pan in grill; pour 2 cups water in pan. Arrange charcoal around pan; heat to medium. Coat grill rack with cooking spray; place rack on grill. Place chickens, breast sides down, on grill rack over foil pan. Cover and grill 1 hour and 15 minutes or until a thermometer registers 180°, turning chickens over halfway through cooking time. Remove chickens from grill; place on a clean cutting surface. Cover with foil; let stand 5 minutes. Discard skin before serving. Garnish with lemon wedges and oregano sprigs, if desired. Yield: 8 servings (serving size: 3 ounces).

CALORIES 149 (28% from fat); FAT 4.7g (sat 1.1g, mono 1.9g, poly 1g); PROTEIN 24.5g; CARB 0.8g; FIBER 0.2g; CHOL 79mg; IRON 1.5mg; SODIUM 308mg; CALC 30mg

Blueberry Granita with Berry Compote

The more frequently you stir granita, the slushier it will be. The less you stir it, the icier it will be.

GRANITA:

- 2 quarts fresh blueberries (about 1½ pounds)
- 1½ cups water, divided
- ¾ cup sugar
- 3 tablespoons lemon juice

COMPOTE:

- 2 cups quartered small strawberries, divided
- ½ cup water
- ⅓ cup sugar
- 1 (2-inch) piece lemon rind (removed with vegetable peeler)
- ¾ cup fresh blueberries
- 1 teaspoon lemon juice

1. To prepare granita, place 2 quarts blueberries in a food processor or blender; process until smooth. With food processor on, slowly add 1 cup water through food chute; process until well blended. Strain blueberry mixture through a fine sieve into a bowl; discard solids.

2. Combine ½ cup water and ¾ cup sugar in a small saucepan over high heat, stirring until sugar dissolves. Stir sugar mixture and 3 tablespoons juice into blueberry mixture. Pour mixture into a 13 x 9-inch glass baking dish; cool to room temperature. Freeze 1½ to 2 hours or until ice crystals begin to form. Remove mixture from freezer; stir well with a fork. Return dish to freezer; freeze 2 hours, stirring every 30 minutes until slushy. Cover and freeze 1 hour.

3. To prepare compote, place 1 cup strawberries in a food processor or blender; process until smooth. Strain strawberry mixture through a fine sieve into a bowl; discard solids.

4. Combine ½ cup water, ⅓ cup sugar, and rind in a medium saucepan over medium-high heat; bring to a boil. Cook 1 minute; remove from heat. Discard rind. Add puréed strawberries, quartered strawberries, ¾ cup blueberries, and 1 teaspoon juice to pan; stir gently to combine. Cool to room temperature. Cover and chill. Spoon compote into each of 8 bowls; top with granita. Yield: 8 servings (serving size: ⅔ cup granita and about ⅓ cup compote).

CALORIES 174 (3% from fat); FAT 0.5g (sat 0g, mono 0g, poly 0.1g); PROTEIN 0.9g; CARB 44.5g; FIBER 3.5g; CHOL 0mg; IRON 0.3mg; SODIUM 7mg; CALC 12mg

Cardamom-Lemon-Polenta Cookie

Serve alongside the Blueberry Granita with Berry Compote (recipe at left).

- ¼ cup blanched almonds, toasted
- 1⅓ cups all-purpose flour
- ½ cup yellow cornmeal
- ½ cup granulated sugar
- 1 tablespoon grated lemon rind
- ¾ teaspoon ground cardamom
- Dash of salt
- 3 tablespoons butter
- 1 tablespoon water
- 1 large egg
- Cooking spray
- 1 tablespoon powdered sugar

1. Preheat oven to 350°.

2. Place almonds in a food processor; pulse until finely ground. Lightly spoon flour into dry measuring cups; level with a knife. Add flour and next 5 ingredients to food processor; process until combined. Add butter, water, and egg; pulse 3 or 4 times or just until combined.

3. Lightly press mixture evenly into bottom of a 9-inch round springform pan coated with cooking spray. Sprinkle with powdered sugar. Bake at 350° for 30 minutes or until lightly browned.

4. Remove sides of pan, and cut cookie into 12 wedges while warm. Yield: 12 servings (serving size: 1 wedge).

CALORIES 150 (29% from fat); FAT 4.9g (sat 1.9g, mono 1g, poly 0.2g); PROTEIN 3g; CARB 24.4g; FIBER 1.2g; CHOL 25mg; IRON 0.9mg; SODIUM 18mg; CALC 12mg

season's best

Blueberry Brunch Cake

Blueberry Brunch Cake, which, despite the name, is perfectly suited for dessert.

At their peak in June, fresh blueberries hold their shape and remain plump during baking.

Blueberry Brunch Cake

(pictured on page 183)

- Cooking spray
- 1 tablespoon all-purpose flour
- ¾ cup granulated sugar
- 6 tablespoons butter, softened
- 1 large egg
- 1 large egg white
- 1⅔ cups all-purpose flour
- ¾ teaspoon baking powder
- ½ teaspoon baking soda
- ½ teaspoon salt
- ½ cup low-fat buttermilk
- ¼ cup orange juice
- 1 teaspoon grated lemon or orange rind
- 1 teaspoon vanilla extract
- 1½ cups fresh blueberries
- 2 tablespoons turbinado sugar
- ⅛ teaspoon ground nutmeg
- ½ cup low-fat sour cream
- 1 teaspoon vanilla extract
- 1 (8-ounce) carton vanilla low-fat yogurt
- ¾ cup fresh blueberries

1. Preheat oven to 350°.

2. Coat bottom of a 10-inch springform pan with cooking spray; line with parchment or wax paper. Coat bottom and sides with cooking spray; dust with 1 tablespoon flour.

3. Combine granulated sugar and butter; beat with a mixer at medium speed until well blended (about 5 minutes). Add egg and egg white; beat well.

4. Lightly spoon 1⅔ cups flour into dry measuring cups; level with a knife. *Continued*

Combine flour, baking powder, baking soda, and salt in a small bowl; stir well with a whisk. Combine buttermilk and next 3 ingredients in a small bowl. Add flour mixture and buttermilk mixture alternately to sugar mixture, beginning and ending with flour mixture. Fold in 1½ cups blueberries. Spoon batter into prepared pan. Combine turbinado sugar and nutmeg in a small bowl; sprinkle over batter.

5. Bake at 350° for 40 minutes or until a wooden pick inserted in center comes out clean. Cool in pan 10 minutes on a wire rack. Remove sides of pan.

6. Combine sour cream, 1 teaspoon vanilla, and yogurt. Serve cake warm or at room temperature with sour cream mixture and ¾ cup blueberries. Yield: 12 servings (serving size: 1 wedge, 2 tablespoons sour cream mixture, and 1 tablespoon blueberries).

CALORIES 235 (31% from fat); FAT 8g (sat 4.7g, mono 1.9g, poly 0.4g); PROTEIN 4.7g; CARB 36.6g; FIBER 1.3g; CHOL 40mg; IRON 1mg; SODIUM 274mg; CALC 87mg

cooking light profile

Healthful Headliner

This CNN anchor has a nose for news— and for good food.

Sophia Choi did not grow up cooking. But in 1994, Choi—now a prime-time anchor for CNN Headline News in Atlanta—married into a Southern family, for whom a home-cooked meal was central to daily life.

"My mother-in-law, Sue Farr, was always in the kitchen, so it was easy to pick up on things," Choi explains. "I stood over her shoulder and watched. Then I'd go home and try it myself."

Today, Choi usually creates her own recipes, a predilection that garnered an invitation to join the prestigious Los Angeles Gourmet Society. Here's one of her recipes.

MAKE AHEAD • FREEZABLE
Ground Turkey Chili

Choi calls this recipe "My Friend Mexene"; she says the Mexene brand chili powder along with the light beer make the flavor of the dish. She likes to prepare a double batch and freeze any leftovers.

 1   tablespoon olive oil
2½ cups chopped onion
 4   garlic cloves, minced
 1   pound ground turkey breast
1½ cups water
 1   tablespoon chili powder (such as Mexene)
 ¼   teaspoon black pepper
 1   (16-ounce) can kidney beans, drained and rinsed
 1   (15.5-ounce) can small red beans, drained and rinsed
 1   (15-ounce) can tomato sauce
 1   (14.5-ounce) can whole tomatoes, undrained and coarsely chopped
 ¾   cup light beer
 ⅓   cup hot brewed coffee

1. Heat oil in a Dutch oven over medium-high heat. Add onion and garlic; sauté 3 minutes. Add turkey. Cook 6 minutes; stir to crumble. Stir in water and next 6 ingredients; bring to a boil. Reduce heat; simmer, uncovered, 45 minutes, stirring occasionally. Stir in beer and coffee; simmer 10 minutes, stirring occasionally. Yield: 6 servings (serving size: 1⅓ cups).

CALORIES 299 (11% from fat); FAT 3.7g (sat 0.5g, mono 1.8g, poly 0.5g); PROTEIN 29g; CARB 36.1g; FIBER 11g; CHOL 47mg; IRON 4mg; SODIUM 748mg; CALC 87mg

lighten up

Sweet Pretender

We reform a cupcake masquerading as a muffin and make it good for breakfast again.

Anne Powell of Boxford, Massachusetts, eyed a recipe for Raspberry-Cream Cheese Muffins in a cookbook her mom gave her. But one look told her it was high in fat. After a failed attempt to lighten the recipe herself, Anne asked for our help.

BEFORE	AFTER
SERVING SIZE	
1 muffin	
CALORIES PER SERVING	
221	142
FAT	
14g	4.7g
PERCENT OF TOTAL CALORIES	
57%	32%

FREEZABLE
Raspberry-Cream Cheese Muffins

 ⅔   cup (5 ounces) ⅓-less-fat cream cheese, softened
 ⅓   cup butter, softened
1½ cups sugar
1½ teaspoons vanilla extract
 2   large egg whites
 1   large egg
 2   cups all-purpose flour
 1   teaspoon baking powder
 ¼   teaspoon baking soda
 ½   teaspoon salt
 ½   cup low-fat buttermilk
 2   cups fresh or frozen raspberries
 ¼   cup finely chopped walnuts

1. Preheat oven to 350°.
2. Combine cream cheese and butter in a large bowl. Beat with a mixer at high speed until well blended. Add sugar; beat until fluffy. Add vanilla, egg whites, and egg; beat well.
3. Lightly spoon flour into dry measuring cups; level with a knife. Combine flour, baking powder, baking soda, and salt. With mixer on low speed, add flour mixture and buttermilk alternately to cream cheese mixture, beginning and ending with flour mixture. Gently fold in raspberries and walnuts.
4. Place 24 foil cup liners in muffin cups. Spoon batter evenly into liners. Bake at 350° for 25 minutes or until a wooden pick inserted in center comes out clean. Remove from pans; cool on a wire rack. Yield: 2 dozen (serving size: 1 muffin).

CALORIES 142 (32% from fat); FAT 4.7g (sat 2.4g, mono 1.3g, poly 0.7g); PROTEIN 2.7g; CARB 22.6g; FIBER 1.1g; CHOL 19mg; IRON 0.7mg; SODIUM 138mg; CALC 31mg

Summer Shrimp Salad with Cilantro,
page 209

Alder-Planked Salmon in an Asian-Style Marinade,
page 205

The Guadalajara, page 197

Seasoned Fries, page 200

Blueberry Brunch Cake, page 179

Grilled Stone Fruit Antipasto Plate,
page 185

Grilled Herbed Chicken, page 178,
Summer Bean Salad, page 177;
and Potato Salad with Olives, Capers,
and Parmesan, page 178

All About Stone Fruits

They're here—cherries, apricots, peaches,
nectarines, and plums—and they're best when fresh.

In the warmth and sunshine of the midyear months, fresh seasonal fruits burst with nectar. Their tooth-breaking seeds give them the family name: stone fruit. These fruits—cherries, apricots, peaches, nectarines, and plums—share thin skins that protect delicate flesh and hard seeds in their centers.

STAFF FAVORITE • QUICK & EASY
Grilled Stone Fruit Antipasto Plate
(pictured on page 184)

Black pepper and vanilla heighten the sweetness of the stone fruit. Firm fruit holds up best on the grill. Serve this dish as an appetizer or a salad. If you can't find pluots, double up on peaches or plums.

DRESSING:
- 3 tablespoons white balsamic vinegar
- 2 tablespoons extravirgin olive oil
- 2 tablespoons fresh lime juice
- 1 tablespoon brown sugar
- 2 teaspoons vanilla extract
- 1/4 teaspoon freshly ground black pepper
- 1/8 teaspoon salt
- 1/8 teaspoon hot sauce

FRUIT:
- 1 pound firm black plums, halved and pitted
- 1 pound firm peaches, halved and pitted
- 1/2 pound firm nectarines, halved and pitted
- 1/2 pound firm pluots, halved and pitted
- Cooking spray
- Chopped fresh mint (optional)

1. Prepare grill.
2. To prepare dressing, combine first 8 ingredients in a small bowl, stirring well with a whisk.

3. To prepare fruit, place fruit on grill rack coated with cooking spray; grill 3 minutes on each side. Remove from grill. Drizzle fruit with dressing. Garnish with mint, if desired. Yield: 8 servings.

CALORIES 129 (29% from fat); FAT 4.1g (sat 0.5g, mono 2.9g, poly 0.4g); PROTEIN 1.4g; CARB 23.8g; FIBER 2.9g; CHOL 0mg; IRON 0.3mg; SODIUM 39mg; CALC 12mg

Mascarpone-Stuffed Apricots

Can't find mascarpone? Substitute crème fraîche for similar rich flavor and creamy texture.

- 1/3 cup (3 ounces) block-style fat-free cream cheese
- 2 tablespoons (1 ounce) mascarpone cheese
- 2 tablespoons honey
- 3 1/2 teaspoons lemon juice, divided
- 1/8 teaspoon ground nutmeg
- 2 tablespoons coarsely chopped walnuts, toasted
- 10 small apricots, halved and pitted
- Chopped fresh mint (optional)

1. Combine cheeses, honey, 1/2 teaspoon lemon juice, and nutmeg, stirring well. Stir in walnuts. Chill 1 hour.
2. Sprinkle cut sides of apricots evenly with 1 tablespoon lemon juice.
3. Spoon about 1 teaspoon cheese mixture into each apricot half; chill 1 hour.

Garnish with mint, if desired. Yield: 10 servings (serving size: 2 apricot halves).

CALORIES 61 (37% from fat); FAT 2.5g (sat 0.9g, mono 0.3g, poly 0.6g); PROTEIN 2.2g; CARB 8.4g; FIBER 0.8g; CHOL 4mg; IRON 0.3mg; SODIUM 49mg; CALC 26mg

Crisp Plum Ravioli with Lemon-Thyme Honey and Yogurt Cheese

Drain the yogurt, make the plum filling, infuse the honey, and assemble the raviolis ahead of time. Bake this special dessert just before you're ready to eat, since it's best straight from the oven. If you're short on time, simply sprinkle the raviolis with powdered sugar.

- 1 (16-ounce) carton vanilla low-fat yogurt
- 4 cups chopped plums (about 2 pounds)
- 3 tablespoons honey
- 3/4 teaspoon ground cinnamon
- 1/8 teaspoon ground nutmeg
- 1 1/2 tablespoons butter
- 60 wonton wrappers
- Cooking spray
- 1/2 cup honey
- 1 teaspoon grated lemon rind
- 1/2 teaspoon chopped fresh thyme

1. Place colander in a medium bowl. Line colander with 4 layers of cheesecloth, allowing cheesecloth to extend over outside edges. Spoon yogurt into colander. Cover loosely with plastic wrap; refrigerate 12 hours. Spoon yogurt cheese into a bowl; discard liquid. Cover and refrigerate.
2. Combine plums and next 3 ingredients in a large saucepan; bring to a boil over medium-high heat. Reduce heat, and simmer 45 minutes, stirring occasionally. Remove from heat. Cool 5 minutes; stir in butter. Cool completely.
3. Preheat oven to 400°.
4. Working with 1 wonton wrapper at a time (cover remaining wrappers with a damp towel to prevent drying), spoon about 1 tablespoon plum mixture into center of wrapper. Moisten edges of dough with water, and top with another
Continued

wrapper. Press 4 edges together to seal. Place ravioli on a large baking sheet coated with cooking spray (cover ravioli with a damp towel to prevent drying). Repeat procedure with remaining wrappers and plum mixture. Bake at 400° for 14 minutes or until golden.

5. Combine ½ cup honey, rind, and thyme in a small saucepan over low heat. Cook 20 minutes (do not boil). Place 3 raviolis on each of 10 plates. Drizzle 2 teaspoons honey mixture over each serving; top with about 1 tablespoon yogurt cheese. Yield: 10 servings.

CALORIES 328 (13% from fat); FAT 4.7g (sat 2.4g, mono 1.4g, poly 0.5g); PROTEIN 7.8g; CARB 65.7g; FIBER 2.2g; CHOL 14mg; IRON 1.9mg; SODIUM 328mg; CALC 116mg

Spiced Duck Breast with Cherry Sauce

Walnut oil subtly flavors the sauce. Feel free to substitute olive oil, if you prefer. Also, try the recipe with chicken or pork tenderloin instead of duck.

SAUCE:

    2   teaspoons walnut oil
    ⅓   cup sliced shallots (about 3 small shallots)
    ¼   teaspoon salt
    ¼   teaspoon fennel seeds
    ¼   teaspoon cumin seeds
    ¼   teaspoon black pepper
    ⅛   teaspoon ground cinnamon
    ⅛   teaspoon ground red pepper
    ⅛   teaspoon ground cloves
    6   cups pitted sweet cherries (about 2 pounds)
    ½   cup dry red wine
    1   tablespoon rice vinegar

DUCK:

    1   tablespoon curry powder
    1   teaspoon ground ginger
    ½   teaspoon salt
    ⅛   teaspoon black pepper
    Dash of ground red pepper
    1½ pounds duck breast, skinned
    Cooking spray

1. To prepare sauce, heat oil in a large saucepan over medium heat. Add shallots; cook 10 minutes or until golden brown, stirring occasionally. Add ¼ teaspoon salt and next 6 ingredients; cook 30 seconds. Add cherries and wine; bring to a boil. Reduce heat, and simmer 30 minutes, stirring occasionally. Remove pan from heat, and stir in vinegar.

2. Preheat oven to 450°.

3. To prepare duck, combine curry powder and next 4 ingredients, stirring well. Rub duck with spice mixture. Place duck on a shallow roasting pan coated with cooking spray.

4. Bake at 450° for 15 minutes or until a thermometer registers 135° (medium-rare) or until desired degree of doneness. Cut duck diagonally across the grain into slices. Serve with sauce. Yield: 4 servings (serving size: 3 ounces duck and ½ cup sauce).

CALORIES 353 (26% from fat); FAT 10.3g (sat 2.7g, mono 2.8g, poly 2.4g); PROTEIN 35.3g; CARB 27.9g; FIBER 4g; CHOL 128mg; IRON 8.8mg; SODIUM 391mg; CALC 42mg

Cumin-Roasted Pork Tenderloin with Plum Chutney

The sweet, tart, and spicy flavors in the Plum Chutney complement pork as well as chicken. Store the remaining chutney in an airtight container in the refrigerator for up to 1 week.

    1   tablespoon ground cumin
    1   teaspoon salt
    ⅛   teaspoon ground red pepper
    ⅛   teaspoon ground cloves
    ⅛   teaspoon freshly ground black pepper
    2   (1-pound) pork tenderloins, trimmed
    Cooking spray
    2   cups Plum Chutney

1. Preheat oven to 375°.

2. Combine first 5 ingredients, stirring well. Rub pork with spice mixture.

3. Place pork on a broiler pan coated with cooking spray. Bake at 375° for 20 minutes or until a thermometer registers 160° (slightly pink). Cut pork into ¼-inch-thick slices. Serve with Plum Chutney. Yield: 8 servings (serving size: 3 ounces pork and ¼ cup chutney).

(Totals include Plum Chutney) CALORIES 173 (27% from fat); FAT 5.2g (sat 1.4g, mono 2.5g, poly 0.6g); PROTEIN 20.7g; CARB 10.7g; FIBER 1.4g; CHOL 51mg; IRON 1.6mg; SODIUM 414mg; CALC 22mg

MAKE AHEAD
PLUM CHUTNEY:

    1   jalapeño pepper
    1   poblano chile
    1   tablespoon olive oil
    1   cup thinly sliced red onion
    2   tablespoons minced peeled fresh ginger
    1   garlic clove, minced
    5   cups chopped plums (about 2½ pounds)
    1   cup chopped seeded tomato
    ¼   cup packed brown sugar
    ¼   cup cider vinegar
    2   teaspoons mustard seeds
    ½   teaspoon salt
    ¼   teaspoon freshly ground black pepper
    ¼   cup chopped fresh cilantro

1. Preheat broiler.

2. Place jalapeño and poblano on a foil-lined baking sheet; broil 10 minutes or until blackened, turning occasionally. Place in a zip-top plastic bag; seal. Let stand 15 minutes. Peel jalapeño and poblano; cut in half lengthwise. Discard seeds and membranes; coarsely chop.

3. Heat oil in a large saucepan over medium-high heat. Add onion, ginger, and garlic; sauté 5 minutes or until tender. Add jalapeño, poblano, plums, and next 6 ingredients; bring to a boil. Cover, reduce heat, and simmer 30 minutes, stirring occasionally. Uncover and simmer an additional 15 minutes or until liquid almost evaporates, stirring occasionally. Cool completely. Stir in cilantro. Yield: 16 servings (serving size: about ¼ cup).

WINE NOTE: Pork goes beautifully with white wines—especially dry Rieslings. Try the Theo Minges Riesling Spätlese "Gleisweiler Hölle" from Pfalz, Germany (the 2000 is $18); this is a deliciously intense Riesling.

CALORIES 51 (23% from fat); FAT 1.3g (sat 0.2g, mono 0.8g, poly 0.2g); PROTEIN 0.7g; CARB 10.4g; FIBER 1.1g; CHOL 0mg; IRON 0.3mg; SODIUM 78mg; CALC 11mg

A Guide to Stone Fruits

Cherries

Cherries open the stone fruit season in late May. Dark red Bing cherries are the popular American standard. But yellow Queen Annes, white and red Rainiers, and sour Montmorencys are widely available. A good rule of thumb among sweet, dark cherries: The darker the fruit, the sweeter it is.

Smaller and more rounded in shape, sour (or tart) cherries are usually destined for pies. Less widely available fresh, most sour cherries are canned, frozen, dried, or used to make juice. Fortunately, nine states help satisfy our nation's cherry obsession, with Michigan the largest grower of sour cherries and California the number one grower of sweet cherries.

Cherries don't ripen after harvest, so once picked, their sweetness is set. Store fresh cherries for up to 1 week in the refrigerator in a bowl lined with paper towels.

Apricots

Spanish missionaries brought apricots to the United States from China in the 18th century. Slightly oval, apricots always contain a pit that is "free," meaning it's not fused to the flesh of the fruit and can be removed easily. When ripe, a gentle scent and slight yield in the flesh trumpet an apricot's sweetness. Its skin is pale yellow, and newer varieties have strong blushes of rouge. The rosy tint indicates which side of the fruit faced the sun as it hung on the tree.

All apricot varieties are interchangeable; their sugar levels are about the same. In these recipes, any ripe variety will work. Store apricots at room temperature to avoid mealiness.

Apricots seldom need peeling. But if you desire to do so, score the base with a small "X," and drop the entire fruit into boiling water for 30 seconds. Remove and quickly transfer to ice water for 2 minutes. The skin will peel away easily, without bruising the delicate flesh.

Peaches

Originating in China, the peach found its way to Greece as early as the 4th century B.C. Spanish settlers brought peaches to America in the 1600s.

Peach season starts in late May in the warmer sections of the United States and runs through late September. There are hundreds of peach varieties, and more than half of the states produce commercial crops. One thing holds true for all peaches: An enticing aroma alerts us to their ripeness. Leave unripe peaches at room temperature for a few days to allow them to develop their full, sweet potential. Refrigeration retards ripening, resulting in flat-tasting, mealy fruit.

It isn't necessary to peel peaches to eat them out of hand. When a recipe calls for peeled chopped peaches, use a vegetable peeler or paring knife for firm fruit; blanch soft, ripe peaches like apricots.

Nectarines

The peach has a fraternal twin—the nectarine, a natural mutation with fuzz-free skin. Otherwise, the two fruits are indistinguishable, with each having red, yellow, or white flesh. White-fleshed varieties are sweeter because they're less acidic, though acid levels in any peach or nectarine decrease as it ripens.

Both peaches and nectarines start the season as clingstones, meaning their meat adheres to their pits. Freestone varieties—the pit easily pulls from the fruit—begin to ripen midseason (late June to early July).

Plums

Believed to have originated in China, plums are multicolored fruits that develop their sweetness on the branch like cherries. The premier eating variety is the Greengage, with its light celadon skin and juicy yellowish meat. Long loved by the British, the plum has one of the lowest acidity levels, which permits its sweetness to come through.

Friar, Fortune, and Angelino are the most widely available varieties in the United States. These plums, with their red and black flesh, are grown primarily in California. They're perfect for chutneys and sauces, and are available from midsummer to early autumn.

A freestone member of this family, the French prune tends to sport an oblong shape, purplish skin, and pale golden meat. This is the variety most often dried to make dried plums (or prunes).

Summer Whites

Peaches, nectarines, and cherries are available in delicate white-fleshed varieties. These taste sweeter because they have lower acidity than the yellow-fleshed fruit. Sweet whites, like all stone fruits, are available during the summer months. Rainier and Queen Anne are common varieties of white-fleshed cherries. The donut peach is a throwback to its Chinese forebears and is a naturally occurring variety. The stone is always free, and its flesh is white. This delicious peach is best eaten out of hand.

Hybrids

Selective breeding and natural mutations have created new "interspecific" varieties of stone fruits. *Interspecific* refers to marrying two species to produce progeny with a desired taste, better texture, unique look, or longer storage life.

Pluot (also known as a plumcot or by its more familiar name, Dinosaur Egg): This union of the plum and apricot is sweeter than either of its parents, with a firm flesh and a mottled plumlike skin.

Aprium: Cross a slightly fuzzy apricot with a plum, and you'll have an aprium, with the best of both parents.

Mango nectarine: Although a hybrid of mango and nectarine, this fruit more closely resembles a nectarine. It's yellow and has a subtle perfumy sweetness when fully ripe.

Deep-Dish Cherry Pie

Cherry pies are traditionally made with sour cherries. Since their availability is limited, we used a combination of Bing cherries and dried sour cherries to lend tart flavor.

CRUST:
- 1 cup all-purpose flour, divided
- 3 tablespoons ice water
- 2 tablespoons sugar
- 1/8 teaspoon salt
- 1/4 cup vegetable shortening

FILLING:
- 3 tablespoons cornstarch
- 1 tablespoon sugar
- 1/4 teaspoon ground cinnamon
- 1/8 teaspoon ground ginger
- 1/8 teaspoon ground allspice
- 4 cups pitted sweet cherries (about 1 1/2 pounds)
- 1 cup dried sour cherries
- 2 tablespoons fresh lemon juice
- Cooking spray

TOPPING:
- 1 tablespoon water
- 1 large egg white
- 2 teaspoons sugar
- 1/4 teaspoon ground ginger

1. Preheat oven to 425°.
2. To prepare crust, lightly spoon flour into a dry measuring cup; level with a knife. Combine 1/4 cup flour and ice water, stirring with a whisk until well blended to form a slurry.
3. Combine 3/4 cup flour, 2 tablespoons sugar, and 1/8 teaspoon salt; cut in shortening with a pastry blender or 2 knives until mixture resembles coarse meal. Add slurry; toss with a fork until moist. Press gently into a 4-inch circle on 2 overlapping sheets of heavy-duty plastic wrap; cover with 2 additional overlapping sheets of plastic wrap. Roll dough, still covered, into an 11-inch circle; chill.
4. To prepare filling, combine cornstarch and next 4 ingredients in a large bowl. Stir in fresh cherries, dried cherries, and lemon juice; toss well to combine. Spoon filling into a 10-inch pie plate coated with cooking spray.

5. Remove top sheets of plastic wrap from dough; place on top of cherry mixture, plastic wrap side up. Remove remaining plastic wrap. Fold edges of dough under, and flute. Cut 6 (1-inch) slits in dough using a sharp knife.
6. To prepare topping, combine 1 tablespoon water and egg white, stirring with a whisk; brush top and edges of dough with egg mixture. Combine 2 teaspoons sugar and 1/4 teaspoon ginger; sprinkle over dough. Place pie on a baking sheet. Bake at 425° for 40 minutes or until golden. Cool completely on a wire rack. Yield: 9 servings.

CALORIES 234 (25% from fat); FAT 6.5g (sat 1.6g, mono 2.7g, poly 1.7g); PROTEIN 3.5g; CARB 40.8g; FIBER 3.3g; CHOL 0mg; IRON 1.1mg; SODIUM 42mg; CALC 22mg

Individual Peach Crisps

In this version of the classic summer dessert, egg whites bind the crisp topping instead of butter. If you prefer, substitute pecans for almonds.

- 1/2 cup regular oats
- 1/3 cup packed brown sugar
- 1/4 cup sliced almonds
- Dash of salt
- 1 teaspoon vanilla extract
- 2 large egg whites
- 6 peaches, peeled, halved, and pitted
- 3 cups vanilla low-fat frozen yogurt

1. Preheat oven to 400°.
2. Combine first 4 ingredients in a medium bowl. Combine vanilla and egg whites in a small bowl; stir with a whisk until foamy. Add egg mixture to oat mixture, stirring until well blended.
3. Spoon about 1 tablespoon oat mixture into each peach half. Arrange peach halves on a baking sheet. Bake at 400° for 13 minutes or until oat mixture is set. Serve with frozen yogurt. Yield: 6 servings (serving size: 2 peach halves and 1/2 cup yogurt).

CALORIES 301 (12% from fat); FAT 3.9g (sat 1.1g, mono 1.8g, poly 0.8g); PROTEIN 9.1g; CARB 60.9g; FIBER 5.5g; CHOL 5mg; IRON 1mg; SODIUM 107mg; CALC 189mg

Nectarine and Raspberry Sorbet

We enjoyed the sweetness of white nectarines, but regular golden nectarines or peaches also work well for this frozen treat.

- 2 cups chopped peeled white nectarines (about 1 1/2 pounds)
- 1 1/3 cups raspberries (about 6 ounces)
- 2 1/2 cups apricot nectar
- 1/2 cup honey
- 1 tablespoon fresh lemon juice

1. Combine nectarines and raspberries in a food processor; process until smooth. Stir in apricot nectar, honey, and lemon juice. Strain mixture through a sieve into a large bowl; discard solids.
2. Pour mixture into freezer can of an ice-cream freezer; freeze according to manufacturer's instructions. Spoon sorbet into a freezer-safe container; cover and freeze 1 hour or until firm. Yield: 5 servings (serving size: 1 cup).

CALORIES 218 (2% from fat); FAT 0.6g (sat 0.1g, mono 0.2g, poly 0.3g); PROTEIN 1.4g; CARB 56.7g; FIBER 3.4g; CHOL 0mg; IRON 0.9mg; SODIUM 5mg; CALC 21mg

Nectarine Clafouti

Chilling the batter allows the protein-rich gluten to rest, ensuring a delicate clafouti. You can also use peaches in this recipe.

- 3/4 cup all-purpose flour
- 1 cup vanilla soy milk
- 3/4 cup sugar
- 1/2 cup plain fat-free yogurt
- 1 teaspoon vanilla extract
- 4 large eggs
- 5 cups coarsely chopped nectarines (about 1 1/2 pounds)
- Cooking spray

1. Preheat oven to 400°.
2. Lightly spoon flour into a dry measuring cup; level with a knife. Combine flour and next 5 ingredients in a blender; process until smooth. Chill 30 minutes.
3. Arrange nectarines in a 13 x 9-inch baking dish coated with cooking spray.

Pour batter over fruit. Bake at 400° for 35 minutes or until set. Yield: 8 servings.

CALORIES 213 (14% from fat); FAT 3.4g (sat 0.8g, mono 1g, poly 0.6g); PROTEIN 6.6g; CARB 41g; FIBER 1.6g; CHOL 107mg; IRON 1.3mg; SODIUM 58mg; CALC 40mg

MAKE AHEAD
Cherry-Pecan Chicken Salad

Purchase silken tofu for the dressing in this recipe; it makes the purée creamy and thick. It typically comes vacuum-packed. Both the firm and the soft varieties will work.

SALAD:
- 3 cups chopped roasted skinless, boneless chicken breast (about 3 breasts)
- 2 cups pitted sweet cherries (about ¾ pound)
- 1 cup chopped peeled English cucumber
- ½ cup frozen green peas, thawed
- ¼ cup chopped celery
- ¼ cup chopped red onion
- ¼ cup chopped carrot
- 3 tablespoons chopped pecans, toasted
- 2 tablespoons sliced green onions
- 2 teaspoons chopped fresh or ½ teaspoon dried tarragon

DRESSING:
- ½ pound soft silken tofu
- ¼ cup red wine vinegar
- 1 tablespoon fresh thyme leaves
- ½ teaspoon salt
- ¼ teaspoon freshly ground black pepper
- ⅛ teaspoon ground red pepper

1. To prepare salad, combine first 10 ingredients in a large bowl.
2. To prepare dressing, combine tofu and remaining 5 ingredients in a blender, and process until smooth. Pour over chicken mixture; toss gently to coat. Cover and chill 1 hour. Yield: 4 servings (serving size: 1½ cups).

CALORIES 277 (29% from fat); FAT 8.9g (sat 1.4g, mono 3.6g, poly 2.9g); PROTEIN 26g; CARB 25g; FIBER 2.5g; CHOL 54mg; IRON 2.4mg; SODIUM 361mg; CALC 76mg

inspired vegetarian
Grilled to a T

Fire up the grill for these tempting tofu and tempeh dishes.

One taste, and you might opt for grilled tofu and tempeh over a steak—both take on irresistible, smoky flavor from the grill.

Grilling Tofu and Tempeh

Grilled tofu and tempeh retain their distinctive taste long after grilling, which means that leftovers can spark salads, soups, and other dishes. Enjoy any left-over patties from the Grilled Tempeh Burgers on a Caesar salad, for example, or crumble them into gazpacho.

You can purchase grill-flavored tofu which is conveniently quick and easy to use. But home grilling gives tofu and tempeh a brighter flavor, especially when they've spent some time marinating.

The best tofu for grilled dishes is the water-packed variety, sold sealed in a plastic tub or pouch. Tofu labeled "silken," which is usually sold in a box and resembles soft custard or bouncy gelatin, falls apart more easily on the grill, even when it's firm or extrafirm. To prepare water-packed tofu for grilling, it's best to draw out some of its mois-ture—either by pressing or oven firm-ing. Both methods compact the tofu, which makes it more chewy and sturdy. Or pick up commercially smoked or baked tofu, available at natural foods stores and some large supermarkets. Both products are already firmed and are sometimes seasoned.

All-soy tempeh has an assertive flavor and is the best choice for burgers. More mellow tempeh varieties—in which a variety of grains, including brown rice and quinoa, are blended with the soybeans—let the flavors in a marinade come through more.

Grilled Tempeh Burgers

Tempeh comes in different varieties, such as five-grain, three-grain, and soy-rice. We like these burgers made with soy tempeh. Chill the tempeh well before slicing so it will be less apt to crumble.

- 2 (8-ounce) packages soy tempeh
- ¾ cup water
- 3 tablespoons low-sodium soy sauce
- 2 teaspoons vegetable oil
- 1 teaspoon grated peeled fresh ginger
- Dash of ground red pepper
- 1 garlic clove, minced
- 4 whole-grain hamburger buns
- Cooking spray
- 2 tablespoons ketchup
- 2 tablespoons spicy brown mustard
- 4 leaf lettuce leaves
- 4 (¼-inch thick) slices tomato
- 4 (⅛-inch thick) slices Vidalia or other sweet onion

1. Split tempeh in half horizontally with a sharp knife; cut each piece in half crosswise. Place tempeh in a heavy-duty zip-top plastic bag. Combine water and next 5 ingredients in a small saucepan; bring to a boil. Pour over tempeh; seal bag. Marinate in refrigerator 3 hours or overnight.
2. Prepare grill.
3. Place buns, cut sides down, on grill rack; grill 1 minute or until toasted.
4. Remove tempeh from bag, reserving marinade. Place tempeh on grill rack coated with cooking spray; grill 2 min-utes on each side or until lightly browned, basting frequently with reserved marinade. Spread 1½ tea-spoons ketchup and 1½ teaspoons mustard evenly over each bun top. Place 1 lettuce leaf on bottom half of each bun; top with 2 tempeh pieces, 1 tomato slice, 1 onion slice, and top half of bun. Yield: 4 servings.

CALORIES 355 (28% from fat); FAT 11.1g (sat 3g, mono 3.3g, poly 4g); PROTEIN 29.9g; CARB 35.8g; FIBER 10.5g; CHOL 0mg; IRON 5.7mg; SODIUM 820mg; CALC 236mg

Tofu Negamaki

Strips of green onions surround seasoned tofu in this appetizer version of the popular Japanese beef dish. You can purchase baked tofu at natural foods stores or large supermarkets—its firm texture makes it ideal for these Asian kabobs. If you can't find baked tofu, purchase water-packed tofu, cut it into cubes, and bake at 375° 25 minutes or until it releases 3 or more tablespoons of liquid.

1½ tablespoons sugar
3 tablespoons low-sodium soy sauce
1 tablespoon mirin (sweet rice wine)
2 teaspoons grated orange rind
1 teaspoon grated peeled fresh ginger
1 teaspoon rice vinegar
16 (4-inch) pieces green onion tops
1 (8-ounce) package baked tofu, cut into 16 (1-inch) cubes
Cooking spray

1. Prepare grill.
2. Combine first 6 ingredients in a small saucepan, and bring to a boil. Cook 1 minute, stirring until sugar dissolves. Cool slightly.
3. Thread 1 onion piece onto a 10-inch skewer, ½ inch from one end of onion. Thread 1 tofu cube onto skewer. Closely wrap onion piece around and over tofu cube; thread other end of onion onto skewer, ½ inch from end of onion. Repeat procedure 3 times to form 1 kabob with 4 tofu cubes and 4 onion slices. Repeat procedure with remaining skewers, onion, and tofu.
4. Brush kabobs with soy sauce mixture; coat kabobs with cooking spray. Place kabobs on grill rack coated with cooking spray. Grill 3 minutes on each side or until browned, basting frequently with soy sauce mixture. Yield: 4 servings (serving size: 1 kabob).

CALORIES 122 (30% from fat); FAT 4.1g (sat 0.7g, mono 0.9g, poly 1.6g); PROTEIN 7.8g; CARB 14.4g; FIBER 1.5g; CHOL 0mg; IRON 1.6mg; SODIUM 222mg; CALC 564mg

---

Vegetarian Pizza Night Menu
serves 6

Fire up the grill and take dinner outside. Have friends help with assembling and grilling the pizzas. The peas can be made ahead and even served chilled.

Grilled Pizza with Smoked Tofu and Roasted Red Peppers

Lemon and mint snap peas*

Green salad

*Cook 3 cups trimmed sugar snap peas in boiling water 2 minutes or until crisp-tender; drain. Combine 1 teaspoon lemon rind, 1 tablespoon fresh lemon juice, 2 teaspoons olive oil, ¼ teaspoon salt, and ¼ teaspoon sugar, stirring with a whisk. Toss peas with lemon mixture and 2 tablespoons chopped fresh mint.

Grilled Pizza with Smoked Tofu and Roasted Red Peppers

With its firm texture, smoked tofu shreds easily and replaces some of the cheese that traditionally tops pizza.

DOUGH:
1 teaspoon sugar
1 package dry yeast (about 2¼ teaspoons)
1 cup warm water (100° to 110°)
2¾ cups all-purpose flour, divided
1 tablespoon olive oil
1 teaspoon salt
Cooking spray

SAUCE:
1 tablespoon olive oil
1 garlic clove, minced
1 (28-ounce) can plum tomatoes, undrained and chopped
¼ teaspoon salt
¼ teaspoon black pepper

REMAINING INGREDIENTS:
2 red bell peppers
2 cups shredded smoked tofu (about 6 ounces)
1½ cups (6 ounces) shredded fresh mozzarella cheese

1. To prepare dough, dissolve sugar and yeast in warm water in a large bowl; let stand 5 minutes. Lightly spoon flour into dry measuring cups; level with a knife. Add 2½ cups flour, 1 tablespoon oil, and 1 teaspoon salt to yeast mixture; stir well to form a stiff dough. Turn dough out onto a lightly floured surface. Knead until smooth and elastic (about 10 minutes); add enough of remaining flour, 1 tablespoon at a time, to prevent dough from sticking to hands (dough will feel tacky). Place dough in a large bowl coated with cooking spray; turn to coat top. Cover; let rise in a warm place (85°), free from drafts, 45 minutes or until doubled in size. (Gently press two fingers into dough. If indentation remains, dough has risen enough.)
2. To prepare sauce, heat 1 tablespoon oil in a medium nonstick skillet over medium-high heat. Add garlic; sauté 1 minute. Add tomatoes; bring to a boil. Reduce heat; simmer 30 minutes or until sauce is thick. Stir in ¼ teaspoon salt and black pepper.
3. Punch dough down. Cover and let rest 5 minutes. Divide dough into 6 equal portions; working with 1 portion at a time, shape each into a ball (cover remaining dough to prevent drying). Roll each ball into a 6-inch circle. Place on baking sheets coated with cooking spray. Lightly coat dough with cooking spray; cover with plastic wrap. Let rest 15 minutes.
4. Prepare grill.
5. Cut bell peppers in half lengthwise; discard seeds and membranes. Place pepper halves, skin sides down, on grill rack coated with cooking spray; grill 15 minutes or until blackened. Place in a zip-top plastic bag; seal. Let stand 15 minutes. Peel and cut into strips.
6. Place dough rounds on grill rack coated with cooking spray; grill 2 minutes or until lightly browned. Turn dough over. Spread ⅓ cup tomato sauce over each dough round, leaving a ½-inch border. Sprinkle ⅓ cup tofu and ¼ cup cheese evenly over each pizza. Divide pepper strips evenly among pizzas. Close grill lid; grill 2 minutes or until cheese melts. Serve immediately. Yield: 6 servings (serving size: 1 pizza).

CALORIES 425 (30% from fat); FAT 14g (sat 5g, mono 5.8g, poly 2.4g); PROTEIN 19.1g; CARB 56.5g; FIBER 4.2g; CHOL 22mg; IRON 4.5mg; SODIUM 908mg; CALC 322mg

Tempeh Fajitas

Use a wire grilling basket for the onion and bell pepper so they don't fall into the grill. If there's enough room on your grill, you can heat the tortillas as the onion mixture and tempeh cook. Wrap in heavy-duty foil, and grill 5 minutes or until thoroughly heated.

    1   (8-ounce) package five-grain
        tempeh
    1   cup pineapple juice
    ¼   cup low-sodium soy sauce
    2   tablespoons fresh lime juice
    2   teaspoons ground cumin
    2   teaspoons canola oil
    ½   teaspoon freshly ground black
        pepper, divided
    1   garlic clove, minced
    2   cups (½-inch) vertically sliced
        onion
 1½   cups (½-inch-thick) slices green
        bell pepper
    Cooking spray
    ¼   teaspoon salt
    4   (8-inch) whole wheat tortillas
    ¼   cup chipotle salsa (such as
        Frontera)

1. Cut tempeh in half horizontally; cut each half lengthwise into 6 strips. Place tempeh in a shallow dish. Combine pineapple juice, soy sauce, lime juice, cumin, oil, ¼ teaspoon black pepper, and garlic in a small saucepan; bring to a boil. Pour juice mixture over tempeh. Marinate at room temperature 30 minutes or up to 2 hours.
2. Prepare grill.
3. Lightly coat onion and bell pepper with cooking spray; sprinkle with salt and ¼ teaspoon black pepper. Arrange onion mixture in a wire grilling basket coated with cooking spray. Place grilling basket on grill rack; grill 5 minutes or until lightly browned, turning occasionally. Remove tempeh from dish, reserving marinade. Place tempeh on grill rack coated with cooking spray; grill 2 minutes on each side or until lightly browned, basting occasionally with reserved marinade.
4. Warm tortillas according to package directions. Arrange 3 tempeh pieces, ½ cup onion mixture, and 1 tablespoon salsa down center of each tortilla; roll up. Yield: 4 servings (serving size: 1 fajita).

CALORIES 259 (18% from fat); FAT 5.1g (sat 0.7g, mono 1.2g, poly 2.2g); PROTEIN 14.6g; CARB 47.3g; FIBER 8g; CHOL 0mg; IRON 3.1mg; SODIUM 712mg; CALC 64mg

Tofu Steaks with Red Wine-Mushroom Sauce and Mashed Grilled Potatoes

In the sauce, miso contributes the rich flavor that's usually provided by meat stock. While the potatoes cook on the grill, firm the tofu in the oven, and then begin preparing the sauce. Oven-firming the tofu gives it the texture of an uncooked chicken breast.

POTATOES:
    Cooking spray
    2   pounds peeled baking potatoes,
        cut into 1-inch pieces
    6   garlic cloves
    ½   cup 2% reduced-fat milk
    ¼   cup fat-free sour cream
    1   tablespoon butter
    ¾   teaspoon salt
    ½   teaspoon freshly ground black
        pepper

TOFU:
    1   (16-ounce) package water-packed
        firm tofu, drained
    ½   teaspoon chopped fresh thyme
    ¼   teaspoon freshly ground black
        pepper

SAUCE:
    ⅓   cup finely chopped shallots
    3   cups sliced cremini mushrooms
        (about 8 ounces)
    3   cups sliced shiitake mushroom
        caps (about 6 ounces)
    1   (5-inch) portobello mushroom
        cap, cut into 1-inch pieces (about
        4 ounces)
 1½   cups dry red wine
    1   cup water, divided
    1   tablespoon red miso (soybean paste)
    ¼   teaspoon salt
    ¼   teaspoon freshly ground black
        pepper
    2   tablespoons chopped fresh parsley

1. Prepare grill.
2. To prepare potatoes, cut an 18 x 12-inch sheet of heavy-duty foil; lightly coat foil with cooking spray. Place potatoes and garlic in center of foil. Gather edges of foil to form a pouch, and tightly seal edges. Pierce foil several times with a fork. Place pouch on grill rack; grill 30 minutes or until potatoes are tender, turning pouch occasionally.
3. Place potatoes and garlic in a large bowl; add milk and next 4 ingredients. Mash with a potato masher to desired consistency; keep warm.
4. Preheat oven to 375°.
5. To prepare tofu, cut tofu lengthwise into 4 slices. Arrange tofu in a single layer on a foil-lined baking sheet coated with cooking spray. Lightly coat tofu slices with cooking spray. Bake at 375° for 25 minutes or until tofu releases 3 or more tablespoons of liquid. Cool slightly.
6. Lightly coat tofu with cooking spray; sprinkle with thyme and ¼ teaspoon pepper. Place tofu on grill rack coated with cooking spray; grill 3 minutes on each side or until browned. Keep warm.
7. To prepare sauce, heat a large non-stick skillet coated with cooking spray over medium-high heat. Add shallots; sauté 1 minute. Add mushrooms; sauté 6 minutes or until moisture evaporates. Remove mushroom mixture from pan. Add wine to pan. Bring to a boil, and cook until reduced to ¾ cup (about 4 minutes).
8. Combine 1 tablespoon water and miso, stirring with a whisk. Add miso mixture, remaining water, mushroom mixture, ¼ teaspoon salt, and ¼ teaspoon pepper to pan. Bring to boil; cook until liquid is reduced to about 1 cup (about 4 minutes). Stir in parsley. Serve sauce with tofu and potatoes. Yield: 4 servings (serving size: 1 tofu steak, 1 cup potatoes, and ½ cup mushroom sauce).

CALORIES 457 (28% from fat); FAT 14g (sat 3.8g, mono 3.3g, poly 6g); PROTEIN 28.2g; CARB 57.8g; FIBER 7.8g; CHOL 11mg; IRON 4.9mg; SODIUM 895mg; CALC 220mg

Vietnamese Lettuce Rolls with Spicy Grilled Tofu

This dish contrasts warm and cold sensations, along with firm, soft, and crunchy textures. The tofu is pressed before grilling so that it becomes firmer. Because the top halves of lettuce leaves are more flexible, they make better wrappers than the bottom halves.

   1   (16-ounce) package water-packed firm tofu, drained
  ½   cup fresh lime juice
  ½   cup honey
  ¼   cup thinly sliced peeled fresh lemongrass
   2   tablespoons low-sodium soy sauce
  ¾   teaspoon chile paste with garlic
  ¼   teaspoon freshly ground black pepper
   3   garlic cloves, minced
Cooking spray
   1   head romaine lettuce
  ½   cup cilantro leaves
   3   tablespoons chopped dry-roasted peanuts
  36   small mint leaves
  36   (2-inch) strips julienne-cut carrot
  12   basil leaves

1. Cut tofu crosswise into 12 (½-inch) slices. Place tofu slices on several layers of heavy-duty paper towels. Cover tofu with additional paper towels. Place a cutting board on top of tofu; place a cast iron skillet on top of cutting board. Let stand 30 minutes to 1 hour. (Tofu is ready when a slice bends easily without tearing or crumbling.) Arrange tofu in a single layer in a 13 x 9-inch baking dish.
2. Combine juice and next 6 ingredients in a small saucepan, and bring to a boil. Cook 1 minute, stirring until honey dissolves. Pour over tofu. Cover and let stand at room temperature 1 hour.
3. Prepare grill.
4. Remove tofu from dish, and reserve marinade. Coat tofu with cooking spray. Place tofu on grill rack coated with cooking spray. Grill 3 minutes on each side or until browned.
5. Remove 12 large outer leaves from lettuce head; reserve remaining lettuce for another use. Remove bottom half of each lettuce leaf; reserve for another use. Place 1 tofu slice on each lettuce leaf top. Top each leaf top with 2 teaspoons cilantro, ¾ teaspoon peanuts, 3 mint leaves, 3 carrot strips, and 1 basil leaf. Wrap leaf around toppings. Serve with reserved marinade. Yield: 4 servings (serving size: 3 lettuce rolls and about ¼ cup sauce).

CALORIES 294 (29% from fat); FAT 9.5g (sat 1.5g, mono 2.5g, poly 4.9g); PROTEIN 14.8g; CARB 44.9g; FIBER 2.8g; CHOL 0mg; IRON 3.5mg; SODIUM 334mg; CALC 157mg

reader recipes

Quick-Change Artist

A reader's favorite strawberry and greens salad has many guises.

As a mother of two-year-old twins and a part-time tutor, Mindy Bennett, of Vernon Hills, Illinois, is always on the lookout for quick, easy meals. She discovered the original recipe for this salad at a luncheon honoring friends. When the host shared how simple it was, Mindy knew she had to have the recipe.

"When I made the salad for the first time, I lightened the dressing and reduced the number of almonds," she says. Soon Mindy realized just how adaptable the salad could be. It can go from a side dish to a main dish just by adding an extra ingredient or two. "I typically make it into an easy weeknight dinner by adding some grilled or roasted chicken, or goat cheese," Mindy says.

"When I make it for other people," she says, "I add different ingredients to give it a new twist." Substituting sugared pecans and walnuts for the almonds works well. And using peaches or blueberries in place of the strawberries is an option. No matter the changes, everyone wants her recipe and her quick-change tips, as well.

Strawberry Salad with Poppy Seed Dressing

   3   tablespoons sugar
   3   tablespoons light mayonnaise
   2   tablespoons fat-free milk
   1   tablespoon poppy seeds
   1   tablespoon white wine vinegar
   1   (10-ounce) bag romaine lettuce
   1   cup sliced strawberries
   2   tablespoons slivered almonds, toasted

1. Combine first 5 ingredients in a small bowl, stirring with a whisk.
2. Place lettuce in a large bowl; add strawberries and almonds, tossing to combine. Divide salad evenly among 6 plates. Drizzle 1 tablespoon dressing over each serving. Yield: 6 servings (serving size: 1½ cups).

CALORIES 78 (35% from fat); FAT 3.3g (sat 0.4g, mono 1g, poly 1.6g); PROTEIN 1.8g; CARB 11.5g; FIBER 1.8g; CHOL 2mg; IRON 0.8mg; SODIUM 45mg; CALC 53mg

Chicken and Asparagus Pasta Toss

"My daughter and I created this recipe together through trial and error. It's good with or without the chicken. If you enjoy spicy food, you'll love it."

—Sandra Wells, Quinton, Virginia

   1   pound uncooked rotini (corkscrew pasta)
   2   teaspoons olive oil
   1   tablespoon butter
   3   cups (1-inch) slices asparagus
   2   cups chopped onion
   1   tablespoon hot sauce
   1   teaspoon crushed red pepper
  ¼   teaspoon salt
  ¼   teaspoon black pepper
   1   (6-ounce) package precooked chicken strips (such as Louis Rich)
   1   (28-ounce) can diced tomatoes, drained
  ¾   cup (3 ounces) preshredded fresh Parmesan cheese
   1   teaspoon paprika

1. Cook pasta according to package directions, omitting salt and fat; drain. Combine pasta and oil in a large bowl, and toss well.

2. Melt butter in a Dutch oven over medium heat; add asparagus, onion, hot sauce, and red pepper. Cook 5 minutes or until asparagus is crisp-tender, stirring frequently. Stir in pasta, salt, black pepper, chicken, and tomatoes; cook 2 minutes or until thoroughly heated. Stir in cheese; sprinkle with paprika. Yield: 7 servings (serving size: 2 cups).

CALORIES 369 (17% from fat); FAT 7.1g (sat 3g, mono 2.3g, poly 0.8g); PROTEIN 19.7g; CARB 57.5g; FIBER 6.1g; CHOL 24mg; IRON 3.4mg; SODIUM 530mg; CALC 170mg

---

QUICK & EASY
Sing-for-Your-Supper Shrimp

"This recipe gets its unusual name because you have to work a little harder to get to the good stuff. But it's worth it. This zesty dish is always a hit, and although it uses a little bit of a lot of spices, it's not time-consuming. Peeling the shrimp can be messy, so just make sure to serve it with plenty of napkins!"

—Heather Mader, Portland, Oregon

½ teaspoon paprika
¼ teaspoon salt
¼ teaspoon dried dill
¼ teaspoon black pepper
¼ teaspoon garlic powder
1 pound medium shrimp, unpeeled
2 teaspoons vegetable oil
½ teaspoon chili oil
1½ teaspoons grated lemon rind
2½ tablespoons fresh lemon juice

1. Combine first 5 ingredients in a large bowl. Add shrimp; toss well.

2. Heat oils and rind in a large nonstick skillet over medium-high heat. Add shrimp; sauté 4 minutes or until shrimp are done. Stir in juice. Yield: 4 servings (serving size: 4 ounces shrimp).

CALORIES 141 (26% from fat); FAT 3.8g (sat 0.8g, mono 1.2g, poly 1.2g); PROTEIN 23.2g; CARB 2.4g; FIBER 0.2g; CHOL 173mg; IRON 2.9mg; SODIUM 343mg; CALC 64mg

---

Mediterranean Grilled Vegetable Tagine

"The idea for this dish came from a favorite restaurant offering. I changed it to fit what I had on hand at the time. I serve the tagine over couscous and top it with the vegetables. My family loves it."

—Patty Lister, Falls Church, Virginia

1 small red onion
2 red bell peppers, quartered
1 green bell pepper, quartered
2 teaspoons balsamic vinegar
½ teaspoon kosher salt, divided
1 teaspoon olive oil, divided
1¾ cups chopped onion
2 garlic cloves, minced
1 teaspoon ground cumin
½ teaspoon fennel seeds, crushed
¼ teaspoon ground cinnamon
1¼ cups water, divided
¼ cup sliced pitted green olives
¼ cup golden raisins
¼ teaspoon freshly ground black pepper
1 (28-ounce) can diced tomatoes, undrained
6 small red potatoes, quartered
Cooking spray
⅔ cup uncooked couscous
¼ cup pine nuts, toasted

1. Cut red onion into 4 wedges, leaving root end intact. Place red onion, bell peppers, vinegar, ¼ teaspoon salt, and ½ teaspoon oil in a zip-top plastic bag. Seal bag; toss well to coat.

2. Prepare grill.

3. Heat ½ teaspoon oil in a large nonstick skillet over medium-high heat. Add chopped onion and garlic; sauté 3 minutes. Add cumin, fennel, and cinnamon; sauté 1 minute. Add ¼ teaspoon salt, ¼ cup water, olives, raisins, black pepper, tomatoes, and potatoes; bring to a boil. Cover, reduce heat, and simmer 25 minutes or until potatoes are just tender.

4. Remove bell peppers and red onion from bag, discarding marinade; place on grill rack coated with cooking spray. Grill 10 minutes, turning frequently.

5. Bring 1 cup water to a boil in a medium saucepan; gradually stir in couscous. Remove from heat; cover and let stand 5 minutes. Fluff with a fork. Serve tomato mixture over couscous. Top with grilled bell peppers and red onions; sprinkle with pine nuts. Yield: 4 servings (serving size: 1¼ cups tomato mixture, ½ cup couscous, ½ cup grilled vegetables, and 1 tablespoon pine nuts).

CALORIES 462 (14% from fat); FAT 7.1g (sat 1g, mono 3.2g, poly 2.2g); PROTEIN 15.8g; CARB 95.5g; FIBER 13.9g; CHOL 0mg; IRON 4.7mg; SODIUM 574mg; CALC 123mg

---

MAKE AHEAD • FREEZABLE
Banana-Blueberry Bread

"This bread is supereasy to make. I like to take it to my daughter's play group and watch the other mothers and toddlers enjoy it. The freshness of the fruit gives a sensational flavor to the bread."

—Kim Leonard, Stamford, Connecticut

1 cup all-purpose flour
½ cup whole wheat flour
¾ cup uncooked quick-cooking grits
½ cup sugar
½ teaspoon salt
½ teaspoon baking powder
¼ teaspoon baking soda
3 tablespoons canola oil
1 cup mashed ripe banana (about 2 bananas)
¾ cup blueberries
2 large eggs, lightly beaten
Cooking spray

1. Preheat oven to 350°.

2. Lightly spoon flours into dry measuring cups; level with a knife. Combine flours, grits, sugar, salt, baking powder, and baking soda in a large bowl; make a well in center of mixture. Combine oil, banana, blueberries, and eggs; add to flour mixture. Stir just until moist.

3. Spoon batter into an 8 x 4-inch loaf pan coated with cooking spray. Bake at 350° for 1 hour or until a wooden pick inserted in center comes out clean. Cool bread in pan 10 minutes on a wire rack. Remove bread from pan, and cool completely on wire rack. Yield: 16 servings (serving size: 1 slice).

CALORIES 145 (25% from fat); FAT 3.6g (sat 0.4g, mono 1.8g, poly 1g); PROTEIN 3g; CARB 25.9g; FIBER 1.4g; CHOL 27mg; IRON 0.9mg; SODIUM 116mg; CALC 15mg

Glazed Spice Cake Cookies

"While visiting Seattle, I noticed that many of the bakeries were selling large cakelike cookies, some topped with a white glaze. They were soft and delicious. After playing around with ratios found in various recipes for cookies and quick-breads from *Cooking Light*, I came up with this recipe."

—Sylvia Lee, Chapel Hill, North Carolina

COOKIES:

1½ cups all-purpose flour
1½ teaspoons baking powder
½ teaspoon salt
½ teaspoon ground cinnamon
½ teaspoon ground nutmeg
½ teaspoon ground allspice
¼ teaspoon ground cloves
1 cup canned pumpkin
1 cup packed brown sugar
¼ cup butter, softened
¼ cup fat-free milk
1½ teaspoons vanilla extract
2 large egg whites
Cooking spray

GLAZE:

¾ cup powdered sugar
1 tablespoon fat-free milk
¼ teaspoon vanilla extract
Dash of ground cinnamon

1. Preheat oven to 375°.
2. To prepare cookies, lightly spoon flour into dry measuring cups; level with a knife. Combine flour and next 6 ingredients; stir well.
3. Combine pumpkin, brown sugar, and butter in a large bowl; beat with a mixer at medium speed until light and fluffy. Add milk, vanilla, and egg whites; beat well. Gradually add flour mixture to pumpkin mixture; stir until combined.
4. Drop dough by heaping tablespoonfuls onto baking sheets coated with cooking spray. Bake at 375° for 10 minutes or until almost firm. Cool on pans 1 minute on a wire rack; remove from pans. Cool completely on wire rack.
5. To prepare glaze, combine powdered sugar and remaining 3 ingredients; stir well with a whisk. Dip tops of cookies in glaze. Place cookies, glaze sides up, on wire racks; allow to set. Yield: 2 dozen cookies (serving size: 1 cookie).

CALORIES 102 (18% from fat); FAT 2g (sat 1.2g, mono 0.6g, poly 0.1g); PROTEIN 1.4g; CARB 19.8g; FIBER 0.6g; CHOL 5mg; IRON 0.7mg; SODIUM 109mg; CALC 34mg

Black Bean Salsa

"I created this recipe for my wife. I used to make summer wraps and top them with feta. My wife suggested adding salsa, so I tried a few, and this one stuck. I make this all summer long and serve it with hot tortilla chips. It's a wonderful break from the same old salsa out of a jar, and we love the texture and spicy flavor."

—Crittenden Kennedy, Killeen, Texas

⅓ cup finely chopped red bell pepper
¼ cup finely chopped red onion
¼ cup chopped cucumber
¼ cup chopped plum tomato
2 tablespoons chopped celery
2 tablespoons chopped seeded jalapeño pepper
2 tablespoons olive oil
2 tablespoons balsamic vinegar
1 tablespoon fresh lime juice
1 tablespoon chopped fresh basil
1½ teaspoons minced fresh or ½ teaspoon dried thyme
½ teaspoon salt
½ teaspoon ground cumin
½ teaspoon chili powder
¼ teaspoon black pepper
3 garlic cloves, minced
2 (15-ounce) cans black beans, rinsed and drained

1. Combine all ingredients in a medium bowl; stir well. Cover and chill 2 hours. Yield: 16 servings (serving size: ¼ cup).

CALORIES 91 (20% from fat); FAT 2g (sat 0.3g, mono 1.3g, poly 0.3g); PROTEIN 4.9g; CARB 13.9g; FIBER 4.9g; CHOL 0mg; IRON 1.3mg; SODIUM 201mg; CALC 19mg

Cajun Scallops

"Crank up your fan—the Cajun seasoning and pepper create smoke when they hit the hot pan."

—Catherine McMichael, Saginaw, Michigan

1 teaspoon olive oil
1 large red onion, thinly sliced and separated into rings
1 teaspoon Cajun seasoning
½ teaspoon black pepper
1 teaspoon butter
1 garlic clove
¾ pound fresh scallops
1 to 2 teaspoons hot sauce

1. Heat oil in a cast iron skillet over high heat. Add onion, Cajun seasoning, and pepper; sauté 3 minutes. Add butter and garlic; sauté 30 seconds. Add scallops; cook 1 minute or until browned. Sprinkle with hot sauce; turn. Cook 3 minutes or until done. Yield: 2 servings (serving size: about 5 ounces scallops).

CALORIES 225 (24% from fat); FAT 5.7g (sat 1.7g, mono 2.3g, poly 0.8g); PROTEIN 29.8g; CARB 12.5g; FIBER 1.8g; CHOL 61mg; IRON 0.9mg; SODIUM 719mg; CALC 65mg

enlightened cook

The Fisherman's Daughter

Sally Calabrese, a third-generation Monterey cook—and granddaughter of the peninsula's pioneering fisherman—reinvents her family's traditional fish barbecue recipes.

Sally uses lower-fat products and techniques to lighten her family's traditional dishes. Except for the grilled fish, these recipes can be made in advance for any gathering. As for the grilling itself, Sally stresses a few basics. "The grill must be nice and hot so the fish doesn't stick," she advises. "Watch the fish closely so that it doesn't overcook. And if you use the broiler, spray the pan with cooking spray. Keep the fish six inches from the heat, and turn it twice."

Breadcrumb-Baked Chicken

Sally's grandmother used homemade leftover Italian bread for the crumbs. To save time, Sally uses store-bought bread (Italian is her favorite). The topping is delicious on chicken, lamb chops, or fish, such as halibut, swordfish, or mahimahi. The chicken is best right out of the oven, but it also tastes good reheated or at room temperature.

- 3 tablespoons olive oil, divided
- 3½ cups (½-inch) cubed Italian bread, toasted (about 6 ounces)
- ⅓ cup finely chopped fresh parsley
- 3 tablespoons grated fresh Parmesan cheese
- 1 tablespoon sugar
- 1 teaspoon salt
- ½ teaspoon freshly ground black pepper
- 4 garlic cloves, minced
- ½ cup all-purpose flour
- 2 large egg whites, lightly beaten
- 1 large egg, lightly beaten
- 8 (6-ounce) skinless, boneless chicken breast halves

1. Preheat oven to 350°.
2. Pour 2 tablespoons oil in a 13 x 9-inch baking dish.
3. Place bread in a food processor; pulse until coarsely ground. Combine breadcrumbs, parsley, and next 5 ingredients in a shallow dish. Place flour in a shallow dish. Combine egg whites and egg in a shallow dish.
4. Dredge 1 chicken breast half in flour; shake off excess flour. Dip in egg mixture; dredge in breadcrumb mixture. Place in prepared dish. Repeat procedure with remaining chicken, flour, egg mixture, and breadcrumb mixture. Drizzle 1 tablespoon oil over chicken. Bake at 350° for 20 minutes or until chicken is done. Yield: 8 servings (serving size: 1 chicken breast half).

CALORIES 311 (26% from fat); FAT 8.9g (sat 2g, mono 4.8g, poly 1.2g); PROTEIN 36.9g; CARB 18.9g; FIBER 0.9g; CHOL 107mg; IRON 2.3mg; SODIUM 573mg; CALC 74mg

STAFF FAVORITE
Grilled Sesame Swordfish with Monterey Bay Pesto

When Sally was growing up, her family liked grilling sardines and mackerel. This was the "pesto" they used, which Sally and her sister use today on grilled shrimp or other fresh fish. Prepare the sauce up to a day ahead, and store it, covered, in the refrigerator. But bring it back to room temperature before serving. The chicken broth and the water replace almost ¼ cup of oil.

SAUCE:
- ½ cup chopped fresh parsley
- ¼ cup chopped fresh basil
- 2½ tablespoons fat-free, less-sodium chicken broth
- 2 tablespoons fresh lemon juice
- 1 tablespoon extravirgin olive oil
- 1 tablespoon water
- ⅛ teaspoon salt
- ⅛ teaspoon freshly ground black pepper
- 3 garlic cloves

FISH:
- 6 (6-ounce) swordfish steaks (about 1 inch thick)
- 1 teaspoon extravirgin olive oil
- 1½ teaspoons sesame seeds
- 1 teaspoon coarse sea salt
  Cooking spray

1. Prepare grill.

2. To prepare sauce, combine first 9 ingredients in a food processor; process until minced.
3. To prepare fish, rub fish with 1 teaspoon oil. Rub sesame seeds and sea salt evenly over fish. Place fish on grill rack coated with cooking spray; grill 4 minutes on each side or until fish flakes easily when tested with a fork. Yield: 6 servings (serving size: 1 steak and about 1 tablespoon sauce).

CALORIES 236 (37% from fat); FAT 9.6g (sat 2.2g, mono 4.8g, poly 1.8g); PROTEIN 32.8g; CARB 1.4g; FIBER 0.3g; CHOL 64mg; IRON 2.8mg; SODIUM 594mg; CALC 21mg

QUICK & EASY
Roma Salad with Capers, Olives, and Mozzarella

Roma tomatoes (also called plum tomatoes) can be found in the supermarket—even in the winter—but any ripe summer tomatoes will work. It's best to dress the salad right before serving, but you can prepare the tomato mixture and vinaigrette ahead of time and store them separately until ready to serve.

- 4 cups (¼-inch-thick) slices plum tomato (about 10 tomatoes)
- 2 cups thinly sliced red onion
- ¼ cup coarsely chopped fresh basil
- 2 tablespoons capers
- 1 tablespoon chopped pitted kalamata olives
- ½ teaspoon coarse sea salt
- ¼ teaspoon freshly ground black pepper
- 2 tablespoons balsamic vinegar
- 1 teaspoon extravirgin olive oil
- ¼ cup (1 ounce) shredded fresh mozzarella cheese

1. Combine first 7 ingredients in a large bowl, tossing gently. Combine vinegar and oil in a small bowl, stirring with a whisk. Drizzle vinegar mixture over tomato mixture; toss gently to combine. Place tomato mixture on each of 6 plates; sprinkle with cheese. Yield: 6 servings (serving size: about 1 cup salad and 2 teaspoons cheese).

CALORIES 68 (38% from fat); FAT 2.9g (sat 0.9g, mono 1.1g, poly 0.3g); PROTEIN 2.4g; CARB 9.5g; FIBER 2g; CHOL 4mg; IRON 0.8mg; SODIUM 340mg; CALC 47mg

Blue Cheese Salad Dressing

Sally uses this as an all-purpose dressing or dip. Sometimes she adds chopped anchovies, and pours it over celery stalks. Other times she adds chopped green onions, and pours it over baked potatoes.

  1 cup low-fat mayonnaise
  2 tablespoons cider vinegar
  1 tablespoon vegetable oil
  ½ teaspoon dried oregano
  ¼ teaspoon salt
  ¼ teaspoon freshly ground black pepper
  1 (8-ounce) carton fat-free sour cream
  1 garlic clove, crushed
  ½ cup (2 ounces) crumbled blue cheese

1. Combine first 8 ingredients, stirring with a whisk. Stir in cheese. Cover and refrigerate at least 3 hours. Yield: 2½ cups (serving size: 1 tablespoon).

CALORIES 24 (45% from fat); FAT 1.2g (sat 0.4g, mono 0.2g, poly 0.4g); PROTEIN 0.6g; CARB 2.7g; FIBER 0g; CHOL 2mg; IRON 0mg; SODIUM 95mg; CALC 17mg

Sautéed Garlicky Artichokes

When Sally was growing up, her father traded fish for artichokes. But now, she grows them in her yard to make this recipe. Sally likes baby artichokes best, but mature ones give a larger yield in less time. Serve them warm or at room temperature.

  4 cups water
  ¼ cup fresh lemon juice (about 2 lemons)
 14 whole artichokes (about 6½ pounds)
  1 tablespoon olive oil
  4 garlic cloves, sliced
  3 cups thinly sliced portobello mushroom caps
  2 tablespoons chopped fresh flat-leaf parsley
  ½ teaspoon salt
  ¼ teaspoon freshly ground black pepper

1. Combine water and juice. Cut off stem of each artichoke to within 1 inch of base; discard stem. Cut off top of each artichoke; discard. Remove bottom leaves and tough outer leaves, leaving tender heart and bottom. Cut each artichoke in half horizontally. Remove fuzzy thistle with a spoon. Cut each artichoke bottom into quarters; dip artichoke quarters in lemon water. Drain.
2. Place artichoke quarters in a medium saucepan; cover with water. Bring to a boil. Reduce heat; simmer 15 minutes or until tender. Drain.
3. Heat oil in a large nonstick skillet over medium-high heat. Add artichoke quarters and garlic; sauté 2 minutes. Add mushrooms; cover and cook 2 minutes or until mushrooms are tender, stirring occasionally. Remove from heat, and stir in parsley, salt, and pepper. Yield: 9 servings (serving size: ½ cup).

CALORIES 191 (17% from fat); FAT 3.6g (sat 0.5g, mono 2.2g, poly 0.5g); PROTEIN 11.5g; CARB 36.5g; FIBER 4g; CHOL 0mg; IRON 4.5mg; SODIUM 438mg; CALC 150mg

Five-Bean Pot

  1 (16-ounce) can cannellini beans or other white beans, undrained
  1 (16-ounce) can chickpeas (garbanzo beans), undrained
  1 (16-ounce) can lima beans, undrained
  1 (16-ounce) can kidney beans, undrained
  1 (16-ounce) can baked beans, undrained
  6 bacon slices
  2 cups chopped onion
  ½ cup packed brown sugar
  ½ cup cider vinegar
  1 teaspoon dry mustard
  1 garlic clove, crushed
    Cooking spray

1. Preheat oven to 350°.
2. Drain beans in a colander over a bowl, reserving 1 cup liquid. Set beans and liquid aside.
3. Cook bacon in a large nonstick skillet over medium heat until crisp. Remove bacon from pan, reserving 3 tablespoons drippings in pan. Crumble bacon. Add onion to drippings in pan; cook over medium heat 10 minutes or until golden brown, stirring frequently. Stir in bacon, sugar, and next 3 ingredients. Cook over medium-low heat until thick and bubbly (about 15 minutes); stir occasionally.
4. Combine beans, reserved bean liquid, and onion mixture in a 3-quart casserole coated with cooking spray. Cover and bake at 350° for 45 minutes, stirring every 15 minutes. Yield: 10 servings (serving size: ¾ cup).

CALORIES 279 (22% from fat); FAT 6.9g (sat 2.5g, mono 2.8g, poly 1.1g); PROTEIN 10.6g; CARB 45.7g; FIBER 10.1g; CHOL 8mg; IRON 3.1mg; SODIUM 524mg; CALC 92mg

Ice Cream with Pear Sauce

The sauce can be made up to 2 days ahead and warmed in the microwave just before serving. You'll get a lot of liquid from the pears after they macerate in the sugar overnight. This sauce is also good served over pound cake.

  5 cups chopped peeled ripe Bartlett pear (about 6 pears)
  ½ cup sugar
  1 lemon, peeled and sectioned
  ¾ cup coarsely chopped walnuts
  ½ cup golden raisins
  ¼ cup dried sweet cherries
  1 navel orange, peeled and sectioned
  6 cups vanilla low-fat ice cream

1. Combine pear and sugar in a zip-top plastic bag; shake well. Seal and refrigerate 8 hours or overnight.
2. Place 2 tablespoons lemon sections in a medium saucepan; reserve remaining lemon sections for another use. Add pear mixture, walnuts, raisins, cherries, and orange to pan. Bring to a simmer over medium heat; cook 30 minutes or until mixture is thick and slightly soft, stirring occasionally. Serve over ice cream. Yield: 12 servings (serving size: ½ cup ice cream and ⅓ cup pear sauce).

CALORIES 267 (23% from fat); FAT 6.8g (sat 1.3g, mono 1.1g, poly 3g); PROTEIN 5.6g; CARB 47.9g; FIBER 4.2g; CHOL 5mg; IRON 0.6mg; SODIUM 48mg; CALC 122mg

Our Best Burgers

When we put out a call for our staff's best burgers, we happily got more than we bargained for.

There are several things at which people often think they're the best. We're all the most skillful and courteous drivers; we can call a game better than any referee; our navigational prowess is unmatched; and the burgers we make are tops. That's how this story came about—conversation among the staff one day turned to how each of us makes the best burgers. We decided to put these assertions to the test, and we're glad we did. When we asked our staff to submit their favorite burger recipes, we got a great mix of recipes—from beef patties to chicken, Asian to Middle Eastern.

The Guadalajara

(pictured on cover and page 183)

"I was in Guadalajara and had a burger similar to this one," Assistant Food Stylist Kathleen Kanen reports. The salsa that topped the burger was a welcome change from the usual tomato and onion slices. Kathleen added tequila to her version. The recipe makes more salsa than you'll need for the burgers; serve the extra on the side with baked tortilla chips.

    1   teaspoon chipotle chile powder
    ½   teaspoon kosher salt
    1   pound ground round
    Cooking spray
    4   (2-ounce) Kaiser rolls
    1⅓ cups Tequila-Spiked Salsa

1. Prepare grill.
2. Combine chile powder, salt, and beef. Divide mixture into 4 equal portions, shaping each into a ½-inch-thick patty.
3. Place patties on grill rack coated with cooking spray; grill 5 minutes on each side or until done. Place rolls, cut sides down, on grill rack; grill 1 minute or until toasted. Place 1 patty on bottom half of each roll; top each serving with ⅓ cup Tequila-Spiked Salsa and top half of roll. Yield: 4 servings.

(Totals include Tequila-Spiked Salsa) CALORIES 405 (35% from fat); FAT 15.9g (sat 5.3g, mono 6.7g, poly 1.7g); PROTEIN 28.5g; CARB 35.3g; FIBER 2.8g; CHOL 77mg; IRON 4.6mg; SODIUM 721mg; CALC 73mg

QUICK & EASY • MAKE AHEAD
TEQUILA-SPIKED SALSA:

    2   cups chopped seeded tomato
    1   cup chopped onion
    ½   cup chopped fresh cilantro
    ⅓   cup chopped peeled avocado
    2   tablespoons fresh lime juice
    2   teaspoons tequila
    ½   teaspoon kosher salt
    2   garlic cloves, minced

1. Combine all ingredients in a bowl; toss gently. Yield: 3 cups (serving size: ⅓ cup).

CALORIES 29 (31% from fat); FAT 1g (sat 0.2g, mono 0.6g, poly 0.2g); PROTEIN 0.7g; CARB 4.4g; FIBER 1.1g; CHOL 0mg; IRON 0.3mg; SODIUM 110mg; CALC 9mg

---

Burger Tips

• Do not overmix ground meat—doing so will make the patties dense.

• Likewise, use a light hand when shaping the burgers so they don't become too compacted.

• To keep meat from sticking to your hands, work with damp hands.

• Resist the urge to press the burgers with a spatula as they cook—you'll press away flavorful juices.

• Freeze uncooked burgers in a heavy-duty zip-top plastic bag up to 3 months; place between sheets of wax paper or plastic wrap so they'll be easy to pry apart.

Smothered Burgers

Associate Food Editor Krista Ackerbloom Montgomery finds many sandwiches too big to eat comfortably. "So I rip them apart, take off the top, and eat them with a knife and fork." Krista has introduced her husband, John, to these open-faced burgers at home. Look for Texas toast, sometimes labeled "barbecue bread," on the bread aisle.

    Cooking spray
    2   cups vertically sliced onion
    2   teaspoons sugar
    ¾   teaspoon salt, divided
    ½   teaspoon freshly ground black
         pepper, divided
    1   (8-ounce) package presliced
         mushrooms
    2   tablespoons Worcestershire sauce
    1   pound ground round
    4   (1-ounce) slices Texas toast
    ½   cup (2 ounces) shredded Swiss
         cheese

1. Prepare grill.
2. Heat a medium nonstick skillet coated with cooking spray over medium heat. Add onion; cover and cook 5 minutes, stirring occasionally. Add sugar, ¼ teaspoon salt, and ¼ teaspoon pepper; cook, uncovered, 5 minutes or until tender, stirring frequently. Remove onion from pan, and keep warm.
3. Heat pan coated with cooking spray over medium-high heat. Add mushrooms and ¼ teaspoon salt; sauté 5 minutes or until tender.
4. Combine ¼ teaspoon salt, ¼ teaspoon pepper, Worcestershire sauce, and beef. Divide mixture into 4 equal portions, shaping each into a ½-inch-thick patty.
5. Preheat broiler.
6. Place patties on grill rack coated with cooking spray; grill 5 minutes on each side or until done. Place bread on grill rack; grill 1 minute on each side or until toasted.
7. Arrange bread on a baking sheet. Top each bread slice with 1 patty, ¼ cup onion, ¼ cup mushrooms, and 2 tablespoons cheese; broil 2 minutes or until cheese melts. Yield: 4 servings.

CALORIES 393 (40% from fat); FAT 17.5g (sat 7.5g, mono 6.7g, poly 1.4g); PROTEIN 31.1g; CARB 27.1g; FIBER 2.5g; CHOL 91mg; IRON 4.4mg; SODIUM 786mg; CALC 204mg

Ham- and Swiss-Stuffed Burgers

Food Stylist Kellie Gerber Kelley says her creation is a variation of the classic bacon cheeseburger, "but all the fun stuff's inside." Kellie's tips: Buy the thinnest slices of ham you can find, then press the patties between two pieces of plastic wrap. Make sure the edges are pinched together well so the cheese can't escape in the cooking process.

 1 tablespoon dried parsley
 1 tablespoon Worcestershire sauce
 ¼ teaspoon salt
 ¼ teaspoon garlic powder
 ¼ teaspoon freshly ground black pepper
 1 pound ground round
 ½ cup (2 ounces) shredded Swiss cheese
 2 ounces thinly sliced 33%-less-sodium smoked deli ham
Cooking spray
 8 (1-ounce) slices sourdough bread
 4 curly leaf lettuce leaves
 8 (¼-inch-thick) slices red onion
 8 (¼-inch-thick) slices tomato

1. Prepare grill.
2. Combine first 6 ingredients. Divide mixture into 8 equal portions, shaping each into a 5-inch oval patty. Top each of 4 patties with 2 tablespoons cheese and ½ ounce ham, leaving a ½-inch border; top with remaining patties. Press edges together to seal.
3. Place patties on grill rack coated with cooking spray; grill 3 minutes on each side or until done. Place bread slices on grill rack; grill 1 minute on each side or until toasted. Top each of 4 bread slices with 1 lettuce leaf, 2 onion slices, 1 patty, 2 tomato slices, and 1 bread slice. Yield: 4 servings.

CALORIES 468 (37% from fat); FAT 19g (sat 8g, mono 7.6g, poly 1.2g); PROTEIN 35.2g; CARB 37.2g; FIBER 2.6g; CHOL 98mg; IRON 4.8mg; SODIUM 808mg; CALC 208mg

Italian Sausage Burgers with Fennel Slaw

Production Manager Liz Rhoades's family had enjoyed Italian sausage burgers for years, a recipe inspired by their Italian neighborhood in Youngstown, Ohio. But the fennel slaw that crowns this recipe came about after Liz accidentally bought fennel instead of celery. Quickly figuring out what to do with the fennel, Liz's mom made a crunchy slaw that went perfectly with the flavorful burgers.

SLAW:
1½ tablespoons cider vinegar
 2 teaspoons sugar
 1 teaspoon extravirgin olive oil
 ¼ teaspoon freshly ground black pepper
 ⅛ teaspoon salt
1½ cups thinly sliced fennel bulb
 1 cup vertically sliced red onion

BURGERS:
 8 ounces hot turkey Italian sausage
 8 ounces ground turkey breast
Cooking spray
 4 (½-ounce) slices provolone cheese
 4 (2-ounce) Kaiser rolls

1. To prepare slaw, combine first 5 ingredients in a medium bowl, stirring with a whisk until sugar dissolves. Add fennel and onion, tossing to combine. Let stand at room temperature 30 minutes to 1 hour, tossing occasionally.
2. Prepare grill.
3. To prepare burgers, remove sausage from casing. Combine sausage and turkey breast. Divide mixture into 4 equal portions, shaping each into a ½-inch-thick patty.
4. Place patties on grill rack coated with cooking spray; grill 5 minutes on each side. Top each patty with 1 cheese slice; grill 1 to 2 minutes or until burgers are done and cheese melts. Place rolls, cut sides down, on grill rack; grill 1 minute or until toasted. Using a slotted spoon, arrange about ½ cup slaw on bottom half of each roll; top each serving with 1 patty and top half of roll. Yield: 4 servings.

CALORIES 413 (30% from fat); FAT 13.9g (sat 4.7g, mono 3.6g, poly 2.8g); PROTEIN 33.9g; CARB 37.5g; FIBER 2.9g; CHOL 97mg; IRON 3.6mg; SODIUM 930mg; CALC 189mg

Smoked Cheddar and Lentil Burgers

When Copy Chief Maria Hopkins gave up eating red meat about a year ago, she missed burgers most. "I created Smoked Cheddar and Lentil Burgers after I fell in love with lentils at taste testing."

2½ cups water
 1 cup dried lentils
 2 bay leaves
 1 teaspoon olive oil
 1 cup finely chopped onion
 ½ cup finely chopped carrot
 1 cup (4 ounces) shredded smoked Cheddar cheese
 ½ cup dry breadcrumbs
 2 teaspoons chopped fresh thyme
1¼ teaspoons salt
 ¾ teaspoon garlic powder
 ¾ teaspoon paprika
 ½ teaspoon freshly ground black pepper
 ¼ teaspoon ground red pepper
 3 large egg whites, lightly beaten
Cooking spray
 8 teaspoons stone-ground mustard
 8 (2-ounce) whole wheat sandwich buns, toasted
 8 (¼-inch-thick) slices tomato
 2 cups trimmed arugula

1. Place first 3 ingredients in a medium saucepan; bring to a boil. Cover, reduce heat, and simmer 30 minutes or until tender; drain. Discard bay leaves. Place lentils in a large bowl; partially mash with a potato masher. Cool slightly.
2. Heat oil in a medium nonstick skillet over medium-high heat. Add onion and carrot; sauté 5 minutes or until tender. Cool slightly.
3. Add onion mixture, cheese, and next 8 ingredients to lentils; stir well to combine. Cover and chill 45 minutes. Divide mixture into 8 equal portions, shaping each into a ½-inch-thick patty.
4. Heat a grill pan coated with cooking spray over medium-high heat. Add half of patties, and cook 5 minutes on each side or until done. Repeat procedure with remaining patties. Spread 1 teaspoon mustard on top half of each bun. Place 1 patty on bottom half of each

bun, and top each serving with 1 tomato slice, ¼ cup arugula, and top half of bun. Yield: 8 servings.

CALORIES 354 (22% from fat); FAT 8.8g (sat 3.5g, mono 2.4g, poly 2g); PROTEIN 19.3g; CARB 50.7g; FIBER 9.8g; CHOL 15mg; IRON 5mg; SODIUM 893mg; CALC 226mg

Kaftah Burgers

Julie Grimes Bottcher, assistant food editor and mom-to-be, cites her pregnancy as the inspiration for this unusual burger recipe. "I had a craving for a burger flavored with Middle Eastern seasonings but with the traditional American accompaniments of yellow mustard and dill pickles."

　1　cup finely chopped onion
　¾　cup chopped fresh flat-leaf parsley
　½　cup dry breadcrumbs
　½　cup chopped fresh cilantro
1½　teaspoons ground cumin
1½　teaspoons ground coriander
1¼　teaspoons salt
　½　teaspoon ground allspice
1¼　pounds ground round
　¾　pound lean ground lamb
　4　garlic cloves, minced
　2　large egg whites, lightly beaten
　　Cooking spray
　8　(2-ounce) onion sandwich buns
　8　teaspoons prepared mustard
16　dill pickle slices
　8　curly leaf lettuce leaves
　8　(¼-inch-thick) slices tomato

1. Prepare grill.
2. Combine first 12 ingredients in a large bowl. Divide mixture into 8 equal portions, shaping each into a ½-inch-thick patty.
3. Place patties on grill rack coated with cooking spray; grill 5 minutes on each side or until done. Place buns, cut sides down, on grill rack; grill 1 minute or until toasted. Spread 1 teaspoon mustard on each bun top. Place 1 patty on bottom half of each bun; top each serving with 2 pickle slices, 1 lettuce leaf, 1 tomato slice, and top half of bun. Yield: 8 servings.

CALORIES 432 (37% from fat); FAT 17.8g (sat 7.3g, mono 6.8g, poly 2g); PROTEIN 29.8g; CARB 37.3g; FIBER 2.6g; CHOL 79mg; IRON 4.8mg; SODIUM 851mg; CALC 119mg

Chicken Burgers with Peanut Sauce

No recipe can offer too much flavor for Assistant Food Editor Ann Taylor Pittman. Her burger is made spicy with Thai chile paste and rounded out with a sweet, creamy Thai-style peanut sauce. Onion sprouts, which look similar to alfalfa sprouts, have a pungent bite. You can find them next to the alfalfa sprouts in many supermarkets.

SAUCE:
　2　tablespoons peanut butter
　2　teaspoons low-sodium soy sauce
1½　teaspoons dark sesame oil
　1　teaspoon water
　1　teaspoon rice vinegar
　1　garlic clove, minced

BURGERS:
　½　cup finely chopped green onions
　1　tablespoon chile paste with garlic
　2　teaspoons grated peeled fresh ginger
　2　teaspoons low-sodium soy sauce
　¼　teaspoon salt
　1　pound skinless, boneless chicken breast, chopped
　　Cooking spray
　4　(2-ounce) sandwich rolls with sesame seeds
　1　cup onion sprouts or alfalfa sprouts

1. To prepare sauce, combine first 6 ingredients, stirring with a whisk until smooth.
2. Prepare grill.
3. To prepare burgers, place onions and next 5 ingredients in a food processor; process until coarsely ground. Divide mixture into 4 equal portions, shaping each into a ½-inch-thick patty.
4. Place patties on grill rack coated with cooking spray; grill 4 minutes on each side or until done. Place rolls, cut sides down, on grill rack; grill 1 minute or until toasted. Place 1 patty on bottom half of each roll; top each serving with ¼ cup sprouts, about 1 tablespoon sauce, and top half of roll. Yield 4 servings.

CALORIES 341 (28% from fat); FAT 10.6g (sat 3.2g, mono 3.5g, poly 3.3g); PROTEIN 28.5g; CARB 32.8g; FIBER 2.5g; CHOL 49mg; IRON 2.7mg; SODIUM 769mg; CALC 67mg

Chicken-Apple-Bacon Burgers

Test Kitchens staffer Kathryn Conrad enjoys this burger with a cold, crisp beer and very little else. "The flavor is in the burger. The best condiment is the residual flavor of the charcoal from grilling," she notes, "and perhaps some honey mustard."

　2　bacon slices
　¼　cup chopped red onion
　1　pound skinless, boneless chicken breast, coarsely chopped
　2　teaspoons chopped fresh sage
　½　teaspoon salt
　½　teaspoon freshly ground black pepper
　　Cooking spray
　1　Granny Smith apple, peeled, cored, and cut crosswise into 8 (¼-inch-thick) slices
　4　(2-ounce) Kaiser rolls

1. Prepare grill.
2. Cook bacon in a large nonstick skillet over medium-high heat until crisp. Remove bacon from pan, and crumble. Add onion to drippings in pan, and sauté 2 minutes or until lightly browned. Cool slightly.
3. Place chicken in a food processor; process until coarsely ground. Combine chicken, bacon, onion, sage, salt, and pepper. Divide chicken mixture into 4 equal portions, shaping each into a ½-inch-thick patty.
4. Place patties on grill rack coated with cooking spray; grill 5 minutes on each side or until done. Place apple slices on grill rack coated with cooking spray, and grill 1 minute on each side. Place rolls, cut sides down, on grill rack; grill 1 minute or until toasted. Place patties on bottom halves of rolls; top each serving with 2 apple slices and top half of roll. Yield: 4 servings.

CALORIES 341 (27% from fat); FAT 10.1g (sat 3.1g, mono 3.9g, poly 2g); PROTEIN 26.4g; CARB 34.4g; FIBER 2g; CHOL 57mg; IRON 2.7mg; SODIUM 740mg; CALC 70mg

Skeen Burgers

"This burger recipe, named after the North Carolina family that created it, was on the fridge at my house for at least 10 years," notes Test Kitchens staffer Tiffany Vickers. "My dad cooks about three things well," she says, "and this is one of them."

1¼ cups crushed reduced-fat round buttery crackers (such as Ritz; about 20 crackers)
½ cup applesauce
1½ teaspoons hot pepper sauce
¼ teaspoon garlic powder
2 pounds ground round
1 (1-ounce) package onion soup mix (such as Lipton)
Cooking spray
10 (1½-ounce) hamburger buns
5 tablespoons ketchup
10 (⅛-inch-thick) slices red onion

1. Prepare grill.
2. Combine first 6 ingredients. Divide mixture into 10 equal portions, shaping each into a ½-inch-thick patty.
3. Place patties on grill rack coated with cooking spray; grill 5 minutes on each side or until done. Place buns, cut sides down, on grill rack; grill 1 minute or until toasted. Spread 1½ teaspoons ketchup on each bun top. Place 1 patty on bottom half of each bun; top each serving with 1 onion slice and top half of bun. Yield: 10 servings.

CALORIES 335 (34% from fat); FAT 12.5g (sat 4.3g, mono 5.3g, poly 1.4g); PROTEIN 22g; CARB 32.7g; FIBER 1.8g; CHOL 62mg; IRON 3.3mg; SODIUM 691mg; CALC 63mg

Turkey and Oat Burgers

Office Manager Rita Kinnamon-Jackson tinkered with her father's original meat loaf-style burger by replacing the ground beef with ground turkey and using chili powder instead of pepper for a flavor boost. The patties might seem a little wet, but they bind together nicely once they begin to cook. Because they're delicate, a grill pan works best.

1 cup regular oats
1 cup finely chopped Vidalia onion
1 tablespoon chili powder
1¼ teaspoons salt
2 large egg whites, lightly beaten
1 (14.5-ounce) can no-salt-added tomatoes, drained and chopped
1½ pounds ground turkey
Cooking spray
6 (2-ounce) onion sandwich buns, toasted
6 curly leaf lettuce leaves
6 (¼-inch-thick) slices tomato

1. Combine first 7 ingredients. Divide mixture into 6 equal portions, shaping each into a ½-inch-thick patty.
2. Heat a grill pan coated with cooking spray over medium-high heat. Add patties; cook 6 minutes on each side or until done. Place 1 patty on bottom half of each roll; top each serving with 1 lettuce leaf, 1 tomato slice, and top half of roll. Yield: 6 servings.

CALORIES 394 (30% from fat); FAT 13.2g (sat 4.7g, mono 4.1g, poly 4.2g); PROTEIN 26.1g; CARB 43.6g; FIBER 4.5g; CHOL 73mg; IRON 4.1mg; SODIUM 946mg; CALC 97mg

Seasoned Fries

(pictured on cover and page 183)

Try varying this simple recipe by adding onion or garlic powder, cumin, paprika, or any favorite seasonings.

1½ pounds baking potatoes, peeled and cut into thin strips
1 tablespoon vegetable oil
½ teaspoon salt
⅛ teaspoon ground red pepper
⅛ teaspoon black pepper

1. Preheat oven to 450°.
2. Combine all ingredients in a bowl; toss well. Arrange potatoes in a single layer on a baking sheet. Bake at 450° for 35 minutes or until golden. Yield: 4 servings.

CALORIES 193 (17% from fat); FAT 3.6g (sat 0.7g, mono 1g, poly 1.7g); PROTEIN 3.3g; CARB 36.6g; FIBER 2.6g; CHOL 0mg; IRON 0.6mg; SODIUM 301mg; CALC 9mg

Cajun Cool Cheeseburgers

Managing Editor Maelynn Cheung combines feta and blue cheese with ground round and ground turkey breast—along with Cajun spices—to create this tasty burger.

3 tablespoons crumbled feta cheese
3 tablespoons crumbled blue cheese
¼ cup dry breadcrumbs
1 teaspoon Creole seasoning (such as Tony Chachere's)
¼ teaspoon paprika
¼ teaspoon ground red pepper
¾ pound ground round
¼ pound ground turkey breast
Cooking spray
4 (1½-ounce) whole wheat hamburger buns
1 cup shredded iceberg lettuce
¾ cup green onion tops, cut into 2-inch julienne strips

1. Prepare grill.
2. Combine cheeses; set aside.
3. Combine breadcrumbs and next 5 ingredients. Divide mixture into 4 equal portions, shaping each into a ½-inch-thick patty.
4. Place patties on grill rack coated with cooking spray; grill 5 minutes on each side. Sprinkle burgers evenly with cheese mixture. Cook 1 to 2 minutes or until burgers are done and cheese melts. Place buns, cut sides down, on grill rack; grill 1 minute or until toasted. Place 1 patty on bottom half of each bun; top each serving with ¼ cup lettuce, 3 tablespoons onions, and top half of bun. Yield: 4 servings.

CALORIES 463 (33% from fat); FAT 17g (sat 7g, mono 5.6g, poly 2.6g); PROTEIN 33.1g; CARB 43.1g; FIBER 2.1g; CHOL 82mg; IRON 5.2mg; SODIUM 956mg; CALC 194mg

Fresh Vegetarian Dinners

Make the most of fresh produce with these vegetarian menus.

Vegetarian Menu 1
serves 4

Greek-Style Stuffed Eggplant

Herbed goat cheese toasts*

Lemon sorbet with almond biscotti

*Combine ½ cup crumbled goat cheese, ¾ teaspoon dried oregano, ½ teaspoon garlic powder, ¼ teaspoon paprika, and ⅛ teaspoon salt; sprinkle evenly over 8 (1-ounce) slices French bread. Broil 2 minutes or until lightly browned.

Game Plan

1. Remove eggplant pulp
2. While eggplant shells cook:
   • Preheat broiler
   • Slice bread
   • Prepare breadcrumb mixture
3. While eggplant filling cooks:
   • Prepare toasts
4. Broil stuffed eggplant shells

QUICK & EASY
Greek-Style Stuffed Eggplant

Leave about ¼-inch eggplant pulp in the shells when you hollow them out. If you're not a fan of eggplant, substitute zucchini; just remember that it will cook a little more quickly.

TOTAL TIME: 41 MINUTES
QUICK TIP: If you don't want to make fresh breadcrumbs, use half the amount of breadcrumbs that come in a can.

2 eggplants, cut in half lengthwise (about 3 pounds)
¼ cup water
Cooking spray
1 cup chopped onion
1 cup chopped plum tomato
¼ cup white wine
3 garlic cloves, minced
1 cup (4 ounces) crumbled feta cheese
½ cup chopped fresh parsley, divided
¾ teaspoon salt, divided
¼ teaspoon freshly ground black pepper
2 (1-ounce) slices French bread
2 tablespoons grated fresh Parmesan cheese

1. Carefully remove pulp from eggplant halves, reserving shells. Coarsely chop pulp to measure 6 cups. Place eggplant shells, cut sides down, in a 10-inch square baking dish. Add ¼ cup water to dish. Cover and microwave at HIGH 5 minutes or until shells are tender. Keep warm.
2. Preheat broiler.
3. Heat a large nonstick skillet coated with cooking spray over medium-high heat. Add eggplant pulp; sauté 7 minutes. Add onion; sauté 2 minutes. Stir in tomato, wine, and garlic; cook 3 minutes or until liquid almost evaporates, stirring occasionally. Remove from heat; stir in feta, ¼ cup parsley, ½ teaspoon salt, and pepper. Spoon ¾ cup onion mixture into each eggplant shell.
4. Place bread slices in food processor; pulse 10 times or until coarse crumbs measure 1 cup. Combine breadcrumbs, ¼ cup parsley, ¼ cup salt, and Parmesan, stirring well. Sprinkle ¼ cup breadcrumb mixture over each stuffed shell. Arrange shells on a baking sheet coated with cooking spray; broil 2 minutes or until lightly browned. Yield: 4 servings (serving size: 1 stuffed eggplant half).

CALORIES 250 (30% from fat); FAT 8.4g (sat 5.1g, mono 1.6g, poly 0.6g); PROTEIN 11.3g; CARB 35.3g; FIBER 10.3g; CHOL 29mg; IRON 2.3mg; SODIUM 906mg; CALC 246mg

Vegetarian Menu 2
serves 4

Onion Bread Pudding

Asparagus salad*

Fresh fruit

*Combine 4 cups (½-inch) cooked asparagus pieces, 1 cup chopped plum tomato, ¼ cup chopped red onion, ¼ cup crumbled feta cheese, 2 tablespoons fresh lemon juice, 2 teaspoons chopped fresh dill, 1 teaspoon olive oil, and ¼ teaspoon salt, stirring well.

Game Plan

1. While oven preheats:
   • Cook onion slices
   • Prepare bread and milk mixture
2. While bread pudding cooks:
   • Prepare asparagus salad

QUICK & EASY
Onion Bread Pudding

Parmesan, fontina, or Monterey Jack would also work well in this recipe.
TOTAL TIME: 40 MINUTES
QUICK TIP: You can assemble the bread pudding ahead of time; cover and refrigerate until you're ready to bake it.

1 Vidalia or other sweet onion, cut into ¼-inch slices
2 cups 2% reduced-fat milk
½ teaspoon salt
½ teaspoon dried thyme
⅛ teaspoon freshly ground black pepper
2 large eggs, lightly beaten
8 cups cubed French bread (about 8 ounces)
¾ cup (3 ounces) shredded Gruyère or Swiss cheese, divided
Cooking spray

1. Preheat oven to 425°.
2. Heat a large nonstick skillet over medium-high heat. Add onion (keep slices intact); cook 3 minutes on each side or until browned.

Continued

3. Combine milk, salt, thyme, pepper, and eggs in a large bowl, stirring with a whisk. Add bread and ½ cup cheese; toss well. Place bread mixture in an 8-inch square baking dish coated with cooking spray. Arrange onion slices on top of bread mixture. Sprinkle with ¼ cup cheese. Bake at 425° for 25 minutes or until set and golden. Yield: 4 servings (serving size: about 1½ cups).

CALORIES 364 (30% from fat); FAT 12.2g (sat 5.7g, mono 3.7g, poly 1.1g); PROTEIN 19.7g; CARB 43.8g; FIBER 3.4g; CHOL 136mg; IRON 2.1mg; SODIUM 806mg; CALC 294mg

---

Vegetarian Menu 3
serves 4

Penne with Tomatoes, Olives, and Capers

Parmesan bread twists*

Green salad

*Combine ¼ cup grated fresh Parmesan cheese and ½ teaspoon black pepper. Unroll 1 (11-ounce) can refrigerated breadstick dough; cut dough along perforations to form 12 breadsticks. Sprinkle cheese mixture over dough, gently pressing into dough. Twist each breadstick, and place on a baking sheet coated with cooking spray. Bake at 375° for 13 minutes or until breadsticks are lightly browned.

Game Plan

1. While oven preheats and water comes to a boil:
- Prepare breadsticks
- Chop tomatoes, olives, and basil
- Grate cheese

2. While tomato mixture cooks:
- Cook pasta, omitting salt and fat
- Toss salad

Penne with Tomatoes, Olives, and Capers

You can use almost any small pasta, such as macaroni, farfalle, rotelle, or tubetti.

TOTAL TIME: 22 MINUTES

QUICK TIP: You'll save time in the kitchen if you buy pitted olives.

1   tablespoon olive oil
¼   teaspoon crushed red pepper
3   garlic cloves, finely chopped
3   cups chopped plum tomato (about 1¾ pounds)
½   cup chopped pitted kalamata olives
1½   tablespoons capers
¼   teaspoon salt
6   cups hot cooked penne (about 4 cups uncooked tube-shaped pasta)
¾   cup (3 ounces) grated fresh Parmesan cheese
3   tablespoons chopped fresh basil

1. Heat oil in a large nonstick skillet over medium-high heat. Add pepper and garlic; sauté 30 seconds. Add tomato, olives, capers, and salt. Reduce heat. Simmer 8 minutes; stir occasionally. Add pasta to pan. Toss gently to coat; cook 1 minute or until thoroughly heated. Remove from heat. Sprinkle with cheese and basil. Yield: 4 servings (serving size: about 1¾ cups).

CALORIES 484 (28% from fat); FAT 15.1g (sat 4.7g, mono 7.7g, poly 1.7g); PROTEIN 19.1g; CARB 67.8g; FIBER 4.3g; CHOL 14mg; IRON 3.9mg; SODIUM 870mg; CALC 287mg

---

Vegetarian Menu 4
serves 4

Rice Noodles with Tofu and Bok Choy

Asian spinach salad*

Iced green tea with mint leaves

*Combine 2 cups fresh spinach, 1 cup grated carrot, and 1 cup bean sprouts. Combine 1 tablespoon fresh lime juice, 1 tablespoon rice vinegar, 2 teaspoons low-sodium soy sauce, ½ teaspoon sugar, and ½ teaspoon sesame oil; stir well. Toss with spinach mixture. Top each serving with 1 teaspoon chopped dry-roasted peanuts.

Game Plan

1. While water comes to a boil:
- Chop vegetables and tofu

2. While noodles cook:
- Prepare soy sauce mixture
- Prepare spinach mixture
- Prepare salad dressing

3. While tofu mixture cooks:
- Slice green onions
- Chop cilantro
- Toss salad with dressing

Rice Noodles with Tofu and Bok Choy

Look for water-packed tofu, which will hold its shape when cooked and tossed with the noodles. If rice noodles are unavailable, substitute angel hair pasta.

TOTAL TIME: 24 MINUTES

QUICK TIP: If you can't find bok choy, almost any quick-cooking crisp vegetable will work. Try snow peas or shredded Napa cabbage.

1   (6-ounce) package rice noodles
¼   cup low-sodium soy sauce
2   tablespoons rice vinegar
1   teaspoon sugar
1   teaspoon dark sesame oil
½   teaspoon crushed red pepper
     Cooking spray
2   cups (¼-inch) red bell pepper strips
5   cups sliced bok choy
½   pound firm water-packed tofu, drained and cut into ½-inch cubes
3   garlic cloves, minced
½   cup thinly sliced green onions
3   tablespoons chopped fresh cilantro

1. Cook noodles in boiling water 6 minutes; drain. Combine soy sauce and next 4 ingredients, stirring well with a whisk.
2. Heat a large nonstick skillet coated with cooking spray over medium-high heat. Add bell pepper strips; sauté 2 minutes. Add bok choy; sauté 1 minute. Add tofu and garlic; sauté 2 minutes. Add noodles and soy sauce mixture; cook 2 minutes or until thoroughly heated, tossing well to coat. Sprinkle with green onions and cilantro. Yield: 4 servings (serving size: 2 cups).

CALORIES 281 (17% from fat); FAT 5.2g (sat 0.8g, mono 0.9g, poly 2.3g); PROTEIN 12.9g; CARB 46.7g; FIBER 4.2g; CHOL 0mg; IRON 3.8mg; SODIUM 575mg; CALC 190mg

Plank Cooking

Grill on a wood plank to keep food moist and impart a mild, smoky flavor. Try it for fish, pork, and beef.

Before you light your grill for the outdoor cooking season, consider adding a new technique to your repertoire. Plank cooking is so simple it's almost foolproof. Unlike plain grilled meats, which can dry out when left over the flames too long, food cooked on a plank is moist, because of the damp smoke from the wood. The smoldering plank also lends a subtle smoky note that complements other flavors without overwhelming them.

Food prepared by plank cooking has become standard fare on restaurant menus across the country. But you don't have to dine out to enjoy the sublime flavor and texture of plank-cooked foods; planks suited for grilling are widely available, conveniently packaged, and sized to fit standard grills. Everything from tuna to tenderloin can be prepared and served on a plank.

Try Something New Menu
serves 6

Fish grilled on a wooden plank takes on a subtle smoky flavor. You can also use skinless, boneless chicken breast for the tacos; the cook time might be longer, so keep checking for doneness.

Cedar-Planked Halibut Tacos with Citrus Slaw

Mango and avocado salad*

Limeade

*Combine 3 cups chopped peeled mango, ½ cup diced peeled avocado, ¼ cup chopped green onions, 2 tablespoons fresh lime juice, 1 tablespoon chopped seeded jalapeño, and ¼ teaspoon salt, tossing gently.

Cedar-Planked Halibut Tacos with Citrus Slaw

If you can't find fresh halibut, use catfish, mahimahi, or snapper. Serve this dish with gazpacho or chilled cucumber soup.

PLANK:

1 (15 x 6½ x ⅜-inch) cedar grilling plank

SLAW:

2 cups shredded napa (Chinese) cabbage
1 cup gourmet salad greens
⅔ cup chopped green onions
¼ cup reduced-fat sour cream
2 tablespoons fresh lime juice
½ teaspoon salt

TACOS:

2 teaspoons chili powder
½ teaspoon black pepper
¼ teaspoon salt
1 (1½-pound) halibut fillet
12 (8-inch) flour tortillas

1. To prepare plank, immerse and soak plank in water 1 hour; drain.
2. Prepare grill, heating one side to medium and one side to high heat.
3. To prepare slaw, combine cabbage and next 5 ingredients; toss well. Chill.
4. To prepare tacos, combine chili powder, pepper, and ¼ teaspoon salt in a small bowl. Sprinkle chili powder mixture over fish. Place plank on grill rack over high heat; grill 5 minutes or until lightly charred. Carefully turn plank over; move to medium heat. Place fish on charred side of plank. Cover and grill 18 minutes or until fish flakes easily when tested with a fork.
5. Warm tortillas according to package directions. Break fish into chunks, and place about 2 ounces fish on each tortilla. Top each taco with ¼ cup slaw; fold tortillas in half. Yield: 6 servings (serving size: 2 tacos).

CALORIES 449 (20% from fat); FAT 9.8g (sat 1.8g, mono 3.7g, poly 1.8g); PROTEIN 34.1g; CARB 55g; FIBER 1.4g; CHOL 40mg; IRON 3.6mg; SODIUM 888mg; CALC 298mg

Plank Cooking 101

1. Submerge the plank in water at least 1 hour before using. Use a can to weigh it down. A water-soaked plank produces maximum smoke and is less likely to burn on the grill.

2. Grill the water-soaked plank over high heat for at least 5 minutes or until it begins to char and smoke. The moist smoke keeps food from drying as it cooks.
3. Turn the plank over so that the charred side faces up.

4. Place food on the charred surface of the plank. Food touching the wood takes on more flavor, so arrange it in a single layer on the plank.
5. Grill large cuts of meat and fish on planks over indirect heat (food isn't placed directly over hot coals) so they cook evenly; use direct heat for smaller quick-cooking foods.
6. Keep the grill lid closed so that smoke surrounds the food and infuses flavor.
7. Keep a spray bottle filled with water handy to douse flare-ups.
8. Serve the food on the plank for an impressive restaurant-style presentation.

Oak-Planked Peppercorn Tuna Steaks with Orange Mayonnaise

The citrus-flavored mayonnaise, which you can make ahead, takes the heat off the spicy peppercorn-crusted tuna. Serve over couscous.

  1 (15 x 6½ x ⅜-inch) oak grilling plank
  ¼ cup low-fat mayonnaise
  ¼ teaspoon grated orange rind
  2 tablespoons fresh orange juice
  2 teaspoons chopped fresh chives
  4 (6-ounce) Bluefin tuna steaks (about 1 inch thick)
Cooking spray
  ½ teaspoon salt
  2 tablespoons mixed peppercorns, crushed

1. Immerse and soak plank in water 1 hour; drain.
2. Prepare grill, heating one side to medium and one side to high heat.
3. Combine mayonnaise, rind, juice, and chives; stir well with a whisk. Chill.
4. Lightly coat top of tuna with cooking spray. Sprinkle tuna with salt; firmly press peppercorns into tuna.
5. Place plank on grill rack over high heat; grill 5 minutes or until lightly charred. Carefully turn plank over; move to medium heat. Place tuna on charred side of plank. Cover and grill 10 minutes or until desired degree of doneness. Serve tuna with orange mayonnaise. Yield: 4 servings (serving size: 1 steak and 1½ tablespoons orange mayonnaise).

CALORIES 245 (25% from fat); FAT 6.7g (sat 1.2g, mono 1.7g, poly 3g); PROTEIN 40.1g; CARB 3.4g; FIBER 0.7g; CHOL 82mg; IRON 1.4mg; SODIUM 528mg; CALC 38mg

Hickory-Planked Pork Tenderloin with Rosemary-Dijon Potatoes

The mustard glaze does double duty on the pork and potatoes. Jump-start the potatoes in the microwave, so they'll come off the grill with the pork.

  1 (15 x 6½ x ⅜-inch) hickory grilling plank
  ¼ cup Dijon mustard
  1 tablespoon honey
  ½ teaspoon freshly ground black pepper
  ½ teaspoon chopped fresh rosemary
  2 garlic cloves, minced
  1 (1-pound) pork tenderloin, trimmed
  2 cups (¼-inch-thick) slices red potato (about 8 ounces)
  1 tablespoon fresh lemon juice

1. Immerse and soak plank in water 1 hour; drain.
2. To prepare grill for indirect grilling, heat one side of grill to high heat.
3. Combine mustard, honey, pepper, rosemary, and garlic, stirring well with a whisk. Brush half of mustard mixture over pork.
4. Place potato in a microwave-safe bowl, and cover with plastic wrap. Microwave at HIGH 1 minute. Add remaining mustard mixture and juice; toss gently to coat.
5. Place plank on grill rack over high heat; grill 5 minutes or until lightly charred. Carefully turn plank over; move to cool side of grill. Place pork in middle of charred side of plank; arrange potato mixture around pork in a single layer. Cover and grill 20 minutes or until a meat thermometer registers 160° (slightly pink). Yield: 4 servings (serving size: 3 ounces pork and ⅓ cup potatoes).

CALORIES 216 (22% from fat); FAT 5.3g (sat 1.4g, mono 2.2g, poly 0.8g); PROTEIN 26g; CARB 16.1g; FIBER 1.3g; CHOL 74mg; IRON 2.3mg; SODIUM 439mg; CALC 37mg

STAFF FAVORITE
Argentinean Oak-Planked Beef Tenderloin with Chimichurri Sauce

This recipe is reminiscent of *churrasco*, a spicy grilled beef dish. Made from fresh herbs, the sauce is a robust accompaniment to the simple tenderloin.

STEAK:
  1 (15 x 6½ x ⅜-inch) oak grilling plank
  4 (4-ounce) beef tenderloin steaks, trimmed (¾ inch thick)
  ½ teaspoon salt
  ¼ teaspoon freshly ground black pepper

SAUCE:
  ¾ cup fresh flat-leaf parsley leaves
  ¼ cup fresh cilantro leaves
  ¼ cup fresh mint leaves
  ¼ cup chopped onion
  ¼ cup fat-free, less-sodium chicken broth
  3 tablespoons sherry vinegar
  2 tablespoons fresh oregano leaves
  1 teaspoon olive oil
  ½ teaspoon salt
  ½ teaspoon freshly ground black pepper
  ½ teaspoon crushed red pepper
  3 garlic cloves

1. Immerse and soak plank in water 1 hour; drain.
2. Prepare grill, heating one side to medium and one side to high heat.
3. To prepare steak, sprinkle steaks with ½ teaspoon salt and ¼ teaspoon black pepper. Place plank on grill rack over high heat; grill 5 minutes or until lightly charred. Carefully turn plank over; move to medium heat. Place steak on charred side of plank. Cover and grill 12 minutes or until desired degree of doneness.
4. To prepare sauce, combine parsley and remaining 11 ingredients in a food processor; process until smooth. Serve with steaks. Yield: 4 servings (serving size: 1 steak and 1½ tablespoons sauce).

CALORIES 159 (31% from fat); FAT 5.5g (sat 1.7g, mono 2.4g, poly 0.1g); PROTEIN 23.3g; CARB 5.7g; FIBER 1.4g; CHOL 60mg; IRON 4.4mg; SODIUM 977mg; CALC 52mg

Alder-Planked Salmon in an Asian-Style Marinade

(pictured on page 182)

1 (15 x 6½ x ⅜-inch) alder grilling plank
½ cup rice vinegar
½ cup low-sodium soy sauce
2 tablespoons honey
1 teaspoon ground ginger
½ teaspoon freshly ground black pepper
3 garlic cloves, minced
1 lemon, thinly sliced
1 (3½-pound) salmon fillet
¼ cup chopped green onions
1 tablespoon sesame seeds, toasted

1. Immerse and soak plank in water 1 hour; drain.
2. To prepare grill for indirect grilling, heat one side of grill to high heat.
3. Combine vinegar and next 6 ingredients in a large zip-top plastic bag; seal. Shake to combine. Add fish; seal. Marinate in refrigerator 30 minutes; turn once.
4. Place plank on grill rack over high heat; grill 5 minutes or until lightly charred. Carefully turn plank over; move to cool side of grill. Remove fish from bag; discard marinade. Place fish, skin side down, on charred side of plank. Cover and grill 15 minutes or until fish flakes easily when tested with a fork. Sprinkle with onions and sesame seeds. Yield: 9 servings (serving size: 5 ounces).

CALORIES 306 (41% from fat); FAT 14.1g (sat 3.3g, mono 6.1g, poly 3.5g); PROTEIN 38.3g; CARB 4.6g; FIBER 0.5g; CHOL 90mg; IRON 0.9mg; SODIUM 353mg; CALC 36mg

superfast

... And Ready in Just About 20 Minutes

Chicken with Lemon and Fennel Seeds, a simple Italian-inspired dish, derives lots of flavor from a few well-chosen ingredients—namely, fennel seeds, lemon rind, and garlic.

Chicken with Lemon and Fennel Seeds

Serve with warm bread and broccoli rabe (rapini) sautéed in olive oil and garlic.

1 tablespoon olive oil
4 (6-ounce) skinless, boneless chicken breast halves
½ teaspoon salt
¼ teaspoon black pepper
3 tablespoons dry white wine
1 teaspoon grated lemon rind
2 tablespoons fresh lemon juice
½ teaspoon fennel seeds
1 garlic clove, crushed

1. Heat oil in a large nonstick skillet over medium-high heat. Sprinkle chicken with salt and pepper. Add chicken to pan, and cook 3 minutes on each side. Add wine and remaining ingredients. Cover, reduce heat, and simmer 5 minutes or until chicken is done. Yield: 4 servings (serving size: 1 chicken breast half and 1½ teaspoons sauce).

CALORIES 229 (22% from fat); FAT 5.5g (sat 1g, mono 3g, poly 0.8g); PROTEIN 39.4g; CARB 1.3g; FIBER 0.2g; CHOL 99mg; IRON 1.4mg; SODIUM 402mg; CALC 26mg

Rosemary Pork Chops

Line the pan with foil for fast cleanup.

2 teaspoons bottled minced garlic
1½ teaspoons chopped fresh rosemary
½ teaspoon salt
¼ teaspoon black pepper
4 (4-ounce) boneless center-cut loin pork chops (about ½ inch thick)
Cooking spray

1. Preheat broiler.
2. Combine first 4 ingredients. Rub mixture over both sides of pork chops. Place pork chops on a broiler pan coated with cooking spray; broil 3 minutes on each side or until desired degree of doneness. Yield: 4 servings (serving size: 1 pork chop).

CALORIES 166 (33% from fat); FAT 6.1g (sat 2.1g, mono 2.7g, poly 0.7g); PROTEIN 25g; CARB 1.4g; FIBER 0.5g; CHOL 62mg; IRON 1.1mg; SODIUM 342mg; CALC 32mg

Shrimp Diablo

8 ounces uncooked angel hair pasta
2 teaspoons vegetable oil
1 pound peeled and deveined large shrimp
½ teaspoon salt
¼ teaspoon black pepper
1 tablespoon bottled minced garlic
1½ tablespoons chile paste with garlic
1 teaspoon ground cumin
1 (14.5-ounce) can diced tomatoes, undrained
½ cup chopped fresh parsley
½ teaspoon crushed red pepper

1. Cook pasta according to package directions, omitting salt and fat. Drain.
2. While pasta cooks, heat oil in a large nonstick skillet over medium-high heat. Sprinkle shrimp with salt and black pepper. Add shrimp to pan, and cook 1 minute on each side or until done. Remove shrimp from pan.
3. Add garlic to pan; sauté 1 minute. Add chile paste, scraping pan to loosen browned bits. Add cumin and tomatoes; simmer 10 minutes, stirring occasionally. Remove pan from heat. Stir in shrimp, parsley, and red pepper. Toss with pasta. Yield: 4 servings (serving size: 2 cups).

CALORIES 332 (15% from fat); FAT 5.5g (sat 0.7g, mono 0.8g, poly 2.1g); PROTEIN 31.4g; CARB 40g; FIBER 3.2g; CHOL 172mg; IRON 5.3mg; SODIUM 933mg; CALC 95mg

Skillet Chicken Pasta

Cream cheese makes the sauce velvety.

1 (9-ounce) package fresh linguine
1 pound chicken breast tenders
¼ teaspoon seasoned salt
⅛ teaspoon black pepper
1 tablespoon butter
1 cup presliced mushrooms
½ cup sliced onion
½ cup dry sherry
1 cup fat-free, less-sodium chicken broth
½ cup (4 ounces) ⅓-less-fat cream cheese

Continued

1. Cook pasta according to package directions, omitting salt and fat. Drain.

2. While pasta cooks, sprinkle chicken with salt and pepper. Melt butter in a large nonstick skillet over medium-high heat. Add chicken, mushrooms, and onion; sauté 7 minutes or until chicken is done. Remove from pan; keep warm.

3. Add sherry to pan, scraping to loosen browned bits. Stir in broth and cheese; bring to a boil. Reduce heat, and simmer until cheese melts (about 3 minutes), stirring constantly. Return chicken mixture to pan, and cook until thoroughly heated. Serve over pasta. Yield: 4 servings (serving size: 1 cup chicken mixture and 1 cup pasta).

CALORIES 500 (19% from fat); FAT 10.4g (sat 5.7g, mono 2.7g, poly 0.6g); PROTEIN 41.3g; CARB 53.3g; FIBER 3.3g; CHOL 90mg; IRON 4.2mg; SODIUM 555mg; CALC 69mg

Bourbon-Glazed Pork Chops and Peaches

The bourbon and honey marinade cooks to become a sauce to serve with the chops. Be sure the marinade comes to a full boil in the microwave.

- ⅓ cup bourbon
- ¼ cup honey
- 3 tablespoons low-sodium soy sauce
- 1 tablespoon vegetable oil
- ½ teaspoon ground ginger
- ¼ teaspoon crushed red pepper
- ¼ teaspoon black pepper
- 4 (4-ounce) boneless center-cut loin pork chops (about ¾ inch thick), trimmed
- 2 peaches, halved and pitted

Cooking spray

1. Combine first 7 ingredients in a large bowl. Add pork chops and peaches; toss well to coat.

2. Heat a nonstick grill pan coated with cooking spray over medium-high heat. Remove pork and peaches from bowl, reserving marinade. Place pork and peaches on grill pan; cook 4 minutes on each side or until pork is done.

3. While pork cooks, place marinade in a microwave-safe bowl; microwave at

HIGH 2 minutes. Spoon over pork and peaches. Yield: 4 servings (serving size: 1 pork chop, 1 peach half, and 2 tablespoons sauce).

CALORIES 285 (29% from fat); FAT 9.3g (sat 3.1g, mono 4.3g, poly 1.1g); PROTEIN 26.4g; CARB 24.3g; FIBER 1.2g; CHOL 73mg; IRON 1.4mg; SODIUM 489mg; CALC 27mg

Creamy Fettuccine with Peas and Ham

There's no need to thaw the green peas. They will have plenty of time to cook in the sauce as it simmers.

- 1 (9-ounce) package fresh fettuccine
- 1 tablespoon butter
- 1 teaspoon bottled minced garlic
- 1 cup frozen green peas
- ⅔ cup half-and-half
- ¼ cup (1 ounce) preshredded fresh Parmesan cheese
- ¼ teaspoon freshly ground black pepper
- 1 cup (4 ounces) thinly sliced reduced-fat ham, cut into ¼-inch-wide strips

1. Cook pasta according to package directions, omitting salt and fat. Drain.

2. While pasta cooks, melt butter in a large nonstick skillet over medium heat. Add garlic; cook 1 minute, stirring constantly. Add peas, half-and-half, cheese, and pepper. Bring to a simmer. Cook 3 minutes, stirring frequently (do not boil). Stir in pasta and ham. Yield: 4 servings (serving size: 1¼ cups).

CALORIES 361 (29% from fat); FAT 11.8g (sat 6.6g, mono 2.8g, poly 0.9g); PROTEIN 19g; CARB 42.2g; FIBER 4.2g; CHOL 94mg; IRON 3.2mg; SODIUM 556mg; CALC 148mg

Chicken, Corn, and Tomato Salad

Cooking spray
- 1½ cups fresh corn kernels (about 3 ears)
- 2 cups chopped cooked chicken breast (such as Purdue Short Cuts)
- 1 cup cherry tomatoes, halved
- ½ cup sliced green onions
- 2 tablespoons red wine vinegar
- 1½ tablespoons olive oil
- 2 teaspoons lemon juice
- 1 teaspoon chopped fresh thyme
- 1 teaspoon bottled minced garlic
- ½ teaspoon Dijon mustard
- ¼ teaspoon salt

1. Heat a large nonstick skillet coated with cooking spray over medium-high heat. Add corn; sauté 3 minutes or until tender. Place corn in a large bowl. Stir in chicken, tomatoes, and onions; set aside.

2. Combine vinegar and remaining 6 ingredients in a small bowl, stirring with a whisk. Drizzle vinegar mixture over chicken mixture, tossing gently to coat. Yield: 4 servings (serving size: 1¼ cups).

CALORIES 231 (28% from fat); FAT 7.3g (sat 0.8g, mono 4g, poly 0.8g); PROTEIN 29g; CARB 14.6g; FIBER 2.6g; CHOL 60mg; IRON 0.6mg; SODIUM 497mg; CALC 6mg

Angel Hair Pasta with Shrimp and Spinach

Serve with ripe tomatoes dressed with oil and vinegar. Substitute finely chopped red onion if you don't have shallots on hand.

- 8 ounces uncooked angel hair pasta
- 1½ pounds peeled and deveined large shrimp
- ¼ teaspoon salt
- ¼ teaspoon black pepper
- 2 tablespoons olive oil
- ¼ cup finely chopped shallots
- ½ cup fat-free, less-sodium chicken broth
- 2 tablespoons lemon juice
- 6 cups coarsely chopped spinach
- 2 tablespoons capers

1. Cook pasta according to package directions, omitting salt and fat. Drain.
2. While pasta cooks, sprinkle shrimp with salt and pepper. Heat oil in a large nonstick skillet over medium-high heat. Add shallots; sauté 30 seconds. Add shrimp; sauté 3 minutes. Remove shrimp mixture from pan. Add broth and juice to pan, scraping pan to loosen browned bits. Add pasta, shrimp mixture, spinach, and capers, and heat 1 minute or until spinach wilts, stirring frequently. Yield: 4 servings (serving size: 1½ cups).

CALORIES 473 (21% from fat); FAT 10.8g (sat 1.6g, mono 5.5g, poly 2.1g); PROTEIN 44.1g; CARB 48.1g; FIBER 2.7g; CHOL 259mg; IRON 7.8mg; SODIUM 652mg; CALC 151mg

Pesto Lamb Chops

The lamb chops will reach about 145° internally (or medium-rare) when they broil.

1   cup fat-free, less-sodium chicken broth
1   cup plus 2 tablespoons uncooked couscous
2½ tablespoons commercial pesto, divided
8   (4-ounce) lamb loin chops, trimmed
2   tomatoes, cut in half crosswise (about 1 pound)
    Cooking spray

1. Preheat broiler.
2. Bring broth to a boil in a medium saucepan; gradually stir in couscous. Remove from heat; cover and let stand 5 minutes or until done. Fluff with a fork.
3. While couscous stands, spread 2 tablespoons pesto over both sides of lamb. Spread 1½ teaspoons pesto over cut sides of tomatoes. Place lamb on a broiler pan coated with cooking spray. Broil 5 minutes; turn lamb chops; add tomatoes to broiler pan, and broil an additional 5 minutes or until desired degree of doneness. Serve with couscous. Yield: 4 servings (serving size: 2 chops, 1 tomato half, and ¾ cup couscous).

CALORIES 515 (32% from fat); FAT 18.3g (sat 6.1g, mono 8.2g, poly 1.7g); PROTEIN 55.3g; CARB 28.6g; FIBER 2.6g; CHOL 153mg; IRON 5.7mg; SODIUM 280mg; CALC 112mg

Grilled Sirloin Salad

Serve with thick slices of garlic bread and ice-cold beer.

1   tablespoon chili powder
2   teaspoons dried oregano
1   teaspoon dried thyme
½   teaspoon salt
½   teaspoon onion powder
½   teaspoon garlic powder
¼   teaspoon black pepper
1   pound lean boneless sirloin steak, trimmed
8   cups spring-blend salad greens
1½ cups red bell pepper strips
1   cup vertically sliced red onion
1   tablespoon chopped fresh parsley
1   tablespoon red wine vinegar
1   teaspoon olive oil
1   teaspoon fresh lemon juice
1   (8¾-ounce) can whole-kernel corn, rinsed and drained

1. Combine first 7 ingredients; rub over both sides of steak. Heat a nonstick grill pan over medium-high heat. Add steak; cook 5 minutes on each side or until desired degree of doneness. Cut steak across the grain into thin slices.
2. While steak cooks, combine salad greens and remaining 7 ingredients in a large bowl; toss well to coat. Top with steak. Yield: 4 servings (serving size: 3 ounces steak and 3 cups salad).

CALORIES 278 (28% from fat); FAT 8.7g (sat 2.7g, mono 3.7g, poly 1g); PROTEIN 30.4g; CARB 22g; FIBER 6.1g; CHOL 76mg; IRON 6.1mg; SODIUM 530mg; CALC 106mg

Creole Pork Chops

Place the chops on red beans and rice, and serve with a simple green salad.

2   teaspoons bottled minced garlic
½   teaspoon salt
½   teaspoon ground thyme
¼   teaspoon ground red pepper
¼   teaspoon black pepper
4   (6-ounce) bone-in center-cut pork chops (about ½ inch thick)
    Cooking spray

1. Combine first 5 ingredients; rub spice mixture over both sides of pork. Heat a large nonstick skillet coated with cooking spray over medium-high heat. Add pork; cook 4 minutes on each side or until done. Yield: 4 servings (serving size: 1 pork chop).

CALORIES 181 (35% from fat); FAT 7.3g (sat 2.7g, mono 3.2g, poly 0.6g); PROTEIN 26.1g; CARB 1.3g; FIBER 0.4g; CHOL 74mg; IRON 1.3mg; SODIUM 345mg; CALC 26mg

Chicken with Mandarin Oranges

Stir chopped cashews and sliced green onions into hot rice for a speedy side dish.

1½ pounds chicken breast tenders
¾   teaspoon salt
½   teaspoon black pepper
1   tablespoon butter
2   teaspoons olive oil
    Cooking spray
½   cup orange marmalade
1   tablespoon cornstarch
1   tablespoon lemon juice
½   teaspoon dry mustard
1   (7-ounce) can mandarin oranges, drained

1. Sprinkle chicken with salt and pepper. Heat butter and oil in a large nonstick skillet coated with cooking spray over medium-high heat. Add chicken to pan; cook 4 minutes on each side or until lightly browned.
2. Combine marmalade, cornstarch, juice, and mustard in a small bowl, stirring well with a whisk. Gently stir in oranges. Add marmalade mixture to pan; cover and simmer 6 minutes or until sauce is slightly thick, stirring once. Yield: 4 servings (serving size: 3 ounces chicken and ½ cup sauce).

CALORIES 364 (18% from fat); FAT 7.4g (sat 2.7g, mono 3g, poly 0.8g); PROTEIN 39.9g; CARB 34.5g; FIBER 1.3g; CHOL 106mg; IRON 1.5mg; SODIUM 599mg; CALC 44mg

Spiced Chicken with Couscous

If you'd prefer, replace the individual spices in the dish with 2 teaspoons of a preblended Asian spice.

- 1 cup water
- ¾ cup uncooked couscous
- 2 teaspoons olive oil
- 1 pound chicken breast tenders
- ½ cup coarsely chopped onion
- 1 teaspoon bottled minced garlic
- 1 cup fat-free, less-sodium chicken broth
- ½ cup raisins
- 1 teaspoon dried thyme
- ½ teaspoon ground cumin
- ¼ teaspoon salt
- ¼ teaspoon ground red pepper
- ¼ teaspoon allspice
- ⅛ teaspoon ground cloves
- 1 (14.5-ounce) can diced tomatoes, drained

1. Bring water to a boil in a small saucepan; gradually stir in couscous. Remove pan from heat; cover and let stand 5 minutes or until done. Fluff couscous with a fork.
2. Heat oil in a large nonstick skillet over medium-high heat. Add chicken, onion, and garlic, and cook 3 minutes, stirring frequently.
3. Add broth and remaining 8 ingredients to chicken mixture; bring to a boil. Reduce heat, and simmer, uncovered, 15 minutes. Serve with couscous. Yield: 4 servings (serving size: 3 ounces chicken, ¾ cup couscous, and ⅔ cup sauce).

CALORIES 360 (10% from fat); FAT 4.1g (sat 0.8g, mono 2g, poly 0.6g); PROTEIN 32.9g; CARB 47.4g; FIBER 4.9g; CHOL 66mg; IRON 2.3mg; SODIUM 471mg; CALC 59mg

The Cook & the Gardener

He cultivates produce; she cultivates recipes. Together, they've discovered the secrets to bringing out the best of both.

Contributing Editor Jean Kressy and her husband, Mike, have been gardening and cooking up the bounty for more than 25 years. Along the way, they've learned that a garden needn't be large to have a big influence on the menu.

QUICK & EASY • MAKE AHEAD
Garden Slaw with Tarragon

This is a great side dish for roast chicken or grilled salmon.

DRESSING:
- ¼ cup low-fat buttermilk
- 3 tablespoons light mayonnaise
- 1 tablespoon fresh lemon juice
- 2 teaspoons sugar
- ¼ teaspoon salt
- ¼ teaspoon coarsely ground black pepper

SALAD:
- 3 cups sliced Savoy cabbage
- 1 cup (1-inch) diagonally cut wax beans, steamed
- ½ cup snow peas, trimmed and cut lengthwise into thin strips
- ½ cup red bell pepper strips
- ⅓ cup shredded carrot
- ¼ cup vertically sliced red onion
- 1 tablespoon chopped fresh tarragon

1. To prepare dressing, combine first 6 ingredients, stirring with a whisk.
2. To prepare salad, combine cabbage and remaining 6 ingredients in a large bowl. Add dressing mixture, tossing to combine. Chill 30 minutes. Yield: 6 servings (serving size: ¾ cup).

CALORIES 62 (39% from fat); FAT 2.7g (sat 0.5g, mono 0.7g, poly 1.3g); PROTEIN 1.9g; CARB 8.6g; FIBER 2.4g; CHOL 3mg; IRON 0.6mg; SODIUM 183mg; CALC 39mg

QUICK & EASY
Chicken Salad with Asparagus and Zucchini

DRESSING:
- ⅔ cup low-fat sour cream
- 2 tablespoons 1% low-fat milk
- ¼ teaspoon salt
- ⅛ teaspoon freshly ground black peppercorns

SALAD:
- 1½ cups (1-inch) diagonally cut asparagus
- 2 cups shredded cooked chicken breast (about 8 ounces)
- 1 cup chopped zucchini
- ⅓ cup thinly sliced radishes
- ⅓ cup finely chopped fresh flat-leaf parsley
- ¼ cup thinly sliced green onions
- 2 teaspoons chopped fresh sage
- 6 cups mixed salad greens

1. To prepare dressing, combine first 4 ingredients, stirring well with a whisk.
2. To prepare salad, steam asparagus, covered, 3 minutes or until crisp-tender. Rinse with cold water; drain. Combine asparagus and next 6 ingredients in a large bowl. Add dressing mixture; toss gently to coat. Serve over greens. Yield: 4 servings (serving size: 1¼ cups chicken mixture and 1 cup greens).

CALORIES 138 (25% from fat); FAT 3.9g (sat 2.8g, mono 0.1g, poly 0.2g); PROTEIN 15.8g; CARB 11.4g; FIBER 4g; CHOL 41mg; IRON 2.8mg; SODIUM 882mg; CALC 162mg

Summer Shrimp Salad with Cilantro

(pictured on page 181)

This light summer salad features a vinaigrette dressing. If you don't have cilantro, the salad's just as good with fresh basil.

DRESSING:

½ cup vegetable broth
1½ teaspoons cornstarch
3 tablespoons fresh lime juice
2 teaspoons extravirgin olive oil
¾ teaspoon sugar
½ teaspoon salt
¼ teaspoon ground cumin
¼ teaspoon freshly ground black peppercorns

SALAD:

1 pound medium shrimp, cooked and peeled
1½ cups julienne-cut yellow squash
1½ cups julienne-cut zucchini
1½ cups cherry tomatoes, halved
1 cup fresh corn kernels (about 2 ears)
2 tablespoons minced fresh cilantro

1. To prepare dressing, combine broth and cornstarch in a small saucepan, stirring with a whisk; bring to a boil. Cook 1 minute, stirring constantly. Remove from heat; stir in juice and next 5 ingredients. Cool.
2. To prepare salad, combine shrimp and remaining 5 ingredients in a large bowl. Add dressing mixture to shrimp mixture, tossing well. Yield: 4 servings (serving size: 1¾ cups).
WINE NOTE: With its fresh seafood and bountiful vegetables, this is just the sort of dish that will convince you how stellar German dry Rieslings can be. Try the 2001 Dr. F. Weins-Prum Riesling Kabinett (the lightest style) from the village and vineyard both known as Wehlener Sonnenuhr; it sells for about $19.

CALORIES 198 (22% from fat); FAT 4.8g (sat 0.7g, mono 2.1g, poly 1.2g); PROTEIN 20.4g; CARB 20.9g; FIBER 3.8g; CHOL 129mg; IRON 3.1mg; SODIUM 559mg; CALC 72mg

Potato Salad with Parsley and Chives

"For years, we grew several varieties of potatoes, but keeping ahead of the beetles was a full-time job. Finally, we decided to call it quits, and we gave up growing potatoes. But we'll never stop eating them."

—Mike Kressy

DRESSING:

¼ cup light mayonnaise
¼ cup fat-free sour cream
2 tablespoons grated Parmesan cheese
1 tablespoon fresh lemon juice
¼ teaspoon salt
⅛ teaspoon freshly ground black peppercorns

SALAD:

4 cups cubed Yukon gold potato (about 1½ pounds)
½ cup chopped celery
⅓ cup finely chopped fresh flat-leaf parsley
¼ cup frozen green peas, thawed
¼ cup chopped fresh chives

1. To prepare dressing, combine first 6 ingredients in a small bowl.
2. To prepare salad, place potato in a saucepan, and cover with water. Bring to a boil, reduce heat, and simmer 9 minutes or until tender. Drain and cool. Combine dressing, potato, celery, parsley, peas, and chives in a large bowl, and toss well. Yield: 5 servings (serving size: about 1 cup).

CALORIES 173 (25% from fat); FAT 4.9g (sat 1.1g, mono 1.4g, poly 2.1g); PROTEIN 5.2g; CARB 27.8g; FIBER 3.1g; CHOL 7mg; IRON 2.4mg; SODIUM 289mg; CALC 79mg

Gazpacho Salad with Cannellini Beans and Feta

If you like gazpacho, you'll love this salad with its piquant dressing and fresh tomatoes, basil, and cucumber.

DRESSING:

3 tablespoons tomato juice
2 tablespoons red wine vinegar
1 tablespoon extravirgin olive oil
1 teaspoon sugar
1 teaspoon Worcestershire sauce
¼ teaspoon salt
¼ teaspoon coarsely ground black pepper
1 garlic clove, minced

SALAD:

6 cups gourmet salad greens
2 cups chopped tomato (about 1 pound)
1 cup chopped cucumber
½ cup thinly sliced fresh basil
⅓ cup (1½ ounces) crumbled feta cheese
⅓ cup chopped green bell pepper
¼ cup thinly sliced green onions
1 (16-ounce) can cannellini beans or other white beans, rinsed and drained

1. To prepare dressing, combine first 8 ingredients, stirring well with a whisk.
2. To prepare salad, combine salad greens and remaining 7 ingredients in a large bowl. Add dressing mixture, tossing gently to combine. Serve immediately. Yield: 4 servings (serving size: 2 cups).

CALORIES 205 (30% from fat); FAT 6.8g (sat 2.2g, mono 3.1g, poly 1.1g); PROTEIN 8.8g; CARB 29g; FIBER 8.4g; CHOL 9mg; IRON 3.7mg; SODIUM 512mg; CALC 157mg

Just-picked vegetables need little more to shine than a piquant vinaigrette dressing.

Dreamy Custard

Homemade custard delivers a wonderful blend of richness and creaminess.

Homemade custards are simple to prepare, and once you try our tempting lineup of silky desserts, you'll find their flavors and versatility can't be matched by the boxed variety.

There are two types of custards: stirred custards, often called stovetop custards, and baked custards. Stirred custards include soft puddings, the luscious vanilla sauce called crème Anglaise, wine-kissed zabaglione, and fillings for icebox pies, such as chocolate and coconut cream. Baked custards range from caramel-glazed flan to silky, elegant crème brûlée.

Stirred or baked, all custards rely on eggs for their texture and richness. When it comes to eggs, remember the saying, "Slow and steady wins the race." Because of the way egg protein cooks, custards require slow, even heat for the best results. For most stovetop custards, this steady cooking is accomplished by tempering (gently introducing hot liquids to cool eggs) and constant stirring to prevent overheating. Baked custards are usually cooked in a water bath to ensure gradual, even, hands-off cooking and creamy results that more than justify the effort.

MAKE AHEAD
Crème Anglaise with Brown-Sugared Strawberries

Silky crème Anglaise is thickened by gently cooking the eggs over moderately low heat while stirring constantly. The custard will be pourable when done and will thicken only slightly when chilled.

- 3 cups halved strawberries
- ⅓ cup packed brown sugar
- ¼ cup granulated sugar
- ¼ teaspoon salt
- 2 large eggs, lightly beaten
- 2 cups whole milk
- 1 teaspoon vanilla extract
- ⅛ teaspoon almond extract
- Mint sprigs

1. Combine strawberries and brown sugar; let stand at room temperature 30 minutes.
2. Combine granulated sugar, salt, and eggs in a large bowl, stirring well with a whisk.
3. Heat milk in a small, heavy saucepan over medium-high heat to 180° or until tiny bubbles form around edge (do not boil). Gradually add milk to egg mixture, stirring constantly with a whisk. Return milk mixture to pan; cook over moderately low heat 5 minutes or until slightly thick and mixture coats the back of a spoon, stirring constantly. Remove from heat, and stir in extracts. Serve warm or chilled over strawberries. Garnish with mint, if desired. Yield: 4 servings (serving size: ¾ cup strawberries and about ⅓ cup crème Anglaise).

CALORIES 270 (23% from fat); FAT 7g (sat 3.4g, mono 2.4g, poly 0.7g); PROTEIN 7.9g; CARB 45.2g; FIBER 2.9g; CHOL 123mg; IRON 1.3mg; SODIUM 247mg; CALC 191mg

MAKE AHEAD
Bittersweet Chocolate Pudding

Adding cornstarch to this homey pudding lessens the possibility of its curdling. To prevent the custard from tipping and taking on ice water, make sure the bowl you use for the ice bath is only slightly larger than the custard bowl.

- ½ cup granulated sugar
- ⅓ cup unsweetened cocoa
- 3 tablespoons cornstarch
- 3 tablespoons dark brown sugar
- ⅛ teaspoon salt
- 4 cups 2% reduced-fat milk
- 3 large egg yolks, lightly beaten
- 2 ounces bittersweet chocolate, chopped
- 1 teaspoon vanilla extract

1. Combine first 5 ingredients in a large saucepan. Gradually add milk, stirring with a whisk. Bring to a boil over medium heat, stirring constantly. Cook 1 minute, stirring constantly.
2. Place egg yolks in a bowl. Gradually add hot milk mixture to egg yolks, stirring constantly. Return milk mixture to pan. Cook over medium heat 5 minutes or until mixture is thick, stirring constantly. Remove mixture from heat, and add chocolate and vanilla, stirring until chocolate melts. Spoon pudding into a small bowl. Place bowl in a large ice-filled bowl 15 minutes or until pudding is cool, stirring occasionally. Remove bowl from ice; cover and chill. Yield: 6 servings (serving size: ¾ cup).

CALORIES 282 (30% from fat); FAT 9.5g (sat 5.1g, mono 2.4g, poly 0.5g); PROTEIN 8.4g; CARB 43g; FIBER 2.4g; CHOL 119mg; IRON 1.2mg; SODIUM 138mg; CALC 222mg

This light yet luscious crème Anglaise enhances ruby-red strawberry halves tossed with sugar.

French Vanilla Summer Trifle

Once you've assembled this dessert, refrigerate it for several hours to allow the peach juices and rich custard to soak into the ladyfingers.

2½ cups finely chopped peeled ripe peaches
2 tablespoons brown sugar
¼ teaspoon ground cinnamon
⅔ cup granulated sugar
2 tablespoons cornstarch
⅛ teaspoon salt
3 large egg yolks
1⅔ cups 2% reduced-fat milk
1 cup evaporated fat-free milk
½ teaspoon vanilla extract
15 cakelike ladyfingers, halved lengthwise

1. Combine peaches, brown sugar, and cinnamon, tossing well to combine; let stand at room temperature 30 minutes.
2. Combine granulated sugar, cornstarch, salt, and egg yolks in a medium bowl, stirring with a whisk until smooth.
3. Heat milks in a medium, heavy saucepan over medium-high heat to 180° or until tiny bubbles form around edge (do not boil). Gradually add hot milk mixture to egg mixture, stirring constantly with a whisk.
4. Return milk mixture to saucepan. Cook over medium heat 2 minutes or until thick and bubbly, stirring constantly. Remove from heat, and stir in vanilla.
5. Spoon custard into a small bowl. Place bowl in a large ice-filled bowl 15 minutes or until custard is cool, stirring occasionally. Remove bowl from ice.
6. Arrange 10 ladyfinger halves, cut sides up, in a single layer on bottom of a 1½-quart soufflé or trifle dish. Spoon half of peach mixture over ladyfingers. Spread half of custard over peach mixture. Arrange 10 ladyfinger halves, standing upright, around side of dish. Arrange 10 ladyfinger halves, cut sides up, on top of custard. Spoon remaining peach mixture over ladyfingers. Spread remaining custard over peach mixture. Cover and refrigerate 4 hours or overnight. Yield: 6 servings (serving size: about 1 cup).

CALORIES 300 (15% from fat); FAT 4.9g (sat 2g, mono 1.5g, poly 0.8g); PROTEIN 8.8g; CARB 56.7g; FIBER 1.7g; CHOL 144mg; IRON 1mg; SODIUM 265mg; CALC 246mg

Ginger Crème Brûlée

A water bath ensures the custards cook slowly and evenly. Line the baking pan with a kitchen towel before adding the ramekins; the towel will also keep them from sliding and will protect the bottoms from the hot pan.

⅓ cup sugar
4 large egg yolks
2 cups 2% reduced-fat milk
2 tablespoons chopped crystallized ginger
½ teaspoon vanilla extract
6 tablespoons sugar

1. Preheat oven to 300°.
2. Combine ⅓ cup sugar and egg yolks in a medium bowl; stir well with a whisk.
3. Combine milk and ginger in a medium saucepan. Heat milk mixture over medium heat to 180° or until tiny bubbles form around edge (do not boil), stirring occasionally. Strain mixture through a sieve into a bowl, and discard solids. Stir in vanilla extract. Gradually add milk mixture to egg mixture, stirring constantly with a whisk.
4. Divide mixture evenly among 6 (4-ounce) ramekins, custard cups, or shallow baking dishes. Place ramekins in a 13 x 9-inch baking pan; add hot water to pan to a depth of 1 inch.
5. Bake at 300° for 45 minutes or until center barely moves when ramekin is touched. Remove ramekins from pan, and cool completely on a wire rack. Cover ramekins, and chill at least 4 hours or overnight.
6. Carefully sift 1 tablespoon sugar evenly over each custard. Holding a kitchen blow torch about 2 inches from top of each custard, heat sugar, moving torch back and forth, until sugar is completely melted and caramelized (about 1 minute). Serve custards immediately or within 1 hour. Yield: 6 servings (serving size: 1 crème brûlée).

NOTE: Sugar topping can be prepared on the stovetop. Place 6 tablespoons sugar and 1 tablespoon water in a small, heavy saucepan. Cook, without stirring, over medium heat until golden (about 5 to 8 minutes). Immediately pour over cold custards, and quickly spread to form a thin layer.

CALORIES 180 (25% from fat); FAT 5g (sat 2g, mono 1.8g, poly 0.5g); PROTEIN 4.6g; CARB 29.8g; FIBER 0g; CHOL 148mg; IRON 0.5mg; SODIUM 46mg; CALC 117mg

How to Test Custard for Doneness

While various factors—including the individual recipe and application—determine a custard's doneness, there are two time-honored guideposts.

For baked custards: When you (carefully) tap the side of the ramekin or pan, the custard should jiggle. If it ripples like water, it's not done. If it doesn't jiggle at all, has shrunk, or is beginning to crack, the custard is overcooked.

For stirred custards: The custard should coat the back of a spoon thickly enough so that when you run a finger across it, the mark remains. If any egg particles appear, the custard is overcooked.

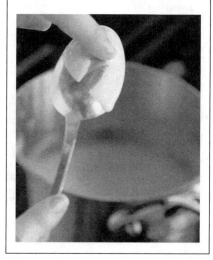

Custard Tips of the Trade

Tempering

Tempering: The process of slowly combining a hot liquid with a cold one is called tempering. In the case of custards, tempering ensures the hot liquid doesn't scramble the eggs. To temper, slowly add the hot liquid to the eggs while whisking constantly.

Stirring: Never stop stirring a recipe that calls for constant stirring. Failure to stir as needed can cause the delicate custard to overheat and curdle. Some chefs insist on a figure eight pattern to maintain constant heat, some claim a zigzag motion does the trick, and some use a simple circular motion. Whatever your preference, keep the mixture moving away from the bottom of the pot.

Ice Bath: It's important that some stove-top custards stop cooking as soon as they become thick. In those cases, an ice bath is necessary: Spoon the hot custard into a bowl, then place the custard bowl into a larger ice-filled bowl.

Water Bath: A water bath (the process of using a shallow pan of warm water in which to cook containers of food) insulates and protects custards from the heat of the oven so they cook slowly and evenly. The depth of the water should be half the height of the custard container (ramekin, cake pan, etc.). If you're baking multiple custards, the pan must be large enough so that the containers don't touch one another.

Ice Bath

Water Bath

Dulce de Leche Flan

1 (14-ounce) can fat-free sweetened condensed milk
½ cup sugar
¼ cup water
Cooking spray
2 cups 2% reduced-fat milk
3 large eggs, lightly beaten
2 large egg whites, lightly beaten
½ teaspoon vanilla extract

1. Preheat oven to 425°.
2. Pour condensed milk into a 1-quart baking dish; cover and place in bottom of a broiler pan. Add hot water to pan to a depth of 1 inch. Bake at 425° for 45 minutes or until milk is thick and caramel colored. Remove dish from pan; uncover and cool to room temperature.
3. Reduce oven temperature to 325°.
4. Combine sugar and ¼ cup water in a small, heavy saucepan, and cook over medium-high heat until sugar dissolves, stirring frequently. Continue cooking 5 minutes or until golden, stirring constantly. Immediately pour into a 9-inch round cake pan coated with cooking spray, tipping quickly until caramelized sugar coats bottom of pan.
5. Spoon condensed milk into a large bowl. Add 2% milk, eggs, egg whites, and vanilla extract; stir with a whisk until well blended. Strain milk mixture through a fine sieve into prepared pan; discard solids.
6. Place cake pan in bottom of broiler pan; add hot water to broiler pan to a depth of 1 inch. Bake at 325° for 40 minutes or until a knife inserted in center comes out clean. Remove from oven, and cool flan to room temperature in water bath. Remove cake pan from water bath, and cover and chill at least 3 hours or overnight. Loosen edges of flan with a knife or rubber spatula. Place a plate, upside down, on top of cake pan; invert flan onto plate. Drizzle any remaining caramelized syrup over flan. Yield: 8 servings (serving size: 1 wedge).

CALORIES 250 (12% from fat); FAT 3.2g (sat 1.3g, mono 1.1g, poly 0.3g); PROTEIN 9.6g; CARB 45.7g; FIBER 0g; CHOL 88mg; IRON 0.3mg; SODIUM 120mg; CALC 223mg

Touch of Honey Custard Pie

Because the pastry crust and low cooking temperature insulate the egg-rich custard, a water bath isn't needed. A little cornmeal helps thicken the filling and gives it a texture similar to that of chess pie. For best results, use finely ground, not coarse-grained, cornmeal.

CRUST:

    1   cup all-purpose flour, divided
    3   tablespoons ice water
    1   teaspoon fresh lemon juice
    2   tablespoons powdered sugar
    ¼   teaspoon salt
    ¼   cup vegetable shortening
        Cooking spray

FILLING:

    1⅓ cups granulated sugar
    2   tablespoons yellow cornmeal
    ¼   teaspoon salt
    ⅓   cup 2% reduced-fat milk
    2   tablespoons honey
    1   tablespoon butter, melted
    ½   teaspoon vanilla extract
    4   large eggs, lightly beaten

1. Preheat oven to 325°.
2. To prepare crust, lightly spoon flour into a dry measuring cup; level with a knife. Combine ¼ cup flour, water, and juice in a small bowl, stirring with a whisk until well blended to form a slurry. Combine ¾ cup flour, powdered sugar, and ¼ teaspoon salt in a medium bowl; cut in shortening with a pastry blender or 2 knives until mixture resembles coarse meal. Add slurry; toss with a fork until moist.
3. Gently press mixture into a 4-inch circle on 2 overlapping sheets of heavy-duty plastic wrap; cover with additional overlapping plastic wrap. Roll dough, still covered, into a 12-inch circle, and freeze 10 minutes. Remove 2 sheets of plastic wrap; let stand 1 minute or until pliable. Fit dough, plastic-wrap side up, into a 9-inch pie plate coated with cooking spray. Remove remaining plastic wrap. Press dough against bottom and up sides of pan. Fold edges under; flute. Freeze 10 minutes.

4. To prepare filling, combine granulated sugar, cornmeal, and ¼ teaspoon salt in a medium bowl; stir well. Combine milk and remaining 4 ingredients in a large bowl, stirring well with a whisk. Add cornmeal mixture, stirring with a whisk until blended. Pour into crust. Bake at 325° for 50 minutes or until just set. Cool completely on a wire rack. Yield: 8 servings (serving size: 1 wedge).

CALORIES 327 (28% from fat); FAT 10.3g (sat 3.3g, mono 3.5g, poly 2g); PROTEIN 5.3g; CARB 53.7g; FIBER 0.6g; CHOL 111mg; IRON 1.2mg; SODIUM 199mg; CALC 28mg

Sherried Zabaglione with Berries

The water that heats the custard must simmer, not boil. Regulate the water before placing the custard on top, and be conservative; once the top is in place, the water tends to heat up. Any berries will work with this tasty sauce. Serve this light custard sauce immediately to enjoy its frothy texture.

    5   tablespoons sugar
    3   tablespoons cream sherry
    2   large eggs, lightly beaten
    3   tablespoons reduced-fat sour cream
    2   cups fresh blackberries

1. Combine first 3 ingredients in top of a double boiler. Cook over simmering water until thick (about 4 minutes) and a thermometer registers 160°, stirring constantly with a whisk. Remove top pan from heat; whisk mixture an additional 2 minutes. Gently whisk in sour cream. Serve zabaglione immediately over berries. Yield: 4 servings (serving size: ½ cup berries and about ¼ cup zabaglione).

CALORIES 157 (24% from fat); FAT 4.2g (sat 1.7g, mono 1.4g, poly 0.6g); PROTEIN 4.2g; CARB 25.9g; FIBER 3.8g; CHOL 112mg; IRON 0.8mg; SODIUM 39mg; CALC 55mg

on hand
The Good Stuff

Stuffing exponentially improves flavor when it involves these sensational ingredients.

Stuffing takes your dish to the next level—or, to borrow a mathematical concept, to the second power. Flavors meld and complement one another.

Shepherd's Pie Peppers

Cooking the peppers in boiling water—or blanching—softens them before stuffing.

    2   large green bell peppers (about
        1 pound)
        Cooking spray
    6   ounces lean boneless leg of lamb
        or lean boneless sirloin steak, cut
        into ¾-inch cubes
    ¾   cup fat-free beef broth
    ⅔   cup frozen peas and carrots
    ⅓   cup chopped onion
    2   tablespoons tomato paste
    1   teaspoon Worcestershire sauce
    ¼   teaspoon black pepper
    ⅛   teaspoon salt
    1   tablespoon cornstarch
    1   tablespoon water
    1   cup frozen mashed potatoes
    ½   cup fat-free milk
    2   teaspoons grated Parmesan cheese
        Dash of paprika

1. Preheat oven to 400°.
2. Cut tops off bell peppers; discard tops, seeds, and membranes. Cook peppers in boiling water 5 minutes; drain and set aside.
3. Heat a large nonstick skillet coated with cooking spray over medium-high heat. Add lamb; cook 6 minutes or until browned, stirring frequently. Drain and pat dry with paper towels. Wipe drippings from pan with a paper towel.
4. Return lamb to pan; add broth and next 6 ingredients. Bring to a boil; cover, reduce heat, and simmer 10 minutes. Combine cornstarch and water; stir well
Continued

with a whisk. Add to lamb mixture; bring to a boil. Cook 1 minute; stir constantly. Divide lamb mixture evenly between peppers. Place stuffed peppers in an 8-inch square baking dish, and set aside.

5. Combine potatoes and milk in a microwave-safe bowl; stir well. Microwave at HIGH 2 minutes; stir after 1 minute. Let stand 2 minutes. Spoon warm potato mixture evenly over tops of stuffed peppers; lightly coat potato mixture with cooking spray. Combine cheese and paprika; sprinkle over potato mixture.

6. Bake at 400° for 20 minutes or until potatoes are golden. Yield: 2 servings (serving size: 1 stuffed pepper).

CALORIES 386 (21% from fat); FAT 9g (sat 3.3g, mono 3.4g, poly 1.1g); PROTEIN 30.1g; CARB 43.3g; FIBER 6.2g; CHOL 66mg; IRON 3.7mg; SODIUM 991mg; CALC 173mg

---

MAKE AHEAD
Parmesan Potato Bites

Using a melon baller to scoop out the potato pulp is easier than using a spoon.

12 small round red potatoes (about 1 pound)
1½ teaspoons olive oil
¾ cup minced fresh onion
¼ cup uncooked chopped turkey bacon (about 2 slices)
⅛ teaspoon freshly ground black pepper
3 garlic cloves, minced
½ cup (2 ounces) grated fresh Parmesan cheese
1 teaspoon rubbed sage

1. Cook potatoes in boiling water 15 minutes or until tender; drain.
2. Heat oil in a nonstick skillet over medium-high heat. Add onion, bacon, pepper, and garlic; sauté 5 minutes or until tender.
3. Preheat broiler.
4. Cut potatoes in half; carefully scoop out pulp, leaving ¼-inch shells. Mash pulp with a fork; stir in cheese and sage. Add to onion mixture, stirring well. Spoon about 1 tablespoon potato mixture into each shell. Arrange stuffed potatoes on a baking sheet, and broil 3 to 4 inches from heat 3 minutes or until

lightly browned. Serve warm. Yield: 12 servings (serving size: 2 stuffed halves).

CALORIES 64 (30% from fat); FAT 2.1g (sat 0.8g, mono 0.9g, poly 0.2g); PROTEIN 3g; CARB 8.2g; FIBER 1g; CHOL 5mg; IRON 0.4mg; SODIUM 93mg; CALC 59mg

---

Mushroom-Stuffed Chicken Breasts with Tomato Sauce

2 teaspoons olive oil, divided
½ cup chopped onion
1 cup sliced mushrooms
1 (10-ounce) package frozen chopped spinach, thawed, drained, and squeezed dry
2 tablespoons grated Asiago or Parmesan cheese
½ teaspoon dried Italian seasoning
¼ teaspoon salt
¼ teaspoon black pepper
4 (6-ounce) skinless, boneless chicken breast halves
½ cup fat-free, less-sodium chicken broth
1 (14.5-ounce) can diced tomatoes with basil, garlic, and oregano, drained

1. Heat 1 teaspoon oil in a large nonstick skillet over medium heat. Add onion; sauté 2 minutes. Add mushrooms; sauté 3 minutes. Stir in spinach; remove from heat. Stir in cheese, Italian seasoning, salt, and pepper.
2. Cut a horizontal slit through thickest portion of each chicken breast half to form a pocket. Stuff ¼ cup mushroom mixture into each pocket. Close opening with a wooden pick. Wipe skillet with paper towels.
3. Heat 1 teaspoon oil in pan over medium-high heat. Add chicken; cook 2 minutes on each side or until browned. Stir in broth and tomatoes; bring to a boil. Cover, reduce heat, and simmer 12 minutes or until chicken is done. Remove chicken from pan. Cook sauce until reduced to 1 cup (about 5 minutes). Yield: 4 servings (serving size: 1 chicken breast half and ¼ cup sauce).

CALORIES 263 (17% from fat); FAT 5.1g (sat 1.4g, mono 2.3g, poly 0.7g); PROTEIN 37.4g; CARB 15.4g; FIBER 4.2g; CHOL 82mg; IRON 3.4mg; SODIUM 968mg; CALC 184mg

---

happy endings
Refreshing Treats

Here are some satisfying snacks sure to please kids—and kids at heart.

It's the time of year when parents sigh, children cheer, and fireflies flicker for their lives. Before you know it, a whole neighborhood's worth of children will appear in your backyard. Tummies will start to rumble, and eventually, they'll come to you asking for a snack. Whether you have a yard full of tots or teens, we have treats that will delight them all.

MAKE AHEAD
Fudgy Sheet Cake

Frosting a cake soon after it cools maintains its moistness. If you must delay that step, wrap the cake in plastic wrap.

CAKE:
½ cup unsweetened cocoa
½ cup boiling water
2 cups sifted cake flour
1 teaspoon baking soda
½ teaspoon salt
1½ cups granulated sugar
⅓ cup vegetable shortening
2 teaspoons vanilla extract
2 large eggs
1 cup low-fat buttermilk
Cooking spray

ICING:
1½ cups sifted powdered sugar
3 tablespoons unsweetened cocoa
2 tablespoons 1% low-fat milk
1 teaspoon butter, softened
½ teaspoon vanilla extract

1. Preheat oven to 350°.
2. To prepare cake, combine ½ cup cocoa and water in a small bowl; cool. Combine flour, baking soda, and salt, stirring well with a whisk. Place granulated sugar, shortening, and 2 teaspoons vanilla in a large bowl; beat with a mixer at medium speed until well blended. Add

eggs, 1 at a time, beating well after each addition. Beat in cocoa mixture. Add flour mixture and buttermilk alternately to sugar mixture, beginning and ending with flour mixture and beating well after each addition.

3. Pour batter into a 13 x 9-inch baking pan coated with cooking spray. Bake at 350° for 30 minutes or until cake springs back when lightly touched. Cool in pan 10 minutes on a wire rack.

4. To prepare icing, combine powdered sugar and 3 tablespoons cocoa in a medium bowl, stirring well with a whisk. Add milk, butter, and ½ teaspoon vanilla; stir with a whisk until smooth. Spread icing over cake. Yield: 12 servings.

CALORIES 294 (24% from fat); FAT 8g (sat 2.4g, mono 3.2g, poly 1.7g); PROTEIN 4.2g; CARB 54.2g; FIBER 1.9g; CHOL 38mg; IRON 2mg; SODIUM 241mg; CALC 39mg

---

MAKE AHEAD

Peanut Butter-Marshmallow Treats

Coating your knife blade with cooking spray lets you cut these into neat squares. Omit the raisins if your kids don't like them.

½ cup sugar
½ cup light-colored corn syrup
½ teaspoon vanilla extract
½ cup chunky peanut butter
3 cups oven-toasted rice cereal
1 cup miniature marshmallows
¾ cup golden raisins
¼ cup peanuts, chopped
Cooking spray

1. Combine sugar, corn syrup, and vanilla in a small saucepan over medium heat, and bring to a boil, stirring constantly. Remove from heat, and add peanut butter, stirring until smooth. Combine cereal, marshmallows, raisins, and peanuts in a large bowl; add peanut butter mixture, stirring well.

2. Press cereal mixture evenly into bottom of an 8-inch square baking dish coated with cooking spray, and cool. Yield: 24 servings (serving size: 1 bar).

CALORIES 112 (24% from fat); FAT 3.4g (sat 0.6g, mono 1.6g, poly 1g); PROTEIN 2.1g; CARB 19.7g; FIBER 0.7g; CHOL 0mg; IRON 0.3mg; SODIUM 68mg; CALC 7mg

---

MAKE AHEAD • FREEZABLE

Multigrain Fruit Bars

Similar to breakfast bars, these are good to pack in a knapsack or bike bag. Use any dried fruit your kids like in place of the apricots—raisins, cranberries, cherries, or even blueberries.

1 cup applesauce
2 cups puffed seven-grain cereal (such as Kashi)
1¼ cups all-purpose flour
¼ cup nonfat dry milk
2 tablespoons toasted wheat germ
1 teaspoon baking soda
1 teaspoon ground cinnamon
¼ teaspoon salt
1 cup fresh or frozen blueberries
¾ cup packed brown sugar
⅓ cup chopped dried apricots
⅓ cup vegetable oil
1 teaspoon vanilla extract
2 large egg whites
Cooking spray

1. Preheat oven to 350°.

2. Spoon applesauce onto several layers of heavy-duty paper towels, and spread to ½-inch thickness. Cover applesauce with additional paper towels, and let stand 5 minutes.

3. Place cereal in a food processor; pulse until coarsely ground. Lightly spoon flour into dry measuring cups, and level with a knife. Add flour and next 5 ingredients to processor, and pulse to combine.

4. Scrape applesauce into processor using a rubber spatula. Add blueberries and next 5 ingredients; pulse just until combined. Spread batter into a 13 x 9-inch baking pan coated with cooking spray. Bake at 350° for 30 minutes or until a wooden pick inserted in center comes out clean. Cool completely on a wire rack. Yield: 2 dozen bars (serving size: 1 bar).

CALORIES 94 (19% from fat); FAT 2g (sat 0.5g, mono 1g, poly 0.5g); PROTEIN 1.7g; CARB 17g; FIBER 1g; CHOL 0mg; IRON 0.7mg; SODIUM 127mg; CALC 20mg

---

MAKE AHEAD

Chocolate Pudding with Bananas

Substitute milk chocolate for bittersweet if you crave a more mellow chocolate flavor.

2¼ cups 1% low-fat milk
⅓ cup sugar
⅓ cup unsweetened cocoa
2 tablespoons cornstarch
⅛ teaspoon salt
2 ounces bittersweet chocolate, finely chopped
1 teaspoon vanilla extract
1½ cups sliced banana (about 2 bananas)

1. Heat milk in a heavy saucepan over medium-high heat to 180° or until tiny bubbles form around edge (do not boil). Remove from heat.

2. Combine sugar and next 4 ingredients in a large bowl. Gradually add hot milk to sugar mixture, stirring constantly with a whisk. Return milk mixture to pan. Cook over medium heat until thick and bubbly (about 5 minutes), stirring constantly. Remove from heat; stir in vanilla.

3. Place banana slices in bottom of a 1½-quart casserole. Spoon pudding over banana slices. Serve warm, or cover with plastic wrap and chill. Yield: 6 servings (serving size: ½ cup).

CALORIES 186 (29% from fat); FAT 5.9g (sat 3.1g, mono 0.5g, poly 0.1g); PROTEIN 5g; CARB 34.1g; FIBER 3.2g; CHOL 4mg; IRON 1.1mg; SODIUM 96mg; CALC 121mg

---

QUICK & EASY

Fresh Banana-Berry Shake

Let your kids help with this smoothie—just remind them to secure the lid before starting the blender. If they find the shake a little too thick to process, suggest adding an extra tablespoon or 2 of juice, scraping the sides of the blender, and reblending.

2 cups sliced banana
1 cup quartered strawberries
¼ cup fresh orange juice
3 cups vanilla low-fat ice cream

Continued

1. Combine first 3 ingredients in a blender, and process until smooth. Add ice cream, and process until smooth. Serve immediately. Yield: 4 cups (serving size: 1 cup).

CALORIES 226 (20% from fat); FAT 4.8g (sat 2.8g, mono 1.3g, poly 0.3g); PROTEIN 4.9g; CARB 44.6g; FIBER 2.8g; CHOL 14mg; IRON 0.5mg; SODIUM 85mg; CALC 150mg

MAKE AHEAD • FREEZABLE
Vanilla-Butter Cookies

Whenever the urge to bake cookies strikes, soften cold butter quickly by heating it in the microwave for about 30 seconds at MEDIUM-LOW.

- ¾ cup sugar
- ⅓ cup butter, softened
- 1 tablespoon light-colored corn syrup
- 2 teaspoons vanilla extract
- ½ teaspoon almond extract
- 1 large egg
- 2 cups all-purpose flour
- 1 teaspoon baking powder
- ¼ teaspoon salt
- Cooking spray

1. Preheat oven to 375°.
2. Combine sugar and butter in a large bowl, and beat with a mixer at medium speed until light and fluffy. Add corn syrup, extracts, and egg; beat well. Lightly spoon flour into dry measuring cups, and level with a knife. Combine flour, baking powder, and salt. Add flour mixture to sugar mixture, and beat at low speed until well blended.
3. Drop dough by level tablespoons 2 inches apart onto baking sheets coated with cooking spray. Flatten cookies with a fork in a crisscross pattern. Bake at 375° for 8 minutes or until cookies are golden brown. Remove cookies from pan, and cool completely on wire racks. Yield: 3 dozen cookies (serving size: 1 cookie).

CALORIES 61 (28% from fat); FAT 1.9g (sat 1.1g, mono 0.6g, poly 0.1g); PROTEIN 0.9g; CARB 10g; FIBER 0.2g; CHOL 6mg; IRON 0.4mg; SODIUM 50mg; CALC 10mg

Picnic Under the Stars

Summer's best sights, sounds, and flavors come together under an evening sky.

Because scores of outdoor evening concerts dot calendars across the country all summer long, we've developed a menu of make-ahead foods that can be easily stored and toted. There's a jazzy jalapeño-infused melon salad and two entrée choices—luxe saffron shrimp or pesto-accented chicken—served with a simple rice salad. Bookend the meal with paprika-spiked white bean dip and a lemon soufflé, and you have ideal fare for taking in music on a summer night. We've even included hot spots for toe-tapping in the park (info on page 218).

Starlit Menu
serves 6

White Bean Dip

Spicy-Sweet Melon Salad

Saffron Shrimp with Fennel Seeds
or
Pesto Chicken Spirals

Italian Rice Salad

Lemon Cloud with Strawberry-Mint Compote

WINE NOTE: A great picnic should include wines for casual sipping. Here are terrific wines worth seeking out:
• Sparkling: Freixenet "Cordon Negro" nonvintage Brut Sparkling Wine from Spain, about $11. It's creamy, dry, and refreshing. Serve it well chilled.
• White: Sokol Blosser Evolution #9, Seventh Edition, nonvintage, about $15. It has super floral and tropical aromas followed by refreshing lime and pear flavors. Bring along ice cubes and club soda to make spritzers.
• Rosé: There are many wonderful dry, snappy rosés on the market; one is Bodegas Nekeas "Vega Sindoa" 2001 from Navarra, Spain, about $8.
• Light Red: A southern French Côtes-du-Rhône will do the trick nicely here. Try the juicy, chocolaty Château du Trignon Rasteau Côtes-du-Rhône Villages 1999, about $17.

MAKE AHEAD
White Bean Dip

- 1 tablespoon olive oil
- 6 garlic cloves, sliced
- 1 tablespoon ground coriander seeds
- 1⅛ teaspoons hot paprika, divided
- 1 (16-ounce) can cannellini beans or other white beans, rinsed and drained
- ¾ cup fat-free, less-sodium chicken broth
- 2 tablespoons chopped fresh flat-leaf parsley
- 20 sesame breadsticks

1. Heat oil in a small saucepan over medium heat. Add garlic, coriander, and 1 teaspoon paprika; cook 2 minutes or until garlic is tender and lightly browned, stirring constantly. Add beans; cook 2 minutes, stirring frequently. Add broth; bring to a boil. Cover, reduce heat, and simmer 15 minutes.
2. Place bean mixture in a food processor; process until smooth. Stir in parsley. Spoon into a medium bowl; chill. Sprinkle with ⅛ teaspoon paprika. Serve with breadsticks. Yield: 20 servings (serving size: 1 breadstick and 1 tablespoon dip).

CALORIES 42 (28% from fat); FAT 1.3g (sat 0.2g, mono 0.5g, poly 0.2g); PROTEIN 1.6g; CARB 5.9g; FIBER 1.1g; CHOL 0mg; IRON 0.6mg; SODIUM 81mg; CALC 13mg

Spicy-Sweet Melon Salad

The longer this salad sits and the flavors meld, the spicier it gets.

- ½ cup sugar
- ½ cup water
- ½ small jalapeño pepper, thinly sliced
- 2 cups cubed peeled honeydew melon
- 2 cups cubed peeled cantaloupe

1. Combine sugar and water in a small saucepan; bring to a boil, stirring until sugar dissolves. Remove from heat; add pepper. Chill.

2. Combine sugar mixture, honeydew cubes, and cantaloupe cubes in a large bowl. Cover and refrigerate 4 hours or overnight. Serve with a slotted spoon. Yield: 6 servings (serving size: ⅔ cup).

CALORIES 104 (2% from fat); FAT 0.2g (sat 0.1g, mono 0g, poly 0.1g); PROTEIN 0.8g; CARB 26.5g; FIBER 0.8g; CHOL 0mg; IRON 0.2mg; SODIUM 11mg; CALC 10mg

Saffron Shrimp with Fennel Seeds

This entrée is great chilled or at room temperature. Sop up the juices with French bread, or serve it over rice. The color and flavor of this dish intensify as it stands.

- 1 cup dry white wine
- 1 tablespoon fennel seeds
- ½ teaspoon saffron threads
- ½ teaspoon salt
- 2 garlic cloves, minced
- 2 pounds large shrimp, peeled and deveined
- ¼ cup chopped fresh flat-leaf parsley

1. Combine first 5 ingredients in a large nonstick skillet; bring to a boil. Cook 5 minutes, and add shrimp. Cover and cook 2 minutes or until shrimp are done; stir occasionally. Spoon into a bowl; chill. Stir in parsley before serving. Yield: 6 servings (serving size: 5 ounces shrimp).

CALORIES 193 (13% from fat); FAT 2.8g (sat 0.5g, mono 0.5g, poly 1g); PROTEIN 31g; CARB 2.7g; FIBER 0.5g; CHOL 229mg; IRON 4mg; SODIUM 422mg; CALC 99mg

Pesto Chicken Spirals

Make these simple chicken "bundles" before your picnic so they'll have plenty of time to chill. They smell so good as they're baking that you may want to eat them straight from the oven. To save time, use bottled pesto in place of the homemade—although the flavors won't be as bright.

PESTO:
- 2 teaspoons extravirgin olive oil
- 6 garlic cloves, crushed
- 1½ cups basil leaves
- 1½ cups chopped fresh flat-leaf parsley
- 2 tablespoons grated Parmesan cheese
- 2 tablespoons fat-free, less-sodium chicken broth
- ¼ teaspoon salt
- ¼ teaspoon black pepper

CHICKEN:
- 12 skinless, boneless chicken thighs
- ¾ teaspoon salt
- ½ teaspoon black pepper
- Cooking spray

1. Preheat oven to 375°.

2. To prepare pesto, combine oil and garlic in a microwave-safe bowl. Microwave at HIGH 40 seconds. Combine garlic mixture, basil and next 5 ingredients in a food processor; process until finely chopped.

3. To prepare chicken, spread 1 teaspoon pesto down center of each thigh, leaving a ¼-inch border on short ends. Roll up jelly-roll fashion, starting with a short end; secure with wooden picks. Sprinkle rolls evenly with ¾ teaspoon salt and ½ teaspoon pepper; arrange rolls ½ inch apart, seam sides down, in a 13 x 9-inch baking dish coated with cooking spray. Bake at 375° for 30 minutes or until a thermometer registers 170°, turning rolls after 15 minutes. Cool and transfer to a serving container using a slotted spoon. Cover and refrigerate overnight. Remove toothpicks; cut each roll crosswise into ¼-inch-thick slices. Yield: 6 servings (serving size: 2 thighs).

CALORIES 276 (27% from fat); FAT 8.4g (sat 2g, mono 3.1g, poly 1.5g); PROTEIN 35g; CARB 13.7g; FIBER 1g; CHOL 116mg; IRON 15mg; SODIUM 568mg; CALC 663mg

Italian Rice Salad

This rice and vegetable dish is a refreshing change from pasta salad. Cool the rice so it won't become gummy, or use 3 cups chilled leftover rice.

- 2 cups water, divided
- 1 cup basmati or long-grain rice
- ¾ teaspoon salt, divided
- 1 (14-ounce) can fat-free, less-sodium chicken broth
- Olive oil-flavored cooking spray
- 1 pound (1-inch) diagonally cut green beans
- 2 tablespoons red wine vinegar
- 2 tablespoons extravirgin olive oil
- 2 cups halved grape tomatoes
- ¾ cup chopped green onions
- ¼ cup (1 ounce) grated fresh pecorino Romano cheese
- ¼ teaspoon ground black pepper

1. Combine 1 cup water, rice, ¼ teaspoon salt, and broth in a large saucepan; bring to a boil. Cover, reduce heat, and simmer 15 minutes or until liquid is absorbed. Coat a large baking sheet with cooking spray. Spread rice in an even layer on baking sheet; cool to room temperature.

2. Bring 1 cup water to a boil in a large pan. Add beans; cover and cook 5 minutes or until crisp-tender. Drain and plunge beans into ice water; drain.

3. Combine vinegar, oil, and ½ teaspoon salt in a large bowl, stirring with a whisk. Add rice, beans, tomatoes, green onions, cheese, and pepper; toss gently to combine. Cover and chill. Yield: 6 servings (serving size: 1⅓ cups).

CALORIES 226 (25% from fat); FAT 6.3g (sat 1.5g, mono 4.1g, poly 0.7g); PROTEIN 6.1g; CARB 36g; FIBER 4g; CHOL 4mg; IRON 0.7mg; SODIUM 474mg; CALC 86mg

Lemon Cloud with Strawberry-Mint Compote

You can substitute any berries for strawberries.

CLOUD:
Cooking spray
¾ cup plus 2 tablespoons sugar, divided
1 tablespoon cornstarch
1 tablespoon grated lemon rind
6 tablespoons fresh lemon juice
2 large egg yolks
4 large egg whites
Dash of salt

COMPOTE:
2 cups quartered small strawberries
2 tablespoons sugar
1 to 2 tablespoons chopped fresh mint

1. To prepare cloud, preheat oven to 350°.
2. Lightly coat a 1½-quart soufflé dish with cooking spray. Sprinkle with 2 tablespoons sugar, shaking out excess. Place dish on a baking sheet.
3. Combine ½ cup sugar and cornstarch in a medium saucepan; stir with a whisk. Stir in lemon rind, juice, and egg yolks. Place over medium heat. Cook 3 minutes or until thick; stir constantly. Remove from heat; immediately scrape mixture into a glass bowl. Cool to room temperature.
4. Place egg whites and salt in a large bowl; beat with a mixer at medium speed 30 seconds or until foamy. Increase mixer speed to high. Gradually add ¼ cup sugar, 1 tablespoon at a time, beating just until stiff peaks form. Gently stir one-fourth of egg white mixture into egg yolk mixture; gently fold in remaining egg white mixture. Spoon into prepared dish. Bake at 350° for 25 minutes or until puffed and lightly browned. Remove from oven, and cool to room temperature on a wire rack. Cover and chill.
5. To prepare compote, combine strawberries, 2 tablespoons sugar, and mint; toss gently. Cover and chill. Serve with lemon cloud. Yield: 6 servings.

CALORIES 187 (9% from fat); FAT 1.9g (sat 0.5g, mono 0.7g, poly 0.3g); PROTEIN 3.8g; CARB 40g; FIBER 1.6g; CHOL 71mg; IRON 0.7mg; SODIUM 65mg; CALC 23mg

Barefoot (and Toe-Tapping) in the Park

Pack up your basket, and head to one of these music events in your neck of the woods. Just be sure to check the rules first (some events prohibit glass bottles, alcohol, coolers, or pets).

Jazz Best

Each summer, Washington, D.C., boasts the Capital Jazz Fest, deemed the "world's largest showcase of contemporary jazz." This two-day festival provides both orchestra seating and a picnic area, along with the opportunity to meet performers like Dianne Reeves and Nancy Wilson (301-322-8100, www.capital jazz.com).

Top Scotts

Scottish performers, Celtic rock groups, and folk entertainers are showcased at the Texas Scottish Festival and Highland Games. Attendees can also enjoy dancing, Celtic athletics, and whiskey tastings (www.texasscottishfestival.com).

Big Apple's Brightest

New York City culture moves outdoors from June through August, when Central Park's SummerStage offers free concerts featuring world music, modern dance, spoken word, electronica, and even opera (www.summerstage.org).

Pickin' for Picnics

The world's oldest continuous annual bluegrass festival marks its 38th year in June 2004 at Bill Monroe's Memorial Music Park and Campground in Bean Blossom, Indiana. Pack a tent along with your picnic if you plan to stay a few days (800-414-4677 or www.beanblossom.com).

International Flavors

Enjoy the tropical sounds of reggae at the International Arts Festival in New Orleans. Carry your blanket to the open field and take along a little cash for the craft booths (888-767-1317 or www.internationalartsfestival.com).

Blues Benefits

Blues fans from around the Midwest flock to Newton, Kansas, for that state's Blues Fest. Held at Harvey County Camp Hawk, the festival benefits the Blues in the Schools program, which gives young Blues musicians from central Kansas the chance to play with professional performers (www.kansas-bluesfest.com).

Rocky Mountain Way

Genuine Jazz in July offers both new-school and traditional jazz styles on two Breckenridge, Colorado, stages—the Main Street Station stage and the floating stage on Maggie Pond (970-453-5579, www.genuinejazz.com).

California Sings

The Live Oak Music Festival is the place to be in Santa Barbara, California. Traditional, folk, blues, bluegrass, classical, jazz, and world music fill the air. A Friday night barn dance and auction kick off the event, which includes activities for kids and a quiet tent where they can sleep while parents enjoy the music (www.liveoakfest.org).

All About Tomatoes

Whatever the color, whatever the kind, tomatoes enchant us.

But even the reddest, plumpest specimens can disappoint when it comes to flavor and juiciness. Finding the best choice, knowing its flavor secrets, and understanding the best way to preserve that flavor will deepen your enthusiasm for one of summer's great tastes.

Open-Faced Bacon, Lettuce, and Fried Green Tomato Sandwiches

Double-breading the tomato slices gives them a crunchy coating. Soaking the tomatoes in hot water draws out their moisture, which helps keep them crisp when cooked. On their own, the fried green tomatoes in this recipe are a classic Southern side dish.

    2   green tomatoes, cut into 12
        (¼-inch-thick) slices (about
        1 pound)
    2   tablespoons fat-free milk
    4   large egg whites, lightly beaten
    1½ cups yellow cornmeal
    ¾   teaspoon salt
    ¼   teaspoon freshly ground black
        pepper
    2   tablespoons olive oil, divided
    5   tablespoons light mayonnaise
    1   teaspoon fresh lemon juice
    ¼   teaspoon hot sauce
    6   (1½-ounce) slices white bread,
        toasted
    6   Bibb lettuce leaves
    9   bacon slices, cooked and cut in
        half
    2   tablespoons chopped fresh
        chives

1. Place tomato slices in a large bowl; cover with hot water. Let stand 15 minutes. Drain and pat dry with paper towels. Combine milk and egg whites, stirring with a whisk. Combine cornmeal, salt, and pepper in a shallow dish, stirring with a whisk. Dip each tomato slice in milk mixture; dredge in cornmeal mixture. Return tomato slices, one at a time, to milk mixture; dredge in cornmeal mixture.

2. Heat 1 tablespoon oil in a large nonstick skillet over medium-high heat. Add half of tomato slices; cook 4 minutes on each side or until crisp and golden. Repeat procedure with remaining oil and tomato slices.

3. Combine mayonnaise, juice, and hot sauce, stirring with a whisk. Spread about 1 tablespoon mayonnaise mixture on each bread slice; top with 1 lettuce leaf, 3 bacon pieces, and 2 tomato slices. Sprinkle each sandwich with 1 teaspoon chives. Serve immediately. Yield: 6 servings (serving size: 1 sandwich).

CALORIES 386 (30% from fat); FAT 12.8g (sat 2.8g, mono 4.5g, poly 2.6g); PROTEIN 12.2g; CARB 56.2g; FIBER 3.9g; CHOL 16mg; IRON 2.2mg; SODIUM 834mg; CALC 44mg

Tomato-Garlic Soup with Parmesan Croutons

Peel the tomatoes for this delicate soup, since the skins can become tough and chewy. Serve with a Caesar salad and a crisp white wine for a light meal.

    4   large tomatoes, cored (about 2½
        pounds)
    2   quarts water
    2   quarts ice water
    1¼ cups uncooked seashell pasta
    4   teaspoons olive oil, divided
    ¾   cup finely chopped red onion
    8   garlic cloves, thinly sliced
    1   cup water
    1   tablespoon chopped fresh flat-leaf
        parsley
    1   tablespoon minced fresh chives
    1   teaspoon minced fresh oregano
    1   teaspoon minced fresh thyme
    2   (14-ounce) cans fat-free,
        less-sodium chicken broth
    1   tablespoon red wine vinegar
    ½   teaspoon freshly ground black
        pepper
    8   (½-ounce) slices diagonally cut
        French bread baguette (about
        1 inch thick)
    ½   cup (2 ounces) grated fresh
        Parmesan cheese
        Thyme sprigs (optional)

1. Score bottom of each tomato with an "X." Bring 2 quarts water to a boil in a Dutch oven. Add tomatoes; cook 30 seconds. Remove tomatoes with a slotted spoon; plunge tomatoes into ice water. Drain and peel. Cut each tomato in half crosswise. Push seeds out of tomato halves using the tip of a knife; discard seeds. Chop tomatoes.

2. Cook pasta according to package directions, omitting salt and fat; drain. Toss pasta with 1 teaspoon oil. Cool completely.

3. Heat 1 tablespoon oil in a Dutch oven over medium-low heat. Add onion; cook 7 minutes, stirring occasionally. Add garlic; cook 3 minutes or until onion is tender, stirring frequently. Stir in tomatoes, 1 cup water, and next 5 ingredients; bring to a boil. Reduce heat, and simmer 20 minutes, stirring occasionally. Add pasta, vinegar, and pepper; cook 1 minute or until thoroughly heated.

4. Preheat broiler.

Continued

5. Place bread slices on a baking sheet, and top each slice with 1 tablespoon cheese. Broil 1½ minutes or until lightly browned. Serve with soup. Garnish with thyme sprigs, if desired. Yield: 4 servings (serving size: 1½ cups soup and 2 croutons).

WINE NOTE: Although it's a bit counterintuitive, tomatoes taste best paired with wines that mirror their high-acid profile. Acidity gives wine a kind of freshness, brightness, and vivacity—just the ticket for tangy tomato dishes. Italians often drink Chianti or Barbera with tomato sauce-based dishes; either would be a good choice with this soup. If you prefer white wines, try Pinot Grigio from Italy; Sauvignon Blanc from New Zealand, California, or Washington State; or, for a twist, Albarino from Spain.

CALORIES 335 (27% from fat); FAT 9.9g (sat 3g, mono 3.8g, poly 1g); PROTEIN 15.3g; CARB 46.6g; FIBER 4.1g; CHOL 11mg; IRON 2.7mg; SODIUM 695mg; CALC 227mg

Rustic Tomato-Basil Tart

(pictured on page 235)

You can use all red tomatoes if you can't find yellow.

- 1½ pounds yellow tomatoes, cut into ¼-inch-thick slices
- 1½ pounds red tomatoes, cut into ¼-inch-thick slices
- 1½ teaspoons salt, divided
- 1 cup fresh corn kernels (about 2 ears)
- 1 tablespoon fresh lemon juice
- 3 tablespoons fat-free sour cream
- 1½ cups all-purpose flour
- ¼ cup yellow cornmeal
- ¼ cup chilled butter, cut into small pieces
- 1 tablespoon yellow cornmeal
- ½ cup thinly sliced fresh basil, divided
- ⅓ cup (1½ ounces) shredded fontina cheese
- 1 tablespoon chopped fresh oregano
- 2 tablespoons all-purpose flour
- ¼ teaspoon cracked black pepper

1. Arrange tomato slices in a single layer on several layers of paper towels; sprinkle with ½ teaspoon salt. Let stand 20 minutes; blot dry with paper towels.

2. Preheat oven to 400°.

3. Place corn, juice, and sour cream in a food processor or blender; process until smooth. Lightly spoon 1½ cups flour into dry measuring cups; level with a knife. Combine 1½ cups flour, ¼ cup cornmeal, and ½ teaspoon salt in a large bowl; stir with a whisk. Cut in butter with a pastry blender or 2 knives until mixture resembles coarse meal. Add corn mixture; stir until a soft dough forms. Knead gently 3 or 4 times.

4. Slightly overlap 2 (16-inch) sheets of plastic wrap on a slightly damp surface. Place dough on plastic wrap; press into a 6-inch circle. Cover with 2 additional sheets of overlapping plastic wrap. Roll dough, still covered, into a 14-inch circle; place on a large baking sheet in freezer 10 minutes or until plastic wrap can be easily removed. Line baking sheet with parchment paper, and sprinkle paper with 1 tablespoon cornmeal. Remove 2 sheets of plastic wrap from dough. Place dough, plastic wrap side up, on baking sheet. Remove top sheets of plastic wrap.

5. Combine ¼ cup basil, cheese, and oregano. Combine 2 tablespoons flour and ½ teaspoon salt. Arrange cheese mixture on dough, leaving a 1½-inch border. Using a sifter or sieve, sift 1 tablespoon flour mixture over cheese mixture. Arrange half of tomatoes over cheese mixture. Sift remaining flour mixture over tomatoes; top with remaining tomatoes. Fold edges of dough toward center; press to seal (dough will only partially cover tomatoes). Bake at 400° for 35 minutes or until crust is brown; let stand 10 minutes. Sprinkle with ¼ cup basil and pepper. Yield: 6 servings (serving size: 1 wedge).

CALORIES 320 (32% from fat); FAT 11.5g (sat 6.4g, mono 3.1g, poly 1.1g); PROTEIN 9.2g; CARB 48g; FIBER 4.7g; CHOL 29mg; IRON 3.1mg; SODIUM 753mg; CALC 80mg

How to Make Tomato-Basil Tart

1. Puréed corn makes a tender crust but also makes the dough a bit sticky. Flour your hands before kneading.

2. A layer of fontina cheese and a dusting of flour keep the juicy tomatoes from making the crust soggy. A second dusting between layers of tomatoes helps, too.

Piadini with Cherry Tomatoes and Smoked Mozzarella

You can substitute store-bought flatbread for the sandwich crust. If you do, heat the bread and melt the cheese before filling the sandwiches so they will stay together.

CRUST:
- 2¼ cups bread flour, divided
- 1 package dry yeast (about 2¼ teaspoons)
- 1 cup plus 2 tablespoons warm water (100° to 110°), divided
- ½ teaspoon salt
- Cooking spray
- ¾ cup (3 ounces) shredded smoked mozzarella cheese, divided

FILLING:

- 1½ cups yellow cherry tomatoes, halved
- 1½ cups red cherry tomatoes, halved
- ½ cup thinly sliced fresh basil
- 3 tablespoons balsamic vinegar
- 1 tablespoon extravirgin olive oil
- ¼ teaspoon salt
- ¼ teaspoon freshly ground black pepper
- 1 garlic clove, minced

1. To prepare crust, lightly spoon flour into dry measuring cups; level with a knife. Dissolve yeast in ½ cup warm water in a large bowl; stir in ½ cup flour. Let stand 30 minutes. Add ½ cup plus 2 tablespoons warm water, 1½ cups flour, and ½ teaspoon salt, stirring to form a soft dough. Turn dough out onto a floured surface. Knead until smooth and elastic (about 8 minutes); add enough of remaining flour, 1 tablespoon at a time, to prevent dough from sticking to hands.
2. Place dough in a large bowl coated with cooking spray, turning to coat top. Cover and let rise in a warm place (85°), free from drafts, 45 minutes or until doubled in size. (Gently press two fingers into dough. If indentation remains, dough has risen enough.) Punch dough down; cover and let rest 5 minutes.
3. Divide dough into 4 equal portions. Working with one portion at a time (cover remaining dough to prevent drying), roll each portion into a 7-inch circle on a lightly floured surface. Heat a large nonstick skillet coated with cooking spray over medium-high heat. Place 1 dough circle in pan. Sprinkle with 3 tablespoons cheese. Cook 3 minutes or until cheese melts and dough is browned on bottom. Repeat procedure with remaining dough circles and cheese.
4. To prepare filling, combine tomatoes and remaining 6 ingredients; toss gently to coat. Spoon ¾ cup tomato mixture onto each crust, and fold over. Yield: 4 servings.

CALORIES 359 (21% from fat); FAT 8.5g (sat 3.6g, mono 2.6g, poly 0.5g); PROTEIN 14.9g; CARB 59g; FIBER 3.7g; CHOL 17mg; IRON 4.6mg; SODIUM 485mg; CALC 143mg

Tomato Q & A

How do you pick a good tomato?
Not by looks. Some of the best-tasting tomatoes happen to be some of the homeliest. Home-grown tomatoes can't be beat. But when you buy tomatoes, smell them—a good tomato should smell like a tomato, especially at the stem end.

How do you make a tomato taste better?
If you have a tomato that's flavorless, drizzle balsamic vinegar or honey over it. Grilling, roasting, and stewing can also give a bland tomato life.

What makes a tomato mealy? How can you tell if a tomato is mealy before slicing?
Cool temperatures can change a tomato's composition, converting its natural sugar to starch and resulting in a tasteless, mealy tomato. For this reason, never refrigerate a tomato. If a tomato feels soft, there's a chance it will be mealy, but, unfortunately, it isn't always possible to tell before slicing.

What is the best way to store tomatoes?
Place them at room temperature in a single layer, shoulder-side up, and out of direct sunlight. For any extended period of time, keep them between 55 and 65 degrees.

My grocer sells little net bags of tomatoes still attached to a vine. Are these really worth their high price?
Unfortunately, they're generally not worth it.

When should you use canned tomatoes?
Opt for canned tomatoes when you want their juice. Otherwise, use fresh tomatoes.

What are the flavor differences among different colors of tomatoes?
Yellow and orange tend to be sweeter than red. Green tomatoes have a tart, citrusy tang. Purple and blackish varieties have a complex flavor similar to red wine.

What's the best way to peel a tomato?

To peel, use a small paring knife to score the bottom of the tomato with an "X," cutting just through the skin but not into the flesh. Place the tomato in boiling water for 30 seconds. Remove it with a slotted spoon; quickly plunge into a bowl of ice water. Once cooled, peel away the skins.

What's the best way to slice and seed tomatoes?

Anyone who's tried to cut a tomato with a dull knife knows the challenge; the skins are tougher than they look. A sharp serrated knife is the best tool for the job.

To seed a tomato, remove the core. Holding the tomato with the core side up, cut the tomato crosswise. Using the tip of a knife, remove and discard the seeds from each tomato half.

Yellow Tomatoes in Spiced Balsamic Vinaigrette

Yellow tomatoes have a low acidity, so they're sweeter than most red tomatoes. Balsamic vinegar brings out the sweetness and adds a mild acidity. Use high-quality vinegar. Serve with steak, lamb, or salmon.

½ cup thinly sliced green onions
1 tablespoon minced seeded jalapeño pepper
8 yellow tomatoes, each cut into 6 wedges (about 2½ pounds)
1½ tablespoons olive oil
¼ cup grated peeled fresh ginger
1 tablespoon ground cumin
1 tablespoon freshly cracked black pepper
2 teaspoons paprika
1 teaspoon ground turmeric
4 garlic cloves, minced
¾ cup balsamic vinegar
3 tablespoons brown sugar
1 teaspoon kosher salt

1. Combine first 3 ingredients in a large bowl.

2. Heat oil in a large saucepan over medium-high heat. Add ginger and next 5 ingredients; sauté 1 minute. Add vinegar, sugar, and salt to pan, stirring to combine. Bring to a boil; cook 1 minute, stirring frequently. Pour spice mixture over tomato mixture; toss gently to coat. Serve at room temperature. Yield: 10 servings (serving size: about ¾ cup).

CALORIES 80 (29% from fat); FAT 2.6g (sat 0.3g, mono 1.6g, poly 0.3g); PROTEIN 1.5g; CARB 14.1g; FIBER 2g; CHOL 0mg; IRON 1.2mg; SODIUM 254mg; CALC 29mg

---

Snappy Italian Menu
serves 6

Broiled Red Snapper with Sicilian Tomato Pesto

Asiago toast*

Steamed green beans

*Place 6 (1½-ounce) slices Italian bread on a baking sheet. Broil 1 minute on each side or until toasted. Rub top of each bread slice with cut side of a halved garlic clove. Drizzle each slice with 1 teaspoon extravirgin olive oil; sprinkle each slice with a dash of salt and black pepper. Top each slice with 2 tablespoons grated Asiago cheese. Broil 1 minute or until cheese melts.

Broiled Red Snapper with Sicilian Tomato Pesto

Plum tomatoes work best in this recipe. No need to seed or peel them. You can make the pesto ahead, and keep it chilled. Stir in the tomatoes just before serving.

PESTO:
2 cups basil leaves
2 tablespoons pine nuts, toasted
2 tablespoons extravirgin olive oil
2 garlic cloves, minced
¼ cup (1 ounce) grated Parmigiano-Reggiano cheese
⅛ teaspoon crushed red pepper
1½ cups chopped plum tomato (about 3 medium)
½ teaspoon salt
½ teaspoon freshly ground black pepper

FISH:
6 (6-ounce) red snapper or other firm, white fish fillets
¼ teaspoon salt
Cooking spray

REMAINING INGREDIENT:
3 cups hot cooked orzo

Tomato Varieties

Beefsteak: Known as a slicing tomato, this large, ribbed, pumpkin-shaped type is common at farmers' markets. Because its characteristic flavor balances sweetness and acidity, it's great for eating raw. It also maintains its shape and flavor when cooked.

Globe: This is the kind you usually find in grocery stores. A medium-sized, firm, juicy tomato, it has a good balance of sweetness and acidity. It's best eaten raw.

Plum: Also called Roma or Italian, this egg-shaped red or yellow tomato isn't as sweet or acidic as the beefsteak and globe varieties. Plum tomatoes have lower water content and fewer seeds, so they're especially good for cooking and canning. Plum are the best year-round supermarket tomatoes.

Heirloom: These tomatoes are old or original tomato varieties that fell out of production and have been reintroduced in recent years. Look for heirloom tomatoes at farmers' markets, or grow your own. Flavors vary widely among the hundreds of types, and there are myriad colors, shapes, and sizes.

Green tomatoes: Picked before ripe, they have a sharp, tart taste and firm flesh, which makes them excellent for frying, broiling, and stewing. You don't want to eat them raw.

Cherry: This term refers to a family of tomatoes, which includes several types and colors, all of which are about an inch in diameter and similar in flavor. The defining difference among the members of this family is their shape. They include the following three varieties:

1. Cherry also refers specifically to a small round type. Available in red, orange, green, or yellow, they taste similar to beefsteak and globe tomatoes but have a more pronounced sweetness. They're often good during winter months. Try them in salads or quick sautés. Use as a garnish, or eat them out of hand. Cut them in half so they'll be easier to eat.

2. Grape tomatoes have a more elliptical shape, similar to a grape, and are almost always red. They have a more intense sweetness than the cherry kind, balanced by subtle acidity. Look for grape tomatoes that are no larger than an inch in diameter. If they're larger, they'll have a higher water content and a diluted taste.

3. Pear tomatoes are shaped liked small pears or teardrops. They're best eaten raw, but you can cook them briefly to finish a sauce or toss with pasta. Pear tomatoes are a bit smaller than cherry and have a flavor similar to grape tomatoes. They're available in yellow, red, and orange.

1. To prepare pesto, combine first 4 ingredients in a food processor; process until smooth. Add cheese and red pepper; process until blended. Transfer mixture to a bowl. Add tomato, ½ teaspoon salt, and black pepper, stirring gently to combine.

2. Preheat broiler.

3. To prepare fish, sprinkle fish with ¼ teaspoon salt. Arrange fish on a broiler pan coated with cooking spray; broil 8 minutes or until fish flakes easily when tested with a fork. Place ½ cup orzo on each of 6 plates; top each serving with 1 fillet and ¼ cup pesto. Yield: 6 servings.

CALORIES 437 (22% from fat); FAT 10.8g (sat 2.4g, mono 4.8g, poly 2g); PROTEIN 44.9g; CARB 38.9g; FIBER 3.1g; CHOL 67mg; IRON 2.9mg; SODIUM 497mg; CALC 156mg

Stewed Chicken with Okra and Tomatoes

This hearty dish calls for canned tomatoes. Soaking the okra gives it a better texture.

    4   cups water
    3   cups okra pods, trimmed (about
        ¾ pound)
   ¼   cup fresh lemon juice
 1¼   teaspoons salt, divided
    1   tablespoon olive oil
    2   chicken breast halves (about 1¾
        pounds), skinned
    2   chicken leg quarters (about 1¾
        pounds), skinned
   ¼   teaspoon freshly ground black
        pepper
   ½   cup thinly sliced red onion
   ½   cup fat-free, less-sodium chicken
        broth
   ½   cup dry white wine
 1½   teaspoons chopped fresh thyme
    1   teaspoon ground cumin
    2   whole cloves
    1   garlic clove, minced
    1   (14.5-ounce) can diced tomatoes,
        undrained
    2   tablespoons chopped fresh
        flat-leaf parsley
   ½   teaspoon red wine vinegar

1. Combine first 3 ingredients and 1 tea-spoon salt. Let mixture stand 1 hour. Drain well, and pat dry with paper towels.

2. Heat oil in a large nonstick skillet over medium-high heat. Sprinkle chicken with ¼ teaspoon salt and pepper. Add chicken to pan, and cook 4 minutes on each side or until browned. Remove from pan. Add okra and onion to pan, and sauté 3 minutes or until lightly browned. Add broth and next 6 ingredients, stirring to combine. Return chicken to pan; bring to a boil. Cover, reduce heat, and simmer 25 minutes or until chicken is done. Remove chicken from pan, and keep warm. Bring tomato mixture to a boil; cook until reduced to 2 cups (about 5 minutes), stirring frequently. Discard cloves. Stir in parsley and vinegar. Serve with chicken. Yield: 4 servings (serving size: about 4 ounces chicken and ½ cup tomato mixture).

CALORIES 311 (30% from fat); FAT 10.3g (sat 1.6g, mono 4g, poly 1.3g); PROTEIN 34.8g; CARB 18.9g; FIBER 4.8g; CHOL 64mg; IRON 2.9mg; SODIUM 681mg; CALC 148mg

STAFF FAVORITE

Grilled Shrimp Skewers with Romesco

Romesco is a classic Spanish sauce made with tomatoes, almonds, bell peppers, and garlic. It's traditionally served with grilled fish or chicken. Here, ancho chiles add a hint of smokiness. The sauce will keep in the refrigerator up to 3 days.

ROMESCO:

    8   plum tomatoes (about 1¼
        pounds)
    4   garlic cloves, unpeeled
  Cooking spray
   ½   cup water
    5   tablespoons red wine vinegar,
        divided
   ¼   teaspoon crushed red pepper
    2   ancho chiles
   ¼   cup whole blanched almonds
    1   (1-ounce) slice French bread or
        other firm white bread, torn into
        small pieces
    2   tablespoons water
    2   teaspoons olive oil
    1   teaspoon salt
   ¾   teaspoon paprika
   ¼   teaspoon freshly ground black
        pepper

SHRIMP:

 2¼   pounds jumbo shrimp, peeled and
        deveined
    3   tablespoons chopped fresh parsley
        (optional)

1. Preheat oven to 350°.

2. To prepare romesco, place tomatoes and garlic in a shallow roasting pan coated with cooking spray. Bake at 350° for 30 minutes or until tender. Cool. Peel and seed tomatoes; peel garlic.

3. Combine ½ cup water, 3 tablespoons vinegar, red pepper, and chiles in a small saucepan; bring to a boil. Cover, reduce heat, and simmer 10 minutes. Remove from heat. Let stand, covered, 30 minutes. Drain. Discard stems and seeds from chiles.

4. Heat a small skillet coated with cooking spray over medium-high heat. Add almonds; cook 2 minutes or until lightly browned, stirring frequently. Remove from pan. Add bread to pan; cook 2 minutes or until lightly browned, stirring frequently. Place tomatoes, garlic, chiles, 2 tablespoons vinegar, almonds, bread, 2 tablespoons water, oil, salt, paprika, and black pepper in a food processor; process until smooth.

5. Prepare grill or broiler.

6. Thread shrimp onto 12 (8-inch) skewers. Place skewers on grill rack or broiler pan coated with cooking spray, and cook 3 minutes on each side or until shrimp are done. Sprinkle shrimp with parsley, if desired. Serve with romesco. Yield: 6 servings (serving size: 2 skewers and ¼ cup sauce).

CALORIES 277 (27% from fat); FAT 8.4g (sat 1.1g, mono 3.5g, poly 2.1g); PROTEIN 37.4g; CARB 13g; FIBER 2.1g; CHOL 259mg; IRON 5.2mg; SODIUM 684mg; CALC 119mg

In-season tomatoes enliven everything from simple sauces to inventive desserts.

MAKE AHEAD
Tomato-Spice
Upside-Down Cake

3 tablespoons brown sugar
2 tablespoons butter
2 teaspoons grated peeled fresh ginger
Cooking spray
1 green tomato, seeded and thinly sliced
1½ cups all-purpose flour
2 teaspoons baking powder
1 teaspoon ground ginger
¼ teaspoon ground cloves
¼ teaspoon ground cinnamon
¼ teaspoon ground mace
⅛ teaspoon salt
¾ cup granulated sugar
5 tablespoons butter, softened
½ cup molasses
2 large egg yolks
1 teaspoon vanilla extract
½ cup fat-free milk
2 large egg whites
1 tablespoon powdered sugar

1. Place first 3 ingredients in a 9-inch round cake pan coated with cooking spray. Place pan over medium-low heat until sugar and butter melt; stir frequently. Arrange tomato slices in a single layer over sugar mixture. Set aside. Preheat oven to 350°.
2. Lightly spoon flour into dry measuring cups; level with a knife. Combine flour, baking powder, and next 5 ingredients; stir with a whisk. Place granulated sugar and 5 tablespoons butter in a bowl; beat with a mixer at medium speed until blended. Add molasses and egg yolks, 1 at a time; beat well after each addition. Beat in vanilla. Add flour mixture and milk alternately to sugar mixture, beginning and ending with flour mixture.
3. Beat egg whites at high speed until stiff peaks form. Fold egg whites into batter; pour into prepared pan. Bake at 350° for 45 minutes or until a wooden pick inserted in center comes out clean. Cool in pan 15 minutes. Place a plate upside down on top of cake; invert onto plate. Cool completely. Sprinkle with powdered sugar. Yield: 12 servings (serving size: 1 wedge).

CALORIES 233 (29% from fat); FAT 7.5g (sat 4.4g, mono 2.2g, poly 0.4g); PROTEIN 3.1g; CARB 39.4g; FIBER 0.5g; CHOL 53mg; IRON 2mg; SODIUM 184mg; CALC 102mg

reader recipes

Sharing the Salsa

An Oregon couple complements their favorite grilled fish with bounty from their garden.

When Tammy and Greg Larsen spot fresh halibut in the supermarket, they nab it. It's their favorite fish and the main ingredient of their favorite recipe, Grilled Halibut and Fresh Mango Salsa.

The Larsens, who are in their early 30s, enjoy an active lifestyle that includes gardening. They hate to see the produce go to waste, so they've experimented with many fresh salsas.

"We worked to create a lively one that would complement the mild flavor of halibut," Tammy says. "After several trials, we came up with this version." Any leftover salsa works wonderfully straight up as an appetizer with chips. And for a complementary wine, she suggests a Washington Fumé Blanc or Oregon Pinot Gris.

QUICK & EASY
Grilled Halibut and Fresh Mango Salsa

2 cups chopped seeded plum tomato
1½ cups diced peeled ripe mango
½ cup chopped onion
½ cup chopped fresh cilantro
2 tablespoons fresh lime juice
1 tablespoon cider vinegar
1 teaspoon sugar
1 teaspoon salt, divided
1 teaspoon black pepper, divided
2 garlic cloves, minced
4 (6-ounce) halibut fillets
1 tablespoon olive oil

1. Prepare grill.
2. Combine first 7 ingredients. Stir in ½ teaspoon salt, ½ teaspoon pepper, and garlic.
3. Rub halibut with oil; sprinkle with ½ teaspoon salt and ½ teaspoon pepper. Place fish on grill rack; grill 3 minutes on

each side or until fish flakes easily when tested with a fork. Serve with mango salsa. Yield: 4 servings (serving size: 1 fillet and ¾ cup salsa).

CALORIES 295 (24% from fat); FAT 7.8g (sat 1.1g, mono 3.9g, poly 1.7g); PROTEIN 37g; CARB 19.5g; FIBER 2.8g; CHOL 54mg; IRON 2.3mg; SODIUM 687mg; CALC 105mg

Swordfish Mexicana

—Sheila Ealden, Sarasota, Florida

SALSA:

1 cup chopped tomato
¼ cup chopped tomatillos
2 tablespoons diced peeled avocado
2 tablespoons chopped fresh cilantro
1½ tablespoons chopped seeded jalapeño pepper
1½ tablespoons fresh lime juice
⅛ teaspoon salt
⅛ teaspoon black pepper
1 garlic clove, minced

FISH:

1 garlic clove, halved
2 (6-ounce) swordfish steaks (about 1 inch thick)
1½ tablespoons fresh lime juice
⅛ teaspoon salt
⅛ teaspoon ground cumin
⅛ teaspoon black pepper
Cooking spray

RICE:

½ teaspoon olive oil
½ cup chopped onion
½ cup uncooked jasmine rice
1 cup fat-free, less-sodium chicken broth
1 teaspoon tomato paste

1. To prepare salsa, combine first 9 ingredients.
2. To prepare fish, rub cut sides of garlic over fish; place fish in a small zip-top plastic bag. Add 1½ tablespoons lime juice to bag; seal. Marinate in refrigerator 30 minutes, turning once.

3. Preheat broiler.

4. To prepare rice, heat oil in a medium saucepan over medium-high heat. Add onion; sauté until tender. Add rice. Cook 2 minutes; stir frequently. Add broth and tomato paste, stirring to dissolve tomato paste; bring to a boil. Cover, reduce heat, and simmer 20 minutes or until liquid is absorbed.

5. Remove fish from marinade, discarding marinade. Sprinkle fish with ⅛ teaspoon salt, cumin, and ⅛ teaspoon black pepper; place fish on a broiler pan coated with cooking spray. Broil 5 minutes on each side or until fish flakes easily when tested with a fork. Yield: 2 servings (serving size: 1 steak, ¾ cup rice, and ⅔ cup salsa).

CALORIES 467 (19% from fat); FAT 10g (sat 2.3g, mono 4.5g, poly 2.1g); PROTEIN 40.3g; CARB 52g; FIBER 4.1g; CHOL 66mg; IRON 2.7mg; SODIUM 684mg; CALC 34mg

QUICK & EASY
Mexican Black Bean and Spinach Pizza

"This recipe is great right out of the oven and even better reheated the next day for lunch."
—Christina Wilson, Lansdowne, Pennsylvania

- 1 (10-ounce) Italian cheese-flavored thin pizza crust (such as Boboli)
- 1 (15-ounce) can black beans, rinsed and drained
- ⅔ cup chopped onion
- 1 teaspoon ground cumin
- 1 teaspoon chili powder
- 1 garlic clove, minced
- ½ cup bottled salsa
- ½ (10-ounce) package frozen chopped spinach, thawed, drained, and squeezed dry
- 2 tablespoons chopped fresh cilantro
- ½ teaspoon hot sauce
- ½ cup (2 ounces) shredded reduced-fat sharp Cheddar cheese
- ½ cup (2 ounces) shredded Monterey Jack cheese

1. Preheat oven to 375°.
2. Place pizza crust on a baking sheet; bake at 375° for 5 minutes or until crisp.
3. Mash beans with a fork; combine beans and next 4 ingredients in a medium bowl, stirring to combine. Spread bean mixture over crust, leaving a 1-inch border. Spoon salsa evenly over bean mixture; top with spinach and cilantro. Drizzle with hot sauce; sprinkle with cheeses. Bake at 375° for 15 minutes or until crust is lightly browned. Yield: 4 servings (serving size: 2 slices).

CALORIES 408 (27% from fat); FAT 12.3g (sat 4.8g, mono 1.3g, poly 1.1g); PROTEIN 22.2g; CARB 51g; FIBER 8.3g; CHOL 23mg; IRON 5.5mg; SODIUM 979mg; CALC 488mg

MAKE AHEAD
Turkey Lasagna

"I began using turkey in lasagna after my husband and I developed health problems."
—Tammie Sanderfer, Chattanooga, Tennessee

- 2 tablespoons vegetable oil
- 1¼ cups chopped onion
- ¾ cup chopped green bell pepper
- 1 (8-ounce) package presliced mushrooms
- 1 garlic clove, minced
- 1 (10-ounce) package thinly sliced deli turkey breast, chopped
- 1 teaspoon dried Italian seasoning
- 1 (26-ounce) bottle tomato-basil pasta sauce (such as Bertoli)
- ¼ cup (1 ounce) grated fresh Parmesan cheese
- ½ teaspoon salt
- ¼ teaspoon black pepper
- 2 large eggs, lightly beaten
- 1 (16-ounce) carton fat-free cottage cheese
- Cooking spray
- 8 cooked lasagna noodles
- 1 cup (4 ounces) shredded part-skim mozzarella cheese

1. Preheat oven to 350°.
2. Heat oil in a large skillet over medium-high heat; add onion, bell pepper, mushrooms, and garlic. Sauté 5 minutes or until tender. Add turkey; cook 10 minutes, stirring frequently. Stir in seasoning and sauce. Reduce heat to medium; simmer 10 minutes, stirring occasionally.
3. Combine Parmesan, salt, black pepper, eggs, and cottage cheese.
4. Spread 1 cup turkey mixture in bottom of a 13 x 9-inch baking dish coated with cooking spray. Arrange 4 noodles over turkey mixture; top with half of Parmesan mixture and 2 cups turkey mixture. Repeat layers, ending with turkey mixture. Sprinkle with mozzarella. Bake at 350° for 45 minutes. Let stand 15 minutes. Yield: 9 servings.

CALORIES 283 (28% from fat); FAT 8.7g (sat 2.8g, mono 2.2g, poly 0.9g); PROTEIN 21.2g; CARB 28.5g; FIBER 6.9g; CHOL 73mg; IRON 1.4mg; SODIUM 838mg; CALC 164mg

season's best
Fresh-Squeezed Lemonade

When it comes to extinguishing summer thirst, syrupy soft drinks are no match for fresh-squeezed lemonade.

For sheer refreshment, you need nothing more than lemons, sugar, water, and a juicer. If it suits your fancy, add a twist of color to the lemonade with a swirl of apricot nectar or puréed sweetened strawberries. And you can spike it for a refreshing cocktail well-suited to sultry nights.

MAKE AHEAD
Fresh-Squeezed Lemonade
(pictured on page 233)

To get the most juice out of your lemons, bring the lemons to room temperature before juicing.

- 3 cups fresh lemon juice (about 20 lemons)
- 2¼ cups sugar
- 12 cups chilled water
- Lemon slices (optional)

1. Combine juice and sugar in a one-gallon container; stir until sugar dissolves. Stir in water. Serve over ice. Garnish with lemon slices, if desired. Yield: 16 servings (serving size: 1 cup).

CALORIES 120 (0% from fat); FAT 0g; PROTEIN 0.2g; CARB 32.1g; FIBER 0.2g; CHOL 0mg; IRON 0.1mg; SODIUM 6mg; CALC 7mg

Scallops with Roasted Pepper-Butter Sauce

One elementary change gives these seafood kabobs new life.

We prepared the recipe as originally directed, but with 14 tablespoons less butter.

BEFORE	AFTER
SERVING SIZE	
5 scallops and ¼ cup sauce	
CALORIES PER SERVING	
443	208
FAT	
36g	5.2g
PERCENT OF TOTAL CALORIES	
73%	23%

Scallops with Roasted Pepper-Butter Sauce

To double-skewer the scallops, just thread the scallops onto a skewer, then run another skewer through the scallops parallel to the first.

30 sea scallops (about 2¼ pounds)
 4 red bell peppers (about 2 pounds)
 2 cups fat-free, less-sodium chicken broth
 ½ cup dry white wine
1½ teaspoons chopped fresh or ½ teaspoon dried basil, crumbled
 2 tablespoons chilled butter, cut into small pieces
 ¼ teaspoon salt
Cooking spray
Basil sprigs (optional)

1. Thread 5 scallops onto each of 6 (12-inch) skewers. Cover and chill.
2. Preheat broiler.
3. Cut peppers in half lengthwise; discard seeds and membranes. Place pepper halves, skin sides up, on a foil-lined baking sheet; flatten with hand. Broil 15 minutes or until blackened. Place in a zip-top plastic bag. Seal and let stand 10 minutes. Peel peppers; discard skins. Place peppers, broth, and wine in a blender; process until smooth. Combine pepper mixture and chopped basil in a skillet. Bring to a boil; cook until reduced to 1½ cups (about 5 minutes). Reduce heat to medium-low; gradually add butter, stirring until melted. Cover and keep warm.
4. Prepare grill.
5. Sprinkle kabobs with salt; place on grill rack coated with cooking spray. Grill 2½ minutes on each side or until done. Serve with bell pepper sauce. Garnish with fresh basil, if desired. Yield: 6 servings (serving size: 5 scallops and ¼ cup sauce).

CALORIES 208 (23% from fat); FAT 5.2g (sat 2.5g, mono 1.2g, poly 0.7g); PROTEIN 29.8g; CARB 9.4g; FIBER 1.6g; CHOL 67mg; IRON 0.9mg; SODIUM 970mg; CALC 52mg

dinner tonight

Salad Stars

Let a fresh, flavorful, and satisfying salad be the star of your meal.

Salad Menu 1
serves 4
Mediterranean Potato Salad with Shrimp and Feta

Garlic toast*

Orange slices

*Rub 4 (1-ounce) French bread slices with cut sides of a halved garlic clove; brush with 1 teaspoon olive oil. Broil 1 minute or until golden.

Game Plan

1. Prepare dressing
2. Cook potatoes
3. While potatoes cook:
 • Prepare garlic toast
4. Toss salad

Mediterranean Potato Salad with Shrimp and Feta
(pictured on page 234)

"Baking" the potatoes in the microwave cuts the cook time in half.

TOTAL TIME: 38 MINUTES

QUICK TIP: You can buy precooked shrimp at the fish counter in large supermarkets.

DRESSING:

1½ tablespoons chopped fresh basil
 1 tablespoon fresh lemon juice
 2 teaspoons extravirgin olive oil
 ¾ teaspoon sugar
 ¼ teaspoon freshly ground black pepper
 ¼ teaspoon Dijon mustard

SALAD:

 5 cups small red potatoes, quartered (about 1½ pounds)
 ½ teaspoon salt
 ¼ teaspoon freshly ground black pepper
 1 pound medium shrimp, cooked and peeled
 3 cups thinly sliced romaine lettuce
 1 cup (¼-inch) strips red bell pepper
 1 cup (¼-inch) strips yellow bell pepper
 1 cup thinly sliced red onion
 ½ cup (2 ounces) crumbled feta cheese
 2 tablespoons chopped pitted kalamata olives

1. To prepare dressing, combine first 6 ingredients, stirring well with a whisk.
2. To prepare salad, arrange potatoes in a single layer on a microwave-safe dish; sprinkle with ½ teaspoon salt and ¼ teaspoon pepper. Microwave at HIGH 15 minutes or until potatoes are tender. Place potatoes in a large bowl.
3. Add shrimp and 1 tablespoon dressing to potatoes; toss gently to combine. Add remaining dressing, lettuce, bell peppers, onion, and cheese; toss gently to coat. Top each serving with 1½ teaspoons olives. Yield: 4 servings (serving size: 2½ cups).

CALORIES 362 (23% from fat); FAT 9.4g (sat 3.1g, mono 3.8g, poly 1.4g); PROTEIN 30.3g; CARB 39.4g; FIBER 5.5g; CHOL 185mg; IRON 5.1mg; SODIUM 740mg; CALC 183mg

Salad Menu 2

serves 4

Grilled Steak Salad with Caper Vinaigrette

Mozzarella and basil toast*

Fresh fruit

*Place 2 (4-inch) Italian cheese-flavored pizza crusts (such as Boboli) on a baking sheet; top each with ¼ cup shredded part-skim mozzarella cheese and ¼ cup chopped fresh basil. Bake at 425° for 8 minutes or until cheese melts. Cut each crust into quarters.

Game Plan

1. While grill heats:
   - Cook green beans
   - Prepare dressing
2. While beef cooks:
   - Prepare toast
3. Combine salad ingredients, and toss

QUICK & EASY

Grilled Steak Salad with Caper Vinaigrette

This salad is great with leftover beef. If you don't like the peppery bite of watercress or just can't find it, use mixed salad greens. Substitute artichoke hearts for the hearts of palm, or just leave them out.

TOTAL TIME: 40 MINUTES

QUICK TIP: Sliced roast beef from the deli counter can cut your prep time in half.

SALAD:

- 1 pound beef tenderloin, trimmed
- Cooking spray
- 4 cups water
- 3 cups (1-inch) cut green beans (about ½ pound)
- 4 cups trimmed watercress (about 1 bunch)
- 1 cup grape tomatoes, halved
- ¾ cup thinly sliced red onion
- 1 (8-ounce) package presliced mushrooms
- 1 (7.75-ounce) can hearts of palm, rinsed and drained

DRESSING:

- ¼ cup red wine vinegar
- 1½ tablespoons fresh lemon juice
- 1 tablespoon capers
- 1 tablespoon honey mustard
- 2 teaspoons extravirgin olive oil
- ½ teaspoon sugar
- ½ teaspoon salt
- ⅛ teaspoon freshly ground black pepper

1. Prepare grill.
2. To prepare salad, place beef on grill rack coated with cooking spray, and grill 7 minutes on each side or until desired degree of doneness. Let stand 10 minutes. Cut beef diagonally across the grain into thin slices. Place in a large bowl.
3. Bring water to a boil in a saucepan; add beans. Cover; cook 3 minutes or until crisp-tender. Rinse with cold water; drain well. Add beans, watercress, and next 4 ingredients to beef; toss gently to combine.
4. To prepare dressing, combine vinegar and remaining 7 ingredients; stir well with a whisk. Drizzle over salad; toss gently to coat. Yield: 4 servings (serving size: 2 cups).

CALORIES 224 (29% from fat); FAT 7.3g (sat 2g, mono 3.3g, poly 0.5g); PROTEIN 27.3g; CARB 16.8g; FIBER 5.2g; CHOL 60mg; IRON 5.7mg; SODIUM 699mg; CALC 114mg

Salad Menu 3

serves 4

Grilled Jamaican Pork Tenderloin Salad

Roasted sweet potato wedges*

Hummus with sesame breadsticks

*Combine 2 pounds sweet potato wedges, 2 tablespoons vegetable oil, ½ teaspoon salt, and ⅛ teaspoon ground red pepper; toss to coat. Arrange wedges on a baking sheet; bake at 425° for 25 minutes or until tender, turning occasionally.

Game Plan

1. While grill heats for pork and oven preheats for potatoes:
   - Prepare dressing
   - Prepare pork
   - Prepare sweet potatoes
2. While pork and potatoes cook:
   - Prepare salad

QUICK & EASY

Grilled Jamaican Pork Tenderloin Salad

If you can't find papaya, use an extra cup of chopped pineapple.

TOTAL TIME: 34 MINUTES

QUICK TIP: Look for cored fresh pineapple in the produce section at the grocery store. You also can buy bottled sliced papaya.

DRESSING:

- 2 tablespoons fresh or 2 teaspoons dried thyme leaves
- 2 tablespoons fresh lime juice
- 1 tablespoon olive oil
- 1 tablespoon minced peeled fresh ginger
- 2 teaspoons brown sugar
- ½ teaspoon salt
- ½ teaspoon ground allspice
- ½ teaspoon ground cinnamon
- ¼ teaspoon freshly ground black pepper
- ¼ teaspoon ground nutmeg
- 1 garlic clove, minced

SALAD:

- 1 (1-pound) pork tenderloin, trimmed
- Cooking spray
- 4 cups salad greens
- 2 cups chopped peeled fresh pineapple
- 1 cup chopped papaya

1. Prepare grill.
2. To prepare dressing, combine first 11 ingredients in a food processor; process until smooth.
3. To prepare pork, slice pork lengthwise, cutting to, but not through, other side. Open halves, laying pork flat. Rub 2 tablespoons dressing on both sides of pork; reserve remaining dressing. Place pork on grill rack coated with cooking spray; cook 10 minutes on each side or until a meat thermometer registers 155°. Let stand 5 minutes. Cut pork into ¼-inch-thick slices; toss with reserved dressing. Place 1 cup greens on each of 4 plates; top with 3 ounces pork, ½ cup pineapple, and ¼ cup papaya. Yield: 4 servings.

CALORIES 263 (30% from fat); FAT 8.7g (sat 2.3g, mono 4.8g, poly 0.9g); PROTEIN 28.4g; CARB 18.3g; FIBER 3.2g; CHOL 69mg; IRON 2.7mg; SODIUM 371mg; CALC 78mg

Cookies and Cream

Grown-ups and children alike will love these cool ice-cream sandwiches.

Gingerbread Ice-Cream Sandwiches

A stand mixer works best for the thick, sticky cookie dough. Save the recipe for these cookies, and make them again for the holidays.

MAKE AHEAD • FREEZABLE

Peppermint Patties

(pictured on page 234)

The peppermint candies should be coarsely crushed in a large zip-top plastic bag by lightly tapping them with a rolling pin or heavy skillet (a food processor would just pulverize them). You can substitute regular unsweetened cocoa powder in the cookies.

COOKIES:

1½ cups all-purpose flour
⅓ cup Dutch process cocoa
½ teaspoon baking soda
¼ teaspoon salt
½ cup granulated sugar
½ cup packed brown sugar
½ cup butter, softened
1 teaspoon vanilla extract
1 large egg
Cooking spray

FILLING:

30 hard peppermint candies, crushed
(about 1 cup)
3 cups vanilla low-fat ice cream, softened

1. To prepare cookies, lightly spoon flour into dry measuring cups; level with a knife. Combine flour, cocoa, baking soda, and salt, stirring with a whisk. Combine sugars and butter in a large bowl, and beat with a mixer at medium speed until well blended. Add vanilla and egg, and beat well. Add flour mixture to sugar mixture, and beat at low speed until well blended.
2. Lightly coat hands with cooking spray. Divide dough in half. Shape each half into a 6-inch log. Wrap logs individually in plastic wrap; freeze 1 hour or until firm.
3. Preheat oven to 350°.
4. Cut each dough log into 24 (¼-inch) slices; place cookies 1 inch apart on baking sheets coated with cooking spray. Bake at 350° for 11 minutes or until set. Cool completely on wire racks.
5. To prepare filling, place crushed candies in a shallow bowl. Spread 2 tablespoons ice cream onto flat side of each of 24 cookies. Top with remaining cookies, flat sides down, pressing gently. Lightly roll sides of each sandwich in candy. Wrap each sandwich tightly in plastic wrap; freeze 4 hours or until firm. Yield: 12 servings (serving size: 2 sandwiches).

CALORIES 321 (30% from fat); FAT 10.6g (sat 6.2g, mono 2.4g, poly 0.4g); PROTEIN 4.3g; CARB 51.6g; FIBER 1.1g; CHOL 56mg; IRON 1.3mg; SODIUM 216mg; CALC 69mg

---

Ice-Cream Sandwiches Made Easy

• Chilling or freezing cookie dough (or batter) may seem time-consuming, but don't skip this step. It makes the sticky dough easier to handle and helps the cookies hold their shape as they bake.
• To soften ice cream, let it stand at room temperature for about 30 minutes. Use a large bowl and a wooden spoon to stir ingredients into store-bought ice cream, or a stand mixer does the trick quickly.
• Some sorbets are smooth and creamy enough to spread straight from the freezer. If yours isn't soft enough to spread, let it stand at room temperature for 20 minutes.
• These ice-cream sandwiches taste great and can be made ahead. With the exception of the Banana Split Ice-Cream Sandwiches (recipe on page 229), you make the recipe, wrap the sandwiches tightly in plastic wrap, and store them in your freezer until you're ready to eat them.

COOKIES:

1¾ cups all-purpose flour
1 teaspoon baking soda
1½ teaspoons ground ginger
⅛ teaspoon baking powder
Dash of salt
½ cup granulated sugar
½ cup packed dark brown sugar
¼ cup butter, softened
½ teaspoon vanilla extract
1 large egg
Cooking spray
1 teaspoon granulated sugar, divided

FILLING:

1 quart vanilla low-fat ice cream, softened
½ cup finely chopped crystallized ginger

1. To prepare cookies, lightly spoon flour into dry measuring cups; level with a knife. Combine flour, baking soda, ground ginger, baking powder, and salt, stirring with a whisk. Place ½ cup granulated sugar, brown sugar, and butter in a large bowl; beat with a mixer at medium speed 3 minutes or until mixture resembles coarse meal. Add vanilla and egg; beat well. Add flour mixture to sugar mixture; beat at low speed until well blended. Divide dough in half; gently press each portion into a 4-inch circle on plastic wrap. Cover and chill 1½ hours.
2. Unwrap each dough portion, and place on 2 sheets of overlapping plastic wrap. Cover each portion with 2 additional sheets of overlapping plastic wrap. Roll, still covered, to a ¼-inch thickness. Place dough in freezer 30 minutes or until plastic wrap can be easily removed.
3. Preheat oven to 350°.
4. Remove plastic wrap from one dough portion; cut dough with a 3-inch gingerbread man cookie cutter to form 12 cookies. Place cookies 1 inch apart on

baking sheets coated with cooking spray. Sprinkle cookies evenly with ½ teaspoon granulated sugar. Bake at 350° for 12 minutes or until set. Remove cookies from baking sheets; cool completely on wire racks. Repeat procedure with remaining dough and ½ teaspoon granulated sugar.

5. To prepare filling, combine ice cream and crystallized ginger, stirring well. Spread 1½ tablespoons ice cream on flat side of each of 12 cookies; top with remaining cookies, flat sides down, pressing gently. Wrap each sandwich tightly in plastic wrap; freeze 4 hours or until firm. Yield: 12 servings (serving size: 1 sandwich).

CALORIES 272 (19% from fat); FAT 5.7g (sat 3.2g, mono 1.3g, poly 0.3g); PROTEIN 4.5g; CARB 50.5g; FIBER 1.2g; CHOL 31mg; IRON 1.4mg; SODIUM 190mg; CALC 93mg

Banana Split Ice-Cream Sandwiches

The vanilla cookies are very thin and are made from a batter that requires chilling before shaping. They'll be soft when warm but light and crisp after they cool. Gooey toppings make this a good knife-and-fork sandwich. Assemble just before serving.

COOKIES:
- 7 tablespoons powdered sugar
- 6 tablespoons sifted all-purpose flour
- ¼ teaspoon vanilla extract
- 1 large egg

FILLING:
- 2 cups vanilla low-fat ice cream, softened
- ¾ cup ripe mashed banana (about 1½ bananas)
- ¼ cup coarsely chopped dry-roasted peanuts

REMAINING INGREDIENTS:
- 6 tablespoons frozen fat-free whipped topping, thawed
- 6 tablespoons chocolate syrup
- 2 tablespoons coarsely chopped dry-roasted peanuts
- 6 maraschino cherries, drained

1. To prepare cookies, combine sugar and flour, stirring with a whisk. Add vanilla and egg, and beat with a mixer at medium speed 2 minutes. Cover and refrigerate 2 hours.

2. Preheat oven to 350°.

3. Cover a large baking sheet with parchment paper. Draw 6 (3-inch) circles on paper. Turn paper over, and secure with masking tape. Spoon about 1 tablespoon batter into center of each drawn circle; spread batter to edge of each circle. Bake at 350° for 6 minutes or until edges begin to brown. Carefully remove cookies from paper, and cool completely on wire racks. Repeat procedure with remaining batter, reusing parchment paper.

4. To prepare filling, combine ice cream, banana, and ¼ cup peanuts, stirring well.

5. Place 1 cookie, flat side up, on each of 6 plates. Carefully spread about ⅓ cup ice cream mixture over each cookie. Top with remaining cookies, flat sides down, pressing gently. Top each sandwich with 1 tablespoon whipped topping, 1 tablespoon chocolate syrup, 1 teaspoon peanuts, and 1 cherry. Serve immediately. Yield: 6 servings (serving size: 1 sandwich).

CALORIES 310 (20% from fat); FAT 7g (sat 1.6g, mono 2.3g, poly 1.6g); PROTEIN 6.9g; CARB 55.9g; FIBER 2.3g; CHOL 39mg; IRON 0.8mg; SODIUM 54mg; CALC 79mg

Coconut Cream Pies

We enjoyed the texture of crunchy oatmeal cookies for this sandwich, but soft oatmeal cookies also will work. If you like coconut, the simple ice cream tastes great on its own, and the recipe doubles easily.

FILLING:
- 1½ cups whole milk
- 1 cup sugar
- 1 tablespoon honey
- ⅛ teaspoon salt
- 1 (14-ounce) can light coconut milk

REMAINING INGREDIENT:
- 32 oatmeal cookies (such as Nabisco Family Favorites)

1. To prepare filling, combine first 5 ingredients in a blender; process until smooth. Pour mixture into freezer can of an ice-cream freezer; freeze according to manufacturer's instructions.

2. Spread about 3 tablespoons filling on flat side of each of 16 cookies; top with remaining cookies, flat sides down, pressing gently. Wrap each sandwich tightly in plastic wrap; freeze 4 hours or until firm. Yield: 16 servings (serving size: 1 sandwich).

CALORIES 242 (30% from fat); FAT 8.1g (sat 2.4g, mono 2.3g, poly 3.1g); PROTEIN 2.8g; CARB 39.6g; FIBER 0g; CHOL 3mg; IRON 0.9mg; SODIUM 170mg; CALC 24mg

Raspberry Sorbet and Meringue Sandwiches

Crisp meringues encase fruity sorbet (any flavor will work). A stint in the freezer hardens the sorbet, ensuring a clean cut.

MERINGUES:
- 1 cup sugar
- 2 teaspoons cornstarch
- ¼ teaspoon salt
- ½ teaspoon cream of tartar
- 5 large egg whites
- 2 teaspoons white vinegar
- ½ teaspoon vanilla extract

FILLING:
- 1 quart raspberry sorbet, softened

1. Preheat oven to 250°.

2. To prepare meringues, cover a large baking sheet with parchment paper. Draw 2 (8 x 12-inch) rectangles on paper. Turn paper over, and secure with masking tape.

3. Combine first 3 ingredients, stirring with a whisk. Place cream of tartar and egg whites in a large bowl, and beat with a mixer at high speed until foamy. Gradually add sugar mixture, 1 tablespoon at a time, beating until stiff peaks form (do not underbeat). Add vinegar and vanilla, and beat until combined. Divide egg white mixture evenly between drawn rectangles; spread to edges of rectangles.

Continued

4. Bake at 250° for 2 hours or until dry. Turn oven off; partially open oven door. Cool meringues in oven 1 hour. Remove from oven. Carefully remove meringues from paper.

5. To prepare sandwiches, spread sorbet over flat side of 1 meringue; top with remaining meringue, flat side down, pressing gently. Wrap sandwich tightly in plastic wrap; freeze 4 hours or until firm. Unwrap and cut sandwich in half lengthwise. Cut each half crosswise into 6 (2 x 4-inch) pieces. Cut each piece in half diagonally to form 24 triangles. Yield: 12 servings (serving size: 2 triangles).

CALORIES 143 (0% from fat); FAT 0g; PROTEIN 1.5g; CARB 34.6g; FIBER 1.3g; CHOL 0mg; IRON 0mg; SODIUM 73mg; CALC 1mg

Pumpkin and Maple Ice-Cream Sandwiches

COOKIES:
2½   cups all-purpose flour
  1   teaspoon baking soda
  ½   teaspoon salt
  ½   teaspoon pumpkin pie spice
  ¾   cup granulated sugar
  ½   cup butter, softened
  ⅓   cup packed brown sugar
  1   cup canned pumpkin purée
  ¼   cup egg substitute
  1   teaspoon vanilla extract
Cooking spray

FILLING:
  1   quart fat-free vanilla ice cream
  ⅓   cup maple syrup

1. Preheat oven to 350°.
2. To prepare cookies, lightly spoon flour into dry measuring cups; level with a knife. Combine flour, baking soda, salt, and pie spice, stirring with a whisk. Place granulated sugar, butter, and brown sugar in a large bowl; beat with a mixer at medium speed until well blended. Add pumpkin, egg substitute, and vanilla; beat well. Gradually add flour mixture to sugar mixture, stirring just until moist.
3. Drop dough by level tablespoons 2 inches apart onto baking sheets coated with cooking spray. With moist hands, flatten cookies into 3-inch circles. Bake

at 350° for 15 minutes or until set. Remove cookies from baking sheets; cool completely on wire racks.
4. To prepare filling, combine ice cream and syrup; cover and freeze 30 minutes or until firm. Spread about ¼ cup ice cream onto flat side of each of 15 cookies. Top with remaining cookies, flat sides down, pressing gently. Wrap each sandwich tightly in plastic wrap; freeze 4 hours or until firm. Yield: 15 servings (serving size: 1 sandwich).

CALORIES 263 (22% from fat); FAT 6.5g (sat 3.9g, mono 1.8g, poly 0.4g); PROTEIN 4.5g; CARB 46.9g; FIBER 1.6g; CHOL 16mg; IRON 1.5mg; SODIUM 213mg; CALC 90mg

S'mores Sandwiches

Make the sandwiches when the ice cream is still soft, just after coming out of the ice-cream freezer. You can eat them right after they're made, or wrap the sandwiches in plastic wrap, freeze them, and enjoy them later.

  1   cup marshmallow creme
 16   sheets honey graham crackers, halved crosswise
  2   cups Chocolate Fudge Ice Cream

1. Spread 1 tablespoon marshmallow creme on flat side of each of 16 cracker halves; spread 2 tablespoons Chocolate Fudge Ice Cream over each. Top with remaining cracker halves, flat sides down, pressing gently. Wrap each sandwich tightly in plastic wrap; freeze 4 hours or until firm. Yield: 8 servings (serving size: 2 sandwiches).

(Totals include Chocolate Fudge Ice Cream) CALORIES 264 (17% from fat); FAT 5g (sat 2g, mono 2g, poly 0.6g); PROTEIN 7.1g; CARB 47.5g; FIBER 1.6g; CHOL 9mg; IRON 1.4mg; SODIUM 227mg; CALC 167mg

CHOCOLATE FUDGE ICE CREAM:
  2   cups whole milk, divided
  ½   cup Dutch process cocoa
  1   cup fat-free sweetened condensed milk
  2   teaspoons vanilla extract
  1   (12-ounce) can evaporated low-fat milk
Dash of salt

1. Heat 1 cup whole milk in a heavy saucepan over medium-high heat to 180° or until tiny bubbles form around edge (do not boil). Remove from heat, and add cocoa, stirring with a whisk until cocoa dissolves. Cool to room temperature.
2. Combine 1 cup whole milk, condensed milk, vanilla, evaporated milk, and salt in a blender, and process until smooth. Add cocoa mixture; blend well. Pour mixture into freezer can of an ice-cream freezer; freeze according to manufacturer's instructions. Yield: 5 cups (serving size: ½ cup).

CALORIES 162 (14% from fat); FAT 2.6g (sat 1.8g, mono 0.6g, poly 0.2g); PROTEIN 7.6g; CARB 26.7g; FIBER 1.1g; CHOL 14mg; IRON 0.6mg; SODIUM 110mg; CALC 231mg

great starts
Power Up

Busy day ahead? Jump-start it with a quick, nutrition-packed breakfast.

Chocolate-Peanut Butter Smoothie

Protein and monounsaturated fat from the peanut butter, potassium from the banana, and protein and calcium from the yogurt will get your day off to a great start. Peel and slice bananas to freeze individually in zip-top bags for smoothies and shakes.

  ½   cup 1% low-fat milk
  2   tablespoons chocolate syrup
  2   tablespoons creamy peanut butter
  1   frozen sliced ripe banana
  1   (8-ounce) carton vanilla low-fat yogurt

1. Place all ingredients in a blender; process until smooth. Yield: 2 servings (serving size: about 1 cup).

CALORIES 332 (29% from fat); FAT 10.8g (sat 3.2g, mono 4.5g, poly 2.3g); PROTEIN 12.7g; CARB 49.8g; FIBER 3.1g; CHOL 8mg; IRON 1mg; SODIUM 194mg; CALC 282mg

Blueberry Power Muffins with Almond Streusel

We call these "power" muffins because they're loaded with B vitamins from whole wheat flour, calcium from milk and yogurt, antioxidants from blueberries, and heart-friendly monounsaturated fat from almonds and canola oil. You can freeze the muffins up to 1 month, then thaw them at room temperature, or microwave each muffin at HIGH 15 to 20 seconds.

MUFFINS:
- 1½ cups all-purpose flour
- 1 cup whole wheat flour
- 1 cup quick-cooking oats
- 1 cup granulated sugar
- 1 tablespoon baking powder
- 1 teaspoon baking soda
- ¼ teaspoon salt
- 2 cups vanilla low-fat yogurt
- ½ cup 2% reduced-fat milk
- 3 tablespoons canola oil
- 2 teaspoons vanilla extract
- 1 large egg, lightly beaten
- 1½ cups fresh blueberries
- Cooking spray

STREUSEL:
- ¼ cup all-purpose flour
- ¼ cup slivered almonds, chopped
- 1 tablespoon brown sugar
- 1 tablespoon butter, melted

1. Preheat oven to 400°.

2. To prepare muffins, lightly spoon flours into dry measuring cups; level with a knife. Combine 1½ cups all-purpose flour, whole wheat flour, and next 5 ingredients in a large bowl, stirring with a whisk. Make a well in center of mixture. Combine yogurt, milk, oil, vanilla, and egg, stirring with a whisk. Add yogurt mixture to flour mixture, and stir just until moist. Fold in blueberries. Spoon 2 rounded tablespoons batter into each of 30 muffin cups coated with cooking spray.

3. To prepare streusel, combine ¼ cup all-purpose flour, almonds, brown sugar, and butter. Sprinkle evenly over batter. Bake at 400° for 15 minutes or until muffins spring back when touched lightly

in center. Cool in pans 10 minutes on a wire rack; remove from pans. Serve warm or at room temperature. Yield: 15 servings (serving size: 2 muffins).

CALORIES 244 (23% from fat); FAT 6.1g (sat 1.3g, mono 2.9g, poly 1.4g); PROTEIN 6.1g; CARB 42.3g; FIBER 2.5g; CHOL 18mg; IRON 1.5mg; SODIUM 260mg; CALC 136mg

Peaches and Yogurt with Sugared Almonds

This dish boasts potassium and vitamin C from the peaches. Be sure to measure the egg white; when we tested the dish with 1 whole egg white, the recipe didn't work.

TOPPING:
- ½ cup sliced almonds
- ½ cup sugar
- 2 tablespoons lightly beaten egg white
- Cooking spray

PEACHES:
- ¼ cup sugar
- ¼ cup water
- 1 teaspoon grated lemon rind
- ½ teaspoon vanilla extract
- 4 cups sliced peeled peaches

REMAINING INGREDIENTS:
- 2 cups vanilla low-fat yogurt
- 2 tablespoons honey

1. Preheat oven to 400°.

2. To prepare topping, combine first 3 ingredients. Spread in an even layer on a jelly roll pan coated with cooking spray. Bake at 400° for 10 minutes or until lightly browned, stirring after 5 minutes. Remove from heat; cool.

3. To prepare peaches, combine ¼ cup sugar, water, and rind in a small saucepan over medium-high heat. Bring to a boil; cook 1 minute. Pour syrup into a large bowl; stir in vanilla. Add peaches, tossing to coat. Let stand 5 minutes; drain.

4. Combine yogurt and honey. Spoon ½ cup yogurt mixture into each of 4 shallow bowls. Top each serving with 1 cup peaches and about 3 tablespoons

topping, and serve immediately. Yield: 4 servings.

CALORIES 394 (18% from fat); FAT 7.7g (sat 1.5g, mono 4.2g, poly 1.6g); PROTEIN 10.5g; CARB 74.9g; FIBER 2.7g; CHOL 6mg; IRON 0.3mg; SODIUM 94mg; CALC 252mg

Honeyed Yogurt and Mixed Berries with Whole-Grain Waffles

As you enjoy this meal, you also enjoy antioxidants, fiber, and vitamin C from the berries; protein and calcium from the yogurt; and protein, fiber, and B vitamins from the waffles.

- 2 cups vanilla low-fat yogurt
- 2 tablespoons honey
- 2 cups fresh raspberries
- 1 cup quartered small strawberries
- 1 cup fresh blackberries
- ⅓ cup sugar
- 2 tablespoons fresh lemon juice
- 4 frozen whole-grain waffles, toasted
- 4 teaspoons toasted wheat germ

1. Drain yogurt in a fine sieve or colander lined with cheesecloth 10 minutes; spoon into a bowl. Add honey, stirring to combine.

2. Combine berries, sugar, and juice; let stand 5 minutes. Place 1 waffle on each of 4 plates; top each serving with 1 cup fruit mixture, about ⅓ cup yogurt mixture, and 1 teaspoon wheat germ. Serve immediately. Yield: 4 servings.

CALORIES 377 (16% from fat); FAT 6.8g (sat 2.3g, mono 2.3g, poly 1.6g); PROTEIN 11.5g; CARB 71.6g; FIBER 8.3g; CHOL 43mg; IRON 1.9mg; SODIUM 214mg; CALC 345mg

Ham and Cheese Breakfast Sandwiches with Mango Chutney

This sandwich packs protein from egg and soy ham, calcium from cheese, and fiber and B vitamins from the whole-grain muffin. If you can't find soy ham, use Canadian bacon or ham.

   Cooking spray
 8 (½-ounce) slices soy ham (such as Lightlife) or Canadian bacon
 4 large eggs
 4 whole-grain English muffins, split and toasted
 8 teaspoons mango chutney
 ¾ cup (3 ounces) shredded reduced-fat sharp Cheddar cheese

1. Preheat broiler.
2. Heat a large nonstick skillet coated with cooking spray over medium-high heat. Add ham; cook 2 minutes on each side or until lightly browned. Remove from pan; keep warm. Reduce heat to medium; recoat pan with cooking spray. Break eggs into hot pan; cook 1 minute on each side or until desired degree of doneness.
3. Place muffin halves, cut sides up, on a baking sheet. Spread 2 teaspoons chutney over bottom half of each muffin; top with 2 ham slices, 1 egg, and 1 tablespoon cheese. Sprinkle 2 tablespoons cheese over top half of each muffin. Broil 1½ minutes or until bubbly. Place top halves of muffins over bottom halves. Yield: 4 servings.

CALORIES 334 (30% from fat); FAT 11g (sat 4.8g, mono 3.7g, poly 1.5g); PROTEIN 24.8g; CARB 34.7g; FIBER 4.7g; CHOL 228mg; IRON 3.4mg; SODIUM 865mg; CALC 380mg

Carrot Quick Bread with Cream Cheese Frosting

This bread is rich in protein. Oats provide soluble fiber. Carrots contribute beta-carotene. Slice the entire loaf, wrap slices individually in foil, and freeze up to 1 month.

BREAD:
 ¾ cup all-purpose flour
 ½ cup whole wheat flour
 ½ cup soy flour
 ¾ cup quick-cooking oats
 2 teaspoons ground cinnamon
 1½ teaspoons baking powder
 ½ teaspoon baking soda
 ¼ teaspoon salt
 ¾ cup packed brown sugar
 2 tablespoons butter, softened
 ½ cup water
 1 large egg
 1 cup whole milk
 1 teaspoon vanilla extract
 1½ cups finely shredded carrot
 ½ cup golden raisins
   Cooking spray

FROSTING:
 1 cup (4 ounces) block-style cream cheese, softened
 ⅓ cup powdered sugar
 2 teaspoons fresh lemon juice

1. Preheat oven to 350°.
2. To prepare bread, lightly spoon flours into dry measuring cups; level with a knife. Combine flours, oats, cinnamon, baking powder, baking soda, and salt.
3. Place brown sugar and butter in a large bowl; beat with a mixer at medium speed until well blended. Add water and egg; beat well. Beat in milk and vanilla. Gradually add flour mixture, stirring just until blended. Fold in carrot and raisins. Spoon batter into a 9 x 5-inch loaf pan coated with cooking spray. Bake at 350° for 1 hour or until a wooden pick inserted in center comes out clean. Cool in pan 10 minutes on a wire rack; remove from pan. Cool completely on wire rack.
4. To prepare frosting, place cream cheese and powdered sugar in a bowl; beat with a mixer at medium speed until fluffy. Beat in lemon juice. Spread frosting over top of cooled bread. Yield: 8 servings (serving size: 1 slice).

CALORIES 393 (27% from fat); FAT 11.9g (sat 6.1g, mono 3.1g, poly 0.9g); PROTEIN 10.2g; CARB 63.9g; FIBER 5.1g; CHOL 54mg; IRON 3.1mg; SODIUM 338mg; CALC 153mg

Crustless Broccoli and Cheese Quiche

Serve this for Sunday brunch, and enjoy high-quality protein from the eggs and egg whites, calcium from the cheese and milk, and vitamin C and folate from the broccoli.

 2 teaspoons olive oil
 ½ cup vertically sliced onion
 1 garlic clove, minced
 5 cups broccoli florets
   Cooking spray
 1¼ cups 1% low-fat milk
 1 cup (4 ounces) shredded reduced-fat Swiss cheese
 2 tablespoons chopped fresh parsley
 2 teaspoons Dijon mustard
 ½ teaspoon salt
 ¼ teaspoon freshly ground black pepper
 ⅛ teaspoon ground nutmeg
 4 large egg whites, lightly beaten
 2 large eggs, lightly beaten
 1 tablespoon grated fresh Parmesan cheese
 6 (1-ounce) slices whole wheat bread, toasted

1. Preheat oven to 350°.
2. Heat oil in a large nonstick skillet over medium-high heat. Add onion and garlic; sauté 1½ minutes. Add broccoli; sauté 1 minute. Spread broccoli mixture in a 9-inch pie plate coated with cooking spray. Combine milk and next 8 ingredients in a large bowl. Pour milk mixture over broccoli mixture; sprinkle with Parmesan. Bake at 350° for 40 minutes or until top is golden and a knife inserted in center comes out clean; let stand 5 minutes. Serve with toast. Yield: 6 servings (serving size: 1 quiche wedge and 1 toast slice).

CALORIES 216 (29% from fat); FAT 6.9g (sat 2.3g, mono 2.9g, poly 0.9g); PROTEIN 17.9g; CARB 22.7g; FIBER 4.1g; CHOL 81mg; IRON 2.1mg; SODIUM 577mg; CALC 354mg

Fresh-Squeezed Lemonade,
page 225

Grilled Mahimahi with Peach and Pink Grapefruit Relish,
page 237

Peppermint Patties, page 228

Mediterranean Potato Salad with Shrimp
and Feta, page 226

Rustic Tomato-Basil Tart, page 220

Pork Tenderloin with Fresh Mango Salsa; Sweet Corn and Roasted-Garlic Custards; and Green and Yellow Wax Beans with Roasted Pepper, page 240

Passion for Peaches

The search for ripe perfection is a journey with a sweet ending.

Unlike many other fruits, which are best plucked and eaten on the spot, a just-picked peach is actually best if left uneaten for at least a couple of days. To get the very best from your prize peaches, let the flavors shine with the following recipes.

Grilled Mahimahi with Peach and Pink Grapefruit Relish

(pictured on page 233)

Onions, peaches, mint, and grapefruit make a cooling, citrusy, sweet relish that pairs well with the delicate fish.

⅓ cup rice vinegar
2 tablespoons brown sugar
½ cup finely chopped red onion
2½ cups chopped peeled ripe peaches (about 1½ pounds)
1½ cups pink grapefruit sections (about 2 large grapefruit)
½ cup small mint leaves
¾ teaspoon salt, divided
½ teaspoon black pepper, divided
6 (6-ounce) mahimahi or other firm, white fish fillets (about ¾ inch thick)
Cooking spray

1. Prepare grill.
2. Place vinegar and sugar in a small saucepan; bring to a boil. Remove from heat. Place onion in a large bowl. Pour vinegar mixture over onion, tossing to coat; cool. Add peaches, grapefruit, mint, ¼ teaspoon salt, and ¼ teaspoon pepper to onion; toss gently.
3. Sprinkle fish with ½ teaspoon salt and ¼ teaspoon pepper. Place fish on grill rack coated with cooking spray, and grill 5 minutes on each side or until fish flakes easily when tested with a fork. Yield: 6 servings (serving size: 1 fillet and about ⅔ cup peach relish).

WINE NOTE: Mint and grapefruit give this dish a cool, tangy quality tailor-made for a crisp Sauvignon Blanc. One that's light and fresh but not too herbal is the 2001 Veramonte, which is from Chile's Casablanca Valley ($10).

CALORIES 226 (5% from fat); FAT 1.4g (sat 0.4g, mono 0.3g, poly 0.4g); PROTEIN 32.8g; CARB 19.3g; FIBER 3.1g; CHOL 124mg; IRON 3.2mg; SODIUM 448mg; CALC 63mg

QUICK & EASY
Fresh Peaches with Sabayon

Sabayon, which is the French version of zabaglione, is a foamy Italian custard made by whisking together egg yolks, wine, and sugar over simmering water.

¼ cup sugar
3 large egg yolks
¼ cup Marsala wine
2 tablespoons water
8 cups sliced peeled peaches (about 4 pounds)
Mint sprigs (optional)

1. Combine sugar and yolks in top of a double boiler, beating with a mixer at medium speed until foamy. Add wine and water. Cook over simmering water until mixture reaches 160° (about 7 minutes), beating with a mixer at medium speed. Serve immediately over peaches. Garnish with fresh mint sprigs, if desired. Yield: 8 servings (serving size: 1 cup peaches and ⅓ cup sabayon).

CALORIES 125 (15% from fat); FAT 2.1g (sat 0.6g, mono 0.8g, poly 0.3g); PROTEIN 2.2g; CARB 25.7g; FIBER 3.4g; CHOL 80mg; IRON 0.4mg; SODIUM 3mg; CALC 17mg

Great Grilled Dinner Menu
serves 6

Here we've used the peach glaze from Peach-Glazed Barbecue Pork Chops and Peaches (recipe below) on 6 skinless, boneless chicken breast halves. Start the potatoes on the grill first; they take longer to cook.

Peach-glazed barbecue chicken

Grilled sweet potato wedges*

Sautéed sugar snap peas with toasted almonds

*Cut each of 4 sweet potatoes (about 3 pounds) into 8 wedges. Toss wedges with 1 tablespoon vegetable oil. Sprinkle with 1 teaspoon salt, ½ teaspoon garlic powder, ¼ teaspoon ground cumin, and ¼ teaspoon ground red pepper; toss to coat. Place on grill rack coated with cooking spray; grill 18 minutes or until tender, turning occasionally.

Peach-Glazed Barbecue Pork Chops and Peaches

The cooking time for the peaches will vary depending on their ripeness. The glaze also works well on chicken (see menu box above).

3 cups chopped peeled peaches (about 1½ pounds)
1 cup dry white wine
¼ cup sugar
1 teaspoon salt, divided
¼ teaspoon black pepper, divided
2 tablespoons white wine vinegar
2 tablespoons molasses
1 teaspoon chili powder
½ teaspoon paprika
¼ teaspoon ground red pepper
6 (6-ounce) bone-in center-cut pork chops (about ½ inch thick), trimmed
6 peaches, halved and pitted
Cooking spray

1. Combine first 3 ingredients in a saucepan; bring to a boil. Cover, reduce heat, and simmer 25 minutes. Uncover and simmer 5 minutes. Place mixture in a food processor; process until smooth. Add ¾ teaspoon salt, ⅛ teaspoon black
Continued

pepper, vinegar, and next 4 ingredients; pulse to combine. Let stand 5 minutes. Place half of mixture in a large heavy-duty zip-top plastic bag; reserve other half for basting. Add chops to bag; seal, and refrigerate 30 minutes to 4 hours.

2. Preheat grill.

3. Remove pork from bag; discard marinade. Sprinkle pork with ¼ teaspoon salt and ⅛ teaspoon black pepper. Place pork and peach halves on grill rack coated with cooking spray, and grill 10 minutes or until pork is done and peaches are tender, turning once. Baste pork and peach halves with reserved peach mixture every 2 minutes during first 6 minutes of cooking. Yield: 6 servings (serving size: 1 chop and 2 peach halves).

WINE NOTE: What's needed with this dish is a wine that's spicy and evocative of peaches—like a dry Gewürztraminer. One that's powerfully vivid and sassy: the 2001 Huia Gewürztraminer from Marlborough, New Zealand ($18).

CALORIES 301 (23% from fat); FAT 7.6g (sat 2.6g, mono 3.4g, poly 0.9g); PROTEIN 26.1g; CARB 33.1g; FIBER 3.5g; CHOL 62mg; IRON 1.7mg; SODIUM 449mg; CALC 34mg

Honeyed Peach and Blackberry Cobbler

2¼ cups all-purpose flour, divided
8 cups chopped peeled peaches (about 4 pounds)
¼ cup honey
3 tablespoons fresh lemon juice
¾ teaspoon salt, divided
3 cups blackberries
Cooking spray
¾ cup granulated sugar
1 tablespoon grated lemon rind
1 teaspoon baking powder
6 tablespoons chilled butter, cut into small pieces
1¼ cups low-fat buttermilk
2 tablespoons turbinado sugar

1. Preheat oven to 400°.

2. Lightly spoon flour into dry measuring cups; level with a knife.

3. Combine ¼ cup flour, peaches, honey, juice, and ¼ teaspoon salt in a large bowl; toss gently. Let stand 15 minutes.

Fold in blackberries. Spoon mixture into a 13 x 9-inch baking dish coated with cooking spray.

4. Combine 2 cups flour, ½ teaspoon salt, granulated sugar, rind, and baking powder in a medium bowl, stirring with a whisk. Cut in butter with a pastry blender or 2 knives until mixture resembles coarse meal. Add buttermilk, and stir just until moist.

5. Drop dough onto peach mixture to form 12 mounds. Sprinkle mounds with turbinado sugar. Bake at 400° for 40 minutes or until bubbly and golden. Yield: 12 servings (serving size: ½ cup cobbler and 1 biscuit).

CALORIES 283 (20% from fat); FAT 6.3g (sat 3.8g, mono 1.8g, poly 0.3g); PROTEIN 4.3g; CARB 56.5g; FIBER 4.7g; CHOL 17mg; IRON 1.5mg; SODIUM 267mg; CALC 63mg

Streusel-Topped Peach Pie

Reserve part of the dough for the streusel.

2⅓ cups all-purpose flour, divided
1 teaspoon salt, divided
½ cup chilled butter, cut into small pieces
¼ cup ice water
1 tablespoon white vinegar
Cooking spray
½ cup regular oats
½ cup packed brown sugar
¾ teaspoon ground cinnamon, divided
⅛ teaspoon ground cloves
6 cups sliced peeled peaches (about 3 pounds)
1 cup granulated sugar
½ cup raisins
1 tablespoon fresh lemon juice

1. Lightly spoon flour into dry measuring cups; level with a knife. Combine 2 cups flour and ½ teaspoon salt in food processor; pulse 2 times or until combined. Add butter; pulse 6 times or until mixture resembles coarse meal. With processor on, slowly pour ice water and vinegar through food chute, processing just until blended (do not allow dough to form a ball).

2. Remove two-thirds of dough, and press into a 4-inch circle on 2 overlapping sheets of plastic wrap. (Leave

remaining dough in processor.) Cover dough circle with 2 additional sheets of overlapping plastic wrap. Roll dough, still covered, into an 11-inch circle. Place rolled dough in freezer 5 minutes or until plastic wrap can be easily removed. Remove top sheets of plastic wrap; fit dough, plastic wrap side up, into a 9-inch pie plate coated with cooking spray. Remove remaining plastic wrap. Fold edges under; flute. Set aside.

3. Add oats, brown sugar, ¼ teaspoon cinnamon, and a dash of cloves to dough in processor; pulse several times or until crumbly. Set aside.

4. Preheat oven to 350°.

5. Combine ⅓ cup flour, ½ teaspoon salt, ½ teaspoon cinnamon, a dash of cloves, peaches, granulated sugar, raisins, and juice in a large saucepan; let stand 10 minutes. Place pan over medium heat; cook 10 minutes or until peaches are soft, stirring occasionally. Spoon peach mixture into crust. Top with oat mixture. Bake at 350° for 50 minutes or until top is browned. Yield: 12 servings (serving size: 1 wedge).

CALORIES 330 (23% from fat); FAT 8.3g (sat 4.9g, mono 2.3g, poly 0.4g); PROTEIN 4.2g; CARB 63.5g; FIBER 3.5g; CHOL 21mg; IRON 2mg; SODIUM 279mg; CALC 22mg

MAKE AHEAD • FREEZABLE
Peach and Muscat Granita

4 cups sliced peaches (about 2 pounds)
1 (375-ml) bottle Muscat wine
3 cups water, divided
¾ cup sugar

1. Combine peaches and wine in a food processor or blender; process until smooth. Strain peach mixture through a sieve into a large bowl; discard solids.

2. Combine 1 cup water and sugar in a small saucepan; bring to a boil, stirring until sugar dissolves. Remove from heat; stir in 2 cups water.

3. Combine peach mixture and sugar mixture in a 13 x 9-inch baking dish, stirring with a whisk. Freeze 6 hours or until firm, stirring twice during first 2 hours. Yield: 8 servings (serving size: 1 cup).

CALORIES 181 (0% from fat); FAT 0.1g (sat 0g, mono 0g, poly 0.1g); PROTEIN 0.7g; CARB 33.7g; FIBER 1.7g; CHOL 0mg; IRON 0.2mg; SODIUM 4mg; CALC 8mg

Dinner at Dusk

Set a place for the Fourth—or any summer soiree—with this fresh outdoor menu.

For a Fourth of July gathering, trade the soda and meal-on-a-bun buffet for cold glasses of white wine and a menu that inspires *ooohs* and *ahhhs* before the fireworks begin. This one mingles savory with sweet, sophisticated with serendipitous. Salty prosciutto lights up a cool melon salad; breadsticks sizzle with peppercorns and sharp pecorino; and ginger sparks roasted fresh plums. This holiday weekend—or any summer weekend, really—is ideal for making memories and sharing food as good as this.

Summer Menu
serves 6

Escarole Salad with Melons and Crispy Prosciutto

Spicy Peppercorn and Pecorino Breadsticks

Pork Tenderloin with Fresh Mango Salsa

Sweet Corn and Roasted-Garlic Custards

Green and Yellow Wax Beans with Roasted Pepper

Roasted Plums with Ginger and Pecans

WINE NOTE: This menu says summertime, and so do the following wines. Begin by pairing the escarole salad with a dry, crisp, and light Italian white, such as a Gavi or Vernaccia di San Gimignano. There are dozens of small producers of both of these, so a wineshop in your area is bound to have one. Next, try a dry Riesling with the pork tenderloin. It will evoke lots of fruity flavors—an ideal accompaniment for the mango and citrus salsa. Germany, Alsace, and Australia all make great dry Rieslings, or try the excellent wine known as "Eroica" from Château Ste. Michelle in Washington State ($20). Finally, pair the roasted plums with a lusciously fruity—but not sugary—dessert wine, such as Quady Electra ($10).

QUICK & EASY
Escarole Salad with Melons and Crispy Prosciutto

4 thin slices prosciutto (about 1.5 ounces), coarsely chopped
3 tablespoons minced shallots
2 tablespoons balsamic vinegar
1 tablespoon red wine vinegar
1½ teaspoons extravirgin olive oil
¼ teaspoon salt
¼ teaspoon freshly ground black pepper
12 cups torn escarole (about 1¼ pounds)
2 cups torn radicchio (about 4 ounces)
2 cups cubed peeled honeydew melon
2 cups cubed peeled cantaloupe
2 tablespoons sliced almonds, toasted

1. Preheat oven to 400°.
2. Arrange prosciutto in a single layer on a baking sheet. Bake at 400° for 6 minutes or until crisp.
3. Combine shallots and next 5 ingredients in a large bowl, stirring with a whisk. Add escarole and radicchio, and toss to coat. Add honeydew and cantaloupe, and toss to combine. Place 2 cups salad on each of 6 plates, and top each serving with about 2 teaspoons prosciutto. Sprinkle each serving with 1 teaspoon almonds. Yield: 6 servings.

CALORIES 105 (32% from fat); FAT 3.7g (sat 0.7g, mono 2.1g, poly 0.6g); PROTEIN 3.6g; CARB 16.4g; FIBER 4g; CHOL 4mg; IRON 1.1mg; SODIUM 228mg; CALC 68mg

---

STAFF FAVORITE • MAKE AHEAD
Spicy Peppercorn and Pecorino Breadsticks

With black and red pepper, these breadsticks pack some heat. If you don't have semolina, you can use cornmeal.

1 package dry yeast (about 2¼ teaspoons)
1⅓ cups warm water (100° to 110°)
3½ cups bread flour, divided
2 tablespoons extravirgin olive oil
2 teaspoons coarsely ground black pepper
1¾ teaspoons salt
¾ teaspoon crushed red pepper
1 cup (4 ounces) grated fresh pecorino Romano cheese
Cooking spray
2 tablespoons ground semolina

1. Dissolve yeast in warm water in a large bowl; let stand 5 minutes. Lightly spoon flour into dry measuring cups; level with a knife. Add ½ cup flour to yeast mixture, stirring with a whisk. Let stand 30 minutes. Add 3 cups flour, oil, black pepper, salt, and red pepper; stir until a soft dough forms. Turn dough out onto a lightly floured surface. Knead until smooth and elastic (about 8 minutes); cover and let rest 10 minutes. Knead in half of cheese; cover and let rest 5 minutes. Knead in remaining cheese.
2. Place dough in a large bowl coated with cooking spray, turning to coat top. Cover and let rise in a warm place (85°), free from drafts, 45 minutes or until doubled in size. (Gently press two fingers into dough. If indentation remains, dough has risen enough.) Punch dough down. Roll dough into a 12 x 8-inch rectangle on a lightly floured surface.
3. Preheat oven to 450°.
4. Sprinkle 1 tablespoon semolina onto each of 2 baking sheets. Cut dough in half lengthwise to form 2 (12 x 4-inch) rectangles. Cut each rectangle crosswise into 12 (1-inch-wide) strips. Working with 1 strip at a time (cover remaining dough to prevent drying), gently roll each strip into a 15-inch-long rope.
Continued

Place 12 ropes on each prepared pan. Cover and let rise 20 minutes.

5. Uncover dough; bake at 450° for 12 minutes. Remove breadsticks from pans; cool completely on wire racks. Yield: 24 servings (serving size: 1 breadstick).

CALORIES 99 (22% from fat); FAT 2.4g (sat 1g, mono 1.2g, poly 0.1g); PROTEIN 4.4g; CARB 15.7g; FIBER 0.7g; CHOL 5mg; IRON 1.1mg; SODIUM 228mg; CALC 52mg

Pork Tenderloin with Fresh Mango Salsa

(pictured on page 236)

Look for mangoes that gently yield to pressure and smell fruity.

2 (1-pound) pork tenderloins, trimmed
1 teaspoon salt
½ teaspoon freshly ground black pepper
1½ cups diced peeled mango (about 2 large)
1 teaspoon grated orange rind
3 tablespoons fresh orange juice
3 tablespoons diagonally sliced green onions
2 teaspoons grated peeled fresh ginger
½ teaspoon ground coriander
¼ teaspoon ground cardamom
1 tablespoon olive oil

1. Cut each tenderloin crosswise into 8 pieces. Place plastic wrap over pork; pound to an even thickness using a meat mallet or rolling pin. Sprinkle evenly with salt and pepper.
2. Combine mango and next 6 ingredients.
3. Heat oil in a large nonstick skillet over medium-high heat. Add half of pork; cook 3 minutes on each side or until done. Remove from pan; repeat procedure with remaining pork. Serve with mango salsa. Yield: 8 servings (serving size: 2 pork medallions and about 3 tablespoons salsa).

CALORIES 195 (22% from fat); FAT 4.7g (sat 1.3g, mono 2.6g, poly 0.5g); PROTEIN 27.5g; CARB 9.9g; FIBER 1.2g; CHOL 67mg; IRON 1.6mg; SODIUM 349mg; CALC 15mg

Sweet Corn and Roasted-Garlic Custards

(pictured on page 236)

The custards are baked in a water bath so that they're gently cooked. The reserved corn is sprinkled around the custards and can be room temperature or warmed in the microwave before garnishing.

1 whole garlic head
2 teaspoons butter
3 cups fresh corn kernels (about 5 ears)
½ cup chopped green onions
½ teaspoon chopped fresh thyme
Cooking spray
1½ cups fat-free milk
3 large eggs
1 large egg yolk
¾ teaspoon salt
½ teaspoon freshly ground black pepper
Thyme sprigs (optional)

1. Preheat oven to 375°.
2. Remove white papery skin from garlic head (do not peel or separate cloves). Wrap head in foil. Bake at 375° for 40 minutes, and cool 10 minutes. Separate cloves; squeeze to extract garlic pulp. Discard skins. Mash pulp.
3. Melt butter in a large nonstick skillet over medium heat. Add corn; cook 4 minutes, stirring occasionally. Remove 1 cup corn, and set aside. Add onions and chopped thyme to corn in pan; cook 1 minute, stirring frequently. Remove from heat; cool slightly.
4. Coat 6 (6-ounce) custard cups with cooking spray. Combine garlic pulp, onion mixture, milk, eggs, egg yolk, salt, and pepper, stirring with a whisk. Divide egg mixture evenly among prepared custard cups. Place cups in a 13 x 9-inch baking pan, and add hot water to pan to a depth of 1 inch.
5. Bake at 375° for 40 minutes or until a knife inserted in center of custards comes out clean. Remove cups from pan, and cool 5 minutes on a wire rack. Loosen edges of custards with a knife or rubber spatula. Place a plate, upside down, on top of each cup, and invert

onto plates. Sprinkle reserved corn evenly around custards. Garnish with thyme sprigs, if desired. Yield: 6 servings.

CALORIES 162 (30% from fat); FAT 5.4g (sat 2g, mono 1.9g, poly 0.8g); PROTEIN 8.4g; CARB 22.5g; FIBER 2g; CHOL 146mg; IRON 1mg; SODIUM 375mg; CALC 104mg

Green and Yellow Wax Beans with Roasted Pepper

(pictured on page 236)

Red and yellow bell peppers and green and yellow beans brighten this side dish. Toasted pine nuts offer a light crunch.

1 yellow bell pepper
1 red bell pepper
¾ pound green beans, trimmed
¾ pound yellow wax beans, trimmed
1 teaspoon olive oil
1 garlic clove, minced
½ teaspoon salt
¼ teaspoon freshly ground black pepper
2 tablespoons pine nuts, toasted
2 teaspoons grated lemon rind
1 tablespoon fresh lemon juice

1. Preheat broiler.
2. Cut bell peppers in half lengthwise; discard seeds and membranes. Place pepper halves, skin sides up, on a foil-lined baking sheet; flatten with hand. Broil 15 minutes or until blackened. Place in a zip-top plastic bag; seal. Let stand 10 minutes. Peel and cut into thin strips.
3. Place green beans in a large saucepan of boiling water; cook 4 minutes. Remove with a slotted spoon. Plunge beans into ice water; drain. Add wax beans to boiling water; cook 4 minutes. Drain and plunge beans into ice water; drain.
4. Heat oil in a large nonstick skillet over medium-high heat. Add bell pepper strips, beans, garlic, salt, and black pepper; sauté 2 minutes or until thoroughly heated. Remove from heat, and add nuts, rind, and juice, tossing gently to coat. Yield: 6 servings (serving size: 1 cup).

CALORIES 70 (31% from fat); FAT 2.4g (sat 0.4g, mono 1.1g, poly 0.8g); PROTEIN 3.2g; CARB 11.6g; FIBER 4.9g; CHOL 0mg; IRON 1.7mg; SODIUM 203mg; CALC 49mg

Roasted Plums with Ginger and Pecans

The warm plums and syrupy sauce are best served immediately. This dessert is also good made with fresh peaches.

- 1 cup Riesling or other sweet white wine
- ⅓ cup dried apricots, chopped
- 3 tablespoons sugar
- 1 tablespoon grated peeled fresh ginger
- 1 tablespoon butter, softened
- 1 large egg yolk, lightly beaten
- 3 tablespoons chopped pecans, toasted
- 9 plums, halved and pitted
- 2 cups vanilla low-fat frozen yogurt

1. Preheat oven to 350°.
2. Bring wine to a simmer in a medium saucepan over medium-high heat. Stir in apricots; cover and remove from heat. Let stand 20 minutes. Drain apricots in a colander over a bowl; reserve wine and apricots separately.
3. Combine sugar, ginger, butter, and egg yolk in a bowl. Stir in apricots and pecans. Fill each plum half with about 1½ teaspoons of apricot filling. Place stuffed plums in a single layer in an 11 x 7-inch baking dish; pour reserved wine around plums. Bake at 350° for 20 minutes or until plums are tender.
4. Remove plums from dish; pour remaining liquid into a small saucepan. Bring to a boil; cook until slightly syrupy and reduced to ¼ cup (about 5 minutes). Serve plum halves with sauce and frozen yogurt. Yield: 6 servings (serving size: 3 plum halves, 2 teaspoons sauce, and ⅓ cup frozen yogurt).

CALORIES 227 (25% from fat); FAT 6.7g (sat 2.3g, mono 2.9g, poly 1g); PROTEIN 4.8g; CARB 36.6g; FIBER 2.4g; CHOL 44mg; IRON 0.6mg; SODIUM 43mg; CALC 119mg

Trail Mix

Mix and match packable high-energy foods to keep you going strong.

QUICK & EASY • MAKE AHEAD
Spicy Red Lentil Dal with Pita Wedges

Dal is a great choice for a hike—it's high in protein and fiber, low in fat, durable, and nonperishable. Pack dal in a heavy-duty zip-top plastic bag separate from pitas. Lentils absorb the liquid as they stand, so there's no need to drain them after cooking.

- 2 cups fat-free, less-sodium chicken broth
- 1 cup dried small red lentils
- 1 tablespoon vegetable oil
- 1½ cups chopped onion
- 1 tablespoon minced fresh garlic
- 1 teaspoon yellow mustard seeds
- ½ teaspoon crushed red pepper
- 1 teaspoon ground cumin
- 1 teaspoon ground turmeric
- ½ teaspoon ground coriander
- ½ teaspoon freshly ground black pepper
- 1 tablespoon tomato paste
- ½ cup light coconut milk
- ½ teaspoon salt
- 2 teaspoons fresh lime juice
- 5 (6-inch) pitas, each cut into 8 wedges

1. Combine broth and lentils in a medium saucepan; bring to a boil. Reduce heat, partially cover, and simmer 10 minutes or until lentils are tender. Remove from heat; cover and set aside.
2. Heat oil in a large nonstick skillet over medium heat. Add onion, garlic, mustard seeds, and red pepper, and cook 5 minutes or until onions are tender and seeds begin to pop, stirring constantly. Add cumin, turmeric, coriander, and black pepper; cook 3 minutes, stirring constantly. Add tomato paste, and cook 3 minutes, stirring constantly. Add lentils, coconut milk, and salt; cook 3 minutes, stirring frequently. Remove from heat; stir in juice. Cool to room temperature. Serve dal with pita wedges. Yield: 5 servings (serving size: ½ cup dal and 8 pita wedges).

CALORIES 375 (13% from fat); FAT 5.5g (sat 1.4g, mono 1g, poly 2.2g); PROTEIN 18.6g; CARB 63.2g; FIBER 14.8g; CHOL 0mg; IRON 5.8mg; SODIUM 746mg; CALC 95mg

Trail-Friendly Foods

When it comes to food for a basic day hike, "almost anything goes, as long as you can pack it and carry it," says Karen Berger, author of *More Everyday Wisdom: Trail-Tested Advice from the Experts.* But to keep things simple, she suggests you look for foods that are easily prepared and eaten, and carry them in lightweight containers with tight-fitting lids, which are crucial to preventing leaks.

Try some of these convenient ideas for easy trail-side snacks and meals:
- Dried meats or sausages and hard cheeses with whole-grain crackers (hard cheeses such as provolone can be safely carried on a day hike; avoid soft cheeses such as goat cheese)
- Nut butter sandwiches with apple chips
- Trail mix that contains nuts and dried fruits (soy nuts are a good addition to trail mix)
- Whole-grain crackers, homemade pita chips, or vegetables with bean spreads or dips (try reconstitutable—"just add water"—black-bean dip and hummus mixes, such as those made by Fantastic Foods)
- Vacuum-packed tuna with crackers
- Roasted, marinated vegetables and hard cheeses with flour tortillas for quick sandwich wraps
- Low-fat granola or granola bars

Summer Garden Lentil and Pasta Salad

Petite green lentils are sometimes labeled "le puy lentils." Other lentils also will work, but the cook time could change, so make sure they're tender before you drain them.

VINAIGRETTE:
2½ tablespoons balsamic vinegar
1½ tablespoons extravirgin olive oil
1 tablespoon minced shallots
1 tablespoon Dijon mustard
1½ teaspoons minced fresh garlic
⅛ teaspoon salt
⅛ teaspoon freshly ground black pepper

SALAD:
1 cup fat-free, less-sodium chicken broth
½ cup dried petite green lentils
1 bay leaf
2 cups uncooked orecchiette pasta ("little ears" pasta)
1 cup chopped zucchini
¾ cup halved cherry tomatoes
½ cup chopped red bell pepper
½ cup chopped yellow bell pepper
½ cup chopped red onion
2 tablespoons chopped fresh basil
2 tablespoons chopped fresh flat-leaf parsley
2 tablespoons grated Parmigiano-Reggiano cheese
1½ teaspoons chopped fresh or ½ teaspoon dried oregano
1½ teaspoons chopped fresh or ½ teaspoon dried thyme
¼ teaspoon salt
¼ teaspoon freshly ground black pepper

1. To prepare vinaigrette, combine first 7 ingredients in a blender or food processor; process until well blended.
2. To prepare salad, combine broth, lentils, and bay leaf in a saucepan; bring to a boil. Reduce heat; simmer 25 minutes or until lentils are tender. Drain; rinse with cold water. Discard bay leaf.
3. Cook pasta according to package directions, omitting salt and fat. Drain and rinse with cold water.

4. Combine lentils, pasta, zucchini, and remaining 11 ingredients. Drizzle with vinaigrette; toss well. Store in an airtight container. Yield: 4 servings (serving size: 1¼ cups).

CALORIES 380 (19% from fat); FAT 7.9g (sat 1.6g, mono 4.4g, poly 1.5g); PROTEIN 16.2g; CARB 63.7g; FIBER 7.6g; CHOL 3mg; IRON 3.9mg; SODIUM 447mg; CALC 97mg

Zesty Black Bean and Corn Salad

This salad is good on its own or as a filling in a Southwestern wrap. Make the salad the night before your hike.

2 teaspoons vegetable oil
Cooking spray
2 garlic cloves, minced
2½ cups fresh corn kernels (about 4 large ears)
¼ cup fresh lime juice (about 2 limes)
1 tablespoon extravirgin olive oil
2 tablespoons red wine vinegar
¾ teaspoon ground cumin
¼ teaspoon salt
1 cup halved grape tomatoes
1 cup chopped red bell pepper
¾ cup chopped red onion
2 tablespoons chopped fresh cilantro
2 tablespoons minced seeded jalapeño pepper
1 tablespoon chopped fresh oregano
1 (19-ounce) can black beans, rinsed and drained

1. Heat vegetable oil in a large nonstick skillet coated with cooking spray over medium-high heat. Add garlic; sauté 30 seconds. Add corn; sauté 8 minutes or until browned. Remove from pan; cool completely.
2. Combine juice and next 4 ingredients, stirring with a whisk. Combine corn mixture, tomatoes, and remaining 6 ingredients. Drizzle juice mixture over corn mixture, and toss gently to coat. Yield: 6 servings (serving size: 1 cup).

CALORIES 164 (26% from fat); FAT 4.8g (sat 0.7g, mono 2.3g, poly 1.5g); PROTEIN 6.5g; CARB 30.3g; FIBER 7.3g; CHOL 0mg; IRON 2.1mg; SODIUM 359mg; CALC 46mg

Herbed White-Bean Spread Open-Faced Sandwiches

Pack the spread, bread, and onion separately, and assemble on site.

SPREAD:
1 teaspoon olive oil
Cooking spray
⅔ cup coarsely chopped shallots
1 tablespoon chopped fresh sage
1 tablespoon chopped fresh thyme
1 teaspoon freshly ground black pepper
2 garlic cloves, minced
1 cup fat-free, less-sodium chicken broth
1 (19-ounce) can cannellini beans, rinsed and drained
¼ cup (1 ounce) shredded Asiago cheese
2 tablespoons chopped fresh flat-leaf parsley
2 tablespoons extravirgin olive oil
1 tablespoon fresh lemon juice

REMAINING INGREDIENTS:
10 (1-ounce) slices diagonally cut French bread (about 1 inch thick)
20 (¼-inch-thick) slices red onion

1. To prepare spread, heat 1 teaspoon oil in a large nonstick skillet coated with cooking spray over medium heat. Add shallots; cook 10 minutes or until tender, stirring frequently. Stir in sage, thyme, pepper, and garlic; sauté 2 minutes. Add broth and beans; reduce heat to low. Cook 5 minutes or until most of liquid is absorbed. Remove from heat; cool to room temperature.
2. Place bean mixture, cheese, parsley, 2 tablespoons oil, and juice in a food processor; process until smooth.
3. Place about 3 tablespoons spread on each bread slice; top each with 2 onion slices. Yield: 5 servings (serving size: 2 open-faced sandwiches).

CALORIES 438 (30% from fat); FAT 14.4g (sat 2.9g, mono 6.4g, poly 3.7g); PROTEIN 12.1g; CARB 65.8g; FIBER 8.6g; CHOL 5mg; IRON 3.2mg; SODIUM 704mg; CALC 109mg

If you have a place to refrigerate the chicken salad, you can combine everything at home. If not, stir in the vacuum-packed chicken just before serving, as the recipe directs.

Chicken Salad with Olive Vinaigrette

Fruit salad with balsamic dressing*

Rosemary focaccia

*Combine 2 cups cubed honeydew melon, 1 cup quartered strawberries, and 1 cup raspberries. Combine ¼ cup half-and-half, 2 tablespoons balsamic vinegar, 1 tablespoon honey, and a dash of salt, stirring with a whisk. Drizzle dressing over fruit; toss gently to coat.

QUICK & EASY • MAKE AHEAD
Chicken Salad with Olive Vinaigrette

You can substitute 2 cups cooked chicken or turkey breast for vacuum-packed chicken.

    1   cup uncooked Israeli couscous
    ¼   cup chopped pitted kalamata olives
    2   tablespoons chopped fresh
        flat-leaf parsley
    2   tablespoons extravirgin olive oil
    1   tablespoon chopped capers
    1   tablespoon fresh lemon juice
    ¼   teaspoon salt
    ¼   teaspoon freshly ground black
        pepper
    1   garlic clove, minced
    2   (7-ounce) packages 98%-fat-free
        chicken breast in water

1. Cook couscous according to package directions, omitting salt and fat. Drain and rinse with cold water.
2. Combine olives and next 7 ingredients in a large bowl, stirring with a whisk. Add couscous to olive mixture; toss gently to coat. Stir in chicken just before serving. Yield: 4 servings (serving size: 1½ cups).

CALORIES 348 (28% from fat); FAT 10.7g (sat 1.2g, mono 6.4g, poly 0.9g); PROTEIN 25g; CARB 34.9g; FIBER 2.4g; CHOL 18mg; IRON 1.9mg; SODIUM 929mg; CALC 66mg

MAKE AHEAD
Wheat Berry Salad with Dried Fruit

Make this salad in advance so the flavors have time to mellow. This salad is high in fiber, flavorful, filling, and easy to pack.

    3   cups water
    1   cup uncooked wheat berries
    ½   cup minced shallots
    ¼   cup cranberry juice
    3   tablespoons raspberry vinegar
    2   tablespoons vegetable oil
    1   tablespoon balsamic vinegar
    2   teaspoons Dijon mustard
    ½   teaspoon salt
    ½   cup coarsely chopped dried
        cranberries
    ½   cup coarsely chopped dried
        cherries
    ½   cup (2 ounces) diced Gouda
        cheese
    ⅓   cup chopped green onions
    ⅓   cup slivered almonds, toasted
    ¼   cup dried currants
    ¼   teaspoon freshly ground black
        pepper

1. Combine water and wheat berries in a medium saucepan; bring to a boil. Cover, reduce heat, and simmer 1 hour. Drain and rinse with cold water.
2. Combine shallots and next 6 ingredients in a large bowl. Let stand 30 minutes.
3. Add wheat berries, cranberries, and remaining ingredients to vinaigrette, and toss to combine. Chill at least 4 hours or overnight. Yield: 6 servings (serving size: 1 cup).

CALORIES 355 (30% from fat); FAT 11.7g (sat 2.7g, mono 4.4g, poly 3.8g); PROTEIN 9.4g; CARB 55.2g; FIBER 7.8g; CHOL 11mg; IRON 2.1mg; SODIUM 332mg; CALC 118mg

MAKE AHEAD
Honey-Roasted Nuts and Fruit

Use any variety of mixed nuts or seeds in this trail mix. Raisins are a concentrated source of carbohydrates, and the nuts add good fats and protein to this snack, which you can pack in bags for the road.

        Cooking spray
    1   teaspoon butter
    ¼   cup honey
    ¼   cup slivered almonds
    ¼   cup chopped hazelnuts
    ¼   cup chopped pecans
    ¼   cup sunflower seeds
    ½   teaspoon ground cinnamon
    ¼   teaspoon ground cardamom
    ¼   teaspoon salt
        Dash of ground cloves
    1   cup raisins

1. Line a baking sheet with parchment paper or foil; coat with cooking spray.
2. Heat butter in a large nonstick skillet over medium-high heat. Stir in honey; cook 2 minutes or until mixture bubbles around edges of pan. Add nuts and next 5 ingredients, and cook over medium heat 8 minutes or until nuts are golden, stirring frequently. Stir in raisins. Immediately spread onto prepared baking sheet; cool completely. Yield: 8 servings (serving size: ¼ cup).

CALORIES 194 (44% from fat); FAT 9.4g (sat 1g, mono 5g, poly 2.8g); PROTEIN 3.4g; CARB 27.8g; FIBER 2.2g; CHOL 2mg; IRON 1mg; SODIUM 82mg; CALC 30mg

Lobster Shack Redux

The secret to snazzy seafood dishes from New York's Pearl Oyster Bar.

Rebecca Charles opened Pearl Oyster Bar, in New York's Greenwich Village, to immediate acclaim in 1997. In time, her upscale take on an old-time Maine lobster shack charmed food critics and made the lobster roll the new must-have on Manhattan menus. Here are some of her recipes.

MAKE AHEAD • FREEZABLE

Lobster Stock

If you're having a lobster dinner, don't toss the shells. Save them to make this simple stock. It's a great way to add fat-free flavor. The stock can be refrigerated up to 2 days and frozen up to 1 month. Any size lobsters totaling about 5 pounds will work.

18 quarts water, divided
6 tablespoons salt
2 (2½-pound) whole lobsters
1 tablespoon olive oil
1 cup coarsely chopped fennel bulb
1 cup coarsely chopped parsnip
1 cup coarsely chopped carrot
½ cup coarsely chopped celery
2 whole garlic heads, halved
   horizontally
1 large onion, quartered
2 cups dry white wine
2 sprigs parsley
2 sprigs thyme

1. Bring 15 quarts of water and salt to a boil in a 19-quart stockpot; plunge lobsters headfirst, 1 at a time, into water. Return to a boil. Cover, reduce heat, and simmer 8 minutes for small lobsters (1 to 1¼ pounds) and 10 minutes for larger lobsters (1½ to 2½ pounds). Drain well; cool completely.
2. Remove meat from cooked lobster tails and claws; reserve meat for another use. Rinse out head portion of lobsters.

Place lobster shells in a large heavy-duty zip-top plastic bag. Coarsely crush shells using a meat mallet or rolling pin.
3. Heat oil in a Dutch oven over medium-high heat. Add fennel and next 5 ingredients; sauté 5 minutes or until vegetables are lightly browned. Add 3 quarts water, crushed shells, wine, parsley, and thyme; bring to a boil. Reduce heat; simmer 1 hour. Strain shell mixture through a sieve over a bowl, reserving stock. Discard solids. Yield: 10 cups (serving size: 1 cup).

CALORIES 25 (50% from fat); FAT 1.4g; (sat 0.2g, mono 1g, poly 0.1g); PROTEIN 0.5g; CARB 0.9g; FIBER 0.2g; CHOL 2mg; IRON 0.1mg; SODIUM 52mg; CALC 5mg

Striped Bass Fillets with Lobster Stock and Aromatic Vegetables

2 carrots, peeled and cut into 3-inch
   pieces
2 small leeks, trimmed and cut into
   3-inch pieces
1 large zucchini, cut into 3-inch
   pieces
4 cups Lobster Stock (recipe at left)
1 tablespoon olive oil
6 (6-ounce) striped bass fillets
½ teaspoon salt, divided
¼ teaspoon black pepper,
   divided
1 tablespoon butter
16 shiitake mushroom caps

1. Cut carrot, leek, and zucchini pieces lengthwise into julienne strips; set aside.
2. Bring Lobster Stock to a simmer in a medium saucepan (do not boil); keep warm over low heat.
3. Heat oil in a large skillet over medium-high heat. Sprinkle fish with ¼ teaspoon salt and ⅛ teaspoon pepper. Add fish to pan; cook 2 minutes on each side. Remove from pan; keep warm. Melt butter in pan over medium-high heat. Add mushrooms and leeks; sauté 2 minutes. Add carrot; sauté 2 minutes. Add zucchini, Lobster Stock, ¼ teaspoon salt, and ⅛ teaspoon pepper. Arrange fish over vegetables; cover and cook 3 minutes or until fish flakes easily when tested with a fork.

4. Place ½ cup vegetables in each of 6 bowls; top each serving with 1 fillet. Ladle ½ cup broth over each serving. Yield: 6 servings.

CALORIES 268 (30% from fat); FAT 8.8g (sat 2.5g, mono 3.6g, poly 1.8g); PROTEIN 34.5g; CARB 11.1g; FIBER 2.6g; CHOL 76mg; IRON 2mg; SODIUM 388mg; CALC 56mg

Pearl Oyster Bar Crab Cakes with Sweet Corn Relish

Top these quintessential crab cakes with a refreshing sweet corn relish.

CRAB CAKES:

1 tablespoon Dijon mustard
1 tablespoon fresh lemon juice
1 teaspoon dry mustard
2 teaspoons chopped fresh chives
½ teaspoon hot pepper sauce (such
   as Tabasco)
½ teaspoon Worcestershire sauce
¼ teaspoon salt
¼ teaspoon black pepper
2 large eggs, lightly beaten
2 tablespoons finely chopped
   seeded plum tomato
1 pound lump crabmeat, drained
   and shell pieces removed
7 tablespoons dry breadcrumbs,
   divided
1½ teaspoons butter

RELISH:

¼ cup water
2¾ cups fresh corn kernels (about
    4 ears)
¼ cup frozen green peas
1½ cups finely chopped seeded plum
    tomato (about 1 pound)
2 tablespoons chopped fresh basil
2 tablespoons chopped fresh chives
1 tablespoon butter
¼ teaspoon salt
⅛ teaspoon black pepper

1. To prepare crab cakes, combine first 9 ingredients in a large bowl, stirring with a whisk. Add 2 tablespoons tomato and crabmeat, tossing gently to coat. Stir in 5 tablespoons breadcrumbs. Cover and chill 30 minutes.

2. Preheat oven to 450°.

3. Fill a ¼-cup measuring cup with crab mixture to form 1 patty. Remove from measuring cup; repeat procedure with remaining crab mixture to form 8 patties. Lightly dredge patties in 2 tablespoons breadcrumbs.

4. Melt 1½ teaspoons butter in a large ovenproof skillet over medium-high heat. Add patties; cook 4 minutes. Turn patties. Place pan in oven; bake at 450° for 5 minutes or until patties are golden brown and thoroughly heated.

5. To prepare relish, bring ¼ cup water to a boil in a medium saucepan. Add corn and peas; cook 2 minutes, stirring frequently. Remove from heat; stir in 1½ cups tomato and remaining 5 ingredients. Serve relish with crab cakes. Yield: 8 servings (serving size: 1 crab cake and ⅓ cup relish).

CALORIES 173 (28% from fat); FAT 5.4g (sat 2g, mono 1.6g, poly 0.9g); PROTEIN 15.1g; CARB 17.5g; FIBER 2.3g; CHOL 103mg; IRON 1.7mg; SODIUM 462mg; CALC 81mg

Mussels with Leeks, Fennel, and Tomatoes

```
3    cups Lobster Stock (recipe on
     page 244)
¾    cup thinly sliced leek
¾    cup thinly sliced fennel bulb
⅔    cup finely chopped shallots
⅓    cup dry white wine
¼    teaspoon black pepper
2    pounds mussels
½    cup chopped seeded tomato
1½   teaspoons chopped fresh chives
```

1. Simmer first 6 ingredients in a Dutch oven over high heat. Add mussels; cover, reduce heat, and cook 4 minutes or until shells open. Remove from heat; discard any unopened shells. Divide mussels and broth evenly between 2 shallow bowls. Sprinkle with tomato and chives. Yield: 2 servings (serving size: about 18 mussels, 2 cups broth, ¼ cup tomato, and ¾ teaspoon chives).

CALORIES 379 (21% from fat); FAT 8.9g (sat 1.6g, mono 3g, poly 2.1g); PROTEIN 37.8g; CARB 30.7g; FIBER 2.8g; CHOL 84mg; IRON 13.5mg; SODIUM 937mg; CALC 143mg

. . . And Ready in Just About 20 Minutes

When your schedule throws you a curve, stay in the game with these dinner recipes.

Three-Step Taco Salad and Greek Dinner Salad are hearty enough to be main dishes (but not too heavy to serve after warm-weather activities). Another refreshing choice is Spiced Shrimp with Peach Salsa. Cook it indoors as the recipe suggests, or skewer the shrimp, and grill them in the same amount of time. You'll also score big with satisfying choices like Shrimp and Sausage Paella and Sesame Pork Rice. Both use convenient boil-in-bag rice. And, since they're all done in 20 minutes or less, everybody wins.

QUICK & EASY
Greek Dinner Salad

This main-dish salad works well with many variations—change the fresh herbs, beans, and cheese to use what you have on hand.

```
¼    cup coarsely chopped fresh
     parsley
3    tablespoons coarsely chopped
     fresh dill
1    tablespoon extravirgin olive oil
1    tablespoon fresh lemon
     juice
1    teaspoon dried oregano
6    cups shredded romaine
     lettuce
3    cups chopped tomato
1    cup thinly sliced red onion
¾    cup (3 ounces) crumbled feta
     cheese
1    tablespoon capers
1    cucumber, peeled, quartered
     lengthwise, and thinly sliced
1    (19-ounce) can chickpeas, rinsed
     and drained
6    (6-inch) whole wheat pitas, each
     cut into 8 wedges
```

1. Combine first 5 ingredients in a large bowl; stir with a whisk. Add lettuce and next 6 ingredients; toss well. Serve with pita wedges. Yield: 6 servings (serving size: 2 cups salad and 8 pita wedges).

CALORIES 388 (29% from fat); FAT 14.8g (sat 3.8g, mono 4.8g, poly 1.4g); PROTEIN 15.7g; CARB 64.9g; FIBER 11.4g; CHOL 17mg; IRON 4.8mg; SODIUM 779mg; CALC 173mg

QUICK & EASY
Sesame Pork Rice

This entrée looks like fried rice—without the eggs. Serve it with a spinach and mushroom salad.

```
2    (3½-ounce) bags boil-in-bag
     long-grain rice
1    pound boneless center-cut loin
     pork chops, cut into bite-sized
     pieces
1½   teaspoons bottled minced garlic,
     divided
1    teaspoon bottled ground fresh
     ginger, divided
1    tablespoon dark sesame oil,
     divided
3    tablespoons low-sodium soy sauce
2    tablespoons hoisin sauce
2    tablespoons rice vinegar
½    cup chopped green onions
1    tablespoon toasted sesame seeds
```

1. Cook rice according to package directions; omit salt. Drain well; set aside.

2. While rice cooks, toss pork with ½ teaspoon garlic and ½ teaspoon ginger. Heat 2 teaspoons oil in a large nonstick skillet over medium-high heat. Add pork; sauté 3 minutes or until done. Remove from pan; keep warm.

3. Heat 1 teaspoon oil in pan over medium-high heat; add 1 teaspoon garlic and ½ teaspoon ginger; sauté 30 seconds. Add rice, soy sauce, hoisin sauce, and vinegar; sauté 2 minutes. Stir in pork; cook 2 minutes or until thoroughly heated. Sprinkle with green onions and sesame seeds. Yield: 4 servings (serving size: 1¼ cups).

CALORIES 438 (25% from fat); FAT 12.1g (sat 3.1g, mono 4.8g, poly 2.4g); PROTEIN 30.1g; CARB 48.6g; FIBER 1g; CHOL 63mg; IRON 5.9mg; SODIUM 593mg; CALC 12mg

Three-Step Taco Salad

We suggest assembling all the ingredients first, and tossing them just before serving to keep the lettuce and chips crisp. Serve pineapple sherbet for dessert.

  1 pound ground sirloin
  1 (1.25-ounce package) taco seasoning
  ¾ cup water
  ⅔ cup fat-free sour cream
  ⅔ cup bottled salsa
  8 cups shredded iceberg lettuce
  4 cups (4 ounces) bite-sized baked tortilla chips
  2 cups chopped fresh tomatoes, drained
  1 cup (4 ounces) shredded reduced-fat sharp Cheddar cheese, divided
  1 (15-ounce) can kidney or black beans, rinsed and drained
  ½ cup sliced ripe olives

1. Cook beef in a large skillet over medium-high heat until browned, stirring to crumble. Stir in taco seasoning and water. Reduce heat, and simmer 5 minutes, stirring occasionally.
2. Combine sour cream and salsa in a small bowl.
3. Combine beef mixture, lettuce, tortilla chips, tomatoes, ½ cup cheese, and beans in a large bowl. Drizzle sour cream mixture over salad, and toss gently. Sprinkle with ½ cup cheese and olives. Serve immediately. Yield: 10 servings (serving size: 2 cups).

CALORIES 217 (24% from fat); FAT 5.7g (sat 2.3g, mono 1.5g, poly 0.7g); PROTEIN 16.8g; CARB 26.1g; FIBER 5g; CHOL 34mg; IRON 2.2mg; SODIUM 757mg; CALC 171mg

Shrimp and Sausage Paella

Just a small amount of saffron gives this dish a golden appearance and a pungent aroma. If you don't have saffron, double the turmeric. Eliminate defrosting by adding the frozen green peas to the rice during the last several minutes of cook time. They'll thaw and cook briefly, leaving them perfectly crisp-tender.

  3 (3½-ounce) bags boil-in-bag long-grain rice
  1 cup frozen green peas
  ¼ cup hot water
  ¼ teaspoon saffron threads
  1 cup (4 ounces) thinly sliced Spanish chorizo sausage
  1½ pounds medium shrimp, peeled and deveined
  1 teaspoon bottled minced garlic
  ½ teaspoon paprika
  ¼ teaspoon ground turmeric
  ¼ teaspoon crushed red pepper
  1 (14.5-ounce) can diced tomatoes with green peppers and oregano

1. Cook rice in boiling water 7 minutes. Add peas; cover and cook 3 minutes. Drain well; set aside.
2. While rice cooks, combine hot water and saffron threads in a small bowl. Heat a large nonstick skillet over medium-high heat. Add chorizo, and cook 3 minutes or until lightly browned, turning once. Add shrimp and next 4 ingredients, and sauté 3 minutes. Add saffron mixture and tomatoes, and bring to a boil. Reduce heat, and simmer 4 minutes, stirring occasionally. Stir in rice and peas. Yield: 6 servings (serving size: 1 cup).

CALORIES 362 (24% from fat); FAT 9.5g (sat 3.2g, mono 3.8g, poly 1.5g); PROTEIN 31.7g; CARB 34.8g; FIBER 2.8g; CHOL 189mg; IRON 5mg; SODIUM 691mg; CALC 86mg

Antipasto Italian Roll-Ups

We used Alessi sun-dried tomato spread. You'll find it in a jar along with other sun-dried tomato products. The blend of herbs, olive oil, and sun-dried tomatoes is also good tossed with pasta or as a topping on grilled beef, pork, or fish.

  1 tablespoon fat-free sour cream
  1 tablespoon sun-dried tomato spread
  2 (6-inch) fat-free flour tortillas
  ½ cup fresh basil leaves
  ⅓ cup chopped bottled roasted red bell peppers
  2 ounces part-skim mozzarella cheese, thinly sliced
  1 ounce thinly sliced reduced-fat salami

1. Combine sour cream and tomato spread. Spread 1 tablespoon tomato mixture down center of each tortilla. Top evenly with basil, bell pepper, mozzarella cheese, and salami; roll up. Yield: 2 servings (serving size: 1 roll-up).

CALORIES 274 (37% from fat); FAT 11.4g (sat 4.5g, mono 1.4g, poly 0.3g); PROTEIN 15.9g; CARB 27.7g; FIBER 1.7g; CHOL 29mg; IRON 1.8mg; SODIUM 824mg; CALC 315mg

Spiced Shrimp with Peach Salsa

PEACH SALSA:
  3½ cups coarsely chopped peeled peaches
  1 cup coarsely chopped red bell pepper
  1 cup coarsely chopped green bell pepper
  ⅓ cup coarsely chopped red onion
  1 jalapeño pepper, seeded and chopped
  ¼ cup fresh cilantro leaves
  1 tablespoon lime juice
  ¼ teaspoon salt

SHRIMP:
  2 teaspoons brown sugar
  1 teaspoon ground cumin
  ¼ teaspoon salt
  ¼ teaspoon black pepper
  1½ pounds large shrimp, peeled and deveined
  1 tablespoon vegetable oil

1. To prepare salsa, place first 8 ingredients in a food processor; pulse 8 times. Set aside.
2. To prepare shrimp, combine sugar, cumin, ¼ teaspoon salt, black pepper, and shrimp in a large bowl; toss gently to coat. Heat oil in a large nonstick skillet over medium-high heat. Add shrimp mixture, and sauté 4 minutes or until shrimp are done. Serve with peach salsa. Yield: 4 servings (serving size: 5 ounces shrimp and 1 cup salsa).

CALORIES 272 (23% from fat); FAT 6.9g (sat 0.8g, mono 2.5g, poly 2.2g); PROTEIN 35.7g; CARB 16.1g; FIBER 2.5g; CHOL 259mg; IRON 4.8mg; SODIUM 612mg; CALC 110mg

All About Soy

In its many guises, soy can star in dishes from appetizers to desserts.

Soy has been a staple in Asian diets for centuries. But just a couple of decades ago, only committed vegetarians in the United States ate tempeh or tofu. Back then, Americans had to venture to health-food stores to buy soy foods. And finding easy, tasty recipes that called for items such as edamame or soy flour was a challenge.

That's all changed. Today, most of us have learned to love soy for what it is. We can be up front with it, no longer sneaking it into recipes in place of something else, or serving it solely as a meat substitute. That's why in this primer, we focus on how to cook with natural soy products such as tofu, soy milk, soybeans, edamame, miso, tempeh, and soy flour.

MAKE AHEAD • FREEZABLE
Spaghetti and Meatballs with Miso-Tomato Sauce
(pictured on page 256)

Not even meat-and-potato diehards are likely to spot the soy in these meatballs. Frozen soy crumbles mix with ground beef for heightened texture and taste; dark red miso gives the sauce a deep richness. Combined, they contribute 4.1 grams of soy protein per serving. To add even more soy, use soy-enriched pasta, such as Soy7. Make a hot hero sandwich with the meatballs and sauce.

MEATBALLS:
- 1 cup frozen soy crumbles, thawed (such as Morningstar Farms)
- ½ cup Italian-seasoned dry breadcrumbs
- ½ cup finely chopped onion
- ¼ cup chopped fresh flat-leaf parsley
- 3 tablespoons 1% low-fat milk
- ½ teaspoon salt
- ⅛ teaspoon freshly ground black pepper
- 1 large egg white, lightly beaten
- 1 garlic clove, minced
- ½ pound ground round

SAUCE:
- 1½ tablespoons olive oil
- 1½ cups finely chopped onion
- 2 garlic cloves, minced
- ¼ cup tomato paste
- 2 tablespoons chopped fresh or 1 teaspoon dried oregano
- 2 (28-ounce) cans diced tomatoes, undrained
- 2 bay leaves
- 2 tablespoons red miso
- 2 tablespoons water
- ¼ teaspoon freshly ground black pepper

REMAINING INGREDIENTS:
- 7 cups hot cooked spaghetti (about 1 pound uncooked pasta)
- ½ cup (2 ounces) grated Parmigiano-Reggiano cheese
- Flat-leaf parsley sprigs (optional)

1. Preheat oven to 375°.
2. To prepare meatballs, combine first 10 ingredients; shape mixture into 24 (¾-inch) meatballs. Arrange meatballs 2 inches apart on a jelly roll pan. Bake at 375° for 12 minutes, turning after 6 minutes. Set aside.
3. To prepare sauce, heat oil in a large nonstick skillet over medium-high heat.

Add 1½ cups onion, and sauté 2 minutes. Add 2 garlic cloves; sauté 1 minute. Add tomato paste, oregano, diced tomatoes, and bay leaves; bring to a boil. Reduce heat, and simmer 15 minutes or until slightly thick.
4. Combine miso and water; stir with a whisk. Add miso mixture and ¼ teaspoon pepper to sauce. Discard bay leaves. Serve sauce over spaghetti and meatballs. Sprinkle with cheese; garnish with parsley sprigs, if desired. Yield: 8 servings (serving size: about 1 cup spaghetti, ¾ cup sauce, 3 meatballs, and 1 tablespoon cheese).

CALORIES 441 (24% from fat); FAT 11.6g (sat 3.6g, mono 4.9g, poly 1.7g); PROTEIN 22.6g; CARB 61.9g; FIBER 8g; CHOL 22mg; IRON 4.8mg; SODIUM 916mg; CALC 174mg

QUICK & EASY
Salmon and Edamame Pasta Salad

Using edamame in a familiar dish is an easy way to incorporate soy into your diet—you get 3.8 grams of soy protein per serving here. This recipe is also a smart use for leftover grilled or poached salmon.

- 1½ cups uncooked farfalle (about 4 ounces bow tie pasta)
- ⅔ cup shelled edamame
- Cooking spray
- 1 (4-ounce) salmon fillet, skinned
- 2 teaspoons olive oil
- 1 cup finely chopped red onion
- 4 ounces baby spinach (about 6 cups)
- ¼ cup chopped fresh dill
- 4 teaspoons whole-grain Dijon mustard
- ½ teaspoon salt
- ¼ teaspoon freshly ground black pepper

1. Cook pasta in boiling water 5 minutes. Add edamame; cook 6 minutes or until tender. Drain and rinse with cold water. Drain and place in a large bowl.
2. Heat a nonstick skillet coated with cooking spray over medium-high heat.
Continued

Add salmon; cook 7 minutes or until fish flakes easily when tested with a fork, turning once. Coarsely chop salmon. Add to pasta mixture; toss gently to combine.

3. Heat oil in pan over medium-high heat. Add onion; sauté 4 minutes or until tender. Add spinach; cook 2 minutes or just until wilted, stirring frequently. Add spinach mixture and dill to pasta mixture; toss gently to combine. Add mustard, salt, and pepper; toss gently to coat. Yield: 4 servings (serving size: 1 cup).

CALORIES 262 (27% from fat); FAT 8g (sat 1.3g, mono 3.2g, poly 2.2g); PROTEIN 17.1g; CARB 31.5g; FIBER 4.8g; CHOL 14mg; IRON 3.6mg; SODIUM 418mg; CALC 137mg

---

MAKE AHEAD

Chipotle-Black Bean Dip with Garlic Pita Chips

The beans in this tasty dip are canned black soybeans. Look for them with organic foods in your supermarket. The dip is thick enough to use as a sandwich spread—try it in a pita pocket with tomato, lettuce, and red onion. One serving contains a fair amount of soy protein—3.2 grams.

CHIPS:

- 6 large garlic cloves, unpeeled
- 2 (6-inch) whole wheat pitas, split in half horizontally
- Olive oil-flavored cooking spray
- ½ teaspoon kosher salt
- ⅛ teaspoon freshly ground black pepper

DIP:

- ⅓ cup bottled salsa
- ¼ cup chopped fresh cilantro
- 3 tablespoons tomato paste
- 1 tablespoon vegetable oil
- 1 teaspoon sugar
- 1 teaspoon ground cumin
- 1 teaspoon dried oregano
- 1 teaspoon minced canned chipotle chile in adobo sauce
- ½ teaspoon kosher salt
- ½ teaspoon onion powder
- 1 (15-ounce) can black soybeans, rinsed and drained
- 1 garlic clove, chopped

1. Preheat oven to 400°.

2. To prepare chips, wrap 6 garlic cloves in foil. Bake at 400° for 45 minutes; cool 10 minutes. Squeeze to extract garlic pulp; discard skins. Spread garlic pulp evenly over pita halves; spray pita halves with cooking spray. Cut each pita half into 8 wedges; arrange on a baking sheet. Sprinkle wedges with ½ teaspoon salt and pepper. Bake at 400° for 7 minutes or until crisp.

3. To prepare dip, combine salsa and remaining 11 ingredients in a food processor; process until smooth, scraping sides of bowl once. Serve dip with chips. Yield: 8 servings (serving size: 3 tablespoons dip and 4 chips).

NOTE: Store dip, covered, up to 4 days in the refrigerator. Store chips in a zip-top plastic bag up to 2 days at room temperature.

CALORIES 107 (24% from fat); FAT 2.8g (sat 0.4g, mono 0.8g, poly 1.3g); PROTEIN 6.1g; CARB 16g; FIBER 4.1g; CHOL 0mg; IRON 2mg; SODIUM 427mg; CALC 42mg

---

Lemon Risotto with Tempeh

Soy and lemon pair elegantly in this golden risotto. Sautéed tempeh adds an earthy flavor reminiscent of chanterelles and provides 6 grams of soy protein per serving. Vary the flavor with Asiago or pecorino cheese.

- Cooking spray
- 4 ounces soy tempeh, cut into ¼-inch cubes
- 4 cups fat-free, less-sodium chicken broth
- 1½ tablespoons butter
- 1 tablespoon olive oil
- ⅓ cup finely chopped shallots
- 1 cup Arborio rice
- ½ cup dry white wine
- 2 teaspoons grated lemon rind
- ½ cup chopped fresh flat-leaf parsley
- 2 tablespoons fresh lemon juice
- ½ cup (2 ounces) grated Parmigiano-Reggiano cheese
- ¼ cup thinly sliced green onions

1. Heat a medium nonstick skillet coated with cooking spray over medium-high

heat. Add tempeh; sauté 4 minutes or until golden brown. Remove from pan; cool slightly.

2. Bring broth to a simmer in a medium saucepan (do not boil). Keep warm over low heat.

3. Heat butter and oil in a large saucepan over medium-high heat until butter melts. Add shallots; sauté 2 minutes or until tender. Add rice; sauté 1 minute. Add wine; cook 1 minute or until liquid is nearly absorbed, stirring constantly. Stir in rind. Add broth, ½ cup at a time, stirring constantly until each portion is absorbed before adding next (about 20 minutes total). Stir in parsley and juice. Remove from heat; stir in cheese. Top with tempeh and green onions. Yield: 4 servings (serving size: 1 cup risotto, 1 ounce tempeh, and 1 tablespoon green onions).

CALORIES 426 (29% from fat); FAT 13.5g (sat 6.3g, mono 5g, poly 0.6g); PROTEIN 19.6g; CARB 53.2g; FIBER 3.5g; CHOL 23mg; IRON 2.1mg; SODIUM 770mg; CALC 278mg

---

Chicken Tonight Menu

serves 4

Miso Chicken Piccata

Broccoli spears tossed in shallot butter*

Orzo

Vanilla ice cream

*Steam 1 pound broccoli spears, covered, 4 minutes. Melt 1 tablespoon butter in a small saucepan over medium heat. Add 2 tablespoons chopped shallots; cook 3 minutes. Remove from heat. Stir in 2 teaspoons balsamic vinegar, 1 teaspoon lemon juice, and ¼ teaspoon salt. Drizzle butter mixture over broccoli, and toss gently to coat.

Miso Chicken Piccata

Salty miso in the classic lemony pan sauce gives this piccata a deeper, richer flavor but isn't a significant source of soy protein (only 1.4 grams per serving in this dish). For more soy, try tofu steaks and vegetable broth in place of the chicken and chicken broth. Serve with orzo or rice to soak up the sauce.

- ¾ cup fat-free, less-sodium chicken broth, divided
- 3 tablespoons yellow miso (soybean paste)
- 4 (6-ounce) skinless, boneless chicken breast halves
- 2 tablespoons all-purpose flour
- 1 tablespoon olive oil
- ½ cup dry white wine
- 1 garlic clove, minced
- ¼ cup fresh lemon juice
- 2 tablespoons capers, rinsed and drained
- ⅛ teaspoon freshly ground black pepper

1. Combine ¼ cup broth and miso, stirring well with a whisk until miso dissolves. Stir in ½ cup broth. Set aside.
2. Place each chicken breast half between 2 sheets of heavy-duty plastic wrap; pound to ¼-inch thickness using a meat mallet or rolling pin. Place flour in a shallow dish; dredge chicken in flour.
3. Heat oil in a large nonstick skillet over medium-high heat. Add chicken; cook 4 minutes on each side or until browned. Remove chicken from pan. Add wine to pan, scraping pan to loosen browned bits. Reduce heat to medium; stir in miso mixture and garlic. Return chicken to pan; cook 3 minutes or until done. Remove from heat; stir in juice, capers, and pepper. Serve immediately. Yield: 4 servings (serving size: 1 chicken breast half and ¼ cup sauce).

CALORIES 263 (21% from fat); FAT 6.2g (sat 1g, mono 3.2g, poly 1.3g); PROTEIN 41.9g; CARB 7.7g; FIBER 0.6g; CHOL 99mg; IRON 1.7mg; SODIUM 880mg; CALC 26mg

---

Getting Your Grams

Consuming 25 grams of soy protein per day, as part of a diet low in saturated fat and cholesterol, might reduce the risk of heart disease, according to the Food and Drug Administration. These are some of the most concentrated sources of soy protein:

Food	Serving size	Grams of soy protein per serving
Tempeh	1 cup	32g
Tofu	1 cup	20g
Yellow soybeans	½ cup	14g
Soy nuts	⅓ cup	13g
Edamame	½ cup	11g
Soy milk (plain, calcium-fortified)	1 cup	10g

Salade Niçoise with Creamy Tofu Dressing

This salad isn't a significant source of soy protein. If you're not an anchovy fan, replace them with a tablespoon of drained capers.

DRESSING:
- 1 tablespoon water
- 1 tablespoon red wine vinegar
- 1 tablespoon fresh lemon juice
- 1 teaspoon chopped fresh thyme
- ¼ teaspoon salt
- ¼ teaspoon freshly ground black pepper
- 4 ounces firm silken tofu
- 2 canned anchovy fillets
- 1 garlic clove, chopped

SALAD:
- 12 ounces small red potatoes
- 12 ounces green beans, trimmed
- 1½ pounds fresh tuna
- ½ teaspoon salt
- ¼ teaspoon freshly ground black pepper
- Cooking spray
- 1 cup thinly sliced red onion, separated into rings
- 2 tomatoes, each cut into ¼-inch-thick wedges
- 1 hard-cooked large egg, cut into 6 wedges
- 2 tablespoons chopped fresh flat-leaf parsley
- 1 tablespoon capers
- 24 green picholine olives, pitted and halved

1. To prepare dressing, place first 9 ingredients in a food processor or blender; process 1 minute or until smooth. Cover and chill.
2. To prepare salad, place potatoes in a saucepan; cover with water. Bring to a boil. Reduce heat; simmer 10 minutes or until tender. Drain and rinse with cold water. Drain and cut potatoes in half. Set aside.
3. Cook beans in boiling water 3 minutes or until crisp-tender. Drain and rinse with cold water; drain. Set aside.
4. Prepare grill or grill pan.
5. Sprinkle fish with ½ teaspoon salt and ¼ teaspoon pepper. Place fish on a grill rack or grill pan coated with cooking spray; cook 4 minutes on each side or until fish flakes easily when tested with a fork. Break fish into large chunks. Arrange fish, beans, and onion in center of a large serving platter; arrange potatoes, tomatoes, and egg around fish mixture. Sprinkle with parsley, capers, and olives. Drizzle with dressing. Yield: 6 servings.

CALORIES 276 (29% from fat); FAT 9g (sat 2g, mono 3.6g, poly 2.3g); PROTEIN 30.8g; CARB 18.3g; FIBER 4g; CHOL 78mg; IRON 3.1mg; SODIUM 781mg; CALC 69mg

Edamame

Served in Japanese restaurants and now offered in many supermarkets, these sweet, bright green soybeans are delicious served in the pod or shelled, like baby limas. Edamame aren't a variety of soybean. They're immature soybeans that are picked green and served fresh. In season, usually from late July to September, you might find fresh edamame at local farmers' markets. Frozen, they're available year-round, both in the pod and shelled. For a snack, boil edamame in the pod, drain, and sprinkle with coarse salt.

Yellow and Black Soybeans

As soybeans mature, they ripen into hard, dry beans. Though most mature soybeans are yellow, there are also black varieties. These dried beans require an overnight soak and about three hours of cooking time to make them tender. Canned yellow or black soybeans, usually found on the organic food aisle, are a fast alternative. They have a slippery texture and a firm bite. Yellow soybeans require assertive seasoning to enhance their bland taste; black soybeans, however, can stand alone in salads and side dishes. Both are good in chili, stews, and soups, and puréed for dip. Rinse canned beans before using.

Tofu

In European writing, the Japanese word *tofu* first appeared in 1603. Today, you find this traditional neutral-tasting soy food in nearly every U.S. supermarket.

Tofu is good in Asian stir-fries, desserts, drinks, dressings, salads, stews, and soups. It's also good tossed on the grill. It varies in texture from creamy and smooth to firm enough to slice. Today, tofu also is sold marinated and smoked, or flavored with seasonings such as teriyaki or garlic and herbs. Selecting the right kind is the key to good tofu dishes.

Silken (*Kinugoshi,* or Japanese-style): Sold in aseptic boxes and available in soft, firm, and extrafirm textures, silken tofu is custardlike and ideal to purée for dressings, soups, desserts, and drinks. It's much too delicate to grill, sauté, or stir-fry.

Regular (*Momen,* or Chinese-style): Also found in soft, firm, and extrafirm textures, this tofu is packed in water in plastic tubs and pouches. Its dense texture makes it ideal to sauté, grill, or broil. Choose soft, water-packed tofu for scrambling and to use in spreads, thick dips, and some desserts; select firm for grilling, sautéing, and stir-frying. Squeezing, pressing, and freezing tofu can enhance its texture.

Tempeh

A fermented food, tempeh is made from partly cooked soybeans inoculated with spores of a friendly mold in a process resembling cheese-making. The mold creates threads that bind the beans into a flat cake. Tempeh is blanched or frozen to slow fermentation and preserve active enzymes. It has a yeasty flavor and firm texture.

Tempeh can be made with soybeans alone, but you often find it composed of soy and a grain, such as rice, barley, or quinoa. All-soy tempeh is highest in protein, has the most pronounced flavor, and is highest in fat. Good grilled, sautéed, pan-crisped, or braised, tempeh is sold at natural-foods stores and in some large supermarkets.

Soy Milk

Soy milk is squeezed from dried soybeans that have been soaked, ground, and cooked. Asian markets sell it just as it comes from the bean, thin and strong-tasting, perhaps sweetened. Soy milk sold in supermarkets and natural-foods stores tastes mild by comparison and is thickened to resemble dairy milk. Besides chocolate and vanilla, it comes in an increasing selection of flavors, such as chai and latte.

Like tofu, which is made from soy milk, it varies significantly by brand in taste, protein, and fat content. (To reduce fat, water is added.) Most soy milk is calcium-fortified to equal dairy milk. A replacement for dairy milk in recipes, unsweetened soy milk is best in desserts and some savory dishes.

Miso

This fermented soybean paste originated in ancient China and migrated throughout Asia, where it's still popular. Chefs love miso, especially for seasoning fish. Made from a blend of soy and grain or with soy alone, it instantly adds rich flavor to all kinds of dishes. It also adds creaminess to sauces and soups, and thickens them slightly.

Resembling peanut butter, miso ranges in color from light to dark and in taste from mildly sweet to very salty. It contains less sodium per serving than salt and regular soy sauce. Miso keeps indefinitely, refrigerated in a glass jar.

Light (Sweet and Mellow White *[Shiro]*, Mellow Beige *[Tanshoku]*): Use with fish, poultry, dressings, creamy soups, and vegetables. Light miso contains the least salt.

Dark (Red *[Aka]*, Barley *[Mugi]*, and all-soy *[Hatcho]*): All dark misos are good with grains and legumes, and in stews, tomato sauce, and gravy.

Soy Flour

Made of finely ground dried soybeans, this high-protein soy food can replace some flour in many recipes. Commercial bakeries often use soy flour in breads and pastries because it retains moisture and gives baked goods longer shelf life. Soy flour also creates a large, fluffy crumb. Adding even a small amount to your favorite bread recipes boosts protein. Using 20 to 30 percent soy flour along with all-purpose works best, because soy flour contains no gluten. Higher amounts can produce a heavy, grainy result. Full-fat soy flour works better than defatted in baking. Store soy flour in a glass jar in the refrigerator or freezer up to 6 months.

Meat Alternatives

From crumbles that resemble ground beef to soy sausage and bacon, these refrigerated and frozen products can replace meat in most recipes. Made with soy protein, they're cholesterol-free and cook quickly.

Spiced-Vanilla Rice Pudding

For this recipe, we used vanilla-flavored soy milk (which adds 3.3 grams of soy protein per serving), but the pudding is also good with chocolate. If you don't have cheesecloth, toss the spices into the rice mixture, and remove them before serving. Short-grain rice is starchier than other varieties; rinsing it removes some of the starch and prevents the dish from becoming chalky.

    ¾ cup uncooked short-grain
       rice
     3 cups water, divided
     3 cardamom pods
     1 whole clove
     1 (2-inch) cinnamon stick
     2 cups vanilla soy milk (such as
       Silk)
    ½ cup sugar
    ⅛ teaspoon salt
     1 large egg yolk
     1 teaspoon vanilla extract
       Ground cinnamon (optional)

1. Place rice in a bowl; cover with water to 1 inch above rice. Stir until water becomes cloudy; drain. Repeat procedure until water no longer becomes cloudy.
2. Place rinsed rice and 2 cups water in a 2-quart saucepan; bring to a boil over medium-high heat. Cover, reduce heat, and simmer 15 minutes or until liquid is absorbed. Remove from heat; let stand 10 minutes. Uncover and stir well.
3. Place cardamom, clove, and cinnamon stick on a double layer of cheesecloth. Gather edges of cheesecloth together; tie securely. Add cheesecloth bag, 1 cup water, milk, sugar, and salt to rice; stir well to combine. Bring to a boil over medium-high heat, stirring frequently. Reduce heat, and simmer until reduced to 4 cups (about 20 minutes). Remove cheesecloth bag; discard.
4. Place egg yolk in a small bowl. Add 1 tablespoon rice mixture; stir well to combine. Stir egg mixture into remaining rice mixture; cook over medium-low heat 3 minutes, stirring constantly. Remove from heat; stir in vanilla. Sprinkle with ground cinnamon, if desired. Serve warm. Yield: 4 servings (serving size: 1 cup).

CALORIES 294 (9% from fat); FAT 3g (sat 0.5g, mono 0.9g, poly 1g); PROTEIN 6.4g; CARB 59.9g; FIBER 1.1g; CHOL 53mg; IRON 1.9mg; SODIUM 123mg; CALC 157mg

Piadini with Garlic Greens

Similar to pitas, Italian *piadini* are quick to make. Soy flour adds a nutty flavor and 2 grams of soy protein per serving. Use full-fat soy flour; low-fat and fat-free flours will yield tough, dry bread. Filling piadini with garlicky greens is common in southern Italy.

PIADINI:
    2¾ cups all-purpose flour
    ¾ cup soy flour
     1 teaspoon salt
    ½ teaspoon baking powder
    ½ teaspoon dried thyme
    ½ teaspoon dried rosemary, crushed
     3 tablespoons extravirgin olive oil
    1¼ cups warm water (100° to 110°)
       Cooking spray

GREENS:
    1½ teaspoons olive oil
     2 garlic cloves, thinly sliced
     1 pound Swiss chard, cut into
       ½-inch strips
     1 (10-ounce) package fresh spinach
     1 teaspoon fresh lemon juice
    ¼ teaspoon freshly ground black
       pepper
    ⅛ teaspoon salt

1. To prepare piadini, lightly spoon flours into dry measuring cups; level with a knife. Combine flours and next 4 ingredients in a large bowl. Add 3 tablespoons oil; stir with a whisk until evenly distributed. Add water, and stir until dough forms. Turn dough out onto a lightly floured surface; knead 2 minutes. Place in a bowl coated with cooking spray. Cover with plastic wrap; let rest at room temperature 30 minutes.
2. To prepare greens, heat 1½ teaspoons oil in a large nonstick skillet over medium heat. Add garlic; cook 2 minutes or until lightly browned, stirring constantly. Add chard; cook 8 minutes or until tender, stirring frequently. Add spinach; cook 3 minutes or just until wilted, stirring frequently. Stir in juice, pepper, and ⅛ teaspoon salt. Remove from heat; keep warm.
3. Divide dough into 24 equal portions; shape each portion into a ball. Working with one portion at a time (cover remaining dough to prevent drying), roll each portion into a 4-inch circle. Stack dough circles between single layers of wax paper to prevent sticking. Heat a large nonstick or cast iron skillet coated with cooking spray over medium-high heat. Add 2 dough circles; cook 1 minute on each side or until golden brown. Cover and keep warm. Repeat procedure with remaining dough circles. Spoon about 2 tablespoons greens onto each flatbread; fold in half. Serve immediately. Yield: 12 servings (serving size: 2 filled piadini).

CALORIES 178 (28% from fat); FAT 5.5g (sat 0.8g, mono 3.2g, poly 1.1g); PROTEIN 6.4g; CARB 26.5g; FIBER 3.1g; CHOL 0mg; IRON 3.3mg; SODIUM 340mg; CALC 71mg

Peach Upside-Down Cake

While soy flour adds only 2 grams soy protein per serving, it produces a moist cake.

     2 tablespoons butter
    ¼ cup packed brown sugar
     4 peeled peaches, halved and pitted
    16 pitted sweet cherries, halved
     1 cup all-purpose flour
    ½ cup soy flour
     2 teaspoons baking powder
    ¼ teaspoon salt
    ⅔ cup granulated sugar
    ¼ cup (2 ounces) block-style fat-free
       cream cheese, softened
     3 tablespoons butter, softened
     1 large egg
     1 large egg white
     1 (6-ounce) can pineapple juice
     1 teaspoon vanilla extract

1. Preheat oven to 350°.
2. Melt 2 tablespoons butter in a 10-inch cast iron skillet over medium heat; sprinkle brown sugar into pan. Remove from heat. Place 1 peach half, cut side

Continued

up, in center of pan; arrange remaining peach halves around center peach half. Arrange cherry halves, cut sides up, around peach halves. Set pan aside.

3. Lightly spoon flours into dry measuring cups; level with a knife. Combine flours, baking powder, and salt; stir with a whisk. Place granulated sugar, cream cheese, and 3 tablespoons butter in a large bowl; beat with a mixer at medium speed 3 minutes. Add egg and egg white; beat well. Add flour mixture and juice alternately to egg mixture, beginning and ending with flour mixture; mix well after each addition. Stir in vanilla. Spoon batter into center of prepared pan; gently spread batter to cover fruit.

4. Bake at 350° for 35 minutes or until cake springs back when lightly touched in center. Cool in pan 10 minutes on a wire rack. Run a knife around edge of cake. Place a plate upside down on top of pan; invert onto plate. Let stand 2 minutes before removing pan. Serve warm. Yield: 8 servings (serving size: 1 wedge).

CALORIES 299 (28% from fat); FAT 9.2g (sat 4.9g, mono 2.6g, poly 1.1g); PROTEIN 6.5g; CARB 48.9g; FIBER 2.8g; CHOL 47mg; IRON 1.8mg; SODIUM 321mg; CALC 120mg

> Soy has gone mainstream with its variety of flavors and textures: the creaminess of tofu, the meaty texture of tempeh, the saltiness of miso, and the nutty crunch of edamame.

Minestrone Soup with Soybeans

This soup features canned yellow soybeans, which give each serving 6.1 grams of soy protein. Using a Tuscan technique, the soup is seasoned with a *battuto*, a paste of turkey bacon and aromatics.

BATTUTO:
- ½ cup coarsely chopped red onion
- ½ cup coarsely chopped carrot
- ⅓ cup coarsely chopped celery
- ¼ cup flat-leaf parsley leaves
- 2 turkey-bacon slices, coarsely chopped
- 1 garlic clove

SOUP:
- 2 teaspoons olive oil
- 4 cups fat-free, less-sodium chicken broth
- 1½ cups coarsely chopped seeded plum tomatoes
- 1½ cups (½-inch) cubed peeled Yukon gold potatoes
- 1 (15-ounce) can yellow soybeans, rinsed and drained
- 1 (3-inch) rosemary sprig
- 1 cup (1-inch) cut green beans
- 1 cup sliced zucchini
- 1 cup cauliflower florets
- ½ teaspoon salt
- ¼ teaspoon freshly ground black pepper
- 1 ounce uncooked spaghetti, broken into 1-inch pieces
- ¼ cup (1 ounce) grated Parmigiano-Reggiano cheese

1. To prepare battuto, combine first 6 ingredients in a food processor; pulse until mixture is almost a paste.

2. To prepare soup, heat oil in a Dutch oven over medium-high heat. Add battuto; sauté 3 minutes. Add broth and next 4 ingredients; bring to a boil. Cover, reduce heat, and simmer 5 minutes. Add green beans and next 5 ingredients. Simmer, uncovered, 20 minutes or until vegetables are tender. Discard rosemary. Top with cheese. Yield: 6 servings (serving size: 1⅓ cups soup and 2 teaspoons cheese).

CALORIES 211 (30% from fat); FAT 7.1g (sat 1.7g, mono 3.3g, poly 1.3g); PROTEIN 13.2g; CARB 25.1g; FIBER 4.8g; CHOL 6mg; IRON 3.9mg; SODIUM 708mg; CALC 172mg

English Muffin Strata with Ham and Cheese

Soy milk, made from only soybeans and water, works best in the savory custard; look for it in boxes on the organic-foods aisle of the supermarket. It provides each serving with 4.2 grams of soy protein.

- 6 English muffins, split
- Cooking spray
- ¾ cup chopped Canadian bacon (about 3 ounces)
- ½ cup (2 ounces) shredded Swiss cheese
- 2½ cups unsweetened soy milk
- 4 teaspoons Dijon mustard
- ½ teaspoon dry mustard
- ¼ teaspoon salt
- ⅛ teaspoon freshly ground black pepper
- Dash of ground red pepper
- 2 large eggs, lightly beaten
- 2 large egg whites, lightly beaten

1. Cut each muffin half into 6 wedges. Arrange half of muffin wedges in bottom of an 8-inch square baking dish coated with cooking spray. Top with bacon. Sprinkle with half of cheese. Arrange remaining muffin wedges over cheese. Top with remaining cheese.

2. Combine milk and remaining 7 ingredients, stirring with a whisk until blended. Pour milk mixture over muffin mixture. Cover and refrigerate 8 hours or overnight.

3. Preheat oven to 325°.

4. Uncover strata, and bake at 325° for 1 hour or until a knife inserted in center comes out clean. Let stand 15 minutes before serving. Yield: 6 servings.

CALORIES 253 (30% from fat); FAT 8.3g (sat 2.7g, mono 2.6g, poly 1.3g); PROTEIN 16.4g; CARB 29.2g; FIBER 3.4g; CHOL 86mg; IRON 2.9mg; SODIUM 652mg; CALC 130mg

Spicy Peanut Noodles with Shrimp, page 260

Beer-Can Chicken with Cola Barbecue Sauce,
page 263

Grilled Asparagus Rafts,
page 261

Caramel Corn Ice Cream, page 265

Creamed Corn with Bacon and Leeks, page 266

White Velvet Soup, page 272

Spaghetti and Meatballs with Miso-Tomato Sauce,
page 247

In the Bag

A family favorite that employs foil cooking gives an Illinois reader more time for fun.

Laura Tucker, of Highland Park, Illinois, contends the best features of her recipe for Sweet-and-Sour Chicken are "a satisfied family and nothing to clean up."

Key to the latter is the use of a foil cooking bag and an outdoor grill. "The steam in the bag helps the flavors blend and the food cook evenly, just as though it was in the oven," she says.

Sweet-and-Sour Chicken

    4   (6-ounce) skinless, boneless
        chicken breast halves
    2   cups teriyaki marinade,
        divided
    2   cups (1-inch) cubed fresh
        pineapple
    2   cups vertically sliced Vidalia or
        other sweet onion
 1 ½   cups yellow or orange bell pepper
        strips
 1 ½   cups red bell pepper strips
    2   cups cherry tomatoes
  ¼   cup chopped fresh cilantro

1. Place chicken in a large zip-top plastic bag; add 1 cup marinade. Seal bag; toss gently to coat. Place pineapple, onion, and bell peppers in another large zip-top plastic bag; add 1 cup marinade. Seal bag; toss gently to coat. Refrigerate bags 2 hours, turning occasionally.
2. Prepare grill.
3. Remove pineapple mixture from bag; discard marinade. Place pineapple mixture and tomatoes in a large foil cooking bag. Remove chicken from bag; discard marinade. Place chicken on top of pineapple mixture. Seal and cut 6 (½-inch) slits in top of cooking bag. Place bag on grill. Grill 25 minutes or until chicken is done. Cut bag open with a sharp knife or kitchen shears. Carefully peel back foil. Sprinkle with cilantro.

Yield: 4 servings (serving size: 1 chicken breast half and 1 cup pineapple mixture).

CALORIES 336 (8% from fat); FAT 3.2g (sat 0.7g, mono 0.6g, poly 0.9g); PROTEIN 43g; CARB 35g; FIBER 7g; CHOL 99mg; IRON 3mg; SODIUM 279mg; CALC 72mg

QUICK & EASY

Scrumptious Shrimp with Artichokes

"The myriad flavors meld to create this 'scrumptious' dish. It can be served over rice or pasta, and tastes even better with a big hunk of crusty bread."

—Mary Bayramian,
Laguna Beach, California

    1   tablespoon olive oil
    1   pound large shrimp, peeled and
        deveined
 1 ½   tablespoons dried red pepper
        flakes
    2   garlic cloves, minced
    2   cups chopped tomato
    2   tablespoons chopped fresh
        flat-leaf parsley
    1   teaspoon paprika
  ¼   teaspoon salt
    1   (14-ounce) can quartered
        artichoke hearts, drained

1. Heat oil in a large nonstick skillet over medium-high heat. Add shrimp, pepper flakes, and garlic; sauté 3 minutes. Add tomato and remaining ingredients; cook 3 minutes or until shrimp are done and mixture is thoroughly heated, stirring frequently. Yield: 4 servings (serving size: 1½ cups).

CALORIES 233 (24% from fat); FAT 6.1g (sat 1g, mono 2.9g, poly 1.4g); PROTEIN 27.8g; CARB 17.9g; FIBER 5.3g; CHOL 172mg; IRON 3.6mg; SODIUM 926mg; CALC 73mg

QUICK & EASY

Salmon with Maple Syrup and Toasted Almonds

"While we were visiting my brother's family, my husband threw this together from what was in the kitchen. The dish was such a huge hit even our finicky teenagers were heading back for seconds."

—Carol Ovios, Newport, Rhode Island

    6   (6-ounce) salmon fillets
        Cooking spray
  ¼   cup packed brown sugar
  ¼   cup maple syrup
    3   tablespoons low-sodium soy sauce
    1   tablespoon Dijon mustard
  ¼   teaspoon black pepper
    4   teaspoons sliced almonds,
        toasted

1. Preheat oven to 425°.
2. Place fillets in a 13 x 9-inch baking dish coated with cooking spray. Combine sugar, syrup, soy sauce, mustard, and black pepper; pour sugar mixture over fillets. Cover with foil; bake at 425° for 10 minutes. Remove foil; sprinkle fillets with almonds. Bake an additional 10 minutes or until fish flakes easily when tested with a fork. Serve with sugar mixture. Yield: 6 servings (serving size: 1 fillet and about 2 tablespoons sugar mixture).

CALORIES 396 (44% from fat); FAT 19.4g (sat 3.8g, mono 7.1g, poly 6.9g); PROTEIN 34.7g; CARB 19.1g; FIBER 0.3g; CHOL 100mg; IRON 1.2mg; SODIUM 435mg; CALC 46mg

Baked Halibut with Vegetables

"I've made this recipe for years but have never kept precise measurements. For this Reader Recipes section, I prepared it and kept notes as I was cooking."

—Betty Snowden, Winchester, Kentucky

    4   (6-ounce) halibut fillets
        Cooking spray
    1   tablespoon lemon juice
    2   teaspoons chopped fresh dill
    1   cup coarsely chopped tomato
  ½   cup sliced green onions
  ½   cup coarsely chopped red bell
        pepper
  ½   cup coarsely chopped green bell
        pepper
  ½   cup coarsely chopped yellow bell
        pepper
  ½   teaspoon salt
  ¼   teaspoon black pepper
  ½   cup (2 ounces) shredded Jarlsberg
        cheese
  ½   cup dry white wine

Continued

1. Preheat oven to 425°.

2. Place fish in a 13 x 9-inch baking dish coated with cooking spray. Drizzle with lemon juice; sprinkle with dill. Top with tomato and next 6 ingredients; sprinkle with cheese. Pour wine into dish; cover with foil. Bake at 425° for 25 minutes or until fish flakes easily when tested with a fork. Yield: 4 servings (serving size: 1 fillet and ½ cup vegetables).

CALORIES 300 (26% from fat); FAT 8.7g (sat 3.5g, mono 2.5g, poly 1.5g); PROTEIN 41.1g; CARB 7.9g; FIBER 1.9g; CHOL 70mg; IRON 2.1mg; SODIUM 435mg; CALC 250mg

---

QUICK & EASY • MAKE AHEAD
Triple Bean Salad

"This salad was inspired by a dish served in a small sandwich shop that my husband and I used to frequent. We loved it so much that I tried my best to re-create it. It can be served as a side dish or over a bed of lettuce as a light lunch."

—Josie Fertig, Selinsgrove, Pennsylvania

½ cup chopped green onions
½ cup chopped green bell pepper
½ cup chopped red bell pepper
1 (15½-ounce) can chickpeas (garbanzo beans), rinsed and drained
1 (15.5-ounce) can kidney beans, rinsed and drained
1 (15.5-ounce) can black beans, rinsed and drained
3 tablespoons red wine vinegar
2 tablespoons olive oil
1 teaspoon freshly ground black pepper
1 teaspoon lemon juice
½ teaspoon salt

1. Combine first 6 ingredients in a large bowl. Combine vinegar, oil, pepper, juice, and salt, stirring with a whisk; pour over bean mixture, stirring to coat. Cover and chill. Yield: 12 servings (serving size: ½ cup).

CALORIES 128 (30% from fat); FAT 4.2g (sat 0.3g, mono 1.7g, poly 0.2g); PROTEIN 5.8g; CARB 20.8g; FIBER 6.3g; CHOL 0mg; IRON 1.6mg; SODIUM 321mg; CALC 34mg

---

MAKE AHEAD
Papaya and Mango Salsa

"This is a great summer salsa. I like to try new stuff at home, and when I brought home a firm, unripe papaya from the local market, I added a few things I had in the house and came up with this. It's so versatile—it can be served with chips, fish, or meat."

—Praba Iyer, San Mateo, California

2 cups shredded peeled firm papaya
2 cups chopped peeled mango
1 cup finely chopped red onion
¼ cup chopped fresh cilantro
¼ cup chopped fresh mint
1½ tablespoons fresh lemon juice
1 tablespoon finely chopped seeded jalapeño pepper
⅛ teaspoon salt
Dash of sugar

1. Combine all ingredients in a large bowl; toss gently to coat. Yield: 8 servings (serving size: ½ cup).

CALORIES 51 (5% from fat); FAT 0.3g (sat 0.1g, mono 0.1g, poly 0.1g); PROTEIN 0.8g; CARB 12.8g; FIBER 2g; CHOL 0mg; IRON 0.5mg; SODIUM 40mg; CALC 23mg

---

season's best

Pesto

Pesto, redolent with fresh basil, garlic, and Parmesan, is a treasure of the summer. And we think this version is as delicious as any we've tried.

It works beautifully in the most traditional manner: stirred into pasta or soup, or served on grilled meats or vegetables. Another way to enjoy it is in a rustic eggplant torte (recipe at right). As a dazzling first course or a light supper unto itself, this make-ahead torte is yet another reason to translate armloads of basil into pesto.

STAFF FAVORITE • QUICK & EASY
MAKE AHEAD
Pesto

When storing, cover the surface of the pesto with plastic wrap. The pesto should keep for 2 weeks in the refrigerator.

4 garlic cloves, peeled
4 cups packed basil leaves (about 2½ ounces)
½ cup (2 ounces) grated fresh Parmesan cheese
¼ cup pine nuts
¾ teaspoon salt
½ teaspoon freshly ground black pepper
½ cup warm water
6 tablespoons extravirgin olive oil

1. Drop garlic through food chute with processor on; process until minced. Add basil and next 4 ingredients to processor; process 10 seconds. Combine water and oil in a measuring cup. With processor on, slowly pour oil mixture through food chute; process just until blended. Yield: 1¼ cups (serving size: 1 tablespoon).

CALORIES 59 (87% from fat); FAT 5.7g (sat 1.2g, mono 3.5g, poly 0.7g); PROTEIN 1.6g; CARB 0.7g; FIBER 0.2g; CHOL 2mg; IRON 0.3mg; SODIUM 134mg; CALC 41mg

---

MAKE AHEAD
Eggplant Torte with Pesto and Sun-Dried Tomatoes

If you don't have a spare baking dish to weigh down the torte, cut a piece of cardboard the size of the pan, and wrap it in foil.

¼ teaspoon salt
2 medium eggplant, cut lengthwise into ½-inch-thick slices
Cooking spray
1 cup boiling water
2 ounces sun-dried tomatoes, packed without oil (about ½ cup)
5 cooked lasagna noodles, cut into thirds
4 ounces thinly sliced provolone cheese
¼ cup Pesto (recipe above)
32 (½-inch-thick) slices diagonally cut French bread baguette, toasted (about 8 ounces)

1. Preheat broiler.

2. Sprinkle salt over 9 eggplant slices; reserve any remaining slices for another use. Place eggplant on a baking sheet coated with cooking spray; broil 10 minutes on each side or until lightly browned. Cool; halve slices crosswise.

3. Combine boiling water and tomatoes; let stand 10 minutes or until soft. Drain and finely chop.

4. Coat an 8½ x 4½-inch baking dish coated with cooking spray; line dish with plastic wrap. Lightly coat plastic wrap with cooking spray. Arrange 5 noodle pieces in bottom of dish; top with half of cheese. Spread half of pesto over cheese; top with 9 eggplant pieces. Sprinkle half of tomato over eggplant. Repeat layers, ending with noodles. Cover with plastic wrap, allowing plastic wrap to extend over edges of dish. Place an empty 8½ x 4½-inch baking dish on top of torte. Place 2 (15-ounce) canned goods upright in dish. Refrigerate overnight.

5. Remove cans, empty baking dish, and top sheet of plastic wrap. Invert torte onto a platter; remove remaining plastic wrap. Cut torte crosswise into 8 slices. Serve at room temperature with bread slices. Yield: 8 servings (serving size: 1 torte slice and 4 bread slices).

CALORIES 246 (30% from fat); FAT 8.3g (sat 3.1g, mono 2.2g, poly 0.8g); PROTEIN 10.3g; CARB 34.6g; FIBER 4.7g; CHOL 11mg; IRON 2.2mg; SODIUM 577mg; CALC 158mg

superfast

. . . And Ready in Just About 20 Minutes

Ingredients straight from the supermarket shelf streamline this month's selections.

Kalamata olives give chicken thighs a Greek flair; marinated artichoke hearts add zest to Israeli couscous and chicken. Peanut noodles with shrimp are fired up, while blueberries shine in a chicken salad and green apples add tartness to a French bread sandwich with turkey and brie.

Chicken Thighs with Tomatoes, Olives, and Capers

Spread the chicken thighs out in the pan so this dish will cook quickly.

- 8   skinless, boneless chicken thighs
- ½   teaspoon salt
- ¼   teaspoon black pepper
- 1   teaspoon vegetable oil
- 1   tablespoon bottled minced garlic
- 1   cup chopped fresh parsley
- ¼   cup chopped pitted kalamata olives
- 2   teaspoons capers
- 1   (14.5-ounce) can no-salt-added diced tomatoes, undrained

1. Sprinkle chicken with salt and pepper. Heat oil in a large nonstick skillet over medium-high heat. Add chicken; cook 4 minutes on each side. Remove chicken from pan; keep warm.

2. Add garlic to pan; sauté 30 seconds. Add parsley and remaining 3 ingredients; scrape pan to loosen browned bits. Return chicken and accumulated juice to pan; reduce heat, and simmer 5 minutes or until chicken is done. Yield: 4 servings (serving size: 2 thighs and about ¼ cup tomato mixture).

CALORIES 174 (28% from fat); FAT 5.5g (sat 1.2g, mono 2.1g, poly 1.2g); PROTEIN 23.9g; CARB 7.2g; FIBER 2.5g; CHOL 94mg; IRON 2.8mg; SODIUM 566mg; CALC 61mg

Smoked Turkey, Brie, Green Apple, and Watercress Sandwich

Serve with a glass of crisp Chardonnay.

- 1½   tablespoons honey
- 1½   tablespoons mustard
- 1   (8-ounce) French bread baguette
- 6   ounces thinly sliced smoked turkey breast
- 4   ounces Brie cheese, thinly sliced
- 1   cup trimmed watercress
- 1   cup thinly sliced peeled Granny Smith apple
- ⅛   teaspoon freshly ground black pepper

1. Preheat oven to 350°.

2. Combine honey and mustard in a small bowl. Cut bread in half horizontally; place on a baking sheet. Spread honey mixture on bottom half of loaf; top with turkey and cheese. Bake at 350° for 5 minutes or until cheese begins to melt.

3. Arrange watercress and apple slices on melted cheese; sprinkle with pepper. Cover with top half of loaf, and cut into 4 portions. Yield: 4 servings (serving size: 1 portion).

CALORIES 337 (29% from fat); FAT 10.7g (sat 5.3g, mono 3.1g, poly 0.7g); PROTEIN 19.4g; CARB 40.8g; FIBER 2.5g; CHOL 45mg; IRON 3.5mg; SODIUM 926mg; CALC 114mg

Tuna and White Bean Salad

Rinsing the white kidney beans, often labeled "cannellini beans," makes them glossy and brightens the salad.

- 1½   cups chopped peeled cucumber (1 medium)
- ½   cup chopped fresh parsley
- ½   cup thinly sliced red onion
- 1½   tablespoons fresh lemon juice
- 1   tablespoon extravirgin olive oil
- ½   teaspoon salt
- ¼   teaspoon black pepper
- 1   (15.5-ounce) can white kidney beans, rinsed and drained
- 2   (6-ounce) cans chunk light tuna, drained
- 1   (2-ounce) jar diced pimiento, drained

1. Combine all ingredients in a large bowl; toss well to coat. Yield: 4 servings (serving size: 1½ cups).

CALORIES 278 (15% from fat); FAT 4.7g (sat 0.8g, mono 2.9g, poly 0.8g); PROTEIN 30.6g; CARB 28.2g; FIBER 6.2g; CHOL 26mg; IRON 5.4mg; SODIUM 574mg; CALC 114mg

Chicken, Endive, and Blueberry Salad with Toasted Pecans

Since Belgian endive is firm and tightly packed, it requires a brief rinse to clean. Remove the outer leaves, and it slices easily.

    4 cups sliced Belgian endive (about
       2 large heads)
 1½ cups chopped roasted skinless,
       boneless chicken breast
    1 cup gourmet salad greens
    1 cup fresh blueberries
 2½ tablespoons apple cider vinegar
 2½ tablespoons honey
   ¾ teaspoon salt
   ¼ teaspoon black pepper
   ½ cup (2 ounces) crumbled goat
       cheese
    2 tablespoons chopped pecans,
       toasted

1. Combine first 4 ingredients in a large bowl. Combine vinegar, honey, salt, and pepper; stir with a whisk. Add dressing to endive mixture; toss gently. Sprinkle with cheese and pecans. Yield: 4 servings (serving size: about 1½ cups).

CALORIES 151 (31% from fat); FAT 5.2g (sat 1.9g, mono 1.9g, poly 0.9g); PROTEIN 13.8g; CARB 13g; FIBER 2.3g; CHOL 34mg; IRON 1.4mg; SODIUM 368mg; CALC 51mg

Spicy Peanut Noodles with Shrimp

(pictured on page 253)

If you don't like spicy food, start with only 1 teaspoon chile paste. If the sauce is too thick, thin it with a little water—it should be the consistency of unwhipped cream.

PEANUT SAUCE:
   ⅓ cup creamy peanut butter
   ¼ to ⅓ cup water
    2 tablespoons low-sodium soy
       sauce
 1½ tablespoons rice vinegar
    1 to 2 teaspoons chile paste with
       garlic
   ½ teaspoon sugar
   ¼ teaspoon salt

SHRIMP:
    1 pound medium shrimp, peeled
       and deveined
   ¼ teaspoon salt
Cooking spray

PASTA:
    8 ounces uncooked thick udon
       noodles or linguine
    1 red bell pepper, cut into julienne
       strips
   ¾ cup chopped seeded cucumber
   ¼ cup diagonally cut green onions
    3 tablespoons chopped roasted
       peanuts
    2 tablespoons cilantro leaves
    4 lime wedges (optional)

1. Cook noodles according to package directions, omitting salt and fat.
2. While noodles cook, prepare peanut sauce. Combine first 7 ingredients; stir with a whisk.
3. To prepare shrimp, toss shrimp with ¼ teaspoon salt. Sauté in a nonstick skillet coated with cooking spray over medium-high heat 3 minutes on each side or until done.
4. To prepare pasta, combine peanut sauce, shrimp, noodles, bell pepper, cucumber, and onions; toss well. Sprinkle with peanuts and cilantro. Serve with lime wedges, if desired. Yield: 4 servings (serving size: 1½ cups).

CALORIES 424 (28% from fat); FAT 13.2g (sat 2.6g, mono 5.6g, poly 3.8g); PROTEIN 25g; CARB 51.1g; FIBER 3.5g; CHOL 129mg; IRON 3mg; SODIUM 765mg; CALC 66mg

Polenta with Sautéed Mushrooms and Asparagus

    2 cups 1% low-fat milk
    2 cups vegetable broth
   ⅛ teaspoon black pepper
   ¾ cup instant polenta
    1 tablespoon butter
Cooking spray
    2 cups sliced mushrooms
    2 teaspoons vegetable oil
 2½ cups (2-inch) sliced asparagus
    1 cup chopped smoked ham
    2 tablespoons grated Parmesan
       cheese

1. Combine first 3 ingredients in a large saucepan. Bring to a simmer; slowly whisk in polenta. Bring to a boil. Cover, reduce heat, and simmer 5 minutes, stirring occasionally. Remove from heat.
2. Melt butter in a large nonstick skillet coated with cooking spray over medium-high heat. Add mushrooms; sauté 5 minutes or until lightly browned. Add oil, asparagus, and ham to pan; sauté 4 minutes or until asparagus is crisp-tender.
3. Serve polenta topped with asparagus mixture; sprinkle with cheese. Yield: 4 servings (serving size: 1 cup polenta, 1 cup asparagus mixture, and 1½ teaspoons cheese).

CALORIES 334 (30% from fat); FAT 11.3g (sat 4.5g, mono 4g, poly 1g); PROTEIN 20.4g; CARB 41.4g; FIBER 2.2g; CHOL 37mg; IRON 1.5mg; SODIUM 1,111mg; CALC 208mg

Couscous with Artichokes, Feta, and Sun-Dried Tomatoes

Though grains of Israeli couscous are larger than those of Moroccan couscous, they still cook faster than rice or pasta.

 2⅓ cups water, divided
   ½ cup sun-dried tomatoes
    1 (14½-ounce) can vegetable
       broth
 1¾ cups uncooked Israeli couscous
    3 cups chopped cooked chicken
       breast
    1 cup chopped fresh flat-leaf
       parsley
   ½ cup (2 ounces) crumbled feta
       cheese
   ¼ teaspoon freshly ground black
       pepper
    2 (6-ounce) jars marinated artichoke
       hearts, undrained

1. Combine 2 cups water and tomatoes in a microwave-safe bowl. Microwave at HIGH 3 minutes or until water boils; cover and let stand 10 minutes or until soft. Drain and chop; set aside.
2. Place ⅓ cup water and broth in a large saucepan; bring to a boil. Stir in couscous. Cover, reduce heat, and

simmer 8 minutes or until tender. Remove from heat; stir in tomatoes, chicken, and remaining ingredients. Yield: 6 cups (serving size: about 1 cup).

CALORIES 419 (30% from fat); FAT 14.1g (sat 3.9g, mono 1.4g, poly 0.8g); PROTEIN 30.2g; CARB 42.5g; FIBER 2.6g; CHOL 64mg; IRON 2.5mg; SODIUM 677mg; CALC 54mg

---

QUICK & EASY
Sautéed Pork Tenderloin with Shallot-Tarragon Sauce

If you prefer, substitute an equal amount of fresh thyme for the tarragon.

1¼ pounds pork tenderloin, trimmed
  2 tablespoons all-purpose flour
  ½ teaspoon salt
  ⅛ teaspoon black pepper
  1 tablespoon vegetable oil
  ½ cup sliced shallots
  ½ cup dry white wine
  ½ cup apple juice
  1 tablespoon Dijon mustard
  1 teaspoon chopped fresh tarragon

1. Cut pork crosswise into 1-inch pieces; flatten each piece to ½-inch thickness using fingertips. Combine flour, salt, and pepper in a large zip-top plastic bag; add pork to bag. Seal and shake to coat.
2. Heat oil in a large nonstick skillet over medium-high heat. Add pork; cook 4 minutes on each side or until browned. Remove pork from pan; keep warm.
3. Add shallots to pan; cook 2 minutes or until lightly browned. Stir in wine, juice, mustard, and tarragon, scraping pan to loosen browned bits. Bring to a boil; reduce heat, and simmer 2 minutes. Serve with pork. Yield: 5 servings (serving size: 3 ounces pork and 2 tablespoons sauce).

CALORIES 196 (30% from fat); FAT 6.5g (sat 1.7g, mono 2.4g, poly 1.8g); PROTEIN 24.8g; CARB 8.6g; FIBER 0.3g; CHOL 74mg; IRON 1.9mg; SODIUM 374mg; CALC 19mg

---

Barbecue U

Where there's smoke, there's fire—and some mighty fine eating.

Grilling guru Steven Raichlen is the author of two dozen cookbooks, including *Miami Spice*, *The Barbecue! Bible*, and the whimsical *Beer Can Chicken*.
  He also hosts the new public television series *Barbecue University with Steven Raichlen*. It's yet another tendril of the "epiphany" he says led him to "follow the fire"—to learn everything he could about live-fire cooking. To do this, he set out to follow the world's barbecue trail, circumnavigating the globe in eight trips during three years, and cataloging the multicultural nuances of the grill. Here are six recipes from Raichlen that we've adapted to help engage both cook and crowd.

QUICK & EASY
Grilled Asparagus Rafts

(pictured on page 254)

Pinning asparagus spears together with skewers makes them easier to flip and grill.

16 thick asparagus spears (about 1 pound)
  1 tablespoon low-sodium soy sauce
  1 teaspoon dark sesame oil
  1 garlic clove, minced
  2 teaspoons sesame seeds, toasted
  ¼ teaspoon black pepper
Dash of salt

1. Prepare grill to high heat.
2. Snap off tough ends of asparagus. Arrange 4 asparagus spears on a flat surface. Thread 2 (3-inch) skewers or wooden picks horizontally through spears 1 inch from each end to form a raft. Repeat procedure with remaining asparagus spears.
3. Combine soy sauce, oil, and garlic; brush evenly over asparagus rafts. Grill 3 minutes on each side or until crisp-tender. Sprinkle evenly with sesame seeds, pepper, and salt. Yield: 4 servings (serving size: 1 asparagus raft).
WINE NOTE: Try Benziger Fumé Blanc 2001, from Sonoma County, California ($13). It has a core of sassy, lemony fruit.

CALORIES 50 (38% from fat); FAT 2.1g (sat 0.2g, mono 0.5g, poly 0.6g); PROTEIN 3.2g; CARB 6.1g; FIBER 2.4g; CHOL 0mg; IRON 3mg; SODIUM 190mg; CALC 26mg

---

Grilled Clams with Sambuca and Italian Sausage

A vegetable grill grate can be used in place of the shellfish grate. Or buy bigger clams; you can set them directly on the grill rack.

  4 ounces hot turkey Italian sausage
  ¼ cup finely chopped onion
  ¼ cup finely chopped green bell pepper
  ¼ cup finely chopped red bell pepper
  ½ teaspoon butter
  1 garlic clove, minced
  1 (1-ounce) slice day-old white bread
  2 tablespoons Sambuca or Pernod (licorice-flavored liqueur)
  ½ teaspoon Worcestershire sauce
  ⅛ teaspoon black pepper
Dash of salt
 36 littleneck clams, cleaned
  6 lemon wedges

1. Remove casing from sausage. Heat a large nonstick skillet over medium heat. Add sausage; cook until browned, stirring to crumble. Add onion, bell peppers, butter, and garlic to pan; cook 5 minutes, stirring frequently.
2. Place bread in a food processor; pulse 5 times or until breadcrumbs form. Add breadcrumbs to sausage mixture; cook 3 minutes, stirring constantly. Pour Sambuca
Continued

into one side of skillet. Ignite Sambuca with a long match, and let flames die down. Stir in Worcestershire sauce, black pepper, and salt.

3. Prepare grill to high heat.

4. Shuck clams; discard top halves of shells and any clams with broken shells or shells that remain open. Place 12 clam halves on shellfish grate. Top each with about 1 teaspoon breadcrumb mixture. Place grate on grill. Cover and cook 4 minutes or until clam juice in shells boils. Remove clams from grate; keep warm. Repeat procedure with remaining clams and breadcrumbs. Serve with lemon wedges. Yield: 6 servings (serving size: 6 clams and 1 lemon wedge).

CALORIES 120 (23% from fat); FAT 3.1g (sat 0.8g, mono 0.8g, poly 0.6g); PROTEIN 15g; CARB 6.2g; FIBER 0.4g; CHOL 44mg; IRON 5.9mg; SODIUM 221mg; CALC 38mg

How to Barbecue Cabbage

Cutting the Core from Cabbage
Place the head of cabbage on a cutting board, core side up. Cut a cone-shaped hole by angling your knife 3 inches into the cabbage about 2 inches from the core. Cut in a circle around the core; remove and discard the core.

Making a Foil Ring for Cabbage
Crumple a 12-inch piece of foil into a ring about 3 inches in diameter. Overlap the ends of the foil where they meet, and crimp them together. Use the ring to hold the cabbage head upright when stuffing and cooking it.

Barbecued Cabbage with Santa Fe Seasonings

To illustrate grilling's versatility, Raichlen cooks a whole head of stuffed cabbage.

    2 cups hickory wood chips
    1 (2-pound) head green cabbage
    ¼ teaspoon black pepper
    ⅛ teaspoon salt
    6 ounces hot turkey Italian sausage
 1½ cups chopped onion
    2 garlic cloves, minced
    2 jalapeño peppers, seeded and
       minced
    ¼ cup barbecue sauce (such as Stubbs)

1. Soak wood chips in water 1 hour.

2. To prepare grill for indirect grilling, place a disposable aluminum foil pan in center of grill. Arrange charcoal around foil pan; heat to medium heat. Crumple a 12-inch-long piece of aluminum foil to form a 3-inch ring. Place foil ring on grill rack over foil pan.

3. Cut core from cabbage to create a cone-shaped cavity about 4 inches wide and 3 inches deep. Discard core. Place cabbage, cavity side up, in foil ring. Sprinkle cavity with pepper and salt.

4. Remove casings from sausage. Cook sausage in a large nonstick skillet over

medium-high heat until browned, stirring to crumble. Add onion, garlic, and jalapeño to pan; sauté 3 minutes or until lightly browned. Stir in barbecue sauce. Spoon sausage mixture into cavity in cabbage. Tent cabbage loosely with additional aluminum foil.

5. Arrange half of wood chips over coals. Cover and grill 40 minutes or until cabbage is tender when pierced with a skewer. Add additional wood chips and charcoal as needed. Remove foil from top of cabbage, and grill 50 minutes or until browned. Remove any dried or charred leaves. Present stuffed cabbage whole, then cut into wedges. Yield: 4 servings (serving size: 1 wedge and about ½ cup sausage mixture).

CALORIES 150 (29% from fat); FAT 4.9g (sat 1.4g, mono 1.7g, poly 1.6g); PROTEIN 11.2g; CARB 17.4g; FIBER 5.4g; CHOL 36mg; IRON 2mg; SODIUM 488mg; CALC 99mg

Tuna "London Broil" with Wasabi Cream

From the Pacific Rim, here's a "London broil" with piquant Asian influences. A cool bite of wasabi dressing finishes the dish.

    2 teaspoons sesame seeds, toasted
    2 teaspoons wasabi powder (dried
       Japanese horseradish)
    2 teaspoons cracked black pepper
    1 teaspoon garlic powder
    ¼ teaspoon salt
    4 (6-ounce) tuna steaks (about
       ¾ inch thick)
    1 tablespoon wasabi powder
    1 tablespoon water
    ¼ cup low-fat mayonnaise
    ¼ cup fat-free sour cream
    1 tablespoon fresh lemon juice
    1 tablespoon low-sodium soy sauce
 Cooking spray
    2 tablespoons sliced green onions

1. Combine first 5 ingredients; rub over tuna. Cover; chill 30 minutes. Combine 1 tablespoon wasabi and water. Let stand 5 minutes. Stir in mayonnaise, sour cream, juice, and soy sauce. Prepare grill to high heat.

2. Place steaks on grill rack coated with cooking spray; grill 5 minutes on each side. Sprinkle with onions. Yield: 4 servings (serving size: 1 steak, 2 tablespoons wasabi cream, and 1½ teaspoons onions).

CALORIES 308 (30% from fat); FAT 10.3g (sat 2.4g, mono 3g, poly 3g); PROTEIN 41.3g; CARB 9.7g; FIBER 0.9g; CHOL 66mg; IRON 4.4mg; SODIUM 500mg; CALC 47mg

Beer-Can Chicken with Cola Barbecue Sauce

(pictured on page 254)

CHICKEN:

1 (12-ounce) can beer
1 cup hickory wood chips
2 teaspoons kosher or sea salt
2 teaspoons brown sugar
2 teaspoons sweet paprika
1 teaspoon coarsely ground black pepper
1 (4-pound) whole chicken
Cooking spray

SAUCE:

½ cup cola
½ cup ketchup
2 tablespoons Worcestershire sauce
1½ teaspoons steak sauce (such as A-1)
½ teaspoon liquid smoke
½ teaspoon instant onion flakes
½ teaspoon instant minced garlic
¼ teaspoon black pepper

1. Open beer can. Carefully pierce top of beer can with "church-key" can opener several times; set aside. To prepare chicken, soak wood chips in water 1 hour. Combine salt, sugar, paprika, and 1 teaspoon (or "coarsely ground") pepper; set aside.

2. To prepare grill for indirect grilling, place a disposable aluminum foil pan in center of grill. Arrange charcoal around foil pan; heat to medium heat.

3. Remove and discard giblets and neck from chicken. Rinse chicken with cold water; pat dry. Trim excess fat. Starting at neck cavity, loosen skin from breast and drumsticks by inserting fingers, gently pushing between skin and meat.

4. Rub 2 teaspoons spice mixture under loosened skin. Rub 2 teaspoons spice mixture in body cavity. Rub 2 teaspoons spice mixture over skin. Slowly add remaining spice mixture to beer can (salt will make beer foam). Holding chicken upright with body cavity facing down, insert beer can into cavity.

5. Drain wood chips. Place half of wood chips on hot coals. Coat grill rack with cooking spray. Place chicken on grill rack over drip pan. Spread legs out to form a tripod to support chicken. Cover and grill 2 hours or until a meat thermometer inserted into meaty portion of thigh registers 180°. Add remaining wood chips after 1 hour and charcoal as needed.

6. Lift chicken slightly using tongs; place spatula under can. Carefully lift chicken and can; place on a cutting board. Let stand 5 minutes. Gently lift chicken using tongs or insulated rubber gloves; carefully twist can, and remove from cavity. Discard skin and can.

7. To prepare sauce, combine cola and remaining 7 ingredients in a saucepan; bring to a boil. Reduce heat, and simmer 6 minutes. Cool. Serve with chicken. Yield: 6 servings (serving size: 3 ounces chicken and about 2 tablespoons sauce).

CALORIES 215 (20% from fat); FAT 4.7g (sat 1.1g, mono 1.4g, poly 1.3g); PROTEIN 31.8g; CARB 10g; FIBER 0.5g; CHOL 100mg; IRON 2.2mg; SODIUM 741mg; CALC 29mg

Grilling Methods

Direct Grilling calls for cooking food right over the fire. This method is generally used to cook small or thin pieces of food, such as steak, chicken, fish, or vegetables.

Indirect Grilling is used to cook larger pieces of meat, such as whole chickens or pork shoulders, and involves cooking foods next to, not directly over, the fire. For gas grills, this generally means lighting only half of the burners. For charcoal grills, it means setting the charcoal up to the sides of the grill and leaving the center open.

To learn more about Steven Raichlen's barbecuing tips, books, and T.V. show, visit www.barbecuebible.com.

How to Make Beer-Can Chicken

Piercing the Can

It's easier to make the vents in flimsy aluminum cans when the can is stabilized by a commercially available beer-can chicken roaster. Place the can in the can holder, close the cage until it snaps in place, and use a can opener to pierce the top.

Stabilizing the Tipsy Chicken

If you don't have a beer-can chicken roaster, you can still set the chicken up by using the can as the third prop of a tripod; spread the drumsticks out to support the chicken.

Sugarcane skewers are doubly functional: They thread the shrimp together and infuse them with sweetness.

Shrimp on Sugarcane with Rum Glaze

Lemony couscous*

Green salad

*Bring 2½ cups water to a boil in a medium saucepan; gradually stir in 1½ cups couscous. Remove from heat; cover and let stand 5 minutes. Fluff with a fork. Stir in ¼ cup chopped green onions, 3 tablespoons lemon juice, ¾ teaspoon salt, and ¼ teaspoon black pepper.

1. Prepare grill to high heat.

2. Combine first 5 ingredients in a large bowl. Add shrimp; toss to coat. Cover and chill 15 minutes.

3. Cut ends of swizzle sticks at a sharp angle. Thread 1 shrimp on each skewer.

4. Combine brown sugar and next 8 ingredients in a saucepan, and bring to a boil. Reduce heat, and simmer 5 minutes or until syrupy.

5. Place shrimp on grill rack coated with cooking spray. Grill 3 minutes on each side or until done, basting generously with glaze. Yield: 6 servings (serving size: 4 shrimp).

WINE NOTE: The sweet, fresh flavor of this dish is terrific with Jekel Riesling 2002 from Monterey, California ($12). Fresh pear, peach, ginger, lavender, and jasmine aromas and flavors, and a streak of acidity nicely counter the shellfish.

CALORIES 273 (22% from fat); FAT 6.8g (sat 1.9g, mono 1.6g, poly 2.3g); PROTEIN 23.6g; CARB 23.3g; FIBER 0.2g; CHOL 177mg; IRON 3.5mg; SODIUM 541mg; CALC 83mg

---

Barbecue Resources

Beer-Can Chicken Roaster ($14.90), Captain Steve's Beer-Can Chicken Roaster; 800-480-4450 (access code: 00), www.beercanchickenroaster.com
Shellfish Griller ($41.45); 877-768-5766 or 401-364-9657, www.greatgrate.com
Grills and Accessories Char-Broil: 800-241-7548, www.charbroil.com; Weber-Stephen Products Company: 800-446-1071, www.weber.com

---

Shrimp on Sugarcane with Rum Glaze

Many of Raichlen's recipes are grilled uncovered over direct heat—they don't rely on smoke to add flavor. Caribbean-influenced shrimp, skewered with sugarcane and basted with a dark rum glaze, rely on high heat to caramelize the glaze and infuse the shrimp from the inside out with the cane's mild sweetness. Look for sugarcane swizzle sticks in the produce section, or order them from www.melissas.com. If you can't find sugarcane, bamboo skewers will do in a pinch.

```
 1   tablespoon vegetable oil
 1   tablespoon fresh lemon juice
 ¼   teaspoon black pepper
 ⅛   teaspoon salt
 1   garlic clove, minced
24   jumbo shrimp, peeled and
     deveined (about 1½ pounds)
 8   sugarcane swizzle sticks, each cut
     into 3 pieces
 ¼   cup packed dark brown sugar
 ¼   cup dark rum
 ¼   cup corn syrup
 3   tablespoons Dijon mustard
 1   tablespoon white vinegar
 1   tablespoon butter
 ¼   teaspoon salt
 ¼   teaspoon ground cinnamon
 ¼   teaspoon black pepper
```
Cooking spray

---

10 Steps to Grade-A Grilling

1. Be organized. Have food, marinade, sauces, and equipment grillside and ready to go before you start cooking.

2. Gauge your fuel. Make sure you have enough gas or charcoal before you start.

3. Keep it hot. "Hot" is a relative term. Not everything grills on high; not everything is grilled directly over the flame. Gas grills take about 10 to 15 minutes to preheat, just like a home oven. Charcoal should have a thin coat of gray ash when it's ready. High heat should be closing in on 500°, and indirect grilling requires a moderate temperature of 350°.

4. Keep it clean. Raichlen recommends cleaning the grill twice: once after preheating the grill, and again when you've finished grilling. Use a combination of a metal spatula and a wire brush to scrape the grates clean.

5. Keep it lubricated. Oil the grate before placing food on it. Quickly run a paper towel that's moist with oil over the grates. This process seasons the grill and helps clean it.

6. Turn, don't stab. Use tongs or a spatula to turn meat; don't use a carving fork.

7. Know when to baste. Too many BBQers ruin great food by basting it too early with sugar-based sauces, which results in charring. To properly caramelize food and prevent burning apply sugar-based sauces toward the end of the cook time. You can baste with yogurt-, citrus-, or oil and vinegar-based sauces throughout cooking. If you use the marinade to baste, stop as you approach the last three minutes of cooking.

8. Keep it covered. When indirectly grilling large pieces of meat, keep the grill covered and resist the temptation to peek. You lose all the built-up heat and add 5 to 10 minutes to your cook time for each peek.

9. Never desert your post. Pay attention. Even though grilling is easy, it requires vigilance for flame-ups and other potential problems. And be organized (see Rule No. 1) to keep from incinerating dinner or your deck.

10. Give it a rest. Meats will taste better and be juicier if given a chance to rest a few minutes after being removed from the flame.

How Sweet It Is

When corn is at its peak, pick any of these recipes to seize its sweetness.

Farmers' markets and roadside stands provide garden-fresh corn, only hours old and at its peak. This is the corn for which these recipes were created, the succulent and sweet cream of the crop.

Corn and Poblano Empanadas

Masa harina—used to make corn tortillas and tamales—yields a more richly flavored and textured dough than that made with flour alone.

 ¾ cup all-purpose flour
 ¾ cup masa harina
 ¾ teaspoon salt, divided
 ½ teaspoon chili powder
 ½ cup water
 2 tablespoons butter, cut into small pieces
 2 poblano peppers
Cooking spray
 2 garlic cloves, minced
 1½ cups fresh corn kernels (about 3 ears)
 ¾ cup (3 ounces) shredded Oaxaca or mozzarella cheese
 1 large egg white, lightly beaten
 1 tablespoon water

1. Lightly spoon flour into dry measuring cups; level with a knife. Combine flour, masa harina, ¼ teaspoon salt, and chili powder in a food processor; pulse 3 times. Add water and butter; pulse until mixture forms a loose ball. Remove from processor; knead until ball completely forms. Divide dough into 8 equal portions. Shape each portion into a ball; flatten each ball into a 3-inch circle on a lightly floured surface. Cover and chill 30 minutes. (Stack dough circles between single layers of wax paper.)
2. Preheat oven to 500°.
3. Place poblanos on a foil-lined baking sheet. Bake at 500° for 20 minutes or until brown and blistered, turning once. Place in a zip-top plastic bag; seal. Let stand 15 minutes. Peel poblanos; cut in half lengthwise. Discard seeds and membranes, and finely chop. Place in a medium bowl.
4. Reduce oven temperature to 425°.
5. Heat a nonstick skillet coated with cooking spray over medium-high heat. Add garlic; sauté 30 seconds. Add ½ teaspoon salt and corn; sauté 3 minutes. Add to poblanos, and let stand 5 minutes. Stir in cheese.
6. Roll each dough portion into a 5-inch circle. Working with 1 circle at a time (cover remaining circles with a damp towel to prevent drying), spoon 3 level tablespoons corn filling into center of each circle. Moisten edges of dough with water; fold dough over filling. Press edges together with a fork or fingers to seal. Place empanadas on a large baking sheet coated with cooking spray. Combine egg white and 1 tablespoon water. Lightly coat tops of empanadas with egg mixture, and pierce with a fork. Bake at 425° for 20 minutes or until lightly browned. Yield: 8 servings (serving size: 1 empanada).

WINE NOTE: Corn and Chardonnay are usually a terrific match, but the heat from the poblanos means the wine must be selected carefully. One without too much oak is best. A great choice: the creamy Jordan Chardonnay 2001 from the Russian River Valley, California ($26), which has light lemon notes.

CALORIES 156 (27% from fat); FAT 4.7g (sat 2.5g, mono 1.3g, poly 0.7g); PROTEIN 5.2g; CARB 25.8g; FIBER 2.6g; CHOL 11mg; IRON 1.3mg; SODIUM 277mg; CALC 58mg

STAFF FAVORITE • QUICK & EASY
Grilled Mexican Corn with Crema

On the streets of Mexico, people line up at vendor carts to buy giant ears of roasted corn dunked in rich *crema Mexicana* and sprinkled with chili powder and lime juice. *Crema Mexicana* is similar to sour cream and can be found in many large supermarkets. If you can't find it, use low-fat sour cream.

 1 teaspoon chipotle chili powder
 ½ teaspoon salt
 ⅛ teaspoon freshly ground black pepper
 6 ears corn
Cooking spray
 ¼ cup crema Mexicana
 6 lime wedges

1. Prepare grill.
2. Combine first 3 ingredients.
3. Place corn on a grill rack coated with cooking spray; cook 12 minutes or until corn is lightly browned, turning frequently. Place corn on a platter; drizzle with crema. Sprinkle with chipotle mixture. Garnish with lime wedges. Yield: 6 servings (serving size: 1 ear).

CALORIES 160 (29% from fat); FAT 5.2g (sat 2.5g, mono 1.5g, poly 1g); PROTEIN 5g; CARB 28.2g; FIBER 4g; CHOL 8mg; IRON 0.8mg; SODIUM 228mg; CALC 24mg

STAFF FAVORITE • MAKE AHEAD
FREEZABLE
Caramel Corn Ice Cream
(pictured on page 255)

The just-frozen ice cream is still soft enough to stir in the melted caramels. For fun, sprinkle with caramel popcorn.

 2 cups fresh corn kernels (about 4 ears)
 1 cup half-and-half
 2 cups 2% reduced-fat milk
 ⅔ cup sugar
Dash of salt
 3 large egg yolks, lightly beaten
 3 tablespoons 2% reduced-fat milk
 12 small soft caramel candies
Continued

1. Combine corn and half-and-half in a food processor; process until smooth (about 1 minute). Strain puréed corn mixture through a sieve into a large bowl; discard solids. Add 2 cups milk, sugar, salt, and egg yolks to bowl; stir with a whisk. Pour mixture into a large saucepan; cook over medium heat 20 minutes or until thick (do not boil), stirring constantly. Remove from heat. Place pan in a large ice-filled bowl 30 minutes or until mixture comes to room temperature, stirring occasionally.

2. Combine 3 tablespoons milk and caramels in a small saucepan. Bring to a simmer, and cook 10 minutes or until caramels melt, stirring frequently. Remove from heat; whisk until smooth. Cool slightly.

3. Pour corn mixture into freezer can of an ice-cream freezer; freeze according to manufacturer's instructions. Stir in caramel mixture. Spoon ice cream into a freezer-safe container; cover and freeze 2 hours. Yield: 7 servings (serving size: ½ cup).

CALORIES 240 (26% from fat); FAT 6.8g (sat 3.1g, mono 1.5g, poly 0.4g); PROTEIN 5.7g; CARB 38.9g; FIBER 0.6g; CHOL 107mg; IRON 0.4mg; SODIUM 113mg; CALC 139mg

STAFF FAVORITE • QUICK & EASY
Creamed Corn with Bacon and Leeks

(pictured on page 255)

Scraping the cut ears of corn releases the remaining starchy milk, giving the creamed corn its thick consistency. Pair this sweet-smoky side dish with grilled chicken.

  6 ears fresh corn
  2 cups 1% low-fat milk
  1 tablespoon cornstarch
  1 teaspoon sugar
  ½ teaspoon salt
  ¼ teaspoon freshly ground black
     pepper
  4 slices bacon
  1 cup chopped leek

1. Cut kernels from ears of corn to measure 3 cups; using dull side of a knife blade, scrape milk and remaining pulp from cobs into a bowl. Place 1½ cups kernels, low-fat milk, cornstarch, sugar,

salt, and pepper in a food processor; process until smooth.

2. Cook bacon in a large cast iron skillet over medium heat until crisp. Remove bacon from pan, reserving 1 teaspoon drippings in pan; crumble bacon. Add leek to pan; cook 2 minutes, stirring constantly. Add puréed corn mixture, 1½ cups corn kernels, and corn milk mixture to pan. Bring to a boil, reduce heat, and simmer 3 minutes or until slightly thick. Stir in crumbled bacon just before serving. Yield: 6 servings (serving size: ⅔ cup).

CALORIES 151 (27% from fat); FAT 4.6g (sat 1.7g, mono 1.9g, poly 0.8g); PROTEIN 7g; CARB 23.1g; FIBER 2.4g; CHOL 9mg; IRON 0.8mg; SODIUM 325mg; CALC 111mg

Sweet Corn Risotto

Purée part of the corn to add sweetness, moisture, and a little body to the risotto. Chanterelles add a nice orange-yellowish color to the dish, but shiitakes work, too.

  3½ cups water
   1 teaspoon salt
   1 (14-ounce) can fat-free,
      less-sodium chicken broth
  1½ cups fresh corn kernels, divided
      (about 3 ears)
   2 tablespoons butter, divided
   1 cup sliced fresh chanterelle
      mushrooms or sliced shiitake
      mushroom caps (about 3½ ounces)
   2 garlic cloves, minced
   ¾ cup finely chopped onion
  1½ cups Arborio or other medium-
      grain rice
  10 tablespoons dry white wine,
      divided
   ½ cup (2 ounces) finely shredded
      Asiago cheese
   2 tablespoons thinly sliced fresh
      basil
   ¼ teaspoon freshly ground black
      pepper

1. Bring first 3 ingredients to a simmer in a medium saucepan (do not boil). Keep warm over low heat.

2. Place ½ cup corn in a food processor; process until smooth. Set aside.

3. Melt 1 tablespoon butter in a large Dutch oven over medium-high heat. Add 1 cup corn and mushrooms; sauté 3 minutes. Add garlic; sauté 1 minute. Remove from pan; set aside.

4. Melt 1 tablespoon butter in pan over medium-high heat. Add onion; sauté 2 minutes. Add rice; sauté 3 minutes or until rice is lightly browned. Stir in ½ cup wine; cook 1 minute or until liquid is nearly absorbed, stirring constantly. Add broth mixture, ½ cup at a time, stirring frequently until each portion of broth mixture is absorbed before adding next (about 22 minutes total). Add puréed corn and mushroom mixture to pan; cook 3 minutes, stirring constantly. Remove from heat; stir in 2 tablespoons wine, cheese, basil, and pepper. Yield: 6 servings (serving size: about 1 cup risotto).

CALORIES 332 (19% from fat); FAT 7g (sat 4.2g, mono 2g, poly 0.5g); PROTEIN 9.5g; CARB 55.9g; FIBER 2.6g; CHOL 19mg; IRON 0.9mg; SODIUM 589mg; CALC 123mg

Kernels of Truth

Selection: For the freshest corn possible, look for ears tightly wrapped in bright green husks that have pale silks with dry brown tips. The cut end should be moist. If the ears feel warm, they're probably no longer utterly fresh: The conversion of sugar to starch generates heat. Peel back the tops of the husks, and use your thumbnail to pierce a kernel; a fresh ear of corn will squirt slightly clouded juice.

Storage: Keep fresh corn as cool as possible. Buy it in the morning, before the summer sun can do its damage, make the trip home quickly, and store the corn in the refrigerator.

Simple Boiled Corn: Fresh corn needs minimal cooking. Place husked ears in a pot of cold water, then bring the water to a boil over high heat. Once the water boils, remove from heat, and let stand 1 minute before serving.

Cutting and Milking Ears: Use a sharp paring knife to cut kernels from the ears directly into a bowl, then scrape the cob to remove the pulp and milk.

Corn and Shrimp Bisque

Nothing goes to waste in this recipe, since the shrimp shells and corn cobs make a delicate stock for the soup.

    2 pounds unpeeled large shrimp
    4 ears corn
    Cooking spray
    2 cups coarsely chopped onion
    5 cups water
    1 bay leaf
    1 thyme sprig
    1 tablespoon butter
    2 tablespoons tomato paste
    ¼ cup dry sherry
    3 tablespoons all-purpose flour
    1¼ teaspoons salt
    ¼ teaspoon white pepper
    1 cup half-and-half

1. Peel and devein shrimp, reserving shells. Coarsely chop shrimp. Cover shrimp, and chill.
2. Remove kernels from ears of corn to measure 2 cups, and set aside. Reserve corn cobs.
3. Heat a stockpot coated with cooking spray over medium-high heat. Add shrimp shells and onion to pan; sauté 5 minutes or until shells turn pink. Add corn cobs, water, bay leaf, and thyme; bring to a boil. Reduce heat, and simmer 30 minutes. Strain shrimp stock through a sieve into a bowl; discard solids.
4. Melt butter in a large nonstick skillet over medium heat. Add corn kernels; cook 2 minutes, stirring frequently. Add tomato paste; cook 2 minutes, stirring frequently. Combine sherry and flour, stirring with a whisk to form a slurry. Add slurry to pan; cook 1 minute, stirring constantly. Add shrimp stock, salt, and pepper; bring to a simmer. Cook 4 minutes or until bisque starts to thicken, stirring frequently. Add shrimp; cook 3 minutes or until shrimp are done. Stir in half-and-half; serve immediately. Yield: 6 servings (serving size: 1¼ cups).

CALORIES 302 (27% from fat); FAT 9.1g (sat 4.4g, mono 2.4g, poly 1.4g); PROTEIN 34.5g; CARB 17.1g; FIBER 1.8g; CHOL 255mg; IRON 4.3mg; SODIUM 764mg; CALC 136mg

Fresh Corn Bread Pudding

Simple ingredients, such as corn, bread, milk, and cheese, render this side dish versatile enough for breakfast with country ham or an elegant dinner with filet mignon and asparagus.

    1 (¾-pound) loaf country-style
       bread (such as Pepperidge Farm
       Hearty Country White)
    2 teaspoons butter
    3 cups fresh corn kernels (about
       6 ears)
    3 garlic cloves, minced
    3 cups fat-free milk
    1 cup egg substitute
    1 teaspoon salt
    ¼ teaspoon freshly ground black
       pepper
    1¼ cups (5 ounces) shredded sharp
       white Cheddar cheese
    Cooking spray

1. Preheat oven to 300°.
2. Trim crust from bread; discard crust. Cut bread into 2-inch cubes. Place bread cubes on a baking sheet. Bake at 300° for 30 minutes or until bread is toasted, turning occasionally.
3. Increase oven temperature to 425°.
4. Heat butter in a large nonstick skillet over medium-high heat. Add corn and garlic to pan; cook 4 minutes or until lightly browned, stirring occasionally. Combine milk, egg substitute, salt, and pepper in a large bowl, stirring with a whisk.
5. Stir corn mixture and cheese into milk mixture. Fold in bread cubes.
6. Pour corn mixture into a 2-quart baking dish coated with cooking spray; let stand 10 minutes. Bake at 425° for 40 minutes or until puffed and set. Yield: 8 servings (serving size: 1 cup).

CALORIES 254 (30% from fat); FAT 8.5g (sat 4.5g, mono 2.2g, poly 0.5g); PROTEIN 15g; CARB 32.5g; FIBER 3.3g; CHOL 23mg; IRON 1.6mg; SODIUM 691mg; CALC 272mg

QUICK & EASY
Sweet Corn Dutch Baby

This is a great option for brunch.

    ½ cup all-purpose flour
    ¾ cup fresh corn kernels (about
       2 ears)
    ¾ cup fat-free milk
    2 tablespoons granulated sugar
    ¼ teaspoon salt
    3 large eggs
    1 tablespoon butter
    1 tablespoon powdered sugar
    ¼ teaspoon ground cinnamon
    1 cup applesauce
    ¼ cup light sour cream

1. Preheat oven to 450°.
2. Place a 9-inch cast iron skillet in oven 10 minutes.
3. Lightly spoon flour into a dry measuring cup; level with a knife. Combine flour, corn, milk, sugar, and salt in a food processor; process until smooth. Add eggs; pulse 5 times to combine.
4. Add butter to preheated pan, tipping to coat bottom and sides of pan. Pour corn mixture into pan. Bake at 450° for 14 minutes or until mixture is set and lightly browned.
5. Sprinkle with powdered sugar and cinnamon. Cut into 4 wedges, and serve with applesauce and sour cream. Yield: 4 servings (serving size: 1 wedge, ¼ cup applesauce, and 1 tablespoon sour cream).

CALORIES 250 (30% from fat); FAT 8.3g (sat 4g, mono 2.4g, poly 0.8g); PROTEIN 9.8g; CARB 35.8g; FIBER 2.1g; CHOL 173mg; IRON 1.5mg; SODIUM 262mg; CALC 110mg

QUICK & EASY
Moist Skillet Corn Bread

    1½ cups all-purpose flour
    1½ cups yellow cornmeal
    2 tablespoons sugar
    1½ teaspoons salt
    1½ teaspoons baking powder
    2½ cups fresh corn kernels (about
       5 ears), divided
    1¼ cups 2% reduced-fat milk
    ¼ cup melted butter, divided
    2 large eggs

Continued

1. Preheat oven to 450°.
2. Lightly spoon flour into dry measuring cups; level with a knife. Sift together flour, cornmeal, sugar, salt, and baking powder; set aside.
3. Place a 9-inch cast iron or ovenproof skillet in oven 10 minutes.
4. Combine 1¼ cups corn, milk, and 2 tablespoons butter in a food processor, and process until smooth. Add eggs, and process until just combined.
5. Add milk mixture to cornmeal mixture; stir until just moist. Stir in 1¼ cups corn.
6. Add 2 tablespoons butter to preheated pan, tipping to coat bottom and sides of pan. Pour corn mixture into pan. Bake at 450° for 25 minutes or until a wooden pick inserted in center comes out clean. Yield: 14 servings (serving size: 1 wedge).

CALORIES 219 (23% from fat); FAT 5.6g (sat 3g, mono 1.7g, poly 0.4g); PROTEIN 5.8g; CARB 37.1g; FIBER 1.7g; CHOL 48mg; IRON 1.7mg; SODIUM 411mg; CALC 54mg

lighten up

Lowcountry Bowl

A few changes streamline a classic crab soup.

Judi Mahoney of Portland, Oregon, makes a point to eat local specialties when she travels. While dining in Savannah, Georgia, she ordered crab soup. Infatuated with the succulent crab in the rich soup, Judi made a second request—for the recipe, which the chef was happy to share.

But Judi knew immediately she'd rarely prepare the Lowcountry specialty; its fat and cholesterol content was too high.

So we offered a solution. Substituting flour browned in a skillet for the roux saved more than 200 calories per serving. To ensure authenticity, we had to maintain the soup's velvety texture, but stirring in two cups of whipping cream—more than 1,500 calories—wasn't the answer. Sautéed carrots, blended with the other vegetables, gave our soup extra body and added subtle flavor compatible with the fresh crab. We finished the soup with whole milk and half-and-half.

BEFORE	AFTER
SERVING SIZE	
1 cup	
CALORIES PER SERVING	
543	151
FAT	
41g	5g
PERCENT OF TOTAL CALORIES	
68%	30%

Savannah-Style Crab Soup

If the flour starts to brown too quickly, remove the skillet from the heat, and stir the flour constantly until it cools.

- ½ cup all-purpose flour
- 1 tablespoon butter
- Cooking spray
- 2 cups chopped carrot
- 1 cup chopped celery
- 1 cup chopped onion
- ¼ cup chopped red bell pepper
- ¼ cup chopped green bell pepper
- 1 garlic clove, minced
- 1 tablespoon Old Bay seasoning
- ¼ teaspoon salt
- ¼ teaspoon black pepper
- ¼ teaspoon dried thyme
- 1 bay leaf
- 4 cups clam juice
- 1½ cups whole milk
- ½ cup half-and-half
- 1 pound lump crabmeat, shell pieces removed
- ⅓ cup dry sherry

1. Place flour in a 9-inch cast iron skillet; cook over medium heat 15 minutes or until brown, stirring constantly with a whisk. Remove from heat.
2. Melt butter in a Dutch oven coated with cooking spray over medium-high heat. Add carrot and next 5 ingredients, and sauté 5 minutes or until vegetables are tender. Add Old Bay seasoning, salt, black pepper, dried thyme, and bay leaf; cook 1 minute. Sprinkle browned flour over vegetable mixture, and cook 1 minute, stirring frequently. Stir in clam juice, and bring to a boil. Reduce heat,

and simmer 10 minutes or until slightly thick, stirring frequently.
3. Stir in milk and half-and-half; cook 4 minutes. Stir in crabmeat and sherry; cook 5 minutes or until soup is thoroughly heated. Discard bay leaf before serving. Yield: 9 servings (serving size: 1 cup).

CALORIES 151 (30% from fat); FAT 5g (sat 2.6g, mono 1.4g, poly 0.4g); PROTEIN 13g; CARB 13.3g; FIBER 1.8g; CHOL 46mg; IRON 2.2mg; SODIUM 835mg; CALC 112mg

dinner tonight

Terrific Tacos

Quick-and-easy tacos solve your dinner dilemma.

Shrimp Taco Menu
serves 4

Shrimp Tacos

Corn and Avocado Salsa*

*Combine 2 cups fresh corn kernels, ⅓ cup diced peeled avocado, ¼ cup finely chopped red onion, 2 tablespoons chopped fresh cilantro, 1 tablespoon fresh lime juice, and ½ teaspoon salt.

Lemon sorbet

Game Plan

1. Peel and devein shrimp
2. Cut limes into quarters
3. Bring cooking water for shrimp to a boil
4. While cooking water comes to a boil:
   - Chop cilantro, avocado, jalapeño, and red onion
   - Cut kernels off corn cobs
   - Juice lime
5. While shrimp cooks:
   - Chop tomato and green onions

Shrimp Tacos

Shredded rotisserie chicken or flaked, cooked fish also works well in these tacos.

TOTAL TIME: 30 MINUTES

QUICK TIP: The Corn and Avocado Salsa (recipe in the Shrimp Taco Menu box on page 268) and these tacos both call for chopped cilantro and fresh lime juice, so measure for both recipes at the same time if you're preparing the entire menu.

- 3 tablespoons black peppercorns
- 3 quarts water
- 1 tablespoon salt
- 1 teaspoon ground red pepper
- 2 limes, quartered
- 1 pound medium shrimp, peeled and deveined
- ½ cup coarsely chopped fresh cilantro
- ¼ cup fresh lime juice
- 1 tablespoon minced seeded jalapeño pepper
- 12 (6-inch) corn tortillas
- ¾ cup chopped peeled tomato
- ½ cup reduced-fat sour cream
- ½ cup chopped green onions

1. Place peppercorns on a double layer of cheesecloth. Gather edges of cheesecloth together, and tie securely. Combine cheesecloth bag, water, salt, red pepper, and lime quarters in a Dutch oven. Bring to a boil; cook 2 minutes. Add shrimp; cook 2 minutes or until done. Drain. Discard cheesecloth bag and lime quarters.

2. Combine shrimp, cilantro, lime juice, and jalapeño pepper, tossing well to coat. Heat tortillas according to package directions. Spoon ⅓ cup shrimp mixture into each tortilla; top each taco with 1 tablespoon tomato, 2 teaspoons sour cream, and 2 teaspoons onions. Yield: 4 servings (serving size: 3 tacos).

CALORIES 358 (20% from fat); FAT 7.8g (sat 3g, mono 0.8g, poly 1.7g); PROTEIN 29.3g; CARB 43.6g; FIBER 5.1g; CHOL 188mg; IRON 4.1mg; SODIUM 612mg; CALC 250mg

Chicken Taco Menu
serves 4

Chicken Soft Tacos with Sautéed Onions and Apples

Spicy coleslaw*

Canned refried beans

*Combine 4 cups shredded cabbage, ⅓ cup thinly sliced red onion, ¼ cup chopped fresh cilantro, 2 tablespoons fresh lime juice, 2 tablespoons apple cider vinegar, ½ teaspoon salt, ¼ teaspoon ground red pepper, and ¼ teaspoon brown sugar, tossing well.

Game Plan

1. While pan preheats:
- Cut chicken into bite-sized pieces

2. While onion mixture cooks:
- Warm refried beans

3. Prepare coleslaw

4. Warm tortillas

Chicken Soft Tacos with Sautéed Onions and Apples

In this recipe, a savory-sweet taco filling is encased in warm flour tortillas.

TOTAL TIME: 35 MINUTES

QUICK TIP: If you're making the Chicken Taco Menu, bagged shredded cabbage will save a preparation step.

- 1 tablespoon olive oil
- 1 pound skinless, boneless chicken breast, cut into bite-sized pieces
- ½ teaspoon salt
- ½ teaspoon ground nutmeg
- ½ teaspoon freshly ground black pepper
- 1 tablespoon butter
- 2 cups thinly sliced onion
- 2 cups thinly sliced peeled Granny Smith apple (about 2 apples)
- 2 garlic cloves, minced
- 8 (6-inch) flour tortillas

1. Heat oil in a large nonstick skillet over medium-high heat. Sprinkle chicken evenly with salt, nutmeg, and pepper. Add chicken to pan; sauté 7 minutes or until golden. Remove chicken from pan; keep warm.

2. Melt butter in pan over medium heat. Add onion; cook 4 minutes or until tender, stirring frequently. Add apple; cook 6 minutes or until golden, stirring frequently. Add garlic; sauté 30 seconds. Return chicken to pan; cook 2 minutes or until thoroughly heated, stirring frequently.

3. Heat tortillas according to package directions. Arrange ½ cup chicken mixture over each tortilla. Yield: 4 servings (serving size: 2 tacos).

CALORIES 454 (25% from fat); FAT 12.6g (sat 3.8g, mono 6.1g, poly 1.5g); PROTEIN 32.9g; CARB 51.5g; FIBER 4.8g; CHOL 73mg; IRON 3.3mg; SODIUM 705mg; CALC 116mg

Pork Taco Menu
serves 4

Red Chile-Pork Tacos with Caramelized Onions (recipe on page 270)

Fruit salsa*

Green salad

*Combine 2 cups sliced banana, ½ cup diced pineapple, ¼ cup chopped fresh cilantro, 1 teaspoon brown sugar, ¼ teaspoon salt, and 2 diced seeded jalapeño peppers.

Game Plan

1. Prepare pork

2. While pork cooks:
- Slice onion
- Chop tomato and green onions
- Prepare salad

3. While onion cooks:
- Prepare salsa

Continued

Red Chile-Pork Tacos with Caramelized Onions

TOTAL TIME: 45 MINUTES

QUICK TIP: Covering the onions helps them caramelize more quickly and requires less oil.

1 tablespoon ancho chile powder
1 teaspoon brown sugar
½ teaspoon salt
1 pound pork tenderloin, trimmed
Cooking spray
1 teaspoon vegetable oil
3 cups thinly sliced onion
8 hard taco shells
½ cup chopped tomato
8 teaspoons chopped green onions

1. Preheat oven to 425°.
2. Combine first 3 ingredients; rub evenly over pork. Place pork on a broiler pan coated with cooking spray. Bake at 425° for 20 minutes or until a thermometer registers 160° (slightly pink). Remove pork from oven; let sit 5 minutes before slicing.
3. While pork cooks, heat oil in a large nonstick skillet coated with cooking spray over medium heat. Add onion; cover and cook 10 minutes or until golden brown, stirring frequently. Uncover and sauté 1 minute.
4. Fill each taco shell with about 2 ounces pork, 3 tablespoons sautéed onion, 1 tablespoon tomato, and 1 teaspoon green onions. Yield: 4 servings (serving size: 2 tacos).

CALORIES 304 (30% from fat); FAT 10.2g (sat 2.2g, mono 5.4g, poly 1.8g); PROTEIN 26.9g; CARB 25g; FIBER 4.5g; CHOL 74mg; IRON 2.1mg; SODIUM 444mg; CALC 46mg

inspired vegetarian

Orient Expressed

Spicy, aromatic flavors from the East enhance all the dishes they grace.

Simple vegetables never tasted so good. Try these dishes and see for yourself.

Stir-Fried Tempeh with Spinach and Thai Basil

Thai basil has small purple leaves and a stronger taste than sweet basil; if unavailable, use the latter. The longer you marinate the tempeh, the more flavorful it will be. We liked this dish best with soy tempeh, but any variety (five-grain, three-grain, soy-rice) will work.

TEMPEH:

3 tablespoons low-sodium soy sauce
1½ tablespoons sake (rice wine)
2 tablespoons minced shallots
1 teaspoon dark sesame oil
1 pound soy tempeh, cut into bite-sized pieces
1½ tablespoons olive oil

SPINACH:

1½ teaspoons olive oil
1½ tablespoons sake (rice wine)
½ teaspoon salt
1 (10-ounce) package fresh spinach

REMAINING INGREDIENTS:

2 tablespoons sugar
3 tablespoons low-sodium soy sauce
3 tablespoons water
2 teaspoons fresh lime juice
1 tablespoon olive oil
3½ cups thinly, vertically sliced red onion (about 3 medium)
3 tablespoons chopped garlic
2 cups loosely packed fresh Thai basil leaves or coarsely chopped sweet basil
4½ cups hot cooked basmati rice

1. To prepare tempeh, combine first 4 ingredients, stirring with whisk. Add tempeh, turning to coat. Let stand at room temperature 20 minutes to 4 hours, turning once. Remove tempeh from marinade; discard marinade.
2. Heat 1½ tablespoons olive oil in a wok or large nonstick skillet over medium-high heat. Add tempeh; sauté 2 minutes. Remove tempeh from pan.
3. To prepare spinach, heat 1½ teaspoons olive oil in pan over medium-high heat. Add 1½ tablespoons sake, salt, and spinach; stir-fry 1 minute or until spinach wilts. Remove spinach from pan with a slotted spoon.
4. Combine sugar and next 3 ingredients; set aside. Heat 1 tablespoon olive oil in pan over medium-high heat. Add onion and garlic; stir-fry 3 minutes or until onion is tender. Add tempeh, sugar mixture, and basil, stirring to combine. Cook 2 minutes or until heated, stirring frequently. Spoon tempeh mixture in center of a serving platter; arrange spinach around tempeh. Serve with rice. Yield: 6 servings (serving size: about ¾ cup tempeh mixture, ⅓ cup spinach, and ¾ cup rice).

CALORIES 416 (26% from fat); FAT 11.9g (sat 2.4g, mono 6.1g, poly 2.7g); PROTEIN 22.6g; CARB 54.7g; FIBER 7.5g; CHOL 0mg; IRON 5.8mg; SODIUM 646mg; CALC 218mg

---

The Spice Is Right Menu
serves 6

The sweet potatoes are cooked in a liquid that's good over rice. It's also great as a vegetable marinade.

Braised Cinnamon-Anise Sweet Potatoes

Pan-fried tofu triangles with ABC sauce*

White rice

Steamed snow peas

*Cut each of 2 (14-ounce) packages of firm tofu into 6 slices; drain on several layers of paper towels. Cut each tofu slice diagonally into 2 triangles. Heat 1 tablespoon peanut oil in a large nonstick skillet over medium-high heat. Add half of tofu; cook 4 minutes on each side or until golden. Repeat with 1 tablespoon oil and remaining tofu. Drizzle each serving with 1 tablespoon Japanese sweet-and-sour sauce (such as ABC).

Braised Cinnamon-Anise Sweet Potatoes

Serve cold or at room temperature. Save liquid for flavoring stir-fries, rice, or tofu.

  1 teaspoon vegetable oil
 ¾ cup (1½-inch) sliced green onions
  2 tablespoons sugar
  1 teaspoon chile paste with garlic
  6 garlic cloves, thinly sliced
  6 (¼-inch) slices peeled fresh ginger, crushed
  2 (3-inch) cinnamon sticks
  1 whole star anise, crushed
  4 cups water
 ⅓ cup low-sodium soy sauce
  3 tablespoons sake (rice wine) or sherry
  2 pounds sweet potatoes, peeled and cut into 2½-inch pieces
  2 tablespoons minced green onions

1. Heat oil in a large Dutch oven over medium-high heat. Add ¾ cup onions and next 6 ingredients; stir-fry 15 seconds. Add water, soy sauce, and sake; bring to a boil. Add potatoes. Reduce heat; simmer 25 minutes or until tender. Cool to room temperature. Remove potatoes from cooking liquid with a slotted spoon. Sprinkle with 2 tablespoons onions. Yield: 6 servings (serving size: ¾ cup).

CALORIES 140 (7% from fat); FAT 1.1g (sat 0.2g, mono 0.2g, poly 0.6g); PROTEIN 2.1g; CARB 30.3g; FIBER 2.2g; CHOL 0mg; IRON 0.7mg; SODIUM 134mg; CALC 25mg

Hoisin-Drenched Tofu and Stir-Fried Vegetables

Use your largest skillet for this dish.

TOFU:
 ¾ cup hoisin sauce
 ⅓ cup sake (rice wine)
  3 tablespoons low-sodium soy sauce
1½ tablespoons minced fresh garlic
  1 teaspoon dark sesame oil
 ¾ teaspoon five-spice powder
1½ pounds firm water-packed tofu, drained and cut into (½-inch thick) slices

STIR-FRY:
3½ tablespoons low-sodium soy sauce
1½ tablespoons sugar
  1 teaspoon dark sesame oil
1½ tablespoons olive oil
  3 tablespoons finely chopped green onion bottoms
  2 tablespoons minced fresh garlic
1½ teaspoons chile paste with garlic
1½ cups red bell pepper strips
1½ cups yellow bell pepper strips
 ½ pound snow peas, trimmed
  2 tablespoons sake (rice wine) or sherry
  2 cups (1-inch) sliced green onion tops
4½ cups hot cooked jasmine rice

1. To prepare tofu, combine first 6 ingredients, stirring well with a whisk. Arrange tofu in a single layer on a foil-lined jelly roll pan; pour hoisin mixture over tofu, turning tofu to coat. Let stand at room temperature 1 hour.
2. Preheat oven to 375°.
3. Bake tofu mixture at 375° for 35 minutes. Discard marinade.
4. To prepare stir-fry, combine 3½ tablespoons soy sauce, sugar, and 1 teaspoon sesame oil.
5. Heat olive oil in a wok or large non-stick skillet over medium-high heat. Add green onion bottoms, 2 tablespoons garlic, and chile paste; stir-fry 15 seconds. Add bell peppers; stir-fry 1 minute. Add peas and 2 tablespoons sake; stir-fry 3 minutes or until peas are tender. Add tofu, soy sauce mixture, and green onion tops; toss gently to combine. Cook 2 minutes or until thoroughly heated. Serve over rice. Yield: 6 servings (serving size: 1 cup stir-fry and ¾ cup rice).
WINE NOTE: This dramatic tofu dish needs an equally bold, mouth-filling wine—one that can counterbalance pungent ingredients like hoisin sauce, five-spice powder, soy sauce, and sesame oil. Try the soft-textured but bold and floral-fruity Echelon Viognier "Esperanza Vineyard" from Clarksburg, California ($14).

CALORIES 427 (28% from fat); FAT 13.4g (sat 2g, mono 4.8g, poly 5.3g); PROTEIN 18.7g; CARB 57.4g; FIBER 5.5g; CHOL 0mg; IRON 5.2mg; SODIUM 736mg; CALC 170mg

Rainbow Salad with Vietnamese Dressing

Serve as a starter or a side dish.

DRESSING:
 ⅔ cup fresh lime juice (about 3 large limes)
 ½ cup hoisin sauce
1½ tablespoons sugar
1¼ teaspoons crushed red pepper
  4 garlic cloves, minced

SALAD:
  6 ounces bean threads (cellophane noodles)
  2 tablespoons water
 ¼ teaspoon salt
  2 large eggs, lightly beaten
  1 teaspoon olive oil, divided
 Cooking spray
  2 cups grated English cucumber
  2 cups grated carrot
  6 tablespoons chopped dry-roasted peanuts
 ¼ cup chopped fresh cilantro
 ¼ cup chopped fresh basil

1. To prepare dressing, combine first 5 ingredients, stirring with a whisk.
2. To prepare salad, cook noodles according to package directions. Drain and rinse with cold water; drain. Set aside.
3. Combine water, salt, and eggs, stirring with a whisk. Heat ½ teaspoon oil in a small nonstick skillet coated with cooking spray over medium-high heat. Pour half of egg mixture into pan; quickly tilt pan in all directions so egg mixture covers pan with a thin film. Cook 1 minute or until done. Place cooked egg on a cutting board. Repeat procedure with ½ teaspoon oil and remaining egg mixture. Cut egg rounds in half, and cut into thin strips.
4. Arrange about 2 tablespoons egg strips, ½ cup cellophane noodles, ⅓ cup cucumber, ⅓ cup carrot, 1 tablespoon peanuts, 2 teaspoons cilantro, and 2 teaspoons basil in separate piles on each of 6 plates. Serve each salad with about 3 tablespoons dressing. Yield: 6 servings.

CALORIES 253 (22% from fat); FAT 6.2g (sat 1g, mono 2.4g, poly 1.2g); PROTEIN 4.9g; CARB 46.1g; FIBER 2.3g; CHOL 71mg; IRON 0.8mg; SODIUM 507mg; CALC 37mg

Is Your Pantry Well-Stocked?

Wondering if your pantry is well-stocked? Well if you have the ingredients for the following recipes, then the answer is an emphatic "yes."

Polenta with Bolognese Sauce

These polenta triangles offer a tasty change of pace from the traditional pasta and sauce dish. You can make extra sauce to freeze and have on hand for busy nights.

SAUCE:

   Cooking spray
   1   cup finely chopped onion
   ¼   cup finely chopped carrot
   ¾   pound ground round
   3   garlic cloves, minced
   ⅓   cup dry red wine
   ¼   teaspoon salt
   ¼   teaspoon fennel seeds
   ¼   teaspoon freshly ground black
        pepper
   1   (28-ounce) can diced tomatoes,
        undrained

POLENTA:

   1½   cups 1% reduced-fat milk
   ½   teaspoon salt
   1   (14-ounce) can fat-free,
        less-sodium chicken broth
   1   cup dry polenta
   ½   cup (2 ounces) finely grated fresh
        Romano or Parmesan cheese, divided
   ¼   cup chopped fresh basil

1. To prepare sauce, heat a large non-stick skillet coated with cooking spray over medium-high heat. Add onion, carrot, beef, and garlic; cook 6 minutes or until beef is browned, stirring to crumble. Add wine; cook 1 minute. Add ¼ teaspoon salt, fennel, pepper, and tomatoes. Bring to a boil; cover, reduce heat, and simmer 40 minutes.

2. To prepare polenta, combine milk, ½ teaspoon salt, and broth in a medium saucepan. Gradually add polenta, stirring constantly with a whisk; bring to a boil. Reduce heat to medium; cook 3 minutes or until thick, stirring constantly. Stir in 6 tablespoons cheese.

3. Spoon polenta into an 8-inch square baking dish coated with cooking spray, spreading evenly. Let stand 10 minutes or until firm. Loosen edges of polenta with a knife. Invert polenta onto a cutting board; cut into 4 squares. Cut each square diagonally into 2 triangles. Place 1 triangle on each of 8 plates; top each serving with ½ cup sauce, ¾ teaspoon cheese, and 1½ teaspoons basil. Yield: 8 servings.

CALORIES 263 (30% from fat); FAT 8.8g (sat 3.8g, mono 3g, poly 0.3g); PROTEIN 15.9g; CARB 28.6g; FIBER 3.7g; CHOL 38mg; IRON 2mg; SODIUM 604mg; CALC 183mg

Chicken Nuggets with Mustard Dipping Sauce

CHICKEN:

   ½   cup low-fat buttermilk
   1½   pounds skinless, boneless chicken
        breast, cut into 40 pieces
   3¾   cups cornflakes
   1   teaspoon paprika
   ½   teaspoon sugar
   ¼   teaspoon salt
   Cooking spray

SAUCE:

   ½   cup prepared mustard
   ¼   cup honey
   ½   teaspoon grated peeled fresh
        ginger

1. To prepare chicken, combine buttermilk and chicken. Marinate in refrigerator 30 minutes; drain.

2. Preheat oven to 375°.

3. Place cornflakes, paprika, sugar, and salt in a food processor; process until cornflakes are finely chopped. Combine chicken and cornflake mixture, tossing well to coat. Place chicken on a baking sheet coated with cooking spray. Bake at 375° for 15 minutes or until done.

4. To prepare sauce, combine mustard, honey, and ginger. Serve with chicken. Yield: 8 servings (serving size: 5 nuggets and 1½ tablespoons sauce).

CALORIES 190 (9% from fat); FAT 1.8g (sat 0.4g, mono 0.6g, poly 0.4g); PROTEIN 21.8g; CARB 21.3g; FIBER 0.8g; CHOL 50mg; IRON 1.3mg; SODIUM 425mg; CALC 40mg

White Velvet Soup

(pictured on page 256)

Celeriac and potatoes are the base of this deceptively rich soup. Serve as the first course of a refined menu.

   4   cups (¼-inch) diced peeled
        celeriac (celery root; about
        1¼ pounds)
   4   cups (¼-inch) diced peeled
        Yukon Gold potato (about
        1¼ pounds)
   3   cups fat-free, less-sodium chicken
        broth
   2   cups water
   2   tablespoons fresh thyme leaves
   4   large garlic cloves, chopped
   ⅓   cup white wine
   ¾   teaspoon salt
   ½   cup 2% reduced-fat milk
   1   tablespoon extravirgin olive oil
   3   tablespoons thinly sliced green
        onions

1. Combine first 6 ingredients in a large stockpot; bring to a boil. Partially cover, reduce heat, and simmer 30 minutes or until vegetables are tender. Place half of potato mixture in a blender; process until smooth. Repeat with remaining potato mixture. Return puréed potato mixture to pan; stir in wine and salt. Cook over medium heat 3 minutes or until thoroughly heated. Remove soup from heat, and stir in milk.

2. Place soup in each of 6 bowls; drizzle oil over soup. Sprinkle with onions. Yield: 6 servings (serving size:1⅓ cups soup, ½ teaspoon oil, and 1½ teaspoons onions).

CALORIES 161 (17% from fat); FAT 3.1g (sat 0.7g, mono 2g, poly 0.4g); PROTEIN 6.4g; CARB 28.5g; FIBER 4.4g; CHOL 2mg; IRON 2.1mg; SODIUM 625mg; CALC 97mg

Mushroom and Fennel-Dusted Pork Tenderloin

Dried mushrooms are a good match for roast pork, but you can omit them.

    2 tablespoons dried porcini
       mushrooms
    1 tablespoon fennel seeds
    ½ teaspoon salt
    1 large garlic clove, minced
    2 pounds pork tenderloin, trimmed
    1 teaspoon olive oil
    ¼ cup fat-free, less-sodium chicken
       broth

1. Preheat oven to 425°.
2. Combine mushrooms and fennel seeds in a food processor or spice grinder; process until finely ground. Combine salt and garlic to make a paste. Rub pork with garlic paste; sprinkle with mushroom mixture.
3. Heat oil in a large cast iron skillet over medium-high heat. Add pork; cook 5 minutes or until browned, turning occasionally.
4. Place pan in oven; bake at 425° for 15 minutes or until a thermometer registers 160° (medium) or desired degree of doneness. Transfer pork to a jelly roll pan, and let stand 10 minutes.
5. Place pork on a cutting board, reserving juices in jelly roll pan. Combine reserved juices and broth in cast iron skillet; bring to a boil, scraping pan to loosen browned bits. Drizzle broth mixture over pork. Yield: 6 servings (serving size: 4 ounces pork).

CALORIES 204 (27% from fat); FAT 6.2g (sat 1.9g, mono 3g, poly 0.7g); PROTEIN 33g; CARB 2.2g; FIBER 0.9g; CHOL 98mg; IRON 2.7mg; SODIUM 290mg; CALC 21mg

Black Bean Stew

    2 teaspoons olive oil
    ½ cup chopped onion
    ⅓ cup uncooked Israeli couscous
    1 cup fat-free, less-sodium chicken
       broth
    1 cup canned black beans, drained
    1 teaspoon minced canned chipotle
       chile in adobo sauce
    1 (14.5-ounce) can stewed
       tomatoes, undrained
    1 tablespoon sliced green onions
    1 tablespoon low-fat sour cream

1. Heat oil in a medium saucepan over medium heat. Add ½ cup onion and couscous; cook 5 minutes, stirring frequently. Add broth; bring to a boil. Cover, reduce heat, and simmer 5 minutes.
2. Add beans, chipotle chile, and tomatoes; cover and simmer 4 minutes or until couscous is tender. Serve with green onions and sour cream. Yield: 2 servings (serving size: 1½ cups stew, 1½ teaspoons green onions, and 1½ teaspoons sour cream).

CALORIES 330 (16% from fat); FAT 5.7g (sat 1g, mono 3.4g, poly 0.5g); PROTEIN 13.7g; CARB 58.6g; FIBER 10.1g; CHOL 3mg; IRON 3.8mg; SODIUM 1,140mg; CALC 162mg

Gnocchi with Broccoli-Fontina Sauce

Because it's vacuum-packed, commercial gnocchi is a good pantry staple.

    14 cups water
    10 cups broccoli florets
     2 (16-ounce) boxes vacuum-packed
        gnocchi (such as Alessi)
     2 teaspoons olive oil
     ¾ cup finely chopped onion
     6 garlic cloves, minced
     1 cup (4 ounces) grated fontina
        cheese
     ½ cup fat-free, less-sodium chicken
        broth
     ¼ teaspoon freshly ground black
        pepper
     ½ cup (2 ounces) grated fresh
        Parmesan cheese

1. Bring water to a boil in a large Dutch oven. Add broccoli and gnocchi; cook 3 minutes or until done. Drain.
2. Heat oil in a large skillet over medium heat. Add onion and garlic; cook 3 minutes or until tender, stirring frequently. Stir in broccoli mixture, fontina, broth, and pepper; cook 1 minute or until thoroughly heated. Sprinkle with Parmesan. Yield: 6 servings (serving size: 1⅓ cups).

CALORIES 480 (24% from fat); FAT 12.9g (sat 6.9g, mono 2.8g, poly 0.7g); PROTEIN 22.8g; CARB 71.1g; FIBER 7.2g; CHOL 42mg; IRON 3.2mg; SODIUM 997mg; CALC 306mg

Risotto Primavera

Serving the vegetables atop the risotto ensures that their flavor isn't lost in the rich, creamy rice.

VEGETABLES:
    1½ teaspoons olive oil
     3 cups (2-inch) diagonally cut
        asparagus
     2 cups chopped yellow squash
     ¼ teaspoon salt
     ¼ teaspoon freshly ground black
        pepper
     1 garlic clove, minced

RISOTTO:
     1 cup water
     2 (14-ounce) cans fat-free,
        less-sodium chicken broth
     1 tablespoon butter
     2 cups chopped leek
    1½ cups Arborio rice
     ½ cup dry white wine
     ½ cup (2 ounces) grated fresh
        Parmesan cheese, divided
    1½ teaspoons chopped fresh thyme
     ½ teaspoon salt

1. To prepare vegetables, heat oil in a large skillet over medium-high heat. Add asparagus and next 4 ingredients; cook 10 minutes or until asparagus is crisp-tender, stirring frequently. Set aside; keep warm.
2. To prepare risotto, bring water and broth to a simmer in a medium saucepan (do not boil). Keep warm over low heat.
Continued

3. Melt butter in a large Dutch oven over medium heat. Add leek; cook 4 minutes or until tender, stirring frequently. Add rice; cook 2 minutes, stirring constantly. Add wine, and cook 1 minute. Stir in 1 cup broth mixture, and cook 4 minutes or until liquid is nearly absorbed, stirring constantly. Add remaining broth mixture, ½ cup at a time, stirring constantly until each portion is absorbed before adding next (about 20 minutes total). Stir in ¼ cup cheese, thyme, and ½ teaspoon salt.

4. Place risotto on each of 6 plates; top each serving with vegetables. Sprinkle servings with cheese. Yield: 6 servings (serving size: ¾ cup risotto, ½ cup vegetables, and 2 teaspoons cheese).

CALORIES 330 (14% from fat); FAT 5.2g (sat 2.6g, mono 2g, poly 0.4g); PROTEIN 10.6g; CARB 54.8g; FIBER 3.5g; CHOL 10mg; IRON 1.9mg; SODIUM 760mg; CALC 149mg

MAKE AHEAD
Pizza Meat Loaves

This recipe is well suited for families who like home-cooked meals but don't always eat together. Store the meat loaves in the refrigerator up to 1 day. Cook them all at once or one at a time.

    2 (1-ounce) slices firm white bread
Cooking spray
    1 cup finely chopped onion
    ⅓ cup bottled roasted red bell
       peppers
    ¼ cup (1 ounce) shredded part-skim
       mozzarella cheese
 1½ teaspoons commercial pesto
    ¾ teaspoon salt
    ¾ pound ground turkey breast
    ¾ pound ground round
    1 large egg
    ⅓ cup pizza sauce

1. Preheat oven to 375°.

2. Place bread slices in a food processor, and pulse 10 times or until fine crumbs measure 1¼ cups. Place breadcrumbs in a bowl; set aside.

3. Heat a medium nonstick skillet coated with cooking spray over medium-high heat. Add onion; sauté 4 minutes or until lightly browned. Place onion in food processor. Add bell peppers, and pulse 10 times or until bell peppers are chopped.

4. Combine breadcrumbs, onion mixture, cheese, pesto, salt, turkey, beef, and egg. Divide beef mixture into 9 equal portions, shaping each into a 3 x 1-inch loaf. Place loaves on a broiler pan coated with cooking spray. Bake at 375° for 18 minutes or until lightly browned. Spoon about 1½ teaspoons sauce over each loaf. Bake an additional 10 minutes or until a thermometer registers 160°. Yield: 9 servings (serving size: 1 meat loaf).

CALORIES 178 (33% from fat); FAT 6.6g (sat 2.5g, mono 2.4g, poly 0.4g); PROTEIN 22.1g; CARB 6g; FIBER 0.6g; CHOL 85mg; IRON 1.9mg; SODIUM 364mg; CALC 44mg

MAKE AHEAD • FREEZABLE
Carrot-Chocolate Cupcakes

Because there is no frosting on these cupcakes, they're great for freezing: Store them (without the powdered sugar) in a heavy-duty zip-top plastic bag. To thaw, wrap each cupcake in a paper towel, and microwave at MEDIUM for 15 to 25 seconds. Or if you have more time, let them sit at room temperature until thawed. Dust with powdered sugar, if desired.

    1 pound carrots, peeled and sliced
 1¾ cups sugar
    6 tablespoons vegetable oil
    ⅓ cup low-fat buttermilk
    3 large eggs, lightly beaten
    2 cups all-purpose flour
    2 teaspoons baking soda
    ½ teaspoon salt
    1 ounce semisweet chocolate, finely
       chopped
    3 tablespoons powdered sugar

1. Preheat oven to 350°.

2. Place carrots in a food processor; process until finely minced.

3. Combine carrots, sugar, oil, buttermilk, and eggs in a large bowl. Lightly spoon flour into dry measuring cups; level with a knife. Combine flour, soda, and salt, stirring with a whisk. Add flour mixture to carrot mixture; stir until smooth. Stir in chocolate.

4. Spoon batter into 22 muffin cups lined with paper liners. Bake at 350° for 22 minutes or until a wooden pick inserted in center comes out clean. Cool in pan 10 minutes on a wire rack, and remove from pan. Cool completely on wire rack. Dust cupcakes with powdered sugar. Yield: 22 servings (serving size: 1 cupcake).

CALORIES 155 (21% from fat); FAT 3.6g (sat 1g, mono 1.5g, poly 0.7g); PROTEIN 2.5g; CARB 28.8g; FIBER 1g; CHOL 29mg; IRON 0.7mg; SODIUM 226mg; CALC 15mg

MAKE AHEAD
Sherry-Braised Roasted Peppers

Serve this side with flank steak, chicken, or tossed with pasta. Keep leftovers in the refrigerator for a few days. Reheat in the microwave or serve at room temperature.

    2 large green bell peppers (about
       1 pound)
    2 large red bell peppers (about
       1 pound)
    2 large yellow bell peppers (about
       1 pound)
    1 tablespoon olive oil
    2 tablespoons capers
    1 teaspoon minced fresh rosemary
    1 teaspoon minced fresh thyme
    2 large garlic cloves, minced
    2 tablespoons medium dry sherry
    ¼ teaspoon salt

1. Preheat broiler.

2. Cut peppers in half lengthwise; discard seeds and membranes. Place pepper halves, skin sides up, on a foil-lined baking sheet; flatten with hand. Broil 10 minutes or until blackened. Place in a zip-top plastic bag; seal. Let stand 10 minutes. Peel and cut pepper halves into ½-inch-wide strips.

3. Heat oil in a large nonstick skillet over medium-high heat. Add capers, rosemary, thyme, and garlic; sauté 1 minute. Reduce heat to medium. Add sherry; cook 1 minute. Add pepper strips and salt; cook 2 minutes or until thoroughly heated. Serve warm or at room temperature. Yield: 6 servings (serving size: ½ cup).

CALORIES 70 (33% from fat); FAT 2.6g (sat 0.4g, mono 1.7g, poly 0.4g); PROTEIN 1.6g; CARB 11.1g; FIBER 2.3g; CHOL 0mg; IRON 0.9mg; SODIUM 186mg; CALC 19mg

Company's Coming

Everyone loves a party. In the following pages, we've wrapped up everything you need for lively entertaining, from fun ways to have guests join you in the kitchen (below) to turning simple dishes into sophisticated fare (page 283).

The Party's in the Kitchen

When your guests pitch in and help with the cooking, the fun starts well before dinner.

When you host a party, everyone usually ends up in the kitchen. Whether they're tossing a salad or pouring wine, being part of the action makes guests feel like family. So since they're already in the kitchen, why not put your guests to work? To suggest ways to do this successfully with minimal fuss, we sought the expertise of Gourmet Gatherings, a San Francisco catering company that specializes in cooking parties. We asked Gourmet Gatherings to devise a menu that would get everyone involved in the kitchen. Follow these tips and recipes for a party that truly cooks.

Getting Started

One of the goals of communal cooking is to make the job fun (and easy).

• Team up with another friend to organize the party.

• E-mail the menu and a recipe to each guest. Help them decide what portions of the recipe to make ahead and what equipment they need to bring.

• Arrange equipment and ingredients for each dish ahead of time. Think through the prep for each recipe, and set out specialty dishes and tools in advance.

• Make a copy of the menu and each recipe for guests to follow.

• Appoint someone to be in charge of each course.

Dinner Party Menu
serves 12

Appetizers

Crostini with Gorgonzola, Caramelized Onions, and Fig Jam
or
Herb-Topped Mussels on the Half Shell

Salad

Spinach Salad with Nectarines and Spicy Pecans

Entrées

Spice-Crusted Salmon with Citrus Sauce
or
Filet Mignon with Peppercorn-Orange Sauce

Sides

Green Beans with Garlic Vinaigrette
or
Wild Rice Cakes with Bacon
or
Fruited Israeli Couscous

Dessert

Coconut Butter Cake with Ginger Ice Milk

Crostini with Gorgonzola, Caramelized Onions, and Fig Jam

The Gorgonzola is great with the jam, but feta or any other soft, pungent cheese will work.

JAM:

1 cup dried Black Mission figs (about 6 ounces)
1 teaspoon lemon juice
2 cups water
2 tablespoons maple syrup
Dash of salt

ONIONS:

Cooking spray
2 cups vertically sliced yellow onion
1 teaspoon balsamic vinegar
½ teaspoon chopped fresh thyme
¼ teaspoon salt
½ cup water (optional)

REMAINING INGREDIENTS:

½ cup (4 ounces) Gorgonzola cheese, softened
24 (1-inch-thick) slices diagonally cut French bread baguette, toasted (about 12 ounces)
1 teaspoon fresh thyme leaves

1. To prepare jam, remove stems from figs. Place figs and juice in a food processor; process until figs are coarsely chopped. Place fig mixture, 2 cups water, syrup, and dash of salt in a medium saucepan; bring to a boil. Reduce heat, and simmer 25 minutes or until thick. Cool completely.

2. To prepare onions, heat a large nonstick skillet coated with cooking spray over medium heat. Add onion, vinegar, ½ teaspoon thyme, and ¼ teaspoon salt; cover and cook 5 minutes. Uncover and cook 20 minutes or until onion is deep golden brown, stirring occasionally. While onion cooks, add ½ cup water, ¼ cup at a time, as needed to keep onion from sticking to pan.

3. Spread 1 teaspoon cheese over each baguette slice. Top each slice with about 1 teaspoon onion mixture and 1 teaspoon jam. Sprinkle evenly with thyme leaves. Yield: 12 servings (serving size: 2 crostini).

CALORIES 106 (29% from fat); FAT 3.4g (sat 1.9g, mono 0.9g, poly 0.3g); PROTEIN 2.9g; CARB 16.3g; FIBER 2.4g; CHOL 8mg; IRON 0.6mg; SODIUM 82mg; CALC 85mg

Game Plan

Gourmet Gatherings devised our menu for an all-out cooking party. With two people on each recipe, the menu can be made in an hour and a half. But cooking every single item may be a bit more than you'd like to tackle. That's why this menu has many make-ahead components. It's also mix-and-match, letting you choose between appetizers, entrées, and sides. Here's the make-ahead strategy:

Crostini with Gorgonzola, Caramelized Onions, and Fig Jam (recipe on page 275)
Make the fig jam and the caramelized onions up to 1 week ahead. One or two guests can slice the baguettes and assemble the appetizers.

Herb-Topped Mussels on the Half Shell (recipe at right)
Making this appetizer will be a novelty for your guests, especially if they've never worked with mussels before. To avoid lugging out the food processor during the party, make the herbed topping and the sauce ahead. Assemble the appetizers, and broil them just before serving.

Spinach Salad with Nectarines and Spicy Pecans (recipe on page 277)
Bake the pecans, whisk the vinaigrette, and sauté the prosciutto ahead. Cut the nectarines, and toss all the ingredients just before serving. With this approach, all you need is a salad bowl, a cutting board, a knife, and salad forks.

Spice-Crusted Salmon with Citrus Sauce (recipe on page 277)
Prepare the sauce up to 2 days ahead. Grinding the spices for the crust is fun, but the mixture can also be made ahead. This leaves only the final prep for the salmon. Cut the salmon into 6-ounce fillets. Dip each fillet into the spice mixture, then sauté and bake just before serving. Line the baking sheet with foil for easy cleanup. You can also crust and sauté the salmon

up to a day ahead, then pop it in the oven to finish just before serving.

Filet Mignon with Peppercorn-Orange Sauce (recipe on page 278)
Give this recipe to the grill-master in the group. Make the sauce up to 3 days ahead, which will leave just a quick turn on the grill or grill pan for the steaks.

Green Beans with Garlic Vinaigrette (recipe on page 278)
Whisk the vinaigrette and toast the almonds up to 3 days ahead, then toss the green beans with the vinaigrette, almonds, and thyme just before serving.

Wild Rice Cakes with Bacon (recipe on page 278)
Depending on the activity in the kitchen, choose either of the following ways to make these ahead. Prepare them completely, and reheat on a baking sheet coated with cooking spray for 10 minutes at 325°. Or make the mixture for the cakes ahead, then sauté them just before serving. Either way, serve immediately.

Fruited Israeli Couscous (recipe on page 279)
Completely prepare this couscous dish a day ahead, and serve it at room temperature.

Coconut Butter Cake with Ginger Ice Milk (recipe on page 279)
If there's one item in this menu that's easily made ahead, this is it. If you don't have a purchased cake container, place the cake on a piece of cardboard covered with aluminum foil. Make up to 2 days ahead. The Ginger Ice Milk is at its creamiest right out of the ice-cream freezer. But you can make the milk mixture ahead, then place it in the ice-cream freezer at the beginning of the evening. It will be ready just in time for dessert. If you make it ahead, let it soften at room temperature for at least 30 minutes before serving.

Herb-Topped Mussels on the Half Shell

24 medium mussels, scrubbed and debearded
Cooking spray
¼ cup chopped leek
2 garlic cloves, minced
¼ cup clam juice
3 tablespoons half-and-half
½ teaspoon grated lemon rind
1 teaspoon fresh lemon juice
1 (1½-ounce) slice white bread
1 tablespoon chopped fresh flat-leaf parsley
2 teaspoons chopped fresh thyme
2 teaspoons olive oil
1 teaspoon chopped fresh oregano
¼ teaspoon freshly ground black pepper
2 bacon slices, cooked and crumbled

1. Preheat oven to 500°.
2. Arrange mussels in a single layer in a 13 x 9-inch baking dish. Bake at 500° for 8 minutes or until shells open; discard any unopened shells. Remove mussels and cooking liquid from dish. Strain cooking liquid through a sieve over a bowl; discard solids. Remove meat from mussels. Reserve 24 shell halves. Discard remaining shells. Arrange reserved shells on a jelly roll pan; place 1 mussel in each shell.
3. Heat a small saucepan coated with cooking spray over medium heat. Add leek; cook 3 minutes or until tender, stirring frequently. Add garlic; cook 30 seconds, stirring frequently. Stir in cooking liquid, clam juice, and half-and-half; bring to a boil. Cook until reduced to ¼ cup (about 3 minutes). Stir in rind and lemon juice.
4. Preheat broiler.
5. Place bread in a food processor; process until fine crumbs measure ¾ cup. Combine breadcrumbs, parsley, and remaining 5 ingredients. Spoon ½ teaspoon sauce over each mussel. Lightly pack 2 teaspoons breadcrumb mixture into each shell. Broil 1½ minutes or until golden. Yield: 12 servings (serving size: 2 stuffed shells).

CALORIES 56 (40% from fat); FAT 2.5g (sat 0.7g, mono 1.1g, poly 0.4g); PROTEIN 4.6g; CARB 3.4g; FIBER 0.1g; CHOL 12mg; IRON 1.5mg; SODIUM 140mg; CALC 21mg

Spinach Salad with Nectarines and Spicy Pecans

This recipe has variations galore. Use almonds or walnuts in place of pecans, and use bacon or ham in place of prosciutto. Substitute any kind of greens, including arugula, field mix, or romaine lettuce.

PECANS:
¼ cup powdered sugar
½ teaspoon salt
¼ teaspoon ground allspice
⅛ teaspoon ground nutmeg
⅛ teaspoon ground red pepper
⅓ cup pecan halves
Cooking spray

VINAIGRETTE:
3 tablespoons finely chopped shallots
3 tablespoons balsamic vinegar
2 teaspoons fresh lemon juice
2 teaspoons extravirgin olive oil
1 teaspoon sugar
1 teaspoon Dijon mustard
¾ teaspoon salt
½ teaspoon freshly ground black pepper

SALAD:
¾ cup very thin slices prosciutto, coarsely chopped (about 2 ounces)
2 (6-ounce) packages fresh baby spinach (about 12 cups)
2 nectarines, each cut into ¼-inch wedges (about ¾ pound)

1. Preheat oven to 350°.
2. To prepare pecans, combine first 5 ingredients in a small bowl. Rinse pecans with cold water; drain (do not allow pecans to dry). Add pecans to sugar mixture, and toss well to coat. Arrange pecan mixture on a jelly roll pan coated with cooking spray. Bake at 350° for 10 minutes, stirring occasionally. Coarsely chop pecans. Set aside.
3. To prepare vinaigrette, combine shallots and next 7 ingredients in a small bowl, stirring with a whisk until blended.
4. To prepare salad, heat a large nonstick skillet coated with cooking spray over medium-high heat. Add prosciutto; sauté 5 minutes or until crisp, and finely chop.

Combine spinach, nectarines, and vinaigrette in a large bowl; toss gently to coat. Sprinkle with pecans and prosciutto. Yield: 12 servings (serving size: 1 cup salad, 1 tablespoon prosciutto, and about 1½ teaspoons pecans).

CALORIES 75 (48% from fat); FAT 4g (sat 0.6g, mono 2g, poly 0.8g); PROTEIN 2.7g; CARB 8.2g; FIBER 1.5g; CHOL 4mg; IRON 1.1mg; SODIUM 369mg; CALC 36mg

Spice-Crusted Salmon with Citrus Sauce

If you can't find *panko* (extracrisp Japanese breadcrumbs), substitute plain, dry breadcrumbs.

SAUCE:
1 (6-ounce) carton plain fat-free yogurt
½ cup fat-free sour cream
½ teaspoon grated orange rind
3 tablespoons fresh orange juice
2 tablespoons finely chopped fresh cilantro
½ teaspoon ground cumin
½ teaspoon crushed red pepper
½ teaspoon grated lemon rind
½ teaspoon grated lime rind
¼ teaspoon salt

SALMON:
2 tablespoons fennel seeds
1 tablespoon coriander seeds
1 tablespoon cumin seeds
¼ cup panko (extracrisp Japanese breadcrumbs)
2½ teaspoons salt
1 teaspoon freshly ground black pepper
12 (6-ounce) salmon fillets (about 1 inch thick), skinned
Cooking spray
Cilantro sprigs (optional)

1. Preheat oven to 400°.
2. To prepare sauce, spoon yogurt onto several layers of heavy-duty paper towels; spread to ½-inch thickness. Cover with additional paper towels; let stand 5 minutes. Scrape into a bowl using a rubber spatula. Add sour cream and next 8 ingredients. Cover and chill.

3. To prepare salmon, place fennel, coriander, and cumin seeds in a spice or coffee grinder; process until finely ground. Combine spice mixture, breadcrumbs, 2½ teaspoons salt, and black pepper in a shallow dish. Dredge skinned side of salmon in spice mixture. Heat a large nonstick skillet coated with cooking spray over medium-high heat. Add half of salmon, crust sides down; cook 3 minutes or until golden brown. Transfer salmon, crust sides up, to a baking sheet lined with aluminum foil. Repeat procedure with remaining salmon. Bake at 400° for 8 minutes or until fish flakes easily when tested with a fork. Serve with sauce. Garnish with cilantro sprigs, if desired. Yield: 12 servings (serving size: 1 fillet and 4 teaspoons sauce).

WINE NOTE: Because salmon is rich, it works especially well with a wine that's crisp and lively enough to act as a counterpoint. Among the great choices: Sauvignon Blanc, dry Riesling, or Pinot Gris (also known as Pinot Grigio). The Sauvignon Blancs from New Zealand are especially terrific thanks to their dramatic raciness and purity. Some suggestions: Spy Valley Sauvignon Blanc 2002 (Marlborough, New Zealand), about $12.

CALORIES 308 (40% from fat); FAT 13.7g (sat 3.2g, mono 5.9g, poly 3.2g); PROTEIN 38.1g; CARB 6.1g; FIBER 0.8g; CHOL 88mg; IRON 1.3mg; SODIUM 643mg; CALC 86mg

---

Small Kitchen?

If your kitchen is small, take some of the work elsewhere. Cook the Filet Mignon with Peppercorn-Orange Sauce (recipe on page 278) on the grill, and toss the Spinach Salad with Nectarines and Spicy Pecans (recipe on page 277) table-side. Use your coffee table, or set a table in the living room with the components for the crostini, and let guests assemble them themselves. Stash the ice-cream freezer in an extra bath or the laundry room to pipe down its noisy hum. Once the ice cream is done, set up the dessert outside or in the living room.

Filet Mignon with Peppercorn-Orange Sauce

Whirling the sauce together in the food processor is a breeze, and it can easily be done before the party.

SAUCE:

- 2 teaspoons grated orange rind
- ¼ cup fresh orange juice
- ¼ cup low-sodium soy sauce
- 2 tablespoons brown sugar
- 2 tablespoons fresh lemon juice
- 2 tablespoons balsamic vinegar
- 2 teaspoons honey
- ½ cup coarsely chopped green onions
- ½ cup coarsely chopped fresh cilantro
- 2 tablespoons drained brine-packed green peppercorns
- 2 teaspoons extravirgin olive oil
- 1 garlic clove, peeled
- 2 teaspoons sesame seeds, toasted
- ½ teaspoon salt

STEAKS:

- 12 (4-ounce) beef tenderloin steaks, trimmed (1 inch thick)
- ½ teaspoon salt
- ½ teaspoon black pepper
- Cooking spray
- Cilantro sprigs (optional)

1. Prepare grill.

2. To prepare sauce, combine first 7 ingredients in a small saucepan; bring to a boil. Cook until reduced to ⅓ cup (about 6 minutes). Cool.

3. Place onions and next 4 ingredients in a food processor; process until finely chopped. Add orange juice mixture, sesame seeds, and ½ teaspoon salt; pulse to combine. Set aside.

4. To prepare steaks, sprinkle beef with ½ teaspoon salt and pepper. Place steaks on a grill rack coated with cooking spray, and grill 3 minutes on each side or until desired degree of doneness. Serve steaks with sauce. Garnish with cilantro sprigs, if desired. Yield: 12 servings (serving size: 1 steak and about 1 tablespoon sauce).

WINE NOTE: Cabernet Sauvignon is the classic accompaniment for steak. Kirralaa Cabernet Sauvignon 2001 (Southeastern Australia), about $15, is a juicy, concentrated, and inexpensive Cabernet to try.

CALORIES 208 (39% from fat); FAT 9.1g (sat 3.1g, mono 3.6g, poly 0.4g); PROTEIN 24.4g; CARB 5.7g; FIBER 0.5g; CHOL 71mg; IRON 3.3mg; SODIUM 497mg; CALC 18mg

---

QUICK & EASY

Green Beans with Garlic Vinaigrette

Toast the almonds in a pie pan at 350° for 5 to 10 minutes.

VINAIGRETTE:

- ½ teaspoon grated lemon rind
- 1 tablespoon fresh lemon juice
- 2 teaspoons extravirgin olive oil
- 1 teaspoon Dijon mustard
- ½ teaspoon salt
- ¼ teaspoon freshly ground black pepper
- 2 garlic cloves, minced

BEANS:

- 2½ pounds green beans, trimmed
- ⅓ cup sliced almonds, toasted
- 1 tablespoon fresh thyme leaves

1. To prepare vinaigrette, combine first 7 ingredients in a small bowl, stirring with a whisk.

2. To prepare beans, cook beans in a large pot of boiling water 4 minutes or until crisp-tender. Drain well. Place beans in a large bowl. Add vinaigrette; toss well to coat. Sprinkle with almonds and thyme. Yield: 12 servings (serving size: 1 cup).

CALORIES 54 (38% from fat); FAT 2.3g (sat 0.2g, mono 1.5g, poly 0.5g); PROTEIN 2.4g; CARB 7.7g; FIBER 3.6g; CHOL 0mg; IRON 1.1mg; SODIUM 113mg; CALC 45mg

---

STAFF FAVORITE • MAKE AHEAD

Wild Rice Cakes with Bacon

Make the rice cakes ahead, then reheat in the oven to free the stovetop for other items.

- 2 teaspoons butter
- 1 cup uncooked brown and wild rice blend
- 1½ teaspoons salt
- 1 (14-ounce) can fat-free, less-sodium chicken broth
- ½ cup all-purpose flour
- 1 large egg, lightly beaten
- 1 large egg white, lightly beaten
- ½ teaspoon baking powder
- 1 cup thinly sliced green onions
- ½ cup slivered almonds, toasted
- 2 teaspoons fresh thyme leaves
- 1 teaspoon fresh lemon juice
- 2 bacon slices, cooked and crumbled
- Cooking spray

1. Melt butter in a large saucepan over medium-high heat. Add rice; cook 1 minute, stirring constantly. Add salt and broth; bring to a boil. Cover, reduce heat, and simmer 40 minutes or until liquid is absorbed and rice is tender. Drain any excess liquid. Cool slightly.

2. Lightly spoon flour into a dry measuring cup; level with a knife. Place egg and egg white in a large bowl; add flour and baking powder, stirring with a whisk. Add rice, green onions, and next 4 ingredients, stirring with a rubber spatula until well blended.

3. Heat a large nonstick skillet coated with cooking spray over medium-high heat. Spoon 3 (¼-cup) mounds rice mixture into pan; flatten slightly with spatula. Cook 2 minutes on each side or until golden brown and thoroughly heated. Repeat procedure with remaining rice mixture. Serve immediately. Yield: 12 servings (serving size: 1 cake).

CALORIES 128 (30% from fat); FAT 4.2g (sat 0.9g, mono 2.1g, poly 0.8g); PROTEIN 4.7g; CARB 17.7g; FIBER 1.6g; CHOL 20mg; IRON 0.8mg; SODIUM 412mg; CALC 28mg

Fruited Israeli Couscous

One person can tackle this recipe, which requires just a saucepan, a cutting board, and a knife. Israeli couscous has bead-sized grains that are much larger than those of regular couscous, and it takes just 15 minutes to cook.

    2   teaspoons butter
    1   cup finely chopped onion
    ½   cup dried currants
    ½   cup diced dried apricots
    ½   teaspoon salt
    3   (14-ounce) cans fat-free,
        less-sodium chicken broth
    3   (3-inch) cinnamon sticks
    2½ cups uncooked Israeli couscous
    ¼   cup chopped fresh cilantro

1. Melt butter in a large saucepan over medium-high heat. Add onion, and sauté 5 minutes. Stir in currants and next 4 ingredients; bring to a boil. Add couscous, and return to a boil. Cover, reduce heat, and simmer 15 minutes. Let couscous mixture stand 5 minutes. Discard cinnamon sticks. Stir in cilantro. Yield: 12 servings (serving size: about ⅔ cup).

CALORIES 190 (4% from fat); FAT 0.9g (sat 0.4g, mono 0.2g, poly 0.1g); PROTEIN 6.5g; CARB 38.2g; FIBER 2.8g; CHOL 2mg; IRON 1mg; SODIUM 297mg; CALC 21mg

Coconut Butter Cake with Ginger Ice Milk

    Cooking spray
    2   tablespoons granulated sugar
    6   tablespoons unsalted butter,
        softened
    1⅓ cups granulated sugar
    2   teaspoons vanilla extract
    3   large egg whites
    2   cups all-purpose flour
    1   teaspoon baking soda
    ½   teaspoon salt
    ¾   cup fat-free milk
    ¾   cup low-fat buttermilk
    ½   cup flaked sweetened
        coconut
    1   tablespoon powdered sugar

1. Preheat oven to 350°.
2. Coat a 9-inch (3 inches deep) spring-form pan with cooking spray; dust with 2 tablespoons sugar. Place butter in a large bowl; beat with a mixer at medium speed until creamy and pale (about 2 minutes); gradually add 1⅓ cups sugar. Beat at high speed 3 minutes or until fluffy. Beat in vanilla. Add egg whites, 1 at a time, beating well after each addition. Lightly spoon flour into dry measuring cups; level with a knife. Combine flour, baking soda, and salt, stirring with a whisk. Combine milk and buttermilk. Add flour mixture and buttermilk mixture alternately to sugar mixture, beginning and ending with flour mixture. Fold in coconut. Pour batter into prepared pan.
3. Bake at 350° for 55 minutes or until a wooden pick inserted in center comes out clean. Cool in pan 15 minutes on a wire rack; remove from pan. Cool completely on wire rack. Sprinkle with powdered sugar. Serve with Ginger Ice Milk. Yield: 12 servings (serving size: 1 slice).

(Totals include Ginger Ice Milk) CALORIES 352 (26% from fat); FAT 10.3g (sat 6.4g, mono 2.8g, poly 0.5g); PROTEIN 7.3g; CARB 58.2g; FIBER 0.8g; CHOL 60mg; IRON 1.3mg; SODIUM 293mg; CALC 121mg

This recipe takes about 20 to 30 minutes to freeze in an electric ice-cream maker.

    2   cups water
    ⅓   cup (¼-inch-thick) slices peeled
        fresh ginger
    3   cups whole milk
    ⅔   cup sugar
    1   vanilla bean, split lengthwise
    2   large eggs, lightly beaten

1. Combine water and ginger in a saucepan; bring to a boil. Drain. Combine ginger mixture, milk, and sugar in a medium saucepan. Scrape seeds from vanilla bean; add seeds and bean to milk mixture. Heat over medium-high heat to 180° or until tiny bubbles form around edge (do not boil). Remove from heat.
2. Place eggs in a large bowl. Gradually add hot milk mixture, stirring constantly with a whisk until blended. Let stand 15 minutes. Strain milk mixture through a sieve into pan; discard solids. Heat milk mixture over medium heat to 160°, stirring constantly with a whisk. Cool completely. Pour mixture into freezer can of an ice-cream freezer, and freeze according to manufacturer's instructions. Yield: 12 servings (serving size: about ¼ cup).

CALORIES 95 (27% from fat); FAT 2.9g (sat 1.5g, mono 1g, poly 0.2g); PROTEIN 3.1g; CARB 14.5g; FIBER 0.1g; CHOL 44mg; IRON 0.2mg; SODIUM 42mg; CALC 78mg

---

Tips from Gourmet Gatherings

Experience taught Bibby Gignillat and Shannan Bishop that they had a rare skill: putting people at ease in the kitchen. The pair founded Gourmet Gatherings in 1999. Two hundred parties and three years later, they have these tips for staging a successful and enjoyable cooking party:

• Have your guests bring (and wash) their own equipment. Mark pieces with colored tape to identify whose is whose.
• Play upbeat music—it relaxes everyone immediately. Gourmet Gatherings' current favorite: classic disco.
• Have something to eat to get the evening underway. Gignillat and Bishop like guests to help themselves to an antipasto platter.
• Make copies of the recipes for each guest. If you're inclined, take digital or Polaroid photos of the guests with the dishes they prepared.
• If you're doing a lot of cooking, team a strong cook with an inexperienced one.
• Remember your sense of humor. If something flops or doesn't look picture perfect, it's not a tragedy. Sometimes great things are born of mistakes.
• Things can never be too simple. Choose a menu with just three recipes, then round it out with the best store-bought items you can find.

Just the Guys

Monday Night Football *turned into a Monday night feast for this group of old friends.*

Twenty-five years ago, a college roommate invited Bruce Aidells and some friends over to watch *Monday Night Football.* "And we're still getting together regularly," Bruce says. "It used to just be about football, but now it's more about the camaraderie and the lively conversation generated by good food and drink."

"Since we moved the meal to the dining table, the food has gotten better; now we drink wine with our meal as often as we drink beer. While we still eat steaks, chops, and roasts, the meat is rarely overcooked, tough, or chewy. Some adventurous hosts make Italian, Mexican, or Middle European dishes. As the only cooking pro in the group, I'm expected to try something exotic."

Here's Bruce's menu for the guys at a recent Monday night football gathering. Perhaps it will serve your fans as well.

Bruce's Tips

• To simplify the menu, pick one of the spicy main dishes and serve it with Saffron Basmati Rice (recipe on page 281) and soothing Raita (recipe on page 282). If time allows, make the Curried Cauliflower (recipe on page 281). Otherwise, prepare a simple salad of diced tomatoes and sweet onions dressed with lime juice and olive oil.

• If you can get *naan*, the traditional Indian bread, serve it. If not, offer warm pita bread.

• We usually enjoy beer with this menu. Some of our favorites are Red Tail Ale, Sierra Nevada Pale Ale, and Anchor Steam.

• Most of the dishes here are improved by making them ahead and then reheating. Only the Saffron Basmati Rice, Raita, and Tomato, Lime, and Onion Salad (recipe on page 282) need to be prepared shortly before serving.

Bruce's Football Spread Menu
serves 8

Warm Spiced Lentils

Beef Curry with Toasted Spices
or
Lamb Shanks with Lime and Cilantro

Saffron Basmati Rice
or
Curried Cauliflower

Raita
Indian Yogurt and Cucumber Condiment

Mango and Mint Chutney

Tomato, Lime, and Onion Salad

MAKE AHEAD
Warm Spiced Lentils

Make the lentils a day ahead and refrigerate, then warm them over low heat. Serve as a side dish or as an appetizer with pita wedges. Try the Tomato, Lime, and Onion Salad (recipe on page 282) as a condiment.

    1 tablespoon olive oil
    2 cups chopped onion
    1 tablespoon finely chopped peeled
       fresh ginger
    ¾ teaspoon salt
    ¾ teaspoon freshly ground black
       pepper, divided
    2 tablespoons minced garlic
    2 teaspoons ground cumin
    2 teaspoons Homemade Curry
       Powder (recipe on page 282)
    1 teaspoon ground coriander
  2½ cups water
    2 cups fat-free, less-sodium chicken
       broth
    2 cups dried lentils
    3 bay leaves
    1 cup plain whole-milk yogurt
    ¾ cup tomato purée

1. Heat oil in a Dutch oven over medium heat. Add onion, ginger, salt, and ½ teaspoon pepper; cover and cook 10 minutes or until soft, stirring occasionally. Stir in garlic, cumin, Homemade Curry Powder, and coriander; cook 1 minute. Stir in water, broth, lentils, and bay leaves; bring to a boil. Reduce heat; cover and simmer 2 hours or until tender. Uncover and cook 5 minutes or until most of liquid is absorbed. Remove from heat; cool slightly. Discard bay leaves. Gradually stir in ¼ teaspoon pepper, yogurt, and purée; cook over low heat 5 minutes or until thoroughly heated. Yield: 12 servings (serving size: ½ cup).

CALORIES 160 (14% from fat); FAT 2.4g (sat 0.6g, mono 1.1g, poly 0.3g); PROTEIN 11.1g; CARB 25g; FIBER 11.1g; CHOL 3mg; IRON 3.6mg; SODIUM 244mg; CALC 60mg

---

MAKE AHEAD
Beef Curry with Toasted Spices
(pictured on page 292)

You can also prepare this recipe with cubed leg of lamb. Find fenugreek seed at an ethnic grocery such as World Market, or order online at www.americanspice.com.

BEEF:

    1 tablespoon Homemade Curry
       Powder (recipe on page 282)
    2 teaspoons freshly ground black
       pepper
  1½ teaspoons salt
  3½ pounds beef stew meat, trimmed
       and cut into bite-sized pieces

TOASTED SPICES:

    2 tablespoons coriander seeds
    1 tablespoon cumin seeds
    2 teaspoons fenugreek seeds
    3 whole cloves
    3 bay leaves
    2 dried hot red chiles
    1 (1-inch) cinnamon stick, broken
    2 tablespoons sugar
    ½ teaspoon ground cardamom
    ¼ teaspoon salt

REMAINING INGREDIENTS:

    1 tablespoon olive oil, divided
    3 cups vertically sliced onion
    3 tablespoons minced peeled fresh
       ginger
    ¼ cup minced garlic
    2 tablespoons Hungarian sweet
       paprika
    2 cups plain low-fat yogurt
  1½ cups low-salt beef broth
    1 cup chopped red bell pepper
    ½ cup minced fresh cilantro stems
    ½ cup tomato purée

1. To prepare beef, combine first 3 ingredients; rub evenly over beef. Cover and chill 2 hours, tossing occasionally.

2. To prepare toasted spices, heat a non-stick skillet over medium-high heat. Add coriander and next 6 ingredients; cook 1 minute or until fragrant, shaking pan constantly. Place coriander mixture, sugar, cardamom, and ¼ teaspoon salt in a spice or coffee grinder; process until finely ground.

3. Heat 1½ teaspoons oil in a Dutch oven over medium-high heat. Add half of beef mixture; sauté 5 minutes or until browned on all sides. Remove from pan with a slotted spoon. Repeat procedure with 1½ teaspoons oil and remaining beef mixture; remove from pan. Reduce heat to medium. Add onion and ginger to pan; cook 6 minutes or until onion is tender, stirring occasionally. Add toasted spice mixture, garlic, and paprika; cook 1 minute, stirring constantly. Add beef, yogurt, and remaining ingredients; bring to a boil. Cover, reduce heat, and simmer 1½ hours or until beef is tender. Yield 12 servings (serving size: about 1 cup).

WINE NOTE: With its bold flavors, Bruce's menu would work nicely with a variety of wines that are bold and spicy themselves. But because beef curry is the centerpiece, try a lip-smacking red that's complex enough to handle lots of flavor nuance. The southern French wine Châteuneuf-du-Pape would be an excellent choice. Domaine de la Charbonnière "Cuvée Mourre des Perdrix" Châteuneuf-du-Pape 1998 (Châteuneuf-du-Pape, Rhone Valley, France), about $29, is a favorite.

CALORIES 262 (38% from fat); FAT 11g (sat 3.9g, mono 5g, poly 0.5g); PROTEIN 27.6g; CARB 12.9g; FIBER 2.1g; CHOL 79mg; IRON 4.1mg; SODIUM 440mg; CALC 118mg

Lamb Shanks with Lime and Cilantro

You can make this a day ahead. To reheat, skim the fat from the top, then place over medium-low heat until thoroughly heated. Serve with Raita (recipe on page 282) and Mango and Mint Chutney (recipe on page 282). Offer guests bowls of peanuts, shredded coconut, raisins plumped in water or brandy, and chopped pineapple to add at will.

4 (1¼-pound) lamb shanks, trimmed
1 tablespoon olive oil, divided
1½ teaspoons ground coriander
1 teaspoon salt
1 teaspoon ground cumin
1 teaspoon freshly ground black pepper
2 cups thinly sliced onion
2 cups (½-inch-thick) slices carrot
1 tablespoon finely chopped garlic
1 tablespoon finely chopped peeled fresh lemongrass
2 teaspoons Homemade Curry Powder (recipe on page 282)
1 cup chopped fresh cilantro leaves, divided
1 cup fat-free, less-sodium chicken broth
½ cup chopped fresh cilantro stems
1 tablespoon grated lime rind
1½ tablespoons fresh lime juice

1. Preheat oven to 350°.

2. Lightly score a diamond pattern into both sides of lamb. Heat 1½ teaspoons oil in a large Dutch oven over medium-high heat. Combine coriander, salt, cumin, and pepper; rub over lamb. Add half of lamb shanks to pan; cook 8 minutes or until browned, turning occasionally. Remove lamb from pan. Repeat procedure with 1½ teaspoons oil and remaining lamb shanks; remove from pan.

3. Reduce heat to medium. Add onion and carrot to pan, and cook 5 minutes or until onion is tender, stirring frequently. Add garlic, lemongrass, and Homemade Curry Powder; sauté 1 minute. Return lamb shanks to pan. Add ½ cup cilantro leaves, broth, cilantro stems, rind, and juice; bring to a boil.

4. Cover and bake at 350° for 1½ hours or until lamb shanks are tender. Skim fat from surface of cooking liquid with a spoon. Stir in ½ cup cilantro leaves. Remove lamb from pan, and cool slightly. Remove meat from bones, and discard bones. Return meat to pan. Yield: 8 servings (serving size: 3 ounces lamb and about ½ cup sauce).

CALORIES 210 (31% from fat); FAT 7.2g (sat 2.1g, mono 3.5g, poly 0.5g); PROTEIN 27.8g; CARB 7.6g; FIBER 2.3g; CHOL 89mg; IRON 2.6mg; SODIUM 427mg; CALC 46mg

Saffron Basmati Rice
(pictured on page 292)

The mildly spiced rice goes with both entrées. Store leftovers separately from the lamb or beef. To reheat the rice, add a teaspoon or 2 of water, and microwave partially covered. The water will rehydrate the grains and make them fluffy again.

5 cups water
1½ teaspoons salt
⅛ teaspoon saffron threads
6 whole cloves
3 cups white basmati rice

1. Bring first 4 ingredients to a boil in a large sauté pan; add rice. Cover, reduce heat, and simmer 15 minutes. Remove from heat; cover and let stand 5 minutes. Discard cloves. Yield: 10 servings (serving size: 1 cup).

CALORIES 216 (0% from fat); FAT 0g; PROTEIN 3.2g; CARB 54.4g; FIBER 1.6g; CHOL 0mg; IRON 1.7mg; SODIUM 352mg; CALC 0mg

Curried Cauliflower

Cooking the cauliflower covered releases enough liquid to steam it and creates a sauce with the spices, yogurt, and tomato.

2 teaspoons olive oil
2 cups thinly sliced onion
2 tablespoons finely chopped peeled fresh ginger
2 tablespoons Mild Curry Powder
1 tablespoon minced garlic
10 cups cauliflower florets (2 medium heads)
1 cup chopped seeded peeled tomato
1 cup whole-milk yogurt
½ cup finely chopped cilantro stems
1 teaspoon salt
8 lemon wedges (optional)
Cilantro sprigs (optional)

1. Heat oil in a Dutch oven over medium-high heat. Add onion and ginger; cover and cook 3 minutes, stirring frequently. Reduce heat to medium. Add Mild Curry Powder and garlic; cook 30 seconds, *Continued*

stirring constantly. Add cauliflower and next 4 ingredients, stirring well to combine. Bring to a boil (yogurt will curdle); cover, reduce heat, and simmer 20 minutes or until cauliflower is tender. Serve with lemon wedges and cilantro sprigs, if desired. Yield: 8 servings (serving size: 1 cup).

(Totals include Mild Curry Powder) CALORIES 83 (29% from fat); FAT 2.7g (sat 0.9g, mono 1.2g, poly 0.4g); PROTEIN 4.4g; CARB 12.9g; FIBER 4.3g; CHOL 4mg; IRON 1.1mg; SODIUM 349mg; CALC 79mg

MILD CURRY POWDER:

Without cloves or mustard and with less red pepper than the Homemade Curry Powder (recipe below), this spice mixture suits delicate vegetables.

    3 tablespoons paprika
    2 teaspoons ground cumin
    1 teaspoon ground ginger
    1 teaspoon ground turmeric
    1 teaspoon ground coriander
    ½ teaspoon ground cardamom
    ½ teaspoon ground red pepper

1. Combine all ingredients. Yield: about ⅓ cup (serving size: 1 teaspoon).

NOTE: Store in an airtight container in a dark, cool place up to 2 months.

CALORIES 6 (45% from fat); FAT 0.3g (sat 0g, mono 0g, poly 0.1g); PROTEIN 0.3g; CARB 1.1g; FIBER 0.5g; CHOL 0mg; IRON 0.5mg; SODIUM 1mg; CALC 6mg

Homemade Curry Powder

In a pinch, Bruce uses Patak's Original Garam Masala Curry Paste, which we agree is a better substitute than a commercial curry powder.

    3 tablespoons Hungarian paprika
    1 tablespoon ground coriander
    1 tablespoon ground turmeric
    2 teaspoons ground cumin
    2 teaspoons ground fennel seed
    2 teaspoons ground yellow or
       brown mustard
    2 teaspoons ground red pepper
    1 teaspoon ground cardamom
    ½ teaspoon ground cinnamon
    ½ teaspoon ground cloves

1. Combine all ingredients. Yield: ½ cup (serving size: 1 teaspoon).

NOTE: Store in an airtight container in a cool, dark place up to 2 months.

CALORIES 6 (45% from fat); FAT 0.3g (sat 0g, mono 0.1g, poly 0g); PROTEIN 0.2g; CARB 0.8g; FIBER 0.5g; CHOL 0mg; IRON 0.3mg; SODIUM 1mg; CALC 8mg

Raita
Indian Yogurt and Cucumber Condiment

A cool, creamy side is a must with spicy Indian food. Whole-milk yogurt soothes the palate and stands up to the spicier dishes. Make this within an hour of serving: It will become watery if it stands too long.

    1 English cucumber, coarsely
       shredded (about 2 cups)
    1 teaspoon kosher salt
    2 cups whole-milk yogurt
    ½ cup finely chopped red
       onion
    ¼ cup coarsely chopped fresh
       cilantro
    2 tablespoons fresh lime
       juice
    ¼ teaspoon ground coriander
    ¼ teaspoon ground cumin
    ⅛ teaspoon freshly ground black
       pepper
       Dash of ground nutmeg
       Dash of ground cinnamon
       Dash of ground cardamom

1. Place cucumber in a colander, and sprinkle with salt. Toss well; drain 30 minutes. Rinse with cold water; drain. Place cucumber on several layers of paper towels; cover with additional paper towels. Let stand 5 minutes, pressing down occasionally. Combine cucumber, yogurt, and remaining ingredients. Yield: 8 servings (serving size: ⅓ cup).

CALORIES 49 (37% from fat); FAT 2g (sat 1.3g, mono 0.6g, poly 0.1g); PROTEIN 2.7g; CARB 5.3g; FIBER 0.7g; CHOL 8mg; IRON 0.3mg; SODIUM 88mg; CALC 86mg

Mango and Mint Chutney

This condiment goes especially well with Beef Curry with Toasted Spices (recipe on page 280). The chutney keeps up to 1 week if covered and in the refrigerator. Use the leftovers as a spread for ham sandwiches.

    1 tablespoon olive oil
    ¼ cup finely chopped red onion
    2 tablespoons minced peeled fresh
       ginger
    1 jalapeño pepper, seeded and finely
       chopped
    ½ cup packed brown sugar
    ½ cup cider vinegar
    ¼ cup raisins
    2 teaspoons Homemade Curry
       Powder (recipe at left)
    ¼ teaspoon ground cloves
    ⅛ teaspoon ground cinnamon
    ⅛ teaspoon ground nutmeg
    ⅛ teaspoon ground allspice
    3¼ cups diced peeled mango
    ¼ cup chopped fresh mint

1. Heat oil in a large nonstick skillet over medium heat. Add onion, ginger, and pepper; cover and cook 7 minutes, stirring occasionally. Stir in sugar and next 7 ingredients; cover and cook 5 minutes. Increase heat to medium-high. Add mango, and cook 4 minutes or until liquid almost evaporates. Stir in mint. Yield: 12 servings (serving size: ¼ cup).

CALORIES 88 (13% from fat); FAT 1.3g (sat 0.2g, mono 0.9g, poly 0.1g); PROTEIN 0.4g; CARB 20.3g; FIBER 1.3g; CHOL 0mg; IRON 0.5mg; SODIUM 6mg; CALC 18mg

Tomato, Lime, and Onion Salad

If you're unable to find good large tomatoes, substitute quartered cherry tomatoes.

    4 cups vertically sliced red onion
    ¼ cup fresh lime juice
    ½ teaspoon kosher salt
    1 cup chopped tomato
    ¼ cup chopped fresh cilantro
    2 teaspoons chopped fresh mint
    1 teaspoon grated lime rind

1. Combine first 3 ingredients in a medium bowl; let stand at room temperature 1 hour. Stir in tomato and remaining ingredients. Yield: 8 servings (serving size: about ⅓ cup).

CALORIES 29 (6% from fat); FAT 0.2g (sat 0g, mono 0g, poly 0.1g); PROTEIN 0.9g; CARB 6.8g; FIBER 1.4g; CHOL 0mg; IRON 0.3mg; SODIUM 122mg; CALC 14mg

From Simple... To Sophisticated

A few ingredients can turn everyday family fare into special meals for company.

Always remember the golden rule of entertaining: Never try something new on guests. Instead, start with a plain, tried-and-true recipe so you have the ins and outs of the dish down pat. Add special touches—a sauce here, extra seasonings there—and presto! An everyday dish can dazzle any upscale audience. Here, we present several basic recipes, and dressed-up versions for company.

QUICK & EASY
Spiced Chicken Thighs

SIMPLE: Instant brown rice makes a fast side for this saucy dish. If you have time, though, basmati rice pairs particularly well with the flavors in the garam masala.

¾ teaspoon olive oil
Cooking spray
1 cup vertically sliced onion
2 teaspoons garam masala
½ teaspoon salt
¼ teaspoon curry powder
8 chicken thighs (about 2¼ pounds), skinned
¼ cup dry red wine
2 tablespoons red wine vinegar
1 cup fat-free, less-sodium chicken broth
3 tablespoons chopped fresh parsley

1. Heat oil in a 12-inch nonstick skillet coated with cooking spray over medium-high heat. Add onion; sauté 3 minutes. Remove from pan.

2. Combine garam masala, salt, and curry powder; sprinkle evenly over chicken. Add chicken to pan; cook over medium-high heat 4 minutes on each side or until browned. Add wine and vinegar; cook 30 seconds, scraping pan to loosen browned bits. Add onion and broth; bring to a boil. Cover, reduce heat, and simmer 20 minutes or until chicken is done; stir in parsley. Yield: 4 servings (serving size: 2 thighs and about ⅓ cup sauce).

CALORIES 203 (30% from fat); FAT 6.7g (sat 1.6g, mono 2.4g, poly 1.5g); PROTEIN 29.9g; CARB 3.9g; FIBER 1.1g; CHOL 121mg; IRON 2.1mg; SODIUM 536mg; CALC 35mg

Chicken with Pancetta and Figs

SOPHISTICATED: Pancetta—Italian unsmoked bacon found in the deli of many supermarkets—adds saltiness to this dish. If you can't find it, substitute lean cooked bacon. If fresh figs are available, stir them in just before serving, omitting the dried figs. Serve over basmati rice in rimmed soup bowls.

¾ teaspoon olive oil
Cooking spray
1 cup vertically sliced onion
1 ounce pancetta, finely chopped
2 teaspoons garam masala
1 teaspoon brown sugar
½ teaspoon salt
¼ teaspoon freshly ground black pepper
8 chicken thighs (about 2¼ pounds), skinned
¼ cup tawny port
2 tablespoons red wine vinegar
1 cup fat-free, less-sodium chicken broth
12 dried Calimyrna figs, quartered
3 tablespoons chopped fresh parsley
1 tablespoon chopped fresh thyme
Thyme sprigs (optional)

1. Heat oil in a 12-inch nonstick skillet coated with cooking spray over medium-high heat. Add onion and pancetta; sauté 3 minutes. Remove from pan.

2. Combine garam masala, sugar, salt, and pepper; sprinkle evenly over chicken.

Add chicken to pan; cook over medium-high heat 4 minutes on each side or until browned. Add port and vinegar; cook 30 seconds, scraping pan to loosen browned bits. Add onion mixture and broth; bring to a boil. Cover, reduce heat, and simmer 10 minutes. Add figs; cover and simmer 8 minutes or until chicken is done. Stir in parsley and chopped thyme. Garnish with thyme sprigs, if desired. Yield: 4 servings (serving size: 2 thighs and about ⅔ cup sauce).

CALORIES 392 (26% from fat); FAT 11.5g (sat 3.2g, mono 4.4g, poly 2.3g); PROTEIN 32.3g; CARB 42.3g; FIBER 8g; CHOL 125mg; IRON 3.5mg; SODIUM 594mg; CALC 125mg

MAKE AHEAD • FREEZABLE
Cranberry-Orange Muffins

SIMPLE: Orange rind and dried cranberries flavor a cake-style muffin that's easy to make and freezes well. Microwave at HIGH 20 to 30 seconds to thaw. When fresh cranberries are available, use them to add a pleasant tartness.

1½ cups all-purpose flour
3 tablespoons yellow cornmeal
1½ teaspoons baking powder
½ teaspoon baking soda
¼ teaspoon salt
¾ cup sugar
¼ cup butter, softened
2 teaspoons grated orange rind
1 large egg
1 large egg white
⅓ cup fat-free buttermilk
¼ cup part-skim ricotta cheese
⅔ cup dried cranberries, coarsely chopped
Cooking spray

1. Preheat oven to 375°.
2. Lightly spoon flour into dry measuring cups; level with a knife. Combine flour and next 4 ingredients, stirring well with a whisk.
3. Place sugar and butter in a large bowl; beat with a mixer at medium speed until well blended (about 2 minutes). Add rind, and beat to combine. Add egg and egg white, 1 at a time, beating well after each addition.

Continued

4. Combine buttermilk and ricotta, stirring well with a whisk. Add flour mixture and buttermilk mixture alternately to sugar mixture, beginning and ending with flour mixture. Fold in cranberries. Spoon batter into 12 muffin cups coated with cooking spray. Bake at 375° for 20 minutes or until a wooden pick inserted in center comes out clean. Cool in pan 10 minutes on a wire rack; remove from pan. Cool completely on wire rack. Yield: 12 servings (serving size: 1 muffin).

CALORIES 184 (24% from fat); FAT 4.9g (sat 2.8g, mono 1.4g, poly 0.3g); PROTEIN 3.5g; CARB 31.6g; FIBER 1g; CHOL 30mg; IRON 1mg; SODIUM 225mg; CALC 63mg

MAKE AHEAD
Cranberry-Orange Gâteau with Cream-Cheese Filling

SOPHISTICATED: A variation of the muffin batter bakes in a cake pan; fill the cake with orange-flavored cream cheese, and spread with orange glaze for a sweet finale.

CAKE:
1½ cups all-purpose flour
3 tablespoons yellow cornmeal
1 teaspoon baking powder
½ teaspoon baking soda
¼ teaspoon salt
¾ cup granulated sugar
¼ cup butter, softened
2 teaspoons grated orange rind
1 large egg
1 large egg white
½ cup fat-free buttermilk
¼ cup part-skim ricotta cheese
⅔ cup dried cranberries
Cooking spray

FILLING:
1 cup sifted powdered sugar
½ cup (4 ounces) ⅓-less-fat cream cheese, softened
2 teaspoons fresh orange juice

GLAZE:
1 cup sifted powdered sugar
1½ tablespoons fresh orange juice

1. Preheat oven to 350°.
2. To prepare cake, lightly spoon flour into dry measuring cups; level with a knife. Combine flour and next 4 ingredients in a bowl, stirring well with a whisk.
3. Place granulated sugar and butter in a large bowl; beat with a mixer at medium speed until well blended (about 2 minutes). Add rind; beat to combine. Add egg and egg white, 1 at a time, beating well after each addition.
4. Combine buttermilk and ricotta, stirring well with a whisk. Add flour mixture and buttermilk mixture alternately to sugar mixture, beginning and ending with flour mixture. Fold in cranberries. Spoon batter into a 9-inch round cake pan coated with cooking spray. Bake at 350° for 35 minutes or until a wooden pick inserted in center comes out clean. Cool in pan 10 minutes on a wire rack; remove from pan. Cool completely on wire rack.
5. To prepare filling, place 1 cup powdered sugar and cream cheese in a bowl; beat with a mixer at medium speed until well blended. Add 2 teaspoons orange juice; beat to combine. Cover; chill 30 minutes.
6. To prepare glaze, combine 1 cup powdered sugar and 1½ tablespoons orange juice, stirring well with a whisk.
7. Split cooled cake in half horizontally using a serrated knife; place bottom layer, cut side up, on a plate. Spread filling over cake layer. Top with remaining cake layer, cut side down. Spread glaze over cake. Yield: 10 servings (serving size: 1 wedge).

CALORIES 329 (23% from fat); FAT 8.3g (sat 5g, mono 1.7g, poly 0.4g); PROTEIN 5.5g; CARB 58.8g; FIBER 1.2g; CHOL 44mg; IRON 1.2mg; SODIUM 298mg; CALC 76mg

QUICK & EASY
Simple Green Salad with Vinaigrette

SIMPLE: Toss any lettuce or field greens you have on hand with this easy dressing.

2 tablespoons minced red onion
1½ tablespoons red wine vinegar
2 teaspoons olive oil
¼ teaspoon salt
¼ teaspoon freshly ground black pepper
¼ teaspoon Dijon mustard
6 cups torn curly leaf lettuce
¼ cup thinly vertically sliced red onion
1 pint cherry tomatoes, halved

1. Combine minced onion and vinegar in a small bowl; let stand 5 minutes. Add oil, salt, pepper, and mustard; stir well with a whisk.
2. Place lettuce, sliced onion, and tomatoes in a large bowl; toss gently to combine. Drizzle vinaigrette over salad; toss gently to coat. Yield: 4 servings (serving size: 2 cups).

CALORIES 49 (44% from fat); FAT 2.4g (sat 0.3g, mono 1.7g, poly 0.3g); PROTEIN 1.5g; CARB 7.2g; FIBER 2.7g; CHOL 0mg; IRON 0.3mg; SODIUM 189mg; CALC 46mg

QUICK & EASY
Mesclun and Romaine Salad with Warm Parmesan Toasts

SOPHISTICATED: Dress up a typical salad by using more refined greens, adding fresh herbs, and tossing it with high-quality olive oil and vinegar. Top the salad with warm slices of cheese-topped baguette. You can substitute chopped red onions for the shallots.

TOASTS:
8 (½-ounce) slices French bread baguette
¼ cup (1 ounce) grated fresh Parmesan cheese

VINAIGRETTE:
2 tablespoons minced shallots
1 tablespoon sherry vinegar
2 teaspoons extravirgin olive oil
¼ teaspoon salt
¼ teaspoon Dijon mustard
⅛ teaspoon freshly ground black pepper

SALAD:
3 cups mesclun (gourmet salad greens)
3 cups torn romaine lettuce
¼ cup thinly vertically sliced red onion
3 tablespoons chopped fresh parsley
3 tablespoons chopped fresh basil
1 pint cherry tomatoes, halved

1. Preheat broiler.

2. To prepare toasts, arrange bread slices on a baking sheet. Broil 1 minute or until lightly browned. Turn bread over; sprinkle each slice with 1½ teaspoons cheese. Broil 1 minute or until cheese begins to melt.

3. To prepare vinaigrette, combine shallots and vinegar in a small bowl; let stand 5 minutes. Add oil, salt, mustard, and pepper; stir well with a whisk.

4. To prepare salad, place salad greens and remaining 5 ingredients in a large bowl; toss gently to combine. Drizzle vinaigrette over salad, and toss gently to coat. Serve with toasts. Yield: 4 servings (serving size: 2 cups salad and 2 toasts).

CALORIES 165 (30% from fat); FAT 5.5g (sat 1.7g, mono 2.6g, poly 0.7g); PROTEIN 7.4g; CARB 23g; FIBER 3.6g; CHOL 5mg; IRON 2.5mg; SODIUM 465mg; CALC 159mg

---

QUICK & EASY
Lemony Green Beans

SIMPLE: A splash of olive oil and fresh lemon juice is an easy dressing for steamed vegetables. It works for everything from green beans to asparagus to broccoli.

  1 pound green beans, trimmed and cut into 2-inch pieces
1½ teaspoons fresh lemon juice
  1 teaspoon olive oil
 ¼ teaspoon salt
 ⅛ teaspoon freshly ground black pepper

1. Steam green beans, covered, 5 minutes or until crisp-tender. Drain and return to pan. Add juice, oil, salt, and pepper; toss to coat. Serve immediately. Yield: 4 servings (serving size: 1 cup).

CALORIES 46 (25% from fat); FAT 1.3g (sat 0.2g, mono 0.8g, poly 0.1g); PROTEIN 2.1g; CARB 8.4g; FIBER 1.3g; CHOL 0mg; IRON 1.2mg; SODIUM 154mg; CALC 43mg

---

QUICK & EASY
Green Beans with Toasted Almond Gremolata

SOPHISTICATED: For a restaurant-caliber presentation, leave the green beans whole, and toss with toasted almonds, garlic, lemon rind, and fresh parsley. The garnish (without the nuts) is called *gremolata* and typically accompanies the veal dish osso buco. But it also can add great flavor to steamed vegetables.

  1 pound green beans, trimmed
  2 tablespoons chopped fresh flat-leaf parsley
  1 tablespoon sliced almonds, toasted
 ¼ teaspoon grated lemon rind
1½ teaspoons fresh lemon juice
  1 teaspoon olive oil
 ¼ teaspoon salt
 ⅛ teaspoon freshly ground black pepper
  1 garlic clove, minced

1. Steam beans, covered, 7 minutes or until crisp-tender. Drain and return to pan. Add parsley and remaining ingredients; toss gently to combine. Serve immediately. Yield: 4 servings (serving size: 1 cup).

CALORIES 59 (35% from fat); FAT 2.3g (sat 0.2g, mono 1.5g, poly 0.4g); PROTEIN 2.6g; CARB 9.1g; FIBER 1.6g; CHOL 0mg; IRON 1.4mg; SODIUM 155mg; CALC 52mg

---

Pasta Dinner Menu
serves 4

Serve this meatless meal as a weeknight dinner or a casual weekend entertaining menu.

Linguine with Garlicky Breadcrumbs

Arugula and hearts of palm salad*

Cantaloupe and honeydew melon

*Divide 6 cups trimmed arugula, 1 cup julienne-cut red bell pepper, 1 cup coarsely chopped jarred hearts of palm, and 1 cup canned garbanzo beans evenly among 4 salad plates. Combine 2 tablespoons sherry vinegar, 2 teaspoons extravirgin olive oil, ¼ teaspoon sea salt, ⅛ teaspoon black pepper, and 1 crushed garlic clove, stirring with a whisk. Drizzle evenly over salads.

Linguine with Garlicky Breadcrumbs

SIMPLE: This dish of pantry staples is a good choice for a hectic weeknight supper. Toast the breadcrumbs in advance to speed preparation later.

  1 slice day-old hearty white bread (such as Pepperidge Farm), torn
  2 tablespoons olive oil, divided
  6 garlic cloves, minced
  8 ounces uncooked linguine
 ¼ cup chopped fresh parsley
  2 teaspoons fresh lemon juice
 ½ teaspoon salt
 ¼ teaspoon freshly ground black pepper

1. Preheat oven to 250°.

2. Place bread in a food processor; pulse 10 times or until coarse crumbs measure ⅔ cup. Place breadcrumbs on a baking sheet. Bake at 250° for 30 minutes or until dry.

3. Heat 1½ tablespoons oil in a large nonstick skillet over medium heat. Add garlic; cook 30 seconds, stirring constantly. Remove from heat, and let stand 5 minutes. Return pan to heat. Stir in breadcrumbs, and cook 6 minutes or until lightly browned, stirring frequently.

4. Cook pasta according to package directions, omitting salt and fat; drain. Place pasta in a large bowl. Add 1½ teaspoons oil, breadcrumbs, parsley, lemon juice, salt, and pepper; toss gently to combine. Serve immediately. Yield: 4 servings (serving size: 1½ cups).

CALORIES 297 (24% from fat); FAT 7.9g (sat 1.2g, mono 5g, poly 0.6g); PROTEIN 8.9g; CARB 49g; FIBER 2.6g; CHOL 0mg; IRON 2.4mg; SODIUM 346mg; CALC 30mg

Gorgonzola-Walnut Fettuccine with Toasted Breadcrumbs

SOPHISTICATED: Toasted walnuts and crumbled Gorgonzola cheese enhance weeknight Linguine with Garlicky Breadcrumbs (recipe on page 285). It's the same easy recipe but with different pasta and a little less garlic and oil, so the cheese and walnuts stand out.

1 slice day-old hearty white bread (such as Pepperidge Farm), torn
1 tablespoon olive oil
4 garlic cloves, minced
8 ounces uncooked fettuccine
¼ cup chopped fresh parsley
¼ cup (1 ounce) crumbled Gorgonzola cheese
3 tablespoons chopped walnuts, toasted
2 teaspoons fresh lemon juice
½ teaspoon salt
¼ teaspoon freshly ground black pepper

1. Preheat oven to 250°.
2. Place bread in a food processor; pulse 10 times or until coarse crumbs measure ⅔ cup. Place breadcrumbs on a baking sheet. Bake at 250° for 30 minutes or until dry.
3. Heat oil in a large nonstick skillet over medium heat. Add garlic, and cook 30 seconds, stirring constantly. Remove from heat, and let stand 5 minutes. Return pan to heat. Stir in breadcrumbs; cook 6 minutes or until lightly browned, stirring frequently.
4. Cook fettuccine according to package directions, omitting salt and fat; drain. Place fettuccine in a large bowl. Add breadcrumb mixture, parsley, and remaining ingredients; toss gently to combine. Serve immediately. Yield: 4 servings (serving size: 1½ cups).

CALORIES 327 (29% from fat); FAT 10.4g (sat 2.5g, mono 3g, poly 3g); PROTEIN 11.1g; CARB 49.5g; FIBER 2.9g; CHOL 6mg; IRON 2.5mg; SODIUM 444mg; CALC 70mg

Thyme-Coated Pork Tenderloin

SIMPLE: Roll pork tenderloin in a mixture of breadcrumbs, thyme, and onion flakes.

1 teaspoon dried thyme
1 teaspoon instant onion flakes
1 slice day-old hearty white bread (such as Pepperidge Farm), torn
2 large egg whites, lightly beaten
1 (1-pound) pork tenderloin, trimmed
¼ teaspoon salt
¼ teaspoon freshly ground black pepper
Cooking spray

1. Preheat oven to 400°.
2. Place thyme, onion, and bread in a food processor; pulse until fine breadcrumbs measure ⅓ cup. Place breadcrumb mixture in a shallow dish. Place egg whites in a shallow dish. Sprinkle pork with salt and pepper. Dip pork in egg whites; dredge in breadcrumb mixture. Place pork on a broiler pan coated with cooking spray. Bake at 400° for 30 minutes or until a thermometer registers 155°. Let stand 5 minutes. Cut into ¼-inch-thick slices. Yield: 4 servings (serving size: 3 ounces).

CALORIES 165 (22% from fat); FAT 4.1g (sat 1.3g, mono 1.5g, poly 0.3g); PROTEIN 25.1g; CARB 5.5g; FIBER 0.8g; CHOL 63mg; IRON 1.7mg; SODIUM 267mg; CALC 17mg

Pork Tenderloin with Hazelnut Crust and Red Wine-Shallot Sauce

SOPHISTICATED: Embellish pork tenderloin with hazelnuts and a red wine sauce.

PORK:
½ cup dry breadcrumbs
3 tablespoons chopped hazelnuts
1 tablespoon chopped fresh thyme
1 teaspoon instant onion flakes
2 large egg whites, lightly beaten
1 (1-pound) pork tenderloin, trimmed
¼ teaspoon salt
¼ teaspoon freshly ground black pepper
Cooking spray

SAUCE:
1 teaspoon olive oil
½ cup thinly sliced shallots
1 cup dry red wine
1 tablespoon red wine vinegar
1½ teaspoons honey
¼ teaspoon salt
¼ teaspoon freshly ground black pepper
¼ cup fat-free milk
1 tablespoon chopped fresh thyme
1½ teaspoons all-purpose flour
Thyme sprigs (optional)

1. Preheat oven to 400°.
2. To prepare pork, place first 4 ingredients in a food processor; pulse until nuts are finely chopped. Place breadcrumb mixture in a shallow dish. Place egg whites in a shallow dish. Sprinkle pork with ¼ teaspoon salt and ¼ teaspoon pepper. Heat a large nonstick skillet coated with cooking spray over medium-high heat. Add pork; cook 6 minutes, browning on all sides. Cool slightly. Dip pork in egg whites; dredge in breadcrumb mixture. Place pork on a broiler pan coated with cooking spray. Bake at 400° for 30 minutes or until a thermometer registers 155°. Let stand 5 minutes. Cut into ¼-inch-thick slices.
3. To prepare sauce, heat oil in a medium saucepan over medium-high heat. Add shallots; sauté 3 minutes or until lightly browned. Stir in wine and next 4 ingredients. Bring to a boil; cook until reduced to ¾ cup (about 3½ minutes). Combine milk, 1 tablespoon thyme, and flour in a small bowl, stirring with a whisk. Add milk mixture to pan; bring to a boil, stirring constantly. Cook 1 minute, stirring constantly. Serve sauce with pork. Garnish with thyme sprigs, if desired. Yield: 4 servings (serving size: 3 ounces pork and ¼ cup sauce).

CALORIES 275 (30% from fat); FAT 9.1g (sat 1.9g, mono 5.2g, poly 1g); PROTEIN 28.1g; CARB 19.5g; FIBER 1.1g; CHOL 63mg; IRON 2.9mg; SODIUM 498mg; CALC 90mg

Potato-Crusted Red Snapper

SIMPLE: Use snapper, cod, orange roughy, or any other white fish in this recipe. Thin, flat fillets work best. The potato crust is first browned over medium-high heat in a skillet, then the fish finishes cooking in a moderate oven to ensure that it stays moist.

 1 cup shredded peeled potato
 1 tablespoon prepared horseradish
 ½ teaspoon salt, divided
 ¼ teaspoon freshly ground black pepper
 4 (6-ounce) red snapper or other firm, white fish fillets
 4 teaspoons olive oil, divided
 Lemon wedges

1. Preheat oven to 375°.
2. Combine potato, horseradish, ¼ teaspoon salt, and pepper. Sprinkle both sides of fillets with ¼ teaspoon salt. Spread ¼ cup potato mixture over 1 side of each fillet, pressing potato mixture onto fish. Heat 2 teaspoons oil in a large ovenproof nonstick skillet over medium-high heat. Add 2 fillets, potato side down, to pan. Cook 3 minutes or until potato mixture is browned. Carefully turn fish over; place on a plate. Repeat procedure with 2 teaspoons oil and remaining fillets. Return fish to pan, potato side up. Bake at 375° for 5 minutes or until fish flakes easily when tested with a fork. Serve with lemon wedges. Yield: 4 servings (serving size: 1 fillet).

CALORIES 234 (26% from fat); FAT 6.8g (sat 1.1g, mono 1.5g, poly 3.4g); PROTEIN 34.3g; CARB 6.9g; FIBER 0.7g; CHOL 60mg; IRON 0.6mg; SODIUM 380mg; CALC 56mg

Potato-and-Herb Crusted Snapper with Yellow Pepper Salsa

SOPHISTICATED: Parmesan cheese and fresh herbs grace the crisp potato crust. An accompanying colorful salsa flavored with capers and herbs gives the dish even more pizzazz for guests.

SALSA:
 1 large yellow bell pepper
 ½ cup chopped onion
 ½ cup chopped seeded plum tomato
 1 tablespoon thinly sliced fresh basil
 1 tablespoon chopped fresh parsley
 1 tablespoon fresh lemon juice
 1½ teaspoons capers
 1 teaspoon extravirgin olive oil
 ⅛ teaspoon salt

FISH:
 1 cup shredded peeled potato
 3 tablespoons grated fresh Parmesan cheese
 2 teaspoons chopped fresh parsley
 2 teaspoons chopped fresh chives
 ¼ teaspoon salt
 ¼ teaspoon freshly ground black pepper
 4 (6-ounce) red snapper or other firm, white fish fillets
 ¼ teaspoon salt
 4 teaspoons olive oil, divided

1. Preheat broiler.
2. To prepare salsa, cut bell pepper in half lengthwise; discard seeds and membranes. Place pepper halves, skin sides up, on a foil-lined baking sheet; flatten with hand. Broil 8 minutes or until blackened. Place in a zip-top plastic bag; seal. Let stand 10 minutes. Peel and coarsely chop. Combine bell pepper, onion, and next 7 ingredients.
3. Preheat oven to 375°.
4. To prepare fish, combine potato and next 5 ingredients. Sprinkle both sides of fillets with ¼ teaspoon salt. Spread ¼ cup potato mixture over 1 side of each fillet; press mixture onto fish. Heat 2 teaspoons oil in a large ovenproof nonstick skillet over medium-high heat. Add 2 fillets, potato side down, to pan. Cook 3 minutes or until browned. Carefully turn fish over; place on a plate. Repeat procedure with 2 teaspoons oil and remaining fillets. Return fish to pan, potato side up. Bake at 375° for 5 minutes or until fish flakes easily when tested with a fork. Serve with salsa. Yield: 4 servings (serving size: 1 fillet and ¼ cup salsa).

CALORIES 284 (29% from fat); FAT 9.2g (sat 2g, mono 2.7g, poly 3.6g); PROTEIN 36.8g; CARB 12.5g; FIBER 2.2g; CHOL 63mg; IRON 1.1mg; SODIUM 548mg; CALC 119mg

reader recipes

Dinner, for Starters

Two restaurant appetizers are transformed into one sensational entrée.

Elizabeth Anderson, from Notre Dame, Indiana, took home more than just leftovers from her favorite Chicago restaurant. She took inspiration.

Two dishes from the tapas bar she once frequented with her husband and friends wowed her. The goat cheese in tomato sauce and the chicken breasts stuffed with goat cheese were so good she started tinkering with them at home. Her result combined the two appetizers into one entrée—Chicken Stuffed with Goat Cheese and Garlic.

Like the restaurant that inspired it, Elizabeth's recipe is unabashedly sociable. She serves the versatile dish to her friends over pasta or sometimes oven-roasted potatoes, with a simple green salad and red wine.

Continued

Go back and forth between these plain and fancy recipes to have plenty of options for stress-free entertaining.

Chicken Stuffed with Goat Cheese and Garlic

Elizabeth Anderson also took inspiration for her recipe from a second source: An Italian acquaintance suggested she simmer garlic cloves in store-bought marinara to add flavor.

4 ounces goat cheese, softened
3 tablespoons thinly sliced fresh basil, divided
1 tablespoon minced garlic
4 (6-ounce) skinless, boneless chicken breast halves
1 (25.5-ounce) jar fat-free Italian herb pasta sauce
3 whole garlic cloves, crushed
3 cups hot cooked fettuccine (about 6 ounces uncooked pasta)

1. Combine goat cheese, 2 tablespoons basil, and minced garlic; set aside.
2. Place each chicken breast half between 2 sheets of heavy-duty plastic wrap, and pound to ¼-inch thickness using a meat mallet or rolling pin. Divide cheese mixture evenly among breast halves. Roll up jelly-roll fashion. Tuck in sides, and secure each roll with wooden picks.
3. Heat pasta sauce and garlic cloves in a large skillet over medium heat; add chicken. Cover and cook 25 minutes or until chicken is done. Serve over pasta. Garnish with 1 tablespoon basil. Yield: 4 servings (serving size: 1 chicken roll, ¾ cup pasta, and ½ cup sauce).

CALORIES 503 (15% from fat); FAT 8.3g (sat 4.7g, mono 1.9g, poly 0.7g); PROTEIN 57.2g; CARB 48.1g; FIBER 5.5g; CHOL 112mg; IRON 3.8mg; SODIUM 785mg; CALC 137mg

QUICK & EASY
Swiss Fruit and Yogurt Muesli

"I have often enjoyed fresh muesli, made with fruit and yogurt, during visits with my husband's family in Germany. It's a quick, easy breakfast loaded with vitamins and calcium. Vary the fruit to create your own favorite blend, or top with chopped walnuts or almonds for extra crunch."

—Sheriann Houtrouw, Glenn, California

1 cup quick-cooking oats
1 cup plain low-fat yogurt
⅓ cup orange juice
2 tablespoons brown sugar
1 cup shredded Red Delicious apple
½ cup sliced banana
¼ cup blueberries

1. Combine first 4 ingredients in a medium bowl. Add apple, banana, and blueberries, stirring gently to combine. Yield: 2 servings (serving size: 1¼ cups).

CALORIES 373 (13% from fat); FAT 5.3g (sat 1.8g, mono 1.5g, poly 0.9g); PROTEIN 13.4g; CARB 72.8g; FIBER 6.7g; CHOL 7mg; IRON 2.6mg; SODIUM 94mg; CALC 269mg

MAKE AHEAD
Pumpkin-Carrot Cake

"I made this as a birthday cake using a low-fat lemon cream-cheese frosting. It was quite a hit."

—Kirsten Quealey, St. Albert, Alberta

½ cup all-purpose flour
½ cup whole wheat flour
1 teaspoon baking powder
½ teaspoon ground cinnamon
¼ teaspoon baking soda
¼ teaspoon salt
1 large egg
1 large egg white
½ cup packed brown sugar
½ cup canned pumpkin
2 tablespoons vegetable oil
2 tablespoons butter, melted
1 tablespoon grated orange rind
¾ cup raisins
½ cup grated carrot
⅓ cup dried cranberries
Cooking spray
2 tablespoons coarsely chopped walnuts

1. Preheat oven to 350°.
2. Lightly spoon flours into dry measuring cups; level with a knife. Combine flours and next 4 ingredients. Place egg and egg white in a large bowl; beat with a mixer at medium speed 30 seconds. Add brown sugar and next 4 ingredients; beat until well blended. Add flour mixture to sugar mixture, stirring just until moist. Stir in raisins, grated carrot, and cranberries. Spoon batter into an 8-inch square baking pan coated with cooking spray. Sprinkle with walnuts. Bake at 350° for 25 minutes or until a wooden pick inserted in center comes out clean. Cool in pan 10 minutes on a wire rack; remove from pan. Cool completely on wire rack. Yield: 9 servings (serving size: 1 square).

CALORIES 219 (26% from fat); FAT 6.4g (sat 2.3g, mono 2.1g, poly 1.5g); PROTEIN 3.7g; CARB 38.2g; FIBER 2.9g; CHOL 31mg; IRON 1.5mg; SODIUM 233mg; CALC 64mg

MAKE AHEAD
Buttermilk Pralines

"This recipe requires your steadfast attention, so try not to get distracted. The periodic stirring prevents it from boiling over."

—Nora Henshaw, Okemah, Oklahoma

1½ cups sugar
½ cup whole buttermilk
1½ tablespoons light-colored corn syrup
½ teaspoon baking soda
Dash of salt
⅔ cup chopped pecans, toasted
1½ teaspoons butter
1 tablespoon vanilla extract

1. Combine first 5 ingredients in a large saucepan. Cook over low heat until sugar dissolves, stirring constantly. Continue cooking over low heat until a candy thermometer registers 234° (about 10 minutes); stir occasionally. Remove from heat; let stand 5 minutes.
2. Stir in nuts, butter, and vanilla; beat with a wooden spoon until mixture begins to lose its shine (about 6 minutes). Drop by teaspoonfuls onto wax paper. Let stand 20 minutes or until set. Yield: 30 servings (serving size: 1 praline).
NOTE: Store pralines in an airtight container up to 2 weeks.

CALORIES 65 (30% from fat); FAT 2.2g (sat 0.4g, mono 1.2g, poly 0.6g); PROTEIN 0.4g; CARB 11.4g; FIBER 0.3g; CHOL 1mg; IRON 0.1mg; SODIUM 36mg; CALC 7mg

Coconut Banana Bread with Lime Glaze, page 304

Eggplant and Onion Noodle Salad with
Warm Soy-Rice Vinaigrette, page 294

Beef Curry with Toasted Spices, page 280,
over Saffron Basmati Rice, page 281

All About Vinegars

Vinegars brighten any dish, from dinner to dessert.

Without adding fat, vinegar can add depth and brightness to dishes. Use it to deglaze pan drippings and add a little acidity to balance a sauce; reduce it into a syrup for drizzling over fruit or vegetables; add it to cooking liquid, and then braise to subdue the bite; or simply use it in a vinaigrette. Here is a round-up of common vinegars for the modern cook's pantry.

STAFF FAVORITE · QUICK & EASY

Sugar-Roasted Plums with Balsamic and Rosemary Syrup

Small, sweet, dark purple plums are ideal for this dessert. Balsamic vinegar, water, and seasonings are reduced to an intense syrupy glaze that contrasts with the sugar-coated plums.

    ½ cup water
    ½ cup balsamic vinegar
    6 tablespoons sugar, divided
   10 black peppercorns
    1 vanilla bean, split
   12 small unpeeled plums (about
        3½ pounds)
    8 fresh rosemary sprigs, divided

1. Preheat oven to 400°.
2. Combine water, vinegar, ¼ cup sugar, and peppercorns, stirring with a whisk until sugar dissolves. Scrape seeds from vanilla bean; add seeds and bean to vinegar mixture. Place plums in a 13 x 9-inch baking dish. Pour vinegar mixture over plums. Nestle 2 rosemary sprigs around plums into vinegar mixture. Sprinkle evenly with 2 tablespoons sugar.
3. Bake at 400° for 20 minutes or until plums are tender (skin will begin to split on some plums).
4. Remove plums with a slotted spoon to a serving platter. Strain vinegar mixture into a small nonaluminum saucepan; discard solids. Bring vinegar mixture to a boil. Reduce heat to medium-high; cook

until reduced to ¾ cup (about 5 minutes). Pour syrup evenly over plums; garnish with 6 rosemary sprigs. Yield: 6 servings (serving size: 2 plums and about 2 tablespoons syrup).

CALORIES 141 (6% from fat); FAT 1g (sat 0g, mono 0g, poly 0.5g); PROTEIN 1.1g; CARB 34.6g; FIBER 2g; CHOL 0mg; IRON 0.2mg; SODIUM 5mg; CALC 6mg

Roasted Sweet-and-Sour Beets, Carrots, and Parsnips

Steam the vegetables to speed up roasting. Serve with ham or roast chicken.

    1 pound small beets, trimmed,
        peeled, and cut into wedges
    1 pound parsnips, cut into
        2-inch-thick slices
    1 pound carrots, cut into
        2-inch-thick slices
       Cooking spray
    ¼ cup maple syrup
    3 tablespoons cider vinegar
    1 lemon
    2 tablespoons olive oil
    2 teaspoons coriander seeds,
        crushed
    2 teaspoons chopped fresh or
    ½ teaspoon dried tarragon
   12 fresh thyme sprigs
    ½ teaspoon salt
    ½ teaspoon freshly ground black
        pepper
       Thyme sprigs (optional)

1. Preheat oven to 400°.
2. Steam first 3 ingredients, covered, 5 minutes. Place in a shallow roasting pan coated with cooking spray.
3. Combine syrup and vinegar; set aside.
4. Squeeze juice from lemon; add lemon halves to beet mixture. Combine juice, oil, coriander, tarragon, and 12 thyme sprigs. Pour over beet mixture; toss well. Sprinkle with salt and pepper. Bake at 400° for 30 minutes. Pour syrup mixture over beet mixture; stir well to coat. Bake an additional 30 minutes or until beets are tender. Discard lemon halves. Garnish with additional thyme sprigs, if desired. Yield: 7 servings (serving size: about 1 cup).

CALORIES 157 (25% from fat); FAT 4.4g (sat 0.6g, mono 3g, poly 0.5g); PROTEIN 2.2g; CARB 29.9g; FIBER 6.3g; CHOL 0mg; IRON 1.4mg; SODIUM 232mg; CALC 62mg

Shrimp Salad with Buttermilk and Tarragon Vinaigrette

This shellfish dish calls for a more subdued vinegar like tarragon. White wine vinegar will also work.

SHRIMP:
    ¼ cup fat-free buttermilk
    2 tablespoons minced Anaheim or
        other mild green chile
    1 tablespoon chopped fresh
        tarragon
    1 teaspoon grated lime rind
    1 tablespoon fresh lime
        juice
    ½ teaspoon salt
    ¼ teaspoon freshly ground black
        pepper
    1 garlic clove, minced
   1½ pounds large shrimp, peeled and
        deveined
       Cooking spray

SALAD:
   12 romaine lettuce leaves
    1 head Bibb lettuce, separated into
        leaves
    2 tomatoes, cut into wedges

Continued

⅓ cup fat-free buttermilk
2 tablespoons tarragon
   vinegar
4 teaspoons finely chopped
   shallots
1 teaspoon minced fresh
   tarragon
1 teaspoon Dijon mustard
½ teaspoon grated lime rind
⅛ teaspoon sugar

1. To prepare shrimp, combine first 8 ingredients in a zip-top plastic bag. Add shrimp, and seal bag. Refrigerate 2 hours, turning bag occasionally. Remove shrimp from bag; discard marinade. Pat shrimp dry.

2. Heat a grill pan coated with cooking spray over medium-high heat. Add half of shrimp to pan, and cook 2 minutes on each side or until done. Repeat procedure with remaining shrimp.

3. To prepare salad, arrange lettuce leaves on a serving platter. Top with tomatoes and shrimp.

4. To prepare vinaigrette, combine ⅓ cup buttermilk and remaining 6 ingredients, stirring with a whisk. Drizzle vinaigrette over salad. Yield: 4 servings (serving size: 5 ounces shrimp and about 2 cups salad).

CALORIES 247 (15% from fat); FAT 4g (sat 0.8g, mono 0.6g, poly 1.5g); PROTEIN 38.3g; CARB 14.8g; FIBER 3.2g; CHOL 260mg; IRON 5.5mg; SODIUM 462mg; CALC 160mg

STAFF FAVORITE • MAKE AHEAD
Vinegar-Braised Beef with Thyme, Carrots, and Onions

You can do much of the work for this dish a day ahead. Prepare the recipe up to straining the cooking liquid in Step 4. Leave the strained liquid and beef in the pan, refrigerate up to 1 day, skim the solidified fat from the surface, and continue with Step 5. Cabernet Sauvignon vinegar is a good choice to balance the fruity wine. Although ½ cup vinegar sounds like a lot, it's not overpowering; vinegar loses much of its pungency when heated.

1 tablespoon minced fresh thyme
1 large garlic clove, minced
1 (3½-pound) beef brisket, trimmed
2 teaspoons olive oil, divided
¾ teaspoon salt, divided
¼ teaspoon freshly ground black
   pepper
1½ cups chopped onion
1 cup chopped carrot
1 cup chopped celery
3 cups low-salt beef broth
½ cup Merlot or other fruity red
   wine
½ cup red wine vinegar
1 bay leaf
1 pound baby carrots with tops
1 pound cipollini or pearl onions,
   peeled
2 tablespoons chopped fresh parsley
1 teaspoon chopped fresh thyme

1. Preheat oven to 350°.

2. Combine 1 tablespoon thyme and garlic. Make 12 small slits in beef, and stuff each with about ¼ teaspoon garlic mixture. Rub beef with 1 teaspoon oil. Sprinkle beef with ¼ teaspoon salt and ¼ teaspoon pepper.

3. Heat a large ovenproof nonstick skillet over medium-high heat. Add beef; cook 2 minutes on all sides or until browned. Remove from pan. Add chopped onion, chopped carrot, and celery to pan; sauté 6 minutes. Add ½ teaspoon salt, broth, wine, vinegar, and bay leaf; bring to a boil. Return beef to pan. Cover and place pan in oven. Bake at 350° for 1 hour. Reduce heat to 325°; turn beef. Cover and bake an additional 1½ hours or until tender, turning beef twice. Remove beef from pan.

4. Strain cooking liquid through a sieve into a bowl, pressing vegetables to extract liquid. Discard solids. Place a zip-top plastic bag inside a 2-cup glass measure. Pour strained liquid into bag; let stand 10 minutes (fat will rise to top). Seal bag; carefully snip off 1 bottom corner of bag. Drain liquid into a bowl, stopping before fat layer reaches opening; discard fat.

5. Preheat oven to 350°.

6. Trim all but 1 inch from green tops of baby carrots. Heat 1 teaspoon oil in a large nonstick skillet over medium-high heat. Add cipollini onions; sauté 3 minutes or until browned. Add beef, cooking liquid, and baby carrots; bring to a boil. Cover and bake at 350° for 1 hour, turning once. Sprinkle with parsley and 1 teaspoon thyme. Serve beef with vegetables and sauce. Yield: 8 servings (serving size: about 3 ounces beef, about 5 onions, about 4 carrots, and about 1½ tablespoons sauce).

CALORIES 327 (26% from fat); FAT 9.3g (sat 2.8g, mono 4.4g, poly 0.6g); PROTEIN 41.5g; CARB 16.4g; FIBER 3.9g; CHOL 113mg; IRON 4.2mg; SODIUM 375mg; CALC 57mg

Eggplant and Onion Noodle Salad with Warm Soy-Rice Vinaigrette
(pictured on page 292)

Rice vinegar is mild and slightly sweet, so it's a good choice to pair with salty soy sauce in this Asian-style vinaigrette. Eggplant easily absorbs large quantities of oil. Salt it before cooking, and use a ridged grill pan to reduce the oil. Serve this salad warm or at room temperature with fish or chicken.

1 pound Japanese eggplant, cut in
   half lengthwise
1 teaspoon kosher salt
1 cup green beans, trimmed
2 tablespoons rice vinegar
2 tablespoons low-sodium soy sauce
1 teaspoon honey
1 teaspoon dark sesame oil
⅛ teaspoon black pepper
1 garlic clove, minced
1 mild red or green chile pepper
   (such as Fresno), seeded and
   minced
Cooking spray
1 cup (½-inch-thick) slices Walla
   Walla or other sweet onion
2½ cups chopped bok choy stalks and
   leaves
2 cups hot cooked wide lo mein
   noodles (about 4 ounces
   uncooked)
1 green onion, cut diagonally into
   1-inch pieces
1 tablespoon toasted sesame seeds
1 tablespoon chopped fresh cilantro

1. Place eggplant halves in a colander, and sprinkle with salt. Toss well; drain 1 hour. Rinse well, and pat dry.

2. Place beans in a large saucepan of boiling water; cook 4 minutes. Drain and plunge into ice water; drain. Place beans in a large bowl.

3. Combine vinegar and next 6 ingredients in a microwave-safe dish, stirring with a whisk. Microwave at HIGH 1 minute.

4. Heat a large nonstick or cast iron grill pan coated with cooking spray over medium-high heat. Add eggplant halves to pan; cook 3 minutes on each side or until just tender. Remove from pan. Add onion to pan; cook 3 minutes on each side or until tender. Remove from pan. Cut eggplant halves diagonally into 1½-inch-wide pieces. Coarsely chop onion. Add eggplant pieces, chopped onion, bok choy, and noodles to green beans; toss to combine. Add vinegar mixture, green onions, sesame seeds, and cilantro; toss well to coat. Yield: 4 servings (serving size: about 1½ cups).

CALORIES 197 (12% from fat); FAT 2.7g (sat 0.4g, mono 0.6g, poly 1.1g); PROTEIN 7.5g; CARB 38.8g; FIBER 6.3g; CHOL 0mg; IRON 2.3mg; SODIUM 334mg; CALC 86mg

Veal Chops with Sage-Balsamic Sauce and Warm Mushroom Salad

Pork chops also work well in this recipe.

VEAL:

¼ cup balsamic vinegar
1 teaspoon grated lemon rind
2 tablespoons fresh lemon juice
2 teaspoons chopped fresh sage
2 teaspoons extravirgin olive oil
¼ teaspoon freshly ground black pepper
2 garlic cloves, minced
4 (8-ounce) veal chops, trimmed
Cooking spray
⅛ teaspoon salt

SALAD:

1 large Walla Walla or other sweet onion, cut into ½-inch-thick slices (about ½ pound)
1 pound portobello mushrooms, stemmed
¼ cup low-sodium soy sauce or tamari
1 tablespoon fresh lemon juice
1 teaspoon honey
1 tablespoon chopped fresh chives
1 tablespoon chopped fresh flat-leaf parsley
¼ teaspoon freshly ground black pepper

SAUCE:

1 cup fat-free, less-sodium chicken broth
1 teaspoon red currant jelly

1. To prepare veal, combine first 7 ingredients in a large heavy-duty zip-top plastic bag. Add chops; seal bag, tossing gently to coat. Refrigerate at least 2 hours, turning occasionally.

2. Preheat broiler.

3. Heat a large nonstick skillet coated with cooking spray over medium-high heat. Remove chops from bag, reserving marinade. Sprinkle chops with salt. Add to pan; cook 4 minutes on each side or until desired degree of doneness. Remove chops from pan.

4. To prepare salad, place onion and mushrooms, gill sides up, on a broiler pan coated with cooking spray. Combine soy sauce, 1 tablespoon juice, and honey; stir with a whisk. Spoon soy sauce mixture evenly over mushrooms and onion. Broil 3 minutes; turn onion. Broil 3 minutes or until onion is tender. Cut mushrooms into thick slices. Combine mushrooms, onion, chives, and parsley. Sprinkle with ¼ teaspoon pepper; toss gently.

5. To prepare sauce, combine reserved marinade, broth, and jelly; add to pan, scraping pan to loosen browned bits. Bring to a boil; cook until reduced to ¼ cup (about 6 minutes), stirring frequently. Yield: 4 servings (serving size: 1 chop, 1 cup salad, and 1 tablespoon sauce).

WINE NOTE: Though the acidic character of distilled vinegar could turn any dish into wine's enemy, a small amount of rich, savory-sweet balsamic vinegar is no problem. (The Italians have been drinking wine with dishes made with balsamic vinegar for centuries.) These veal chops, with their luxurious, earthy flavors, beg for a good Pinot Noir. Try Morgan Pinot Noir 2000 (Santa Lucia Highlands, California) $22, or for a very special treat, try the Morgan Pinot Noir 2000 "Rosella's Vineyard," $38.

CALORIES 391 (29% from fat); FAT 12.7g (sat 4.3g, mono 5.8g, poly 0.9g); PROTEIN 48.2g; CARB 18.8g; FIBER 3.1g; CHOL 123mg; IRON 4.7mg; SODIUM 721mg; CALC 90mg

Pickled Cherries in Red Wine Vinegar with Cinnamon

Juicy red Bing cherries are ideal with duck, ham, or a cheese course. They'll keep for at least 1 year. After a few months in the refrigerator, the almond flavor of the cherry stones pervades the pickling liquid, which is then good for using in marinades.

2½ pounds sweet cherries
3½ cups red wine vinegar
1½ cups sugar
1 teaspoon black peppercorns
4 whole cloves
2 (3-inch) cinnamon sticks
2 bay leaves
1 (10 x ½-inch) lemon rind strip

1. Wash and pat cherries dry. Pierce each cherry several times with a fork; set aside.
2. Place vinegar and remaining 6 ingredients in a nonaluminum saucepan; bring to a boil. Stir to dissolve sugar. Reduce heat; simmer 5 minutes. Remove from heat; let stand 30 minutes. Strain vinegar mixture through a sieve over a bowl; discard solids. Return vinegar mixture to pan; bring to a boil.
3. Spoon cherries evenly into hot jars; cover evenly with hot vinegar mixture, leaving ¼-inch head space. Cover jars with metal lids; screw on bands. Cool. Refrigerate at least 2 weeks before serving. Yield: 20 servings (serving size: about 8 cherries).

CALORIES 100 (5% from fat); FAT 0.6g (sat 0.1g, mono 0.2g, poly 0.2g); PROTEIN 0.7g; CARB 24.6g; FIBER 1.3g; CHOL 0mg; IRON 0.5mg; SODIUM 4mg; CALC 11mg

---

Versatile Vinegar

• If a recipe tastes flat, stir in 1 or 2 teaspoons of vinegar to perk it up.
• Add a little vinegar to water when poaching eggs to keep them compact.
• To check if baking soda is still active, combine ¼ teaspoon baking soda with 2 teaspoons vinegar. If the baking soda bubbles, it still works.
• Dissolve hard deposits in a teapot by steeping a solution of 1 part vinegar to 6 parts water in the pot overnight.

Chicken with Fennel, Tomato, and Tarragon Vinegar

Tarragon vinegar provides this hearty stew-like dish with the delicate flavors of white wine and herbs. Whipping cream stirred in at the end rounds out the sauce, but it's not necessary. Serve over rice.

1 teaspoon olive oil
8 skinless, boneless chicken thighs (about 1 pound)
½ teaspoon salt, divided
¼ teaspoon freshly ground black pepper, divided
2 fennel bulbs, trimmed and quartered
3 garlic cloves, minced
1 (14-ounce) can fat-free, less-sodium chicken broth
⅓ cup tarragon vinegar
2 fresh tarragon sprigs
2 cups chopped seeded peeled tomato
1 tablespoon whipping cream
½ teaspoon sugar
Tarragon sprigs (optional)

1. Heat oil in a large nonstick skillet over medium-high heat. Sprinkle chicken with ¼ teaspoon salt and ⅛ teaspoon pepper. Add chicken to pan; cook 3 minutes on each side. Remove from pan. Add fennel; cook 5 minutes, turning to brown. Remove from pan. Add garlic; sauté 30 seconds. Add broth, vinegar, and 2 tarragon sprigs, scraping pan to loosen browned bits. Bring to a boil. Add fennel; cover, reduce heat, and simmer 7 minutes. Add chicken; cover and simmer 10 minutes. Remove chicken and fennel from pan, and keep warm.
2. Add ¼ teaspoon salt, ⅛ teaspoon pepper, tomato, cream, and sugar to pan; bring to a boil. Cook until reduced to 1 cup (about 10 minutes), stirring frequently. Serve over chicken and fennel. Garnish with additional tarragon sprigs, if desired. Yield: 4 servings (serving size: 2 thighs, 2 fennel quarters, and ¼ cup sauce).

CALORIES 227 (30% from fat); FAT 7.5g (sat 2.2g, mono 2.6g, poly 1.3g); PROTEIN 26g; CARB 14.6g; FIBER 4.7g; CHOL 99mg; IRON 2.5mg; SODIUM 650mg; CALC 81mg

---

Pickled Cipollini Onions in Sherry

Serve these traditional English-style sweet-sour-spicy pickled onions whole as a first course with cheese, sliced or chopped in a salad, or thinly sliced and heated with a ribeye steak. Boiling the onions in salted water keeps them crisp. Let them sit 1 month to absorb the subtleties of the pickling liquid. Keep the spices whole to prevent clouding and sediment.

2 cups water, divided
⅓ cup kosher salt
1 pound peeled cipollini or pearl onions
1 cup sherry vinegar
1 cup malt vinegar
½ cup cream sherry
3 tablespoons brown sugar
1½ teaspoons mustard seeds
½ teaspoon fennel seeds
½ teaspoon black peppercorns
1 dried hot red chile
2 bay leaves
1 fresh rosemary sprig

1. Combine 1½ cups water, salt, and onions in a bowl. Cover and refrigerate overnight.
2. Combine ½ cup water, sherry vinegar, and next 7 ingredients in a nonaluminum saucepan, and bring to a boil, stirring to dissolve sugar. Reduce heat, and simmer 5 minutes. Remove mixture from heat, and let stand 1 hour.
3. Drain onions. Rinse onions, and pat dry. Add onions to vinegar mixture, and bring to a boil.
4. Reduce heat, and simmer 3 minutes. Place onions, bay leaves, and rosemary in a hot 1-quart jar; cover onion mixture with hot vinegar mixture, leaving ¼-inch head space.
5. Cover jar with a metal lid, and screw on band. Cool completely. Refrigerate at least 1 month before serving. Yield: 16 servings (serving size: about ¼ cup).

CALORIES 37 (2% from fat); FAT 0.1g (sat 0g, mono 0.1g, poly 0g); PROTEIN 0.4g; CARB 8.2g; FIBER 0.1g; CHOL 0mg; IRON 0mg; SODIUM 246mg; CALC 14mg

Red and White Wine Vinegar

These are the stalwarts in the modern kitchen because they're versatile and work well in just about any dish. Wine vinegars, like wine itself, vary in flavor according to the type of grape from which they're made, where the grapes are grown, and how the vinegar is stored and aged. Generally, the more expensive the vinegar, the better. Try fine, well-aged vinegar made from the Cabernet Sauvignon grape, Italian Chianti or Barolo vinegars, or a robust Spanish Rioja vinegar, all of which have more rounded flavors than other varieties.

Wine vinegars that don't refer to a particular wine on the label are often made from undistinguished wine blends or grape juice. These are what you'll usually find at the supermarket and are fine for most recipes. We used Maître Jacques White Wine Vinegar in testing our recipes.

If you want to splurge, look for wine vinegar made by the ancient Orleans process, named for the French town most commonly associated with producing fine vinegar. Aging in barrels adds smoky, nutty, woodsy flavors.

Use red wine vinegar in Greek and Italian vinaigrettes, drizzle it over hot soups, and add it to wine sauces. Use white wine vinegar with foods that you would pair with white wine—chicken and fish. Champagne produces a light, mild white vinegar, which is excellent for seafood salads. Herb vinegar is often made with white wine vinegar as the base. We tested tarragon vinegar recipes with Maître Jacques Tarragon Vinegar.

Balsamic Vinegar

Few of us drink fine wine every day or consider it for cooking. It's the same with balsamic vinegar. Some traditionally produced balsamic vinegars (balsamico tradizionale) are aged for decades and become increasingly concentrated and syrupy over time. These are the equivalent of vintage port or a perfectly constructed, well-aged wine, and they're phenomenally expensive—sometimes more than $100 per bottle. The best are made on a small, artisanal scale in and around Modena in northern Italy. Reserve these for drizzling over berries and vegetables, as they stand on their own and don't need other ingredients to mask their intense flavor. The commercially produced balsamics found in supermarkets (balsamico industriale) aren't as well rounded or deep but are perfectly fine for cooking. We used a middle-of-the-road balsamic: Alessi 4-year Balsamic Vinegar. Try balsamics in marinades, vinaigrettes, tomato sauces, and soups.

Cider Vinegar

Before gourmet vinegars came around, cider vinegar was the choice for most recipes and is common in many traditional American dishes. Made from the juice of apples (or apple cider), it's light brown in color and has sweet fruit flavor and gentler acidity than most white wine vinegars, though it's still quite sharp. It's an excellent everyday vinegar to use in pickling, salad dressings, and barbecue sauces. Unlike other vinegars, which have begotten many gourmet siblings, cider vinegar remains simple and true to its roots. Unadorned Heinz Cider Vinegar works just fine.

Rice Vinegar

Colorless and very mild, vinegar made from fermented white rice is essential to many Asian recipes. White rice vinegar is a key ingredient in the seasoned rice that gives Japanese sushi its name. The sweet-and-sour mildness makes it suitable for Asian dipping sauces and salad dressings. Try it in fruit and vegetable salsas, and with cucumber or seafood salads when you want a little acidity but not the citrus flavor of lemon or lime juice. Because it's not harsh, rice vinegar is excellent for making quick pickles. We used Marukan and Nakano vinegars, standard supermarket brands.

Dark Chinese and Japanese rice vinegars are very different. They have complex, savory, and smoky flavors, and are excellent in braised meat dishes or in dipping sauces for bland foods, such as tofu, noodles, and steamed dumplings. Combine dark rice vinegars with a little sweet soy sauce or with salty tamari or miso to use in dressings for rice or cooked vegetable salads. The best dark rice vinegars come from Zhejiang, in northern China.

Rice wine vinegar is made from fermented rice wines, like sake and mirin, and is sweeter than rice vinegar. It's a good choice when you want a combined sweet-and-sour flavor without the acidic "heat" of a stronger vinegar, such as white wine vinegar.

Sherry Vinegar

In Spain, people have used sherry vinegar for years, but it's just now becoming popular here. Sherry makes a strong but mellow concentrated vinegar with powerful acidity and great depth of taste. The best ones age in oak barrels and have rounded, distinct notes of hazelnut. A dash of sherry vinegar is traditionally used in gazpacho, but the vinegar also works well in salad dressings, especially ones with nut oils. Use it when making Spanish or Mexican nut-based salsas or moles. It's also good for deglazing the pan after cooking poultry or game, and it's delicious on grilled vegetable salads, especially those with zucchini, bell peppers, and chiles.

The flavors of sherry vinegar and balsamic vinegar are very different, so they're not interchangeable; cider vinegar is a closer match to sherry vinegar. Sherry vinegar isn't readily available in supermarkets, but you can find it in many specialty food stores. We tested with Columela Reserva Solera Sherry Vinegar.

Chicken Marsala Makes the Cut

A North Carolina family gives a thumbs-up to our lightened recipe.

Judy Frederick, of Greensboro, North Carolina, is creating a cookbook filled with tried-and-true healthy family favorites to pass on to her kids and their families. "We gather about eight recipes and try them out each month for dinner," she says. When Chicken Marsala was on the lineup, Judy found her heart sinking as she prepared the recipe, which called for an enormous amount of clarified butter.

To help Judy out, we lightly dusted the chicken breasts with flour, and easily pan-seared them in only 3 tablespoons of butter, saving more than 20 grams of fat and 200 calories per serving. We doubled the Marsala in the sauce to replace the volume lost by reducing the butter. The Marsala also added authentic flavor with zero fat. Our savings allowed us to finish the sauce in the same rich way as the original. Swirling 2 tablespoons of half-and-half and 1 tablespoon of butter into the sauce delivered the creamy texture Judy wanted.

BEFORE	AFTER
SERVING SIZE	
1 chicken breast half, 1 cup pasta, and ¼ cup sauce	
CALORIES PER SERVING	
793	585
FAT	
37.3g	15.3g
PERCENT OF TOTAL CALORIES	
42%	24%

Chicken Marsala

(pictured on page 290)

Clarified butter (butter without the milk solids) is ideal for searing meats because it can be heated to a high temperature without burning. Although you can purchase clarified butter, we detail how to make it below in the first step.

      4   tablespoons butter, divided
  Cooking spray
      1   (8-ounce) package presliced mushrooms
      2   tablespoons finely chopped shallots
      1   tablespoon minced fresh garlic
      4   (6-ounce) skinless, boneless chicken breast halves
   ¼   teaspoon salt, divided
   ¼   teaspoon black pepper, divided
      3   tablespoons all-purpose flour
   ¾   cup fat-free, less-sodium chicken broth
   ½   cup dry Marsala wine
   ½   cup frozen green peas
      2   tablespoons half-and-half
      4   cups hot cooked fettuccine (about 8 ounces uncooked pasta)

1. Place 3 tablespoons butter in a small glass measuring cup. Microwave butter at MEDIUM-HIGH 45 seconds or until melted. Let stand 1 minute. Skim foam from surface; discard. (Mixture will appear separated.) Pour melted butter through a fine sieve over a small bowl; discard milk solids. Set clarified butter aside.
2. Heat a large nonstick skillet coated with cooking spray over medium-high heat; add mushrooms, shallots, and garlic. Cook 3 minutes or until moisture evaporates; remove mushroom mixture from pan. Set aside.
3. Place each chicken breast half between 2 sheets of heavy-duty plastic wrap; pound to ¼-inch thickness using a meat mallet or rolling pin. Sprinkle both sides of chicken with ⅛ teaspoon salt and ⅛ teaspoon pepper. Place flour in a shallow dish; dredge chicken breast halves in flour.
4. Add clarified butter to pan, and place over medium-high heat. Add chicken; cook 3 minutes on each side or until lightly browned. Remove chicken from

pan. Return mushroom mixture to pan; add broth and Marsala, scraping pan to loosen browned bits. Bring mixture to a boil, reduce heat, and simmer 5 minutes or until reduced to 1 cup. Stir in peas; cook 1 minute. Add 1 tablespoon butter, ⅛ teaspoon salt, ⅛ teaspoon pepper, and half-and-half, stirring until butter melts. Return chicken to pan; cook until thoroughly heated. Serve chicken and sauce over pasta. Yield: 4 servings (serving size: 1 chicken breast half, 1 cup pasta, and ¼ cup sauce).

CALORIES 585 (24% from fat); FAT 15.3g (sat 8.4g, mono 4.1g, poly 1g); PROTEIN 51.4g; CARB 55g; FIBER 3.7g; CHOL 133mg; IRON 4.4mg; SODIUM 469mg; CALC 57mg

Kidding Around

Coax children to eat healthier by incorporating new foods into familiar favorites.

Most kids like some sorts of vegetarian food: pizza, pasta, soups, sandwiches, nut butters, and cut-up fruits and vegetables. The golden rule of vegetarian cooking for kids is "keep it simple." What tastes like a symphony of flavors to you may overwhelm a young, sensitive palate. Fortunately, this simplifies cooking. It's why these dishes are based on basic flavors, using ingredients like peanut butter, bananas, tomatoes, cheese, and other foods kids like.

QUICK & EASY
Peanut Butter-Banana Spirals

   ½   cup reduced-fat peanut butter
   ⅓   cup vanilla low-fat yogurt
      1   tablespoon orange juice
      2   ripe bananas, sliced
      4   (8-inch) fat-free flour tortillas
      2   tablespoons honey-crunch wheat germ
   ¼   teaspoon ground cinnamon

1. Combine peanut butter and yogurt, stirring until smooth. Drizzle juice over bananas; toss gently to coat.

2. Spread about 3 tablespoons peanut butter mixture over each tortilla, leaving ½-inch borders. Arrange banana slices in a single layer over peanut butter mixture. Combine wheat germ and cinnamon; sprinkle evenly over banana slices. Roll up tortillas. Slice each roll into 6 pieces. Yield: 6 servings (serving size: 4 pieces).

CALORIES 245 (28% from fat); FAT 7.7g (sat 1.5g, mono 3.8g, poly 2.4g); PROTEIN 9.1g; CARB 31.3g; FIBER 3.9g; CHOL 1mg; IRON 0.8mg; SODIUM 275mg; CALC 37mg

G.I. Joes

Adults who like spicy food can add hot sauce at the table.

```
  1  cup boiling water
  ½  cup sun-dried tomatoes, packed
     without oil
  1  tablespoon olive oil
1 ½  cups chopped onion
  1  cup chopped red bell pepper
  2  garlic cloves, minced
  1  tablespoon low-sodium soy sauce
  1  tablespoon balsamic vinegar
  1  teaspoon sugar
  1  teaspoon chili powder
  1  teaspoon dried oregano
  ½  teaspoon ground cumin
  ½  teaspoon black pepper
  ⅛  teaspoon salt
  1  (28-ounce) can crushed tomatoes,
     undrained
  1  (12-ounce) bag frozen soy crumbles,
     thawed (such as Morningstar Farms)
  6  (2-ounce) Kaiser rolls or
     hamburger buns
```

1. Combine boiling water and sun-dried tomatoes in a bowl, and let stand 5 minutes or until tomatoes are soft. Drain and chop tomatoes.

2. Heat oil in a large nonstick skillet over medium-high heat. Add onion, bell pepper, and garlic; sauté 3 minutes or until vegetables are tender. Stir in sun-dried tomatoes, soy sauce, and next 8 ingredients. Bring to a boil; reduce heat, and simmer 20 minutes or until slightly thick,

stirring occasionally. Stir in soy crumbles; cook 2 minutes or until thoroughly heated, stirring frequently. Spoon about ⅔ cup crumbles mixture onto bottom half of each roll; top with top halves of rolls. Yield: 6 servings.

CALORIES 393 (27% from fat); FAT 11.7g (sat 2.4g, mono 4.7g, poly 3.8g); PROTEIN 20.9g; CARB 51.7g; FIBER 8.3g; CHOL 0mg; IRON 7.7mg; SODIUM 999mg; CALC 164mg

Kid-Friendly Fiesta Menu
serves 6

To keep this menu kid-friendly, we've included a nonalcoholic frozen beverage.

Chili-Cheese-Black Bean Enchiladas

Fizzy frozen mock-a-rita*

Tortilla chips and bottled salsa

*Place 1 (10-ounce) bag frozen strawberries, 1 (6-ounce) can frozen limeade, and 1 (12-ounce) can lemon-lime soda in a blender; process until smooth.

Chili-Cheese-Black Bean Enchiladas

Soy crumbles stand in for ground beef in this simple vegetarian entrée. If can't find soy crumbles, chop thawed veggie burgers. Look for red enchilada sauce in the Mexican food section of your supermarket.

```
     Cooking spray
  ½  cup chopped onion
  ½  teaspoon ground cumin
  ½  teaspoon dried oregano
  ½  teaspoon chili powder
  2  garlic cloves, minced
  1  (15-ounce) can black beans,
     rinsed and drained
  1  (12-ounce) bag frozen soy crumbles,
     thawed (such as Morningstar Farms)
  ¾  cup bottled salsa
  ⅓  cup (3 ounces) block-style fat-free
     cream cheese, softened
  1  cup (4 ounces) shredded reduced-
     fat extrasharp Cheddar cheese,
     divided
 12  (6-inch) corn tortillas
  1  (10-ounce) can enchilada sauce
```

1. Preheat oven to 350°.

2. Heat a large nonstick skillet coated with cooking spray over medium-high heat. Add onion; sauté 4 minutes or until tender. Stir in cumin and next 5 ingredients, and cook 2 minutes; stir frequently.

3. Stir in salsa, and cook 1 minute. Remove from heat, and add cream cheese and ½ cup Cheddar cheese, stirring until cheese melts.

4. Warm tortillas according to package directions. Spread ⅓ cup enchilada sauce in bottom of a 13 x 9-inch baking dish coated with cooking spray. Spoon about ⅓ cup black bean mixture down center of each tortilla, and roll up. Arrange enchiladas, seam sides down, crosswise in dish. Pour remaining enchilada sauce evenly over enchiladas, and sprinkle with ½ cup Cheddar. Bake at 350° for 20 minutes or until thoroughly heated. Yield: 6 servings (serving size: 2 enchiladas).

CALORIES 386 (30% from fat); FAT 12.9g (sat 4g, mono 3.8g, poly 3.4g); PROTEIN 26.8g; CARB 43.9g; FIBER 10.7g; CHOL 17mg; IRON 5.4mg; SODIUM 995mg; CALC 390mg

MAKE AHEAD
Tofu Bites

Serve cold or at room temperature with toothpicks.

```
  1  pound extrafirm reduced-fat
     water-packed tofu, drained and
     cut into ½-inch cubes
1 ½  teaspoons vegetable oil
  1  teaspoon dark sesame oil
  2  tablespoons low-sodium soy sauce
  1  tablespoon rice vinegar
```

1. Place tofu on several layers of heavy-duty paper towels. Cover tofu with additional paper towels, and let stand 5 minutes, pressing occasionally.

2. Heat oils in a large nonstick skillet over medium-high heat. Add tofu; sauté 7 minutes or until browned. Place in a bowl. Drizzle with soy sauce and vinegar; toss gently to coat. Cover and chill at least 1 hour, stirring occasionally. Yield: 6 servings (serving size: ⅓ cup).

CALORIES 51 (49% from fat); FAT 2.8g (sat 0.3g, mono 1.1g, poly 1.2g); PROTEIN 4.8g; CARB 1.4g; FIBER 0g; CHOL 0mg; IRON 0.8mg; SODIUM 241mg; CALC 37mg

Orange-Banana Smoothie

This creamy, refreshing drink is great for breakfast, after a workout, or as a midday pick-me-up. Use any flavored yogurt you like—strawberry makes the smoothie pink, while blueberry turns it purple.

> 1 cup orange juice
> 1 cup vanilla low-fat yogurt
> 1/8 teaspoon ground cinnamon
> Dash of salt
> 1 ripe banana, sliced

1. Place all ingredients in a blender; process until smooth. Yield: 2 servings (serving size: 1 1/4 cups).

CALORIES 206 (9% from fat); FAT 2g (sat 1.1g, mono 0.5g, poly 0.2g); PROTEIN 7.2g; CARB 42.1g; FIBER 1.7g; CHOL 6mg; IRON 0.5mg; SODIUM 150mg; CALC 212mg

Cheddar-Jack Crackers

Get your young bakers to help with rolling and cutting the dough—use a pizza cutter instead of a knife for safety. Roll out the dough on parchment paper, then transfer it to a baking sheet. If you don't have enough time to roll out all the dough, refrigerate the remainder for up to 2 days or freeze for up to 2 weeks.

> 2/3 cup all-purpose flour
> 1/4 cup stone-ground yellow cornmeal
> 1/2 teaspoon sugar
> 1/4 teaspoon baking soda
> 1/4 teaspoon salt
> 1/8 teaspoon ground red pepper
> 2 tablespoons chilled butter, cut into small pieces
> 1/2 cup (2 ounces) shredded Cheddar-Jack cheese
> 1/4 cup ice water
> 1 tablespoon white vinegar
> 2 teaspoons poppy seeds, divided

1. Lightly spoon flour into a dry measuring cup, and level with a knife. Combine flour and next 5 ingredients in a large bowl, stirring with a whisk. Cut in butter with a pastry blender or 2 knives until mixture resembles coarse meal. Add cheese, water, and vinegar; stir until mixture just comes together. Divide dough into 4 equal portions, shaping each into a ball. Wrap each ball in plastic wrap; cover and freeze 30 minutes.

2. Preheat oven to 375°.

3. Roll 1 ball into an 8-inch circle on parchment paper on a lightly floured surface (dough will be very thin). Sprinkle dough with 1/2 teaspoon seeds, and lightly press seeds into dough. Cut dough into 8 wedges (do not separate wedges). Place dough on a large baking sheet. Repeat procedure with remaining dough and seeds, arranging on 2 baking sheets. Bake at 375° for 10 minutes or until crackers are brown and crispy. Cool completely on a wire rack. Separate into wedges. Yield: 32 crackers (serving size: 2 crackers).

CALORIES 54 (47% from fat); FAT 2.8g (sat 1.7g, mono 0.5g, poly 0.2g); PROTEIN 1.6g; CARB 5.8g; FIBER 0.3g; CHOL 7mg; IRON 0.4mg; SODIUM 95mg; CALC 34mg

Tomato Alphabet Soup

On chilly autumn afternoons, nothing warms you more than a good bowl of creamy tomato soup and a grilled cheese sandwich. Pureed alphabet pasta, instead of cream, thickens the soup in this version.

> 2 tablespoons butter
> 1 cup chopped onion
> 1 cup chopped carrot
> 1/3 cup chopped celery
> 1 1/2 cups vegetable broth
> 1 teaspoon dried basil
> 1/4 teaspoon black pepper
> 1 (28-ounce) can diced tomatoes, undrained
> 2 cups cooked alphabet pasta (about 1 cup uncooked pasta), divided
> 1 cup 2% reduced-fat milk

1. Melt butter in a saucepan over medium-high heat. Add onion, carrot, and celery; sauté 4 minutes or until tender. Add broth, basil, pepper, and tomatoes, and bring to a boil. Reduce heat; simmer 15 minutes. Stir in 1/2 cup pasta. Remove from heat; let stand 5 minutes.

2. Place half of tomato mixture in a blender, and process until smooth. Pour puréed soup into a large bowl. Repeat procedure with remaining tomato mixture. Return puréed soup to pan; stir in 1 1/2 cups pasta and milk. Cook over medium-high heat 2 minutes or until thoroughly heated, stirring frequently (do not boil). Yield: 6 servings (serving size: about 1 cup).

CALORIES 175 (27% from fat); FAT 5.2g (sat 2.9g, mono 1.3g, poly 0.2g); PROTEIN 6.1g; CARB 27.9g; FIBER 4g; CHOL 13mg; IRON 1.3mg; SODIUM 492mg; CALC 93mg

dinner tonight

Speedy Flank Steak

Take versatile flank steak home for speedy suppers.

Flank Steak Menu 1
serves 4

Rosemary-Merlot Flank Steak (recipe on page 301)

Garlic-roasted new potatoes*

Tossed salad

*Combine 1 tablespoon olive oil, 1/2 teaspoon salt, 1/4 teaspoon dried Italian seasoning, 1/4 teaspoon paprika, 1/4 teaspoon black pepper, 4 minced garlic cloves, and 1 1/2 pounds quartered small red potatoes on a jelly roll pan coated with cooking spray. Bake at 500° for 25 minutes or until tender, stirring every 10 minutes.

Game Plan

1. While oven heats for potatoes:
- Prepare marinade
- Marinate steak
- Toss potatoes with seasonings

2. While potatoes bake:
- Prepare salad
- Cook steak
- Prepare sauce

Rosemary-Merlot Flank Steak

(pictured on page 291)

If you don't have dried Italian seasoning on hand, use ⅛ teaspoon dried basil and ⅛ teaspoon dried oregano. You can also substitute 1 teaspoon dried rosemary for the fresh.

TOTAL TIME: 37 MINUTES

QUICK TIP: Prepare marinade up to 1 day in advance, and store in an airtight container in the refrigerator.

1 cup finely chopped onion
¾ cup low-salt beef broth
¾ cup Merlot or other dry red wine
1 tablespoon chopped fresh rosemary
½ teaspoon salt
¼ teaspoon dried Italian seasoning
2 garlic cloves, minced
1 (1-pound) flank steak, trimmed
Cooking spray
1 tablespoon tomato paste
2 teaspoons Dijon mustard

1. Prepare grill or broiler.
2. Combine first 7 ingredients in a large zip-top plastic bag. Add steak; seal bag. Marinate in refrigerator 20 minutes, turning once. Remove steak from bag, reserving marinade.
3. Place steak on grill rack or broiler pan coated with cooking spray; cook 6 minutes on each side or until desired degree of doneness. Let stand 5 minutes. Cut steak diagonally across the grain into thin slices; keep warm.
4. While steak cooks, combine reserved marinade, tomato paste, and mustard in a medium saucepan over medium-high heat, stirring well with a whisk. Bring to a boil, and cook until reduced to 1 cup (about 7 minutes). Serve sauce with steak. Yield: 4 servings (serving size: 3 ounces steak and ¼ cup sauce).

CALORIES 203 (39% from fat); FAT 8.8g (sat 3.6g, mono 3.5g, poly 0.5g); PROTEIN 23.8g; CARB 6.1g; FIBER 1.1g; CHOL 54mg; IRON 2.7mg; SODIUM 445mg; CALC 32mg

---

Flank Steak Menu 2

serves 4

Greek Steak Pitas with Dill Sauce

Grape tomato salad*

Prepared hummus with baby carrots

*Place 2 cups grape tomatoes, 1¼ cups chopped English cucumber, and 2 tablespoons chopped green onions in a medium bowl; toss gently to combine. Combine ¼ cup balsamic vinegar, 1 teaspoon sugar, 2 teaspoons olive oil, ¼ teaspoon black pepper, and ⅛ teaspoon salt, stirring with a whisk. Drizzle vinaigrette over salad; toss gently to coat.

Game Plan

1. While steak marinates, prepare sauce
2. While steak cooks, prepare salad

Greek Steak Pitas with Dill Sauce

The lemon-juice marinade quickly penetrates the steak, so a 10-minute soak is enough to flavor the meat. Try crumbled goat or blue cheese in place of the feta.

TOTAL TIME: 40 MINUTES

QUICK TIP: Use bagged hearts of romaine lettuce, which you don't have to wash and dry.

SAUCE:
½ cup plain fat-free yogurt
2 teaspoons chopped fresh dill
¼ teaspoon salt
¼ teaspoon black pepper
1 garlic clove, minced

STEAK:
½ cup fresh lemon juice
1 teaspoon dried oregano
½ teaspoon black pepper
2 garlic cloves, minced
1 (1-pound) flank steak, trimmed
Cooking spray

REMAINING INGREDIENTS:
4 (6-inch) pitas, cut in half
4 romaine lettuce leaves, halved
¼ cup (1 ounce) crumbled feta cheese

---

1. Prepare grill or broiler.
2. To prepare sauce, combine first 5 ingredients, stirring with a whisk.
3. To prepare steak, combine juice and next 4 ingredients in a large zip-top plastic bag; seal. Marinate in refrigerator 10 minutes, turning once. Remove steak from bag; discard marinade.
4. Place steak on grill rack or broiler pan coated with cooking spray; cook 6 minutes on each side or until desired degree of doneness. Let stand 5 minutes. Cut steak diagonally across the grain into thin slices. Line each pita half with 1 lettuce leaf half. Divide steak evenly among pita halves. Spoon 1 tablespoon sauce and 1½ teaspoons cheese into each pita half. Yield: 4 servings (serving size: 2 stuffed pita halves).

CALORIES 386 (25% from fat); FAT 10.9g (sat 4.9g, mono 3.9g, poly 0.7g); PROTEIN 31.6g; CARB 38.4g; FIBER 1.7g; CHOL 64mg; IRON 4.2mg; SODIUM 643mg; CALC 165mg

---

Flank Steak Menu 3

serves 6

Thai Beef Salad (recipe on page 302)

Coconut rice*

Strawberry sorbet

*Bring ½ cup water, ¼ teaspoon salt, and 1 (14-ounce) can light coconut milk to a simmer in a medium saucepan. Add 1 cup jasmine rice; cover and simmer 20 minutes or until liquid is absorbed.

Game Plan

1. While water for rice comes to a boil:
• Prepare marinade
• Marinate steak
• Slice onion
• Cut tomatoes into wedges
2. While rice cooks:
• Cook steak
• Prepare lettuce, cucumber, and mint for the salad

Thai Beef Salad

The salad gets its heat from 2 tablespoons of chile paste. If you prefer milder food, use half.

TOTAL TIME: 42 MINUTES

QUICK TIP: English cucumbers work well for quick meals because they're virtually seedless.

 ½ cup fresh lime juice
 ¼ cup chopped fresh cilantro
 2 tablespoons brown sugar
 2 tablespoons Thai fish sauce
 2 tablespoons chile paste with garlic
 2 garlic cloves, minced
 1 (1½-pound) flank steak, trimmed
 Cooking spray
 1½ cups vertically sliced red onion
 4 plum tomatoes, each cut into 6 wedges
 6 cups torn romaine lettuce
 1¼ cups thinly sliced English cucumber
 2 tablespoons chopped fresh mint

1. Prepare grill or broiler.
2. Combine first 6 ingredients, stirring until sugar dissolves; set half of lime mixture aside. Combine remaining half of lime mixture and steak in a large zip-top plastic bag; seal. Marinate in refrigerator 10 minutes, turning once. Remove steak from bag; discard marinade.
3. Place steak on grill rack or broiler pan coated with cooking spray; cook 6 minutes on each side or until desired degree of doneness. Let stand 5 minutes. Cut steak diagonally across the grain into thin slices.
4. Heat a large nonstick skillet coated with cooking spray over medium-high heat. Add onion; sauté 3 minutes. Add tomatoes; sauté 2 minutes. Place onion mixture, lettuce, cucumber, and mint in a large bowl; toss gently to combine. Divide salad evenly among 6 plates. Top each serving with 3 ounces steak; drizzle each serving with 1 tablespoon reserved lime mixture. Yield: 6 servings.

CALORIES 219 (35% from fat); FAT 8.6g (sat 3.6g, mono 3.3g, poly 0.5g); PROTEIN 24.1g; CARB 12.3g; FIBER 2.2g; CHOL 54mg; IRON 3.1mg; SODIUM 456mg; CALC 44mg

baking

Banana Appeal

America's number one fruit is at its best in America's favorite quick bread.

With barely a chance to cool down, moist, tender banana bread gets snatched up faster than you can say, "Pass the butter." If you're lucky, you might be able to stash away a few loaves in the freezer for last-minute homemade gifts, bake-sale contributions, or your personal fix.

Fortunately, banana bread is simple to make. Choose bananas that are very ripe—the browner they are, the more flavor they impart. Banana bread is a perfect application for squishy, speckled bananas, whose soft texture helps them blend well and mash easily.

To ensure a light, tender crumb, be careful not to overmix the batter after adding the flour. Once all the ingredients are incorporated, put the bread in the oven right away. If the batter rests for more than a few minutes, the baking soda will start to lose its leavening power.

Finally, use the right-sized loaf pan (see "The Right Pan for the Job," below). If the pan is too small, the batter will slump over the edges. If it's too large, your bread will look more like a doorstop.

The Right Pan for the Job

Most of these recipes call for an 8½ x 4½-inch loaf pan. If your pan is labeled 8 x 4-inches, it's probably the right size. To tell for sure, measure the length and width of the pan from the top inside edges.

We tested these recipes in dull metal pans. If you're using dark metal, nonstick, or glass pans, decrease the baking time by 5 to 10 minutes.

Marbled-Chocolate Banana Bread

Chocolate and bananas are a natural pair. Toast and top with a spoonful of peanut butter for breakfast.

 2 cups all-purpose flour
 ¾ teaspoon baking soda
 ½ teaspoon salt
 1 cup sugar
 ¼ cup butter, softened
 1½ cups mashed ripe banana (about 3 bananas)
 ½ cup egg substitute
 ⅓ cup plain low-fat yogurt
 ½ cup semisweet chocolate chips
 Cooking spray

1. Preheat oven to 350°.
2. Lightly spoon flour into dry measuring cups, and level with a knife. Combine flour, baking soda, and salt, stirring with a whisk.
3. Place sugar and butter in a large bowl; beat with a mixer at medium speed until well blended (about 1 minute). Add banana, egg substitute, and yogurt; beat until blended. Add flour mixture; beat at low speed just until moist.
4. Place chocolate chips in a medium microwave-safe bowl, and microwave at HIGH 1 minute or until almost melted, stirring until smooth. Cool slightly. Add 1 cup batter to chocolate, stirring until well combined. Spoon chocolate batter alternately with plain batter into an 8½ x 4½-inch loaf pan coated with cooking spray. Swirl batters together using a knife. Bake at 350° for 1 hour and 15 minutes or until a wooden pick inserted in center comes out clean. Cool 10 minutes in pan on a wire rack; remove from pan. Cool completely on wire rack. Yield: 1 loaf, 16 slices (serving size: 1 slice).

CALORIES 183 (23% from fat); FAT 4.7g (sat 2.8g, mono 1.4g, poly 0.2g); PROTEIN 3.1g; CARB 33.4g; FIBER 1.3g; CHOL 8mg; IRON 1.1mg; SODIUM 180mg; CALC 18mg

Blueberry-Lemon Banana Bread with Cream-Cheese Glaze

BREAD:

    2 cups all-purpose flour
    ¾ teaspoon baking soda
    ½ teaspoon salt
    1 cup granulated sugar
    ¼ cup butter, softened
    1 cup mashed ripe banana (about
       2 bananas)
    ½ cup egg substitute
    ⅓ cup reduced-fat sour cream
    1 teaspoon vanilla extract
    1 cup fresh blueberries
    1 tablespoon grated lemon rind
Cooking spray

GLAZE:

    ¼ cup (2 ounces) block-style
       ⅓-less-fat cream cheese, softened
    3 tablespoons powdered sugar
    1 tablespoon fresh lemon juice
    2 teaspoons water

1. Preheat oven to 350°.
2. To prepare banana bread, lightly spoon flour into dry measuring cups, and level with a knife. Combine flour, baking soda, and salt, stirring with a whisk.
3. Place granulated sugar and butter in a large bowl; beat with a mixer at medium speed until mixture is well blended (about 1 minute). Add banana, egg substitute, sour cream, and vanilla; beat until blended. Add flour mixture; beat at low speed just until moist. Gently fold in blueberries and lemon rind. Spoon batter into an 8½ x 4½-inch loaf pan coated with cooking spray. Bake at 350° for 1 hour and 15 minutes or until a wooden pick inserted in center comes out clean. Cool 10 minutes in pan on a wire rack; remove from pan. Cool completely on wire rack.
4. To prepare glaze, combine cream cheese, powdered sugar, lemon juice, and water, stirring with a whisk until smooth. Drizzle glaze over cooled bread. Yield: 1 loaf, 16 servings (serving size: 1 slice).

CALORIES 176 (24% from fat); FAT 4.6g (sat 2.7g, mono 1.1g, poly 0.2g); PROTEIN 3.2g; CARB 31.3g; FIBER 1.1g; CHOL 13mg; IRON 1mg; SODIUM 194mg; CALC 19mg

Cardamom Banana Bread with Pistachios

    2 cups all-purpose flour
    ¾ teaspoon baking soda
    ½ teaspoon salt
    ½ cup granulated sugar
    ½ cup packed brown sugar
    ¼ cup butter, softened
    2 large eggs
 1½ cups mashed ripe banana (about
       3 bananas)
    ⅓ cup reduced-fat sour cream
    ½ teaspoon ground cardamom
    ⅓ cup finely chopped pistachios
Cooking spray

1. Preheat oven to 350°.
2. Lightly spoon flour into dry measuring cups, and level with a knife. Combine flour, baking soda, and salt, stirring with a whisk.
3. Place sugars and butter in a large bowl, and beat with a mixer at medium speed until well blended (about 1 minute). Add eggs, 1 at a time, beating well after each addition. Add banana, sour cream, and cardamom; beat until blended. Add flour mixture; beat at low speed just until moist. Stir in pistachios. Spoon batter into a 9 x 5-inch loaf pan coated with cooking spray. Bake at 350° for 1 hour or until a wooden pick inserted in center comes out clean. Cool 10 minutes in pan on a wire rack; remove from pan. Cool completely on wire rack. Yield: 1 loaf, 16 servings (serving size: 1 slice).

CALORIES 185 (27% from fat); FAT 5.5g (sat 2.6g, mono 1.7g, poly 0.6g); PROTEIN 3.4g; CARB 31.3g; FIBER 1.3g; CHOL 37mg; IRON 1.2mg; SODIUM 175mg; CALC 25mg

Classic Banana Bread

Banana bread should form a crack down the center as it bakes—a sign the baking soda is doing its job.

    2 cups all-purpose flour
    ¾ teaspoon baking soda
    ½ teaspoon salt
    1 cup sugar
    ¼ cup butter, softened
    2 large eggs
 1½ cups mashed ripe banana (about
       3 bananas)
    ⅓ cup plain low-fat yogurt
    1 teaspoon vanilla extract
Cooking spray

1. Preheat oven to 350°.
2. Lightly spoon flour into dry measuring cups; level with a knife. Combine flour, baking soda, and salt, stirring with a whisk.
3. Place sugar and butter in a large bowl, and beat with a mixer at medium speed until well blended (about 1 minute). Add eggs, 1 at a time, beating well after each addition. Add banana, yogurt, and vanilla; beat until blended. Add flour mixture; beat at low speed just until moist. Spoon batter into an 8½ x 4½-inch loaf pan coated with cooking spray. Bake at 350° for 1 hour or until a wooden pick inserted in center comes out clean. Cool 10 minutes in pan on a wire rack; remove from pan. Cool completely on wire rack. Yield: 1 loaf, 14 servings (serving size: 1 slice).

CALORIES 187 (21% from fat); FAT 4.3g (sat 2.4g, mono 1.2g, poly 0.3g); PROTEIN 3.3g; CARB 34.4g; FIBER 1.1g; CHOL 40mg; IRON 1mg; SODIUM 198mg; CALC 20mg

Freezing Tips

• To freeze a whole loaf, wrap tightly in plastic wrap, then in heavy-duty aluminum foil. Freeze for up to 1 month. To thaw, let stand at room temperature.
• To freeze individual slices, place in small, heavy-duty zip-top plastic bags.

Remove excess air from bags; seal and freeze for up to 1 month. Or wrap slices in plastic wrap and aluminum foil as noted above. Thaw at room temperature, or microwave at HIGH for 15 to 30 seconds.

Orange Banana-Nut Bread

Orange rind and juice delicately flavor this bread. For a quick breakfast, spread toasted slices of this bread with reduced-fat cream cheese and top with thinly sliced strawberries, peaches, or kiwi.

    2   cups all-purpose flour
    ¾   teaspoon baking soda
    ½   teaspoon salt
    1   cup sugar
    ¼   cup butter, softened
    2   large eggs
 1½   cups mashed ripe banana (about
        3 bananas)
 1½   tablespoons grated orange rind
    3   tablespoons fresh orange juice
    ⅓   cup chopped walnuts
        Cooking spray

1. Preheat oven to 350°.
2. Lightly spoon flour into dry measuring cups, and level with a knife. Combine flour, baking soda, and salt, stirring with a whisk.
3. Place sugar and butter in a large bowl; beat with a mixer at medium speed until well blended (about 1 minute). Add eggs, 1 at a time, beating well after each addition. Add banana, rind, and juice; beat until blended. Add flour mixture; beat at low speed just until moist. Stir in walnuts; spoon batter into an 8½ x 4½-inch loaf pan coated with cooking spray. Bake at 350° for 1 hour and 5 minutes or until a wooden pick inserted in center comes out clean. Cool 10 minutes in pan on a wire rack; remove from pan. Cool completely on wire rack. Yield: 1 loaf, 16 servings (serving size: 1 slice).

CALORIES 178 (27% from fat); FAT 5.4g (sat 2.2g, mono 1.3g, poly 1.5g); PROTEIN 3.1g; CARB 30.5g; FIBER 1.2g; CHOL 34mg; IRON 1mg; SODIUM 170mg; CALC 11mg

Molasses-Oat Banana Bread

Molasses gives this bread a rich, deep brown color and distinctly old-fashioned taste. Because of the whole wheat flour and oats, the chewy loaf won't rise very high.

    1   cup all-purpose flour
    ½   cup whole wheat flour
    ⅔   cup regular oats
    1   teaspoon baking soda
    1   teaspoon ground cinnamon
    ½   teaspoon salt
    ⅔   cup sugar
    ¼   cup butter, softened
    ⅓   cup dark molasses
    2   large eggs
    1   cup mashed ripe banana (about
        2 bananas)
    ⅓   cup plain low-fat yogurt
    1   teaspoon vanilla extract
        Cooking spray

1. Preheat oven to 350°.
2. Lightly spoon flours into dry measuring cups; level with a knife. Combine flours, oats, baking soda, cinnamon, and salt, stirring with a whisk.
3. Place sugar, butter, and molasses in a large bowl; beat with a mixer at medium speed until well blended (about 1 minute). Add eggs, 1 at a time, beating well after each addition. Add banana, yogurt, and vanilla; beat until blended. Add flour mixture; beat at low speed just until moist. Spoon batter into an 8½ x 4½-inch loaf pan coated with cooking spray. Bake at 350° for 1 hour and 5 minutes or until a wooden pick inserted in center comes out clean. Cool 10 minutes in pan on a wire rack; remove from pan. Cool completely on wire rack. Yield: 1 loaf, 14 servings (serving size: 1 slice).

CALORIES 177 (23% from fat); FAT 4.6g (sat 2.4g, mono 1.3g, poly 0.4g); PROTEIN 3.5g; CARB 31.9g; FIBER 1.6g; CHOL 40mg; IRON 2mg; SODIUM 224mg; CALC 61mg

Coconut Banana Bread with Lime Glaze

(pictured on page 289)

The tangy lime glaze cuts the sweetness of the bread. Substitute apple juice for the rum if you prefer.

    2   cups all-purpose flour
    ¾   teaspoon baking soda
    ½   teaspoon salt
    1   cup granulated sugar
    ¼   cup butter, softened
    2   large eggs
 1½   cups mashed ripe banana (about
        3 bananas)
    ¼   cup plain low-fat yogurt
    3   tablespoons dark rum
    ½   teaspoon vanilla extract
    ½   cup flaked sweetened coconut
        Cooking spray
    1   tablespoon flaked sweetened
        coconut
    ½   cup powdered sugar
 1½   tablespoons fresh lime or lemon
        juice

1. Preheat oven to 350°.
2. Lightly spoon flour into dry measuring cups, and level with a knife. Combine flour, baking soda, and salt, stirring with a whisk.
3. Place granulated sugar and butter in a large bowl; beat with a mixer at medium speed until well blended (about 1 minute). Add eggs, 1 at a time, beating well after each addition. Add banana, yogurt, rum, and vanilla; beat until blended. Add flour mixture; beat at low speed just until moist. Stir in ½ cup coconut. Spoon batter into a 9 x 5-inch loaf pan coated with cooking spray; sprinkle with 1 tablespoon coconut. Bake at 350° for 1 hour or until a wooden pick inserted in center comes out clean. Cool 10 minutes in pan on a wire rack; remove from pan. Combine powdered sugar and juice, stirring with a whisk; drizzle over warm bread. Cool bread completely on wire rack. Yield: 1 loaf, 16 servings (serving size: 1 slice).

CALORIES 193 (21% from fat); FAT 4.6g (sat 2.8g, mono 1.1g, poly 0.3g); PROTEIN 2.9g; CARB 35g; FIBER 1.1g; CHOL 35mg; IRON 1mg; SODIUM 179mg; CALC 15mg

Let Time Do the Work

When it's hot outside, turn to cold, marinated dishes that taste even better the next day.

The following recipes use various marinating techniques to create flavors that, like good cheese and fine wine, improve with time. The dishes are prepared in advance, then stay in the refrigerator overnight to allow their flavors to mellow and marry. They're easy to make and ideal for casual cookouts or picnics. Simply prepare them the day before and carry them to the patio when it's mealtime.

MAKE AHEAD
Rum-Soaked Sponge Cake with Tropical Fruit
(pictured on page 291)

Both the cake and fruit mixture chill overnight so the cake can absorb the rum and the sugar can soften and sweeten the fruit.

CAKE:
Cooking spray
1 cup all-purpose flour
¼ teaspoon vanilla extract
Dash of salt
4 large eggs
½ cup sugar
¼ cup dark rum
1 (14-ounce) can fat-free sweetened condensed milk
1 (5-ounce) can evaporated fat-free milk

FRUIT:
1 cup cubed pineapple
1 cup cubed peeled kiwifruit
1 cup cubed peeled ripe mango
1 tablespoon sugar

CUSTARD:
¼ cup egg substitute
2 tablespoons sugar
1 tablespoon cornstarch
½ cup fat-free milk
¼ teaspoon vanilla extract

1. Preheat oven to 375°.
2. To prepare cake, coat a 9-inch round cake pan with cooking spray. Line bottom of pan with wax paper; coat wax paper with cooking spray. Set pan aside.
3. Lightly spoon flour into a dry measuring cup; level with a knife. Place ¼ teaspoon vanilla, salt, and eggs in a large bowl; beat with a mixer at high speed 2 minutes. Gradually add ½ cup sugar, beating until thick and pale (about 3 minutes). Sift flour over egg mixture, ¼ cup at a time; fold in. Spoon batter into prepared pan. Bake at 375° for 20 minutes or until cake springs back when touched lightly in center. Cool cake in pan on a wire rack.
4. Combine rum, condensed milk, and evaporated milk in a small saucepan over medium-high heat. Bring to a boil, stirring constantly. Remove from heat; cool to room temperature. Pierce top of entire cake with a skewer. Pour rum mixture evenly over top of cake in two batches, beginning at outer edge and working inward. Cool to room temperature. Cover and refrigerate overnight. Run a knife or spatula around outside edge of cake. Place a serving plate upside down on top of cake; invert onto plate.
5. To prepare fruit, combine pineapple, kiwifruit, mango, and 1 tablespoon sugar. Cover and refrigerate overnight.
6. To prepare custard, place egg substitute in a bowl, and set aside. Combine 2 tablespoons sugar and cornstarch in a small saucepan. Gradually add ½ cup fat-free milk; stir with a whisk until blended. Bring to a boil over medium heat; cook 1 minute, stirring constantly. Remove from heat; gradually stir one-fourth of hot-milk mixture into egg substitute. Add to remaining hot-milk mixture; stir constantly. Cook over medium heat 1 minute or until thick. Remove from heat. Spoon custard into a bowl; place bowl in a large ice-filled bowl 10 minutes or until custard comes to room temperature, stirring occasionally.
7. Remove bowl from ice. Stir in ¼ teaspoon vanilla; spread custard over cake. Serve with fruit mixture. Yield: 12 servings (serving size: 1 cake wedge and about ¼ cup fruit mixture).

CALORIES 255 (8% from fat); FAT 2.2g (sat 0.6g, mono 0.7g, poly 0.4g); PROTEIN 8.2g; CARB 48.2g; FIBER 1.2g; CHOL 74mg; IRON 1mg; SODIUM 98mg; CALC 158mg

MAKE AHEAD
Macerated Berries

Macerating is similar to marinating, but it usually refers to soaking fruit in alcohol. Ripe berries give up their own juices until they swim in a sweet liquid. These are great on their own or over vanilla ice cream or plain yogurt.

2 cups sliced strawberries
2 cups fresh blueberries
1 cup fresh raspberries
3 tablespoons fresh lemon juice
3 tablespoons Grand Marnier (orange-flavored liqueur)
1 tablespoon sugar

1. Combine all ingredients, stirring gently. Cover and refrigerate at least 2 hours or overnight, stirring occasionally. Yield: 4 servings (serving size: 1 cup).

CALORIES 133 (5% from fat); FAT 0.8g (sat 0.1g, mono 0.1g, poly 0.4g); PROTEIN 1.3g; CARB 28.4g; FIBER 6g; CHOL 0mg; IRON 0.6mg; SODIUM 6mg; CALC 24mg

MAKE AHEAD
Scallop Seviche

The acidity of the citrus juices "cooks" the scallops. If you'd prefer, poach them for about 2 minutes before marinating. Serve this appetizer with tortilla chips for a refreshing start to a summer meal.

1 pound sea scallops
1 cup fresh lime juice (about 4 limes)
¾ cup chopped onion
¼ cup fresh orange juice
1 tablespoon chopped fresh cilantro
½ teaspoon salt
1 serrano pepper, thinly sliced

1. Cut each scallop horizontally into 3 even slices. Place scallops in a nonaluminum dish. Add lime juice and remaining ingredients; toss to coat. Cover and refrigerate at least 6 hours or overnight, stirring occasionally. Serve scallops cold using a slotted spoon. Yield: 8 servings (serving size: about 2 ounces scallops).

CALORIES 68 (7% from fat); FAT 0.5g (sat 0.1g, mono 0g, poly 0.2g); PROTEIN 9.9g; CARB 6.3g; FIBER 0.5g; CHOL 19mg; IRON 0.2mg; SODIUM 239mg; CALC 21mg

Chicken with Fruit and Olives

This dish really marinates twice. Chicken soaks in a vinegar-oil-garlic mixture before it's cooked, then it chills in the cooking juices, making for very tender meat.

- ¼ cup red wine vinegar
- 3 tablespoons extravirgin olive oil
- ½ teaspoon salt
- ¼ teaspoon freshly ground black pepper
- 4 garlic cloves, minced
- ½ cup pitted prunes, chopped
- ½ cup dried apricots, chopped
- ½ cup pitted green olives, halved
- 3 pounds skinless, bone-in chicken breasts
- 1 cup dry white wine
- ½ cup finely chopped fresh flat-leaf parsley

1. Combine first 5 ingredients in a 13 x 9-inch baking dish, stirring with a whisk. Add prunes, apricots, and olives; toss well to coat. Add chicken; turn to coat. Cover and chill at least 6 hours or overnight.
2. Preheat oven to 450°.
3. Pour wine around, but not over, chicken; let stand 15 minutes. Bake at 450° for 35 minutes or until chicken is done; let stand 15 minutes. Sprinkle with parsley. Cover and refrigerate at least 2 hours or overnight. Remove chicken from bones; discard bones. Return chicken to fruit mixture; let stand 15 minutes. Serve with a slotted spoon. Yield: 6 servings (serving size: about 4 ounces chicken and about ¼ cup fruit mixture).

CALORIES 328 (26% from fat); FAT 9.6g (sat 1.7g, mono 5.4g, poly 1.7g); PROTEIN 38.2g; CARB 19g; FIBER 2.4g; CHOL 102mg; IRON 2.7mg; SODIUM 393mg; CALC 42mg

Couscous Chicken Salad

The couscous cooks in a little less liquid than normal, and the broth simmers instead of boils. That allows the couscous to absorb the seasonings while it chills overnight and to maintain a fluffy texture.

- 1½ cups fat-free, less-sodium chicken broth
- 12 ounces skinless, boneless chicken breast
- 1 (10-ounce) package couscous
- 1 cup chopped fresh basil
- ¼ cup extravirgin olive oil
- 3 tablespoons sherry vinegar
- ¾ teaspoon salt
- ¼ teaspoon freshly ground black pepper
- 1 garlic clove, minced
- 1½ cups halved cherry tomatoes
- 1 cup sliced green onions
- 1 (15½-ounce) can chickpeas (garbanzo beans), rinsed and drained

1. Bring broth to a boil in a medium saucepan. Add chicken; cover, reduce heat, and simmer 10 minutes or until chicken is done. Remove chicken using a slotted spoon; set aside. Cool slightly; coarsely chop.
2. While chicken cools, add couscous to broth; stir well. Cover and let stand 10 minutes. Place couscous in a large bowl; cool completely. Fluff with a fork. Stir in basil and next 5 ingredients. Add chopped chicken, tomatoes, onions, and chickpeas; toss gently to combine. Cover and refrigerate at least 2 hours or overnight. Yield: 8 servings (serving size: about 1 cup).

CALORIES 322 (23% from fat); FAT 8.1g (sat 1.1g, mono 5.3g, poly 1g); PROTEIN 18.5g; CARB 42.8g; FIBER 4.9g; CHOL 25mg; IRON 1.9mg; SODIUM 502mg; CALC 42mg

Grilled Vegetable Antipasto

Grilling the zucchini and the eggplant makes them more absorbent, which allows them to soak up more of the vinaigrette.

- 2 red bell peppers
- 2 zucchini (about 1 pound), each cut in half lengthwise
- 2 Japanese eggplant (about 8 ounces), each cut in half lengthwise
- ¼ cup chopped fresh parsley
- ¼ cup balsamic vinegar
- 1 tablespoon extravirgin olive oil
- ¼ teaspoon salt
- 6 garlic cloves, peeled and crushed

1. Prepare grill.
2. Place peppers on grill rack; grill 15 minutes or until charred, turning occasionally. Place peppers in a zip-top plastic bag; seal and let stand 15 minutes. Peel peppers; discard seeds and membranes. Coarsely chop peppers; place in a large zip-top plastic bag. Place zucchini and eggplant on grill rack; grill 10 minutes, turning occasionally. Remove zucchini and eggplant from grill; let stand 10 minutes. Coarsely chop zucchini and eggplant; add to chopped peppers.
3. Combine parsley and remaining 4 ingredients, stirring with a whisk. Pour parsley mixture over pepper mixture. Seal bag; toss gently to coat. Refrigerate at least 2 hours or overnight. Yield: 4 servings (serving size: 1 cup).

CALORIES 122 (30% from fat); FAT 4g (sat 0.6g, mono 2.5g, poly 0.6g); PROTEIN 3.9g; CARB 21.1g; FIBER 6.7g; CHOL 0mg; IRON 1.7mg; SODIUM 163mg; CALC 52mg

Pan Bagnat

The salad-like ingredients of this French sandwich are wrapped tightly for a few hours so the flavors can blend.

- 4 (4-ounce) round rustic rolls
- 3 tablespoons sherry vinegar
- 2 tablespoons extravirgin olive oil
- 2 garlic cloves, minced
- 3 tablespoons fresh lemon juice
- 2 tablespoons chopped fresh parsley
- ¼ teaspoon black pepper
- 1 (12-ounce) can solid white tuna in water, drained
- 1 (12-ounce) bottle roasted red bell peppers, drained and sliced
- 4 plum tomatoes, cut into ¼-inch-thick slices
- 24 spinach leaves
- 8 canned anchovy fillets, chopped (about ¾ ounce)
- 4 thin red onion slices

1. Split rolls in half. Hollow out top and bottom halves of rolls, leaving ½-inch-thick shells; reserve torn bread for another use. Combine vinegar, oil, and garlic; stir with a whisk. Spoon vinegar mixture evenly over cut sides of rolls.

2. Combine juice, parsley, black pepper, and tuna. Spoon ½ cup tuna mixture on bottom half of each roll. Layer bell pepper slices, tomato slices, spinach leaves, anchovies, and onion evenly over tuna mixture. Cover with tops of rolls. Wrap each roll tightly with plastic wrap, and refrigerate 2 hours or overnight. Yield: 4 servings (serving size: 1 sandwich).

CALORIES 540 (27% from fat); FAT 16.3g (sat 4.4g, mono 6.8g, poly 3.6g); PROTEIN 34.6g; CARB 64.6g; FIBER 4.4g; CHOL 40mg; IRON 6.4mg; SODIUM 1,111mg; CALC 96mg

superfast

. . . And Ready in Just About 20 Minutes

No need to wait for the pizza guy—the two pies in this month's offering are faster than delivery.

Pork Medallions with Red Peppers and Artichokes

Two-ounce pork chops are wafer thin and often referred to as "breakfast chops." If your chops are thicker, you'll need to cook them longer.

2 teaspoons olive oil
Cooking spray
8 (2-ounce) boneless center-cut loin pork chops
¼ teaspoon dried Italian seasoning
⅛ teaspoon salt
⅛ teaspoon coarsely ground black pepper
2 cups red bell pepper strips
1 cup fat-free, less-sodium chicken broth
2 tablespoons tomato paste
¼ teaspoon dried thyme
¼ teaspoon dried rubbed sage
1 (14-ounce) can artichoke hearts, drained

1. Heat oil in a large nonstick skillet coated with cooking spray over medium-high heat. Sprinkle pork with Italian seasoning, salt, and black pepper. Add pork to pan, and cook 1 minute on each side or until lightly browned. Remove from pan. Add bell pepper to pan; sauté 2 minutes.
2. Combine broth, tomato paste, thyme, and sage, stirring with a whisk.
3. Return pork to pan, and add broth mixture and artichoke hearts. Cover, reduce heat, and simmer 8 minutes or until thoroughly heated. Remove pork from pan, and keep warm. Increase heat to medium-high; cook 2 minutes or until artichoke mixture is slightly thickened. Spoon artichoke mixture over pork. Yield: 4 servings (serving size: 2 pork chops and 1 cup artichoke mixture).

CALORIES 245 (22% from fat); FAT 6.3g (sat 1.7g, mono 3.4g, poly 0.7g); PROTEIN 29.8g; CARB 17.4g; FIBER 5.7g; CHOL 74mg; IRON 2.5mg; SODIUM 782mg; CALC 22mg

Chicken Puttanesca Pizza

If you use leftover cooked chicken instead of packaged, you'll need about 1 cup.

1 (10-ounce) Italian cheese-flavored pizza crust (such as Boboli)
1⅓ cups mushroom-and-olive pasta sauce (such as Classico)
2 teaspoons capers
¼ teaspoon crushed red pepper
1 (6-ounce) package Italian-style cooked chicken breast (such as Louis Rich)
¾ cup (3 ounces) shredded part-skim mozzarella cheese

1. Preheat oven to 450°.
2. Place pizza crust on a baking sheet. Spread pasta sauce over crust, leaving a 1-inch border; top with capers, pepper, and chicken. Sprinkle with cheese. Bake at 450° for 12 minutes or until crust is crisp. Cut into 4 wedges. Yield: 4 servings (serving size: 1 wedge).

CALORIES 342 (25% from fat); FAT 9.6g (sat 2.3g, mono 1g, poly 0.1g); PROTEIN 24.3g; CARB 38.5g; FIBER 1.4g; CHOL 39mg; IRON 1.8mg; SODIUM 1,178mg; CALC 343mg

Chicken with Cranberry-Port Sauce

Serve this dish with quick-cooking wild rice and a spinach salad.

2 teaspoons olive oil
Cooking spray
4 (6-ounce) skinless, boneless chicken breast halves
1½ tablespoons Italian-seasoned breadcrumbs
½ cup fat-free, less-sodium chicken broth
¼ cup tawny port or other sweet red wine
¼ cup cranberry chutney (such as Crosse and Blackwell)
1 teaspoon cornstarch
⅛ teaspoon coarsely ground black pepper
⅛ teaspoon dried rubbed sage

1. Heat oil in a large nonstick skillet coated with cooking spray over medium-high heat. Dredge chicken in breadcrumbs. Add to pan, and cook 2 minutes on each side or until lightly browned.
2. Combine broth and remaining 5 ingredients, stirring with a whisk. Add to pan; reduce heat to medium. Cover and cook 10 minutes or until chicken is done.
3. Remove chicken from pan. Bring broth mixture to a boil, and cook until reduced to ½ cup (about 1 minute). Spoon sauce over chicken. Yield: 4 servings (serving size: 1 chicken breast half and 2 tablespoons sauce).

CALORIES 262 (15% from fat); FAT 4.5g (sat 0.9g, mono 2.2g, poly 0.7g); PROTEIN 40g; CARB 12.6g; FIBER 0.1g; CHOL 99mg; IRON 1.4mg; SODIUM 234mg; CALC 25mg

Pan-Seared Scallops with Cilantro-Celery Mayonnaise

When done, scallops should feel soft to the touch. They should also flake easily when tested with a fork and appear moist inside.

- ¼ cup low-fat mayonnaise
- 2 tablespoons minced celery
- 2 teaspoons minced fresh cilantro
- ¼ teaspoon salt
- ⅛ teaspoon black pepper
- 1 teaspoon olive oil
- Cooking spray
- 1½ pounds sea scallops
- ¼ cup Italian-seasoned breadcrumbs
- 4 lime wedges

1. Combine first 5 ingredients.
2. Heat oil in a large nonstick skillet coated with cooking spray over medium-high heat. Dredge scallops in breadcrumbs. Add scallops to pan; cook 4 minutes. Turn scallops; cook 3 minutes or until done. Serve with mayonnaise mixture and lime wedges. Yield: 4 servings (serving size: 5 ounces scallops, 1 tablespoon mayonnaise mixture, and 1 lime wedge).

CALORIES 216 (16% from fat); FAT 3.8g (sat 0.3g, mono 0.9g, poly 0.5g); PROTEIN 29.3g; CARB 14.7g; FIBER 0.8g; CHOL 56mg; IRON 0.8mg; SODIUM 743mg; CALC 58mg

Three-Cheese Pizza with Mushrooms and Basil

- Cooking spray
- 1 (8-ounce) package presliced mushrooms
- ½ cup part-skim ricotta cheese
- ¼ cup (1 ounce) preshredded fresh Parmesan cheese
- 1 (10-ounce) Italian cheese-flavored pizza crust (such as Boboli)
- 1 cup chunky vegetable pasta sauce (such as Ragú)
- ½ cup (2 ounces) preshredded part-skim mozzarella cheese
- 2 tablespoons thinly sliced fresh basil

1. Preheat oven to 450°.
2. Heat a large nonstick skillet coated with cooking spray over medium-high heat. Add mushrooms; sauté 5 minutes. Remove from heat.
3. Combine ricotta and Parmesan cheeses. Place pizza crust on a baking sheet. Spread pasta sauce over crust; leave a 1-inch border. Dollop ricotta cheese mixture evenly over sauce; top with mushrooms. Sprinkle with mozzarella. Bake at 450° for 12 minutes or until crust is crisp. Sprinkle with basil; cut into 4 wedges. Yield: 4 servings (serving size: 1 wedge).

CALORIES 356 (26% from fat); FAT 10.1g (sat 4g, mono 1.8g, poly 0.2g); PROTEIN 19.4g; CARB 42g; FIBER 2g; CHOL 21mg; IRON 2.2mg; SODIUM 1,033mg; CALC 445mg

Open-Faced Mushroom, Tomato, and Goat-Cheese Sandwiches

To soften the goat cheese for easy spreading, microwave it at MEDIUM for 1 minute.

- ½ teaspoon olive oil
- Cooking spray
- 1 cup thinly sliced onion, separated into rings
- 1 cup thinly sliced red bell pepper
- 1 (6-ounce) package portobello mushroom caps, thinly sliced
- 2 teaspoons red wine vinegar
- 1 teaspoon capers
- ¼ teaspoon salt
- ⅛ teaspoon black pepper
- 3 ounces goat cheese
- 3 (2-ounce) slices sourdough bread, toasted
- 9 (⅛-inch-thick) slices tomato

1. Heat oil in a large nonstick skillet coated with cooking spray over medium heat. Add onion and bell pepper; sauté 4 minutes. Add mushroom caps, and sauté 5 minutes or until tender. Remove pan from heat. Stir in vinegar, capers, salt, and black pepper.
2. Spread about 2 tablespoons cheese over each bread slice, and top each with 3 tomato slices and ⅔ cup mushroom mixture. Yield: 3 servings (serving size: 1 sandwich).

CALORIES 410 (22% from fat); FAT 10.2g (sat 4.9g, mono 3.1g, poly 1.1g); PROTEIN 16.7g; CARB 63.5g; FIBER 6.4g; CHOL 13mg; IRON 4mg; SODIUM 922mg; CALC 133mg

season's best

Buttery Apple Crumble

Autumn's glory is never more evident than in the apples abundant in September.

Buttery Apple Crumble

Whole wheat flour adds an unexpected nutty flavor to the oatmeal topping. Removing the foil halfway through baking allows the topping to become crisp and browned.

- ¾ cup whole wheat flour
- 1¼ cups regular oats
- ½ cup packed brown sugar
- 1 teaspoon ground cinnamon
- ½ teaspoon salt
- ½ cup butter, melted
- 2 teaspoons vanilla extract, divided
- ½ cup apple cider
- ¼ cup granulated sugar
- 1½ teaspoons cornstarch
- Dash of salt
- 10 cups sliced peeled baking apples
- Cooking spray

1. Preheat oven to 375°.
2. Lightly spoon flour into a dry measuring cup, and level with a knife. Combine flour, oats, brown sugar, cinnamon, and ½ teaspoon salt in a small bowl. Add butter and 1 teaspoon vanilla; stir with a fork until moist and crumbly.
3. Combine 1 teaspoon vanilla, cider, granulated sugar, cornstarch, and dash of salt in a large bowl; stir with a whisk until sugar dissolves and mixture is smooth. Add apples; toss to coat. Spoon apple mixture into a 13 x 9-inch baking dish coated with cooking spray. Sprinkle with oat mixture. Cover with foil; bake at 375° for 30 minutes. Uncover and bake 30 minutes or until browned and bubbly. Yield: 9 servings (serving size: ⅔ cup).

CALORIES 356 (31% from fat); FAT 12.2g (sat 6.6g, mono 3.4g, poly 1.1g); PROTEIN 5.3g; CARB 59.6g; FIBER 6g; CHOL 27mg; IRON 1.8mg; SODIUM 257mg; CALC 36mg

Italian-American Comes of Age

Fresh interpretations of classic recipes

Spurned by restaurant chefs and dismissed as cliché—the fare of mediocre chain restaurants and the Mafia in the media—Italian-American cooking is finally receiving recognition as a cuisine in its own right.

A bumper crop of cookbooks, with titles like *Lidia's Italian-American Kitchen*, by Lidia Matticchio Bastianich, *The Italian-American Cookbook*, by John and Galina Mariani, and *Italian Comfort Food*, by the Marion Scotto family, has fueled new interest in Italian cooking in the United States. These and other books—from which the following recipes were adapted—offer fresh interpretations of classic recipes, including spaghetti with meatballs, shrimp scampi, minestrone, and pizza.

STAFF FAVORITE • QUICK & EASY
Chicken Cacciatore "Pronto"

"I took the classic theme of chicken cacciatore and re-created it with a minimum of ingredients and cooking time. The result is lots of flavor from using only chicken thighs and a base layer of seasoning from dried porcini mushrooms—a perfect weeknight or 'everyday' meal."
–Michael Chiarello (Recipe adapted from *Michael Chiarello's Casual Cooking*, by Michael Chiarello; Chronicle Books, 2002.)

    1   (½-ounce) package dried porcini
        mushrooms
    1   cup boiling water
    2   teaspoons olive oil
    8   skinless, boneless chicken thighs
        (about 1 pound)
    1   teaspoon salt
    ½   teaspoon freshly ground black
        pepper
    3   garlic cloves, minced
    3   tablespoons minced fresh parsley,
        divided
    ¾   cup canned crushed tomatoes
    ½   cup fat-free, less-sodium chicken
        broth
    ½   cup water

1. Combine mushrooms and boiling water in a bowl; cover and let stand 30 minutes. Remove mushrooms with a slotted spoon. Finely chop mushrooms; set aside. Strain soaking liquid into a bowl through a sieve lined with cheesecloth or paper towels. Discard solids; reserve soaking liquid.

2. Heat oil in a large nonstick skillet over medium-high heat. Sprinkle chicken with salt and pepper. Add chicken to pan; cook 4 minutes on each side or until browned. Remove chicken from pan. Reduce heat to medium. Add garlic to pan; sauté 2 minutes or until golden. Add 2 tablespoons parsley; sauté 30 seconds. Add chopped mushrooms; sauté 30 seconds. Stir in reserved soaking liquid, tomatoes, broth, and ½ cup water; bring to a simmer. Return chicken to pan, and reduce heat to low. Cover and cook 10 minutes or until chicken is done.

3. Remove chicken; keep warm. Increase heat to medium-high; cook until sauce is reduced to 1 cup (about 5 minutes). Spoon sauce over chicken; sprinkle with 1 tablespoon parsley. Yield: 4 servings (serving size: 2 chicken thighs and ¼ cup sauce).

CALORIES 263 (29% from fat); FAT 8.5g (sat 1.7g, mono 3.7g, poly 1.8g); PROTEIN 33.6g; CARB 11.7g; FIBER 3.5g; CHOL 115mg; IRON 5.7mg; SODIUM 771mg; CALC 32mg

Pork Scaloppine Perugina

"The origins of this dish lie in the Italian university town of Perugia. But many of the ingredients and the cooking technique—cutting the meat into scaloppine and sautéing it in a wine and caper sauce—are Italian-American."
–Mario Batali (Recipe adapted from *Simple Italian Food: Recipes from My Two Villages*, by Mario Batali; Clarkson Potter, 1998.)

    4   (4-ounce) boneless center-cut loin
        pork chops (about ¾ inch thick)
    ¼   cup all-purpose flour
    ½   teaspoon freshly ground black
        pepper
    4   teaspoons olive oil, divided
    1   tablespoon capers, rinsed and
        drained
    2   ounces very thin slices prosciutto,
        cut into ¼ inch strips
    2   garlic cloves, thinly sliced
    ½   cup fat-free, less-sodium chicken
        broth
    1   teaspoon all-purpose flour
    1½ cups dry white wine
    1½ tablespoons grated lemon rind
    1   teaspoon finely chopped fresh
        sage
    4   canned anchovy fillets, drained,
        rinsed, and chopped
    4   cups hot cooked fresh fettuccine
        (1 [9-ounce] package)

1. Place each piece of pork between 2 sheets of heavy-duty plastic wrap; pound each piece to ½-inch thickness using a meat mallet or rolling pin. Combine ¼ cup flour and pepper in a shallow dish. Dredge pork in flour mixture; set aside.

2. Heat 1 teaspoon oil in a large nonstick skillet over medium-high heat. Add capers, prosciutto, and garlic; sauté 3 minutes. Combine broth and 1 teaspoon flour, stirring well with a whisk. Add broth mixture, wine, rind, sage, and anchovies to pan, and cook 10 minutes, stirring occasionally. Pour sauce into a bowl; keep warm. Wipe pan clean with a paper towel.

Continued

3. Heat 1 tablespoon oil in pan over medium-high heat. Add pork to pan; cook 2 minutes on each side or until done. Add sauce to pan; cook 30 seconds or until thoroughly heated, stirring constantly. Remove pork from pan. Add pasta to pan; toss well to coat. Place 1 cup pasta on each of 4 plates; top each serving with 1 chop. Yield: 4 servings.

CALORIES 421 (30% from fat); FAT 14.4g (sat 4g, mono 6.8g, poly 1.2g); PROTEIN 30.6g; CARB 26.5g; FIBER 1.7g; CHOL 74mg; IRON 2.7mg; SODIUM 592mg; CALC 54mg

QUICK & EASY
Linguine with Clam Sauce

"This is a classic Italian-American dish, but it's also a dish we eat in Italy every summer. It's so fresh and simple. But you absolutely have to use fresh clams."
–Marion Scotto (Recipe adapted from *Italian Comfort Food*, by Marion Scotto, Rosanna Scotto, Anthony Scotto Jr., and Elaina Scotto; HarperCollins, 2002.)
Use the larger amount of red pepper for a zestier dish.

- ¼ cup olive oil, divided
- 2 garlic cloves, minced
- ⅓ cup clam juice
- ¼ cup chopped fresh flat-leaf parsley
- ½ to ¾ teaspoon crushed red pepper
- ½ teaspoon salt
- ¼ teaspoon freshly ground black pepper
- 3 dozen littleneck clams
- 8 cups hot cooked linguine (about 1 pound uncooked pasta)

1. Heat 2 tablespoons oil in a large skillet over medium heat. Add garlic; cook 3 minutes or until golden, stirring frequently. Stir in clam juice and next 5 ingredients. Cover and cook 10 minutes or until clams open. Discard any unopened clams.
2. Place pasta in a large bowl. Add 2 tablespoons oil; toss well to coat. Add clam mixture to pasta; toss well. Yield: 6 servings (serving size: 1⅓ cups pasta mixture and about 6 clams).

CALORIES 398 (24% from fat); FAT 10.6g (sat 1.6g, mono 6.7g, poly 0.9g); PROTEIN 17.4g; CARB 58.4g; FIBER 2.6g; CHOL 19mg; IRON 10.3mg; SODIUM 258mg; CALC 46mg

Butternut Squash Risotto

"Here's a perfect example of a traditional Italian dish and cooking technique adapted to an American ingredient. Where the recipe originated in Italy, the Italian pumpkin, *zucca barucca*, is used. But here in the States, I use butternut squash. In fact, I have served this risotto as a first course for our Thanksgiving."
–Giuliano Hazan (Recipe adapted from *Every Night Italian*, by Giuliano Hazan; Scribner, 2000.)

- 2 cups water, divided
- 2 (14¼-ounce) cans low-salt beef broth
- 2 teaspoons olive oil
- ½ cup finely chopped yellow onion
- 3 cups (¾-inch) cubed peeled butternut squash (about 1 pound)
- ½ teaspoon salt
- ¼ teaspoon freshly ground black pepper
- 1½ cups Arborio rice or other short-grain rice
- ½ cup (2 ounces) grated Parmigiano-Reggiano cheese
- 3 tablespoons unsalted butter
- 2 tablespoons finely chopped fresh parsley

1. Bring 1½ cups water and broth to a simmer in a large saucepan (do not boil). Keep warm over low heat.
2. Heat oil in a Dutch oven over medium heat. Add onion; cook 8 minutes or until golden, stirring frequently. Add ½ cup water, squash, salt, and pepper; cook 10 minutes or until squash is tender and water has almost evaporated. Add rice; stir until combined. Stir in ½ cup broth mixture; cook until liquid is nearly absorbed, stirring constantly. Add remaining broth mixture, ½ cup at a time, stirring constantly until each portion of broth is absorbed before adding next (about 30 minutes total). Stir in cheese, butter, and parsley. Serve immediately. Yield: 8 servings (serving size: ⅔ cup).

CALORIES 272 (25% from fat); FAT 7.6g (sat 4g, mono 2.8g, poly 0.5g); PROTEIN 7.9g; CARB 41.4g; FIBER 2.8g; CHOL 15mg; IRON 1mg; SODIUM 275mg; CALC 119mg

> # The enduring love affair between Americans and Italian food is unlikely to diminish.

QUICK & EASY
Shrimp Scampi

"This is an example of how Italian-American restaurant cooks adapt a basic Italian food idea. *Scampi* is a Venetian dialect word for a local prawn, rarely found in American markets. So Italian-American cooks use shrimp instead, cooking it with a little garlic."
–John Mariani (Recipe adapted from *The Italian-American Cookbook*, by John and Galina Mariani; Harvard Common Press, 2000.)

- 2 teaspoons olive oil
- 28 large shrimp, peeled and deveined (about 1½ pounds)
- 3 garlic cloves, minced
- ⅓ cup Sauvignon Blanc or other dry white wine
- ½ teaspoon salt
- ¼ teaspoon freshly ground black pepper
- ¼ cup chopped fresh flat-leaf parsley
- 1 tablespoon fresh lemon juice

1. Heat oil in a large skillet over medium-high heat. Add shrimp; sauté 1 minute. Add garlic; sauté 1 minute. Stir in wine, salt, and pepper; bring mixture to a boil. Reduce heat to medium; cook 30 seconds. Add parsley and juice; toss well to coat. Cook 1 minute or until shrimp are done. Yield: 4 servings (serving size: 7 shrimp).

CALORIES 220 (21% from fat); FAT 5.2g (sat 0.9g, mono 2.1g, poly 1.3g); PROTEIN 34.9g; CARB 3.1g; FIBER 0.2g; CHOL 259mg; IRON 4.5mg; SODIUM 546mg; CALC 100mg

Spaghetti and Meatballs

"I don't remember having spaghetti and meatballs as a child at home; we had *polpette*, which had the shape of crab cakes. Spaghetti and meatballs, on the other hand, is a big Italian-American dish, a cuisine born out of the early Italian immigrants adapting to the New World."
–Lidia Matticchio Bastianich (Recipe adapted from *Lidia's Italian-American Kitchen*, by Lidia Matticchio Bastianich; Knopf, 2001.)

SAUCE:

  5 (14.5-ounce) cans no-salt-added whole tomatoes, undrained
  1 tablespoon olive oil
  1 cup chopped onion
  1 teaspoon crushed red pepper
  ¾ teaspoon salt
  ¼ teaspoon freshly ground black pepper
  2 bay leaves

MEATBALLS:

  1 (1-ounce) slice white bread
  ⅓ cup (about 1½ ounces) grated Parmigiano-Reggiano cheese
  ¼ cup milk
  ¼ cup chopped fresh flat-leaf parsley
  ½ teaspoon salt
  ¼ teaspoon freshly ground black pepper
  1 pound ground sirloin
  2 garlic cloves, peeled and minced
  1 large egg white
Cooking spray

REMAINING INGREDIENTS:

  1 pound uncooked spaghetti
  ⅓ cup (about 1½ ounces) grated Parmigiano-Reggiano cheese

1. To prepare sauce, place half of tomatoes in a blender or food processor, and process until smooth. Pour puréed tomatoes into a large bowl. Repeat procedure with remaining tomatoes.
2. Heat olive oil in a Dutch oven over medium heat. Add onion; sauté 4 minutes. Stir in puréed tomatoes, red pepper, salt, black pepper, and bay leaves; bring to a boil. Reduce heat, and simmer 30 minutes, stirring occasionally. Remove

from heat. Discard bay leaves. Keep sauce warm.
3. Preheat oven to 400°.
4. To prepare meatballs, place bread in a food processor; pulse 10 times or until coarse crumbs measure ½ cup. Combine breadcrumbs, ⅓ cup cheese, and next 7 ingredients. Shape mixture into 24 (1-inch) meatballs, and place on a broiler pan coated with cooking spray. Bake at 400° for 15 minutes or until done. Add meatballs to sauce; cook over low heat 15 minutes or until thoroughly heated.
5. Cook pasta according to package directions, omitting salt and fat. Drain pasta; return to pot. Spoon about 2 cups tomato sauce (leaving meatballs in pan) into pasta, and toss well to coat. Transfer pasta mixture to a platter; top with remaining sauce and meatballs. Sprinkle with ⅓ cup cheese. Yield: 8 servings (serving size: about ¾ cup pasta mixture, ½ cup sauce, and 3 meatballs).

CALORIES 449 (25% from fat); FAT 12.5g (sat 4.9g, mono 5.1g, poly 0.6g); PROTEIN 27.4g; CARB 58.3g; FIBER 4.9g; CHOL 50mg; IRON 4.8mg; SODIUM 633mg; CALC 239mg

---

Wine Note

There are very few meals (with the exception of breakfast) that Italians eat without an accompanying glass of wine. From a culinary standpoint, wine, with its acidity and tannin, works as a textural counterpoint to dishes that are made with olive oil. Lots of wines work well with Italian fare—and not just obvious choices such as Chianti, a red wine made principally from Sangiovese grapes. Italian whites, such as Pinot Grigio and Vernaccia di San Gimignano, for instance, can be just the ticket. Or for a more flavorful white, consider wines like Tocai Friulano or Gavi. Good non-Italian options, both white and red, include California Sauvignon Blanc (with the Shrimp Scampi [recipe on page 310] or the Linguine with Clam Sauce [recipe on page 310], for example), California Pinot Noir, and even Zinfandel.

---

inspired vegetarian

Hearty Fall Soups

Simple, soulful, and satisfying soups warm you from the inside out.

Grano and Chickpea Soup with Parmesan-Herb Topping

Grano, polished durum wheat, is new to the United States (to find out more about it, visit www.sunnylandmills.com). If you have trouble finding grano, substitute wheat berries that have been soaked overnight or pearl barley.

  1 tablespoon olive oil
  2¼ cups chopped onion
  ½ cup chopped celery
  2 garlic cloves, minced
  2 tablespoons tomato paste
  ¾ cup dry white wine
  1½ quarts water
  1 cup grano
  1 teaspoon sea salt
  ½ teaspoon freshly ground black pepper
  1 teaspoon chopped fresh basil
  1 (15½-ounce) can chickpeas (garbanzo beans), drained
  1 (14.5-ounce) can diced tomatoes, undrained
  ½ cup (2 ounces) grated fresh Parmesan cheese
  2 tablespoons chopped fresh parsley
  2 tablespoons chopped fresh basil
  1 garlic clove, minced
  1 tablespoon extravirgin olive oil

1. Heat 1 tablespoon olive oil in a large Dutch oven over medium-high heat. Add onion, celery, and 2 garlic cloves; sauté 5 minutes. Reduce heat to medium, and cook 5 minutes or until lightly browned, stirring frequently. Stir in tomato paste. Add wine; cook 2 minutes, stirring frequently. Add water, grano,
Continued

salt, and pepper. Cover and simmer 30 minutes. Add 1 teaspoon basil, chickpeas, and tomatoes. Cook 5 minutes or until thoroughly heated.

2. Combine cheese, parsley, 2 tablespoons basil, and 1 garlic clove. Ladle 1⅓ cups soup into each of 6 bowls. Drizzle each serving with ½ teaspoon extravirgin olive oil; top each serving with about 2 tablespoons cheese mixture. Yield: 6 servings.

CALORIES 291 (26% from fat); FAT 8.4g (sat 2.2g, mono 4.5g, poly 1.1g); PROTEIN 11.1g; CARB 40.6g; FIBER 6.2g; CHOL 6mg; IRON 2.5mg; SODIUM 751mg; CALC 165mg

---

MAKE AHEAD • FREEZABLE
Late Fall Garden Soup with Kale and Rice

If you can find black kale (cavalo nero), try it in place of regular kale. Serve with a grilled Swiss cheese sandwich on sourdough bread with sliced tomato or a grilled fontina sandwich with roasted red bell peppers.

  2 teaspoons olive oil
  2 cups sliced leek (about 2 large)
  2 cups cubed baking potato
  5 cups water, divided
  2 cups thinly sliced kale
  ¼ cup uncooked long-grain rice
  ¾ teaspoon sea salt
  ½ teaspoon dried thyme
  ¼ teaspoon freshly ground black pepper
  1 garlic clove, minced
  2 vegetable-flavored dry bouillon cubes
  ½ cup (2 ounces) grated Asiago cheese

1. Heat oil in a large Dutch oven over medium heat. Add leek and potato; cook 8 minutes or until leek is tender, stirring frequently. Add ⅓ cup water, kale and next 5 ingredients; cook 5 minutes or until kale wilts, stirring frequently. Add 4⅔ cups water and bouillon cubes; bring to a boil. Reduce heat, and simmer 20 minutes. Sprinkle each serving with 2 tablespoons cheese. Yield: 4 servings (serving size: 1½ cups).

CALORIES 222 (28% from fat); FAT 6.9g (sat 3g, mono 2.8g, poly 0.6g); PROTEIN 8.5g; CARB 33.1g; FIBER 2.7g; CHOL 13mg; IRON 2.9mg; SODIUM 832mg; CALC 225mg

---

STAFF FAVORITE • MAKE AHEAD
Butternut Squash Soup with Sautéed Radicchio

A topping of sautéed radicchio tossed with balsamic vinegar and topped with grated Parmesan cheese provides a slightly bitter, sharp contrast to the creamy, sweet soup.

  3 pounds butternut squash (about 2 medium)
     Cooking spray
  5 teaspoons olive oil, divided
  5½ cups finely chopped onion (about 2 large)
  ¼ cup chopped fresh parsley
  2 tablespoons chopped fresh or ½ tablespoon dried sage
  ½ teaspoon chopped fresh or ⅛ teaspoon dried thyme
  4½ cups water
  1½ teaspoons sea salt, divided
  ½ teaspoon coarsely ground black pepper, divided
  2 garlic cloves, minced
  6 cups thinly sliced radicchio (about 1¼ pounds)
  1 tablespoon balsamic vinegar
  6 tablespoons (about 1½ ounces) grated fresh Parmesan cheese

1. Preheat oven to 375°.

2. Cut squash in half lengthwise; remove seeds. Place squash halves, cut sides down, on a foil-lined baking sheet coated with cooking spray. Bake at 375° for 30 minutes or until tender. Scoop out pulp; set aside. Discard skins.

3. Heat 2 teaspoons oil in a large Dutch oven over medium heat. Add onion, parsley, sage, and thyme; cook 15 minutes or until lightly browned, stirring frequently. Add squash, water, 1¼ teaspoons salt, ¼ teaspoon pepper, and garlic; bring to a boil. Partially cover, reduce heat, and simmer 25 minutes. Place about 2½ cups squash mixture in a blender, and process until smooth. Pour puréed soup into a large bowl. Repeat procedure with remaining squash mixture, 2½ cups at a time.

4. Heat 1 tablespoon oil in a large nonstick skillet over medium-high heat. Add radicchio, ¼ teaspoon salt, and ¼ teaspoon pepper; sauté 5 minutes or until

lightly browned. Remove from heat; drizzle with vinegar, tossing to coat. Ladle 1⅓ cups soup into each of 6 bowls. Top each serving with ⅓ cup radicchio and 1 tablespoon cheese. Yield: 6 servings.

CALORIES 217 (26% from fat); FAT 6.2g (sat 1.8g, mono 3.4g, poly 0.6g); PROTEIN 6.9g; CARB 38.1g; FIBER 9.6g; CHOL 5mg; IRON 2.2mg; SODIUM 712mg; CALC 224mg

---

MAKE AHEAD
Creamy Mushroom Soup with Tarragon

The bread disappears into the soup to give it body. Dried mushrooms enhance the flavor of the fresh mushrooms. For a nice presentation, sauté some additional sliced button mushrooms to use as a garnish with the chives.

  2 teaspoons butter
  1¾ cups chopped onion
  ⅓ cup dried porcini mushrooms (about ½ ounce)
  1 teaspoon minced fresh tarragon
  ½ teaspoon chopped fresh thyme
  1 bay leaf
  2 garlic cloves, minced
  ½ cup dry white wine
  1½ teaspoons sea salt, divided
  ½ teaspoon cracked black pepper
  1 (8-ounce) package button mushrooms, chopped
  1 (8-ounce) package cremini mushrooms, chopped
  1 (1¼-ounce) slice whole wheat bread
  5½ cups water
  1 vegetable-flavored or mushroom-flavored dry bouillon cube
  ⅔ cup half-and-half
  2 tablespoons chopped fresh chives

1. Melt butter in a large Dutch oven over medium-high heat. Add onion and next 4 ingredients; sauté 10 minutes or until onion is lightly browned. Add garlic, and cook 2 minutes, stirring frequently. Add wine, scraping pan to loosen browned bits. Add 1 teaspoon salt, pepper, button mushrooms, and cremini mushrooms. Cook 10 minutes, stirring occasionally.

2. Place bread in a food processor; pulse 5 times or until crumbly. Add breadcrumbs, water, and bouillon cube to pan. Reduce heat; simmer 20 minutes. Discard bay leaf.

3. Place about 2½ cups mushroom mixture in a blender; process until smooth. Pour puréed soup into a large bowl. Repeat procedure with remaining mushroom mixture, 2½ cups at a time. Stir in ½ teaspoon salt and half-and-half. Top each serving with 1 teaspoon chives. Yield: 6 servings (serving size: 1⅓ cups).

WINE NOTE: In Europe, rich soups such as this creamy, earthy mushroom soup are often served with a dry amontillado Sherry. Osborne Amontillado "Coquinero" Sherry nonvintage from Jerez, Spain ($16) is a great choice.

CALORIES 150 (29% from fat); FAT 4.8g (sat 2.7g, mono 1.6g, poly 0.3g); PROTEIN 7.6g; CARB 16.1g; FIBER 4g; CHOL 17mg; IRON 2.9mg; SODIUM 767mg; CALC 61mg

MAKE AHEAD • FREEZABLE

Pressure Cooker Bean and Pasta Soup

Use a pressure cooker to make this soup in less than 1 hour, even if you haven't soaked the beans. We top each serving with fruity extravirgin olive oil.

- 2 cups dried cannellini beans or other white beans
- 4 quarts water, divided
- 2 tablespoons olive oil
- 2 cups cubed peeled baking potato
- 1½ cups chopped onion
- 1½ tablespoons minced fresh or 1 teaspoon dried crushed rosemary
- 2 garlic cloves, chopped
- ½ teaspoon freshly ground black pepper
- 1 (3-inch) piece Parmigiano-Reggiano cheese rind
- 2 cups uncooked whole wheat seashell pasta
- 2½ teaspoons sea salt
- 1 (14.5-ounce) can diced tomatoes, undrained
- ½ cup (2 ounces) grated Parmigiano-Reggiano cheese
- 2 tablespoons balsamic vinegar
- 4 teaspoons extravirgin olive oil

1. Sort and wash beans. Combine beans and 2 quarts water in a 6-quart pressure cooker. Close lid securely; bring to high pressure over high heat. Adjust heat to medium or level needed to maintain high pressure; cook 3 minutes. Remove from heat; place pressure cooker under cold running water. Remove lid. Drain beans. Place beans in a bowl; wipe pan dry with paper towels.

2. Heat 2 tablespoons oil in pan over medium-high heat. Add potato, onion, rosemary, and garlic; sauté 3 minutes. Add beans, 2 quarts water, pepper, and cheese rind to pan. Close lid securely; bring to high pressure over high heat. Adjust heat to medium or level needed to maintain high pressure; cook 40 minutes. Remove from heat; place pressure cooker under cold running water. Remove lid. Remove and discard cheese rind.

3. Cook pasta according to package directions, omitting salt and fat. Add pasta, salt, and tomatoes to soup. Ladle 1¼ cups soup into each of 8 bowls, and top each serving with 1 tablespoon grated cheese, ¾ teaspoon vinegar, and ½ teaspoon extravirgin olive oil. Yield: 8 servings.

CALORIES 372 (21% from fat); FAT 8.5g (sat 2.2g, mono 4.8g, poly 0.9g); PROTEIN 17.7g; CARB 59.4g; FIBER 13.3g; CHOL 5mg; IRON 4mg; SODIUM 910mg; CALC 198mg

---

Soup and Salad Supper Menu

serves 6

Snuggle by the fire and cozy up to this satisfying meal.

Lentil Soup with Chard

Gourmet greens with oranges and raisins*

Dinner rolls

*Arrange 1½ cups gourmet salad greens on each of 6 plates. Top each serving with ⅓ cup canned mandarin orange slices, 2 tablespoons chopped red onion, and 1 tablespoon raisins. Drizzle each serving with 1 tablespoon bottled low-fat balsamic vinaigrette.

MAKE AHEAD • FREEZABLE

Lentil Soup with Chard

Lentils are good with all kinds of greens—from sweet spinach and chard to pungent broccoli rabe, turnip greens, and mustard greens. Adding the greens toward the end of cooking keeps their color bright.

- 1¾ cups dried brown lentils
- 2 quarts water
- 1 cup chopped carrot
- 1¾ teaspoons sea salt
- Dash of dried thyme
- 2 garlic cloves, crushed
- 2 parsley sprigs
- 2 bay leaves
- 2 tablespoons butter
- 3 cups chopped onion
- 1 teaspoon ground cumin
- 6 cups torn Swiss chard
- 1 tablespoon fresh lemon juice
- ½ teaspoon freshly ground black pepper
- 6 tablespoons plain whole yogurt

1. Sort and wash lentils. Combine lentils, water, and next 6 ingredients in a large Dutch oven; bring to a boil. Cover, reduce heat, and simmer 45 minutes or until tender.

2. Melt butter in a large nonstick skillet over medium-high heat. Add onion and cumin; sauté 10 minutes or until browned. Stir onion mixture into lentil mixture. Discard bay leaves and parsley. Add chard to soup; simmer, uncovered, 10 minutes or until chard is tender. Remove soup from heat. Stir in juice and pepper. Ladle 1⅓ cups soup into each of 6 bowls; top each serving with 1 tablespoon yogurt. Yield: 6 servings.

CALORIES 283 (17% from fat); FAT 5.2g (sat 2.8g, mono 1.4g, poly 0.5g); PROTEIN 18.2g; CARB 43.9g; FIBER 20g; CHOL 12mg; IRON 6.2mg; SODIUM 810mg; CALC 95mg

Red Onion Soup

Attempting to make a vegetarian French onion soup is a challenge because most versions rely on beef broth. Red wine, tomato paste, and fresh herbs flavor this soup. Don't be tempted to use sweet yellow onions—besides being too sweet, they're also watery.

> 2 teaspoons butter
> Cooking spray
> 4 red onions, quartered and thinly sliced crosswise (about 2½ pounds)
> 1 teaspoon sea salt
> ¼ teaspoon freshly ground black pepper
> 1 cup dry red wine
> 2 tablespoons tomato paste
> 1 quart water
> 1 cup canned diced tomatoes, drained
> 1 teaspoon minced fresh rosemary
> ½ teaspoon chopped fresh thyme
> 4 parsley sprigs
> 2 bay leaves
> 1 tablespoon low-sodium soy sauce
> 6 (½-inch-thick) slices diagonally cut French bread baguette
> ¾ cup (3 ounces) shredded Gruyère cheese
> ⅓ cup (1½ ounces) grated Asiago cheese

1. Melt butter in a large Dutch oven coated with cooking spray over medium heat. Add onion, salt, and pepper; cover and cook over low heat 30 minutes or until onion is browned, stirring occasionally.
2. Increase heat to medium-high; stir in wine and tomato paste. Cook until wine almost evaporates (about 5 minutes). Add water and next 5 ingredients; bring to a boil. Cover, reduce heat, and simmer 20 minutes. Stir in soy sauce; discard parsley and bay leaves.
3. Preheat broiler.
4. Ladle 1⅓ cups soup into each of 6 ovenproof bowls. Place bowls on a baking sheet. Top each serving with 1 bread slice, and sprinkle each bread slice with 2 tablespoons Gruyère and about 1 tablespoon Asiago. Broil 3 minutes or until cheese melts. Yield: 6 servings.

CALORIES 264 (30% from fat); FAT 8.7g (sat 4.9g, mono 2.6g, poly 0.6g); PROTEIN 10.8g; CARB 30.6g; FIBER 5g; CHOL 26mg; IRON 1.4mg; SODIUM 732mg; CALC 276mg

Broccoli Rabe and White Bean Soup

Collard or mustard greens are good alternatives for the broccoli rabe.

> 8 ounces broccoli rabe (rapini)
> 1 tablespoon olive oil
> 2 cups coarsely chopped onion
> ¼ teaspoon crushed red pepper
> 2 garlic cloves, minced
> ½ teaspoon sea salt
> 5 cups water
> 1 (3-inch) piece Parmigiano-Reggiano cheese rind
> 1 (16-ounce) can cannellini beans or other white beans, rinsed and drained
> 5 (1-ounce) slices whole wheat bread, toasted
> 1 garlic clove, halved
> ½ cup (2 ounces) grated Parmigiano-Reggiano cheese

1. Remove and discard tough ends from broccoli rabe stems; coarsely chop broccoli rabe.
2. Heat oil in a large Dutch oven over medium heat. Add onion; cook 5 minutes, stirring frequently. Add red pepper and 2 garlic cloves; sauté 1 minute. Add broccoli rabe and salt, and sauté 30 seconds. Add water and cheese rind. Increase heat to medium-high; bring to a boil. Reduce heat; simmer 15 minutes. Add beans, and simmer 5 minutes. Discard cheese rind.
3. Rub both sides of toasted bread with cut sides of halved garlic clove. Tear toasts into bite-sized pieces; divide toast pieces evenly among 4 bowls. Ladle 1½ cups soup over toast pieces in each bowl; top each serving with 2 tablespoons grated cheese. Yield: 4 servings.

CALORIES 267 (30% from fat); FAT 9g (sat 3.1g, mono 4.2g, poly 1.1g); PROTEIN 13.6g; CARB 35.2g; FIBER 6.6g; CHOL 10mg; IRON 2.8mg; SODIUM 875mg; CALC 245mg

lighten up

Currying Favor

After an update, a traditional Indian chicken dish finds a home in California.

As a journalist in the Middle East, Joan Borsten spent her free days with a family that had immigrated from New Delhi. The father, a retiree from the Indian Army, introduced Joan to Indian cuisine. "He had a specific blend of masala, or spices, that was unwritten. So before he would throw the spices into a dish," Joan says, "I would have him put them into a bowl so I could measure them." Joan returned to America with an accurate recipe for Colonel Benjamin's Curry Chicken. But with weight control a priority in her life, she knew this high-calorie recipe needed help.

The most significant change was to use skinless chicken thighs instead of a whole chicken. The dark meat added richness and provided a simple portion control solution for Joan. We drastically reduced the oil for cooking the vegetables from ⅓ cup to only 1 teaspoon. The small amount is adequate, but it requires frequent stirring to prevent overbrowning. We wanted to keep the dish authentic, so we left Colonel Benjamin's spices unchanged.

Joan believes Colonel Benjamin's family would approve.

BEFORE	AFTER
SERVING SIZE	
2 thighs, 1 cup potato curry, and ½ cup rice	
CALORIES PER SERVING	
731	449
FAT	
35g	7g
PERCENT OF TOTAL CALORIES	
43%	14%

Colonel Benjamin's Curry Chicken

Colonel Benjamin used many spices, rather than a premixed curry powder.

    1   teaspoon salt
    1   teaspoon ground coriander
    1   teaspoon ground cumin
    1   teaspoon chili powder
    1   teaspoon grated peeled fresh ginger
    ¼   teaspoon ground turmeric
    1   teaspoon vegetable oil
    4   cups finely chopped onion
    2   garlic cloves, minced
    3½ cups coarsely chopped peeled
        tomato (about 1½ pounds)
    2   tablespoons fresh lemon juice
    12 chicken thighs (about 3 pounds),
        skinned
    ½   teaspoon salt
    1½ pounds peeled baking potatoes,
        cut into 1-inch pieces
    2   tablespoons chopped fresh
        cilantro
    3   cups hot cooked rice
        Cilantro sprigs

1. Combine first 6 ingredients.
2. Heat oil in a Dutch oven over medium-high heat. Add onion and garlic; cook 15 minutes, stirring frequently. Add cumin mixture, tomato, and juice. Reduce heat to medium, and cook 10 minutes, stirring occasionally.
3. Sprinkle chicken with ½ teaspoon salt. Add chicken and potatoes to pan; stir in chopped cilantro. Bring to a boil; cover, reduce heat, and simmer 50 minutes or until chicken is done. Serve over rice, and garnish with cilantro sprigs. Yield: 6 servings (serving size: 2 thighs, 1 cup potato curry, and ½ cup rice).

CALORIES 449 (14% from fat); FAT 7g (sat 1.6g, mono 2.1g, poly 1.8g); PROTEIN 34g; CARB 62.6g; FIBER 5.8g; CHOL 115mg; IRON 3.9mg; SODIUM 735mg; CALC 67mg

reader recipes

Majority Rules

One woman's vegetarian creation pleases two out of three picky eaters, and one meat-lover.

Susan Gelb's family calls her "a health nut." That's fine with her as long as she can get a healthful dinner on the table in good time. A physician—and the wife of a physician—she's also mother to three daughters younger than 13. So making the most of her dinner hour is critical.

When Gelb tried vegetarian cooking one night in her Pittsburgh, Pennsylvania, kitchen, she was "searching for something different that everyone in the family would enjoy." What emerged was a mélange of mushrooms, shallots, and other pantry ingredients mounded in red bell pepper shells. She christened the dish Vegetarian Stuffed Peppers.

"I love the combination of mushrooms and shallots, and that was the basis for the recipe," she explains. At its debut, the dish that also includes nuts, smoky chile powder, and sharp cheese pleased two out of three picky young eaters—and one adult meat-lover.

MAKE AHEAD
Vegetarian Stuffed Peppers

(pictured on page 327)

    6   red bell peppers
    1   teaspoon olive oil
    ¾   cup finely chopped shallots
    4   cups chopped mushrooms
    1   cup chopped fresh parsley
    ¼   cup slivered almonds, toasted
    3   tablespoons dry sherry
    1½ teaspoons ancho chile powder
    2½ cups hot cooked brown rice
    1   cup tomato juice
    ½   teaspoon freshly ground black
        pepper
    ½   teaspoon garlic powder
    ¼   teaspoon salt
    ¼   cup (1 ounce) grated fresh
        Parmesan cheese

1. Preheat oven to 350°.
2. Cut tops off bell peppers; discard tops, seeds, and membranes. Cook peppers in boiling water 5 minutes; drain.
3. Heat oil in a large nonstick skillet over medium-high heat. Add shallots; sauté 3 minutes or until tender. Add mushrooms; sauté 4 minutes or until tender. Add parsley, almonds, sherry, and chile powder; sauté 3 minutes. Add rice, juice, black pepper, garlic powder, and salt; sauté 3 minutes. Spoon ¾ cup rice mixture into each bell pepper. Top each bell pepper with 2 teaspoons cheese. Place stuffed bell peppers in a 13 x 9-inch baking dish; bake at 350° for 15 minutes. Yield: 6 servings (serving size: 1 stuffed pepper).

CALORIES 234 (23% from fat); FAT 5.9g (sat 1.2g, mono 2.9g, poly 1.3g); PROTEIN 8.4g; CARB 39.2g; FIBER 6.7g; CHOL 3mg; IRON 3.3mg; SODIUM 402mg; CALC 112mg

QUICK & EASY • MAKE AHEAD
Poppy Seed Fruit Salad

"Although I always try to cook light, I love the flavor and convenience of bottled salad dressings. But unfortunately they're often high in fat. I've found that I can dramatically lighten these dressings just by mixing them with fat-free ingredients. The creamy dressing for this fruit salad is one of my adaptations."
—Nancy Rucinski, Crown Point, Indiana

    3   tablespoons orange-mango
        fat-free yogurt (such as Dannon)
    3   tablespoons poppy seed salad
        dressing
    2   cups halved strawberries
    2   cups cubed pineapple
    1   cup honeydew melon balls
    1   cup cantaloupe balls
    12 Boston lettuce leaves

1. Combine yogurt and salad dressing; stir well with a whisk. Combine strawberries, pineapple, and melon balls in a large bowl, tossing gently. Line each of 6 plates with 2 lettuce leaves; spoon 1 cup fruit mixture onto each plate. Drizzle each salad with 1 tablespoon dressing. Serve immediately. Yield: 6 servings.

CALORIES 106 (31% from fat); FAT 3.6g (sat 0.4g, mono 0.1g, poly 0.3g); PROTEIN 1.5g; CARB 18.5g; FIBER 3g; CHOL 3mg; IRON 1mg; SODIUM 62mg; CALC 25mg

Baked Oatmeal

"Since I'm the only oatmeal lover in my family, I make this dish for myself—it's a satisfying breakfast. Once I enjoy that first serving, I can then cover and refrigerate the leftovers. Small portions reheat easily in the microwave."

—Susan Baldwin, Eatontown, New Jersey

  2   cups uncooked quick-cooking oats
  ½   cup packed brown sugar
  ⅓   cup raisins
  1   tablespoon chopped walnuts
  1   teaspoon baking powder
1½   cups fat-free milk
  ½   cup applesauce
  2   tablespoons butter, melted
  1   large egg, beaten
Cooking spray

1. Preheat oven to 375°.
2. Combine first 5 ingredients in a medium bowl. Combine milk, applesauce, butter, and egg. Add milk mixture to oat mixture; stir well. Pour oat mixture into an 8-inch square baking dish coated with cooking spray. Bake at 375° for 20 minutes. Serve warm. Yield: 5 servings (serving size: ⅔ cup).

CALORIES 281 (24% from fat); FAT 7.6g (sat 2.8g, mono 1.5g, poly 0.9g); PROTEIN 7g; CARB 48.8g; FIBER 3.4g; CHOL 47mg; IRON 0.8mg; SODIUM 171mg; CALC 148mg

---

MAKE AHEAD
Frosted Pumpkin Cake

"I can no longer find reduced-fat cake mix, so I use a regular mix and healthier choices for the added ingredients."

—Robin Holland, Lexington, Kentucky

CAKE:
Cooking spray
  1   tablespoon all-purpose flour
  ¾   cup egg substitute
  ⅓   cup granulated sugar
  ⅓   cup applesauce
  1   (15-ounce) can pumpkin
  2   teaspoons pumpkin-pie spice
  1   (18.25-ounce) package yellow cake mix (such as Betty Crocker)

FROSTING:
  ⅔   cup (6 ounces) tub-style light cream cheese
1¼   teaspoons vanilla extract
3½   cups powdered sugar

1. Preheat oven to 350°.
2. Coat a 13 x 9-inch baking pan with cooking spray; dust with flour.
3. To prepare cake, place egg substitute, granulated sugar, applesauce, and pumpkin in a large bowl; beat with a mixer at high speed 1 minute. Add pie spice and cake mix, beating at high speed 2 minutes. Pour batter into prepared pan. Bake at 350° for 35 minutes or until a wooden pick inserted in center comes out clean. Cool cake completely on a wire rack.
4. To prepare frosting, place cream cheese and vanilla in a large bowl; beat at medium speed until smooth. Gradually add powdered sugar, beating just until blended. (Do not overbeat.) Spread frosting evenly over top of cake. Yield: 24 servings (serving size: 1 piece).

CALORIES 202 (16% from fat); FAT 3.7g (sat 1.2g, mono 1.1g, poly 1g); PROTEIN 2.6g; CARB 40g; FIBER 1g; CHOL 4mg; IRON 1mg; SODIUM 236mg; CALC 47mg

---

QUICK & EASY • MAKE AHEAD
Pumpkin Dip

"When my kids were young, they would beg for the typical junk food they were often served at parties. I began making this treat for their parties years ago, and the whining stopped. My girls are now in college, and they still devour it."

—Lynne Bouton, Roswell, Georgia

  ¾   cup (6 ounces) ⅓-less-fat cream cheese
  ½   cup packed brown sugar
  ½   cup canned pumpkin
  2   teaspoons maple syrup
  ½   teaspoon ground cinnamon
 24   apple slices

1. Place first 3 ingredients in a medium bowl; beat with a mixer at medium speed until well blended. Add syrup and cinnamon, and beat until smooth. Cover dip, and chill 30 minutes. Serve with apple.

Yield: 12 servings (servings size: 2 tablespoons dip and 2 apple slices).

CALORIES 107 (27% from fat); FAT 3.2g (sat 2g, mono 0.9g, poly 0.1g); PROTEIN 2g; CARB 18.3g; FIBER 1.4g; CHOL 10mg; IRON 1mg; SODIUM 87mg; CALC 35mg

---

dinner tonight

Featuring Fall Produce

These quick menus feature hearty, comforting meals filled with fall produce.

Menu 1
serves 3

Chicken Potpies

Spinach and orange salad*

Chocolate low-fat ice cream with graham crackers

*Combine 5 cups packaged baby spinach, 1 cup drained mandarin oranges in light syrup, and ¼ cup slivered red onion. Combine 2 tablespoons balsamic vinegar, 1 tablespoon honey, 2 teaspoons Dijon mustard, 1 teaspoon olive oil, ⅛ teaspoon salt, and ⅛ teaspoon black pepper, stirring with a whisk. Drizzle vinaigrette over salad; toss gently to coat.

Game Plan

1. While oven preheats for piecrusts:
  • Prepare flour mixture for chicken
  • Cut chicken into bite-sized pieces
  • Prepare vinaigrette for salad
2. While crusts bake:
  • Cook chicken mixture
  • Prepare salad

Chicken Potpies

Because the piecrust topping cooks on a baking sheet and is then placed over the filling, you don't need to use ovenproof bowls for the pies. Use a bowl or ramekin as a guide for cutting the dough.

TOTAL TIME: 32 MINUTES

QUICK TIP: Use 2 cups chopped leftover chicken in place of chicken breast tenders.

- ½ (15-ounce) package refrigerated pie dough (such as Pillsbury)
- Cooking spray
- ⅛ teaspoon salt
- 2 tablespoons all-purpose flour
- 1 teaspoon dried rubbed sage
- ¼ teaspoon salt
- ¼ teaspoon black pepper
- 8 ounces chicken breast tenders, cut into bite-sized pieces
- 1¼ cups water
- 1½ cups frozen mixed vegetables
- 1 cup mushrooms, quartered
- 1 (10½-ounce) can condensed reduced-fat, reduced-sodium cream of chicken soup

1. Preheat oven to 425°.

2. Cut 3 (4-inch) circles out of dough; discard remaining dough. Place dough circles on a baking sheet coated with cooking spray. Lightly coat dough circles with cooking spray; sprinkle evenly with ⅛ teaspoon salt. Pierce top of dough with a fork. Bake at 425° for 8 minutes or until golden.

3. Combine flour, sage, ¼ teaspoon salt, and pepper in a zip-top plastic bag; add chicken. Seal bag, and toss to coat. Heat a large nonstick skillet coated with cooking spray over medium-high heat. Add chicken mixture; cook 5 minutes, browning on all sides. Stir in water, scraping pan to loosen browned bits. Stir in vegetables, mushrooms, and soup; bring to a boil. Reduce heat, and cook 10 minutes. Spoon 1 cup chicken mixture into each of 3 (1-cup) ramekins or bowls; top each serving with 1 piecrust. Yield: 3 servings (serving size: 1 pie).

CALORIES 374 (27% from fat); FAT 11.4g (sat 4.8g, mono 4.2g, poly 1.2g); PROTEIN 24.1g; CARB 42.6g; FIBER 4.6g; CHOL 58mg; IRON 1.9mg; SODIUM 882mg; CALC 38mg

---

Menu 2
serves 4

Pork Loin Chops with Cinnamon Apples

Buttered poppy seed noodles*

Green peas

*Cook 8 ounces wide egg noodles according to package directions, omitting salt and fat; drain. Place noodles in a large bowl. Add 2 tablespoons chopped fresh parsley, 1½ tablespoons butter, 2 teaspoons poppy seeds, ¼ teaspoon salt, and ¼ teaspoon pepper; toss to combine.

Game Plan

1. While water for noodles comes to a boil:
- Peel and slice apples
- Sprinkle pork with sage mixture

2. While noodles cook:
- Cook pork and apples
- Prepare peas
- Chop parsley for noodles

QUICK & EASY
Pork Loin Chops with Cinnamon Apples
(pictured on page 327)

Pork and apples are simply meant for each other. Tart Granny Smiths balance the caramel sweetness of brown sugar.

TOTAL TIME: 22 MINUTES

QUICK TIP: To quickly peel the apples, use a vegetable peeler instead of a paring knife.

- 1 teaspoon dried rubbed sage
- ½ teaspoon salt
- ¼ teaspoon freshly ground black pepper
- 4 (4-ounce) boneless center-cut loin pork chops (about ½ inch thick)
- ½ teaspoon vegetable oil
- Cooking spray
- 1 teaspoon butter
- 4 cups (½-inch) slices peeled Granny Smith apples (about 4 medium)
- 1 tablespoon brown sugar
- 1 teaspoon fresh lemon juice
- ½ teaspoon ground cinnamon
- Dash of salt

1. Combine first 3 ingredients, and sprinkle over pork. Heat oil in a large nonstick skillet coated with cooking spray over medium heat. Add pork; cook 3 minutes on each side or until done. Remove pork from pan. Cover and keep warm.

2. Melt butter in pan over medium heat. Add apple and remaining 4 ingredients, and cook 5 minutes or until tender, stirring frequently. Serve with pork. Yield: 4 servings (serving size: 1 pork chop and ¾ cup apple mixture).

CALORIES 251 (30% from fat); FAT 8.3g (sat 3.1g, mono 3.3g, poly 0.9g); PROTEIN 24.1g; CARB 20.2g; FIBER 2.3g; CHOL 67mg; IRON 0.9mg; SODIUM 388mg; CALC 38mg

---

Menu 3
serves 8

Quick Fall Minestrone (recipe on page 318)

Monterey Jack and roasted red-pepper quesadillas*

Cantaloupe, grape, and honeydew fruit salad

*Preheat broiler. Place 8 (6-inch) fat-free flour tortillas on a large baking sheet coated with cooking spray. Sprinkle each tortilla evenly with 2 tablespoons shredded Monterey Jack cheese and 2 tablespoons chopped bottled roasted red bell peppers. Top each prepared tortilla with another (6-inch) fat-free flour tortilla; coat tops with cooking spray. Broil 3 minutes or until lightly browned. Carefully turn over; coat tops with cooking spray. Broil an additional 3 minutes or until lightly browned. Cut each quesadilla into 4 wedges; serve 4 wedges per person.

Game Plan

1. While broiler preheats for quesadillas:
- Chop vegetables for soup
- Shred cheese
- Chop bell peppers for quesadillas

2. While soup cooks:
- Broil quesadillas
- Grate cheese for soup

Continued

Quick Fall Minestrone

This easy soup brims with fresh vegetables; canned beans and orzo make it hearty and filling.

TOTAL TIME: 35 MINUTES

QUICK TIP: To quickly remove the skin from the squash, use a vegetable peeler.

- 1 tablespoon vegetable oil
- 1 cup chopped onion
- 2 garlic cloves, minced
- 6 cups vegetable broth
- 2½ cups (¾-inch) cubed peeled butternut squash
- 2½ cups (¾-inch) cubed peeled baking potato
- 1 cup (1-inch) cut green beans (about ¼ pound)
- ½ cup chopped carrot
- 1 teaspoon dried oregano
- ½ teaspoon freshly ground black pepper
- ¼ teaspoon salt
- 4 cups chopped kale
- ½ cup uncooked orzo (rice-shaped pasta)
- 1 (16-ounce) can cannellini beans or other white beans, rinsed and drained
- ½ cup (2 ounces) grated fresh Parmesan cheese

1. Heat oil in a large Dutch oven over medium-high heat. Add onion and garlic; sauté 2½ minutes or until tender. Add broth and next 7 ingredients; bring to a boil. Reduce heat, and simmer 3 minutes. Add kale, orzo, and beans; cook 5 minutes or until orzo is done and vegetables are tender. Sprinkle with cheese. Yield: 8 servings (serving size: 1½ cups soup and 1 tablespoon cheese).

CALORIES 212 (21% from fat); FAT 5g (sat 1.6g, mono 1g, poly 1.2g); PROTEIN 9.6g; CARB 36g; FIBER 3.9g; CHOL 5mg; IRON 1.9mg; SODIUM 961mg; CALC 164mg

Menu 4
serves 4

Sweet-Spicy Glazed Salmon

Baked sweet potatoes with brown sugar-pecan butter*

Steamed broccoli spears

*Pierce 4 (8-ounce) sweet potatoes with a fork. Microwave at HIGH 12 minutes or until done. Combine 2 tablespoons softened butter, 2 tablespoons brown sugar, and 1½ tablespoons finely chopped toasted pecans. Top each potato with about 1 tablespoon butter mixture.

Game Plan

1. While oven preheats for salmon:
- Prepare glaze for salmon
- Scrub sweet potatoes
- Prepare butter mixture for sweet potatoes
2. While salmon cooks:
- Cook sweet potatoes
- Prepare broccoli

Sweet-Spicy Glazed Salmon

Chinese-style hot mustard has a sharp bite similar to that of wasabi. If you can't find it, use Dijon mustard or 1 teaspoon of a dry mustard such as Coleman's.

TOTAL TIME: 22 MINUTES

- 3 tablespoons dark brown sugar
- 4 teaspoons Chinese-style hot mustard
- 1 tablespoon low-sodium soy sauce
- 1 teaspoon rice vinegar
- 4 (6-ounce) salmon fillets (about 1 inch thick)
- Cooking spray
- ¼ teaspoon salt
- ¼ teaspoon freshly ground black pepper

1. Preheat oven to 425°.
2. Combine first 4 ingredients in a saucepan; bring to a boil. Remove from heat.

3. Place fillets on a foil-lined jelly roll pan coated with cooking spray; sprinkle with salt and pepper. Bake at 425° for 12 minutes. Remove from oven.
4. Preheat broiler.
5. Brush sugar mixture evenly over fillets; broil 3 inches from heat 3 minutes or until fish flakes easily when tested with a fork. Yield: 4 servings (serving size: 1 fillet).

CALORIES 252 (37% from fat); FAT 10.3g (sat 2.3g, mono 4.4g, poly 2.5g); PROTEIN 27.7g; CARB 11g; FIBER 0.1g; CHOL 65mg; IRON 0.9mg; SODIUM 470mg; CALC 33mg

well equipped
Cool Crockpot

Chef Jesse Cool found that an old crockpot is good for more than just chili. Here are some of her favorite recipes.

Pesto Lasagna with Spinach and Mushrooms

Use 2 (10-ounce) packages of frozen chopped spinach in place of fresh, if you prefer. Also, any mushroom will work.

- 4 cups torn spinach
- 2 cups sliced cremini mushrooms
- ½ cup commercial pesto
- ¾ cup (3 ounces) shredded part-skim mozzarella cheese
- ¾ cup (3 ounces) shredded provolone cheese
- 1 (15-ounce) carton fat-free ricotta cheese
- 1 large egg, lightly beaten
- ¾ cup (3 ounces) grated fresh Parmesan cheese, divided
- 1 (25.5-ounce) bottle fat-free tomato-basil pasta sauce
- 1 (8-ounce) can tomato sauce
- Cooking spray
- 1 (8-ounce) package precooked lasagna noodles (12 noodles)

1. Arrange spinach in a vegetable steamer; steam, covered, 3 minutes or until spinach wilts. Drain, squeeze dry, and coarsely chop. Combine spinach, mushrooms, and pesto in a medium bowl; set aside.

2. Combine mozzarella, provolone, ricotta, and egg in a medium bowl, stirring well. Stir in ¼ cup Parmesan, and set aside. Combine pasta sauce and tomato sauce in a medium bowl.

3. Spread 1 cup pasta sauce mixture in bottom of a 6-quart oval electric slow cooker coated with cooking spray. Arrange 3 noodles over pasta sauce mixture; top with 1 cup cheese mixture and 1 cup spinach mixture. Repeat layers once, ending with spinach mixture. Arrange 3 noodles over spinach mixture; top with remaining cheese mixture and 1 cup pasta sauce mixture. Place 3 noodles over sauce mixture; spread remaining sauce mixture over noodles. Sprinkle with ½ cup Parmesan. Cover with lid; cook on LOW 5 hours or until done. Yield: 8 servings.

CALORIES 398 (41% from fat); FAT 18.2g (sat 7.8g, mono 6.6g, poly 2.3g); PROTEIN 22.2g; CARB 38.5g; FIBER 2g; CHOL 56mg; IRON 2.8mg; SODIUM 1,036mg; CALC 407mg

---

Crockpot Considerations

•Consult old crockpot cookbooks. Their charts should still hold up. Use them as a jumping-off point for new recipes.

•Don't brown meats first. Sacrificing appearance for convenience and efficiency is more important.

•Season foods in your crockpot cautiously. Add fresh herbs at the end, which adds a bright, flavorful finish.

•All the ingredients for a dish don't have to go in at once. Grains such as rice, bulgur, or barley thicken and give body to many recipes; but cook them separately and add them at the last minute. Otherwise, their starch cooks into the recipe, which clouds the juices and changes the consistency. Add quick-cooking vegetables, such as corn or peas, as well as shellfish such as shrimp, clams, and mussels during the last half-hour of cooking.

•Little liquid escapes during cooking. The juices of the ingredients will come out, so add liquid judiciously.

MAKE AHEAD
Slow-Cooker Meat Loaf with Shiitake Mushrooms

Because no evaporation takes place, the crockpot makes an especially moist and tender meat loaf. The mushrooms add moisture as well.

 2 (1-ounce) slices whole wheat bread
 ¾ pound ground round
 ¾ pound ground turkey
 1½ cups sliced shiitake mushrooms
 ½ cup grated fresh onion
 1 teaspoon dried Italian seasoning
 ¾ teaspoon salt
 2 large eggs, lightly beaten
 1 garlic clove, minced
 2 tablespoons ketchup
 1½ teaspoons Dijon mustard
 ⅛ teaspoon ground red pepper

1. Place bread in a food processor, and pulse 10 times or until crumbs measure 1⅓ cups. Combine crumbs, beef, and next 7 ingredients in a large bowl, and shape meat mixture into a 9 x 6-inch loaf. Place loaf in an electric slow cooker.
2. Combine ketchup, mustard, and pepper in a small bowl, stirring with a fork. Spread ketchup mixture evenly over top of loaf. Cover with lid; cook on LOW 5 hours. Yield: 6 servings (serving size: 4 ounces).

CALORIES 265 (43% from fat); FAT 12.7g (sat 4.2g, mono 5.1g, poly 1.7g); PROTEIN 25.2g; CARB 12.7g; FIBER 1.9g; CHOL 152mg; IRON 3mg; SODIUM 545mg; CALC 41mg

---

MAKE AHEAD
Walnut-Stuffed Slow-Cooked Apples

Serve these apples warm from the crockpot with low-fat frozen yogurt.

 ¼ cup coarsely chopped walnuts
 3 tablespoons dried currants
 2½ tablespoons brown sugar
 ¾ teaspoon ground cinnamon, divided
 4 Granny Smith apples, cored
 1 cup packed brown sugar
 ¾ cup apple cider

1. Combine first 3 ingredients in a small bowl; stir in ¼ teaspoon cinnamon. Peel top third of each apple; place apples in an electric slow cooker. Spoon walnut mixture evenly into cavities of apples.
2. Combine ½ teaspoon cinnamon, 1 cup brown sugar, and apple cider in a small bowl. Pour over apples. Cover with lid; cook on LOW 2 hours and 45 minutes. Remove apples with a slotted spoon. Spoon ¼ cup cooking liquid over each serving. Yield: 4 servings (serving size: 1 apple and ¼ cup cooking liquid).

CALORIES 310 (14% from fat); FAT 4.9g (sat 0.5g, mono 0.7g, poly 3.6g); PROTEIN 1.9g; CARB 70g; FIBER 3.8g; CHOL 0mg; IRON 1.6mg; SODIUM 23mg; CALC 60mg

---

MAKE AHEAD
Turkey Thighs with Olives and Dried Cherries

This recipe is adapted from *Your Organic Kitchen*, by Jesse Ziff Cool. Turkey thighs are easy to find, but you also can use a cut-up chicken, if you prefer. This dish is great served with couscous.

 1 cup thinly sliced leek (about 1 large)
 1 cup ruby port or other sweet red wine
 ¾ cup dried cherries
 ¾ cup pitted kalamata olives
 ⅓ cup fresh orange juice (about 1 orange)
 1 teaspoon paprika
 1 teaspoon crushed red pepper
 4 thyme sprigs
 1 (3-inch) cinnamon stick
 1½ teaspoons salt, divided
 3½ pounds turkey thighs, skinned
 1 tablespoon ground cumin

1. Combine first 9 ingredients in an electric slow cooker. Stir in ½ teaspoon salt.
2. Rinse turkey with cold water; pat dry. Sprinkle with 1 teaspoon salt and cumin. Place in slow cooker. Cover with lid, and cook on LOW 6 hours. Discard cinnamon stick. Yield: 8 servings (serving size: 3 ounces turkey and about ⅓ cup liquid).

CALORIES 314 (34% from fat); FAT 12.1g (sat 3.5g, mono 4.1g, poly 3.1g); PROTEIN 24.4g; CARB 17.3g; FIBER 2.2g; CHOL 76mg; IRON 3.1mg; SODIUM 1,090mg; CALC 46mg

Green Acres

When Marion Winik traded city life for country digs, she found her inner cook.

Five years ago, Marion Winik, author and NPR commentator, fell in love while traveling on business, then married and moved with her sons from Austin, Texas, to rural Glen Rock, Pennsylvania. Moving to the country changed her life in many ways. But the biggest change happened in her kitchen.

Before, Marion avoided many aspects of cooking, particularly making things from scratch. Now, with a quieter social calendar, and fewer traffic lights, she finds more time and patience for making home-cooked meals. Here are some of her specialties.

MAKE AHEAD • FREEZABLE
Marion's Baguettes

Marion's bread recipe is a starting point for her signature sandwich, consisting of mustard greens, wasabi mayonnaise, and tomato. Pouring water into the bottom of the oven creates steam and gives the bread a crisp crust.

    1   package dry yeast (about 2¼ teaspoons)
    2   tablespoons sugar
    2½ cups warm water (100° to 110°)
    3¾ cups bread flour, divided
    2   cups whole wheat flour
    ½   cup semolina or pasta flour
    1½ tablespoons salt
        Cooking spray
    1   tablespoon cornmeal
    ¼   cup water

1. Dissolve yeast and sugar in warm water in a large bowl; let stand 5 minutes. Lightly spoon flours into dry measuring cups; level with a knife. Add 3½ cups bread flour, wheat flour, semolina, and salt to yeast mixture; stir with a whisk until well blended.
2. Turn dough out onto a lightly floured surface. Knead until smooth and elastic (about 10 minutes); add enough of remaining bread flour, 1 tablespoon at a time, to prevent dough from sticking to hands (dough will feel tacky).
3. Place dough in a large bowl coated with cooking spray, turning to coat top.

Cover and let rise in a warm place (85°), free from drafts, 45 minutes or until doubled in size. (Gently press two fingers into dough. If indentation remains, dough has risen enough.) Punch dough down; cover and let rest 5 minutes. Divide into thirds. Working with one portion at a time (cover remaining dough to prevent drying), roll each portion into a 16-inch rope on a floured surface. Place ropes on a large baking sheet sprinkled with cornmeal. Cover and let rise 40 minutes or until ropes are doubled in size. Uncover dough. Cut 3 slits in top of each rope.
4. Preheat oven to 425°.
5. Pour ¼ cup water onto floor of oven (avoiding heating element). Place baking sheet in oven. Quickly close oven door. Bake at 425° for 30 minutes or until loaves are golden brown and sound hollow when tapped. Remove from pan, and cool on wire racks. Cut each loaf into 12 slices. Yield: 3 loaves, 36 slices (serving size: 1 slice).

CALORIES 82 (4% from fat); FAT 0.4g (sat 0.1g, mono 0g, poly 0.2g); PROTEIN 2.9g; CARB 17g; FIBER 1.3g; CHOL 0mg; IRON 1mg; SODIUM 292mg; CALC 5mg

Jerk Chicken

"This version of jerk chicken was taught to me by our cook in Jamaica, where we vacationed annually. It starts out with bottled jerk sauce, which simplifies matters."

    1   cup vertically sliced onion
    ¼   cup fresh lemon juice
    ¼   cup jerk sauce
    ¼   teaspoon salt
    ¼   teaspoon black pepper
    3   garlic cloves, chopped
    4   chicken breast halves (about 1½ pounds), skinned
    4   chicken thighs (about 1 pound), skinned
    ½   cup light beer
    ¼   cup jerk sauce
    3   tablespoons ketchup
    1   tablespoon hot sauce
        Cooking spray
        Julienne-cut green onions

1. Combine first 6 ingredients in a large zip-top plastic bag. Add chicken to bag; seal. Marinate in refrigerator overnight, turning occasionally. Remove chicken from bag; discard marinade.
2. Prepare grill to medium-high heat.
3. Combine beer, ¼ cup jerk sauce, ketchup, and hot sauce.
4. Place chicken on grill rack coated with cooking spray; grill 20 minutes or until done, turning and basting frequently with beer mixture. Garnish chicken with green onions, if desired. Yield: 6 servings (serving size: about 4 ounces).

CALORIES 245 (20% from fat); FAT 5.4g (sat 1.1g, mono 1.3g, poly 1.1g); PROTEIN 42.4g; CARB 6g; FIBER 1.3g; CHOL 129mg; IRON 1.9mg; SODIUM 589mg; CALC 26mg

Breakfast Soft Tacos with Persimmon Salsa

Inspired by Marion Winik's passion for salsa, we developed a persimmon version to pair with her soft tacos. If you can't find persimmon, use mango or peaches.

SALSA:
    1¾ cups chopped peeled ripe persimmon (about 2 medium)
    ⅓   cup finely chopped red onion
    2   tablespoons fresh lime juice
    1   tablespoon minced fresh cilantro
    ¼   teaspoon salt
    1   jalapeño pepper, seeded and diced

TACOS:

3¼ cups cubed peeled baking potato
Cooking spray
½ cup (2 ounces) shredded
Monterey Jack cheese with
jalapeño peppers
6 large eggs, lightly beaten
6 (8-inch) flour tortillas

1. To prepare salsa, combine first 6 ingredients; set aside.
2. To prepare tacos, place potato in a microwave-safe bowl. Cover with plastic wrap; microwave at HIGH 5 minutes.
3. Heat a large nonstick skillet coated with cooking spray over medium-high heat. Add potato; cook 5 minutes, stirring occasionally. Stir in cheese and egg; cook 3 minutes or until soft-scrambled, stirring constantly. Warm tortillas according to package directions. Spoon about ⅔ cup egg mixture down center of each tortilla. Top each with ⅓ cup salsa; roll up tortillas. Yield: 6 servings (serving size: 1 taco).

CALORIES 337 (30% from fat); FAT 11.2g (sat 3.9g, mono 3.3g, poly 1.2g); PROTEIN 14.6g; CARB 45.2g; FIBER 1.9g; CHOL 223mg; IRON 2mg; SODIUM 476mg; CALC 196mg

---

Ziti with Chard

"Armed with a hefty bag of chard from our first garden, I pulled out my old vegetarian cookbooks and came up with this pasta dish, inspired by Mollie Katzen's *Sundays at Moosewood*."

2 tablespoons olive oil
8 cups chopped Swiss chard
4 garlic cloves, minced
4 cups hot cooked ziti (about
8 ounces uncooked pasta)
2 cups grape or cherry tomatoes,
halved
¼ cup chopped pitted kalamata
olives
2 tablespoons fresh lemon
juice
¾ teaspoon kosher salt
½ teaspoon freshly ground black
pepper
¼ cup (1 ounce) shaved fresh
Romano cheese

1. Heat oil in a large nonstick skillet over medium-high heat. Add chard and garlic; sauté 2 minutes. Combine chard mixture, pasta, and next 5 ingredients, tossing well. Top with cheese. Yield: 4 servings (serving size: about 2 cups).

CALORIES 336 (28% from fat); FAT 10.5g (sat 2.4g, mono 6.2g, poly 0.8g); PROTEIN 12g; CARB 51g; FIBER 4.2g; CHOL 7mg; IRON 3.9mg; SODIUM 665mg; CALC 132mg

---

Veggie-Surimi Sushi

This is a great introduction to sushi. The ingredients are familiar, and the flavor is mild. Kids love it.

2 cups sushi rice or other
short-grain rice
⅓ cup seasoned rice vinegar
1½ teaspoons salt
6 nori (seaweed) sheets
12 (¼-inch) slices peeled avocado
12 (¼-inch) julienne-cut carrot strips
12 (¼-inch) julienne-cut seeded
peeled cucumber strips
6 imitation crab sticks, halved
lengthwise

1. Prepare rice according to package directions. Stir in vinegar and salt; cool.
2. Cut off top quarter of nori sheets along short end. Discard remaining pieces. Place 1 nori sheet, shiny side down, on a sushi mat covered with plastic wrap, with long end toward you. Pat 1 cup rice over nori with moist hands, leaving a 1-inch border on one long end of nori.
3. Arrange 2 avocado slices, 2 carrot strips, 2 cucumber strips, and 2 crab halves along top third of rice-covered nori.
4. Lift edge of nori closest to you; fold over filling. Lift bottom edge of sushi mat; roll toward top edge, pressing firmly on sushi roll. Continue rolling to top edge; press mat to seal sushi roll. Let rest, seam side down, 5 minutes. Slice crosswise into 8 pieces. Repeat procedure with remaining nori, rice, avocado, carrot, cucumber, and crab sticks. Yield: 6 servings (serving size: 8 pieces).

CALORIES 345 (11% from fat); FAT 4.4g (sat 0.7g, mono 2.5g, poly 0.7g); PROTEIN 10.4g; CARB 64.7g; FIBER 3.9g; CHOL 19mg; IRON 3.4mg; SODIUM 883mg; CALC 32.6mg

---

No-Delivery Chinese Menu
serves 6

Beef-Broccoli Lo Mein

Egg rolls with spicy-sweet
dipping sauce*

Fortune cookies

*Bake 6 frozen white-meat chicken egg rolls (such as Pagoda) according to package directions. While egg rolls bake, combine 1 tablespoon minced green onions, 2 tablespoons low-sodium soy sauce, 2 tablespoons duck sauce, 1 tablespoon rice vinegar, and 1 teaspoon sriracha or hot sauce (such as Tabasco). Serve sauce with egg rolls.

Beef-Broccoli Lo Mein

"When my sons requested beef lo mein, I had no idea how easy it was to make."

4 cups hot cooked spaghetti (about
8 ounces uncooked pasta)
1 teaspoon dark sesame oil
1 tablespoon peanut oil
1 tablespoon minced peeled fresh
ginger
4 garlic cloves, minced
3 cups chopped broccoli
1½ cups vertically sliced onion
1 (1-pound) flank steak, trimmed
and cut across the grain into long,
thin strips
3 tablespoons low-sodium soy sauce
2 tablespoons brown sugar
1 tablespoon oyster sauce
1 tablespoon chile paste with garlic

1. Combine pasta and sesame oil, tossing well to coat.
2. Heat peanut oil in a large nonstick skillet over medium-high heat. Add ginger and garlic; sauté 30 seconds. Add broccoli and onion; sauté 3 minutes. Add steak, and sauté 5 minutes or until done. Add pasta mixture, soy sauce, and remaining ingredients; cook 1 minute or until lo mein is thoroughly heated, stirring constantly. Yield: 6 servings (serving size: 1⅓ cups).

CALORIES 327 (26% from fat); FAT 9.3g (sat 3g, mono 3.6g, poly 1.6g); PROTEIN 21.7g; CARB 39.1g; FIBER 2.9g; CHOL 36mg; IRON 3.6mg; SODIUM 382mg; CALC 47mg

. . . And Ready in Just About 20 Minutes

October's recipes feature warming, ample meals that offer full-bodied tastes.

Included are an Asian soup, beef tenderloins with a red wine sauce, and seared lamb chops with toasted sesame seeds and a fragrant honey-raisin sauce. For vegetarians, we offer chickpea stew with buttered polenta or barley pilaf topped with grated Parmesan. For a seafood dinner, you'll find halibut or cod—both of which cook in spicy broths that partner well with crusty bread.

The finished dishes might appear time-consuming but, as always, require mere minutes.

QUICK & EASY
Sesame Lamb Chops with Honey-Raisin Sauce

The simmering in Step 2 takes the lamb chops to medium-rare. Simmer a minute less for rare or a minute more for medium. Serve with hot cooked couscous.

Cooking spray
- 8 (4-ounce) lamb loin chops, trimmed
- ½ teaspoon salt, divided
- ⅓ cup diced shallots
- 1 cup fat-free, less-sodium chicken broth
- ⅓ cup golden raisins
- 2 tablespoons honey
- ½ teaspoon cumin seeds
- ½ teaspoon ground cinnamon
- 1 tablespoon sesame seeds, toasted

1. Heat a large skillet coated with cooking spray over medium-high heat. Sprinkle lamb chops evenly with ¼ teaspoon salt. Add lamb chops to pan; cook 5 minutes on each side. Remove lamb chops from pan.

2. Recoat pan with cooking spray. Add ¼ teaspoon salt and shallots; sauté 1 minute. Stir in broth and next 4 ingredients. Add lamb, turning to coat. Simmer 3 minutes or until desired degree of doneness. Sprinkle with sesame seeds. Yield: 4 servings (serving size: 2 lamb chops, 3 tablespoons sauce, and ¾ teaspoon sesame seeds).

CALORIES 195 (22% from fat); FAT 4.8g (sat 1.3g, mono 1.5g, poly 0.4g); PROTEIN 15.6g; CARB 22.7g; FIBER 0.8g; CHOL 40mg; IRON 5.5mg; SODIUM 379mg; CALC 30mg

QUICK & EASY
Thai Shrimp and Chicken Soup

The minced ginger, minced garlic, mushrooms, and snow peas in this recipe require no preparation time at all. Find all those ingredients in your supermarket's produce department.

- 3 cups fat-free, less-sodium chicken broth
- 1 cup bottled clam juice
- 1 tablespoon fish sauce
- 2 teaspoons bottled minced garlic
- 1½ teaspoons bottled minced fresh ginger
- ¾ teaspoon red curry paste
- 1 (8-ounce) package presliced mushrooms
- ½ pound peeled and deveined large shrimp
- ½ pound skinless, boneless chicken breast, cut into 1-inch pieces
- 1 (3-ounce) package trimmed snow peas
- ¼ cup fresh lime juice
- 2 tablespoons sugar
- 2 tablespoons (½-inch) sliced green onion tops
- 2 tablespoons chopped fresh cilantro
- 1 (13.5-ounce) can light coconut milk

1. Combine first 6 ingredients in a large Dutch oven, stirring with a whisk. Add mushrooms, and bring to a boil. Reduce heat, and simmer 4 minutes. Add shrimp, chicken, and snow peas, and bring to a boil. Cover, reduce heat, and simmer 3 minutes.
2. Stir in lime juice and remaining ingredients. Cook 2 minutes or until thoroughly heated. Yield: 4 servings (serving size: about 2 cups).

CALORIES 262 (24% from fat); FAT 7.1g (sat 3.8g, mono 0.3g, poly 0.6g); PROTEIN 30g; CARB 18.3g; FIBER 1.8g; CHOL 121mg; IRON 3.3mg; SODIUM 973mg; CALC 64mg

QUICK & EASY
Cod Poached in Spicy Tomato Broth

You may substitute flounder or sole for the cod, if you prefer.

- 1 tablespoon olive oil
- 1½ teaspoons bottled minced garlic
- 1 cup water
- ¾ cup dry white wine
- 2 tablespoons capers
- ¾ teaspoon crushed red pepper
- 1 (14.5-ounce) can diced tomatoes with basil, garlic, and oregano
- 4 (6-ounce) cod fillets
- 10 kalamata olives, pitted and chopped

1. Heat oil in a large nonstick skillet over medium-high heat. Add garlic; sauté 1 minute or until lightly browned. Add water and next 4 ingredients; bring to a boil. Reduce heat, and simmer 2 minutes. Add fillets; cover and simmer 5 minutes or until fish flakes easily when tested with a fork. Top with olives. Yield: 4 servings (serving size: 1 fillet and about ⅔ cup sauce).

CALORIES 272 (23% from fat); FAT 7.1g (sat 1g, mono 4.6g, poly 1g); PROTEIN 32.4g; CARB 11.4g; FIBER 1.3g; CHOL 73mg; IRON 2.5mg; SODIUM 907mg; CALC 104mg

> ### Consider Cod
> The darling of New England, cod is a flaky white fish with mild, sweet flavor—so mild in fact, those who are wary of seafood tend to gravitate to it. Now rebounding from shortages in the Atlantic, cod is plentiful year-round. A 4½-ounce serving has 134 calories and 1.1 grams of fat.

Getting dinner on the table in minutes does not mean you are sacrificing flavor.

QUICK & EASY
Halibut in Tomato-Shiitake Broth

A little red curry paste delivers complex flavors to the shiitake mushroom broth. Look for it in jars or foil packets in the Asian section of your supermarket.

    8   ounces uncooked udon noodles
        (thick, round fresh Japanese wheat
        noodles) or spaghetti
    1   teaspoon olive oil
    1   teaspoon bottled minced garlic
 1½   cups bottled clam juice
    2   teaspoons red curry paste
    4   cups thinly sliced shiitake
        mushroom caps (about ½ pound
        mushrooms)
  ⅔   cup canned diced tomatoes,
        undrained
  ¼   teaspoon crushed red pepper
    4   (6-ounce) halibut fillets
  ¼   cup chopped fresh basil
  ⅛   teaspoon salt

1. Cook noodles according to package directions, omitting salt and fat.
2. While noodles cook, heat oil in a large nonstick skillet over medium heat. Add garlic; sauté 1½ minutes or until tender. Add clam juice and curry paste, stirring with a whisk until smooth. Add mushrooms, tomatoes, and pepper to pan; bring to a simmer. Add fillets; sprinkle with basil and salt. Cover and cook 5 minutes or until fish flakes easily when tested with a fork. Serve over noodles. Yield: 4 servings (serving size: 1 fillet, ¾ cup noodles, and ½ cup clam juice mixture).

CALORIES 392 (14% from fat); FAT 5.9g (sat 0.7g, mono 2.2g, poly 1.4g); PROTEIN 41.5g; CARB 38.2g; FIBER 1.2g; CHOL 57mg; IRON 3.3mg; SODIUM 811mg; CALC 130mg

QUICK & EASY
Beef Tenderloin Steaks with Red Wine-Tarragon Sauce

If these steaks are cut from a whole tenderloin, ask the butcher to cut them about an inch thick from the middle portion. Packaged beef tenderloin steaks are often labeled "filet mignon."

  ¼   cup low-salt beef broth
  ¼   cup dry red wine
  ½   teaspoon all-purpose
        flour
  ¼   teaspoon salt
  ¼   teaspoon dried tarragon
  ⅛   teaspoon black pepper
        Cooking spray
    2   (4-ounce) beef tenderloin
        steaks
    2   tablespoons chopped
        shallots
    1   teaspoon chopped fresh
        parsley

1. Combine first 6 ingredients, stirring with a whisk.
2. Heat a nonstick skillet coated with cooking spray over medium-high heat. Add steaks, and cook 3 minutes on each side or until desired degree of doneness. Remove from pan, and keep warm. Add shallots to pan, and sauté 1 minute. Add broth mixture; bring to a boil. Cook until reduced to ¼ cup (about 1 minute). Serve sauce with steaks. Sprinkle with parsley. Yield: 2 servings (serving size: 1 steak, about 2 tablespoons sauce, and ½ teaspoon parsley).

CALORIES 228 (42% from fat); FAT 10.6g (sat 4.1g, mono 4.2g, poly 0.4g); PROTEIN 24g; CARB 2.9g; FIBER 0.2g; CHOL 72mg; IRON 3.3mg; SODIUM 358mg; CALC 16mg

QUICK & EASY
Chickpea Stew Scented with Lemon and Cumin

The garbanzo beans provide plenty of protein for this meatless meal. Polenta gives the dish a creamy base and balances the spicy sauce.

    4   cups water
    1   cup instant dry polenta
    1   tablespoon butter
    1   tablespoon olive oil
    1   cup chopped onion
 1½   teaspoons bottled minced
        garlic
  ¼   cup lemon juice
    1   teaspoon ground cumin
  ¼   teaspoon black pepper
    2   (15-ounce) cans chickpeas
        (garbanzo beans), drained
    2   (14.5-ounce) cans diced tomatoes,
        undrained
  ½   cup chopped green onions
  ¾   cup reduced-fat sour cream

1. Bring water to a boil in a medium saucepan. Gradually add polenta, stirring constantly with a whisk. Reduce heat, and simmer 3 minutes, stirring frequently. Remove from heat; stir in butter. Cover and set aside.
2. While polenta cooks, heat oil a large nonstick skillet over medium-high heat. Add onion and garlic; sauté 3 minutes. Add lemon juice, cumin, pepper, chickpeas, and tomatoes; bring to a boil. Reduce heat, and simmer 6 minutes. Stir in green onions. Serve stew over polenta. Top with sour cream. Yield: 6 servings (serving size: 1⅓ cups stew, ⅔ cup polenta, and 2 tablespoons sour cream).

CALORIES 400 (22% from fat); FAT 9.6g (sat 4g, mono 2.6g, poly 1g); PROTEIN 12.9g; CARB 68g; FIBER 9.8g; CHOL 21mg; IRON 2.8mg; SODIUM 838mg; CALC 180mg

Tortilla Soup

1 tablespoon olive oil
1 cup chopped onion
1 teaspoon bottled minced garlic
2 tablespoons fajita seasoning (such as McCormick)
2¼ cups water
2 (15-ounce) cans pinto beans, rinsed and drained
1 (28-ounce) can diced tomatoes, undrained
1 (14-ounce) can fat-free, less-sodium chicken broth
2 (4-ounce) cans chopped green chiles
3 tablespoons fresh lime juice
1½ cups (6 ounces) shredded reduced-fat Cheddar cheese
¾ cup crushed baked tortilla chips

1. Heat oil in a large nonstick skillet over medium-high heat. Add onion and garlic; sauté 3 minutes. Add fajita seasoning, and cook 1 minute. Stir in water and next 4 ingredients; bring to a boil. Reduce heat, and simmer 10 minutes. Stir in juice. Top each serving with cheese and chips. Yield: 6 servings (serving size: 2 cups soup, ¼ cup cheese, and 2 tablespoons tortilla chips).

CALORIES 292 (18% from fat); FAT 5.8g (sat 1.8g, mono 2.6g, poly 0.9g); PROTEIN 18.5g; CARB 43.8g; FIBER 9.3g; CHOL 6mg; IRON 2.4mg; SODIUM 1,262mg; CALC 264mg

Vietnamese-Spiced Pork Chops

These pork chops are best served with rice.

4 (4-ounce) boneless center-cut loin pork chops (about ½ inch thick)
2 tablespoons brown sugar
1 tablespoon bottled minced fresh ginger
2 teaspoons paprika
2 teaspoons ground coriander
2 teaspoons bottled minced garlic
¾ teaspoon salt
½ teaspoon crushed red pepper
Cooking spray
Sliced green onions (optional)

1. Lightly score a diamond pattern on both sides of pork. Combine sugar and next 6 ingredients; rub evenly over pork.
2. Heat a large nonstick skillet coated with cooking spray over medium-high heat. Add pork; cook 4 minutes on each side or until done. Garnish with green onions, if desired. Yield: 4 servings (serving size: 1 pork chop).

CALORIES 199 (29% from fat); FAT 6.4g (sat 2.1g, mono 2.7g, poly 1g); PROTEIN 25.3g; CARB 9.2g; FIBER 1.1g; CHOL 62mg; IRON 1.4mg; SODIUM 491mg; CALC 42mg

Udon Noodles with Sesame and Tofu

Peeling the cucumber in this recipe is a matter of preference. If the cucumbers are unwaxed, we leave the peel on.

8 ounces udon noodles
2 tablespoons seasoned rice or cider vinegar
1½ tablespoons low-sodium soy sauce
1 tablespoon dark sesame oil
1 teaspoon bottled minced garlic
1 teaspoon bottled minced fresh ginger
¼ teaspoon crushed red pepper
1½ cups diced cucumber
1 cup shredded carrot
¼ cup (1-inch) diagonally cut green onions
2 teaspoons sesame seeds, toasted
¼ teaspoon salt
1 (8-ounce) package baked Asian-style tofu (such as White Wave), drained and diced

1. Cook noodles according to package directions, omitting salt and fat.
2. While noodles cook, combine vinegar and next 5 ingredients in a small bowl, stirring with a whisk. Drain noodles. Combine cooked noodles, cucumber, and remaining 5 ingredients in a large bowl. Drizzle with vinegar mixture; toss well. Yield: 4 servings (serving size: 2 cups).

CALORIES 344 (29% from fat); FAT 11g (sat 1.5g, mono 1.4g, poly 1.5g); PROTEIN 18.1g; CARB 41.2g; FIBER 2.7g; CHOL 0mg; IRON 4.3mg; SODIUM 938mg; CALC 64mg

cooking light profile

Keeping the Faith

How one hard-working Mom took on Atlanta and gave Mother Nature a helping hand.

For nine-plus years, Sally Bethea has been *the* Riverkeeper, which is to say she is the boss of the Atlanta-based upper Chattahoochee Riverkeeper—an organization devoted to the protection and stewardship of the Chattahoochee River.

Grilled Lemon-Soy Salmon

Make sure to coat the fish with cooking spray before turning it so it won't stick to the grill.

3 tablespoons dry white wine
3 tablespoons fresh lemon juice
1½ tablespoons low-sodium soy sauce
1½ teaspoons olive oil
½ teaspoon salt
1 garlic clove, minced
4 (6-ounce) salmon fillets (about 1 inch thick)
Cooking spray
Sliced green onions (optional)

1. Combine first 6 ingredients in a large heavy-duty zip-top plastic bag. Add salmon to bag; seal. Marinate in refrigerator 40 minutes, turning once.
2. Prepare grill.
3. Remove fillets from bag, and reserve marinade. Place fillets on grill rack coated with cooking spray, skin sides down; grill 5 minutes. Brush with reserved marinade; discard remaining marinade. Lightly coat fillets with cooking spray. Turn fish over; grill 3 minutes or until fish flakes easily when tested with a fork. Garnish with onions, if desired. Yield: 4 servings (serving size: 1 fillet).

CALORIES 216 (44% from fat); FAT 10.6g (sat 2.4g, mono 4.9g, poly 2.5g); PROTEIN 27.4g; CARB 10.1g; FIBER 0g; CHOL 65mg; IRON 0.5mg; SODIUM 308mg; CALC 18mg

Darjeeling-Chocolate Layer Cake,
page 340

Hunter's Stew, page 337

Vegetarian Stuffed Peppers, page 315

Pork Loin Chops with Cinnamon Apples,
page 317

Sweet Potato and Canadian Bacon Hash,
page 329

All About Potatoes

How to choose and best prepare America's favorite vegetable.

When potatoes were first introduced to Europe in the late 16th century, people feared they were poisonous. South America's Incas knew better, as they had been cultivating the tubers for some 2,000 years. Potatoes eventually caught on in Europe and steadily grew in popularity. Today in this country they're the ultimate comfort food. What Sunday dinner would be complete without fluffy mashed potatoes or a cheesy potato gratin?

Potatoes boast a tapestry of tints, tastes, and textures—red, blue, white, and purple; nutty and earthy; starchy, waxy, firm, and creamy. Although most people stick to the basics, working with red-skinned, white, baking, and sometimes Yukon gold potatoes, there are now a number of varieties available. Here are classic potato dishes and a few new twists, along with types, tips, and techniques, all guaranteed to put potatoes front and center at any meal.

MAKE AHEAD
Chilean Beef and Purple Potato Salad

Purple potatoes combine with South American flavors for an exciting main-dish salad. Boiling the potatoes whole allows them to retain their brilliant color; letting them stand before they're cut "sets" the color.

BEEF:
- 1 tablespoon chili powder
- 1 tablespoon fresh lime juice
- 1 teaspoon olive oil
- ½ teaspoon salt
- ¼ teaspoon ground cumin
- ⅛ teaspoon garlic powder
- 1½ pounds flank steak, trimmed

VEGETABLES:
- 2 pounds purple potatoes
- 1½ cups fresh corn kernels (about 3 ears)
- 1 cup chopped red bell pepper
- ½ cup thinly sliced celery
- 3 tablespoons chopped green onions

DRESSING:
- 3 tablespoons fresh lime juice
- 1 tablespoon olive oil
- 1 teaspoon cumin seeds, toasted
- ½ teaspoon salt
- ¼ teaspoon freshly ground black pepper
- ¼ teaspoon hot sauce

REMAINING INGREDIENTS:
- Cooking spray
- 2 tablespoons chopped fresh cilantro

1. To prepare beef, combine first 6 ingredients in a large zip-top plastic bag. Add steak to bag; seal. Marinate in refrigerator 1 hour, turning occasionally.
2. To prepare vegetables, place potatoes in a saucepan; cover with water. Bring to a boil. Reduce heat; simmer 20 minutes or just until tender (do not overcook). Drain and let stand 30 minutes. Peel potatoes. Quarter lengthwise. Combine potato, corn, bell pepper, celery, and onions.
3. Preheat broiler.
4. To prepare dressing, combine 3 tablespoons juice and next 5 ingredients, stirring with a whisk.
5. Remove steak from bag; discard marinade. Place steak on a broiler rack coated with cooking spray. Broil 6 minutes on each side or until desired degree of doneness. Let stand 5 minutes. Cut steak in half lengthwise. Cut each half diagonally across the grain into thin slices. Add steak to potato mixture. Drizzle with dressing; toss well to coat. Sprinkle with cilantro. Yield: 6 servings (serving size: 1½ cups).

CALORIES 384 (30% from fat); FAT 12.6g (sat 4.3g, mono 5.9g, poly 1g); PROTEIN 27.6g; CARB 41.5g; FIBER 5g; CHOL 57mg; IRON 3.5mg; SODIUM 494mg; CALC 28mg

STAFF FAVORITE
Sweet Potato and Canadian Bacon Hash
(pictured on page 328)

Don't boil the potatoes too long; remove them from the water while they're al dente.

- 4 cups (¾-inch) diced peeled sweet potato (about 1 pound)
- 2 cups (¾-inch) diced red potato (about 8 ounces)
- 2 tablespoons vegetable oil
- 1 cup diced Canadian bacon (about 8 ounces)
- 1 cup chopped green bell pepper
- ⅔ cup chopped green onions
- ¾ teaspoon salt
- ½ teaspoon celery seed
- ½ teaspoon freshly ground black pepper
- ⅛ teaspoon grated whole nutmeg
- ¼ cup fat-free, less-sodium chicken broth
- 1 tablespoon cider vinegar

1. Place potatoes in a saucepan, and cover with water. Bring to a boil. Reduce heat, and simmer 5 minutes. Drain.
2. Heat oil in a large cast iron or non-stick skillet over medium heat. Add bacon; cook 4 minutes, stirring frequently. Add bell pepper and onions; cook 2 minutes, stirring frequently. Add potatoes, salt, celery seed, black pepper, and nutmeg; cook 4 minutes, gently stirring occasionally. Stir in broth and vinegar. Toss gently until liquid is absorbed. Yield: 6 servings (serving size: about 1 cup).

CALORIES 207 (30% from fat); FAT 6.8g (sat 1.4g, mono 2.1g, poly 3g); PROTEIN 8.8g; CARB 28g; FIBER 3g; CHOL 19mg; IRON 1.4mg; SODIUM 711mg; CALC 32mg

Chunky Potato-Crab Chowder

This easy New England-style chowder lets red-skinned potatoes shine. Cream-style corn is a surprise ingredient that adds a little sweetness and contributes to the creamy texture.

    2   tablespoons butter
    1   cup chopped onion
    ¾   cup chopped celery
    1   garlic clove, minced
    3½ cups (1-inch) cubed red potato
        (about 1 pound)
    3   tablespoons all-purpose flour
    2½ cups 2% reduced-fat milk
    2   teaspoons chopped fresh
        thyme
    ½   teaspoon freshly ground black
        pepper
    ¼   teaspoon grated whole nutmeg
    1   (14¾-ounce) can cream-style
        corn
    1   (14-ounce) can fat-free,
        less-sodium chicken broth
    8   ounces lump crabmeat, shell
        pieces removed
    3   tablespoons chopped fresh
        parsley
    1   teaspoon salt

1. Melt butter in a large saucepan over medium-high heat. Add onion, celery, and garlic; sauté 4 minutes. Add potato; sauté 1 minute. Sprinkle with flour; sauté 1 minute. Stir in milk and next 5 ingredients. Bring to a simmer over medium heat, stirring frequently. Cover, reduce heat, and simmer 20 minutes or until potato is tender, stirring occasionally. Stir in crab, parsley, and salt; cook 5 minutes, stirring occasionally. Yield: 6 servings (serving size: 1½ cups).

CALORIES 265 (23% from fat); FAT 6.8g (sat 3.8g, mono 1.9g, poly 0.6g); PROTEIN 16.3g; CARB 36.5g; FIBER 3.1g; CHOL 47mg; IRON 1.5mg; SODIUM 968mg; CALC 176mg

Potato, Ham, and Spinach Gratin

Peel and slice the potatoes just before assembly. Using a "V" slicer or mandoline really helps to make uniformly thin slices.

    2   teaspoons olive oil
    ½   cup thinly sliced shallots
    2   garlic cloves, minced
    1   cup chopped reduced-fat ham
        (about 4 ounces)
    1   teaspoon salt, divided
    ¾   teaspoon freshly ground black
        pepper, divided
    ⅛   teaspoon grated whole nutmeg
    1   (10-ounce) package frozen
        chopped spinach, thawed,
        drained, and squeezed dry
    2   cups 1% low-fat milk
    ⅓   cup all-purpose flour
    7   cups (⅛-inch-thick) slices peeled
        Yukon gold potato (about 2½
        pounds)
    Cooking spray
    ¾   cup (3 ounces) shredded Gruyère
        cheese

1. Preheat oven to 375°.
2. Heat oil in a small nonstick skillet over medium-high heat. Add shallots and garlic; sauté 2 minutes or until tender. Remove from heat; stir in ham, ¼ teaspoon salt, ¼ teaspoon pepper, nutmeg, and spinach. Combine milk, flour, ¼ teaspoon salt, and ½ teaspoon pepper, stirring with a whisk.
3. Arrange half of potato slices in an 8-inch square baking pan coated with cooking spray; sprinkle with ¼ teaspoon salt. Spread spinach mixture over potato slices. Arrange remaining potato slices over spinach mixture; pour milk mixture over top. Sprinkle with ¼ teaspoon salt. Cover with foil coated with cooking spray. Bake at 375° for 1 hour and 15 minutes or until potato is tender. Uncover and sprinkle with cheese; bake an additional 15 minutes.
4. Preheat broiler.
5. Broil gratin 2 minutes or until cheese is lightly browned. Yield: 8 servings.

CALORIES 240 (24% from fat); FAT 6.3g (sat 2.9g, mono 2.5g, poly 0.5g); PROTEIN 12.8g; CARB 34g; FIBER 3g; CHOL 22mg; IRON 1.7mg; SODIUM 581mg; CALC 235mg

Ajiaco
Potato, Corn, and Chicken Stew

Use the small holes on a box grater to shred the baking potatoes for this traditional Columbian dish; if you shred them coarsely, they won't dissolve into the broth.

    1   tablespoon olive oil, divided
    12   chicken thighs (about 3 pounds),
         skinned
    ½   cup chopped onion
    ½   cup thinly sliced carrot
    3   cups fat-free, less-sodium
         chicken broth
    1   cup fresh corn kernels (about 2 ears)
    1½   teaspoons chopped fresh oregano
    1   teaspoon chopped fresh thyme
    2½   cups finely shredded peeled
         baking potato
    2½   cups cubed peeled Yukon gold
         potato (about 1 pound)
    ¼   cup chopped fresh cilantro
    1   tablespoon fresh lime juice
    1   teaspoon salt
    ½   teaspoon hot pepper sauce
    ¼   teaspoon freshly ground black
         pepper

1. Heat 1½ teaspoons oil in a large Dutch oven over medium-high heat. Add half of chicken; cook 5 minutes, browning on all sides. Remove chicken from pan. Repeat procedure with 1½ teaspoons oil and remaining chicken. Remove from pan; cover and keep warm.
2. Add onion and carrot to pan; sauté 2 minutes. Stir in broth, corn, oregano, and thyme; bring to a simmer. Stir in shredded potato and chicken; cover and simmer 20 minutes, stirring frequently to keep potato from sticking to pan. Add cubed potato; cover and simmer 20 minutes, stirring frequently. Stir in cilantro and remaining ingredients, and cook, uncovered, 5 minutes, stirring frequently. Yield: 6 servings (serving size: 2 thighs and 1 cup broth mixture).
WINE NOTE: This stew is wonderful with a soft, silky red. For one with a Spanish connection, try Muga Rioja Reserva 1997 from Rioja, Spain ($17).

CALORIES 331 (21% from fat); FAT 7.8g (sat 1.7g, mono 3.3g, poly 1.6g); PROTEIN 30.3g; CARB 34.4g; FIBER 3.7g; CHOL 107mg; IRON 2mg; SODIUM 744mg; CALC 34mg

Potato Varieties

Baking Potatoes

These long, dusky brown tubers with numerous eyes are the gold standard for potatoes: starchy, floury, large, and slightly nutty. Some call them "Idaho" potatoes because that state traditionally grows more than any other; today Idaho produces almost a third of the country's potato crop.
Varieties: Generic, hybridized baking potatoes have begun showing up in markets, but the preferred choice is the ashen-skinned russet, with its unique balance of starch and moisture. Certain dishes, like gnocchi, call specifically for russets. There are different strains—including the russet Burbank, undoubtedly the best baking potato—but stores rarely label potatoes so exactly.
Uses: Despite the name, baking potatoes are also great for making gratins, mashed potatoes, and gnocchi.

White-Fleshed Potatoes

Characterized by pale-beige skin and white flesh, these medium- to low-starch potatoes are oblong (usually grown in California or Arizona) or spherical (most often from Maine). Some old-fashioned cookbooks refer to them as "boiling" potatoes, but because they're moist yet firm, they're also good braised and stewed.
Varieties: Irish Cobblers and California long whites, excellent all-around potatoes, are the most common type—they're slightly dry, very firm, and mildly earthy in taste. Sweeter Katahdins and Kennebecs from Maine also serve many purposes, although they may have too much starch for successful roasting. They become crisp on the outside but stay very creamy inside. If you enjoy this textural contrast—irresistible to some, cloying to others—try white creamers: tiny, velvety spheres with a woody taste that take on an unbelievable creaminess when roasted in their skins.
Uses: Try white-fleshed potatoes boiled, roasted, or steamed in gratins, salads, and scalloped dishes. They're also excellent

wrapped in foil and placed in the embers of a charcoal fire.

Red-Skinned Potatoes

Once called "new" potatoes—probably because of their small size, although some of the smallest take the longest to mature—red-skinned potatoes are waxy, meaning they have very little starch. They're the workhorses of potatoes: great most ways, with less fuss than high-starch potatoes, which can scorch and burn. Red-skinned potatoes have the thinnest skins of any type, so they're usually cooked unpeeled.
Varieties: Red-skinned potatoes encompass far more than Red Bliss, the variety most commonly thought of as a new potato. Nutty and drier exotics, like Desirees, French fingerlings, and Red La Sodas, are often available at local farmers' markets, where labeling produce exactly is a passion.
Uses: Red potatoes shine when boiled, roasted, steamed, or tossed in salads or soups.

Yellow-Fleshed Potatoes

These buttery, creamy potatoes have a good balance of starchiness and waxiness, so they work well in complicated dishes. They're also quite good prepared simply—steamed or boiled, for example. Their flesh has too much moisture and starch, however, for baking or roasting; the skins rarely get crisp, and the insides turn mushy. Yellow-fleshed potatoes store exceptionally well.
Varieties: By far the most common is the Yukon gold, developed in Canada in the 1980s. A wonderful addition to stews or braised dishes, it also pairs with greens like spinach and dandelion. Other varieties, like Ozettes, Rattes, and Charlottes, are waxier and even drier—and do best with butter or olive oil.
Uses: These work well in gratins and stews, and they make mashed potatoes that look like they've already been buttered.

Purple Potatoes

These ancient potatoes are most closely related to those the Incas were cultivating when the Spanish landed in the New World. Today, most purple potatoes still grow in South America. They have a strong, distinct flavor: nutty, earthy, and a little bitter. They run the gamut from medium-starchy to quite waxy, and from deep purple to bright blue. Many varieties turn gray when cooked. Most will stain your hands, so wear rubber gloves while peeling.
Varieties: Blues and purple Peruvians have the nuttiest taste, but because they're dry, add fat to enhance their flavor and texture. Caribes have purple skin and white flesh; their skins are quite bitter, almost metallic, while the flesh is creamy and delicate.
Uses: Purple potatoes are good to roast or mash, and are delicious in salads.

Sweet Potatoes

Sweet potatoes are actually members of the morning glory family—they're warm-weather plants, happy in the Caribbean and other hot, humid climates. Several years ago, Southern marketers tried to paste the name "yam" onto their sweet potatoes as a way to distinguish them from the Irish potato—but that seems to have only added confusion. A true yam is native to West Africa and Asia, and is entirely different botanically.
Varieties: Sweet potatoes range from red to orange. The most familiar are Red Garnets, a favorite at Thanksgiving. There are also white sweet potatoes—most are quite dry, better in stews or gratins with lots of added moisture. A few white sweet potatoes are Asian varieties that turn gelatinous when grated.
Uses: Their high moisture content means sweet potatoes are best for mashing or tossing into soups and stews, though many people also enjoy them baked or roasted.

Creamy Herbed Mashed Potatoes

Mash the potatoes by hand just until creamy—overworking the potatoes will make them gummy.

 4 cups cubed peeled Yukon gold potato (about 2 pounds)
 ½ cup 2% reduced-fat milk
 ¼ cup low-fat sour cream
 3 tablespoons butter
 3 tablespoons chopped fresh chives
 2 tablespoons chopped fresh parsley
 ½ teaspoon salt
 ¼ teaspoon freshly ground black pepper

1. Place potato in a saucepan; cover with water. Bring to a boil; cover, reduce heat, and simmer 10 minutes or until tender. Drain. Return potato to pan. Add milk and remaining ingredients; mash with a potato masher to desired consistency. Yield: 6 servings (serving size: ¾ cup).

CALORIES 215 (30% from fat); FAT 7.1g (sat 4.5g, mono 1.8g, poly 0.3g); PROTEIN 4.5g; CARB 34.5g; FIBER 2.4g; CHOL 20mg; IRON 0.7mg; SODIUM 280mg; CALC 51mg

How to Bake Potatoes

1. Position the rack in the bottom third of the oven; preheat oven to 400°.
2. Scrub and prick the potatoes.
3. Sprinkle with a little kosher or sea salt, if desired.
4. Bake at 400° for 1 hour or until tender when pierced with a knife.
5. For maximum fluffiness, cut an "X" into each cooked potato, then press on the ends to push the flesh up and out. This prevents steam from building up and making the flesh dense.

For faster results, prick the potato in several places and microwave at HIGH 3 minutes. (Cook 1 minute extra for each additional spud.) Transfer to a 400° oven and bake 30 minutes or until crunchy outside and soft inside.

Meat and Potatoes Menu
serves 4

This simple meal is a snap to pull together. Place the potatoes in the oven after the pork has cooked for 10 minutes so that everything is done at the same time.

Simple Roasted Fingerlings

Mustard-rubbed pork tenderloin*

Frozen creamed spinach

Strawberries drizzled with balsamic vinegar

*Rub 1 tablespoon coarse-ground mustard evenly over 1 (1-pound) trimmed pork tenderloin. Sprinkle evenly with ½ teaspoon dried crushed rosemary, ½ teaspoon salt, and ¼ teaspoon black pepper. Place pork on a broiler pan coated with cooking spray. Bake at 400° for 30 minutes or until thermometer registers 160° (slightly pink). Let stand 5 minutes before slicing.

Simple Roasted Fingerlings

Small fingerlings become deliciously fluffy inside when roasted. We like the texture of kosher salt, but you can also use ½ teaspoon regular table salt. Red-fleshed fingerling potatoes are waxier than yellow-fleshed, so they crisp on the outside; use whatever variety you can find, since either will work.

 1 tablespoon olive oil
 1½ pounds red- or yellow-fleshed fingerling potatoes
 Cooking spray
 ¾ teaspoon kosher salt
 ½ teaspoon freshly ground black pepper
 ⅛ teaspoon ground red pepper

1. Preheat oven to 400°.
2. Combine oil and potatoes on a jelly roll pan coated with cooking spray, tossing to coat. Sprinkle with salt and peppers; toss to coat. Bake at 400° for 20 minutes or until tender when pierced with a knife. Yield: 4 servings.

CALORIES 196 (17% from fat); FAT 3.6g (sat 0.6g, mono 2.5g, poly 0.4g); PROTEIN 4.5g; CARB 36.7g; FIBER 4g; CHOL 0mg; IRON 1.9mg; SODIUM 367mg; CALC 32mg

Stir-Fried Potatoes with Vinegar and Hot Peppers

Waxy white potatoes stay firm and hold their shape when cooked. Cut the potatoes for this stir-fry into threads using a mandoline or food processor fitted with a julienne blade to quickly cut the potatoes. Sauté just a few minutes so they're still a bit crunchy.

 3 tablespoons rice vinegar
 4 teaspoons low-sodium soy sauce
 1 tablespoon dry sherry
 1½ teaspoons sugar
 ¼ teaspoon salt
 4 cups (1-inch) julienne-cut peeled white potato (about 1½ pounds)
 1 tablespoon peanut oil
 ⅓ cup thinly sliced green onions
 1 tablespoon grated peeled fresh ginger
 2 garlic cloves, minced
 1 to 2 Thai chiles, thinly sliced

1. Combine first 5 ingredients; set aside.
2. Soak potato in cold water 5 minutes. Drain and pat dry.
3. Heat oil in a large nonstick skillet over medium-high heat. Add onions, ginger, garlic, and chiles; stir-fry 30 seconds. Add potato; stir-fry 4 minutes or until crisp-tender. Add vinegar mixture, and stir-fry 1 minute. Serve immediately. Yield: 4 servings (serving size: 1 cup).

CALORIES 207 (16% from fat); FAT 3.6g (sat 0.6g, mono 1.6g, poly 1.2g); PROTEIN 3.8g; CARB 40.3g; FIBER 3.1g; CHOL 0mg; IRON 0.8mg; SODIUM 336mg; CALC 13mg

Fingerling Fact

The term *fingerling* refers to a potato's long, thin shape rather than to a type of tuber. Red-skinned, yellow-fleshed, white, and purple fingerlings vary in texture from waxy to starchy. Because they're most often cultivated in small batches, fingerlings tend to have a pronounced flavor.

Roasted-Garlic Pierogi with Shallot-Browned Butter

Pierogi are Polish dumplings. Unfortunately, they often contain lots of cream or chicken fat to help make the potato filling creamy. Starchy russets, however, break down and provide a creaminess that allows you to forego the fat.

FILLING:
 1 pound baking potatoes
 1 small whole garlic head
 1 teaspoon olive oil
 ¼ cup fat-free sour cream
 ½ teaspoon salt
 ¼ teaspoon freshly ground black pepper

DOUGH:
 ½ cup plain fat-free yogurt
 ½ teaspoon salt
 2 large eggs, lightly beaten
 3 cups all-purpose flour
 12 cups water

BROWNED BUTTER:
 4 tablespoons butter
 ⅔ cup finely chopped shallots

1. Preheat oven to 400°.
2. To prepare filling, pierce potatoes with a fork; place potatoes on a baking sheet. Remove white papery skin from garlic head (do not peel or separate cloves). Drizzle garlic head with oil, and wrap in foil. Place garlic on baking sheet. Bake potato and garlic at 400° for 1 hour or until tender. Cool slightly. Peel potatoes; discard skins. Place potatoes in a large bowl. Separate garlic cloves; squeeze to extract garlic pulp. Add garlic to potatoes, and mash with a potato masher until smooth. Stir in sour cream, ½ teaspoon salt, and pepper. Set aside.
3. To prepare dough, combine yogurt, ½ teaspoon salt, and eggs in a large bowl. Lightly spoon flour into dry measuring cups; level with a knife. Add flour to yogurt mixture; stir well. Turn dough out onto a lightly floured surface; knead until smooth. Divide dough into 24 equal portions, shaping each into a ball. Working with 1 portion at a time (cover remaining dough to prevent drying), roll

each ball into a 3½-inch circle on a lightly floured surface. Spoon 1 rounded tablespoon filling onto half of each circle. Fold dough over filling; press edges together to seal.
4. Bring 12 cups water to a boil in a large Dutch oven. Add half of pierogi; cook 6 minutes or until tender. Remove pierogi with a slotted spoon; place in a colander. Repeat procedure with remaining pierogi.
5. To prepare browned butter, melt butter in a large nonstick skillet over medium heat; cook 10 minutes or until lightly browned (be careful not to burn). Add shallots; cook 1 minute. Add pierogi; cook 2 minutes, tossing to coat. Yield: 6 servings (serving size: 4 pierogi).
WINE NOTE: This recipe works best with Alsace Pinot Gris, a full-bodied, dry, lightly spicy white made without any oak influence. Try Pierre Sparr Pinot Gris Reserve 2000 from Alsace, France ($15).

CALORIES 435 (23% from fat); FAT 10.9g (sat 5.5g, mono 3.4g, poly 0.9g); PROTEIN 12.2g; CARB 72.1g; FIBER 3.1g; CHOL 93mg; IRON 3.8mg; SODIUM 516mg; CALC 80mg

---

MAKE AHEAD • FREEZABLE
Potato-Dill Bread

Use dried, not fresh, dill so it slowly infuses the bread as it bakes. The loaf is great for sandwiches—try one with smoked turkey, Havarti cheese, sliced cucumber, and a little light mayonnaise mixed with dried dill.

 ½ cup warm water (100° to 110°)
 1 tablespoon sugar
 1 tablespoon dried dill
 1 teaspoon salt
 1 package dry yeast (about 2¼ teaspoons)
 ⅔ cup mashed baking potatoes
 2 tablespoons canola oil
 2¼ cups all-purpose flour, divided
   Cooking spray

1. Combine first 5 ingredients in a large bowl. Let stand 5 minutes. Stir in potatoes and oil.
2. Lightly spoon flour into dry measuring cups; level with a knife. Add 2 cups flour to potato mixture; stir until a soft dough forms. Turn dough out onto a floured surface. Knead dough until

smooth and elastic (about 10 minutes); add enough of remaining flour, 1 tablespoon at a time, to prevent dough from sticking to hands.
3. Place dough in a large bowl coated with cooking spray, turning to coat top. Cover and let rise in a warm place (85°), free from drafts, 55 minutes or until doubled in size. (Gently press two fingers into dough. If indentation remains, dough has risen enough.)
4. Punch dough down. Let rest 5 minutes. Roll into a 14 x 7-inch rectangle on a lightly floured surface. Roll up tightly, starting with a short edge, pressing firmly to eliminate air pockets. Pinch seam and ends to seal. Place roll, seam side down, in an 8 x 4-inch loaf pan coated with cooking spray. Coat dough with cooking spray. Cover and let rise 35 minutes or until doubled in size.
5. Preheat oven to 350°.
6. Uncover dough. Bake at 350° for 30 minutes or until loaf is browned on top and sounds hollow when tapped. Remove loaf from pan. Cool on a wire rack 15 minutes. Yield: 10 servings (serving size: 1 slice).

CALORIES 144 (21% from fat); FAT 3.3g (sat 0.4g, mono 1.7g, poly 1g); PROTEIN 3.3g; CARB 24.7g; FIBER 1.1g; CHOL 0mg; IRON 1.6mg; SODIUM 251mg; CALC 10mg

---

The Best Baked Potato

Nothing inspires culinary rivalries like the simple task of baking a potato. Follow these tips for success:
• Use only baking potatoes, preferably russet Burbanks that weigh 8 to 10 ounces each.
• Prick the potato in a few places with a fork before baking. Doing so lets excess moisture escape, rendering a fluffier inside and preventing the skin from cracking.
• Don't wrap the potato in aluminum foil: The skin will steam instead of becoming crunchy.
• Don't insert an aluminum potato nail into the flesh. It lets too much moisture escape and creates a rift of tough, fibrous flesh in the potato's center.

Ten Great Baked Potato Toppings

1. Chicken salad and sliced celery

2. Mozzarella cheese and purchased marinara or pizza sauce

3. Any low-fat salad dressing, including Ranch, Russian, or a fruity vinaigrette

4. Guacamole and salsa

5. Pesto made from any herb, including sage, basil, or cilantro

6. Bottled condiments, including Thai peanut sauce, mango chutney, or barbecue sauce

7. Steamed vegetables, including broccoli, cauliflower, or asparagus

8. Shredded rotisserie chicken tossed with hoisin sauce, chopped green onions, and grated peeled fresh ginger

9. Sautéed mushrooms and chives

10. Cooked shrimp and cocktail sauce

Potato Gnocchi in Mushroom Broth

Use only high-starch, dry-textured russet potatoes to make these light Italian dumplings. Serve the potato pillows in a delicate broth for a comforting fall soup. Bake the potatoes while the broth simmers, or make the broth up to 1 day ahead.

BROTH:

- 6 cups water
- 3 cups sliced cremini mushrooms
- 2 cups thinly sliced carrot
- 2 cups thinly sliced leek
- 1½ cups thinly sliced celery
- ½ teaspoon salt
- ½ teaspoon freshly ground black pepper
- 12 dried shiitake mushroom caps (about 1 ounce)
- 5 thyme sprigs
- 1 tablespoon low-sodium soy sauce
- 1 tablespoon butter
- 2 cups thinly sliced cremini mushrooms
- 1 cup (1-inch) julienne-cut leek
- 1 cup (1-inch) julienne-cut carrot

GNOCCHI:

- 1¾ pounds baking potatoes
- 1½ cups all-purpose flour, divided
- 1 teaspoon salt
- 1 large egg yolk
- Cooking spray
- 12 cups water
- 2 tablespoons chopped fresh chives

1. To prepare broth, combine first 9 ingredients in a Dutch oven; bring to a boil. Cover, reduce heat, and simmer 45 minutes. Strain through a sieve into a bowl; discard solids. Stir in soy sauce.

2. Preheat oven to 400°.

3. Melt butter in a large nonstick skillet over medium heat. Add 2 cups mushrooms, 1 cup leek, and 1 cup carrot; cook 10 minutes or until tender, stirring occasionally. Set aside.

4. To prepare gnocchi, pierce potatoes with a fork; bake at 400° for 1 hour or until tender. Cool slightly. Peel potatoes; mash. Lightly spoon flour into dry measuring cups, and level with a knife. Combine potatoes, 1¼ cups flour, 1 teaspoon salt, and egg yolk. Stir well to form a smooth dough. Turn dough out onto a lightly floured surface. Knead until smooth; add enough of remaining flour, 1 tablespoon at a time, to prevent dough from sticking to hands. Divide dough into 4 equal portions, and shape each portion into a 15-inch-long rope. Cut each rope into 15 (1-inch) pieces, and roll each piece into a ball. Drag a fork's tines over each ball, forming a concave shape. Place gnocchi on a baking sheet coated with cooking spray. Cover and set aside.

5. Bring water to a boil in a large Dutch oven. Add half of gnocchi; cook 1½ minutes or until gnocchi float. (Do not overcook or gnocchi will fall apart.) Remove gnocchi with a slotted spoon; place in a colander. Repeat procedure with remaining gnocchi. Bring broth to a simmer; stir in mushroom mixture. Place 10 gnocchi in each of 6 soup bowls. Ladle 1 cup broth mixture into each bowl; sprinkle with chives. Serve immediately. Yield: 6 servings.

CALORIES 261 (11% from fat); FAT 3.3g (sat 1.5g, mono 0.9g, poly 0.4g); PROTEIN 7g; CARB 51.4g; FIBER 3.6g; CHOL 41mg; IRON 2.7mg; SODIUM 713mg; CALC 32mg

A Chicken for Every Pot

Sunday Dinner Menu
serves 4

Garden Salad with Honey Vinaigrette

Sage Pesto-Rubbed Roast Chicken

Cheddar Grit Cakes with Roasted Peppers

Garlicky Lemon Broccoli

Pear-Amaretti Crumble

QUICK & EASY • MAKE AHEAD
Garden Salad with Honey Vinaigrette

- 6 cups gourmet salad greens
- 1 cup halved grape tomatoes
- 1 cup thinly sliced cucumber
- ½ cup shredded carrot
- ¼ cup chopped red onion
- ¼ cup Honey Vinaigrette

1. Combine first 5 ingredients in a large bowl. Drizzle with Honey Vinaigrette, and toss gently to coat. Yield: 4 servings (serving size: about 1¼ cups).

(Totals include Honey Vinaigrette) CALORIES 61 (31% from fat); FAT 2.4g (sat 0.3g, mono 1.4g, poly 0.4g); PROTEIN 2.3g; CARB 9.4g; FIBER 3g; CHOL 0mg; IRON 1.5mg; SODIUM 171mg; CALC 60mg

HONEY VINAIGRETTE:

Use leftover vinaigrette as a marinade for chicken or to dress a salad later in the week.

- ¼ cup fat-free, less-sodium chicken broth
- 1½ tablespoons olive oil
- 1½ tablespoons white balsamic or white wine vinegar
- 1 tablespoon honey
- 1 tablespoon minced shallots
- 2 teaspoons minced fresh tarragon
- 2 teaspoons Dijon mustard
- ½ teaspoon salt
- ½ teaspoon freshly ground black pepper

1. Combine all ingredients, stirring well with a whisk. Cover and chill at least 30 minutes. Yield: about ⅔ cup (serving size: 1 tablespoon).

NOTE: Store, covered, in the refrigerator up to 1 week.

CALORIES 26 (66% from fat); FAT 1.9g (sat 0.3g, mono 1.4g, poly 0.2g); PROTEIN 0.2g; CARB 2.2g; FIBER 0g; CHOL 0mg; IRON 0.1mg; SODIUM 141mg; CALC 4mg

Sage Pesto-Rubbed Roast Chicken

PESTO:

- ⅓ cup fat-free, less-sodium chicken broth
- ⅓ cup chopped fresh parsley
- ¼ cup chopped fresh sage
- 2 tablespoons chopped walnuts, toasted
- 1 teaspoon extravirgin olive oil
- ½ teaspoon salt
- 3 garlic cloves, peeled

CHICKEN:

- 1 (7-pound) roasting chicken
  Cooking spray

1. Preheat oven to 450°.
2. To prepare pesto, combine first 7 ingredients in a blender or food processor; process until smooth.
3. To prepare chicken, remove and discard giblets and neck from chicken. Rinse chicken with cold water; pat dry. Trim excess fat. Starting at neck cavity, loosen skin from breast and drumsticks by inserting fingers, gently pushing between skin and meat. Rub pesto under loosened skin and over breast and drumsticks. Lift wing tips up and over back; tuck under chicken. Place chicken, breast side up, on a broiler pan coated with cooking spray; bake at 450° for 30 minutes. Reduce oven temperature to 350° (do not remove chicken from oven); bake an additional 1½ hours or until a thermometer registers 180°. Let stand 10 minutes. Discard skin. Yield: 6 servings (serving size: about 5 ounces).

CALORIES 298 (39% from fat); FAT 12.9g (sat 3.1g, mono 4.7g, poly 3.4g); PROTEIN 42.1g; CARB 1.2g; FIBER 0.3g; CHOL 126mg; IRON 2mg; SODIUM 345mg; CALC 38mg

Cheddar Grit Cakes with Roasted Peppers

Prepare the peppers up to 1 day ahead, then reheat them in the microwave before serving. This frees the oven so you can roast the chicken.

GRITS:

- 1 cup 1% low-fat milk
- 1 (14-ounce) can fat-free, less-sodium chicken broth
- ¾ cup uncooked quick-cooking grits
- 2 teaspoons minced jalapeño pepper
- ½ cup (2 ounces) shredded extrasharp Cheddar cheese
  Cooking spray

PEPPERS:

- 3 red or orange bell peppers
- 2 teaspoons extravirgin olive oil
- 1 teaspoon balsamic vinegar
- ½ teaspoon ground coriander
- ¼ teaspoon salt

1. To prepare grits, bring milk and broth to a boil in a medium saucepan. Stir in grits and jalapeño. Cover, reduce heat, and simmer 5 minutes or until thick. Stir in cheese; cook until cheese melts. Spread grits into a 9-inch square baking pan coated with cooking spray; cover and refrigerate 8 hours or until set.
2. To prepare peppers, cut bell peppers in half lengthwise; discard seeds and membranes. Place pepper halves, skin sides up, on a foil-lined baking sheet, and flatten with hand. Broil 15 minutes or until blackened. Place in a zip-top plastic bag; seal. Let stand 15 minutes. Peel and cut into 1-inch strips. Combine peppers, oil, vinegar, coriander, and salt; toss well.
3. Invert grits onto a cutting board. Cut grits into 4 (4½-inch) squares. Cut each square diagonally into 2 triangles. Heat a large nonstick skillet coated with cooking spray over medium-high heat. Add triangles; cook 4 minutes on each side or until lightly browned. Serve pepper mixture over grit cakes. Yield: 4 servings (serving size: 2 grit cakes and ½ cup pepper mixture).

CALORIES 247 (30% from fat); FAT 8.2g (sat 3.8g, mono 3.3g, poly 0.6g); PROTEIN 10.3g; CARB 33.1g; FIBER 2.5g; CHOL 17mg; IRON 0.9mg; SODIUM 457mg; CALC 189mg

Garlicky Lemon Broccoli

This simple vegetable side dish also pairs well with pork and beef.

- 1½ pounds broccoli spears
- ½ cup water
- 2 teaspoons butter
- ¼ teaspoon salt
- ¼ teaspoon black pepper
- 2 garlic cloves, chopped
- 1 teaspoon grated lemon rind
- 2 teaspoons fresh lemon juice

1. Peel broccoli stems using a vegetable peeler. Combine broccoli and water in a large nonstick skillet; cover and cook over medium-high heat 6 minutes or until crisp-tender. Remove broccoli from pan; wipe pan with a paper towel.
2. Melt butter in pan over medium heat. Add salt, pepper, and garlic; cook 2 minutes, stirring frequently. Add broccoli, and toss to coat. Sprinkle broccoli mixture with rind; drizzle with lemon juice. Yield: 4 servings (serving size: 1 cup).

CALORIES 67 (34% from fat); FAT 2.5g (sat 1.3g, mono 0.6g, poly 0.4g); PROTEIN 5.2g; CARB 9.6g; FIBER 5.1g; CHOL 5mg; IRON 1.5mg; SODIUM 212mg; CALC 85mg

Pear-Amaretti Crumble

This dessert is pretty when it's baked and served in individual dishes, but a 9-inch pie plate also works.

- 2¾ cups thinly sliced pear
- 2 tablespoons brown sugar
- 1 teaspoon grated lemon rind
- 1 tablespoon fresh lemon juice
- ¼ cup dry Marsala wine
- ¼ cup amaretti cookie crumbs (about 4 cookies)
- 4 teaspoons chilled butter, cut into small pieces
- 1⅓ cups vanilla low-fat frozen yogurt

1. Preheat oven to 500°.

Continued

2. Combine first 4 ingredients, tossing to coat. Divide pear mixture evenly among 4 (8-ounce) ramekins; drizzle each serving with 1 tablespoon Marsala. Spoon 1 tablespoon crumbs over each serving; top each serving with 1 teaspoon butter.

3. Bake at 500° for 8 minutes or until filling bubbles and topping browns. Top each serving with ⅓ cup frozen yogurt. Yield: 4 servings.

CALORIES 226 (22% from fat); FAT 5.5g (sat 2.9g, mono 1.4g, poly 0.3g); PROTEIN 3.7g; CARB 39.1g; FIBER 2.8g; CHOL 14mg; IRON 0.5mg; SODIUM 81mg; CALC 122mg

enlightened cook

Father Knows Best

Chef Charles Holmes dishes up sophisticated breakfasts for guests at the Gaige House Inn in Glen Ellen, California, so he can be home for dinner with his children.

Holmes's creations—like the Seared Salmon with Avocado, Shrimp, and Mango Salsa, and the Crisp Polenta Rounds with Fresh Figs, Raspberries, and Maple Syrup featured here—will surely tempt your guests, too.

Seared Salmon with Avocado, Shrimp, and Mango Salsa

Holmes serves salmon for brunch often and says it's a big hit at the Gaige House Inn—particularly when it's hot outside. Since most of the guests have been hiking or walking by the time they show up for brunch, they appreciate a substantial meal. Salmon and avocado contribute heart-healthy monounsaturated fats.

SALMON:
  Cooking spray
  4 (6-ounce) salmon fillets (about
      1 inch thick)
  ¼ teaspoon salt
  ¼ teaspoon black pepper

SALSA:
  1 cup cubed peeled ripe
      mango
  ½ cup medium shrimp, cooked and
      peeled
  ¼ cup chopped red onion
  2 tablespoons chopped fresh
      cilantro
  2 tablespoons fresh lime
      juice
  1 tablespoon olive oil
  1 jalapeño pepper, seeded and
      chopped

SALAD:
  6 cups gourmet salad greens
  2 tablespoons fresh lime juice
  ¼ teaspoon salt
  ⅛ teaspoon freshly ground black
      pepper
  1 peeled avocado, cut into ¼-inch
      wedges

1. To prepare salmon, heat a large non-stick skillet coated with cooking spray over medium heat. Sprinkle fillets with ¼ teaspoon salt and ¼ teaspoon black pepper. Add fillets to pan, and cook 9 minutes or until fish flakes easily when tested with a fork, turning once.

2. To prepare salsa, combine mango and next 6 ingredients in a medium bowl, and toss well.

3. Combine salad greens, juice, ¼ teaspoon salt, ⅛ teaspoon black pepper, and avocado wedges in a large bowl; toss gently. Arrange 1½ cups salad mixture on each of 4 plates; top each with ½ cup salsa and a salmon fillet. Yield: 4 servings.

CALORIES 500 (54% from fat); FAT 30g (sat 5.5g, mono 14g, poly 8.2g); PROTEIN 42g; CARB 15g; FIBER 5g; CHOL 155mg; IRON 3.2mg; SODIUM 482mg; CALC 92mg

Crisp Polenta Rounds with Fresh Figs, Raspberries, and Maple Syrup

Charles Holmes cooks with the seasons, and in summer he makes this dish with peaches and apricots. In winter, he uses dates and dried plums. Holmes typically uses *fromage blanc*, but we substituted yogurt and sour cream.

  2 tablespoons reduced-fat sour
      cream
  2 tablespoons plain low-fat yogurt
  2 teaspoons olive oil
  ¼ cup finely chopped onion
  1 cup dry polenta
  4 cups water
  1 teaspoon salt
  Cooking spray
 20 fresh raspberries
  6 fresh figs, sliced
  ½ cup maple syrup
  Rosemary sprigs (optional)

1. Combine sour cream and yogurt in a small bowl, stirring with a whisk. Cover and chill.

2. Heat oil in a medium saucepan over medium heat; add onion. Cook 5 minutes or until tender, stirring frequently; add polenta. Cook 1 minute, stirring constantly. Add water and salt; stir with a whisk until polenta begins to absorb water (about 2 minutes). Reduce heat to low; cover and cook 25 minutes, stirring occasionally. Pour polenta into an 11 x 7-inch baking dish coated with cooking spray. Refrigerate, uncovered, 30 minutes or until cool.

3. Preheat oven to 400°.

4. Cut polenta into 8 pieces with a 2-inch round cutter, and discard excess polenta. Arrange rounds on a baking sheet coated with cooking spray. Bake at 400° for 40 minutes, turning after 20 minutes. Cool completely on a wire rack.

5. Arrange 2 polenta rounds on each of 4 plates; top each serving with 5 raspberries and 3 fig slices. Drizzle 2 tablespoons maple syrup over each serving; top each with 1 tablespoon sour cream mixture. Garnish with rosemary sprigs, if desired. Yield: 4 servings.

CALORIES 377 (11% from fat); FAT 4.4g (sat 0.7g, mono 2.4g, poly 0.2g); PROTEIN 8g; CARB 80g; FIBER 3.3g; CHOL 3mg; IRON 0.9mg; SODIUM 601mg; CALC 84mg

The Harvest Table

For the Barretts of Chateau Montelena, the perfect blend is family, winemaking, and dinner.

In Calistoga, which is the northernmost town in California's Napa Valley, at the Chateau Montelena Winery, proprietor Jim Barrett tastes and stirs his aromatic Hunter's Stew for a Sunday family supper. Try it on your family, too. But keep in mind that the stew, according to Jim, is always better the second day.

Casual Harvest Dinner Menu
serves 8

Set out bowls of purchased olives, hummus dip, cheese, and breadsticks to start this rustic meal.

Caesar Salad with Crisp Croutons

Hunter's Stew

Fall Pear Galette

Caesar Salad with Crisp Croutons

The Barretts serve Hunter's Stew (recipe at right) with this classic Caesar salad. The Crisp Croutons do double duty—on the stew and the salad.

    ¼   cup egg substitute
    1   tablespoon fresh lemon juice
    3   tablespoons extravirgin olive oil
    3   tablespoons red wine vinegar
    1½ teaspoons anchovy paste
    1   teaspoon Worcestershire sauce
    ½   teaspoon freshly ground black
        pepper
    ¼   teaspoon fine sea salt
    2   garlic cloves, minced
    18 cups torn romaine and hearty field
        greens
    2   cups Crisp Croutons (recipe at
        right)
    ¼   cup (1 ounce) grated fresh
        Parmesan cheese

1. Combine egg substitute and juice; gradually add oil, whisking constantly.

Stir in vinegar and next 5 ingredients. Place greens, croutons, and cheese in a large bowl. Add dressing; toss well to coat. Yield: 12 servings (serving size 1½ cups).

(Totals include Crisp Croutons) CALORIES 75 (48% from fat); FAT 4.4g (sat 0.9g, mono 2.8g, poly 0.5g); PROTEIN 3g; CARB 6g; FIBER 2g; CHOL 2mg; IRON 2mg; SODIUM 210mg; CALC 63mg

QUICK & EASY • MAKE AHEAD

CRISP CROUTONS:

    6   cups (½-inch) cubed sourdough
        or French bread (6 ounces)
    1   tablespoon butter, melted
    1   teaspoon paprika
    1   teaspoon onion powder

1. Preheat oven to 350°.
2. Combine all ingredients in a jelly roll pan; toss well. Bake at 350° for 20 minutes or until toasted, turning once. Yield: 6 cups.

CALORIES 24 (26% from fat); FAT 0.7g (sat 0.4g, mono 0.2g, poly 0.1g); PROTEIN 0.7g; CARB 4g; FIBER 0.2g; CHOL 1mg; IRON 0.2mg; SODIUM 48mg; CALC 6mg

MAKE AHEAD
Hunter's Stew

(pictured on page 326)

An avid hunter, Jim Barrett devised this stew to showcase his catch, which is usually duck. A combination of chicken and supermarket duck is a fine substitute, or use all chicken. Preparing this stew 1 day ahead allows the flavors to blossom and makes it easier to skim the fat from the top. Use reserved Crisp Croutons (recipe above) to top the stew.

    1   pound dried cranberry, Great
        Northern, or navy beans
    11 cups water, divided
    2½ cups (1-inch) chopped peeled
        rutabaga or turnip
    3   cups (1-inch) cubed red or Yukon
        gold potato
    3   cups quartered cremini or button
        mushrooms (about ½ pound)
    2   cups chopped onion
    1   cup chopped carrot
    1   cup chopped celery
    1   (5¾- to 6¼-pound) dressed
        domestic duck, fresh or thawed
    2   chicken drumsticks (about
        ¾ pound)
    2   chicken thighs (about ¾ pound)
    9   ounces sweet turkey Italian
        sausage or smoked turkey and
        duck sausages (such as Gerhard's)
    3   cups Cabernet or other dry red
        wine, divided
    ½   cup chopped fresh flat-leaf
        parsley
    2   tablespoons red wine vinegar
    1½ teaspoons dried summer savory
    1½ teaspoons dried thyme
    1½ teaspoons salt
    1½ teaspoons black pepper
    1   (14¼-ounce) can fat-free,
        less-sodium beef broth
    2   cups Crisp Croutons (recipe at
        left)
    Parsley sprigs (optional)

1. Sort and wash beans, and place in a large Dutch oven. Cover with water to 2 inches above beans, and bring to a boil. Cook 2 minutes. Remove from heat. Cover and let stand 1 hour. Drain beans, and return to pan. Add 8 cups water; bring to a boil. Cover and cook 1 hour or until just slightly firm. Drain and set aside.
2. Place 3 cups water in a large stockpot; bring to a boil. Add rutabaga, and cook 5 minutes. Add potato, mushrooms, onion, carrot, and celery, and return to a boil. Reduce heat; simmer 15 minutes or until crisp-tender. Set aside (do not drain).
3. Remove and discard giblets and neck from duck. Rinse duck with cold water; pat dry. Trim excess fat. Cut duck into 8 pieces. Heat a large nonstick skillet over medium-high heat. Add duck pieces; *Continued*

sauté 5 minutes on each side or until well browned. Remove from pan. Add chicken pieces; sauté 5 minutes on each side or until well browned. Remove from pan. Add sausage; sauté 10 minutes, browning on all sides. Remove from pan, and let cool. Slice sausage into 24 (¾-inch) pieces.

4. Carefully add ¼ cup wine, scraping pan to loosen browned bits, and add pan drippings to stockpot with vegetables. Add beans, duck, chicken, sausage, 2¾ cups wine, chopped parsley, and next 6 ingredients, and bring to a boil. Reduce heat, and simmer 30 minutes. Cover stew, and chill 8 to 24 hours.

5. Skim solidified fat from surface; discard. Reheat over medium heat, stirring frequently to prevent scorching. Bring to a boil. Reduce heat, and simmer 10 minutes. Sprinkle stew with Crisp Croutons, and garnish with parsley sprigs, if desired. Yield: 12 servings (serving size: about 2 cups stew, 1 poultry piece, 2 sausage pieces, and about 2 tablespoons Crisp Croutons).

(Totals include Crisp Croutons) CALORIES 548 (27% from fat); FAT 16.1g (sat 5.6g, mono 4g, poly 3g); PROTEIN 55g; CARB 41g; FIBER 12g; CHOL 195mg; IRON 8mg; SODIUM 659mg; CALC 128mg

Fall Pear Galette

For a fitting end to a hearty autumn meal, serve this free-form tart featuring pears, Cheddar, and caramel. You can make the galette a day ahead, but drizzle the caramel over it just 1 or 2 hours before you serve it.

GALETTE:
  Cooking spray
  ½ (15-ounce) package refrigerated pie dough (such as Pillsbury)
  ½ cup (2 ounces) shredded aged sharp Cheddar cheese
  5 ripe Bartlett or D'Anjou pears, peeled, cored, and cut into 1-inch slices
  1 tablespoon lemon juice
  ⅛ teaspoon ground nutmeg
  ¼ cup packed brown sugar
  3 tablespoons all-purpose flour

CARAMEL:
  ⅓ cup granulated sugar

1. Preheat oven to 400°.
2. To prepare galette, line a jelly roll pan with foil, and coat foil with cooking spray. Roll dough into an 11-inch circle; place on baking sheet. Sprinkle crust with cheese, leaving a 1-inch border.
3. Combine pears, juice, and nutmeg in a large bowl; toss well. Add brown sugar and flour; toss gently. Arrange pear mixture on dough, leaving a 2-inch border. (Pears will be piled high on dough.) Fold edges of dough toward center, pressing gently to seal (dough will only partially cover pears). Bake at 400° for 30 minutes or until crust is lightly browned (filling may leak slightly during cooking). Cool galette on a wire rack.
4. To prepare caramel, heat granulated sugar in a small heavy saucepan over medium heat until sugar dissolves, stirring to dissolve sugar evenly (about 4 minutes). Cook 1 minute or until golden. Remove from heat. Drizzle over galette. Yield: 8 servings.

CALORIES 292 (30% from fat); FAT 9.7g (sat 4.3g, mono 0.1g, poly 0.1g); PROTEIN 4g; CARB 50g; FIBER 3g; CHOL 12mg; IRON 0.6mg; SODIUM 146mg; CALC 71mg

season's best

Chocolate Spiderweb Cookies

In October, the air becomes crisp and cool, leaves begin to fall, and we enjoy the turn of season. Halloween and its treats are just ahead.

Among our favorite treats are spiderweb cookies. Whether you spend Halloween at a party or meandering from house to house, they're ideal. The chocolaty crunch and white glaze make them a delicious treat for all sorts of ghouls and goblins. Don't worry about creating perfect webs. The more imperfect, the scarier the effect.

Chocolate Spiderweb Cookies

For the glaze, snip a very small hole in the corner of the plastic bag. If it's too small, you can always make it bigger.

  1 cup all-purpose flour
  ⅓ cup unsweetened cocoa
  ½ teaspoon baking soda
  ⅛ teaspoon salt
  ⅓ cup vegetable shortening
  ⅔ cup granulated sugar
  1 teaspoon vanilla extract
  1 large egg white
  Cooking spray
  2 cups powdered sugar, sifted
  3 tablespoons 2% reduced-fat milk

1. Lightly spoon flour into a dry measuring cup; level with a knife. Combine flour, cocoa, baking soda, and salt, stirring well with a whisk. Place shortening in a large mixing bowl; beat with a heavy-duty mixer at medium speed until light and fluffy. Gradually add granulated sugar, 1 tablespoon at a time, beating until well blended. Add vanilla and egg white; beat well. Add flour mixture; beat until well blended.
2. Turn dough out onto wax paper; shape into a 6-inch log. Wrap log in wax paper. Freeze 2 hours or until very firm.
3. Preheat oven to 350°.
4. Cut log into 24 (¼-inch) slices, and place slices 1 inch apart on baking sheets coated with cooking spray. Bake at 350° for 10 minutes or until set. Remove from pans; cool completely on wire racks.
5. Combine powdered sugar and milk in a medium bowl; stir with a whisk until smooth. Spoon into a small zip-top plastic bag; seal. Snip a tiny hole in 1 corner of bag. Working with 1 cookie at a time, pipe 3 concentric circles onto each cookie. Starting at center circle, pull a wooden pick through other circles at regular intervals to create a "web." Yield: 2 dozen cookies (serving size: 1 cookie).

CALORIES 102 (26% from fat); FAT 2.9g (sat 0.8g, mono 1g, poly 0.7g); PROTEIN 1g; CARB 19g; FIBER 1g; CHOL 0mg; IRON 0mg; SODIUM 42mg; CALC 5mg

Camping Cuisine

You can eat well on the trail—scout's honor.

Trail Tips

Here are some tips for great food outside:

- Minimize pots. Think skillet dinners, stews, and grilled items.
- Mix dry ingredients together, and pack them in heavy-duty zip-top plastic bags with directions and cooking times.
- Make extra soups and stews to freeze for camping trips. The frozen dinners pull double duty as block ice in the cooler.
- Stock a kitchen box with utensils, cookware, and staples so you can just grab and go.
- Choose dishes with short cooking times. Less time spent cooking means more time for hiking through wildflower-studded mountain meadows and savoring breathtaking views.

Orange-Ginger Skillet Chicken

1 cup chopped orange sections
½ cup orange juice
¼ cup chopped green onions
¼ cup low-sodium soy sauce
3 tablespoons fresh lemon juice
2 tablespoons olive oil
1 tablespoon honey
2 teaspoons grated peeled fresh ginger
1 teaspoon ground coriander seeds
1½ pounds chicken breast tenders
8 cups cooked rotini (about 1 pound uncooked corkscrew pasta)

1. At home, combine first 9 ingredients in a large heavy-duty zip-top plastic bag; seal. Place chicken and cooked pasta in separate large heavy-duty zip-top plastic bags; seal.
2. At campsite, add chicken to marinade; seal bag. Marinate in cooler 3 hours. Heat a large cast iron skillet over hot coals (or over medium-high heat if at home). Add chicken mixture, and cook 15 minutes. Add pasta, and simmer 5 minutes or until chicken is done and pasta is thoroughly heated. Yield: 6 servings (serving size: 2 cups).

CALORIES 473 (14% from fat); FAT 7.3g (sat 1.2g, mono 3.8g, poly 1.2g); PROTEIN 36.2g; CARB 63.7g; FIBER 3.7g; CHOL 66mg; IRON 3.8mg; SODIUM 433mg; CALC 45mg

---

QUICK & EASY

Barbecued Lime Shrimp and Corn

⅓ cup fresh lime juice
¼ cup fresh orange juice
2 tablespoons low-sodium soy sauce
2 tablespoons honey
2 teaspoons grated peeled fresh ginger
2 tablespoons sugar
1 teaspoon ground coriander seeds
¼ teaspoon black pepper
2 garlic cloves, minced
2 ears corn, each cut crosswise into 4 pieces
1½ pounds large shrimp, peeled and deveined
4 cups cooked couscous

1. At home, combine first 9 ingredients in a heavy-duty zip-top plastic bag, and seal. Place corn, shrimp, and couscous in separate heavy-duty zip-top plastic bags, and seal bags. Place shrimp in cooler.
2. At campsite, place lime mixture, corn, and shrimp in a foil oven bag. Place directly on hot coals (or in a 450° oven if at home); cook 10 minutes. Serve over couscous. Yield: 4 servings (serving size: 5 ounces shrimp, 2 pieces corn, and 1 cup couscous).

CALORIES 473 (7% from fat); FAT 3.9g (sat 0.7g, mono 0.6g, poly 1.5g); PROTEIN 42.8g; CARB 66.7g; FIBER 4g; CHOL 259mg; IRON 5.3mg; SODIUM 534mg; CALC 115mg

---

QUICK & EASY • MAKE AHEAD

Vegetable-Couscous Salad

Prepare this recipe at home, and pack in a plastic bag. The flavors develop over time.

DRESSING:

⅓ cup water
¼ cup sherry or balsamic vinegar
1 tablespoon olive oil
1 (.6-ounce) envelope Italian dressing mix (such as Good Seasons)

SALAD:

1½ cups water
1 cup uncooked couscous
2 cups chopped red bell pepper
2 cups chopped tomato
½ cup (2 ounces) crumbled feta cheese
½ cup finely chopped green onions
¼ cup chopped pitted kalamata olives
¼ cup chopped fresh parsley

1. Combine first 4 ingredients in a jar. Cover tightly, and shake vigorously.
2. Bring 1½ cups water to a boil in a medium saucepan; gradually stir in couscous. Remove from heat. Cover and let stand 5 minutes. Fluff with a fork. Combine couscous, bell pepper, and remaining 5 ingredients in a large bowl. Add dressing mixture. Toss gently to coat. Yield: 8 servings (serving size: 1 cup).

CALORIES 169 (30% from fat); FAT 5.6g (sat 1.6g, mono 3.1g, poly 0.6g); PROTEIN 4.7g; CARB 25.1g; FIBER 2.7g; CHOL 6mg; IRON 0.9mg; SODIUM 446mg; CALC 53mg

---

S'Mores the Score

If you think the only legitimate reason to go camping is s'mores, you'll like these fresh twists on the campfire classic.

- Lightened Traditional Version: Low-fat honey graham crackers, chocolate, marshmallows
- Chocolate Mint: Chocolate graham crackers, marshmallows, Andes mints
- Peanut Butter and Jelly: Oat graham crackers, reduced-fat peanut butter, all-fruit jam, marshmallows
- Cinnamon Apple: Low-fat cinnamon graham crackers, marshmallows, apple slices

Vegetarian Cashew Chili

- 3 cups chopped onion
- 2½ cups chopped red bell pepper
- 1½ cups chopped celery
- 3 garlic cloves, minced
- ⅓ cup red wine vinegar
- 1 tablespoon molasses
- 1½ teaspoons dried basil
- 1½ teaspoons dried oregano
- 1 teaspoon ground cumin
- ½ teaspoon salt
- ½ teaspoon chili powder
- ½ teaspoon black pepper
- 1 bay leaf
- 2 tablespoons olive oil
- 2 (15.5-ounce) cans red kidney beans, undrained
- 1 (28-ounce) can whole tomatoes, undrained and chopped
- 1 (15-ounce) can pinto beans, undrained
- ⅔ cup cashews, coarsely chopped

1. At home, place first 4 ingredients in a heavy-duty zip-top plastic bag. Combine vinegar and next 8 ingredients in a heavy-duty zip-top plastic bag. Place bags in cooler or backpack.
2. At campsite, heat oil in a large Dutch oven over hot coals (or in a Dutch oven over medium-high heat if at home). Add onion, bell pepper, celery, and garlic; sauté 8 minutes or until tender. Add vinegar mixture, kidney beans, tomatoes, and pinto beans; cook 20 minutes, stirring frequently. Discard bay leaf. Stir in cashews. Yield: 7 servings (serving size: about 1½ cups).

CALORIES 350 (28% from fat); FAT 10.9g (sat 1.9g, mono 6.6g, poly 1.7g); PROTEIN 15.6g; CARB 51.7g; FIBER 13.4g; CHOL 0mg; IRON 5.3mg; SODIUM 882mg; CALC 178mg

Thyme-Leek Braised Pork Tenderloin

- 2 cups chopped leek
- 1 cup Riesling or other slightly sweet white wine
- 2 tablespoons butter
- 2 tablespoons honey
- 2 tablespoons Dijon mustard
- 2 tablespoons prepared horseradish
- 1 tablespoon olive oil
- ¾ teaspoon freshly ground black pepper
- ½ teaspoon salt
- 4 thyme sprigs
- 3 garlic cloves, minced
- 2 (1-pound) pork tenderloins, trimmed
- 8 (1-ounce) slices French bread

1. At home, combine first 11 ingredients in a large zip-top plastic bag; add pork. Seal and marinate in cooler 2 to 12 hours.
2. At campsite, place pork and marinade in a foil oven bag. Place directly on hot coals (or in a 450° oven if at home) 25 minutes. Serve with bread. Yield: 8 servings (serving size: 3 ounces pork, ¼ cup leek mixture, and 1 slice bread).

CALORIES 294 (30% from fat); FAT 9.7g (sat 3.6g, mono 4.3g, poly 1g); PROTEIN 27.1g; CARB 24g; FIBER 1.5g; CHOL 81mg; IRON 2.9mg; SODIUM 519mg; CALC 54mg

Trail Stew

Pack the ground round frozen; it acts as an ice pack to keep other foods cold.

- 2 cups chopped onion
- 2 garlic cloves, minced
- 5 cups peeled baking potato, cut into 1-inch pieces
- 2 cups sliced carrot
- 1 cup chopped red bell pepper
- 1 (1-ounce) package onion soup mix, such as Lipton
- 2 pounds lean ground round
- 2 (14¼-ounce) cans low-salt beef broth
- 2 cups frozen green beans
- 2 cups frozen whole-kernel corn
- ½ teaspoon salt
- ½ teaspoon black pepper

1. At home, combine onion and garlic in a heavy-duty zip-top plastic bag; seal. Combine potato, carrot, bell pepper, and soup mix in a heavy-duty zip-top plastic bag; seal. Place bags in cooler.
2. At campsite, cook beef, onion, and garlic in a large Dutch oven over hot coals (or in a Dutch oven over medium-high heat if at home) 10 minutes or until browned; stir to crumble. Add potato mixture and broth; cook 15 minutes or until vegetables are tender. Add beans, corn, salt, and black pepper; simmer 10 minutes. Yield: 8 servings (serving size: 2 cups).

CALORIES 391 (30% from fat); FAT 13.2g (sat 5g, mono 5.6g, poly 0.8g); PROTEIN 28.7g; CARB 40.8g; FIBER 5.9g; CHOL 81mg; IRON 3.5mg; SODIUM 539mg; CALC 59mg

happy endings

Tea Cakes

Subtly flavored with brewed tea, these cakes are not just for afternoon tea.

Darjeeling-Chocolate Layer Cake

(pictured on page 325)

While Darjeeling is a strong black tea, in this cake its flavor is muted so that it enhances the deep chocolate flavor.

CAKE:
- Cooking spray
- ⅔ cup boiling water
- 6 tablespoons loose Darjeeling tea
- 2 cups sifted cake flour
- 1 teaspoon baking soda
- ¼ teaspoon salt
- ⅔ cup unsweetened cocoa
- ⅔ cup boiling water
- ¼ cup plain fat-free yogurt
- 2 teaspoons vanilla extract
- 1¼ cups granulated sugar
- ¾ cup packed brown sugar
- ¼ cup butter, softened
- 3 large egg whites
- 1 large egg

ICING:

½ cup boiling water
5 tablespoons loose Darjeeling tea
⅔ cup (6 ounces) ⅓-less-fat cream cheese, softened
2½ cups powdered sugar
½ cup unsweetened cocoa

REMAINING INGREDIENT:

2 tablespoons chopped hazelnuts, toasted

1. Preheat oven to 350°.

2. To prepare cake, coat 2 (9-inch) round cake pans with cooking spray; line bottoms of pans with wax paper. Coat wax paper with cooking spray; set aside.

3. Pour ⅔ cup boiling water over 6 tablespoons tea leaves in a bowl; steep 5 minutes. Strain through a fine sieve into a bowl; cool to room temperature.

4. Lightly spoon flour into dry measuring cups; level with a knife. Sift together flour, baking soda, and salt; set aside.

5. Combine ⅔ cup cocoa and ⅔ cup boiling water, stirring with a whisk. Cool in freezer 10 minutes, and stir in brewed tea, yogurt, and vanilla.

6. Place granulated sugar, brown sugar, and butter in a large bowl; beat with a mixer at medium speed until well blended (about 5 minutes). Add egg whites and egg, 1 at a time, beating well after each addition. Add flour mixture and brewed tea mixture alternately to sugar mixture, beginning and ending with flour mixture. Pour batter into prepared cake pans; sharply tap pans once on counter to remove air bubbles. Bake at 350° for 30 minutes or until a wooden pick inserted in center comes out clean. Cool in pans 10 minutes on a wire rack; remove from pans. Carefully remove and discard wax paper. Cool completely on wire rack.

7. To prepare icing, pour ½ cup boiling water over 5 tablespoons tea leaves in a bowl; steep 5 minutes. Strain through a fine sieve into a bowl; cool to room temperature. Place cream cheese in a large bowl, and beat with a mixer at medium speed until fluffy (about 1 minute). Sift together powdered sugar and ½ cup cocoa. Gradually add cocoa mixture and 2½ to 3 tablespoons brewed tea to cream cheese. Beat just until smooth.

(Do not overbeat or icing will be too thin.) Discard any remaining tea.

8. Place 1 cake layer on a plate; spread with ½ cup icing. Top with another cake layer. Spread remaining icing over top and sides of cake. Sprinkle with hazelnuts. Store cake loosely covered in refrigerator. Yield: 16 servings (serving size: 1 slice).

CALORIES 305 (21% from fat); FAT 7.1g (sat 3.9g, mono 2.3g, poly 0.4g); PROTEIN 4.7g; CARB 60.3g; FIBER 2.5g; CHOL 29mg; IRON 1.9mg; SODIUM 212mg; CALC 33mg

---

MAKE AHEAD • FREEZABLE
Black Currant Pound Cake

Black currant tea's naturally sweet, fruity flavor and aroma stand out in this cake but don't overpower it. If you don't want to pour all the glaze over the cake, drizzle some over individual slices.

CAKE:

⅔ cup boiling water
6 black currant tea bags (such as Twinings)
⅓ cup fat-free sour cream
3 cups all-purpose flour
1 teaspoon baking powder
¼ teaspoon salt
2 cups granulated sugar
¾ cup butter, softened
3 large eggs
2 teaspoons vanilla extract
Cooking spray

GLAZE:

¼ cup boiling water
1 black currant tea bag (such as Twinings)
¾ cup powdered sugar
½ teaspoon fresh lemon juice

1. Preheat oven to 350°.

2. To prepare cake, pour ⅔ cup boiling water over 6 tea bags in a bowl; steep 10 minutes. Remove and discard tea bags; cool tea to room temperature. Stir in sour cream.

3. Lightly spoon flour into dry measuring cups; level with a knife. Combine flour, baking powder, and salt, stirring with a whisk. Place granulated sugar and butter in a large bowl; beat with a mixer

at medium speed until well blended (about 5 minutes). Add eggs, 1 at a time, beating well after each addition. Beat in vanilla. Add flour mixture and brewed tea mixture alternately to sugar mixture, beginning and ending with flour mixture; mix after each addition. Spoon batter into a 10-inch tube pan coated with cooking spray. Bake at 350° for 1 hour and 10 minutes or until a wooden pick inserted in center comes out clean. Cool in pan 15 minutes on a wire rack. Remove from pan; cool completely on wire rack.

4. To prepare glaze, pour ¼ cup boiling water over 1 tea bag in a medium bowl; steep 5 minutes. Remove and discard tea bag. Add powdered sugar and juice to brewed tea, stirring well with a whisk. Drizzle glaze over cake. Yield: 16 servings (serving size: 1 slice).

CALORIES 300 (29% from fat); FAT 9.8g (sat 5.7g, mono 2.8g, poly 0.5g); PROTEIN 3.9g; CARB 49.6g; FIBER 0.6g; CHOL 63mg; IRON 1.3mg; SODIUM 171mg; CALC 35mg

---

MAKE AHEAD • FREEZABLE
Chai-Buttermilk Spice Cake

Chai tea is an Indian black tea perfumed with spices, such as cardamom, cinnamon, ginger, and cloves. Here, it delicately flavors a snack cake made tender by the addition of beaten egg whites.

½ cup boiling water
6 chai tea bags
2½ cups all-purpose flour
1 teaspoon baking soda
¼ teaspoon salt
¼ teaspoon ground cinnamon
⅓ cup (3 ounces) block-style fat-free cream cheese, softened
¼ cup butter, softened
½ cup granulated sugar, divided
½ cup packed light brown sugar
¼ cup vegetable oil
1 cup fat-free buttermilk
2 large egg whites
½ teaspoon cream of tartar
Cooking spray
¼ cup powdered sugar

Continued

1. Preheat oven to 350°.

2. Pour boiling water over tea bags in a bowl; steep 5 minutes. Remove and discard tea bags; cool to room temperature.

3. Lightly spoon flour into dry measuring cups; level with a knife. Combine flour, baking soda, salt, and cinnamon, stirring with a whisk. Place cream cheese and butter in a large bowl; beat with a mixer at medium speed until well blended (about 3 minutes). Add ¼ cup granulated sugar and brown sugar; beat until well combined. Beat in brewed tea and vegetable oil. Add flour mixture and buttermilk alternately to sugar mixture, beginning and ending with flour mixture; mix after each addition.

4. Using clean, dry beaters, beat egg whites with a mixer at high speed until foamy. Add cream of tartar; beat until soft peaks form. Add ¼ cup granulated sugar, 1 tablespoon at a time, beating until stiff peaks form. Gently stir one-third of egg white mixture into batter; gently fold in remaining egg white mixture. Spoon batter into a 9-inch square baking pan coated with cooking spray. Bake at 350° for 35 minutes or until a wooden pick inserted in center comes out clean. Cool in pan on a wire rack. Sprinkle with powdered sugar. Yield: 12 servings (serving size: 1 piece).

CALORIES 263 (29% from fat); FAT 8.6g (sat 3.1g, mono 2.2g, poly 2.9g); PROTEIN 5.1g; CARB 41.4g; FIBER 0.7g; CHOL 12mg; IRON 1.4mg; SODIUM 261mg; CALC 59mg

Green Tea-Almond Cake with Green Tea Sorbet

Because green tea is more delicate than black tea, use very hot, rather than boiling, water. Bring the water to the point where it's just about to boil, and then pour it over the tea to steep. Although the cake tends to sink a bit in the center as it cools, it tastes great.

SORBET:
- ¾ cup very hot water
- 6 green tea bags
- 1½ cups water
- 1 cup sugar
- 1 tablespoon honey

CAKE:
- Cooking spray
- ½ cup very hot water
- 7 green tea bags
- 1 cup whole blanched almonds
- 1 cup sugar, divided
- 2 tablespoons cornstarch
- ⅛ teaspoon salt
- 3 large egg yolks
- 5 large egg whites
- ½ teaspoon cream of tartar

1. To prepare sorbet, pour ¾ cup hot water over 6 tea bags in a bowl; steep 5 minutes. Remove and discard tea bags; cool tea to room temperature.

2. Combine 1½ cups water, 1 cup sugar, and honey in a saucepan; bring to a boil. Cook until sugar dissolves; remove from heat. Pour sugar mixture into a medium bowl; stir in tea. Cover and chill.

3. Pour mixture into freezer can of an ice-cream freezer; freeze according to manufacturer's instructions. Spoon sorbet into a freezer-safe container; cover and freeze 3 hours or until firm.

4. Preheat oven to 350°.

5. To prepare cake, coat bottom of a 9-inch springform pan with cooking spray. Line bottom of pan with wax paper; coat wax paper with cooking spray.

6. Pour ½ cup hot water over 7 tea bags in a bowl; steep 5 minutes. Remove and discard tea bags; cool tea to room temperature. Set aside.

7. Combine almonds, 2 tablespoons sugar, cornstarch, and salt in food processor; process until finely ground (about 1 minute).

8. Place egg yolks in a large bowl; beat with a mixer at high speed 2 minutes. Gradually add 14 tablespoons sugar, beating until thick and pale (about 2 minutes). Place egg whites in a large bowl. Using clean, dry beaters, beat egg whites with mixer at high speed until foamy. Add cream of tartar; beat until stiff peaks form. Gently fold egg whites into egg yolk mixture. Gently fold almond mixture and brewed tea into egg white mixture. Spoon batter into prepared pan.

9. Bake at 350° for 30 minutes or until cake is lightly browned and a wooden pick inserted in center comes out clean. Cool cake completely in pan on a wire rack. Remove sides from springform pan. Loosen bottom of cake from pan using a spatula. Carefully remove and discard wax paper. Yield: 10 servings (serving size: 1 cake slice and ¼ cup sorbet).

CALORIES 278 (29% from fat); FAT 8.9g (sat 1g, mono 5.3g, poly 2g); PROTEIN 5.8g; CARB 46.5g; FIBER 1.5g; CHOL 64mg; IRON 0.8mg; SODIUM 64mg; CALC 40mg

English Breakfast Angel Food Cake

English breakfast tea is actually a combination of several black teas.

- ½ cup boiling water
- ¼ cup loose English breakfast tea leaves
- 1 cup plus 2 tablespoons sifted cake flour
- 1½ cups sugar, divided
- 12 large egg whites
- 1 teaspoon cream of tartar
- ¼ teaspoon salt

1. Preheat oven to 325°.

2. Pour boiling water over tea leaves in a bowl; steep 5 minutes. Strain through a fine sieve into a bowl; cool tea to room temperature.

3. Combine flour and ¾ cup sugar, stirring with a whisk. Place egg whites in a large bowl; beat with a mixer at high speed until foamy. Add cream of tartar and salt; beat until soft peaks form. Add ¾ cup sugar, 2 tablespoons at a time, beating until stiff peaks form. Beat in brewed tea.

4. Sift about ¼ cup flour mixture over egg white mixture; fold in. Repeat procedure with remaining flour mixture, ¼ cup at a time.

5. Spoon batter into an ungreased 10-inch tube pan, spreading evenly. Break air pockets by cutting through batter with a knife. Bake at 325° for 50 minutes or until cake springs back when lightly touched. Invert pan, and cool completely. Loosen cake from sides of pan using a narrow metal spatula. Invert cake onto a plate. Yield: 12 servings (serving size: 1 slice).

CALORIES 147 (1% from fat); FAT 0.1g (sat 0g, mono 0g, poly 0.1g); PROTEIN 4.3g; CARB 32.5g; FIBER 0.2g; CHOL 0mg; IRON 0.7mg; SODIUM 105mg; CALC 4mg

Covered-Dish Delights

If your holidays require traveling with food, these road-tested dishes will stay the course.

MAKE AHEAD • FREEZABLE
Garlic and Rosemary Cloverleaf Rolls
(pictured on page 361)

These rolls freeze well. Bake, cool completely, wrap in heavy-duty foil, and freeze up to 1 month. Thaw completely, and reheat in foil at 375° for 15 minutes or until warm. The recipe doubles easily, too.

 1 whole garlic head
 1 package dry yeast (about
    2¼ teaspoons)
 1 cup warm 2% reduced-fat milk
    (100° to 110°)
3⅓ cups all-purpose flour, divided
 2 tablespoons butter, softened
 2 tablespoons sugar
 1 teaspoon salt
 1 large egg
 1 tablespoon finely chopped fresh or
    1 teaspoon crushed dried rosemary
Cooking spray
 1 tablespoon butter, melted

1. Preheat oven to 350°.
2. Remove white papery skin from garlic head (do not peel or separate cloves). Wrap head in foil. Bake at 350° for 1 hour; cool slightly. Separate cloves; squeeze to extract garlic pulp. Discard skins.
3. Dissolve yeast in milk in a large bowl; let stand 5 minutes. Add garlic pulp. Lightly spoon flour into dry measuring cups; level with a knife. Add 1 cup flour, 2 tablespoons butter, sugar, salt, egg, and rosemary to yeast mixture; beat with a mixer at medium speed until combined. Add 2 cups flour, and beat until smooth. Turn dough out onto a floured surface.

Knead until smooth and elastic (about 8 minutes); add enough of remaining flour, 1 tablespoon at a time, to prevent dough from sticking to hands (dough will feel tacky).
4. Place dough in a large bowl coated with cooking spray; turn to coat top. Cover; let rise in a warm place (85°), free from drafts, 1 hour or until doubled in size. (Gently press two fingers into dough. If indentation remains, dough has risen enough.)
5. Punch dough down. Divide into 12 equal portions. Divide each portion into 3 pieces; shape each piece into a ball. Coat 12 muffin cups with cooking spray; place 3 balls in each muffin cup. Cover and let rise in a warm place (85°), free from drafts, 30 minutes or until doubled in size.
6. Preheat oven to 400°.
7. Uncover dough, and brush tops with 1 tablespoon melted butter. Bake at 400° for 12 minutes or until browned. Remove from pans; serve warm. Yield: 12 servings (serving size: 1 roll).

CALORIES 181 (20% from fat); FAT 4.1g (sat 2.2g, mono 1.1g, poly 0.3g); PROTEIN 5.2g; CARB 30.5g; FIBER 1.1g; CHOL 27mg; IRON 1.9mg; SODIUM 241mg; CALC 39mg

---

Wine Note

As a gift for hosts of a party, bring a bottle you think they haven't tried. A wine that fits the bill: Guenoc Victorian Claret from North Coast, California. The 1998 is $21.50. With its vanilla and mocha aroma, this blend has a flavor that's somewhere between cherry strudel and blackberry pie. Beautifully refined, it tastes like it costs a lot more than it does.

MAKE AHEAD
Bay-Scented Lentil Salad with Pancetta
(pictured on page 361)

This hearty salad is good chilled or at room temperature. Dressing the salad in advance gives the lentils time to imbibe the vinaigrette. Prepare and chill in a pretty serving bowl up to 1 day ahead; store the cooked pancetta separately in the refrigerator. Stir the salad well, and top with pancetta just before serving.

 2 cups dried petite green lentils
 2 bay leaves
 4 ounces pancetta, finely chopped
    (about 1 cup)
 6 cups finely chopped red cabbage
 ⅓ cup white wine vinegar
 2 tablespoons Dijon mustard
1½ teaspoons chopped fresh rosemary
 1 teaspoon salt
 ¼ teaspoon freshly ground black
    pepper
 3 garlic cloves, minced

1. Place lentils and bay leaves in a large saucepan. Cover with water to 2 inches above lentils; bring to a boil. Reduce heat, and simmer 18 minutes or until tender; drain. Discard bay leaves.
2. Heat a large nonstick skillet over medium-high heat. Add pancetta; sauté 2 minutes or until browned. Remove pancetta with a slotted spoon. Add cabbage to drippings in pan; sauté 5 minutes or until tender. Combine lentils and cabbage in a large bowl. Combine vinegar and remaining ingredients, stirring with a whisk. Drizzle vinaigrette over lentil mixture; toss well to coat. Sprinkle with pancetta just before serving. Yield: 12 servings (serving size: ¾ cup salad and 1½ teaspoons pancetta).

CALORIES 169 (30% from fat); FAT 5.6g (sat 2g, mono 2.5g, poly 0.7g); PROTEIN 8.9g; CARB 21.1g; FIBER 5.6g; CHOL 6mg; IRON 2.2mg; SODIUM 340mg; CALC 53mg

Pissaladière Tartlets

Present *pissaladière*—a classic French onion, anchovy, and olive pie—in miniature form. Make the tart shells and the filling a day ahead, and store separately in airtight containers—the shells at room temperature and the filling in the refrigerator. Assemble at the party or dinner. Use trimmed crusts to make fresh bread-crumbs: Place in a food processor, and process to form coarse crumbs. Freeze in a zip-top plastic bag up to 6 months.

        1 tablespoon olive oil
       10 cups thinly vertically sliced onion
           (about 4 medium)
        ¼ teaspoon salt
        3 canned anchovy fillets, chopped
        ¼ cup balsamic vinegar
        1 teaspoon chopped fresh thyme
        ¼ cup niçoise olives, pitted and
           chopped
       24 (½-ounce) slices very thin white
           bread (such as Pepperidge Farm)
           Cooking spray
        ¼ teaspoon thyme leaves

1. Heat olive oil in a large nonstick skillet over medium-high heat. Add onion, and sauté 10 minutes. Stir in salt and anchovies; sauté 10 minutes. Stir in vinegar and chopped thyme. Reduce heat to medium-low; cook 3 minutes or until liquid is absorbed, stirring frequently. Stir in olives. Cool to room temperature.
2. Preheat oven to 375°.
3. Trim crusts from bread; reserve crusts for another use. Lightly coat both sides of bread with cooking spray. Place 1 slice into each of 24 miniature muffin cups, pressing bread into pan to form cups (bread tips will stick up). Bake at 375° for 10 minutes or until dry and golden. Carefully remove bread cups from pan; cool on a wire rack. Spoon 1 heaping tablespoon onion mixture into each bread cup. Sprinkle evenly with whole thyme leaves. Yield: 12 servings (serving size: 2 tartlets).

CALORIES 122 (30% from fat); FAT 4g (sat 0.4g, mono 2.5g, poly 0.4g); PROTEIN 2.9g; CARB 18.3g; FIBER 1.8g; CHOL 1mg; IRON 0.8mg; SODIUM 281mg; CALC 39mg

Creamy Winter Squash Gratin

Kabocha squash has a pale green rind and light orange flesh. Substitute butternut squash or pumpkin, if you'd prefer. Prepare the gratin 1 day ahead, and refrigerate; store the breadcrumb topping separately. Bake at 400° for 30 minutes or until heated through.

        8 cups cubed peeled kabocha
           squash (about 3 pounds)
           Cooking spray
        2 teaspoons butter
        2 cups thinly sliced leek (about
           2 large)
        1 teaspoon salt
      3½ cups 1% low-fat milk
        ⅓ cup all-purpose flour
        1 cup (4 ounces) shredded
           Gruyère cheese
        ¼ teaspoon freshly ground black
           pepper
        ¼ teaspoon ground nutmeg
        2 (1-ounce) slices white bread
        2 teaspoons chopped fresh parsley
        1 garlic clove, minced

1. Preheat oven to 400°.
2. Arrange squash in a single layer on a baking sheet coated with cooking spray. Bake at 400° for 25 minutes or until squash is tender.
3. Melt butter in a large nonstick skillet over medium heat. Add leek and salt; cook 4 minutes or until tender, stirring frequently. Combine milk and flour, stirring well with a whisk. Add milk mixture to pan; bring to a boil. Cook 1 minute or until thick, stirring constantly. Remove from heat. Add cheese, pepper, and nutmeg; stir until cheese melts. Gently stir in squash. Spoon mixture into a 2-quart baking dish coated with cooking spray.
4. Place bread in a food processor; pulse 10 times or until coarse crumbs measure 1¼ cups. Add parsley and garlic; pulse twice to combine. Sprinkle mixture evenly over squash mixture. Bake at 400° for 20 minutes or until golden brown. Yield: 8 servings (serving size: about 1 cup).

CALORIES 222 (29% from fat); FAT 7.2g (sat 4.1g, mono 2.1g, poly 0.6g); PROTEIN 10.6g; CARB 31.2g; FIBER 4.8g; CHOL 22mg; IRON 1.9mg; SODIUM 453mg; CALC 358mg

Cheesecake with Cranberry-Maple Topping

Prepare and refrigerate the topping and the cheesecake up to 3 days ahead, but take the cheesecake to your gathering in the springform pan. To serve it, remove the springform ring, slice the cheesecake, and pass the topping.

TOPPING:

        1 cup maple syrup
        2 (8-ounce) packages fresh cranberries

CHEESECAKE:

       15 gingersnaps
       24 cinnamon graham crackers (6 full
           cracker sheets)
        2 tablespoons butter, melted
           Cooking spray
      1¼ cups sugar
      1½ teaspoons vanilla extract
        2 (8-ounce) blocks ⅓-less-fat cream
           cheese, softened
        1 (8-ounce) block fat-free cream
           cheese, softened
        4 large egg whites

1. To prepare topping, combine syrup and cranberries in a saucepan; bring to a boil. Reduce heat; simmer 15 minutes, stirring occasionally. Cover and chill.
2. Preheat oven to 375°.
3. To prepare cheesecake, place gingersnaps and graham crackers in a food processor; process until fine crumbs measure 1¾ cups. Drizzle with butter; pulse 2 times or until moist. Firmly press mixture into bottom and 1 inch up sides of a 9-inch springform pan coated with cooking spray.
4. Place sugar, vanilla, and cheeses in a large bowl. Beat with a mixer at high speed until smooth. Add egg whites, 1 at a time, beating well after each addition. Pour into prepared pan. Bake at 375° for 35 minutes or until center barely moves when pan is touched. Remove from oven, and run a knife around outside edge. Cool to room temperature. Cover and chill at least 8 hours. Serve with topping. Yield: 16 servings (serving size: 1 wedge and 2½ tablespoons topping).

CALORIES 283 (30% from fat); FAT 9.3g (sat 5.3g, mono 2.9g, poly 0.6g); PROTEIN 6.6g; CARB 43.7g; FIBER 1.5g; CHOL 28mg; IRON 1mg; SODIUM 288mg; CALC 84mg

Layered Mashed Potatoes with Duxelles

For a splurge, replace 1 tablespoon butter in the potatoes with 1 tablespoon truffle oil. Remove and discard stems from the shiitake mushrooms. Assemble and chill the dish up to 1 day ahead; microwave at HIGH 10 minutes or until heated.

DUXELLES:

    6 ounces cremini mushrooms
    6 ounces shiitake mushroom caps
    1 tablespoon butter
1¼ cups finely chopped onion
    ½ teaspoon chopped fresh thyme
    ¼ teaspoon salt
    ¼ teaspoon freshly ground black pepper
    4 garlic cloves, minced
    ½ cup 2% reduced-fat milk
    1 tablespoon all-purpose flour

POTATOES:

3½ pounds cubed peeled Yukon gold potato
    ¾ cup 2% reduced-fat milk
    3 tablespoons butter
    1 teaspoon salt
    ¼ teaspoon freshly ground black pepper
    1 large egg, lightly beaten
Cooking spray
Chopped fresh flat-leaf parsley (optional)

1. To prepare duxelles, place mushrooms in a food processor, and process until finely chopped.
2. Melt 1 tablespoon butter in a large nonstick skillet over medium heat. Add onion, and cook 3 minutes, stirring frequently. Add mushrooms, thyme, ¼ teaspoon salt, ¼ teaspoon pepper, and garlic, and cook 5 minutes, stirring occasionally. Combine ½ cup milk and flour, stirring with a whisk. Add milk mixture to pan; bring to a boil. Cook 1 minute or until thick, stirring constantly.
3. To prepare potatoes, place potato in a medium saucepan, and cover with water. Bring to a boil. Reduce heat, and simmer 15 minutes or until tender. Drain and return potato to pan. Add ¾ cup milk,

3 tablespoons butter, 1 teaspoon salt, ¼ teaspoon pepper, and egg; mash with a potato masher.
4. Spread half of potato mixture evenly into a 2-quart microwave-safe baking dish coated with cooking spray, and top with mushroom mixture. Spread remaining potato mixture over mushroom mixture. Cover with plastic wrap, and vent. Microwave at HIGH 8 minutes or until thoroughly heated. Garnish with parsley, if desired. Yield: 9 servings (serving size: about 1 cup).

CALORIES 246 (24% from fat); FAT 6.5g (sat 3.8g, mono 1.9g, poly 0.4g); PROTEIN 6.6g; CARB 41.6g; FIBER 4.3g; CHOL 40mg; IRON 1.2mg; SODIUM 418mg; CALC 68mg

Butternut, Goat Cheese, and Walnut Spread

Pungent goat cheese, sweet butternut squash, and slightly bitter walnuts create an unusual spread for crostini. Toast the baguette slices a day ahead, and store at room temperature in a zip-top plastic bag. Prepare and chill the spread up to 1 day ahead; serve at room temperature.

    1 medium butternut squash (about 1½ pounds)
Cooking spray
    1 whole garlic head
    2 tablespoons fresh lemon juice
    ½ teaspoon salt
    1 (3-ounce) package goat cheese
    ¼ cup chopped walnuts, toasted
  36 (½-inch-thick) slices French bread baguette, toasted (about 8 ounces)

1. Preheat oven to 400°.
2. Cut squash in half lengthwise; remove and discard seeds and membrane. Place squash halves, cut sides down, on a foil-lined jelly roll pan coated with cooking spray. Remove white papery skin from garlic head (do not peel or separate cloves). Wrap garlic head in foil. Place garlic on pan with squash. Bake at 400° for 30 minutes or until squash is tender. Cool slightly. Scoop out pulp from squash, and discard skins. Separate garlic cloves,

and squeeze to extract garlic pulp. Discard skins.
3. Place squash, garlic, juice, salt, and cheese in a food processor; process until smooth. Spoon mixture into a bowl, and sprinkle evenly with nuts. Serve with baguette slices. Yield: 12 servings (serving size: about 2½ tablespoons spread and 3 baguette slices).

CALORIES 114 (28% from fat); FAT 3.5g (sat 1.3g, mono 0.8g, poly 1.2g); PROTEIN 4.1g; CARB 17.5g; FIBER 2.4g; CHOL 3mg; IRON 1.1mg; SODIUM 251mg; CALC 54mg

Green Beans with Caramelized-Shallot Butter

To make this dish ahead, plunge the beans into ice water after boiling, then drain and refrigerate up to 1 day ahead. Prepare and chill the shallot mixture up to 2 days ahead. To serve, place the beans and shallot mixture in a large microwave-safe bowl, cover with plastic wrap, and microwave at HIGH 3 minutes or until heated. Toss well before serving.

2½ tablespoons butter
    1 cup sliced shallots
    ⅓ cup balsamic vinegar
    2 teaspoons chopped fresh thyme
    1 teaspoon grated lemon rind
    ¾ teaspoon salt
    ¼ teaspoon freshly ground black pepper
    2 pounds green beans, trimmed (about 10 cups)

1. Melt butter in a saucepan over medium-high heat. Add shallots; sauté 4 minutes or until golden. Stir in vinegar; cook 1½ minutes. Remove from heat. Stir in thyme, rind, salt, and pepper.
2. Cook beans in boiling water 3 minutes or until crisp-tender; drain. Place beans in a large bowl. Stir in shallot mixture; toss well to coat. Yield: 10 servings (serving size: 1 cup).

CALORIES 90 (29% from fat); FAT 2.9g (sat 1.8g, mono 0.8g, poly 0.1g); PROTEIN 2.8g; CARB 14.8g; FIBER 3.3g; CHOL 8mg; IRON 1.1mg; SODIUM 207mg; CALC 49mg

Triple-Cranberry Sauce with Dried Apricots and Apples

This easy-to-prepare sauce holds up well in the refrigerator up to 5 days.

    2   cups chopped dried apples
    1   cup chopped dried apricots
    1   cup sweetened dried cranberries
    2   cups cranberry juice cocktail
    ⅔   cup sugar
    ½   cup white wine vinegar
    1   (8-ounce) package fresh
        cranberries
    1   tablespoon grated lemon rind

1. Combine first 7 ingredients in a large saucepan; bring to a boil. Cover, reduce heat, and simmer 25 minutes. Add rind, and simmer 2 minutes. Cover and chill. Yield: 4 cups (serving size: ¼ cup).

CALORIES 127 (1% from fat); FAT 0.1g (sat 0g, mono 0g, poly 0.1g); PROTEIN 0.5g; CARB 32.1g; FIBER 2.2g; CHOL 0mg; IRON 0.7mg; SODIUM 8mg; CALC 9mg

---

Lazy-Day Breakfast Menu
serves 6

To make this menu even easier, pick up precut mixed fruit in the produce section of the supermarket. You'll have extra rolls to freeze.

Fig-Pecan Rolls with Maple Butter

Ham and egg scramble*

Fruit salad

*Heat 2 tablespoons butter in a large non-stick skillet over medium-high heat. Add 1½ cups frozen hash brown potatoes; cook 2 minutes, stirring frequently. Add ¾ cup chopped green onions, ½ cup chopped ham, and 1 teaspoon minced garlic; cook potato mixture 8 minutes or until golden, stirring frequently. Combine ¾ teaspoon salt, ¼ teaspoon black pepper, 5 eggs, and 3 egg whites in a bowl, stirring with a whisk. Add eggs to pan; cook 3 minutes or until set, stirring occasionally.

Fig-Pecan Rolls with Maple Butter

These dense rolls start with a sponge that needs 24 hours to develop its yeasty yet slightly tangy flavor. Freeze the rolls up to 1 month; thaw completely, and reheat in foil at 375° for 15 minutes or until warm. Make and refrigerate the maple butter up to 1 week ahead. Seal well, as butter can easily pick up other aromas from the fridge.

ROLLS:

    1   package dry yeast (about
        2¼ teaspoons)
    1   cup warm water (100° to 110°)
    3   cups all-purpose flour, divided
    2   tablespoons sugar
    1   teaspoon salt
    1   cup dried Mission figs, chopped
    ⅓   cup chopped pecans, toasted
        Cooking spray

BUTTER:

    ⅓   cup butter, softened
    ⅓   cup maple syrup

1. To prepare rolls, dissolve yeast in warm water in a large bowl; let stand 5 minutes. Lightly spoon flour into dry measuring cups; level with a knife. Add 1½ cups flour to yeast mixture. Cover with a damp towel; let stand at room temperature 24 hours.
2. Add 1¼ cups flour, sugar, and salt to yeast mixture; stir well to form a stiff dough. Turn dough out onto a lightly floured surface. Knead until smooth and elastic (about 8 minutes); add enough of remaining flour, 1 tablespoon at a time, to prevent dough from sticking to hands. Let dough rest 5 minutes. Knead in figs and pecans.
3. Place dough in a large bowl coated with cooking spray, turning to coat top. Cover and let rise in a warm place (85°), free from drafts, 1½ hours or until doubled in size. (Gently press two fingers into dough. If indentation remains, dough has risen enough.) Punch dough down; cover and let rest 5 minutes.
4. Divide dough into 20 equal portions. Working with 1 portion at a time (cover remaining dough to prevent drying),

---

shape each into a ball. Arrange balls on a baking sheet lined with parchment paper. Let rise in a warm place (85°), free from drafts, 1 hour or until dough is doubled in size.
5. Preheat oven to 425°.
6. Bake rolls at 425° for 10 minutes or until lightly browned. Cool rolls on a wire rack.
7. To prepare butter, place butter in a small bowl; beat with a mixer at high speed until light and fluffy. Slowly add maple syrup, beating until blended. Serve butter with rolls. Yield: 20 servings (serving size: 1 roll and about 1 teaspoon butter).

CALORIES 154 (28% from fat); FAT 4.8g (sat 2.1g, mono 1.7g, poly 0.7g); PROTEIN 2.6g; CARB 26.1g; FIBER 2g; CHOL 8mg; IRON 1.3mg; SODIUM 150mg; CALC 23mg

---

Streusel-Topped Pear Pie

In this recipe, part of the homemade pie dough becomes the crust, and the rest, with the addition of oats and brown sugar, becomes the streusel topping. Keep the skins on the pears so they maintain their shape; the skins also give the pie a rustic quality. Bake the pie up to 2 days ahead, and serve at room temperature.

    2   cups all-purpose flour
    ¾   teaspoon salt, divided
    ½   cup chilled butter, cut into small
        pieces
    ⅓   cup ice water
        Cooking spray
    ½   cup regular oats
    ⅓   cup packed dark brown sugar
    7   cups thinly sliced ripe Bartlett
        pears (about 6 pears)
    ½   cup granulated sugar
    3   tablespoons all-purpose flour
    3   tablespoons finely chopped
        crystallized ginger
    1   teaspoon ground cinnamon

1. Lightly spoon 2 cups flour into dry measuring cups, and level with a knife. Combine 2 cups flour and ½ teaspoon salt in a food processor; pulse 2 times to combine. Add butter, and pulse 6 times or until mixture resembles coarse meal.

With processor on, slowly pour ice water through food chute, processing just until blended (do not allow dough to form a ball).

2. Remove two-thirds of dough, and press into a 4-inch circle on 2 overlapping sheets of plastic wrap. (Leave remaining dough in processor.) Cover dough with 2 additional sheets of overlapping plastic wrap. Roll dough, still covered, into an 11-inch circle. Place dough in freezer 5 minutes or until plastic wrap can be easily removed.

3. Remove top sheets of plastic wrap, and fit dough, plastic wrap side up, into a 9-inch pie plate coated with cooking spray. Remove remaining plastic wrap. Fold edges under; flute. Refrigerate until ready to use.

4. Add oats and brown sugar to dough in food processor; pulse 4 times or until crumbly. Cover and chill.

5. Preheat oven to 375°.

6. Combine pear, granulated sugar, 3 tablespoons flour, ginger, cinnamon, and ¼ teaspoon salt; toss well to combine. Spoon pear mixture into crust. Bake at 375° for 25 minutes. Sprinkle oat mixture over pear mixture. Bake an additional 25 minutes or until top of pie is browned. Cool at least 2 hours. Yield: 10 servings (serving size: 1 wedge).

CALORIES 325 (28% from fat); FAT 10g (sat 5.8g, mono 2.8g, poly 0.6g); PROTEIN 3.9g; CARB 57.1g; FIBER 3.6g; CHOL 25mg; IRON 2mg; SODIUM 273mg; CALC 31mg

reader recipes

Practice What You Preach

How one reader was inspired to teach others that living well means eating well.

Rebecca Averill of Beverly, Massachusetts, created the recipe for Thai Cabbage Slaw after indulging her passion for Thai food at a local restaurant. As an eight-year cancer survivor, Rebecca counsels other women about the importance of practicing healthy eating habits. This recipe is just one she recommends.

Thai Cabbage Slaw

Serve with grilled flank steak, roast chicken, or fajitas.

    3   tablespoons fresh lime juice
    3   tablespoons rice vinegar
    2   tablespoons fish sauce
    1   tablespoon water
    1   tablespoon creamy peanut butter
    1   teaspoon chile paste with garlic
    1   garlic clove, minced
    6   cups shredded napa (Chinese) cabbage
    2   cups shredded red cabbage
    1   cup red bell pepper strips
    1   cup shredded carrot
    2   tablespoons chopped dry-roasted peanuts
    1   tablespoon chopped fresh cilantro
    1   tablespoon chopped fresh mint

1. Combine first 7 ingredients in a large bowl, stirring with a whisk until blended. Add cabbages, bell pepper, and carrot, and toss gently to coat. Cover and marinate in refrigerator 1 hour. Stir in peanuts, cilantro, and mint just before serving. Yield: 8 servings (serving size: ¾ cup).

CALORIES 66 (34% from fat); FAT 2.5g (sat 0.4g, mono 1.1g, poly 0.8g); PROTEIN 2.9g; CARB 10g; FIBER 3.2g; CHOL 0mg; IRON 0.9mg; SODIUM 540mg; CALC 55mg

QUICK & EASY
South-of-the-Border Chicken

"This is my dinnertime solution when I haven't had time to stop by the grocery store. I always keep chicken in the freezer."
—Louisa Gordy, Germantown, Tennessee

    1   cup water
    ½   cup uncooked basmati rice
    ⅛   teaspoon ground red pepper
    1   (16-ounce) can pinto beans, rinsed and drained
    1   (10-ounce) can diced tomatoes and green chiles, drained
    4   (6-ounce) skinless, boneless chicken breast halves
    ¼   teaspoon salt
    ¼   teaspoon black pepper
    ¼   teaspoon ground cumin
        Cooking spray

1. Bring 1 cup water to a boil in a medium saucepan, and stir in rice and red pepper. Cover, reduce heat, and simmer 20 minutes or until liquid is absorbed. Stir in beans and tomatoes; keep warm.

2. Sprinkle chicken with salt, black pepper, and cumin. Heat a large nonstick skillet coated with cooking spray over medium-high heat. Add chicken; cook 4 minutes on each side or until done. Serve chicken with rice mixture. Yield: 4 servings (serving size: 1 chicken breast half and 1 cup rice mixture).

CALORIES 347 (7% from fat); FAT 2.8g (sat 0.7g, mono 0.6g, poly 0.7g); PROTEIN 44.4g; CARB 35.7g; FIBER 4.6g; CHOL 99mg; IRON 3.2mg; SODIUM 740mg; CALC 64mg

MAKE AHEAD • FREEZABLE
Rosemary-Apple Bread

"I enjoy fresh rosemary from my herb garden year-round. Apple keeps the bread moist. It's even better the second day."
—Elaine Collins, Pensacola, Florida

    3   cups all-purpose flour, divided
    1¼   teaspoons salt
    1   teaspoon finely chopped fresh rosemary
    1   package quick-rise yeast (about 2¼ teaspoons)
    1   cup warm water (100° to 110°)
    1   cup diced peeled Granny Smith apple (about 1 small)
         Cooking spray
    2   teaspoons butter, melted

1. Lightly spoon flour into dry measuring cups; level with a knife. Combine 2¾ cups flour, salt, rosemary, and yeast in a large bowl, stirring with a whisk. Add water, stirring until a soft dough forms. Turn dough out onto a floured surface. Knead until smooth and elastic (about 8 minutes); add enough of remaining flour, 1 tablespoon at a time, to prevent dough from sticking to hands. Cover and let rest 5 minutes. Knead in apple. Place dough in a large bowl coated with cooking spray, turning to coat top. Cover and let rest 10 minutes.

2. Shape dough into a loaf; place dough in an 8½ x 4½-inch loaf pan coated with *Continued*

cooking spray. Gently press dough into pan; cover. Let rise in a warm place (85°), free from drafts, 30 minutes or until doubled in size.

3. Preheat oven to 375°.

4. Uncover and bake at 375° for 45 minutes or until bread is lightly browned and sounds hollow when tapped. Brush top with butter. Cool in pan 5 minutes. Remove from pan; cool on a wire rack. Yield: 16 servings (serving size: 1 slice).

CALORIES 95 (10% from fat); FAT 0.7g (sat 0.3g, mono 0.2g, poly 0.1g); PROTEIN 2.6g; CARB 19.1g; FIBER 0.9g; CHOL 1mg; IRON 1.2mg; SODIUM 188mg; CALC 5mg

---

QUICK & EASY
Turkey Burritos

"The filling can be stuffed into a burrito, as it is here, or spooned into crispy taco shells. Either way, it's delicious. Served with Spanish rice, it's an easy and fun dinner."
—Melinda Moon, Brewster, Massachusetts

Cooking spray
½ cup chopped onion
2 garlic cloves, minced
1 pound ground turkey breast
½ cup water
3 tablespoons bottled salsa
2 teaspoons dried oregano
2 teaspoons ground cumin
1½ teaspoons chili powder
1 (4.5-ounce) can chopped green chiles, undrained
6 (8-inch) flour tortillas
1 cup (4 ounces) preshredded reduced-fat Mexican blend cheese

1. Heat a large nonstick skillet coated with cooking spray over medium heat. Add chopped onion and minced garlic, and cook 3 minutes or until onion and garlic are tender, stirring frequently. Add ground turkey breast, and cook mixture 10 minutes or until turkey is browned, stirring to crumble. Stir in water and next 5 ingredients. Cover mixture, and cook 5 minutes over medium heat.

2. Warm flour tortillas according to package directions. Spoon 2½ tablespoons Mexican blend cheese down center of each tortilla. Top each tortilla with

½ cup turkey mixture; roll up. Yield: 6 servings (serving size: 1 burrito).

CALORIES 329 (30% from fat); FAT 11.1g (sat 3.3g, mono 4.2g, poly 2.1g); PROTEIN 24.2g; CARB 32.5g; FIBER 4.2g; CHOL 63mg; IRON 3.2mg; SODIUM 513mg; CALC 160mg

---

Weeknight Italian Menu
serves 8

You can assemble the pasta dish ahead, and bake it when you're ready for dinner.

Baked Pasta with Sausage, Tomatoes, and Cheese

Quick Caesar salad*

Vanilla ice cream

*Cut 2 ounces French bread into ½-inch cubes; toss with 1 tablespoon extravirgin olive oil, ¼ teaspoon salt, and ¼ teaspoon black pepper. Bake at 400° for 12 minutes or until golden. Place 1 cup torn romaine lettuce on each of 8 salad plates. Top each serving with 1 tablespoon grated Parmesan cheese; drizzle each serving with 1 tablespoon bottled light Caesar salad dressing. Divide croutons evenly among salads.

STAFF FAVORITE • MAKE AHEAD
Baked Pasta with Sausage, Tomatoes, and Cheese

"This easy-to-make dish is comforting and convenient. It makes a lot, and leftovers reheat well."
—Marilina Ackerbloom, Windermere, Florida

1 (1-pound) package uncooked ziti (short tube-shaped pasta)
1 pound hot turkey Italian sausage links
1 cup chopped onion
2 garlic cloves, minced
1 tablespoon tomato paste
¼ teaspoon salt
¼ teaspoon black pepper
2 (14.5-ounce) cans petite-diced tomatoes, undrained
¼ cup chopped fresh basil
Cooking spray
1 cup (4 ounces) shredded fresh mozzarella cheese
1 cup (4 ounces) grated fresh Parmesan cheese

1. Preheat oven to 350°.

2. Cook pasta according to package directions, omitting salt and fat. Drain pasta, and set aside.

3. Remove casings from sausage. Cook sausage, onion, and garlic in a large nonstick skillet over medium heat until browned, stirring to crumble. Add tomato paste, salt, pepper, and tomatoes, and bring to a boil. Cover, reduce heat, and simmer 10 minutes, stirring occasionally.

4. Combine cooked pasta, sausage mixture, and basil. Place half of pasta mixture in a 4-quart casserole coated with cooking spray. Top with half of mozzarella and half of Parmesan. Repeat layers. Bake at 350° for 25 minutes or until bubbly. Yield: 8 servings (serving size: 1½ cups).

CALORIES 413 (26% from fat); FAT 11.8g (sat 6.1g, mono 2.2g, poly 1g); PROTEIN 24.1g; CARB 53g; FIBER 4.5g; CHOL 49mg; IRON 7.9mg; SODIUM 941mg; CALC 265mg

---

inspired vegetarian

Celebrating the Harvest

A creamy fall vegetable lasagna takes center stage in this satisfying holiday dinner.

Vegetarian Thanksgiving Menu
serves 8

Crispy Butternut Won Tons with Spicy Tomato Sauce

Green Apple and Celery Salad with Mustard Vinaigrette

Cauliflower-Leek Potage

Lasagna with Fall Vegetables, Gruyère, and Sage Béchamel

Pear-Cranberry Crisp

Cranberry-Orange Compote with Port

Lemon-Poppy Seed Pan Rolls

Crispy Butternut Won Tons with Spicy Tomato Sauce

You'll only use 1 cup of the cooked squash; mash the remaining squash with a little butter, salt, and pepper to serve another day. Prepare the won ton filling up to 1 day ahead, and the sauce up to 2 days in advance.

SAUCE:

1½ teaspoons olive oil
1½ cups thinly sliced leek (about 2 medium)
1 garlic clove, minced
¼ teaspoon crushed red pepper
⅛ teaspoon sea salt
⅛ teaspoon freshly ground black pepper
1 (14.5-ounce) can whole tomatoes, undrained and chopped
1 (3-inch) orange rind strip
1 bay leaf
1 tarragon sprig

WON TONS:

1 small butternut squash (about 1½ pounds)
½ cup water
½ cup ricotta cheese
3 tablespoons grated fresh Parmesan cheese
2 tablespoons dry breadcrumbs
¼ teaspoon sea salt
¼ teaspoon freshly ground black pepper
⅛ teaspoon ground nutmeg
1 teaspoon water
1 large egg, lightly beaten
24 won ton wrappers
Cooking spray

1. To prepare sauce, heat oil in a large nonstick skillet over medium heat. Add leek and garlic; cook 8 minutes or until tender (do not brown), stirring frequently. Increase heat to medium-high. Add red pepper and next 6 ingredients; bring to a boil. Reduce heat to low; simmer 15 minutes or until thick. Discard rind, bay leaf, and tarragon.

2. Preheat oven to 375°.

3. To prepare won tons, cut squash in half lengthwise; discard seeds and membrane. Place squash halves, cut sides down, in a 2-quart baking dish; add ½ cup water. Bake at 375° for 45 minutes or until squash is tender when pierced with a fork; cool. Scoop out pulp to measure 1 cup, and reserve remaining pulp for another use. Combine 1 cup pulp, ricotta, and next 5 ingredients, stirring until well combined.

4. Combine 1 teaspoon water and egg, stirring with a whisk. Working with 1 won ton wrapper at a time (cover remaining wrappers with a damp towel to prevent drying), spoon about 2 teaspoons squash mixture into center of each wrapper. Brush edges of dough with egg mixture; bring 2 opposite corners together. Press edges together to seal, forming a triangle.

5. Place won tons on a large baking sheet coated with cooking spray, and brush lightly with remaining egg mixture. Bake at 375° for 17 minutes or until golden and crisp. Serve with sauce. Yield: 8 servings (serving size: 3 won tons and 3 tablespoons sauce).

CALORIES 157 (26% from fat); FAT 4.6g (sat 2.1g, mono 1.7g, poly 0.4g); PROTEIN 6.8g; CARB 22.3g; FIBER 2g; CHOL 38mg; IRON 1.8mg; SODIUM 385mg; CALC 100mg

---

MAKE AHEAD
Green Apple and Celery Salad with Mustard Vinaigrette

This crunchy salad can chill up to 1 hour before serving. If you want to get a head start on the preparation, slice the celery, chop the parsley, and toast the nuts in advance.

3 tablespoons fresh lemon juice
3 tablespoons Dijon mustard
2 tablespoons honey
½ teaspoon sea salt
1½ teaspoons extravirgin olive oil
¼ teaspoon freshly ground black pepper
1 garlic clove, minced
6 cups sliced peeled Granny Smith apple (about 3 apples)
4 cups thinly sliced celery (about 6 stalks)
¼ cup chopped fresh flat-leaf parsley leaves
3 tablespoons coarsely chopped walnuts, toasted

1. Combine first 7 ingredients in a large bowl, stirring well with a whisk. Add apple and remaining ingredients, and toss well to combine. Yield: 8 servings (serving size: 1 cup).

CALORIES 108 (30% from fat); FAT 3.6g (sat 0.4g, mono 1.1g, poly 1.7g); PROTEIN 1.5g; CARB 20.6g; FIBER 3g; CHOL 0mg; IRON 0.7mg; SODIUM 340mg; CALC 42mg

---

MAKE AHEAD
Cauliflower-Leek Potage

Make the soup up to 1 day ahead, and store in the refrigerator. Reheat over medium-low heat, stirring frequently.

2 tablespoons fresh lemon juice
7 cups cauliflower florets (about 2½ pounds)
1½ tablespoons butter, divided
Cooking spray
3 cups thinly sliced leek (about 2 large)
¼ teaspoon sea salt
2 (14-ounce) cans vegetable broth, divided
⅛ teaspoon white pepper
Dash of ground nutmeg
4 teaspoons minced fresh chives

1. Bring 4 quarts water to a boil in a Dutch oven, and stir in juice. Add cauliflower, reduce heat, and simmer 15 minutes or until tender. Drain.

2. Melt 1½ teaspoons butter in a large nonstick skillet coated with cooking spray over medium heat. Add leek and salt; cover and cook 5 minutes, stirring occasionally. Reduce heat to medium-low; cook 5 minutes or until tender (do not brown), stirring occasionally. Combine leek and cauliflower.

3. Place half of cauliflower mixture and 1 cup broth in a blender; process until smooth. Pour puréed mixture into a large bowl. Repeat procedure with remaining cauliflower mixture and 1 cup broth.

4. Melt 1 tablespoon butter over medium heat in Dutch oven. Cook 3 minutes or until lightly browned, stirring occasionally. Add cauliflower purée and remaining broth. Simmer 5 minutes. Stir in pepper and nutmeg. Sprinkle each
Continued

serving with ½ teaspoon chives. Yield: 8 servings (serving size: ¾ cup).

CALORIES 83 (33% from fat); FAT 3g (sat 1.4g, mono 0.6g, poly 0.3g); PROTEIN 4.2g; CARB 13.4g; FIBER 4.2g; CHOL 6mg; IRON 1.3mg; SODIUM 565mg; CALC 52mg

MAKE AHEAD

Lasagna with Fall Vegetables, Gruyère, and Sage Béchamel

Prepare and refrigerate the béchamel, covered, up to 2 days ahead. Refrigerate the mushroom-sweet potato mixture and the spinach mixture separately up to 2 days.

BÉCHAMEL:

⅔ cup all-purpose flour
6 cups fat-free milk
½ cup finely chopped onion
¼ cup chopped fresh sage
2 tablespoons finely chopped shallots
½ teaspoon sea salt
1 bay leaf

FILLING:

1 tablespoon olive oil, divided
2½ cups finely chopped onion
3 garlic cloves, minced
1 teaspoon sea salt, divided
1 (10-ounce) package fresh spinach
8 cups chopped portobello mushroom caps (about 1½ pounds)
6 cups (½-inch) cubed peeled sweet potato (about 2½ pounds)
Cooking spray
1 cup (4 ounces) shredded Gruyère cheese
¾ cup (3 ounces) grated fresh Parmesan cheese

NOODLES:

12 precooked lasagna noodles
2 cups warm water

1. Preheat oven to 450°.
2. To prepare béchamel, lightly spoon flour into a dry measuring cup; level with a knife. Place flour in a Dutch oven, and gradually add milk, stirring with a whisk. Add ½ cup onion, sage, shallots, ½ teaspoon salt, and bay leaf. Bring mixture to a boil; cook 1 minute or until thick.

Strain béchamel through a sieve over a bowl, and discard solids. Set béchamel aside.
3. To prepare filling, heat 1½ teaspoons olive oil in a large nonstick skillet over medium-high heat. Add 2½ cups onion and garlic; sauté 3 minutes. Add ½ teaspoon salt and spinach; sauté 2 minutes or until spinach wilts. Set aside.
4. Combine 1½ teaspoons oil, ½ teaspoon salt, mushroom, and sweet potato on a jelly roll pan coated with cooking spray. Bake at 450° for 15 minutes.
5. Combine cheeses; set aside.
6. To prepare noodles, soak noodles in 2 cups warm water in a 13 x 9-inch baking dish 5 minutes. Drain.
7. Spread ¾ cup béchamel in bottom of a 13 x 9-inch baking dish coated with cooking spray. Arrange 3 noodles over béchamel; top with half of mushroom mixture, 1½ cups béchamel, and ⅓ cup cheese mixture. Top with 3 noodles, spinach mixture, 1½ cups béchamel, and ⅓ cup cheese mixture. Top with 3 noodles, remaining mushroom mixture, 1½ cups béchamel, and 3 noodles. Spread remaining béchamel over noodles. Bake at 450° for 20 minutes. Sprinkle with remaining cheese; bake an additional 10 minutes. Let stand 10 minutes before serving. Yield: 9 servings.

CALORIES 418 (20% from fat); FAT 9.5g (sat 4.5g, mono 3.2g, poly 1g); PROTEIN 22.3g; CARB 62.7g; FIBER 6.4g; CHOL 24mg; IRON 3.7mg; SODIUM 703mg; CALC 505mg

MAKE AHEAD

Pear-Cranberry Crisp

This seasonal dessert doesn't take a lot of work. Prepare the topping earlier in the day, and refrigerate in a zip-top plastic bag.

FILLING:

6 cups sliced peeled pear (about 3 pounds)
1 teaspoon cornstarch
½ cup fresh cranberries
½ cup apple juice
¼ cup maple syrup
1 teaspoon vanilla extract
¾ teaspoon ground ginger
⅛ teaspoon sea salt
Cooking spray

TOPPING:

¾ cup regular oats
¾ cup whole wheat pastry flour
¼ cup sugar
¼ cup chopped pecans
¼ cup butter, melted
1 teaspoon vanilla extract
¼ teaspoon sea salt

1. Preheat oven to 375°.
2. To prepare filling, place pear in a large bowl. Sprinkle with cornstarch; toss well to coat. Stir in cranberries and next 5 ingredients. Spoon pear mixture into a 2-quart baking dish coated with cooking spray.
3. To prepare topping, combine oats and remaining 6 ingredients, tossing until moist. Sprinkle topping in an even layer over pear mixture. Cover with foil; bake at 375° for 40 minutes. Uncover and bake an additional 20 minutes or until topping is golden and fruit mixture is bubbly. Yield: 8 servings (serving size: about ¾ cup).

CALORIES 310 (30% from fat); FAT 10.2g (sat 3.9g, mono 3.4g, poly 1.3g); PROTEIN 4.2g; CARB 55.4g; FIBER 4.8g; CHOL 15mg; IRON 1.1mg; SODIUM 168mg; CALC 40mg

QUICK & EASY • MAKE AHEAD

Cranberry-Orange Compote with Port

Prepare and refrigerate up to 5 days ahead.

1 cup port or other sweet red wine
½ cup honey
6 cups fresh cranberries
1 cup sugar
1 tablespoon grated orange rind
¼ teaspoon ground cinnamon
⅛ teaspoon ground cloves
⅛ teaspoon freshly ground black pepper

1. Combine port and honey in a large saucepan; bring to a boil. Add cranberries; cook 6 minutes or until cranberries begin to pop, stirring occasionally. Stir in sugar and remaining ingredients; cook 5 minutes or until sugar dissolves. Cover and chill. Yield: 4 cups (serving size: ¼ cup).

CALORIES 110 (1% from fat); FAT 0.1g (sat 0g, mono 0g, poly 0.1g); PROTEIN 0.2g; CARB 26.7g; FIBER 1.6g; CHOL 0mg; IRON 0.2mg; SODIUM 2mg; CALC 5mg

MAKE AHEAD • FREEZABLE

Lemon-Poppy Seed Pan Rolls

If you can't find whole wheat pastry flour, substitute all-purpose flour. Make and freeze the rolls up to 1 month ahead. Follow the instructions for freezing and reheating in the Garlic and Rosemary Cloverleaf Rolls recipe (recipe on page 343).

1½ cups warm 2% reduced-fat milk (100° to 110°)
1 tablespoon honey
1 package dry yeast (about 2¼ teaspoons)
3 cups all-purpose flour, divided
1 cup whole wheat pastry flour
2½ teaspoons poppy seeds, divided
1½ teaspoons salt
3 tablespoons butter, melted
4 teaspoons grated lemon rind
1 large egg, lightly beaten
Cooking spray
1 teaspoon water
1 large egg, lightly beaten

1. Combine first 3 ingredients in a large bowl, and let stand 5 minutes. Lightly spoon flours into dry measuring cups; level with a knife. Combine 2¾ cups all-purpose flour, pastry flour, 2 teaspoons poppy seeds, and salt; stir with a whisk. Add flour mixture to milk mixture; stir until a soft dough forms. Add butter, rind, and 1 egg. Turn dough out onto a lightly floured surface. Knead until smooth and elastic (about 10 minutes); add enough of remaining flour, 1 tablespoon at a time, to prevent dough from sticking to hands (dough will feel tacky).
2. Place dough in a large bowl coated with cooking spray, turning to coat top. Cover and let rise in a warm place (85°), free from drafts, 1 hour or until doubled in size. (Gently press two fingers into dough. If indentation remains, dough has risen enough.) Punch dough down; cover and let rise 1 hour or until doubled in size.
3. Turn dough out onto a floured surface. Lightly dust dough with flour; pat into an 8 x 10-inch rectangle. Divide dough by making 3 lengthwise cuts and 4 crosswise cuts to form 20 equal pieces; shape each piece into a ball. Arrange balls in a 13 x 9-inch baking pan coated with cooking spray. Combine water and 1 egg, stirring with a whisk. Lightly brush rolls with egg mixture; sprinkle with ½ teaspoon poppy seeds. Cover with plastic wrap, and let rise in a warm place (85°), free from drafts, 20 minutes.
4. Preheat oven to 400°.
5. Uncover dough. Bake at 400° for 20 minutes or until golden. Remove from heat; cool in pan 5 minutes. Serve warm, or cool completely on a wire rack. Yield: 20 servings (serving size: 1 roll).

CALORIES 127 (21% from fat); FAT 3g (sat 1.5g, mono 0.9g, poly 0.4g); PROTEIN 4.2g; CARB 20.8g; FIBER 1.4g; CHOL 27mg; IRON 1.3mg; SODIUM 210mg; CALC 36mg

passport

Festival of Lights

For an illuminating party, try great food and customs drawn from one of India's most important holidays.

Festival of Lights Menu

Lentil and Spinach Puffs with Plum-Date Dip
Roasted-Garlic Puppodums
Goan Duck Vindaloo in Hot-and-Sour Cayenne Sauce
Jheega Shrimp and Squash in Creamy Mustard Sauce
Saffron Pilaf
Brussels Sprouts with Toasted Spices
Cranberry Chutney
Cinnamon-Scented Sweet Potato Chapati
Indian Rice Pudding
Sweet Semolina Pudding with Ginger Topping
Indian Summer
Caramelized Cayenne Almonds
Pistachio Brittle

MAKE AHEAD

Lentil and Spinach Puffs with Plum-Date Dip

The lentil puffs, studded with spinach and cilantro, are a specialty in the northern and western parts of India, where they're enjoyed with various sauces. Make these up to 1 hour ahead. To reheat, lightly cover and place in a 250° oven for 12 minutes or until warmed.

PUFFS:
¾ cup dried small red lentils
3 tablespoons water
3½ cups coarsely chopped fresh spinach (about 5 ounces)
2 tablespoons thinly sliced green onions
1 tablespoon finely chopped fresh cilantro
1 tablespoon finely chopped seeded serrano chile
2 teaspoons all-purpose flour
¾ teaspoon kosher salt
⅛ teaspoon baking powder
1 garlic clove, minced
3 tablespoons peanut oil, divided

DIP:
½ cup water
2 tablespoons lemon juice
1½ teaspoons sugar
½ teaspoon ground cumin
½ teaspoon ground ginger
¼ teaspoon kosher salt
⅛ teaspoon ground red pepper
4 pitted prunes
4 whole pitted dates

REMAINING INGREDIENT:
Cilantro sprigs (optional)

1. To prepare puffs, sort and wash lentils; place in a bowl. Cover with water to 2 inches above lentils. Cover and refrigerate 8 hours or overnight. Drain well. Place lentils and 3 tablespoons water in a food processor; process until smooth, scraping bowl occasionally. Combine puréed lentils, spinach, and next 7 ingredients, stirring well.
2. Heat 1 tablespoon oil in a large nonstick skillet over medium-high heat.

Continued

Drop lentil mixture by heaping table-spoons into pan. Cook 2 minutes on each side or until lightly browned. Remove from pan. Cover and keep warm. Repeat procedure with remaining oil and lentil mixture.

3. To prepare dip, combine ½ cup water and next 8 ingredients in a blender; process until well blended. Serve with puffs. Garnish with cilantro sprigs, if desired. Yield: 10 servings (serving size: 3 puffs and about 1 tablespoon dip).

CALORIES 136 (29% from fat); FAT 4.4g (sat 0.7g, mono 1.9g, poly 1.4g); PROTEIN 4.7g; CARB 21.5g; FIBER 6.9g; CHOL 0mg; IRON 1.8mg; SODIUM 206mg; CALC 27mg

Roasted-Garlic Puppodums

Puppodum, a wafer-thin bread, is popular throughout India. Look for it with the Indian foods in your supermarket. To add smoky flavor, add ½ teaspoon toasted cumin seeds, lightly crushed, to the garlic spread.

2 large whole garlic heads
¼ cup minced fresh cilantro
2 tablespoons tomato paste
1 tablespoon olive oil
2 finely chopped seeded serrano chiles
8 Indian puppodums (such as Sharwood's)

1. Preheat oven to 400°.
2. Remove white papery skin from garlic heads (do not peel or separate cloves). Wrap each head separately in foil. Bake at 400° for 45 minutes; cool 10 minutes. Separate cloves; squeeze to extract garlic pulp. Discard skins.
3. Combine garlic, cilantro, tomato paste, oil, and chiles.
4. Microwave 1 puppodum at a time at HIGH 40 to 50 seconds or until edges curl and entire puppodum is cream col-ored, turning as necessary to avoid uncooked spots. Spread 1 tablespoon garlic spread over each puppodum. Yield: 8 servings (serving size: 1 puppodum).

CALORIES 39 (42% from fat); FAT 1.8g (sat 0.2g, mono 1.3g, poly 0.2g); PROTEIN 1.2g; CARB 4.9g; FIBER 0.7g; CHOL 0mg; IRON 0.3mg; SODIUM 50mg; CALC 19mg

MAKE AHEAD
Goan Duck Vindaloo in Hot-and-Sour Cayenne Sauce

This dish originated in Goa, a coastal west Indian state. *Vindaloo* is typically the hottest of curries, but the spices here mit-igate the heat. Found in specialty markets, fenugreek seed plays a prominent role in southern Asian cooking. Vindaloo can be made up to 2 days ahead and refrigerated. To reheat, place over medium-low heat, and stir often.

2 teaspoons cumin seeds
2 teaspoons mustard seeds
½ teaspoon black peppercorns
½ teaspoon fenugreek seeds
2 teaspoons minced peeled fresh ginger
2 teaspoons minced fresh garlic
1 teaspoon ground red pepper
½ teaspoon ground cinnamon
⅓ cup white wine vinegar
2 pounds skinless, boneless duck breast halves
1 teaspoon vegetable oil
1½ cups minced fresh onion
1 tablespoon ground coriander
1 teaspoon ground turmeric
1 cup water
3 tablespoons tomato paste
2 teaspoons kosher salt
1 pound small red potatoes, cut into 1-inch pieces
1 teaspoon sugar

1. Combine first 4 ingredients in a spice grinder; process until powdered. Place in a small bowl; stir in ginger, garlic, red pepper, and cinnamon. Add vinegar, stir-ring until combined. Place vinegar mix-ture and duck in a large zip-top plastic bag; seal. Marinate in refrigerator 4 hours or overnight.
2. Heat vegetable oil in a large nonstick skillet over medium-high heat. Add onion, and sauté 6 minutes or until browned. Add coriander and turmeric; sauté 1 minute.
3. Add duck to pan; cook 3 minutes on each side. Stir in water, tomato paste, salt, and potatoes, and bring to a boil. Cover, reduce heat, and simmer 20 minutes or until duck is done and pota-toes are tender. Remove from heat. Remove duck from pan; cut duck diago-nally into ½-inch-wide slices. Add sugar to pan; stir to combine. Return duck to pan; stir to combine. Yield: 6 servings (serving size: about 3 ounces duck and about ⅓ cup potatoes).

CALORIES 216 (25% from fat); FAT 6.1g (sat 1.6g, mono 1.8g, poly 1.1g); PROTEIN 25g; CARB 14.1g; FIBER 2.6g; CHOL 87mg; IRON 6.4mg; SODIUM 546mg; CALC 34mg

MAKE AHEAD
Jheega Shrimp and Squash in Creamy Mustard Sauce

This celebratory dish has an abundance of shrimp and aromatic flavors; use your largest skillet to hold it all.

2½ tablespoons vegetable oil, divided
1½ tablespoons dry mustard
1½ tablespoons ground cumin
1½ tablespoons minced fresh garlic
¾ teaspoon ground red pepper
3 pounds large shrimp, peeled and deveined
3 cups (½-inch) cubed peeled butternut squash (about 1½ pounds)
¼ cup julienne-cut peeled fresh ginger
¼ teaspoon ground cloves
½ cup water, divided
¾ cup chopped green onions
3 tablespoons Dijon mustard
1 teaspoon kosher salt
1 tablespoon fresh lemon juice
¼ cup chopped fresh cilantro

1. Combine 1 tablespoon oil, dry mus-tard, cumin, garlic, and red pepper in a large bowl. Add shrimp; toss gently to coat. Let stand 15 minutes.
2. Combine squash, ginger, cloves, and ¼ cup water in a large nonstick skillet over medium-high heat; bring to a boil. Cover, reduce heat, and simmer 3 min-utes or until squash is crisp-tender. Remove squash mixture from pan.
3. Add 1½ tablespoons oil to pan; increase heat to medium-high. Add green onions to pan, and sauté 1 minute. Add

Festival of Lights Party Planner

Four weeks ahead:
- Make a shopping list for the menu.
- Invite guests.
- Stock up on staples and specialty ingredients, such as saffron, cardamom, nuts, dried fruit, tamarind concentrate, rum, and wine.
- Purchase supplies such as candles, brocade, tissue paper, and gold and silver ribbon or string.

One week ahead:
- Prepare Pistachio Brittle (recipe on page 355) and Caramelized Cayenne Almonds (recipe on page 355); wrap in tissue and fabric tied with ribbon.

Two days ahead:
- Prepare Cranberry Chutney (recipe on page 354), Plum-Date Dip (recipe on page 351) (to serve with Lentil and Spinach Puffs [recipe on page 351]), and Indian Rice Pudding (recipe on page 354); store, covered, in the refrigerator.

One day ahead:
- Decorate the house with candles.
- Set the table and bar.
- Make Goan Duck Vindaloo in Hot-and-Sour Cayenne Sauce (recipe on page 352) and Sweet Semolina Pudding (recipe on page 354); store, covered, in the refrigerator.
- Clean, peel, and devein shrimp; cut and cook squash, and trim Brussels sprouts.

Day of Celebration:
- Prepare Cinnamon-Scented Sweet Potato Chapati (recipe on page 354) and Lentil and Spinach Puffs (recipe on page 351); wrap in foil, and keep warm in oven.
- Prepare Saffron Pilaf (recipe below), Jheega Shrimp and Squash in Creamy Mustard Sauce (recipe on page 352), and Brussels Sprouts with Toasted Spices (recipe below); cover pans and keep warm over low heat on stovetop.
- Prepare Ginger Topping (recipe on page 355) for Sweet Semolina Pudding (recipe on page 354); store in the refrigerator until ready to serve.
- Reheat Goan Duck Vindaloo.
- Prepare Roasted-Garlic Puppodums (recipe on page 352).
- Prepare Indian Summer (recipe on page 355).
- Open wines, and light candles.

---

shrimp; sauté 3 minutes. Stir in squash mixture, ¼ cup water, Dijon mustard, and salt; bring to a boil. Cover and cook 2 minutes. Stir in juice, and sprinkle with cilantro. Yield: 8 servings (serving size: 6 ounces shrimp and about ⅓ cup squash mixture).

CALORIES 272 (29% from fat); FAT 8.7g (sat 1.2g, mono 1.6g, poly 3.8g); PROTEIN 36.6g; CARB 11.2g; FIBER 2.8g; CHOL 259mg; IRON 5.4mg; SODIUM 637mg; CALC 147mg

---

MAKE AHEAD
Saffron Pilaf

1 tablespoon warm water
½ teaspoon saffron threads, crumbled
1⅓ cups uncooked basmati rice
2 cups cold water
1 teaspoon vegetable oil
3 whole cloves
2 bay leaves
2¼ cups fat-free, less-sodium chicken broth
2 tablespoons raisins
¾ teaspoon salt
2 tablespoons sliced almonds, toasted

1. Combine warm water and saffron.
2. Rinse rice well; drain. Combine rice and 2 cups cold water in a bowl, and let stand 30 minutes to 2 hours. Drain.
3. Heat oil in a large saucepan over medium-high heat. Add cloves and bay leaves; cook 1½ minutes, stirring occasionally (be careful not to burn bay leaves). Stir in saffron mixture, rice, broth, raisins, and salt; bring to a boil. Reduce heat; simmer 5 minutes or until liquid is absorbed. Reduce heat to low. Cover and cook 5 minutes. Remove from heat; let stand 5 minutes. Fluff with a fork. Discard cloves and bay leaves; sprinkle with almonds. Yield: 8 servings (serving size: ⅔ cup).

CALORIES 147 (8% from fat); FAT 1.3g (sat 0.2g, mono 0.6g, poly 0.5g); PROTEIN 3g; CARB 32.9g; FIBER 1.1g; CHOL 0mg; IRON 1mg; SODIUM 345mg; CALC 5mg

---

QUICK & EASY • MAKE AHEAD
Brussels Sprouts with Toasted Spices

To trim a Brussels sprout, cut a small portion from the stem, and pull off the yellow leaves. Carrots, green beans, and cauliflower will also work. Nigella seeds, also called black onion seeds, have a nutty, peppery flavor.

1½ pounds small Brussels sprouts, trimmed
1 tablespoon vegetable oil
2 small dried hot red chiles
½ teaspoon mustard seeds
½ teaspoon cumin seeds
½ teaspoon fennel seeds
¼ teaspoon nigella seeds
1½ cups vertically sliced red onion
½ teaspoon ground turmeric
1 teaspoon kosher salt
½ teaspoon sugar
2 tablespoons chopped fresh cilantro
1 tablespoon unsweetened grated coconut
2 teaspoons fresh lemon juice

1. Cut a shallow "X" in stem end of each sprout. Cook sprouts in boiling water 7 minutes or until tender; drain.
2. Heat oil in a large skillet over medium heat. Add chiles; cook 1 minute or until browned, shaking pan frequently. Add seeds; cook, partially covered, 1 minute or until mustard seeds begin to pop, shaking pan frequently. Add onion and turmeric; sauté 5 minutes or until lightly browned. Add sprouts, salt, and sugar; cook 3 minutes or until thoroughly heated. Stir in *Continued*

cilantro, coconut, and juice. Yield: 8 servings (serving size: ½ cup).

CALORIES 68 (32% from fat); FAT 2.4g (sat 0.5g, mono 0.5g, poly 1.1g); PROTEIN 3.3g; CARB 10.6g; FIBER 3.8g; CHOL 0mg; IRON 1.5mg; SODIUM 260mg; CALC 44mg

MAKE AHEAD
Cranberry Chutney

For the best results, make the chutney at least 1 day ahead to let the flavors blend. Let stand at room temperature for about 1 hour before serving. Partially covering the pan keeps the mustard seeds from popping out.

- 2 cups fresh or frozen cranberries (about 8 ounces)
- ¾ cup packed brown sugar
- ¾ cup fresh orange juice
- 2 tablespoons fresh lemon juice
- 2 tablespoons finely chopped seeded serrano chile
- 1 tablespoon julienne-cut peeled fresh ginger
- 1 teaspoon ground cumin
- ¾ teaspoon kosher salt
- ½ teaspoon ground cinnamon
- 1 teaspoon vegetable oil
- 1 teaspoon mustard seeds
- ¾ cup dried Mission figs, coarsely chopped
- ¼ cup pistachios

1. Combine first 9 ingredients.
2. Heat oil in a medium saucepan over medium-high heat. Add mustard seeds, and cook, partially covered, 1 minute or until seeds pop, shaking pan frequently. Add cranberry mixture, and bring to a boil. Reduce heat, and simmer 15 minutes or until cranberries pop and mixture thickens. Stir in figs and pistachios; cook 3 minutes. Remove from heat, and cool. Spoon into a bowl. Cover and chill. Yield: 8 servings (serving size: ¼ cup).

CALORIES 182 (14% from fat); FAT 2.8g (sat 0.4g, mono 1.1g, poly 1g); PROTEIN 1.9g; CARB 40.3g; FIBER 4.3g; CHOL 0mg; IRON 1.2mg; SODIUM 188mg; CALC 59mg

MAKE AHEAD
Cinnamon-Scented Sweet Potato Chapati

To reheat the chapati, wrap the bread rounds in foil, and place them in a 350° oven for 8 minutes. Turn off the oven, and leave the foil-wrapped bread for about 30 minutes.

- 1½ cups whole wheat flour
- ½ cup barley flour
- 1 cup mashed cooked sweet potato
- 1 tablespoon butter, melted
- 1 teaspoon salt
- ½ teaspoon ground cinnamon
- ¼ cup water

1. Lightly spoon flours into dry measuring cups; level with a knife. Combine flours, potato, butter, salt, and cinnamon in a large bowl; mix well. Add water; press mixture together with hands. Turn dough out onto a lightly floured surface; knead until smooth (about 2 minutes).
2. Divide dough into 16 equal portions, shaping each into a ball. Working with 1 ball at a time (cover remaining dough to prevent drying), roll into a 4-inch circle on a lightly floured surface (circles will be very thin).
3. Heat a medium cast iron skillet over medium-high heat until very hot. Place 1 dough circle in pan, and cook 2 minutes or until brown spots appear, turning after 1 minute. Place bread on a cooking rack over eye of a gas burner. Hold bread over flame with tongs, turning until both sides of bread are puffed and brown spots appear. (Some chapatis will puff more than others). Repeat procedure with remaining dough. Yield: 8 servings (serving size: 2 chapatis).

CALORIES 151 (13% from fat); FAT 2.1g (sat 1g, mono 0.5g, poly 0.3g); PROTEIN 4.5g; CARB 31.1g; FIBER 4.3g; CHOL 4mg; IRON 1.3mg; SODIUM 312mg; CALC 18mg

MAKE AHEAD
Indian Rice Pudding

Make this cardamom-infused pudding up to 2 days ahead and store, covered, in the refrigerator. Serve in martini glasses for a sophisticated presentation.

- ⅔ cup uncooked basmati rice
- 5 cups 2% reduced-fat milk
- ¼ cup sugar
- 2 tablespoons flaked sweetened coconut
- ½ teaspoon ground cardamom
- 2 tablespoons sliced almonds, toasted
- 2 tablespoons raisins

1. Rinse rice; drain well. Combine rice and milk in a medium saucepan; bring to a boil over medium-high heat, stirring frequently. Reduce heat; simmer 30 minutes or until rice is tender and creamy, stirring frequently. Stir in sugar, coconut, and cardamom; chill. Sprinkle with almonds and raisins. Yield: 8 servings (serving size: about ⅓ cup).

CALORIES 183 (20% from fat); FAT 4.1g (sat 2.2g, mono 1.3g, poly 0.3g); PROTEIN 6.4g; CARB 31.6g; FIBER 0.8g; CHOL 11mg; IRON 0.7mg; SODIUM 80mg; CALC 191mg

MAKE AHEAD
Sweet Semolina Pudding with Ginger Topping

Set out all the ingredients for this fast-paced recipe before you begin cooking. *Ghee* is clarified butter that's been simmered to remove the moisture and brown the milk solids. The result is a nutty, caramel flavor and aroma. To make ghee, simmer 2 tablespoons butter over medium heat until milk solids stop crackling and turn amber (about 5 minutes), stirring occasionally. Turn off heat, and let the residue settle to the bottom of the pan. Pour the clear butter fat into a small bowl. The pudding can be made a day ahead and stored, covered, in the refrigerator.

PUDDING:
- 2½ tablespoons golden raisins
- 2 tablespoons chopped cashews
- 1 tablespoon ghee (Indian clarified butter)
- ½ cup semolina
- 1 cup plus 3 tablespoons water
- ¼ cup granulated sugar
- ¼ teaspoon saffron threads
- ⅛ teaspoon ground cardamom

TOPPING:

½ cup plain fat-free yogurt
½ cup fat-free sour cream
1 tablespoon powdered sugar
1½ teaspoons vodka
1 tablespoon finely chopped crystallized ginger

1. To prepare pudding, combine first 3 ingredients in a large saucepan over medium-high heat; sauté 1½ minutes or until raisins puff. Stir in semolina, and sauté 3 minutes or until golden brown. Add water, granulated sugar, saffron, and cardamom; cook 1 minute, stirring rapidly to prevent lumps. Reduce heat to medium-low; cook 4 minutes or until semolina is soft, stirring frequently. Divide mixture evenly among 16 miniature muffin cups. Cool completely. Place a plate upside down on top of pan, and invert puddings onto plate.

2. To prepare topping, combine yogurt, sour cream, powdered sugar, and vodka in a medium bowl, and stir until smooth. Fold in ginger. Serve with pudding. Yield: 16 servings (serving size: 1 pudding mold and 1 tablespoon topping).

CALORIES 61 (21% from fat); FAT 1.4g (sat 0.6g, mono 0.5g, poly 0.1g); PROTEIN 1.7g; CARB 10.6g; FIBER 0.3g; CHOL 3mg; IRON 0.3mg; SODIUM 21mg; CALC 27mg

QUICK & EASY
Indian Summer

This drink comes from the sultry plains of New Delhi. Gin was originally used, but preferences have lately changed to milder-tasting vodka. This recipe serves 2 but is easy to multiply. For testing, we used Laxmi Natural Tamarind Concentrate, available in ethnic markets.

¼ cup vodka
1 tablespoon sugar
3 tablespoons water
2 tablespoons fresh lime juice
1 teaspoon tamarind concentrate
⅔ cup crushed ice
2 orange slices, cut into quarters
2 pineapple slices, cut into quarters

1. Combine first 5 ingredients, stirring until sugar dissolves. Divide vodka mixture, ice, orange quarters, and pineapple quarters between 2 glasses. Serve immediately Yield: 2 servings.

CALORIES 202 (1% from fat); FAT 0.3g (sat 0g, mono 0g, poly 0.1g); PROTEIN 1.3g; CARB 36.4g; FIBER 7.8g; CHOL 0mg; IRON 0.6mg; SODIUM 4mg; CALC 68mg

MAKE AHEAD
Caramelized Cayenne Almonds

Make these ahead, cool, and store in an airtight container. Serve this spicy-sweet snack with beverages before dinner.

1 cup sugar
⅓ cup water
1¼ teaspoons ground red pepper
2 teaspoons fresh lemon juice
½ teaspoon salt
½ teaspoon ground cumin
2 cups blanched almonds
Cooking spray

1. Preheat oven to 325°.
2. Combine first 6 ingredients in a medium, heavy saucepan over medium-high heat. Bring to a boil, stirring occasionally. Add nuts to pan, and cook 22 minutes or until sugar mixture thickens and coats nuts, stirring occasionally. Immediately spread nut mixture in a single layer on a jelly roll pan coated with cooking spray. Bake at 325° for 20 minutes. Separate nuts with 2 forks. Cool completely. Yield: 2 cups (serving size: 2 tablespoons).

CALORIES 152 (51% from fat); FAT 8.6g (sat 0.6g, mono 5.5g, poly 1.9g); PROTEIN 3.6g; CARB 15.9g; FIBER 1.6g; CHOL 0mg; IRON 0.7mg; SODIUM 75mg; CALC 44mg

MAKE AHEAD
Pistachio Brittle

Place the jelly roll pan in the oven at the lowest setting for 3 minutes before pouring out the brittle. Once prepared, wrap the brittle pieces in tissue paper, and then in a piece of pretty fabric; secure with gold and silver ribbon or string. If it's humid, wrap it in wax paper first. Use ⅛ teaspoon saffron for a light yellow brittle with a subtle saffron flavor.

1¼ cups unsalted pistachios
¼ cup unsalted sunflower seed kernels
½ teaspoon ground cardamom
⅛ to ¼ teaspoon saffron threads
2 cups sugar
¾ cup light-colored corn syrup
½ cup water
Dash of kosher salt
2 teaspoons unsalted butter
1½ teaspoons baking soda
Cooking spray

1. Combine first 4 ingredients, tossing to coat.
2. Combine sugar, syrup, water, and salt in a heavy saucepan. Cook over medium heat, stirring until sugar dissolves. Cook 25 minutes or until golden and a candy thermometer registers 340°, stirring occasionally. Stir in pistachio mixture and butter, stirring rapidly. Remove from heat; stir in baking soda (mixture will bubble). Rapidly spread mixture onto a jelly roll pan coated with cooking spray. Cool completely, and break into small pieces. Yield: 24 servings.

CALORIES 141 (25% from fat); FAT 3.9g (sat 0.6g, mono 1.8g, poly 1.4g); PROTEIN 1.6g; CARB 26.7g; FIBER 0.9g; CHOL 1mg; IRON 0.4mg; SODIUM 96mg; CALC 9mg

Festival Food

Enticing foods with appealing aromas are the hallmark of Festival of Lights.

The appetizers will satisfy guests well enough so they'll have ample time to mingle, and you'll have plenty of time to organize dinner. These nibbles are great with cocktails; wines such as Shiraz, Pinot Noir, or Riesling; and beer.

The duck, shrimp, rice pilaf, and desserts are all classic dishes at festival banquets in India.

Several weeks before the festival, sweets are prepared with nuts, fruits, coconut milk, clarified butter, and sugar. Packed in gift boxes or wrapped in brocade, they're given with good wishes for the coming year.

Simple Intimate Dinner

This festive menu suits a small gathering of friends.

MAKE AHEAD
Turkey Tenderloins with Mushroom Stuffing

1½ cups boiling water
1 cup dried porcini mushrooms (about 1 ounce)
1 tablespoon butter
¼ cup finely chopped shallots
1½ cups finely chopped cremini or button mushrooms (about 3 ounces)
¾ teaspoon salt, divided
¼ teaspoon freshly ground black pepper, divided
2 tablespoons Madeira or port wine
1½ teaspoons chopped fresh thyme
2 (10-ounce) turkey tenderloins
1½ tablespoons all-purpose flour, divided
2 teaspoons olive oil
½ cup fat-free, less-sodium chicken broth
½ cup 1% low-fat milk

1. Place 1½ cups boiling water and porcini in a bowl. Cover and let stand 30 minutes or until tender. Drain through a sieve over a bowl, reserving soaking liquid. Finely chop porcini; set aside.
2. Melt butter in a large nonstick skillet over medium-high heat. Add shallots, and sauté 3 minutes. Add cremini; sauté 3 minutes. Sprinkle cremini mixture with ¼ teaspoon salt and ⅛ teaspoon pepper. Add wine, and cook 1 minute or until liquid evaporates. Remove from heat; stir in ¼ cup porcini and thyme.
3. Cut a horizontal slit through thickest portion of each tenderloin to form a pocket. Fill pockets evenly with cremini mixture, and secure at 1-inch intervals with twine. Sprinkle tenderloins with ¼ teaspoon salt and ⅛ teaspoon pepper. Dredge tenderloins in 1½ teaspoons flour.
4. Heat oil in a large nonstick skillet over medium-high heat. Add turkey; cook 4 minutes on each side or until browned. Add reserved soaking mixture and broth, and bring to a boil. Cover, reduce heat, and simmer 8 minutes. Remove turkey; keep warm. Cook broth mixture until reduced to ¾ cup (about 5 minutes). Combine 1 tablespoon flour and milk, stirring with a whisk. Add milk mixture to broth mixture; bring to a boil. Reduce heat, and simmer 2 minutes. Stir in ¼ teaspoon salt and remaining porcini.
5. Remove twine from tenderloins; slice turkey diagonally. Serve with sauce. Yield: 4 servings (serving size: 4 ounces turkey and ¼ cup sauce).

CALORIES 269 (26% from fat); FAT 7.7g (sat 2.9g, mono 3.4g, poly 1g); PROTEIN 37.9g; CARB 10.8g; FIBER 1.6g; CHOL 78mg; IRON 2.1mg; SODIUM 620mg; CALC 49mg

Caramelized Pearl Onions

To peel pearl onions easily, slice off the root ends and drop into boiling water for less than 1 minute. Drain and rinse with cold water. Pinch the stem end of each, and a peeled onion will pop out.

1 teaspoon olive oil
1 teaspoon butter
1 (10-ounce) package pearl onions, peeled
⅓ cup water
1 teaspoon sugar
1 tablespoon chopped fresh thyme
2 tablespoons dry white wine
¼ teaspoon salt
⅛ teaspoon black pepper

1. Heat oil in a medium nonstick skillet over medium heat. Melt butter in pan. Add onions, and cook 5 minutes or until lightly browned, shaking pan frequently. Add water and sugar, and bring to a boil. Cover, reduce heat, and simmer 8 minutes. Uncover and cook 2 minutes or until liquid evaporates. Stir in thyme and remaining ingredients; cook 1 minute. Yield: 4 servings (serving size: ¼ cup).

CALORIES 55 (36% from fat); FAT 2.2g (sat 0.8g, mono 1.1g, poly 0.2g); PROTEIN 0.9g; CARB 7.4g; FIBER 1.4g; CHOL 3mg; IRON 0.3mg; SODIUM 158mg; CALC 18mg

MAKE AHEAD
Roasted-Corn Bread Stuffing

2 strips center-cut bacon, chopped (such as Oscar Mayer)
½ cup fresh corn kernels (1 ear yellow corn)
¼ cup chopped onion
¼ cup chopped celery
⅓ cup water
2 Corn Bread Muffins
1 (1½-ounce) slice hearty white bread
2 teaspoons chopped fresh sage
2 teaspoons chopped fresh thyme
¼ teaspoon black pepper
⅛ teaspoon salt
¼ cup fat-free, less-sodium chicken broth
Cooking spray

1. Preheat oven to 350°.
2. Cook bacon in a large saucepan over medium heat until crisp. Remove bacon from pan, reserving 1 teaspoon of drippings in pan; crumble bacon. Set aside.

Add corn, chopped onion, and celery to pan; cook 2 minutes, stirring occasionally. Stir in water, and bring to a boil. Cover, reduce heat, and simmer 5 minutes.

3. Crumble 2 Corn Bread Muffins into a large bowl. Place white bread in a food processor; pulse until coarse crumbs form. Stir into crumbled Corn Bread Muffins. Add corn mixture, sage, thyme, pepper, salt, and bacon; stir to combine. Add broth; stir gently to coat. Place mixture in a (1-quart) baking dish coated with cooking spray. Bake at 350° for 30 minutes. Yield: 4 servings (serving size: ²/₃ cup).

(Totals include 2 Corn Bread Muffins) CALORIES 171 (30% from fat); FAT 5.7g (sat 2.5g, mono 2g, poly 0.7g); PROTEIN 5.7g; CARB 25.5g; FIBER 2.4g; CHOL 28mg; IRON 1.4mg; SODIUM 396mg; CALC 77mg

MAKE AHEAD

CORN BREAD MUFFINS:
Plan an easy chili, soup, or stew dinner for Thanksgiving Eve, and enjoy this tasty corn bread hot from the oven. Save two muffins for the dressing.

  1   cup yellow cornmeal
  ³/₄ cup all-purpose flour
  1½ teaspoons baking powder
  ¼   teaspoon baking soda
  ¼   teaspoon salt
  1   cup low-fat buttermilk
  2   tablespoons butter, melted
  1   large egg, lightly beaten
  Cooking spray

1. Preheat oven to 400°.
2. Lightly spoon cornmeal and flour into measuring cups; level with a knife. Combine cornmeal, flour, baking powder, baking soda, and salt in a large bowl, stirring with a whisk. Combine buttermilk, butter, and egg. Pour buttermilk mixture into cornmeal mixture; stir just until moist.
3. Spoon batter evenly into 6 muffin cups coated with cooking spray. Bake at 400° for 20 minutes or until a wooden pick inserted in center comes out clean. Cool on a wire rack. Yield: 6 muffins (serving size: 1 muffin).

CALORIES 205 (25% from fat); FAT 5.6g (sat 2.9g, mono 1.5g, poly 0.5g); PROTEIN 6.1g; CARB 32.1g; FIBER 2.1g; CHOL 48mg; IRON 1.1mg; SODIUM 345mg; CALC 111mg

QUICK & EASY
Braised Peas with Green Onions

  8   green onions
  1   tablespoon butter
  ¼   teaspoon black pepper
  2   cups fresh or frozen green peas, thawed
  ¼   cup water
  1   teaspoon chopped fresh or
  ¼   teaspoon dried marjoram
  ⅛   teaspoon salt

1. Remove green tops from green onions; reserve for another use. Cut white portion of each onion into ½-inch pieces.
2. Melt butter in a medium skillet over medium heat. Add onion pieces and pepper; cover and cook 3 minutes. Stir in peas and water, and bring to a boil. Cover and cook 5 minutes or until peas are tender. Uncover and cook 2 minutes or until liquid evaporates. Remove from heat; stir in marjoram and salt. Yield: 4 servings (serving size: ½ cup).

CALORIES 97 (30% from fat); FAT 3.2g (sat 1.8g, mono 0.9g, poly 0.3g); PROTEIN 4.7g; CARB 13.7g; FIBER 4.8g; CHOL 8mg; IRON 1.9mg; SODIUM 191mg; CALC 55mg

MAKE AHEAD
Wild Rice and Walnut Pilaf

  1   teaspoon butter
  ¼   cup finely chopped onion
  2½ cups water
  ³/₄ cup long-grain brown and wild rice blend (such as Lundberg's)
  ½   teaspoon salt, divided
  2   tablespoons chopped fresh parsley
  1   tablespoon chopped fresh chives
  1   tablespoon fresh lemon juice
  1   teaspoon olive oil
  2   tablespoons chopped walnuts, toasted

1. Melt butter in a small saucepan over medium heat. Add onion; cook 3 minutes, stirring frequently. Stir in water, rice, and ¼ teaspoon salt; bring to a boil. Cover, reduce heat, and simmer 40 minutes or until liquid is absorbed. Remove from heat; stir in ¼ teaspoon salt, parsley, chives, juice, and oil. Sprinkle each serving with walnuts. Yield: 4 servings (serving size: ²/₃ cup rice mixture and 1½ teaspoons walnuts).

CALORIES 177 (28% from fat); FAT 5.5g (sat 1.2g, mono 1.8g, poly 2.3g); PROTEIN 3.5g; CARB 29g; FIBER 1.7g; CHOL 3mg; IRON 0.9mg; SODIUM 308mg; CALC 24mg

STAFF FAVORITE • MAKE AHEAD
FREEZABLE
Apple and Ice Cream Pie

Similar to apple pie à la mode, this frozen dessert has an easy-to-make graham cracker crust. Layer the apple filling with vanilla frozen yogurt spiced with cinnamon, caramel syrup, and chopped pecans.

CRUST:
  10 reduced-fat graham cracker sheets
  2   tablespoons brown sugar
  2   tablespoons butter, melted
  1   large egg white
  Cooking spray

FILLING:
  1   tablespoon butter
  5   cups thinly sliced peeled Granny Smith apple (about 2 pounds)
  ³/₄ cup water
  1   tablespoon brown sugar
  1¼ teaspoons ground cinnamon, divided
  ¼   teaspoon ground nutmeg
  4   cups reduced-fat vanilla frozen yogurt, softened
  6   tablespoons caramel topping, divided
  1   reduced-fat graham cracker sheet, coarsely crumbled
  1   tablespoon chopped pecans, toasted

1. Preheat oven to 350°.
2. To prepare crust, place crackers in a food processor; process until fine crumbs form. Add 2 tablespoons sugar, 2 tablespoons melted butter, and egg white; pulse 8 times or until moist. Press crumb mixture into a 9-inch pie plate coated with cooking spray. Bake at 350° for
Continued

8 minutes; cool on a wire rack. Freeze 30 minutes to overnight.

3. To prepare filling, melt 1 tablespoon butter in a large nonstick skillet over medium heat. Add apple; cook 10 minutes or until lightly browned, stirring frequently. Add water; bring to a boil. Cover, reduce heat, and simmer 15 minutes. Stir in 1 tablespoon brown sugar, ¼ teaspoon cinnamon, and nutmeg; cook, uncovered, 3 minutes or until liquid evaporates. Remove from pan. Cover and chill 2 hours.

4. Place frozen yogurt in a chilled bowl. Stir in 1 teaspoon cinnamon and ¾ cup apple mixture. Cover and chill 30 minutes. Spread half of yogurt mixture into frozen crust (keep remaining yogurt mixture in freezer). Top yogurt mixture with remaining apple mixture. Drizzle with ¼ cup caramel topping. Cover and freeze 1 hour. Carefully spread reserved yogurt mixture over caramel. Top with graham cracker crumbs and pecans. Drizzle with 2 tablespoons caramel topping. Freeze overnight or until solid. Place pie in refrigerator 30 minutes before serving. Yield: 8 servings (serving size: 1 slice).

CALORIES 314 (21% from fat); FAT 7.3g (sat 3.8g, mono 2g, poly 0.5g); PROTEIN 6.2g; CARB 59.1g; FIBER 3.9g; CHOL 17mg; IRON 0.8mg; SODIUM 204mg; CALC 184mg

enlightened cook

Beyond the Bird

After the last pan from Thanksgiving dinner has been washed and put away, the best part arrives—leftovers.

Stock On

All but one of the following recipes calls for considerable amounts of chicken broth. Our Rich Turkey Stock (recipe on page 383) is great to substitute for the chicken broth and will give these recipes even more flavor.

Turkey Magiritsa

This is a variation of the classic Greek soup *magiritsa*, which is typically made from lamb, chicken broth, egg, and lemon, and is served to end the Lenten fast. Here, it's transformed into a fine fall dish using turkey leftovers.

—Jim Botsacos
Molyvos, New York, New York

　2　tablespoons fresh lemon juice
　½　teaspoon all-purpose flour
　2　large eggs
　7　cups fat-free, less-sodium chicken broth, divided
　2　tablespoons olive oil
2½　cups finely chopped onion
　　Dash of salt
1½　cups shredded leftover cooked turkey (light and dark meat)
　1　cup cooked short-grain rice
　1　cup shredded romaine lettuce
　½　cup sliced green onions
　1　tablespoon chopped fresh dill
　½　teaspoon fresh lemon juice
　¼　teaspoon salt
　¼　teaspoon freshly ground black pepper

1. Combine 2 tablespoons lemon juice and flour in a bowl; whisk until smooth. Add eggs; whisk until combined.

2. Bring 1 cup broth to a simmer in a medium saucepan over medium-high heat. Gradually add hot broth to egg mixture, stirring constantly with a whisk. Return egg mixture to pan. Cook 2 minutes or until slightly thick, whisking constantly. Remove from heat; set aside.

3. Heat oil in a large saucepan over medium-high heat. Add onion and dash of salt, and sauté 8 minutes or until tender. Add 6 cups broth; bring to boil. Reduce heat, and simmer 5 minutes. Add turkey, and simmer 2 minutes. Add rice, and slowly whisk in egg mixture. Keep warm over low heat. Add remaining ingredients immediately before serving. Yield: 6 servings (serving size: 1⅓ cups).

CALORIES 232 (35% from fat); FAT 9.1g (sat 1.9g, mono 4.9g, poly 1.3g); PROTEIN 18g; CARB 17g; FIBER 2g; CHOL 98mg; IRON 1.5mg; SODIUM 697mg; CALC 34mg

Roasted Squash Soup with Turkey Croquettes

Leftover turkey, breadcrumbs, and egg combine to make crisp croquettes that nestle in velvety squash soup. Panko breadcrumbs are extracrisp, but you can use plain dry breadcrumbs, if you prefer.

—Gary Mennie
Conoe Restaurant, Atlanta, Georgia

SOUP:
　2　pounds butternut or kabocha squash, or pumpkin
　1　tablespoon honey
　¼　teaspoon kosher salt
　¼　teaspoon freshly ground black pepper
　1　teaspoon canola oil
　¾　cup finely chopped onion
　½　cup finely chopped carrot
　¼　cup finely chopped celery
　3　garlic cloves, minced
　4　cups fat-free, less-sodium chicken broth
　1　cup 2% reduced-fat milk
　¼　teaspoon kosher salt
　　Dash of freshly ground black pepper

CROQUETTES:
　2　cups finely chopped leftover cooked turkey (light and dark meat)
1¾　cups panko breadcrumbs, divided
　2　tablespoons 2% reduced-fat milk
1½　teaspoons chopped fresh sage
　½　teaspoon salt
　　Dash of freshly ground black pepper
　1　large egg, lightly beaten
　1　egg white
2½　tablespoons canola oil, divided
　　Sage leaves (optional)

1. Preheat oven to 400°.

2. To prepare soup, cut squash in half lengthwise. Discard seeds and membrane. Place squash, cut sides up, on a foil-lined baking sheet. Drizzle with honey; sprinkle with ¼ teaspoon salt and ¼ teaspoon pepper. Bake at 400° for 1 hour or until tender; cool. Scoop out squash with a spoon; discard skin.

3. Heat 1 teaspoon oil in a saucepan over medium-high heat. Add onion, carrot, celery, and garlic; sauté 10 minutes or until tender. Remove ¾ cup vegetables;

set aside. Add broth to pan; cook over medium heat 12 minutes. Stir in squash. Reduce heat; simmer 15 minutes. Place soup in food processor; process until smooth. Add 1 cup milk, ¼ teaspoon salt, and dash of pepper; set aside.

4. To prepare croquettes, combine reserved vegetables, turkey, ¼ cup breadcrumbs, and next 6 ingredients. Cover and refrigerate 30 minutes or until firm. Shape into 12 (1-inch-thick) patties; press 1½ cups breadcrumbs onto patties.

5. Heat 3¾ teaspoons oil in a nonstick skillet over medium heat. Add 6 patties to pan; cook 3 minutes on each side or until golden brown. Remove croquettes from pan; keep warm. Repeat procedure with remaining oil and patties.

6. Reheat soup over medium heat. Divide among 4 bowls; top with croquettes. Garnish with sage leaves, if desired. Yield: 4 servings (serving size: about 1½ cups soup and 3 croquettes).

CALORIES 602 (28% from fat); FAT 18g (sat 3.5g, mono 8.6g, poly 4.6g); PROTEIN 33g; CARB 77g; FIBER 11g; CHOL 100mg; IRON 4.5mg; SODIUM 1,375mg; CALC 282mg

Post-Turkey Day Posole

This Mexican stew is traditionally topped with shredded cabbage, sliced radishes, cilantro, and lime wedges.

—Greg Higgins
Higgins Restaurant, Portland, Oregon

    1 tablespoon olive oil
    1 canned chipotle chile in adobo
      sauce
    ¾ cup finely chopped onion
    ¾ cup finely chopped celery
    ¾ cup finely chopped carrot
    2 tablespoons minced fresh garlic
    2 teaspoons chili powder
    2 cups shredded leftover cooked
      turkey (light and dark meat)
    3 cups fat-free, less-sodium chicken
      broth
    ½ cup tomato purée
    ½ teaspoon salt
    ¼ teaspoon freshly ground black
      pepper
    1 (15.5-ounce) can white hominy,
      drained

1. Heat oil in a large heavy saucepan over medium-high heat. Finely chop chile. Add chile and next 5 ingredients, and sauté 5 minutes or until tender. Add remaining ingredients, and bring to a simmer.

2. Cover and cook 45 minutes or until slightly thick, stirring occasionally. Yield: 4 servings (serving size: 1¼ cups).

CALORIES 286 (29% from fat); FAT 9g (sat 1.8g, mono 4.2g, poly 1.9g); PROTEIN 22g; CARB 29g; FIBER 5.5g; CHOL 41mg; IRON 2.5mg; SODIUM 1,121mg; CALC 66mg

Warm Turkey and Spinach Salad with Crispy Pancetta and Cranberry Vinaigrette

You can substitute bacon for the pancetta.

—Jan Birnbaum
Catahoula Restaurant, Calistoga, California

SALAD:

    2 small poblano peppers
    4 cups chopped leftover cooked
      turkey (light and dark meat)
    6 cups prewashed spinach
    2 cups torn Boston lettuce

VINAIGRETTE:

    2 ounces pancetta
    ½ cup minced shallots
    1 garlic clove, minced
    ½ cup whole-berry cranberry sauce
      or leftover cranberry relish
    2 tablespoons Champagne vinegar
    2 tablespoons olive oil
    ½ teaspoon salt
    ¼ teaspoon black pepper

1. To prepare salad, preheat broiler. Cut peppers in half lengthwise; discard seeds and membranes. Place pepper halves, skin sides up, on a foil-lined baking sheet; flatten with hand. Broil 15 minutes or until blackened. Place in a zip-top plastic bag; seal. Let stand 5 minutes. Peel and chop peppers.

2. Combine peppers, turkey, spinach, and lettuce in a large bowl.

3. To prepare vinaigrette, cook pancetta in a skillet over medium-high heat until crisp. Remove pancetta from pan; chop and set aside. Reserve 1 tablespoon drippings in pan. Add shallots and garlic to pan, and sauté 1 minute or until tender. Stir in cranberry sauce, vinegar, olive oil, salt, and pepper. Cook over medium-low heat 2 minutes or until warm. Pour warm vinaigrette over salad; toss. Top with pancetta. Serve immediately. Yield: 5 servings (serving size: about 2 cups).

CALORIES 349 (46% from fat); FAT 17g (sat 4.9g, mono 8.7g, poly 2.7g); PROTEIN 29g; CARB 15g; FIBER 1.7g; CHOL 75mg; IRON 2.6mg; SODIUM 433mg; CALC 70mg

Turkey Pot-au-Feu

Pot-au-feu is a simple French dish of meat and vegetables simmered together.

—Johnathan Sundstrom
Earth and Ocean Restaurant,
Seattle, Washington

    1 tablespoon olive oil, divided
    1 cup quartered mushrooms
    ½ cup chopped carrot
    ½ cup chopped leek
    ½ cup chopped peeled rutabaga
    ½ cup chopped peeled turnips
    1 garlic clove, thinly sliced
    ½ cup dry white wine
    4 cups fat-free, less-sodium chicken
      broth
    2 cups chopped leftover cooked
      turkey (light and dark meat)
    1 teaspoon chopped fresh thyme
    ½ teaspoon salt
    Dash of black pepper
    Thyme sprigs (optional)

1. Heat 1½ teaspoons oil in a large saucepan over medium-high heat. Add mushrooms; sauté 5 minutes or until golden. Remove mushrooms from pan.

2. Heat 1½ teaspoons oil in pan over medium-high heat. Add carrot and next 4 ingredients; sauté 5 minutes. Add wine, and cook until reduced to ¼ cup (about 1 minute). Add mushrooms, broth, turkey, chopped thyme, salt, and pepper. Bring to a boil, reduce heat, and simmer 15 minutes or until vegetables are tender. Garnish with thyme sprigs, if desired. Yield: 6 servings (serving size: 1 cup).

CALORIES 139 (33% from fat); FAT 5.1g (sat 1g, mono 2.5g, poly 0.9g); PROTEIN 13g; CARB 5g; FIBER 1g; CHOL 27mg; IRON 1mg; SODIUM 534mg; CALC 28mg

Warm Gingerbread with Lemon Glaze

When the cool temperatures and early evenings of late fall draw us indoors, the lure of a warm kitchen is simply irresistible.

MAKE AHEAD • FREEZABLE
Warm Gingerbread with Lemon Glaze

⅓ cup butter, cut into small pieces
⅔ cup hot water
1 cup light or dark molasses
1 large egg
2¾ cups all-purpose flour
1½ teaspoons baking soda
1½ teaspoons ground ginger
1 teaspoon ground cinnamon
½ teaspoon salt
¼ teaspoon ground cloves
Cooking spray
1½ cups powdered sugar
6 tablespoons fresh lemon
   juice
1 cup frozen reduced-fat whipped
   topping, thawed
Ground cinnamon (optional)
Lemon slices (optional)

1. Preheat oven to 350°.
2. Combine butter and hot water in a large bowl, stirring with a whisk until butter melts. Add molasses and egg, and stir with a whisk until blended. Lightly spoon flour into dry measuring cups, and level with a knife. Combine flour, baking soda, ginger, cinnamon, salt, and cloves. Add flour mixture to molasses mixture, stirring just until moist.
3. Spoon batter into a 9-inch cake pan coated with cooking spray. Bake at 350° for 30 minutes or until a wooden pick inserted in center comes out clean.
4. Combine sugar and lemon juice, stirring until well blended. Pierce top of gingerbread liberally with a wooden skewer. Pour glaze over gingerbread.
5. Top each serving with whipped topping. Sprinkle gingerbread with cinnamon and garnish with lemon slices, if desired. Yield: 12 servings (serving size: 1 gingerbread slice and about 1½ tablespoons whipped topping).

CALORIES 296 (20% from fat); FAT 6.5g (sat 3.7g, mono 1.7g, poly 0.4g); PROTEIN 3.6g; CARB 57.3g; FIBER 1g; CHOL 35mg; IRON 2.8mg; SODIUM 322mg; CALC 68mg

Cake with Character

Donna Garvin, of Waltham, Massachusetts, turned to us for a remake of one of her favorite cakes.

Here's a healthier version of Orange Marmalade Layer Cake.

MAKE AHEAD
Orange Marmalade Layer Cake

After the cake layers are drenched with fresh orange syrup, they become moist and delicate.

Cooking spray
3 cups sifted cake flour
1½ teaspoons baking soda
¾ teaspoon salt
9 tablespoons butter,
   softened
2 cups sugar, divided
1 tablespoon grated orange rind
1 tablespoon vanilla extract
4 large egg whites
1¼ cups low-fat buttermilk
1 cup fat-free milk
½ cup fresh orange
   juice
1 (12-ounce) jar orange marmalade,
   melted and cooled
¼ cup low-fat sour cream
1½ cups frozen reduced-calorie
   whipped topping, thawed

1. Preheat oven to 350°.
2. Coat 2 (9-inch) round cake pans with cooking spray, and line bottoms of pans with wax paper.
3. Combine sifted flour, baking soda, and salt, stirring with a whisk. Place butter in a large bowl, and beat with a mixer at medium speed until light and fluffy (about 2 minutes). Gradually add 1¾ cups sugar, 1 tablespoon at a time, beating until well blended. Beat in orange rind and vanilla. Add egg whites, 1 at a time, beating well after each addition.
4. Combine buttermilk and milk. Add flour mixture and buttermilk mixture alternately to butter mixture, beginning and ending with flour mixture. Pour batter into prepared pans; sharply tap pans once on counter to remove air bubbles. Bake at 350° for 25 minutes or until a wooden pick inserted in center comes out clean. Cool in pans 20 minutes on a wire rack; remove from pans. Cool completely on wire rack.
5. Combine juice and ¼ cup sugar; stir until sugar dissolves. Pierce cake layers liberally with a wooden pick. Slowly drizzle juice mixture over cake layers.
6. Carefully place 1 layer on a plate; spread with ⅓ cup marmalade. Top with remaining layer; spread remaining marmalade on top of cake. Fold sour cream into whipped topping; spread over sides of cake. Cover and chill at least 2 hours. Yield: 16 servings (serving size: 1 slice).

CALORIES 309 (23% from fat); FAT 7.8g (sat 4.7g, mono 1.9g, poly 0.3g); PROTEIN 3.9g; CARB 57.7g; FIBER 0.4g; CHOL 23mg; IRON 1.5mg; SODIUM 350mg; CALC 61mg

	BEFORE	AFTER
SERVING SIZE		
	1 slice	
CALORIES PER SERVING		
	439	309
FAT		
	17g	7.8g
PERCENT OF TOTAL CALORIES		
	35%	23%

Garlic and Rosemary Cloverleaf Rolls, page 343 and Bay-Scented Lentil Salad with Pancetta, page 343

Farmhouse Roast Turkey with Rosemary Gravy, page 375,
Sausage and Mushroom Stuffing, page 376,
Mashed Honey-Roasted Sweet Potatoes, page 376,
Broccoli and Carrots with Toasted Almonds, page 376,
Gingered Cranberry Sauce, page 376

Red Chile Potatoes, page 389

Sparkling White-Sangría Salad, page 375

Chocolate-Walnut Meringue Pie, page 392

All About Pork

From pork chops to prosciutto, savor the versatility and flavor of pork.

Pork Saltimbocca with Polenta

Traditional *saltimbocca* is made with thin slices of pounded veal, but lean pork chops update the recipe and provide more flavor. The butternut overtones of fontina cheese are also a pleasant addition. Top with a whole sage leaf for a handsome presentation.

PORK:

- 6 (4-ounce) boneless center-cut loin pork chops, trimmed
- 6 very thin slices prosciutto (about 2 ounces)
- 6 large sage leaves
- ⅓ cup (about 1½ ounces) shredded fontina cheese
- ¼ teaspoon freshly ground black pepper
- ⅛ teaspoon salt
- 2 tablespoons all-purpose flour
- 1 tablespoon olive oil
- ½ cup dry white wine
- 1 cup fat-free, less-sodium chicken broth
- 1 tablespoon thinly sliced fresh sage

POLENTA:

- 2 cups 2% reduced-fat milk
- 1 (14-ounce) can fat-free, less-sodium chicken broth
- 1 cup instant polenta
- ½ teaspoon salt

1. To prepare pork, place each chop between 2 sheets of heavy-duty plastic wrap; pound to ¼-inch thickness using a meat mallet or rolling pin. Arrange 1 prosciutto slice over each chop; top with 1 sage leaf and about 1 tablespoon cheese. Fold chops in half to sandwich filling, and secure with wooden picks. Sprinkle both sides of chops with pepper and ⅛ teaspoon salt. Place flour in a shallow dish; dredge stuffed chops in flour.

2. Heat oil in a large nonstick skillet over medium-high heat. Add chops, and cook 3 minutes on each side or until done. Remove chops from pan; cover and keep warm.

3. Add wine to pan, scraping pan to loosen browned bits; cook until reduced to ¼ cup (about 2 minutes). Add 1 cup broth; bring to a boil. Cook until reduced to ½ cup (about 5 minutes). Stir in 1 tablespoon sage. Reduce heat to medium. Return chops to pan; cook 2 minutes or until thoroughly heated, turning once.

4. To prepare polenta, bring milk and 1 can broth to a boil. Gradually stir in polenta and ½ teaspoon salt. Cover, reduce heat to medium-low, and cook 2 minutes. Serve polenta immediately with pork chops and sauce. Yield: 6 servings (serving size: 1 stuffed chop, about 4 teaspoons sauce, and ½ cup polenta).

CALORIES 404 (30% from fat); FAT 13.3g (sat 5.3g, mono 6g, poly 1g); PROTEIN 34.9g; CARB 30.8g; FIBER 2.8g; CHOL 85mg; IRON 1.6mg; SODIUM 733mg; CALC 172mg

MAKE AHEAD

Prosciutto-Wrapped Shrimp on Artichoke, Fennel, and Tomato Salad

Suitable for a dinner party, most of this recipe can be made ahead and finished quickly by cooking the shrimp at the last minute. Paper-thin prosciutto wraps easily around the shrimp.

DRESSING:

- 1 teaspoon grated lemon rind
- 1 tablespoon fresh lemon juice
- 1 tablespoon fresh lime juice
- 1 tablespoon extravirgin olive oil
- 1 teaspoon paprika
- ¼ teaspoon sugar
- ⅛ teaspoon freshly ground black pepper
- 1 garlic clove, minced

SALAD:

- 4 cups water
- ⅓ cup fresh lemon juice
- 8 medium artichokes (about 8 ounces each)
- 1 cup thinly sliced fennel bulb
- 1 cup grape or cherry tomatoes, halved
- ½ cup thinly sliced bottled roasted red bell peppers
- 2 tablespoons thinly sliced fresh basil
- 1 tablespoon large capers

SHRIMP:

- 1½ tablespoons butter
- 2 garlic cloves, minced
- 1 teaspoon grated lemon rind
- 1 tablespoon fresh lemon juice
- 1½ teaspoons Dijon mustard
- 1 teaspoon Worcestershire sauce
- ½ teaspoon hot sauce (such as Tabasco)
- 3 ounces very thin slices prosciutto
- 1 pound jumbo shrimp, peeled and deveined
- Cooking spray

1. To prepare dressing, combine first 8 ingredients, stirring with a whisk; set aside.

2. To prepare salad, combine water and ⅓ cup lemon juice in a Dutch oven. Cut off stem of each artichoke to within ½ inch of base; peel stem. Cut 1 inch off tops of artichokes. Remove bottom leaves and tough outer leaves, leaving tender heart and bottom. Cut artichokes lengthwise into quarters; place in lemon water. Bring to a boil; reduce heat, and simmer 20 minutes or until tender. Drain and plunge into cold water. Drain well. Remove fuzzy thistles from bottoms with a spoon.

3. Combine artichokes, fennel, and next 4 ingredients in a large bowl. Drizzle dressing over salad; toss gently to coat. Set aside.

Continued

4. To prepare shrimp, melt butter in a small saucepan over low heat. Add 2 minced garlic cloves; cook 1 minute, stirring frequently. Add rind and next 4 ingredients, stirring with a whisk.

5. Preheat broiler.

6. Cut prosciutto slices lengthwise into ½-inch strips. Wrap prosciutto strips around shrimp. Arrange shrimp on a broiler pan coated with cooking spray. Brush shrimp with half of butter mixture; broil 3 minutes. Remove pan from oven. Turn shrimp; brush with remaining butter mixture. Broil an additional 3 minutes or until shrimp are done.

7. Arrange 1½ cups salad on each of 4 plates. Top each serving with about 4 ounces prosciutto-wrapped shrimp. Yield: 4 servings.

CALORIES 384 (29% from fat); FAT 12.5g (sat 4.3g, mono 5.1g, poly 1.9g); PROTEIN 37.7g; CARB 36.1g; FIBER 6.5g; CHOL 196mg; IRON 7.2mg; SODIUM 975mg; CALC 207mg

Pork Tenderloin on a Bed of Spinach, Piquillo Peppers, and Prosciutto

Look for jarred or canned *piquillo* peppers in specialty stores or upscale groceries. They add bittersweet notes deeper than those of roasted red bell peppers or pimientos, although either makes a fine substitute. Similarly, using smoked paprika in the rub adds depth to an already great main dish.

    2 teaspoons paprika
    2 teaspoons finely chopped fresh
       rosemary
    1 teaspoon salt
    1 teaspoon black pepper
 1½ pounds pork tenderloin, trimmed
    Cooking spray
    2 teaspoons olive oil
  ½ cup finely chopped red onion
    2 ounces very thin slices prosciutto,
       cut into thin strips
    1 garlic clove, minced
    1 (10-ounce) package fresh spinach
    2 tablespoons water
    1 tablespoon sherry vinegar
    1 tablespoon honey
  ½ cup bottled piquillo peppers, cut
       into ¼-inch strips

1. Preheat oven to 450°.

2. Combine first 4 ingredients; rub over pork. Heat a large nonstick skillet coated with cooking spray over medium-high heat. Add pork; cook 5 minutes, browning on all sides. Wrap handle of skillet with foil; place pan in oven. Bake at 450° for 20 minutes or until a thermometer registers 155° (slightly pink). Remove pork from pan, and let stand 10 minutes. Cut pork tenderloin crosswise into ½-inch-thick slices.

3. Heat oil in a Dutch oven over medium heat. Add onion; cook 5 minutes, stirring frequently. Add prosciutto and garlic; sauté 1 minute. Add spinach, tossing to combine. Add water, vinegar, and honey; cook 2 minutes or until spinach wilts, tossing frequently. Stir in piquillo peppers. Arrange about ⅓ cup spinach mixture on each of 6 plates; top each serving with 3 ounces pork. Yield: 6 servings.

CALORIES 202 (29% from fat); FAT 6.6g (sat 1.9g, mono 3.3g, poly 0.8g); PROTEIN 27.8g; CARB 7.6g; FIBER 0.9g; CHOL 79mg; IRON 3.1mg; SODIUM 697mg; CALC 64mg

STAFF FAVORITE • MAKE AHEAD
Ham Hocks and White Beans

This dish may take a couple of days to make, but it's worth the time and effort. Chilling the stock overnight allows you to skim off the fat. Similarly, refrigerating the ham hocks makes separating the meat from the fat easier. Soak the beans overnight while the stock and hocks chill. Serve with rice for an authentic Louisiana-style meal. Note that the beans should be moist, but not soupy.

HAM HOCKS:

    1 medium onion
    3 whole cloves
  10 cups water
    1 teaspoon black peppercorns
    6 smoked ham hocks (about 3 pounds)
    4 bay leaves
    3 cups coarsely chopped leek greens
    3 garlic cloves
    2 celery stalks, coarsely chopped
    1 carrot, coarsely chopped
    1 thyme sprig

BEANS:

 1½ cups dried Great Northern or
       other small white beans
    2 teaspoons chopped fresh thyme
    1 teaspoon fennel seeds, crushed
  ½ teaspoon dried marjoram
    6 sun-dried tomato halves, chopped
    1 tablespoon olive oil
    2 cups chopped leek bottoms
 1½ cups chopped onion
    1 cup chopped carrot
  ½ cup chopped celery
    2 garlic cloves, minced
  ½ teaspoon freshly ground black
       pepper
  ¼ teaspoon salt

GARNISH:

    2 tablespoons chopped fresh parsley
    2 tablespoons chopped fresh basil
    2 tablespoons finely chopped green
       onions

1. To prepare ham hocks, stud onion with cloves. Place onion, water, and next 8 ingredients in a stockpot; bring to a boil. Reduce heat; simmer 3 hours. Remove hocks from stock. Strain stock through a sieve into a large bowl; discard solids. Cool stock to room temperature. Cover and chill hocks and stock separately 8 hours or overnight. Remove meat from bones; finely chop. Discard bones, skin, and fat. Skim solidified fat from surface of stock; discard fat. Reserve 4 cups stock.

2. To prepare beans, sort and wash beans; place in a large Dutch oven. Cover with water to 2 inches above beans. Cover and let stand 8 hours or overnight. Drain.

3. Combine beans and reserved stock in a Dutch oven. Add chopped thyme, fennel seeds, marjoram, and tomato; bring to a boil. Reduce heat; simmer 1 hour and 15 minutes or until beans are tender.

4. While beans simmer, heat oil in a nonstick skillet over medium heat. Add leek bottoms, chopped onion, 1 cup carrot, ½ cup celery, and 2 garlic cloves; cover. Cook 10 minutes; stir occasionally. Add vegetable mixture, ham, ground pepper, and salt to bean mixture.

5. To prepare garnish, combine parsley, basil, and green onions; sprinkle over bean mixture. Yield: 6 servings (serving size: about 1 cup bean mixture and 1 tablespoon garnish).

CALORIES 366 (28% from fat); FAT 11.5g (sat 3.6g, mono 5.5g, poly 1.3g); PROTEIN 23.5g; CARB 40.1g; FIBER 11.7g; CHOL 46mg; IRON 4.5mg; SODIUM 402mg; CALC 137mg

Apple and Corn Bread-Stuffed Pork Loin

The double-butterfly method used to flatten the pork for stuffing creates an attractive pinwheel pattern.

  Cooking spray
  ½ cup finely chopped onion
  ¼ cup finely chopped celery
  1¼ teaspoons freshly ground black
       pepper, divided
  ½ cup diced peeled Granny Smith
       apple
  1½ cups corn bread stuffing mix
       (such as Pepperidge Farm)
  1⅓ cups apple juice or cider, divided
  1½ teaspoons dried rubbed sage,
       divided
  1 large egg, lightly beaten
  1 (4-pound) boneless center-cut
       pork loin roast, trimmed
  1½ teaspoons salt, divided
  3 Granny Smith apples, peeled,
       cored, and cut into 1-inch wedges
  2 teaspoons cornstarch
  1 (14-ounce) can fat-free,
       less-sodium chicken broth

1. Preheat oven to 450°.
2. Heat a nonstick skillet coated with cooking spray over medium heat. Add onion, celery, and ⅛ teaspoon pepper; cover and cook 10 minutes or until tender, stirring occasionally. Add diced apple; cook 1 minute, stirring constantly. Place apple mixture in a large bowl, and cool slightly. Stir in stuffing mix, ⅓ cup juice, ½ teaspoon sage, and egg; set aside.
3. Starting off-center, slice pork lengthwise, cutting to, but not through, other side. Open butterflied portions, laying pork flat. Turning knife blade parallel to surface of cutting board, slice larger portion of pork in half horizontally, cutting to, but not through, other side; open flat.

Place plastic wrap over pork; pound to 1-inch thickness using a meat mallet or rolling pin. Sprinkle with ½ teaspoon salt.
4. Spread stuffing over pork, leaving a ½-inch margin around outside edges. Roll up pork, jelly roll fashion, starting with a long side. Secure at 2-inch intervals with twine. Combine 1 teaspoon pepper, 1 teaspoon sage, and 1 teaspoon salt; rub over pork.
5. Arrange apple wedges in a single layer in bottom of a broiler pan coated with cooking spray; place pork on apples. Bake at 450° for 20 minutes. Reduce oven temperature to 325° (do not remove pork from oven). Bake an additional 1 hour and 15 minutes or until a thermometer registers 155°. Remove pork from pan; cover and let stand 10 minutes. Discard apple wedges.
6. Combine 1 cup juice, cornstarch, and broth in a small saucepan; stir with a whisk. Bring broth mixture to a boil. Reduce heat, and simmer 5 minutes. Stir in ⅛ teaspoon black pepper. Cut pork into ½-inch-thick slices, and serve with sauce. Yield: 12 servings (serving size: about 5 ounces stuffed pork and about 2½ tablespoons sauce).

CALORIES 249 (30% from fat); FAT 8.3g (sat 2.9g, mono 3.6g, poly 0.8g); PROTEIN 24.3g; CARB 18.2g; FIBER 2.6g; CHOL 81mg; IRON 1.5mg; SODIUM 567mg; CALC 40mg

---

Bountiful Autumn Menu
serves 4

You'll need to start a day ahead if you let the pork chops brine overnight.

Molasses-Brined Pork Chops

Roasted butternut squash and onion wedges*

Toasted almond rice pilaf (such as Near East)

Pumpernickel bread

*Peel and cube 1 (2-pound) butternut squash. Cut 1 medium red onion into 8 wedges. Place squash and onion in a 13 x 9-inch baking dish coated with cooking spray. Drizzle with 1 tablespoon olive oil; sprinkle with ½ teaspoon sugar, ½ teaspoon salt, and ¼ teaspoon ground red pepper. Toss to coat. Bake at 425° for 20 minutes or until tender, stirring occasionally.

Molasses-Brined Pork Chops

Pork chops that are even the slightest bit overdone can be dry and tough. Two tricks will help to prevent this from happening: First, choose thick chops; there's less risk of overcooking. Second, brine the pork chops before cooking, which makes them tender and juicy, even if you inadvertently overcook them.

BRINE:
  3½ cups water
  ¼ cup kosher salt
  3 tablespoons dark brown sugar
  2 tablespoons molasses
  ½ teaspoon vanilla extract
  1 cup ice cubes
  4 (6-ounce) bone-in center-cut pork
       chops (about 1-inch thick)

RUB:
  1 tablespoon finely chopped fresh
       or 1 teaspoon dried rubbed sage
  2 teaspoons freshly ground black
       pepper
  ½ teaspoon ground cloves
  ½ teaspoon ground nutmeg
  ¼ teaspoon ground cardamom
  ¼ teaspoon ground cinnamon
  3 garlic cloves, minced

REMAINING INGREDIENTS:
  2 tablespoons all-purpose flour
  2 teaspoons olive oil

1. To prepare brine, combine water and salt in a large bowl, stirring until salt dissolves. Add sugar, molasses, and vanilla; stir until sugar dissolves. Stir in ice. Add chops; cover and refrigerate 8 hours or overnight. Remove chops from brine; pat dry. Discard brine.
2. To prepare rub, combine sage and next 6 ingredients; rub over both sides of chops. Refrigerate 30 minutes.
3. Place flour in a shallow dish; dredge chops in flour. Heat oil in a large nonstick skillet over medium-high heat. Add chops; cook 5 minutes on each side or until done. Yield: 4 servings (serving size: 1 chop).

CALORIES 218 (38% from fat); FAT 9.3g (sat 2.9g, mono 4.8g, poly 0.7g); PROTEIN 26.1g; CARB 6.2g; FIBER 0.7g; CHOL 69mg; IRON 1.4mg; SODIUM 617mg; CALC 43mg

Cooking Lean Pork

Of all today's red meats, pork has experienced the most significant fat reduction. In just 20 years, growers have reduced the amount of intramuscular fat by more than 50 percent. No longer are 300-pound-plus hogs sent to market. Today's pig weighs in at a svelte 240 pounds, on average. He's not just lighter, but because of selective breeding, he's more muscular, with considerably less back and belly fat.

Two important reasons explain this drastic change. Shortening and cooking oils replaced lard as the primary cooking fat, so farmers no longer raised their pigs to have thick layers of back fat.

Nutritional concerns have had an even more pronounced effect. Pork growers have responded to recommendations that people should eat less animal fat; today's pork has a fat content so low that it favorably compares to chicken. The leanest cuts, such as loin chops, loin roasts, and tenderloins, have less overall fat, saturated fat, and cholesterol than equal amounts of skinless chicken thighs.

Except for fattier cuts like the Boston butt, spare ribs, and blade shoulder chops, pork has little or no marbling; it must be cooked carefully so it won't dry out. In Grandma's day, pork was cooked beyond well done to temperatures of 170° to 180°. Cooking today's lean cuts to these temperatures will yield dry, hard results. Instead, cook to 150° to 155°. Perfect pork will have a faint pink blush. Let it stand for 10 to 15 minutes after cooking to reabsorb juices and to allow the meat to finish cooking (raising the internal temperature by 5° to 10°; the USDA recommends cooking pork to 160°).

Another good way to improve flavor and juiciness is to brine pork overnight in a solution of water, salt, sugar, and other flavors. The brined meat will remain juicy even if slightly overcooked.

Pork Shoulder Braised in Milk

Caramel and lemon flavors combine in this traditional Bolognese recipe. Although the sauce will look curdled, the dish tastes delicious. Cover and keep the pork warm while reducing the milk mixture. Add any juices the pork releases as it stands to the milk mixture before serving. To get a long strip of lemon rind, use a vegetable peeler; aside from making the job easier, it will ensure that you don't dig into the bitter white pith.

　1　(3-pound) boneless pork shoulder
　　　roast (Boston butt)
　1　teaspoon salt
　½　teaspoon dried rubbed sage
　½　teaspoon dried thyme
　½　teaspoon freshly ground black
　　　pepper
　　　Cooking spray
　1　tablespoon minced fresh garlic
　4　cups whole milk
　2　tablespoons fresh lemon juice
　4　sage leaves
　2　bay leaves
　1　thyme sprig
　1　(10 x ¾-inch) strip lemon rind
　8　cups hot cooked brown rice

1. Preheat oven to 325°.
2. Unroll pork; trim and discard fat. Reroll pork; secure at 2-inch intervals with twine. Combine salt, dried sage, dried thyme, and pepper; rub salt mixture over pork.
3. Heat a Dutch oven coated with cooking spray over medium-high heat. Add pork, and cook 7 minutes, browning on all sides. Remove pork from pan. Add garlic to pan, and sauté 30 seconds. Add milk and next 5 ingredients; bring to a boil, stirring frequently. Return pork to pan. Cover and bake at 325° for 45 minutes. Uncover. Turn pork; bake, uncovered, at 325° for 45 minutes. Turn pork; bake an additional 30 minutes or until pork is fork-tender. Remove from pan; cover and keep warm.
4. Place pan on stovetop over medium-high heat, and bring milk mixture to a boil. Cook until mixture is reduced to 2 cups (about 20 minutes), stirring frequently. Discard lemon rind, sage leaves, bay leaves, thyme sprig, and twine. Cut pork into ½-inch slices; serve with sauce and rice. Yield: 10 servings (serving size: 3 ounces pork, about 3 tablespoons sauce, and about ¾ cup rice).

CALORIES 404 (29% from fat); FAT 12.8g (sat 5.1g, mono 5.3g, poly 1.5g); PROTEIN 29.5g; CARB 41g; FIBER 3g; CHOL 89mg; IRON 2.2mg; SODIUM 377mg; CALC 152mg

Gingersnap-Crusted Ham with Apricot-Mustard Sauce

Whole hams usually weigh at least 15 pounds; ham halves, which are labeled either "shank" or "butt end," are more manageable. A bone-in shank is easier to carve than the butt end, which contains part of the hipbone.

HAM:

　1　(8-pound) 33%-less-sodium
　　　smoked, fully cooked ham
　　　half
　2　tablespoons apricot preserves
　2　tablespoons Dijon mustard
　½　cup brown sugar
　½　cup gingersnap crumbs (about
　　　9 cookies, finely crushed)

SAUCE:

　1½　cups apricot preserves
　½　cup dry Marsala wine
　3　tablespoons Dijon mustard
　½　teaspoon ground allspice

1. Preheat oven to 325°.
2. To prepare ham, line a broiler pan with foil. Trim fat and rind from ham. Score outside of ham in a diamond pattern. Place ham on prepared pan. Bake at 325° for 1 hour. Remove ham from oven, and cool slightly. Increase oven temperature to 375°.
3. Combine 2 tablespoons preserves and 2 tablespoons mustard, stirring with a whisk. Combine sugar and crumbs. Brush preserves mixture over ham. Carefully press crumb mixture onto preserves mixture (some crumb mixture will fall onto pan). Bake at 375° for 45 minutes or until a thermometer registers 145°. Place ham on a platter; let stand 15 minutes before slicing.

4. To prepare sauce, combine 1½ cups preserves and remaining ingredients in a small saucepan. Bring to a boil; cook 5 minutes. Serve sauce with ham. Yield: 24 servings (serving size: about 3½ ounces ham and 2 teaspoons sauce).

CALORIES 233 (24% from fat); FAT 6.3g (sat 1.9g, mono 2.9g, poly 0.7g); PROTEIN 21.2g; CARB 22.4g; FIBER 0.4g; CHOL 53mg; IRON 1.9mg; SODIUM 1,076mg; CALC 23mg

Bacon, Ham, and Lentil Soup

Most legume soups benefit from being made a day ahead so their flavors meld. Substitute green split peas for the lentils, if you prefer; they take less time to cook, so monitor the soup accordingly.

    5 slices thick-sliced bacon, cut
       crosswise into ½-inch strips
 1½ cups (½-inch) cubed ham (about
       8 ounces)
    1 cup chopped onion
    1 cup chopped fennel bulb
    1 cup chopped celery
    ½ cup chopped leek
    ½ cup chopped carrot
    3 (14-ounce) cans fat-free,
       less-sodium chicken broth
    2 cups water
    1 teaspoon chopped fresh or
       ¼ teaspoon dried thyme
    ½ teaspoon freshly ground black
       pepper
    1 cup canned diced tomatoes with
       basil, garlic, and oregano
    1 pound dried lentils
    2 bay leaves
    ¼ cup chopped fresh chives

1. Cook bacon strips in a Dutch oven over medium heat until crisp. Remove from pan, reserving 2 tablespoons drippings in pan; set bacon aside. Add ham to drippings in pan; cook 2 minutes, stirring frequently. Add onion and next 4 ingredients; cover and cook 10 minutes, stirring occasionally. Add broth and next 6 ingredients. Bring to a boil; cover, reduce heat, and simmer 30 minutes or until lentils are tender. Discard bay leaves; sprinkle with bacon and chives

just before serving. Yield: 8 servings (serving size: 1¾ cups).

CALORIES 359 (28% from fat); FAT 11g (sat 4g, mono 4.8g, poly 1.4g); PROTEIN 25.2g; CARB 40.6g; FIBER 18.9g; CHOL 21mg; IRON 6.1mg; SODIUM 956mg; CALC 72mg

Linguine with Pancetta and Swiss Chard

Use any greens—turnip or collard greens, kale, or curly endive.

    1 pound Swiss chard
    3 ounces pancetta, diced
    ¼ cup finely chopped onion
    2 tablespoons minced fresh garlic
    ½ to 1 teaspoon crushed red pepper
    1 pound uncooked linguine
    ¾ cup (3 ounces) grated fresh
       Parmesan cheese, divided
    ¼ cup chopped fresh flat-leaf parsley
    ¼ teaspoon salt
    ¼ teaspoon freshly ground black
       pepper

1. Rinse and drain chard; pat dry with paper towels. Remove stems and center ribs from chard, and cut ribs and stems crosswise into ¼-inch slices. Cut chard leaves into 1-inch strips.
2. Heat a Dutch oven over medium heat. Add pancetta; cook 6 minutes or until browned. Add onion and garlic, and cook 10 minutes or until lightly browned, stirring frequently. Add chard ribs and stems, and cook 3 minutes, stirring frequently. Add chard leaves and red pepper; cook 5 minutes or until chard wilts, tossing frequently.
3. Cook pasta according to package directions, omitting salt and fat. Drain pasta in a colander over a bowl; reserve ¼ cup pasta water. Add reserved pasta water and pasta to chard mixture; cook over medium-high heat 1 minute, stirring frequently. Stir in ¼ cup cheese. Add parsley, salt, and black pepper; toss well to combine. Sprinkle with cheese. Yield: 6 servings (serving size: 1⅓ cups pasta mixture and 4 teaspoons cheese).

CALORIES 426 (28% from fat); FAT 13.1g (sat 5.7g, mono 4.8g, poly 1.1g); PROTEIN 17.7g; CARB 60.1g; FIBER 3.5g; CHOL 19mg; IRON 3.6mg; SODIUM 511mg; CALC 212mg

---

Pork Safety

There was a time when folks worried about nematodes in fresh pork, and therefore overcooked it to eliminate those fears. Trichinosis, the disease caused by the nematodes, has been all but eliminated from commercial pork. But even when an infestation is present, spores are killed when the meat reaches an internal temperature of 137°, well below the doneness recommended to produce juicy pork.

dinner tonight

Change of Pace

These menus offer a change of pace from typical autumn fare.

Menu 1
serves 4

Caribbean Pork and Plantain Hash (recipe on page 370)

Tomato and hearts of palm salad*

Mango slices drizzled with lime juice

*Cut each of 4 plum tomatoes lengthwise into 8 wedges; place in a medium bowl. Drain 1 (14-ounce) can hearts of palm; cut each heart of palm lengthwise into quarters. Cut each heart of palm quarter in half crosswise; add to tomato wedges. Add ½ cup thinly vertically sliced red onion, 1 tablespoon chopped cilantro, 1½ tablespoons fresh lime juice, 1 teaspoon olive oil, ¼ teaspoon salt, and ¼ teaspoon black pepper. Toss well.

Game Plan

1. While pork cooks:
   • Chop onion
   • Chop bell pepper and plantains for hash
2. While plantain mixture cooks:
   • Mince garlic
   • Prepare salad
   • Prepare mango

Continued

Caribbean Pork and Plantain Hash

Use semiripe plantains—not green or soft, ripe black ones. The plantains brown better if not stirred too much as they cook. Serve leftovers with poached eggs for breakfast.

TOTAL TIME: 35 MINUTES

 1 tablespoon low-sodium soy sauce
 ¾ teaspoon salt, divided
 ¾ teaspoon dried thyme
 ¼ teaspoon ground ginger
 ¼ teaspoon ground red pepper
 ⅛ teaspoon ground allspice
 1 pound pork tenderloin, trimmed and cut into ½-inch pieces
 1½ tablespoons vegetable oil, divided
 1 tablespoon butter
 1½ cups coarsely chopped onion
 1 cup chopped green bell pepper
 2 large yellow plantains, chopped (about 3 cups)
 ½ teaspoon black pepper
 4 garlic cloves, minced
 1 teaspoon habanero hot pepper sauce
 2 tablespoons chopped fresh cilantro

1. Combine soy sauce, ¼ teaspoon salt, thyme, and next 4 ingredients; toss well to coat. Heat 1½ teaspoons oil in a large nonstick skillet over medium-high heat. Add pork mixture; sauté 4 minutes or until done. Remove from pan; keep warm. Add remaining 1 tablespoon oil and butter to pan. Add onion, bell pepper, plantains, ½ teaspoon salt, and black pepper; cook 6 minutes, stirring occasionally. Stir in garlic; sauté 2 minutes or until plantains are tender. Return pork mixture to pan. Drizzle with hot sauce; stir well. Sprinkle with cilantro. Yield: 4 servings (serving size: about 1½ cups).

CALORIES 384 (29% from fat); FAT 12.5g (sat 4g, mono 3.8g, poly 3.7g); PROTEIN 26.8g; CARB 44.9g; FIBER 4.7g; CHOL 81mg; IRON 2.8mg; SODIUM 674mg; CALC 38mg

---

Menu 2

serves 4

Falafel-Stuffed Pitas

Grape and walnut salad*

Iced mint tea

*Combine ½ cup plain low-fat yogurt, 2 tablespoons brown sugar, and a dash of ground cinnamon in a bowl. Add 3 cups halved red seedless grapes and 3 tablespoons chopped walnuts; stir well to combine.

Game Plan

1. Prepare grape salad; cover and chill
2. While falafel patties cook:
 • Prepare sauce
 • Slice tomato
 • Wash lettuce
 • Prepare tea

Falafel-Stuffed Pitas

TOTAL TIME: 30 MINUTES

QUICK TIP: To prevent the falafel mixture from sticking to your hands, dip your hands in water before forming the patties.

FALAFEL:

 ¼ cup dry breadcrumbs
 ¼ cup chopped fresh cilantro
 1½ teaspoons ground cumin
 ½ teaspoon salt
 ¼ teaspoon ground red pepper
 2 garlic cloves, crushed
 1 large egg
 1 (15-ounce) can chickpeas (garbanzo beans), drained
 1 tablespoon olive oil

SAUCE:

 ½ cup plain low-fat yogurt
 2 tablespoons fresh lemon juice
 2 tablespoons tahini (sesame-seed paste)
 1 garlic clove, minced

REMAINING INGREDIENTS:

 4 (6-inch) whole wheat pitas, cut in half
 8 curly leaf lettuce leaves
 16 (¼-inch-thick) slices tomato

1. To prepare falafel, place first 8 ingredients in a food processor; process mixture until smooth. Divide mixture into 16 equal portions, and shape each portion into a ¼-inch-thick patty. Heat olive oil in a large nonstick skillet over medium-high heat. Add patties, and cook 5 minutes on each side or until patties are browned.

2. To prepare sauce, combine yogurt, lemon juice, tahini, and 1 garlic clove, stirring mixture with a whisk. Spread about 1½ tablespoons tahini sauce into each pita half. Fill each pita half with 1 lettuce leaf, 2 tomato slices, and 2 patties. Yield: 4 servings (serving size: 2 stuffed pita halves).

CALORIES 403 (28% from fat); FAT 12.6g (sat 1.9g, mono 5.6g, poly 3.9g); PROTEIN 15g; CARB 59g; FIBER 6.8g; CHOL 56mg; IRON 4.4mg; SODIUM 901mg; CALC 188mg

---

Menu 3

serves 4

Greek Salad with Shrimp

Oregano pita crisps*

Vanilla low-fat yogurt topped with honey and sliced almonds

*Preheat oven to 400°. Cut each of 2 (6-inch) pitas into 8 wedges; arrange pita wedges in a single layer on a baking sheet. Lightly coat pita wedges with cooking spray. Combine ½ teaspoon dried oregano, ⅛ teaspoon salt, ⅛ teaspoon garlic powder, and ⅛ teaspoon black pepper; sprinkle evenly over pita wedges. Lightly coat pita wedges again with cooking spray. Bake at 400° for 10 minutes or until golden.

Game Plan

1. While oven preheats for pita crisps and water for shrimp comes to a boil:
 • Peel and devein shrimp
 • Prepare lettuce
 • Prepare herb mixture for pita crisps
2. While pita crisps bake:
 • Cook shrimp
 • Prepare remaining salad ingredients

Greek Salad with Shrimp

Use shredded rotisserie chicken in place of the shrimp, if you'd prefer.

TOTAL TIME: 25 MINUTES

QUICK TIP: For quick suppers, keep a bag of cooked, peeled, and deveined shrimp in the freezer. Set the shrimp in a colander, and rinse with cool water to thaw quickly.

- 4 quarts water
- 1½ pounds large shrimp, peeled and deveined
- 6 cups torn romaine lettuce
- 1½ cups halved cherry tomatoes
- 1 cup (¼-inch-thick) slices red onion, separated into rings
- 1 cup cucumber, halved lengthwise and cut into ¼-inch slices
- 1 tablespoon chopped fresh flat-leaf parsley
- 3 tablespoons red wine vinegar
- 2 teaspoons Dijon mustard
- 1 teaspoon extravirgin olive oil
- ¾ teaspoon dried oregano
- ¼ teaspoon salt
- ¼ teaspoon black pepper
- 2 garlic cloves, minced
- ½ cup (2 ounces) crumbled feta cheese
- 8 kalamata olives, pitted and halved
- 4 pepperoncini peppers

1. Bring water to a boil in a large saucepan. Add shrimp; cook 2 minutes or until done. Drain and rinse with cold water. Place shrimp in a bowl; cover and chill.
2. Place lettuce, tomatoes, onion, and cucumber in a large bowl; toss gently to combine. Combine parsley and next 7 ingredients, stirring with a whisk. Spoon 1 tablespoon dressing over shrimp; toss to combine. Add shrimp mixture and remaining dressing to lettuce mixture; toss gently to coat. Spoon about 2¾ cups salad onto each of 4 plates. Top each serving with 2 tablespoons cheese, 4 olive halves, and 1 pepperoncini pepper. Yield: 4 servings.

CALORIES 296 (30% from fat); FAT 9.8g (sat 3.2g, mono 3.6g, poly 1.8g); PROTEIN 39.4g; CARB 12.1g; FIBER 3.2g; CHOL 271mg; IRON 6mg; SODIUM 849mg; CALC 219mg

---

Menu 4
serves 4

Herbed Chicken Parmesan
Roasted lemon-garlic broccoli*
Hot cooked orzo

*Preheat oven to 425°. Combine 6 cups broccoli florets, 1 teaspoon grated lemon rind, 2 teaspoons olive oil, ¼ teaspoon salt, ⅛ teaspoon black pepper, and 2 thinly sliced garlic cloves on a jelly roll pan coated with cooking spray. Bake at 425° for 15 minutes or until crisp-tender and lightly browned, stirring occasionally.

Game Plan

1. While oven preheats for broccoli and water for orzo comes to a boil:
- Prepare broccoli mixture
- Combine breadcrumb mixture
- Grate provolone cheese
2. While broccoli bakes:
- Cook chicken
- Cook orzo
- Heat pasta sauce

Herbed Chicken Parmesan

We recommend rice-shaped orzo pasta with this saucy entrée.

TOTAL TIME: 28 MINUTES

- ⅓ cup (1½ ounces) grated fresh Parmesan cheese, divided
- ¼ cup dry breadcrumbs
- 1 tablespoon minced fresh parsley
- ½ teaspoon dried basil
- ¼ teaspoon salt, divided
- 1 large egg white, lightly beaten
- 1 pound chicken breast tenders
- 1 tablespoon butter
- 1½ cups bottled fat-free tomato-basil pasta sauce (such as Muir Glen Organic)
- 2 teaspoons balsamic vinegar
- ¼ teaspoon black pepper
- ⅓ cup (1½ ounces) shredded provolone cheese

1. Preheat broiler.
2. Combine 2 tablespoons Parmesan, breadcrumbs, parsley, basil, and ⅛ teaspoon salt in a shallow dish. Place egg white in a shallow dish. Dip each chicken tender in egg white; dredge in breadcrumb mixture. Melt butter in a large nonstick skillet over medium-high heat. Add chicken; cook 3 minutes on each side or until done. Set aside.
3. Combine ⅛ teaspoon salt, pasta sauce, vinegar, and pepper in a microwave-safe bowl. Cover with plastic wrap; vent. Microwave mixture at HIGH 2 minutes or until thoroughly heated. Pour over chicken in pan. Sprinkle evenly with remaining Parmesan and provolone cheese. Wrap handle of pan with foil; broil 2 minutes or until cheese melts. Yield: 4 servings.

CALORIES 308 (30% from fat); FAT 10.4g (sat 5.7g, mono 3g, poly 0.6g); PROTEIN 35.9g; CARB 16.2g; FIBER 1.8g; CHOL 88mg; IRON 2.3mg; SODIUM 808mg; CALC 249mg

---

happy endings

Vanilla

Once reserved for royalty, vanilla adds extraordinary aroma and taste to any dish.

Some of the following desserts feature beans, others feature extract, and some use both, which provides layers of flavor.

MAKE AHEAD
Angel Food Cake with Fall Fruit Compote

We liked the fruit for the compote in bigger pieces, but you can chop it, if you'd like.

CAKE:
- 1 cup sifted cake flour
- 1½ cups sugar, divided
- 12 large egg whites
- 1 teaspoon cream of tartar
- ¼ teaspoon salt
- 1 tablespoon vanilla extract

Continued

COMPOTE:

3 cups water
¼ cup sugar
1 vanilla bean, split lengthwise
½ cup dried cranberries
8 dried figs, halved (about 4 ounces)
2 (7-ounce) packages dried mixed fruit

REMAINING INGREDIENT:

¾ cup crème fraîche

1. Preheat oven to 325°.
2. To prepare, combine cake flour and ¾ cup sugar. Beat egg whites with a mixer at high speed until foamy. Add cream of tartar and salt; beat until soft peaks form. Add ¾ cup sugar, 2 tablespoons at a time, beating until stiff peaks form. Fold in vanilla. Sift flour mixture over egg white mixture, 3 tablespoons at a time; fold in.
3. Spoon batter into an ungreased 10-inch tube pan, spreading evenly. Break air pockets by cutting through batter with a knife. Bake at 325° for 50 minutes or until cake springs back when lightly touched. Invert pan, and cool completely. Loosen cake from sides of pan using a narrow metal spatula. Invert cake onto plate. Cut cake into 12 slices.
4. To prepare compote, combine water, ¼ cup sugar, and vanilla bean in a medium saucepan. Bring to a boil over medium heat, stirring until sugar dissolves. Cover, reduce heat, and simmer 15 minutes. Add dried fruits; cover and simmer 25 minutes or until fruit is tender, stirring once. Remove from heat. Remove vanilla bean. Let bean stand 5 minutes. Scrape seeds from vanilla bean; stir seeds into fruit mixture. Discard bean. Cool to room temperature. Spoon compote over cake slices, and top with crème fraîche. Yield: 12 servings (serving size: 1 cake slice, ⅓ cup compote, and 1 tablespoon crème fraîche).

CALORIES 346 (15% from fat); FAT 5.9g (sat 3.5g, mono 1.7g, poly 0.3g); PROTEIN 5.9g; CARB 70g; FIBER 4.3g; CHOL 20mg; IRON 2mg; SODIUM 117mg; CALC 41mg

Hazelnut-Raisin Pound Cake

After soaking the raisins, about a tablespoon of Frangelico (hazelnut-flavored liqueur) will remain. Use it in the cake, adding it with the vanilla.

Cooking spray
⅓ cup dry breadcrumbs
½ cup raisins, finely chopped
½ cup Frangelico (hazelnut-flavored liqueur)
3 cups all-purpose flour
1 teaspoon baking powder
½ teaspoon salt
½ teaspoon ground mace
¾ cup butter, softened
2⅓ cups granulated sugar, divided
2 teaspoons vanilla extract
3 large eggs
1 cup fat-free milk
1 teaspoon grated lemon rind
¼ cup sifted powdered sugar

1. Coat a 12-cup Bundt pan with cooking spray, and dust with breadcrumbs. Tap out excess crumbs; set aside.
2. Place raisins in a bowl. Bring liqueur to a boil in a small saucepan over medium-high heat; pour over raisins. Cover and let stand 30 minutes.
3. Preheat oven to 350°.
4. Lightly spoon flour into dry measuring cups; level with a knife. Sift together flour, baking powder, salt, and mace.
5. Place butter in a large bowl; beat with a mixer at medium speed 1 minute or until smooth. Add ⅓ cup granulated sugar and vanilla; beat 1 minute. Add 2 cups granulated sugar, ⅓ cup at a time, beating well after each addition. Add eggs, 1 at a time, beating 1 minute after each addition. With mixer at low speed, add flour mixture and milk alternately to sugar mixture, beginning and ending with flour mixture. Beat just until smooth. Stir in raisin mixture and rind. Pour batter into prepared pan.
6. Bake at 350° for 55 minutes or until cake springs back when lightly touched in center. Cool in pan on a wire rack 20 minutes. Invert pan, remove cake, and cool completely on wire rack. Sprinkle with powdered sugar. Yield 18 servings (serving size: 1 slice).

CALORIES 316 (25% from fat); FAT 8.8g (sat 5.1g, mono 2.6g, poly 0.5g); PROTEIN 4.1g; CARB 52g; FIBER 0.9g; CHOL 56mg; IRON 1.4mg; SODIUM 126mg; CALC 46mg

Double-Chocolate Soufflé with Vanilla Custard Sauce

This soufflé doesn't rise over the edge of the dish, but it's rich and delicious.

SAUCE:

1¼ cups 1% low-fat milk
½ vanilla bean, split lengthwise
3 tablespoons sugar
2 large egg yolks
Dash of salt

SOUFFLÉ:

Cooking spray
¾ cup sugar, divided
1 cup 1% low-fat milk
½ vanilla bean, split lengthwise
½ cup Dutch process cocoa
1 tablespoon cornstarch
⅛ teaspoon salt
2 ounces bittersweet chocolate, finely chopped
2 large egg yolks
6 large egg whites
½ teaspoon cream of tartar

1. To prepare sauce, heat 1¼ cups milk and ½ vanilla bean in a small, heavy saucepan over medium heat to 180° or until tiny bubbles form around edge (do not boil), stirring frequently. Remove from heat; let stand 30 minutes. Scrape seeds from vanilla bean, and add seeds to milk. Discard bean.
2. Combine 3 tablespoons sugar, 2 egg yolks, and dash of salt in a medium bowl, stirring with a whisk. Gradually add milk mixture to egg mixture, stirring constantly with a whisk. Return milk mixture to pan. Heat milk mixture over medium heat to 180° or until tiny bubbles form around edge (do not boil), stirring constantly with a whisk. Reduce heat; cook 2 minutes or until slightly thick and mixture coats back of a spoon, stirring constantly. Cover and chill.

3. To prepare soufflé, lightly coat a 2-quart soufflé dish with cooking spray. Coat with 2 tablespoons sugar; set aside.

4. Heat 1 cup milk and ½ vanilla bean over medium heat in a small, heavy saucepan to 180° or until tiny bubbles form around edge (do not boil), stirring frequently. Remove from heat; let stand 30 minutes.

5. Preheat oven to 400°.

6. Scrape seeds from vanilla bean. Stir seeds into milk; discard bean. Add ½ cup sugar, cocoa, cornstarch, and ⅛ teaspoon salt to milk mixture, stirring with a whisk. Bring to a boil over medium heat, stirring frequently. Cook 1 minute or until thick, stirring constantly. Remove from heat, and stir in chocolate until melted. Let cool 5 minutes. Place 2 egg yolks in a large bowl; stir with a whisk. Gradually add chocolate mixture to egg yolks, stirring constantly with a whisk.

7. Place egg whites and cream of tartar in a large bowl; beat with a mixer at high speed until soft peaks form. Gradually add 2 tablespoons sugar, 1 tablespoon at a time, beating until stiff peaks form. Gently stir one-fourth of egg white mixture into chocolate mixture; gently fold in remaining egg white mixture. Spoon into prepared dish. Bake at 400° for 10 minutes. Reduce oven temperature to 375° (do not remove soufflé from oven); bake an additional 25 minutes or until puffy and set. Serve immediately, and top each serving with two tablespoons sauce. Yield: 10 servings.

CALORIES 181 (24% from fat); FAT 4.9g (sat 2.4g, mono 1.2g, poly 0.3g); PROTEIN 6.2g; CARB 28.1g; FIBER 1.3g; CHOL 88mg; IRON 1.8mg; SODIUM 108mg; CALC 78mg

Vanilla Custard Crumble with Mixed Berries

CRUMBLE:

- 45 reduced-fat vanilla wafers
- 2 tablespoons chilled butter, cut into small pieces
- 1 tablespoon vanilla extract
- 1 large egg white
- Cooking spray

CUSTARD:

- 2 cups 2% reduced-fat milk
- 1 vanilla bean, split lengthwise
- ⅔ cup sugar
- 2 tablespoons cornstarch
- ⅛ teaspoon salt
- 2 large egg yolks, lightly beaten
- 1 teaspoon butter
- ⅓ cup raspberries
- ⅓ cup blueberries
- ⅓ cup blackberries

1. Preheat oven to 300°.

2. To prepare crumble, place wafers in a food processor; pulse 15 times or until fine crumbs form. Add 2 tablespoons butter; pulse 4 times or until mixture resembles coarse meal. Add extract and egg white; pulse just until moist. Spread mixture onto a baking sheet coated with cooking spray, pressing gently. Bake at 300° for 27 minutes or until golden; let stand 10 minutes. Crumble and set aside.

3. To prepare custard, heat milk and vanilla bean over medium-high heat in a large, heavy saucepan to 180° or until tiny bubbles form around edge (do not boil), stirring frequently. Remove from heat, and let stand 30 minutes. Remove vanilla bean from pan. Scrape seeds from bean, and add seeds to milk mixture. Discard bean. Add sugar, cornstarch, and salt to milk mixture, stirring with a whisk. Bring to a boil over medium-high heat, stirring frequently. Cook 1 minute, stirring constantly. Remove from heat.

4. Place egg yolks in a medium bowl, and stir with a whisk. Gradually add hot milk mixture to egg yolks, stirring constantly with a whisk. Return milk mixture to pan. Bring to a boil, and cook 1 minute, stirring constantly. Remove from heat; add 1 teaspoon butter, stirring until butter melts. Place pan in a large ice-filled bowl 30 minutes or until mixture comes to room temperature, stirring occasionally. Cover and chill 8 hours or until set. Combine berries. Place ¼ cup crumble in each of 8 (8-ounce) custard cups, and top each serving with ¼ cup custard. Spoon 2 tablespoons berry mixture over each serving. Yield: 8 servings.

CALORIES 234 (30% from fat); FAT 7.9g (sat 3.5g, mono 2.8g, poly 1g); PROTEIN 4.4g; CARB 36.7g; FIBER 1.2g; CHOL 74mg; IRON 0.7mg; SODIUM 165mg; CALC 94mg

Vanilla Bean Crème Brûlée

To prevent skins from forming while the custards cool, gently press plastic wrap to the top of each.

- 2 cups 2% reduced-fat milk
- ¾ cup nonfat dry milk
- 1 vanilla bean, split lengthwise
- ½ cup sugar, divided
- 4 large egg yolks
- Dash of salt

1. Combine milks and vanilla bean in a medium saucepan. Heat mixture over medium heat to 180° or until tiny bubbles form around edge (do not boil), stirring occasionally. Remove mixture from heat. Cover and steep 30 minutes. Scrape seeds from vanilla bean into milk mixture; reserve bean for another use.

2. Preheat oven to 300°.

3. Combine ¼ cup sugar, egg yolks, and salt in a medium bowl, stirring well with a whisk. Gradually add milk mixture to egg yolk mixture, stirring constantly with a whisk. Strain mixture through a sieve into a bowl; discard solids.

4. Divide mixture evenly among 4 (4-ounce) ramekins, custard cups, or shallow baking dishes. Place ramekins in a 13 x 9-inch baking pan; add hot water to pan to a depth of 1 inch.

5. Bake at 300° for 25 minutes or until center barely moves when ramekin is touched. Remove ramekins from pan; cool completely on a wire rack. Cover with plastic wrap, and chill at least 4 hours or overnight.

6. Sift 1 tablespoon sugar evenly over each custard. Holding a kitchen blow torch about 2 inches from top of each custard, heat sugar, moving torch back and forth, until sugar is completely melted and caramelized (about 1 minute). Serve crème brûlée immediately or within 1 hour. Yield: 4 servings.

NOTE: If you don't have a kitchen blow torch, you can make the sugar topping on the stovetop. Place ¼ cup sugar and 1 tablespoon water in a small, heavy

Continued

saucepan. Cook over medium heat 5 to 8 minutes or until golden. (Resist the urge to stir, since doing so may cause the sugar to crystallize.) Immediately pour sugar mixture evenly over cold custards, spreading to form a thin layer.

CALORIES 262 (26% from fat); FAT 7.5g (sat 3.1g, mono 2.6g, poly 0.8g); PROTEIN 11g; CARB 37.8g; FIBER 0g; CHOL 224mg; IRON 0.7mg; SODIUM 177mg; CALC 328mg

If you're hosting your first Thanksgiving dinner, here's a traditional menu with tips to make everything easy.

MAKE AHEAD
Poached Pears in Vanilla Sauce

Vanilla seeds perfume the syrup, making this simple yet elegant dessert a standout. Refrigerate extra poaching liquid up to three months; serve it over ice cream or pancakes.

    4   cups water
    1   cup sugar
    1   vanilla bean, split lengthwise
    1   (3-inch) cinnamon stick
    4   small firm Bosc pears

1. Combine water and sugar in a medium saucepan; bring to a boil, stirring until sugar dissolves. Add vanilla bean and cinnamon. Cover, reduce heat, and simmer 15 minutes.
2. Peel and core pears, leaving stems intact. Cut about ¼-inch from base of each pear so they will sit flat. Add pears to sugar mixture. Cover and cook over medium heat 10 minutes or until tender. Remove pears with a slotted spoon; chill thoroughly. Discard cinnamon stick. Scrape seeds from vanilla bean, and stir seeds into sugar mixture. Discard bean. Set aside 2 cups sugar mixture; reserve remaining mixture for another use.
3. Return 2 cups sugar mixture to pan; bring to a boil over high heat. Cook until slightly syrupy and reduced to ½ cup (about 12 minutes). Chill thoroughly. Serve sauce with pears at room temperature or chilled. Yield: 4 servings (serving size: 1 pear and 2 tablespoons sauce).

CALORIES 227 (2% from fat); FAT 0.6g (sat 0g, mono 0.1g, poly 0.1g); PROTEIN 0.5g; CARB 58.5g; FIBER 3.3g; CHOL 0mg; IRON 0.4mg; SODIUM 0mg; CALC 16mg

---

First-Timer's Thanksgiving Menu
serves 12

Creamy Salsa Dip

Sparkling White-Sangría Salad

Farmhouse Roast Turkey with Rosemary Gravy

Sausage and Mushroom Stuffing

Mashed Honey-Roasted Sweet Potatoes

Gingered Cranberry Sauce

Broccoli and Carrots with Toasted Almonds

Classic Pumpkin Pie

WINE NOTE: A traditional menu that's easy to prepare deserves a traditional wine that's easy to love. Thick, soft, bold, and juicy, Zinfandel is a wine that bridges the multitude of flavors inherent in a Thanksgiving dinner—from stuffing to sweet potatoes to the bird itself. Any wine shop will have loads of Zins to choose from, but here are two suggestions:
• Ridge "Lytton Springs" Zinfandel 2001 from Dry Creek Valley, California ($30): Complex and structured with a muscular grip on the end.
• Beaulieu Vineyard "BV" Zinfandel 2001 from Napa Valley, California ($14): A terrific price for this juicy Zin, which has spiced cherry jam and black currant flavors.

MAKE AHEAD
Creamy Salsa Dip

Make this spicy appetizer up to 2 days ahead, and sprinkle with cilantro right before serving. Serve the dip with baked tortilla chips.

    2   teaspoons olive oil
    ½   cup finely chopped onion
    2   garlic cloves, minced
    1   finely chopped seeded jalapeño pepper
    1   (14.5-ounce) can diced tomatoes, undrained
    3   tablespoons chopped fresh cilantro, divided
    1   teaspoon habanero hot pepper sauce or any hot pepper sauce
    1   (16-ounce) carton low-fat sour cream

1. Heat oil in a large nonstick skillet over medium heat. Add onion, garlic, and jalapeño; cover and cook 3 minutes or until onion is tender. Add tomatoes; bring to a boil. Reduce heat, and simmer, uncovered, 5 minutes. Cool completely. Stir in 2 tablespoons cilantro, pepper sauce, and sour cream. Cover and chill. Sprinkle with remaining 1 tablespoon cilantro. Yield: 16 servings (serving size: ¼ cup).

CALORIES 45 (48% from fat); FAT 2.4g (sat 1.5g, mono 0.4g, poly 0.1g); PROTEIN 1.2g; CARB 5.5g; FIBER 0.6g; CHOL 9mg; IRON 0.1mg; SODIUM 68mg; CALC 43mg

Sparkling White-Sangría Salad

(pictured on page 363)

To many families, it isn't a holiday dinner without a gelatin salad. This rendition uses Riesling, but for a nonalcoholic version, substitute sparkling white grape juice. Make up to 1 day ahead, and refrigerate. To make the salad easier to unmold, dip the covered mold into a bowl of warm water 5 seconds.

    2   envelopes unflavored gelatin
1 ½   cups Riesling, divided
1 ½   cups white grape juice
    ¼   cup sugar
1 ½   cups orange sections
    1   cup seedless green grapes, halved
    ¾   cup fresh raspberries
Cooking spray

1. Sprinkle gelatin over ½ cup wine, and let stand 5 minutes.
2. Combine 1 cup wine, juice, and sugar in a medium saucepan; bring to a boil over medium-high heat. Remove from heat; add gelatin mixture, stirring until gelatin dissolves. Place pan in a large ice-filled bowl; let stand 20 minutes or until thick but not set, stirring occasionally. Whisk gelatin mixture to form small bubbles; fold in orange sections, grapes, and raspberries. Spoon gelatin mixture into a 5-cup decorative mold coated with cooking spray. Cover and chill at least 4 hours. Place a plate upside down on top of mold; invert mold onto plate. Yield: 12 servings (serving size: 1 slice).

CALORIES 82 (2% from fat); FAT 0.2g (sat 0.1g, mono 0g, poly 0.1g); PROTEIN 1.5g; CARB 14.7g; FIBER 1.2g; CHOL 0mg; IRON 0.3mg; SODIUM 6mg; CALC 20mg

Farmhouse Roast Turkey with Rosemary Gravy

(pictured on page 362)

Basting promotes browning, and hot drippings help seal the skin to hold in juices and keep the turkey moist. You'll have plenty of rosemary gravy to go over the stuffing and potatoes, and to use on open-faced turkey sandwiches later.

    1   (12-pound) fresh or frozen turkey, thawed
    2   cups coarsely chopped onion
    1   cup coarsely chopped celery
    2   tablespoons chopped fresh rosemary, divided
1 ¾   teaspoons salt, divided
    ¾   teaspoon black pepper, divided
Cooking spray
    2   tablespoons butter, melted
    5   cups Homemade Turkey Stock (recipe at right), divided
    ⅓   cup all-purpose flour
    ¼   cup water
    2   tablespoons cornstarch

1. Preheat oven to 325°.
2. Remove heart, gizzard, liver, and neck from turkey; reserve neck, heart, and gizzard for Homemade Turkey Stock. Discard liver. Rinse turkey thoroughly with cold water; pat dry. Trim excess fat. Combine onion, celery, 1 tablespoon rosemary, ½ teaspoon salt, and ¼ teaspoon pepper. Stuff mixture into body cavity. Tie ends of legs with twine. Lift wing tips up and over back; tuck under bird.
3. Place a roasting rack coated with cooking spray in a roasting pan. Place turkey, breast side up, on rack. Brush with butter; sprinkle evenly with 1 teaspoon salt and ¼ teaspoon pepper. Pour 1 cup Homemade Turkey Stock in bottom of pan. Insert a meat thermometer into meaty part of thigh, making sure not to touch bone. Cover turkey breast tightly with foil. Bake at 325° for 2 hours, basting with ⅓ cup Homemade Turkey Stock every 30 minutes (1⅓ cups total). Remove foil; bake an additional 1½ hours or until thermometer registers 180°, basting with ⅓ cup Homemade Turkey Stock every 30 minutes (⅔ cup total). Remove turkey from oven; let stand 30 minutes. Discard skin.
4. Place a zip-top plastic bag inside a 2-cup glass measure. Pour pan drippings into bag; let stand 10 minutes (fat will rise to top). Seal bag, and snip off 1 bottom corner of bag. Drain pan drippings into a measuring cup, stopping before fat layer reaches opening. Reserve 2 tablespoons fat, and discard remaining fat. Combine pan drippings with 2 cups Homemade Turkey Stock.

5. Heat 2 tablespoons reserved fat in bottom of roasting pan over medium heat. Add flour, stirring with a whisk. Cook 1 minute, stirring constantly. Stir in pan drippings mixture. Combine water and cornstarch, stirring with a whisk. Add cornstarch mixture to pan, stirring with a whisk. Bring to a boil, stirring frequently. Add 1 tablespoon rosemary. Reduce heat, and simmer 5 minutes or until sauce thickens. Stir in ¼ teaspoon salt and ¼ teaspoon pepper. Serve gravy with turkey. Yield: 12 servings (serving size: 6 ounces turkey and ⅓ cup gravy).

CALORIES 440 (26% from fat); FAT 12.6g (sat 3.8g, mono 3g, poly 3g); PROTEIN 71g; CARB 5.4g; FIBER 0.6g; CHOL 221mg; IRON 5.5mg; SODIUM 574mg; CALC 56mg

Homemade Turkey Stock

Giblets is the general term for a turkey's heart, gizzard, and liver. Take the neck, heart, gizzard, and canned chicken broth and turn them into a rich stock to enhance the gravy and stuffing. Don't use livers in the stock—they make it bitter and cloudy. A cleaver works best to chop the neck. Make the stock 1 or 2 days ahead so it will be ready to use in the Farmhouse Roast Turkey with Rosemary Gravy (recipe at left), Sausage and Mushroom Stuffing (recipe on page 376), and Broccoli and Carrots with Toasted Almonds (recipe on page 376).

    2   teaspoons vegetable oil
    1   turkey neck
    1   turkey heart
    1   turkey gizzard
    ½   cup chopped onion
    ½   cup chopped celery
    ½   cup chopped carrot
    8   cups cold water
    2   (14-ounce) cans fat-free, less-sodium chicken broth
    ½   teaspoon dried thyme
    ¼   teaspoon black peppercorns
    3   parsley sprigs
    1   bay leaf

1. Heat oil in a large stockpot or Dutch oven over medium-high heat. Chop neck, heart, and gizzard into 2-inch pieces; add
Continued

to pan. Cook 5 minutes or until browned, stirring occasionally. Add onion, celery, and carrot; cook 4 minutes or until tender, stirring frequently. Stir in water and broth; bring to a boil. Add thyme, peppercorns, parsley, and bay leaf. Reduce heat, and simmer 2 hours. Strain mixture through a sieve over a large bowl; discard solids. Cool to room temperature. Cover and chill overnight. Skim solidified fat from surface, and discard fat. Yield: 7 cups (serving size: 1 cup).

NOTE: Refrigerate leftover stock in an airtight container up to 1 week, or freeze up to 3 months.

CALORIES 27 (33% from fat); FAT 1g (sat 0.2g, mono 0.2g, poly 0.5g); PROTEIN 2.9g; CARB 0.9g; FIBER 0.1g; CHOL 8mg; IRON 0.3mg; SODIUM 217mg; CALC 3mg

Sausage and Mushroom Stuffing

(pictured on page 362)

Make the croutons ahead. When you take the turkey out of the oven, increase the temperature to 350° for the stuffing.

  5 cups (1-inch) cubed white bread (about 7 [1-ounce] slices)
  5 cups (1-inch) cubed whole wheat bread (about 7 [1-ounce] slices)
  1 pound turkey Italian sausage
Cooking spray
  1 teaspoon vegetable oil
  3 cups finely chopped onion
1½ cups finely chopped celery
  1 (8-ounce) package presliced mushrooms (about 2 cups)
  1 teaspoon dried thyme
  1 teaspoon dried rubbed sage
  1 teaspoon dried rosemary
  ½ teaspoon dried marjoram
  ½ teaspoon black pepper
  ⅓ cup chopped fresh parsley
1½ cups Homemade Turkey Stock (recipe on page 375)

1. Preheat oven to 250°.
2. Place bread in a single layer on 2 baking sheets. Bake at 250° for 1 hour or until dry. Set aside.
3. Remove casings from sausage. Cook sausage in a large nonstick skillet coated with cooking spray over medium heat until browned, stirring to crumble. Place sausage in a large bowl.
4. Heat oil in pan over medium heat. Add onion, celery, and mushrooms; cover and cook 10 minutes or until vegetables are tender, stirring occasionally. Remove from heat; stir in thyme and next 4 ingredients. Add onion mixture, bread, and parsley to sausage; toss gently to combine. Add Homemade Turkey Stock, and stir until moist.
5. Increase oven temperature to 350°.
6. Spoon bread mixture into a 13 x 9-inch baking dish coated with cooking spray. Cover and bake at 350° for 15 minutes. Uncover and bake 20 minutes or until top is crusty. Yield: 12 servings (serving size: about ¾ cup).

CALORIES 187 (28% from fat); FAT 5.9g (sat 1.6g, mono 2g, poly 1.5g); PROTEIN 12.4g; CARB 21.6g; FIBER 2.9g; CHOL 38mg; IRON 2.5mg; SODIUM 460mg; CALC 52mg

MAKE AHEAD
Mashed Honey-Roasted Sweet Potatoes

(pictured on page 362)

Prepare this dish up to 1 day ahead, and store, covered, in the refrigerator. To reheat, bake at 350°, covered, for 45 minutes.

  6 pounds sweet potatoes, peeled and cut into (1-inch) cubes
Cooking spray
  5 tablespoons honey, divided
  4 tablespoons unsalted butter
  ¾ teaspoon salt

1. Preheat oven to 375°.
2. Place potatoes in a single layer on 2 large baking sheets coated with cooking spray. Lightly spray potatoes with cooking spray. Bake at 375° for 1 hour or until tender, stirring occasionally. Place potatoes, ¼ cup honey, butter, and salt in a large bowl, and beat with a mixer at medium speed until smooth. Drizzle with 1 tablespoon honey. Yield: 12 servings (serving size: ½ cup).

CALORIES 140 (25% from fat); FAT 3.9g (sat 2.4g, mono 1.1g, poly 0.2g); PROTEIN 1.4g; CARB 26.2g; FIBER 2.4g; CHOL 10mg; IRON 0.4mg; SODIUM 154mg; CALC 24mg

QUICK & EASY • MAKE AHEAD
Gingered Cranberry Sauce

(pictured on page 362)

Make up to 1 week ahead, and store, covered, in the refrigerator.

1½ cups sugar
  ½ cup water
  ⅓ cup chopped crystallized ginger (1 [2.7-ounce] bottle)
  1 (12-ounce) package fresh cranberries

1. Combine all ingredients in a medium saucepan. Bring to a boil; reduce heat, and simmer 9 minutes or until cranberries pop. Cool completely. Serve at room temperature. Yield: 12 servings (serving size: ¼ cup).

CALORIES 112 (0% from fat); FAT 0g; PROTEIN 0.2g; CARB 29g; FIBER 1.2g; CHOL 0mg; IRON 0.1mg; SODIUM 1.2mg; CALC 3mg

QUICK & EASY • MAKE AHEAD
Broccoli and Carrots with Toasted Almonds

(pictured on page 362)

Toast the almonds and blanch the vegetables a day ahead. If you would rather not make the Homemade Turkey Stock (recipe on page 375), substitute fat-free, less-sodium chicken broth.

  ⅓ cup sliced almonds
  1 pound (1-inch) diagonally cut carrots (about 3 cups)
  1 (12-ounce) bag broccoli florets (about 6 cups)
  1 tablespoon butter
  ¼ cup finely chopped shallots
  ½ cup Homemade Turkey Stock (recipe on page 375)
  ½ teaspoon salt
  ¼ teaspoon freshly ground black pepper

1. Preheat oven to 350°.
2. Spread almonds in a single layer in a shallow pan. Bake at 350° for 7 minutes or until lightly browned and fragrant; stir occasionally. Cool completely; set aside.
3. Place carrots in a large saucepan of boiling water; cook 3 minutes. Remove with a slotted spoon. Plunge into ice

water, and drain. Place broccoli in boiling water; cook 2 minutes. Drain and plunge into ice water; drain.

4. Melt butter in a 12-inch nonstick skillet over medium-high heat. Add shallots; sauté 2 minutes or until tender. Reduce heat to medium. Add carrots, broccoli, Homemade Turkey Stock, salt, and pepper; cover and cook 6 minutes or until carrots and broccoli are crisp-tender. Sprinkle with almonds. Serve immediately. Yield: 12 servings (serving size: ½ cup).

CALORIES 54 (43% from fat); FAT 2.6g (sat 0.7g, mono 1.1g, poly 0.4g); PROTEIN 2.5g; CARB 6.3g; FIBER 2.3g; CHOL 5mg; IRON 0.6mg; SODIUM 130mg; CALC 36mg

Classic Pumpkin Pie

Bake the pie in the lower third of the oven.

FILLING:
¾ cup packed brown sugar
1¾ teaspoons pumpkin pie spice
¼ teaspoon salt
1 (12-ounce) can evaporated low-fat milk
2 large egg whites
1 large egg
1 (15-ounce) can unsweetened pumpkin

CRUST:
½ (15-ounce) package refrigerated pie dough (such as Pillsbury)
Cooking spray

TOPPING:
¼ cup whipping cream
1 tablespoon amaretto (almond-flavored liqueur)
2 teaspoons powdered sugar

1. Position oven rack to lowest position.
2. Preheat oven to 425°.
3. To prepare filling, combine first 6 ingredients in a bowl; stir with a whisk. Add pumpkin; stir with a whisk until smooth.
4. To prepare crust, roll dough into an 11-inch circle; fit into a 9-inch pie plate coated with cooking spray. Fold edges under, and flute.
5. Pour pumpkin mixture into crust. Place pie plate on a baking sheet. Place baking sheet on lowest oven rack. Bake at 425° for 10 minutes. Reduce oven temperature to 350° (do not remove pie from oven); bake an additional 50 minutes or until almost set. Cool completely on a wire rack.
6. To prepare topping, beat cream with a mixer at high speed until stiff peaks form. Add amaretto and powdered sugar, and beat until blended. Serve with pie. Yield: 12 servings (serving size: 1 wedge pie and about 1 tablespoon topping).

CALORIES 222 (30% from fat); FAT 7.4g (sat 3.7g, mono 0.7g, poly 0.1g); PROTEIN 4.1g; CARB 35.3g; FIBER 3g; CHOL 32mg; IRON 0.8mg; SODIUM 241mg; CALC 104mg

Prompt Pumpkin

These seven recipes show why nutrition-packed canned pumpkin deserves to be more than a once-a-year pie filling.

MAKE AHEAD
Pumpkin Pudding with Candied Pecans

PUDDING:
6 ounces firm silken tofu
6 tablespoons fat-free sweetened condensed milk
¼ cup maple syrup
1 teaspoon vanilla extract
1 teaspoon ground cinnamon
⅛ teaspoon ground cardamom
⅛ teaspoon grated whole nutmeg
Dash of salt
1 (15-ounce) can pumpkin
1 cup frozen fat-free whipped topping, thawed

PECANS:
½ cup pecans
2 tablespoons sugar
⅛ teaspoon salt

REMAINING INGREDIENT:
6 tablespoons frozen fat-free whipped topping, thawed

1. To prepare pudding, place tofu on several layers of heavy-duty paper towels. Cover tofu with additional paper towels, and let stand 10 minutes. Combine tofu, condensed milk, syrup, and vanilla extract in a blender, and process until smooth. Add cinnamon and next 4 ingredients; process until smooth. Pour pumpkin mixture into a large bowl, and fold in 1 cup whipped topping. Cover and chill at least 8 hours or overnight.
2. To prepare pecans, heat a medium nonstick skillet over medium heat. Add pecans, sugar, and ⅛ teaspoon salt. Cook 3 minutes or until sugar melts and coats pecans, shaking pan to evenly coat. Pour pecans onto a parchment-lined baking sheet. Let pecans cool, and coarsely chop.
3. To assemble desserts, spoon ⅔ cup pudding into each of 6 (6-ounce) custard cups; top each serving with 1 tablespoon whipped topping. Sprinkle about 1½ tablespoons pecans over each serving. Yield: 6 servings.

CALORIES 240 (29% from fat); FAT 7.7g (sat 0.8g, mono 4.1g, poly 2.3g); PROTEIN 5.2g; CARB 38.2g; FIBER 3.2g; CHOL 1mg; IRON 1.7mg; SODIUM 133mg; CALC 103mg

Warm Pumpkin-Cheese Dip

The unusual combination of goat cheese and pumpkin was a surprise hit in our Test Kitchens. Serve the dip with crisp bread-sticks, bagel chips, or toasted French or sourdough baguette slices.

1¼ cups plain low-fat yogurt
½ teaspoon butter
1 cup thinly sliced leek
2 teaspoons chopped fresh or ½ teaspoon dried thyme
1 teaspoon salt
¾ cup (3 ounces) goat cheese
⅓ cup evaporated fat-free milk
1 (15-ounce) can pumpkin
3 large egg whites

1. Preheat oven to 375°.

2. Spoon yogurt onto several layers of heavy-duty paper towels; spread to ½-inch thickness. Cover with additional paper towels; let stand 5 minutes. Scrape into a large bowl using a rubber spatula.

3. Melt butter in a skillet over medium-high heat. Add leek; sauté 5 minutes or until tender. Remove from heat, and stir in thyme and salt. Place strained yogurt, goat cheese, and remaining 3 ingredients in a large bowl, and beat with a mixer at medium speed just until smooth. Stir in leek mixture. Spoon pumpkin mixture into a 1-quart baking dish. Bake at 375° for 25 minutes or until dip is bubbly and lightly browned. Serve warm. Yield: 3½ cups (serving size: ¼ cup).

CALORIES 57 (36% from fat); FAT 2.3g (sat 1.6g, mono 0.5g, poly 0.1g); PROTEIN 3.9g; CARB 5.5g; FIBER 1g; CHOL 7mg; IRON 0.7mg; SODIUM 306mg; CALC 81mg

---

STAFF FAVORITE • MAKE AHEAD
Pumpkin Biscuits with Orange-Honey Butter

Serve at breakfast or dinner with baked ham or pork chops.

  2   cups all-purpose flour
  3   tablespoons sugar
  2   teaspoons baking powder
  1   teaspoon ground cinnamon
  ½   teaspoon baking soda
  ½   teaspoon salt
  ¼   teaspoon ground nutmeg
  ¼   cup chilled butter, cut into small pieces
  ¾   cup fat-free buttermilk
  ½   cup canned pumpkin
Cooking spray
  ¼   cup Orange-Honey Butter

1. Preheat oven to 450°.

2. Lightly spoon flour into dry measuring cups, and level with a knife. Combine flour and next 6 ingredients; cut in chilled butter with a pastry blender or 2 knives until mixture resembles coarse meal. Add buttermilk and pumpkin; stir just until moist. Turn dough out onto a lightly

---

floured surface; knead lightly 5 times. Roll dough to about ½-inch thickness. Cut into 12 biscuits with a 2½-inch biscuit cutter. Place biscuits on a baking sheet coated with cooking spray. Bake at 450° for 11 minutes or until golden. Serve warm with Orange-Honey Butter. Yield: 12 servings (serving size: 1 biscuit and 1 teaspoon butter).

(Totals include ¼ cup Orange-Honey Butter) CALORIES 153 (33% from fat); FAT 5.6g (sat 3.4g, mono 1.6g, poly 0.3g); PROTEIN 2.9g; CARB 23.1g; FIBER 1g; CHOL 15mg; IRON 1.2mg; SODIUM 311mg; CALC 68mg

---

MAKE AHEAD
ORANGE-HONEY BUTTER:

Store in the refrigerator up to 2 weeks.

  ½   cup butter, softened
  ½   cup honey
  ½   teaspoon grated orange rind

1. Combine all ingredients in a medium bowl; beat with a mixer at medium speed until well blended. Yield: 1¼ cups (serving size: 1 teaspoon).

CALORIES 22 (61% from fat); FAT 1.5g (sat 0.9g, mono 0.5g, poly 0.1g); PROTEIN 0g; CARB 2.3g; FIBER 0g; CHOL 4mg; IRON 0mg; SODIUM 16mg; CALC 1mg

---

Pumpkin-Cream Cheese Soufflés

These individual desserts are creamy from both the pumpkin and the cream cheese.

Cooking spray
  1   tablespoon granulated sugar
  ¼   cup all-purpose flour
  1   cup evaporated fat-free milk, divided
  ⅔   cup granulated sugar, divided
  ½   cup (4 ounces) ⅓-less-fat cream cheese, softened
  1   teaspoon ground cinnamon
  1   teaspoon vanilla extract
  ¼   teaspoon grated whole nutmeg
  ⅛   teaspoon ground allspice
Dash of salt
  1   (15-ounce) can pumpkin
  3   large egg whites
  1   tablespoon powdered sugar

---

1. Preheat oven to 375°.

2. Lightly coat 6 (8-ounce) ramekins with cooking spray; sprinkle evenly with 1 tablespoon granulated sugar.

3. Lightly spoon flour into a dry measuring cup; level with a knife. Place flour in a bowl; add ½ cup milk, stirring well with a whisk. Set aside.

4. Combine ½ cup milk, ⅓ cup granulated sugar, and cream cheese in a medium saucepan. Cook over medium heat until cheese almost melts, stirring constantly. Stir in flour mixture, and cook 2 minutes or until thick, stirring constantly. (Cheese may not appear completely melted.) Spoon mixture into a large bowl. Add cinnamon and next 5 ingredients; beat with a mixer at medium speed until smooth.

5. Using clean beaters, beat egg whites with a mixer at high speed until foamy. Gradually add ⅓ cup granulated sugar, 1 tablespoon at a time, until stiff peaks form. Stir one-fourth of egg whites into pumpkin mixture. Gently fold in remaining egg whites. Divide pumpkin mixture evenly among prepared ramekins. Place ramekins on a baking sheet. Bake at 375° for 25 minutes or until soufflés are puffy and set. Sprinkle evenly with powdered sugar. Serve immediately. Yield: 6 servings.

CALORIES 236 (18% from fat); FAT 4.8g (sat 3g, mono 1.3g, poly 0.2g); PROTEIN 8.2g; CARB 41.3g; FIBER 2.4g; CHOL 16mg; IRON 1.6mg; SODIUM 180mg; CALC 164mg

---

QUICK & EASY
Pumpkin-Sage Polenta

Serve this with pan-sautéed ham steaks.

  2½ cups 1% low-fat milk
  2   cups water
  ¾   cup canned pumpkin
  1¼ teaspoons salt
  1¼ cups instant dry polenta
  ¾   cup (3 ounces) grated fresh Parmesan cheese
  2   tablespoons ⅓-less-fat cream cheese, softened
  1   tablespoon chopped fresh sage
  ¼   cup (1 ounce) shaved fresh Parmesan

1. Bring milk and water to a boil in a large saucepan over medium heat. Add pumpkin and salt; stir with a whisk. Reduce heat to low, and gradually whisk in polenta; cook 1 minute or until thick. Remove from heat. Add ¾ cup grated Parmesan, cream cheese, and sage; stir until cheeses melt. Top with shaved Parmesan. Serve immediately. Yield: 8 servings (serving size: ¾ cup).

CALORIES 197 (21% from fat); FAT 4.7g (sat 3g, mono 1.4g, poly 0.1g); PROTEIN 10.1g; CARB 28.7g; FIBER 3.2g; CHOL 14mg; IRON 1mg; SODIUM 614mg; CALC 253mg

Savory Pumpkin-Chestnut Stuffing

For best results, use firm, sturdy bread such as French bread, and dry it in the oven at a low temperature. Or let it sit out overnight. To prevent the foil from sticking to the stuffing during baking, coat one side of foil with cooking spray, and place it, coated side down, over the stuffing.

    8   ounces firm white bread, cut into
        1-inch cubes (about 8 cups)
    1   tablespoon butter
    2   cups chopped onion
    2   cups sliced cremini mushrooms
    1   cup chopped celery
 1½   cups chopped Granny Smith
        apple
    ½   cup sweetened dried cranberries
    1   cup coarsely chopped bottled
        chestnuts
    ⅓   cup chopped fresh flat-leaf parsley
    2   tablespoons chopped fresh sage
    2   tablespoons chopped fresh or
        1 teaspoon dried thyme
 1¼   cups canned pumpkin
    ½   cup fat-free, less-sodium chicken
        broth
    1   teaspoon salt
    ½   teaspoon black pepper
    2   large eggs
        Cooking spray

1. Preheat oven to 250°.
2. Place bread cubes on a large baking sheet. Bake at 250° for 1 hour or until dry, tossing occasionally.
3. Increase oven temperature to 350°.

4. Melt butter in a large nonstick skillet over medium-high heat. Add onion, mushrooms, and celery to pan, and sauté 5 minutes. Add apple and cranberries; sauté 5 minutes. Add chestnuts; sauté 1 minute. Remove from heat; stir in parsley, sage, and thyme.
5. Combine pumpkin and next 4 ingredients in a large bowl. Add bread and mushroom mixture; stir gently to combine. Spoon mixture into a 13 x 9-inch baking dish coated with cooking spray; cover with foil. Bake at 350° for 45 minutes; uncover and bake an additional 15 minutes or until top is crisp. Yield: 8 servings (serving size: about 1 cup).

CALORIES 226 (20% from fat); FAT 4.6g (sat 1.8g, mono 1.4g, poly 0.5g); PROTEIN 6.6g; CARB 40g; FIBER 4.6g; CHOL 60mg; IRON 2.5mg; SODIUM 532mg; CALC 72mg

Pasta with Mushrooms and Pumpkin-Gorgonzola Sauce

Any short pasta will work in this dish. We recommend our favorite brand of cheese: Saladena Gorgonzola; it gave the sauce a luscious consistency.

    1   pound uncooked pennette (small
        penne)
    1   tablespoon olive oil
    5   cups thinly sliced shiitake
        mushroom caps (about ¾ pound
        whole mushrooms)
    4   cups vertically sliced onion
    4   garlic cloves, minced
    1   teaspoon chopped fresh sage
    1   (12-ounce) can evaporated milk
 1½   tablespoons cornstarch
 1½   tablespoons cold water
    ½   cup (2 ounces) crumbled
        Gorgonzola cheese
    ½   cup canned pumpkin
    1   teaspoon salt
    ½   teaspoon freshly ground black
        pepper
    ⅛   teaspoon grated whole nutmeg
        Sage sprigs (optional)

1. Cook pasta according to package directions, omitting salt and fat. Keep pasta warm.

2. Heat oil in a Dutch oven over medium-high heat. Add mushrooms, onion, and garlic; cover and cook 3 minutes. Uncover; cook 5 minutes or until tender, stirring occasionally.
3. Combine chopped sage and milk in a medium saucepan over medium heat. Bring to a simmer. Combine cornstarch and water, stirring with a whisk. Add cornstarch mixture and cheese to milk mixture, stirring with a whisk. Cook 2 minutes or until thick and smooth, stirring constantly. Remove from heat; stir in pumpkin, salt, pepper, and nutmeg.
4. Add pasta and pumpkin mixture to mushroom mixture; toss well to combine. Garnish with sage sprigs, if desired. Yield: 6 servings (serving size: 1½ cups).

CALORIES 462 (13% from fat); FAT 6.5g (sat 2.8g, mono 1.7g, poly 0.4g); PROTEIN 19.9g; CARB 83.1g; FIBER 7.3g; CHOL 11mg; IRON 3.7mg; SODIUM 636mg; CALC 265mg

in season

Particular Parsnips

Sweeter than a carrot, starchy as a potato, parsnips can stand in for either.

Glazed Parsnips

    1   tablespoon unsalted butter
    3   cups (2-inch-long) julienne-cut
        peeled parsnip
    ¼   cup packed dark brown sugar
    2   tablespoons tomato juice
    ¼   teaspoon kosher salt
    ⅛   teaspoon freshly ground black pepper

1. Melt butter in a large nonstick skillet over medium heat. Add parsnip and remaining ingredients; stir until well blended. Cover and cook 7 minutes or until tender, stirring occasionally. Yield: 4 servings (serving size: ½ cup).

CALORIES 153 (18% from fat); FAT 3.1g (sat 1.8g, mono 0.9g, poly 0.2g); PROTEIN 1.3g; CARB 31.7g; FIBER 5g; CHOL 8mg; IRON 0.9mg; SODIUM 157mg; CALC 49mg

Mock Crab Salad

This salad works well with pork or poultry and is terrific with a turkey sandwich.

2 cups shredded peeled parsnip
¼ cup finely chopped celery
¼ cup chopped pimiento-stuffed olives
¼ cup fat-free mayonnaise
2 tablespoons minced fresh onion
2 tablespoons 1% low-fat milk
⅛ teaspoon kosher salt
⅛ teaspoon freshly ground black pepper
1 (4-ounce) jar diced pimiento, drained

1. Combine all ingredients, tossing well. Yield: 4 servings (serving size: ½ cup).

CALORIES 86 (21% from fat); FAT 1.6g (sat 0.3g, mono 0.8g, poly 0.2g); PROTEIN 1.5g; CARB 17.4g; FIBER 4.6g; CHOL 2mg; IRON 1.2mg; SODIUM 277mg; CALC 48mg

Roasted Parsnips

The natural sweetness of parsnips comes alive when they're roasted and caramelized. This is a great side dish to serve with ham or pork tenderloin.

3 tablespoons balsamic vinegar
1 tablespoon brown sugar
2 teaspoons chopped fresh rosemary
2 pounds (2-inch-thick) slices peeled parsnip
1 large red onion, peeled and quartered
Cooking spray
1 tablespoon olive oil
½ teaspoon salt
¼ teaspoon freshly ground black pepper

1. Combine first 5 ingredients in a large zip-top plastic bag; seal and marinate in refrigerator 1 hour, turning twice. Remove parsnip and onion; discard marinade.
2. Preheat oven to 500°.
3. Place parsnip and onion in a shallow roasting pan coated with cooking spray. Drizzle with oil, and toss to coat. Sprinkle with salt and pepper. Bake at

500° for 30 minutes or until parsnip is tender, stirring often. Yield: 4 servings (serving size: about 1 cup).

CALORIES 235 (16% from fat); FAT 4.2g (sat 0.6g, mono 2.8g, poly 0.4g); PROTEIN 3.2g; CARB 49.3g; FIBER 11.9g; CHOL 0mg; IRON 1.7mg; SODIUM 319mg; CALC 97mg

Spice Cake with Caramel Icing

One way to make certain you get your veggies is to put them in a cake. Just like carrots do for carrot cake, parsnips make this aromatic spice cake moist.

CAKE:
1 pound (1-inch-thick) slices peeled parsnip
1 cup packed dark brown sugar
½ cup granulated sugar
5 tablespoons butter, melted
1 teaspoon vanilla extract
½ cup apple juice
3 cups all-purpose flour
2 teaspoons baking soda
1 teaspoon ground cinnamon
1 teaspoon ground nutmeg
½ teaspoon salt
¾ cup 1% low-fat milk
Cooking spray

ICING:
1 cup packed dark brown sugar
½ cup 1% low-fat milk
2 tablespoons butter
¼ teaspoon salt
1½ cups sifted powdered sugar
½ teaspoon vanilla extract
¼ cup chopped pecans, toasted

1. Preheat oven to 350°.
2. To prepare cake, place parsnip in a saucepan; cover with water. Bring to a boil, reduce heat, and simmer over medium heat 20 minutes or until tender. Drain.
3. Place parsnip, 1 cup brown sugar, granulated sugar, 5 tablespoons butter, and 1 teaspoon vanilla in a food processor, and process until smooth, scraping sides of bowl occasionally. With processor on, slowly add apple juice through food chute, processing until well combined. Place parsnip mixture in a large bowl.

4. Lightly spoon flour into dry measuring cups; level with a knife. Combine flour, baking soda, cinnamon, nutmeg, and ½ teaspoon salt, stirring well with a whisk. Add flour mixture and ¾ cup milk alternately to parsnip mixture, beginning and ending with flour mixture. Pour batter into 2 (9-inch) round cake pans lightly coated with cooking spray. Bake at 350° for 30 minutes or until a wooden pick inserted in center comes out clean. Cool in pans 10 minutes on a wire rack; remove from pans. Cool completely on wire rack.
5. To prepare icing, combine 1 cup brown sugar, ½ cup milk, 2 tablespoons butter, and ¼ teaspoon salt in a medium saucepan. Bring to a boil over medium-high heat, stirring constantly. Reduce heat, and simmer until slightly thick (about 5 minutes), stirring occasionally. Remove from heat. Add powdered sugar and ½ teaspoon vanilla; beat with a mixer at medium speed until icing is smooth and only slightly warm. (Icing will continue to thicken as it cools.)
6. Place 1 cake layer on a plate. Working quickly, spread layer with half of icing, and top with remaining layer. Spread remaining icing over top layer, and sprinkle with toasted pecans. Cool to room temperature. Store cake loosely covered in refrigerator. Yield: 18 servings (serving size: 1 slice).

CALORIES 309 (17% from fat); FAT 6g (sat 3g, mono 2g, poly 0.6g); PROTEIN 3.2g; CARB 61.8g; FIBER 2.1g; CHOL 12mg; IRON 1.7mg; SODIUM 303mg; CALC 59mg

Mashed Potatoes and Parsnips

Cut the parsnips smaller than the potatoes so they'll finish cooking at the same time. Also, because the parsnip pieces are small, they're easier to mash.

2 cups chopped peeled parsnip
2 cups cubed peeled baking potato
½ cup half-and-half
2 teaspoons butter
¾ teaspoon kosher salt
¼ teaspoon coarsely ground black pepper

1. Place parsnip and potato in a saucepan; cover with water. Bring to a boil. Reduce heat; simmer 10 minutes or until very tender. Drain and return to pan. Add remaining ingredients; mash with a potato masher to desired consistency. Yield: 4 servings (serving size: about 1¼ cups).

CALORIES 164 (29% from fat); FAT 5.2g (sat 3.2g, mono 1.6g, poly 0.1g); PROTEIN 3g; CARB 26.2g; FIBER 4.2g; CHOL 20mg; IRON 0.7mg; SODIUM 397mg; CALC 68mg

Pork Stew with Parsnips and Apricots

Classic cool-weather flavors, such as pork, onion, and celery, meet summer's dried fruits and herbs.

    1   tablespoon olive oil
  1½   pounds boneless pork loin, cut into ½-inch pieces
  1½   cups chopped onion
    1   cup thinly sliced celery
    2   tablespoons water
    ¼   cup tomato paste
    2   teaspoons dried rubbed sage
    1   teaspoon dried thyme
    ¾   teaspoon kosher salt
    ¼   teaspoon coarsely ground black pepper
    3   (14-ounce) cans fat-free, less-sodium chicken broth
    2   bay leaves
    4   cups (½-inch-thick) slices peeled parsnip
    ¾   cup dried apricots, finely chopped
    2   tablespoons chopped fresh flat-leaf parsley

1. Heat oil in a Dutch oven over medium-high heat. Add pork, and cook 6 minutes or until browned, stirring occasionally. Remove pork from pan, and wipe pan with a paper towel, leaving browned bits on bottom of pan. Add onion, celery, and water; cook 3 minutes, scraping pan to loosen browned bits. Return pork to pan. Add tomato paste and next 6 ingredients, and bring stew to a boil. Cover, reduce heat, and simmer 1 hour.
2. Stir in parsnip and apricots; bring to a boil. Cover, reduce heat, and simmer 30 minutes or until pork is tender. Discard bay leaves; sprinkle with parsley. Yield: 6 servings (serving size: about 1⅓ cups).

CALORIES 349 (23% from fat); FAT 9.1g (sat 2.6g, mono 4.7g, poly 1g); PROTEIN 29.6g; CARB 36.3g; FIBER 7.4g; CHOL 67mg; IRON 2.9mg; SODIUM 696mg; CALC 86mg

Parsnip-Caraway Bread

Grated parsnips add moisture and earthy sweetness; caraway supplies a bitter zip. This bread rises three times, which gives it a complex flavor and texture.

    1   package dry yeast (about 2¼ teaspoons)
    ¾   cup warm water (100° to 110°)
    ¼   cup rye flour
  2¼   cups bread flour, divided
    1   cup finely grated peeled parsnip
    2   teaspoons caraway seeds
    1   teaspoon salt
    ⅛   teaspoon white pepper
        Cooking spray
    1   tablespoon yellow cornmeal
    1   teaspoon water
    1   large egg white, lightly beaten
    ¼   teaspoon kosher salt

1. Dissolve yeast in warm water in a large bowl; let stand 5 minutes. Lightly spoon flours into dry measuring cups, and level with a knife. Add rye flour and parsnip to yeast mixture, and stir well to form a sponge. Cover and let rest at room temperature 30 minutes.
2. Add 2 cups bread flour, caraway seeds, 1 teaspoon salt, and pepper to parsnip mixture; stir until a soft dough forms. Turn dough out onto a lightly floured surface. Knead until smooth and elastic (about 8 minutes); add enough of remaining bread flour, 1 tablespoon at a time, to prevent dough from sticking to hands (dough will feel tacky).
3. Place dough in a large bowl coated with cooking spray, turning to coat top. Cover and let rise in a warm place (85°), free from drafts, 45 minutes or until doubled in size. (Gently press two fingers into dough. If indentation remains, dough has risen enough.) Punch dough down, and lightly spray surface of dough with cooking spray. Cover and let rise a second time, 45 minutes or until doubled in size. Punch dough down; cover and let rest 5 minutes. Shape dough into an (8-inch-long) oval; place on a baking sheet sprinkled with cornmeal. Lightly spray surface of dough with cooking spray. Cover and let rise in a warm place (85°), free from drafts, 30 minutes or until doubled in size.
4. Preheat oven to 400°.
5. Combine 1 teaspoon water and egg white, and brush over loaf. Sprinkle loaf with kosher salt. Bake at 400° for 30 minutes or until dough is browned on bottom and sounds hollow when tapped. Cool on a wire rack. Yield: 12 servings (serving size: 1 slice).

CALORIES 116 (5% from fat); FAT 0.6g (sat 0.1g, mono 0.1g, poly 0.2g); PROTEIN 4.1g; CARB 23.3g; FIBER 1.8g; CHOL 0mg; IRON 1.4mg; SODIUM 240mg; CALC 12mg

Brown Rice Pilaf with Parsnips and Celery

Instant rice cuts the cooking time in half.

    1   tablespoon olive oil
  1½   cups chopped peeled parsnip
    ½   cup (¼-inch-thick) sliced celery
  1½   cups uncooked instant brown rice
    ⅓   cup water
    ½   teaspoon kosher salt
    ¼   teaspoon dried thyme
    ⅛   teaspoon freshly ground black pepper
    1   (14-ounce) can fat-free, less-sodium chicken broth
    3   tablespoons sliced almonds, toasted

1. Heat oil in a large saucepan over medium heat. Add parsnip and celery, and cook 4 minutes, stirring occasionally. Add rice and next 5 ingredients, and bring to a boil. Cover, reduce heat, and simmer 10 minutes. Stir in almonds. Yield: 6 servings (serving size: ⅔ cup).

CALORIES 184 (23% from fat); FAT 4.6g (sat 0.4g, mono 2.6g, poly 0.6g); PROTEIN 4.2g; CARB 31.5g; FIBER 3.7g; CHOL 0mg; IRON 0.8mg; SODIUM 291mg; CALC 40mg

Cream of Parsnip Soup

This soup is sweeter than potato soup. We found that using a blender instead of a food processor yielded a more velvety consistency.

- 1 tablespoon butter
- 1 cup chopped onion
- ½ cup chopped celery
- 1 pound sliced peeled parsnip
- ¼ cup dry white wine
- 2 cups water
- ½ teaspoon salt
- ⅛ teaspoon freshly ground black pepper
- 2 (14-ounce) cans fat-free, less-sodium chicken broth
- 1 pound peeled baking potatoes, cubed
- 1 bay leaf
- 2 teaspoons fresh lemon juice
- 6 tablespoons reduced-fat sour cream
- 1 tablespoon finely chopped fresh parsley

1. Melt butter in a Dutch oven over medium-high heat. Add onion, celery, and parsnip; sauté 10 minutes. Stir in wine, scraping pan to loosen browned bits. Add water, salt, pepper, broth, potato, and bay leaf. Bring to a boil; reduce heat to medium. Cook 20 minutes or until vegetables are tender. Discard bay leaf.

2. Place one-third of vegetable mixture in a blender, and process until smooth. Pour puréed vegetable mixture into a large bowl. Repeat procedure with remaining vegetable mixture. Stir in lemon juice. Spoon 1 cup soup into each of 6 bowls; top each serving with 1 tablespoon sour cream and ½ teaspoon parsley. Yield: 6 servings.

CALORIES 169 (12% from fat); FAT 2.2g (sat 1.2g, mono 0.6g, poly 0.1g); PROTEIN 5.5g; CARB 32.9g; FIBER 5.9g; CHOL 8mg; IRON 1.2mg; SODIUM 496mg; CALC 71mg

Parsnip Slaw with Grapes

Crunchy parsnips complement juicy grapes. Serve with pork or a ham sandwich.

- 3½ cups shredded peeled parsnip
- 1 cup seedless red grapes, halved
- ¼ cup light mayonnaise
- ¼ cup plain fat-free yogurt
- 2 tablespoons chopped fresh flat-leaf parsley
- 2 tablespoons fresh lemon juice
- 2 teaspoons sugar
- ¼ teaspoon kosher salt
- ¼ teaspoon freshly ground black pepper

1. Combine all ingredients, tossing well. Yield: 6 servings (serving size: ⅔ cup).

CALORIES 113 (18% from fat); FAT 2.3g (sat 0.4g, mono 0.6g, poly 1.2g); PROTEIN 1.8g; CARB 23g; FIBER 4.2g; CHOL 3mg; IRON 0.6mg; SODIUM 145mg; CALC 54mg

Parsnip-Potato Latkes with Horseradish Cream

Pressing the patties firmly between your hands helps bind all the ingredients together.

- ½ cup fat-free sour cream
- ¼ teaspoon prepared horseradish
- 2½ cups shredded peeled baking potato (about 1 pound)
- 2½ cups shredded peeled parsnip
- 1 cup grated carrot
- 1 teaspoon salt, divided
- ½ cup chopped red onion
- ¼ cup all-purpose flour
- ¼ teaspoon freshly ground black pepper
- 2 tablespoons vegetable oil, divided

1. Combine sour cream and horseradish; cover and chill.

2. Combine potato, parsnip, and carrot; spread evenly onto several layers of paper towels. Sprinkle with ¾ teaspoon salt; let stand 30 minutes. Cover with additional paper towels, and press down to absorb liquid. Place parsnip mixture in a large bowl. Add onion, flour, and pepper; toss to combine.

3. Preheat oven to 400°.

4. Divide parsnip mixture into 10 equal portions (about ¼ cup per portion), shaping each into a ½-inch-thick patty.

5. Heat 1 tablespoon oil in a large non-stick skillet over medium heat. Add 5 patties; cook 2 minutes on each side or until golden brown. Place cooked patties on a baking sheet. Repeat procedure with remaining oil and uncooked patties. Bake latkes at 400° for 20 minutes, turning after 10 minutes. Sprinkle evenly with ¼ teaspoon salt. Serve latkes with horseradish cream. Yield: 5 servings (serving size: 2 latkes and about 1½ tablespoons horseradish cream).

CALORIES 201 (17% from fat); FAT 3.9g (sat 0.9g, mono 1.9g, poly 0.9g); PROTEIN 3.9g; CARB 37.6g; FIBER 5.3g; CHOL 5mg; IRON 1.1mg; SODIUM 571mg; CALC 71mg

Parsnip Gratin

White sauce and golden buttered bread-crumbs lend elegance to parsnips in this dish. Use a shallow 1½-quart baking dish or a gratin dish to get the most surface area for the crisp topping. Serve with roast beef or, for a vegetarian meal, with a big salad and bread.

- 2 pounds (1-inch-thick) slices peeled parsnip
- Cooking spray
- ½ cup chopped onion
- 2 garlic cloves, minced
- ¼ cup all-purpose flour
- 2 cups 2% reduced-fat milk, divided
- ½ teaspoon salt
- ⅛ teaspoon black pepper
- Dash of ground nutmeg
- 1 teaspoon chopped fresh sage
- 1 (1-ounce) slice white bread
- 1 tablespoon butter, melted

1. Place parsnip in a saucepan, and cover with water. Bring to a boil, reduce heat, and simmer over medium heat 20 minutes or until tender. Drain. Place parsnip in a bowl, and mash with a potato masher until smooth.

2. Preheat oven to 400°.

3. Heat a large nonstick skillet coated with cooking spray over medium-high heat. Add onion and garlic; sauté 3 minutes or until onion is tender. Add flour, stirring to coat onions. Gradually add ½ cup milk; stir constantly with a whisk until blended. Add remaining milk; cook over medium heat until thick (about 8 minutes), stirring constantly. Remove from heat; stir in salt, pepper, and nutmeg. Add milk mixture and sage to mashed parsnip; stir to combine. Place parsnip mixture in a shallow 1½-quart baking dish coated with cooking spray.

4. Place bread in a food processor; pulse 10 times or until coarse crumbs measure ½ cup. Combine breadcrumbs and butter, and sprinkle evenly over parsnip mixture. Bake at 400° for 25 minutes or until golden brown. Yield: 4 servings (serving size: about ¾ cup).

CALORIES 245 (22% from fat); FAT 6g (sat 3.4g, mono 1.7g, poly 0.3g); PROTEIN 7.5g; CARB 41.7g; FIBER 7.2g; CHOL 17mg; IRON 1.5mg; SODIUM 438mg; CALC 213mg

technique

Stock Options

Make the most of your turkey by turning it into flavorful stock for soups and sauces.

MAKE AHEAD • FREEZABLE
Rich Turkey Stock

The secret to rich stock is roasting the bones and vegetables. To encourage caramelization, cut the carcass into pieces that lie as flat as possible in the pan. If your turkey was larger than 12 pounds, you may have to cut it into smaller pieces than the recipe instructs.

    Carcass and skin from a cooked
        12-pound turkey
  2 carrots, each cut in half crosswise
  1 celery stalk, cut in half crosswise
  1 large onion, quartered
  1 whole garlic head, halved
  5 cups water
  3 (14-ounce) cans fat-free,
        less-sodium chicken broth
  ¼ teaspoon black peppercorns

1. Preheat oven to 425°.

2. Cut turkey carcass into quarters. Place carcass, skin, carrot, celery, onion, and garlic on a jelly roll pan or shallow roasting pan. Bake at 425° for 45 minutes, stirring once.

3. Place bones and vegetable mixture, water, broth, and peppercorns in a large stockpot. Bring to a boil; cover, reduce heat, and simmer 2 hours. Strain mixture through a sieve into a bowl, reserving stock. Discard solids. Cover and chill stock 8 hours or overnight. Skim solidified fat from surface; discard fat. Yield: 9 cups (serving size: 1 cup).

NOTE: Store the turkey stock in an airtight container in the refrigerator up to 1 week, or freeze up to 3 months.

CALORIES 53 (34% from fat); FAT 2g (sat 0.6g, mono 0.6g, poly 0.5g); PROTEIN 7.3g; CARB 0.5g; FIBER 0g; CHOL 17mg; IRON 0.4mg; SODIUM 257mg; CALC 5mg

MAKE AHEAD • FREEZABLE
Broccoli Rabe, Butternut Squash, and White Bean Soup

To make this simple-to-prepare soup even easier, look for chopped peeled squash in the produce section of your supermarket. If you're unable to find broccoli rabe, substitute escarole.

  2 cups (¾-inch) cubed peeled
        butternut squash
    Cooking spray
  1 tablespoon olive oil, divided
  8 ounces broccoli rabe (rapini),
        trimmed
  ½ cup finely chopped onion
  1 garlic clove, minced
  4½ cups Rich Turkey Stock (recipe at
        left)
  1 (16-ounce) can cannellini beans
        or other white beans, rinsed and
        drained
  ¼ teaspoon salt

1. Preheat oven to 450°.

2. Arrange squash in a single layer on a jelly roll pan coated with cooking spray. Drizzle with 1½ teaspoons oil; toss well to coat. Bake at 450° for 25 minutes or until lightly browned. Set aside.

3. Cut broccoli rabe crosswise into thirds. Cook broccoli rabe in boiling water 5 minutes; drain. Set aside.

4. Heat 1½ teaspoons oil in a large saucepan over medium heat. Add onion and garlic; cook 5 minutes, stirring frequently. Add squash, stock, and beans; cook 10 minutes. Place 1½ cups vegetable mixture in a blender or food processor; process until smooth. Return puréed mixture to pan; stir in broccoli rabe and salt. Cook 5 minutes or until thoroughly heated. Yield: 4 servings (serving size: 1¾ cups).

CALORIES 195 (28% from fat); FAT 6g (sat 1.1g, mono 3.2g, poly 0.9g); PROTEIN 15.4g; CARB 26g; FIBER 6.9g; CHOL 19mg; IRON 2.2mg; SODIUM 756mg; CALC 100mg

MAKE AHEAD
Curried Couscous, Spinach, and Roasted Tomato Soup

Israeli couscous is toasted semolina pasta; each grain is about half the size of a green pea. Even in hot soup, this kind of couscous retains al dente firmness for a long time.

  4 plum tomatoes, each cut into 8
        wedges (about ¾ pound)
  1 teaspoon olive oil
  1 teaspoon butter
  1 cup finely chopped onion
  ½ cup uncooked toasted Israeli
        couscous
  1½ teaspoons curry powder
  ¼ teaspoon salt
  1 garlic clove, minced
  4½ cups Rich Turkey Stock (recipe at
        left)
  1 (6-ounce) package fresh baby
        spinach

1. Preheat oven to 450°.

2. Combine tomato wedges and oil on a baking sheet lined with foil, tossing well to coat. Bake at 450° for 15 minutes or until tender and lightly browned.

3. Melt butter in a large saucepan over medium-high heat. Add onion, and sauté 3 minutes. Add couscous, curry, salt, and garlic; sauté 3 minutes. Add tomato

Continued

wedges and stock, and bring to a boil. Reduce heat, and simmer 7 minutes or until couscous is almost tender. Stir in spinach, and cook 2 minutes or just until spinach wilts. Yield: 4 servings (serving size: 1½ cups).

CALORIES 339 (15% from fat); FAT 5.8g (sat 1.5g, mono 1.9g, poly 1.3g); PROTEIN 18.6g; CARB 55.1g; FIBER 4.8g; CHOL 21mg; IRON 3.3mg; SODIUM 486mg; CALC 64mg

MAKE AHEAD
Blond Gravy

This light-colored gravy pairs nicely with pork, veal, or poultry. Quick-mixing flour dissolves in hot liquids without lumps. Look for it on the baking aisle of your grocery store.

    1   teaspoon butter
    ½   cup finely chopped onion
    ⅛   teaspoon fennel seeds
    1   garlic clove, halved
    ⅓   cup dry white wine
    1½ cups Rich Turkey Stock (recipe on
        page 383)
    2   (5-inch) thyme sprigs
    1   tablespoon quick-mixing flour
        (such as Wondra or Pillsbury
        Shake and Blend)
    ¼   teaspoon salt

1. Melt butter in a small saucepan over medium heat. Add onion; cook 4 minutes or until tender, stirring frequently. Add fennel and garlic; sauté 1 minute. Stir in wine; cook 1 minute. Add stock and thyme; bring to a boil. Reduce heat; simmer 10 minutes. Strain mixture through a sieve into a bowl; discard solids.
2. Return reserved liquid to pan. Gradually add flour and salt, stirring with a whisk. Bring to a boil; cook 1 minute or until slightly thick, stirring constantly with a whisk. Yield: 6 servings (serving size: about ¼ cup).

CALORIES 32 (31% from fat); FAT 1.1g (sat 0.5g, mono 0.3g, poly 0.2g); PROTEIN 2g; CARB 1.2g; FIBER 0g; CHOL 6mg; IRON 0.2mg; SODIUM 169mg; CALC 3mg

MAKE AHEAD • FREEZABLE
Escarole, Endive, and Pasta Soup

Save Parmesan cheese rind to flavor this simple Italian soup. Any small pasta, such as orecchiette, radiatore, or rotelle, works well in place of the seashells.

    1   tablespoon olive oil
    1   cup chopped carrot
    2   garlic cloves, minced
    6   cups Rich Turkey Stock (recipe on
        page 383)
    3   cups coarsely chopped escarole
    3   cups coarsely chopped curly
        endive
    1½ cups uncooked small seashell
        pasta
    ½   teaspoon salt
    1   (3-inch) piece Parmigiano-
        Reggiano cheese rind

1. Heat oil in a large saucepan over medium-low heat. Add carrot; cook 5 minutes, stirring occasionally. Add garlic; sauté 30 seconds. Stir in stock and remaining ingredients; bring to a boil. Cover, reduce heat, and simmer 7 minutes or until shells are tender. Discard rind. Yield: 4 servings (serving size: about 1½ cups).

CALORIES 258 (25% from fat); FAT 7.1g (sat 1.4g, mono 3.5g, poly 1.4g); PROTEIN 16.4g; CARB 31.2g; FIBER 4.4g; CHOL 25mg; IRON 2.6mg; SODIUM 707mg; CALC 64mg

MAKE AHEAD • FREEZABLE
Barley-Mushroom Soup

Sautéing the barley toasts it, which yields a light, nutty flavor.

    1½ teaspoons olive oil
    1½ cups chopped onion
    1   cup thinly sliced carrot
    1   (8-ounce) package presliced
        mushrooms
    ½   cup uncooked pearl barley
    4¾ cups Rich Turkey Stock (recipe on
        page 383)
    ⅓   cup finely chopped celery
    ½   teaspoon salt
    ½   teaspoon chopped fresh or
        ¼ teaspoon dried thyme

1. Heat oil in a large saucepan over medium-high heat. Add onion, carrot, and mushrooms; sauté 7 minutes or until golden brown. Stir in barley, and sauté 2 minutes. Add stock, celery, and salt, and bring to a boil. Cover, reduce heat, and simmer 20 minutes. Add thyme; cook 5 minutes. Yield: 4 servings (serving size: 1½ cups).

CALORIES 217 (19% from fat); FAT 4.7g (sat 1g, mono 2.1g, poly 1g); PROTEIN 13.9g; CARB 31.1g; FIBER 6.8g; CHOL 20mg; IRON 2mg; SODIUM 624mg; CALC 42mg

MAKE AHEAD
Porcini Mushroom Sauce

Dried porcini mushrooms impart a lot of flavor to this simple sauce, which pairs well with steak. Break large mushrooms into smaller pieces for easier measuring.

    2   tablespoons dried porcini
        mushrooms (about ⅛ ounce)
    ⅓   cup boiling water
    2   teaspoons butter
    ¼   cup finely chopped shallots
    ¼   cup medium dry sherry
    1¼ cups Rich Turkey Stock (recipe on
        page 383)
    ½   teaspoon minced fresh or
        ¼ teaspoon dried thyme
    1   tablespoon quick-mixing flour
        (such as Wondra or Pillsbury
        Shake and Blend)
    ¼   teaspoon salt
    ⅛   teaspoon freshly ground
        pepper

1. Combine mushrooms and ⅓ cup boiling water in a bowl; cover and let stand 15 minutes. Drain mushrooms in a colander over a bowl, reserving ¼ cup liquid. Rinse and drain mushrooms; finely chop.
2. Melt butter in a small saucepan over medium heat. Add shallots; cook 3 minutes or until tender, stirring frequently. Add sherry; cook 1 minute. Add mushrooms, reserved mushroom liquid, stock, and thyme; bring to a boil. Reduce heat; simmer 10 minutes. Gradually add flour, stirring with a whisk. Bring to a boil; cook 1 minute or until slightly thick, stirring constantly with a whisk. Stir in

salt and pepper. Yield: 6 servings (serving size: ¼ cup).

CALORIES 49 (33% from fat); FAT 1.8g (sat 0.9g, mono 0.6g, poly 0.2g); PROTEIN 2.8g; CARB 3.9g; FIBER 0.6g; CHOL 7mg; IRON 0.9mg; SODIUM 167mg; CALC 7mg

Leek and Potato Stew

If you're looking for a new version of potato soup, this recipe is for you. Part of the cooked potatoes are puréed, and then added to the stew to thicken it.

    2 bacon slices
    3 cups chopped leek
 4½ cups Rich Turkey Stock (recipe on page 383)
    4 cups cubed peeled Yukon gold potato
  ½ teaspoon salt
  ½ teaspoon chopped fresh or ¼ teaspoon dried thyme
    2 tablespoons chopped fresh flat-leaf parsley

1. Cook bacon in a large saucepan over medium-high heat until crisp. Add leek; cover, reduce heat to medium-low, and cook 3 minutes. Add stock, potato, salt, and thyme; bring to a boil. Reduce heat; simmer 15 minutes or until potato is tender. Remove 1 cup potato with a slotted spoon; place in a blender. Add ½ cup cooking liquid to blender; process until smooth. Return puréed mixture to pan. Sprinkle with parsley. Yield: 4 servings (serving size: 2 cups).

CALORIES 312 (26% from fat); FAT 9.1g (sat 3.1g, mono 3.7g, poly 1.5g); PROTEIN 13.4g; CARB 44.5g; FIBER 4.3g; CHOL 26mg; IRON 2.5mg; SODIUM 686mg; CALC 59mg

Turkey Caldo Tlalpeno

Named after a community on the outskirts of Mexico City—Tlalpan—this is a simple brothy soup studded with bits of turkey and chickpeas. If you've already eaten all the leftover turkey, chop some rotisserie chicken. Adjust the spice level to your taste by using more or less chipotle. We liked it spicy.

 1½ teaspoons olive oil
 1½ cups chopped onion
  ⅔ cup grape or cherry tomatoes, halved
    1 garlic clove, minced
 4½ cups Rich Turkey Stock (recipe on page 383)
    1 to 2 teaspoons minced canned chipotle chiles in adobo sauce
    1 (15½-ounce) can chickpeas (garbanzo beans), rinsed and drained
 1½ cups chopped cooked turkey
  ½ teaspoon salt
  ¼ cup thinly sliced green onions
    4 lime wedges

1. Heat oil in a large saucepan over medium heat. Add onion; cook 5 minutes or until tender, stirring frequently. Add tomato and garlic; cook 2 minutes, stirring frequently.
2. Add stock, chipotle, and chickpeas; bring to a simmer. Stir in turkey and salt. Cook 1 minute or until thoroughly heated. Top each serving with 1 tablespoon green onions. Serve with lime wedges. Yield: 4 servings (serving size: 2 cups soup and 1 lime wedge).

CALORIES 275 (27% from fat); FAT 8.4g (sat 1.8g, mono 3.2g, poly 2.5g); PROTEIN 27.8g; CARB 21g; FIBER 4.9g; CHOL 59mg; IRON 2.8mg; SODIUM 818mg; CALC 61mg

superfast

. . . And Ready in Just About 20 Minutes

Recipes with long ingredient lists can cook quickly. As proof, we offer Cashew Sweet-and-Sour Pork, and our Spinach, Chicken, and Feta Salad.

While each recipe has more than 15 ingredients, most are staples already on your pantry shelf. Try Coriander Chicken with Tomato-Corn Salad; despite the number of ingredients, two preparation steps are all you need to have supper on the table.

Cashew Sweet-and-Sour Pork

Stir-frying is fast but requires constant attention. To succeed, the ingredients must be ready to go before cooking begins. Once you start, keep stirring the food, maintaining medium-high heat.

    1 (3½-ounce) bag boil-in-bag long-grain rice
    2 tablespoons cornstarch, divided
    1 tablespoon sherry
    1 (1-pound) pork tenderloin, trimmed and cut into ½-inch pieces
  ⅓ cup water
  ¼ cup sugar
  ¼ cup cider vinegar
    3 tablespoons low-sodium soy sauce
    3 tablespoons ketchup
    1 tablespoon peanut oil
  ⅓ cup finely chopped unsalted dry-roasted cashews
  ¼ cup chopped green onions
    2 teaspoons bottled minced fresh ginger
    1 teaspoon bottled minced garlic
  ½ pound snow peas, trimmed
    1 (8-ounce) can pineapple chunks in juice, drained

1. Cook rice according to package directions, omitting salt and fat.
2. Combine 1 tablespoon cornstarch, sherry, and pork, tossing well. Combine 1 tablespoon cornstarch, water, sugar, vinegar, soy sauce, and ketchup, stirring with a whisk.
3. Heat peanut oil in a large nonstick skillet over medium-high heat. Add pork mixture; stir-fry 3 minutes. Add cashews, green onions, ginger, and garlic; stir-fry 1 minute. Add snow peas and pineapple; stir-fry 3 minutes or until snow peas are crisp-tender.
4. Add vinegar mixture to pan; bring to a boil. Cook 1 minute, stirring frequently. Serve pork mixture over rice. Yield: 4 servings (serving size: 1 cup pork mixture and ½ cup rice).

CALORIES 468 (25% from fat); FAT 13g (sat 3g, mono 6.5g, poly 2.6g); PROTEIN 30.4g; CARB 58.2g; FIBER 3.1g; CHOL 74mg; IRON 4.8mg; SODIUM 603mg; CALC 51mg

Asian Pork and Pineapple Salad

Arugula is widely available in ready-to-use salad packages. It's highly perishable, so check the package date for freshness.

- 1 (15¼-ounce) can pineapple chunks in juice, undrained
- 2 tablespoons fresh lime juice
- 1½ tablespoons fish sauce
- 1 teaspoon sugar
- 2 teaspoons bottled minced garlic
- ½ cup vertically sliced red onion
- ½ cup chopped fresh basil
- 1 tablespoon low-sodium soy sauce
- 1 teaspoon minced pickled jalapeños
- ½ teaspoon bottled minced fresh ginger
- 1 (1-pound) pork tenderloin, trimmed and cut into ¾-inch pieces
- 2 teaspoons vegetable oil
- 8 cups trimmed arugula or spinach (about 4 ounces)

1. Drain pineapple, reserving 1 tablespoon juice. Discard remaining pineapple juice. Set pineapple aside. Combine reserved pineapple juice, lime juice, fish sauce, sugar, and garlic.
2. Place reserved pineapple chunks, onion, and next 4 ingredients in a large bowl. Drizzle 2 tablespoons lime juice mixture over onion mixture; toss gently. Combine remaining lime juice mixture with pork, stirring well.
3. Heat oil in a large nonstick skillet over medium-high heat. Add pork, and sauté 3 minutes or until done. Add pork to onion mixture; toss well. Serve over arugula. Yield: 4 servings (serving size: 1 cup pork mixture and 2 cups arugula).

CALORIES 251 (24% from fat); FAT 6.6g (sat 1.7g, mono 2.3g, poly 1.9g); PROTEIN 26.3g; CARB 23g; FIBER 2.1g; CHOL 74mg; IRON 2.6mg; SODIUM 741mg; CALC 105mg

Spinach, Chicken, and Feta Salad

As the red onions in this salad cook, they become translucent, an appealing contrast to the dark green spinach.

- ¼ cup fat-free, less-sodium chicken broth
- ½ teaspoon grated lemon rind
- 1 tablespoon fresh lemon juice
- 1 tablespoon balsamic vinegar
- 1 teaspoon sugar
- 1 teaspoon bottled minced garlic
- 1 teaspoon Dijon mustard
- 1 teaspoon olive oil
- ½ teaspoon salt
- Cooking spray
- 1 pound skinless, boneless chicken breast
- ¼ teaspoon black pepper
- 1½ cups chopped red onion
- 1¼ cups (1-inch) pieces yellow bell pepper
- ½ cup (2 ounces) crumbled feta cheese
- 1 (15½-ounce) can chickpeas (garbanzo beans), rinsed and drained
- 1 (7-ounce) package prewashed baby spinach

1. Combine first 9 ingredients, stirring with a whisk.
2. Heat a large nonstick skillet coated with cooking spray over medium-high heat. Sprinkle chicken with black pepper. Add chicken to pan; cook 4 minutes. Turn chicken. Add onion; cook 4 minutes or until chicken is done and onion is tender, stirring onion frequently. Cut chicken into ½-inch-thick slices. Combine chicken, onion, bell pepper, cheese, chickpeas, and spinach in a large bowl. Drizzle vinaigrette over salad; toss gently to coat. Yield: 4 servings (serving size: 3 cups).

CALORIES 369 (29% from fat); FAT 11.8g (sat 3.4g, mono 3.1g, poly 1.7g); PROTEIN 37.1g; CARB 37.1g; FIBER 8g; CHOL 82mg; IRON 4.2mg; SODIUM 873mg; CALC 211mg

Fennel and Black Pepper-Crusted Lamb Chops

Crush the fennel seeds with a mortar and pestle, or use a heavy-duty zip-top plastic bag and a rolling pin.

- Cooking spray
- 1½ teaspoons fennel seeds, lightly crushed
- 1 teaspoon ground coriander
- ½ teaspoon salt
- ¾ teaspoon cracked black pepper
- ¼ teaspoon garlic powder
- 4 (4-ounce) lamb loin chops, trimmed

1. Heat a grill pan coated with cooking spray over medium-high heat until hot. Combine fennel seeds, coriander, salt, pepper, and garlic powder. Press mixture onto both sides of lamb. Add lamb to pan, and cook 5 minutes on each side or until desired degree of doneness. Yield: 2 servings (serving size: 2 lamb chops).

CALORIES 159 (40% from fat); FAT 7.1g (sat 2.4g, mono 2.9g, poly 0.4g); PROTEIN 20.7g; CARB 2g; FIBER 1.3g; CHOL 64mg; IRON 2mg; SODIUM 645mg; CALC 42mg

Ale-Steamed Mussels with French Bread

A pale ale, such as Sierra Nevada, is ideal for this juicy entrée because it's fruity and just a little bitter.

- 1 cup chopped tomato
- 1 cup ale or beer
- ½ cup bottled clam juice
- ⅓ cup chopped fresh parsley
- 2 tablespoons fresh lemon juice
- 1 tablespoon bottled minced garlic
- 2 pounds mussels, scrubbed and debearded (about 40 mussels)
- 4 (½-inch-thick) slices diagonally cut French bread baguette

1. Combine first 6 ingredients in a large stockpot; cover and bring to a boil. Add mussels; cover and cook 4 minutes or until shells open. Remove from heat; discard any unopened shells.

2. Place mussels and broth in each of 2 shallow bowls, and serve with bread. Yield: 2 servings (serving size: about 20 mussels, about 1 cup broth, and 2 bread slices).

CALORIES 434 (19% from fat); FAT 9.1g (sat 1.7g, mono 2.2g, poly 3.1g); PROTEIN 35.2g; CARB 43.8g; FIBER 3.2g; CHOL 73mg; IRON 10.4mg; SODIUM 780mg; CALC 80mg

Chicken Fattoosh Salad

The toasted pita pieces in this Middle Eastern salad add a toothsome crunch, much like croutons.

  2 (7-inch) pitas, cut into ½-inch pieces
  2 teaspoons olive oil
  1 pound chicken breast tenders, cut into ½-inch pieces
  ¼ teaspoon salt
  ¼ teaspoon black pepper
  1 cup ready-to-eat shelled soybeans (such as Melissa's)
  ¼ cup finely chopped cherry tomatoes
  ¼ cup dry white wine
  ¼ cup lemon juice
  1 teaspoon bottled minced garlic
  2 cups halved cherry tomatoes
  ½ cup vertically sliced Vidalia or other sweet onion
  3 tablespoons chopped fresh mint

1. Preheat broiler.
2. Arrange pitas in a single layer on a baking sheet, and broil 2 minutes or until toasted.
3. Heat oil in a large nonstick skillet over medium-high heat. Sprinkle chicken with salt and pepper. Add chicken to pan; sauté 2 minutes or until done. Add soybeans, chopped tomatoes, wine, lemon juice, and garlic; cook 1 minute or until thoroughly heated, stirring constantly. Combine chicken mixture, toasted pitas, halved tomatoes, onion, and mint, tossing gently. Yield: 4 servings (serving size: 1½ cups).

CALORIES 370 (21% from fat); FAT 8.7g (sat 1.3g, mono 2.9g, poly 2.9g); PROTEIN 38.6g; CARB 33.1g; FIBER 5.2g; CHOL 66mg; IRON 4.5mg; SODIUM 400mg; CALC 184mg

Cajun Shrimp and Rice

Bagged frozen vegetables work great in this spicy application. To thaw the vegetables quickly, place them in a colander, and rinse with hot water. Before sautéing, drain the thawed vegetables on paper towels.

  1 (3½-ounce) bag boil-in-bag long-grain rice
  2 tablespoons olive oil, divided
  2 pounds peeled and deveined large shrimp
  1 tablespoon salt-free Cajun seasoning
  1 tablespoon bottled minced garlic
  1 cup frozen bell pepper stir-fry (such as Bird's Eye), thawed
  ¼ cup chopped green onions
  ¼ teaspoon dried thyme
  ½ cup canned Italian-style stewed tomatoes, undrained
  ½ teaspoon salt
  ⅛ teaspoon black pepper

1. Cook rice according to package directions, omitting salt and fat.
2. While rice cooks, heat 1 tablespoon oil in a large nonstick skillet over medium-high heat. Sprinkle shrimp with Cajun seasoning; toss to coat. Add shrimp to pan; sauté 4 minutes or until done. Remove from pan; keep warm.
3. Heat 1 tablespoon oil in pan over medium-high heat. Add garlic; sauté 30 seconds. Add pepper stir-fry, green onions, and thyme; sauté 3 minutes or until tender. Stir in cooked rice, shrimp, tomatoes, salt, and pepper, and cook 1 minute or until thoroughly heated. Yield: 4 servings (serving size: 1¼ cups).

CALORIES 354 (25% from fat); FAT 9.8g (sat 1.5g, mono 5.4g, poly 1.8g); PROTEIN 37.4g; CARB 27g; FIBER 1.1g; CHOL 259mg; IRON 5.3mg; SODIUM 658mg; CALC 106mg

Coriander Chicken with Tomato-Corn Salad

Assemble all the ingredients, then start cooking the chicken. As the chicken sizzles, make the salad.

CHICKEN:
  1 tablespoon olive oil
  1½ teaspoons ground coriander
  ½ teaspoon salt
  ½ teaspoon ground cumin
  ¼ teaspoon chili powder
  ⅛ teaspoon ground cinnamon
  ⅛ teaspoon black pepper
  4 (6-ounce) skinless, boneless chicken breast halves

SALAD:
  2 cups cherry tomatoes, halved
  ¼ cup sliced green onion tops
  2 tablespoons thinly sliced fresh basil
  1 tablespoon balsamic vinegar
  1 teaspoon olive oil
  ¼ teaspoon salt
  ⅛ teaspoon black pepper
  1 (7-ounce) can whole-kernel corn, drained

1. To prepare chicken, heat 1 tablespoon oil in a large nonstick skillet over medium-high heat. Combine coriander and next 5 ingredients; rub evenly over both sides of chicken. Add chicken to pan; cook 5 minutes on each side or until done.
2. To prepare salad, combine tomato and remaining 7 ingredients, tossing well. Slice chicken; serve over salad. Yield: 4 servings (serving size: about 4½ ounces chicken and ¾ cup salad).

CALORIES 296 (23% from fat); FAT 7.4g (sat 1.3g, mono 4g, poly 1.1g); PROTEIN 42g; CARB 14.7g; FIBER 3.6g; CHOL 99mg; IRON 3.6mg; SODIUM 664mg; CALC 111mg

Sausage and Pepper Subs

Serve this sandwich with a knife and fork.

  1 teaspoon olive oil
  12 ounces sweet Italian turkey sausage, cut into ½-inch pieces
  2 teaspoons bottled minced garlic
  ¼ teaspoon fennel seeds, crushed
  3 cups frozen bell pepper stir-fry (such as Bird's Eye), thawed
  1 (12-ounce) bottle marinara sauce
  1 teaspoon balsamic vinegar
  4 (2½-ounce) hoagie rolls, split lengthwise

Continued

1. Heat oil in a large nonstick skillet over medium-high heat. Add sausage, and cook 7 minutes or until lightly browned, stirring occasionally. Add garlic and fennel to pan; sauté 30 seconds. Stir in bell pepper stir-fry and marinara sauce, and bring to a boil. Reduce heat, and simmer 5 minutes. Stir in vinegar.

2. Spoon 1 cup sausage mixture into each hoagie roll. Yield: 4 servings (serving size 1 sandwich).

CALORIES 403 (29% from fat); FAT 13.2g (sat 3.4g, mono 5.7g, poly 3.2g); PROTEIN 22.9g; CARB 47.8g; FIBER 4.3g; CHOL 72mg; IRON 4.7mg; SODIUM 1,160mg; CALC 165mg

---

QUICK & EASY

Hoisin Barbecue Chicken Breasts

The basting sauce for this dish is sticky. Line the broiler pan with aluminum foil, and coat with cooking spray for easy cleanup. Serve with basmati rice and a spinach salad sprinkled with sesame seeds.

¼ cup hoisin sauce
2 tablespoons honey
1 tablespoon rice vinegar
1 teaspoon dark sesame oil
2 teaspoons cornstarch
2 teaspoons water
¼ teaspoon salt
¼ teaspoon garlic powder
¼ teaspoon ground ginger
¼ teaspoon black pepper
⅛ teaspoon five-spice powder
4 (6-ounce) skinless, boneless chicken breast halves
Cooking spray

1. Preheat broiler.

2. While broiler heats, combine hoisin, honey, vinegar, and oil in a small saucepan; bring to a boil over medium-high heat. Combine cornstarch and water; add to hoisin mixture, stirring with a whisk. Bring to a boil; cook 1 minute, stirring constantly. Remove mixture from heat.

3. Combine salt and next 4 ingredients; rub evenly over both sides of chicken. Place chicken on a broiler pan coated with cooking spray, and broil 5 minutes. Brush with hoisin mixture, and broil

4 minutes. Turn chicken; brush with hoisin mixture. Broil 4 minutes or until done, basting frequently with hoisin mixture. Yield: 4 servings (serving size: 1 chicken breast half).

CALORIES 273 (13% from fat); FAT 3.8g (sat 0.8g, mono 1.1g, poly 1.2g); PROTEIN 39.9g; CARB 17.8g; FIBER 0.6g; CHOL 99mg; IRON 1.6mg; SODIUM 515mg; CALC 26mg

---

QUICK & EASY

Chicken Cordon Bleu Pasta

The flavors of the classic French recipe are recast in this simple pasta dish. We used roasted chicken purchased in the meat department to speed things up.

8 ounces uncooked medium egg noodles
¼ cup all-purpose flour
2 cups fat-free milk, divided
1 tablespoon Dijon mustard
1½ cups (6 ounces) shredded Jarlsberg cheese
2 cups chopped roasted skinless, boneless chicken breast
1 cup frozen peas, thawed
1 cup (4 ounces) diced lean deli ham
¼ teaspoon black pepper

1. Cook noodles according to package directions, omitting salt and fat.

2. While noodles cook, lightly spoon flour into a dry measuring cup, and level with a knife. Combine flour and ¼ cup milk in a heavy saucepan, stirring with a whisk until smooth. Place pan over medium heat; whisk in 1¾ cups milk and mustard. Cook 6 minutes or until mixture begins to thicken, stirring frequently. Reduce heat to low. Add cheese, stirring until melted. Stir in chicken, peas, ham, and pepper. Serve over noodles. Yield: 4 servings (serving size: 1¼ cups chicken mixture and 1 cup noodles).

CALORIES 587 (25% from fat); FAT 16.5g (sat 8.5g, mono 4g, poly 1.3g); PROTEIN 48.6g; CARB 59.7g; FIBER 3.6g; CHOL 146mg; IRON 3.9mg; SODIUM 731mg; CALC 593mg

---

Southwestern Holiday Brunch

Let hot chiles, fresh tortillas, and creamy refried beans define your next family gathering.

Southwestern Holiday Brunch Menu
serves 8

New Mexican Hot Chocolate

Green Chile-Chicken Casserole

Pork Marinated in Chile Colorado

Red Chile Potatoes

Refried Beans

Sautéed Spinach with Chopped Egg

Tere's White Flour Tortillas

Bread Pudding with Colby Cheese

QUICK & EASY

New Mexican Hot Chocolate

½ cup water
⅓ cup honey
5 tablespoons unsweetened cocoa
½ teaspoon ground cinnamon
⅛ teaspoon ground nutmeg
¼ teaspoon salt
4 cups 2% reduced-fat milk
1 teaspoon vanilla extract

1. Combine first 6 ingredients in a large, heavy saucepan. Bring to a boil over medium-high heat, stirring constantly. Gradually add milk and extract, stirring constantly with a whisk. Heat to 180° or until tiny bubbles form around edge, stirring with a whisk (do not boil). Yield: 8 servings (serving size: about ⅔ cup).

CALORIES 117 (23% from fat); FAT 3g (sat 1.8g, mono 0.2g, poly 0g); PROTEIN 4.8g; CARB 19.9g; FIBER 1.2g; CHOL 10mg; IRON 0.6mg; SODIUM 137mg; CALC 132mg

Green Chile-Chicken Casserole

Just about every New Mexican home has a favorite version of this recipe. In the old days, canned soup wasn't available, but now cooks have the convenience of canned cream of chicken soup. Leftover turkey works in this recipe, too. If you assemble the casserole the day before, cover it with cooking spray-coated foil. When ready to serve, bake 1 hour; then uncover and bake an additional 30 minutes or until the cheese is bubbly and begins to brown.

1⅓ cups fat-free, less-sodium chicken broth
1 cup canned chopped green chiles, drained
1 cup chopped onion
1 cup fat-free sour cream
¾ teaspoon salt
½ teaspoon ground cumin
½ teaspoon freshly ground black pepper
2 (10½-ounce) cans condensed 98%-fat-free cream of chicken soup, undiluted (such as Campbell's)
1 garlic clove, minced
Cooking spray
24 (6-inch) corn tortillas
4 cups shredded cooked chicken breast (about 1 pound)
2 cups (8 ounces) finely shredded sharp Cheddar cheese

1. Preheat oven to 350°.
2. Combine first 9 ingredients in a large saucepan, stirring with a whisk. Bring to a boil, stirring constantly. Remove from heat.
3. Spread 1 cup soup mixture in a 13 x 9-inch baking dish coated with cooking spray. Arrange 6 tortillas over soup mixture, and top with 1 cup chicken and ½ cup cheese. Repeat layers 3 times, ending with cheese. Spread remaining soup mixture over cheese. Bake at 350° for 30 minutes or until bubbly. Yield: 12 servings (serving size: about ¾ cup).

CALORIES 335 (29% from fat); FAT 10.8g (sat 5.9g, mono 2.7g, poly 1.2g); PROTEIN 23.9g; CARB 34.3g; FIBER 3.2g; CHOL 66mg; IRON 1.5mg; SODIUM 693mg; CALC 270mg

Pork Marinated in Chile Colorado

Serve this as an entrée wrapped in warm flour tortillas, or pair it with eggs cooked over easy and potatoes for breakfast.

4 cups Chile Colorado (recipe on page 390)
1 teaspoon dried oregano
½ teaspoon salt
2 pounds boneless pork loin, trimmed and cut into ½-inch strips
Cooking spray

1. Combine first 3 ingredients in a large zip-top plastic bag. Add pork; toss to coat. Marinate in refrigerator overnight, turning occasionally.
2. Preheat oven to 300°.
3. Place pork and marinade in an 11 x 7-inch baking dish coated with cooking spray; cover with foil. Bake at 300° for 1 hour. Increase oven temperature to 350° (do not remove pork from oven); remove foil, and bake 30 minutes. Remove pork from oven; shred with 2 forks. Yield: 8 servings (serving size: about ½ cup).

CALORIES 223 (33% from fat); FAT 8.1g (sat 2.8g, mono 3.4g, poly 1g); PROTEIN 25.8g; CARB 11.6g; FIBER 4.4g; CHOL 62mg; IRON 1.9mg; SODIUM 660mg; CALC 26mg

Red Chile Potatoes
(pictured on page 363)

3 pounds red potatoes, cut into 1-inch pieces (about 10 cups)
3 tablespoons vegetable oil, divided
½ cup chopped green onions
½ cup Chile Colorado (recipe on page 390)
1¼ teaspoons salt

1. Place potato in a Dutch oven. Cover with water; bring to a boil. Reduce heat; simmer 20 minutes or until tender. Drain.
2. Heat 1½ tablespoons vegetable oil in a large nonstick skillet over medium-high heat. Add half of potato; sauté 8 minutes or until lightly browned. Remove from pan. Repeat procedure with remaining oil and potato. Place potato, onions, Chile Colorado, and salt

in pan, and cook over medium heat 1 minute or until thoroughly heated, stirring constantly. Yield: 8 servings (serving size: 1 cup).

CALORIES 177 (28% from fat); FAT 5.5g (sat 0.4g, mono 3g, poly 1.7g); PROTEIN 3.7g; CARB 28.9g; FIBER 3.6g; CHOL 0mg; IRON 1.5mg; SODIUM 437mg; CALC 23mg

Refried Beans

These beans can be made ahead and frozen either whole or refried. They taste great as a side dish, or in tacos, burritos, quesadillas, or nachos. They're best when they've sat overnight.

3 cups dried pinto beans
20 cups water, divided
2 ounces salt pork
2 large garlic cloves, minced
1¼ teaspoons salt
1½ cups (6 ounces) shredded sharp Cheddar cheese

1. Sort and wash beans; place in a pressure cooker. Add 10 cups water. Close lid securely; bring to high pressure over high heat (about 7 minutes). Cook 3 minutes. Remove from heat; place pressure cooker under cold running water. Remove lid. Drain beans, discarding liquid.
2. Return beans to pressure cooker. Add 10 cups water, salt pork, and garlic. Close lid securely; bring to high pressure over high heat (about 7 minutes). Adjust heat to medium or level to maintain high pressure; cook 1 hour. Remove from heat; place pressure cooker under cold running water. Remove lid.
3. Discard salt pork. Cool beans to room temperature.
4. Drain beans, reserving 1 cup cooking liquid. Heat a large nonstick skillet over medium heat. Add beans, reserved cooking liquid, and salt. Mash bean mixture with a potato masher to desired consistency. Cook 5 minutes or until thoroughly heated. Sprinkle with cheese. Yield: 12 servings (serving size: ½ cup).
NOTE: To prepare in a pan: Sort and wash beans, and place in a large Dutch oven.
Continued

Cover with water to 2 inches above beans; bring to a boil. Cook 2 minutes; remove from heat. Cover and let stand 1 hour. Drain beans. Add beans, 10 cups water, salt pork, and garlic to pan; bring to a boil. Cover, reduce heat, and simmer 1 hour and 45 minutes or until beans are tender. Continue with Steps 3 and 4.

CALORIES 242 (28% from fat); FAT 7.5g (sat 4.3g, mono 1g, poly 0.4g); PROTEIN 13.2g; CARB 30.8g; FIBER 11.8g; CHOL 17mg; IRON 2.9mg; SODIUM 373mg; CALC 160mg

MAKE AHEAD

Sautéed Spinach with Chopped Egg

3   large eggs
1   teaspoon vegetable oil, divided
1   cup chopped onion, divided
1   teaspoon crushed red pepper, divided
5   (6-ounce) packages fresh baby spinach, divided
¾   teaspoon salt
¼   teaspoon freshly ground black pepper

1. Place eggs in a large saucepan. Cover with water to 1 inch above eggs, and bring just to a boil. Remove from heat. Cover and let stand 15 minutes. Drain and rinse with cold running water until cool. Remove shells. Cut 2 eggs in half lengthwise, and remove and discard yolks. Coarsely chop egg whites and remaining egg.
2. Heat ½ teaspoon oil in a large Dutch oven over medium-high heat. Add ½ cup onion, and sauté 5 minutes or until browned. Add ½ teaspoon red pepper; sauté 30 seconds. Add half of spinach, and sauté 3 minutes or until wilted. Remove from pan. Repeat procedure with remaining oil, onion, red pepper, and spinach. Place spinach mixture in a colander; drain well. Return spinach mixture to pan; stir in salt and black pepper. Sauté over medium-high heat 2 minutes or until thoroughly heated. Sprinkle with chopped egg. Yield: 8 servings (serving size: about ⅓ cup).

CALORIES 52 (29% from fat); FAT 1.7g (sat 0.3g, mono 0.6g, poly 0.4g); PROTEIN 5g; CARB 5.8g; FIBER 3.4g; CHOL 27mg; IRON 3mg; SODIUM 326mg; CALC 114mg

Tere's White Flour Tortillas

4   cups all-purpose flour
2   teaspoons baking powder
2   teaspoons salt
6   tablespoons vegetable shortening
1½ cups hot water
1   tablespoon nonfat dry milk

1. Lightly spoon flour into dry measuring cups; level with a knife. Combine flour, baking powder, and salt in a large bowl. Cut in shortening with a pastry blender or 2 knives until mixture resembles coarse meal; make a well in center of mixture. Combine hot water and dry milk, and add to flour mixture. Stir until blended. Cover and let rest 20 minutes.
2. Divide dough into 18 equal portions, shaping each portion into a ball (cover remaining dough to prevent drying). Working with one ball at a time, roll ball into a 7-inch round. Heat a cast iron skillet over medium-high heat. Cook round 1 minute on each side or until lightly browned. Yield: 18 tortillas (serving size: 1 tortilla).

CALORIES 126 (29% from fat); FAT 4g (sat 1g, mono 1.3g, poly 1g); PROTEIN 2.8g; CARB 20.6g; FIBER 0.7g; CHOL 0mg; IRON 1.3mg; SODIUM 306mg; CALC 30mg

Bread Pudding with Colby Cheese

1¼ cups hot water
1   cup raisins
1   cup packed brown sugar
1½ teaspoons ground cinnamon
1   tablespoon butter
14 ounces dense white bread, toasted and cubed
    Cooking spray
1¾ cups (7 ounces) shredded colby or white Cheddar cheese
⅓   cup heavy cream
    Powdered sugar (optional)

1. Preheat oven to 350°.
2. Combine water and raisins; let stand 10 minutes or until raisins plump. Drain raisins over a bowl, reserving soaking liquid. Combine soaking liquid, brown sugar, and cinnamon in a large saucepan; bring to a boil. Reduce heat; simmer 15 minutes. Stir in butter.
3. Arrange half of bread in bottom of a 13 x 9-inch baking dish coated with cooking spray. Top with half of cheese and half of raisins. Repeat layers, ending with raisins. Pour sugar liquid over bread. Cover with foil coated with cooking spray. Bake at 350° for 1 hour or until set.
4. Place cream in a medium bowl, and beat with a mixer at high speed until stiff peaks form. Sprinkle bread pudding with powdered sugar, if desired, and serve with whipped cream. Yield: 14 servings (serving size: about ⅔ cup bread pudding and about 1½ teaspoons whipped cream).

CALORIES 244 (30% from fat); FAT 8.2g (sat 4.8g, mono 2.2g, poly 0.3g); PROTEIN 6.3g; CARB 39.7g; FIBER 2.1g; CHOL 25mg; IRON 1.2mg; SODIUM 250mg; CALC 141mg

MAKE AHEAD

Chile Colorado

½   pound dried New Mexico chiles
5   cups fat-free, less-sodium chicken broth, divided
4   garlic cloves, peeled
1   teaspoon salt

1. Preheat broiler.
2. Remove stems and seeds from chiles; discard. Rinse chiles with cold water; drain. Arrange chiles in a single layer on a baking sheet. Broil 20 seconds on each side or until lightly toasted (be careful not to burn chiles).
3. Bring 4 quarts water to a boil in a large Dutch oven over medium-high heat. Stir in chiles, and cover. Remove from heat, and let stand 30 minutes or until soft. Drain.
4. Place half of chiles, 2½ cups broth, and garlic in a blender; process until smooth. Pour puréed mixture into a large bowl; repeat procedure with remaining chiles and broth. Strain chile mixture through a sieve into a large saucepan, and discard solids. Stir in salt. Cook over medium heat 30 minutes, stirring occasionally. Yield: 5 cups (serving size: ½ cup).

CALORIES 61 (13% from fat); FAT 0.9g (sat 0.1g, mono 0.1g, poly 0.5g); PROTEIN 3.2g; CARB 11.5g; FIBER 2g; CHOL 0mg; IRON 0.9mg; SODIUM 474mg; CALC 9mg

New Flavors for the Holiday

Give this Italian-inspired menu a try.

Nontraditional Thanksgiving Menu

serves 8

Orange, Arugula, and Kalamata Olive Salad

Herb, Garlic, and Mustard-Crusted Fillet of Beef

Creamy Two-Cheese Polenta

Ciabatta

Chocolate-Walnut Meringue Pie

Sautéed Leeks and Broccolini with Balsamic Vinegar

WINE NOTE: This menu needs two wines—a fresh, crisp white to accompany the orange-olive salad, and a well structured, powerful red for the beef. For the white, try St. Supéry Sauvignon Blanc 2002 from Napa Valley, California ($16); for the red, Château St. Jean Cabernet Sauvignon 2000 from Sonoma County, California ($22).

QUICK & EASY
Orange, Arugula, and Kalamata Olive Salad

Use blood oranges if you can find them.

- 2 tablespoons fresh lemon juice
- 1½ teaspoons extravirgin olive oil
- ½ teaspoon salt
- ⅛ teaspoon freshly ground black pepper
- 8 cups trimmed arugula (about 8 ounces)
- 2 cups thinly sliced fennel bulb
- ¾ cup vertically sliced red onion
- 12 sliced pitted kalamata olives
- 2 cups coarsely chopped orange sections (about 2 pounds)

1. Combine first 4 ingredients. Combine arugula, fennel, onion, and olives in a large bowl. Drizzle lemon mixture over arugula mixture; toss gently to coat. Top with orange sections. Yield: 8 servings (serving size: about 1¼ cups).

CALORIES 62 (38% from fat); FAT 2.6g (sat 0.3g, mono 1.8g, poly 0.3g); PROTEIN 1.4g; CARB 9.4g; FIBER 2.3g; CHOL 0mg; IRON 0.6mg; SODIUM 254mg; CALC 65mg

Herb, Garlic, and Mustard-Crusted Fillet of Beef

To make a sauce for the beef, deglaze the pan with red wine, and reduce it.

- 1 (2-pound) beef tenderloin, trimmed
- Cooking spray
- ¾ teaspoon salt
- ¼ teaspoon freshly ground black pepper
- 3 tablespoons Dijon mustard
- ¼ cup chopped fresh basil
- ¼ cup chopped fresh parsley
- 1 tablespoon chopped fresh thyme
- 1 tablespoon chopped fresh oregano
- 3 garlic cloves, minced

1. Preheat oven to 400°.
2. Place beef on broiler pan coated with cooking spray, and sprinkle with salt and pepper. Spread mustard evenly over beef. Combine remaining ingredients; pat evenly over beef.
3. Insert a meat thermometer into thickest portion of beef. Bake at 400° for 40 minutes or until thermometer registers 145° (medium-rare) or desired degree of doneness.

4. Transfer beef to a cutting board. Cover loosely with foil, and let stand 10 minutes before slicing. Yield: 8 servings (serving size: 3 ounces).

CALORIES 154 (43% from fat); FAT 7.4g (sat 2.6g, mono 2.8g, poly 0.4g); PROTEIN 19.8g; CARB 1.4g; FIBER 0.3g; CHOL 57mg; IRON 2.8mg; SODIUM 404mg; CALC 23mg

---

STAFF FAVORITE • MAKE AHEAD
Creamy Two-Cheese Polenta

If you're not serving this immediately, keep the polenta warm by covering it and placing it over very low heat. Stir occasionally.

- 4 cups 1% low-fat milk
- 1 cup water
- 1¼ teaspoons salt
- ¼ teaspoon freshly ground black pepper
- 1¼ cups instant dry polenta
- ⅓ cup (about 2½ ounces) mascarpone cheese
- ⅓ cup (about 1½ ounces) grated Parmigiano-Reggiano cheese

1. Combine first 4 ingredients in a medium saucepan over medium-high heat. Bring to a boil; gradually add polenta, stirring constantly with a whisk. Cook 2 minutes or until thick, stirring constantly. Remove from heat; stir in cheeses. Serve immediately. Yield: 8 servings (serving size: about ⅔ cup).

CALORIES 206 (28% from fat); FAT 6.4g (sat 3.7g, mono 0.7g, poly 0.1g); PROTEIN 8.5g; CARB 28.7g; FIBER 2.5g; CHOL 19mg; IRON 0.6mg; SODIUM 493mg; CALC 207mg

---

MAKE AHEAD
Ciabatta

This bread gets its name from its shape; *ciabatta* is Italian for "slipper."

SPONGE:
- 1 cup bread flour
- ½ cup warm fat-free milk (100° to 110°)
- ¼ cup warm water (100° to 110°)
- 1 tablespoon honey
- 1 package dry yeast (about 2¼ teaspoons)

Continued

DOUGH:

3½ cups bread flour, divided
½ cup semolina or pasta flour
¾ cup warm water (100° to 110°)
½ cup warm fat-free milk (100° to 110°)
1½ teaspoons salt
1 package dry yeast (about 2¼ teaspoons)
3 tablespoons semolina or pasta flour, divided

1. To prepare sponge, lightly spoon 1 cup flour into a dry measuring cup; level with a knife. Combine 1 cup flour and next 4 ingredients in a large bowl, stirring well with a whisk. Cover; chill 12 hours.
2. To prepare dough, let sponge stand at room temperature 30 minutes. Lightly spoon 3½ cups bread flour and ½ cup semolina flour into dry measuring cups, and level with a knife. Add 3 cups bread flour, ½ cup semolina flour, ¾ cup warm water, ½ cup warm milk, salt, and 1 package yeast to sponge, and stir well to form a soft dough. Turn dough out onto a floured surface. Knead until smooth and elastic (about 8 minutes), and add enough of remaining bread flour, 1 tablespoon at a time, to prevent dough from sticking to hands. Divide dough in half.
3. Working with 1 portion at a time (cover remaining dough to prevent drying), roll each into a 13 x 5-inch oval. Place, 3 inches apart, on a large baking sheet sprinkled with 2 tablespoons semolina flour. Taper ends of dough to form a "slipper." Sprinkle 1 tablespoon semolina flour over dough. Cover and let rise in a warm place (85°), free from drafts, 45 minutes or until doubled in size.
4. Preheat oven to 425°.
5. Uncover dough. Bake at 425° for 18 minutes or until loaves are lightly browned and sound hollow when tapped. Remove from pan, and cool on a wire rack. Yield: 2 loaves, 16 servings (serving size: 1 slice).

CALORIES 150 (1% from fat); FAT 0.1g (sat 0g, mono 0.1g, poly 0g); PROTEIN 6.3g; CARB 32.1g; FIBER 1.3g; CHOL 0mg; IRON 2.1mg; SODIUM 227mg; CALC 21mg

MAKE AHEAD

Chocolate-Walnut Meringue Pie

(pictured on page 364)

Place plastic wrap over the filling to keep it warm while you make the meringue. Spreading the meringue over warm filling helps it adhere. Use a knife dipped in hot water to slice the pie.

CRUST:

1½ cups low-fat graham cracker crumbs (about 10 cookie sheets)
½ cup finely ground walnuts
¼ cup butter, melted
Cooking spray

FILLING:

¾ cup sugar
3½ tablespoons cornstarch
Dash of salt
2 cups evaporated fat-free milk
4 ounces semisweet chocolate, finely chopped
3 large egg yolks, lightly beaten
1 teaspoon vanilla extract

MERINGUE:

4 large egg whites
¼ teaspoon cream of tartar
¼ teaspoon salt
½ cup sugar
1 teaspoon vanilla extract

1. Preheat oven to 350°.
2. To prepare crust, combine first 3 ingredients, tossing well. Press into bottom and up sides of a 9-inch pie plate coated with cooking spray. Bake at 350° for 15 minutes or until lightly browned. Cool completely on a wire rack.
3. To prepare filling, combine ¾ cup sugar, cornstarch, and dash of salt in a medium saucepan; whisk in milk and chocolate. Bring to a boil over medium heat, stirring constantly. Cook 1 minute, stirring constantly. Remove from heat. Gradually add ½ cup chocolate mixture to egg yolks, stirring constantly with a whisk. Return egg mixture to pan. Cook over medium heat until thick (about 4 minutes), stirring constantly. Stir in 1 teaspoon vanilla. Spread into prepared crust. Cover surface of mixture with plastic wrap.

4. Reduce oven temperature to 325°.
5. To prepare meringue, place egg whites, cream of tartar, and ¼ teaspoon salt in a large bowl. Beat with a mixer at high speed until foamy. Add ½ cup sugar, 1 tablespoon at a time; beat until stiff peaks form. Add 1 teaspoon vanilla; beat just until blended. Remove plastic wrap from filling. Spread meringue evenly over filling, sealing to edge of crust.
6. Bake at 325° for 25 minutes. Cool 1 hour on a wire rack. Chill 3 hours or until pie is set. Yield: 12 servings (serving size: 1 wedge).

CALORIES 344 (30% from fat); FAT 11.4g (sat 5g, mono 2.9g, poly 2g); PROTEIN 8.5g; CARB 53.5g; FIBER 1.7g; CHOL 65mg; IRON 1.3mg; SODIUM 218mg; CALC 146mg

QUICK & EASY

Sautéed Leeks and Broccolini with Balsamic Vinegar

To enjoy it at its best, prepare this dish last, and serve immediately.

4 center-cut bacon slices
1 pound broccolini, trimmed and cut in half crosswise
2 leeks, halved lengthwise and cut diagonally into 2-inch pieces (about 1 pound)
¼ teaspoon dried oregano
¼ teaspoon crushed red pepper
4 garlic cloves, thinly sliced
¼ cup fat-free, less-sodium chicken broth
1½ tablespoons balsamic vinegar
¾ teaspoon salt

1. Cook bacon in a large nonstick skillet over medium-high heat until crisp. Remove bacon from pan; reserve 2 teaspoons drippings in pan. Crumble bacon; set aside. Add broccolini and leeks to drippings in pan; sauté 4 minutes. Add oregano, pepper, and garlic; sauté 3 minutes. Stir in remaining ingredients; cook 30 seconds or until liquid almost evaporates. Sprinkle with crumbled bacon. Serve immediately. Yield: 8 servings (serving size: about ¾ cup).

CALORIES 81 (32% from fat); FAT 2.9g (sat 1.1g, mono 1.2g, poly 0.4g); PROTEIN 3.8g; CARB 10.6g; FIBER 1.5g; CHOL 4mg; IRON 1.5mg; SODIUM 316mg; CALC 70mg

Honoring Hanukkah

Celebrate the holiday of light with this make-ahead menu for eight.

Vegetarian Hanukkah Menu
serves 8

Sweet-and-Sour Beet, Cabbage, and Tomato Soup

Multigrain Honey Bread

Eggplant and Green Pepper Kugel

Carrot-Wheat Berry Salad with Cumin and Raisins

Mashed Potato Latkes with Zucchini and Dill

Pear Applesauce

Poached Figs in Wine

MAKE AHEAD
Sweet-and-Sour Beet, Cabbage, and Tomato Soup

This soup is similar to the Polish and Russian soup borscht. Serve hot or cold.

4½ cups water
6 cups shredded cabbage (about 1 pound)
2 cups chopped onion
2 cups diced peeled beets (about 1 pound)
1½ cups canned petite diced tomatoes, undrained
½ cup tomato sauce
¼ cup chopped peeled celeriac (celery root)
1 tablespoon brown sugar
¼ teaspoon salt
¼ teaspoon freshly ground black pepper
2 tablespoons golden raisins
1 tablespoon fresh lemon juice
½ cup sour cream
4 teaspoons grated lemon rind

1. Bring water to a boil in a Dutch oven. Add cabbage and next 8 ingredients; bring to a boil. Cover, reduce heat, and simmer 1 hour, stirring occasionally. Stir in raisins and juice. Simmer, partially covered, 15 minutes. Top with sour cream and rind. Yield: 8 servings (serving size: about 1 cup soup, 1 tablespoon sour cream, and ½ teaspoon rind).

CALORIES 114 (27% from fat); FAT 3.4g (sat 1.9g, mono 0.9g, poly 0.3g); PROTEIN 3.4g; CARB 20g; FIBER 4.8g; CHOL 6mg; IRON 1.3mg; SODIUM 295mg; CALC 75mg

MAKE AHEAD • FREEZABLE
Multigrain Honey Bread

Oats, whole wheat flour, bran flakes, and wheat germ make this bread full flavored.

⅓ cup honey
2 packages dry yeast (about 4½ teaspoons)
4 cups warm water (100° to 110°)
8 cups all-purpose flour, divided
2 cups whole wheat flour
2 cups regular oats
1 cup wheat bran flakes cereal (such as Bran Flakes)
1 cup toasted wheat germ
4 teaspoons salt
Cooking spray

1. Dissolve honey and yeast in warm water in a large bowl; let stand 5 minutes. Lightly spoon flours into dry measuring cups; level with a knife. Add 7 cups all-purpose flour, whole wheat flour, and next 4 ingredients to yeast mixture; stir well to form a stiff dough. Turn dough out onto a floured surface. Knead until smooth and elastic (about 8 minutes); add enough of remaining all-purpose flour, 1 tablespoon at a time, to prevent dough from sticking to hands (dough will feel tacky).
2. Place dough in a large bowl coated with cooking spray, turning to coat top. Cover and let rise in a warm place (85°), free from drafts, 45 minutes or until doubled in size. (Gently press two fingers into dough. If indentation remains, dough has risen enough.)

3. Punch dough down; cover and let rest 5 minutes. Divide in half. Working with one portion at a time (cover remaining dough to prevent drying), roll into a 15 x 8-inch rectangle on a floured surface. Roll up rectangle tightly, starting with a short edge, pressing firmly to eliminate air pockets; pinch seam and ends to seal. Place rolls, seam sides down, in 2 (9 x 5-inch) loaf pans coated with cooking spray. Cover and let rise 45 minutes or until doubled in size.
4. Preheat oven to 350°.
5. Uncover dough; bake at 350° for 40 minutes or until loaves are browned on bottom and sound hollow when tapped. Remove from pans; cool on wire racks. Yield: 2 loaves, 18 slices per loaf (serving size: 1 slice).

CALORIES 166 (6% from fat); FAT 1.1g (sat 0.2g, mono 0.2g, poly 0.5g); PROTEIN 5.6g; CARB 34.2g; FIBER 2.7g; CHOL 0mg; IRON 2.4mg; SODIUM 270mg; CALC 12mg

Eggplant and Green Pepper Kugel

Kugel is traditionally a baked pudding made with potato or noodles. This version uses matzo meal and eggplant for a more savory flavor and heartier texture.

1 large eggplant (about 2 pounds)
2 teaspoons vegetable oil
3 cups finely chopped onion
1½ cups finely chopped green bell pepper
3 tablespoons pine nuts
1 teaspoon salt
½ teaspoon freshly ground black pepper
2 large eggs, lightly beaten
¾ cup matzo meal
Cooking spray
1 teaspoon paprika

1. Preheat oven to 450°.
2. Pierce eggplant several times with a fork; place on a foil-lined baking sheet.
Continued

Bake at 450° for 20 minutes or until tender. Cool slightly; peel and chop. Place in a large bowl.

3. Heat oil in a large nonstick skillet over medium-high heat. Add onion, bell pepper, and nuts. Cook 6 minutes or until onion is tender. Add onion mixture, salt, black pepper, and eggs to eggplant; stir well to combine. Add matzo meal; toss gently to combine. Spoon mixture into an 11 x 7-inch baking dish coated with cooking spray. Sprinkle with paprika. Bake at 450° for 30 minutes or until thoroughly heated and golden brown. Yield: 8 servings (serving size: about ¾ cup).

CALORIES 136 (30% from fat); FAT 4.5g (sat 0.9g, mono 2g, poly 1.1g); PROTEIN 5.4g; CARB 21g; FIBER 5g; CHOL 53mg; IRON 1.5mg; SODIUM 315mg; CALC 32mg

Carrot-Wheat Berry Salad with Cumin and Raisins

Fresh lemon juice and cumin make a zesty, savory dressing for this robust salad. Make and chill up to 2 days ahead; sprinkle with herbs just before serving.

  ½ cup uncooked wheat berries (hard winter wheat)
1½ teaspoons salt, divided
  2 pounds carrots, chopped
  ½ cup fresh lemon juice
  2 teaspoons ground cumin
  2 teaspoons paprika
  ¼ teaspoon ground red pepper
  2 garlic cloves, minced
  ⅓ cup golden raisins
  2 tablespoons extravirgin olive oil
  3 tablespoons chopped fresh parsley
  2 tablespoons chopped fresh cilantro

1. Place wheat berries and ½ teaspoon salt in a medium saucepan; cover with water to 2 inches above wheat berries. Bring to a boil. Reduce heat; cook, uncovered, 50 minutes or until tender. Drain.
2. Cook half of carrots in a large pot of boiling water 2 minutes or until crisp-tender. Remove with a slotted spoon. Rinse with cold water; drain. Repeat procedure with remaining carrots. Combine carrots and wheat berries in a large bowl;

add 1 teaspoon salt, juice, cumin, paprika, pepper, and garlic. Stir in raisins and oil; toss well to combine. Cover and refrigerate 1 hour or until chilled. Sprinkle with parsley and cilantro. Yield: 8 servings (serving size: about ⅔ cup).

CALORIES 145 (25% from fat); FAT 4g (sat 0.5g, mono 2.5g, poly 0.4g); PROTEIN 3.2g; CARB 26.5g; FIBER 4.6g; CHOL 0mg; IRON 1.5mg; SODIUM 409mg; CALC 44mg

Mashed Potato Latkes with Zucchini and Dill

These potato cakes are made with mashed potatoes instead of traditional shredded potatoes. They're great with Pear Applesauce (recipe at right). Combine and refrigerate the potato mixture up to 1 day ahead; dredge in matzo meal, and sauté just before serving.

  4 cups cubed peeled Yukon gold potato (about 1¾ pounds)
  2 cups cubed zucchini
  1 cup diced leek
  ¼ cup cornstarch
  2 teaspoons minced fresh dill
1½ teaspoons salt
  ½ teaspoon freshly ground black pepper
  1 large egg, lightly beaten
  ½ cup matzo meal
  3 tablespoons vegetable oil, divided

1. Place potato in a saucepan; cover with water. Bring to a boil. Reduce heat; simmer 15 minutes. Add zucchini and leek; cook 6 minutes or until tender. Drain. Return mixture to pan; mash with a potato masher. Cool slightly. Stir in cornstarch and next 4 ingredients.
2. Divide potato mixture into 16 equal portions, shaping each into a ½-inch-thick patty. Dredge in matzo meal.
3. Heat 2¼ teaspoons oil in a large nonstick skillet over medium-high heat. Add 4 patties; sauté 2 minutes on each side or until browned. Repeat procedure with remaining oil and patties. Yield: 8 servings (serving size: 2 patties).

CALORIES 185 (29% from fat); FAT 6g (sat 1g, mono 1.4g, poly 3.1g); PROTEIN 3.7g; CARB 30.4g; FIBER 2.6g; CHOL 27mg; IRON 1.1mg; SODIUM 456mg; CALC 24mg

Pear Applesauce

Cook the fruit unpeeled to add flavor and a pink hue. Then pass through a sieve or food mill. Or cool the fruit slightly, remove and discard the peels, and pulse in a food processor. Refrigerate up to 5 days.

  ½ cup apple juice
  2 pounds Fuji apples, cored and cut into wedges
  2 pounds red Bartlett pears, cored and cut into wedges
  2 (3-inch) cinnamon sticks
  ½ lemon, cut into 2 pieces
  ¼ cup packed brown sugar

1. Combine first 5 ingredients in a large saucepan; bring to a boil. Cover, reduce heat, and simmer 45 minutes or until fruit is tender. Discard cinnamon sticks and lemon. Press fruit mixture through a sieve over a bowl using the back of a spoon; discard skins. Stir in sugar. Serve at room temperature or chilled. Yield: 16 servings (serving size: ¼ cup).

CALORIES 80 (5% from fat); FAT 0.4g (sat 0.1g, mono 0.1g, poly 0.1g); PROTEIN 0.3g; CARB 20.7g; FIBER 1.6g; CHOL 0mg; IRON 0.2mg; SODIUM 2mg; CALC 12mg

Poached Figs in Wine

Serve this dessert in wine stems or sherbet glasses. Prepare the fig mixture up to 2 days ahead; cover and chill. Whip the cream at the last minute so it will remain fluffy. Sprinkle with grated lemon rind for extra zip.

  3 cups dried figs, halved (about 1 pound)
  2 cups port or other sweet red wine
  ½ cup dry red wine
  ½ cup packed brown sugar
  1 teaspoon grated orange rind
  6 whole cloves
  1 whole star anise
  1 (3-inch) cinnamon stick
  ½ cup whipping cream
  ½ cup slivered almonds, toasted

1. Combine first 8 ingredients in a large saucepan; bring to a boil. Cover. Reduce heat; simmer over low heat 40 minutes. Place mixture in a glass bowl; cover and chill. Discard cloves, anise, and cinnamon.

2. Place cream in a medium bowl; beat with a mixer at high speed until soft peaks form. Top each serving of fig mixture with whipped cream and almonds. Yield: 8 servings (serving size: ½ cup fig mixture, 2 tablespoons whipped cream, and 1 tablespoon almonds).

CALORIES 337 (26% from fat); FAT 9.6g (sat 3.8g, mono 3.9g, poly 1.4g); PROTEIN 3.6g; CARB 55.9g; FIBER 7.7g; CHOL 20mg; IRON 1.9mg; SODIUM 20mg; CALC 123mg

dinner tonight

Mexican Meals

Spice up your weeknight repertoire.

Mexican Menu 1
serves 5

White Bean-Rajas Soup

Chicken and cheese quesadillas*

Green salad with bottled salsa

*Heat a medium nonstick skillet coated with cooking spray over medium heat. Working with 1 (6-inch) corn tortilla at a time, place tortilla in pan; cook 30 seconds. Turn tortilla; sprinkle 1 tablespoon shredded queso chihuahua on half of tortilla. Top cheese with 2 tablespoons shredded cooked chicken breast and 1 teaspoon chopped green onions. Sprinkle 1 tablespoon shredded queso chihuahua evenly over onions. Fold tortilla in half; turn and cook 1 minute or until lightly browned and cheese melts. Repeat procedure to yield 5 quesadillas. Cut each quesadilla into 3 wedges.

Game Plan

1. While broth mixture simmers:
- Squeeze lime juice
- Shred cheese for soup and quesadillas
- Preheat skillet for quesadillas

2. While soup stands for 5 minutes:
- Prepare quesadillas
- Spoon salsa over salads

QUICK & EASY • MAKE AHEAD
White Bean-Rajas Soup
(pictured on page 397)

This soup derives its spiciness from the poblanos. Sour cream helps mellow the heat and rounds out the flavors. The soup gets its name from the cooked peppers that are called *rajas* in Spanish.

QUICK TIP: To save time, use bagged chopped onions, found in the produce section of most supermarkets.

Cooking spray
2 cups chopped white onion
2 cups chopped seeded poblano chile
1 cup chopped red bell pepper
4 garlic cloves, minced
2 (14-ounce) cans fat-free, less-sodium chicken broth
2 (15-ounce) cans navy beans, rinsed and drained
¼ cup fresh lime juice
2 tablespoons ground cumin
1 cup (4 ounces) shredded queso chihuahua or Monterey Jack cheese
2½ tablespoons reduced-fat sour cream

1. Heat a Dutch oven coated with cooking spray over medium-high heat. Add onion, chile, red bell pepper, and garlic; sauté 5 minutes. Add broth; bring to a boil. Cover, reduce heat, and simmer 10 minutes. Remove from heat. Add beans, juice, and cumin. Cover and let stand 5 minutes. Ladle about 1½ cups soup into each of 5 bowls; top each serving with about 3 tablespoons cheese and 1½ teaspoons sour cream. Yield: 5 servings.

CALORIES 373 (22% from fat); FAT 9.2g (sat 5.1g, mono 2g, poly 0.7g); PROTEIN 22.8g; CARB 52.5g; FIBER 12.1g; CHOL 28mg; IRON 5.1mg; SODIUM 968mg; CALC 291mg

---

Mexican Menu 2
serves 4

Scallops with Chipotle-Orange Sauce

Yellow pepper rice*

Steamed broccoli spears

*Prepare 1 (3½-ounce) bag boil-in-bag white rice according to package directions. Heat 1 tablespoon olive oil in a large nonstick skillet coated with cooking spray over medium heat. Add 2 cups thinly sliced yellow bell pepper; cook 10 minutes or until golden brown, stirring frequently. Add cooked rice and ¼ teaspoon salt; cook 2 minutes, stirring constantly.

Game Plan

1. While rice cooks in boiling water:
- Slice yellow bell peppers
- Chop green onions and chipotle

2. While yellow bell peppers cook:
- Heat skillet to cook scallops
- Boil water to cook broccoli

3. While scallops cook in skillet:
- Steam broccoli spears
- Finish preparing rice

QUICK & EASY
Scallops with Chipotle-Orange Sauce

Chipotle peppers are smoked jalapeños that are often canned in sauce; use more or less than we call for here, depending on your tolerance for heat.

QUICK TIP: Heat your pan while you prep the ingredients.

2 tablespoons butter, divided
Cooking spray
1½ pounds large sea scallops
½ teaspoon paprika
¼ teaspoon salt, divided
½ cup fresh orange juice
1 tablespoon finely chopped canned chipotle chile in adobo sauce
¼ cup chopped green onions

1. Melt 1 tablespoon butter in a large skillet coated with cooking spray over
Continued

medium-high heat. Sprinkle scallops with paprika and ⅛ teaspoon salt. Add to pan; cook 3 minutes on each side or until browned. Remove from pan; keep warm. **2.** Add juice and chile to pan, scraping pan to loosen browned bits. Bring to a boil; cook until reduced to ¼ cup (about 1 minute). Add 1 tablespoon butter and ⅛ teaspoon salt, stirring with a whisk until smooth. Serve with scallops; garnish with onions. Yield: 4 servings (serving size: about 4½ ounces scallops, about 1 table-spoon sauce, and 1 tablespoon onion).

CALORIES 218 (29% from fat); FAT 7.1g (sat 3.7g, mono 1.7g, poly 0.7g); PROTEIN 28.9g; CARB 8.1g; FIBER 0.4g; CHOL 72mg; IRON 0.6mg; SODIUM 488mg; CALC 47mg

---

Mexican Menu 3
serves 4

Border-Style Shrimp

Potatoes Bravas*

Bagged coleslaw mix with bottled vinaigrette

*Heat 1 tablespoon olive oil in a large non-stick skillet over medium-high heat. Add 1 (20-ounce) package refrigerated prepared potato wedges (such as Simply Potatoes); cook 5 minutes or until lightly browned, stirring occasionally. Add ½ teaspoon ground cumin, ½ teaspoon crushed red pepper, and 1 (14.5-ounce) can diced tomatoes, drained; cook 5 minutes, stirring frequently. Stir in 2 teaspoons lime juice and ½ teaspoon coarse salt.

Game Plan

1. While skillets preheat for potatoes and shrimp:
  • Chop onion, mince garlic, and squeeze lime juice
  • Measure spices for potatoes and shrimp
2. While shrimp and potatoes cook:
  • Prepare coleslaw

QUICK & EASY
Border-Style Shrimp

Serve over yellow rice or Spanish rice.

QUICK TIP: Have the seafood counter at your supermarket peel and devein the shrimp while you finish shopping.

Cooking spray
1½ cups chopped white onion
 1 teaspoon ground cumin
 1 teaspoon chili powder
1½ pounds medium shrimp, peeled and deveined
 2 garlic cloves, minced
 2 tablespoons butter
 ½ teaspoon salt
 ⅛ teaspoon hot pepper sauce
 ¼ cup fresh lime juice
 ¼ cup finely chopped green onions
Lime wedges (optional)

1. Heat a large nonstick skillet coated with cooking spray over medium-high heat. Add onion; sauté 3 minutes. Add cumin, chili powder, shrimp, and garlic; sauté 4 minutes. Remove from heat; add butter, salt, and hot sauce. Stir until butter melts. Stir in juice and green onions. Garnish with lime wedges, if desired. Yield: 4 servings (serving size: about 1 cup shrimp).

CALORIES 266 (30% from fat); FAT 9g (sat 4.1g, mono 2.1g, poly 1.4g); PROTEIN 35.6g; CARB 9.7g; FIBER 1.8g; CHOL 274mg; IRON 4.5mg; SODIUM 618mg; CALC 113mg

---

QUICK & EASY
Cumin-Spiced Pork with Avocado-Tomatillo Salsa

The lemon juice in the salsa keeps the avo-cado green. Pile the sliced pork and salsa on warm flour tortillas, and roll up for soft tacos.

QUICK TIP: Substitute ½ cup chopped drained canned tomatillos or ½ cup chopped green tomatoes for fresh tomatillos.

PORK:
 1 teaspoon ground cumin
 1 teaspoon chili powder
 ½ teaspoon paprika
 ½ teaspoon lemon pepper
 ⅛ teaspoon salt
 1 (1-pound) pork tenderloin, trimmed

SALSA:
 2 tomatillos
 ½ cup diced peeled avocado
 ½ cup chopped peeled cucumber
 ¼ cup chopped fresh cilantro
 1 teaspoon lemon rind
 2 tablespoons fresh lemon juice
 ¼ teaspoon salt
 1 minced seeded jalapeño pepper

1. Preheat oven to 425°.
2. To prepare pork, combine first 5 ingre-dients; rub over pork. Place pork on a jelly roll pan. Bake at 425° for 25 minutes or until a thermometer registers 160° (slightly pink). Let stand 5 minutes before slicing.
3. Discard husks and stems from tomatil-los. Finely chop tomatillos; place in a bowl. Add avocado and remaining 6 ingre-dients; toss well. Yield: 4 servings (serving size: 3 ounces pork and about ⅓ cup salsa).

CALORIES 182 (36% from fat); FAT 7.2g (sat 1.9g, mono 3.6g, poly 1g); PROTEIN 24.7g; CARB 4.5g; FIBER 2g; CHOL 74mg; IRON 2.1mg; SODIUM 343mg; CALC 20mg

---

Mexican Menu 4
serves 4

Cumin-Spiced Pork with Avocado-Tomatillo Salsa

Seasoned black beans*

Warm flour tortillas

*Heat 1 tablespoon olive oil in a saucepan over medium heat. Add ¾ cup chopped onion, 1 tablespoon chopped jalapeño, and 2 teaspoons minced garlic; cook 5 minutes or until tender, stirring frequently. Add 1 tablespoon red wine vinegar, ¼ tea-spoon dried oregano, and 1 (15-ounce) can black beans; cook 5 minutes or until thoroughly heated, stirring frequently.

Game Plan

1. While oven preheats:
  • Combine spice mixture
  • Chop salsa and black bean ingredients
2. While pork bakes:
  • Prepare black beans
  • Combine salsa ingredients
3. While pork rests:
  • Warm tortillas according to package directions

Chocolate Decadence, page 425

White Bean-Rajas Soup, page 395

Pork Loin with Olivada, Spinach,
and Rice Stuffing, page 402

Hot Grand Marnier Soufflés,
page 409

Orange-Basmati Salad with Pine
Nuts and Pomegranate Seeds,
page 407

Tunisian-Spiced Turkey with Garlic Couscous
and Harissa Gravy, page 401

The *Cooking Light* Holiday Cookbook

This time of year brings a host of decisions. Our Holiday Cookbook sets out to make one group of them—namely, what to serve, when, and how—a little easier.

Within these pages, you'll find recipes tailored to the reasons you cook now. From simple suppers for busy nights to glamorous holiday dinners, the ideas here can ensure that the time you spend in the kitchen is, indeed, time well-spent.

This cookbook features enlightened versions of familiar favorites as well as exciting new takes. Technique photos illustrate many of the recipes, both to speed prep time and to reassure you that you're on the right track. What's more, we offer a generous helping of make-ahead tips and menu suggestions.

Entrées for Entertaining

Don your apron, turn on the music, and bake, braise, and stir your way to eight memorable, company-worthy entrées.

Tunisian-Spiced Turkey with Garlic Couscous and Harissa Gravy
(pictured on page 400)

Prepare the spice paste and the yogurt mixture up to 1 day ahead; store separately in the refrigerator.

TURKEY:
- 1½ tablespoons black peppercorns
- 1 tablespoon whole cloves
- 1 tablespoon cardamom pods
- 1 tablespoon olive oil
- 1½ teaspoons ground cinnamon
- 1 teaspoon salt
- ½ teaspoon ground nutmeg
- 1 (12-pound) fresh or frozen turkey, thawed
- Cooking spray
- 2 (14-ounce) cans fat-free, less-sodium chicken broth

GRAVY:
- ⅓ cup water
- 2 tablespoons cornstarch
- 2 teaspoons coriander seeds
- 1 teaspoon caraway seeds
- 1 teaspoon cumin seeds
- 2 teaspoons crushed red pepper
- 2 red jalapeño or Fresno peppers, seeded and chopped
- 2 garlic cloves, minced
- ¾ cup plain low-fat yogurt
- ½ teaspoon salt
- ¼ teaspoon freshly ground black pepper

COUSCOUS:
- 1 tablespoon olive oil
- 8 garlic cloves, crushed
- 1 cup water
- 2 (14-ounce) cans fat-free, less-sodium chicken broth
- 2½ cups uncooked couscous
- ½ cup dried currants
- ¼ cup chopped fresh flat-leaf parsley
- ¼ cup chopped fresh cilantro
- ½ teaspoon salt
- ¼ teaspoon freshly ground black pepper

1. Preheat oven to 400°.

2. To prepare turkey, place first 3 ingredients in a small skillet, and cook over medium-low heat 2 minutes or until toasted and fragrant, shaking pan frequently. Place peppercorn mixture in a spice or coffee grinder; process until finely ground. Place mixture in a small bowl. Stir in 1 tablespoon oil, cinnamon, 1 teaspoon salt, and nutmeg to form a paste.

3. Remove and discard giblets and neck from turkey. Rinse turkey with cold water; pat dry. Trim excess fat. Starting at neck cavity, loosen skin from breast and drumsticks by inserting fingers, gently pushing between skin and meat. Rub spice paste under loosened skin, and rub over breast and drumsticks. Lift wing tips up and over back; tuck under turkey.

4. Place turkey, breast side down, on rack of a broiler pan or roasting pan coated with cooking spray. Pour 2 cans broth into shallow roasting pan; place rack in pan. Bake at 400° for 45 minutes. Carefully turn over (breast side up); bake 1 hour and 15 minutes or until a thermometer inserted in thigh registers 180°. Let stand 10 minutes.

5. To prepare gravy, place a heavy-duty zip-top plastic bag inside a 2-cup glass measure. Pour pan drippings into bag; let stand 10 minutes (fat will rise to the top). Seal bag; carefully snip off 1 bottom corner of bag. Drain drippings into a medium saucepan, stopping before fat layer reaches

Continued

opening; discard fat. Bring to a boil. Reduce heat; simmer 5 minutes. Combine ⅓ cup water and cornstarch, stirring with a whisk. Stir cornstarch mixture into drippings; bring to a boil. Reduce heat; simmer 3 minutes or until slightly thick.

6. Place coriander, caraway, and cumin in a small skillet; cook over medium-low heat 2 minutes or until toasted and fragrant, shaking pan frequently. Place mixture in a spice or coffee grinder; process until finely ground. Add crushed red pepper, jalapeños, and 2 garlic cloves; process until a paste forms. Remove spice paste from grinder; combine spice paste and yogurt. Add yogurt mixture to drippings mixture; simmer 3 minutes. Stir in ½ teaspoon salt and ¼ teaspoon black pepper.

7. To prepare couscous, heat 1 tablespoon oil in a large nonstick saucepan over medium-high heat. Add 8 garlic cloves; sauté 1 minute. Add 1 cup water and 2 cans broth to pan; bring to a boil. Stir in couscous and currants. Cover, remove from heat; let stand 8 minutes. Fluff with a fork. Stir in parsley, cilantro, ½ teaspoon salt, and ¼ teaspoon black pepper. Serve turkey with couscous and gravy. Discard skin before serving. Yield: 12 servings (serving size: 6 ounces turkey, about ¾ cup couscous, and about 2 tablespoons gravy).

CALORIES 521 (24% from fat); FAT 13.7g (sat 4g, mono 4.6g, poly 3.2g); PROTEIN 57.8g; CARB 38.1g; FIBER 3.2g; CHOL 132mg; IRON 4.4mg; SODIUM 771mg; CALC 105mg

How to Turn a Turkey

Insert long-handled tongs or a heavy spatula into the cavity to support the weight of the turkey, and use another set of tongs or a spatula to turn the bird.

Beef Tenderloin with Parsnip-Mushroom Ragoût
(menu on page 418)

The sweet parsnips and woodsy porcini mushrooms create a flavorful sauce for beef tenderloin. If you don't have an ovenproof skillet, wrap your pan's handle with foil to protect it from the heat.

RAGOÛT:

1½ cups boiling water
 2 cups dried porcini mushrooms (about 2 ounces)
 2 teaspoons butter
 ½ cup chopped shallots
 3 tablespoons minced garlic
 1 teaspoon minced fresh or ¼ teaspoon dried thyme
 3 cups coarsely chopped parsnips (about 1 pound)
12 cups quartered button mushrooms (about 1½ pounds)
 ½ cup port wine
 2 tablespoons chopped fresh parsley
 ½ teaspoon salt
 ½ teaspoon freshly ground black pepper

BEEF:

 ½ teaspoon salt
 ½ teaspoon freshly ground black pepper
 1 (3-pound) beef tenderloin, trimmed and cut in half crosswise
Cooking spray

SAUCE:

 1 teaspoon butter
 ⅓ cup (2-inch) julienne-cut carrot
 ⅓ cup vertically sliced shallots
 ¼ cup port wine
 1 (14-ounce) can low-salt beef broth
 ¼ teaspoon salt
 ¼ teaspoon freshly ground black pepper

1. To prepare ragoût, pour boiling water over porcini; let stand 20 minutes. Strain through a sieve into a bowl; reserve liquid. Finely chop porcini; divide in half.
2. Melt 2 teaspoons butter in a large nonstick skillet over medium heat. Add ½ cup shallots, garlic, and thyme; cook

1 minute, stirring frequently. Add parsnips; cook 2 minutes, stirring occasionally. Add button mushrooms; cook 10 minutes, stirring occasionally. Add half of porcini and ½ cup wine; bring to a boil. Cover, reduce heat, and cook 15 minutes or until parsnips are tender. Stir in parsley, ½ teaspoon salt, and ½ teaspoon pepper. Set aside; keep warm.

3. Preheat oven to 450°.
4. To prepare beef, rub ½ teaspoon salt and ½ teaspoon pepper over tenderloin. Heat a large ovenproof skillet coated with cooking spray over medium-high heat. Add tenderloin; cook 5 minutes, browning on all sides. Bake at 450° for 20 minutes or until a thermometer registers 140° (medium-rare) or desired degree of doneness. Place tenderloin on a cutting board; cover loosely with foil. Let stand 10 minutes. (Temperature of tenderloin will increase 5° upon standing.)
5. To prepare sauce, melt 1 teaspoon butter in pan over medium-high heat. Add carrot and ⅓ cup shallots; sauté 3 minutes. Add reserved porcini liquid, remaining porcini, ¼ cup wine, and broth; bring to a boil. Cook until reduced to 1½ cups (about 10 minutes). Stir in ¼ teaspoon salt and ¼ teaspoon pepper. Cut beef into thin slices; serve with ragoût and sauce. Yield: 12 servings (serving size: 3 ounces tenderloin, ⅔ cup ragoût, and 2 tablespoons sauce).

WINE NOTE: A California Merlot is an ideal companion. Try Benziger Merlot 2000 from Sonoma County ($19).

CALORIES 265 (35% from fat); FAT 10.3g (sat 3.9g, mono 3.8g, poly 0.6g); PROTEIN 28.8g; CARB 14.1g; FIBER 3.4g; CHOL 74mg; IRON 5.2mg; SODIUM 330mg; CALC 36mg

Pork Loin with Olivada, Spinach, and Rice Stuffing
(pictured on page 398)

This roast can be assembled and refrigerated up to 2 days ahead. To cook, let stand at room temperature 30 minutes, then proceed with baking instructions. Overnight brining tenderizes the pork and keeps it juicy. Jasmine rice is soft, slightly sticky aromatic grain and holds together when the pork is sliced.

BRINE:

8 cups water
¾ cup sugar
¾ cup kosher salt
2 tablespoons grated lemon rind
2 tablespoons chopped fresh oregano
2 garlic cloves, crushed
1 (3½-pound) center-cut boneless pork loin roast, trimmed

STUFFING:

¾ cup uncooked jasmine rice
1 (6-ounce) package fresh baby spinach
½ teaspoon salt
½ cup pitted kalamata olives, finely chopped
1 teaspoon crushed red pepper
1 teaspoon grated lemon rind
2 teaspoons fresh lemon juice

REMAINING INGREDIENT:

1 tablespoon freshly ground black pepper

1. To brine pork, combine first 6 ingredients in a large nonaluminum bowl or pan; stir until sugar and salt dissolve. Add pork. Cover; refrigerate 8 hours or overnight. Remove pork from bowl; discard brine.
2. Preheat oven to 325°.
3. Starting off-center, slice pork lengthwise, cutting to, but not through, other side. Open uneven portions, laying pork flat. Turning knife blade parallel to surface of cutting board, slice larger portion of pork in half horizontally, cutting to, but not through, other side; open flat. Place plastic wrap over pork; pound to an even thickness using a meat mallet or rolling pin. Refrigerate until ready to use.
4. To prepare stuffing, cook rice according to package directions, omitting salt and fat. Add spinach and ½ teaspoon salt to hot rice, stirring until spinach wilts. Stir in olives, red pepper, 1 teaspoon rind, and juice.
5. Spread rice mixture over pork, leaving a ½-inch border. Roll up pork, jelly roll fashion, starting with a long side. Secure both ends with twine; secure middle at 2-inch intervals with twine. Rub black pepper over pork. Place pork on a broiler pan. Bake at 325° for 1 hour 20 minutes or until a thermometer registers

155°. Let pork stand 10 minutes before slicing. Yield: 12 servings (serving size: 1 [6-ounce] slice stuffed pork).

CALORIES 232 (33% from fat); FAT 8.5g (sat 3g, mono 3.9g, poly 0.7g); PROTEIN 25.2g; CARB 12.2g; FIBER 0.8g; CHOL 68mg; IRON 1.7mg; SODIUM 780mg; CALC 44mg

How to Tie a Roast

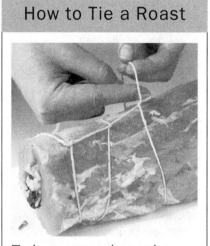

Tie the roast at 2-inch intervals to ensure that it keeps its round shape.

Honey-Basted Duck with Balsamic Lentils

Fall-off-the-bone tenderness and a Provençal sweetness are the hallmarks of this dish. Because duck has a thick layer of fat that melts as it cooks, drain the roasting pan a couple of times during cooking. Allow the herbs to penetrate the meat overnight for the best flavor—but the dish is still good if you don't have time to do so.

DUCK:

1 tablespoon chopped fresh or 1 teaspoon dried thyme
1 tablespoon dried herbes de Provence
2 teaspoons freshly ground black pepper
1 teaspoon salt
3 garlic cloves, minced
2 (5-pound) whole ducks
½ cup honey
2 tablespoons balsamic vinegar
1 tablespoon dried herbes de Provence

LENTILS:

1 shallot, peeled and cut in half
2 whole cloves
4 cups water
2 cups petite green lentils
2 garlic cloves, peeled
1 cup balsamic vinegar
1 tablespoon Dijon mustard
¼ teaspoon salt
1 teaspoon olive oil
1 cup finely chopped shallots
½ cup finely chopped carrot
2 teaspoons chopped fresh thyme
¼ teaspoon freshly ground black pepper
Thyme sprig (optional)

1. To prepare duck, combine first 5 ingredients. Remove and discard giblets and neck from ducks. Cut off wing tips. Rinse ducks with cold water; pat dry. Trim excess fat. Starting at neck cavity, loosen skin from breast and drumsticks by inserting fingers, gently pushing between skin and meat. Rub herb mixture under loosened skin; rub over breast and drumsticks. Cover and refrigerate 8 hours or overnight.
2. Preheat oven to 325°.
3. Combine honey, 2 tablespoons vinegar, and 1 tablespoon herbes de Provence; set aside.
4. Score duck skin several times with a paring knife (do not cut into meat). Place ducks in a roasting pan, breast side up. Cover pan tightly with foil. Bake at 325° for 1½ hours. Carefully remove ducks from pan. Drain and discard drippings from pan. Carefully place ducks in pan, breast side down. Cover and bake at 325° for 1½ hours.
5. Carefully remove ducks from pan, and discard drippings. Cool ducks slightly. Remove and discard skin. Carefully place ducks in pan, breast side up. Baste with honey mixture. Bake, uncovered, at 325° for 30 minutes, basting every 10 minutes. Let stand 10 minutes. Reserve drumsticks. Remove remaining meat from bones; discard bones.
6. To prepare lentils, stud shallot halves with cloves. Combine shallot halves, water, lentils, and 2 garlic cloves in a *Continued*

large saucepan; bring to a boil. Cover, reduce heat, and simmer 20 minutes or until lentils are tender. Remove from heat; let stand 10 minutes. Drain and discard shallot halves.

7. Bring 1 cup vinegar to a boil in a small saucepan. Cook until reduced to ¼ cup (about 10 minutes). Stir in mustard and ¼ teaspoon salt; set aside.

8. Heat oil in a large nonstick skillet over medium-high heat. Add chopped shallots, carrot, 2 teaspoons thyme, and ¼ teaspoon pepper; sauté 3 minutes. Add shallot mixture and mustard mixture to lentils, and toss well. Place lentils on a platter. Arrange drumsticks around lentils, and top lentils with pulled meat. Garnish with thyme sprig, if desired. Yield: 8 servings (serving size: about 4 ounces duck and ⅔ cup lentil mixture).

CALORIES 498 (25% from fat); FAT 13.7g (sat 4.9g, mono 4.7g, poly 1.8g); PROTEIN 38.8g; CARB 55.8g; FIBER 8g; CHOL 101mg; IRON 6.9mg; SODIUM 518mg; CALC 101mg

How to Score a Duck

Scoring the duck skin helps much of the fat drain off during cooking.

STAFF FAVORITE
Seafood Lasagna

You can always splurge on fresh crabmeat, but we tested with canned Chicken of the Sea lump crabmeat. Shrimp shells render a quick stock to flavor the sauce. To save prep time, we used oven-ready lasagna noodles.

  2 teaspoons olive oil
  5 cups finely chopped mushrooms (about 1 pound)
1½ cups chopped onion
  2 tablespoons chopped fresh thyme
  2 garlic cloves, minced
  ¼ cup dry white wine
  2 (6.5-ounce) cans lump crabmeat
  1 pound uncooked large shrimp
  2 cups water
1½ teaspoons celery salt
  1 teaspoon fennel seeds
1¼ cups (5 ounces) crumbled goat or feta cheese
  1 cup 2% reduced-fat cottage cheese
  ¼ cup finely chopped fresh basil
  1 tablespoon fresh lemon juice
  1 garlic clove, minced
  ¼ cup all-purpose flour
  1 cup 1% low-fat milk
  ¼ cup (1 ounce) grated fresh Parmesan cheese
    Cooking spray
  1 (8-ounce) package precooked lasagna noodles
  2 cups (8 ounces) shredded part-skim mozzarella cheese
  ¼ cup chopped fresh flat-leaf parsley

1. Preheat oven to 375°.

2. Heat oil in a large nonstick skillet over medium heat. Add mushrooms, onion, thyme, and 2 garlic cloves; cook 10 minutes, stirring occasionally. Add wine. Bring to a boil; cook 1½ minutes or until liquid almost evaporates. Remove from heat; stir in crabmeat. Set aside.

3. Peel and devein shrimp, reserving shells. Cut each shrimp in half lengthwise; cover and refrigerate. Combine reserved shrimp shells, 2 cups water, celery salt, and fennel seeds in a small saucepan. Bring to a boil; cook until reduced to 1½ cups shrimp stock (about 15 minutes). Strain stock through a sieve into a bowl; discard solids. Set stock aside.

4. Combine goat cheese, cottage cheese, basil, juice, and 1 garlic clove; set aside.

5. Lightly spoon flour into a dry measuring cup, and level with a knife. Place flour in a small saucepan; gradually add

milk, stirring with a whisk. Stir in shrimp stock; bring to a boil. Reduce heat; simmer 5 minutes or until thick. Remove from heat; stir in Parmesan cheese.

6. Spread ½ cup sauce in bottom of a 13 x 9-inch baking dish coated with cooking spray. Arrange 4 noodles, slightly overlapping, over sauce; top with one-third goat cheese mixture, one-third crab mixture, one-third shrimp, ⅔ cup sauce, and ⅔ cup mozzarella. Repeat layers twice, ending with mozzarella. Bake at 375° for 40 minutes or until golden. Let stand 15 minutes. Sprinkle with parsley. Yield: 8 servings.

CALORIES 428 (29% from fat); FAT 13.9g (sat 7.7g, mono 2.5g, poly 1.1g); PROTEIN 40.1g; CARB 33.6g; FIBER 3.6g; CHOL 143mg; IRON 4.1mg; SODIUM 934mg; CALC 414mg

Bourbon-Brown Sugar Salmon with Onion Sauce

(menu on page 418)

Cereal nuggets create a crunchy topping for meaty salmon. Serve with roasted potatoes and asparagus.

  1 (2¼-pound) salmon fillet
  3 cups thinly sliced onion
  ½ cup packed brown sugar
  ½ cup water
  ½ cup bourbon
  1 tablespoon low-sodium soy sauce
  1 teaspoon freshly ground black pepper
  ¾ teaspoon salt
  6 tarragon sprigs
  4 thyme sprigs
  ⅓ cup nutlike cereal nuggets (such as Grape-Nuts)
  ¼ cup chopped pecans
    Cooking spray
  ¾ teaspoon salt
  2 tablespoons packed brown sugar
  2 tablespoons honey
1½ teaspoons water

1. Place salmon in a 13 x 9-inch baking dish. Combine onion and next 8 ingredients; pour over salmon. Cover and marinate in refrigerator 2 hours, turning occasionally.

2. Preheat oven to 350°.

3. Place cereal and pecans in a baking pan. Bake at 350° for 7 minutes or until toasted. Place mixture in a food processor; pulse 4 times or until finely chopped.

4. Remove salmon from dish; reserve marinade. Arrange salmon diagonally on a broiler pan coated with cooking spray. Sprinkle with ¾ teaspoon salt. Combine 2 tablespoons sugar, honey, and 1½ teaspoons water, stirring with a whisk. Spread honey mixture over salmon; sprinkle with cereal mixture, gently pressing into salmon. Bake at 350° for 20 minutes or until fish flakes easily when tested with a fork.

5. While salmon bakes, place reserved marinade in a small saucepan. Discard tarragon and thyme. Bring marinade to a boil over medium-high heat; cook until reduced to ¾ cup (about 10 minutes). Serve sauce with salmon. Yield: 6 servings (serving size: about 4½ ounces salmon and 2 tablespoons sauce).

CALORIES 437 (30% from fat); FAT 14.7g (sat 2.9g, mono 6.8g, poly 3.8g); PROTEIN 32.2g; CARB 39.5g; FIBER 2.2g; CHOL 72mg; IRON 3.2mg; SODIUM 793mg; CALC 57mg

Squash-Stuffed Cannelloni with Roasted-Shallot Sauce and Hazelnuts

(menu on page 418)

Prepare the filling up to 1 day in advance. For a vegetarian version, use vegetable broth in place of chicken broth; sauté the shallots and garlic in oil, omitting the bacon.

FILLING:

10 cups (½-inch) cubed butternut squash (about 4 pounds)
¼ cup chopped shallots
2 tablespoons chopped fresh sage
Cooking spray
1 tablespoon butter, melted
½ cup fat-free sour cream
¼ cup half-and-half
¼ teaspoon salt
¼ teaspoon freshly ground black pepper

SAUCE:

3 slices applewood smoked bacon, chopped
½ pound shallots, peeled and halved
2 garlic cloves, crushed
½ cup dry white wine
1 (14-ounce) can fat-free, less-sodium chicken broth
2 tablespoons half-and-half
¼ teaspoon salt
¼ teaspoon freshly ground black pepper

REMAINING INGREDIENTS:

16 cooked lasagna noodles
¾ cup (3 ounces) shredded fontina cheese
¼ cup chopped blanched hazelnuts, toasted

1. Preheat oven to 400°.

2. To prepare filling, combine first 3 ingredients on a jelly roll pan coated with cooking spray. Drizzle with butter; toss to coat. Bake at 400° for 25 minutes or until lightly browned, stirring occasionally. Place squash mixture in a large bowl; mash with a potato masher. Stir in sour cream and next 3 ingredients.

3. To prepare sauce, cook bacon in a Dutch oven over medium-high heat until crisp. Remove bacon from pan, reserving 2 teaspoons drippings in pan; set bacon aside. Add ½ pound shallots and garlic to drippings in pan; sauté 5 minutes or until browned. Bake at 400° for 25 minutes, stirring occasionally. Place pan on stovetop over medium-high heat. Add wine, scraping pan to loosen browned bits. Add broth; bring to a boil. Reduce heat; simmer 5 minutes. Remove from heat; stir in 2 tablespoons half-and-half, ¼ teaspoon salt, and ¼ teaspoon pepper.

4. Spread ¼ cup filling over each noodle, leaving a ½-inch border on each short end. Beginning with a short end, roll up noodles jelly roll fashion. Place rolls, seam sides down, in a 13 x 9-inch baking pan coated with cooking spray. Pour sauce over noodles; sprinkle evenly with cheese. Bake at 400° for 25 minutes or until cheese is golden. Sprinkle with

bacon and hazelnuts. Yield: 8 servings (serving size: 2 cannelloni).

CALORIES 349 (29% from fat); FAT 11.4g (sat 5g, mono 4.5g, poly 1g); PROTEIN 12.2g; CARB 51.8g; FIBER 7.8g; CHOL 26mg; IRON 3mg; SODIUM 414mg; CALC 206mg

Chicken Braised with Figs on Wilted Escarole

Serve this saucy braise over couscous or rice in shallow bowls. Substitute spinach for escarole, if desired.

CHICKEN:

1 cup port or other sweet red wine
1 cup dried figs, halved
¼ cup all-purpose flour
¾ teaspoon salt, divided
½ teaspoon freshly ground pepper, divided
4 chicken thighs (about 1 pound), skinned
4 chicken drumsticks (about 1 pound), skinned
2 chicken breast halves (about 1 pound), skinned
2 tablespoons olive oil, divided
¾ pound small shallots, peeled
1 tablespoon minced fresh thyme
½ teaspoon ground fennel seeds
2 garlic cloves, crushed
1 (14-ounce) can fat-free, less-sodium chicken broth
¼ cup honey
¼ cup cider vinegar

ESCAROLE:

1 tablespoon olive oil
1½ pounds escarole, coarsely chopped
½ cup fat-free, less-sodium chicken broth
¼ teaspoon salt
¼ teaspoon freshly ground pepper

1. Preheat oven to 350°.

2. To prepare chicken, bring port to a boil in a medium saucepan. Add figs; remove from heat. Let stand, covered, 30 minutes or until soft.

3. Combine flour, ½ teaspoon salt, and ¼ teaspoon pepper in a large zip-top plastic bag; add chicken. Seal and shake to coat.

Continued

Heat 1 tablespoon oil in a large Dutch oven over medium-high heat. Add half of chicken to pan, and cook 5 minutes on each side or until lightly browned. Remove chicken from pan. Repeat procedure with 1 tablespoon oil and remaining chicken. Return chicken to pan. Add fig mixture, ¼ teaspoon salt, ¼ teaspoon pepper, shallots, and next 4 ingredients. Cover and bake at 350° for 25 minutes. Stir in honey. Uncover; bake at 350° for 25 minutes. Stir in vinegar; place mixture in a large bowl. Cover; keep warm.

4. To prepare escarole, heat 1 tablespoon oil in pan over medium heat. Add escarole; cook 5 minutes or until escarole begins to wilt. Add ½ cup broth; cover and cook 5 minutes or until tender. Stir in ¼ teaspoon salt and ¼ teaspoon pepper. Serve chicken mixture over escarole. Yield: 6 servings (serving size: 1 breast half or 1 thigh and 1 drumstick, about ¾ cup sauce, and about ½ cup escarole).

CALORIES 423 (24% from fat); FAT 11.4g (sat 2g, mono 6.2g, poly 1.8g); PROTEIN 33.9g; CARB 48.7g; FIBER 8.6g; CHOL 97mg; IRON 4mg; SODIUM 694mg; CALC 151mg

Choosing Sides

Any of these 10 simple side dishes can make your meal a success.

Braised Fennel with Orange

Serve this slightly sweet side with ham, pork chops, or roasted pork tenderloin.

- 4 large fennel bulbs, each cut into 8 wedges (about 1½ pounds)
- 1 tablespoon olive oil
- 2 teaspoons sugar
- 1 cup fat-free, less-sodium chicken broth
- 1 tablespoon grated orange rind
- ⅓ cup fresh orange juice (about 1 orange)
- 2 teaspoons sherry vinegar
- ½ teaspoon salt
- ⅛ teaspoon freshly ground black pepper
- 2 tablespoons chopped fennel fronds

1. Bring 2 quarts of water to a boil in a large saucepan. Add fennel wedges. Cook 5 minutes or until crisp-tender, and drain.
2. Heat oil in a large nonstick skillet over medium-high heat. Add fennel wedges and sugar, and sauté 3 minutes. Add chicken broth and next 5 ingredients. Reduce heat, and simmer 25 minutes or until liquid almost evaporates. Sprinkle with fennel fronds. Yield: 6 servings (serving size: 1 cup).

CALORIES 85 (28% from fat); FAT 2.6g (sat 0.3g, mono 1.7g, poly 0.2g); PROTEIN 2.6g; CARB 14.8g; FIBER 5g; CHOL 0mg; IRON 1.2mg; SODIUM 353mg; CALC 81mg

Red Cabbage, Cranberry, and Apple Slaw

The slaw marinates in the refrigerator for a couple of hours, allowing the vinaigrette to permeate the cabbage and plump the cranberries. Stir in apples just before serving to keep them bright.

- 5 cups thinly sliced red cabbage (about 1½ pounds)
- ½ cup dried cranberries
- ⅓ cup rice vinegar
- ⅓ cup sugar
- 2 tablespoons white wine vinegar
- 2 teaspoons olive oil
- ¾ teaspoon salt
- ½ teaspoon freshly ground black pepper
- 2¼ cups thinly sliced Granny Smith apple
- ¼ cup chopped pecans, toasted

1. Combine cabbage and cranberries in a large bowl. Combine vinegar and next 5 ingredients, stirring with a whisk; drizzle over cabbage mixture, tossing gently to coat. Cover and chill 2 hours. Add apple, and toss well to combine. Sprinkle with pecans. Yield: 8 servings (serving size: 1 cup).

CALORIES 131 (29% from fat); FAT 4.2g (sat 0.4g, mono 2.4g, poly 1g); PROTEIN 1.7g; CARB 23.6g; FIBER 3.8g; CHOL 0mg; IRON 0.7mg; SODIUM 236mg; CALC 46mg

STAFF FAVORITE
Potato-Gorgonzola Gratin

To easily create uniformly thin potato slices, use a mandoline or the slicing blade of a food processor. Substitute fontina or Monterey Jack for the blue cheese, if you like.

- 2 tablespoons butter
- 2½ tablespoons all-purpose flour
- 1 teaspoon chopped fresh thyme
- 2½ cups fat-free milk
- ¾ cup (3 ounces) crumbled Gorgonzola or other blue cheese
- 1½ teaspoons salt
- ¼ teaspoon freshly ground black pepper
- 3 pounds baking potatoes, peeled and cut into ⅛-inch-thick slices
- Cooking spray
- ⅓ cup (1½ ounces) grated Parmigiano-Reggiano cheese

1. Preheat oven to 375°.
2. Melt butter in a small saucepan over medium-high heat. Add flour, and cook 2 minutes, stirring constantly with a whisk. Stir in thyme. Gradually add milk, stirring with a whisk; cook over medium heat until slightly thick (about 3 minutes), stirring constantly. Stir in Gorgonzola; cook 3 minutes or until cheese melts, stirring constantly. Stir in salt and pepper. Remove from heat.
3. Arrange one-fourth of potatoes in bottom of a 13 x 9-inch baking dish coated with cooking spray; spoon about ¾ cup sauce over potatoes. Repeat layers twice; arrange remaining potatoes over sauce. Sprinkle with Parmigiano-Reggiano. Cover and bake at 375° for 30 minutes. Uncover and bake 40 minutes or until potatoes are tender. Remove from oven; let stand 10 minutes before serving. Yield: 8 servings (serving size: about 1 cup).

CALORIES 254 (28% from fat); FAT 7.9g (sat 5g, mono 2g, poly 0.2g); PROTEIN 10.6g; CARB 36.8g; FIBER 2.8g; CHOL 22mg; IRON 1.5mg; SODIUM 751mg; CALC 228mg

Brussels Sprouts with Crisp Prosciutto

3 cups trimmed halved Brussels
  sprouts (about 1½ pounds)
¼ cup chopped prosciutto (about
  1½ ounces)
Cooking spray
1 tablespoon butter
½ teaspoon salt
¼ teaspoon freshly ground black
  pepper
1 tablespoon fresh lemon juice

1. Cook Brussels sprouts in boiling water 3 minutes or until crisp-tender; drain.
2. Heat a large nonstick skillet over medium heat; add prosciutto. Cook 6 minutes or until crisp, stirring occasionally. Remove from pan; set aside.
3. Heat pan coated with cooking spray over medium-high heat. Add Brussels sprouts; sauté 3 minutes or until lightly browned. Add butter, salt, and pepper, stirring until butter melts. Remove from heat; drizzle with juice. Add prosciutto; toss to combine. Yield: 6 servings (serving size: about ¾ cup).

CALORIES 79 (33% from fat); FAT 2.9g (sat 1.5g, mono 0.9g, poly 0.3g); PROTEIN 5.5g; CARB 10.4g; FIBER 4.3g; CHOL 9mg; IRON 1.7mg; SODIUM 350mg; CALC 50mg

Green Beans and Red Onion with Warm Mustard Vinaigrette

The simple vinaigrette is briefly warmed to bring out the mustard's hot bite. You can also heat the dressing in a microwave-safe bowl at HIGH 1 minute.

1½ pounds green beans,
  trimmed
1 cup vertically sliced red onion
3 tablespoons red wine vinegar
2 tablespoons Dijon mustard
1 tablespoon extravirgin olive oil
¼ teaspoon salt
¼ teaspoon black pepper

1. Cook green beans in boiling water 6 minutes or until crisp-tender; drain.

Combine green beans and onion in a large bowl.
2. Heat a small saucepan over medium heat. Add vinegar, Dijon mustard, olive oil, salt, and black pepper; cook over medium heat 30 seconds or until thoroughly heated, stirring vinaigrette constantly with a whisk. Drizzle vinaigrette over bean mixture; toss well to coat. Serve immediately. Yield: 6 servings (serving size: 1 cup).

CALORIES 69 (38% from fat); FAT 2.9g (sat 0.4g, mono 1.8g, poly 0.4g); PROTEIN 2.6g; CARB 10.4g; FIBER 4.3g; CHOL 0mg; IRON 1.5mg; SODIUM 232mg; CALC 54mg

Barley Risotto with Caramelized Leeks and Mushrooms
(menu on page 418)

Cooking the leeks over moderately low heat results in a buttery-soft texture and sweet flavor. As with any risotto, serve immediately for the creamiest texture.

2 tablespoons olive oil
3 cups chopped leek (about 3 large)
3 cups sliced cremini mushrooms
  (about 8 ounces)
1 cup uncooked pearl barley
1 teaspoon salt
¼ teaspoon freshly ground black
  pepper
2 (14-ounce) cans fat-free,
  less-sodium chicken broth
2 tablespoons chopped fresh
  flat-leaf parsley

1. Heat oil in a large saucepan over medium heat. Add leek; cook 20 minutes or until tender and golden, stirring occasionally. Add mushrooms; cook 5 minutes or until tender, stirring occasionally. Add barley, salt, and pepper; cook 1 minute, stirring constantly. Add broth; bring to a boil. Cover, reduce heat, and simmer 30 minutes, stirring occasionally. Uncover and cook 5 minutes or until liquid is absorbed. Stir in parsley. Yield: 6 servings (serving size: about ⅔ cup).

CALORIES 208 (22% from fat); FAT 5g (sat 0.7g, mono 3.4g, poly 0.6g); PROTEIN 7.3g; CARB 34.1g; FIBER 6.9g; CHOL 0mg; IRON 2.2mg; SODIUM 661mg; CALC 38mg

Orange-Basmati Salad with Pine Nuts and Pomegranate Seeds
(pictured on page 399)

Although best served immediately, this dish can be covered and chilled for a couple of hours. Try it with roasted chicken. Pomegranate juice stains, so be careful when extracting the seeds. Here's our favorite way to seed a pomegranate: Carefully cut the fruit in half, submerge in a large bowl of water, and slowly turn the shell inside out to dislodge the seeds.

2 cups water
1 cup uncooked basmati rice
1 teaspoon salt, divided
¼ cup white wine vinegar
2 teaspoons grated orange rind
¼ cup fresh orange juice
1½ tablespoons extravirgin olive oil
¼ teaspoon freshly ground black
  pepper
2 cups orange sections (about 3
  oranges)
½ cup pomegranate seeds
¼ cup pine nuts, toasted
3 tablespoons chopped fresh
  flat-leaf parsley

1. Bring water to a boil in a medium saucepan over medium-high heat. Add rice and ¾ teaspoon salt; cover, reduce heat, and simmer 15 minutes or until liquid is absorbed. Remove from heat; fluff rice with a fork. Cool completely.
2. Combine ¼ teaspoon salt, vinegar, and next 4 ingredients, stirring with a whisk. Combine rice, vinegar mixture, orange sections, and remaining ingredients; toss gently to combine. Yield: 6 servings (serving size: about ⅔ cup).

CALORIES 225 (27% from fat); FAT 6.8g (sat 1.1g, mono 3.7g, poly 1.7g); PROTEIN 4.8g; CARB 38g; FIBER 2.1g; CHOL 0mg; IRON 1.1mg; SODIUM 393mg; CALC 35mg

Purée of Roasted Garlic and White Vegetables

Turnips and celeriac turn ordinary mashed potatoes into a dish that can stand up to lamb, pork, or beef.

 1 whole garlic head
 3¼ cups chopped peeled baking potato (about 1¾ pounds)
 3 cups chopped peeled turnip
 2½ cups chopped peeled celeriac (celery root; about ¾ pound)
 1 cup chopped onion
 2 tablespoons butter
 ¼ cup whipping cream
 1½ tablespoons white wine vinegar
 1 teaspoon salt
 ½ teaspoon freshly ground black pepper

1. Preheat oven to 350°.
2. Remove white, papery skin from garlic head (do not peel or separate cloves). Wrap garlic head in foil. Bake at 350° for 1 hour; cool 10 minutes. Separate garlic cloves; squeeze to extract garlic pulp. Discard skins.
3. Place potato, turnip, celeriac, and onion in a large Dutch oven; cover with water. Bring to a boil, reduce heat, and simmer 15 minutes or until vegetables are tender. Drain. Place half of vegetables in a food processor; process until smooth. Pour puréed vegetables into a bowl. Repeat procedure with remaining vegetables.
4. Melt butter in pan over medium heat. Stir in garlic pulp, puréed vegetables, and cream; cook 5 minutes or until thoroughly heated, stirring frequently. Stir in vinegar, salt, and pepper. Yield: 8 servings (serving size: ¾ cup).

CALORIES 181 (29% from fat); FAT 5.9g (sat 3.6g, mono 1.7g, poly 0.4g); PROTEIN 3.5g; CARB 30.1g; FIBER 3.9g; CHOL 18mg; IRON 0.9mg; SODIUM 406mg; CALC 58mg

---

QUICK & EASY
Wilted Cabbage with Toasted Cumin

Savoy cabbage has crinkled, pale green leaves and mellow flavor; you can also use napa (Chinese) cabbage. If you can't find sherry vinegar, substitute cider vinegar.

 2 teaspoons olive oil
 12 cups coarsely chopped Savoy cabbage (about 2 pounds)
 ½ cup water
 ½ teaspoon salt
 ¼ teaspoon freshly ground black pepper
 1 teaspoon cumin seeds
 1 tablespoon sherry vinegar

1. Heat olive oil in a Dutch oven over medium heat. Add cabbage and water. Cook 6 minutes or until cabbage wilts; stir occasionally. Stir in salt and black pepper.
2. Place cumin seeds in a small nonstick skillet; cook over medium heat 1 minute or until seeds are toasted and fragrant, shaking pan frequently. Add toasted cumin seeds and vinegar to cabbage; cook 6 minutes or until tender, stirring mixture occasionally. Yield: 6 servings (serving size: 1 cup).

CALORIES 58 (28% from fat); FAT 1.8g (sat 0.2g, mono 1.2g, poly 0.2g); PROTEIN 3.1g; CARB 9.9g; FIBER 4.8g; CHOL 0mg; IRON 1mg; SODIUM 239mg; CALC 59mg

---

Marsala-Glazed Winter Vegetables

(menu on page 418)

For the best flavor, use freshly grated nutmeg instead of bottled ground.

 3 cups (½-inch) cubed peeled rutabaga (about ½ pound)
 1⅓ cups (½-inch-thick) slices parsnip (about ½ pound)
 1¼ cups pearl onions, peeled (about ½ pound)
 1 cup (½-inch-thick) slices carrot (about ½ pound)
 1½ cups trimmed halved Brussels sprouts (about ½ pound)
 Cooking spray
 1 tablespoon butter
 1 tablespoon extravirgin olive oil
 2 teaspoons chopped fresh or ½ teaspoon dried thyme
 ½ teaspoon salt
 ¼ teaspoon freshly ground black pepper
 ⅛ teaspoon ground nutmeg
 ½ cup dry Marsala wine

1. Preheat oven to 450°.
2. Bring 2 quarts water to a boil in a Dutch oven. Add rutabaga, parsnip, onions, and carrot; cook 4 minutes. Add Brussels sprouts, and cook 1 minute. Drain and place vegetables in a large roasting or jelly roll pan coated with cooking spray. Add butter and next 5 ingredients, stirring mixture until butter melts. Pour wine over vegetables; cover pan with foil. Bake vegetables at 450° for 30 minutes. Uncover and stir vegetables (do not remove pan from oven). Bake an additional 15 minutes or until vegetables are tender, stirring after 8 minutes. Yield: 6 servings (serving size: 1 cup).

CALORIES 149 (28% from fat); FAT 4.6g (sat 1.5g, mono 2.2g, poly 0.4g); PROTEIN 3.1g; CARB 23.7g; FIBER 4.3g; CHOL 5mg; IRON 1.3mg; SODIUM 256mg; CALC 71mg

---

Dazzling Desserts

How to finish a memorable evening? Our collection of sweets will make the grand finale unforgettable.

MAKE AHEAD • FREEZABLE
Cream Puffs

This classic dessert is easily made ahead. Bake the shells up to a month in advance, then freeze in an airtight container. Several hours before serving, top off the frozen shells with the custard filling and refrigerate. In the refrigerator, the shells will thaw but remain crisp.

FILLING:
 1½ cups 2% low fat milk, divided
 ¼ cup granulated sugar
 3 tablespoons cornstarch
 ⅛ teaspoon salt
 2 large eggs, lightly beaten
 1 teaspoon chilled butter, cut into small pieces
 2 teaspoons vanilla extract
 1 cup frozen fat-free whipped topping, thawed

SHELLS:
- 1 cup water
- 3 tablespoons butter
- 2 teaspoons granulated sugar
- ¼ teaspoon salt
- 1 cup all-purpose flour
- 2 large eggs
- 2 large egg whites
- 1 teaspoon powdered sugar

1. To prepare filling, heat 1¼ cups milk in a medium, heavy saucepan to 180° or until tiny bubbles form around edge (do not boil). Combine ¼ cup milk, ¼ cup granulated sugar, cornstarch, ⅛ teaspoon salt, and 2 eggs in a medium bowl, stirring well with a whisk. Gradually add hot milk to sugar mixture, stirring constantly. Pour milk mixture into pan. Add 1 teaspoon butter; cook over medium heat until thick and bubbly (about 3 minutes), stirring constantly. Reduce heat to low, and cook 2 minutes, stirring constantly. Strain mixture through a sieve into a bowl; stir in vanilla. Place plastic wrap directly on surface of custard, and refrigerate 2 hours or until chilled. Fold in whipped topping. Cover filling, and chill.

2. Preheat oven to 425°.

3. To prepare shells, cover a large, heavy baking sheet with parchment paper. Combine water, 3 tablespoons butter, 2 teaspoons granulated sugar, and ¼ teaspoon salt in a large, heavy saucepan over medium-high heat, stirring occasionally with a wooden spoon. Bring to a boil; remove from heat. Lightly spoon flour into a dry measuring cup; level with a knife. Add flour to water mixture, stirring well until smooth and mixture pulls away from sides of pan. Return pan to heat; cook 30 seconds, stirring constantly. Remove from heat. Add eggs and egg whites, 1 at a time, beating with a mixer at medium speed just until combined. Beat 1 minute at medium speed.

4. Drop dough into 10 mounds (about ¼ cup each), 2 inches apart, onto prepared baking sheet. Bake at 425° for 20 minutes; reduce oven temperature to 350° (do not open oven door). Bake an additional 20 minutes. Turn oven off; partially open oven door. Pierce top of

each puff with a knife; cool puffs in oven 20 minutes. Remove from oven; cool completely on a wire rack.

5. Cut top third off puffs, and fill each puff with about 1 tablespoon filling. Replace tops, and sprinkle with powdered sugar. Yield: 10 servings (serving size: 1 cream puff).

CALORIES 177 (33% from fat); FAT 6.6g (sat 3.4g, mono 2.1g, poly 0.5g); PROTEIN 5.8g; CARB 22.4g; FIBER 0.4g; CHOL 98mg; IRON 0.9mg; SODIUM 185mg; CALC 58mg

Hot Grand Marnier Soufflés

(pictured on page 399; menu on page 418)

This dessert is beautiful, dramatic, and perfect for holiday dinner parties. It's not make-ahead, but to ensure it comes together quickly, separate the eggs, coat the ramekins with sugar, and measure out all the ingredients in advance.

- Cooking spray
- ¾ cup granulated sugar, divided
- 4 large egg yolks
- 3 tablespoons Grand Marnier (orange-flavored liqueur)
- ¾ teaspoon vanilla extract
- 6 large egg whites
- ¼ teaspoon cream of tartar
- ⅛ teaspoon salt
- 1 teaspoon powdered sugar

1. Preheat oven to 400°; place a heavy baking sheet on middle rack.

2. Coat 6 (8-ounce) ramekins with cooking spray; sprinkle each dish with 2 teaspoons granulated sugar, shaking and turning to coat.

3. Place egg yolks in a large bowl; beat with a mixer at medium-high speed 5 minutes or until thick and pale. Gradually add ¼ cup granulated sugar; beat 2 minutes. Beat in liqueur and vanilla.

4. Place egg whites in a large bowl; using clean, dry beaters, beat with a mixer at high speed 1 minute or until foamy. Add cream of tartar and salt, and beat until soft peaks form. Gradually add ¼ cup granulated sugar, 1 tablespoon at a time, beating until stiff peaks form. Gently stir one-fourth of egg white mixture

into liqueur mixture. Gently fold in remaining egg white mixture, and divide evenly among prepared ramekins.

5. Place soufflé dishes on baking sheet in oven; bake at 400° for 10 minutes or until tall and golden brown (soufflés will rise 1½ to 2 inches above the dish rim). Quickly dust soufflés with powdered sugar. Serve immediately. Yield: 6 servings.

CALORIES 167 (18% from fat); FAT 3.4g (sat 1.1g, mono 1.3g, poly 0.5g); PROTEIN 5.4g; CARB 27.2g; FIBER 0g; CHOL 142mg; IRON 0.4mg; SODIUM 109mg; CALC 18mg

Cranberry-Speckled White Chocolate Cheesecake

Making yogurt cheese is effortless but slow. Purchase a yogurt with no added starch, gelatin, or gums. Also, make sure it's not labeled "extracreamy." We used Dannon.

YOGURT CHEESE:
- 1 (32-ounce) container plain fat-free yogurt

CRUST:
- 2 cups graham cracker crumbs (about 9 cookie sheets)
- 2 tablespoons butter, melted
- Cooking spray

CRANBERRY JAM:
- 1 cup dried cranberries
- ½ cup sugar
- ⅓ cup water
- 3 tablespoons fresh lemon juice

FILLING:
- 1 (3.5-ounce) bar premium white chocolate, chopped
- 2 tablespoons fat-free milk
- 1 tablespoon vanilla extract
- 1 cup sugar
- ¼ cup cornstarch
- ¼ teaspoon salt
- 1 (8-ounce) block ⅓-less-fat cream cheese
- 1 (8-ounce) carton reduced-fat sour cream
- 2 large eggs

Continued

1. To prepare yogurt cheese, place a colander in a medium bowl. Line colander with 2 layers of cheesecloth, allowing cheesecloth to extend over outside edge. Spoon yogurt into colander. Cover loosely with plastic wrap; refrigerate 12 hours. Spoon yogurt cheese into a bowl; discard liquid. Cover and refrigerate.

2. Preheat oven to 350°.

3. To prepare crust, combine cracker crumbs and butter, tossing with a fork until moist. Press into bottom of a 9-inch springform pan coated with cooking spray. Bake at 350° for 10 minutes; cool on a wire rack. Reduce oven temperature to 300°.

4. To prepare cranberry jam, combine cranberries and next 3 ingredients in a medium, heavy saucepan. Bring to a boil over medium-high heat. Cover, reduce heat to medium-low, and simmer 10 minutes or until cranberries are soft. Remove from heat; cool slightly. Place cranberry mixture in a food processor; process 2 minutes or until almost smooth. Set aside.

5. To prepare filling, place chocolate and milk in top of a double boiler. Cook over simmering water 5 minutes or until chocolate melts and mixture is smooth, stirring constantly. Remove from heat; stir in vanilla. Set aside.

6. Place yogurt cheese, 1 cup sugar, and next 4 ingredients in a large bowl; beat with a mixer at low speed 1 minute. Beat at medium-high speed 2 minutes or until smooth, scraping bowl occasionally. Beat in chocolate mixture. Add eggs, 1 at a time, beating well after each addition. Scrape bowl; beat 30 seconds. Fold in cranberry jam. Pour over crust, and smooth top. Loosely cover with aluminum foil.

7. Bake at 300° for 1 hour and 10 minutes. Turn oven off; remove foil. Cool cheesecake in closed oven 1 hour and 15 minutes. Remove cheesecake from oven; run a knife around outside edge. Cool to room temperature. Cover and chill at least 8 hours. Yield: 16 servings (serving size: 1 slice).

CALORIES 310 (31% from fat); FAT 10.8g (sat 5.4g, mono 3.2g, poly 0.4g); PROTEIN 6.7g; CARB 48.2g; FIBER 0.6g; CHOL 49mg; IRON 0.8mg; SODIUM 286mg; CALC 49mg

MAKE AHEAD
Overnight Meringue Torte

Look for pasteurized whites or cartons of pasteurized eggs in your supermarket's dairy case. Or you can order them directly from Eggology (888-669-6557, www.eggology.com). If you use pasteurized eggs, whipping the whites to soft peaks will take slightly longer than the recipe specifies.

1½ cups pasteurized egg whites (such as Eggology)
¼ teaspoon salt
½ teaspoon cream of tartar
2½ cups sugar
1½ teaspoons vanilla extract
2 teaspoons butter
3 (10-ounce) packages frozen raspberries in light syrup, thawed and undrained
1½ cups frozen reduced-calorie whipped topping, thawed

1. Preheat oven to 450°.

2. Place egg whites and salt in a large bowl, and beat with a mixer at medium speed until foamy. Add cream of tartar; beat 1 minute. Gradually add 2½ cups sugar, 1 tablespoon at a time, beating until well blended (about 8 minutes). Add vanilla. Increase mixer speed to high; beat 5 minutes or until soft peaks form. (Do not underbeat.) Coat inside of a 10-inch springform pan with butter, and add meringue, spreading evenly. Break air pockets by cutting through meringue with a knife.

3. Place pan in 450° oven. Turn oven off, and cool in closed oven at least 24 hours.

4. Drain raspberries, reserving ¼ cup liquid. Place raspberries in a food processor, and process until smooth. Press raspberry mixture through a fine sieve into a bowl to measure 1¼ cups. Discard solids. Stir in reserved raspberry liquid. Spoon cooled meringue into bowls. Drizzle with raspberry mixture, and top with whipped topping. Yield: 16 servings (serving size: about 1 cup meringue, 1½ tablespoons raspberry mixture, and 1½ tablespoons whipped topping.)

CALORIES 200 (6% from fat); FAT 1.3g (sat 0.7g, mono 0.1g, poly 0.1g); PROTEIN 2.8g; CARB 46.2g; FIBER 2.3g; CHOL 5mg; IRON 0.4mg; SODIUM 80mg; CALC 9mg

MAKE AHEAD
Rich Chocolate Soufflé Cakes with Crème Anglaise
(menu on page 418)

These don't need to be served immediately (although they can be). We loved their fudgy, dense texture when chilled. The crème anglaise is good warmed or chilled.

SOUFFLÉ CAKES:
Cooking spray
8 teaspoons sugar
⅔ cup sugar
½ cup water
2 ounces semisweet chocolate, chopped
1 ounce unsweetened chocolate, chopped
½ cup Dutch process cocoa
3 tablespoons cornstarch
⅛ teaspoon salt
2 large egg yolks
1 teaspoon vanilla extract
4 large egg whites
¼ teaspoon cream of tartar
3 tablespoons sugar

CRÈME ANGLAISE:
3 large egg yolks, lightly beaten
⅛ teaspoon salt
⅓ cup sugar
1 cup 1% low-fat milk
2 teaspoons vanilla extract

1. Preheat oven to 350°.

2. To prepare soufflé cakes, lightly coat 8 (4-ounce) ramekins with cooking spray. Sprinkle each with 1 teaspoon sugar.

3. Combine ⅔ cup sugar and ½ cup water in a medium, heavy saucepan. Bring to a boil over medium heat, stirring to dissolve sugar. Remove from heat. Add chocolates, stirring with a whisk until chocolates melt. Combine ½ cup cocoa, 3 tablespoons cornstarch, and ⅛ teaspoon salt. Add cocoa mixture to chocolate mixture, stirring with a whisk. Whisk in 2 egg yolks and 1 teaspoon vanilla.

4. Place egg whites and cream of tartar in a large bowl; beat with a mixer at medium speed until soft peaks form. Gradually add 3 tablespoons sugar, 1 tablespoon at a time, beating at high

speed until stiff peaks form. Gently stir one-fourth of egg white mixture into chocolate mixture; fold in remaining egg white mixture. Spoon chocolate mixture into prepared ramekins. Place ramekins in a large baking dish; add hot water to dish to a depth of ¾ inch.

5. Bake at 350° for 15 minutes or until puffy and slightly cracked. Remove ramekins from dish.

6. To prepare crème anglaise, combine 3 egg yolks and ⅛ teaspoon salt in a medium bowl. Gradually add ⅓ cup sugar, whisking until thick and pale yellow (about 3 minutes).

7. Heat milk in a heavy saucepan over medium heat to 180° or until tiny bubbles form around edge (do not boil). Remove from heat.

8. Gradually add hot milk to egg yolk mixture, stirring with a whisk. Return egg yolk mixture to pan; cook over medium-low heat 5 minutes or until slightly thick and mixture coats back of a spoon, stirring constantly (do not boil). Remove from heat. Stir in 2 teaspoons vanilla. Serve with soufflé cakes. Yield: 8 servings (serving size: 1 soufflé cake and about 1 tablespoon sauce).

CALORIES 271 (27% from fat); FAT 8.2g (sat 4g, mono 2.2g, poly 0.5g); PROTEIN 6.4g; CARB 47.1g; FIBER 2.7g; CHOL 134mg; IRON 1.4mg; SODIUM 123mg; CALC 63mg

MAKE AHEAD
Espresso Layer Cake

If the intense aroma of freshly ground coffee causes you to swoon, make this cake. It's a big, two-layer cake that's impressive on a dressy cake stand.

CAKE:
  Cooking spray
  ¼ cup hot water
  2 tablespoons finely ground espresso
2¼ cups all-purpose flour
  1 teaspoon baking soda
  ½ teaspoon salt
  1 cup granulated sugar
  ¼ cup packed brown sugar
  ½ cup vegetable shortening
  1 teaspoon vanilla extract
  3 large eggs
  1 cup low-fat buttermilk

FROSTING:
  ¼ cup butter
  ½ cup packed brown sugar
  7 tablespoons evaporated fat-free milk
  2 teaspoons finely ground espresso
1½ teaspoons vanilla extract
  3 cups powdered sugar
  Whole coffee beans (optional)

1. Preheat oven to 350°.

2. To prepare cake, coat 2 (9-inch) round cake pans with cooking spray; line bottom of pans with wax paper. Coat wax paper with cooking spray; set aside.

3. Combine hot water and 2 tablespoons espresso in a small bowl; stir to dissolve. Set aside. Lightly spoon flour into dry measuring cups; level with a knife. Sift together flour, baking soda, and salt; set aside.

4. Combine granulated sugar and ¼ cup brown sugar. Place ¼ cup sugar mixture, shortening, and vanilla in a large bowl; beat with a mixer at low speed 30 seconds or until well combined. Increase speed to medium; add remaining sugar mixture, ¼ cup at a time, beating 15 seconds after each addition. Scrape sides of bowl; beat 5 minutes. Add eggs, 1 at a time, beating 1 minute after each addition. Add espresso mixture, beating until well combined. Add flour mixture and buttermilk alternately to egg mixture, beginning and ending with flour mixture. Pour batter into prepared pans. Bake at 350° for 30 minutes or until a wooden pick inserted in center comes out clean. Cool in pans 10 minutes on a wire rack; remove from pans. Cool completely on wire rack. Discard wax paper.

5. To prepare frosting, melt butter in a medium, heavy saucepan over medium heat. Add ½ cup brown sugar; cook 3 minutes or until mixture is smooth, stirring frequently with a whisk. Stir in evaporated milk, 1 tablespoon at a time; cook 3 minutes or until mixture resembles caramel sauce. Remove from heat; stir in 2 teaspoons espresso. Cool to room temperature. Stir in vanilla. Gradually add powdered sugar, stirring with a whisk until smooth.

6. Place 1 cake layer on a plate; spread with ½ cup frosting. Top with remaining cake layer; spread remaining frosting over

top and sides of cake. Arrange coffee beans around top edge of cake, if desired. Let stand 1 hour or until frosting is set. Yield: 18 servings (serving size: 1 slice).

CALORIES 309 (26% from fat); FAT 9g (sat 3.3g, mono 2.9g, poly 1.6g); PROTEIN 3.7g; CARB 53.4g; FIBER 0.4g; CHOL 43mg; IRON 1.1mg; SODIUM 197mg; CALC 50mg

MAKE AHEAD
Pear-Almond Upside-Down Cake

An ovenproof nonstick skillet works as well as cast iron. You can substitute apples for the pears to vary the flavor of this cake.

  ¼ cup blanched almonds
  1 tablespoon powdered sugar
  2 tablespoons light-colored corn syrup
  1 tablespoon butter
  ½ cup packed brown sugar
  3 peeled Anjou or Bosc pears, cored and each cut into 8 wedges
  ⅓ cup dried tart cherries
  ⅔ cup granulated sugar
  ⅓ cup butter, softened
  2 large eggs
  1 cup all-purpose flour
1¼ teaspoons baking powder
  ¼ teaspoon salt
  ½ cup low-fat buttermilk
  1 teaspoon vanilla extract
  ¼ teaspoon almond extract

1. Preheat oven to 350°.

2. Combine almonds and powdered sugar in a food processor; pulse 8 times or until finely chopped.

3. Heat corn syrup and 1 tablespoon butter in a 10-inch cast iron skillet over medium heat until butter melts. Stir in brown sugar; cook 1 minute or until bubbly. Remove from heat. Arrange pear slices spokelike in pan, working from center of pan to edge; sprinkle with cherries. Cook over medium heat 15 minutes or until syrupy, gently shaking pan occasionally (do not stir).

4. While pears cook, place granulated sugar and ⅓ cup butter in a large bowl; beat with a mixer at medium speed 4 minutes or until well blended. Add eggs,
Continued

1 at a time, beating well after each addition. Lightly spoon flour into a dry measuring cup; level with a knife. Combine almond mixture, flour, baking powder, and salt, stirring well with a whisk. Add flour mixture and buttermilk alternately to egg mixture, beginning and ending with flour mixture; stir with a rubber spatula just until blended. Stir in extracts. Gently spoon batter over pears, spreading evenly. Bake at 350° for 30 minutes or until golden brown. Run a sharp knife around edge of pan to loosen cake. Place a plate upside down on top of pan; carefully invert cake onto plate. Yield: 10 servings (serving size: 1 wedge).

CALORIES 302 (31% from fat); FAT 10.4g (sat 5g, mono 3.7g, poly 0.9g); PROTEIN 4.1g; CARB 49.7g; FIBER 2g; CHOL 62mg; IRON 1.3mg; SODIUM 217mg; CALC 62mg

Party Fare

Whether you host an open house or cocktail party, offer these appetizers for afternoon or evening entertaining.

Party Fare Menu
serves 12

Many of these dishes can be prepared ahead and assembled the morning of the party. They hold up beautifully on the buffet, requiring only that you replenish as needed.

Pomegranate Cocktail

Curried Crab Spread

Warm Mushroom Spread

Chicken and Lemon Pot Stickers with Soy-Scallion Dipping Sauce

Poached Shrimp with Bay Leaves and Lemon

Apple Cider-Glazed Pork Tenderloin on Buttermilk-Chive Biscuits

Swiss Chard Spanakopita Casserole

Lemon-Ginger Biscotti (recipe on page 416)

Pomegranate Cocktail

Fresh orange juice is a great substitute for blood orange juice in this recipe. Garnish with a lime twist, if desired.

    2   cups pomegranate juice
    1½ cups vodka
    1   cup grenadine
    1   cup fresh blood orange juice
        (about 2 oranges)
    ½   cup fresh lime juice (about 2 limes)

1. Combine all ingredients in a pitcher. Serve over ice. Yield: 12 servings (serving size: ½ cup).

CALORIES 171 (1% from fat); FAT 0.1g (sat 0g, mono 0g, poly 0.1g); PROTEIN 0.2g; CARB 28.3g; FIBER 0.1g; CHOL 0mg; IRON 0.2mg; SODIUM 14mg; CALC 6mg

QUICK & EASY • MAKE AHEAD
Curried Crab Spread

This cold crab spread can be made a couple of days ahead. To make the crostini ahead, let the slices cool completely on a wire rack, then place them in a zip-top plastic bag.

    ½   cup minced celery
    ½   cup minced green bell pepper
    ½   cup minced red bell pepper
    ½   cup ⅓-less-fat cream cheese
    ⅓   cup light mayonnaise
    1   teaspoon curry powder
    1   teaspoon hot sauce
    ½   teaspoon salt
    ½   teaspoon grated lemon rind
    ¼   teaspoon dry mustard
    ¼   teaspoon black pepper
    1   pound lump crabmeat, shell pieces
        removed
    36 (¼-inch-thick) slices diagonally
        cut French bread baguette (about
        18 ounces)
    1   tablespoon olive oil

1. Combine first 11 ingredients in a large bowl, stirring until well combined. Gently fold in crabmeat.
2. Preheat broiler.
3. Place bread slices in a single layer on a baking sheet. Brush 1 side of bread slices evenly with olive oil. Broil 1 minute or until lightly brown. Serve with spread.

Yield: 18 servings (serving size: about 2 tablespoons spread and 2 bread slices).

CALORIES 156 (27% from fat); FAT 4.6g (sat 1g, mono 1.4g, poly 0.8g); PROTEIN 7.6g; CARB 21g; FIBER 1.8g; CHOL 22mg; IRON 0.8mg; SODIUM 359mg; CALC 33mg

MAKE AHEAD
Warm Mushroom Spread
(menu on page 418)

Before chopping portobello mushrooms, use a spoon to scrape away the dark brown gills on the undersides. Prepare and refrigerate the dip up to 1 day in advance. Then pop in the microwave for a couple minutes to reheat. Toast the crostini up to 3 days prior to the party, and store them at room temperature in a zip-top plastic bag. Use truffle oil on the bread, if desired.

    32 (½-inch-thick) slices diagonally
        cut French bread baguette (about
        1 pound)
    2   tablespoons olive oil, divided
    ½   cup finely chopped shallots
    1   garlic clove, minced
    4   cups chopped portobello
        mushrooms (about 1 pound)
    4   cups chopped shiitake mushrooms
        (about 1 pound)
    1   cup Madeira wine
    ⅓   cup chopped fresh parsley
    1   teaspoon dried thyme
    1   teaspoon salt
    ¼   teaspoon freshly ground black
        pepper
    ⅓   cup reduced-fat sour cream
    1½ teaspoons balsamic vinegar
    1   tablespoon chopped fresh parsley

1. Preheat broiler.
2. Place bread slices in a single layer on a large baking sheet. Brush 1 side of bread slices evenly with 1 tablespoon oil. Broil 1 minute or until lightly brown.
3. Heat 1 tablespoon oil in a large nonstick skillet over medium-high heat. Add shallots and garlic; sauté 1 minute. Add mushrooms; sauté 5 minutes or until tender. Add wine, ⅓ cup parsley, thyme, salt, and pepper; bring to a boil. Cook 15 minutes or until liquid almost evaporates. Remove from heat; stir in sour cream and vinegar. Spoon into a serving

bowl, and sprinkle with 1 tablespoon parsley. Yield: 16 servings (serving size: 2 bread slices and 2 tablespoons spread).

CALORIES 190 (24% from fat); FAT 5g (sat 1g, mono 2.1g, poly 1.5g); PROTEIN 3.9g; CARB 27.3g; FIBER 2.5g; CHOL 2mg; IRON 1.3mg; SODIUM 331mg; CALC 18mg

MAKE AHEAD

Chicken and Lemon Pot Stickers with Soy-Scallion Dipping Sauce

(menu on page 418)

Make the filling and sauce 1 day ahead, but assemble the pot stickers just before cooking. They're just as good at room temperature as they are when warm. Sprinkle the baking sheet with cornstarch to keep the bottoms of the pot stickers crisp.

POT STICKERS:
- ½ cup dry sherry
- ½ cup water
- ½ ounce dried shiitake mushrooms
- ¾ cup finely chopped bok choy (about ½ pound)
- ⅓ cup chopped green onions
- ¼ cup finely chopped water chestnuts
- 1 tablespoon low-sodium soy sauce
- 2 teaspoons minced peeled fresh ginger
- 2 teaspoons grated lemon rind
- 1 teaspoon salt
- 1 teaspoon dark sesame oil
- Dash of hot sauce
- ½ pound ground chicken or turkey
- 24 wonton wrappers
- 2 tablespoons cornstarch
- ¼ cup vegetable oil, divided
- 1 cup water, divided

SAUCE:
- 5 tablespoons mirin (sweet rice wine)
- ¼ cup low-sodium soy sauce
- ¼ cup seasoned rice vinegar
- 3 tablespoons chopped green onions
- 1 teaspoon chile paste with garlic

1. To prepare pot stickers, bring sherry and ½ cup water to a boil in a small saucepan. Remove from heat; add mushrooms. Cover and let stand 30 minutes or until mushrooms are tender. Drain and discard liquid. Finely chop mushrooms. Combine mushrooms, bok choy, and next 9 ingredients, stirring well.
2. Working with 1 won ton wrapper at a time (cover remaining wrappers with a damp towel to prevent drying), spoon about 1½ teaspoons chicken mixture into center of each wrapper. Moisten edges of dough with water; bring 2 opposite corners to center, pinching points to seal. Bring remaining 2 corners to center, pinching points to seal. Pinch 4 edges together to seal. Place pot stickers on a large baking sheet sprinkled with cornstarch.
3. Heat 2 tablespoons oil in a large non-stick skillet over medium-high heat. Add half of pot stickers; cook 2 minutes or until bottoms are golden brown. Carefully add ½ cup water to pan; cover and cook 4 minutes. Uncover and cook 3 minutes or until liquid evaporates. Repeat procedure with 2 tablespoons oil, remaining pot stickers, and ½ cup water.
4. To prepare sauce, combine mirin and remaining 4 ingredients. Serve with pot stickers. Yield: 12 servings (serving size: 2 pot stickers and about 2 teaspoons sauce).

CALORIES 196 (19% from fat); FAT 4.2g (sat 0.8g, mono 1.7g, poly 0.9g); PROTEIN 4.4g; CARB 32g; FIBER 2.6g; CHOL 2mg; IRON 1.4mg; SODIUM 567mg; CALC 49mg

MAKE AHEAD

Poached Shrimp with Bay Leaves and Lemon

If you love shrimp cocktail, this is for you. Prepare and chill several hours in advance.

- 3 quarts water
- 1½ tablespoons salt
- 1 tablespoon mustard seeds
- 6 whole black peppercorns
- 6 bay leaves
- 1 celery stalk, halved
- 1 carrot, halved
- 2 pounds medium shrimp, peeled and deveined
- 2 teaspoons grated lemon rind
- ½ cup fresh lemon juice
- 1 tablespoon extravirgin olive oil
- ½ teaspoon salt
- ¼ teaspoon freshly ground black pepper

1. Combine first 7 ingredients in a Dutch oven; bring to a boil. Reduce heat; simmer 15 minutes. Add shrimp; cook 3 minutes. Drain shrimp. Place shrimp mixture in a shallow dish.
2. Combine lemon rind and remaining ingredients. Add to warm shrimp mixture; toss well. Cover and chill until ready to serve. Yield: 12 servings (serving size: 3 ounces).

CALORIES 94 (24% from fat); FAT 2.5g (sat 0.4g, mono 1.1g, poly 0.6g); PROTEIN 15.4g; CARB 1.7g; FIBER 0.1g; CHOL 115mg; IRON 1.9mg; SODIUM 313mg; CALC 46mg

Apple Cider-Glazed Pork Tenderloin

(menu on page 418)

Its small size makes pork tenderloin a good choice for buffet biscuit sandwiches. Reduce apple cider and chicken broth to a flavorful syrup to brush over the cooked pork. Serve apple chutney and coarse-grain mustard alongside the pork and Buttermilk-Chive Biscuits (recipe on page 414).

- 2 tablespoons dried rosemary, crushed
- 1 tablespoon minced peeled fresh ginger
- 1 tablespoon grated orange rind
- 1 tablespoon olive oil
- ½ teaspoon salt
- ¼ teaspoon freshly ground black pepper
- 6 garlic cloves, minced
- 3 (1-pound) pork tenderloins, trimmed
- 3 cups apple cider
- 3 whole cloves
- 2 bay leaves
- 1 cup fat-free, less-sodium chicken broth

1. Combine first 7 ingredients, and rub evenly over pork. Place pork in a dish; cover and chill 1 hour.
2. Combine cider, cloves, and bay leaves in a large skillet; bring to a boil over medium-high heat. Cook until reduced to 1½ cups (about 10 minutes). Add broth; bring to a boil. Add pork; cover and simmer 20 minutes or until done. Remove pork from pan. Bring cooking
Continued

liquid to a boil. Cook until reduced to ¾ cup (about 8 minutes). Strain cooking liquid through a fine sieve into a bowl; discard solids. Spoon sauce over pork. Cut pork into thin slices. Yield: 12 servings (serving size: 3 ounces).

CALORIES 183 (25% from fat); FAT 5.1g (sat 1.5g, mono 2.6g, poly 0.5g); PROTEIN 24.2g; CARB 8.7g; FIBER 0.4g; CHOL 74mg; IRON 1.6mg; SODIUM 198mg; CALC 17mg

Cut the phyllo stacks so they fit in and up the long sides of the baking dish.

Arrange folded sections against short edges of dish to encase filling.

Swiss Chard Spanakopita Casserole

(menu on page 418)

A casserole version of the classic individual pastries, this recipe is much quicker to assemble with less fuss, and is just as tasty.

Cooking spray
2¼ cups minced white onion
¾ cup minced green onions
3 garlic cloves, minced
9 cups chopped trimmed Swiss chard (about 1½ pounds)
6 tablespoons chopped fresh parsley
3 tablespoons minced fresh mint
1 cup (4 ounces) crumbled feta cheese
½ cup (2 ounces) freshly grated Parmesan cheese
½ teaspoon salt
¼ teaspoon black pepper
3 large egg whites, lightly beaten
10 (18 x 14-inch) sheets frozen phyllo dough, thawed

1. Preheat oven to 350°.
2. Heat a large nonstick skillet coated with cooking spray over medium-high heat. Add white onion; sauté 7 minutes or until golden. Add green onions and garlic, and sauté 1 minute. Stir in chard; cook 2 minutes or until chard wilts. Stir in parsley and mint, and cook 1 minute. Place in a large bowl; cool slightly. Stir in cheeses, salt, pepper, and egg whites.
3. Place 1 phyllo sheet on a large cutting board (cover remaining phyllo to prevent drying), and coat with cooking spray. Top with 1 phyllo sheet, and coat with cooking spray. Repeat procedure with 3 additional sheets.
4. Cut phyllo stack into a 14-inch square. Place square in center of a 13 x 9-inch baking dish coated with cooking spray, allowing phyllo to extend up long sides of dish. Cut 14 x 4-inch piece into 2 (7 x 4-inch) rectangles. Fold each rectangle in half lengthwise. Place each rectangle against an empty side at short ends of dish. Spread chard mixture evenly over phyllo. Repeat Step 3 with remaining phyllo sheets. Place 18 x 14-inch phyllo stack over chard mixture. Fold overhanging phyllo edges to center. Coat with cooking spray. Score phyllo by making 2 lengthwise cuts and 3 crosswise cuts to form 12 rectangles. Bake at 350° for 40 minutes or until golden. Yield: 12 servings.

CALORIES 121 (35% from fat); FAT 4.7g (sat 2.8g, mono 1.4g, poly 0.3g); PROTEIN 6.1g; CARB 13.6g; FIBER 1.6g; CHOL 14mg; IRON 1.3mg; SODIUM 449mg; CALC 134mg

MAKE AHEAD
Buttermilk-Chive Biscuits

(menu on page 418)

Replace the chives with an equal amount of any of your favorite fresh herbs, if desired. Bake the biscuits up to 3 days ahead, and store in an airtight container. To reheat, place in a 300° oven for 10 minutes. To maximize the number of biscuits, gather the dough scraps after cutting and gently reroll to a ½-inch thickness. A light hand with the dough will ensure tender biscuits.

2 cups all-purpose flour
1 tablespoon baking powder
½ teaspoon baking soda
½ teaspoon salt
¼ cup chilled butter, cut into small pieces
¾ cup low-fat buttermilk
1 large egg, lightly beaten
¼ cup chopped fresh chives

1. Preheat oven to 400°.
2. Lightly spoon flour into dry measuring cups; level with a knife. Combine flour, baking powder, baking soda, and salt in a large bowl; cut in butter with a pastry blender or 2 knives until mixture resembles coarse meal. Combine buttermilk and egg, and stir in chives. Add buttermilk mixture to flour mixture, and stir just until moist.
3. Turn dough out onto a heavily floured surface; knead lightly 5 times. Roll dough to a ½-inch thickness; cut with a 2-inch biscuit cutter. Place dough rounds, 1 inch apart, on a baking sheet. Bake at 400° for 12 minutes or until golden. Serve warm or at room temperature. Yield: 20 biscuits (serving size: 1 biscuit).

CALORIES 74 (33% from fat); FAT 2.7g (sat 1.6g, mono 0.8g, poly 0.2g); PROTEIN 2g; CARB 10.2g; FIBER 0.4g; CHOL 17mg; IRON 0.7mg; SODIUM 199mg; CALC 56mg

Gifts from the Kitchen

From ready-to-make pancakes to exotic preserved lemons, these gifts will be well received.

MAKE AHEAD
Preserved Lemons

This classic Moroccan condiment brings lemony zing to lamb and poultry dishes. We've added saffron for earthy flavor and beautiful golden-orange color. Pack in a wide-mouth glass pint container. Attach this recipe suggestion to the gift: For subtle lemon-saffron flavor, stir 2 chopped preserved lemon slices into 2 cups cooked basmati rice.

    1   tablespoon kosher salt
    ½   teaspoon saffron threads, crushed
    2   cups thinly sliced lemon (about 3
        lemons)
    ¼   cup fresh lemon juice
    1   tablespoon olive oil

1. Combine salt and saffron. Place one lemon slice in bottom of a wide-mouth 2-cup glass container. Sprinkle with a dash of salt mixture. Repeat layers with remaining lemon slices and salt mixture. Cover and let stand at room temperature 3 days.

2. After 3 days, press lemon slices down with a spoon. Pour juice and oil over lemon slices. Place a ramekin, custard cup, or clean decorative stone on top of lemon slices (to weigh them down). Cover and let stand at room temperature 5 days. Yield: 1 cup (serving size: 1 tablespoon).

NOTE: Preserved lemons can be stored at room temperature up to 1 month, or refrigerated up to 6 months.

CALORIES 11 (74% from fat); FAT 0.9g (sat 0.1g, mono 0.6g, poly 0.1g); PROTEIN 0.1g; CARB 1g; FIBER 0.2g; CHOL 0mg; IRON 0.1mg; SODIUM 353mg; CALC 2mg

How to Cut the Dough

Floss or thread cuts the dough roll much more quickly and easily than a knife.

MAKE AHEAD • FREEZABLE
Freezer Cinnamon-Fruit Rolls

These frozen rolls are good for busy mornings—let them stand at room temperature 30 minutes, then bake 20 minutes. Make them in disposable foil pans for easy gift-giving; present the glaze in a small jar with instructions to microwave at HIGH 15 to 30 seconds, stir until smooth, and drizzle over warm rolls.

DOUGH:

    1   package dry yeast (about 2¼
        teaspoons)
    ¼   cup warm water (100° to 110°)
    ½   cup fat-free milk
    ⅓   cup granulated sugar
    ¼   cup butter, melted
    1   teaspoon vanilla extract
    ½   teaspoon salt
    1   large egg, lightly beaten
    3¾ cups all-purpose flour, divided
        Cooking spray

FILLING:

    ⅔   cup packed brown sugar
    ½   cup golden raisins
    ½   cup chopped dried apricots
    ½   cup chopped pecans
    1   tablespoon ground cinnamon
    2   tablespoons butter, melted

GLAZE:

    1   cup powdered sugar
    2   tablespoons fat-free milk

1. Dissolve yeast in warm water in a large bowl; let stand 5 minutes. Stir in ½ cup milk and next 5 ingredients. Lightly spoon flour into dry measuring cups; level with a knife. Add 3½ cups flour to yeast mixture, stirring until blended. Turn dough out onto a floured surface. Knead until smooth and elastic (about 10 minutes); add enough of remaining flour, 1 tablespoon at a time, to prevent dough from sticking to hands (dough will feel sticky).

2. Place dough in a large bowl coated with cooking spray, turning to coat top. Cover and let rise in a warm place (85°), free from drafts, 1 hour or until doubled in size. (Gently press two fingers into dough. If indentation remains, dough has risen enough.) Punch dough down; cover and let rest 5 minutes.

3. To prepare filling, combine brown sugar and next 4 ingredients.

4. Roll dough into an 18 x 10-inch rectangle on a floured surface. Brush 2 tablespoons melted butter over dough. Sprinkle 1½ cups filling over dough, leaving a ½-inch border. Beginning with a long side, roll up dough jelly-roll fashion; pinch seam to seal (do not seal ends of roll).

5. Place a long piece of dental floss or thread under dough ¾ inch from end of roll. Cross ends of floss over top of dough roll; slowly pull ends to cut through dough. Repeat procedure to make 24 rolls. Coat 2 (9-inch) square foil baking pans with cooking spray. Sprinkle remaining filling evenly into bottom of pans. Place 12 rolls, cut sides up, in each prepared pan. Cover and let rise 1½ hours or until doubled in size.

6. Preheat oven to 350°.

7. Uncover rolls. Bake at 350° for 20 minutes or until browned. Invert onto a serving platter.

8. To prepare glaze, combine powdered sugar and 2 tablespoons milk, stirring until smooth. Drizzle over warm rolls. Yield: 24 servings (serving size: 1 roll).

TO FREEZE UNBAKED ROLLS: Prepare through Step 5. Cover with plastic wrap. Wrap tightly with heavy-duty foil. Store in freezer up to 2 months.

Continued

Remove rolls from freezer; let stand at room temperature 30 minutes. Uncover and bake at 350° for 20 minutes or until browned.

CALORIES 193 (24% from fat); FAT 5.1g (sat 2g, mono 1.9g, poly 0.8g); PROTEIN 3.1g; CARB 34.4g; FIBER 1.4g; CHOL 17mg; IRON 1.5mg; SODIUM 87mg; CALC 28mg

MAKE AHEAD
Croquant

Instead of high-fat pralines, toffee, or brittle, give *croquant* (French for "crisp")—a cream- and butter-free combination of caramelized sugar and almonds. Package in a paper-lined confection box or pretty bowl with a note to crumble over ice cream, layer into parfaits, or simply eat like brittle. Be careful not to burn yourself when pouring the hot mixture into the jelly roll pan. The color of the sugar mixture (rather than temperature) is the best cue for doneness. The darker the color, the more bitter the candy—aim for a golden honey color. If your pan is too dark to gauge the color of the caramel, very carefully lift a small amount of the mixture with a wooden spoon and drop it onto a piece of white paper—the level of caramelization will be evident.

    3 cups sugar
    ¾ cup water
    1½ cups sliced almonds,
         toasted
    Cooking spray

1. Combine sugar and water in a medium, heavy saucepan, being careful not to splash sides of pan. Stir gently over high heat just until sugar dissolves (do not stir beyond this point). Using a clean pastry brush dipped in water, brush inside walls of pan to loosen any sugar particles.
2. Cook sugar mixture over high heat until light golden brown (about 10 to 15 minutes; do not leave unattended). Remove pan from heat; gently stir in almonds. Immediately pour almond mixture onto a jelly roll pan coated with cooking spray. Cool completely; break into pieces. Yield: 20 servings (serving size: about 1½ ounces).

NOTE: Store in an airtight container up to 5 days.

CALORIES 159 (20% from fat); FAT 3.6g (sat 0.3g, mono 2.3g, poly 0.9g); PROTEIN 1.5g; CARB 31.3g; FIBER 0.7g; CHOL 0mg; IRON 0mg; SODIUM 0mg; CALC 19mg

MAKE AHEAD
Lemon-Ginger Biscotti
(menus on pages 412 and 418)

Seal these crunchy cookies in a tin, and give them with your recipient's favorite coffee, tea, or bottle of port. Or pile the biscotti in a jumbo latte cup with the recipe tied to the handle.

    2½ cups all-purpose flour
    1 cup sugar
    1 teaspoon baking soda
    ½ teaspoon ground ginger
    ¼ teaspoon salt
    ¼ cup finely chopped crystallized
         ginger
    2 tablespoons grated lemon
         rind
    1 tablespoon fresh lemon
         juice
    3 large eggs, lightly beaten
    Cooking spray
    1 tablespoon water
    1 large egg white, lightly beaten
    1 tablespoon sugar

1. Preheat oven to 350°.
2. Lightly spoon flour into dry measuring cups; level with a knife. Combine flour and next 4 ingredients in a large bowl, stirring with a whisk. Stir in crystallized ginger. Combine rind, juice, and 3 eggs; add to flour mixture, stirring until well blended (dough will be crumbly). Turn dough out onto a lightly floured surface; knead lightly 7 or 8 times. Divide dough in half. Shape each portion into a 9-inch-long roll. Place rolls 6 inches apart on a baking sheet coated with cooking spray; flatten each roll to a 1-inch thickness. Combine water and egg white; brush over rolls. Sprinkle rolls evenly with 1 tablespoon sugar.
3. Bake at 350° for 20 minutes. Remove rolls from baking sheet; cool 10 minutes on a wire rack. Cut each roll diagonally into 15 (¾-inch) slices. Carefully stand slices upright on baking sheet. Reduce oven temperature to 325°; bake 20 minutes (cookies will be slightly soft in center but will harden as they cool). Remove from baking sheet; cool completely on a wire rack. Yield: 2½ dozen (serving size: 1 biscotto).

CALORIES 77 (7% from fat); FAT 0.6g (sat 0.2g, mono 0.2g, poly 0.1g); PROTEIN 1.8g; CARB 16.1g; FIBER 0.3g; CHOL 21mg; IRON 0.6mg; SODIUM 70mg; CALC 6mg

MAKE AHEAD
Sugared Cranberries

Because of the contrast between the tart cranberries and sugary coating, the flavor of this snack pops in your mouth. The berries are steeped in hot sugar syrup to tame their tangy bite. When entertaining, serve these in place of nuts. For gift-giving, package in parchment-lined tins. Present with a small bottle of the reserved cranberry cooking syrup for the recipient to use as a cocktail mixer. If you can't find superfine sugar, make your own by processing granulated sugar in a food processor for 1 minute.

    2 cups granulated sugar
    2 cups water
    2 cups fresh cranberries
    ¾ cup superfine sugar

1. Combine granulated sugar and water in a small saucepan over low heat, stirring until sugar dissolves. Bring to a simmer; remove from heat. (Do not boil or cranberries may pop when added.) Stir in cranberries; pour mixture into a bowl. Cover and refrigerate 8 hours or overnight.
2. Drain cranberries in a colander over a bowl, reserving liquid, if desired. Place superfine sugar in a shallow dish. Add cranberries, rolling to coat. Spread cranberries in a single layer on a baking sheet; let stand at room temperature 1 hour or until dry. Yield: 9 servings (serving size: about ⅓ cup).

NOTE: Store in an airtight container in a cool place up to 1 week.

CALORIES 118 (0% from fat); FAT 0g; PROTEIN 0.1g; CARB 30.4g; FIBER 0.9g; CHOL 0mg; IRON 0.1mg; SODIUM 0mg; CALC 2mg

Cheddar-Asiago Potato Bread

Mashed potatoes make an especially tender bread that's great for sandwiches. This recipe makes two loaves. Keep one for yourself, and wrap the other in a pretty kitchen towel secured with a ribbon or raffia.

    3 cups cubed peeled baking potato
       (about 1 pound)
    1 package dry yeast (about 2¼
       teaspoons)
 5½ cups all-purpose flour, divided
    2 teaspoons salt
    ¾ teaspoon freshly ground black
       pepper
    1 cup (4 ounces) shredded
       extra-sharp Cheddar cheese
    ¾ cup (3 ounces) grated Asiago cheese
 Cooking spray

1. Place potato in a saucepan; cover with water. Bring to a boil. Reduce heat; simmer 15 minutes or until tender. Drain in a colander over a bowl, reserving 1¼ cups cooking liquid. Cool liquid to 110°. Mash potato with a potato masher to measure 2 cups; set aside.
2. Combine warm cooking liquid and yeast in a large bowl; let stand 5 minutes. Stir in mashed potato. Lightly spoon flour into dry measuring cups; level with a knife. Gradually stir 5 cups flour, salt, and pepper into potato mixture to form a stiff dough.
3. Turn dough out onto a lightly floured surface. Knead until smooth and elastic (about 10 minutes); add enough of remaining flour, 1 tablespoon at a time, to prevent dough from sticking to hands. Gently knead in cheeses.
4. Place dough in a large bowl coated with cooking spray, turning to coat top. Cover and let rise in a warm place (85°), free from drafts, 30 minutes or until doubled in size. (Gently press two fingers into dough. If indentation remains, dough has risen enough.) Punch dough down; cover and let rest 5 minutes. Divide dough in half. Working with one portion at a time (cover remaining dough to prevent drying), roll each portion into an 11 x 7-inch rectangle on a floured

surface. Roll up each rectangle tightly, starting with a short edge, pressing firmly to eliminate air pockets; pinch seam and ends to seal. Place rolls, seam sides down, in 2 (8 x 4-inch) loaf pans coated with cooking spray. Cover and let rise 45 minutes or until doubled in size.
5. Preheat oven to 375°.
6. Uncover dough; bake at 375° for 1 hour or until loaves are browned on bottom and sound hollow when tapped. Remove from pans; cool on a wire rack. Yield: 2 loaves, 12 slices per loaf (serving size: 1 slice).

CALORIES 151 (17% from fat); FAT 2.8g (sat 1.5g, mono 0.8g, poly 0.3g); PROTEIN 5.5g; CARB 25.7g; FIBER 1.1g; CHOL 8mg; IRON 1.6mg; SODIUM 270mg; CALC 67mg

Apple Butter
(menu on page 418)

This treat needs to be refrigerated; a clear glass jar with a secure lid will work best. To decorate, tie a cinnamon stick and star anise to the jar with ribbon or raffia. It's a spicy partner for toasted slices of Cheddar-Asiago Potato Bread (recipe at left).

    4 pounds Granny Smith apples,
       peeled, cored, and quartered
    1 cup apple cider
    ¼ cup packed dark brown sugar
    1 tablespoon fresh lemon juice
    ¼ teaspoon salt
 Dash of ground cloves
    2 (3-inch) cinnamon sticks
    1 star anise

1. Combine apples and cider in a large stockpot; bring to a boil. Reduce heat; simmer, partially covered, 30 minutes or until apples are tender.
2. Place mixture in a food processor; pulse 6 times or until chunky. Return to pan.
3. Stir in sugar and remaining ingredients. Cook over low heat 1 hour or until thick, stirring occasionally. Discard cinnamon and star anise. Cover and chill. Yield: 4 cups (serving size: ¼ cup).
NOTE: Store in an airtight container in refrigerator up to 1 month.

CALORIES 76 (4% from fat); FAT 0.3g (sat 0.1g, mono 0g, poly 0.1g); PROTEIN 0.2g; CARB 19.6g; FIBER 1.8g; CHOL 0mg; IRON 0.1mg; SODIUM 40mg; CALC 7mg

Vanilla Bean Pancakes

Prepare through Step 1, and package with a recipe card.

    2 cups all-purpose flour
    1 tablespoon sugar
    ½ teaspoon baking soda
    ¼ teaspoon salt
    1 vanilla bean
 1½ cups low-fat buttermilk
    2 large eggs, lightly beaten
 Cooking spray

1. Lightly spoon flour into dry measuring cups; level with a knife. Combine flour, sugar, baking soda, and salt, stirring with a whisk; add vanilla bean. Store in an airtight container at least 2 days. Remove bean; reserve for another use.
2. Combine buttermilk and eggs in a large bowl, stirring with a whisk. Add flour mixture to buttermilk mixture, stirring with a whisk until well combined.
3. Heat a nonstick griddle or large nonstick skillet coated with cooking spray over medium heat. Spoon a scant ¼ cup batter onto griddle for each pancake. Turn pancakes when tops are covered with bubbles and edges look cooked (about 3 minutes). Yield: 6 servings (serving size: 2 pancakes).

CALORIES 209 (11% from fat); FAT 2.6g (sat 0.9g, mono 0.8g, poly 0.4g); PROTEIN 8.4g; CARB 37g; FIBER 1.1g; CHOL 73mg; IRON 2.2mg; SODIUM 289mg; CALC 86mg

Maple-Blueberry Syrup

    2 cups maple syrup
    1 (12-ounce) bag frozen blueberries
    1 tablespoon fresh lemon juice

1. Combine syrup and blueberries in a medium saucepan. Bring to a boil over medium-high heat, stirring occasionally. Remove from heat; stir in juice. Pour into a bowl; cover and chill. Serve warm. Yield: 3 cups (serving size: about 3 tablespoons).
NOTE: Store in refrigerator up to 2 weeks.

CALORIES 116 (2% from fat); FAT 0.2g (sat 0g, mono 0g, poly 0.1g); PROTEIN 0.1g; CARB 29.6g; FIBER 0.6g; CHOL 0mg; IRON 0.5mg; SODIUM 4mg; CALC 29mg

Potato Pancakes with Chive Yogurt Cheese

(menu below)

Give these as a Hanukkah present—potato pancakes reheat easily in the oven. Give the frozen pancakes with a package of smoked salmon for a terrific brunch option.

YOGURT CHEESE:

- 2 cups plain low-fat yogurt
- ⅓ cup chopped fresh chives
- ¼ teaspoon salt
- ⅛ teaspoon freshly ground black pepper

POTATO PANCAKES:

- 6 cups shredded baking potato (about 2 pounds)
- 1 cup grated fresh onion
- 2 tablespoons all-purpose flour
- 1 teaspoon salt
- ½ teaspoon freshly ground black pepper
- 2 large eggs, lightly beaten
- 2½ tablespoons vegetable oil, divided

1. To prepare yogurt cheese, place a colander or sieve in a 2-quart glass measure or medium bowl. Line colander with 4 layers of cheesecloth, allowing cheesecloth to extend over outside edge. Spoon yogurt into colander. Cover loosely with plastic wrap; refrigerate 12 hours. Spoon yogurt cheese into a bowl; discard liquid. Stir in chives, ¼ teaspoon salt, and ⅛ teaspoon pepper. Cover and refrigerate.

2. To prepare potato cakes, spread potato and onion between several layers of paper towels; let stand 15 minutes or until barely moist, pressing occasionally. Combine flour, 1 teaspoon salt, ½ teaspoon pepper, and eggs in a large bowl. Stir in potato and onion.

3. Heat about 2 teaspoons oil in a large nonstick skillet over medium-high heat. Spoon 2 tablespoons potato mixture for each of 6 pancakes onto pan. Cook 2 minutes on each side or until golden. Repeat procedure with remaining oil and potato mixture. Serve with yogurt cheese. Yield: 8 servings (serving size: 3 pancakes and 2 tablespoons yogurt cheese).

NOTE: To freeze, let cooked pancakes cool completely. Stack in an airtight container between layers of wax paper; freeze up to 2 months. To reheat, place on a baking sheet. Bake at 350° for 15 minutes.

CALORIES 187 (30% from fat); FAT 6.3g (sat 1.4g, mono 1.7g, poly 2.7g); PROTEIN 6.7g; CARB 27g; FIBER 2g; CHOL 56mg; IRON 1.4mg; SODIUM 417mg; CALC 104mg

---

Six Holiday Menus

To make meal planning easier, we composed six all-occasion menus with dishes from our holiday cookbook.

Holiday Dinner Menu

Garden salad

Beef Tenderloin with Parsnip-Mushroom Ragoût
(recipe on page 402)

Long grain and wild rice

Green beans

Buttermilk-Chive Biscuits
(recipe on page 414)

Rich Chocolate Soufflé Cakes with Crème Anglaise
(recipe on page 410)

Brunch Menu

Potato Pancakes with Chive Yogurt Cheese
(recipe above)

Smoked salmon

Grapes

Reduced-fat refrigerated crescent rolls

Apple Butter
(recipe on page 417)

Mimosas

Sunday Dinner Menu

Apple Cider-Glazed Pork Tenderloin
(recipe on page 413)

Barley Risotto with Caramelized Leeks and Mushrooms
(recipe on page 407)

Broccoli spears

Cranberry sauce

Dinner rolls

Vanilla ice cream

Dinner Party Menu

Warm Mushroom Spread
(recipe on page 412)

Green salad

Squash-Stuffed Cannelloni with Roasted-Shallot Sauce and Hazelnuts
(recipe on page 405)

Garlic breadsticks

Hot Grand Marnier Soufflés
(recipe on page 409)

Weeknight Supper Menu

Pan sautéed pork chops

Marsala-Glazed Winter Vegetables
(recipe on page 408)

Swiss Chard Spanakopita Casserole
(recipe on page 414)

Whole wheat dinner rolls

Lemon sorbet

Try Something New Menu

Chicken and Lemon Pot Stickers with Soy-Scallion Dipping Sauce
(recipe on page 413)

Bourbon-Brown Sugar Salmon with Onion Sauce
(recipe on page 404)

White rice

Sugar snap peas

Lemon-Ginger Biscotti
(recipe on page 416)

Green tea

All About Holiday Spices

Spices traditionally associated with holiday dishes add a festive touch year-round.

Holiday spices offer a variety of great contemporary flavor combinations, and in the following descriptions and recipes, you'll find ideas to further explore their versatility.

STAFF FAVORITE
Chicken and Basmati Rice Pilau with Saffron, Spinach, and Cardamom

The cardamom in the pilaf is left whole, so the pods need to be bruised or crushed slightly to allow the flavor to escape. The delicate scent of basmati rice works well with saffron and cardamom. Serve this dish with yogurt and cilantro relish flavored with a little crushed garlic and ground, toasted cumin. If you don't have a nonstick skillet large enough to hold 10 cups, use a Dutch oven.

1½ cups uncooked basmati rice
¾ cup dried lentils
Cooking spray
10 skinless, boneless chicken thighs (about 1¼ pounds)
2 cups vertically sliced onion
2 teaspoons chopped peeled fresh ginger
1 cup shredded carrot
4 cardamom pods, lightly crushed
½ teaspoon grated orange rind
½ cup fresh orange juice (about 1 orange)
1 teaspoon salt
¼ teaspoon black pepper
2½ cups warm fat-free, less-sodium chicken broth
⅛ teaspoon saffron threads, crushed
1 (6-ounce) package fresh baby spinach, coarsely chopped
1 teaspoon butter
½ cup blanched almonds

1. Cover rice with cold water. Let stand 20 minutes. Drain and rinse with cold water. Drain.
2. Sort and rinse lentils. Place lentils in a small saucepan; cover with water 2 inches above lentils. Bring to a boil. Reduce heat; simmer 20 minutes or until almost tender. Drain.
3. Heat a large nonstick skillet coated with cooking spray over medium-high heat. Add chicken; cook 4 minutes on each side or until lightly browned. Remove chicken from pan. Add onion and ginger to pan; sauté 7 minutes or until tender. Add carrot and cardamom; sauté 2 minutes. Return chicken to pan. Add rice, lentils, rind, juice, salt, and pepper. Combine broth and saffron; stir until saffron is dissolved. Add saffron mixture to pan; bring to a simmer. Cover and cook 15 minutes or until rice is almost tender and liquid is absorbed. Stir in spinach. Remove from heat. Cover with a towel; place lid over towel. Let stand 10 minutes.
4. Melt butter in a small skillet over medium heat. Add almonds; cook 5 minutes or until lightly browned, stirring frequently. Sprinkle almonds over chicken mixture. Yield: 5 servings (serving size: 2 cups).

CALORIES 601 (19% from fat); FAT 12.7g (sat 2.2g, mono 6.1g, poly 2.8g); PROTEIN 40.1g; CARB 85.8g; FIBER 14.5g; CHOL 96mg; IRON 7.4mg; SODIUM 837mg; CALC 119mg

Pasta with Spinach, Nutmeg, and Shrimp

Musky nutmeg combines naturally with spinach and pasta in this simple supper dish. For maximum flavor, always use freshly grated nutmeg.

12 ounces uncooked penne pasta
1 (10-ounce) package fresh spinach
2 tablespoons butter, divided
1½ pounds large shrimp, peeled and deveined
½ teaspoon salt, divided
2½ cups chopped Vidalia or other sweet onion
1 cup vegetable broth
¼ cup dry vermouth
1 teaspoon finely grated fresh lemon rind
½ cup (4 ounces) ⅓-less-fat cream cheese
½ teaspoon freshly grated nutmeg
¼ teaspoon freshly ground black pepper

1. Prepare pasta according to package directions, omitting salt and fat. Drain well; return to pan. Stir in spinach; toss well until spinach wilts.
2. Melt 1 tablespoon butter in a large nonstick skillet over medium-high heat. Add shrimp. Sprinkle with ¼ teaspoon salt; sauté 2 minutes or until shrimp are done. Remove shrimp from pan; set aside. Melt 1 tablespoon butter in pan over medium heat. Add onion; cook 10 minutes or until tender, stirring frequently.
3. Stir in broth, vermouth, and rind. Increase heat to medium-high; cook 8 minutes or until mixture begins to thicken. Reduce heat to medium. Add cheese; stir until well blended. Stir in ¼ teaspoon salt, nutmeg, and pepper; remove from heat. Add shrimp and onion mixture to pasta mixture; toss to combine. Yield: 6 servings (serving size: about 2 cups).

CALORIES 496 (21% from fat); FAT 11.8g (sat 5.6g, mono 2.7g, poly 1.2g); PROTEIN 35.3g; CARB 59.2g; FIBER 4.8g; CHOL 197mg; IRON 14.6mg; SODIUM 685mg; CALC 150mg

Saffron and Raisin Breakfast Bread

This recipe employs the technique of steeping saffron in hot liquid to release its color and aroma. Serve toasted or plain with honey for a special holiday breakfast or brunch.

1⅓ cups warm fat-free milk (100° to 110°)
¼ teaspoon saffron threads, crushed
1 package dry yeast (about 2¼ teaspoons)
1 teaspoon sugar
½ cup warm water (100° to 110°)
5¼ cups bread flour, divided
1½ cups raisins
¼ cup sugar
3 tablespoons butter, melted and cooled
1 teaspoon salt
Cooking spray

1. Combine milk and saffron; let stand 10 minutes.

2. Dissolve yeast and 1 teaspoon sugar in warm water in a large bowl; let stand 5 minutes or until foamy. Stir in milk mixture. Lightly spoon flour into dry measuring cups; level with a knife. Add 5 cups flour, raisins, ¼ cup sugar, butter, and salt to milk mixture, stirring to form a soft dough. Turn dough out onto a floured surface. Knead until smooth and elastic (about 8 minutes); add enough of remaining flour, 1 tablespoon at a time, to prevent dough from sticking to hands (dough will feel sticky).

3. Place dough in a large bowl coated with cooking spray, turning to coat top. Cover and let rise in a warm place (85°), free from drafts, 1½ hours or until doubled in size. (Gently press two fingers into dough. If indentation remains, dough has risen enough.) Punch dough down; cover and let rest 5 minutes. Divide in half. Shape each portion into a 5-inch round loaf. Place loaves, 3 inches apart, on a large baking sheet coated with cooking spray. Make 2 diagonal cuts ¼-inch-deep across top of each loaf using a sharp knife. Cover and let rise 30 minutes or until doubled in size.

4. Preheat oven to 375°.

5. Uncover dough. Bake at 375° for 30 minutes or until loaves are browned on bottom and sound hollow when tapped. Remove from pan; cool on wire racks. Yield: 2 loaves, 20 servings (serving size: 1 slice).

CALORIES 199 (11% from fat); FAT 2.4g (sat 1.2g, mono 0.6g, poly 0.3g); PROTEIN 5.4g; CARB 39.5g; FIBER 1.4g; CHOL 5mg; IRON 1.9mg; SODIUM 145mg; CALC 33mg

Lamb Tagine with Cinnamon, Saffron, and Dried Fruit

Warm cinnamon and saffron combine with coriander and cumin to lend complex flavor to this Moroccan-style dish. Adding the spice paste in two stages gives depth and brightens the flavor. Leaving the cinnamon whole keeps its influence subtle. Moroccan tagines tend to be warmly and sweetly spiced rather than hot. A *tagine* is named after the earthenware, conical-lidded dish in which it is traditionally cooked. This festive dish is served over couscous to soak up the delicious gravy.

¼ cup diced seeded Anaheim chile
1 teaspoon cumin seeds, toasted
1 teaspoon coriander seeds, toasted
1 teaspoon grated peeled fresh ginger
½ teaspoon salt
½ teaspoon paprika
¼ teaspoon freshly ground black peppercorns
2 garlic cloves, minced
Cooking spray
1 (1½-pound) boneless leg of lamb, trimmed and cubed
3 cups chopped onion
½ cup tomato purée
2½ cups water
2¾ cups green bell pepper, cut into 1-inch-thick strips
2 cups cubed butternut squash
1 cup cubed carrot
¼ teaspoon saffron threads
1 (3-inch) cinnamon stick
⅔ cup dried apricots, cut into ¼-inch strips
4½ cups cooked couscous
¼ cup minced fresh cilantro

1. Preheat oven to 325°.

2. Combine first 8 ingredients.

3. Heat a large nonstick skillet coated with cooking spray over medium-high heat. Add lamb; cook 8 minutes on all sides or until browned. Remove lamb from pan. Add onion to pan; cook 5 minutes or until tender, stirring frequently. Stir in half of chile mixture and tomato purée; cook 3 minutes, stirring occasionally. Stir in lamb and water; bring to a boil. Reduce heat; simmer 5 minutes.

4. Wrap handle of skillet with foil, and bake, covered, at 325° for 1 hour. Stir in bell pepper, squash, carrot, saffron, and cinnamon. Cover and bake an additional 40 minutes. Stir in remaining chile mixture and apricots. Cover and bake an additional 15 minutes. Remove cinnamon stick; serve tagine over couscous. Sprinkle with cilantro. Yield: 6 servings (serving size: about 1 cup tagine and ¾ cup couscous).

WINE NOTE: Because their spices are deep, complex, and warming—not fiery hot—Morrocan-inspired dishes have many potential wine partners. In particular, the soft, thick fruitiness of Zinfandel works well. Try the Beaulieu Vineyard "BV" Zinfandel 2001 from Napa Valley, California ($30), a juicy Zin with spiced cherry jam and black-currant flavors.

CALORIES 420 (13% from fat); FAT 5.9g (sat 1.9g, mono 2.2g, poly 0.8g); PROTEIN 31.4g; CARB 61g; FIBER 8.3g; CHOL 73mg; IRON 4.9mg; SODIUM 372mg; CALC 91mg

How to Get the Best from Spices

The finer you crush, grind, or mill spices, the more powerful and pervasive their effect on the finished dish will be. Freshly ground spices have a fresher, "sweeter" flavor than off-the-shelf ground spices. This is especially true with cinnamon, cloves, and nutmeg. For the subtlest effect, use spices whole; for more flavor, bruise or crush them lightly; for the most impact, grind them finely.

Pear and Ginger Crisp

The slight heat of ground ginger brings out the sweetness of the pears. Ground gingerroot is far more intense and peppery than fresh gingerroot. If you prefer only a hint of ginger, omit it from the topping. When it's fresh out of the oven and still hot, this is especially good with ice cream.

¼ cup packed brown sugar
¼ cup water
1½ teaspoons grated lemon rind
2 tablespoons fresh lemon juice
½ teaspoon ground ginger
2½ pounds pears, peeled, cored and sliced
Cooking spray
¾ cup all-purpose flour
½ cup packed brown sugar
1½ teaspoons ground ginger
¼ teaspoon salt
3 tablespoons chilled butter, cut into small pieces
1½ (1-ounce) slices white bread
¼ cup slivered almonds, ground
¼ cup finely chopped pecans

1. Preheat oven to 350°.
2. Heat a large nonstick skillet over medium heat. Add first 6 ingredients; cook 5 minutes, stirring occasionally.
3. Place pear mixture in a 2-quart casserole lightly coated with cooking spray.
4. Lightly spoon flour into a dry measuring cup; level with a knife. Combine flour, ½ cup brown sugar, 1½ teaspoons ginger, and salt; cut in butter with a pastry blender or 2 knives until mixture resembles coarse meal.
5. Place bread in a food processor; pulse 10 times or until crumbs measure ¾ cup. Stir breadcrumbs and nuts into flour mixture.
6. Sprinkle flour mixture evenly over pear mixture. Bake at 350° for 40 minutes or until filling is bubbly and topping is golden. Yield: 8 servings (serving size: about ¾ cup).

CALORIES 305 (28% from fat); FAT 9.6g (sat 3.1g, mono 4g, poly 1.6g); PROTEIN 3.4g; CARB 55.1g; FIBER 4.7g; CHOL 12mg; IRON 1.8mg; SODIUM 155mg; CALC 53mg

Cranberry and Orange Tartlets with Spiced Crust

Cinnamon and cloves are traditional in holiday cooking, and both have a natural affinity with orange. The tartness of the fruit is offset by the sweet, sultry spiciness of the crust. You can purchase a kitchen blow torch and small ceramic tartlet dishes at kitchen supply shops; serve the tartlets straight from those dishes.

CRUSTS:
1½ cups graham cracker crumbs
2 tablespoons brown sugar
3 tablespoons butter, melted
1 tablespoon water
½ teaspoon ground cinnamon
¼ teaspoon ground cloves
Cooking spray

FILLING:
½ cup (4 ounces) ⅓-less-fat cream cheese, softened
½ cup reduced-fat sour cream
3 tablespoons granulated sugar
½ teaspoon grated orange rind
Dash of ground cloves

TOPPING:
1 cup fresh orange juice (about 2 oranges)
½ cup granulated sugar
2 cups fresh cranberries

REMAINING INGREDIENTS:
20 orange sections (about 3 oranges)
5 teaspoons granulated sugar

1. Preheat oven to 350°.
2. To prepare crusts, combine first 6 ingredients, tossing well. Spoon about 3 tablespoons crumb mixture into each of 10 (3 x 1-inch) ceramic tart dishes coated with cooking spray. Press crumbs into bottom and up sides of dishes. Place dishes on a baking sheet. Bake at 350° for 12 minutes or until lightly browned. Cool completely on a wire rack.
3. To prepare filling, beat cream cheese with a mixer at high speed until smooth. Add sour cream and next 3 ingredients; beat until well blended. Chill.
4. To prepare topping, combine orange juice and ½ cup granulated sugar in a large saucepan. Cook over medium-high heat, stirring until sugar dissolves. Add cranberries; bring to a boil. Reduce heat; simmer until thick and reduced to 1 cup (about 15 minutes). Cool completely.
5. Spread about 1½ tablespoons filling into bottom of each crust; top each tartlet with about 1½ tablespoons topping. Just before serving, top each tart with 2 orange sections. Sprinkle ½ teaspoon granulated sugar over each serving. Holding a kitchen blow torch about 2 inches from top of each tartlet and moving torch back and forth, heat sugar until completely melted and caramelized (about 30 seconds). Serve within 30 minutes (do not refrigerate or caramel will melt). Yield: 10 servings.

CALORIES 240 (32% from fat); FAT 8.4g (sat 4.6g, mono 2.5g, poly 0.8g); PROTEIN 3.2g; CARB 39.7g; FIBER 2.4g; CHOL 21mg; IRON 0.9mg; SODIUM 153mg; CALC 54mg

Grinding Spices

A mortar and pestle are the best tools for coarsely crushing spices. But it is difficult to crush such hard spices as cinnamon and cloves in a mortar. A small, deep mortar is better than a wide, shallow one, from which the spices tend to shoot out.

A coffee grinder crushes most spices, especially tough, woody ones such as cinnamon and cloves. Clean the mill afterward by grinding a small piece of bread or a couple of tablespoons of raw rice. For cardamom- or cinnamon-flavored coffee, grind a cardamom pod or a ½- to 1-inch piece of cinnamon stick with the coffee beans.

Bruising (barely breaking the outer seed coat or husk) enhances flavor and aroma. Bruise soft spices like cardamom pods and juniper berries by pressing down with the blade of a chef's knife.

To make spice pastes, roast and grind the dry spices first before adding the wet or fresh ingredients. This lets the spices properly incorporate.

Fresh Pineapple, Chile, and Black Pepper Salsa

Black pepper brings out the sweetness of the pineapple. Serve with shrimp, pork, or chicken. Remove the seeds from the jalapeño if you want a less spicy salsa.

1 cup chopped fresh pineapple
½ cup chopped peeled kiwifruit
2 tablespoons finely chopped jalapeño pepper
2 tablespoons finely chopped red onion
2 tablespoons chopped fresh cilantro
1 tablespoon seasoned rice vinegar
½ teaspoon sugar
½ teaspoon grated lime rind
¼ teaspoon freshly ground black pepper
⅛ teaspoon ground cardamom
Dash of salt

1. Combine all ingredients, tossing gently. Let stand 1 hour. Yield: 6 servings (serving size: ¼ cup).

CALORIES 28 (6% from fat); FAT 0.2g (sat 0g, mono 0g, poly 0.1g); PROTEIN 0.4g; CARB 6.8g; FIBER 1g; CHOL 0mg; IRON 0.2mg; SODIUM 77mg; CALC 8mg

Orange, Date, and Endive Salad with Lemon-Cardamom Dressing

This refreshing, North African-inspired salad is a good antidote to the richness of traditional holiday fare and is excellent with cold turkey, chicken, and duck. It's also good with feta and other fresh cheeses. Lightly toasting the cardamom seeds develops their citrusy fragrance.

DRESSING:

½ teaspoon cardamom seeds, toasted
¼ cup low-fat buttermilk
1 tablespoon extravirgin olive oil
2 teaspoons chopped fresh mint
1 teaspoon grated lemon rind
¼ teaspoon salt
¼ teaspoon freshly ground black pepper

SALAD:

12 Belgian endive leaves
3 cups blood orange sections
1 cup thinly sliced radish
1 cup thinly vertically sliced red onion
½ cup thinly sliced pitted dates (about 5 whole)
4 teaspoons chopped fresh mint

1. To prepare dressing, place cardamom in a spice or coffee grinder; process until finely ground. Combine cardamom, buttermilk and next 5 ingredients.

2. To prepare salad, arrange 3 endive leaves on each of 4 salad plates. Top each with ¾ cup orange, ¼ cup radish, ¼ cup onion, 2 tablespoons dates, and 1 teaspoon mint. Drizzle each serving with 1 tablespoon dressing. Yield: 4 servings.

CALORIES 187 (20% from fat); FAT 4.1g (sat 0.7g, mono 2.8g, poly 0.4g); PROTEIN 3.2g; CARB 38.2g; FIBER 7g; CHOL 1mg; IRON 1mg; SODIUM 179mg; CALC 112mg

Pork Meatballs with Garlic and Allspice

Allspice works well with pork. The grated zucchini in this recipe helps lighten these spicy meatballs and keeps them extra-moist. Serve over pasta.

MEATBALLS:

2 cups shredded zucchini (about 8 ounces)
1 teaspoon salt, divided
⅓ cup plain dry breadcrumbs
1 tablespoon finely chopped fresh parsley
1 tablespoon finely chopped fresh oregano
1 teaspoon grated lemon rind
½ teaspoon ground allspice
½ teaspoon chili powder
½ teaspoon freshly ground black pepper
1¼ pounds lean ground pork
2 garlic cloves, minced
Cooking spray

SAUCE:

2 (16-ounce) cans plum tomatoes, undrained
1⅓ cups chopped onion
1 cup chopped carrot
½ teaspoon crushed red pepper
2 garlic cloves, minced
½ cup dry red wine
½ teaspoon salt
½ teaspoon black pepper
1 tablespoon chopped fresh oregano
1 tablespoon finely chopped fresh parsley

1. To prepare meatballs, combine zucchini and ½ teaspoon salt in a colander; let stand 30 minutes. Squeeze moisture from zucchini.

2. Combine zucchini, ½ teaspoon salt, breadcrumbs, and next 8 ingredients. Shape mixture into 24 (1-inch) meatballs.

3. Heat a large nonstick skillet coated with cooking spray over medium-high heat. Add meatballs; cook 6 minutes or until done, turning to brown all sides. Drain well.

4. To prepare sauce, drain 1 can tomatoes; discard liquid.

5. Heat a medium saucepan coated with cooking spray over medium heat. Add onion and carrot; cook 10 minutes or until tender, stirring occasionally. Add red pepper and 2 garlic cloves; cook 2 minutes, stirring frequently. Stir in drained tomatoes, undrained tomatoes, wine, ½ teaspoon salt, and ½ teaspoon black pepper.

6. Place half of tomato mixture in food processor; process until smooth. Place in a large bowl. Repeat procedure with remaining tomato mixture. Return tomato purée to pan; bring to a boil. Reduce heat; simmer 25 minutes. Add meatballs and 1 tablespoon oregano to pan; cook 5 minutes or until thoroughly heated. Sprinkle with 1 tablespoon parsley. Yield: 6 servings (serving size 4 meatballs and about ¾ cup sauce).

CALORIES 216 (17% from fat); FAT 4g (sat 1.3g, mono 1.7g, poly 0.6g); PROTEIN 23.4g; CARB 19.3g; FIBER 3.9g; CHOL 61mg; IRON 3.1mg; SODIUM 710mg; CALC 100mg

Roasted Spiced-Pork Tenderloin with Beet, Apple, and Caraway Salsa

Combining Thai and north European flavors may seem odd, but the sweet beet, apple, and caraway work remarkably well with the salty hotness of Thai spicing. Try this with rice or in flatbreads with low-fat sour cream and chopped cilantro or scallions.

PORK:

½   cup water
⅓   cup fresh orange juice
¼   cup fresh lime juice
2½ tablespoons chopped peeled fresh lemongrass
1   tablespoon minced fresh cilantro
1   tablespoon Thai fish sauce
1   tablespoon low-sodium soy sauce
1   teaspoon brown sugar
1   teaspoon grated peeled fresh ginger
2   garlic cloves, minced
1   (1-pound) pork tenderloin, trimmed
    Cooking spray

SALSA:

2   cups diced Granny Smith apple
1   cup diced, cooked beets
¼   cup sliced green onions
¼   cup diced seeded Anaheim chile
1   tablespoon chopped fresh mint
2   teaspoons rice vinegar
½   teaspoon caraway seeds, crushed
½   teaspoon brown sugar
¼   teaspoon salt
¼   teaspoon freshly ground black pepper

1. To prepare pork, combine first 11 ingredients in a large zip-top plastic bag; seal. Marinate in refrigerator 4 to 12 hours, turning bag occasionally.
2. Preheat oven to 450°.
3. Heat a large nonstick skillet coated with cooking spray over medium-high heat. Remove pork from bag, reserving marinade. Pat pork dry with paper towels. Add pork to pan; cook 6 minutes, browning on all sides. Remove pork from pan; place on a broiler pan coated with cooking spray. Place reserved marinade in a small saucepan; bring to a boil.

Remove from heat. Bake pork at 450° for 25 minutes or until a thermometer registers 155° (slightly pink), basting occasionally with reserved marinade. Let stand 5 minutes; cut into thin slices.
4. To prepare salsa, combine apple and remaining 9 ingredients. Serve with pork. Yield: 4 servings (serving size: 3 ounces pork and about ½ cup salsa).

CALORIES 225 (17% from fat); FAT 4.3g (sat 1.4g, mono 1.8g, poly 0.5g); PROTEIN 25.7g; CARB 21.5g; FIBER 3.1g; CHOL 74mg; IRON 2.5mg; SODIUM 721mg; CALC 35mg

Lemon and Dill Fish with Red Cabbage and Caraway over Mashed Potatoes

The caraway is left whole in this recipe so that its flavor is gentle. Caraway, dill, and lemon give this complete meal a Scandinavian feel. Any thick cut of a white fish, such as halibut, snapper, or haddock, is a good choice.

FISH:

1   tablespoon chopped fresh dill
1   teaspoon grated lemon rind
¼   teaspoon salt
¼   teaspoon freshly ground black pepper
4   (6-ounce) skinless halibut or other firm white fish fillets

POTATOES:

5   cups cubed red potato (about 1¾ pounds)
½   cup 2% reduced-fat milk
¼   cup chopped fresh chives
2   teaspoons prepared horseradish
¾   teaspoon salt
½   teaspoon freshly ground black pepper

CABBAGE:

1   teaspoon vegetable oil
½   cup finely chopped onion
½   teaspoon caraway seeds
1   cup shredded peeled Granny Smith apple (about ¾ pound)
6   cups very thinly sliced red cabbage
¼   teaspoon salt
¼   teaspoon freshly ground black pepper

REMAINING INGREDIENTS:

    Cooking spray
1½ tablespoons fresh lemon juice

1. To prepare fish, combine first 4 ingredients, and rub over fish. Cover and chill 1 hour.
2. To prepare potatoes, place potatoes in a large saucepan; cover with water. Bring to a boil; cook 12 minutes or until very tender. Drain. Return potato to pan. Add milk and next 4 ingredients; mash with a potato masher to desired consistency. Keep warm.
3. To prepare cabbage, heat oil in a large nonstick skillet over medium-high heat. Add onion and caraway; sauté 3 minutes. Add apple; sauté 2 minutes. Add cabbage, ¼ teaspoon salt, and ¼ teaspoon pepper; cover and cook 5 minutes or just until tender. Keep warm.
4. Preheat broiler.
5. Place fish on a broiler pan coated with cooking spray; broil 10 to 12 minutes or until fish flakes easily when tested with a fork. Drizzle lemon juice over fish. Serve with potatoes and cabbage. Yield: 4 servings (serving size: 1 fillet, 1 cup potato, and 1 cup cabbage).

CALORIES 423 (14% from fat); FAT 6.5g (sat 1.5g, mono 2g, poly 1.8g); PROTEIN 42.6g; CARB 49g; FIBER 7.6g; CHOL 58mg; IRON 3.9mg; SODIUM 875mg; CALC 223mg

Spiced Beef with Onion and Allspice Gratin

This is a good, subtle use of a strong spice. Use the side of knife's blade to crush the allspice easily.

BEEF:

½   teaspoon kosher salt
½   teaspoon chopped fresh thyme
¼   teaspoon crushed whole allspice
¼   teaspoon freshly ground black pepper
1   garlic clove, chopped
1   (1-pound) flank steak, trimmed

Continued

GRATIN:

- 1 baking potato, peeled and cut into ⅛-inch-thick slices (about ½ pound)
- Cooking spray
- 4 cups chopped Vidalia or other sweet onion
- 1 cup fat-free, less-sodium chicken broth
- 1 tablespoon red wine vinegar
- 1 teaspoon chopped fresh thyme
- ½ teaspoon kosher salt
- ½ teaspoon crushed whole allspice
- ¼ teaspoon freshly ground black pepper
- ½ cup (4 ounces) block-style fat-free cream cheese
- ½ cup reduced-fat sour cream
- ⅓ cup dry breadcrumbs
- ¼ cup (1 ounce) grated fresh Parmesan cheese

1. To prepare beef, combine first 5 ingredients; rub evenly over beef. Cover and chill 2 hours.

2. To prepare gratin, preheat oven to 400°.

3. Arrange potato in a single layer on a jelly roll pan coated with cooking spray; coat potato with cooking spray. Bake at 400° for 15 minutes or until soft. Set aside.

4. Heat a large nonstick skillet coated with cooking spray over medium heat. Add onion; cook 10 minutes or until lightly browned, stirring frequently. Stir in broth and next 5 ingredients; cook 3 minutes, stirring occasionally. Remove from heat.

5. Add cream cheese to onion mixture; stir until well blended. Stir in sour cream. Add potato to pan; stir gently to combine. Place mixture in a shallow 1-quart casserole coated with cooking spray. Combine breadcrumbs and Parmesan cheese; spoon evenly over onion mixture. Lightly coat surface of gratin with cooking spray. Bake at 400° for 30 minutes or until golden brown.

6. Preheat broiler.

7. Place beef on broiler pan coated with cooking spray; cook 3 minutes on each side or until desired degree of doneness. Cut steak diagonally across grain into thin slices. Yield: 4 servings (serving size: 4 ounces beef and about 1 cup gratin).

CALORIES 472 (28% from fat); FAT 14.8g (sat 7.2g, mono 5.2g, poly 0.8g); PROTEIN 35.8g; CARB 49.2g; FIBER 4.4g; CHOL 72mg; IRON 4.2mg; SODIUM 1,005mg; CALC 255mg

---

MAKE AHEAD

Caramelized Rice Pudding with Pears and Raisins

This method of slow-baking gives a rich, caramelized flavor to the rice pudding and is based on a technique from cookery writer Sue Kreitzman. It takes some time to make, so prepare the rice pudding the day before. Cool the rice pudding before caramelizing the sugar topping.

- 4 cups 2% reduced-fat milk
- 1 cup Arborio rice or other short-grain rice
- 3 tablespoons sugar
- 3 tablespoons nonfat dry milk
- ¼ teaspoon ground nutmeg
- ⅛ teaspoon salt
- 1 (3-inch) cinnamon stick
- 1 (3-inch) piece vanilla bean, split lengthwise
- ½ cup heavy cream
- 3½ cups chopped peeled Bosc pears
- ½ cup raisins
- ¼ cup apple juice
- 3 tablespoons sugar
- 1 (3-inch) cinnamon stick
- ½ cup sugar

1. Preheat oven to 300°.

2. Combine first 7 ingredients in a 3-quart casserole. Scrape seeds from vanilla bean; add seeds and bean to rice mixture. Place dish in a 13 x 9-inch baking pan; add hot water to pan to a depth of 1 inch. Bake at 300°, uncovered, 2½ hours or until rice is tender, stirring occasionally. Discard cinnamon stick and vanilla bean; stir in cream. Cool.

3. Combine pears and next 4 ingredients in a small saucepan; bring to a boil. Reduce heat; simmer 10 minutes or until tender. Discard cinnamon stick. Spoon about ⅓ cup pear mixture into bottom of each of 8 (8-ounce) ramekins. Top each serving with about ⅓ cup rice pudding. Just before serving, sprinkle 1 tablespoon sugar over each serving. Holding a kitchen blow torch about 2 inches over rice pudding and moving torch back and forth, heat sugar until completely melted and caramelized (about 45 seconds). Serve within 30 minutes. (Do not refrigerate or caramel will melt.) Yield: 8 servings.

CALORIES 385 (19% from fat); FAT 8.2g (sat 4.9g, mono 2.3g, poly 0.4g); PROTEIN 7.5g; CARB 71.5g; FIBER 2.7g; CHOL 30mg; IRON 0.7mg; SODIUM 114mg; CALC 201mg

---

Chinese Beef-and-Mushroom Stew with Whole Spices

Whole cinnamon, anise, cloves, and peppercorns subtly flavor this slow-cooked stew of beef and dried Chinese black mushrooms. Use brisket, chuck, or blade steak for this melt-in-the-mouth dish. Remove the hard stems from the mushrooms and use just the caps.

- 2 cups boiling water
- 1 cup dried black mushrooms
- Cooking spray
- 1 (1½-pound) beef brisket, trimmed and cubed
- 1½ cups chopped green onions, divided
- 1 teaspoon grated peeled fresh ginger
- 4 garlic cloves, minced
- 1¼ cups water
- 3 tablespoons low-sodium soy sauce
- 2 tablespoons sake (rice wine)
- 2 tablespoons brown sugar
- ½ teaspoon mixed peppercorns
- 3 star anise
- 3 whole cloves
- 2 dried red chiles
- 1 (14¼-ounce) can low-salt beef broth
- 1 (3-inch) cinnamon stick
- 1 teaspoon dark sesame oil
- 2½ cups hot cooked basmati rice

1. Combine boiling water and dried mushrooms. Cover and let stand 30 minutes. Remove mushrooms with a slotted spoon. Chop mushrooms; set aside. Strain soaking liquid through a cheesecloth- or paper towel-lined sieve into a bowl. Discard solids; reserve 1 cup soaking liquid.

2. Heat a large Dutch oven coated with cooking spray over medium-high heat. Add beef; cook 8 minutes on all sides or until browned. Add ¾ cup onion, ginger, and garlic; cook 1 minute, stirring frequently. Stir in reserved soaking liquid, 1¼ cups water, and next 9 ingredients; bring to a boil. Cover, reduce heat, and simmer 1 hour. Stir in mushrooms. Cover and simmer 40 minutes or until beef is tender. Remove beef mixture with a slotted spoon. Discard star anise, cloves, dried chiles, and cinnamon stick. Bring liquid to a boil; cook 3 minutes or until reduced to 1 cup. Stir in ¾ cup onion and oil. Serve beef mixture over rice with sauce. Yield: 5 servings (serving size: ⅔ cup beef mixture, about 3 tablespoons sauce, and ½ cup rice).

CALORIES 379 (24% from fat); FAT 10.1g (sat 3.1g, mono 4.4g, poly 0.9g); PROTEIN 34.1g; CARB 33g; FIBER 1.9g; CHOL 80mg; IRON 4.2mg; SODIUM 460mg; CALC 33mg

---

Roasting and Toasting Spices

Heat whole spices in a dry pan to release their natural volatile oils and bring out optimal aroma and flavor. Use a small, heavy skillet. Add the whole spices (roasting ground spices tends to turn them bitter, so is best avoided) and place over a gentle heat. Shake the pan, or stir with a wooden spatula, to keep the spices on the move, and toast gently for 1 to 3 minutes.

Some spices—like mustard and poppy seeds—"pop" when they are ready, others darken. The essential sign is that the spice becomes aromatic and smells toasty. Tip into a bowl to cool before grinding.

---

lighten up

A Little Slice of Heaven

We convert a tempting dessert from sinner to saint.

Nancy Lee Page of Wilmington, North Carolina, and her husband, John, take pride in eating a nutritious, well-balanced diet. But like most of us, they have a favorite indulgence—chocolate. She writes, "My husband does not care what he has for dessert so long as it is some form of chocolate." Nancy Lee's recipe for Chocolate Decadence—dark chocolate pudding cakes, with warm fudgy centers—is their all-time favorite dessert. It's a snap to make, but after considering how this enticing cake tipped the scales of their eating plan, Nancy Lee decided to ask for help.

We scaled back the solid chocolate and butter, eliminating 231 calories and 28 grams of fat per serving. The savings allowed us to layer the chocolate batter with straight semisweet chocolate, providing the dessert with that fudgy burst of flavor Nancy Lee and John crave.

STAFF FAVORITE
Chocolate Decadence
(pictured on page 397)

If you don't have 2-ounce ramekins, you can make the dessert in a regular-sized muffin pan.

Cooking spray
½ cup plus 3 tablespoons sugar, divided
¼ cup 2% reduced-fat milk
8 teaspoons unsweetened cocoa
1½ tablespoons butter
½ ounce unsweetened chocolate, chopped
5 tablespoons all-purpose flour
½ teaspoon vanilla extract
⅛ teaspoon salt
1 large egg white, lightly beaten
8 teaspoons semisweet chocolate chips

1. Preheat oven to 350°.

2. Lightly coat 4 (2-ounce) ramekins with cooking spray, and sprinkle ¾ teaspoon sugar into each, shaking and turning to coat. Set prepared ramekins aside.

3. Combine ½ cup plus 2 tablespoons sugar, milk, and cocoa in a small saucepan, stirring well with a whisk. Bring to a boil over medium heat. Cook 30 seconds or until sugar dissolves, stirring constantly. Remove from heat; add butter and unsweetened chocolate. Stir until chocolate melts and mixture is smooth. Cool chocolate mixture 10 minutes.

4. Add flour, vanilla, salt, and egg white to chocolate mixture, stirring with a whisk just until blended. Spoon 2 tablespoons chocolate mixture into each prepared ramekin, and top with 2 teaspoons chocolate chips. Divide remaining chocolate mixture evenly among ramekins, spreading to cover chocolate chips. Bake at 350° for 20 minutes or until barely set. Cool 10 minutes. Invert onto dessert plates. Serve warm. Yield: 4 servings.

CALORIES 315 (31% from fat); FAT 11g (sat 5.7g, mono 2.8g, poly 0.8g); PROTEIN 4.1g; CARB 52.1g; FIBER 1.6g; CHOL 13mg; IRON 2.2mg; SODIUM 140mg; CALC 27mg

BEFORE	AFTER
SERVING SIZE	
1 ramekin	
CALORIES PER SERVING	
546	315
FAT	
39g	11g
PERCENT OF TOTAL CALORIES	
64%	31%

Hot Date

Striking a balance between elegant entrées and family-friendly fare is child's play for this mom.

Mary Alayne Long and her husband, Rick, of Vestavia Hills, Alabama, have been going to their favorite restaurant on a weekly date night for most of their 10-year marriage. But now with two children, it's not that easy to do. So Mary Alayne put their favorite ingredients together to create a creamy risotto. Now, they have a family version of date night that they all enjoy.

Risotto with Fresh Mozzarella, Grape Tomatoes, and Basil

- 3 tablespoons balsamic vinegar
- 4½ cups fat-free, less-sodium chicken broth
- 2 tablespoons extravirgin olive oil, divided
- 2 cups chopped leek
- 1½ cups Arborio rice or other medium-grain rice
- ⅓ cup dry white wine
- ¼ cup half-and-half
- 1 teaspoon salt
- ¼ teaspoon freshly ground black pepper
- 1 cup halved grape tomatoes
- ¼ cup chopped fresh basil
- 5 ounces fresh mozzarella cheese, finely diced

1. Place vinegar in a small, heavy saucepan; bring to a boil over medium heat. Cook until slightly syrupy and reduced to 1 tablespoon (about 4 minutes). Set aside.
2. Bring broth to a simmer in a medium saucepan (do not boil). Keep warm over low heat.
3. Heat 1 tablespoon oil in a large saucepan over medium-high heat. Add leek; sauté 3 minutes or until tender. Add rice; cook 2 minutes, stirring constantly. Stir in wine; cook 1 minute or until liquid is nearly absorbed, stirring constantly. Stir in 1 cup broth; cook 5 minutes or until liquid is nearly absorbed, stirring constantly. Reduce heat to medium. Add remaining broth, ½ cup at a time, stirring constantly until each portion of broth is absorbed before adding next (about 25 minutes total). Stir in half-and-half, salt, and pepper; cook 2 minutes. Remove from heat; stir in tomatoes, basil, and cheese. Place about 1 cup risotto into each of 6 shallow serving bowls, and drizzle each with ½ teaspoon balsamic syrup and ½ teaspoon olive oil. Yield: 6 servings.

CALORIES 378 (29% from fat); FAT 12.1g (sat 5.2g, mono 4.1g, poly 1g); PROTEIN 13.2g; CARB 51.6g; FIBER 1.6g; CHOL 24mg; IRON 1.3mg; SODIUM 777mg; CALC 178mg

QUICK & EASY
Southwest Sausage and Rice

"This easy rice dish is a simplified takeoff of a *Cooking Light* risotto made with yellow bell peppers and sausage. The saffron rice mix gave me the yellow color of the roasted bell peppers, and the plain rice eliminated the need to constantly stir the dish."

—Renee Canuso, Villa Park, California

- 1 (5-ounce) package saffron rice mix (such as Mahatma)
- 2 (4-ounce) links turkey Italian sausage
- 2 cups frozen whole-kernel corn
- 1 garlic clove, minced
- ¼ cup (1 ounce) grated fresh Parmesan cheese
- ½ teaspoon chili powder
- ¼ teaspoon ground cumin
- ¼ teaspoon black pepper
- Dash of salt
- Minced fresh cilantro (optional)

1. Cook rice according to package directions, omitting salt and fat.
2. Remove casings from sausage. Cook sausage in a large skillet over medium-high heat until browned, stirring to crumble. Remove from pan with a slotted spoon.
3. Add corn and garlic to pan; cook over medium heat 3 minutes, stirring frequently. Stir in rice, sausage, cheese, chili powder, cumin, pepper, and salt. Reduce heat to low; cook, stirring constantly, until thoroughly heated. Sprinkle with cilantro, if desired. Yield: 5 servings (serving size: 1 cup).

CALORIES 253 (24% from fat); FAT 6.7g (sat 2.3g, mono 2.3g, poly 1.4g); PROTEIN 14.8g; CARB 37g; FIBER 2.7g; CHOL 37mg; IRON 1.8mg; SODIUM 795mg; CALC 105mg

QUICK & EASY
Quick Roasted-Vegetable Fajitas

"This recipe uses four vegetables that are available nearly everywhere year-round."
—Nancy Byron, Dublin, Ohio

- 2½ cups julienne-cut zucchini
- 2 cups julienne-cut yellow squash
- 2 cups red bell pepper strips
- 1½ cups vertically sliced red onion
- 3 tablespoons vegetable soup and dip mix (such as Lipton Recipe Secrets)
- 4 teaspoons olive oil
- 8 (8-inch) flour tortillas
- 1 (16-ounce) can fat-free refried beans
- 2 cups shredded leaf lettuce
- 1 cup (4 ounces) reduced-fat shredded Cheddar cheese
- 1 cup chopped tomato
- ½ cup bottled salsa

1. Preheat oven to 450°.
2. Place first 4 ingredients in a large zip-top plastic bag. Add vegetable soup mix and oil to bag; seal and shake to coat. Place vegetable mixture in a 13 x 9-inch baking dish. Bake at 450° for 20 minutes, stirring once.
3. Heat tortillas and beans according to package directions.
4. Spread 3 tablespoons beans over each tortilla; top each with ½ cup vegetable mixture and ¼ cup lettuce. Sprinkle each serving with 2 tablespoons cheese, 2 tablespoons tomato, and 1 tablespoon salsa. Roll up. Yield: 8 servings (serving size: 1 fajita).

CALORIES 309 (21% from fat); FAT 7.1g (sat 1.8g, mono 3.8g, poly 0.9g); PROTEIN 13.7g; CARB 48.6g; FIBER 7.8g; CHOL 3mg; IRON 3.8mg; SODIUM 748mg; CALC 133mg

Chunky Vegetarian Chili

"This is a great way to get kids to eat fiber-rich foods. We take it on camping trips, and my son even takes it for school lunches."

—Denice French, Redmond, Washington

1 tablespoon vegetable oil
2 cups chopped onion
½ cup chopped yellow bell pepper
½ cup chopped green bell pepper
2 garlic cloves, minced
1½ tablespoons chili powder
1 tablespoon brown sugar
1 teaspoon ground cumin
1 teaspoon dried oregano
½ teaspoon salt
½ teaspoon black pepper
2 (16-ounce) cans stewed tomatoes, undrained
2 (15-ounce) cans black beans, rinsed and drained
1 (15-ounce) can kidney beans, rinsed and drained
1 (15-ounce) can pinto beans, rinsed and drained

1. Heat oil in a Dutch oven over medium-high heat. Add onion, bell peppers, and garlic; sauté 5 minutes or until tender. Add chili powder and remaining ingredients; bring to a boil. Reduce heat, and simmer 30 minutes. Yield: 8 servings (serving size: 1 cup).

CALORIES 257 (9% from fat); FAT 2.7g (sat 0.3g, mono 0.5g, poly 1.2g); PROTEIN 12.8g; CARB 48.8g; FIBER 14.2g; CHOL 0mg; IRON 4.5mg; SODIUM 876mg; CALC 150mg

Lime-Spiked Black Bean Dip

"This dip is best served at room temperature."

—Sara Szunyogh, North Olmsted, Ohio

2 (15-ounce) cans black beans, rinsed and drained
1 cup grated carrot
½ cup fresh lime juice (about 2 limes)
¼ cup finely chopped green onion
¼ cup chopped fresh cilantro
1 teaspoon minced garlic
¼ teaspoon salt
⅛ teaspoon ground red pepper

1. Place beans in a food processor; pulse until almost smooth. Combine beans, carrot, and remaining ingredients in a medium bowl, stirring until well blended. Let stand 30 minutes. Serve with baked tortilla chips. Yield: 40 servings (serving size: 2 tablespoons).

CALORIES 19 (5% from fat); FAT 0.1g (sat 0g, mono 0.1g, poly 0g); PROTEIN 1.2g; CARB 3.9g; FIBER 1.3g; CHOL 0mg; IRON 0.3mg; SODIUM 61mg; CALC 8mg

Crisp Potato Hash Browns

"My love of fried food didn't fit into my healthy-eating lifestyle, so I came up with this recipe using nonstick aluminum foil. It requires high heat but no oil."

—Thomas Hale, Portsmouth, Ohio

4 cups shredded peeled baking potato (about 1¼ pounds)
¼ cup thinly sliced green onions
¼ cup chopped green bell pepper
2 tablespoons cornstarch
¼ teaspoon salt
¼ teaspoon black pepper
¼ teaspoon onion powder
Cooking spray

1. Preheat oven to 475°.
2. Place potato in a large bowl; cover with cold water. Let stand 5 minutes. Drain and rinse potato. Dry thoroughly in a salad spinner or pat dry with paper towels. Combine potato, onion, and bell pepper in bowl. Add cornstarch, salt, pepper, and onion powder; toss well to coat.
3. Line a baking sheet with nonstick aluminum foil; coat thoroughly with cooking spray. Place a 3-inch biscuit cutter on prepared baking sheet. Fill biscuit cutter with ½ cup potato mixture (do not pack). Carefully remove cutter, leaving potato patty intact. Repeat procedure with remaining potato mixture. Coat tops of potato patties with cooking spray. Bake at 475° for 20 minutes. Turn patties over, and bake an additional 15 minutes or until golden brown. Yield: 8 servings (serving size: 1 patty).

CALORIES 97 (6% from fat); FAT 0.7g (sat 0.2g, mono 0g, poly 0.3g); PROTEIN 2.2g; CARB 21.1g; FIBER 1.7g; CHOL 0mg; IRON 1.1mg; SODIUM 97mg; CALC 12mg

Orange-Glazed Carrots and Onions

—Trisha Kruse, Boise, Idaho

1½ cups thinly sliced onion
1 cup fat-free, less-sodium chicken broth
3 tablespoons low-sodium soy sauce
1 pound baby carrots
1 garlic clove, minced
2 tablespoons orange marmalade
¼ teaspoon salt
¼ teaspoon freshly ground black pepper

1. Combine first 5 ingredients in a medium saucepan; bring to a simmer over medium heat. Cover; simmer 10 minutes or until onion is tender. Stir in marmalade, salt, and pepper. Cook, uncovered, 30 minutes or until liquid is reduced to ¼ cup (about 30 minutes); stir frequently. Yield: 6 servings (serving size: ½ cup).

CALORIES 63 (7% from fat); FAT 0.5g (sat 0.1g, mono 0g, poly 0.2g); PROTEIN 1.8g; CARB 13.9g; FIBER 2g; CHOL 0mg; IRON 0.8mg; SODIUM 381mg; CALC 28mg

Waldorf Coleslaw

—Kristen Laise, Washington, D.C.

3 cups shredded cabbage
3 cups diced Granny Smith apple
6 tablespoons raisins
3 tablespoons coarsely chopped walnuts
3 tablespoons plain fat-free yogurt
2 tablespoons fat-free mayonnaise
1 tablespoon honey
1 teaspoon prepared horseradish
¼ teaspoon salt
¼ teaspoon black pepper

1. Combine first 4 ingredients in a bowl. Combine yogurt and remaining 5 ingredients; stir well with a whisk. Pour over cabbage mixture; toss well. Cover; chill 2 hours. Yield: 10 servings (serving size: ½ cup).

CALORIES 69 (23% from fat); FAT 1.8g (sat 0.2g, mono 0.2g, poly 1.1g); PROTEIN 1.3g; CARB 14.1g; FIBER 1.9g; CHOL 1mg; IRON 0.5mg; SODIUM 91mg; CALC 27mg

Running with a Mission

In a club committed to running and community service, everyone's a winner.

With Mark Brody, resistance is futile. In the five years since he started the Running/Walking/Eating/Volunteering Club, Brody has cheered countless couch potatoes over marathon finish lines, convinced an army of volunteers they could make a difference, and created a new social venue in Baltimore. Here's one of his favorite recipes.

Quick Vegetarian Chili

1 tablespoon olive oil
½ cup chopped onion
2 garlic cloves, minced
1½ cups chopped zucchini
1 cup chopped red bell pepper
1 cup chopped green bell pepper
4 cups chopped tomatoes (about 1¾ pounds)
1 tablespoon chili powder
1 teaspoon Old Bay seasoning
¼ teaspoon black pepper
2 (5.5-ounce) cans spicy-hot vegetable juice
1 (15-ounce) can black beans, rinsed and drained
1 (15-ounce) can kidney beans, rinsed and drained
1 jalapeño pepper, minced

1. Heat oil in a Dutch oven over medium-high heat; add onion and garlic. Cook 2 minutes or until tender, stirring constantly. Add zucchini and bell peppers; cook 5 minutes, stirring frequently. Add tomatoes and remaining ingredients, stirring well. Cover, reduce heat, and simmer 20 minutes, stirring occasionally. Yield: 6 servings (serving size: 1⅓ cups).

CALORIES 200 (18% from fat); FAT 3.6g (sat 0.4g, mono 1.8g, poly 0.5g); PROTEIN 10g, CARB 36.2g, FIBER 12g, CHOL 0mg; IRON 3.2mg, SODIUM 573mg, CALC 71mg

Cabin Fever

Leave the crowds behind and share New Year's Eve and one of these simple menus with someone special.

You could go to that crowded New Year's Eve party your neighbors are planning. But perhaps you would prefer an escape to a quiet cabin in the woods.

These menus are rustic, but each dish has a simple, straightforward elegance. And you can prepare everything with the basic equipment that you'll find in a cabin's cabinets—a skillet, a saucepan, a baking dish, and a baking sheet.

Filet Mignon Menu

Tomato Crostini

Pepper-Crusted Filet Mignon with Horseradish Cream

Spicy Roasted Potatoes and Asparagus

Sautéed Apple over Ice Cream

Cornish Hen Menu

Tomato Crostini

Roasted Cornish Hens

Rice Pilaf with Shallots and Parmesan

Garlicky Green Beans

Sautéed Apple over Ice Cream

WINE NOTE: For the filet mignon or Cornish hen, a structured but soft and magnificently rich red is in order. Splurge on Robert Mondavi Merlot (about $35) from the Stags Leap District of California's Napa Valley. And no New Year's Eve should be spent without some bubbly. Try a superdelicious California sparkler that's easy on the pocketbook: Gloria Ferrer Sonoma Brut nonvintage (about $18). It's fresh and tingly with hints of vanilla and baked apples.

Tomato Crostini

Plum tomatoes usually have better flavor and are less watery than other tomatoes available during winter. If you're without a baking sheet, carefully arrange the bread slices directly on the oven rack.

½ cup chopped plum tomato
1 tablespoon chopped fresh basil
1 tablespoon chopped pitted green olives
1 teaspoon capers
½ teaspoon balsamic vinegar
½ teaspoon olive oil
⅛ teaspoon sea salt
Dash of freshly ground black pepper
1 garlic clove, minced
4 (1-inch-thick) slices French bread baguette
Cooking spray
1 garlic clove, halved

1. Preheat oven to 375°.
2. Combine first 9 ingredients.
3. Lightly coat both sides of bread slices with cooking spray, and arrange bread slices in a single layer on a baking sheet. Bake at 375° for 4 minutes on each side or until lightly toasted.
4. Rub 1 side of each bread slice with halved garlic; top evenly with tomato mixture. Yield: 2 servings (serving size: 2 bread slices and about ⅓ cup tomato mixture).

CALORIES 109 (23% from fat); FAT 2.8g (sat 0.4g, mono 1.5g, poly 0.7g); PROTEIN 3.1g; CARB 18g; FIBER 1.4g; CHOL 0mg; IRON 1mg; SODIUM 373mg; CALC 30mg

Pepper-Crusted Filet Mignon with Horseradish Cream

2 (4-ounce) beef tenderloin steaks, trimmed (about ¾ inch thick)
½ teaspoon sea salt
¼ teaspoon freshly ground black pepper
1 teaspoon butter
Cooking spray
1 garlic clove, minced
¼ cup fat-free sour cream
½ teaspoon prepared horseradish

1. Sprinkle both sides of steaks with salt and pepper.
2. Melt butter in a nonstick skillet coated with cooking spray over medium heat. Add steaks; cook 3 minutes on each side or until desired degree of doneness. Sprinkle steaks evenly with garlic; cook 1 minute on each side over medium-low heat.
3. Combine sour cream and horseradish; serve with steaks. Yield: 2 servings (serving size: 1 steak and 2 tablespoons horseradish cream).

CALORIES 231 (44% from fat); FAT 11.3g (sat 4.8g, mono 4g, poly 0.5g); PROTEIN 25.2g; CARB 5.6g; FIBER 0.1g; CHOL 78mg; IRON 3.3mg; SODIUM 684mg; CALC 58mg

Roasted Cornish Hens

You can also rub rosemary or a combination of fresh herbs under the loosened skin of the hens.

  2 (1¼-pound) Cornish hens
  ¼ teaspoon sea salt
  ¼ teaspoon freshly ground black
      pepper
  4 thyme sprigs
  2 garlic cloves, halved and crushed
  ⅓ cup dry white wine

1. Preheat oven to 350°.
2. Remove and discard giblets and necks from hens. Rinse hens with cold water; pat dry.
3. Starting at neck cavity, loosen skin from breast by inserting fingers, gently pushing between skin and meat. Combine salt and pepper; rub under loosened skin. Insert 2 thyme sprigs and 2 garlic halves under loosened skin of each hen. Lift wing tips up and over backs; tuck under hens.
4. Place hens, breast sides up, in an 11 x 7-inch baking dish. Pour white wine over hens.
5. Bake at 350° for 55 minutes or until a thermometer registers 180°, basting occasionally with wine. Let stand 5 minutes. Discard skin. Yield: 2 servings (serving size: 1 hen).

CALORIES 221 (26% from fat); FAT 6.3g (sat 1.6g, mono 2g, poly 1.5g); PROTEIN 38.1g; CARB 0.7g; FIBER 0.1g; CHOL 173mg; IRON 1.5mg; SODIUM 394mg; CALC 26mg

Rice Pilaf with Shallots and Parmesan

Cooked basmati rice smells like popcorn and has a delicate texture, but you can use any long-grain white rice in this recipe.

  2 teaspoons butter
  2 tablespoons minced shallots
  1 garlic clove, minced
  ½ cup basmati rice
  1 cup fat-free, less-sodium chicken
      broth
  ¼ cup dry white wine
  2 tablespoons grated fresh Parmesan
      cheese
  2 tablespoons minced fresh parsley
  ⅛ teaspoon freshly ground black
      pepper
  Dash of sea salt

1. Melt butter in a small saucepan over medium-high heat. Add shallots and garlic; sauté 1 minute. Stir in rice; sauté 1 minute. Stir in broth and wine; bring to a boil. Cover, reduce heat; simmer 15 minutes.
2. Remove from heat; stir in cheese, parsley, pepper, and salt. Yield: 2 servings (serving size: about ¾ cup).

CALORIES 266 (21% from fat); FAT 6.3g (sat 3.8g, mono 1.8g, poly 0.4g); PROTEIN 8.4g; CARB 43.9g; FIBER 0.6g; CHOL 15mg; IRON 0.8mg; SODIUM 455mg; CALC 100mg

Garlicky Green Beans

If you can find them, use haricots verts (thin, tender green beans). Because this recipe is so simple, coarse freshly ground sea salt and black peppercorns really count. Pack disposable salt and pepper grinders, such as Alessi's Tip 'N' Grind Coarse Sea Salt and McCormick's Black Peppercorn Grinder, available in the spice section of supermarkets.

  2 cups green beans, trimmed
  1 teaspoon butter
  Cooking spray
  ⅛ teaspoon sea salt
  ⅛ teaspoon freshly ground black
      pepper
  1 garlic clove, minced

1. Cook beans in boiling water 2 minutes. Drain and plunge beans into ice water; drain.
2. Melt butter in a small nonstick skillet coated with cooking spray over medium heat. Add beans, salt, pepper, and garlic; cook 2 minutes or until heated. Yield: 2 servings (serving size: 1 cup).

CALORIES 54 (35% from fat); FAT 2.1g (sat 1.2g, mono 0.6g, poly 0.1g); PROTEIN 2.1g; CARB 8.4g; FIBER 3.8g; CHOL 5mg; IRON 1.2mg; SODIUM 170mg; CALC 45mg

Spicy Roasted Potatoes and Asparagus

Move the potatoes to one side of the dish before you add the asparagus so the spears can cook in a single, even layer.

  2 teaspoons olive oil, divided
  ¼ teaspoon sea salt, divided
  ¼ teaspoon chopped fresh or
      ⅛ teaspoon dried thyme
  ⅛ teaspoon freshly ground black
      pepper
  ⅛ teaspoon crushed red pepper
  6 small red potatoes (about ¾
      pound), quartered
  Cooking spray
  2 tablespoons grated fresh Parmesan
      cheese
  1 teaspoon minced garlic, divided
  ½ pound asparagus spears

1. Preheat oven to 450°.
2. Combine 1 teaspoon oil, ⅛ teaspoon salt, thyme, peppers, and potatoes in an 11 x 7-inch baking dish coated with cooking spray. Bake at 450° for 20 minutes, stirring occasionally. Stir in cheese and ½ teaspoon garlic.
3. Snap off tough ends of asparagus. Combine 1 teaspoon oil, ⅛ teaspoon salt, ½ teaspoon garlic, and asparagus. Add asparagus mixture to dish. Bake 10 minutes or until asparagus is crisp-tender. Yield: 2 servings.

CALORIES 223 (27% from fat); FAT 6.8g (sat 1.9g, mono 3.9g, poly 0.6g); PROTEIN 9.1g; CARB 34.2g; FIBER 4.6g; CHOL 5mg; IRON 3.6mg; SODIUM 419mg; CALC 136mg

Sautéed Apple over Ice Cream

Use your favorite brandy in this dessert, then enjoy sipping the rest alongside it.

1 tablespoon butter
1½ cups sliced peeled Fuji apple
3 tablespoons brandy
1 tablespoon sugar
¼ teaspoon fresh lemon juice
⅛ teaspoon ground ginger
1 cup vanilla reduced-fat ice cream

1. Melt butter in a small nonstick skillet over medium heat. Add apple; cook 5 minutes or until lightly browned, stirring frequently.
2. Add brandy, sugar, juice, and ginger; cook over medium-low heat 2 minutes or until apple is tender, stirring occasionally. Serve warm over ice cream. Yield: 2 servings (serving size: about ½ cup apple and ½ cup ice cream).

CALORIES 316 (23% from fat); FAT 8.2g (sat 4.7g, mono 1.7g, poly 0.4g); PROTEIN 3.3g; CARB 46.9g; FIBER 3.8g; CHOL 21mg; IRON 0.2mg; SODIUM 104mg; CALC 108mg

superfast
...And Ready in Just About 20 Minutes

Mustard and Herb-Crusted Trout

Serve with mashed potatoes and a green vegetable.

1½ (1-ounce) slices sourdough bread, torn
4 (3-ounce) rainbow trout fillets
Cooking spray
1 tablespoon Dijon mustard
½ teaspoon dried tarragon
¼ teaspoon paprika
2 lemon wedges

1. Preheat oven to 450°.
2. Place bread in a food processor; pulse until crumbly. Place trout, skin side down, on a jelly roll pan coated with cooking spray. Combine mustard and tarragon; spread over top of fish. Sprinkle fish with breadcrumbs and paprika; lightly coat with cooking spray. Bake at 450° for 10 minutes or until fish flakes easily when tested with a fork. Serve with lemon wedges. Yield: 2 servings (serving size: 2 fillets).

CALORIES 297 (32% from fat); FAT 10.5g (sat 2.8g, mono 3.1g, poly 3.4g); PROTEIN 37.8g; CARB 11g; FIBER 0.9g; CHOL 100mg; IRON 1.4mg; SODIUM 357mg; CALC 145mg

Moroccan Shrimp with Couscous

Drain the yogurt to thicken it and concentrate its flavor. If you don't have time, skip this step.

¾ cup plain low-fat yogurt
1 teaspoon paprika
¾ teaspoon salt
½ teaspoon ground cumin
½ teaspoon curry powder
⅛ teaspoon ground red pepper
⅛ teaspoon ground cinnamon
½ cup dried mixed fruit bits or golden raisins
¼ cup water
1 (14-ounce) can fat-free, less-sodium chicken broth
1 cup uncooked couscous
1 tablespoon butter
1½ pounds peeled and deveined large shrimp
6 cilantro sprigs (optional)

1. Spoon yogurt onto several layers of heavy-duty paper towels; spread to ½-inch thickness. Cover with additional paper towels; let stand 5 minutes. Scrape into a bowl using a rubber spatula. Cover and refrigerate.
2. While yogurt stands, combine paprika and next 5 ingredients. Bring 1½ teaspoons paprika mixture, dried fruit, water, and broth to a boil in a medium saucepan; gradually stir in couscous. Remove from heat; cover and let stand 5 minutes. Fluff with a fork.
3. While couscous stands, melt butter in a large nonstick skillet over medium-high heat. Sprinkle shrimp with remaining paprika mixture. Add shrimp to pan; sauté 5 minutes or until done. Spoon ½ cup couscous in center of each of 6 plates. Top each with ½ cup shrimp and 1 tablespoon yogurt. Garnish with cilantro sprigs, if desired. Yield: 6 servings.

CALORIES 318 (13% from fat); FAT 4.7g (sat 1.9g, mono 1g, poly 1g); PROTEIN 30.7g; CARB 36.9g; FIBER 2.3g; CHOL 179mg; IRON 4.1mg; SODIUM 554mg; CALC 140mg

Linguine and Spinach with Gorgonzola Sauce

This rich-tasting pasta dish comes together in a flash.

1 (9-ounce) package fresh linguine
1 tablespoon butter
1 tablespoon all-purpose flour
1 (12-ounce) can evaporated low-fat milk
¾ cup (3 ounces) crumbled Gorgonzola cheese
¾ teaspoon salt
¼ teaspoon black pepper
1 (6-ounce) bag fresh baby spinach (about 6 cups)

1. Cook pasta according to package directions, omitting salt and fat.
2. While pasta cooks, melt butter in a medium saucepan over medium heat. Add flour; cook 1 minute, stirring constantly with a whisk. Gradually add milk, stirring constantly with a whisk. Increase heat to medium-high; bring to a boil, stirring constantly. Reduce heat, and simmer 3 minutes or until sauce thickens slightly, stirring frequently. Remove from heat; stir in cheese, salt, and pepper. Combine sauce, pasta, and spinach, tossing gently to coat. Yield: 4 servings (serving size: 1¼ cups).

CALORIES 379 (29% from fat); FAT 12.2g (sat 7.5g, mono 1.5g, poly 0.8g); PROTEIN 19.6g; CARB 48.3g; FIBER 4.6g; CHOL 80mg; IRON 3.7mg; SODIUM 898mg; CALC 411mg

Sausage, Kale, and Bean Soup

Sausage spices up a simple five-ingredient soup.

    4   ounces Cajun smoked sausage,
        chopped (such as Conecuh)
    3   cups fat-free, less-sodium chicken
        broth
    1   (14.5-ounce) can no-salt-added
        diced tomatoes, undrained
    6   cups coarsely chopped kale (about
        8 ounces)
    1   (16-ounce) can navy beans,
        drained and rinsed

1. Heat a large saucepan over medium-high heat. Add sausage; cook 2 minutes, stirring occasionally. Add broth and tomatoes; bring to a boil over high heat. Stir in kale. Reduce heat; simmer 4 minutes or until kale is tender. Stir in beans; cook 1 minute or until thoroughly heated. Yield: 4 servings (serving size: 1¾ cups).

CALORIES 280 (29% from fat); FAT 9g (sat 3.2g, mono 3.8g, poly 1.4g); PROTEIN 17g; CARB 33.6g; FIBER 2.8g; CHOL 20mg; IRON 3.4mg; SODIUM 924mg; CALC 153mg

Turkey Breast Cutlets in Port Wine Sauce

Slicing the tenderloins ensures even cooking.

    1   pound turkey tenderloins
    ⅔   cup low-sodium beef broth,
        divided
    ¼   cup port wine
    2   tablespoons chopped dried cherries
    2   teaspoons black cherry fruit
        spread (such as Polaner)
    1   teaspoon Worcestershire sauce
    ½   teaspoon balsamic vinegar
    ¼   teaspoon black pepper
    1   teaspoon cornstarch
    1   teaspoon butter
    3   tablespoons chopped shallots
    1   teaspoon chopped fresh
        rosemary

1. Heat a large nonstick skillet over medium-high heat.

2. Cut tenderloin diagonally across grain into 1-inch-thick slices. Pound each slice to ½-inch thickness, using a meat mallet or rolling pin. Combine ½ cup broth, wine, and next 5 ingredients. Combine remaining broth and cornstarch, stirring with a whisk.

3. Melt butter in pan. Add shallots and rosemary; sauté 3 minutes. Add turkey; cook 3 minutes. Turn turkey over; cook 1 minute. Add wine mixture; bring to a boil. Cook 2 minutes. Add cornstarch mixture; boil 1 minute. Yield: 4 servings (serving size: about 3 ounces turkey and about ¼ cup sauce).

CALORIES 194 (9% from fat); FAT 2g (sat 0.9g, mono 0.5g, poly 0.3g); PROTEIN 29.3g; CARB 9.7g; FIBER 0.5g; CHOL 73mg; IRON 1.8mg; SODIUM 195mg; CALC 22mg

One-Dish Rosemary Chicken and White Beans

A spinach salad spiked with slivered red onions and drizzled with red wine vinaigrette complements this dish nicely.

    2   teaspoons olive oil
    1½ teaspoons dried rosemary
    ¼   teaspoon salt
    ¼   teaspoon black pepper
    8   skinless, boneless chicken thighs
        (about 1 pound)
    1   (14.5-ounce) can stewed tomatoes,
        undrained
    1   (15-ounce) can navy beans,
        drained
    ¼   cup chopped pitted kalamata
        olives

1. Heat oil in a large skillet over medium-high heat. Combine rosemary, salt, and pepper; sprinkle evenly over one side of chicken. Place chicken in pan, seasoned side down; cook 3 minutes. Reduce heat to medium; turn chicken. Add tomatoes and beans; cover and simmer 10 minutes or until chicken is done. Stir in olives. Yield: 4 servings (serving size: 2 thighs and ¾ cup bean mixture).

CALORIES 316 (23% from fat); FAT 8.1g (sat 1.7g, mono 3.7g, poly 1.5g); PROTEIN 31.2g; CARB 30.2g; FIBER 6.8g; CHOL 94mg; IRON 4.2mg; SODIUM 978mg; CALC 109mg

Focaccia Pastrami Sandwich

For a hot sandwich, bake the focaccia halves in a 350° oven 5 minutes or until toasted.

    3   tablespoons fat-free mayonnaise
    2   tablespoons stone-ground mustard
    1   (8-inch) round focaccia loaf
        (about 9 ounces)
    1½ cups trimmed watercress
    ¾   cup sliced bottled roasted red bell
        peppers
    8   ounces turkey pastrami

1. Combine mayonnaise and mustard. Cut loaf in half horizontally; spread mayonnaise mixture evenly over cut sides of bread. Arrange watercress, peppers, and pastrami over bottom half of loaf; top with remaining half. Cut loaf into 4 wedges. Yield: 4 servings (serving size: 1 wedge).

CALORIES 273 (23% from fat); FAT 7g (sat 2.1g, mono 2.2g, poly 2.1g); PROTEIN 16g; CARB 35.7g; FIBER 2.4g; CHOL 31mg; IRON 2.8mg; SODIUM 1,130mg; CALC 43mg

Corn and Scallop Chowder

Chunks of tender potatoes are the hallmark of New England-style chowders. To save time, use packaged diced potatoes and onion.

    1   tablespoon butter
    1   cup thinly sliced leek
    1   cup thinly sliced celery
    2   tablespoons all-purpose flour
    3   cups refrigerated diced potato
        with onion (such as Simply
        Potatoes)
    2   cups frozen whole-kernel corn
    ½   teaspoon salt
    ¼   teaspoon dried thyme
    ⅛   teaspoon black pepper
    2   (14-ounce) cans fat-free,
        less-sodium chicken broth
    ¾   pound bay scallops
    ½   cup half-and-half
    1   tablespoon chopped fresh parsley

Continued

1. Melt butter in a Dutch oven over medium-high heat. Add leek and celery; sauté 2 minutes. Sprinkle with flour, stirring to coat. Add potato and next 5 ingredients. Bring to a simmer over medium heat. Reduce heat to low. Cover and cook 6 minutes or until thoroughly heated. Add scallops; cook 2 minutes or until scallops are done. Stir in half-and-half and parsley. Yield: 4 servings (serving size: 2 cups).

CALORIES 352 (20% from fat); FAT 7.8g (sat 4.1g, mono 2.1g, poly 0.9g); PROTEIN 23.7g; CARB 48.9g; FIBER 4.9g; CHOL 47mg; IRON 2.4mg; SODIUM 919mg; CALC 92mg

QUICK & EASY
Sirloin Steak and Pasta Salad

Jump-start dinner by using leftover steak.

    2 cups uncooked penne or
       mostaccioli (tube-shaped pasta)
  ¼ pound green beans, trimmed
    1 (¾-pound) boneless sirloin steak,
       trimmed
    1 tablespoon salt-free garlic-pepper
       blend (such as Spice Hunter)
1½ cups thinly sliced red onion
1½ cups thinly sliced red bell pepper
  ¼ cup chopped fresh basil
    3 tablespoons Dijon mustard
    2 tablespoons balsamic vinegar
    1 teaspoon extravirgin olive oil
    1 teaspoon bottled minced garlic
  ¼ teaspoon salt
  ¼ teaspoon black pepper
  ¼ cup (1 ounce) crumbled blue cheese

1. Preheat broiler.
2. While broiler preheats, bring 3 quarts water to a boil in a large Dutch oven. Add pasta; cook 5½ minutes. Add beans; cook 3 minutes or until pasta is done. Drain and rinse with cold water. Drain.
3. Sprinkle steak with garlic-pepper blend. Place steak on a broiler pan; broil 3 inches from heat 10 minutes or until desired degree of doneness, turning after 5 minutes. Let stand 5 minutes. Cut steak diagonally across grain into thin slices.
4. Combine onion and next 8 ingredients in a large bowl. Add pasta mixture and beef; toss well to coat. Sprinkle with

cheese. Yield: 4 servings (serving size: about 1½ cups).

CALORIES 437 (24% from fat); FAT 11.8g (sat 4.3g, mono 4.5g, poly 0.8g); PROTEIN 29.4g; CARB 54.4g; FIBER 4.4g; CHOL 54mg; IRON 4.5mg; SODIUM 582mg; CALC 100mg

QUICK & EASY
Wasabi Salmon

Heat the skillet while the fish marinates.

    2 tablespoons low-sodium soy sauce
    1 teaspoon wasabi powder (dried
       Japanese horseradish)
    1 teaspoon bottled minced fresh
       ginger
  ½ teaspoon dark sesame oil
    4 (6-ounce) skinless salmon fillets
       (about 1 inch thick)
Cooking spray

1. Combine first 4 ingredients in a large zip-top plastic bag; add fish. Seal and marinate at room temperature 5 minutes, turning bag occasionally to coat. Remove fish from bag, reserving marinade.
2. Heat a large nonstick skillet coated with cooking spray over medium-high heat. Add fish; cook 3 minutes. Turn fish over. Reduce heat to medium; cook 8 minutes or until done. Add reserved marinade; cook 1 minute, turning fish to coat. Yield: 4 servings (serving size: 1 fillet).

CALORIES 283 (43% from fat); FAT 13.6g (sat 3.2g, mono 5.9g, poly 3.4g); PROTEIN 36.6g; CARB 0.9g; FIBER 0.1g; CHOL 87mg; IRON 0.8mg; SODIUM 347mg; CALC 23mg

MAKE AHEAD
Cranberry Liqueur

    2 cups sugar
    1 cup water
    1 (12-ounce) package fresh
       cranberries
    3 cups vodka

1. Combine sugar and water in a medium saucepan; cook over medium heat 5 minutes or until sugar dissolves, stirring constantly. Remove from heat, and cool completely.
2. Place cranberries in a food processor; process 2 minutes or until finely chopped. Combine sugar mixture and cranberries in a large bowl; stir in vodka.
3. Pour cranberry mixture into clean jars; secure with lids. Let stand 3 weeks in a cool, dark place, shaking every other day.
4. Strain cranberry mixture through a cheesecloth-lined sieve into a bowl, and discard solids. Carefully pour liqueur into clean bottles or jars. Yield: 4½ cups (serving size: ¼ cup).
NOTE: Liqueur can be stored refrigerated or at room temperature up to 1 year.

CALORIES 193 (0% from fat); FAT 0g; PROTEIN 0.1g; CARB 25g; FIBER 0.8g; CHOL 0mg; IRON 0.1mg; SODIUM 1mg; CALC 2mg

CRANBERRY COSMOPOLITANS:
Place crushed ice in a martini shaker. Add ½ cup Cranberry Liqueur, ¼ cup Cointreau, and 2 tablespoons lime juice; strain into martini glasses. Yield: 2 cocktails.

season's best
Cranberry Liqueur

To celebrate the holidays, we present you with an indisputably evocative recipe.

Drench homemade fruitcake with the liqueur. Drizzle it over ice cream and fruit for an instantly glamorous dessert. Give it away in small decanters or glass bottles, if you can bear to do so. Or just sip it, chilled, in liqueur glasses.

Recipe Title Index

An alphabetical listing of every recipe title that appeared
in the magazine in 2003. See page 448 for the General Recipe Index.

Month-by-Month Index

A month-by-month listing of every food story with recipe titles that appeared in the magazine in 2003. See page 448 for the General Recipe Index.

General Recipe Index

A listing by major ingredient and food category
for every recipe that appeared in the magazine in 2003.

HOW TO USE IT AND WHY Glance at the end of any *Cooking Light* recipe, and you'll see how committed we are to helping you make the best of today's light cooking. With six chefs, four registered dietitians, three home economists, and a computer system that analyzes every ingredient we use, *Cooking Light* gives you authoritative dietary detail like no other magazine. We go to such lengths so you can see how our recipes fit into your healthful eating plan. If you're trying to lose weight, the calorie and fat figures will probably help most. But if you're keeping a close eye on the sodium, cholesterol, and saturated fat in your diet, we provide those numbers, too. And because many women don't get enough iron or calcium, we can also help there, as well. Finally, there's a fiber analysis for those of us who don't get enough roughage.

Here's a helpful guide to put our nutrition analysis numbers into perspective. Remember, one size doesn't fit all, so take your lifestyle, age, and circumstances into consideration when determining your nutrition needs. For example, pregnant or breast-feeding women need more protein, calories, and calcium. And men over 50 need 1,200mg of calcium daily, 200mg more than the amount recommended for younger men.

IN OUR NUTRITIONAL ANALYSIS, WE USE THESE ABBREVIATIONS:

sat	saturated fat	**CHOL**	cholesterol
mono	monounsaturated fat	**CALC**	calcium
poly	polyunsaturated fat	**g**	gram
CARB	carbohydrates	**mg**	milligram

Your Daily Nutrition Guide

	WOMEN AGES 25 TO 50	WOMEN OVER 50	MEN OVER 24
Calories	2,000	2,000 or less	2,700
Protein	50g	50g or less	63g
Fat	65g or less	65g or less	88g or less
Saturated Fat	20g or less	20g or less	27g or less
Carbohydrates	304g	304g	410g
Fiber	25g to 35g	25g to 35g	25g to 35g
Cholesterol	300mg or less	300mg or less	300mg or less
Iron	18mg	8mg	8mg
Sodium	2,400mg or less	2,400mg or less	2,400mg or less
Calcium	1,000mg	1,200mg	1,000mg

The nutritional values used in our calculations either come from The Food Processor, Version 7.5 (ESHA Research), or are provided by food manufacturers.

Credits

CONTRIBUTING RECIPE DEVELOPERS:

Bruce Aidells
Patricia Baird
Mary Corpening Barber
Melanie Barnard
Jim Barrett
Peter Berley
Jan Birnbaum
Carole Bloom
David Bonom
Jim Botsacos
Lora Brody
Barbara Seelig Brown
Maureen Callahan
Suzanne Carreiro
Rebecca Charles
Barbara Chernetz
Michael Chiarello

Katherine Cobbs
Jesse Cool
Lorrie Hulston Corvin
Natalie Danford
Derrin Davis
John DeMers
Cynthia DePersio
Abby Duchin Dinces
Crescent Dragonwagon
Melissa Dupree
Judith Fertig
Allison Fishman
Jim Fobel
Brian Glover
Gourmet Gatherings
Ken Haedrich
Jessica B. Harris
Julie Hasson
Greg Higgins

Charles Holmes
Lia Mack Huber
Nancy Hughes
Dana Jacobi
Bill Jamison
Cheryl Alters Jamison
David Joachim
Lisa E. Kobs
Jean Kressy
Mike Kressy
Sarah Doyle Lacamoire
Barbara Lauterbach
Jeanne Lemlin
Karen Levin
Stephen Lewandowski
Alison Lewis
Hannah Lucy
Karen MacNeil
Deborah Madison

Elaine Magee
Donata Maggipinto
Domenica Marchetti
Theresa Marquez
Jennifer Martinkus
Don Mauer
Alice Medrich
Andrew Meek
Gary Mennie
Joan Nathan
Michel Nischan
Greg Patent
Jean Patterson
Marge Perry
Jim Peterson
Steve Petusevsky
Kathleen Prisant
Steven Raichlen
Rick Rodgers

Richard Ruben
Julie Sahni
Sharon Sanders
Mark Scarbrough
Nina Simonds
Angie Sinclair
Allen Smith
Lisë Stern
Johnathan Sundstrom
Sandy Szwarc
Elizabeth Taliaferro
Robin Vitetta-Miller
Robyn Webb
Bruce Weinstein
Joanne Weir
Sara Corpening Whiteford
Karen Wilcher
Marion Winik
Lisa Zwirn